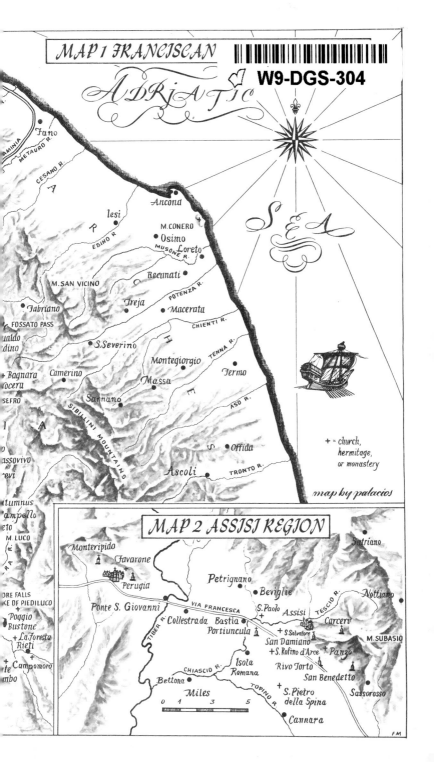

ST. FRANCIS OF ASSISI

Writings and
Early Biographies

ST. FRANCIS OF ASSISI
WRITINGS AND EARLY BIOGRAPHIES

*English Omnibus of the Sources
for the Life of St. Francis*

Translations by
Raphael Brown, Benen Fahy, Placid Hermann,
Paul Oligny, Nesta de Robeck, Leo Sherley-Price,
with a Research Bibliography by R. Brown

**Edited by
MARION A. HABIG**

Fourth Revised Edition
including *A New Fioretti*
by John R. H. Moorman, D.D.
and *Francis of Assisi: Writer*
by Marion A. Habig O.F.M.

FRANCISCAN HERALD PRESS
Publishers of Franciscan Literature
Chicago, Illinois 60609

ST. FRANCIS OF ASSISI, WRITINGS AND EARLY BIOGRA-
PHIES: ENGLISH OMNIBUS OF THE SOURCES FOR THE
LIFE OF ST. FRANCIS, edited by Marion A. Habig.

Copyright © 1983
FRANCISCAN HERALD PRESS
1434 W. 51st Street
Chicago, Illinois 60609

All rights reserved. No part of this book may be reproduced or copied in
any form or by any means — graphic, electronic, or mechanical, including
photocopying, recording, taping or information storage and retrieval sys-
tems — without written permission of the publisher.

Library of Congress Cataloging in Publication Data
Main entry under title:

St. Francis of Assisi: writings and early biographies.

"Including A new Fioretti by John R.H. Moorman, D.D. and
Francis of Assisi: writer by Marion A. Habig O.F.M."
  Bibliography: p.
  Includes indexes.
  1. Francis, of Assisi, Saint, 1182-1226.
2. Christian saints — Italy — Assisi — Biography.
3. Assisi (Italy) — Biography. I. Habig, Marion
Alphonse, 1901-   II. Title: Saint Francis of Assisi.
BX4700.F6S663   1983   271'.3'024 [B]   83-1730
ISBN 0-8199-0862-2

Nihil Obstat:
  MARK P. HEGENER O.F.M.
  Censor Deputatus

Imprimatur:
  MSGR. RICHARD A. ROSEMEYER, J.C.D.
  Vicar General, Archdiocese of Chicago

December 5, 1972

*"The Nihil Obstat and Imprimatur are official declarations that a book
or pamphlet is free of doctrinal error. No indication is contained therein
that those who have granted the Nihil Obstat and Imprimatur agree with
the contents, opinions, or statements expressed."*

Sixth printing, 1983 — total of 22,000

MADE IN THE UNITED STATES OF AMERICA

FOREWORD

To commemorate the seventh centenary of the death of St. Francis of Assisi, Pope Pius XI issued the encyclical *Rite Expiatis* on April 30, 1926. In it the Supreme Pontiff wrote: "While it is presumptuous to make comparisons between the heroes of sanctity who have been called to their heavenly home and whom the Holy Spirit has chosen, one for this task, another for that purpose here below — comparisons which, arising as they generally do from inordinate motives, are altogether futile and even offensive to God, the author of sanctity — still it would appear that in no one has the image of Christ our Lord, and the ideal of Gospel life, been more faithfully and strikingly expressed than in Francis. For this reason, while he called himself 'the Herald of the Great King,' he has been justly styled 'the second Christ,' because he appeared like Christ reborn to his contemporaries no less than to later ages, with the result that he lives today in the eyes of men and will live unto posterity."

Among all the saints of post-apostolic times, it is generally conceded, none seems to have exercised a more profound influence upon the Church and the world, not only in his own age, but also during the subsequent centuries down to our own day, than the Little Poor Man of Assisi. None had and still has so many devoted followers and ardent admirers within the fold of the Catholic Church as well as outside it. None has been the subject of so many biographies and other books, written and printed in every major language of the world.

In the field of historical research, interest in St. Francis seems to have attained a higher degree in modern times than ever before. During the past century especially, numerous scholars, Franciscans and others, have busied themselves with discovering, collecting, and analyzing all existing historical documents concerning St.

Francis and subjecting them to minute critical study and careful examination.

Besides collections of these sources in the original Latin, translations of them into modern languages have also been published in single large volumes. The first omnibus of this kind was the Spanish work of 897 pages which appeared in the *Biblioteca de Autores Cristianos* series in 1945 and has been reprinted in its fourth edition in 1965.[1]

A similar, more critical and comprehensive volume of 1599 pages in the French language, with introductions, notes, and a concordance, made its appearance in 1968.[2]

Following the plan of the latter along general lines, we now present an omnibus of English versions of the sources for the life of St. Francis. Some of these are new and better translations which have been published during the past twelve years in five separate volumes. Two of them, the biographies of St. Francis written by St. Bonaventure and the so-called ancient Legend of Perugia, are new translations which have not been previously published. Added to these is Raphael Brown's "Research Bibliography," which has been described as "the most complete and systematic bibliography ever compiled on St. Francis."[3] Originally forming a part of the second English edition of Omer Englebert's life of St. Francis,[4] it is now offered in a revised and updated form.

To introduce the reader to our English omnibus, it will be well to acquaint him with its contents by means of a short précis.

In the first place, as is meet, are the recognized, authentic *Writings* of St. Francis, with the addition of a few whose authenticity is questioned.

These are followed by the principal early biographies of St. Francis. They are undoubtedly of an historical nature despite the use of the term "Legenda." This word signifies exactly what the Latin means, namely "a narrative designed to be read (in public)"; it is not synonymous with the modern meaning of "legend." Included in our omnibus are the following: Thomas of Celano's *First Life,* completed in 1228; Celano's *Second Life,* completed before July 13, 1247, the date of a general chapter held at Lyons; selections from Celano's *Treatise on the Miracles of Blessed*

Francis, written in 1253; St. Bonaventure's *Major Legend* or Life, completed before 1263 when a general chapter was held at Pisa; his *Minor Legend* of the same date; excerpts from his other works (St. Bonaventure died July 15, 1274). Not included are: Celano's *Legenda ad usum chori,* a summary of his *First Life* for use in choir, written c. 1230; Julian of Speyer's short life of St. Francis which is based on Celano's *First Life* and was written 1232-1239; Henry d'Avranches' *Legenda versificata,* a versified form of Celano's *First Life,* written c. 1232-1234; a little treatise by Bernard of Besse, St. Bonaventure's secretary, *De laudibus beati Francisci* (On the praises of St. Francis); several other short sketches of the life of St. Francis written during the thirteenth century.

The three "legends" which follow in our omnibus are compilations extracted from earlier writings. The compilations themselves were made and distributed during the early fourteenth century; but the authorship and date of composition of their contents are questions concerning which there is no unanimity among research scholars. They have given rise to the so-called "Franciscan Question," which has been discussed at great length by experts in the field. Today, however, it is generally admitted that a large part of the compilations is taken from the writings of Brother Leo, companion of St. Francis, who died in the 1270's. The so-called *Legend of the Three Companions* was compiled during the first years of the fourteenth century; the *Legend of Perugia,* probably in 1311; and the *Mirror of Perfection,* probably in 1318. The Introductions which precede these compilations are not meant to be the last word concerning them; they present the deductions and opinions of the writers whose names are given.[5]

It will be well to add that the *Legend of Perugia* is not identical with *Anonymous of Perugia* which probably is a later elaboration of the *Legend of the Three Companions. Anonymous of Perugia* it not included in our omnibus.

However, we do present excellent modern English versions of two additional important works which may be classified as belles-lettres rather than history, although much of their contents is historical. The first is the very popular *Little Flowers of St. Francis,* a fourteenth-century collection of stories about St. Francis and his first followers, some of which are of a legendary character. The original Latin work, entitled *Actus Beati Francisci et Sociorum Ejus,* was written by Ugolino Boniscambi di Monte Santa Maria, apparently between 1327 and 1342 — at least the greater part. It received the title of *Little Flowers* in the anonymous Italian version and condensation, *I Fioretti di San Francesco,* made between 1370-1385. The translator added the "Considerations on the Holy Stigmata," which are based on earlier writers including Celano and St. Bonaventure. Our omnibus includes the latter and all of the *Little Flowers* with the exception of the Life of Brother Juniper and the Life and Sayings of Brother Giles.

The other and final work is the *Sacrum Commercium,* a short allegorical epic which develops the theme of the spiritual marriage of St. Francis and his first companions with Lady Poverty. It may have come from the facile pen of Thomas of Celano as early as 1227, but some are of the opinion that it was not written until the 1260's.

Lastly, to make our thesaurus of sources on St. Francis complete, we have appended English translations of a series of short thirteenth-century testimonies. Those of Cardinal Jacques de Vitry are especially striking and valuable.

We are confident that this English omnibus will find a ready welcome, not only among writers and scholars, but also by the general reading public, including those who have already read one or more biographies of the Poverello. It will enable all to "go back to the sources" — something which is repeatedly recommended in our post-conciliar age — and so become better acquainted with the real St. Francis.

— M. A. H.

NOTES

1. *San Francisco de Asis: Sus Escritos, Las Florecillas, Biografias del Santo por Celano, San Buenaventura, y los Tres Cpmpañeros, Espejo de Perfeccion,* edited by Fr. Juan R. de Legísima O.F.M. and Fr. Lino Gómez Canedo O.F.M., xxxix-758 pp. (Madrid, 1965).
2. *Saint François d'Assise: Documents, Écrits et Premières Biographies,* edited and annotated by Fr. Théophile Desbonnets O.F.M. and Fr. Damien Vorreux O.F.M., 1599 pp. (Paris, 1968).
3. *Archivum Franciscanum Historicum,* vol. 60 (1967), p. 255.
4. Omer Englebert, *Saint Francis of Assisi; A Biography,* a new translation by Eve Marie Cooper, 2nd English ed. revised and augmented

by Ignatius Brady O.F.M. and Raphael Brown, with introduction, appendices, and comprehensive bibliography covering modern research, xii-616 pp. (Franciscan Herald Press, Chicago, 1965).

5. Cf. the lengthy review and discussion of the French omnibus edited by Fr. Desbonnets and Fr. Vorreux in the article, "A Francisco Legendarum ad Franciscum Historicum, Quaestio Franciscana et vita S. Francisci duplici opere illustratae," by Fr. Octavian Schmucki O.F.M.Cap., published in *Collectanea Franciscana,* vol. 38 (1968), pp. 373-392. Of great importance is also Fr. Kajetan Esser's *Anfänge und ursprüngliche Zielsetzungen des Ordens der Minderbrüder,* xvi-296 pp. (Leiden, Netherlands, 1966), of which an English translation, entitled *Franciscan Origins,* was published in 1970 by Franciscan Herald Press, Chicago.

CHRONOLOGY

This chronological table of the life of St. Francis was prepared by Omer Englebert and Raphael Brown. The references in parentheses are to the Appendices in O. Englebert, *Saint Francis of Assisi: A Biography,* 2nd English edition (Chicago, 1965), pp. 347-458.

1181, summer or fall (?) — Born in Assisi (App. II, 6). Baptized Giovanni di Pietro di Bernardone, renamed Francesco by father. (App. III, IV, V).

1198, January 8. — Innocent III elected Pope.

1198, spring. — Duke Conrad of Urslingen's Rocca fortress besieged, taken, and razed by people of Assisi, as he yields Duchy of Spoleto to Innocent III (App. VI, 1).

1199-1200. — Civil war in Assisi; destruction of feudal nobles' castles; families of later St. Clare & Brother Leonardo move to Perugia (App. VI,2).

1202, November. — War between Perugia & Assisi. Latter's army is defeated at Battle of Collestrada. Francis spends a year in prison in Perugia, until ransomed by father as ill (App. VI,3 & 4).

1204. — Long illness.

1204 end, or spring 1205 (?) — Francis sets out for war in Apulia, but returns the next day, after a vision and message in Spoleto. Beginning of the gradual process of conversion (App. II,5; & VI,5).

1205, June. — Gautier de Brienne dies in southern Italy (App. VI, 5).

1205, fall & end. — Message of the Crucifix of San Damiano. Conflict with father.

1206, — Jan. or Feb. — Bishop's trial (App. II,5).

1206, spring. — Francis in Gubbio, nursing victims of leprosy (App. II,5).

1206, summer, probably July. — Returns to Assisi, assumes hermit's habit, and begins to repair San Damiano (App. II,5): end of conversion process; beginning of Thomas of Celano's "years of conversion" chronology (App. II,5).

1206, summer, to Jan. or early Feb. **1208**. — Repairs San Damiano, San Pietro, and Portiuncula (App. II,7).

1208, Feb. 24 . — Francis hears Gospel of St. Mathias Mass. Changes from hermit's habit to that of barefoot preacher; begins to preach (App. II,7).

1208, April 16 — Brothers Bernard and Peter Catanii join Francis. On April 23 Brother Giles is received at the Portiuncula (App. II,7).

1208, spring. — First Mission: Francis and Giles go to the Marches of Ancona. (App.II,7).

1208, summer. — Three more, including Philip, join them (App. VII,1).

1208, fall & winter. — Second Mission: all seven go to Poggio Bustone in the Valley of Rieti (App. II,7). After being assured of the remission of his sins and the future growth of the Order, Francis sends the six, plus a new seventh follower, on the Third Mission, two by two. Bernard & Giles go to Florence (App. II,7).

1209, early. — The eight return to the Portiuncula. Four more join them (App. VII,2).

1209, spring. — Francis writes brief Rule and goes to Rome with his eleven first companions. There he obtains the approval of Pope Innocent III. (App. II,8; Ch. 5, Notes 23 & 28). On the way back, they stay a while at Orte, then settle at Rivo Torto.

1209, Sept. — German Emperor-elect Otto IV passes by Rivo Torto (App. II,8).

1209 or **1210**. — The friars move to the Portiuncula.

1209-1210 (?) — Possible beginning of Third Order.

1211, summer (?) — Francis goes to Dalmatia and returns.

1212, March 18/19. — On Palm Sunday night, reception of St. Clare at the Portiuncula (App. II,9).

1212, May (?) — After a few days at S. Paolo and a few weeks at Panzo Benedictine convents, Clare moves to San Damiano (App. II,9).

1213, May 8. — At San Leo, near San Marino, Count Orlando offers Mount La Verna to Francis as a hermitage.

1213/14 or **1214/15** (?) — Francis travels to Spain and back.

1215, November. — Fourth Lateran General Council. Francis in Rome

1216, July 16. — Pope Innocent III dies in Perugia. July 18: Honorius III elected. French Archbishop Jacques de Vitry at Perugia.

1216, summer. — Francis obtains the Portiuncula Indulgence from Pope Honorius in Perugia.

1217, May 5. — Pentecost General Chapter at the Portiuncula. First missions beyond the Alps and overseas. Giles leaves for Tunis,

Elias for Syria, & Francis for France, but Cardinal Hugolin meets him in Florence & persuades him to stay in Italy.

1219, May 26. — Chapter. First martyrs leave for Morocco. On June 24, Francis sails from Ancona for Acre and Damietta.

1219, fall. — Francis visits Sultan. November 5, Damietta taken by Crusaders.

1220, Jan. — First martyrs killed in Morroco.

1220, early. — Francis goes to Acre & Holy Land.

1220, spring or summer (?) — Francis returns to Italy, landing at Venice (App. II,10). Cardinal Hugolin appointed Protector of the Order.

1220, (or **1217, 1218**) (?) — Francis resigns (App. II,11). Peter Catanii vicar.

1221, March. — Peter Catanii dies.

1221, May 30. — Chapter. First Rule. Elias vicar.

1221. — Rule of Third Order approved by Honorius III.

1221/1222 (?) — Francis on a preaching tour in southern Italy.

1222, Aug. 15. — Francis preaches in Bologna.

1223, early. — At Fonte Colombo Francis composes Second Rule. Chapter on June 11 discusses it. Fall: further discussion in Rome.

1223, Nov 29. — Pope Honorius III approves Rule of 1223.

1223, December 24/25. — Christmas Crib Midnight Mass at Greccio.

1224, June 2. — Chapter sends mission to England.

1224, end of July or early August (?) — In Foligno, Elias is given message in vision that Francis has only two years to live (App. II,13).

1224, Aug. 15-Sept. 29 (Assumption to St. Michael's Day). — Francis fasts at La Verna, receiving the Stigmata about Sept 14.

1224, Oct & early Nov. — Francis returns to the Portiuncula via Borgo San Sepolcro, Monte Casale, & Città di Castello.

1224/1225, Dec.-Feb. (?) — Riding on a donkey, he makes a preaching tour in Umbria & the Marches (App. II,12).

1225, Mar. (?) — On a visit to St. Clare at San Damiano, his eye-sickness suddenly turns much worse. Almost blind, he has to stay there in a cell in or by the chaplain's house. At the insistence of Brother Elias, at last consents to receive medical care, but weather is too cold and treatment is postponed.

1225, Apr.-May (?) — Still at San Damiano, undergoes treatment without improvement. Receives divine promise of eternal life and composes Canticle of Brother Sun.

1225, June (?) — Adding to the Canticle, reconciles feuding bishop and podestà of Assisi. Summoned by a letter from Cardinal Hugolin, leaves San Damiano for Rieti Valley.

1225, early July (?) — Welcomed in Rieti by Hugolin and papal court (there from June 23 to February 6). Goes to Fonte Colombo to undergo eye treatment urged by Hugolin, but has it postponed owing to absence of Brother Elias.

1225, July-Aug. (?) — Doctor cauterizes the Saint's temples at Fonte Colombo, without improvement.

1225, Sept. — Francis moves to San Fabiano near Rieti to be treated by other doctors, who pierce his ears. Restores the trampled vineyard of the poor priest.

1225/1226, Oct.-Mar. (?) — In either Rieti or Fonte Colombo.

1226, April. — Francis is in Siena for further treatment.

1226, May or June (?) — Returns to the Portiuncula via Cortona.

1226, July-Aug. — In summer heat, he is taken to Bagnara in the hills near Nocera.

1226, late Aug. or early Sept. — His condition growing worse, he is taken via Nottiano to the palace of the bishop in Assisi. Bishop Guido is absent on a pilgrimage to Monte Gargano.

1226, Sept. — Knowing that his death is imminent, Francis insists on being carried to the Portiuncula.

1226, Oct. 3. — He dies there. Sunday, Oct. 4, is buried in San Giorgio Church.

1227, Mar. 19. — His friend Hugolin becomes Pope Gregory IX.

1228, July 16. — In Assisi Gregory IX canonizes St. Francis.

1230, May 25. — Translation of the Saint's remains to his new basilica, San Francesco.

ABBREVIATIONS

Fior	*Fioretti* or *Little Flowers of St. Francis*
FrFr	*La France franciscaine*
FS	*Franziskanische Studien*
Herm	St. Francis' *Rule for Hermitages*
Inf	St. Francis' *Prayer in Time of Sickness*
Lds	The *Lauds* or Praises written by St. Francis, added to his paraphrase of the Our Father
1Let to 13Let	The thirteen *Letters* of St. Francis (nos. 8-13 in the Appendix to his *Writings*)
LM	*Major Life of St. Francis* by St. Bonaventure
Lm	*Minor Life of St. Francis* by St. Bonaventure
LP	*Legend of the Perugian* (*Anonymus Perusinus*)
1Mat	Matins of the first schema in St. Francis' *Office of the Passion*
MF	*Miscellanea Francescana*
MGH	*Monumenta Germaniae Historica*
3Non	None of the third schema in St. Francis' *Office of the Passion*
NRT	*Nouvelle revue théologique*
OCH	*Opuscules de critique historique* by Paul Sabatier (Paris, 1901-1919) 3 v.
Pat	*Paraphrase of the Our Father,* by St. Francis
PBV	*Prayer to the Blessed Virgin,* by St. Francis
PG	*Patrologie Grecque* (Migne)
PL	*Patrologie Latine* (Migne)
PLeo	*Praises of God for Brother Leo,* by St. Francis
1Pri	Prime of the first schema in St. Francis' *Office of the Passion*
PSD	*Prayer before the Crucifix of San Damiano,* by St. Francis
RCL	*Rule for St. Clare,* by St. Francis
1Reg	*First Rule* of St. Francis
2Reg	*Second Rule* of St. Francis
RHE	*Revue d'histoire ecclésiastique*
RHF	*Revue d'histoire franciscaine* (Paris)
RMAL	*Revue du Moyen Age Latin*

SBV   *Salutation to the Blessed Virgin Mary,* by St. Francis

Sp   *Speculum Perfectionis, Mirror of Perfection*

SV   *Salutation of the Virtues,* by St. Francis

3Sxt   Sext of the third schema in St. Francis' *Office of the Passion*

1Tce   Terce of the first schema in St. Francis' *Office of the Passion*

Test   *Testament* of St. Francis

TestSi   *Testament* of St. Francis, of Siena

5Vesp   Vespers of the fifth schema in St. Francis' *Office of the Passion*

CONTENTS

THE WRITINGS
OF ST. FRANCIS

Translated by Benen Fahy O.F.M.
with Introduction and Notes
by Placid Hermann O.F.M.

First published in 1964 by Burns & Oates, London (Catalogue No.: 55223), and Franciscan Herald Press, Chicago. SBN: 8199-0106-7.

Introduction

THERE IS something paradoxical about the fact that the Little Poor Man of Assisi, who sought only obscurity, should have become so widely known and universally loved as he is today. But paradoxical or not, the truth of the matter is that St Francis has entered deeply into the hearts of men during these past seven and one half centuries since his death. Men of all faiths have come to admire and respect him. Biographers have turned out book after book to recount his life. Students have pored over his words and writings and actions to discover his spirit. Painters have immortalized his life on their canvases, and poets have sung his praises in their verses century after century as the years have gone by. Countless men and women of all lands have embraced his way of life and many have attained a degree of perfection that has enrolled them in the catalogue of saints and blessed. And there is no sign today that his popularity will not continue or that his influence will grow less. As a matter of fact, both seem to be increasing rather than diminishing.

There is indeed a reason for all this, and the reason is to be found in Francis himself, in the spirit that prompted him to lead the life he did, and in the way of life he bequeathed to those who would follow in his footsteps. Of these things we must understand at least something, if we are to understand his popularity and the influence he has exerted and continues to exert upon the many who have found in him the inspiration to a more perfect life in Christ, the King and Centre of the World.

I. THE SPIRIT OF ST FRANCIS

When St Francis of Assisi knelt before the crucifix in the church of San Damiano and heard the words of the crucified Christ, "Go, Francis, and repair my house", there took place in his heart a complete transformation that left him ever after

5

burning with compassion for his crucified Master. Francis' first biographer, Thomas of Celano, records this transformation in these words: "From then on compassion for the crucified was rooted in his holy soul, and, as it can be piously supposed, the stigmata of the venerable passion were deeply imprinted in his heart, though not as yet upon his flesh. . . . And from then on he could never keep himself from weeping, even bewailing in a loud voice the passion of Christ which was always, as it were, before his mind. He filled the ways with his sighs. He permitted himself no consolation, remembering the wounds of Christ."[1]

So great indeed was the love that welled up in Francis' heart that thereafter he wanted nothing more than to become like to Christ, to imitate him as perfectly as he could, to become one with him. St Bonaventure wrote later: "Jesus Christ crucified reposed continually on the breast of Francis like a bouquet of myrrh, and the fire of love with which he burned made him desire to be entirely transformed into Jesus."[2] And Thomas of Celano said: "He was always occupied with Jesus; Jesus he bore in his heart, Jesus in his mouth, Jesus in his ears, Jesus in his eyes, Jesus in his hands, Jesus in the rest of his members."[3]

It was this love for Christ that impelled Francis to put aside everything that could keep him from perfect union with Christ and to embrace complete and unrestricted poverty. Poverty had accompanied Christ throughout his earthly life, from the first moment of his existence in the womb of his mother to the last moment of his life on the hill of Calvary.[4] So Francis too

[1] *II Cel.*, 10-11. The quotations from Thomas of Celano are taken from the English translation of his *Lives of St Francis*, entitled *St Francis of Assisi*, Placid Hermann, O.F.M., translator, Franciscan Herald Press, 1963.

[2] St Bonaventure, *Legenda Major S. Francisci*, in *Analecta Franciscana*, vol. 10, IX, 2.

[3] *I Cel.*, 115.

[4] See the *Sacrum Commercium Sancti Francisci Cum Domina Paupertate*, anon., Quaracchi edition, 1929. Ubertino da Casale adds this interesting thought: "Yes, when, because the cross was so high, your very Mother —and such a Mother!—could not reach you (though she cherished you faithfully even then and remained in union with your sufferings with anguished affection)—then, I say, Lady Poverty was there like a most welcome handmaiden with all her privations to enfold you more tightly than ever and to share the more feelingly in your torment." See *The Words of St Francis*, James Meyer, O.F.M., Franciscan Herald Press, 1952, p. 10.

"gathered her to himself with chaste embraces," as Celano puts it, "and not even for an hour did he allow himself not to be her husband. This, he would tell his sons, is the way to perfection, this the pledge and earnest of eternal riches. . . . Indeed, from the very beginning of his religious life unto his death he was rich in having only a tunic, a cord, and drawers, and he had nothing else."[1]

But Francis' poverty was not restricted to material poverty, to the mere renunciation of ownership of material goods, or even to austerity in the simple use of things. His poverty included also a complete renunciation of self in the deepest humility, "the guardian and the ornament of all virtues".[2] Francis' renunciation was absolute, a total immolation of himself. He gave his body back to God by the most perfect chastity, and he renounced his own will by the most unselfish obedience. Mindful of the words of Christ, *every one of you who does not renounce all that he possesses, cannot be my disciple* (Lk. 14: 33), he crucified himself with Christ so that in renouncing everything that was his own he could become a most perfect disciple of Christ.[3]

Accordingly, when Francis' first followers began to gather round him, they found in him the only norm of life they needed, for in imitating him they were imitating Christ, and that was the way of life that would lead them to union with Christ. But, as their number grew, Francis saw that he himself could not for long remain their only norm of life; he saw that their way of life would have to be more precisely determined. Accordingly he set down in words what "the Rule and life" of the brothers should be.

But this Rule and life was not to be something elaborate. Francis found what he wanted and what suited his whole inclination in the book of the holy Gospel, the revelation of the teachings and the life of his divine Master. And so he chose as the cardinal point of his Rule this basic principle: "to follow

[1] *II Cel.*, 55.

[2] *Ibid.*, 140.

[3] He succeeded to such an extent that in 1224, two years before his death, he was marked with the stigmata on Mount La Verna. Many people spoke of him as the "Christ of Umbria". Nearly all the Scripture quotations in this volume are from the Confraternity of Christian Doctrine edition, 1941.

the teachings and the footsteps of Christ." He wanted his brothers to live according to Christ's teachings and to walk, as it were, in the very prints where Christ's feet had trod. But their following of Christ was not to be something purely external. It was to be an imitation of Christ that would lead to a total transformation interiorly, a complete submission of the spirit of the flesh to the spirit of Christ, a seraphic love of him who is *the way, and the truth, and the life* (Jn 14: 6).

But Francis, who was a man completely Catholic and wholly apostolic, wholly devoted to the Apostolic See, wanted the Rule and life of his followers to be from the beginning under the direction and protection of the Catholic Church, for he knew that only in this way could they be sure they were following the teachings and the footsteps of Christ. Consequently, as soon as the number of his followers had reached eleven, he set out with them for Rome to ask the Holy See to give its approbation on his Rule of life.

This attained, Francis' Order grew rapidly during the next years, from the first follower, who did not persevere and is not even known by name,[1] to the thousands who were present a decade or so later at the Chapter of Mats.[2] But what character-ized these early friars above all else was their love for Christ, Christ in the crib, Christ on the cross, and Christ in the Blessed

---

[1] *I Cel.*, 24.

[2] It is impossible to date precisely what is generally called the Chapter of Mats. Neither is it possible to be sure of the meaning of the term nor of the number of friars present. It is likely that this chapter was held in 1221 or 1222, though some authors have insisted it was as early as 1218 (See: J. R. H. Moorman, *The Sources for the Life of St Francis of Assisi*, Manchester University Press, 1940, p. 29). Various Latin terms are used to describe the chapter, most of them meaning in one way or another *mats* or *rushes*, and all of them commonly taken to mean temporary shelters made of rushes. The Latin term, however, *sestorium, sextorium, sistoriorum,* might also be a corruption of *consistorium,* implying the mean-ing of a house of assembly, as Rosalind Brooke notes in her *Early Franciscan Government, Elias to Bonaventure* (Cambridge University Press, 1959, pp. 288-291). She also favours the date of 1222, though Brother Jordan of Giano dates it 1221 in his *Chronicle* (See: *XIIIth Century Chronicles,* Placid Hermann, O.F.M., translator, Franciscan Herald Press, 1961, pp. 30-31). Brother Jordan says that three thousand friars were present. Other sources give five thousand.

Eucharist; their deep spirit of brotherliness; their love for poverty, which, like their father, they personified as Lady Poverty; their humility; their devotedness to prayer and to work; their wholehearted submission to obedience. As a result, they were a happy band of friars, happy with the supernatural joy that radiates from a heart that has renounced itself completely and given itself in an abiding attachment to Christ, its King.[1]

2. THE WRITINGS OF ST FRANCIS

(a) Manuscript Collections

The early sources of Franciscan history, in particular the two biographies of St Francis by Thomas of Celano, make frequent allusions to the writings of the saint. Celano, for instance, alludes to or quotes directly snatches from such writings as Francis' *Admonitions*, his two *Rules*, the *Testament*, his various letters, and his *Canticle of Brother Sun*. On the other hand, Celano makes no attempt to give an account of these writings, to collect them, or even to quote them precisely or in full. Still it is evident that he was well acquainted with them and that he could call upon them for reference with ease.

Who it was that made the first collection of Francis' writings is not known. But it is clear that this collecting was begun rather soon after the saint's death. What is undoubtedly the oldest collection, and also the most important, is found in a manuscript known as the Assisi codex, MS. 338. This manuscript was formerly in the library of the Franciscans at the Sacro Convento in Assisi, but it is now in the municipal library of that city.

This manuscript is not confined to the writings of St Francis. It contains, in addition, some liturgical notes, some selections

[1]See the series of articles by Fr Cajetan Esser, O.F.M., entitled *The Order of St Francis*, in *Franciscan Herald and Forum*, vols. 34 and 35. Fr Cajetan concludes: "Our search for the spirit and essence of the Franciscan Order leads to this conclusion: The disciples of Saint Francis are a brotherhood, a family of brothers who in living charity, follow literally and without gloss the sacred footprints of Christ; who, filled with the Spirit of the Lord, must ever be *minores*; who, experiencing even in this life the bliss of the love of the Eternal Father, are ready to communicate that love to all men in word and deed."

from the *Legendae* or biographies of St Francis, in particular the *Legenda Versificata S. Francisci*, and some writings about St Clare. The writings of St Francis that are included in this manuscript occur in this order: The Second Rule (fol. 12r-15v); the Testament (fol. 16r-18r); the Admonitions (fol. 18r-23v); three letters (fol. 23v-32v), to All the Faithful, to the General Chapter, and to All Clerics; the Salutation of the Virtues (fol. 32v-33r); the Canticle of Brother Sun (fol. 33r-34r); the paraphrase of the Lord's Prayer (fol. 34r-34v); the Office of the Passion (fol. 34v-42r); and Religious Life in Hermitages (fol. 43). This manuscript, therefore, contains ten of the writings of St Francis that are considered authentic and the dubiously authentic paraphrase of the Lord's Prayer.[1]

The question naturally arises concerning the age of this codex, and, in particular, the age of the section containing the writings of St Francis. All are agreed that the codex goes back at least to the early part of the fourteenth century. But, as some have pointed out, there seems to be good reason for believing that the collection of writings of St Francis contained in it is of an earlier date. Fr Cajetan Esser, O.F.M., for instance, in an article in *Franziskanische Studien*, 1939, argued for a date around the middle of the thirteenth century and concluded his reasoning with the assertion that it is certain that the second part of the Assisi MS. 338, that is, the part containing the writings of St Francis, dates back to the third quarter of the thirteenth century, and that it is almost certain that it dates back to the latter part of the first half of that century.[2] This dating seems reasonable, although other recent authors argue for a date towards the end of the thirteenth century.[3]

[1]See the *Archivum Franciscanum Historicum*, Vol. 5, pp. 237-239, for a description of the MS. 338, by Benvenuto Bughetti, O.F.M. There are a number of other manuscripts closely related to this Assisi MS.: Vatican MS. 4354; Berlin MS. 196; Lemberg MS. 131; Liegnitz MS. 12; Mazarin MSS. 989 and 1743; Duesseldorf MS. 132. These same writings are found also in the *Chronicle* of Mariano of Florence, written about 1500, and in the fourteenth-century compilation known as the *Fac secundum exemplar* from the opening words of the prologue.

[2]"Die Aelteste Handschrift des Opuscula des Hl. Franziskus (cod. 338 von Assisi)", *Franziskanische Studien*, vol. 26, 1939, pp. 121-142.

[3]See *Archivum Franciscanum Historicum*, Vol, 41, p. 26.

A second collection of the writings of St Francis is found in another group of early manuscripts, represented especially by the important codex known as the Ognissanti MS., because it was found in the Franciscan convent of All Saints (Ognissanti) in Florence, Italy. This manuscript, described at length by Paul Sabatier,[1] contains the following writings of St Francis: the First Rule; the Testament; a letter to a certain Minister General concerning friars who sin mortally; the letter to all clerics (concerning reverence to the Blessed Eucharist); the Admonitions; the Praises before the Office (*Sanctus, sanctus, sanctus*); the Praises of the Most High God (*Tu es Sanctus Dominus Deus*); the Salutation of the Virtues; the Salutation of the Blessed Virgin; the letter to the General Chapter and to all the friars; the letter to all Christians; Religious Life in Hermitages; the Blessing of Brother Leo.[2] This manuscript dates back to the fourteenth century and was compiled probably about 1370.[3]

(b) *Editions of the Writings*

Early in the sixteenth century two works were published that contained, among other things, some of the writings of St Francis. The first of these was called *Speculum B. Francisci et Sociorum Ejus*. It was printed first in Venice in 1504 and then again in Metz in 1509. It contained the First Rule of the Order and several of St Francis' prayers. The second work appeared first at Rouen in 1509 under the title *Speculum Minorum*, again at Salamanca in 1511 under the title *Monumenta Ordinis Minorum*, and the next year at Paris under the title *Firmamenta Trium Ordinum B. Francisci*. This second work also contained some of the writings of St Francis, slightly more in

[1]*Le Speculum Perfectionis*, Manchester, The University Press, 1931, Vol. II, pp. 8-17.

[2]This manuscript contains also the *Speculum Perfectionis*, the *Legenda Trium Sociorum*, and a few other items.

[3]Other manuscripts related to the Ognissanti MS. are: Codex 1/25 at the College of St Isidore in Rome; Vatican MS. 7650; the codex at the Capuchin monastery at Foligno. See also Bartholomew of Pisa, *Liber de Conformitate Vitae Beati Francisci ad Vitam Domini Jesu* (*Liber Conformitatum*), written between 1385 and 1390, *Analecta Franciscana*, IV, Fructus XII. The collection of writings in this second group of manuscripts differs in some minor points from the Assisi MS. 338.

number than those contained in the first work mentioned.[1]

But the most important of the early editions of the writings of St Francis was that of Fr Luke Wadding, O.F.M., published in Antwerp in 1623 under the title *B.P. Francisci Assisiatis Opuscula*.[2] Wadding divided his work into three parts. The first part contained seventeen letters, some prayers, and the Testament of St Francis. The second part contained the two Rules. The third part contained some twenty-eight conferences, the Office of the Passion, and various minor items called apophthegms or maxims, colloquies, prophecies, parables, and other sayings.

Wadding's edition, however, valuable though it was at the time, was not a truly critical edition of the writings. It contained, in addition to authentic writings of the saint, some writings too that could be attributed to him only doubtfully and some sayings that could not be considered writings. Nevertheless, Wadding's edition formed the basis for a number of other editions through the years that followed his work, and, as a matter of fact, it still has value for students of Franciscana.

Today, however, the most important edition of the writings of St Francis is the one published in 1904 and republished again in 1949 by the Fathers of St Bonaventure's College at Quaracchi, entitled *Opuscula Sancti Patris Francisci Assisiensis*. This truly critical edition was based upon the early manuscripts, and it contains, for the most part, only the authenticated writings of St Francis. The *Canticle of Brother Sun*, however, is omitted, not because the Quaracchi editors considered it of doubtful authenticity, but because they wanted to include only such writings as are in the Latin language.[3] This edition is the basis for this present English translation of *The Writings of Saint Francis*.

Since the publication of the first Quaracchi edition in 1904

[1] For example, in the *Monumenta Ordinis Minorum* are found: the First Rule, the Testament, an Explanation of the Faith, the Letter to All Christians, and a part of a letter to all the friars.

[2] See also *Scriptores Ordinis Minorum*, Luke Wadding, O.F.M., reprinted in *Supplementum ad Scriptores Ordinis Minorum*, Joannes Hyacinthus Sbaralea, O.F.M. Conv., Rome, 1906.

[3] One Italian version of the *Canticle of Brother Sun* can be found in *Via Seraphica*, Placid Hermann, O.F.M., Franciscan Herald Press, 1959, p. 32.

much additional work has been done on these writings. Even today discussion continues with regard to certain of the writings, and the attempt to date them more precisely still goes on. In 1951 a German translation of the writings was published by Dr Cajetan Esser and Dr Lothar Hardick, both Franciscans, under the title *Die Schriften Des Hl. Franziskus von Assisi*,[1] and in 1959 a new French translation appeared, edited by Alexandre Masseron.[2] Both these editions make use of the most critical thought about the writings and both are valuable for any new version of the writings.

(c) The Lost Writings of St Francis

It is obvious from the early Franciscan authors that other writings of St Francis were known to them, though there is no record of them in the early manuscripts. Francis' first biographer, Thomas of Celano, and the chronicler of the activities of the first friars in England, Thomas of Eccleston, both refer to letters written by St Francis that are no longer extant.

In his *First Life of St Francis* Thomas of Celano makes mention of certain letters that Francis wrote to Cardinal Ugolino, the bishop of Ostia and the first official protector of the Order.[3] In these letters, according to Celano, Francis foretold, in a way, that Ugolino would one day be pope, for he used this salutation: *To the Reverend Father, or the Lord Hugo, Bishop of the Whole World*.[4] It is regrettable that these letters have been lost; they would surely throw additional light upon Francis' relations with the cardinal.[5]

Thomas of Eccleston, too, in his *De Adventu Fratrum Minorum in Angliam*,[6] makes mention of two letters that were written by St Francis at about the same time. Both, however, are lost. The

[1]Dietrich Coelde-Verlag, Werl i. Westfalen, 1951.

[2]*Oeuvres de saint François d'Assise*, Paris, Editions Albin Michel, 1959.

[3]Ugolino was appointed Cardinal Protector of the Order probably in 1220 or 1221. He became Pope Gregory IX in 1227 and lived on until 1241.

[4]*I Cel.*, 100.

[5]Ugolino had much to do with the writing of the Rule of 1223, as he himself said later in the Bull *Quo elongati* of 1230.

[6]An English translation of Eccleston's work can be found in *XIIIth Century Chronicles*.

one, he says, was written by Francis at a general chapter,[1] "standing in the rain, but without getting wet", and it was addressed "to the minister and brothers of France that, seeing his letter, they should rejoice and sing praises to the Triune God, saying: 'We bless Thee, Father, Son, and Holy Ghost.'"[2] The second letter was written shortly thereafter to the people of Bologna. In it Francis foretold the coming of an earthquake. "This earthquake", Eccleston adds, "happened before the war of Frederick and lasted for forty days, so that all the mountains of Lombardy were shaken."[3] Eccleston notes that this letter was written in "bad Latin". Nothing more, however, is known of either of these letters.

In a work of later date entitled *Speculum Perfectionis* or *Mirror of Perfection*,[4] several additional writings of St Francis are recorded. These too have been otherwise lost. The first is the short piece known as the "Short Testament of St Francis". The anonymous author of the *Speculum Perfectionis* records that when Francis was ill at Siena towards the end of his life,[5] he sent for Brother Benedict of Pirato[6] and gave him the gist of what he wanted him to write down. "Write down", the saint said, "that I bless all my brothers in the order and who will enter the order to the end of the world. And because I am not able to speak much because of my weakness and the pain of my illness, I make known briefly my will and intention to all my brothers present and future in these three words. Namely, that as a sign that they remember me, my blessing, and my testament, they always love one another as I have loved them and do love

[1]This was probably the Chapter of Mats, 1221/1222. See also *II Cel.*, 57.

[2]*The Coming of the Friars Minor to England*, Chapter 6, p. 126 in the English translation.

[3]Probably in 1222. Other chroniclers also record the event. *Loc. cit.*

[4]There were two redactions of this work. The first, edited by Fr Leonard Lemmens, O.F.M. (*Documenta Antiqua Franciscana*, Pars.II, Quaracchi, 1901), was written sometime between 1277 and 1300. The second, edited by Paul Sabatier (*Le Speculum Perfectionis*, two volumes, 1928, 1931, Manchester, The University Press), was written probably in 1318.

[5]Francis was in Siena in April or May of 1226. He died October 3/4, 1226.

[6]Or Prato, in the Lemmens redaction.

them; that they always love and respect our Lady Poverty; and that they always remain faithful and obedient to the prelates and the clergy of holy Mother Church."[1] There is, however, no other record of this Siena pre-Testament, as it is sometimes called.

In this same *Speculum Perfectionis* there is recorded too that after Francis had composed the *Canticle of Brother Sun*, "he wrote also some holy words with a melody to comfort and edify the Poor Ladies, knowing that they were in great sorrow over his illness". In this letter that he sent to the Poor Clares by one of his brothers he exhorted them to live and converse humbly, and to be of one mind in charity. For, he said, he "saw that their conversion and holy life were not only a source of glory for the Order of the brothers, but also a very great edification to the whole Church". He exhorted them to continue the strict life of poverty they had led from the beginning and asked that the Lord would grant them the grace to persevere in holy charity, poverty, and obedience until death. He admonished them especially to provide for their bodily needs out of the alms the Lord gave them, and to do so with joy and thankfulness. Finally, he said that those who were healthy should be patient in caring for the sick and those who were sick should be patient in their illness. Written as it was after the writing of the *Canticle of Brother Sun*, this letter was written during the summer of 1225, or not long thereafter. There is, however, no record of it in the early manuscripts.[2]

A third piece of writing recorded in the *Speculum Perfectionis*, but which, like the other two, is no longer extant in any other source, is the letter written by St Francis to St Clare during the last week of his life,[3] as the *Speculum* indicates. Clare was sick at the time and thought she might die before Francis,[4] and she longed to see Francis before she would die. Accordingly she sent word of this to Francis. But Francis could do no more than send her a letter to comfort her and to extend to her his blessing,

[1]Translated from Sabatier's edition of the *Speculum*, Chapter 87, pp. 259-260.

[2]*Ibid.*, Chapter 90, pp. 265-266.

[3]Between September 27 and October 3. *Ibid.*, Chapter 108, pp. 309-310.

[4]She lived on, however, until 1253.

15

promising her, however, that before she would die she and her sisters would have an opportunity to see him. His promise was indeed fulfilled, but it was only after he had died, for his brothers carried his body to San Damiano, the home of Clare and her sisters, when they were taking his body to be buried.[1]

We can only regret that these, and other, writings of St Francis have been lost, except for the partial record of them in some of the early sources. Undoubtedly they would have given us a deeper insight into Francis and a better understanding of his ideal of the Franciscan way of life.

3. THE VALUE OF FRANCIS' WRITINGS

The average boy of the Middle Ages received his early schooling at one of the ecclesiastical schools attached either to the cathedral or to the local parish church. For the most part, the curriculum consisted of grammar and training in the Catholic religion. Grammar, however, meant the study of Latin, but a study that extended to speaking and writing Latin as well as to learning the basic rules of grammar.[2] And the training in religion included not only a knowledge of doctrine and practice of the sacraments but also an understanding of the liturgy and an acquaintance with Holy Scripture.

St Francis received this early education at the ecclesiastical school connected with the church of San Giorgio in Assisi, not far from his home. How long he attended this school, or how proficient were his teachers, or how proficient he became himself during these days, is not known. It is obvious, however, from his whole life and in particular from his writings, that he was not the *idiota*, or completely unlettered person, he called himself.[3]

[1] Francis was first buried in the church of San Giorgio in Assisi. In 1230 his remains were translated to the new basilica dedicated to him.

[2] See *The Medieval University*, L. J. Daly, S.J., Sheed and Ward, N.Y., 1961. Brother Salimbene degli Adami, the famous chronicler of the Franciscan Order, in his *Chronicle*, written between 1282-1288, says that he himself spent fifteen years in the study of grammar before being admitted into the Order in 1238. See the Parma edition of his *Chronicle*, 1856, p. 120.

[3] In his simplicity and humility Francis was always inclined to underestimate himself.

Francis' more formal education, moreover, was supplemented by his contact with the troubadours and the jongleurs so often found in cities like Assisi in those days. The troubadours were inventors of rhymes or poems,[1] and they sang their songs of knightly love and knightly exploits in the Provençal tongue.[2] The jongleurs, on the other hand, were not inventors; they simply sang the songs of others, the songs of the troubadours. But they too were important in the life of the day, for they were constantly called upon to entertain at the courts and castles, or at the crossroads and in the public squares of the cities. They sang of Charlemagne, the Holy Grail, Queen Guinevere, and Merlin the magician. They were the popular story-tellers of the day and they brought to the ordinary people a form of culture for which they were hungry.

In addition, Francis was trained also in the ways of the merchants. His father, Pietro Bernardone, was a cloth merchant. He imported his wares from France and apparently did a flourishing business with the wealthier citizens of Assisi. Like many another father, he was anxious to see his son grow up to carry on his business and he tried to instil in Francis a love of the business as well as some of his own astuteness in buying and selling.

Francis, therefore, had a background of training that was at least adequate for the average young man of his day. But once he had turned his heart and mind to God and once the young men of Assisi and of the neighbouring towns began to follow his way of life, he had time for little else but to seek his own perfection and the perfection of those who followed him in one way or another. Whatever he wrote was written to benefit his fellow men and to bring them closer to Almighty God.

Some of his writings, particularly the Rules, were called forth by the necessity of the moment. But in addition to these, there were other writings that welled up and burst forth from

[1] The Italian *trovatori*, from which troubadours is derived, means *finders* or *inventors*.

[2] The Provence was the area along the Mediterranean Sea between the Pyrenees and the Alps. The Provençal tongue was the language spoken in this area. Latin, of course, was the more formal language of the learned, though most had at least some acquaintance with it.

an inner urgency to do good to others and, like the *Canticle of Brother Sun*, to express the depths of gratitude he felt towards the Creator of the world. His writings, however, fill only a comparatively small volume, and most of these, it will be noted, were the product of the last years of his life, when he felt, perhaps more than at any other time, the need to do something while he yet could for the salvation of his fellow men. All the writings that are known to be his and that are accepted as certainly authentic are included in this present volume, along with some in the Appendix that are of doubtful authenticity, and the Rule of the Third Order, which, as it has come down to us, was written, not by Francis himself, but by Cardinal Ugolino, but which undoubtedly embodies the substance of the way of life Francis envisioned for those who are not able to leave the world and live in community, yet wish to follow a more perfect way of life.

Francis' writings were, as a rule, dictated to an amanuensis or secretary, most probably Brother Leo, either in Latin or in the Umbrian dialect. Two pieces of writing, however, have come down to us as autographs, namely, the *Letter to Brother Leo* and the *Praises of God* written for Brother Leo. These two pieces of writing, therefore, are most characteristic of Francis' style and method, though undoubtedly the rest of the writings too, while they are touched up to a certain degree by the secretary or others (as in the case of the Rules), also represent Francis' way of expressing himself. His Latin is sometimes deficient, or even "bad", as Eccleston says of the letter written to the people of Bologna, and he is often repetitious. But his whole method of expression is lighted up with an inner urgency and a deep knowledge of human nature that make the practical advice he offers valuable and even indispensable for a life in Christ and for Christ. And in at least one piece of writing, the *Canticle of Brother Sun*, he rose to such poetic heights that he became an inspiration to many later poets, in particular to the greatest of them all, Dante Alighieri.

It is obvious from his writings that Francis had a wide acquaintance with Holy Scripture and at least a passing acquaintance with some other writings. He quotes, or at least alludes to, passages of Holy Scripture more than two hundred times. Apart from the Office of the Passion, which is made up almost entirely of passages from the Psalms, Francis quotes or alludes to fourteen books of the Old Testament some thirty-nine times and from nineteen books of the New Testament some two hundred times. He quotes most frequently the Gospel according to St Matthew; then that of St Luke; then that of St John.[1] In addition, Francis quotes from such other sources as the Rule of St Benedict.[2]

St Francis' concern for others was not limited, of course, to concern for his closest followers in the three Orders he founded. As a matter of fact, his concern reached out to all clerics and to all the faithful the world over. This is apparent especially from the various letters he wrote, though indeed his other writings too have application to others besides his immediate followers.

But Francis was not a philosopher given to abstract reasoning. He was rather a poet and an apostle, taken up with the concrete here and now of the lives of his followers and of the faithful in general. That is why we do not find in his writings an organized compendium of ascetical or mystical theology, but rather day-by-day admonitions and exhortations to a better life. Still, though he was not a philosopher in the strictest sense of the term, he understood well the aspirations of the human heart and its needs in its struggle towards salvation and sanctification.

There are many things in the writings of St Francis that meet these needs: reverence for the sacred presence in the Blessed Eucharist; lively faith in the reception of Holy Communion; sincere confession of sin; the practice of penance and mortification, and of the virtues of patience, humility, simplicity, purity, and obedience; prayer and confidence in God; love for and

---

[1]St Matthew he quoted sixty-two times; St Luke, forty times; St John, thirty-two times. See Willibrord Lampen, O.F.M., *Archivum Franciscanum Historicum*, Vol. 17, 1924, pp. 443-445.

[2]For instance, in the First Rule, Chapter VII, "Idleness is the enemy of the soul", though this can also be found in St Anselm, *Epistola* 49. He also quoted at least one proverb: "Necessity knows no law" in Chapter 9. He quotes St Bernard several times, for instance, in the *Praises before the Office*: "Tu es bonum, omne bonum, summum bonum". He quotes also from the liturgy.

devotion to the Blessed Mother. All of these things, and many more, are found in Francis' writings, all welling up from the sincerity of a heart filled with love of God and of fellow men. It is for this reason that his writings, even after seven hundred and fifty years, have a freshness that appeals to everyone and an urgency that can lift the heart to union with Christ in love.

Ever since the day in 1894 when Paul Sabatier published his life of St Francis, there has been renewed study of the question: just what did St Francis intend in founding his Order? And, in an effort to solve this problem, various writers have searchingly re-examined the sources for the history of St Francis and his Order and in particular the writings of St Francis.

Sabatier contended that the writings of St Francis are the best source of information about the saint and that the only genuine expression of Francis' will is to be found in the primitive Rule of 1209/1210. The Rule of 1223, he maintained, had little in common with this primitive Rule, except the name; and the reason for this, he said, was that the latter Rule represented, not what Francis wanted for his Order, but what Cardinal Ugolino and the Church forced upon Francis.[1] Hence he saw the *Testament* as in reality a revocation of the Rule of 1223.

Another critic, Walter Goetz, a contemporary of Sabatier, agreed in the main with Sabatier and insisted that the *Testament* was more in line with Francis' thought in the Rule of 1221 than in the Rule of 1223, since the latter shows the strong imprint of Cardinal Ugolino's influence on Francis. Goetz, however, avoided Sabatier's insistence that Francis was victimized by the selfishness of the cardinal, but he did insist, with Sabatier, that the *Testament* was the primary statement of Francis' ideals for his Order. J. R. H. Moorman, too, writing in 1940, considered the Rule of 1223 as but a poor shadow of Francis' real wishes and even the Rule of 1221 as running counter to his ideals.[2]

The *Testament*, however, was not intended to be in any way a complete survey of Francis' ideal of the way of life his friars should live. It did not touch on certain points of observance,

---

[1]More will be said about this under the Rules of the Order.

[2]See the study of this question in *Franciscan Poverty*, M. D. Lambert, London, S.P.C.K., 1961, pp. 1-30. See also Moorman, *The Sources for the Life of St Francis of Assisi*, p. 31 and the following.

though it stressed in a special way the strong prohibition not to seek favours at the papal court and the equally strong prohibition not to put glosses on the Rule. But it did not so much as mention the capital precept of the Rule not to accept coins or money.[1] The *Testament*, therefore, cannot be given the pre-eminence given it by these earlier critics, but it must be considered simply for what it is: not another Rule, but simply a reminder, admonition, exhortation, and testament or last will of St Francis.[2]

The fact is, as will be noted again in the discussion of the several forms of the Rule, there were not three Rules, but only one. The so-called First Rule of 1221 was simply the primitive Rule expanded by additions that became necessary during the first decade of the Order's existence. The Rule of 1223 was the Rule of 1221 stated in more precise and more legal terminology. And the *Testament* was the final appeal of St Francis for a perfect observance of the Franciscan Rule and the Franciscan way of life.

Both the Rule and the *Testament*, therefore, are important for a complete understanding of what Francis intended his Order to be. And so too are the rest of Francis' writings. It is true, of course, that there is little of a biographical nature in any of these writings. They simply were not intended for anything like that. Still, it would be a great mistake to disregard these writings in constructing a biography of the saint. For, while they do not yield any statistical information, they do reveal his personality and spirit. That is why his first biographer, Thomas of Celano, referred so frequently to his writings and quoted from them. And what they do reveal of Francis is the fact that he was completely human, yet just as completely transformed into a saint and mystic. They show that his mind understood the truths of his religion and the principles of the ascetical life. But they show even more that his heart was bound to the heart of his Master and that, united inseparably with his Master, he yearned for the salvation of his fellow men.

Francis' writings have an enduring value for everyone: for the Christian seeking his salvation amid the distractions of the

[1]See Chapter 4, Rule of 1223.
[2]See Francis' *Testament.*

21

world; for the religious striving after perfection in community life; for the priest occupied with the cares of his parish; for the biographer, the writer, the poet; and even for little children going about their task of learning how to love God. For St Francis is everybody's saint and everybody's inspiration to a better life and to a fuller realization of that life in Christ, the King and Centre of the universe.

— Fr. Placid Hermann O.F.M.

CHAPTER TITLES

24

Part One

"THE RULE AND LIFE OF THE FRIARS MINOR"

—Rule of 1223

1. The Rule of 1221[1]

EARLY in the year 1206 Francis of Assisi made his final break with the world.[2] His ways just before this had greatly disturbed his father, Pietro Bernardone, particularly the fact that he had sold some bolts of cloth and had disposed of the money.[3] In the hope of recovering the money and of winning his son back from what he considered his errant ways, Francis' father cited him to appear before the civil authorities of Assisi. But Francis refused to appear there, on the plea that he had already entered the service of the Lord and was therefore no longer subject to the civil officials. His father then cited him to appear before the bishop of Assisi instead. Francis respected this summons, and there, in the presence of his father and the bishop, he stripped off his garments and cast them at the feet of his father, saying: "From now on I can freely say *Our Father who art in heaven*, not *father Peter Bernardone*."[4]

Thereafter, Francis gave himself wholly to the service of God. During the next several years, he laboured to restore several churches in the neighbourhood, first the church of San Damiano, then that of San Pietro, not far from Assisi,[5] then the little church of St Mary of the Angels, deep in the woods near Assisi. By the time he had finished this work, he was within the third year of his conversion, as Thomas of Celano says.[6]

[1]The First Rule is found in the important Ognissanti MS. (14th century) and in a number of other early manuscripts, especially the codex at the College of St Anthony in Rome (14th cent.), the codex 1/25 at the College of St Isidore in Rome (14th cent.). There can be no question concerning its authenticity.

[2]The date is based upon Celano's statement that Francis died in the twentieth year after his conversion. *I Cel.*, 119.

[3]*I Cel.*, 9.

[4]*Ibid.*, 14-15, and *II Cel.*, 12.

[5]At that time just outside the walls of the city, now within the city.

[6]*I Cel.*, 21.

About this time, he attended Mass one day at St Mary of the Angels, or the Porziuncola, as it was called. There he heard the Gospel of the Mass read that admonished: *And as you go, preach the message, "The kingdom of heaven is at hand." Cure the sick, raise the dead, cleanse the lepers, cast out devils. Freely have you received, freely give. Do not keep gold, or silver, or money in your girdles, no wallet for your journey, nor two tunics, nor sandals, nor staff; for the labourer deserves his living* (Mt. 10: 7-12).[1] This, Francis said, is what I want. And immediately he exchanged the hermit's garment he was wearing[2] for a rough tunic of a simple peasant, a rope about his waist, and his feet unshod.[3]

Soon, however, other young men took notice of Francis and asked to join him in his way of life. The first of these was Bernard of Quintavalle, then Peter Catani, then Giles of Assisi.[4] And by April of the next year, 1209, the number of those who had joined Francis had reached eleven.[5] At first Francis had no thought of following a particular rule of life. But when he saw that the number of his followers was growing steadily, he realized that some rule of life would be necessary and that this rule of life would need the approval of the Church.

Accordingly, he put together a short Rule and had it written down in simple and few words, made up for the most part of passages from Holy Scripture, with some other things added that were necessary for a proper norm of living.[6] Then he went with his companions to Rome to seek the approbation of the Holy See. There, after some delay and some discussion, he was able to persuade Pope Innocent III to approve orally the Rule he had drawn up. This was April 16, 1209. This short Rule, however, is no longer extant in its original form.[7] But it was the norm of life

---

[1] Most probably this was the feast of St Matthias, February 28, 1208.

[2] *I Cel.*, 21. He probably wore a tunic, a leather girdle, and shoes, and carried a staff.

[3] *Ibid.*, 22.

[4] *Ibid.*, 24-25.

[5] *Ibid.*, 32-33.

[6] *Ibid.*, 32.

[7] Various attempts have been made to reconstruct the early Rule. One of the most successful is that of Fr Dominic Mandic, O.F.M., in *De Legislatione Antiqua O.F.M. 1210-1221*, Mostar, 1924, pp. 122-123.

for the friars for the next decade or so, supplemented by the constant example of Francis himself.

As time went on, though, and the number of friars grew and their activity began to extend to other countries beyond Italy, some additions to this primitive Rule became necessary. These additions were made at the general chapters of the friars,[1] where new problems were discussed and solutions adopted with the advice and approval of representatives of the Holy See who were present at these chapters.[2]

The *Legend of the Three Companions* tells us that at these general chapters too Francis gave the friars "admonitions, corrections, and precepts, as it seemed good to him according to the counsel of the Lord".[3] Among other things he admonished them especially to show reverence to the Blessed Eucharist and towards priests, to recite the Divine Office with reverence and devotion, not to judge those who live sumptuously, to have respect for one another, to walk in the world in such a way as to glorify God and not to provoke others to anger and scandal, and not to be overly severe in their own practice of penance. Some of these things found their way into the first revision of the Rule in 1221.

Moreover, Thomas of Celano makes mention of one admonition in particular that was incorporated into the Rule. He says: "So much, however, did he love a man who was full of spiritual joy that he had these words written down as an admonition to all at a certain general chapter: 'Let the brothers beware lest they show themselves outwardly gloomy and sad hypocrites; but let

[1] In the early days of the Order, a general chapter was a meeting of all the friars at the Porziuncola twice each year, at Pentecost and on the Feast of St Michael, the Archangel. See the *Legend of the Three Companions*, Chapter 14. But the first Rule determined: "All the ministers are bound to attend the chapter at St Mary's of the Porziuncola at Pentecost, those from overseas or beyond the Alps once every three years, and the others once each year, unless the Minister General . . . has made some other arrangements." But it made allowance also for the provincial ministers to meet each year on the feast of St Michael with the friars of their own province. The Rule of 1223 provided for a general chapter every three years and for a provincial chapter once in the same year after the Pentecost general chapter.

[2] See the discussion of this point in Fr Dominic Mandic's book mentioned in the last note but one, pp. 53-59.

[3] See the *Legend of the Three Companions*, Chapter 14.

them show themselves joyful in the Lord, cheerful and suitably gracious.' "[1] And at least two additions were made to the primitive Rule by order of Pope Honorius III, namely, the obligation of the year of the novitiate[2] and the prohibition against roaming "about the world beyond the limits of obedience".[3]

By 1221, therefore, there was need for revising the Rule and for putting greater order into it. The Order had been divided into provinces in 1217 and the office of minister provincial instituted.[4] Moreover, certain abuses had crept in, especially while Francis was in the Orient in 1219.[5] There was need, therefore, to determine more precisely the office of the ministers and to make the Rule a more effective instrument for the direction of the members of the Order.[6] Accordingly, Francis set about during the years 1220 and 1221 to draw up a revision of the original Rule and to bring it into harmony with the needs of the day.

When he had finished the revision, he gave it to Brother Caesar of Speyer to check it over and to embellish it with quotations from Holy Scripture.[7] Brother Caesar did this, and the result was the so-called *First Rule of 1221*. It was not, however, presented to the Holy See for approbation, in part at least because it was in

[1] *II Cel.*, 128. Also Chapter 7, of the First Rule.

[2] First Rule, Chapter 2.

[3] *Ibid.* This provision and the preceding one were contained in the Bull of Honorius III *Cum secundum consilium*, Sept. 22, 1220.

[4] In the Franciscan Order a minister general rules the whole Order. The single provinces of the Order are ruled by a provincial minister. At times, especially in the earlier days of the Order, a province was divided into custodies for more efficient government and a custos ruled each custody, but under the provincial minister of the whole area. The individual friaries are ruled by guardians; the smaller houses by a praeses.

[5] At a chapter held under Brother Matthew of Narni and Brother Gregory of Naples, Francis' representatives while he was in the Orient, some new constitutions were introduced not in accordance with the Rule. Moreover, Brother Philip had been seeking privileges from the Holy See for the Poor Clares, and Brother John Capella wanted to found an Order for lepers, both male and female. See Brother Jordan of Giano, *Chronicle*, English translation in *XIIIth Century Chronicles*, nos. 11-13.

[6] The First Rule, however, speaks only of the Minister General and of *ministers* in general; in the Second Rule appears the term *provincial minister*.

[7] See Brother Jordan's *Chronicle*, no. 15.

essence the same Rule approved orally in 1209, with some additions, and in part, no doubt, because it was not considered set in sufficiently legal terminology to satisfy the Holy See as a final expression of the Rule of a young Order.

This Rule, of course, has no legal standing today.[1] But it does have an importance and real value, especially for the members of the Franciscan Order and the students of its spirit, for, without a doubt, it set down at some length and in detail Francis' ideal of the way of life he would have his friars live.

THE RULE OF 1221

IN THE NAME of the Father and of the Son and of the Holy Spirit. Amen. This is the life Brother Francis asked to be permitted him and approved by the lord Pope Innocent. The Pope granted his request and approved the Rule for him and for his friars, present and to come.

Brother Francis and his successors as head of this Order must promise obedience and reverence to his holiness Pope Innocent and his successors. The other friars are bound to obey Brother Francis and his successors.

Chapter 1. *The friars are to live in obedience, without property, and in chastity*

The Rule and life of the friars is to live in obedience, in chastity and without property, following the teaching and the footsteps of our Lord Jesus Christ who says, *If thou wilt be perfect, go, sell what thou hast, and give to the poor, and thou shalt have treasure in heaven; and come, follow me* (Mt. 19: 21); and, *If anyone wishes to come after me, let him deny himself, and take up his cross, and follow me* (Mt. 16: 24). Elsewhere he says, *If anyone comes to me and does not hate his father and mother, and wife and children, and brothers and sisters, yes, and even his own life, he cannot be my disciple* (Lk. 14: 26). *And everyone who has left house, or brothers, or sisters, or father, or mother, or wife, or children, or lands, for my name's*

---

[1]It was soon revised again and superseded by the final Rule of 1223.

sake, shall receive a hundredfold, and shall possess life everlasting (Mt. 19: 29).

Chapter 2. *Of the reception and clothing of the friars*

If anyone is inspired by God to live our life and comes to our brothers, they should welcome him; and if they see that he is determined to profess our Rule, they should bring him to their minister as soon as possible, being very careful not to interfere in his temporal affairs in any way. The minister, for his part, should receive him kindly and encourage him and tell him all about our way of life. When that has been done, the candidate should sell all his possessions and give the money to the poor, if he is willing and able to do so in conscience and without hindrance. The friars and their ministers, however, should be careful not to interfere in his affairs in any way; they must not accept any money from him, either personally or through an intermediary. But if they are in want, the friars could accept other material goods for their needs, just like the rest of the poor, but not money.

When the postulant returns, the minister should clothe him as a novice for a year, giving him two tunics without a hood, a cord and trousers, and a caperon[1] reaching to the cord. When the year fixed for the novitiate is over, he should be allowed to profess obedience; and once that has been done, he may not change to another Order, or wander about beyond the limits of obedience, as the pope has commanded.[2] The Gospel tells us, *No one, having put his hand to the plough and looking back, is fit for the kingdom of God* (Lk. 9: 62).

If anyone who seeks admission to the Order cannot dispose of his property without hindrance, although he is spiritually minded to do so, he should leave it all behind him, and that is enough.

[1]The caperon was a kind of upper garment extending down to the cord. All that remains of it today is a narrow strip of cloth that is attached to the front of the novice's capuche.

[2]In the Bull *Cum secundum consilium*, 1220.

No candidate may be received contrary to the norms and prescriptions of the Church.

The friars who have already made their profession of obedience may have one habit with a hood and, if necessary, another without a hood. They may also have a cord and trousers. All the friars must wear poor clothes and they can patch them with pieces of sackcloth and other material, with God's blessing. As our Lord tells us in the Gospel, *Those who wear fine clothes and live in luxury are in the houses of kings* (Lk. 7: 25).

And even though people may call them hypocrites, the friars should never cease doing good. They should avoid expensive clothes in this world in order that they may have something to wear in the kingdom of heaven (Mt. 22: 11).

Chapter 3. The Divine Office and fasting

Our Lord tells us in the Gospel, *This kind* [of evil spirits] *can be cast out in no way except by prayer and fasting* (Mk 9: 28), and in another place, *When you fast, do not look gloomy like the hypocrites* (Mt. 6: 16). And so all the friars, both clerics and lay brothers, must say the Divine Office[1] with the praises and prayers, as they are obliged to.

The clerics should celebrate the liturgy, praying for the

[1]The whole question of the early liturgical practice in the Order is involved with many historical difficulties. The first friars, with the exception of Sylvester, who had been a priest in Assisi, and Peter Catani, who had been a canon of a cathedral, had only the first tonsure. Most of them, therefore, did not know how to say the Office. Still Francis said in his *Testament*: "Those of us who were clerics said the Office like other clerics, while the lay brothers said the *Our Father*". Undoubtedly they said some form of Office from the beginning, though of course there was no question of chanting the Office in choir, since for many years they had no choirs. After Francis had become a deacon (sometime between 1209 and 1216, according to Michael Bihl, O.F.M. See *Archivum Franciscanum Historicum*, Vol. 20, 1927, pp. 193-196), he, like Sylvester and Peter and the other clerics who were joining the Order, had to say the prescribed Office of clerics and priests. But, as the number of clerics increased, they and the more educated among the lay brothers wanted portos or portable breviaries to say the Office. The Rule of 1221 is rather confused in the way it prescribes the liturgical prayers to be

living and the dead, like the clerics of the Roman Curia. Each day they should say the *Miserere* (Psalm 50) and one *Our Father* for the faults and failings of the friars, together with the *De Profundis* (Psalm 129) and an *Our Father* for the dead friars.

They may have only those books which are necessary for their religious exercises. The lay brothers who can read the psalter may have a copy of it, but those who cannot read are not allowed to have one.

The lay brothers are to say the *Creed* and twenty-four *Our Fathers* with the *Glory be to the Father* for Matins. For Lauds they are to say five; for Prime the *Creed* and seven *Our Fathers* together with the *Glory be to the Father*. For Terce, Sext, and None they are to say seven; for Vespers, twelve; and for Compline, the *Creed* followed by seven *Our Fathers* with the *Glory be to the Father*. For the dead they must say seven *Our Fathers* with the prayer *Eternal rest*, and each day they are to say three *Our Fathers* for the faults and failings of the friars.

All the friars without exception must fast from the feast of All Saints until Christmas, and from Epiphany, when our Lord began his fast, until Easter. The friars are not bound by the Rule to fast at other times, except on Friday. In obedience to the Gospel, they may eat any food put before them (cf. Lk. 10:8).

Chapter 4. *The relations between the ministers and the other friars*

It is the duty of the friars who are elected ministers, and therefore servants of the other friars, to assign their subjects to

said by the various groups in the Order, but it seems to come down to this. Educated clerics had to say the canonical hours prescribed by Canon Law and tradition (including the Gradual and Penitential Psalms for the living, and the Office of the dead). Uneducated clerics and the uneducated lay brothers were to say the *Our Father* principally. Educated lay brothers who could read the psalter (a book in common use among lay people) could have one and could read from it the psalms of the day. (See n. 1, p. 59). See Stephan Van Dijk, O.F.M., "Liturgical Legislation of the Franciscan Rules", *Franciscan Studies*, 1952. Also his book, together with J. Hazelden Walker, *The Origins of the Modern Roman Liturgy*, 1960 (see Bibliography).

the various houses of their provinces. Afterwards they must visit them often, giving them encouragement and spiritual advice. My other beloved brothers must all obey them in all that concerns the salvation of their souls, and is not contrary to our way of life.

The friars should behave towards one another the way the Lord tells us: *Therefore all that you wish men to do to you, even so do you also to them* (Mt. 7: 12); and, *What you do not want done to you, do not do to anyone else* (Tob. 4: 16). The ministers who are servants should remember the words of our Lord, *The Son of Man has not come to be served but to serve* (Mt. 20: 28). They should remember, too, that they have been entrusted with the care of the souls of the friars. If any one of them is lost through their fault or bad example, they must account for it before our Lord Jesus Christ on the day of Judgement.

Chapter 5. *The correction of the friars who have fallen into sin*

It is a fearful thing to fall into the hands of the living God (Heb. 10: 31), and so the ministers must keep close watch over their own souls and those of their friars. A friar is not bound to obey if a minister commands anything that is contrary to our life or his own conscience, because there can be no obligation to obey if it means committing sin.

Moreover, the friars who are subject to the ministers, who are their servants, should examine the behaviour of their ministers and servants in the light of reason and in a spirit of charity. If they see that any of them is leading a worldly and not a religious life, as the perfection of our life demands, they should warn him three times. Then, if he has failed to amend, they must denounce him to the Minister General, who is the servant of the whole Order, at the Chapter of Pentecost, notwithstanding any opposition.

If a friar is clearly determined to live according to the flesh and not according to the spirit,[1] no matter where he is, the others are bound to warn, instruct and correct him with humble charity. After he has been warned for the third time, if he still refuses to do anything about it, the friars must send him as quickly as possible to their minister and servant, or at least tell him all about it. The minister can do with him whatever he thinks right, in the sight of God.

All the friars, both the ministers, who are servants, and their subjects, should be careful not to be upset or angry when anyone falls into sin or gives bad example; the devil would be only too glad to ensnare many others through one man's sin. They are bound, on the contrary, to give the sinner spiritual aid, as best they can. *It is not the healthy who need a physician, but they who are sick* (Mt. 9: 12).

All the friars without exception are forbidden to wield power or authority, particularly over one another. Our Lord tells us in the Gospel that *the rulers of the Gentiles lord it over them, and their great men exercise authority over them* (Mt. 20: 25). That is not to be the way among the friars. Among them *whoever wishes to become great shall be their servant, and whoever wishes to be first shall be their minister* (Mt. 28: 26-28), and he is their servant. *Let him who is the greatest among you become as the youngest* (Lk. 22: 26).

Far from doing or speaking evil to one another, the friars should be glad to serve and obey one another in a spirit of charity. This is the true, holy obedience of our Lord Jesus Christ. The friars who withdraw from obedience and disobey God's commandments, wandering about from place to place,

[1]St Francis follows St Paul: *We have not received the spirit of the world, but the spirit that is from God, that we may know the things that have been given us by God* (1 Cor. 2: 12). Again: *The prudence of the flesh is death, but the prudence of the spirit is life and peace* (Rom. 8: 6). For Francis, therefore, the carnal, the flesh, the body meant what savoured of the earthly, of self-seeking. The spirit of the Lord, of course, is not the Holy Spirit, but the grace of God inspiring one to a proper estimate of what is of God and to follow it. See *The Marrow of the Gospel*, Ignatius Brady, O.F.M., pp. 198-199, and *Die Schriften des h. Franziskus*, Esser-Hardick, O.F.M., pp. 168-172.

can be sure that they are under a curse as long as they remain obstinately in their sin. But if they keep God's commandments as they have promised according to the Gospel and our life, they can be sure that they are really obedient and have God's blessing.

Chapter 6. *Recourse to the ministers, and let none of the friars be called "Prior"*

The friars who cannot observe the Rule, no matter where they are, must have recourse to their minister as soon as possible and tell him all about it. The minister should do his best to provide for them as he would like provision to be made for himself, if he were in similar circumstances.

No one is to be called "Prior". They are all to be known as "Friars Minor" without distinction, and they should be prepared to wash one another's feet.

Chapter 7. *Work and the service of others*

The friars who are engaged in the service of lay people for whom they work should not be in charge of money or of the cellar. They are forbidden to accept positions of authority in the houses of their employers, or to take on any job which would give scandal or make them lose their own souls. They should be the least and subordinate to everyone in the house.

The friars who have a trade should work at it, provided that it is no obstacle to their spiritual progress and can be practised without scandal. The Psalmist tells us, *You shall eat the fruit of your handiwork; happy shall you be, and favoured* (127: 2); and St Paul adds, *If any man will not work, neither let him eat* (2 Thess. 3: 10). Everyone should remain at the trade and in the position in which he was called. In payment they may accept anything they need, except money. If necessary, they can go for alms like the rest of the friars. They are allowed to have the tools which they need for their trade.

All the friars must work hard doing good, as it has been said,

"Always be doing something worthwhile; then the devil will always find you busy",[1] and, "Idleness is the enemy of the soul".[2] And so those who serve God should be always busy praying or doing good.

No matter where they are, in hermitages or elsewhere, the friars must be careful not to claim the ownership of any place, or try to hold it against someone else. Everyone who comes to them, friend or foe, rogue or robber, must be made welcome.

And all the friars, no matter where they are or in whatever situation they find themselves, should, like spiritually minded men, diligently show reverence and honour to one another *without murmuring* (1 Pet. 4: 9). They should let it be seen that they are happy in God, cheerful and courteous, as is expected of them, and be careful not to appear gloomy or depressed like hypocrites.

Chapter 8. *The friars are forbidden to take money*

Our Lord tells us in the Gospel, *Take heed and guard yourselves from all covetousness* (Lk. 12: 15) and malice; and *Take heed of the cares of this life* (Lk. 21: 34) and the anxieties of the world. And so all the friars, no matter where they are or where they go, are forbidden to take or accept money in any way or under any form, or have it accepted for them, for clothing or books, or as wages, or in any other necessity, except to provide for the urgent needs of those who are ill. We should have no more use or regard for money in any of its forms than for dust. Those who think it is worth more or who are greedy for it, expose themselves to the danger of being deceived by the devil. We have left everything we had behind us; we must be very careful now not to lose the kingdom of heaven for so little. If ever we find money somewhere, we should think no more of it than of the dust we trample under our feet, for it is vanity of vanities, and all vanity (Eccles. 1: 2).

If any of the friars collects or keeps money, except for the

[1] St Jerome, Epistle 125.
[2] St Anselm, Epistle 49.

needs of the sick, the others must regard him as a fraud and a thief and a robber and a traitor, who keeps a purse,[1] unless he is sincerely sorry. The friars are absolutely forbidden to take money as alms, or have it accepted for them; so too they cannot ask for it themselves, or have others ask for it, for their houses or dwelling places. It is also forbidden to accompany anyone who is collecting money for their houses.

The friars are free to engage in any other activity which is not contrary to our Rule, with God's blessing. But if there are lepers in urgent need, the friars may beg alms for them, only they must be on their guard against money. So too, they should not undertake long journeys for mere temporal reasons.

Chapter 9. Begging alms

The friars should be delighted to follow the lowliness and poverty of our Lord Jesus Christ, remembering that of the whole world we must own nothing; *but having food and sufficient clothing, with these let us be content* (1 Tim. 6: 8), as St Paul says. They should be glad to live among social outcasts, among the poor and helpless, the sick and the lepers, and those who beg by the wayside. If they are in want, they should not be ashamed to beg alms, remembering that our Lord Jesus Christ, the Son of the living, all-powerful God *set his face like a very hard rock* (Is. 50: 7) and was not ashamed. He was poor and he had no home of his own and he lived on alms, he and the Blessed Virgin and his disciples.

If people insult them and refuse to give them alms, they should thank God for it, because they will be honoured before the judgement-seat of our Lord Jesus Christ for these insults. The shame will be imputed to those who cause it, not to those who suffer it. Alms are an inheritance and a right which is due to the poor because our Lord Jesus Christ acquired this inheritance for us. The friars who are busy begging alms will receive a great reward themselves, besides enriching those who give

[1]Therefore one like Judas.

them. Everything people leave after them in this world is lost, but for their charity and almsgiving they will receive a reward from God.

The friars should have no hesitation about telling one another what they need, so that they can provide for one another. They are bound to love and care for one another as brothers, according to the means God gives them, just as a mother loves and cares for her son. As St Paul says: *Let not him who eats despise him who does not eat, and let not him who does not eat judge him who eats* (Rom. 14: 3). In case of necessity the friars, no matter where they are, can eat any ordinary food, just as our Lord tells us about King David who *ate the loaves of proposition, which he could not lawfully eat, but only the priests* (Mk 2: 26). And they should remember those other words of the Lord: *Take heed to yourselves, lest your hearts be overburdened with self-indulgence and drunkenness and the cares of this life, and that day come upon you suddenly as a snare. For come it will upon all who dwell on the face of all the earth* (Lk. 21: 34-35).

In times of urgent need, the friars may provide for themselves as God gives them the opportunity, because necessity knows no law.[1]

Chapter 10. *The sick*

If a friar falls ill, no matter where he is, the others may not leave him, unless someone has been appointed to look after him as they should like to be looked after themselves.

In case of grave necessity, however, they can leave him with some lay person who undertakes to care for his illness.

I beg the friar who is sick to thank God for everything; he should be content to be as God wishes him to be, in sickness or in health, because it is those *who were destined for eternal life* (Acts 13: 48) that God instructs by sickness and affliction and the spirit of compunction. He tells us himself, *those whom I love I rebuke and chastise* (Ap. 3: 19). But if the sick friar lets his illness upset him and becomes angry with God or with the other friars,

[1] An ancient proverb.

always looking for medicine in an effort to relieve the body that is soon to die and is the enemy of the soul, it is a result of evil in him and a sign that he is a carnal person; he does not seem to be a real friar, because he cares more for his body than for his soul.

Chapter 11. *The friars must love one another; detraction or speaking injuriously of one another is forbidden*

Far from indulging in detraction or disputing in words (2 Tim. 2: 14) the friars should do their best to avoid talking, according as God gives them the opportunity. There must be no quarrelling among themselves or with others, and they should be content to answer everyone humbly, saying, *We are unprofitable servants* (Lk. 17: 10). They must not give way to anger because the Gospel says: *Everyone who is angry with his brother shall be liable to judgment; and whoever says to his brother, "Raca", shall be liable to the Sanhedrin; and whoever says, "Thou fool!", shall be liable to the fire of Gehenna* (Mt. 5: 22).

The friars are bound to love one another because our Lord says, *This is my commandment, that you love one another as I have loved you* (Jn 15: 12). And they must prove their love by deeds, as St John says: *Let us not love in word, neither with the tongue, but in deed and in truth* (1 Jn 3: 18).

They are to speak *evil of none* (Tit. 3: 2); there must be no complaining, no slander; it is written, "Whisperers and detractors are people hateful to God" (cf. Rom. 1: 29). And let them be *moderate, showing all mildness to all men* (Tit. 3: 2), without a word of criticism or condemnation; as our Lord says, they must give no thought even to the slightest faults of others (cf. Mt. 7: 3; Lk. 6: 41), but rather count over their own in the bitterness of their soul (cf. Is. 38: 15). They must *strive to enter by the narrow gate* (Lk. 13: 24), because in the words of the Gospel, *How narrow the gate and close the way that leads to life! And few there are who find it* (Mt. 7: 14).

Chapter 12. *Evil relations with women must be avoided*

No matter where they are or where they go, the friars are bound to avoid the sight or company of women, when it is evil. No one should speak to them alone. Priests may speak to them in confession or when giving spiritual direction, but only in such a way as not to give scandal. The friars are absolutely forbidden to allow any woman to profess obedience to them. Once they have given her advice, they should let her go and lead a life of penance wherever she likes.

We must keep a close watch over ourselves and let nothing tarnish the purity of our senses, because our Lord says: *Anyone who so much as looks with lust at a woman has already committed adultery with her in his heart* (Mt. 5: 28).

Chapter 13. *The penalty for incontinence*

If a friar is tempted and commits fornication, he must be deprived of the habit. By his wickedness he has lost the right to wear it and so he must lay it aside completely and be dismissed from the Order. Then he should do penance for his sins.

Chapter 14. *How the friars are to travel*

As they go about the country, the friars are to take nothing with them for their journey, *neither staff, nor wallet, nor bread, nor money* (Lk. 9: 3). When they enter a house, they are to say first of all, *Peace to this house* (Lk. 10: 5). And they should *remain in the same house, eating and drinking what they have* (Lk. 10: 7).

They should not offer resistance to injury; if a man strikes them on the right cheek, they should turn the other cheek also towards him (cf. Mt. 5: 39). If a man would take away their cloak, they should not grudge him their coat along with it. They should give to every man who asks, and if a man takes what is theirs, they should not ask him to restore it (cf. Lk. 6: 29-30).

Chapter 15. *The friars may not keep animals or ride horseback*

The friars, both clerics and lay brothers, whether travelling about the country or attached to a certain place, are forbidden to have animals of any kind, either in their own keeping or in the keeping of others, or in any other way. They are also forbidden to ride horseback, unless they are forced to it by sickness or real necessity.

Chapter 16. *Missionaries among the Saracens and other unbelievers*

Our Lord told his apostles: *Behold, I am sending you forth like sheep in the midst of wolves. Be therefore wise as serpents, and guileless as doves* (Mt. 10: 16). And so the friars who are inspired by God to work as missionaries among the Saracens and other unbelievers must get permission to go from their minister, who is their servant. The minister, for his part, should give them permission and raise no objection, if he sees that they are suitable; he will be held to account for it before God, if he is guilty of imprudence in this or any other matter.

The brothers who go can conduct themselves among them spiritually in two ways. One way is to avoid quarrels or disputes and *be subject to every human creature for God's sake* (1 Pet. 2: 13), so bearing witness to the fact that they are Christians. Another way is to proclaim the word of God openly, when they see that is God's will, calling on their hearers to believe in God almighty, Father, Son, and Holy Spirit, the Creator of all, and in the Son, the Redeemer and Saviour, that they may be baptized and become Christians, because *unless a man be born again of water, and the Spirit, he cannot enter into the kingdom of God* (Jn 3: 5.)

They may tell them all that and more, as God inspires them, because our Lord says in the Gospel: *Everyone who acknowledges me before men, I also will acknowledge him before my Father in heaven* (Mt. 10: 32); and: *Whoever is ashamed of me and my words, of him will the Son of Man be ashamed when he comes in his glory and that of the Father and of the holy angels* (Lk. 9: 26).

No matter where they are, the friars must always remember that they have given themselves up completely and handed over their whole selves to our Lord Jesus Christ, and so they should be prepared to expose themselves to every enemy, visible or invisible, for love of him. He himself tells us, *He who loses his life for my sake will save it* (Mk 8: 35), for eternal life. *Blessed are they who suffer persecution for justice' sake, for theirs is the kingdom of heaven* (Mt. 5: 10). *If they have persecuted me, they will persecute you also* (Jn 15: 20). *When they persecute you in one town, flee to another* (Mt. 10: 23). *Blessed are you when men reproach you, and persecute you, and, speaking falsely, say all manner of evil against you, for my sake* (Mt. 5: 11). *Rejoice on that day and exult, for behold your reward is great in heaven* (Lk. 6: 23). *I say to you, my friends: Do not be afraid of those who kill the body, and after that have nothing more that they can do* (Lk. 12, 4). *Take care that you do not be alarmed* (Mt. 24: 6). *By your patience you will win your souls* (Lk. 21: 19). *He who has persevered to the end will be saved* (Mt. 10: 22).

Chapter 17. Preachers

No friar may preach contrary to Church law or without the permission of his minister. The minister, for his part, must be careful not to grant permission indiscriminately. All the friars, however, should preach by their example.

The ministers and preachers must remember that they do not have a right to the office of serving the friars or of preaching, and so they must be prepared to lay it aside without objection the moment they are told to do so. In that love which is God (cf. 1 Jn 4: 8), I entreat all my friars, whether they are given to preaching, praying, or manual labour, to do their best to humble themselves at every opportunity; not to boast or be self-satisfied, or take pride in any good which God says or does or accomplishes in them or by them; as our Lord himself put it, *Do not rejoice in this, that the spirits are subject to you* (Lk. 10: 20).

We must be firmly convinced that we have nothing of our own, except our vices and sins. And so we should be glad when we *fall into various trials* (Jam. 1: 2), and when we suffer anguish of soul or body, or affliction of any kind in this world, for the sake of life eternal. We must all be on our guard against pride and empty boasting and beware of worldly or natural wisdom. A worldly spirit loves to talk a lot but do nothing, striving for the exterior signs of holiness that people can see, with no desire for true piety and interior holiness of spirit. It was about people like this that our Lord said, *Amen I say to you, they have received their reward* (Mt. 6: 2). The spirit of God, on the other hand, inspires us to mortify and despise our lower nature and regard it as a source of shame, worthless and of no value. Humility, patience, perfect simplicity,[1] and true peace of heart are all its aim, but above everything else it desires the fear of God, the divine wisdom and the divine love of the Father, Son, and Holy Spirit.

We must refer every good to the most high supreme God, acknowledging that all good belongs to him; and we must thank him for it all, because all good comes from him. May the most supreme and high and only true God receive and have and be paid all honour and reverence, all praise and blessing, all thanks and all glory, for to him belongs all good and *no one is good but only God* (Lk. 18: 19). And when we see or hear people speaking or doing evil or blaspheming God, we must say and do good, praising God, who is blessed for ever.

Chapter 18. *The ministers in chapter*

Each year, on the feast of St Michael the Archangel, the ministers and their friars may hold a chapter wherever they wish, to treat of the things of God. All the ministers are bound to attend the chapter at St Mary's of the Porziuncola at Pentecost, those from overseas or beyond the Alps once every

[1] A man of holy simplicity is a man who is not affected by human speculations; he does not calculate nor scheme to realize his purposes; his heart is not divided between God and the world.

45

three years, and the others once each year, unless the Minister General, who is the servant of the whole Order, has made some other arrangements.

Chapter 19. *The friars must be Catholics*

All the friars are bound to be Catholics, and live and speak as such. Anyone who abandons the Catholic faith or practice by word or deed must be absolutely excluded from the Order, unless he repents. We must regard all other clerics and religious as our superiors in all that concerns the salvation of the soul and is not contrary to the interests of our religious life. We must respect their position and office, together with their ministry.

Chapter 20. *The friars' confessions and of the reception of Holy Communion*

My friars, both clerics and lay brothers, are to confess to priests of the Order. If this is impossible, they may confess to any other qualified Catholic priest and they should be convinced that once they have received penance and absolution from any Catholic priest their sins are forgiven, provided that they perform the penance enjoined on them, humbly and faithfully. If they cannot find a priest there and then, they should confess to one another, as St James says, *Confess, therefore, your sins to one another* (Jam. 5: 16). However, this does not excuse them from going to a priest afterwards, because the power of binding and loosing has been given to priests alone.

And when they have confessed their sins with due contrition, they should receive the Body and Blood of our Lord Jesus Christ with great humility and reverence, remembering the words of our Lord himself, *He who eats my flesh and drinks my blood has life everlasting* (Jn 6: 55), and, *Do this in remembrance of me* (Lk. 22: 19).

Chapter 21. *The praise and exhortation which the friars may announce*

Whenever they see fit my friars may exhort the people to praise God with words like these: Fear him and honour him, praise him and bless him, thank and adore him, the Lord almighty, in Trinity and Unity, Father, Son, and Holy Spirit, Creator of all. *Repent, for the kingdom of heaven is at hand* (Mt. 3: 2); remember we must soon die. *Forgive, and you shall be forgiven; give, and it shall be given to you* (Lk. 6: 38); *if you do not forgive, neither will your Father in heaven forgive you your offences* (Mk 11: 26). Confess all your sins.

It is well for those who die repentant; they shall have a place in the kingdom of heaven. Woe to those who die unrepentant; they shall be children of the devil whose work they do, and they shall go into everlasting fire. Be on your guard and keep clear of all evil, standing firm to the last.

Chapter 22. *An exhortation to the friars*

Remember the words of our Lord, *Love your enemies, do good to those who hate you* (Mt. 5: 44). Our Lord Jesus Christ himself, in whose footsteps we must follow (cf. 1 Pet. 2: 21), called the man who betrayed him his friend, and gave himself up of his own accord to his executioners. Therefore, our friends are those who for no reason cause us trouble and suffering, shame or injury, pain or torture, even martyrdom and death. It is these we must love, and love very much, because for all they do to us we are given eternal life.

We must hate our lower nature with its vices and sins; by living a worldly life, it would deprive us of the love of our Lord Jesus Christ and of eternal life, dragging us down with it into hell. By our own fault we are corrupt, wretched, strangers to all good, willing and eager only to do evil, as our Lord says in the Gospel: *Out of the heart of men, come evil thoughts, adulteries, immorality, murders, thefts, covetousness, wickedness, deceit, shamelessness, jealousy, blasphemy, pride, foolishness. All these things come from within*, from the heart of man, and it is these that make a man unclean (Mk 7: 21-22).

We have left the world now and all we have to do is to be careful to obey God's will and please him. We must be very careful, or we will turn out to be like the earth by the wayside, or the stony or thorn-choked ground, as our Lord tells us in the Gospel: *The seed is the word of God. And those by the wayside are they who have heard; then the devil comes and takes away the word from their heart, that they may not believe and be saved. Now those upon the rock are they who, when they have heard, receive the word with joy; and these have no root, but believe for a while, and in time of temptation fall away. And that which fell among thorns, these are they who have heard, and as they go their way are choked by the cares and riches and pleasures of life, and their fruit does not ripen. But that upon good ground, these are they who, with a right and good heart, having heard the word, hold it fast, and bear fruit in patience* (Lk. 8: 11-15).

And so we friars should *leave the dead to bury their own dead* (Mt. 8: 22), as the Lord says. We should beware especially of the malice and wiles of Satan; his only desire is to prevent man from raising his mind and heart to his Lord and God. He goes about, longing to steal man's heart away under the pretext of some good or useful interest, and obliterate the words and commandments of God from his memory. By the anxieties and worries of this life he tries to dull man's heart and make a dwelling for himself there, as our Lord put it: *But when the unclean spirit has gone out of man, he roams through dry places in search of rest, and finds none. Then he says, "I will return to my house which I have left"; and when he has come to it, he finds the place unoccupied, swept and decorated. Then he goes and takes with him seven other spirits more evil than himself, and they enter in and dwell there; and the last state of that man becomes worse than the first* (Mt. 12: 43-45). And so we must all keep close watch over ourselves or we will be lost and turn our minds and hearts from God, because we think there is something worth having or doing, or that we will gain some advantage.

In that love which is God (cf. 1 Jn 4: 16), I entreat all my friars, ministers and subjects, to put away every attachment, all care and solicitude, and serve, love, honour, and adore our Lord and God with a pure heart and mind;[1] this is what he

[1]With a pure heart, with a pure mind, imply freedom from all self-seeking and attachment to earthly goods, not freedom from the guilt of

seeks above all else. We should make a dwelling-place within ourselves where he can stay, he who is the Lord God almighty, Father, Son, and Holy Spirit. He himself tells us: *Watch, then, praying at all times, that you may be accounted worthy to escape all these things that are to be, and to stand before the Son of Man* (Lk. 21: 36). *When you stand up to pray* (Mk 11: 25), say *Our Father who art in heaven* (Mt. 6: 9). Let us adore him with a pure heart for *we must always pray and not lose heart* (Lk. 18: 1); it is such men as these the Father claims for his worshippers. *God is spirit, and they who worship him must worship in spirit and truth* (Jn 4: 24). We should turn to him as to *the shepherd and guardian of our souls* (1 Pet. 2: 25). He says, *I am the good shepherd* (Jn 10: 11). I feed my sheep and *I lay down my life for my sheep* (Jn 10: 15). *All you are brothers. And call no one on earth your father; for one is your Father, who is in heaven. Neither be called masters; for one only is your Master, the Christ* (Mt. 23: 8-10) who is in heaven.

If you abide in me, and if my words abide in you, ask whatever you will and it shall be done to you (Jn 15: 7). *For where two or three are gathered together for my sake, there am I in the midst of them.* (Mt. 18: 20). *Behold I am with you even unto the consummation of the world* (Mt. 28: 20). *The words that I have spoken to you are spirit and life* (Jn 6: 64). *I am the way, and the truth, and the life* (Jn 14: 6). And so we must hold fast to the words, the life, the teaching, and the holy Gospel of our Lord Jesus Christ. Of his own goodness, he prayed to his Father for us and made his name known to us, as he said: Father, *I have manifested thy name to the men whom thou hast given me; because the words that thou hast given me, I have given to them. And they have received them, and have known of a truth that I came forth from thee, and they have believed that thou didst send me. I pray for them; not for the world do I pray, but for those whom thou hast given me, because they are thine, and all things that are mine are thine.*

Holy Father, keep in thy name those whom thou hast given me, that

---

sin. A man is pure if he lives for God alone, if there is no room in his heart for the desires of the Ego or attachment to the world and worldly goods.

they may be one even as we are. These things I speak in the world, in order that they may have my joy made full in themselves. I have given them thy word; and the world has hated them because they are not of the world, even as I am not of the world. I do not pray that thou take them out of the world, but that thou keep them from evil. Sanctify them in truth. Thy word is truth.

Even as thou hast sent me into the world, so I also have sent them into the world. And for them I sanctify myself, that they also may be sanctified in truth. Yet not for these only do I pray, but for those also who through their word are to believe in me, that they may be perfectly made one, *and that the world may know that thou hast sent me, and that thou hast loved them even as thou hast loved me.* I will reveal thy name to them *in order that the love with which thou hast loved me be in them, and I in them. Father, I will that where I am, they also whom thou hast given me may be with me in order that they may behold my glory* (Jn 17: 6-26) in thy kingdom.

Chapter 23. Prayer, praise, and thanksgiving

Almighty, most high and supreme God, Father, holy and just, Lord, King of heaven and earth, we give you thanks for yourself. Of your own holy will you created all things spiritual and physical, made us in your own image and likeness, and gave us a place in paradise, through your only Son, in the Holy Spirit. And it was through our own fault that we fell. We give you thanks because, having created us through your Son, by that holy love with which you loved us, you decreed that he should be born, true God and true man, of the glorious and ever blessed Virgin Mary and redeem us from our captivity by the blood of his passion and death. We give you thanks because your Son is to come a second time in the glory of his majesty and cast the damned, who refused to do penance and acknowledge you, into everlasting fire; while to all those who acknowledged you, adored you, and served you by a life of penance, he will say: *Come, blessed of my Father, take possession of the kingdom prepared for you from the foundation of the world* (Mt. 25: 34).

We are all poor sinners and unworthy even to mention your name, and so we beg our Lord Jesus Christ, your beloved Son, *in whom* you are *well pleased* (Mt. 17: 5), and the Holy Spirit, to give you thanks for everything, as it pleases you and them; there is never anything lacking in him to accomplish your will, and it is through him that you have done so much for us.

And we beg his glorious mother, blessed Mary, ever Virgin, Saints Michael, Gabriel, Raphael, and all the choirs of blessed spirits, Seraphim, Cherubim, Thrones and Dominations, Principalities and Powers; we beg all the choirs of Angels and Archangels, St John the Baptist, John the Evangelist, Saints Peter and Paul, all the holy Patriarchs, Prophets, Innocents, Apostles, Evangelists, Disciples, Martyrs, Confessors, Virgins, blessed Elias and Enoch and the other saints, living and dead or still to come, we beg them all most humbly, for love of you, to give thanks to you, the most high, eternal God, living and true, with your Son, our beloved Lord Jesus Christ, and the Holy Spirit, the Comforter, for ever and ever. Amen.

We Friars Minor, servants and worthless as we are, humbly beg and implore everyone to persevere in the true faith and in a life of penance; there is no other way to be saved. We beseech the whole world to do this, all those who serve our Lord and God within the holy, catholic, and apostolic Church, together with the whole hierarchy, priests, deacons, subdeacons, acolytes, exorcists, lectors, porters, and all clerics and religious, male or female; we beg all children, big and small, the poor and the needy, kings and princes, labourers and farmers, servants and masters; we beg all virgins and all other women, married or unmarried; we beg all lay folk, men and women, infants and adolescents, young and old, the healthy and the sick, the little and the great, all peoples, tribes, families and languages, all nations and all men everywhere, present and to come; we Friars Minor beg them all to persevere in the true faith and in a life of penance.

With all our hearts and all our souls, all our minds and all our strength, all our power and all our understanding, with every faculty (cf. Dt. 6: 5) and every effort, with every affection and all our emotions, with every wish and desire, we should love our Lord and God who has given and gives us everything, body and soul, and all our life; it was he who created and redeemed us and of his mercy alone he will save us; wretched and pitiable as we are, ungrateful and evil, rotten through and through, he has provided us with every good and does not cease to provide for us.

We should wish for nothing else and have no other desire; we should find no pleasure or delight in anything except in our Creator, Redeemer, and Saviour; he alone is true God, who is perfect good, all good, every good, the true and supreme good, and he alone is good, loving and gentle, kind and understanding; he alone is holy, just, true, and right; he alone is kind, innocent, pure, and from him, through him, and in him is all pardon, all grace, and all glory for the penitent, the just, and the blessed who rejoice in heaven.

Nothing, then, must keep us back, nothing separate us from him, nothing come between us and him. At all times and seasons, in every country and place, every day and all day, we must have a true and humble faith, and keep him in our hearts, where we must love, honour, adore, serve, praise and bless, glorify and acclaim, magnify and thank, the most high supreme and eternal God, Three and One, Father, Son, and Holy Spirit, Creator of all and Saviour of those who believe in him, who hope in him, and who love him; without beginning and without end, he is unchangeable, invisible, indescribable and ineffable, incomprehensible, unfathomable, blessed and worthy of all praise, glorious, exalted, sublime, most high, kind, lovable, delightful and utterly desirable beyond all else, for ever and ever.

In the name of God I entreat the friars to grasp the meaning of all that is written in this Rule for the salvation of our souls, and recall it to mind again and again. I beg almighty God, Three and One, to bless those who teach, learn, or have by them this Rule, keeping it fresh in their memory and putting it into practice, as they repeat and perform what is written in it for our salvation. Prostrate at their feet, I beg them all to love, observe, and treasure this Rule. In virtue of obedience, I, Brother Francis, on behalf of almighty God, and his holiness the Pope, absolutely forbid anything to be added to this Rule or subtracted from it; and I command the friars to follow this Rule and no other.

Glory be to the Father and to the Son and to the Holy Spirit. As it was in the beginning, is now, and ever shall be, world without end. Amen.

2. *The Rule of 1223* [1]

THE FIRST RULE of 1221 did not meet the expectations of the friars, especially the ministers and the more learned brothers, for the most part because it was not presented in sufficiently legal terminology and because its regulations were not sufficiently precise. Some pressure, therefore, was brought upon Francis to re-write the Rule, no doubt with the additional advice that, as it stood, it could not hope to be found acceptable to the precise thinking of the Roman Curia as an enduring Rule for a religious Order.

Accordingly, Francis set about the task of producing a more acceptable form of the Rule. The *Speculum Perfectionis* records that he employed the services of his close friend Brother Leo as companion and secretary in the work and Brother Bonizo of Bologna, a canon lawyer, to assure the legal aspects of the work. [2]

[1] The Rule of 1223 is preserved with the papal Bull in the sacristy of the Sacro Convento in Assisi.

[2] The prologue of the *Speculum Perfectionis*, Sabatier edition, p. 1. Ubertino da Casale, *Arbor vitae crucifixae Jesu Christi* (*c.* 1305), says the two companions were Brother Leo and Brother Rufino (bk. 5, c. 5). The *Speculum* says, "after the second Rule written by blessed Francis had been lost", he went to Fonte Colombo, near Rieti, to write another. The ministers, fearing Francis would make his Rule too strict, urged Brother Elias to go to him and tell him in their name that they would not observe it. Elias at first refused to go, but eventually yielded to their urging. When he had explained the situation to Francis, all present heard the voice of Christ saying: "Francis, nothing in the Rule is yours; it is all mine. I want the Rule observed to the letter, to the letter, without a gloss, without a gloss." With regard to the Rule that was lost, St Bonaventure records that when Francis came down from the mountain he gave the Rule to his vicar, who, after a few days, asserted that it had been lost through carelessness (*per incuriam*). Francis then went on to re-write it and eventually presented it to Pope Honorius for final approbation (*Leg. Maj.*, IV, 11). Whatever the case may have been, whether the first version of the Second Rule was lost by accident or by design, it does seem certain that Francis did write a shorter Rule after the First Rule of 1221 and before the final version of the Rule of 1223. See Brady, *The Marrow of the Gospel*, for a discussion of the various Rules.

The revision went on during 1221 and 1222, and by the spring of 1223 Francis was ready to take it to Cardinal Ugolino to get his help in putting it into its final shape.[1] When they had completed their work on it, Francis presented it to the Pentecost Chapter of June 11, 1223. No doubt the Chapter discussed it and made minor changes in it. But what came of it all was a Rule that expressed in briefer and more precise legal form the spirit and the statutes of the Rule of 1221.[2]

This Rule, generally called the Second Rule, was approved by Pope Honorius III in the Bull *Solet annuere*, November 29, 1223. For this reason it is often called the *Regula Bullata*. But it must be emphasized that the Second Rule was by no means a new Rule. Pope Honorius indicated as much in the Bull of approbation when he said: "We, in virtue of the Apostolic authority, confirm, and by these letters present, sanction with our protection, the Rule of your Order, approved by Pope Innocent, our Predecessor of happy memory." In a sense, therefore, the Franciscan Order has had but one Rule, for the Rule of 1221 likewise was simply the original Rule, with additions that were found necessary during the intervening years. Or, to put it another way, the original Rule of 1209, the First Rule of 1221, and the Second

[1] We know that Cardinal Ugolino had a part in the production of this final Rule. He himself says this in his Bull of 1230 *Quo elongati*, after he had become Gregory IX: "We gave assistance [to Francis] in preparing the aforementioned Rule, and in obtaining confirmation of it from the Apostolic See, when We were still holding a lesser office", namely, as Cardinal Bishop of Ostia and Protector of the Order.

[2] That Francis had additional help in constructing the Rule is evident from its style, for the style has an elegance and fluency that are not found in the other writings of Francis. One need only read the Latin passage in praise of poverty that occurs in Chapter 6 to appreciate the artistry of the style: *Haec est illa celsitudo altissimae paupertatis, quae vos, carissimos fratres meos, heredes et reges regni caelorum instituit, pauperes rebus fecit, virtutibus sublimavit (II Regula, Opuscula*, Quaracchi, 1949, pp. 68-69). Or the artistic expression of the exhortation to fraternal charity in the same chapter: *quia si mater nutrit et diligit filium suum carnalem, quanto diligentius debet quis diligere et nutrire fratrem suum spiritualem (loc. cit.)*. Contrast the Latin of this second passage with what Francis wrote in the same vein in the First Rule, Chapter 10: *Et quilibet diligat et nutriat fratrem suum, sicut mater nutrit et diligit filium suum, in quibus ei Dominus gratiam largietur (Opuscula*, p. 39). For a further discussion of this point see *The Marrow of the Gospel*, Brady.

Rule of 1223 were but stages in the development of the one Rule of the Friars Minor.[1]

If we examine the Rule of 1223, we will see that the most important chapters in it are the first and the last. The first chapter sets forth in brief fashion what is explained in detail in the chapters that follow: "The Rule and life of the Friars Minor is this, namely, to observe the holy Gospel of our Lord Jesus

[1]Mention should be made here of the false interpretation some have placed upon Francis' relationship with the Church in these days of the writing of the Second Rule and during the years that followed. Paul Sabatier, in his life of St Francis, took the position that the only true expression of Francis' ideal with regard to his Order is found in the primitive Rule (of 1210, according to Sabatier) and that whatever changes were introduced during the years that followed, up to and including the final redaction of the Rule in 1223, were forced upon an unwilling Francis by the authorities of the Church. According to this view, adopted by some other writers, the heavy hand of the Church interfered with and hindered the fulfilment of Francis' ideal and reduced Francis to a frustrated genius during the last years of his life and made him a rebel against the authority of the Church. Actually, there is no justification for a view like this in any of the original sources. From the beginning it was Francis who took the initiative with regard to the Church. In 1209 he set out of his own accord for Rome to get the papal approbation for his Rule. It was Francis who asked the Pope (Honorius III), probably in late 1220, to give official sanction to the role of Protector of the Order that Ugolino had assumed probably as early as 1217 or 1218 unofficially at the request of Francis. It was no doubt at Francis' insistence, too, that Ugolino assisted Francis in the writing of the final Rule of 1223. Francis' last years were indeed marked by sufferings and trials. He was a sick man physically and he was undoubtedly disturbed by the attitude of some of the friars with regard to religious observance and by the changing conditions within the Order under its growth numerically and geographically, conditions that called for legal restrictions to ensure greater stability for his Order and better living conditions under which a more stable religious life could flourish. But with it all, Francis remained ever a *vir catholicus et totus apostolicus*, a man Catholic and wholly devoted to the Apostolic See (in the meaning of *totus apostolicus*), as the first antiphon of the Office of St Francis, composed by Caesar of Speyer, says. And what is more, the evidence shows that Francis reached the peak of his spiritual happiness during these last years, a happiness that welled up to mystical heights at the stigmatization on Mount La Verna in 1224 and that found expression in his singularly triumphant *Canticle of Brother Sun*, written during the year before his death. See also the study of the question in *Franciscan Poverty*. M. D. Lambert, pp. 1-30.

Christ by living in obedience. without property, and in chastity."
And the final chapter sums up the whole in one sentence: "And
so, firmly established in the Catholic faith, we may live always
according to the poverty, and the humility, and the Gospel of
our Lord Jesus Christ, as we have solemnly promised."

St Francis always felt that the Rule of his Order was given to
him by God himself. In his *Testament* he said: "When God gave
me some friars, there was no one to tell me what I should do; but
the Most High himself made it clear to me that I must live the
life of the Gospel." And he called the Rule "the book of life, the
hope of salvation, the marrow of the Gospel, the way of perfection, the key to paradise, the agreement of a perpetual covenant."[1]

THE RULE OF 1223

Chapter 1. *In the name of the Lord begins the life of the Friars Minor*[2]

The Rule and life of the Friars Minor is this, namely, to
observe the Holy Gospel of our Lord Jesus Christ by living in
obedience, without property, and in chastity. Brother Francis
promises obedience and reverence to his holiness Pope Honorius
and his lawfully elected successors and to the Church of Rome.
The other friars are bound to obey Brother Francis and his
successors.

[1] *II Cel.*, 208.

[2] These words of the papal Bull are prefaced to the Rule: "Honorius
Bishop, servant of the servants of God. To our beloved sons Brother
Francis and the other brothers of the Order of Friars Minor, health and
apostolic benediction. The Apostolic See is accustomed to comply with
the pious wishes and to bestow a benevolent regard on the laudable
desires of petitioners. Wherefore, beloved children in the Lord, moved
by your pious prayers, We, in virtue of the Apostolic authority, confirm,
and by these letters present, sanction with our protection, the Rule of
your Order, approved by Pope Innocent, our Predecessor of happy
memory. Which Rule is as follows."

Chapter 2. Of those who wish to take up this life and how they are to be received

If anyone wants to profess our Rule and comes to the friars, they must send him to their provincial minister, because he alone, to the exclusion of others, has permission to receive friars into the Order. The ministers must carefully examine all candidates on the Catholic faith and the sacraments of the Church. If they believe all that the Catholic faith teaches and are prepared to profess it loyally, holding by it steadfastly to the end of their lives, and if they are not married; or if they are married and their wives have already entered a convent or after taking a vow of chastity have by the authority of the bishop of the diocese been granted this permission; and the wives are of such an age that no suspicion can arise concerning them: let the ministers tell them what the holy Gospel says (Mt. 19: 21), that they should go and sell all that belongs to them and endeavour to give it to the poor. If they cannot do this, their good will is sufficient.

The friars and their ministers must be careful not to become involved in the temporal affairs of newcomers to the Order, so that they may dispose of their goods freely, as God inspires them. If they ask for advice, the ministers may refer them to some God-fearing persons who can advise them how to distribute their property to the poor.

When this has been done, the ministers should clothe the candidates with the habit of probation, namely, two tunics without a hood, a cord and trousers, and a caperon reaching to the cord, unless the ministers themselves at any time decide that something else is more suitable. After the year of the novitiate, they should be received to obedience, promising to live always according to this life and Rule. It is absolutely forbidden to leave the Order, as his holiness the Pope has laid down.[1] For the Gospel tells us, *No one, having put his hand to the plough and looking back, is fit for the kingdom of God* (Lk. 9: 62).

The friars who have already vowed obedience may have one

[1] Bull *Cum secundum consilium*, Honorius III, Sept. 22, 1220.

tunic with a hood and those who wish may have another without a hood. Those who are forced by necessity may wear shoes. All the friars are to wear poor clothes and they can use pieces of sackcloth and other material to mend them, with God's blessing.

I warn all the friars and exhort them not to condemn or look down on people whom they see wearing soft or gaudy clothes and enjoying luxuries in food or drink; each one should rather condemn and despise himself.

Chapter 3. *Of the Divine Office and fasting, and how the friars are to travel about the world*

The clerics are to recite the Divine Office according to the rite of the Roman Curia,[1] except the psalter; and so they may have breviaries.[2] The lay brothers are to say twenty-four *Our*

[1]See n. 1, p. 33. The prescriptions of the Rule of 1223 are very precise: clerics are to say the Divine Office; laics the *Our Father*. The Divine Office was to be said according to the order (*ordo*) of the Holy Roman Church, that is, the use of the papal court, developed especially under the direction of Pope Innocent III. The psalter, however, was to be, not the Roman Psalter used at the papal court, but the so-called Gallican Psalter which was used outside of Rome (the version drawn up by St Jerome with the help of Origen's Hexapla). Undoubtedly, the new prescriptions caused some difficulties, for all clerics, lettered or unlettered, were to say the Divine Office; and all laics, even the educated laics like Brother Elias, Francis' vicar, were to say the *Our Father*. These facts seem to have given rise to considerable disapproval and discussion during the next several years, and some friars wanted to bring about some change in the new rulings. In 1224, Francis wrote a letter to the General Chapter (see Part Two of this volume) in which he asked that the Rule be observed exactly with regard to the Office, and in his *Testament* of 1226 he returned to the subject and branded as "not Catholics" those who wanted to introduce changes into the office. See the article by Van Dijk mentioned earlier and especially his book in collaboration with J. H. Walker mentioned in the same place (under n. 1, p, 33).

[2]Various interpretations have been given to the phrase, *ex quo habere poterunt breviaria*. The four Masters of Paris (during the generalate of Haymo of Faversham, 1240-1244) rendered it as *ex quo tempore* ("from which time"). St Bonaventure as *ex quo officio* ("as a result of this obligation"; *Expositio Regulae*). Angelo of Clareno as *quando* ("when they can have breviaries"). Van Dijk: "because they will have breviaries" (see his

Fathers for Matins and five for Lauds; for Prime, Terce, Sext, and None, for each of these, they are to say seven; for Vespers twelve and for Compline seven. They should also say some prayers for the dead.

All the friars are to fast from the feast of All Saints until Christmas. Those who voluntarily fast for forty days after Epiphany have God's blessing, because this is the period our Lord sanctified by his holy fast (cf. Mt. 4: 2). However, those who do not wish to do so, should not be forced to it. All the friars are bound to keep the Lenten fast before Easter, but they are not bound to fast at other times, except on Fridays. However, in case of manifest necessity, they are not obliged to corporal fasting.

And this is my advice, my counsel, and my earnest plea to my friars in our Lord Jesus Christ that, when they travel about the world, they should not be quarrelsome or take part in disputes with words (cf. 2 Tim. 2: 14) or criticize others; but they should be gentle, peaceful, and unassuming, courteous and humble, speaking respectfully to everyone, as is expected of them. They are forbidden to ride on horseback, unless they are forced to it by manifest necessity or sickness. *Whatever house* they *enter*, they should *first say*, "*Peace to this house*" (Lk. 10: 5), and in the words of the Gospel they *may eat what is set before* them (Lk. 10: 8).

Chapter 4. *The friars are forbidden to accept money*

I strictly forbid all the friars to accept money in any form, either personally or through an intermediary. The ministers and superiors, however, are bound to provide carefully for the needs of the sick and the clothing of the other friars, by having recourse to spiritual friends, while taking into account differences of place, season, or severe climate, as seems best to

---

works referred to in the previous note). Others: "wherefore they may have breviaries". The rendering chosen for the present translation, "and so they may have breviaries", seems to be in line with St Bonaventure's understanding of the words.

them in the circumstances. This does not dispense them from the prohibition of receiving money in any form.

Chapter 5. *The manner of working*

The friars to whom God has given the grace of working should work in a spirit of faith and devotion and avoid idleness, which is the enemy of the soul, without however extinguishing the spirit of prayer and devotion, to which every temporal consideration must be subordinate. As wages for their labour they may accept anything necessary for their temporal needs, for themselves or their brethren, except money in any form. And they should accept it humbly as is expected of those who serve God and strive after the highest poverty.

Chapter 6. *That the friars are to appropriate nothing for themselves; on seeking alms; and on the sick friars*

The friars are to appropriate nothing for themselves, neither a house, nor a place, nor anything else. As *strangers and pilgrims* (1 Pet. 2: 11) in this world, who serve God in poverty and humility, they should beg alms trustingly. And there is no reason why they should be ashamed, because God made himself poor for us in this world. This is the pinnacle of the most exalted poverty, and it is this, my dearest brothers, that has made you heirs and kings of the kingdom of heaven, poor in temporal things, but rich in virtue. This should be your portion, because it leads to the land of the living. And to this poverty, my beloved brothers, you must cling with all your heart, and wish never to have anything else under heaven, for the sake of our Lord Jesus Christ.

Wherever the friars meet one another, they should show that they are members of the same family. And they should have no hesitation in making known their needs to one another. For if a mother loves and cares for her child in the flesh, a friar should certainly love and care for his spiritual brother all the more tenderly. If a friar falls ill, the others are bound to look after him as they would like to be looked after themselves.

Chapter 7. *Of the penance to be imposed on friars who fall into sin*

If any of the friars, at the instigation of the enemy, fall into mortal sin, they must have recourse as soon as possible, without delay, to their provincial ministers, if it is a sin for which recourse to them has been prescribed for the friars. If the ministers are priests, they should impose a moderate penance on such friars; if they are not priests, they should see that a penance is imposed by some priest of the Order, as seems best to them before God. They must be careful not to be angry or upset because a friar has fallen into sin, because anger or annoyance in themselves or in others makes it difficult to be charitable.

Chapter 8. *The election of the Minister General of the Order and the Pentecost Chapter*

The friars are always bound to have a member of the Order as Minister General, who is the servant of the whole fraternity, and they are strictly bound to obey him. At his death the provincial ministers and the custodes are to elect a successor at the Pentecost Chapter, at which the provincial ministers are bound to assemble in the place designated by the Minister General. This chapter should be held once every three years, or at a longer or shorter interval, if the Minister General has so ordained.

If at any time it becomes clear to all the provincial ministers and custodes that the Minister General is incapable of serving the friars and can be of no benefit to them, they who have the power to elect must elect someone else as Minister General.

After the Pentecost Chapter, the provincial ministers and custodes may summon their subjects to a chapter in their own territory once in the same year, if they wish and it seems worthwhile.

Chapter 9. *Of preachers*

The friars are forbidden to preach in any diocese, if the bishop objects to it. No friar should dare to preach to the people unless he has been examined and approved by the Minister General of the Order and has received from him the commission to preach.

Moreover, I advise and admonish the friars that in their preaching, their words should be examined and chaste. They should aim only at the advantage and spiritual good of their listeners, telling them briefly about vice and virtue, punishment and glory, because our Lord himself kept his words short on earth.

Chapter 10. *On admonishing and correcting the friars*

The ministers, who are the servants of the other friars, must visit their subjects and admonish them, correcting them humbly and charitably, without commanding them anything that is against their conscience or our Rule. The subjects, however, should remember that they have renounced their own wills for God's sake. And so I strictly command them to obey their ministers in everything that they have promised God and is not against their conscience and our Rule. The friars who are convinced that they cannot observe the Rule spiritually, wherever they may be, can and must have recourse to their ministers. The ministers, for their part, are bound to receive them kindly and charitably, and be so sympathetic towards them that the friars can speak and deal with them as employers with their servants. That is the way it ought to be; the ministers should be the servants of all the friars.

With all my heart, I beg the friars in our Lord Jesus Christ to be on their guard against pride, boasting, envy, and greed, against the cares and anxieties of this world, against detraction and complaining. Those who are illiterate should not be anxious to study. They should realize instead that the only thing they should desire is to have the spirit of God at work within them, while they pray to him unceasingly with a heart free from self-interest. They must be humble, too, and patient in persecution or illness, loving those who persecute us by blaming us or bringing charges against us, as our Lord tells us, *Love your enemies, pray for those who persecute and calumniate you* (Mt. 5: 44). *Blessed are those who suffer persecution for justice' sake, for theirs is the kingdom of heaven* (Mt. 5: 10). *He who has persevered to the end will be saved* (Mt. 10: 22).

Chapter 11. *The friars are forbidden to enter the monasteries of nuns*

I strictly forbid all the friars to have suspicious relationships or conversations with women. No one may enter the monasteries of nuns, except those who have received special permission from the Apostolic See. They are forbidden to be sponsors of men or women lest scandal arise amongst or concerning the friars.

Chapter 12. *Of those who wish to go among the Saracens and other unbelievers*

If any of the friars is inspired by God to go among the Saracens or other unbelievers, he must ask permission from his provincial minister. The ministers, for their part, are to give permission only to those whom they see are fit to be sent.

The ministers, too, are bound to ask the Pope for one of the cardinals of the holy Roman Church to be governor, protector, and corrector of this fraternity, so that we may be utterly subject and submissive to the Church. And so, firmly established in the Catholic faith, we may live always according to the poverty, and the humility, and the Gospel of our Lord Jesus Christ, as we have solemnly promised.[1]

[1]The following words of the papal Bull bring the Rule to a close: "To no one, therefore, be it allowed to infringe on this page of our confirmation or to oppose it with rash temerity. But if any one shall have presumed to attempt this, be it known to him that he will incur the indignation of Almighty God and of his holy Apostles Peter and Paul. Given at the Lateran on the 29th of November, in the 8th year of Our pontificate."

3. The Testament of St Francis[1]

IN HIS LAST illness St Francis dictated what he himself called "a reminder, admonition, exhortation,· and my testament". This was done very probably during the month of September, or perhaps even on the first or second day of October, just before Francis died, October 3, 1226.[2] Pope Gregory IX, who quotes from·the *Testament* in his Bull *Quo elongati*,[3] says that it was written *circà ultimum vitae suae*, near the end of his life. The *Testament* is mentioned by the early historians of the Order, particularly by Thomas of Celano[4] and by St Bonaventure.[5]

Contrary to the opinion of some authors, as was mentioned in the general introduction to this volume, the *Testament* is in no way a "revocation of the Rule of 1223". That it was such a revocation was the opinion of Paul Sabatier, who held that the Rule of 1223 did not express Francis' ideals and was forced upon him against his will and that the *Testament* was an emphatic proclamation of·his personal ideals. There is, however, nothing in the history of the last years·of Francis' life or in the *Testament* to support such an opinion.

The *Testament* makes no attempt to give a complete summary of St Francis' ideals. It contains no reference, for instance, to the

[1]The *Testament* is found in both the Assisi MS. 338 and the Ognissanti MS. Numerous other manuscripts also have it.

[2]Francis died shortly after sundown on Saturday, 1226. The day was October 4, according to the reckoning of the time, since the day was reckoned from sundown to sundown. According to our reckoning, it would have been October 3.

[3]This Bull can be found conveniently in *Via Seraphica*, Placid Hermann, O.F.M.

[4]Celano quotes directly from the *Testament* (I: 17, 23; II: 163) and refers to it in several other places.

[5]St Bonaventure (*Leg. Maj.*, III, 2) quotes Francis' greeting, "God give you peace", and recalls that Francis said this greeting had been revealed to him by God.

capital precept of the Rule, the prohibition of money. On the other hand, certain of its expressions are more emphatic than any found in the Rule. For instance he says: "In virtue of obedience, I strictly forbid the friars, wherever they may be, to petition the Roman Curia, either personally or through an intermediary, for a papal brief." Again: "I strictly forbid any of my friars, clerics or lay brothers, to interpret the Rule or these words, saying, 'This is what they mean'."

Perhaps the circumstances under which the *Testament* was written account for the unusual severity on the part of St Francis. It was written under the stress of serious illness and when death was approaching and, apparently, under the persuasion that some of his brothers were tending to seek privileges from the Apostolic See and to explain away some of the obligations of the Rule. Ill as he was, and worried too over the future of his Order, he spoke more severely here than was his custom.

As a result of the wording of parts of the *Testament* some doubt arose shortly after Francis' death concerning the obligation of observing this last will of the founder. The question was proposed to Pope Gregory IX in 1230, along with certain doubts concerning parts of the Rule, whether or not the *Testament* should be considered as binding in conscience. The Pope's reply in the negative was given in the Bull *Quo elongati*.[1] The Holy Father, of course, did not deny the spiritual value of the *Testament*, nor did he deny that it deserves the respect of all the friars as the last will of their dying founder. He simply declared that it carried with it no obligation in conscience. Still, the friars of those early days who were inclined to rigorism (the gradually developing body of Spirituals) clung to their opinion that the *Testament* obliged them seriously as the only proper norm for interpreting the Rule of the Order. This opinion, however, has long since been abandoned; but the *Testament* is held in great respect as an expression of the deep wisdom and spirituality of St Francis and of his fatherly concern for those who would come after him.

[1] ". . . *ad mandatum illud vos* [scl. the Testament], *dicimus, non teneri; quod sine consensu Fratrum, maxime Ministrorum, quos universos tangebat, obligare nequivit: nec successorem suum quomodolibet obligavit; cum non habet imperium par in parem.*"

THE TESTAMENT OF ST FRANCIS

THIS IS HOW God inspired me, Brother Francis, to embark upon a life of penance. When I was in sin, the sight of lepers nauseated me beyond measure; but then God himself led me into their company, and I had pity on them.[1] When I had once become acquainted with them, what had previously nauseated me became a source of spiritual and physical consolation for me. After that I did not wait long before leaving the world.

And God inspired me with such faith in his churches that I used to pray with all simplicity, saying, "We adore you, Lord Jesus Christ, here[2] and in all your churches in the whole world, and we bless you, because by your holy cross you have redeemed the world."

God inspired me, too, and still inspires me with such great faith in priests who live according to the laws of the holy Church of Rome, because of their dignity, that if they persecuted me, I should still be ready to turn to them for aid. And if I were as wise as Solomon and met the poorest priests of the world, I would still refuse to preach against their will in the parishes in which they live. I am determined to reverence, love and honour priests and all others as my superiors. I refuse to consider their sins, because I can see the Son of God in them and they are better than I. I do this because in this world I cannot see the most high Son of God with my own eyes, except for his most holy Body and Blood which they receive and they alone administer to others.

Above everything else, I want this most holy Sacrament to be honoured and venerated and reserved in places which are richly ornamented. Whenever I find his most holy name or writings containing his words in an improper place, I make a point of picking them up, and I ask that they be picked up and put aside in a suitable place. We should honour and venerate

[1] *I Cel.*, 17. Bonaventure, *Leg. Maj.*, II, 6.
[2] Some manuscripts omit *here*, as does *I Cel.*, 45. Obviously, however, the sense of these words implies *here* too.

theologians, too, and the ministers of God's word, because it is they who give us spirit and life.

When God gave me some friars, there was no one to tell me what I should do; but the Most High himself made it clear to me that I must live the life of the Gospel. I had this written down briefly and simply and his holiness the Pope confirmed it for me. Those who embraced this life gave everything they had to the poor. They were satisfied with one habit which was patched inside and outside, and a cord, and trousers. We refused to have anything more.

Those of us who were clerics said the Office like other clerics, while the lay brothers said the *Our Father*, and we were only too glad to find shelter in abandoned churches. We made no claim to learning and we were submissive to everyone. I worked with my own hands and I am still determined to work; and with all my heart I want all the other friars to be busy with some kind of work that can be carried on without scandal. Those who do not know how to work should learn, not because they want to get something for their efforts, but to give good example and to avoid idleness. When we receive no recompense for our work, we can turn to God's table and beg alms from door to door. God revealed a form of greeting to me, telling me that we should say, "God give you peace".

The friars must be very careful not to accept churches or poor dwellings for themselves, or anything else built for them, unless they are in harmony with the poverty which we have promised in the Rule; and they should occupy these places only as strangers and pilgrims.

In virtue of obedience, I strictly forbid the friars, wherever they may be, to petition the Roman Curia, either personally or through an intermediary, for a papal brief, whether it concerns a church or any other place, or even in order to preach, or because they are being persecuted. If they are not welcome somewhere, they should flee to another country where they can lead a life of penance, with God's blessing.

I am determined to obey the Minister General of the Order

and the guardian whom he sees fit to give me. I want to be a captive in his hands so that I cannot travel about or do anything against his command or desire, because he is my superior. Although I am ill and not much use, I always want to have a cleric with me who will say the Office for me, as is prescribed in the Rule.

All the other friars, too, are bound to obey their guardians in the same way, and say the Office according to the Rule. If any of them refuse to say the Office according to the Rule and want to change it, or if they are not true to the Catholic faith, the other friars are bound in virtue of obedience to bring them before the custos nearest the place where they find them. The custos must keep any such friar as a prisoner day and night so that he cannot escape from his hands until he personally hands him over to his minister. The minister, then, is strictly bound by obedience to place him in the care of friars who will guard him day and night like a prisoner until they present him before his lordship the Bishop of Ostia,[1] who is the superior, protector, and corréctor of the whole Order.

The friars should not say, this is another Rule. For this is a reminder, admonition, exhortation, and my testament which I, Brother Francis, worthless as I am, leave to you, my brothers, that we may observe in a more Catholic way the Rule we have promised to God. The Minister General and all the other ministers and custodes are bound in virtue of obedience not to add anything to these words or subtract from them. They should always have this writing with them as well as the Rule and at the chapters they hold, when the Rule is read, they should read these words also.

In virtue of obedience, I strictly forbid any of my friars, clerics or lay brothers, to interpret the Rule or these words, saying, "This is what they mean". God inspired me to write the Rule and these words plainly and simply, and so you too must understand them plainly and simply, and live by them, doing good to the last.

[1]Cardinal Ugolino at this time.

And may whoever observes all this be filled in heaven with the blessing of the most high Father, and on earth with that of his beloved Son, together with the Holy Spirit, the Comforter, and all the powers of heaven and all the saints. And I, Brother Francis, your poor worthless servant, add my share internally and externally to that most holy blessing. Amen.

4. *Religious Life in Hermitages* [1]

FROM THE VERY early days of the Church there were both cenobites and hermits among the various groups of religious. The cenobites lived as monks in community life. The hermits lived in retirement to pray and meditate alone. So too from the very early days of the Franciscan Order there were small hermitages where the friars could retire to give themselves more completely to a life of prayer and meditation.

Francis himself always felt drawn to remote places. Even as a young man he liked to go with a certain unnamed companion to a grotto or cave near Assisi where they could talk undisturbed and where Francis could pour out his heart to God. [2] After he had renounced the world at the court of the Bishop of Assisi, he spent the next several years living as a hermit, wearing the garments of a hermit. [3] And when Francis and his eleven companions returned to the Spoleto valley from Rome after their Rule had been approved in 1209, they first discussed among themselves whether they should live strictly as hermits or live a mixed life of prayer and work for the salvation of souls. [4]

But, even while they chose the mixed life of prayer and the apostolate, Francis still wanted a number of places of retirement, called hermitages, where some at least of the friars could lead a life of seclusion and to which others could retire at least occasionally. [5] Thomas of Celano makes mention of such places a number of times, sometimes without giving their location, [6] at other times speaking more precisely of the hermitage of St Urban, Sarteano,

---

[1] This short work is found in various codices, especially: Ognissanti (14th cent.); the manuscript at the Capuchin monastery at Foligno (15th cent.); the Vatican MS. 7650 (15th cent.); and others.

[2] *I Cel.*, 6.

[3] *Ibid.*, 21.

[4] *Ibid.*, 35.

[5] *II Cel.*, 71.

[6] *I Cel.*, 63, 92; *II Cel.*, 46, 168.

Rieti, Poggio Bustone, Greccio, La Verna, and one even in Spain.[1]

The brief instruction entitled *Religious Life in Hermitages* very probably dates from the year 1222 or 1223. The reason for dating it from this time is the fact that it uses the technical term *custos*, or superior of a smaller division of a larger province. It may be that the term came into use shortly after the division of the Order into provinces in 1217, but it does not yet appear in the Rule of 1221. It is only in the Rule of 1223 that the office of provincial minister and of custos are mentioned specifically. Accordingly, it is more likely that this little work was written at a time when the term *custos* was in more common use, hence about 1222 or 1223.

RELIGIOUS LIFE IN HERMITAGES

NOT MORE THAN three or at most four friars should go together to a hermitage to lead a religious life there. Two of these should act as mothers, with the other two, or the other one, as their children. The mothers are to lead the life of Martha; the other two, the life of Mary Magdalen.[2]

Those who live the life of Mary are to have a separate enclosure and each should have a place to himself, so that they are not forced to live or sleep together. At sunset they should say Compline of the day. They must be careful to keep silence and say their Office, rising for Matins. Their first care should be *to seek the kingdom of God and his justice* (Lk. 12: 31). Prime and Terce should be said at the proper time, and after Terce the silence ends and they can speak and go to their mothers. If they wish, they may beg alms from them for the love of the Lord God, like any ordinary poor people. Afterwards, they should say Sext and None, with Vespers at the proper time.

They are forbidden to allow anyone to enter the enclosure where they live, and they must not take their meals there.

[1] *I Cel.*, 61, 94; *II Cel.*, 44, 49, 59, 61, 64, 116, 131, 167, 178-179.
[2] The life of Mary is symbolic of the contemplative life; that of Martha of the active life.

The friars who are mothers must be careful to stay away from outsiders and in obedience to their custos keep their sons away from them, so that no one can speak to them.[1] The friars who are sons are not to speak to anyone except their mother or their custos,[2] when he chooses to visit them, with God's blessing. Now and then, the sons should exchange places with the mothers, according to whatever arrangement seems best suited for the moment. But they should all be careful to observe what has been laid down for them, eagerly and zealously.

[1]The Assisi MS. has *sui ministri* instead of *sui custodi* in this passage.

[2]The Assisi MS. has *cum ministro et custode suo* here instead of simply *cum custode suo*.

5. *Francis'* Form of Life *and* Last Will *for St Clare*[1]

CLARE OF ASSISI, the daughter of Faverone di Offreduccio and his wife Ortolana, was born in 1194. About the year 1212 Clare became acquainted with the new way of life of St Francis, who encouraged her to break with the world and enter upon a life of complete dedication to Christ. In that year, on Palm Sunday morning, March 18, she attended the liturgical functions in the cathedral of San Rufino in Assisi, dressed in all her finery. But that night she slipped away from her home and was received by Francis into her chosen life of poverty at St Mary of the Angels, or the Porziuncola. She then went to live for a short time with a community of Benedictine nuns at the monastery of San Paolo at Bastia, and then at San Angelo di Panza near Assisi. But Francis soon got her a home at San Damiano, where, as her biographer Thomas of Celano says, "she fixed the anchor of her soul".[2] Others gradually came to join her in her new way of life.

Clare herself tells us in her Rule that "when the Blessed Father saw that we feared no poverty, toil, sorrow, humiliation, or the contempt of the world, but rather that we held these in great delight, moved by love he wrote for us a form of life". This *forma vivendi*, or form of life, Clare gives in the words of the first selection given below.[3] She then goes on to add: "And that we and

[1] The extracts given here are found in the Rule of St Clare. The original Latin text of the Bull of Innocent IV (dated August 9, 1253) and of the Rule of St Clare was found in the spring of 1893 by the Mother Abbess of Santa Chiara wrapped in a habit of St Clare and hidden in a reliquary box. The authenticity of the extracts, therefore, is guaranteed.

[2] Thomas of Celano, *Legenda S. Clarae*, 10.

[3] Pope Gregory IX in a letter to Blessed Agnes of Prague, dated May 11, 1238, makes mention of this and uses the term *formula vitae*: "After Clare and some other pious women in the Lord had chosen to serve the Lord in religion, the blessed Francis gave them a formula of life." *Bullarium Franciscanum*, I, 243.

those who were to come after us might never fall away from the highest poverty which we had chosen, shortly before his death he again wrote to us his last will''. This "last will" is given in the second selection below.[1]

Francis himself was the model and way of life for St Clare. Still, Francis undoubtedly gave her and her followers some brief Rule of life from the very beginning. It is not likely, however, that the few words quoted by St Clare in her Rule were the entire *forma vivendi* or pattern of life given her by St Francis, though they probably do contain the substance of what he gave her. The Rule of St Clare, as it has come down to us, is the final Rule prepared by Clare herself towards the end of her life.[2] It is obvious from this Rule that she followed very closely the pattern of Francis' Rule of 1223 for the Friars Minor, for even the wording is frequently identical.

The first of the two selections given here, or the form of life, dates from the early days of St Clare's religious life. The second,

---

[1]See *The Legend and Writings of Saint Clare of Assisi*, Ignatius Brady, O.F.M., The Franciscan Institute, St Bonaventure, N.Y., 1953, pp. 73-74.

[2]St Clare wanted two things above all: first, to live a life of perfect poverty, in accordance with the holy Gospel and Francis' example; and second, to be guided by the spiritual direction of the Friars Minor. Pope Innocent III confirmed for her the privilege of the "highest poverty" in 1215/1216, a privilege that included not only personal poverty, but also, as with St Francis and the Friars Minor, the privilege of owning nothing in common. The original text of this confirmation is no longer extant, but Thomas of Celano makes mention of it in his life of St Clare (IX, 14). Pope Gregory IX confirmed this privilege on September 17, 1228. In 1218/1219 Cardinal Ugolino prepared a Rule for all the Poor Clares, not only for those living at San Damiano; it did not, however, prove satisfactory, though Clare did incorporate some of its prescriptions in her own final Rule. In 1245 Innocent IV proclaimed the Rule of Ugolino obligatory on all Poor Clares but two years later recalled this proclamation and himself wrote a new Rule for them. But since this Rule allowed common ownership of goods, Clare refused to accept it. Finally she prepared her own Rule and ultimately it was approved by Innocent IV, orally, when he visited Clare on her deathbed (between August 1 and 8, 1253) and again by the Bull *Solet annuere*, dated August 9. See *Bullarii Franciscani Epitome et Supplementum*, Sbaralea-Eubel, 1908, pp. 241, 251. Also: *Archivum Franciscanum Historicum*, Vol. 5, 1912, pp. 181-209, 413-447, and Brady, *op. cit.*

or Francis' last will for the Poor Clares, dates from the last years of his life, as St Clare indicates. It is not possible to date them any more precisely than this.

FRANCIS' *FORM OF LIFE* AND *LAST WILL* FOR ST CLARE

(1) The *Form of Life*

Because it was God who inspired you to become daughters and handmaids of the most high supreme King and Father of heaven and to espouse yourselves to the Holy Spirit by choosing to live according to the perfection of the holy Gospel, I desire and promise you personally and in the name of my friars that I will always have the same loving care and special solicitude for you as for them.

(2) The *Last Will*

I, little Brother Francis, wish to live according to the life and poverty of our most high Lord Jesus Christ and his most holy Mother and to persevere in this to the last. And I beseech you, my Ladies, and I exhort you to live always in this most holy life and poverty. Keep close watch over yourselves so that you never abandon it through the teaching or advice of anyone.

6. The Admonitions[1]

The Words of Admonition of Our Holy Father Francis, as the complete title reads in the Quaracchi edition of the *Opuscula*, contains twenty-eight rather short exhortations or reminders to the early friars concerning various points of the ascetical life. They form a kind of *mirror of perfection* for anyone called to follow the Franciscan way of life, for Francis presents in them his ideal of Franciscan observance in the various points covered. They are replete with a knowledge of human nature and with practical good sense.

It is impossible to say how or when exactly the *Admonitions* were first composed, but it is quite likely that they were not gathered together until after the death of the saint. It is known from the *Legend of the Three Companions*[2] and from other sources that at the early general chapter meetings of the friars held at the Porziuncola near Assisi St Francis used to give "admonitions, corrections, and precepts" to the friars. These *Admonitions*, as they have come down to us, may be a collection of these sayings and exhortations given at these chapters, augmented by others given at other times. Paul Sabatier preferred to consider them notes of Cardinal Ugolino and St Francis left over from the original draft of the Rule or not belonging properly to such a Rule.[3] They should, however, be considered rather as a collection of words of advice given by Francis at various times during his life.

THE ADMONITIONS

I. The Blessed Sacrament

Our Lord Jesus told his disciples, *I am the way, and the truth,*

[1]The *Admonitions* are found in the Assisi MS. 338, the Ognissanti MS., a thirteenth-century MS. in the Laurentian library at Florence, and in some twenty-one other manuscripts. Since the manuscripts are unanimous in attributing them to St Francis, there can be no question of their authenticity.

[2]Chapter XIV.   [3]See Goetz, *op. cit.*, pp. 41-47.

and the life. No one comes to the Father but through me. If you had known me, you would also have known my Father. And henceforth you do know him, and you have seen him. Philip said to him, Lord, show us the Father and it is enough for us. Jesus said to him, Have I been so long a time with you, and you have not known me? Philip, he who sees me sees also the Father (Jn 13: 6-9).

Sacred Scripture tells us that the Father dwells in *light inaccessible* (1 Tim. 6: 16) and that *God is spirit* (Jn 4: 24), and St John adds, *No one at any time has seen God* (Jn 1: 18). Because God is a spirit he can be seen only in spirit; *It is the spirit that gives life; the flesh profits nothing* (Jn 6: 64). But God the Son is equal to the Father and so he too can be seen only in the same way as the Father and the Holy Spirit. That is why all those were condemned who saw our Lord Jesus Christ in his humanity but did not see or believe in spirit in his divinity, that he was the true Son of God. In the same way now, all those are damned who see the sacrament of the Body of Christ which is consecrated on the altar in the form of bread and wine by the words of our Lord in the hands of the priest, and do not see or believe in spirit and in God that this is really the most holy Body and Blood of our Lord Jesus Christ. It is the Most High himself who has told us, This is my Body and Blood *of the new covenant* (Mk 14: 22-24), and, *He who eats my flesh and drinks my blood has life everlasting* (Jn 6: 55).

And so it is really the Spirit of God who dwells in his faithful who receive the most holy Body and Blood of our Lord. Anyone who does not have this Spirit and presumes to receive him *eats and drinks judgement to himself* (1 Cor. 11: 29). And so we may ask in the words of Scripture, *Men of rank, how long will you be dull of heart?* (Ps. 4: 3). Why do you refuse to recognize the truth *and believe in the Son of God?* (Jn 9: 35) Every day he humbles himself just as he did when he came from his *heavenly throne* (Wis. 18: 15) into the Virgin's womb; every day he comes to us and lets us see him in abjection, when he descends from the bosom of the Father into the hands of the priest at the altar. He shows himself to us in this sacred bread just as he once appeared to his apostles in real flesh. With their own eyes they saw only his flesh, but they believed that he was God, because they contemplated him with the eyes of the spirit. We, too, with our own eyes, see only bread and wine, but we must see further and firmly believe that this is his most holy Body and Blood, living and true. In this way our Lord remains continually with his followers, as he promised, *Behold, I am with you all days, even unto the consummation of the world* (Mt. 28: 20).

II. The Evil of Self-will

God told Adam: *From every tree of the garden you may eat; but from the tree of the knowledge of good and evil you must not eat* (Gen. 2: 16-17). Adam, then, could eat his fill of all the trees in the garden, and as long as he did not act against obedience, he did not sin. A man eats of the tree that brings knowledge of good when he claims that his good will comes from himself alone and prides himself on the good that God says and does in him. And so, at the devil's prompting and by transgressing God's command, the fruit becomes for him the fruit that brings knowledge of evil, and it is only right that he should pay the penalty.

III. Perfect and Imperfect Obedience

Our Lord tells us in the Gospel, *Everyone of you who does not renounce all that he possesses cannot be my disciple* (Lk. 14: 33), and, *He who would save his life will lose it* (Mt. 16: 25). A man takes leave of all that he possesses and loses both his body and his life when he gives himself up completely to obedience in the hands of his superior. Any good that he says or does which he knows is not against the will of his superior is true obedience. A subject may realize that there are many courses of action that would be better and more profitable to his soul than what his superior commands. In that case he should make an offering of his own will to God, and do his best to carry out what the superior has enjoined. This is true and loving obedience which is pleasing to God and one's neighbour.

If a superior commands his subject anything that is against his conscience, the subject should not spurn his authority, even though he cannot obey him. If anyone persecutes him because of this, he should love him all the more, for God's sake. A religious who prefers to suffer persecution rather than be separated from his confrères certainly perseveres in true obedience, because he lays down his life for his brethren (cf. Jn 15: 13). There are many religious who under the pretext of doing something more perfect than what their superior commands look behind and go back to their own will that they have given up (cf. Prov. 26: 11). People like that are murderers, and by their bad example they cause the loss of many souls.

IV. No one should claim the office of superior as his own

I did *not come to be served but to serve* (Mt. 20: 28), our Lord tells us. Those who are put in charge of others should be no prouder of their office than if they had been appointed to wash the feet of their confrères. They should be no more upset at the loss of their authority than they would be if they were deprived of the task of washing feet. The more they are upset, the greater the risk they incur to their souls.

V. No one should give way to pride but boast only in the cross of the Lord

Try to realize the dignity God has conferred on you. He created and formed your body in the image of his beloved Son, and your soul in his own likeness (cf. Gen. 1: 26). And yet every creature under heaven serves and acknowledges and obeys its Creator in its own way better than you do. Even the devils were not solely responsible for crucifying him; it was you who crucified him with them and you continue to crucify him by taking pleasure in your vices and sins.

What have you to be proud of? If you were so clever and learned that you knew everything and could speak every language, so that the things of heaven were an open book to you, still you could not boast of that. Any of the devils knew more about the things of heaven, and knows more about the things of earth, than any human being, even one who might have received from God a special revelation of the highest wisdom. If you were the most handsome and the richest man in the world, and could work wonders and drive out devils, all that would be something extrinsic to you; it would not belong to you and you could not boast of it. But there is one thing of which we can all boast; we can boast of our humiliations (cf. 2 Cor. 12: 15) and in taking up daily the holy cross of our Lord Jesus Christ.

VI. The Imitation of Christ

Look at the Good Shepherd, my brothers. To save his sheep he endured the agony of the cross. They followed him in trials and persecutions, in ignominy, hunger, and thirst, in humiliations and temptations, and so on. And for this God rewarded them with eternal life. We ought to be ashamed of ourselves; the saints endured all that, but we who are servants of God try to win honour and glory by recounting and making known what they have done.

VII. Good works must follow knowledge

St Paul tells us, *The letter kills, but the spirit gives life* (2 Cor. 3: 6). A man has been killed by the letter when he wants to know quotations only so that people will think he is very learned and he can make money to give to his relatives and friends. A religious has been killed by the letter when he has no desire to follow the spirit of Sacred Scripture, but wants to know what it says only so that he can explain it to others. On the other hand, those have received life from the spirit of Sacred Scripture who, by their words and example, refer to the most high God, to whom belongs all good, all that they know or wish to know, and do not allow their knowledge to become a source of self-complacency.

VIII. *Beware the sin of envy*

St Paul tells us, *No one can say Jesus is Lord, except in the Holy Spirit* (1 Cor. 12: 3) and, *There is none who does good, no, not even one* (Rom. 3: 12). And so when a man envies his brother the good God says or does through him, it is like committing a sin of blasphemy, because he is really envying God, who is the only source of every good.

IX. *Charity*

Our Lord says in the Gospel, *Love your enemies* (Mt. 5: 44). A man really loves his enemy when he is not offended by the injury done to himself, but for love of God feels burning sorrow for the sin his enemy has brought on his own soul, and proves his love in a practical way.

X. *Exterior mortification*

Many people blame the devil or their neighbour when they fall into sin or are offended. But that is not right. Everyone has his own enemy in his power and this enemy is his lower nature which leads him into sin. Blessed the religious who keeps this enemy a prisoner under his control and protects himself against it. As long as he does this no other enemy, visible or invisible, can harm him.

XI. *No one should be scandalized at another's fall*

Nothing should upset a religious except sin. And even then, no matter what kind of sin has been committed, if he is upset or angry for any other reason except charity, he is only drawing blame upon himself. A religious lives a good life and avoids sin when he is never angry or disturbed at anything. Blessed the man who keeps nothing for himself, but renders *to Caesar the things that are Caesar's, and to God the things that are God's* (Mt. 22: 21).

XII. How to know the spirit of God

We can be sure that a man is a true religious and has the spirit of God if his lower nature does not give way to pride when God accomplishes some good through him, and if he seems all the more worthless and inferior to others in his own eyes. Our lower nature is opposed to every good.

XIII. Patience

We can never tell how patient or humble a person is when everything is going well with him. But when those who should co-operate with him do the exact opposite, then we can tell. A man has as much patience and humility as he has then, and no more.

XIV. Poverty of spirit

Blessed are the poor in spirit, for theirs is the kingdom of heaven (Mt. 5: 3). There are many people who spend all their time at their prayers and other religious exercises and mortify themselves by long fasts and so on. But if anyone says as much as a word that implies a reflection on their self-esteem or takes something from them, they are immediately up in arms and annoyed. These people are not really poor in spirit. A person is really poor in spirit when he hates himself and loves those who strike him in the face (cf. Mt. 5: 39).

XV. The peacemakers

Blessed are the peacemakers, for they shall be called the children of God (Mt. 5: 9). They are truly peacemakers who are able to preserve their peace of mind and heart for love of our Lord Jesus Christ, despite all that they suffer in this world.

XVI. Purity of heart

Blessed are the clean of heart, for they shall see God (Mt. 5: 8). A man is really clean of heart when he has no time for the things of this world but is always searching for the things of heaven, never failing to keep God before his eyes and always adoring him with a pure heart and soul.

XVII. *The humble religious*

Blessed the religious who takes no more pride in the good that God says and does through him, than in that which he says and does through someone else. It is wrong for anyone to be anxious to receive more from his neighbour than he himself is willing to give to God.

XVIII. *Compassion for one's neighbour*

Blessed the man who is patient with his neighbour's shortcomings as he would like him to be if he were in a similar position himself.

XIX. *The happy and the unhappy religious*

Blessed the religious who refers all the good he has to his Lord and God. He who attributes anything to himself hides *his master's money* (Mt. 25: 18) in himself, and *even what he thinks he has shall be taken away* (Lk. 8: 18).

XX. *The virtuous and humble religious*

Blessed the religious who has no more regard for himself when people praise him and make much of him than when they despise and revile him and say that he is ignorant. What a man is before God, that he is and no more.[1] Woe to that religious who, after he has been put in a position of authority by others, is not anxious to leave it of his own free will. On the other hand, blessed is that religious who is elected to office against his will but always wants to be subject to others.

[1]In his *Legenda Major S. Francisci* (VI, 1), St Bonaventure says: Francis "had these words continually in his mouth: 'What a man is before God, that he is and no more.' "

XXI. *The happy and the silly religious*

Blessed that religious who finds all his joy and happiness in the words and deeds of our Lord and uses them to make people love God gladly. Woe to the religious who amuses himself with silly gossip, trying to make people laugh.

XXII. *The talkative religious*

Blessed that religious who never says anything just for what he can get out of it. He should never be *hasty in his words* (Prov. 29: 20) or open his heart to everyone, but he should think hard before he speaks. Woe to that religious who does not keep the favours God has given him to himself; people should see them only through his good works, but he wants to tell everybody about them, hoping he will get something out of it. In this way he has received his reward, and it does not do his listeners any good.

XXIII. *True correction*

Blessed that religious who takes blame, accusation, or punishment from another as patiently as if it were coming from himself. Blessed the religious who obeys quietly when he is corrected, confesses his fault humbly and makes atonement cheerfully. Blessed the religious who is in no hurry to make excuses, but accepts the embarrassment and blame for some fault he did not commit.

XXIV. *True humility*

Blessed that person who is just as unassuming among his subjects as he would be among his superiors. Blessed the religious who is always willing to be corrected. A man is a *faithful and prudent servant* (Mt. 24: 45) when he is quick to atone for all his offences, interiorly by contrition, exteriorly by confessing them and making reparation.

XXV. *True Love*

Blessed that friar who loves his brother as much when he is sick and can be of no use to him as when he is well and can be of use to him. Blessed that friar who loves and respects his brother as much when he is absent as when he is present and who would not say anything behind his back that he could not say charitably to his face.

XXVI. *Religious should be respectful towards the clergy*

Blessed is that servant of God who has confidence in priests who live according to the laws of the holy Roman Church. Woe to those who despise them. Even if they fall into sin, no one should pass judgement on them, for God has reserved judgement on them to himself. They are in a privileged position because they have charge of the Body and Blood of our Lord Jesus Christ, which they receive and which they alone administer to others, and so anyone who sins against them commits a greater crime than if he sinned against anyone else in the whole world.

XXVII. *Virtue and Vice*

Where there is Love and Wisdom,
   there is neither Fear nor Ignorance.
Where there is Patience and Humility,
   there is neither Anger nor Annoyance.
Where there is Poverty and Joy,
   there is neither Cupidity nor Avarice.
Where there is Peace and Contemplation,
   there is neither Care nor Restlessness.
Where there is the Fear of God to guard the dwelling,
   there no enemy can enter.
Where there is Mercy and Prudence,
   there is neither Excess nor Harshness.

XXVIII. Virtue should be concealed or it will be lost

Blessed the religious who treasures up for heaven (cf. Mt. 6: 20) the favours God has given him and does not want to show them off for what he can get out of them. God himself will reveal his works to whomsoever he pleases. Blessed the religious who keeps God's marvellous doings to himself.

Part Two

"I DECIDED TO SEND YOU A LETTER"

—Letter to All the Faithful

1. Letter to All the Faithful [1]

THERE IS RECORD of a number of letters written by St Francis. Not all of them, however, have come down to us[2] and not all of those that are at times listed are authentic.[3] But among those considered certainly authentic is the *Letter to All the Faithful*. One of the oldest manuscripts gives it the sub-title, "A Warning and Exhortation".

This letter is an earnest appeal to all the faithful to sanctify themselves by prayer, by the use of the sacraments, by mortification, and by the practice of justice, charity, and humility; to establish peace by the forgiveness of enemies and by love for them; to observe the commandments and precepts of Christ; to show respect for the Blessed Eucharist; and to live the Catholic life in all its fullness. It is especially noteworthy for its graphic description of the last moments of an impenitent possessor of ill-gotten goods.

It is not possible to date this letter precisely. But, in the opening words, Francis indicates that it was written at a time when he was ill and was not able to do any extensive travelling to preach to the people in person: "Realizing, however, that because of my sickness and ill-health I cannot personally visit each one individually, etc.".

Thomas of Celano tells us that Francis made two unsuccessful attempts to go to the Orient, the first "in the sixth year of his conversion", and the second a short time later, "after a not very long time". The first time, late in 1212, he was turned back by an ill wind that drove the ship to the region of Slavonia. The

[1]This *Letter* is found in the Assisi MS. 338, in the Ognissanti MS., and in many other of the early codices. All admit the authenticity of this *Letter* because its thought and spirit are in complete harmony with the rest of Francis' writings.

[2]See the general introduction concerning the lost writings of Francis.

[3]Wadding lists seventeen letters, but less than half of these can be considered genuinely authentic.

second time he was forced to abandon the trip in Spain because of illness.[1] By the time he got back to the Porziuncola it was late in 1214. Some have said, therefore, that this *Letter to All the Faithful* was written during this illness.[2]

In 1219, however, Francis did actually go to the Orient.[3] On this trip he was present at the fall of Damietta to the Moslems on August 29, 1219, and during the temporary peace that followed this battle he met and preached to the sultan, Melek el-Khamil.[4] From Egypt Francis went to Syria and returned to Italy probably early in 1220. This time he again was very ill. Brother Jordan of Giano records in his *Chronicle* that he was very weak from the journey when he returned.[5] Some, therefore, place this letter during this period of Francis' life, on the added consideration too that it contains some similarities in content and expression to the First Rule of 1221.

There was, of course, the third period of serious illness in Francis' life, and that was the period of the last two years of his life, from the stigmatization in 1224 to the end of his life in 1226. It is probable that the letter was written at this time, particularly because it has much in common with the *Letter to All Clerics*, generally conceded to have been written at this later date, and with Francis' final *Testament* of 1226. These last several years were perhaps the most fruitful years of Francis' writings. It seems proper, therefore, to assign this letter to these last years of his life.

The *Letter to All the Faithful* has been called the most beautiful and most vivid of all Francis' writings. It is replete with quota-

---

[1]*I Cel.*, 55-56.

[2]Wadding gives the date as 1213. Fr Paschal Robinson, O.F.M., *The Writings of St Francis of Assisi*, 1905, gives the date as 1215. Some writers choose an earlier date because they prefer to see in this letter a preliminary sketch, as it were, of the Rule for the Third Order. It does express Francis' thought for such a life; yet the later date seems preferable, 1224-1226.

[3]*I Cel.*, 57.

[4]*Loc. cit.* Also Brother Jordan's *Chronicle*, no. 10. Melek el-Khamil was sultan 1217-1238. The crusaders had been fighting since May 9, 1218, at Damietta. After the battle of August 29, 1219, Francis took advantage of the peace that had been arranged between the Christians and the Saracens to visit the sultan.

[5]Jordan's *Chronicle*, no. 17. Francis contracted an eye disease and seems to have suffered also the effects of malaria.

tions from Holy Scripture, particularly those passages that seem to have been particularly dear to Francis. The more than ordinary elegance of its style suggests that it has been touched up.

LETTER TO ALL THE FAITHFUL

TO ALL CHRISTIANS, religious, clerics and layfolk, men and women; to everyone in the whole world, Brother Francis, their servant and subject, sends his humble respects, imploring for them true peace from heaven and sincere love in God.

I am the servant of all and so I am bound to wait upon everyone and make known to them the fragrant words of my Lord. Realizing, however, that because of my sickness and ill-health I cannot personally visit each one individually, I decided to send you a letter bringing a message with the words of our Lord Jesus Christ, who is the Word of the Father, and of the Holy Spirit, whose words are *spirit and life* (Jn 6: 64).

Our Lord Jesus Christ is the glorious Word of the Father, so holy and exalted, whose coming the Father made known by St Gabriel the Archangel to the glorious and blessed Virgin Mary, in whose womb he took on our weak human nature. He was rich beyond measure and yet he and his holy Mother chose poverty.

Then, as his passion drew near, he celebrated the Pasch with his disciples and, taking bread, he *blessed and broke, and gave to his disciples, and said, Take and eat; this is my body. And taking a cup, he gave thanks and gave it to them, saying, This is my blood of the new covenant, which is being shed for many unto the forgiveness of sins* (Mt. 26: 26-29). And he prayed to his Father, too, saying, *Father, if it is possible, let this cup pass away from me* (Mt. 26: 39); and his sweat fell to the ground like thick drops of blood (cf. Lk. 22: 44). Yet he bowed to his Father's will and said, *Father, thy will be done; yet not as I will, but as thou willest* (Mt. 26: 42 and 39). And it was the Father's will that his blessed and glorious Son, whom he gave to us and who was born for our sake, should offer himself by his own blood as a sacrifice and victim on the altar of the cross; and this, not for himself, through whom *all things were made* (Jn 1: 3), but for our sins, *leaving* us *an example that* we *may follow in his steps* (1 Pet. 2: 21). It is the Father's will that we should all be saved by the Son, and that we should receive him with a pure heart and chaste body. But very few are anxious to receive him, or want to be saved by him, although his *yoke is easy, and* his *burden light* (Mt. 11: 30).

All those who refuse to *taste and see how good the Lord is* (Ps. 33: 9) and who love *the darkness rather than the light* (Jn. 3: 19) are under a curse. It is God's commandments they refuse to obey and so it is of them the Prophet says, *You rebuke the accursed proud who turn away from your commands* (Ps. 118: 21). On the other hand, those who love God are happy and blessed. They do as our Lord himself tells us in the Gospel, *Thou shalt love the Lord thy God with thy whole heart, and with thy whole soul, . . . and thy neighbour as thyself* (Mt. 22: 37-39). We must love God, then, and adore him with a pure heart and mind, because this is what he seeks above all else, as he tells us, *True worshippers will worship the Father in spirit and in truth* (Jn 4: 23). All *who worship him must worship him in spirit and in truth* (Jn 4: 24). We should praise him and pray to him day and night, saying, *Our Father, who art in heaven* (Mt. 6: 9), because we *must always pray and not lose heart* (Lk. 18: 1).

And moreover, we should confess all our sins to a priest and receive from him the Body and Blood of our Lord Jesus Christ. The man who does not eat his flesh and drink his blood cannot enter into the kingdom of God (cf. Jn 6: 54). Only he must eat and drink worthily because *he who eats and drinks unworthily, without distinguishing the body, eats and drinks judgement to himself* (1 Cor. 11: 29); that is, if he sees no difference between it and other food.

Besides this, we must *bring forth therefore fruits befitting repentance* (Lk. 3: 8) and love our neighbours as ourselves. Anyone who will not or cannot love his neighbour as himself should at least do him good and not do him any harm.

Those who have been entrusted with the power of judging

others should pass judgement mercifully, just as they themselves hope to obtain mercy from God. *For judgement is without mercy to him who has not shown mercy* (James 2: 13). We must be charitable, too, and humble, and give alms, because they wash the stains of sin from our souls. We lose everything which we leave behind us in this world; we can bring with us only the right to a reward for our charity and the alms we have given. For these we shall receive a reward, a just retribution from God.

We are also bound to fast and avoid vice and sin, taking care not to give way to excess in food and drink, and we must be Catholics. We should visit churches often and show great reverence for the clergy, not just for them personally, for they may be sinners, but because of their high office, for it is they who administer the most holy Body and Blood of our Lord Jesus Christ. They offer It in sacrifice at the altar, and it is they who receive It and administer It to others. We should realize, too, that no one can be saved except by the Blood of our Lord Jesus Christ and by the holy words of God, and it is the clergy who tell us his words and administer the Blessed Sacrament, and they alone have the right to do it, and no one else.

Religious especially are bound to make greater efforts, without neglecting the duties of ordinary Christians, because they have left the world.

Our lower nature, the source of so much vice and sin, should be hateful to us. Our Lord says in the Gospel, It is from the heart of man that all vice and sin comes (cf. Mt. 15: 18-19), and he tells us, *Love your enemies; do good to those who hate you* (Lk. 6: 27). We are bound to order our lives according to the precepts and counsels of our Lord Jesus Christ, and so we must renounce self and bring our lower nature into subjection under the yoke of obedience; this is what we have all promised God. However, no one can be bound to obey another in anything that is sinful or criminal.

The man who is in authority and is regarded as the superior should become the least of all and serve his brothers, and he should be as sympathetic with each one of them as he would wish others to be with him if he were in a similar position. If one of his brothers falls into sin, he should not be angry with him; on the contrary, he should correct him gently, with all patience and humility, and encourage him.

It is not for us to be wise and calculating in the world's fashion; we should be guileless, lowly, and pure. We should hold our lower nature in contempt, as a source of shame to us, because through our own fault we are wretched and utterly corrupt, nothing more than worms, as our Lord tells us by the Prophet, *I am a worm, not a man; the scorn of men, despised by the people* (Ps. 21: 7). We should not want to be in charge of others; we are to be servants, and should *be subject to every human creature for God's sake* (1 Pet. 2: 13). On all those who do this and endure to the last the Spirit of God will rest (cf. Is. 11: 2); he will make his dwelling in them and there he will stay, and they will be *children of your Father in heaven* (Mt. 5: 45) whose work they do. It is they who are the brides, the brothers and the mothers of our Lord Jesus Christ. A person is his bride when his faithful soul is united with Jesus Christ by the Holy Spirit; we are his brothers when we do the will of his Father who is in heaven (cf. Mt. 12: 50), and we are mothers to him when we enthrone him in our hearts and souls by love with a pure and sincere conscience, and give him birth by doing good. This, too, should be an example to others.

How glorious, how holy and wonderful it is to have a Father in heaven. How holy it is, how beautiful and lovable to have in heaven a Bridegroom. How holy and beloved, how pleasing and lowly, how peaceful, delightful, lovable and desirable above all things it is to have a Brother like this, who laid down his life for his sheep (cf. Jn 10: 15), and prayed to his Father for us, saying: Holy Father, in your name keep those whom you have given me. Father, all those whom you gave me in the world, were yours and you gave them to me. And the words you have given me, I have given to them. And they have received them and have known truly that I have come forth from you, and they have believed that you have sent me. I am praying for them, not for the world: Bless and sanctify them. And for them I sanctify myself, that they may be sanctified in their unity, just as we are. And, Father, I wish that where I am, they also may be with me, that they may see my splendour in your kingdom (cf. Jn 17: 6-24).

Every creature in heaven and on earth and in the depths of the sea should give God praise and glory and honour and blessing (cf. Ap. 5: 13); he has borne so much for us and has done and will do so much good to us; he is our power and our strength, and he alone is good (cf. Lk. 18: 19), he alone most high, he alone all-powerful, wonderful, and glorious; he alone is holy and worthy of all praise and blessing for endless ages and ages. Amen.

All those who refuse to do penance and receive the Body and Blood of our Lord Jesus Christ are blind, because they cannot see the true light, our Lord Jesus Christ. They indulge their vices and sins and follow their evil longings and desires, without a thought for the promises they made. In body they are slaves of the world and of the desires of their lower nature, with all the cares and anxieties of this life; in spirit they are slaves of the devil. They have been led astray by him and have made themselves his children, dedicated to doing his work. They lack spiritual insight because the Son of God does not dwell in them, and it is he who is the true wisdom of the Father. It is of such men as these that Scripture says, *their skill was swallowed up* (Ps. 106: 27). They can see clearly and are well aware what they are doing; they are fully conscious of the fact that they are doing evil, and knowingly lose their souls.

See, then, you who are blind, deceived by your enemies, the world, the flesh, and the devil, our fallen nature loves to commit sin and hates to serve God; this is because vice and sin come from the heart of man, as the Gospel says. You have no good in this world and nothing to look forward to in the next. You imagine that you will enjoy the worthless pleasures of this life indefinitely, but you are wrong. The day and the hour will come, the day and the hour for which you have no thought and of which you have no knowledge whatever. First sickness, then death, draws near; friends and relatives come and advise the dying man, "Put your affairs in order". Wife and children, friends and relatives, all pretend to mourn. Looking about, he sees them weeping. An evil inspiration comes to him. Thinking to himself, he says, "Look, I am putting my body and soul and all that I have in your hands". Certainly a man who would do a thing like that is under a curse, trusting and leaving his body and his soul and all that he has defenceless in such hands. God tells us by his Prophet, *Cursed shall he be that puts his trust in man* (Jer. 17: 5). There and then, they call a priest; he says to the sick man, "Do you want to be absolved from all your sins?" And the dying man replies, "I do". "Are you ready then to make restitution as best you can out of your property for all that you have done, all the fraud and deceit you practised towards your fellow men?" the priest asks him. "No", he replies. And the priest asks, "Why not?" "Because I have left everything in the hands of my relatives and friends", is the answer. Then his speech begins to fail and so the unfortunate man dies an unhappy death.

We should all realize that no matter where or how a man dies, if he is in the state of mortal sin and does not repent, when he could have done so and did not, the devil tears his soul from his body with such anguish and distress that only a person who has experienced it can appreciate it. All the talent and ability, all the learning and wisdom which he thought his own, are taken away from him, while his relatives and friends bear off his property and share it among themselves. Then they say, "A curse on his soul; he could have made more to leave to us and he did not". And the worms feast on his body. So he loses both body and soul in this short life and goes to hell, where he will be tormented without end.

In the name of the Father and of the Son and of the Holy Spirit. Amen.

In that love which is God (cf. 1 Jn 4: 16), I, Brother Francis, the least of your servants and worthy only to kiss your feet, beg and implore all those to whom this letter comes to hear these words of our Lord Jesus Christ in a spirit of humility and love, putting them into practice with all gentleness and observing them perfectly. Those who cannot read should have them read to them often and keep them ever before their eyes, by persevering in doing good to the last, because they are *spirit and life* (Jn 6: 64). Those who fail to do this shall be held to account for it before the judgement-seat of Christ at the last day. And may God, Father, Son, and Holy Spirit, bless those who welcome them and grasp them and send copies to others, if they persevere in them to the last (cf. Mt. 10: 22).

2. *Letter to All Clerics*[1]

THIS SHORT PIECE of writing of St Francis is placed among his letters by Fr Luke Wadding, O.F.M., in his collection of the saint's writings. It seems to fit better here than among the writings concerning the Rule and life of the Friars Minor. Wadding prefaces it with an opening salutation: "To my reverend masters in Christ; to all the clerics who are in the world." The older codices, however, do not have this salutation.[2]

This letter concerns itself mainly with devotion to the Blessed Eucharist and the need for proper sacred vessels. It contains an admonition to have respect for the names of Christ and written words.

The content of the letter seems to indicate a date towards the end of Francis' life, the time when the Blessed Eucharist occupied so much of his thinking. Much of it is very similar in thought to the thoughts expressed in his *Testament*. Moreover, the Wadding prefatory salutation adds: "Since because of my infirmities I cannot address you personally, I beg you to receive, with all love and charity, this remembrance of me and this brief exhortation I send you". This too would indicate the period of Francis' last illness as the time of its composition.

LETTER TO ALL CLERICS

WE CLERICS cannot overlook the sinful neglect and ignorance some people are guilty of with regard to the holy Body and Blood of our Lord Jesus Christ. They are careless,

[1]This piece of writing is found in the Assisi MS. 338 and in a number of old codices. Fr Livarius Oliger, O.F.M., discovered an old text of it in a missal of the Subiaco Abbey, the Codex B 24 Vallicellanus; it dates back at least to 1238, and possibly to an earlier date, and may have been copied from Francis' autograph. See his article in *Archivum Franciscanum Historicum*, Vol. 6, 1913, pp. 1-12. There is no question of the authenticity of this writing.

[2]The Quaracchi edition of the *Opuscula* does not place it among the letters, but gives it under the title: *Concerning Reverence for the Body of Christ and Cleanliness of the Altar*.

too, about his holy name and the writings which contain his words, the words that consecrate his Body. We know his Body is not present unless the bread is first consecrated by these words. Indeed, in this world there is nothing of the Most High himself that we can possess and contemplate with our eyes, except his Body and Blood, his name and his words, by which we were created and by which we have been brought back from death to life.

Those who are in charge of these sacred mysteries, and especially those who are careless about their task, should realize that the chalices, corporals and altar linens where the Body and Blood of our Lord Jesus Christ are offered in sacrifice should be completely suitable. And besides, many clerics reserve the Blessed Sacrament in unsuitable places, or carry It about irreverently, or receive It unworthily, or give It to all-comers without distinction. God's holy name, too, and his written words are sometimes trodden underfoot, because *the sensual man does not perceive the things that are of the Spirit of God* (1 Cor. 2: 14).

Surely we cannot be left unmoved by loving sorrow for all this; in his love, God gives himself into our hands; we touch him and receive him daily into our mouths. Have we forgotten that we must fall into his hands?

And so we must correct these and all other abuses. If the Body of our Lord Jesus Christ has been left abandoned somewhere contrary to all the laws, It should be removed and put in a place that is prepared properly for It, where It can be kept safe. In the same way, God's name and his written words should be picked up, if they are found lying in the dirt, and put in a suitable place. We all know that we are bound to do this, according to the law of God and the prescriptions of Mother Church. Anyone who refuses to obey should realize that he will have to account for it before our Lord Jesus Christ on the day of judgement.

Anyone who has this writing copied, so that it may be obeyed more widely, can be sure that he has God's blessing.

3. *Letter to a General Chapter*[1]

THERE IS SOME difficulty in assigning a precise date for the *Letter to a General Chapter*. Ubertino da Casale, in his *Arbor vitae crucifixae Jesu Christi*, completed in 1305, places the letter "at the end of the days" of St Francis. The Assisi manuscript says that it was written when Francis was sick.

It seems certain that the letter was written after the approbation of the final Rule, November 29, 1223, since in speaking of the obligation of the recitation of the Divine Office, it refers only to "clerics". Moreover, most versions of the letter say it is addressed to a "general chapter". If this is so, then the letter should be dated 1224, since that was the last year in which a general chapter was held before Francis' death in 1226. The Assisi manuscript says only that it was addressed to a chapter, not specifically a general chapter. If this is so, then it should be dated some time after the general chapter of 1224. Many local or provincial chapters were held at that time, and Brother Elias, the Minister General or vicar of Francis, could be said to preside over them as the official visitor of the provinces. In any case, the letter must be dated close to the end of Francis' life, and more probably shortly before the general chapter at Pentecost of 1224.

The letter concerns itself primarily with respect for the Blessed Eucharist, and in particular with the proper celebration of Holy Mass and the proper recitation of the Divine Office. In these

[1]This letter is found in many of the ancient manuscripts, including the Assisi MS. 338 and the Florence manuscript (Ognissanti). The Assisi MS. adds in the address: to Brother A, minister general. Some therefore have speculated that the intended minister general was either Albert of Pisa (1239-1240) or Aymo (Haymo) of Faversham (1240-1244). This, however, would destroy the authenticity of the letter, and there is no doubt about its having been written by Francis. Most likely the *A* is intended as indicating the name of the current minister general or of any who would succeed in the office in later days. The Brother *H* towards the end of the letter is undoubtedly Brother Elias (Helias).

liturgical functions Francis insists upon the importance of a pure intention, one that is without any ulterior motives, but only for the honour of God. And the reasons he offers for such reverence in celebrating these sacred functions are truly inspiring. He is most urgent in his insistence upon a devout recitation of the Divine Office, particularly in the choral recitation of the Office.[1] His humble confession with regard to his own weaknesses is characteristic of his whole approach to the spiritual life. Many of the things he says in this letter are stressed again in his *Testament* of 1226.

The letter closes with a fervent prayer for the grace to follow in the footsteps of Christ and so come to eternal happiness with God, the Most High.[2]

LETTER TO A GENERAL CHAPTER

A letter which St Francis sent to a general chapter and to all the friars towards the end of his life.

IN THE NAME of the most high Trinity and holy Unity, Father, Son, and Holy Spirit. Amen.

To all the friars, so reverend, so well-beloved; to the Minister General of the Order of Minors and to his successors; to all the ministers and custodes; to the ordinary priests of the Order in Christ, and to all the friars who are obedient and without pretensions, to first and last, Brother Francis, the least of your servants, worthless and sinful, sends greetings in him who redeemed and cleansed us in his precious Blood. At the sound of his name you should fall to the ground and adore him with

---

[1] Choral recitation of the Office was undoubtedly introduced wherever possible soon after the Rule of 1223. This is evident from what Francis says here. The obligation of choral Office was, however, of later date, probably 1250, during the generalate of John of Parma (Bull of Innocent IV, *Cum tamquam veri*, April 5, 1250).

[2] This prayer is placed thus at the end of this letter in several of the manuscripts, including the Assisi MS. 338. Other manuscripts, however, place it before the letter. Wadding places it separately. The content of the letter suggests that it belongs at the end, for it is a kind of summary of the content.

fear and reverence; the Lord Jesus Christ, Son of the Most High, is his name, and he is blessed for ever. Amen.

Listen, then, sons of God and my friars, and *give ear to my words* (Acts 2: 14). Give hearing (cf. Is. 55: 3) with all your hearts and obey the voice of the Son of God. Keep his commandments wholeheartedly and practise his counsels with all your minds. *Give thanks to the Lord, for he is good* (Ps. 135: 1); *extol* him *in your works* (Tob. 13: 6). This is the very reason he has sent you all over the world, so that by word and deed you might bear witness to his message and convince everyone *that there is no other almighty God besides him* (Tob. 13: 4). Be well disciplined then and patient under holy obedience, keeping your promises to him generously and unflinchingly. *God deals with you as with sons* (Heb. 12: 7).

Kissing your feet with all the love I am capable of, I beg you to show the greatest possible reverence and honour for the most holy Body and Blood of our Lord Jesus Christ through whom *all things, whether on the earth or in the heavens*, have been brought to peace and reconciled with Almighty God (cf. Col. 1: 20). And I implore all my friars who are priests now or who will be priests in the future, all those who want to be priests of the Most High, to be free from all earthly affection when they say Mass, and offer singlemindedly and with reverence the true sacrifice of the most holy Body and Blood of our Lord Jesus Christ, with a holy and pure intention, not for any earthly gain or through human respect or love for any human being, *not serving to the eye as pleasers of men* (Eph. 6: 6). With the help of God's grace, their whole intention should be fixed on him, with a will to please the most high Lord alone, because it is he alone who accomplishes this marvel in his own way. He told us, *Do this in remembrance of me* (Lk. 22: 19), and so the man who acts otherwise is a traitor like Judas, and he *will be guilty of the body and blood of the Lord* (1 Cor. 11: 27).

All of you who are priests should remember what is written of the law of Moses; all those who violated it even in externals died *without any mercy* (Heb. 10: 28), by God's own decree. *How much worse punishments do you think he deserves who has trodden under foot the Son of God, and has regarded as unclean the blood of the covenant through which he was sanctified, and has insulted the Spirit of grace?* (Heb. 10: 29). A man despises, defiles, and tramples under foot the Lamb of God when, as St Paul says, he sees no difference between the bread which is Christ and other food (cf. 1 Cor. 11: 29), or between receiving It and any other employment, and receives It unworthily, or even if he is in the state of grace, receives It without faith or proper devotion. God tells us by the Prophet Jeremy, *Cursed be he that doth the work of the Lord deceitfully* (Jer. 48: 10). He spurns the priests who refuse to take this to heart with the words, *I will curse your blessings* (Mal. 2: 2).

Listen to this, my brothers: If it is right to honour the Blessed Virgin Mary because she bore him in her most holy womb; if St John the Baptist trembled and was afraid even to touch Christ's sacred head; if the tomb where he lay for only a short time is so venerated; how holy, and virtuous, and worthy should not a priest be; he touches Christ with his own hands, Christ who is to die now no more but enjoy eternal life and glory, upon whom the *angels desire to look* (1 Pet. 1: 12). A priest receives him into his heart and mouth and offers him to others to be received.

Remember your dignity, then, my friar-priests. *You shall make and keep yourselves holy*, because God is holy (Lev. 11: 44). In this mystery God has honoured you above all other human beings, and so you must love, revere, and honour him more than all others. Surely this is a great pity, a pitiable weakness, to have him present with you like this and be distracted by anything else in the whole world. Our whole being should be seized with fear, the whole world should tremble and heaven rejoice, when Christ the Son of the living God is present on the altar in the hands of the priest. What wonderful majesty! What stupendous condescension! O sublime humility! O humble sublimity! That the Lord of the whole universe, God and the Son of God, should humble himself like this and hide under the form of a little

105

bread, for our salvation. Look at God's condescension, my brothers, and *pour out your hearts before him* (Ps. 61: 9). Humble yourselves that you may be exalted by him (cf. 1 Pet. 5: 6). Keep nothing for yourselves, so that he who has given himself wholly to you may receive you wholly.

And so this is my advice, this is my earnest request in the Lord: That in the places where the friars live only one Mass a day be said in the rite of the holy Church. If there are several priests in a place, each should be glad for the love of charity to have assisted at the celebration of the other.[1] Our Lord Jesus Christ will fill both present and absent with his grace, if they are worthy. We see that he is present in numerous different places, yet he remains indivisible and suffers no loss; everywhere he is one and the same, and he is at work in his own way with God the Father and the Holy Spirit, the Comforter, for ever and ever. Amen.

[1]It should be stressed that "the one Mass" was to be said according to the rite of the holy Church, that is, the Roman rite. Such a Mass was longer and more elaborate, with tropes, sequences, etc., as distinguished from the private Mass, which was shorter and less elaborate. In the private Mass of those days the celebrant was free to insert personal prayers. Francis, on one occasion, gave this admonition to Brother Leo: "Celebrate your Mass devoutly, and do not take too much time in celebrating and conform yourself to other priests. But if the Lord gives you the grace, go to your cell after Mass and there meditate and enjoy the divine consolation, if it is given you by heaven. I think it is better and safer to do it this way. For because of those who attend your Mass it could easily happen that you have vainglory or some other fault. . . . Otherwise the devil may profit of it by taking away your merit, not to speak of the assistants at your Mass, who may become weary of waiting for you." (*Liber exemplorum fratrum minorum*, 12th cent., ed. by L. Oliger, *Antonianum*, 1927, 203-276.) Some have interpreted this passage, including the words that follow, to mean that Francis wanted only one Mass in his friaries, and they render the following passage as "when there are several priests, one should be content to hear the Mass of another". (See Van Dijk and Walker, *The Origin of the Modern Roman Liturgy*, 1960.) However, there is good reason, as the *Opuscula* editors emphasize, to stress the one Mass as being understood of the Roman rite, the longer type. And, if there are several priests in the friary, then each should be *contented*, that is, happy, glad, eager, to attend each other's Masses, for the Latin *alter . . . alterius* implies reciprocal action. (See *The Words of St Francis*, James Meyer, O.F.M., p. 322.)

Writings of St. Francis

He who is of God hears the words of God (Jn 8: 47), and so we who are called to serve God in a more special way are bound not merely to listen to and carry out what he commands; we must give proof in ourselves of the greatness of our Creator and of our subjection to him by keeping the liturgical books and anything else which contains his holy words with great care. I urge all my friars and I encourage them in Christ to show all possible respect for God's words wherever they may happen to find them in writing. If they are not kept properly or if they lie thrown about disrespectfully, they should pick them up and put them aside, paying honour in his words to God who spoke them. God's words sanctify numerous objects, and it is by the power of the words of Christ that the sacrament of the altar is consecrated.

I confess all my sins to God, Father, Son, and Holy Spirit; to blessed Mary ever Virgin and all the saints in heaven and on earth; to the Minister General of our Order, my reverend superior; to all the priests of the Order and all my other friars. I have sinned in many ways, through my own most grievous fault, and in particular by not keeping the Rule which I promised to God, and by not saying the Office, as the Rule prescribes, through carelessness or sickness, or because I am ignorant and have never studied.

And so I beseech the Minister General, my superior, to see that the Rule is observed inviolably by all, and that the clerics say the Office devoutly,[1] not concentrating on the melody of the chant, but being careful that their hearts are in harmony so that their words may be in harmony with their hearts and their hearts with God. Their aim should be to please God by purity of heart, not to soothe the ears of the congregation by their sweet singing. I myself promise to observe this strictly, as God gives me the grace, and I will hand it on to the friars who are with me so that they too may put it into practice in the Office and in other prescriptions of the Rule. If a friar refuses to do this, I will not regard him as a Catholic or as one of my friars

[1] Concerning the Divine Office, see n.1, p. 33 and n. 1, p. 59.

and I even refuse to see or speak with him until he repents. I say the same of all those others who go wandering about with no thought for regular discipline. Our Lord Jesus Christ gave his life rather than fail in the obedience he owed his most holy Father.

Through our Lord Jesus Christ, I, Brother Francis, worthless as I am and an unworthy creature of the Lord God, command Brother Elias, Minister General of the Order, and all his successors, with the other superiors and guardians, present and to come, to keep a copy of this letter and put it into practice, preserving it carefully. I beseech them to observe scrupulously all that is written in it and to see that it is observed by others, according to the good pleasure of almighty God, now and forever, as long as the world lasts.

May you who do this be blessed by God and may God be ever with you. Amen.

Almighty, eternal, just and merciful God, grant us in our misery that we may do for your sake alone what we know you want us to do, and always want what pleases you; so that, cleansed and enlightened interiorly and fired with the ardour of the Holy Spirit, we may be able to follow in the footsteps of your Son, our Lord Jesus Christ, and so make our way to you, Most High, by your grace alone, you who live and reign in perfect Trinity and simple Unity, and are glorified, God all-powerful, for ever and ever. Amen.

4. Letter to a Minister[1]

THE CONTENT of the *Letter to a Minister* indicates that it was written before the approbation of the Second Rule in 1223, for the letter states that "we shall make one chapter out of all the chapters of the Rule that speak of mortal sin". This can refer only to the First Rule, since it alone contains several chapters that speak of mortal sin (Chapters 5, 13, 20). Moreover, this passage also speaks of impending changes in the Rule, and such changes could not have been considered after the final approbation of the Rule by papal Bull in 1223. Hence the letter must be dated between 1221 and 1223, and probably late in 1222 or early in 1223, since it says that these changes will be proposed at the coming Pentecost chapter.

Most probably the letter was written to one of the provincial ministers. This seems likely since the letter says to him: "You will attend the chapter with your friars". This would hardly refer to the Minister General, or rather Francis' vicar, at this time Brother Elias. Obviously, the minister was having some difficulties in his province regarding what should be done about friars who fall into sin and perhaps some difficulties too with outsiders. As a result, he seems to have requested permission to withdraw to a quiet and peaceful hermitage to give more time to his spiritual life. Francis' answer gives us a glimpse into his deep, personal holiness and into his understanding of the difficulties of a superior and of the importance of bearing these difficulties out of obedience and resignation to the will of God. In speaking of those who sin he reveals the depths of his love for his brethren, even for sinful brothers; and the depth of feeling he pours out in his words

[1]This letter is found in various manuscripts, especially: the Florence MS. (14th cent., Ognissanti), the MS. 1/25 at the College of St Isidore, Rome (14th cent.), Vatican MS. 7652 (15th cent.), the MS. at the Capuchin monastery at Foligno (15th cent.). Two of the various manuscripts say it was written to the "minister general"; but most of them say "To Brother N . . ., minister.")

reveals his anxiety to bring them all to a true love for Christ.

LETTER TO A MINISTER

To Brother N . . . , Minister. May God bless you.

This is my advice with regard to the state of your soul. As I see it, you should consider everything that makes it difficult for you to love God as a special favour, even if other persons, whether friars or not, are responsible for it, or even if they go so far as to do you physical violence. This is the way you should want it to be, and you can take this as a command from God and from me. I am convinced that this is true obedience. You must love those who behave like this towards you, and you should want nothing else from them, except what God permits to happen to you. You can show your love for them by wishing that they should be better Christians. This should be of greater benefit to you than the solitude of a hermitage.

I should like you to prove that you love God and me, his servant and yours, in the following way. There should be no friar in the whole world who has fallen into sin, no matter how far he has fallen, who will ever fail to find your forgiveness for the asking, if he will only look into your eyes. And if he does not ask forgiveness, you should ask him if he wants it. And should he appear before you again a thousand times, you should love him more than you love me, so that you may draw him to God; you should always have pity on such friars. Tell the guardians, too, that this is your policy.

At the Pentecost Chapter, with God's help and the advice of the friars, we shall make one chapter out of all the chapters in the Rule that speak of mortal sin. It will go like this:

If a friar is tempted and falls into mortal sin, he is bound by obedience to have recourse to his guardian. The other friars who know that he has sinned should not embarrass him by speaking about it. They should have the greatest sympathy for him and keep their brother's fall a secret. *It is not the healthy who need a physician, but they who are sick* (Mt. 9: 12).

They are obliged by obedience to send him to their superior, in the company of another friar. The superior, in his turn, is bound to provide compassionately for him, just as he would wish provision to be made for him if he were in a similar position. A friar who falls into venial sin should confess to a confrère who is a priest; if there is no priest present, he should confess to another friar, until he meets a priest who can absolve him sacramentally, as has been said.[1] The other friars have no authority to impose a penance, but must be content with the advice, *Go thy way, and from now on sin no more* (Jn 8: 11).

Keep this letter until Pentecost, so that it may be more faithfully observed. You will attend the chapter with your friars. With the help of God, you will see that these and other points not provided for in the Rule are fulfilled.

[1]See the Rule of 1221, Chapter 20.

5. *Letter to All Superiors of the Friars Minor* [1]

THIS LETTER IS addressed to all the "custodes" of the Franciscan Order, but the term, as it is used here, means "superiors" in the general sense rather than in the sense of the more technical meaning of the term in the Rule of 1223. [2]

Fr Luke Wadding, O.F.M., in his collection of the writings of St Francis, translated this letter into Latin from a Spanish version, the only text he knew. In more recent years, however, a Latin manuscript of the letter came to light and this manuscript was edited by Paul Sabatier. This manuscript dates back to the fourteenth century.

Again in this letter Francis returns to his favourite subject, proper respect for the Blessed Eucharist, for writings that bear the name of Christ or of his Body, and for the sacred vessels and ornaments associated with the Blessed Eucharist. It contains an admonition to preach repentance and to have copies of the letter made for preachers and superiors.

There does not seem to be any reason to doubt the authenticity of this letter. The style is similar to Francis' other writings, and the content is characteristic of his fervent devotion to the Blessed Eucharist. The whole letter is similar in many ways to the thought of the *Letter to a General Chapter* and Francis' *Testament*. It cannot be dated precisely, but it is obviously a work of the latter days of St Francis.

---

[1] This letter exists in the Codex 225 of the Guarnacci Library at Volterra, Italy (14th century).
[2] See n. 4, p. 30.

LETTER TO ALL SUPERIORS OF
THE FRIARS MINOR

To all superiors of the Friars Minor who receive this letter, Brother Francis, your poor worthless servant in God, sends greetings, with new portents in heaven and on earth,[1] which are very significant in the eyes of God, but are disregarded by the majority of people, including religious.

With everything I am capable of and more, I beg you to ask the clergy with all humility, when it is called for and you think it is a good idea, to have the greatest possible reverence for the Body and Blood of our Lord Jesus Christ, together with his holy name and the writings which contain his words, those words which consecrate his body. They should set the greatest value, too, on chalices, corporals, and all the ornaments of the altar that are related to the holy Sacrifice. If the Body of our Lord has been left in a poverty-stricken place, they should put It somewhere that is properly prepared for It, according to Church law, so that It will be kept safe. They should carry It about with the greatest reverence and be discreet in administering It to others. If the name of God or the writings that contain his words are found lying in the dust, they should be picked up and put in a suitable place.

In all your sermons you shall tell the people of the need to do penance, impressing on them that no one can be saved unless he receives the Body and Blood of our Lord.[2] When the priest is offering sacrifice at the altar or the Blessed Sacrament is being carried about, everyone should kneel down and give praise, glory, and honour to our Lord and God, living and true.

When you are preaching, too, tell the people about the glory that is due to him, so that at every hour and when the bells are rung, praise and thanks may be offered to almighty God by everyone all over the world.

My friars and superiors who receive this letter can be sure that they have God's blessing and mine, if they copy and keep

[1] The reference is to the Blessed Eucharist.
[2] See John 6: 54.

113

it, and have copies made for the friars who are devoted to preaching or are superiors, and if they preach all that is contained in it to the last. These directions should be regarded by them as true commands of holy obedience. Amen.

6. Letter to the Rulers of the People[1]

ST FRANCIS was concerned not only for the proper functioning of his Order and for the spiritual welfare of his friars, but also for the spiritual well-being of public officials because of the difficulties of their positions. But since he could not visit them personally, he addressed a letter to them, urging them not to let the cares of their offices keep them from remembering their obligations towards God. In his characteristic way, he urged them to receive the Body and Blood of Christ and to worry at least as much about the welfare of their souls as about their official duties.

There is little known, though, about the origin of this letter or about the date of its writing; apparently, however, it was written sometime during the last years of his life. Wadding accepted the letter among the writings of St Francis, and for its authenticity he made reference to the fact that the one-time Minister General of the Order, Francis Gonzaga (1579-1587), said in his work concerning the origin of the Franciscan Order[2] that the Minister General John Parenti (1227-1232) had brought a copy of it to Spain. Wadding translated the letter from a Spanish copy and inserted it into his collection of Francis' writings. No other copy of the letter is known.

LETTER TO THE RULERS OF THE PEOPLE

TO ALL MAGISTRATES and consuls, to all judges and governors all over the world and to everyone else who receives this letter, Brother Francis, your poor worthless servant in the Lord God, sends greetings and peace.

[1]The only known copy of this letter is the one Wadding transcribed into his collection of Francis' writings. But its authenticity is accepted by all because its style and content are in harmony with the style and content of his other writings.

[2]*De Origine Seraphicae Religionis Franciscanae*, Venice, 1603.

Consider and realize that the day of death is approaching.[1] I therefore beg of you with all the respect I am capable of that you do not forget God or swerve from his commandments because of the cares and anxieties of this world which you have to shoulder. For all who forget him and *turn away from* his *commandments* (Ps. 118: 21) *shall be forgotten* by him (Ez. 33: 13). When the day of death comes, all that they thought their own will be taken away from them.[2] The more wisdom and power they enjoyed in this life, the greater the torments they will have to endure in hell.[3]

And so, my lords, this is my advice. Put away all worry and anxiety and receive the holy Body and Blood of our Lord Jesus Christ fervently in memory of him. See to it that God is held in great reverence among your subjects; every evening, at a signal given by a herald or in some other way, praise and thanks should be given to the Lord God almighty by all the people. If you refuse to see to this, you can be sure that you will be held to account for it at the day of judgement before Jesus Christ, your Lord and God.

Those who keep a copy of this letter and put its prescriptions into practice can rest assured that they have God's blessing.

[1] Cf. Gen. 47: 29.
[2] Cf. Lk. 8: 18.
[3] Cf. Wis. 6: 7.

7. *Letter to Brother Leo*[1]

THIS SHORT *Letter to Brother Leo*[2] is preserved in Francis' own handwriting. The only other such autograph is the sheet on which Francis wrote the *Praises for Brother Leo* and his personal blessing to his friend.[3] Up until the year 1860 this letter was in the possession of the Franciscan Conventuals in Spoleto. But after the dissolution of that friary in that year, it disappeared for a time. Later, in the 1890's, it turned up in the possession of a priest of Spoleto, who wanted to sell it in America. But Mgr Faloci-

[1] The salutation of this *Letter to Brother Leo* is: *F. Leo, F. Francisco tuo salutem et pacem.* Some have questioned the grammar of this salutation, saying that as it stands it gives the impression of a letter of Brother Leo to Francis, since the dative case is used with *Francisco tuo*. Of course this could be just another example of Francis' "bad Latin". But, as others have pointed out, Francis, instead of sending a greeting to Leo, is asking Leo to bless him. Hence: "Brother Leo, send greetings and peace to your Brother Francis". This seems more likely.

[2] The date of Brother Leo's birth is not known. He was probably from Assisi, like Francis, and was among the first to join Francis after the approbation of the primitive Rule in 1209. He was perhaps already a priest at the time, and he soon became Francis' confessor and secretary. From about 1220 on, he was Francis' constant companion and, along with Brother Angelo, nursed him in his last illness. He was with Francis on Mount La Verna when Francis received the stigmata and was able to give an accurate account of this event, though he was not a direct witness to it. Francis had a great love for him. He called Leo his "little sheep", spoke of him as an ideal friar because of his simplicity and purity, and gave him his tunic when he was about to die. In 1244, Leo and several other friars replied to the request of the Minister General for information about Francis by gathering as much material as they could. Later he wrote a short piece about Francis' intention in the Rule (*Sanctissimi Patris Nostri Francisci Intentio Regulae, Documenta Antiqua Franciscana,* Pars I, Scripta Fratris Leonis, ed. by Fr Leonardus Lemmens, O.F.M., 1901, Quaracchi). He also gathered other materials about the saint, much of which he entrusted to the safekeeping of the Poor Clares of Assisi. He died November 15, 1271, and was buried near St Francis' own tomb in the basilica in Assisi.—*Analecta Franciscana,* III, pp. 65-74.

[3] See Part Three of this volume.

Pulignani, an energetic student of Franciscana, persuaded Pope Leo XIII to get hold of the document. The Holy Father acquired it by granting the priest a life-annuity of 200 lire in payment for it. Later the Holy Father presented the document to the city of Spoleto, where, in accordance with his wish, it is preserved since 1902 in the cathedral of that city.[1]

The letter cannot be dated precisely. Some think it should be dated about 1220, before Brother Leo became the constant companion of Francis. Others suggest a date after the stigmatization of Francis. The former date seems preferable,[2] for it would hardly be necessary for Francis to send a letter to Brother Leo at a time when he was almost continually with Francis. Moreover, it speaks of a journey they made together. This would seem to indicate a date before the stigmatization, when they would have been more likely to make such a journey.

Since the letter is an autograph, it gives an excellent example of Francis' personal style, untouched by anyone else. Typical of Francis' style is the constant repetition of "et".

LETTER TO BROTHER LEO

Brother Leo, send greetings and peace to your Brother Francis.

As a mother to her child, I speak to you, my son. In this one word, this one piece of advice, I want to sum up all that we said on our journey, and, in case hereafter you still find it necessary to come to me for advice, I want to say this to you: In whatever way you think you will best please our Lord God and follow

---

[1]This account is taken from the Esser-Hardick German translation of the writings, *Die Schriften des Hl. Franziskus von Assisi*, pp. 14-13. Other writers simply say that the letter was in the possession of the conventual church of San Simeone until it was alienated from the Order in 1893 and became an institute for the orphans of State officials. See, for instance, *Assisi and Umbria Revisited*, Edward Hutton, Hollis & Carter and David McKay Company, Inc., 1953, p. 76, or *L'Umbria Francescana*, P. Nicola Cavanna, O.F.M., Perugia, Unione Tip. Cooperativa, 1910, pp. 340-341.

[2]See Ubald D'Alencon's introduction to the writings in the English translation by Lady de la Warr, *The Writings of St Francis of Assisi*, 1907.

in his footsteps and in poverty, take that way[1] with the Lord God's blessing and my obedience. And if you find it necessary for your peace of soul or your own consolation and you want to come to me, Leo, then come.

[1]The Latin plural is used here: *faciatis*. This usage may be a familiar usage following Italian usage, as some suggest. Or it may be simply an example of what Eccleston calls Francis' "bad Latin".

Part Three

"THE SPIRIT OF HOLY PRAYER AND DEVOTION"

—Rule of 1223

1. Praises of God[1]

THOMAS OF CELANO gives the following account of how Francis came to write the *Praises of God* for Brother Leo. Once, when Francis and Leo were together at Mount La Verna, Leo "longed with a great desire to have something encouraging from the words of the Lord noted down briefly in the hand of St Francis. For he believed he would escape by this means a serious temptation that troubled him, not indeed of the flesh but of the spirit, or at least that he would be able to resist it more easily. Languishing with such a desire, he nevertheless was afraid to make known the matter to the most holy father. But what man did not tell Francis, the Spirit revealed to him. One day Blessed Francis called this brother and said : 'Bring me some paper and ink, for I want to write down the words of the Lord and his praises which I have meditated upon in my heart.' After these things he had asked for were quickly brought to him, he wrote down with his own hand the *Praises of God* and the words he wanted, and lastly a blessing for that brother, saying: 'Take this paper and guard it carefully till the day of your death.' Immediately every temptation was put to flight, and the writing was kept and afterwards it worked wonderful things."[2]

The original sheet of paper with these *Praises* is preserved today in a reliquary in the Basilica of St Francis in Assisi. On the one side of the paper is the text of the *Praises of God*. It is in the handwriting of St Francis, but it is difficult to read, for quite obviously Brother Leo followed the advice of Francis and kept it with him, but in a folded state. Consequently, the various manuscripts give varying readings of the text.

On the reverse side of the paper is the blessing St Francis gave

[1]The *Praises* are in part in the handwriting of Francis himself. Because of the difficulty of reading the text of the autograph, the Quaracchi editors of the *Opuscula* used especially the Codex 344 of the fourteenth century.

[2]*II Cel.*, 49.

to Brother Leo. It is the formula of the blessing with which the high-priest Aaron was accustomed to bless the children of Israel.[1] Francis dictated this blessing to Brother Leo, and it is therefore in the handwriting of the latter. Beneath it, though, are Francis' words of personal blessing to Leo written in his own handwriting and signed with the letter *Tau* or T.[2]

Moreover, on this reverse side of the paper Brother Leo made additional notations of his own. In the upper margin he wrote in red ink: "Blessed Francis two years before his death kept a Lent in the place of Mount La Verna in honour of the Blessed Virgin Mary, the Mother of the Lord, and of the blessed Michael, the Archangel, from the feast of the Assumption of the holy Virgin Mary until the September feast of St Michael. And the hand of the Lord was laid upon him; after the vision and speech of the Seraph and the impression of the stigmata of Christ in his body, he made and wrote with his own hand the *Praises* written on the other side of this sheet, giving thanks to the Lord for the benefits conferred upon him."

Below this notation comes the Biblical blessing and below the latter Brother Leo wrote: "Blessed Francis wrote this blessing with his own hand for me, Brother Leo". And a final notation at the bottom says: "In like manner he made this sign *Tau* together with the head in his own hand". All the writing on this second side is clearly legible.[3]

The large *Tau* with which Francis signed his blessing is drawn between the letters *e* and *o* of the name *Leo*. This seems to have been a customary practice, and it indicates very clearly that the blessing was meant for Leo. It may be noted that the text of the

[1]Numbers 6: 24-26.

[2]Celano says that Francis frequently used this sign on letters and on the walls of cells. *Tractatus de Miraculis*, 3. St Bonaventure says that Francis had a great reverence for this sign, that he often praised it in his conversations, and that he used it to sign his letters. *Leg. Maj.*, IV, 9.

[3]What Brother Leo says is a "head" is a bit difficult to decipher as such. But the *Tau* undoubtedly is a symbol of the cross. Perhaps the head is a symbol of Mount Calvary (the bare skull) upon which Christ's cross stood. The whole, therefore, would also be a symbol of Francis' stigmatization. One lone author sees in the head a rough picture of Mount La Verna. But in this case, too, the whole would still symbolize Francis' stigmatization.

blessing reads: May God bless, Leo, you. Someone has suggested that it is as though Francis looked up to Leo at this point in his writing and nodded to him, pronouncing and recording his name in this way.

The *Praises of God* illustrates the mystical heights to which Francis had attained in and after the stigmatization.

PRAISES OF GOD

You are holy, Lord, the only God,
    and your deeds are wonderful.
You are strong.
    You are great.
    You are the Most High,
    You are almighty.
    You, holy Father, are
    King of heaven and earth.
You are Three and One,
    Lord God, all good.
    You are Good, all Good, supreme Good,
    Lord God, living and true.
You are love,
    You are wisdom.
    You are humility,
    You are endurance.
    You are rest,
    You are peace.
    You are joy and gladness.
    You are justice and moderation.
    You are all our riches,
    And you suffice for us.
You are beauty.
    You are gentleness.
    You are our protector,
    You are our guardian and defender.
    You are courage.
    You are our haven and our hope.

You are our faith,
    Our great consolation.
You are our eternal life,
    Great and wonderful Lord,
    God almighty,
    Merciful Saviour.

THE BLESSING FOR BROTHER LEO

God bless you and keep you.
    May God smile on you, and be merciful to you;
May God turn his regard towards you
    and give you peace.

May God bless you, Brother Leo.

2. *The Canticle of Brother Sun*[1]

SOMEONE HAS SAID that a poet is a man with keen vision, exquisite sensitivity, a great heart, and a deep conviction of the eternal values. Beyond a doubt, St Francis had all these qualities, and many more besides. Francis Thompson, a poet who understood the spirit of St Francis, pinpointed the essential element of Francis' poetry when he said that though the saint was sworn to poverty, he did not forswear beauty, but that, on the other hand, he discerned through the lamp Beauty the Light God.

Francis saw the tiny worm lying in his path, and he stooped to pick it up, because it was a creature of the Almighty. He saw the wild flowers of the fields, but even more he saw the hand of God that made them. He beheld the moon and the stars in the heavens at night, and the sun at midday, and he beheld the love of God reaching down along their beams to embrace the children He had created. Even in suffering, to use the phrase Francis Thompson used many years later, he saw "the shade of His hand outstretched caressingly".[2] But always he saw, more than anything else, that all things were intended to touch the hearts of men and lift them to God.[3]

[1] Thomas of Celano refers to the *Canticle* several times in his biographies of St Francis (e.g., I, 80, 109; II, 213, 217). It is found in various ancient manuscripts, particularly the Assisi MS. 338. It is found also in the *Speculum Perfectionis* (120) and in the *Liber Conformitatum* (*Analecta Franciscana*, V, pp. 261-262). The Quaracchi edition of the *Opuscula* omits it, but only because it was not written in Latin. Its authenticity is universally accepted.

[2] *The Hound of Heaven.*

[3] St Bonaventure wrote: "In all things fair, he beheld him who is most fair, and by his footprints in created things he found his Beloved everywhere, making a ladder of all things by which to ascend to him who is all lovely. With a feeling of unwonted love, he tasted that fountain of all goodness in all creatures, as in so many rivulets; and in the harmonious powers and functions given them by God, he perceived, as it were, a celestial symphony, and, like the prophet David, he fondly exhorted them to praise the Lord." (*Leg. Maj.*, IX, 1.)

All of this is evident in the several poems St Francis left us. But among these, one stands out particularly as representative of Francis' poetic nature, and this one is the *Canticle of Brother Sun*. Written in the Umbrian dialect, it is thought to be the oldest extant poem in any modern language.[1] The theme of the *Canticle* is that God, and God alone, deserves praise and deserves it from every source. Accordingly, he calls upon all creatures, the sun, the moon, the stars, the elements, even suffering and death itself, to pour forth their praise to God. It is a counterpart, as Celano points out, of the canticle of the three young men in the fiery furnace recorded by the prophet Daniel.[2]

Francis began the *Canticle* in the summer of 1225, at a time indeed when he was deep in suffering, but when he had already attained the mystical heights in his experience on Mount La Verna.[3] But the joy he had experienced in that great privilege was tempered by the thought of how men were greatly offending their Creator by misusing the creature world God had given them. "For his praise," he said, "I want to compose a new hymn about the Lord's creatures, of which we make daily use, without which we cannot live, and with which the human race greatly offends its Creator."[4]

The first part of the *Canticle*, up to the verses about pardon and peace, he composed in the garden of the Poor Clares' convent at San Damiano, where he lay sick and in intense suffering for some six or seven weeks.[5] He then composed a melody for it and frequently urged his brothers to sing it when they were out preaching. The second part, consisting of the next two verses about pardon and peace, he composed a short time later in an effort to restore

---

[1] J. R. H. Moorman, *The Sources for the Life of St Francis of Assisi*, p. 17.

[2] *I Cel.*, 80: "For as of old the three youths in the fiery furnace invited all the elements to praise and glorify the Creator of the universe, so also this man, filled with the spirit of God, never ceased to glorify, praise, and bless the Creator and Ruler of all things in all the elements and creatures." See Daniel, Chapter 3.

[3] The stigmatization in 1224.

[4] *Speculum Perfectionis*, 100.

[5] *Loc. cit.* See also the rubric of the Assisi MS. 338: Here begin the Praises of the Creatures, which the Blessed Francis composed for the praise and honour of God while he lay sick at San Damiano. *Archivum Franciscanum Historicum*, Vol. 24, 1931, p. 551.

peace between the quarrelling parties in a dispute between the civil and religious authorities of Assisi.[1] The final verses about Sister Death Francis added shortly before his own death, after Brother Leo and Brother Angelo had sung the *Canticle* at his request. Celano adds that his last words were: "Welcome, my Sister Death".[2]

The *Canticle*, for all the depth of feeling it displays towards creatures, is nonetheless an earnest prayer. What makes it all the more remarkable is the fact that, written though it was during his last illness and amid intense suffering, it displays a heart filled with joy and happiness and a heart filled with the deepest gratitude towards Almighty God, even for suffering and for Sister Death.

The *Canticle* was written in the Umbrian dialect of the people. Yet, a great deal of poetic artistry can be perceived in it. There is, indeed, no specific rhythm in it, such as we are accustomed to in most of our English poetry; but there is in it the broader rhythm of the spoken language. The fluency of its movement is somewhat akin to the movement of what Gerard Manley Hopkins much later called *sprung rhythm*. The various verses of the poem are made up of two hemistiches each, and they are organized on the basis of assonance,[3] rather than on the basis of perfect rhyme.[4] Furthermore, the rhythmic beauty of the poem is enhanced by the constantly recurring *o*-sounds and the sounds of the liquid *l* and *r* and by the strong accents of the words. All in all, it is a

[1]The bishop of Assisi had excommunicated the podesta of Assisi, and the latter retaliated by preventing the people from selling anything to the bishop. Peace was re-established when Francis' *Canticle* was sung. See *Speculum Perfectionis*, 101.

[2]*II Cel.*, 217.

[3]That is, correspondence of the vowel sounds in the accented syllables, the consonants being different. For instance, the *Signore* and *benedizione* in these two verses: "Altissimo, onnipotente,/ bon Signore,// tue so le laude,/ la gloria e l'onore e onne benedizione". See the study of the *Canticle* by Vittore Branca, *Il Cantico Di Frate Sole*, in *Archivum Franciscanum Historicum*, Vol. 41, 1949, pp. 1-87.

[4]Several almost perfect rhymes do occur, for instance, the *Stelle* and *belle* in these two verses: "Laudato si, mi Signore,/ per sora Luna e le Stelle:// in cielo l'hai formate clarite/ e preziose e belle". Branca, *loc. cit.*

poem truly comparable to the song of the three young men in
the fiery furnace.[1]

THE CANTICLE OF BROTHER SUN

Most high, all-powerful, all good, Lord!
>All praise is yours, all glory, all honour
>And all blessing.

To you, alone, Most High, do they belong.
>No mortal lips are worthy
>To pronounce your name.

All praise be yours, my Lord, through all that you have made,
>And first my lord Brother Sun,
>Who brings the day; and light you give to us through him.

How beautiful is he, how radiant in all his splendour!
>Of you, Most High, he bears the likeness.

All praise be yours, my Lord, through Sister Moon and Stars;
>In the heavens you have made them, bright
>And precious and fair.

All praise be yours, my Lord, through Brothers Wind and Air,
>And fair and stormy, all the weather's moods,
>By which you cherish all that you have made.

All praise be yours, my Lord, through Sister Water,
>So useful, lowly, precious and pure.

All praise be yours, my Lord, through Brother Fire,
>Through whom you brighten up the night.
>How beautiful is he, how gay! Full of power and strength.

[1]For a proper understanding of the poem it should be kept in mind
that the praise is not directed to the creatures, nor is the praise directed
to Almighty God for the creatures, that is, for giving them to us. The
prepositions *cun* and *per* are used in the meaning of instrumentality, that
is, *by means of* or *through*. In his *Essays in Criticism* Matthew Arnold pointed
this out already in 1875, though he used *of* as a simpler way of saying
by means of or *through*. This is in accordance with the Italian meaning of
these prepositions. The German translation of the poem in the Esser-
Hardick edition uses *durch*, as does also a more recent study by Erhard
Platzek, O.F.M. (*Das Sonnenlied des Heiligen Franziskus von Assisi*, 1956).
The present English translation follows this thought. See also *The
Words of Saint Francis*, James Meyer, O.F.M., note, pp. 339-340.

All praise be yours, my Lord, through Sister Earth, our mother,
    Who feeds us in her sovereignty and produces
    Various fruits with coloured flowers and herbs.
All praise be yours, my Lord, through those who grant pardon
    For love of you; through those who endure
    Sickness and trial.
Happy those who endure in peace,
    By you, Most High, they will be crowned.
All praise be yours, my Lord, through Sister Death,
    From whose embrace no mortal can escape.
Woe to those who die in mortal sin!
    Happy those She finds doing your will!
    The second death can do no harm to them.
Praise and bless my Lord, and give him thanks,
    And serve him with great humility.

3. *The Praises of the Virtues* [1]

IN HIS *Second Life of St Francis* Thomas of Celano speaks eloquently of the virtue of holy "simplicity, the daughter of grace, the sister of wisdom, the mother of justice",[2] and concludes with a reference to Francis' little poetic composition called the *Praises of the Virtues* or *Salute to the Virtues*: "Therefore, in the *Praises of the Virtues* he composed, he says this: 'Hail, Queen Wisdom! The Lord save you, with your sister, pure, holy Simplicity'."[3] This is the opening verse of the short piece that has come down to us under the title *Salutatio Virtutum*.[4]

In the *Praises* Francis stresses the need for self-denial, dying to self, as the basis of virtues; and he points out how the virtues all hang together: "The man who practises one and does not offend against the others possesses all; the man who offends against one, possesses none and violates all". He then goes on to point out the characteristics of the single virtues. The fact that he stresses obedience at greater length than any of the other virtues has led some to conclude that the *Praises* are addressed to the friars more than to the other faithful.

No precise date can be given for this little work.

THE PRAISES OF THE VIRTUES

Hail, Queen Wisdom! The Lord save you,
    with your sister, pure, holy Simplicity.
Lady Holy Poverty, God keep you,
    with your sister, holy Humility.

[1] The *Praises of the Virtues* is found in most of the ancient manuscripts, including the Assisi MS. 338 (13th cent.) and the Ognissanti MS. (14th cent.). Its authenticity is solidly established.
[2] *II Cel.*, 189.
[3] *Loc. cit.*
[4] The Quaracchi *Opuscula* uses this title.

Lady Holy Love, God keep you,
    with your sister, holy Obedience.
All holy virtues,
    God keep you,
    God, from whom you proceed and come.
In all the world there is not a man
    who can possess any one of you
    without first dying to himself.
The man who practises one and does not offend against
the others
    possesses all;
The man who offends against one,
    possesses none and violates all.
Each and every one of you
    puts vice and sin to shame.
Holy Wisdom puts satan
    and all his wiles to shame.
Pure and holy Simplicity puts
    all the learning of this world,
    all natural wisdom, to shame.
Holy Poverty puts to shame
    all greed, avarice,
    and all the anxieties of this life.
Holy Humility puts pride to shame,
    and all the inhabitants of this world
    and all that is in the world.
Holy Love puts to shame all the temptations
    of the devil and the flesh
    and all natural fear.
Holy Obedience puts to shame
    all natural and selfish desires.
It mortifies our lower nature
    and makes it obey the spirit
    and our fellow men.

Obedience subjects a man
    to everyone on earth,
And not only to men,
    but to all the beasts as well
    and to the wild animals,
So that they can do what they like with him,
    as far as God allows them.

4. *Salutation of the Blessed Virgin*[1]

THOMAS OF CELANO tells us in his *Second Life of St Francis*: "Towards the Mother of Jesus he [Francis] was filled with an inexpressible love, because it was she who made the Lord of Majesty our brother. He sang special *Praises* to her, poured out prayers to her, offered her his affections, so many and so great that the tongue of man cannot recount them."[2] The *Praises* that Celano speaks of, or, as it is commonly known, the *Salutation of the Blessed Virgin*, forms in some of the early manuscripts an addition to the *Praises of the Virtues*. The closing passage of the *Salutation* is the reason for this juxtaposition, since it contains a greeting to all holy virtues. It rounds off, therefore, the *Praises*. Still, it can stand separately, and today it is generally given separately.

The *Salutation*, along with the antiphon *Holy Virgin Mary*,[3] shows St Francis' deep and warm devotion to the Mother of God.[4] Many of the titles he uses in his address to her are based upon the sacred liturgy. No date, however, can be assigned to this work.

SALUTATION
OF THE BLESSED VIRGIN

Hail, holy Lady,
> Most holy Queen,
> Mary, Mother of God,
> Ever Virgin;

[1] This *Salutation* is found in all the early manuscripts except the Assisi MS. 338. Its authenticity is accepted by all.

[2] *II Cel.*, 198.

[3] See the *Office of the Passion* in this volume.

[4] *II Cel.*, 198. Celano adds here: "But what delights us most, he made her the advocate of the order and placed under her wings the sons he was about to leave that she might cherish them and protect them to the end". See also *II Cel.*, 19.

Chosen by the most holy Father in heaven,
 Consecrated by him,
  With his most holy beloved Son
  And the Holy Spirit, the Comforter.
On you descended and in you still remains
 All the fulness of grace
  And every good.
Hail, his Palace.
Hail, his Tabernacle.
Hail, his Robe.
Hail, his Handmaid.
Hail, his Mother.
And Hail, all holy Virtues,
 Who, by the grace
  And inspiration of the Holy Spirit,
  Are poured into the hearts of the faithful
  So that, faithless no longer,
  They may be made faithful servants of God
  Through you.

5. The Praises Before the Office[1]

IN MANY ANCIENT and modern collections of the writings of St Francis, including the Quaracchi edition of 1949, the prayer called *The Praises* is preceded by a paraphrase of the *Our Father*. A rubric in the oldest manuscript, Assisi MS. 338, reads: "Here begin the praises which our most blessed father Francis arranged and recited at every Hour of the day and night and before the Office of the Blessed Virgin Mary. They begin thus: *Our Most Holy Father, who art in heaven*, etc., with the *Glory*. After that are said the Praises, *Holy, Holy, Holy*, etc."[2]

Of recent years authors tend more and more to doubt the authenticity of the paraphrase of the *Our Father*. The paraphrase, as a matter of fact, does not begin, "*Our Most Holy Father, who art in heaven*", but after *Our Most Holy Father*, or as one manuscript has it, simply, *Our Father*,[3] the paraphrase goes on: "Creator, Redeemer, Saviour and Comforter". The paraphrase, therefore, does not seem to be the prayer spoken of in the rubric of the ancient manuscript. Accordingly, since there is good reason to doubt the authenticity of the paraphrase, it is omitted here, but it is included as a work of doubtful authenticity in the Appendix of this volume.

The prayer entitled *The Praises*, however, is considered by all to be an authentic writing of St Francis.[4] As with the other prayers

[1]The *Lauds* or *Praises* (before the Office) is found in many of the ancient manuscripts, including the Assisi MS. 338 and the Ognissanti MS. At times what is called the *Paraphrase of the Our Father* is found prefixed to these *Praises*, sometimes the *Paraphrase* is found alone, and the *Praises* alone. The *Paraphrase* is assigned to Brother Giles by MS. 1/73 at St Isidore's College, Rome (14th cent.). Many doubt the authenticity of the *Paraphrase* today, but not of the *Praises*.

[2]Quaracchi edition of the *Opuscula*, p. 119.

[3]The MS. 1/73.

[4]This may be the song Francis referred to when he wrote to the brothers in France and exhorted them to sing the praises of the Divine Trinity. Eccleston, *De Adventu*, Chapter 6. See also the *Speculum Perfectionis*, 82.

of St Francis, this one too is made up of passages from Holy Scripture and from the liturgy. It is a song of praise to God for all his works. The prayer that follows the praises is in the same vein. No date, however, can be assigned for its composition.

THE PRAISES BEFORE THE OFFICE

"Holy, holy, holy, the Lord God almighty,
  Who was, and who is, and who is coming." (Ap. 4: 8)
R7. Let us praise and glorify him for ever.

"Worthy art thou, O Lord our God,
  to receive glory and honour and power." (Ap. 4: 11)
R7. Let us praise and glorify him for ever.

"Worthy is the Lamb who was slain
  to receive power and divinity
  and wisdom and strength
  and honour and glory and blessing." (Ap. 5: 12)
R7. Let us praise and glorify him for ever.

Let us bless the Father and the Son and the Holy Spirit.
R7. Let us praise and glorify him for ever.

"Bless the Lord, all you works of the Lord." (Dan. 3: 57)
R7. Let us praise and glorify him for ever.

"Praise our God, all you his servants,
  and you who fear him, the small and the great."
                                                    (Ap. 19: 5)
R7. Let us praise and glorify him for ever.

Praise him in his glory, heaven and earth, "and every creature that is in heaven and on the earth and under the earth, and such as are on the sea, and all that are in them".
                                                    (Ap. 5: 13)
R7. Let us praise and glorify him for ever.

Glory be to the Father, and to the Son, and to the Holy Spirit.

R⁊. Let us praise and glorify him for ever.

As it was in the beginning, is now, and ever shall be, world without end. Amen.

R⁊. Let us praise and glorify him for ever.

Prayer

All-powerful, all holy, most high and supreme God, sovereign good, all good, every good, you who alone are good, it is to you we must give all praise, all glory, all thanks, all honour, all blessing; to you we must refer all good always. Amen.

6. *The Office of the Passion*[1]

IN HIS *Legend of St Clare* Thomas of Celano says of that saint: "She learned the Office of the Cross as Francis, the lover of the Cross, had composed it, and prayed it often with like affection".[2] The words "Office of the Cross", as Wadding concluded, refer undoubtedly to *The Office of the Passion*. St Francis was the author of this Office, but he did not intend it to take the place of the Divine Office.

The psalms of this Office of the Passion are composed of verses or parts of verses from scattered places in the Book of Psalms. Now and then a phrase or verse is taken from some other part of the Bible, and occasionally a few of Francis' own words are added. In the text below, the number of the psalm is indicated together with the number of the respective verse. Where a verse is taken from some other source, this source is indicated. Francis' own words are given in italics.

The Office is arranged for five different parts of the year: (1) for the last two days of Holy Week and the weekdays of the year; (2) for the Easter season; (3) for the Sundays and principal feasts of the year; (4) for Advent; (5) for the Christmas season to the close of the octave of Epiphany. The cycle of the year begins with Compline of Holy Thursday, "because on that night our Lord Jesus Christ was betrayed and taken prisoner".[3] The Office for the single days begins with Compline and extends through the Vespers, with the exception that on Christmas it begins with the First Vespers and runs through the Second Vespers.

The initial rubric in the Assisi MS. 338 explains how Francis

[1]This Office is found in various manuscripts, including the Assisi MS. 338.

[2]*Legenda S. Clarae*, XX, 30. See *The Legend and Writings of St Clare of Assisi*, p. 40.

[3]The Quaracchi edition of the *Opuscula*, p. 126.

said this Office: "First he would say the prayer the Lord and Master taught us: *Our Most Holy Father*, etc., together with the praises, namely, *Holy, Holy, Holy*. When he had finished the praises together with the prayer, he would say the first part of the antiphon, namely, *Holy Mary*. Then he would first say the psalms of the holy Mary; in addition, he would recite other psalms, as he chose, and at the end of all the psalms he would say, he would recite the psalms of the Passion. Then he would say the antiphon, namely, *Holy Virgin Mary*. With the recitation of this antiphon, the Office was finished."[1]

The whole Office of the Passion is filled with the warmth and devotion of a deeply earnest man of prayer. No date, however, can be given for its composition.

THE OFFICE OF THE PASSION

(The First Office is for Compline of Holy Thursday, for Good Friday, and for Holy Saturday through Vespers; for all weekdays beginning with Compline of Trinity Sunday and up to Compline of the Saturday before the first Sunday of Advent; from Compline of the octave day of the feast of Epiphany through the Vespers of Holy Thursday.)[2]

COMPLINE

Antiphon: Holy Virgin Mary.

Psalm

My wanderings you have counted; my tears are stored in your flask; are they not recorded in your book? (55: 9).

All my foes whisper together against me (40: 8); and take counsel together (70: 10).

They repaid me evil for good and hatred for my love (108: 5).

In return for my love they slandered me, but I prayed (108: 4).

My holy Father, King of heaven and earth, be not far from me,

[1]*Loc. cit.*

[2]The rubrics here are shortened from the rubrics given in the Assisi MS. See the Quaracchi edition of the *Opuscula*.

for I am in distress; be near, for I have no one to help me (21: 12).

Then do my enemies turn back, when I call upon you; now I know that God is with me (55: 10).

My friends and my companions stand back because of my affliction (37: 12).

You have taken my friends away from me; you have made me an abomination to them; I am imprisoned, and I cannot escape (87: 9).

Holy Father, be not far from me; *O my God*, hasten to aid me 1: 20).

Make haste to help me, O Lord my salvation! (37:23).

Glory be to the Father, etc.

Antiphon: Holy Virgin Mary, among all the women of the world there is none like you; you are the daughter and handmaid of the most high King and Father of heaven; you are the mother of our most holy Lord Jesus Christ; you are the spouse of the Holy Spirit. Pray for us, with St Michael the archangel and all the powers of heaven and all the saints, to your most holy and beloved Son, our Lord and Master.

Glory be to the Father, etc.

> (*This antiphon is said at all the hours, including Matins. It serves as an antiphon, chapter, hymn, verse, and prayer. To bring the Office to a close St Francis used always to say:* Let us bless our Lord and God, living and true; to him we must attribute all praise, glory, honour, blessing, and every good for ever. Amen.)

MATINS

Ant.: Holy Virgin Mary.

Psalm

O Lord, my God, by day I cry out, at night I clamour in your presence. Let my prayer come before you; incline your ear to my call for help (87: 2-3).

Come and ransom my life; as an answer for my enemies, redeem me (68: 19).

You have been my guide since I was first formed, my security at my mother's breast. To you I was committed at birth, from my mother's womb you are my God. Be not far from me (21: 10-12).

You know my reproach, my shame and my ignominy; before you are all my foes.

Insult has broken my heart, and I am weak; I looked for sympathy, but there was none; for comforters, and I found none (68: 20-21).

O God, the haughty have risen up against me, and the company of fierce men seeks my life, nor do they set you before their eyes (85: 14).

I am numbered with those who go down into the pit; I am a man without strength.

My couch is among the dead (87: 5-6).

You are my most holy Father, my King and my God.

Make haste to help me, O Lord my salvation! (37: 23).

PRIME

Ant.: Holy Virgin Mary.

Psalm

Have pity on me, O God; have pity on me, for in you I take refuge. In the shadow of your wings I take refuge, till harm pass by.

I call to *my most holy Father*, the Most High, to God, my benefactor.

May he send from heaven and save me; may he make those a reproach who trample upon me (56: 2-4).

He rescued me from my mighty enemy and from my foes, who were too powerful for me (17: 18).

They have prepared a net for my feet; they have bowed me down; they have dug a pit before me, but they fall into it.

My heart is steadfast, O God; my heart is steadfast; I will sing and chant praise.

Awake, O my soul; awake, lyre and harp! I will wake the dawn.

I will give thanks to you among the peoples, O Lord, I will chant your praise among nations.

For your kindness towers to the heavens, and your faithfulness to the skies.

Be exalted above the heavens, O God; above all the earth be your glory! (56: 7-12).

TERCE

Ant.: Holy Virgin Mary.

Psalm

Have pity on me, O God, for men trample upon me; all the day they press their attack against me.

My adversaries trample upon me all the day; yes, many fight against me (55: 2-3).

All my foes whisper together against me; against me they imagine the worst (40: 8).

They who keep watch against my life take counsel together (70: 10).

When they leave they speak to the same purpose (40: 7).

All who see me scoff at me; they mock me with parted lips, they wag their heads (21: 8).

But I am a worm, not a man; the scorn of men, despised by the people (21: 7).

For all my foes I am an object of reproach, a laughingstock to my neighbours, and a dread to my friends (30: 12).

Holy Father, be not far from me; hasten to my aid (21: 20).

Make haste to help me, O Lord my salvation! (37: 23).

SEXT

Ant.: Holy Virgin Mary.

Psalm

With a loud voice I cry out to the Lord; with a loud voice I beseech the Lord.

My complaint I pour out before him; before him I lay bare my distress.

When my spirit is faint within me, you know my path.

In the way along which I walk they have hid a trap for me.

I look to the right to see, but there is no one who pays heed.

I have lost all means of escape; there is no one who cares for my life (141: 2-5).

Since for your sake I bear insult, and shame covers my face,

I have become an outcast to my brothers, a stranger to my mother's sons,

Because, *Holy Father*, zeal for your house consumes me, and the insults of those who blaspheme you fall upon me (68: 8-10).

Yet when I stumbled they were glad and gathered together; they gathered together striking me unawares (34: 15).

Those outnumber the hairs of my head who hate me without cause. Too many for my strength are they who wrongfully are my enemies. Must I restore what I did not steal? (68: 5).

Unjust witnesses have risen up; things I knew not of, they lay to my charge. They have repaid me evil for good, bringing bereavement to my soul (34: 11-12).

Those who repay evil for good harass me for pursuing good (37: 21).

You are my most holy Father, my King and my God.

Make haste to help me, O Lord my salvation! (37: 23).

NONE

Ant.: Holy Virgin Mary.

Psalm

O all ye that pass by the way, attend, and see if there be any sorrow like to my sorrow (Lam. 1: 12).

Indeed, many dogs surround me, a pack of evildoers closes in upon me (21: 17).

They look on and gloat over me; they divide my garments among them, and for my vesture they cast lots (21: 18-19).

They have pierced my hands and my feet; I can count all my bones (21: 17-18).

They open their mouths against me like ravening and roaring lions (21: 14).

I am like water poured out; all my bones are racked. My heart has become like wax melting away within my bosom.

My throat is dried up like baked clay, my tongue cleaves to my jaws (21: 15-16).

They put gall in my food, and in my thirst they gave me vinegar to drink (68: 22).

To the dust of death you have brought me down (21: 16).

For they kept after him whom you smote, and added to the pain of him you wounded (68: 27).

When I lie down in sleep, I wake again, *and my Father, most holy, has raised me up in glory* (3: 6).

Holy Father, with your counsel you guide me, and in the end you will receive me in glory.

Whom else have I in heaven? And when I am with you, the earth delights me not (72: 24-25).

Desist! and confess that I am God, exalted among the nations, exalted upon the earth (45: 11).

But the Lord redeems the lives of his servants *with his own most precious blood*; no one incurs guilt who takes refuge in him (33: 23).

He comes to rule the world with justice and the peoples with his constancy (95: 13).

VESPERS

Ant.: Holy Virgin Mary.

Psalm

All you peoples, clap your hands, shout to God with cries of gladness,

For the Lord, the Most High, the awesome, is the great king over all the earth (46: 2-3).

The Father of heaven, most holy, our King, sent his beloved Son from on high before all the ages, the doer of saving deeds on earth (73: 12).

Let the heavens be glad and the earth rejoice; let the sea and what fills it resound; let the plains be joyful and all that is in them (95: 11).

Sing to the Lord a new song; sing to the Lord, all you lands (95: 1).

For great is the Lord and highly to be praised; awesome is he, beyond all gods (95: 4).

Give to the Lord, you families of nations, give to the Lord glory and praise; give to the Lord the glory due his name! (95: 7-8).

Prepare your hearts and take up his holy cross; live by his holy commandments to the last.

Tremble before him, all the earth; say among the nations: The Lord is king (95 9-10).

> (*The psalm is said thus far from Good Friday to Ascension Thursday. On Ascension Thursday the following verses are added.*)

He ascended into heaven, and sits at the right hand of the most holy Father in heaven.

Be exalted above the heavens, O God; above all the earth be your glory! (56: 12).

He comes to rule the earth. He shall rule the world with justice (95: 13).

> (*This last psalm is said daily at Vespers from Ascension Thursday until Advent. The others are said daily during the seasons indicated, except on Sundays and the principal feasts.*)

SECOND OFFICE
Holy Saturday

COMPLINE

Ant.: Holy Virgin Mary.

Psalm

Deign, O God, to rescue me; O Lord, make haste to help me.
Let them be put to shame and confounded who seek my life.
Let them be turned back in disgrace who desire my ruin.
Let them retire in their shame who say to me, "Aha, aha!"
But may all who seek you exult and be glad in you. And may
those who love your salvation say ever, "God be glorified!"
But I am afflicted and poor; O God, hasten to me! You are
my help and my deliverer; O Lord, hold not back! (69).

> (*This psalm is said daily at Compline until the octave of
> Pentecost.*)

Easter Sunday

MATINS

Ant.: Holy Virgin Mary.

Psalm

Sing to the Lord a new song, for he has done wondrous deeds;
His right hand, his holy arm *sanctified his Son*.
The Lord has made his salvation known: in the sight of the
nations he has revealed his justice (97: 1-2).
By day the Lord bestows his grace, and at night I have his
song (41: 9).
This is the day the Lord has made; let us be glad and rejoice
in it (117: 24).
Blessed is he who comes in the name of the Lord; the Lord
is God, and he has given us light (117: 26-27).
Let the heavens be glad and the earth rejoice; let the sea and
what fills it resound; let the plains be joyful and all that is in
them! (95: 11-12).

Give to the Lord, you families of nations, give to the Lord glory and praise; give to the Lord the glory due his name! (95: 7-8).

(This psalm is said from Easter Sunday to Ascension at all the hours except Vespers, Compline, and Prime. On the night of Ascension Thursday the following verses are added.)

You kingdoms of the earth, sing to God, chant praise to the Lord who rides on the heights of the ancient heavens.

Behold, his voice resounds, the voice of power: "Confess the power of God!" Over Israel is his majesty; his power is in the skies.

Awesome in his sanctuary is God, the God of Israel; he gives power and strength to his people. Blessed be God! (67: 33-36).

(This psalm is said daily at Matins, Terce, Sext, and None from Ascension until the octave of Pentecost. It is said at Matins only on the Sundays and principal feasts from the octave of Pentecost until Holy Thursday. At Matins and Vespers Psalm 29, "Give to the Lord, you sons of God", may be said instead, but only from Easter until Ascension.)

PRIME

Ant.: Holy Virgin Mary.

Psalm

Have pity on me, O God; . . . (*as at Prime of the First Office*).

TERCE, SEXT, NONE

Ant.: Holy Virgin Mary.

Psalm

Sing to the Lord a new song . . . (*as at Matins of the Second Office*).

VESPERS

Ant.: Holy Virgin Mary.

149

Psalm

All you peoples, clap your hands . . . (*as at Vespers of the First Office*).

THIRD OFFICE

(*On the Sundays and principal feasts from the octave of Epiphany until Holy Thursday and from the octave of Pentecost until Advent.*)

COMPLINE

Ant.: Holy Virgin Mary.

Psalm

Deign, O God, to rescue me . . . (*as at Compline of the Second Office*).

MATINS

Ant.: Holy Virgin Mary.

Psalm

Sing to the Lord a new song . . . (*as at Matins of the Second Office*).

PRIME

Ant.: Holy Virgin Mary.

Psalm

Have pity on me, O God . . . (*as at Prime of the First Office*).

TERCE

Ant.: Holy Virgin Mary.

Psalm

Shout joyfully to God, all you on earth, sing praise to the glory of his name; proclaim his glorious praise.

Say to God, "How tremendous are your deeds! for your great strength your enemies fawn upon you.

Let all the earth worship and sing praise to you, sing praise to your name!" (65: 1-4).

Hear now, all you who fear God, while I declare what he has done for me.

When I appealed to him in words, praise was on the tip of my tongue (65: 16-17).

From his temple he heard my voice, and my cry to him reached his ears (17: 7).

Bless our God, you peoples, loudly sound his praise (65: 8).

In him shall all the tribes of the earth be blessed; all the nations shall proclaim his happiness.

Blessed be the Lord, the God of Israel, who alone does wondrous deeds.

And blessed forever be his glorious name; may the whole earth be filled with his glory. Amen. Amen (71: 17-19).

SEXT

Ant.: Holy Virgin Mary.

Psalm

The Lord answer you in time of distress; the name of the God of Jacob defend you!

May he send you help from the sanctuary, from Sion may he sustain you.

May he remember all your offerings and graciously accept your holocaust.

May he grant you what is in your heart and fulfil your every plan.

May we shout for joy at your victory and raise the standards in the name of our God. The Lord grant all your requests!

Now I know that the Lord has given *his Son Jesus Christ to judge all peoples faithfully* (19: 2-7).

The Lord is a stronghold for the oppressed, a stronghold in times of distress. They trust in you who cherish your name, for you forsake not those who seek you (9: 10-11).

But I will sing of your strength; you have been my stronghold, my refuge in the day of distress (58: 17).

NONE

Ant.: Holy Virgin Mary.

Psalm

In you, O Lord, I take refuge; let me never be put to shame.

In your justice rescue me, and deliver me; incline your ear to me, and save me.

Be my rock of refuge, a stronghold to give me safety (70: 1-3).

For you are my hope, O Lord; my trust, O God, from my youth.

On you I depend from birth; from my mother's womb you are my strength; constant has been my hope in you (70: 5-6).

My mouth shall be filled with your praise, with your glory day by day (70: 8).

Answer me, O Lord, for bounteous is your kindness; in your great mercy turn towards me.

Hide not your face from your servant; in my distress, make haste to answer me (68: 17-18).

Blessed be the Lord my God; you have been my stronghold, my refuge in the day of distress.

Your praise will I sing; for you, O God, are my stronghold, my gracious God! (58: 17-18).

VESPERS

Ant.: Holy Virgin Mary.

Psalm

All you peoples, clap your hands . . . (*as at Vespers of the First Office*).

FOURTH OFFICE

(*Advent until the Vigil of Christmas*)

COMPLINE

Ant.: Holy Virgin Mary.

Psalm

How long, O Lord? Will you utterly forget me? How long will you hide your face from me?

How long shall I harbour sorrow in my soul, grief in my heart day after day? How long will my enemy triumph over me?

Look, answer me, O Lord, my God! Give light to my eyes that I may not sleep in death lest my enemy say, "I have overcome him";

Lest my foes rejoice at my downfall though I trusted in your kindness.

Let my heart rejoice in your salvation; let me sing of the Lord, "He has been good to me" (12).

MATINS

Ant.: Holy Virgin Mary.

Psalm

I will give thanks to you, O Lord, *most holy Father, King of heaven and earth*; that you have comforted me (85: 12 and 17).

You are God my saviour (24: 5); I will act with confidence and have no fear (Is. 12: 2).

My strength and my courage is the Lord, and he has been my saviour (117: 14).

Your right hand, O Lord, has mightily shown its power, your right hand, O Lord, has struck the enemy; in your plenteous glory you have put down my adversaries (Ex. 15: 6-7).

See, you lowly ones, and be glad; you who seek God, may your hearts be merry! (68: 33).

Let the heavens and the earth praise him, the seas and whatever moves in them! (68: 35).

For God will save Sion and rebuild the cities of Juda. They shall dwell in the land and own it, and the descendants of his servants shall inherit it, and those who love his name shall inhabit it (68: 36-37).

PRIME

Ant.: Holy Virgin Mary.

Psalm

Have pity on me, O God . . . (*as at Prime of the First Office*).

TERCE

Ant.: Holy Virgin Mary.

Psalm

Shout joyfully to God . . . (*as at Terce of the Third Office*).

SEXT

Ant.: Holy Virgin Mary.

Psalm

The Lord answer you in distress . . . (*as at Sext of the Third Office*).

NONE

Ant.: Holy Virgin Mary.

Psalm

In you, O Lord, I take refuge . . . (*as at None of the Third Office*).

VESPERS

Ant.: Holy Virgin Mary.

Psalm

All you peoples, clap your hands . . . (*as at Vespers of the First Office*).

(*This psalm is said only up to verse* 8, *then* Glory be to the Father, *etc., is added immediately.*)

FIFTH OFFICE

(*At all hours from Christmas until the Octave of Epiphany*)

Ant.: Holy Virgin Mary.

Psalm

Sing joyfully to God our strength (80: 2); *cry jubilee to the Lord, the true and living God, with a voice of exultation.*

For the Lord, the Most High, the awesome, is the great King over all the earth (46: 3).

Our most holy Father of heaven, our King, before time was, sent his beloved Son from on high and he was born of the blessed and holy Virgin Mary.

He shall say of me, "You are my father," and I will make him the first-born, highest of the kings of the earth (88: 27-28).

By day the Lord bestows his grace, and at night I have his song (41: 9).

This is the day the Lord has made; let us be glad and rejoice in it (117: 24).

To our race this most holy and well loved son is given, for our sakes a child is born on the wayside and laid in a manger because there was no room for *him* in the inn (Lk. 2: 7).

Glory to God in the highest, and on earth peace among men of good will (Lk. 2: 14).

Let the heavens be glad and the earth rejoice, let the sea and what fills it resound; let the plains be joyful and all that is in them (95: 11-12).

Sing to the Lord a new song; sing to the Lord, all you lands (95: 1).

For great is the Lord and highly to be praised; awesome is he, beyond all gods (95: 4).

Give to the Lord, you families of nations, give to the Lord glory and praise; give to the Lord the glory due his name! (95: 7-8).

Prepare your hearts and take up his cross; live by his holy commandments to the last.

Appendix

1. Two Prayers

THE FOLLOWING two prayers are often attributed to St Francis, but modern writers raise serious objections to their authenticity.

(a) *The Paraphrase of the Our Father*[1]

In a number of manuscripts this Paraphrase precedes the *Praises Before the Office*. In others, however, it is omitted altogether. Furthermore, the style of the work seems to indicate that the work came from the pen of a man who had studied in the Schools. These reasons have led a number of recent critics to exclude it from the genuine works of St Francis.[2]

Our Father: Most holy, our Creator and Redeemer, our Saviour and our Comforter.

Who art in heaven: In the angels and the saints. You give them light so that they may have knowledge, because you, Lord, are light. You inflame them so that they may love, because you, Lord, are love. You live continually in them and you fill them so that they may be happy, because you, Lord, are the supreme good, the eternal good, and it is from you all good comes, and without you there is no good.

Hallowed be thy name: May our knowledge of you become ever clearer, so that we may realize the extent of your benefits, the steadfastness of your promises, the sublimity of your majesty and the depth of your judgments.

Thy kingdom come: So that you may reign in us by your grace and bring us to your kingdom, where we shall see you clearly, love you perfectly, be happy in your company and enjoy you for ever.

[1]See what was said about the *Praises Before the Office* (no. 5, Part Three).

[2]It may well be that this is a prayer that Francis knew and taught to the friars, and in that way can be said to be his prayer.

Thy will be done on earth as it is in heaven: That we may love you with our whole heart by always thinking of you; with our whole mind by directing our whole intention towards you and seeking your glory in everything; and with all our strength by spending all our energies and affections of soul and body in the service of your love alone. And may we love our neighbours as ourselves, encouraging them all to love you as best we can, rejoicing at the good fortune of others, just as if it were our own, and sympathizing with their misfortunes, while giving offence to no one.

Give us this day our daily bread: Your own beloved Son, our Lord Jesus Christ, to remind us of the love he showed for us and to help us understand and appreciate it and everything that he did or said or suffered.

And forgive us our trespasses: In your infinite mercy, and by the power of the Passion of your Son, our Lord Jesus Christ, together with the merits and the intercession of the Blessed Virgin Mary and all your saints.

As we forgive those who trespass against us: And if we do not forgive perfectly, Lord, make us forgive perfectly, so that we may really love our enemies for love of you, and pray fervently to you for them, returning no one evil for evil, anxious only to serve everybody in you.

And lead us not into temptation: Hidden or obvious, sudden or unforeseen.

But deliver us from evil: Present, past, or future. Amen.

(b) *The Prayer* Absorbeat[1]

THERE is so little manuscript support for this short prayer and its form is so stylized and so different from Francis' way of writing that it cannot be attributed to Francis with any certainty. It does, however, resemble broadly a short invocation attributed to St

---

[1]The Quaracchi editors of the *Opuscula* said: To prove the authenticity of this prayer we can adduce nothing but what Wadding said, namely, that St Bernardine (his works, II, serm. 60) and Ubertino da Casale (*Arbor vitae*) said Francis was its author. It too may be a prayer that Francis knew and taught to the friars.

Francis by Thomas of Celano in his *Second Life of St Francis*.[1]

May the power of your love, O Lord, fiery and sweet as honey, wean my heart from all that is under heaven, so that I may die for love of your love, you who were so good as to die for love of my love.

---

[1]*II Cel.*, 196: "The love of him," he said, "who loved us much is much to be loved."

2. *Letter to St Anthony*[1]

PERHAPS AS EARLY as 1219 the Friars Minor opened a house of studies in the university city of Bologna.[2] Not long after that date, it would seem, the friars asked St Anthony to undertake the task of teaching the young brothers their theology.[3] But, according to the account in the *Chronica XXIV Generalium*,[4] St Anthony, being a holy man, "did not presume to teach, no matter how urgent was the request of the friars, without first getting permission from Blessed Francis".

The chronicle implies that the permission was requested and then goes on to say that Francis "is said to have given" his

[1]This letter is contained in five related manuscripts that are known as the *Avignon Compilation*, in the so-called *Liber Miraculorum s. Antonii*, and in the *Chronica XXIV Generalium*. The *Compilation* has the introduction called *Fac secundum exemplar*, in which the author (a student at Avignon) explains that he put together this collection of texts for his own edification and to overcome laziness, and he says that he made some changes in them. He says too that he wrote in certain little-known things about St Anthony, among which may have been this letter. Whether he simply copied the letter, or put it together from the sources he had, is not really known. See *Archivum Franciscanum Historicum*, Vol. 45, pp. 474-492.

[2]St Anthony was born in Lisbon in 1195. Around 1210 he became an Augustinian canon. Shortly after he had seen the bodies of the first Franciscan martyrs (martyred in Morocco, January 16, 1220) brought to Portugal he became a novice in the Franciscan Order, 1220-1221. From 1221-1222 he lived as a hermit at Montepaolo. In the autumn of 1222 he was sent to preach in the province of Romagna. He was appointed first lector of theology in the Order in 1223 or 1224. Later, in 1224, he was sent to preach in France. In 1227 he returned to Italy, and after 1228 he lived in Padua. On June 13, 1231, he died, and on May 30, 1232, he was canonized. On June 16, 1946, he was declared a doctor of the Church.

[3]Eventually the friars' school of theology became the theological faculty of the university of Bologna (*c.* 1360).

[4]*Analecta Franciscana*, Vol. III, p. 132.

favourable answer in writing.[1] The text of the short reply is given in the words of the letter quoted below, with the exception that in place of the salutation "To Brother Anthony, my bishop" it says: "To my very dear Brother Anthony Brother Francis extends greetings in Christ."[2] It was Francis' first biographer, Thomas of Celano, who made mention of a letter that Francis wrote to St Anthony which began, "To Brother Anthony, my bishop", and it is this salutation that is usually given in connection with the letter quoted below.

That Francis wrote a letter to St Anthony, therefore, is certain. But the authenticity of the text of the letter as it has been handed down is very often called into question. As a matter of fact, the *Chronica XXIV Generalium* does speak with a certain amount of doubt implied by the verb *fertur*, "it is said", or, "it is narrated". Evidently the author of the chronicle did not see the letter, but only reported what he had heard. The text as he gives it, therefore, can only be a matter of hearsay. Much the same thing can be said of the text as it is reported in the various other manuscripts that contain the letter.[3]

The result has been that many writers have rejected the authenticity of the letter or at least have doubted its authenticity. Others, on the other hand, have advanced various arguments in support of its authenticity. But the Quaracchi editors of St Francis' writings were not convinced of its authenticity and

[1]That is, *fertur*.

[2]It is not surprising that Francis should use the term *bishop* for a learned theologian. The Fourth Lateran Council (1215) had said that the office of teaching pertains to the bishop; and Francis had asked that Ugolino be given to him as his *pope*, that is, as Cardinal Protector of his Order. See *II Cel.*, 163, for his reference to this letter. Bartholomew of Pisa, *Liber Conformitatum* (*Analecta Franciscana*, IV, p. 270), knew the salutation "my bishop", but he did not record the letter: he says that Anthony was much loved by St Francis, and he called Anthony "his bishop because of the great reverence he had towards him".

[3]The *Chronica XXIV Generalium* gives the letter as follows: *Hic autem vir sanctus Antonius legere non praesumpsit, quantumcumque rogatur fratribus, nisi beati Francisci praehabita voluntate. Qui tale in scriptis fertur dedisse responsum: "Carissimo meo fratri Antonio frater Franciscus salutem in Christo. Placet mihi, quod sacram theologiam leges fratribus, dummodo propter hujusmodi studium sanctae orationis et devotionis spiritum non extinguant, sicut in regula continetur. Vale."* *Analecta Franciscana*, III, p. 132.

therefore omitted it from their edition of the writings. In rather recent years a new study of the matter was undertaken by Fr Cajetan Esser, O.F.M.[1] After a brief examination of the manuscripts in question and of the text as it has been handed down in the various sources, he concluded that there can hardly be any further doubt about the authenticity of the text of the letter as we know it. However, about three years later, Fr Ottokar Bonmann, O.F.M., took up the question again by way of reply to Fr Cajetan.[2] He made a more thorough examination of the manuscripts and the text and concluded that, to date, no one had as yet given an objectively valid argument in support of the letter's authenticity. And there the matter stands, still unresolved, though many writers at the present time are becoming more and more inclined to accept its authenticity.[3]

The most likely date for the letter, if indeed it was written by St Francis, would be late 1223 or early 1224, since this date would correspond better to the known activities of St Anthony at this time.

LETTER TO ST ANTHONY

To BROTHER ANTHONY, my bishop, Brother Francis sends greetings.

It is agreeable to me that you should teach the friars sacred theology, so long as they do not extinguish the spirit of prayer and devotedness over this study, as is contained in the Rule. Farewell.

[1] *Franziskanische Studien*, Vol. 31, 1949, pp. 135-151. Fr Cajetan based his argument upon the history of the manuscripts, the text derived from the three most ancient traditions (*Chronica XXIV Generalium, Liber Miraculorum S. Antonii*, the manuscripts of the Avignon compilation; the *Liber*, however, derives its text from the *Chronica XXIV Generalium*).

[2] *Archivum Franciscanum Historicum*, Vol. 45, 1952, pp. 474-492.

[3] Fr Bonmann concludes: "If one wants to hold that the compiler of Avignon reconstructed the letter, there are good reasons to support him, though they do not prove it conclusively. But no one as yet has given any objectively valid argument to prove that St Francis wrote this particular letter to St Anthony." *Loc. cit.*

3. The Rule of the Third Order (1221)[1]

AFTER FRANCIS and his first followers had obtained papal approbation of their Rule in 1209, they first lived for a short time in a deserted place near Orte and then went on to live in the Spoleto valley.[2] At this point in his narrative of the life of St Francis, Thomas of Celano introduces the following account of Francis' activity: "Francis, therefore, the most valiant knight of Christ, went about the towns and villages announcing the kingdom of God, preaching peace, teaching salvation and penance unto the remission of sins. . . . He acted boldly in all things, because of the apostolic authority granted to him, using no words of flattery or seductive blandishments. . . . Men ran, women too ran, clerics hurried, and religious hastened that they might see and hear the holy man of God who seemed to all to be a man of another world. Every age and every sex hurried to see the wonderful things that the Lord was newly working in the world through his servant. It seemed at that time, whether because of the presence of St Francis or through his reputation, that a new light had been sent from heaven upon this earth, shattering the widespread darkness that had so filled almost the whole region that hardly anyone knew where to go. For so profound was the forgetfulness of God and the sleep of neglect of his commandments

[1]With some slight modifications, the present translation of the Third Order Rule is that of Fr James Meyer, O.F.M., prepared for *The Words of St Francis*, Franciscan Herald Press, 1952. It is based upon the so-called Venice version of the Rule, which was discovered unexpectedly in the library of Landau in Codex 225-226. This codex dates back to the thirteenth century or at the latest the fourteenth century. The Third Order Rule forms the second part of this codex (fol. 183r-185v). See the description of the codex and the text of the Rule in *Archivum Franciscanum Historicum*, Vol. 14, pp. 109-121.

[2]*I Cel.*, 34-35. Celano says they lived near Orte for fifteen days.

oppressing almost everyone that they could hardly be aroused even a little from their old and deeply rooted sins.

"Francis shone forth like a brilliant star in the obscurity of the night and like the morning spread upon the darkness. And thus it happened that in a short time the face of the region was changed, and it took on a more cheerful aspect everywhere, once the former foulness had been laid aside. . . . Many of the people, both noble and ignoble, cleric and lay, impelled by divine inspiration, began to come to St Francis, wanting to carry on the battle constantly under his discipline and under his leadership. All of these the holy man of God, like a plenteous river of heavenly grace, watered with streams of gifts; he enriched the field of their hearts with flowers of virtue, for he was an excellent craftsman; and, according to his plan, rule, and teaching, proclaimed before all, the Church is being renewed in both sexes, and the threefold army of those to be saved is triumphing. To all he gave a norm of life, and he showed in truth the way of salvation in every walk of life."[1]

Traditionally, the date for the founding of the Third Order is given as 1221.[2] Nevertheless, the words of Celano point to an

---

[1]*Ibid.*, 36-37.

[2]Among the older sources the *Chronica XXIV Generalium* (*c.* 1370) gives the date of the founding of the Third Order as 1221 (*Analecta Franciscana*, III, p. 27). The *Liber Conformitatum* (*c.* 1390) does not give the year but says that it was founded about the fourteenth year after Francis' conversion (*Analecta*, IV, pp. 360-361). Julian of Speyer (*Vita S. Francisci*, *c.* 1232), says that Francis founded, in addition to the First and Second Orders, the Third Order of Penitents for clerics and lay, for virgins and married of both sexes, but without giving any date. Like Celano, whose *First Life* he follows, he inserts the founding of the three Orders immediately after his account of the return of Francis and his followers to the Spoleto valley (*Analecta*, X, p. 346. See also his rhythmic Office for the feast of St Francis, *ibid.*, p. 380). St Bonaventure, *Legenda Major S. Francisci* (*c.* 1262), inserts the account of the Third Order just after the account of Francis' moving from Rivo Torto to the Porziuncola (*Analecta*, X, p. 573). The *Legenda Trium Sociorum* (probably early 14th century) puts it in about the same place (Chapter XIV). In his Bull of December 16, 1221, *Significatum est*, Pope Honorius III gave orders to the bishop of Rimini to take the Brothers of Penance of Faenza, near Rimini, and of the neighbouring towns and villages under his protection; this would indicate that the Third Order was already well established by 1221 (*Bullarium*, I, 8). Originally the Third Order was called "Order of

earlier date. It is true, of course, that in this passage Celano is looking forward a bit rather than giving a strictly chronological sequence of events. This is obvious from the fact that he speaks here of "the threefold army", including therefore also the Order of Poor Clares, which was founded in 1212, after the events mentioned here.[1] Still, there is every reason to believe that Francis did not wait until 1221 to found the Third Order, for Celano's account shows very definitely that the response to Francis' preaching was remarkably great from the very beginning and that many people wanted, from the beginning, to follow a life similar to that of Francis and his early followers.

Undoubtedly, Francis very early drew up some kind of short Rule of life for these people who could not leave the world yet wanted to strive after perfection as he was striving after perfection. Quite likely, he did this as early as 1209 or 1210, but certainly before 1221. In 1221, however, Cardinal Ugolino, the Protector of the Franciscan Order and Francis' close friend, took Francis' original short Rule and set it up in more legal form. This Rule, then, was approved orally in that year by Pope Honorius III.[2]

During the years that followed considerable confusion grew around the Third Order Rule by reason of the divergent local versions of it that came into existence and by reason of the addition of various local statutes. In 1289, therefore, Pope

---

Penance," and the members were called "Brothers and Sisters of Penance" (those turning to God from a sinful and idle life) or "Brothers and Sisters of Continence" (those refraining from certain things). The name "Third Order" seems to have been first used by Pope Gregory IX in 1230 in a letter addressed to all the bishops of Italy.

[1] The older biographers did not feel themselves always bound to adhere to the strict chronological order of events. Already in paragraphs 18-20 Celano speaks of the founding of the Poor Clares, and at the end of paragraph 50 he says: "But now let us return to what we were speaking of above and observe again the historical order."

[2] Fr Cuthbert, in his *The Life of St Francis of Assisi* (1912, p. 283) quotes the author of the *Vita Gregorii IX* as saying that Cardinal Ugolino instituted the Third Order and the Poor Clares. Bernard of Besse (*Liber de Laudibus, Analecta*, III, p. 686) is certainly more correct in saying that Ugolino supplied what was wanting to Francis in composing the Rule of the Third Order.

Nicholas IV issued a universally uniform Rule[1] that remained in force until Pope Leo XIII adapted it to more modern conditions in 1883.[2] Pope Leo's adaptation of the Rule is the Rule of the Third Order today, supplemented by the General Constitutions approved in 1957.[3]

The original Rule that Francis drew up for the Third Order is no longer extant. But the Rule that Cardinal Ugolino drew up in 1221 contained, undoubtedly, the substance of that original Rule. Cardinal Ugolino's Rule is preserved in four ancient versions: (a) the Venice Rule, which dates back beyond 1228; (b) the Koenigsberg Rule, also before 1228; (c) the Capistrano Rule, from about 1228; and (d) the Mariano Rule, from about 1234 or later.[4] The translation given here is a translation of the Venice Rule.

FIRST RULE OF THE THIRD ORDER

Here begins the Rule of the Continent Brothers and Sisters

IN THE NAME of the Father and of the Son and of the Holy Spirit. Amen.

The memorial of what is proposed for the Brothers and Sisters of Penance living in their own homes, begun in the year of our Lord 1221, is as follows.

Chapter I: Daily Life

1. The men belonging to this brotherhood shall dress in humble,

[1] In twenty chapters. Bull *Supra montem.*

[2] Reduced to three chapters. Bull *Misericors Dei Filius.*

[3] Pope Leo X issued a basic Rule for the Third Order Regular, *Inter cetera*, 1521. This Rule was superseded by a new basic Rule in 1927, *Rerum conditio*, Pius XI.

[4] An English translation of the Capistrano Rule can be found in *The Rules of the Third Order of St Francis*, Maximus Poppy, O.F.M., Franciscan Institute, St Bonaventure, N.Y., 1945. A description of the other versions of the Rule can be found in *Archivum Franciscanum Historicum*: in Vol. 6, pp. 242-250, the Koenigsberg Rule; in Vol. 13, pp. 3-77, the Mariano Rule; in Vol. 14, pp. 109-121, the Venice Rule. See also the excellent article on the founding of the Third Order by Fr Marion Habig, O.F.M., in *Franciscan Herald and Forum*, April 1959, "Seven Hundred and Fifty Years."

undyed cloth, the price of which is not to exceed six Ravenna soldi an ell, unless for evident and necessary cause a temporary dispensation be given. And breadth and thinness of the cloth are to be considered in said price.

2. They shall wear their outer garments and furred coats without open throat, sewed shut or uncut but certainly laced up, not open as secular people wear them; and they shall wear their sleeves closed.

3. The sisters in turn shall wear an outer garment and tunic made of cloth of the same price and humble quality; or at least they are to have with the outer garment a white or black underwrap or petticoat, or an ample linen gown without gathers, the price of an ell of which is not to exceed twelve Pisa denars. As to this price, however, and the fur cloaks they wear a dispensation may be given according to the estate of the woman and the custom of the place. They are not to wear silken or dyed veils and ribbons.

4. And both the brothers and the sisters shall have their fur garments of lamb's wool only. They are permitted to have leather purses and belts sewed in simple fashion without silken thread, and no other kind. Also other vain adornments they shall lay aside at the bidding of the Visitor.

5. They are not to go to unseemly parties or to shows or dances. They shall not donate to actors, and shall forbid their household to donate.

Chapter II: Abstinence

6. All are to abstain from meat save on Sundays, Tuesdays, and Thursdays, except on account of illness or weakness, for three days at blood-letting, in travelling, or on account of a specially high feast intervening, namely, the Nativity for three days, New Year's, Epiphany, the Pasch of the Resurrection for three days, the holy Apostles Peter and Paul, St John the Baptist, the Assumption of the glorious Virgin Mary, the solemnity of All Saints and of St Martin. On the other days, when there is no fasting, they may eat cheese and eggs. But when they are with

religious in their convent homes, they have leave to eat what is
served to them. And except for the feeble, the ailing, and those
travelling, let them be content with dinner and supper. Let the
healthy be temperate in eating and drinking.

7. Before their dinner and supper let them say the Lord's prayer
once, likewise after their meal, and let them give thanks to God.
Otherwise let them say three *Our Fathers*.

Chapter III: Fasting

8. From the Pasch of the Resurrection to the feast of All Saints
they are to fast on Fridays. From the feast of All Saints until
Easter they are to fast on Wednesdays and Fridays, but still
observing the other fasts enjoined in general by the Church.

9. They are to fast daily, except on account of infirmity or any
other need, throughout the fast of St Martin from after said day
until Christmas, and throughout the greater fast from Carnival
Sunday until Easter.

10. Sisters who are pregnant are free to refrain until their
purification from the corporal observances except those regarding their dress and prayers.

11. Those engaged in fatiguing work shall be allowed to take
food three times a day from the Pasch of the Resurrection until
the Dedication feast of St Michael. And when they work for
others it will be allowed them to eat everything served to them,
except on Fridays and on the fasts enjoined in general by the
Church.

Chapter IV: Prayer

12. All are daily to say the seven canonical Hours, that is,
Matins, Prime, Terce, Sext, None, Vespers, and Compline.
The clerics are to say them after the manner of the clergy.
Those who know the Psalter are to say the *Deus in nomine tuo*
and the *Beati immaculati* up to the *Legem pone* for Prime, and the
other psalms of the Hours, with the *Glory be to the Father*; but
when they do not attend church, they are to say for Matins the
psalms the Church says or any eighteen psalms; or at least to

say the *Our Father* as do the unlettered at any of the Hours.

The others say twelve *Our Fathers* for Matins and for every one of the other Hours seven *Our Fathers* with the *Glory be to the Father* after each one. And those who know the *Creed* and the *Miserere mei Deus* should say it at Prime and Compline. If they do not say that at the Hours indicated, they shall say three *Our Fathers*.

13. The sick are not to say the Hours unless they wish.

14. All are to go to Matins in the fast of St Martin and in the great fast, unless inconvenience for persons or affairs should threaten.

Chapter V: The Sacraments, Other Matters

15. They are to make a confession of their sins three times a year and to receive Communion at Christmas, Easter, and Pentecost. They are to be reconciled with their neighbours and to restore what belongs to others. They are to make up for past tithes and pay future tithes.

16. They are not to take up lethal weapons, or bear them about, against anybody.

17. All are to refrain from formal oaths unless where necessity compels, in the cases excepted by the Sovereign Pontiff in his indult, that is, for peace, for the Faith, under calumny, and in bearing witness.

18. Also in their ordinary conversations they will do their best to avoid oaths. And should anyone have sworn thoughtlessly through a slip of the tongue, as happens where there is much talking, he should the evening of the same day, when he is obliged to think over what he has done, say three *Our Fathers* in amends of such oaths. Let each member fortify his household to serve God.

Chapter VI: Special Mass and Meeting Each Month

19. All the brothers and sisters of every city and place are to foregather every month at the time the ministers see fit, in a

church which the ministers will make known, and there assist
at Divine services.

20. And every member is to give the treasurer one ordinary
denar. The treasurer is to collect this money and distribute it
on the advice of the ministers among the poor brothers and
sisters, especially the sick and those who may have nothing for
their funeral services, and thereupon among other poor; and
they are to offer something of the money to the aforesaid
church.

21. And, if it be convenient at the time, they are to have some
religious who is informed in the words of God to exhort them
and strengthen them to persevere in their penance and in performing the works of mercy. And except for the officers, they are
to remain quiet during the Mass and sermon, intent on the
Office, on prayer, and on the sermon.

Chapter VII: Visiting the Sick, Burying the Dead

22. Whenever any brother or sister happens to fall ill, the
ministers, if the patient let them know of it, shall in person or
through others visit the patient once a week, and remind him
of penance; and if they find it expedient, they are to supply
him from the common fund with what he may need for the
body.

23. And if the ailing person depart from this life, it is to be
published to the brothers and sisters who may be present in the
city or place, so that they may gather for the funeral; and they
are not to leave until the Mass has been celebrated and the body
consigned to burial. Thereupon each member within eight days
of the demise shall say for the soul of the deceased: a Mass, if he
is a priest; fifty psalms, if he understands the Psalter, or if not
then fifty *Our Fathers* with the *Requiem aeternam* at the end of each.

24. In addition, every year, for the welfare of the brothers and
sisters living and dead, each priest is to say three Masses, each
member knowing the Psalter is to recite it, and the rest shall say

one hundred *Our Fathers* with the *Requiem aeternam* at the end of each.[1]

25. All who have the right are to make their last will and make disposition of their goods within three months after their profession, lest anyone of them die intestate.

26. As regards making peace among the brothers and sisters or non-members at odds, let what the ministers find proper be done; even, if it be expedient, upon consultation with the Lord Bishop.

27. If contrary to their right and privileges trouble is made for the brothers and sisters by the mayors and governors of the places where they live, the ministers of the place shall do what they shall find expedient on the advice of the Lord Bishop.

28. Let each member accept and faithfully exercise the ministry of other offices imposed on him, although anyone may retire from office after a year.

29. When anybody wishes to enter this brotherhood, the ministers shall carefully inquire into his standing and occupation, and they shall explain to him the obligations of the brotherhood, especially that of restoring what belongs to others. And if he is content with it, let him be vested according to the prescribed way, and he must make satisfaction for his debts, paying money according to what pledged provision is given. They are to reconcile themselves with their neighbours and to pay up their tithes.

30. After these particulars are complied with, when the year is up and he seems suitable to them, let him on the advice of some discreet brothers be received on this condition: that he promise he will all the time of his life observe everything here written, or to be written or abated on the advice of the brothers, unless on occasion there be a valid dispensation by the ministers; and that he will, when called upon by the ministers, render satisfaction as the Visitor shall ordain if he have done anything contrary to this condition. And this promise is to be put in writing

[1]This paragraph ends with this added incomplete statement: "Otherwise let them duplicate. . . ."

then and there by a public notary. Even so nobody is to be received otherwise, unless in consideration of the estate and rank of the person it shall seem advisable to the ministers.

31. No one is to depart from this brotherhood and from what is contained herein, except to enter a religious Order.

32. No heretic or person in bad repute for heresy is to be received. If he is under suspicion of it, he may be admitted if otherwise fit, upon being cleared before the bishop.

33. Married women are not to be received except with the consent and leave of their husbands.

34. Brothers and sisters ejected from the brotherhood as incorrigible are not to be received in it again except it please the saner portion of the brothers.

Chapter VIII: Correction, Dispensation, Officers

35. The ministers of any city or place shall report public faults of the brothers and sisters to the Visitor for punishment. And if anyone proves incorrigible, after consultation with some of the discreet brothers he should be denounced to the Visitor, to be expelled by him from the brotherhood, and thereupon it should be published in the meeting. Moreover, if it is a brother, he should be denounced to the mayor or the governor.

36. If anyone learns that scandal is occurring relative to brothers and sisters, he shall report it to the ministers and shall have opportunity to report it to the Visitor. He need not be held to report it in the case of husband against wife.

37. The Visitor has the power to dispense all the brothers and sisters in any of these points if he finds it advisable.

38. When the year has passed, the ministers with the counsel of the brothers are to elect two other ministers; and a faithful treasurer, who is to provide for the need of the brothers and sisters and other poor; and messengers who at the command of the ministers are to publish what is said and done by the fraternity.

39. In all the above mentioned points no one is to be obligated under guilt, but under penalty; yet so that if after being

admonished twice by the ministers he should fail to discharge the penalty imposed or to be imposed on him by the Visitor, he shall be obligated under guilt as contumacious.

Here ends the Rule of the Continent.[1]

---

[1]At the end of the Venice Rule, as with the other versions of the Rule, local *items* are added, things of special obligation for the local fraternities.

FIRST AND SECOND LIFE
OF ST. FRANCIS
with selections from
TREATISE ON THE MIRACLES
OF BL. FRANCIS
by Thomas of Celano

Translated from the Latin, with
Introduction and Notes by
Placid Hermann O.F.M.

First published in 1963 by Franciscan Herald
Press, Chicago. Library of Congress Catalog
Card Number: 62-22288. Illustrated edition,
xxviii-245 pp.; SBN: 8199-0097-4. Paper, liv-405
pp. SBN: 8199-0098-2.

INTRODUCTION

1

THE AUTHOR

Brother Thomas, the first biographer of St. Francis of Assisi, was born in the little town of Celano in central Italy.[1] Accordingly, he is always known as Brother Thomas of Celano. The year of his birth, however, is not known with any degree of certainty. A recent writer in *Ecclesia* (1960), a monthly publication from the Vatican, expressed the opinion that Brother Thomas was born in 1185. Though this cannot as yet be regarded as certain, it may at least be close to the actual date, for we know from the other facts of his life that he was born some time during the closing years of the twelfth century. The name of his family is likewise unknown.

It is very probable that Brother Thomas entered the Franciscan Order between the years 1213 and 1216, and quite likely in the year 1215. This conclusion seems to follow from what he himself says in his *First Life of St. Francis,* numbers 56-57. There, after telling of Francis' unsuccessful attempt to go to Morocco as a missionary, he implies that Almighty God had his own personal welfare in view in thus frustrating Francis' desire to carry the word of God to that country and his desire for martyrdom. Brother Thomas writes: "But the good God, whom it pleased in his kindness to be mindful of me and of many others, *withstood him to his face* (Gal. 2, 11) when he had traveled as far as Spain; and, that he might not go any farther, he recalled him from the journey he had begun by a prolonged illness."[2] Brother Thomas then goes on to tell how very shortly after Francis' return to the Portiuncula, "some educated and noble men"[3] were received into the order. Most authors think that Brother Thomas was among these men. Accordingly, since Francis' unsuccessful journey to Morocco took place most probably during the winter of 1213-1214,[4] and since he was turned back while he was in Spain, he must have returned to the Portiuncula late in 1214 or early in 1215. Not long thereafter[5] Thomas was received into the order along with the other educated and noble men of whom he speaks. Some think that he had already been ordained a priest before his entry into the order.

Nothing is known of the life of Brother Thomas during the first years he was a member of the Franciscan Order. The first information we get concerning him comes to us from the *Chronicle of Brother Jordan of Giano.*[6] Brother Jordan tells us that among the brothers chosen to undertake the founding of the order in Germany in 1221 was "Thomas of Celano, who later wrote both a first and a second *Legenda* of St. Francis."[7] These brothers were chosen at the general chapter of 1221, held at Assisi,[8] and they left for Germany about three months later, in September 1221. On October 16 they arrived at Augsburg under the leadership of Brother Caesar of Speyer, who had been appointed at that same chapter the first minister provincial of Germany. The following year, 1222, Brother Caesar held a provincial chapter at Worms, and in this chapter Brother Thomas of Celano was appointed custos of Mainz, Worms, Cologne, and Speyer.[9] In 1223 Brother Caesar appointed Brother Thomas to serve as vicar provincial in Germany while he himself attended the general chapter of the order at Assisi.[10] This general chapter relieved Brother Caesar of his office and appointed Brother Albert of Pisa to succeed him as minister provincial of Germany.

Brother Thomas was still in Germany on September 8, 1223, because, on the authority of Brother

Jordan,[11] he was present at the provincial chapter held at Speyer on that day. Apparently he was relieved of his office of custos at this time. The German province was divided in this chapter into four custodies, according to Brother Jordan, who gives the names of the four who were appointed custodes and of the four custodies over which they were to preside. Brother Thomas is not named among them.[12] It is quite generally assumed that Brother Thomas left Germany about this time, or shortly thereafter, and returned to Italy. He is not mentioned anymore in connection with the German province,[13] but he is known to have been in Italy a little later.

Apparently Brother Thomas did not have any really close contact with St. Francis during the last years of the saint's life. True, he does give a rather complete account of these last years, especially 1224-1226; but his account is based only in part upon what he himself experienced, and otherwise, as he himself says, upon what he could learn from others.[14] However, his description of the ceremonies of Francis' canonization gives the impression that he was present for that solemn ceremony on July 16, 1228. It was on this occasion too, or perhaps somewhat earlier, that Pope Gregory IX commissioned Brother Thomas to write his *First Life of St. Francis.*

In 1230 Brother Thomas was living in Assisi. It was there that Brother Jordan of Giano visited him after he had completed his business with the minister general[15] on behalf of the minister provincial of the Rhine.[16] Brother Thomas gave some relics of St. Francis to Brother Jordan to take back to Germany.[17] No doubt, Brother Thomas was present that year at the translation ceremonies, when St. Francis' body was taken from the church of St. George in Assisi, where he was first buried, to the new basilica of St. Francis.[18]

Brother Thomas is not heard of in the early sources of Franciscan history for the next fourteen years. Then, at the general chapter of the order held at Genoa in 1244, the newly elected minister general, Crescentius of Jesi,[19] asked Brother Thomas to write a second life of St. Francis, and he issued an order that whatever material could be gathered together by the brothers concerning the life and miracles of St. Francis should be sent to the minister general.[20] The response to this order was generous, and Brother Thomas used this material for the writing of his second life of St. Francis.

Several years later, probably shortly before 1250, Brother Thomas was again asked to write about St. Francis, this time by the new minister general, John of Parma.[21] The new work, the *Treatise on the Miracles of Blessed Francis*, was written between the years 1250-1253. Most likely Brother Thomas was living at Assisi during the writing of this treatise as well as during the writing of the earlier *Second Life*. And it is quite likely that he was still living in that city when he wrote his last work, the *Legenda Sanctae Clarae*, during the years 1255-1256. This life of St. Clare was written at the order of Pope Alexander IV.[22]

It seems that Brother Thomas spent the last years of his life, with the exception of the years spent at Assisi writing the life of St. Clare, in Tagliacozzo, in the custody of the Marches. Apparently he had charge of the Poor Clare nuns of the monastery of St. John of Varro. He died in 1260 or not long thereafter and was buried in the Poor Clare monastery. However, the Poor Clares gave up this monastery in 1476; and in 1506, by order of Pope Julian II, it became the property of the Friars Minor Conventual. In 1516 Brother Thomas' body was laid to rest behind the high altar of their church, and at the beginning of the eighteenth century it was clothed in the habit of the Friars Minor Conventual and laid to rest under the high altar at Tagliacozzo. The tomb is marked with this inscription:

B. THOMAS DE CELANO S.F.D.
SCRIPTOR CRONICAR ET SEQUENTIAE
MORTUOR[23]

2
THE WORKS OF THOMAS OF CELANO

The *First Life of St. Francis*

On April 29, 1228, Pope Gregory IX issued a Bull authorizing the building of a church to honor St. Francis of Assisi.[24] This was done in anticipation of the canonization of the saint, three months later, July 16, 1228. It is likely that already at this time Pope Gregory commissioned Thomas of Celano to write the first biography of the new saint. In any case he did so at some time during the months that followed, or at least on the day of the canonization itself. Celano himself tells us that he wrote the *First Life of St. Francis* "at the command of our lord, the gloriously reigning Pope Gregory."[25]

Brother Thomas must have set to work immediately on this first life of the founder of the order, for, if we can trust a note in one manuscript of the work, the completed biography was presented to the pope and received his approbation seven months later, on February 25, 1229. This, the Paris manuscript, dating back to at least the fourteenth century, says: *Apud Perusium felix dominus papa Gregorius nonus secundo gloriosi pontificatus sui anno quinto Kal. martii legendam hanc recepit, confirmavit, et censuit fore tenendum.*[26] At any rate, whether this statement of the Paris manuscript is correct or not, the biography must certainly have been completed before May 25, 1230, for it does not make mention of the very important event that took place on that day, namely, the translation of the remains of St. Francis from the church of St. George in Assisi to the new basilica that was being erected to honor the saint.

Just why Pope Gregory IX chose Brother Thomas of Celano for this task is not known. However, he was admirably suited for the task. He was a learned man, probably one of those "educated and noble men" who were admitted into the order shortly after Francis' return from Spain. The work itself shows that the author was both a skilled literary craftsman and a painstaking artist.[27] Whether or not he had become known by reason of some other literary work and for that reason drew the attention of the holy father is not known. There is a possibility, in no way proven however, that he might have been the author of the *Sacrum Commercium S. Francisci cum Domina Paupertate*,[28] a little allegorical work that is dated 1227. If this were so, there would then be at hand an excellent reason why Pope Gregory should have chosen him from among many others for this task, for the *Sacrum Commercium* is a literary gem.

The *First Life* is prefaced by a Prologue in which Brother Thomas tells briefly of the command of Pope Gregory IX to write the life and how he intends to proceed. The life itself is divided into three *opuscula* or books. The first book, which "follows the historical order,"[29] tells of the years of Francis' early youth, his conversion, the founding of the order, his holy life and teaching; and it concludes with an account of Francis' celebration of Christmas at Greccio in 1223. The historical order, however, is followed only in a general way, not with precision. The second book gives an account of the last two years of Francis' life on earth and covers above all the stigmatization, the death, and the burial of the saint. The third book consists of two parts. The first part tells of the canonization of St. Francis on July 16, 1228, and the second part recounts the miracles that were accepted and read as a part of that colorful ceremony of canonization. The life closes with a short Epilogue in which the author asks to be remembered before God by the reader.

Brother Thomas used as his sources for this *First Life* his own personal experience and the testimony of reliable witnesses.[30] He himself, however, could not have spent too much time in the company of St. Francis, as is evident from the brief chronology of his life given above. Hence he had to rely to a great extent on the testimony of others. These others, no doubt, included many of Francis' early companions who were still living, men like Brother Leo, Brother Rufino, Brother Angelo, and many others, as the occasion arose. He could also consult Brother Elias, who had been Francis' vicar from 1221 until the election of John Parenti as minister general in 1227. He could also consult Pope Gregory IX, who already as Cardinal Hugolino had been a close friend of the saint. Bishop Guido, too, of Assisi, and St. Clare, Francis' first daughter, and her companions were likewise available.

Furthermore, Brother Thomas had access to Francis' own writings, which he seems to have had at hand, since he quotes from or alludes to them quite frequently, such things as the Rule of 1221, the Rule of 1223, the *Testament, The Canticle of our Brother the Sun,* the admonitions of St. Francis, and other writings. He used also Brother Elias' letter announcing the death of St. Francis to the brothers around the world and the Bull of Canonization. Whether or not he was able to make use of the official *Acta* of the process of canonization, we do not know; these

185

official *Acta* are no longer extant. However, the fact that he did make use of such *Acta* in writing his life of St. Clare leads us to believe that he did surely make use of them for his life of St. Francis, at least if they were at all available to him. There were, of course, no other *legendae* in existence at this time concerning St. Francis' life, since Celano's was the first biography of the saint.[31]

This *First Life,* no doubt, is the most important document concerning St. Francis and things Franciscan that we have, written as it was so soon after the saint's death and presented as the official biography of the saint, commissioned by Pope Gregory IX, for the general edification of the faithful.

The *Second Life of St. Francis*

In the general chapter of the order held at Genoa in 1244 the minister general, Crescentius of Jesi, "commanded all the friars to send to him in writing whatever they could know with certainty about the life, signs, and wonders of Blessed Francis."[32] The response to this appeal was generous. Brother Leo, Brother Rufino, and Brother Angelo, in particular, gathered together what they could from their own experience and from the experience of others of the early companions of St. Francis and transmitted this material to the minister general along with a covering letter explaining what they had done.

This letter is addressed to the minister general, "our reverend father and brother in Christ, by the grace of God minister general," by "Brother Leo, Brother Rufino, and Brother Angelo, onetime companions, though unworthy, of the most blessed Francis." These companions refer to the command issued at the general chapter of Genoa and then go on to describe their procedure:

it seemed good to us who lived with him
for a long time, though we were unworthy,
to present to your holiness a few things we
are sure of from among the many things he
did, things which we ourselves saw or which
we could learn from other holy brothers,
and especially from Brother Philip, the
visitor of the Poor Ladies, Brother
Illuminato of Rieti, Brother Masseo of
Marignano, and Brother John, the companion of the venerable Brother Giles, who
had learned many things from that same
Brother Giles and from Brother Bernard
of blessed memory, the first companion of
the blessed Francis.

The three companions then go on to say that they
are not writing these things "after the fashion of a
legend, since legends have already been written about
his life and the miracles the Lord performed through
him." On the contrary, they say they are presenting
these things as so many "flowers gathered from a
delightful meadow," flowers they regard as more
beautiful than the rest. "We are not offering, therefore," they go on to say, "a continuous story, for we
have omitted many things that have already been
written in the legends mentioned before in so truthful and brilliant a style."[33] Apparently the three
companions were not looking forward to an entirely
new life of St. Francis, for they added: "these few
things which we have written you can insert in the
legends already mentioned, if your discretion sees
fit to do so." They closed their letter with this
thought: "We believe that if these things had been
known to the venerable men who wrote the legends
mentioned before, they would certainly not have
passed them by, but would have embellished them
with their own style and handed them down for a
remembrance to those who would come after them."

The letter is dated: Greccio, August 11, 1246.[34]

Some time after the command of the minister general in this matter had been issued, Crescentius also asked Brother Thomas of Celano to undertake the writing of a second life of St. Francis. This may have been at that same general chapter of 1244 or at some time during the following two years. The chronicler Brother Salimbene, writing between 1282 and 1288, says: "He [Crescentius] ordered Brother Thomas of Celano, who had written the first legend of Blessed Francis, to write another book, inasmuch as many things had been uncovered about the blessed Francis that had not been written down."[35] Moreover, Brother Thomas himself refers to this command in the Prologue of the *Second Life*: "It has pleased the entire holy assembly of the past general chapter and you, Most Reverend Father, not without the disposition of divine wisdom, to enjoin upon our littleness that we set down in writing ... the deeds and also the words of our glorious father Francis, inasmuch as they were better known to us than to the rest because of our close association with him and our mutual intimacy. We hasten to obey with humble devotion the holy injunctions which we cannot pass over."[36]

The companions of St. Francis forwarded this material to the minister general, as was indicated, on August 11, 1246. This material was then given to Brother Thomas to be used in the composition of a new life of St. Francis. It need not be supposed, however, that Brother Thomas relied solely on this material. It would have been only natural for him to have gathered material himself ever since he had completed the *First Life*, for he must have realized that much could be added to the things he had been able to learn at that time. Furthermore, the command of the minister general had been issued to all the brothers, not merely to those who had been close companions of St. Francis. It may well be, therefore, that Brother Thomas received other material too, in addition to what he received from the three companions, either by word of mouth or in writing.

In any case, Brother Thomas set to work on a new life of St. Francis. It is evident especially from the Prologue of the *Life* and from the prayer that concludes it that Brother Thomas regarded himself as being rather the spokesman of the brothers who had supplied most of the material than as writing simply in his own name. In the Prologue quoted above he is speaking in the first person plural and in the name of those who were close associates and intimates of St. Francis. Furthermore, in the so-called *Prayer of Francis' Companions to Him*,[37] the first person plural is used consistently, as though the several companions and Brother Thomas were speaking as one.

Nevertheless, there can be no doubt at all about Celano being really the sole author of the whole. Already in the Prologue he refers to himself as the author when he says that the present work contains certain things that were not included in the earlier work because "they had not come to the notice of the author."[38] Again, throughout the work, when the first person is used, it is always, with few exceptions,[39] the first person singular.[40] Finally, it is evident from the third section of the concluding prayer that Thomas alone is the author, for though this prayer is put upon the lips of the several companions in a rather elaborate apostrophe, it has a very personal reference to the one author: "We beseech you also with all the affection of our hearts, most kind Father, for this your son who now and earlier has devotedly written your praises. He, together with us, offers and dedicates this little work." Beyond a doubt, therefore, Thomas of Celano is the sole author of the

Second Life, even though, in a sense, he regards himself as the spokesman for those who supplied the material for the new life.

The *Second Life* is often call the *Memoriale in Desiderio Animae* from the opening words of Book One. The whole work begins with the aforementioned Prologue, which tells how the life came to be written and closes with a dedication to the minister general. The dedication consists of a play on the name *Crescentius:* "so that the things that are approved as well said by your learned judgment may indeed grow together with your name *Crescentius* and be multiplied in Christ. Amen." The life itself is divided into two books. The first book is comparatively short and covers much the same period that was covered in the first book of the *First Life*: the naming of Francis at baptism, the conversion of Francis, the founding of the order, the appointment of Cardinal Hugolino as protector of the order. However, it is evident that Brother Thomas is writing this section only as a supplement to what had already been said in the *First Life,* for it repeats little, but only adds details. The second book treats a variety of subjects in a rather systematic and logical arrangement of the material. As Brother Thomas says, it is his intention to bring out "what was the good and acceptable will of Francis both for himself and for his followers in every practice of heavenly discipline and in zeal for the highest perfection which he ever had toward God in his sacred affections and toward men in his examples."[41] Certain miracles are inserted, "as occasion for inserting them presents itself."[42] The latter part of this second book returns again to the chronological order and treats of Francis' illnesses, his stigmatization, death, canonization, and translation. However, the latter part of this section is missing and nothing actually is said concerning the translation of his remains from the church of St. George to the lower church of the new basilica. But one can easily return to the *First Life* to supply the conclusion of the canonization ceremonies and to the *Legenda ad usum chori* for at least a brief note concerning the translation.[43]

As was said, Brother Thomas dedicated the *Second Life* to the minister general who had asked him to write it, Crescentius of Jesi. No doubt, when Brother Thomas had completed the life, he forwarded it to the minister general. However, Crescentius did not go personally to the next general chapter, July 13, 1247, and he was released from his office "because of his insufficiencies."[44] Still, he did forward to the chapter Brother Thomas' work; and John of Parma, who was elected minister general at this chapter, confirmed the *Second Life* either at the chapter itself or not long thereafter.[45] Obviously, therefore, the *Second Life* was written for the most part between August 11, 1246, the date on which the three companions sent their material to the minister general, and July 13, 1247, the date of the general chapter held at Lyons.

During the past seventy-five years or so there has been much discussion over the relationship between the material submitted to the minister general by the three companions and the several works that are in one way or another dependent upon that material, especially the *Second Life* of Celano, the so-called *Legenda Trium Sociorum* (or *The Legend of the Three Companions*), and the *Speculum Perfectionis* (or *Mirror of Perfection*). The letter of the three companions, spoken of above, is generally found as a preface to the *Legenda Trium Sociorum*. Obviously it does not belong there, for the eighteen or so chapters of this legend are written after the fashion of a legend and not merely as a collection of "flowers gathered from a delightful meadow," contrary to what the three companions say in their letter.

Up to 1894, however, the *Legenda Trium Sociorum* was quite generally accepted as the authentic work of Brothers Leo, Rufino, and Angelo. Even so, some doubt arose when Stanislaus Melchiorri published in 1856 an Italian text of the work that dated back to the sixteenth century,[46] which in its turn was a copy of a still older text. This text contained much additional material over what was contained in the traditional Latin text.[47] But the editor explained this material as additions made by the copyist from Thomas of Celano, St. Bonaventure, Bartholomew of Pisa, and the *Speculum Vitae*.

When Paul Sabatier published his life of St. Francis in 1894,[48] he proposed the theory that the *Legenda Trium Sociorum*, as we know it today, is only a fragment; and, in his characteristic way, he said that the minister general Crescentius of Jesi was responsible for deleting what is missing because he was not in sympathy with the thought of Brother Leo and his companions. Two Franciscans, Marcellino da Civezza and Teofilo Domenichelli, pursued the thought of Sabatier that the legend was only a fragment. They took Melchiorri's Italian text, translated it into Latin, added the Latin texts from the other authors mentioned (Celano, Bonaventure, Bartholomew of Pisa, the *Speculum Vitae*), and published the whole as the complete *Legenda Trium Sociorum*.

In 1900 Franciscus Van Ortroy, writing in the *Analecta Bollandiana*, showed that the *Legenda Trium Sociorum* contains passages borrowed from later writings, like St. Bonaventure's *Legenda Major Sancti Francisci* and Bernard of Bessa's *Liber de Laudibus S. Francisci*.[49] He argued therefore rather conclusively that it was necessarily a later work, probably of the latter part of the thirteenth century or of the early part of the fourteenth century, and could not therefore be the work of the three companions of St. Francis. The letter prefaced to the work accordingly belongs elsewhere. The discussion has continued, but today the opinion is rather general that the *Legenda Trium Sociorum,* though it may derive some of its material from the contributions of the three companions in 1246, is a work of the early fourteenth century and that the letter of the three companions is very probably the covering letter for the material they sent to the minister general in 1246. The material itself, however, is lost, probably for good.[50]

Meanwhile Sabatier happened upon a manuscript that bore the title *Speculum vitae S. Francisci et sociorum ejus* and dated back to about 1445. It was a rather formless collection of material, first issued in Venice in 1504. Sabatier extracted from this mass of material whatever seemed to harmonize with the style of the *Legenda Trium Sociorum,* believing that here he had found the missing part of the *Legenda.* He was especially struck by the rather frequent occurrence of the phrase, "we who were with him," a phrase that is very similar to the phrase used by the three companions in their letter to the minister general, "we who, though unworthy, lived with him for a long time." However, just about this time he came upon another manuscript in the Mazarin Library, Paris, that contained the very same material he had culled from the *Speculum Vitae* manuscript, but bearing the title *Speculum Perfectionis Fratris Minoris.*

Sabatier, however, was misled by an error in the dating of this manuscript into thinking that it was the oldest of all the legends about St. Francis. The date given was *anno domini MCCXXVIII,* that is, 1228, or, according to the old Pisan reckoning of the years, 1227. He therefore published his material as a separate work under the title *Speculum Perfectionis, legenda antiquissima auctore fratre Leone.* But the fact that he was in error about the date seemed obvious to others, and their surmise was confirmed shortly thereafter by the discovery of another manuscript of the *Speculum Perfectionis* which bore the correct date of 1318.[51]

A little later Fr. Leonard Lemmens O.F.M. edited a manuscript of the *Speculum Perfectionis* that was found in the archives of the Franciscan convent of St. Isidore in Rome, dating back to the fourteenth century.[52] This is a comparatively short work as compared to the *Speculum Perfectionis* edited by Sabatier; it has only forty-five numbered paragraphs as against 124 chapters in the latter. This manuscript opens with these words: "In the name of the Lord begins the Mirror of Perfection, of the rule and profession, the life and vocation of the true Friar Minor according to the will of Christ and the intention of Blessed Francis, composed from certain things found in the writings of Brother Leo, the companion of Blessed Francis, and of other of his companions, which are not in the common legend."

Some saw in this comparatively short work the original material sent to the minister general in 1246 by the three companions. This is not the case; but, as the manuscript says, it was compiled from this same material. Fr. Lemmens, taking note of the opening words just quoted, concluded that it was compiled after the *Legenda Major* of St. Bonaventure had become, by decree, the *legenda communis,* the common or standard legend for the order; and, as is indicated in those opening words, that it was written as a kind of supplement to that legend. Since therefore it precedes in time the *Speculum Perfectionis* published by Sabatier, it is often referred to as the *first redaction,* or, as some prefer, the *earlier red-*

action, considering the original material of the three companions to be the *first redaction.* Sabatier's edition, therefore, is a later redaction and is primarily an expansion of the earlier *Speculum Perfectionis* by the addition of material that had come to light during the intervening years.

As is to be expected, the *Speculum Perfectionis* in both redactions contains much material that was contained in the *Second Life* of Brother Thomas of Celano, for all of these writings derive at least in some part from the original material given to the minister general by the three companions in 1246. Thus all but the very last paragraph of the earlier redaction is found in the second redaction; and forty-four of the 124 chapters of the second redaction are contained in the Second Life of Celano. This, of course, has reference to substance, not to precise wording.

In summary, this can be said. The three companions named in the letter to the minister general, namely, Brothers Leo, Rufino, and Angelo, forwarded to Crescentius of Jesi the material they were able to gather between the general chapter of Genoa in 1244 and the date of their letter, August 11, 1246. This material was then used by Brother Thomas of Celano for his *Second Life of St. Francis.* It was again used by later writers for the separate redactions of the *Speculum Perfectionis.* The *Legenda Trium Sociorum* does not belong with the letter with which it is generally associated, but is a later compilation, probably of the early fourteenth century.[53]

The *Treatise on the Miracles of Blessed Francis*

In the *Second Life of St. Francis* Brother Thomas of Celano had included only a few miracles, inserting them here and there as occasion presented itself; and these were only such miracles as were performed through St. Francis while he was yet alive.[54] In this, the *Second Life* was considered deficient, for even the *First Life* had included a special section on the miracles that had been accepted and read for the process of canonization. Consequently, John of Parma, minister general 1247-1257, commanded Brother Thomas of Celano to correct this defect. The *Chronica XXIV Generalium* tells of this command: "This general [John of Parma] commanded Brother Thomas of Celano in repeated letters to complete the *Life of Blessed Francis,* which was called the *Ancient Legend,*[55] because mention had been made in the first treatise,[56] compiled at the order of the minister general Crescentius, only of his life and words, the miracles being omitted"[57]

The *Treatise on the Miracles of Blessed Francis* (*Tractatus de Miraculis B. Francisci*) was written, therefore, by Thomas of Celano during the term of office of John of Parma, and most probably during the middle years of that term, 1250-1253.[58] When the work was completed, Brother Thomas sent it to the minister general together with a letter that began with the words: *Religiosa vestra sollicitudo,*[59] a letter, however, that has not come down to us. The treatise was accepted and approved in the next general chapter, most probably, at Metz in 1254.

The *Treatise on the Miracles of the Blessed Francis* is not divided into books, as were both the *First* and *Second Life,* but the 198 numbered paragraphs of the work are distributed over nineteen chapters, the last of which is an epilogue. The opening chapter treats of the miraculous beginnings of the order. The second chapter treats of the stigmata of St. Francis and of the miracles related to these wounds. The rest of the chapters, with the exception of Chapter VI, recount the various miracles wrought through St. Francis, some of them during his life, but most of them after his death. Chapter VI, however, concerns itself with the visit of Lady Jacoba of Settesoli to Francis just before the death of the saint.

Much of the *Treatise on the Miracles* is not new material; about one third of it is contained already in the earlier *Lives*.[60] Nevertheless, and despite the fact that most of the miracles narrated are miracles that were wrought after St. Francis' death, the *Treatise on the Miracles* has a value for the biography of the saint. Forty-one of its 198 numbered paragraphs refer to things that happened while Francis was still alive. Although most of these paragraphs are contained already in the two *Lives,* thirteen contain material that is new. These thirteen paragraphs are of special value for the biography of St. Francis. They are included in Part III of this English volume.

Other Works

1   The *Legenda Sanctae Clarae Assisiensis.* — St. Clare of Assisi was the founder, under St. Francis, of the Order of Poor Clares. Born in 1194, she left her home in 1212 and was given a habit and a way of life by St. Francis.[61] All her life, however, she had to carry on a struggle to maintain her ideal of highest or absolute poverty. Pope Innocent III had confirmed for her this "privilege of seraphic poverty" in 1215 or 1216. But in 1218 or 1219 Cardinal Hugolino prepared a new rule of life for St. Clare and her followers, in which the rule of absolute poverty was softened. St. Clare insisted, however, that the highest poverty would be observed at least in the convent at St. Damian's church.

In 1245 Pope Innocent IV[62] confirmed this rule of Cardinal Hugolino for all the monasteries of the Poor

Clares; but two years later he wrote a new rule for them, which he hoped would prove more satisfactory. This new rule, however, was even more lenient than Cardinal Hugolino's and St. Clare refused to accept it. Instead, she set herself the task of writing her own rule. This rule was approved orally by Pope Innocent IV when he visited her on her deathbed, and it was approved by papal Bull August 9, 1253, just two days before her death.

Pope Innocent IV died December 7, 1254. One of the early acts of the new pope, Alexander IV,[63] was the canonization of St. Clare, August 15, 1255. In accordance with custom, he commissioned a biography or legend to be written to celebrate the new saint. For many years it had been thought that St. Bonaventure was the author of this legend, the *Legenda Sanctae Clarae Assisiensis*. Now, however, it is quite generally accepted that Brother Thomas of Celano was the author of this legend too. The work indeed has all the characteristics of style that the earlier works of Celano have, and there is no longer any reason to doubt his authorship.

The life opens with a Prologue that has the form of a letter addressed to the pope, Alexander IV. In it the author recalls the fact that he had been asked to write the life: "It has pleased Your Holiness to enjoin on my lowliness to review the *Acta* of Saint Clare and form therefrom a Legend."[64] It may be noted that Brother Thomas is also indicating here his chief source for this life, namely, the official *Acta*, that is, the acts of the canonical process of canonization and the Bull of canonization. The author adds that he "deemed it unwise to rely on incomplete records, and had recourse to the companions of Blessed Francis and even to the community of the virgins of Christ," for "none should write history save those who had seen for themselves or who had received their knowledge from eyewitnesses."[65]

The *Legenda Sanctae Clarae Assisiensis* was therefore started by Brother Thomas of Celano in 1255 and finished probably within a year or so.

2   The *Legenda ad Usum Chori* (Legend for Use in Choir). In the opening paragraph of this brief legend the author addresses himself to a certain Brother Benedict who had asked for a shortened form of the *First Life of St. Francis* for use in choir service: "You asked me, Brother Benedict, to excerpt some things from the legend of our most blessed father Francis and to arrange them in a series of nine lessons, so that they might be placed in our breviaries and be had by all by reason of their brevity."[66]

It is not known definitely who this Brother Benedict was, but some think it may have been Brother Benedict of Arezzo, a rather noteworthy person who was minister provincial in Greece from 1221 to 1237.[67] It is possible that he met Brother Thomas at the general chapter held at Assisi in 1230 on the occasion of the translation of St. Francis' remains to the new basilica and made his request at that time for a brief condensation of the *First Life*.

While the author of this brief legend does not identify himself by name, nevertheless the opening words (quoted above) give much the same impression as would the words *"de Legenda mea,"* from *my* legend, and therefore point to Brother Thomas as the author. Furthermore, almost the entire legend is based upon the *First Life;* it is literally excerpted from it, words, phrases, clauses taken over and tied together to make a very compact and concise summary of that *First Life*.[68] The style too has the same artistic touches as the two *Lives*.

There are, however, several new items in this short *Legenda ad Usum Chori*. In the first place, the day of Francis' death is more precisely indicated by add-

ing these several words: *die sabbati in sero,* Saturday
evening.[69] Moreover, the translation of Francis' remains from the church of St. George to the new
basilica is given.[70] This was not contained in the
First Life in as much as that life had been completed
before this event. Likewise, some new miracles are
added that were not known to the author at the time
of the writing of the *First Life.* These miracles are
further expanded in the later *Treatise on the Miracles of Blessed Francis.*

Brother Thomas is undoubtedly the author of this
brief legend which was written quite certainly in
1230 or immediately thereafter.

3   The liturgical sequence, *Dies Irae.* — According
to a long standing tradition that goes back at least to
the fourteenth century, Thomas of Celano was the
author of this well known and highly poetic sequence
of the Requiem Mass, the *Dies Irae.*[71] That Brother
Thomas was the author also of the two other
sequences, *Sanctitatis nova signa* and *Fregit victor,*
is very doubtful.[72]

3

THE LITERARY CHARACTER OF THE *LIVES*

Brother Thomas of Celano had no intention, of
course, of writing a biography of St. Francis in the
way we understand that term today. Neither did he
intend to write an exhaustive study of the saint. In
the Prologue of the *First Life* he says: "No one can
retain fully in his memory all the things that Francis
did and taught." And a little later in that same life:[73]
"Many more things happened too which we could
not tell adequately even at great length."

What Brother Thomas did intend to write was a
legenda or legend in the medieval understanding of

that term, namely, a book or record of the deeds of a saint. The emphasis was upon the word *saint,* and accordingly the supernatural elements in the life of the subject were emphasized, often at the expense of the human side of his life. The medieval writer of a legend was careful to avoid any purely human detail that might in any way lessen the estimate of the sanctity of the saint, while at the same time he played up strongly what might be considered a supernatural explanation of something that actually could be explained naturally. This does not mean that the writers of the middle ages were poor and unreliable biographers. They wrote the truth as they saw and understood it, but they also followed the practice of their times and were inclined to stress the supernatural and often to suppress the natural and distinctly human. It may well be, for all of that, that they were more reliable than some modern biographers who only too often tend to stress the natural and human at the expense of the supernatural.

It is readily apparent from a study of Brother Thomas' two lives of St. Francis that the author was a skilled literary craftsman and a painstaking artist. His style is vigorous and forceful, elegant, and even poetic. He makes use of figurative language freely, metaphors, similes, plays on words.[74] He uses contrast and antithesis to good effect.[75] He quotes countless passages from Holy Scripture[76] and now and then he inserts a passage from classical writers[77] and from early Christian writers.[78]

One artistic device in particular that Brother Thomas uses deserves a little more extended treatment since it is such a constant factor of his writing. This is the device known as the *cursus,* or periodic cadence, or end-pattern. Both ancient and medieval Latin writers strove to follow a certain rhythmic pattern, particularly at the end of each sentence.

This practice was governed by the laws of the so-called *cursus* or end-pattern. In the course of time these end-patterns came to be reduced to the three that Brother Thomas uses throughout his works, namely:[79]

    a. the *cursus planus*: a u / u a u
    b. the *cursus tardus*: a u / u a u u
    c. the *cursus velox*: a u u / u u a u

To illustrate Brother Thomas' use of these end-patterns, we might take as an example the first paragraph of Chapter I of the *First Life*. The words given below are the final words of each sentence of that paragraph. The syllables not in italics indicate the position of the word accent; the letter following each phrase indicates which *cursus* is being used in each case.

    *insolen*tior est ef*fectus* — c.
    stu*deant* edu*care* — c.
    *ope*rari co*gun*tur — a.
    sub*jacet* disci*plinis* — c.
    ma*la* se*quun*tur — a.
    *cess*ere fe*licius* — b.
    *ope*ra dila*bun*tur — c.
    *regu*lam ae*quitatis* — c.
    fi*eri* ar*bit*raris — c.
    *flagi*tiis de*servire* — c.
    no*mine* se *tuen*tur — c.
    innocentiores exis*tunt* — a.

The painstaking care with which Brother Thomas observes these patterns is evidence in itself that he was a true artist.

4

THE HISTORICAL VALUE OF THE *LIVES*

During the past seventy years or so there has been much discussion as to the historical value of Brother Thomas' lives of St. Francis. Opinions have varied, but the harshest have been the opinions of Paul Sabatier and those who have followed his lead.[80] Sabatier noted, in the first place, that Brother Thomas made no mention in his *First Life* of the general chapters of the order or of the fact that St. Francis was opposed to the friars seeking privileges at the Roman curia. Sabatier concluded that Celano deliberately omitted these things because he was dominated by Brother Elias and wanted to gain favor with him; and Elias had no use for general chapters[81] and was at the time seeking privileges from the Pope for the new basilica of St. Francis that was then under construction. Some add to this also that Brother Thomas was dominated similarly by Pope Gregory IX who more or less told him what he was to include in the life and what he was to omit. There is, however, no evidence of any of this either in the *First Life* or in any contemporary sources, and the omission of such things can very readily be explained by the fact that Brother Thomas's whole intent was to present to a reading audience that extended far beyond the order itself a picture of Francis, the saint, not a history of the order. The things omitted were simply not relevant to that picture.[82]

Another accusation leveled against Brother Thomas is that of inconsistency and, as a consequence, of unreliability as an historian and biographer.[83] This accusation grows out of Brother Thomas' handling of the case of Brother Elias in the *First Life* and again later in the *Second Life*. The situation is as follows. By actual count Elias is mentioned by name in six paragraphs of the *First Life*.[84] Each time he is mentioned, the wording of the narrative is such that it has a ring of good feeling about it concerning Elias. To give but one example, six months before Francis' death, when he was staying at Siena to get some much needed medical care, "Brother Elias hurried to him with great haste from a distant place."[85] Almost immediately, Francis began to improve and soon was well enough to go with Brother Elias to Le Celle near Cortona. But there his illness took a turn for the worse again, and Francis asked Elias to take him back to Assisi. Brother Thomas says, "this good son did what his gracious father asked."[86] There is a kindly feeling on the part of Brother Thomas throughout the telling of this incident. The same is true wherever Elias is mentioned in this *First Life*.

Unquestionably, however, there is a difference in the way Brother Elias is treated in the *Second Life*. Not once is he mentioned by name there. Twice he is referred to as the *vicar* of Francis.[87] Once there is a veiled reference to him.[88] Once he is simply referred to as "another of the brothers."[89] In this last instance Brother Thomas tells how Elias artfully managed to satisfy his curiosity about the wound in Francis' side and how by a bit of maneuvering he became the only brother to see that wound while Francis was yet alive. The telling of the incident is in sharp contrast to the brief note about it in the *First Life* where it was simply said: "But happy was Elias who, while the saint lived, merited to see this wound."[90] In the *Second Life* the words and the whole tone of the narrative are cold and almost contemptuous.

It is not difficult to understand the changed attitude of Brother Thomas in the *Second Life* and the changed tone of his writing about Brother Elias. When he wrote the *First Life*, Brother Elias was still in good standing with his confreres and with the Church. He had been an efficient vicar for Francis and, as a matter of fact, had been highly regarded by Francis, as Francis was by him. Francis relied heavily upon him during the last years of his life, and Elias in turn had a deep regard and a deep concern for his father. These things are evident from the *First Life.*[91]

But after Francis' death, Elias was entrusted by Pope Gregory IX with the task of building a new basilica to honor St. Francis, a work that was carried out under papal auspices. But Elias angered the rest of the friars by insisting that the various provinces supply funds for the new building.[92] However, had this been the only thing, it is quite likely that it would have been overlooked, for the brothers as such were undoubtedly in sympathy with the goal for which the funds were being collected.

Of even more serious concern to the friars was Brother Elias' personal conduct as minister general.[93] He lived in luxury, maintained two residences for himself,[94] rode horseback, kept a private cook to serve his tastes at table, ate but seldom with other friars, and so on. Furthermore, he apparently refused to hold any general chapters. In the end, the friars, led by such outstanding brothers as Alexander of Hales, John of La Rochelle, and Haymo of Faversham, moved against him and succeeded in having him deposed from his office of minister general in 1239. Shortly thereafter Elias joined the excommunicated emperor Frederick II and was himself excommunicated. In 1244 he was summoned to appear at the general chapter of Genoa, but when he failed to appear, he was again excommunicated.[95]

In the light of these circumstances of Elias' life, Brother Thomas' attitude toward him is not at all surprising. When he wrote the *First Life,* Elias was in good standing, had been a friend and confidant of St. Francis, had been Francis' vicar for about six years, and had been known for his kindness and consideration toward Francis as well as for his efficiency as an administrator. Why then should Thomas have felt anything but sympathy and kindliness toward him? But by the time he wrote the *Second Life* Elias had fallen from grace, and proved himself a tyrannical ruler, had abandoned the order, and had been excommunicated. Should he have continued his sympathetic attitude toward him? As a matter of fact, the only proper attitude he could have taken toward him was the attitude he did in reality take. True, that attitude did of necessity weaken the picture of Elias' relationship toward Francis in the *Second Life*. That, however, could not matter. Elias had fallen, as all the friars knew; and to depict him with the same sympathy with which he had depicted him in the *First Life* would have been a scandal to all.

Of particular concern to some writers is the way Brother Thomas handled the blessing that St. Francis imparted to those about him on his deathbed. That there is considerable difference between the narrative of the *First Life* and that of the *Second Life* on this matter will be readily apparent from a comparison of the relevant passages.

In the *First Life* Francis is presented as imparting his blessing twice to his brothers. The first blessing was given while Francis was staying at the palace of the bishop of Assisi. He summoned some of his brothers about him and, like the patriarch Jacob of old, blessed them. Elias was seated at the left of Francis and Francis reached over and put his right hand on Elias' head and spoke the following blessing:

> You, my son, I bless *above all and throughout all*;[96] and, just as the Most High has multiplied my brothers and sons in your hands, so also I bless them all upon you and

in you. May God, the King of all, bless you
in heaven and upon earth. I bless you as
much as I can and more than I can, and
what I cannot, may He who can do all
things do in you. May the Lord be mindful
of your work and of your labor, and may a
share be reserved for you in the reward of
the just. May you find every blessing you
desire, and may whatever you ask worthily be granted to you.[97]

Then to the rest of the brothers Francis said:

Farewell, all you my sons, *in the fear of
God*,[98] and may you remain in him always,
for a very great trial will come upon you
and a great tribulation is approaching.
Happy will they be who will persevere in
the things they have begun; from them
future scandals will separate some. I am
hastening to the Lord and I am confident
that I will go to my God *whom I serve*
devoutly *in my spirit*.[99]

Francis then asked the brothers to take him to St.
Mary's of the Portiuncula. There, on the day of his
death, he was asked by Brother Elias to bless all the
brothers present and absent. And Francis did so,
saying:

Behold, my son, I am called by God; I forgive my brothers, both present and absent,
all their offenses and faults, and, in as far
as I am able, I absolve them; I want you
to announce this to them and to bless them
all on my behalf.[100]

In the *Second Life*, however, there is only one
blessing, and while it is not clear just where it took
place, the supposition is that it was at the Portiuncula. Brother Thomas relates that Francis placed his
right hand upon the head of each one present, be-

ginning with his vicar, and then said:

> Farewell, all you my sons, *in the fear of the
> Lord,*[101] and may you remain in him al-
> ways! And because a future temptation and
> tribulation is approaching, happy will they
> be who will persevere in the things they
> have begun. I am hastening to the Lord,
> to whose grace I commend you all.[102]

Then Francis blessed them, we are told, those present
and all his brothers who were in the world and who
would come after them unto the end of the world.
He then took bread and broke it and gave to each a
share. Then he had a portion of the Gospel of St.
John read to him and thereafter spent the remaining
days in praising Christ.

Apart from the fact that in the *First Life* two distinct occasions are indicated upon which Francis
gave the brothers a blessing and in the *Second Life*
no such distinction is made, the only essential difference between the two narratives is the omission in
the *Second Life* of the special blessing imparted to
Brother Elias.[103] The same facts indicated above
apply here, namely, that it is the changed circumstances surrounding Elias that account for Brother
Thomas' handling the same blessings in a different
manner in the *Second Life*. Again, because of the
scandals that accompanied Elias' actions, he wants
to keep Elias in the background, and again too, there
was nothing else for him to do. Of course it should
also be kept in mind that the *Second Life* was written
as a complement to the *First Life* and accordingly
Brother Thomas was in no way obliged to repeat all
the details that were given already in the *First Life*.

In it all, however, there is no reason to blame
Brother Thomas or to call into question either his
honesty or his reliability as an historian. He acted
as anyone else would act under similar circumstances.

His *Second Life,* like the first, was about St. Francis; and, while it was necessary that Brother Elias should come into the narrative, there was no need to include details of a relationship with St. Francis that had become tarnished by Elias' subsequent defection and excommunication. The fact that he allowed touches of his personal feelings toward Elias to enter in does not lessen in any way his reputation as an historian. On the contrary, to anyone who reads the *Lives* with a mind unprejudiced by what some critics have said the legends have a ring of truthfulness and accuracy about them that makes one sure that here are reliable accounts of the life of St. Francis, and of the early days of the Franciscan Order as well; in fact, accounts so reliable that they are indispensable to both the biographer of St. Francis and the historian of the Franciscan Order.

5
THE LATER FATE OF THE *LIVES*

By the time St. Bonaventure came to be minister general of the order,[104] there were in existence the three major writings of Brother Thomas of Celano: the *First Life of St. Francis,* the *Second Life of St. Francis,* and the *Treatise on the Miracles of Blessed Francis.* In addition there were several short legends in existence, principally: Brother Thomas' *Legend for Use in Choir;* Julian of Speyer's short *Life of St. Francis* based on Brother Thomas' *First Life;* a very short life of St. Francis by a certain Bartholomew of Trent, a Dominican; and a life of St. Francis in verse (*Legenda Versificata*) by Henry of Avranches.

The short treatises served a purpose, but they could not be considered in any way an adequate narrative of the life of St. Francis. On the other hand, the three main works of Brother Thomas of Celano were separate works, none of which was complete in itself; and even taken together, they did not constitute a unified whole. As a result of these many legends, there was a growing confusion over the life and deeds of the founder of the order among the friars of the later generation, and these men were finding it difficult to come to know St. Francis as he should be known. The superiors of the order recognized these facts and in due time took action to remedy the situation.

In the general chapter of the order held at Narbonne in 1260, the minister general, St. Bonaventure, was asked by the members of the chapter to prepare a new life of St. Francis to take the place of the existing *legendae* as the official life of the saint. Bonaventure himself refers to this request in the Prologue of his life where he says that he "would not by any means have attempted the task of describing the life of St. Francis"[105] had not the insistence of the general chapter induced him to do so, for he considered himself unworthy and incapable of the task.[106]

Bonaventure, however, despite his feelings of inadequacy, carried out the wishes of the general chapter and completed the *Vita B. Francisci* by 1262 or 1263.[107] The Quaracchi editors think that it was then presented to the general chapter of Pisa in 1263, where it was received with enthusiasm, and that then some thirty-four copies were ordered made, a copy for each of the ministers provincial of the order.[108]

Three years later, at the general chapter at Paris, 1266, the new *legenda* was again discussed; and at this time there was issued that much discussed decree, under obedience, that "all the *legendae* about St. Francis that had been made in the past should be destroyed." Likewise, the decree went on to say, that wherever these *legendae* could be located outside of the order, they should be given the same treatment.

Thereafter, "that *Legenda* that had been made by the minister general," since it had been compiled in accordance with what he could learn from the mouths of those who had been close to St. Francis,[109] was to be henceforth the standard biography of St. Francis.[110]

The results of this decree of the general chapter of Paris, whatever may have been the motivation behind it,[111] were catastrophic as far as the works of Brother Thomas of Celano were concerned. These were lost sight of almost completely for many years thereafter. Gradually, however, manuscripts of these works have been rediscovered. In all, twenty manuscripts of the *First Life* have been found, five of which are complete, and four others fairly complete. Eight of these manuscripts were found in Cistercian monasteries, three in Benedictine monasteries, but only one among the Franciscans themselves. It is perhaps not too surprising that so many were found among the Cistericans, for in 1259, at the request of St. Bonaventure, their general chapter accepted the feast of St. Francis for their whole order, and St. Bonaventure gave them a copy of the *First Life.* Apparently this life was copied many times by the Cistercians for their various monasteries, and since they were outside the Franciscan Order, these copies more easily escaped the effects of the decree of the general chapter of Paris. The Benedictines, too, used the *First Life* in their liturgy. The friars themselves, however, seem to have done a rather complete job of carrying out the decree of the general chapter. The *Second Life* and the *Treatise on the Miracles* did not fare as well as the *First Life.* Only two complete copies of the former have survived,[112] and only one of the latter.[113]

Since the middle of the eighteenth century there have been a number of editions of these works of

Brother Thomas. In 1768 the *First Life* was published for the first time in the *Acta Sanctorum* by Constantine Suysken S.J. In 1806 the *First* and *Second Life* were published together by Stephen Rinaldi O.F.M. Conv. In 1904 H. G. Rosedale published an edition of all three works, which, however, was very imperfect and uncritical. In 1906 Edward d'Alencon published a much better edition of these works. But the best edition of all is that of the Fathers of St. Bonaventure's College, Quaracchi, published in the *Analecta Franciscana*, X. It is this edition that was used for this present English translation.

— Fr. Placid Hermann O.F.M.

Celano, Chapter Titles

CHAPTER TITLES

PART I
The First Life of St. Francis

213

BOOK TWO (I-X, 88-118)
About the contents of this book, about the time of

PART II
The Second Life of St. Francis

Celano, Chapter Titles

PART III
Treatise on the Miracles of Blessed
Francis, Selections

223

PART I

The First Life of St. Francis
by
Thomas of Celano

PROLOGUE

In the Name of the Lord. Amen

HERE BEGINS THE PROLOGUE OF
THE LIFE OF BLESSED FRANCIS

1   It is my desire to relate in an orderly manner, with pious devotion and with truth as my first consideration and guide, the acts and the life of our most blessed father Francis. But in as much as no one can retain fully in his memory all the things that Francis *did and taught,*[1] I have tried, at the command of our lord, the gloriously reigning Pope Gregory,[2] to set forth as well as I can, though indeed with unskilled words, at least those things that I have heard from his own mouth or that I have gathered from faithful and trustworthy witnesses. I wish, however, that I might truly deserve to be a disciple of him who always avoided enigmatic ways of saying things and who knew nothing of the ornaments of language!

2   I have divided the things I have been able to gather concerning the blessed Francis into three books, arranging everything in separate chapters, so that the many occasions when these things were done will not confuse the order and lead to doubt about their truth. The first book follows the historical order and is given over, for the most part, to the purity of his conduct and life,[3] to his holy striving after virtue, and to his salutary teachings. In it, too, are inserted a few of the many miracles which the Lord our God deigned to perform through him while he was *in the flesh.*[4] — The second book tells what happened from the second last year of his life until his happy death.[5] The third book relates many of the miracles this most glorious saint worked here upon earth while reigning with Christ in heaven,

though it omits many more. It also records the reverence, honor, praise, and glory which the happy Pope Gregory, along with the cardinals of the holy Roman Church, heaped upon him when they enrolled him in the catalogue of saints.[6] Thanks be to Almighty God, who shows himself in his saints always worthy of admiration and love.

THUS ENDS THE PROLOGUE

BOOK ONE

To the Praise and Glory of Almighty God,
the Father, Son, and Holy Spirit. Amen

HERE BEGINS THE LIFE
OF OUR MOST BLESSED FATHER FRANCIS

CHAPTER I

How Francis lived in the world before his conversion

1   In the city of Assisi, which lies at the edge of
the Spoleto valley,[1] *there was a man*[2] by the name of
Francis, who from his earliest years was brought up
by his parents proud of spirit, in accordance with
the vanity of the world; and imitating their wretched
life and habits for a long time, he became even more
vain and proud. For this very evil custom has grown
up everywhere among those who are considered
Christians in name, and this pernicious teaching has
become so established and prescribed, as though by
public law, that people seek to educate their children
from the cradle on very negligently and dissolutely.
For, indeed, when they first begin to speak or stammer, children, just hardly born, are taught by signs
and words to do certain wicked and detestable things;
and when they come to be weaned, they are forced
not only to speak but also to do certain things full of
lust and wantonness. Impelled by a fear that is
natural to their age, none of them dares to conduct
himself in an upright manner, for if he were to do so
he would be subjected to severe punishments. Therefore, a secular poet says well: "Because we have
grown up amid the practices of our parents, we therefore pursue all evil things from our childhood on."[3]
This testimony is true, for so much the more injurious to their children are the desires of the parents, the more successfully they work out. But when
the children have progressed a little in age, they always sink into worse deeds, following their own

impulses. For from a corrupt root a corrupt tree will grow,[4] and what has once become wickedly depraved can hardly ever be brought into harmony with the norms of uprightness. But when they begin to enter the portals of adolescence, how do you think they will turn out? Then, indeed, tossed about amid every kind of debauchery, they give themselves over completely to shameful practices, in as much as they are permitted to do as they please. For once they have become the slaves of sin by a voluntary servitude, they give over all their members to be instruments of wickedness;[5] and showing forth in themselves nothing of the Christian religion either in their lives or in their conduct, they take refuge under the mere name of Christianity. These miserable people very often pretend that they have done even worse things than they have actually done, lest they seem more despicable the more innocent they are.

2   These are the wretched circumstances among which the man whom we venerate today as a saint, for he is truly a saint, lived in his youth; and almost up to the twenty-fifth year of his age, he squandered and wasted his time miserably.[6] Indeed, he outdid all his contemporaries in vanities and he came to be a promoter of evil[7] and was more abundantly zealous for all kinds of foolishness.[8] He was the admiration of all and strove to outdo the rest in the pomp of vainglory, in jokes, in strange doings, in idle and useless talk, in songs, in soft and flowing garments, for he was very rich, not however avaricious but prodigal, not a hoarder of money but a squanderer of his possessions, a cautious business man but a very unreliable steward. On the other hand, he was a very kindly person, easy and affable, even making himself foolish because of it; for because of these qualities many ran after him, doers of evil and promoters of crime. And thus overwhelmed by a host of evil com-

panions, proud and high-minded, he walked about the streets of Babylon[9] until the *Lord looked down from heaven*[10] and for his own name's sake removed his *wrath far off* and for his praise bridled Francis lest he should perish.[11] *The hand of the Lord* therefore came *upon him*[12] and a change was wrought by the right hand of the Most High, that through him an assurance might be granted to sinners that they had been restored to grace and that he might become an example to all of conversion to God.[13]

CHAPTER II

How God touched the heart of Francis by sickness and by a vision

3   For, indeed, while this man was still in the glow of youthful passion, and the age of wantonness was urging him on immoderately to fulfill the demands of youth; and while, not knowing how to restrain himself, he was stirred by the venom of the serpent of old, suddenly the divine vengeance, or, perhaps better, the divine unction, came upon him and sought first to recall his erring senses by visiting upon him mental distress and bodily suffering, according to the saying of the prophet: *Behold I will hedge up thy way with thorns, and I will stop it up with a wall.*[14] Thus, worn down by a long illness, as man's stubbornness deserves when it can hardly be corrected except by punishments, he began to think of things other than he was used to thinking upon. When he had recovered somewhat and had begun to walk about the house with the support of a cane to speed the recovery of his health, he went outside one day and began to look about at the surrounding landscape with great interest. But the beauty of the fields, the pleasantness of the vineyards, and whatever else was beautiful to look upon, could stir in him no de-

light. He wondered therefore at the sudden change that had come over him, and those who took delight in such things he considered very foolish.

4   From that day on, therefore, he began to despise himself and to hold in some contempt the things he had admired and loved before. But not fully or truly, for he was not yet freed from the *cords of vanity*[15] nor had he shaken off from his neck the yoke of evil servitude.[16] It is indeed very hard to give up things one is accustomed to, and things that once enter into the mind are not easily eradicated; the mind, even though it has been kept away from them for a long time, returns to the things it once learned; and by constant repetition vice generally becomes second nature.[17] So Francis still tried to flee the hand of God, and, forgetting for a while his paternal correction, he thought, amid the smiles of prosperity, of *the things of the world;*[18] and, ignorant of the *counsel of God,*[19] he still looked forward to accomplishing great deeds of worldly glory and vanity. For a certain nobleman of the city of Assisi was preparing himself in no mean way with military arms, and, puffed up by a gust of vainglory, vowed that he would go to Apulia[20] to increase his wealth and fame. Upon hearing this, Francis, who was flighty and not a little rash, arranged to go with him; he was inferior to him in nobility of birth, but superior in generosity, poorer in the matter of wealth, but more lavish in giving things away.

5   On a certain night, therefore, after he had given himself with all deliberation to the accomplishment of these things, and while, burning with desire, he longed greatly to set about the journey, he who had struck him with the rod of justice visited him in the sweetness of grace by means of a nocturnal vision; and because Francis was eager for glory, he

enticed him and raised his spirits with a vision of the heights of glory. For it seemed to Francis that his whole home was filled with the trappings of war, namely, saddles, shields, lances, and other things; rejoicing greatly, he wondered silently within himself what this should mean. For he was not accustomed to see such things in his home, but rather piles of cloth to be sold. When, accordingly, he was not a little astonished at this sudden turn of events, the answer was given him that all these arms would belong to him and to his soldiers. When he awoke, he arose in the morning with a glad heart, and considering the vision an omen of great success, he felt sure that his journey to Apulia would come out well. *He did not know what to say*[21] and he did not as yet recognize the task given him from heaven. Nevertheless, he might have understood that his interpretation of the vision was not correct, for while the vision bore some resemblance to things pertaining to war, his heart was not filled with his usual happiness over such things. He had to use some force on himself to carry out his designs and to complete the proposed journey. It is indeed quite fitting that mention be made of arms in the beginning and it is quite opportune that arms should be offered to the soldier about to engage one strongly armed, that like another David he might free Israel from the long-standing reproach of its enemies[22] in *the name of the Lord God of hosts.*[23]

CHAPTER III

How, changed in mind but not in body, Francis spoke of the treasure he had found and of his spouse in allegory

6 Changed, therefore, but in mind, not in body, he refused to go to Apulia and he strove to bend his own will to the will of God. Accordingly, he with-drew for a while from the bustle and the business of the world and tried to establish Jesus Christ dwell-ing within himself.[24] Like a prudent business man, he hid the treasure he had found from the eyes of the deluded, and, having sold all his possessions, he tried to buy it secretly.[25] Now since there was a certain man in the city of Assisi whom he loved more than any other because he was of the same age as the other, and since the great familiarity of their mutual affec-tion led him to share his secrets with him,[26] he often took him to remote places, places well-suited for counsel, telling him that he had found a certain precious and great treasure. This one rejoiced and, concerned about what he heard, he willingly accom-panied Francis whenever he was asked. There was a certain grotto near the city where they frequently went and talked about this treasure. The man of God, who was already holy by reason of his holy purpose, would enter the grotto, while his compan-ion would wait for him outside; and filled with a new and singular spirit, he would pray to his Father in secret. He wanted no one to know what he did within, and taking the occasion of the good to wisely conceal the better, he took counsel with God alone concerning his holy proposal. He prayed devoutly that the eternal and true God would direct his way and teach him to do his will. He bore the greatest sufferings in mind and was not able to rest until he should have completed in deed what he had conceiv-ed in his heart; various thoughts succeeded one an-other and their importunity disturbed him greatly. He was afire within himself with a divine fire and he was not able to hide outwardly the ardor of his mind; he repented that he had sinned so grievously and had offended *the eyes of* God's *majesty,*[27] and neither the past evils nor those present gave him any delight. Still he had not as yet won full confidence that he would be able to guard himself against them in the future. Consequently, when he came out again to his companion, he was so exhausted with the strain, that one person seemed to have entered, and another to have come out.

7   One day, however, when he had begged for the mercy of God most earnestly, it was shown to him by God what he was to do. Accordingly, he was so filled with joy that he could not contain himself, and, though he did not want to, he uttered some things to the ears of men. But, though he could not keep silent because of the greatness of the joy that filled him, he nevertheless spoke cautiously and *in an obscure manner.*[28] For, while he spoke to his special friend of a hidden treasure, as was said, he tried to speak to others only figuratively; he said that he did not want to go to Apulia, but he promised that he would do noble and great things in his native place. People thought he wished to take to himself a wife, and they asked him, saying: "Francis, do you wish to get married?" But he answered them, saying: "I shall take a more noble and more beautiful spouse than you have ever seen; she will surpass all others in beauty and will excel all others in wisdom." Indeed, the immaculate spouse of God is the true religion which he embraced; and the hidden treasure is the kingdom of heaven, which he sought with such great desire; for it was extremely necessary that the Gospel calling be fulfilled in him who was to be the minister of the Gospel in faith and in truth.

CHAPTER IV

Francis sold all his goods and despised the money given him

8   Behold, when the blessed servant of the Most

High was thus disposed and strengthened by the Holy
Spirit, now that the opportune time had come, he
followed the blessed impulse of his soul, by which
he would come to the highest things, trampling
worldly things under foot. He could not delay any
longer, because a deadly disease had grown up everywhere to such an extent and had so taken hold of all
the limbs of many that, were the physician to delay
even a little, it would snatch away life, shutting off
the life-giving spirit. He rose up, therefore, fortified
himself with the sign of the cross, got his horse ready
and mounted it, and taking with him some fine cloth
to sell, he hastened to the city called Foligno.[29] There,
as usual, he sold everything he had with him, and,
successful as a merchant, he left behind even the
horse he was riding, after he had received payment
for it; and, free of all luggage, he started back, wondering with a religious mind what he should do with
the money. Soon, turned toward God's work in a
wondrous manner, and accordingly feeling that it
would be a great burden to him to carry that money
even for an hour, he hastened to get rid of it, considering the advantage he might get from it as so
much sand. When, therefore, he neared the city of
Assisi, he discovered a certain church along the way
that had been built of old in honor of St. Damian
but which was now threatening to collapse because
it was so old.[30]

9 When this new soldier of Christ came up to
this church, moved with pity over such great need,
he entered it with fear and reverence. And when he
found there a certain poor priest, he kissed his sacred
hands with great faith, and offered him the money
he had with him, telling him in order what he proposed to do. The priest was astonished and, wondering over a conversion so incredibly sudden, he refused to believe what he heard. And because he

thought he was being deceived, he refused to keep the money offered him. For he had seen him just the day before, so to say, living in a riotous way *among his relatives and acquaintances*[31] and showing greater foolishness than the rest. But Francis persisted obstinately and tried to gain credence for what he said, asking earnestly and begging the priest to suffer him to remain with him for the sake of the Lord. In the end the priest acquiesced to his remaining there, but out of fear of the young man's parents, he did not accept the money; whereupon this true contemner of money threw it upon a window sill, for he cared no more for it than for the dust. He wanted to possess that wisdom that is better than gold and to acquire that prudence that is more precious than silver.[32]

CHAPTER V

How his father persecuted Francis and put him in chains

10   So while the servant of the most high God was staying in the aforesaid place, his father[33] went about everywhere, like a persistent spy, wanting to learn what had happened to his son. And when he learned that he was living in such a way at that place, *being touched inwardly with sorrow of heart*,[34] he was *troubled exceedingly*[35] at the sudden turn of events, and calling together his friends and neighbors, he hurried to the place where the servant of God was staying. But he, the new athlete of Christ, when he heard of the threats of those who were pursuing him and when he got knowledge of their coming, wanting to *give place to wrath*,[36] hid himself in a certain secret pit which he himself had prepared for just such an emergency. That pit was in that house and was known probably to one person alone; in it he hid so continuously for one month that he hardly dared

leave it to provide for his human needs. Food, when it was given to him, he ate in the secrecy of the pit, and every service was rendered to him by stealth. Praying, he prayed always with a torrent of tears that the Lord would deliver him from the hands of those who were persecuting his soul,[37] and that he would fulfill his pious wishes in his loving kindness; *in fasting and in weeping*[38] he begged for the clemency of the Savior, and, distrusting his own efforts, he *cast* his whole *care upon the Lord.*[39] And though he was in a pit and *in darkness,*[40] he was nevertheless filled with a certain exquisite joy of which till then he had had no experience; and catching fire therefrom, he left the pit and exposed himself openly to the curses of his persecutors.

11 He arose, therefore, immediately, active, eager, and lively; and, bearing the shield of faith to fight for the Lord, armed with a great confidence, he took the way toward the city; aglow with a divine fire, he began to accuse himself severely of laziness and cowardice. When those who knew him saw this, they compared what he was now with what he had been; and they began to revile him miserably. Shouting out that he was mad and demented, they threw the mud of the streets and stones at him. They saw that he was changed from his former ways and greatly worn down by mortification of the flesh, and they therefore set down everything he did to exhaustion and madness. But since a patient man is better than a proud man, the servant of God showed himself deaf to all these things and, neither broken nor changed by any of these injuries, he gave thanks to God for all of them. In vain does the wicked man persecute one striving after virtue, for the more he is buffeted, the more strongly will he triumph. As someone says, indignity strengthens a generous spirit.[41]

12   Now when the noise and the shouting of this kind concerning Francis had been going on for a long time through the streets and quarters of the city, and the sound of it all was echoing here and there, among the many to whose ears the report of these things came was finally his father. When he heard the name of his son mentioned, and understood that the commotion among the citizens turned about his son, he immediately arose, not indeed to free him but rather to destroy him; and, with no regard for moderation, he rushed upon him like a wolf upon a sheep, and looking upon him with a fierce and savage countenance, he laid hands upon him and dragged him shamelessly and disgracefully to his home. Thus, without mercy, he shut him up in a dark place for several days, and thinking to bend his spirit to his own will, he first used words and then blows and chains. But Francis became only the more ready and more strong to carry out his purpose; but he did not abandon his patience either because he was insulted by words or worn out by chains. For he who is commanded to rejoice in tribulation[42] cannot swerve from the right intention and position of his mind or be led away from Christ's flock, not even by scourgings and chains; neither does he waver *in a flood of many waters*,[43] whose refuge from oppression is the Son of God, who, lest our troubles seem hard to us, showed always that those he bore were greater.

CHAPTER VI

How Francis' mother freed him, and how he stripped himself before the bishop of Assisi

13   It happened, however, when Francis' father had left home for a while on business and the man of God remained bound in the basement of the house, his mother, who was alone with him and who did

not approve of what her husband had done, spoke kindly to her son. But when she saw that he could not be persuaded away from his purpose, she was moved by motherly compassion for him, and loosening his chains, she let him go free. He, however, giving thanks to Almighty God, returned quickly to the place where he had been before. But now, after he had been proved by temptations, he allowed himself greater liberty, and he took on a more cheerful aspect because of the many struggles he had gone through. From the wrongs done him he acquired a more confident spirit, and he went about everywhere freely with higher spirits than before. Meanwhile his father returned, and not finding Francis, he turned to upbraid his wife, heaping sins upon sins. Then, raging and blustering, he ran to that place hoping that if he could not recall him from his ways, he might at least drive him from the province. But, because it is true that *in the fear of the Lord is confidence*,[44] when this child of grace heard his carnally minded[45] father coming to him, confident and joyful he went to meet him, exclaiming in a clear voice that he cared nothing for his chains and blows. Moreover, he stated that he would gladly undergo evils for the name of Christ.

14   But when his father saw that he could not bring him back from the way he had undertaken, he was roused by all means to get his money back. The man of God had desired to offer it and expend it to feed the poor and to repair the buildings of that place. But he who had no love for money could not be mislead by any aspect of good in it; and he who was not held back by any affection for it was in no way disturbed by its loss. Therefore, when the money was found, which he who hated the things of this world so greatly and desired the riches of heaven so much had thrown aside in the dust of the window

sill, the fury of his raging father was extinguished a little, and the thirst of his avarice was somewhat allayed by the warmth of discovery. He then brought his son before the bishop of the city,[46] so that, renouncing all his possessions into his hands, he might give up everything he had. Francis not only did not refuse to do this, but he hastened with great joy to do what was demanded of him.

15   When he was brought before the bishop, he would suffer no delay or hesitation in anything; indeed, he did not wait for any words nor did he speak any, but immediately putting off his clothes and casting them aside, he gave them back to his father. Moreover, not even retaining his trousers, he stripped himself completely naked before all. The bishop, however, sensing his disposition and admiring greatly his fervor and constancy, arose and drew him within his arms and covered him with the mantle he was wearing. He understood clearly that the counsel was of God, and he understood that the actions of the man of God that he had personally witnessed contained a mystery. He immediately, therefore, became his helper and cherishing him and encouraging him, he embraced him in the bowels of charity. Behold, now he wrestles naked with his naked adversary,[47] and having put off everything that is of this world, he thinks only *about the things of the Lord.*[48] He seeks now so to despise his own life, putting off all solicitude for it, that he might find peace in his harassed ways,[49] and that meanwhile only the wall of flesh should separate him from the vision of God.

CHAPTER VII

How Francis was seized by robbers and cast into the snow, and how he served the lepers

16   He who once wore fine garments now went

about clad only in scanty garments. As he went through a certain woods singing praises to the Lord in the French language, robbers suddenly rushed out upon him. When they asked him in a ferocious tone who he was, the man of God replied confidently in a loud voice: "I am the herald of the great King. What is that to you?" But they struck him and cast him into a ditch filled with deep snow, saying: "Lie there, foolish herald of God!" But he rolled himself about and shook off the snow; and when they had gone away, he jumped out of the ditch, and, glad with great joy, he began to call out the praises of God in a loud voice throughout the grove. At length, coming to a certain cloister of monks,[50] he spent several days there as a scullion, wearing a ragged shirt and being satisfied to be filled only with broth. But, when all pity was withdrawn from him and he could not get even an old garment, he left the place, not moved by anger, but forced by necessity; and he went to the city of Gubbio,[51] where he obtained a small tunic from a certain man who once had been his friend.[52] Then, after some time had elapsed, when the fame of the man of God was beginning to grow and *his name was spread abroad*[53] among the people, the prior of the aforementioned monastery recalled and realised how the man of God had been treated and he came to him and begged pardon for himself and for his monks out of reverence for the Savior.

17   Then the holy lover of complete humility went to the lepers and lived with them, serving them most diligently for God's sake; and washing all foulness from them, he wiped away also the corruption of the ulcers, just as he said in his *Testament*: "When I was in sins, it seemed extremely bitter to me to look at lepers, and the Lord himself led me among them and I practiced mercy with them."[54] So greatly loathsome was the sight of lepers to him at one time, he used to

242

say, that, in the days of his vanity, he would look at their houses only from a distance of two miles and he would hold his nostrils with his hands. But now, when by the grace and the power of the Most High he was beginning to think of holy and useful things, while he was still clad in secular garments, he met a leper one day and, made stronger than himself, he kissed him. From then on he began to despise himself more and more, until, by the mercy of the Redeemer, he came to perfect victory over himself. Of other poor, too, while he yet remained in the world and still followed the world, he was the helper, stretching forth a hand of mercy to those who had nothing, and showing compassion to the afflicted. For when one day, contrary to his custom, for he was a most courteous person, he upbraided a certain poor man who had asked an alms of him, he was immediately sorry; and he began to say to himself that it was a great reproach and a shame to withhold what was asked from one who had asked in the name of so great a King. He therefore resolved in his heart never in the future to refuse any one, if at all possible, who asked for the love of God. This he most diligently did and carried out, until he sacrificed himself entirely and in every way; and thus he became first a practicer before he became a teacher of the evangelical counsel: *To him who asks of thee,* he said, *give; and from him who would borrow of thee, do not turn away.*[55]

CHAPTER VIII

How Francis built the church of St. Damian; and of the life of the Ladies who dwelt in that place

18 The first work that blessed Francis undertook after he had gained his freedom from the hand of his carnally minded father was to build a house of God.

He did not try to build one anew, but he repaired an old one, restored an ancient one. He did not tear out the foundation, but he built upon it, ever reserving to Christ his prerogative, though he was not aware of it, *for other foundation no one can lay, but that which has been laid, which is Christ Jesus.*[56] When he had returned to the place where, as has been said, the church of St. Damian had been built in ancient times, he repaired it zealously within a short time with the help of the grace of the Most High. This is the blessed and holy place, where the glorious religion and most excellent order of Poor Ladies and holy virgins had its blessed origin about six years after the conversion of St. Francis and through that same blessed man. Of it, the Lady Clare,[57] a native of the city of Assisi, the most precious and the firmest stone of the whole structure, was the foundation. For when, after the beginning of the Order of Brothers, the said lady was converted to God through the counsel of the holy man, she lived unto the advantage of many and as an example to a countless multitude. She was of noble parentage, but she was more noble by grace; she was a virgin in body, most chaste in mind; a youth in age, but mature in spirit; steadfast in purpose and most ardent in her desire for divine love; endowed with wisdom and excelling in humility; Clare by name,[58] brighter in life, and brightest in character.

19   Over her arose a noble structure of most precious pearls, whose *praise is not from men but from God,*[59] since neither is our limited understanding sufficient to imagine it, nor our scanty vocabulary to utter it. For above everything else there flourishes among them that excelling virtue of mutual and continual charity, which so binds their wills into one that, though forty or fifty of them dwell together in one place, agreement in likes and dislikes moulds

one spirit in them out of many.[60] Secondly, in each one there glows the gem of humility, which so preserves the gifts and good things bestowed from heaven,[61] that they merit other virtues too. Thirdly, the lily of virginity and chastity so sprinkles them with a wondrous odor that, forgetful of earthly thoughts, they desire to meditate only on heavenly things; and so great a love for their eternal Spouse arises in their hearts from the fragrance of that lily that the integrity of that holy affection excludes from them every habit of their former life. Fourthly, they have all become so conspicuous by the title of the highest poverty that their food and clothing hardly at all or never come together to satisfy extreme necessity.

20   Fifthly, they have so attained the singular grace of abstinence and silence that they need exert hardly any effort to check the movements of the flesh and to restrain their tongues; some of them have become so unaccustomed to speak that when necessity demands that they speak, they can hardly remember how to form the words as they should. Sixthly, with all these things, they are adorned so admirably with the virtue of patience, that no adversity of tribulations or injury of vexations ever breaks their spirit or changes it. Seventhly, and finally, they have so merited the height of contemplation that in it they learn everything they should do or avoid; and happily they know how to be *out of mind for God,*[62] persevering night and day in praising him and in praying to him. May the eternal God deign by his holy grace to bring so holy a beginning to an even more holy end. And let this suffice for the present concerning these virgins dedicated to God and the most devout handmaids of Christ, for their wondrous life and their glorious institutions, which they received from the lord Pope Gregory, at that time Bishop of Ostia,[63] requires a work of its

own and leisure in which to write it.[64]

CHAPTER IX

How Francis, having changed his habit, rebuilt the church of St. Mary of the Portiuncula, and how, upon hearing the Gospel, he left all things, and how he designed and made the habit the brothers wear

21   Meanwhile the holy man of God, having put on a new kind of habit and having repaired the aforesaid church, went to another place near the city of Assisi, where he began to rebuild a certain dilapidated and well-nigh destroyed church, and he did not leave off from his good purpose until he had brought it to completion.[65] Then he went to another place, which is called the Portiuncula,[66] where there stood a church of the Blessed Virgin Mother of God that had been built in ancient times, but was now deserted and cared for by no one. When the holy man of God saw how it was thus in ruins, he was moved to pity, because he burned with devotion toward the mother of all good; and he began to live there in great zeal. It was the third year of his conversion when he began to repair this church. At this time he wore a kind of hermit's dress, with a leather girdle about his waist; he carried a staff in his hands and wore shoes on his feet.

22   But when on a certain day the Gospel was read in that church,[67] how the Lord sent his disciples out to preach, the holy man of God, assisting there, understood somewhat the words of the Gospel; after Mass he humbly asked the priest to explain the Gospel to him more fully. When he had set forth for him in order all these things, the holy Francis, hearing that the disciples of Christ should not possess gold or silver or money; nor carry along the way scrip, or wallet, or bread, or a staff; that they should

not have shoes, or two tunics;[68] but that they should preach the kingdom of God and penance,[69] immediately cried out exultingly: "This is what I wish, this is what I seek, this is what I long to do with all my heart."[70] Then the holy father, *overflowing with joy,*[71] hastened to fulfill that salutary word he had heard, and he did not suffer any delay to intervene before beginning devoutly to perform what he had heard. He immediately put off his shoes from his feet, put aside the staff from his hands, was content with one tunic, and exchanged his leather girdle for a small cord. He designed for himself a tunic that bore a likeness to the cross, that by means of it he might beat off all temptations of the devil; he designed a very rough tunic so that by it he might crucify the flesh with all its vices and sins;[72] he designed a very poor and mean tunic, one that would not excite the covetousness of the world. The other things that he had heard, however, he longed with the greatest diligence and the greatest reverence to perform. For he was not a deaf hearer of the Gospel, but committing all that he had heard to praiseworthy memory, he tried diligently to carry it out to the letter.

CHAPTER X

Of his preaching of the Gospel and his announcing peace and of the conversion of the first six brothers

23   From then on he began to preach penance to all with great fervor of spirit and joy of mind, edifying his hearers with his simple words and his greatness of heart. His words was like a *burning fire,*[73] penetrating the inmost reaches of the heart, and it filled the minds of all the hearers with admiration. He seemed completely different from what he had been, and, looking up to the heavens, he disdained to look upon the earth. This indeed is wonderful,

that he first began to preach where as a child he had first learned to read and where for a time he was buried amid great honor,[74] so that the happy beginning might be commended by a still happier ending. Where he had learned he also taught, and where he began he also ended. In all his preaching, before he proposed the word of God to those gathered about, he first prayed for peace for them, saying: "The Lord give you peace."[75] He always most devoutly announced peace to men and women, to all he met and overtook. For this reason many who had hated peace and had hated also salvation embraced peace, through the cooperation of the Lord, with all their heart and were made children of peace and seekers after eternal salvation.

24   Among these, a certain man from Assisi, of pious and simple spirit, was the first to devoutly follow the man of God.[76] After him, Brother Bernard,[77] embracing the delegation of peace,[78] ran eagerly after the holy man of God to purchase the kingdom of heaven.[79] He had often given the blessed father hospitality, and, having had experience of his life and conduct and having been refreshed by the fragrance of his holiness, he conceived a fear and brought forth the spirit of salvation.[80] He noticed that Francis would pray all night, sleeping but rarely, praising God and the glorious Virgin Mother of God, and he wondered and said: "In all truth, this man is from God." He hastened therefore to sell all his goods and gave the money to the poor, though not to his parents; and laying hold of the title to the way of perfection, he carried out the counsel of the holy Gospel: *If thou wilt be perfect, go, sell what thou hast, and give to the poor, and thou shalt have treasure in heaven; and come, follow me.*[81] When he had done this, he was associated with St. Francis by his life and by his habit, and he was always with him

until, after the number of the brothers had increased, he was sent to other regions by obedience to his kind father.[82] His conversion to God was a model to others in the manner of selling one's possessions and giving them to the poor. St. Francis rejoiced with very great joy over the coming and conversion of so great a man, in that the Lord was seen to have a care for him by giving him a needed companion and a faithful friend.[83]

25   But immediately another man of the city of Assisi followed him; he deserves to be greatly praised for his conduct, and what he began in a holy way, he completed after a short time in a more holy way.[84] After a not very long time, Brother Giles followed him; he was *a simple and upright man,* and one *fearing* God.[85] He lived a long time, leading a holy life, *justly and piously,*[86] and giving us examples of perfect obedience, manual labor, solitary life, and holy contemplation.[87] After another one had been added to these, Brother Philip brought the number to seven.[88] The Lord touched his lips with a purifying coal,[89] that he might speak pleasing things of him and utter sweet things. Understanding and interpreting the sacred Scriptures, though he had not studied,[90] he became an imitator of those whom the leaders of the Jews alleged to be ignorant and unlearned.[91]

CHAPTER XI

Of the spirit of prophecy of St. Francis and of his admonitions

26   Therefore the blessed father Francis was being daily filled with the consolation and the grace of the Holy Spirit; and with all vigilance and solicitude he was forming his new sons with new learning, teaching them to walk with undeviating steps the way of holy poverty and blessed simplicity. One day, when he was wondering over the mercy of the Lord with regard to the gifts bestowed upon him, he wished that the course of his own life and that of his brothers might be shown him by the Lord; he sought out a place of prayer, as he had done so often, and he persevered there for a long time *with fear and trembling*[92] standing *before the Lord of the whole earth,*[93] and he thought *in the bitterness of his soul*[94] of the years he had spent wretchedly, frequently repeating this word: *O God, be merciful to me the sinner.*[95] Little by little a certain unspeakable joy and very great sweetness began to flood his innermost heart. He began also to stand aloof from himself, and, as his feelings were checked and the darkness that had gathered in his heart because of his fear of sin dispelled, there was poured into him a certainty that all his sins had been forgiven and a confidence of his restoration to grace was given him. He was then caught up above himself, and absorbed in a certain light; the capacity of his mind was enlarged and he could see clearly what was to come to pass. When this sweetness finally passed, along with the light, renewed in spirit, he seemed changed into another man.

27   And then, coming back, he said with joy to his brothers: *"Be strengthened,* dear brothers, *and rejoice in the Lord,*[96] and do not be sad because you seem so few; and do not let either my simplicity or your own dismay you, for, as it has been shown me in truth by the Lord, God will make us grow into a very great multitude and will make us increase to the ends of the world. For your profit I am compelled to tell you what I have seen, though I would much rather remain silent, were it not that charity urges me to tell you. I saw a great multitude of men coming to us and wanting to live with us in the habit of our

250

way of life and under the rule of our blessed religion. And behold, the sound of them is in my ears as they go and come according to the command of holy obedience. I have seen, as it were, the roads filled with their great numbers coming together in these parts from almost every nation. Frenchmen are coming, Spaniards are hastening, Germans and Englishmen are running, and a very great multitude of others speaking various tongues are hurrying." When the brothers had heard this, they were filled with a salutary joy, both because of the grace the Lord God gave to his holy one and because they were ardently thirsting for the advantages to be gained by their neighbors, whom they wished to grow daily in numbers and to be saved thereby.

28   And the holy one said to them: "Brothers, in order that we may give thanks to the Lord our God faithfully and devoutly for all his gifts, and that you may know what kind of life the present and future brothers are to live, understand the truth of the things that are to come. We will find now, at the beginning of our life, fruits that are extremely sweet and pleasant to eat; but a little later some that are less sweet and less pleasant will be offered; and lastly, some that are full of bitterness will be given, which we will not be able to eat, for because of their bitterness they will be inedible to all, though they will manifest some external fragrance and beauty. And, in truth, as I have told you, the Lord will give us increase unto *a great nation*.[97] In the end, however, it will so happen just as though a man were to cast his nets into the sea or into some lake and *enclose a great number of fishes*,[98] and, when he has put them all into his boat, not liking to carry them all because of their great number, he gathers the bigger ones and those that please him into his vessels and throws the rest away."[99] It is apparent to those who, in the spirit

251

of truth, consider all these things which the holy man of God predicted, how greatly they shine forth for their truth and how manifestly they were fulfilled. Behold how the spirit of prophecy rested on St. Francis.

CHAPTER XII

How Francis sent them into the world two by two, and how they came together again after a short time

29 At this same time also, when another good man had entered their religion, their number rose to eight.[100] Then the blessed Francis called them all together, and telling them many things concerning the kingdom of God, the contempt of the world, the renunciation of their own will, and the subduing of their own body, he separated them into four groups of two each and said to them: "Go, my dearest brothers, two by two into the various parts of the world, announcing to men peace and repentance unto the forgiveness of sins;[101] and *be patient in tribulation*,[102] confident that the Lord will fulfill his purpose and his promise. To those who put questions to you, reply humbly; bless those who persecute you; give thanks to those who injure you and calumniate you; because for these things there is prepared for you an eternal kingdom."[103] But they, accepting the command of holy obedience *with joy* and great *gladness*,[104] cast themselves upon the ground before St. Francis. But he embraced them and said to each one with sweetness and affection: "Cast thy thought upon the Lord, and he will nourish you."[105] This word he spoke whenever he transferred any brothers in obedience.

30 Then Brother Bernard made a journey with Brother Giles to St. James.[106] St. Francis, however, with one companion chose another part of the world; the four others went two by two to other regions.

But, after a short time had elapsed, St. Francis, wanting to see them all, prayed to the Lord, who *gathers the dispersed of Israel*,[107] that he would deign to bring them together within a short time. And thus it happened that within a short time they came together as he wished and without any human intervention, and they gave thanks to God. When they had gathered together, they rejoiced greatly at seeing their kind shepherd; and they wondered that they had thus come together by a common desire. They then gave an account of the good things the merciful Lord had done for them; and, if they had been negligent and ungrateful in any way, they humbly begged and willingly received correction and punishment from their holy father. For thus they had always been accustomed to act when they came to him, and they did not hide from him the least thought or the first impulses of their hearts; and when they had fulfilled all things that had been commanded them, they considered themselves unprofitable servants.[108] For the spirit of purity so filled that first school of the blessed Francis that, though they knew how to do useful, holy, and just works, they knew not at all how to rejoice vainly over them. But the blessed father, embracing his sons with exceedingly great love, began to make known to them his purpose and to show them what the Lord had revealed to him.[109]

31   Immediately, however, four other good and suitable men were numbered among them and they followed the holy man of God.[110] Then a great stir arose among the people and the fame of the man of God began to be spread farther about. There was indeed at that time a great rejoicing and a singular joy among St. Francis and his brothers whenever one of the faithful, no matter who he might be or of what quality, rich or poor, noble or ignoble, despised or valued, prudent or simple, cleric or unlettered or lay,

led on by the spirit of God, came to put on the habit
of holy religion. There was also great wonder among
the people of the world over all these things and the
example of humility led them to amend their way of
life and to do penance for their sins. Not even low-
ness of birth or any condition of poverty stood in the
way of building up the work of God in those in whom
God wished to build it up, God who delights to be
with the outcasts of the world and with the simple.

CHAPTER XIII

*How Francis first wrote a rule when he had eleven
brothers, and how the lord pope confirmed it; and
how he had a vision of a great tree*

32   When Blessed Francis saw that the Lord God
was daily adding to their number,[111] he wrote for himself and his brothers, present and to come, simply and
with few words,[112] a form of life and rule, using for
the most part the words of the holy Gospel, for the
perfection of which alone he yearned. But he did insert a few other things that were necessary to provide
for a holy way of life. He then came to Rome with
all the aforementioned brothers, desiring very much
that what he had written should be confirmed by the
Lord Pope Innocent III.[113] At that time the venerable bishop of Assisi was at Rome, Guido by name,[114]
who honored Francis and all his brothers in all things
and venerated them with special affection. When he
saw St. Francis and his brothers, he was grievously
annoyed at their coming, not knowing the reason for
it; for he feared that they might wish to leave their
native region where the Lord had already begun to
work very great things through his servants. He rejoiced greatly to have such great men in his diocese,
on whose life and conduct he was relying greatly.
But when he had heard the reason for their coming

and understood their purpose, he rejoiced greatly in the Lord, promising to give them his advice and help in these things. St. Francis also approached the lord bishop of Sabina, John of St. Paul by name,[115] who of all the other princes and great ones at the Roman curia was seen to despise earthly things and love heavenly things. He received Francis kindly and charitably, and praised highly his will and purpose.

33   Indeed, because he was a prudent and discreet man, he began to ask Francis about many things and urged him to turn to the life of a monk or hermit.[116] But St. Francis refused his counsel, as humbly as he could, not despising what was counselled, but in his pious leaning toward another life, he was inspired by a higher desire. The lord bishop wondered at his fervor, and, fearing that he might decline from so great a purpose, he showed him ways that would be easier to follow. In the end, overcome by Francis' constancy, he acquiesced to his petition and strove from then on to further his aims before the lord pope. It was Pope Innocent III who was at that time at the head of the Church, a famous man, greatly learned, renowned in discourse, burning with zeal for justice in the things that the cause of the Christian faith demanded. When he had come to know the wishes of these men of God, he first examined the matter, then gave assent to their request and carried out all that had to be done;[117] exhorting them concerning many things and admonishing them, he blessed St. Francis and his brothers and said to them: "Go with the Lord, brothers, and as the Lord will deign to inspire you, preach penance to all. Then, when the almighty Lord shall give you increase in number and in grace, return to me with joy, and I will add many more things to these and entrust greater things to you with greater confidence."

In all truth the Lord was with St. Francis wherever

he went, cheering him with revelations and encouraging him by his gifts. For one night after he had given himself to sleep, it seemed to him that he was walking along a certain road, at the side of which stood a tree of great height. The tree was beautiful and strong, thick and exceedingly high. It happened as he drew near to it, and was standing beneath it, admiring its beauty and its height, that suddenly the holy man himself grew to so great a height that he touched the top of the tree, and taking hold of it with his hand, he bent it to the ground. And so indeed it happened, for the lord Innocent, the highest and loftiest tree in the world, graciously stooped to Francis' petition and desire.

CHAPTER XIV

Concerning Francis' return from the city of Rome to the Spoleto valley and how he stopped along the way

34   Greatly rejoicing over the gift and the grace of so great a father and lord, St. Francis gave thanks with his brothers to Almighty God, who *setteth up the humble on high* and *comforteth with health those that mourn*.[118] Immediately he went to visit the shrine of St. Peter; and, when he had finished his prayer, he left the city, and taking up his journey, he proceeded toward the Spoleto valley.

While they were going along the way, they talked with one another about the number and the quality of the gifts the most kind God had bestowed upon them, and about how they had been received most kindly by the vicar of Christ, the lord and father of the whole Christian world; about how they might be able to fulfill his admonitions and commands; about how they could sincerely observe the rule they had taken upon themselves and keep it without failure; about how they should walk in all sanctity and religion before the Most High; and finally, about how their life and conduct might be an example to their neighbors by an increase of holy virtues.

By the time the new disciples of Christ had sufficiently discussed these things in the school of humility, the day was far spent and the *hour* was *already late.* They came then to a *desert place*[119] greatly fatigued from their journey and hungry, but they could find no refreshment because that place was far removed from any dwelling of men. Immediately, the grace of God providing, a man met them bearing in his hand some bread, which he gave them and departed. But they did not know him and they wondered in their hearts and devoutly admonished one another to place even greater trust in the divine mercy. After they had eaten the food and were strengthened not a little, they went to a certain place near the city of Orte[120] and stayed there for fifteen days. Some of them would go into the city and get the necessary food, and what little they could get by begging from door to door, they would bring back to the other brothers; and they all ate *with all thankfulness*[121] and *joy of heart.*[122] If anything was left over, since they could not give it to anyone, they stowed it away in a certain sepulcher that had at one time held the bodies of the dead, that they might eat of it again. That place was deserted and abandoned and visited by few or no people at all.[123]

35   There was great rejoicing among them when they saw and had nothing that might give them vain or carnal pleasure. They began therefore to have in that place commerce with holy poverty; and comforted exceedingly in the absence of all things that are of this world, they resolved to cling to poverty everywhere just as they were doing here. And because once they had put aside solicitude for earthly things, only the divine consolation gave them joy,

they decreed and confirmed that they would not depart from its embraces no matter by what tribulations they might be shaken or by what temptations they might be led on. But, though the pleasantness of that place, which could contribute not a little toward a weakening of their true strength of mind, did not detain their affections, they nevertheless withdrew from it, lest a longer stay might entangle them even in some outward show of ownership; and, following their happy father, they went at that time to the Spoleto valley. They all conferred together, as true followers of justice, whether they should dwell among men or go to solitary places. But St. Francis, who did not trust in his own skill, but had recourse to holy prayer before all transactions, chose not to live for himself alone, but for him *who died for all,*[124] knowing that he was sent for this that he might win for God the souls the devil was trying to snatch away.

CHAPTER XV

Concerning the fame of the blessed Francis and the conversion of many to God; how the order was called the Order of Friars Minor, and how Blessed Francis formed those entering religion

36   Francis, therefore, the most valiant knight of Christ, went about *the towns and villages*[125] announcing the kingdom of God, preaching peace, teaching salvation and penance unto the remission of sins, *not in the persuasive words of* human *wisdom,*[126] but with the learning and power of the Spirit. He *acted boldly* in all things,[127] because of the apostolic authority granted to him, using no words of flattery or seductive blandishments. He did not know how to make light of the faults of others, but he knew well how to cut them out; neither did he encourage the life of sinners, but he struck hard at them with sharp

reproof, for he had first convinced himself by practicing himself what he wished to persuade others to do by his words; and fearing not the censurer, he spoke the truth boldly, so that even the most learned men, men enjoying renown and dignity, wondered at his words and were struck with wholesome fear by his presence. Men ran, and women too ran, clerics hurried, and religious hastened that they might see and hear the holy man of God who seemed to all to be a man of another world. Every age and every sex hurried to see the wonderful things that the Lord was newly working in the world through his servant. It seemed at that time, whether because of the presence of St. Francis or through his reputation, that a new light had been sent from heaven upon this earth, shattering the widespread darkness that had so filled almost the whole region that hardly anyone knew where to go. For so profound was the forgetfulness of God and the sleep of neglect of his commandments oppressing almost everyone that they could hardly be aroused even a little from their old and deeply rooted sins.

37   Francis shone forth like a brilliant star in the *obscurity of the night*[128] and *like the morning spread upon the* darkness.[129] And thus it happened that in a short time the face of the region was changed, and it took on a more cheerful aspect everywhere, once the former foulness had been laid aside. The former dryness was routed and the crops sprang up quickly in the neglected field. Even the untended vine began to sprout shoots of the fragrance of the Lord and, after producing blossoms of sweetness, it brought forth fruits of *honor and riches.*[130] *Thanksgiving and voice of praise*[131] resounded everywhere so that many put aside wordly cares and gained knowledge of themselves from the life and teaching of the most blessed Francis, and they longed to attain love and reverence

for their Creator.[132] Many of the people, both noble and ignoble, cleric and lay, impelled by divine inspiration, began to come to St. Francis, wanting to carry on the battle constantly under his discipline and under his leadership. All of these the holy man of God, like a plenteous river of heavenly grace, watered with streams of gifts; he enriched the field of their hearts with flowers of virtue, for he was an excellent craftsman; and, according to his plan, rule, and teaching, proclaimed before all, the Church is being renewed in both sexes, and the threefold army of those to be served is triumphing.[133] To all he gave a norm of life, and he showed in truth the way of salvation in every walk of life.

38   But our first concern here is with the order of which he was the founder and preserver both by charity and by profession. What shall we say? He himself first planted the Order of Friars Minor and accordingly gave it this name. For he wrote in the rule, "and let them be lesser brothers," and when these words were spoken, indeed in that same hour, he said: "I wish that this fraternity should be called the Order of Friars Minor."[134] And indeed they were lesser brothers, who, being subject to all, always sought a place that was lowly and sought to perform a duty that seemed in some way to be burdensome to them so that they might merit to be founded solidly in true humility and that through their fruitful disposition a spiritual structure of all virtues might arise in them. Truly, upon the foundation of constancy a noble structure of charity arose, in which the living stones, gathered from all parts of the world, were erected into a dwelling place of the Holy Spirit. O with what ardor of charity the new disciples of Christ burned! How great was the love that flourished in the members of this pious society! For whenever they came together anywhere, or met one another along the way, as the custom is, there a shoot of spiritual love sprang up, sprinkling over all love the seed of true affection. What more shall I say? Chaste embraces, gentle feelings, a holy kiss, pleasing conversation, modest laughter, joyous looks, a *single eye*,[135] a submissive spirit, a *peacable tongue*,[136] a *mild answer*,[137] oneness of purpose, ready obedience, unwearied hand, all these were found in them.

39   And indeed, since they despised all earthly things and did not love themselves with a selfish love, pouring out their whole affection on all the brothers, they strove to give themselves as the price of helping one another in their needs. They came together with great desire; they remained together with joy; but separation from one another was sad on both sides, a bitter divorce, a cruel estrangement. But these most obedient knights dared put nothing before holy obedience; before the command of obedience was even uttered, they prepared themselves to fulfill the order; knowing not how to misinterpret the commands, they put aside every objection and hastened to fulfill what was commanded. Followers of most holy poverty, because they had nothing, loved nothing, they feared in no way to lose anything. They were content with one tunic, patched at times within and without;[138] in it was seen no refinement, but rather abjectness and cheapness, so that they might seem to be completely crucified to the world. Girt with a cord, they wore poor trousers, and they had the pious intention of remaining like this, and they wished to have nothing more. They were, therefore, everywhere secure, kept in no suspense by fear; distracted by no care, they awaited the next day without solicitude,[139] nor were they in anxiety about the night's lodging, though in their journeyings they were often placed in great danger. For, when they frequently lacked the necessary lodging amid the coldest weather, an oven sheltered them, or at least they lay hid for the night humbly in grottos or caves. During the day, those who knew how labored with their hands,[140] staying in the houses of lepers, or in other decent places, serving all humbly and devotedly. They did not wish to exercise any position from which scandal might arise,[141] but always doing what is holy and just, honest and useful, they led all with whom they came into contact to follow their example of humility and patience.

40 The virtue of patience so took hold of them that they sought rather to be where they might suffer persecution of their bodies than where they might be lifted up by the favor of the world, when their holiness was known or praised. For many times when they were insulted and ridiculed, stripped naked, beaten, bound, imprisoned, they did not protect themselves by means of anyone's patronage, but they bore all things so courageously that nothing but the voice of praise and thanksgiving resounded in their mouths. Scarcely at all, or really never, did they let up in their praise of God and in their prayers; but recalling by constant discussion what they had done, they gave thanks to God for what they had done well; for what they had neglected or incautiously committed, they poured forth groans and tears. They thought they were forsaken by God if they did not find themselves to be constantly visited in their devotions by their accustomed piety. For when they wanted to give themselves to prayer, they made use of certain means lest sleep should take hold of them: some were held erect by hanging ropes lest their prayers should be disturbed by sleep stealing over them; others put instruments of iron about their bodies, and others wore wooden girdles of penance. If, as it can happen, their sobriety were disturbed by an abundance of food or drink, or if because they were tired from a journey, they surpassed even a little the bounds of necessity, they mortified themselves very sharply by an abstinence of many days. Lastly, they tried to repress the promptings of the flesh with such great mortification that often they did not refrain from stripping themselves naked in the coldest weather and from piercing their bodies all over with the points of thorns, even to causing the blood to flow.

41   They despised all wordly things so keenly that they hardly permitted themselves to receive even the necessaries of life; and they were separated from bodily comforts for so long a time that they did not shrink from anything difficult. Amid all these things they strove for *peace* and gentleness *with all men*,[142] and always conducting themselves modestly and peaceably, they avoided all scandals with the greatest zeal. They hardly spoke even when necessary; neither did anything scurrilous or idle proceed from their mouths, in order that nothing immodest or unbecoming might be found in their life and conversation. Their every action was disciplined, their every movement modest; all their senses were so mortified that they would hardly permit themselves to hear or see anything except what their purpose demanded. With their eyes directed toward the ground, they clung to heaven with their minds. No envy, no malice, no rancor, no abusive speech, no suspicion, no bitterness found any place in them; but great concord, continual quiet, thanksgiving, and the voice of praise were in them. These were the teachings of their beloved father, by which he formed his new sons, not by words alone and tongue, but above all *in deeds and in truth*.[143]

CHAPTER XVI

Of Francis' stay at Rivo Torto and of the observance of poverty

42 Blessed Francis betook himself with the rest of his brothers to a place near Assisi called Rivo Torto.[144] In that place there was a certain abandoned hovel in the shelter of which these most ardent despisers of great and beautiful homes lived; and there they kept themselves safe from the rains. For, as a certain saint said,[145] from a hovel one ascends more quickly to heaven than from a palace. All his sons and brothers lived in this same place with their blessed father, working much, lacking everything; very often they were entirely deprived of the comfort of bread, and they were content with turnips which they begged here and there over the plain of Assisi. That place was so very cramped that they could hardly sit down or rest in it. But no murmur was heard over these things, no complaint; but with a serene heart and a mind filled with joy they kept their patience.[146] St. Francis most diligently examined himself and his brothers daily, even continually; and, suffering nothing in them of wantonness, he drove every negligence from their hearts. Strict in discipline, he was watchful of his trust at all hours. For if, as happens, a temptation of the flesh at times assailed him, he would hurl himself into a ditch full of ice, when it was winter, and remain in it until every vestige of anything carnal had departed. And indeed the others most fervently followed his example of such great mortification.

43 He taught them not only to mortify vices and repress carnal movements, but also to restrain the exterior senses themselves, for through them death enters the soul. When at that time the Emperor Otto was passing through the place with much clamor and pomp to receive the crown of his earthly empire,[147] the most holy father, who was living with his brothers in that hovel close to the road on which the emperor would pass, did not even go out to watch; and he did not let any one else do so except one who continuously called out to the emperor that his glory would last but a short time.[148] for the glorious saint, withdrawn within himself and walking in the broadness of his heart, had prepared within himself a dwelling fit for God, and therefore the outward clamor did not catch his ears, nor could any sound drive out or interrupt the great business he had at hand. The apostolic authority[149] was strong in him, and he therefore refused entirely to offer flattery to kings and princes.

44 He attended always to holy simplicity and he did not permit the straitened circumstances of that place to impede the greatness of his heart. He therefore wrote the names of his brothers on the beams of their dwelling so that each one, if he wished to pray or to rest, would know his place, and that the smallness of the place might not disturb the silence of the mind. While they were dwelling there, it happened that one day a certain man came leading an ass to the shelter where the man of God was staying with his brothers; and lest he suffer repulse, the man, exhorting his ass to enter, spoke these words: "Go in, for we will do well for this place."[150] When St. Francis heard this, he took it very ill, knowing what the man's intention was; for the man thought the brothers wanted to stay there to enlarge the place and to *join house to house.*[151] Immediately St. Francis went away from there, and abandoning the hovel because of what the peasant had said, he went to another place not far from there, which is called the Portiuncula, where, as was said above,[152] the church of St. Mary had been built and had been repaired by him. He wanted to have nothing to do with ownership, in order that he might possess all things more fully in God.

CHAPTER XVII

How Blessed Francis taught his brothers to pray; and of the obedience and purity of the brothers

45 At that time, *walking in simplicity* of spirit,[153] they did not know as yet the ecclesiastical office.[154] He said to them:*"When you pray, say Our Father,*[155] *and We adore thee, Christ, here and in all thy churches which are in the whole world, and we bless thee, because by thy holy cross thou hast redeemed the world."*[156] But this the brothers strove to observe with the greatest diligence as disciples of their beloved master, for they strove to carry out most efficaciously not only those things which the blessed father Francis said to them in fraternal advice or fatherly command, but also the things that were in his mind or on which he was meditating, if in some way they would come to know them. For the blessed father himself said to them that true obedience consists not only in doing things that are commanded in word, but even those merely thought of; not only in doing things commanded, but even things desired; for, "if a brother, subject to a brother superior, not only hears his voice, but even understands his will, he must immediately give himself entirely to obedience and do what he understands him to will by some sign or other."[157]

Moreover, if a church were standing in any place whatsoever, even though the brothers were not present there but could only see it from some distance, they were to prostrate themselves upon the ground in its direction and, having bowed low with body and soul,[158] they were to adore Almighty God, saying,

We adore thee, Christ, here and in all thy churches, as the holy father had taught them. And, what is no less to be admired, wherever they saw a crucifix or the mark of a cross, whether upon the ground, or upon a wall, or on trees, or in the hedges along the way, they were to do the same thing.

46   For holy simplicity had so filled them, innocence of life was so instructing them, purity of heart so possessed them, that they knew nothing of duplicity of mind. For, as there was one faith in them, so was there one spirit in them, one will, one love; there was unity of souls among them, harmony of behavior, the practice of virtues, conformity of minds, and piety of actions.

At one time, when they were often confessing their sins to a certain secular priest who was very infamous, as he deserved, and was despised by all because of the enormity of his crimes, and they were made aware of his iniquity by many people, they did not want to believe it and they did not on that account omit confessing their sins to him as usual; and they did not refuse him the reverence due him.[159] Indeed, when one day, he, or another priest, said to a certain one of the brothers, "See, Brother, that you be not a hypocrite," that brother immediately believed that he was a hypocrite, because of the word of the priest. Because of this he wept day and night, moved by excessive grief. When, however, the brothers asked him why he was so filled with grief and why he mourned in such an unusual way, he replied: "A certain priest spoke such a word to me and it caused me so much grief I can hardly think of anything else." The brothers consoled him and admonished him not to believe such a thing. But he said to them: "What is this you say, brothers? It was a priest who spoke this word to me. Can a priest lie? Since therefore a priest cannot lie, we must believe that what he said

is true." And then he continued for a long time in
this simplicity; but at last he gave in at the words of
the most blessed father, who explained to him the
word of the priest and wisely excused the priest's intention.[160] It was hardly possible for any of the brothers to be troubled to such an extent in mind that
every cloud would not be dispersed at Francis' glowing words and serenity return.

CHAPTER XVIII

*Of the fiery chariot, and of the knowledge the blessed
Francis had of those who were absent*

47   Walking in simplicity before God and in confidence before men, the brothers merited at this
time to be filled with gladness by means of a divine
revelation.[161] For while, kindled by the fire of the
Holy Spirit, they chanted the *Pater Noster*, not only
at the appointed hours, but at all hours, with suppli-
ant and melodious voice, being little occupied with
earthly solicitude and troublesome anxiety of cares,
the most blessed father Francis absented himself one
night from them in body. And behold, about midnight, when some of the brothers were resting and
some were praying in silence with great devotion, a
most splendid fiery chariot entered through the door
of the house and turned around two or three times
here and there inside the house; a huge globe of
light rested above it, much like the sun, and it lit
up the night. The watchers were dazed, and those
who had been asleep were frightened; and they felt
no less a lighting up of the heart than a lighting up
of the body. Gathering together, they began to ask
one another what it was; but by the strength and
grace of that great light each one's conscience was
revealed to the others. Finally they understood and
knew that it was the soul of their holy father that

was shining with such great brilliance and that, on account of the grace of his understanding purity and his great tenderness for his sons, he merited to receive such a blessing from God.

48 And indeed they had found proof of this by manifest tokens and had experienced that the secrets of their hearts were not hidden from their most holy father. O how often, without any man telling him, but by means of a revelation of the Holy Spirit, Francis knew the actions of his absent brothers, laid open the secrets of their hearts, and explored their consciences! O how many he admonished in their sleep, commanded them things to be done, forbade things not to be done! Of how many did he not predict future evils, though their present conduct seemed good! Thus, knowing in many cases that certain brothers would end their evil ways, he foretold the future grace of salvation for them. Even more, if anyone merited to be distinguished by his spirit of purity and simplicity, he enjoyed the singular consolation of seeing Francis in a way not experienced by the rest. I will give one example from among many, which I know from reliable witnesses. When at one time Brother John of Florence,[162] who had been appointed by St. Francis minister of the brothers in the Provence,[163] was celebrating a chapter of the brothers in that same province,[164] the Lord God, in his customary mercy, opened unto him the door of speech[165] and he made all the brothers well disposed and attentive to his words. Among the brothers was one, a priest of great renown but of more splendid life, Monaldo by name;[166] his virtue was grounded in humility, aided by frequent prayer, and preserved by the shield of patience. Brother Anthony[167] was also present at this chapter, he whose mind the Lord opened[168] that he might understand the Scriptures and speak among all the people words about Jesus that were sweeter than syrup or honey from the comb.[169] While he was preaching very fervently and devoutly to the brothers on this topic, *"Jesus of Nazareth, King of the Jews,"*[170] the aforementioned Brother Monaldo looked toward the door of the house in which there were many other brothers gathered and he saw there with his bodily eyes Blessed Francis raised up into the air, his arms extended as though upon a cross, and blessing the brothers. And they all were seen to be filled *with the consolation of the Holy Spirit,*[171] and, from the joy of salvation they felt, what they were told concerning the vision and the presence of their most glorious father seemed entirely believable.

49 To show that Francis knew the secrets of the hearts of others, I will mention from among the many cases experienced by many one case about which no doubt can arise. A certain brother, Riccerio by name,[172] a noble by birth but even more noble in his conduct, one who loved God and despised himself, was led by a pious spirit and a great desire to attain and possess perfectly the favor of holy father Francis; but he feared greatly that St. Francis despised him for some secret reason and therefore made him a stranger to the favor of his affection. That brother thought, in as much as he was a God-fearing man, that whomever St. Francis loved with an intimate love would merit to be worthy of the divine favor; but, on the other hand, he to whom St. Francis did not show himself well disposed and kind would, he thought, incur the anger of the heavenly judge. These things that brother revolved in his mind and spoke about frequently within himself, but he did not reveal the secret of his thoughts to anyone.

50 For the rest, when on a certain day the blessed father was praying in his cell and Brother Riccerio had come to that place, disturbed by his usual thoughts, the holy man of God became aware of his coming and of what was going on in his mind. Immediately he sent for him and said to him: "Let no temptation disturb you, son; let no thought exasperate you; for you are very dear to me. Know that among those who are especially dear to me you are worthy of my affection and intimacy. Come to me with confidence whenever you wish and talk with me with great familiarity." The brother was filled with the greatest admiration at this; and as a result was even more reverent; and, as he grew in the favor of his father, so did he begin to *open wide*[173] in his trust in the mercy of God.

How sadly, holy father, must not they take your absence who despair of ever finding anyone like you upon earth. Help, we pray, by your intercession those whom you see mired in the harmful contagion of sin. Though you were already filled with the spirit of all the just, foreseeing the future and knowing the present, you always kept before you the image of holy simplicity in order that you might shun all boastfulness.

But now let us return to what we were speaking of above and observe again the historical order.

CHAPTER XIX

Of the watchfulness of Francis over his brothers; and of his contempt of self and of his true humility

51   The most blessed Francis returned to his brothers in body, from whom, as has been said, he never withdrew in spirit. Scrutinizing the actions of all his brothers with cautious and diligent examination, he was concerned about his subjects out of a kindly curiosity; and he left nothing unpunished if he found something done that was less than good. He first

settled spiritual failings, then he judged concerning bodily things, and lastly he rooted out all occasions that open the way to sins.

With all zeal, with all solicitude, he guarded holy Lady Poverty, not permitting any vessel of any kind [174] to be in the house, lest it lead to superfluous things, when he could in some way avoid being subject to extreme necessity without it. For, he used to say, it is impossible to satisfy necessity and not give in to pleasure. Cooked foods he permitted himself scarcely at all or very rarely; and if he did allow them, he either mixed them with ashes or destroyed their flavor with cold water. O how often, when he was going about the world preaching the *Gospel of God,*[175] if he were invited to dinner by great princes who venerated him with wonderful affection, he would taste a bit of the meat in observance of the holy Gospel[176] and then, making a pretense of eating by raising his hand to his mouth, lest anyone should perceive what he was doing, he would drop the rest in his lap. But what can I say of his drinking of wine, when he would not allow himself to drink enough water to quench his thirst?

52   Francis would not allow his resting place to be laid over with covers or garments when he received hospitality, but the bare ground received his bare limbs, with only a tunic between. When at times he refreshed his small body with sleep, he very often slept sitting up, and in no other position, using a piece of wood or a stone as a pillow. When his appetite for something particular was aroused, as often happens, he seldom ate that thing afterwards. Once, when in an infirmity he had eaten a little chicken, after he regained his strength of body he entered the city of Assisi; and when he had come to the gate of the city, he commanded a certain brother who was with him to tie a rope about his neck and to drag him in this way like a robber through the entire city and to shout in the voice of a herald, saying: "Behold the glutton who has grown fat on the meat of chickens which he ate without your knowing about it." Many therefore ran to see so great a spectacle, and weeping together with great sighs, they said: "Woe to us miserable ones, whose whole life is spent in blood and who nourish our hearts and bodies with uncleanness and drunkenness." And thus, *pierced to the heart*,[177] they were moved to a better way of life by so great an example.

53   Many other things like these he did very often that he might learn to despise himself perfectly and that he might entice others to seek eternal honor. He had become to himself *like a vessel that is destroyed*,[178] and, burdened by no fear or solicitude for his body, he most zealously subjected it to affronts, lest he be driven by love of his body to desire eagerly some temporal things. Despising himself in all truth, he taught others by his word and example to despise themselves.

What then? He was *honored by all*[179] and extolled by all, with praiseworthy judgment; and he alone considered himself the most vile among men, he alone despised himself most severely. For often, when he was honored by all, he suffered the deepest sorrow; and rejecting the favor of men, he would see to it that he would be rebuked by some one. He would call some brother to him, saying to him: "In obedience, I say to you, revile me harshly and speak the truth against the lies of these others." And when that brother, though unwilling, would say he was a boor, a hired servant, a worthless being, Francis, smiling and applauding very much, would reply: "May the Lord bless you, for you have spoken most truly; it is becoming that the son of Peter of Bernardone[180] should hear such things." So saying, he would recall the conditions of his humble origin.

54 That he might show himself in every way contemptible and give an example to the rest of true confession, Francis was not ashamed, when he had failed in something, to confess his failing in his preaching before all the people. Indeed, if it happened that he had had an evil thought about anyone, or if he had on occasion spoken an angry word, he would immediately confess his sins with all humility to the one about whom he had had the evil thought and beg his pardon. His conscience, which was a witness to his complete innocence, guarding itself with all solicitude, would not let him rest until it had gently healed the wound in his heart. Certainly he wanted to make progress in every kind of good deed, but he did not want to be looked up to on that account, but he fled admiration in every way, lest he ever become vain. But woe to us, who have lost you, worthy father, model of every good deed and of humility. By a just judgment, in truth, we have lost him whom we did not care to know when we had him.

CHAPTER XX

Of Francis' desire for martyrdom and his trip first to Spain, then to Syria; and how God delivered the sailors from peril through him by multiplying the provisions

55 Glowing with love for God, the most blessed father Francis sought always to put his hand to courageous deeds; and walking the way of the commandments of God with a generous heart, he longed to attain the height of perfection. In the sixth year of his conversion,[181] burning intensely with the desire for holy martyrdom, he wanted to take ship for the regions of Syria to preach the Christian faith and penance to the Saracens and infidels. When he had gone on board a certain ship to go there, contrary winds arose and he found himself with the rest of his shipmates in the region of Slavonia.[182] But when he saw that he was deprived of attaining his great desire, after a short period of time he begged some sailors who were going to Ancona[183] to take him with them, because it would hardly be possible for any other ship to sail for Syria that year. But they obstinately refused since Francis could not pay the expenses; the holy man of God, however, trusting very much in the goodness of the Lord, stowed away on the boat with his companion. However, by Divine Providence, there was a certain man who had come on board without anyone knowing it and who carried with him the necessary provisions; and he called one of the crew members who feared God and said to him: "Take these things with you and give them faithfully to those poor men hiding on your boat when they have need of them." And thus it happened that, when a great storm arose and the men had been working hard at rowing for many days, they consumed all the food, and only the provisions of the poor Francis were left. These, by divine grace and power, were multiplied to such an extent that, though the voyage was to last through several more days, they had enough to take care of their needs generously all the way to the port of Ancona. Therefore, when the sailors saw that they had escaped the dangers of the sea through the servant of God Francis, they thanked Almighty God who always shows himself wonderful and lovable in his servants.

56   The servant of the most high God, Francis, leaving the sea, walked over the land, and ploughing it up with the word, he sowed the seed of life and brought forth blessed fruit. For immediately quite a few good and suitable men, clerics and lay, fleeing from the world and manfully crushing the devil, fol-

lowed Francis devoutly in his life and purpose
through the grace and the will of the Most High.
Still, though the branch of the Gospel[184] produced
an abundance of the choicest fruits, the sublime purpose of attaining martyrdom and the ardent desire
for it in no way grew cold in him. After a not very
long time he started on a journey toward Morocco,
to preach the Gospel of Christ to Miramamolin and
his people.[185] He was carried along by so great a desire, that at times he left his companion on the trip
behind and hurried to accomplish his purpose, drunk,
as it were, in spirit. But the good God, whom it
pleased in his kindness to be mindful of me and of
many others, *withstood him to his face*[186] when he
had traveled as far as Spain; and, that he might not
go any farther, he recalled him from the journey he
had begun by a prolonged illness.

57   Not long after he had returned to the church
of St. Mary of the Portiuncula,[187] some educated and
noble men very gratifyingly joined him. These, since
Francis was a most noble and discreet man in spirit,
he treated with honor and dignity and he most generously gave each one his due. In truth, since he was
endowed with outstanding discretion, he prudently
considered in all the dignity of each one's station.
But he was not able to rest without following even
more fervently the impulse of his soul. Accordingly,
in the thirteenth year of his conversion[188] he set out
for Syria, at a time when great and severe battles
were raging daily between the Christians and the
pagans; he took with him a companion,[189] and he did
not fear to present himself before the sultan of the
Saracens.[190] But who can narrate with what great
steadfastness of mind he stood before him, with what
strength of spirit he spoke to him, with what eloquence and confidence he replied to those who insulted the Christian law? For before he gained access

to the sultan, though he was captured by the sultan's soldiers, was insulted and beaten, still he was not frightened; he did not fear the threats of torture and, when death was threatened, he did not grow pale. But though he was treated shamefully by many who were quite hostile and hateful toward him, he was nevertheless received very honorably by the sultan. The sultan honored him as much as he was able, and having given him many gifts, he tried to bend Francis' mind toward the riches of the world. But when he saw that Francis most vigorously despised all these things as so much dung, he was filled with the greatest admiration, and he looked upon him as a man different from all others. He was deeply moved by his words and he listened to him very willingly. Still, in all these things the Lord did not fulfill Francis' desire for martyrdom, reserving for him the prerogative of a singular grace.[191]

CHAPTER XXI

How Francis preached to the birds and of the obedience of creatures

58   Meanwhile, while many were joining the brothers, as was said, the most blessed father Francis was making a trip through the Spoleto valley. He came to a certain place near Bevagna[192] where a very great number of birds of various kinds had congregated, namely, doves, crows, and some others popularly called daws.[193] When the most blessed servant of God, Francis, saw them, being a man of very great fervor and great tenderness toward lower and irrational creatures, he left his companions in the road and ran eagerly toward the birds. When he was close enough to them, seeing that they were waiting expectantly for him, he greeted them in his usual way. But, not a little surprised that the birds did not rise in flight, as they usually do, he was filled with great

joy and humbly begged them to listen to the word of
God. Among the many things he spoke to them were
these words that he added: "My brothers, birds, you
should praise your Creator very much and always
love him; he gave you feathers to clothe you, wings
so that you can fly, and whatever else was necessary
for you. God made you noble among his creatures,
and he gave you a home in the purity of the air;
though you neither sow nor reap, he nevertheless
protects and governs you without any solicitude on
your part."[194] At these words, as Francis himself
used to say and those too who were with him, the
birds, rejoicing in a wonderful way according to their
nature, began to stretch their necks, extend their
wings, open their mouths and gaze at him. And
Francis, *passing through their midst, went on his
way*[195] and returned, touching their heads and bodies
with his tunic. Finally he blessed them, and then,
after he had made the sign of the cross over them, he
gave them permission to fly away to some other place.
But the blessed father went his way with his companions, rejoicing and giving thanks to God, whom
all creatures venerate with humble acknowledgement.
But now that he had become simple by grace, not
by nature, he began to blame himself for negligence
in not having preached to the birds before, seeing
that they had listened to the word of God with such
great reverence. And so it happened that, from that
day on, he solicitously admonished all birds, all animals and reptiles, and even creatures that have no
feeling, to praise and love their Creator, for daily,
when the name of the Savior had been invoked, he
saw their obedience by personal experience.

59   When he came one day to a city called
Alviano[196] to preach the word of God, he went up
to a higher place[197] so that he could be seen by all
and he began to ask for silence. But when all the

people had fallen silent and were standing reverently at attention, a flock of swallows, chattering and making a loud noise, were building nests in that same place. Since the blessed Francis could not be heard by the people over the chattering of the birds, he spoke to them saying: "My sisters, swallows, it is now time for me to speak, for you have already spoken enough. Listen to the word of the Lord and be silent and quiet until the word of the Lord is finished." And those little birds, to the astonishment and wonder of the people standing by, immediately fell silent, and they did not move from that place until the sermon was finished. When these men therefore saw this miracle, they were filled with the greatest admiration and said: "Truly this man is a saint and a friend of the Most High." And they hastened with the greatest devotion to at least touch his clothing, *praising and blessing God*.[198] It is indeed wonderful how even irrational creatures recognized his affection for them and felt his tender love for them.

60   Once when he was staying at the town of Greccio,[199] a little rabbit[200] that had been caught in a trap was brought alive to him by a certain brother. When the most blessed man saw it, he was moved to pity and said: "Brother rabbit, come to me. Why did you allow yourself to be deceived like this?" And as soon as the rabbit had been let go by the brother who held it, it fled to the saint, and, without being forced by anyone, it lay quiet in his bosom as the safest place possible. After he had rested there a little while, the holy father, caressing it with motherly affection, released it so it could return free to the woods. But when it had been placed upon the ground several times and had returned each time to the saint's bosom, he finally commanded it to be carried by the brothers to the nearby woods. Something similar happened with a certain rabbit, by nature a very

wild creature, when he was on an island in the lake of Perugia.[201]

61   He was moved by the same tender affection toward fish, too, which, when they were caught, and he had the chance, he threw back into the water, commanding them to be careful lest they be caught again.[202] Once when he was sitting in a boat near a port in the lake of Rieti,[203] a certain fisherman, who had caught a big fish popularly called a *tinca*,[204] offered it kindly to him. He accepted it joyfully and kindly and began to call it *brother;* then placing it in the water outside the boat, he began devoutly to bless the name of the Lord. And while he continued in prayer for some time, the fish played in the water beside the boat and did not go away from the place where it had been put until his prayer was finished and the holy man of God gave it permission to leave. For thus did the glorious father Francis, walking in the way of obedience and embracing perfectly the yoke of obedience to God, acquire great dignity in the sight of God in that creatures obeyed him. For even water was turned into wine for him, when on one occasion he was grievously ill at the hermitage of St. Urban.[205] At the taste of it he became well so easily that it was thought to be a miracle by all, as it really was. And truly he is a saint whom creatures obey in this way,[206] and at whose nod the elements change themselves to other uses.

CHAPTER XXII

Of Francis' preaching at Ascoli; and how the sick were healed by touching things his hand had touched, though he himself was absent

62   At that time, when, as has been said, the venerable father Francis preached to the birds,[207] going about the cities and towns and everywhere scattering

the seeds of his blessings, he came to the city of Ascoli.[208] There, when he preached the word of God very fervently, as was his custom, almost all the people were filled with such great grace and devotion, through a change brought about by the right hand of the Most High, that they trampled on one another in their eagerness to hear and see him. For at that time thirty men, clerics and lay, received the habit of religion from him.

So great was the faith of the men and women, so great their devotion toward the holy man of God, that he pronounced himself happy who could but touch his garment. When he entered any city, the clergy rejoiced, the bells were rung, the men were filled with happiness, the women rejoiced together, the children clapped their hands; and often, taking branches from the trees, they went to meet him singing. The wickedness of heretics was confounded, the faith of the Church exalted; and while the faithful rejoiced, the heretics slipped secretly away. For such great signs of sanctity were evident in him that no one dared to oppose his words, while the great assembly of people looked only upon him. In the midst of all these things and above everything else, Francis thought that the faith of the holy Roman Church was by all means to be preserved, honored, and imitated, that faith in which alone is found the salvation of all who are to be saved. He revered priests and he had a great affection for every ecclesiastical order.

63   The people would offer Francis bread to bless, which they would then keep for a long time; and upon eating it, they were cured of various illnesses. So also they very often cut off parts of his tunic in their very great faith, so much so that he sometimes was left almost naked. And what is even more wonderful, if the holy father would touch any object with his hand, health returned to many by means of that object. Thus when a certain woman from a little village near Arezzo was pregnant[209] and the time had come for her to be delivered, she was in labor through several days and thereby in incredible suffering, hanging between life and death. Her neighbors and her relatives heard that the blessed Francis was going to pass through that village on his way to a certain hermitage. But, while they were waiting for him, it happened that Francis went to that place by another way. He was riding a horse because he was weak and ill. When he had come to that place, he sent the horse back by a certain brother, Peter by name, to the man who had let him have it out of charity. Brother Peter, bringing the horse back, passed through that village where the suffering woman lay. When the men of the village saw him, they ran quickly to him, thinking he was the blessed Francis himself; when they saw it was not Francis, they were exceedingly sad. Finally, they began to ask each other if they might be able to find something that Francis had touched with his hand. After looking for a long time, they found the reins which he had held in his hands while riding. And taking the bit from the mouth of the horse upon which Francis had sat, they put the reins he had touched with his hands upon the woman; immediately the danger was gone and she bore her child with joy in safety.

64   Walfried, who lived in Città della Pieve,[210] *a devout and God-fearing man, as was all his household,*[211] had a cord with which the blessed Francis had been girded at one time. It happened that in this place many men and not a few women were afflicted with various illnesses and fevers. This man, after dipping the cord in water or mixing some strands of the cord with the water, would give the water to the sick to drink; and thus all of them were healed in Christ's name. These things took place in the absence

of Blessed Francis, and many more things happened too which we could not tell adaquately even at great length. Now we will insert in this work a few things that the Lord Our God deigned to work through his presence.

CHAPTER XXIII

How Francis healed a cripple at Toscanella and a paralytic at Narni

65 Once when the holy man of God Francis was going about through various regions to preach the kingdom of God, he came to a certain city called Toscanella.[212] There, when he was sowing the seed of life[213] in his usual way, a certain soldier of that city gave him hospitality; he had an only son who was lame and weak of body. Though he was a young child, he had passed the years of weaning; still he remained in a cradle. When the father of the boy saw the great sanctity of the man of God, he humbly cast himself at his feet, begging from him health for his son. But Francis, who considered himself useless and unworthy of such great power and grace, refused for a long time to do this. But finally overcome by the insistence of his petitions, he prayed and then put his hand upon the boy and, blessing him, raised him up. Immediately, with all present looking on and rejoicing, the boy arose completely restored and began to walk here and there about the house.

66 Once when the man of God Francis had come to Narni[214] and was staying there for a number of days, a certain man of that city, Peter by name, lay in bed paralyzed. For a period of five months he had been so deprived of the use of all his limbs that he could not rise at all or move himself even a little; and thus having completely lost the use of his feet and hands and head, he could only move his tongue and open his eyes. When he heard that Francis had come to Narni, he sent a messenger to the bishop of that city to ask him for the love of God to send the servant of the most high God to him, confident that he would be freed from the illness from which he suffered at the sight and presence of Francis. And it so happened that, when the blessed Francis had come to him and had made the sign of the cross over him from his head to his feet, he was immediately healed and restored to his former health.

CHAPTER XXIV

How Francis gave sight to a blind woman; and how at Gubbio he straightened the hands of a crippled woman

67 A certain woman from the city mentioned just above,[215] who had been struck blind, merited to receive immediately the sight she desired when the blessed Francis drew the sign of the cross upon her eyes. At Gubbio there was a woman both of whose hands were so crippled that she could do no work at all with them. When she learned that St. Francis had entered the city, she immediately ran to him; and with her face covered with misery and sadness, she showed her crippled hands to him and began to ask him to touch them. Moved to pity he touched her and healed her. Immediately the woman went home full of joy, made a kind of cheese cake with her own hands, and offered it to the holy man. He took a little of it in his kindness and commanded the woman to eat the rest of it with her family.

CHAPTER XXV

How Francis freed one of the brothers from the falling sickness or from a devil; and how he freed a possessed woman at the city of San Gemini

68   One of the brothers suffered frequently from a very serious infirmity and one horrible to see; I do not know by what name it is called, though some think it is an evil spirit. Frequently he was cast upon the ground and he turned about foaming at the mouth and with a terrible look upon his face; at times his limbs were drawn up, at other times they were extended; now they were folded up and twisted, again they were rigid and hard. Sometimes, when he was stretched out and rigid, he would be raised up into the air to the height of a man's stature, with his feet even with his head, and then would fall back to the ground. Pitying his grievous illness the holy father Francis went to him and, after praying, signed him and blessed him. Suddenly he was cured and he did not again suffer in the least from the tortures of this illness.

69   One day when the most blessed father Francis was passing through the diocese of Narni, he came to a certain city called San Gemini,²¹⁶ and preaching there the kingdom of God, he was entertained along with three of his brothers by a certain man of good repute in that region who feared and worshipped God. But his wife was *beset by a devil,*²¹⁷ as was known to all who lived in that town. Her husband interceded with St. Francis for her, confident that she could be freed by his merits. But because Francis preferred in his simplicity to be held in contempt rather than be praised by the world because of a demonstration of his sanctity, he refused firmly to do this. Finally, because God was concerned in the case, and because so many were begging him to do it, he consented, overcome by their prayers. He called the three brothers who were with him and, placing each one in a corner of the house, he said to them: "Let us pray to the Lord, brothers, for this woman that God may strike the yoke of the devil from her unto his own praise and glory. Let us stand separately in the corners of the house lest that evil spirit be able to escape us or deceive us by getting into the hiding places of the corners." When the prayer was finished, blessed Francis went up to the woman, who was being miserably tormented and who was clamoring horribly, and, with the power of the Holy Spirit, he said: "In the name of the Lord Jesus Christ, I command you in holy obedience, evil spirit, to go out of her and never dare to hinder her again." He had hardly finished the words when the devil left that woman so very quickly and with such anger and racket that, because of the sudden healing of the woman and the very quick obedience of the devil, the holy father thought he perhaps had been deceived. He immediately left that place in shame, divine providence so arranging things that he would not be able to glory vainly in any way. Whence it happened that blessed Francis was passing through the same place on another occasion, and Brother Elias was with him; and behold, that woman, when she heard of his coming, immediately arose; and running through the street, she cried out after him that he should deign to speak to her. But he did not want to speak to her, knowing that she was the woman from whom he had once cast out a devil by the power of God. But she *kissed the steps of his feet*,[218] giving thanks to God and to his servant St. Francis who had freed her *out of the hand of death*.[219] Finally, Brother Elias urged the saint by his prayers, and he spoke to her after he had been assured by the people of her illness, as was said, and of her cure.

CHAPTER XXVI

How Francis also cast out a devil at Città di Castello

70   Also at Citta di Castello[220] there was a woman obsessed by the devil. When the most blessed father Francis was in this city, the woman was brought to the house where he was staying. That woman, standing outside, began to gnash her teeth and, her face twisted, she began to set up a great howl, as unclean spirits do. Many people of both sexes from that city came and pleaded with St. Francis in her behalf, for that evil spirit had long tormented and tortured her and had disturbed them with his loud cries. The holy father then sent to her a brother who was with him, wishing to discover whether it was really a devil or deception on the part of the woman. When that woman saw him, she began to deride him, knowing that it was not Francis who had come out. The holy father was inside praying. He came out when he had finished his prayer. But the woman, unable to stand his power, began to tremble and roll about on the ground. St. Francis called to her and said: "In virtue of obedience, I command you, unclean spirit, to go out of her." Immediately he left her, without injuring her, but departing in great anger. Thanks be to God, who does everything according to his will.

But since we have not undertaken to narrate miracles, which indeed do not make sanctity, but only manifest it, but rather to speak of the excellence of Francis' life and his most pure conduct, we will omit the miracles because of their great number and tell of his works for eternal salvation.

CHAPTER XXVII

Of the clarity and constancy of Francis' mind, and of his preaching before Pope Honorius; and how he committed himself and his brothers to the lord Hugo, Bishop of Ostia

71   The man of God Francis had been taught not to seek his own,[221] but to seek especially what in his eyes would be helpful toward the salvation of others; but above everything else he desired *to depart and to be with Christ*.[222] Therefore, his greatest concern was to be free from everything of this world, lest the serenity of his mind be disturbed even for an hour by the taint of anything that was mere dust. He made himself insensible to all external noise, and, bridling his external senses with all his strength and repressing the movements of his nature, he occupied himself with God alone. *In the clefts of the rock* he would build his nest and *in the hollow places of the wall* his dwelling.[223] With fruitful devotion he frequented only heavenly dwellings,[224] and he who had totally emptied himself remained so much the longer in the wounds of the Savior. He therefore frequently chose solitary places so that he could direct his mind completely to God; yet he was not slothful about entering into the affairs of his neighbors, when he saw the time was opportune, and he willingly took care of things pertaining to their salvation. For his safest haven was prayer; not prayer of a single moment, or idle or presumptuous prayer, but prayer of long duration, full of devotion, serene in humility. If he began late, he would scarcely finish before morning. Walking, sitting, eating, or drinking, he was always intent upon prayer. He would go alone to pray at night in churches abandoned and located in deserted places, where, under the protection of divine grace, he overcame many fears and many dis-

turbances of mind.

72 He fought hand to hand with the devil, for in such places the devil not only struck at him with temptations but discouraged him by ruining and destroying things. But the most valiant soldier of God, knowing that his Lord can do all things everywhere, did not give in to fright, but said within his heart: "You can no more rattle the weapons of your wickedness against me here, O evil one, than if we were in public before all the people." Indeed, he was extremely steadfast, and he paid no attention to anything except what pertained to the Lord. For when he so very often preached the word of God to thousands of people, he was as sure of himself as though he were speaking with a familiar companion. He looked upon the greatest multitude of people as one person and he preached to one as he would to a multitude. Out of the purity of his mind he provided for himself security in preaching a sermon and, without thinking about it beforehand, he spoke wonderful things to all and things not heard before. When he did give some time to meditation before a sermon, he at times forgot what he had meditated upon when the people had come together, and he knew nothing else to say. Without embarrassment he would confess to the people that he had thought of many things but could remember nothing at all of them; and suddenly he would be filled with such great eloquence that he would move the souls of the hearers to admiration. At times, however, knowing nothing to say, he would give a blessing and dismiss the people feeling that from this alone they had received a great sermon.

73 But when at one time he had come to Rome because the interests of his order demanded it, he longed greatly to speak before Pope Honorius and the venerable cardinals.[225] When the lord Hugo,[226] the glorious bishop of Ostia, who venerated the holy man of God with a special affection, understood this, he was filled with both fear and joy, admiring the fervor of the holy man but conscious of his simple purity. But confident of the mercy of the Almighty, which in the time of need never fails those who trust in it, the bishop brought Francis before the lord pope and the reverend cardinals; and standing before such great princes, after receiving their permission and blessing, he began to speak fearlessly. Indeed, he spoke with such great fervor of spirit, that, not being able to contain himself for joy, when he spoke the words with his mouth, he moved his feet as though he were dancing, not indeed lustfully, but as one burning with the fire of divine love, not provoking laughter, but drawing forth tears of grief. For many of them were *pierced to the heart*[227] in admiration of divine grace and of such great constancy in man. But the venerable lord bishop of Ostia was kept in suspense by fear and he prayed with all his strength to the Lord that the simplicity of the blessed man would not be despised, since the glory of the saint would reflect upon himself as would his disgrace, in as much as he had been placed over Francis' family as a father.[228]

74 For St. Francis had clung to him as a son to his father and as an only son to his mother, sleeping and resting securely upon the bosom of his kindness. In truth, the bishop held the place and did the work of a shepherd, but he left the name of shepherd to the holy man. The blessed father provided what provisions were necessary, but the kindly lord bishop carried them into effect. O how many, above all when these things were first taking place, were plotting to destroy the new Order that had been planted! O how many were trying to choke off this new *chosen vine-*

yard[229] that the hand of the Lord had so kindly planted in the world! How many there were who were trying to steal and consume its first and purest fruits! But they were all *slain by the sword*[230] of the reverend father and lord who *brought* them to *nothing*.[231] For he was a river of eloquence, a wall of the Church, a champion of truth, and a lover of the humble. Blessed that day, therefore, and memorable, on which the holy man of God committed himself to such a venerable lord. For once when that lord was exercising the office of legate for the holy see, as he often did, in Tuscany,[232] Blessed Francis, who as yet did not have many brothers but wanted to go to France, came to Florence where the aforementioned bishop was staying at the time. As yet they were not joined in that extraordinary familiarity, but only the fame of Francis' blessed life joined them in mutual affection and charity.

75   For the rest, because it was blessed Francis' custom upon entering any city or country to go to the bishops or priests, hearing of the presence of so great a bishop, he presented himself to his clemency with great reverence. When the lord bishop saw him, he received him with humble devotion, as he always did those who professed holy religion, those particularly who loved the noble insignia of blessed poverty and holy simplicity. And because he was solicitous in providing for the wants of the poor and in handling their business with special care, he diligently asked Francis the reason for his coming and listened to his proposal with great kindness. When he saw that Francis despised all earthly things more than the rest and that he was alight with that fire that Jesus had sent upon earth,[233] his soul was from that moment knit with the soul of Francis and he devoutly asked his prayers and most graciously offered his protection to him in all things. Then he ad-

monished Francis not to finish the journey he had
begun but to give himself solicitously to the care of
and watchfulness over those whom the Lord had
committed to him. But St. Francis, seeing such a
venerable lord conducting himself so kindly, giving
such warm affection and such efficacious advice, rejoiced with a very great joy; and then, *falling at his
feet*,[234] he handed himself over and entrusted himself and his brothers to him with a devout mind.[235]

CHAPTER XXVIII

*Concerning Francis' spirit of charity and compassion
toward the poor; and how he treated a sheep and
some lambs*

76 The father of the poor, the poor Francis, conforming himself to the poor in all things, was grieved
when he saw some one poorer than himself, not because he longed for vainglory, but only from a feeling of compassion. And, though he was content with
a tunic that was quite poor and rough, he very frequently longed to divide it with some poor person.[236]
But that this very rich poor man, drawn on by a
great feeling of affection, might be able to help the
poor in some way, he would ask the rich of this
world, when the weather was cold, to give him a
mantle or some furs. And when, out of devotion, they
willingly did what the most blessed father asked of
them, he would say to them: "I will accept this from
you with this understanding that you do not expect
ever to have it back again." And when he met the
first poor man, he would clothe him with what he
had received with joy and gladness.[237] He bore it very
ill if he saw a poor person reproached or if he heard
a curse hurled upon any creature by anyone.

Once it happened that a certain brother uttered
a word of invective against a certain poor man who

had asked for an alms, saying to him: "See, perhaps you are a rich man and pretending to be poor." Hearing this, the father of the poor, St. Francis, was greatly saddened, and he severely rebuked the brother who had said such a thing and commanded him to strip himself before the poor man and, kissing his feet, beg pardon of him. For, he was accustomed to say: "Who curses a poor man does an injury to Christ, whose noble image he wears, the image of him who made himself poor for us in this world." Frequently, therefore, when he found the poor burdened down with wood or other things, he offered his own shoulders to help them, though his shoulders were very weak.

77   Francis abounded in the spirit of charity; he was filled with compassion not only toward men in need, but even toward dumb animals, reptiles, birds, and other creatures, sensible and insensible. But, among all the various kinds of animals, he loved little lambs with a special predilection and more ready affection, because in the sacred scriptures the humility of our Lord Jesus Christ is more frequently likened to that of the lamb and best illustrated by the simile of a lamb.[238] So, all things, especially those in which some allegorical similarity to the Son of God could be found, he would embrace more fondly and look upon more willingly. Once, when he made a trip through the Marches of Ancona[239] and had preached the word of God in that same city and had taken up his journey toward Osimo[240] with a certain Brother Paul whom he had appointed minister of all the brothers in that province,[241] he found a certain shepherd feeding a herd of she-goats and he-goats in the fields. Among the great number of these goats there was one little lamb going along and feeding humbly and quietly. When blessed Francis saw it, he stopped and, *touched inwardly with sorrow of*

heart[242] and groaning deeply, he said to the brother who was with him: "Do you not see this sheep that walks so meekly among the goats? I tell you that our Lord Jesus Christ walked in the same way meekly and humbly among the pharisees and chief priests. Therefore I ask you, my son, for love of him, to have pity with me on this little sheep. Let us pay the price and lead her away from among these goats."

78   Brother Paul, wondering over Francis' grief, began himself to be filled with sorrow. But since they had nothing but the poor tunics with which they were clothed and while they were worrying about the price of buying the sheep, immediately a certain merchant on a journey was there and offered the price desired. Thanking God, they took the sheep and went on to Osimo. There, entering the house of the bishop of the city, they were received by him with great reverence. But the lord bishop wondered about the sheep which the man of God was leading and about his affection for it. But when the servant of Christ had recounted the long parable of the sheep of the Gospel, touched to the heart the bishop gave thanks to God for the purity of the man of God. The next day, however, when he was leaving the city and wondering what he should do with the sheep, he took the advice of his companion and brother and gave it over to a certain monastery of handmaids of Christ at San Severino[243] to be cared for. The venerable handmaids of Christ accepted the sheep with joy as a great gift to them by God. They watched over it carefully for a long time, and they made a tunic out of its wool and sent it to the blessed father Francis at St. Mary of the Portiuncula at the time of a certain chapter. The holy man of God took it with great reverence and joy of spirit, and, embracing it, he kissed it and invited all who stood by to share his happiness.

79   Another time when he was passing through the same marches, with the same brother serving gladly as his companion, he met a certain man who had two little lambs hanging bound over his shoulder, taking them to the market to sell them. When blessed Francis heard them bleating, he was filled with pity; and, coming close, he touched them and showed his compassion for them like a mother over her weeping child. And he said to the man: "Why are you torturing my brother lambs tied up and hanging like this?" Answering, he said: "I am taking them to the market to sell them, because I need the money." The saint said: "What will happen to them then?" He answered: "Those who buy them will kill them and eat them." "God forbid," replied the saint; "this must not happen. Take the mantle I am wearing as their price and give the lambs to me." He quickly gave him the lambs and took the mantle, for the mantle was of much greater value. Now the saint had borrowed the mantle that day from a certain faithful man to ward off the cold. For the rest, the saint, after receiving the lambs, considered carefully what he should do with them; and, at the advice of his companion, he gave them to that man to take care of them; and he commanded him not to sell them at any time, nor to do them any harm, but to keep them, feed them, and take care of them conscientiously.

CHAPTER XXIX

Of the love Francis bore all creatures on account of their Creator; a description of the inner and outer man[244]

80   It would take too long and it would be impossible to enumerate and gather together all the things the glorious Francis did and taught while he

was living in the flesh. For who could ever give expression to the very great affection he bore for all things that are God's? Who would be able to narrate the sweetness he enjoyed while contemplating in creatures the wisdom of their Creator, his power and his goodness? Indeed, he was very often filled with a wonderful and ineffable joy from this consideration while he looked upon the sun, while he beheld the moon, and while he gazed upon the stars and the firmament. O simple piety and pious simplicity! Toward little worms even he glowed with a very great love, for he had read this saying about the Savior: *I am a worm, not a man.*[245] Therefore he picked them up from the road and placed them in a safe place, lest they be crushed by the feet of the passersby. What shall I say of the lower creatures, when he would see to it that the bees would be provided with honey in the winter, or the best wine, lest they should die from the cold? He used to praise in public the perfection of their works and the excellence of their skill, for the glory of God, with such encomiums that he would often spend a whole day in praising them and the rest of creatures. For as of old the three youths in the fiery furnace[246] invited all the elements to praise and glorify the Creator of the universe, so also this man, filled with the spirit of God, never ceased to glorify, praise, and bless the Creator and Ruler of all things in all the elements and creatures.[247]

81   How great a gladness do you think the beauty of the flowers brought to his mind[248] when he saw the shape of their beauty and perceived the odor of their sweetness? He used to turn the eye of consideration immediately to the beauty of that flower that comes *from the root of Jesse*[249] and gives light *in the days of spring*[250] and by its fragrance has raised innumerable thousands from the dead. When he found

an abundance of flowers, he preached to them and invited them to praise the Lord as though they were endowed with reason. In the same way he exhorted with the sincerest purity cornfields and vineyards, stones and forests and all the beautiful things of the fields, fountains of water and the green things of the gardens, earth and fire, air and wind, to love God and serve him willingly. Finally, he called all creatures *brother,* and in a most extraordinary manner, a manner never experienced by others, he discerned the hidden things of nature with his sensitive heart, as one who had already escaped *into the freedom of the glory of the sons of God.*[251] O good Jesus, he is now praising you as admirable in heaven with all the angels, he who on earth preached you as lovable to every creature.

82 For he was filled with love that surpasses all human understanding when he pronounced your holy name, O holy Lord; and carried away with joy and purest gladness, he seemed like a new man, one from another world. Therefore, whenever he would find anything written, whether about God or about man,[252] along the way, or in a house, or on the floor, he would pick it up with the greatest reverence and put it in a sacred or decent place, so that the name of the Lord would not remain there or anything else pertaining to it. One day when he was asked by a certain brother why he so diligently picked up writings even of pagans or writings in which there was no mention of the name of the Lord, he replied: "Son, because the letters are there out of which the most glorious name of the Lord God could be put together. Whatever is good there does not pertain to the pagans, nor to any other men, but to God alone, to whom belongs every good." And what is no less to be admired, when he had caused some letters of greeting or admonition to be written, he would not allow even a single letter or syllable to be deleted, even though they had often been placed there superfluously or in error.

83   O how beautiful, how splendid, how glorious did he appear in the innocence of his life, in the simplicity of his words, in the purity of his heart, in his love for God, in his fraternal charity, in his ardent obedience, in his peaceful submission, in his angelic countenance![253] He was charming in his manners, serene by nature, affable in his conversation, most opportune in his exhortations, most faithful in what was entrusted to him, cautious in counsel, effective in business, gracious in all things. He was serene of mind, sweet of disposition, sober in spirit, raised up in contemplation, zealous in prayer, and in all things fervent. He was constant in purpose, stable in virtue, persevering in grace, and unchanging in all things. He was quick to pardon, slow to become angry, ready of wit, tenacious of memory, subtle in discussion, circumspect in choosing, and in all things simple. He was unbending with himself, understanding toward others, and discreet in all things.

He was a most eloquent man, a man of cheerful countenance, of kindly aspect; he was immune to cowardice, free of insolence. He was of medium height, closer to shortness; his head was moderate in size and round, his face a bit long and prominent, his forehead smooth and low; his eyes were of moderate size, black and sound;[254] his hair was black, his eyebrows straight, his nose symmetrical, thin and straight; his ears were upright, but small; his temples smooth. His speech was peaceable,[255] fiery and sharp; his voice was strong, sweet, clear, and sonorous. His teeth were set close together, even, and white; his lips were small and thin; his beard black, but not bushy. His neck was slender, his shoulders straight, his arms short, his hands slender, his fingers long, his nails extended; his legs were thin, his feet small. His skin was delicate, his flesh very spare. He wore rough garments, he slept but very briefly, he gave most generously. And because he was very humble, he showed *all mildness to all men*,[256] adapting himself usefully to the behavior of all. The more holy amongst the holy, among sinners he was as one of them. Therefore, most holy father, help the sinners, you who loved sinners, and deign, we beg of you, most kindly to raise up by your most glorious intercession those whom you see lying in the mire of their sins.

CHAPTER XXX

Of the manger Francis made on the day of the Lord's birth

84   Francis' highest intention, his chief desire, his uppermost purpose was to observe the holy Gospel in all things and through all things and, with perfect vigilance, with all zeal, with all the longing of his mind and all the fervor of his heart, "to follow the teaching and the footsteps of our Lord Jesus Christ."[257] He would recall Christ's words through persistent meditation and bring to mind his deeds through the most penetrating consideration. The humility of the incarnation and the charity of the passion occupied his memory particularly, to the extent that he wanted to think of hardly anything else. What he did on the birthday of our Lord Jesus Christ near the little town called Greccio[258] in the third year before his glorious death[259] should especially be noted and recalled with reverent memory. In that place there was a certain man by the name of John, of good reputation and an even better life, whom blessed Francis loved with a special love, for in the place where he lived he held a noble and honorable position in as much as he had trampled upon the

nobility of his birth and pursued nobility of soul. Blessed Francis sent for this man, as he often did, about fifteen days before the birth of the Lord, and he said to him: "If you want us to celebrate the present feast of our Lord at Greccio, go with haste and diligently prepare what I tell you. For I wish to do something that will recall to memory the little Child who was born in Bethlehem and set before our bodily eyes in some way the inconveniences of his infant needs, how he lay in a manger, how, with an ox and an ass standing by, he lay upon the hay where he had been placed." When the good and faithful man heard these things, he ran with haste and prepared in that place all the things the saint had told him.

85   But the day of joy drew near, the time of great rejoicing came. The brothers were called from their various places. Men and women of that neighborhood prepared with glad hearts, according to their means, candles and torches to light up that night that has lighted up all the days and years with its gleaming star. At length the saint of God came, and finding all things prepared, *he saw it and was glad.*[260] The manger was prepared, the hay had been brought, the ox and ass were led in. There simplicity was honored, poverty was exhalted, humility was commended, and Greccio was made, as it were, a new Bethlehem. The night was lighted up like the day, and it delighted men and beasts. The people came and were filled with new joy over the new mystery. The woods rang with the voices of the crowd and the rocks made answer to their jubilation. The brothers sang, paying their debt of praise to the Lord, and the whole night resounded with their rejoicing. The saint of God stood before the manger, uttering sighs, overcome with love, and filled with a wonderful happiness. The solemnities of the Mass were celebrated over the manger and the priest experienced a new

consolation.

86 The saint of God was clothed with the vestments of the deacon, for he was a deacon, and he sang the holy Gospel in a sonorous voice. And his voice was a strong voice, a sweet voice, a clear voice, a sonorous voice,[261] inviting all to the highest rewards. Then he preached to the people standing about, and he spoke charming words concerning the nativity of the poor King and the little town of Bethlehem. Frequently too, when he wished to call Christ *Jesus,* he would call him simply the *Child of Bethlehem,* aglow with overflowing love for him; and speaking the word *Bethlehem,* his voice was more like the bleating of a sheep. His mouth was filled more with sweet affection than with words. Besides, when he spoke the name *Child of Bethlehem* or *Jesus,* his tongue licked his lips, as it were, relishing and savoring with pleased palate the sweetness of the words. The gifts of the Almighty were multiplied there, and a wonderful vision was seen by a certain virtuous man. For he saw a little child lying in the manger lifeless, and he saw the holy man of God go up to it and rouse the child as from a deep sleep. This vision was not unfitting, for the Child Jesus had been forgotten in the hearts of many; but, by the working of his grace, he was brought to life again through his servant St. Francis and stamped upon their fervent memory. At length the solemn night celebration was brought to a close, and each one returned to his home with holy joy.

87 The hay that had been placed in the manger was kept, so that the Lord might save the beasts of burden and other animals through it as he multiplied his holy mercy.[262] And in truth it so happened that many animals throughout the surrounding region that had various illnesses were freed from their illnesses after eating of this hay. Indeed, even women laboring for a long time in a difficult birth, were delivered safely when some of this hay was placed upon them; and a large number of persons of both sexes of that place, suffering from various illnesses, obtained the health they sought. Later, the place on which the manger had stood was made sacred by a *temple of the Lord*,[263] and an altar was built in honor of the most blessed father Francis over the manger and a church was built, so that where once the animals had eaten the hay, there in the future men would eat unto health of soul and body the flesh of the *lamb without blemish and without spot*,[264] our Lord Jesus Christ,[265] who in highest and ineffable love gave himself to us, who lives and reigns with the Father and the Holy Spirit, God, eternally glorious, forever and ever. Amen. Alleluja, Alleluja.

HERE ENDS THE FIRST BOOK ABOUT THE LIFE AND ACTS OF BLESSED FRANCIS

BOOK TWO

HERE BEGINS THE SECOND BOOK WHICH TELLS OF THE LAST TWO YEARS OF THE LIFE OF OUR MOST BLESSED FATHER FRANCIS AND ABOUT HIS HAPPY DEATH

CHAPTER I

[About the contents of this book, about the time of Francis' death, and about his progress in perfection][1]

88   In the first part of this work, which, with the help of the grace of the Savior, we have brought to a fitting conclusion, we wrote about the life and acts of our most blessed father Francis up to the eighteenth year of his conversion.[2] We will now add to this work briefly the rest of the things he did from the second last year of his life on, in so far as we have been able to get proper knowledge of them; and at present we intend to note down only those things which were of greater importance, so that they who wish to say more about them may always be able to find something they can add.

In the year of our Lord's incarnation 1226, in the fourteenth indiction,[3] on Sunday, October 4,[4] our blessed father Francis went forth from the prison of the flesh and took flight most happily to the mansions of the heavenly spirits, consummating perfectly what he had begun. He died in the city of Assisi, where he was born and at St. Mary of the Portiuncula where he first planted the Order of Friars Minor, twenty years after he had given himself perfectly to Christ, following the life and the footsteps of the Apostles. His sacred and holy body was laid to rest and honorably buried with hymns and praises in that city, and there, by reason of many miracles, it shines radiantly unto the glory of Almighty God. Amen.

89   Since this man had received little or no in-

struction in the way of God and in knowledge of him
when he was young, he remained for no short time in
his natural simplicity and under the sway of vices;
but *he was justified from sin*[5] *by a change of the right
hand of the Most High,*[6] and by the grace and *power
of the Most High*[7] he was filled with divine wisdom
above all others of his time. For when the teachings
of the Gospel, not indeed in every respect, but taken
generally, had everywhere failed to be put into practice, this man was sent by God to bear *witness to the
truth*[8] throughout the whole world in accordance
with the example of the Apostles. And thus it came
to pass that his teaching showed that *the wisdom of
this world* is most evidently *turned to foolishness,*[9]
and within a short period of time brought it, under
the guidance of Christ, to the true wisdom of God
by the foolishness of his *preaching.*[10] For in this *last
time*[11] this new evangelist, like one of the rivers that
flowed out of paradise, diffused the waters of the
Gospel over the whole world by his tender watering,
and preached by his deeds the way of the Son of God
and the doctrine of truth. Accordingly, in him and
through him there arose throughout the world an
unlooked for happiness and a holy newness, and a
shoot of the ancient religion suddenly brought a great
renewal to those who had grown calloused and to the
very old. A new spirit was born in the hearts of the
elect, and a saving unction was poured out in their
midst, when the servant and holy man of Christ, like
one of the lights of the heavens, shone brilliantly
with a new rite and with new signs. Through him the
miracles of ancient times were renewed, while there
was planted in the desert of this world, by a new order but in an ancient way, a fruitful vine bearing
flowers of sweetness unto the odor of holy virtues by
extending everywhere the branches of a sacred
religion.

90   For, though he was a man *subject to the same infirmities* as we ourselves,[12] he was not content with observing the common precepts, but overflowing with the most ardent charity, he set out upon the way of total perfection; he aimed at the heights of perfect sanctity, and he saw the *end of all perfection.*[13] Therefore, every order, every sex, every age has in him a visible pattern of the way of salvation and has outstanding examples of holy works. If any propose to set their hand to difficult things and to *strive after the greater gifts*[14] of the more excellent way, let them look into the mirror of his life and learn every perfection. If any take to the lower and easier way, fearing to walk the difficult way and fearing the ascent to the top of the mountain, on this plain too they will find in him suitable guidance. If any, finally, seek signs and wonders, let them petition his sanctity and they will get what they seek. And indeed the glorious life of this man sheds a more brilliant light upon the perfection of the saints who preceded him. The passion of Jesus Christ proves this and his cross shows it most clearly. For in truth, the venerable father was marked in five parts of his body with the marks of the passion and of the cross as though he had hung upon the cross with the Son of God. *This is a great mystery*[15] and shows forth the majesty of the prerogative of love. But a secret counsel lies hidden therein and therein is concealed an awe-inspiring mystery which we believe is known to God alone and revealed only in part by the saint himself to a certain person. Therefore it is not expedient to attempt much in praise of him whose praise is from him who is the praise of all, the source and highest honor, giving the rewards of light. Blessing, therefore, the holy, true, and glorious God, let us return to our narrative.

CHAPTER II

Concerning Blessed Francis' greatest desire; and how he understood the Lord's will in his regard through the opening of a book

91 At a certain time the blessed and venerable father Francis left behind the crowds of the world that were coming together daily with the greatest devotion to hear and see him, and he sought out a quiet and secret place of solitude, desiring to spend his time there with God and to cleanse himself of any dust that may have clung to him from his association with men.[16] It was his custom to divide up the time given him to merit grace, and, as seemed necessary to him, to give part of it to working for the good of his neighbors and the rest to the blessed retirement of contemplation. He therefore took with him just the very few companions to whom his holy life was better known than it was to the rest, so that they might protect him from the invasion and *disturbance of men*[17] and respect and preserve his quiet in all things. After he had remained there for a while and had acquired in an inexpressible way familiarity with God by his constant prayer and frequent contemplation, he longed to know what might be more acceptable to the eternal King concerning himself or in himself or what might happen. Most carefully he sought out and most piously longed to know in what manner, by what way, and by what desire he might cling perfectly to the Lord God according to his counsel and according to the good pleasure of his will. This was always his highest philosophy; this very great desire always flamed in him while he lived, namely, to seek out from the simple, from the wise, from the perfect and imperfect, how he might attain the way of truth and come to his highest good.

92 For, though he was the most perfect of the

perfect, he denied that he was perfect and considered himself entirely imperfect. For he had tasted and seen how sweet,[18] how delightful and *how good is God to Israel, to them who are of a right heart*[19] and who seek him in pure *simplicity*[20] and true purity. The infused sweetness and serenity, which he felt had been given him from on high, such as is but rarely given even to the very rarest of men, compelled him to renounce himself completely, and, filled with great joyfulness, he wished to pass over completely to that state to which, going beyond his own strength, he had already gone in part. Filled with *the Spirit of God*,[21] he was ready to suffer every distress of mind and to bear every bodily torment, if only his wish might be granted, that the will of the Father in heaven might be mercifully fulfilled in him. One day therefore he went before the holy altar which was erected in the hermitage where he was staying, and taking the book in which the holy Gospel was written, he reverently placed it upon the altar. Then he prostrated himself in prayer to God, not less in heart than in body, and he asked in humble prayer that the good God, *the Father of mercies and the God of all comfort*,[22] would deign to make known his will to him, and that he might be able to carry out what he had earlier begun simply and devoutly; and he prayed that it might be shown to him at the first opening of the book what was more fitting for him to do. For he was led by the spirit of the saints and of the most perfect men, who, we read, did the same thing with pious devotion in their desire for sanctity.[23]

93 Then rising from his prayer, in a spirit of humility and with a contrite heart[24] and signing himself with the sign of the holy cross, he took the book from the altar and opened it with reverence and fear. But it happened that when he had opened the book the passion of our Lord Jesus Christ was the first thing that met his eye, and that part of it that said he would suffer tribulation.[25] But that there could be no suspicion that this had happened by chance, he opened the book a second and a third time, and each time he found the same passage or a similar one written there. Then the man filled with the Spirit of God understood that it was for him *to enter the kingdom of God*[26] through many tribulations, many trials, and many struggles. But the very strong soldier of the Lord was not disturbed at the struggles at hand, nor was he shaken, he who was about to fight the battles of the Lord on the battlefields of this world. It is not likely that a man would succumb to an enemy who has labored long, even beyond the measure of human strength, not to give in to himself. In truth, he was most fervent, and if in the past centuries there had been anyone who equaled him in his purpose, there was no one who was superior to him in his desire. For since he knew it was easier for him to do perfect things than to talk about them, he always put his zeal and his efforts not in words, which do not accomplish good but only give evidence of it, but in holy deeds. He remained therefore unshaken and happy, and he sang songs of happiness in his heart to himself and to God. Accordingly, he was considered worthy of a greater revelation who had so rejoiced over the least, and *faithful in a very little*,[27] he was *set over many*.[28]

CHAPTER III

Concerning the vision of the man in the likeness of a crucified seraph

94   Two years before Francis gave his soul back to heaven, while he was living in the hermitage which was called Alverna,[29] after the place on which it stood, he saw *in the vision of God*[30] a man standing above him, like a seraph with six wings, his hands extended and his feet joined together and fixed to a cross. Two of the wings were extended above his head, two were extended as if for flight, and two were wrapped around the whole body.[31] When the blessed servant of the Most High saw these things, he was filled with the greatest wonder, but he could not understand what this vision should mean. Still, he was filled with happiness and he rejoiced very greatly because of the kind and gracious look with which he saw himself regarded by the seraph, whose beauty was beyond estimation; but the fact that the seraph was fixed to a cross and the sharpness of his suffering filled Francis with fear. And so he arose, if I may so speak, sorrowful and joyful, and joy and grief were in him alternately. Solicitously he thought what this vision could mean, and his soul was in great anxiety to find its meaning. And while he was thus unable to come to any understanding of it and the strangeness of the vision perplexed his heart, the marks of the nails began to appear in his hands and feet, just as he had seen them a little before in the crucified man above him.

95   His hands and feet seemed to be pierced through the middle by nails, with the heads of the nails appearing in the inner side of the hands and on the upper sides of the feet and their pointed ends on the opposite sides. The marks in the hands were round on the inner side, but on the outer side they were elongated; and some small pieces of flesh took on the appearance of the ends of the nails, bent and driven back and rising above the rest of the flesh. In the same way the marks of the nails were impressed upon the feet and raised in a similar way above the rest of the flesh. Furthermore, his right side was as though it had been pierced by a lance and had a wound in

it that frequently bled so that his tunic and trousers were very often covered with his sacred blood. Alas, how few indeed merited to see the wound in his side while this crucified servant of the crucified Lord lived! But happy was Elias who, while the saint lived, merited to see this wound;[32] and no less happy was Rufino who touched the wound with his own hands.[33] For when this Brother Rufino once put his hand upon the bosom of this most holy man to rub him, his hand fell down to the right side of Francis, as it can happen; and it happened to touch the precious wound. The holy man of God was not a little grieved at this touch, and pushing his hand away, he cried out to the Lord to forgive Rufino. For he made every effort to hide this wound from those outside the order, and he hid it with such great care from those close to him that even the brothers who were always at his side and his most devoted followers did not know of this wound for a long time. And though the servant and friend of the Most High saw himself adorned with so many and such great pearls, as with the most precious gems, and endowed in a wonderful manner above the glory and honor of all other men,[34] he did not become vain in heart nor did he seek to please anyone out of thirst for vainglory; but, lest human favor should steal any of the grace given him, he strove in every way he could to hide it.

96   It was Francis' custom to reveal his great secret but rarely or to no one at all, for he feared that his revealing it to anyone might have the appearance of a special affection for him, in the way in which special friends act, and that he would thereby suffer some loss in the grace that was given him. He therefore carried about in his heart and frequently had on his lips this saying of the prophet: *Thy words have I hidden in my heart, that I may not sin against thee.*[35] Francis had given a sign to his brothers and sons who

310

lived with him, that whenever any lay people would come to him and he wanted to refrain from speaking with them, he would recite the aforementioned verse and immediately they were to dismiss with courtesy those who had come to him. For he had experienced that it is a great evil to make known all things to every one, and that he cannot be a spiritual man whose secrets are not more perfect and more numerous than the things that can be read on his face and completely understood by men. For he had found some who outwardly agreed with him but inwardly disagreed with him, who applauded him to his face, but ridiculed him behind his back, who acquired credit for themselves, but made the upright suspect to him. For wickedness often tries to blacken purity, and because of a lie that is familiar to many, the truth spoken by a few is not believed.

CHAPTER IV

Of the fervor of Blessed Francis and of the infirmity of his eyes

97   During the course of this same period of time Francis' body began to be burdened with various and more serious sicknesses than before. For he suffered frequent infirmities in as much as he had chastised his body and brought it into subjection[36] during the many years that had preceded. For during the space of eighteen years, which was now completed,[37] his body had had little or no rest while he traveled through various very large regions so that that willing spirit,[38] that devoted spirit, that fervent spirit that dwelt within him might scatter everywhere the seeds of the word of God.[39] He filled the whole earth with the Gospel of Christ, so that often in one day *he made a circuit of*[40] four or five villages and even cities, *preaching the kingdom of God*[41] to every one;

and edifying his hearers not less by his example than
by his word, he made a tongue out of his whole body.
For so great was the harmony of his body toward his
spirit, so great its obedience, that while his spirit
tried to lay hold of all sanctity, his body nevertheless
did not only not resist, but tried even to outrun his
spirit, according to what was written: *For thee my
soul hath thirsted; for thee my flesh, O how many
ways*.[42] Persistence in subjection had made the flesh
willing, and he attained his position of such great
virtue by daily conquering himself, for custom is
often turned into second nature.[43]

98   But since according to the laws of nature and
the constitution of man it is necessary that our outer
man decay day by day, though the inner man is being
renewed,[44] that most precious vessel in which the
heavenly treasure was hidden began to break up and
to suffer the loss of all its powers. Because indeed,
when a man hath done, then shall he begin: *and
when he leaveth off*,[45] then shall he work, his spirit
became more willing as his flesh became weak.[46] So
much did he value the salvation of souls and thirst
for the advancement of his neighbors that, since he
could no longer walk, he went about the country
riding on an ass.

Frequently the brothers admonished him, suggesting to him with great urgency in their entreaties, that
he should seek to restore his infirm and greatly weakened body in some measure with the help of doctors.
But Francis, with his noble spirit fixed on heaven
and wanting only *to depart and to be with Christ*,[47]
refused entirely to do this. In truth, because he had
not yet filled *up in his flesh what* was *lacking of the
suffering of Christ*,[48] though he bore *the marks of the
Lord Jesus in his body*,[49] he incurred a very severe
infirmity of the eyes, according as God had multiplied
his mercy to him.[50] But when the infirmity increased

day by day and seemed to be aggravated daily from a lack of care, Brother Elias, whom Francis had chosen to take the place of a mother in his own regard and to take the place of a father for the rest of the brothers,[51] finally compelled him not to abhor medicine but to accept it *in the name of the Son of God*[52] by whom it was created, as it is written: *The Most High hath created medicines out of the earth, and a wise man will not abhor them.*[53] The holy father then graciously acquiesced and humbly complied with the words of his adviser.

CHAPTER V

How Francis was received at Rieti by the lord Hugo, bishop of Ostia, and how the saint foretold that Hugo would be bishop of the whole world

99   But it happened that, when many were coming to help Francis with their medicines and no remedy was found, he went to the city of Rieti where a man was said to live who was very skilful in curing this disease. When he arrived there, he was received quite kindly and respectfully by the whole Roman curia, which was staying at that time in that city,[54] and especially by the lord Hugo, bishop of Ostia, who was greatly conspicuous for his virtue and holiness.

The blessed father Francis had chosen him, with the consent and at the will of the lord Pope Honorius,[55] to be father and lord over the whole religion and order of his brothers in as much as blessed poverty was very pleasing to him and holy simplicity was held in great reverence by him.[56] This lord conformed himself to the ways of the brothers, and in his desire for sanctity he was simple with the simple, humble with the humble, poor with the poor. He was a brother among the brothers, the least among the lesser brothers; and he strove to conduct himself in his life and manners, in so far as it was permissible for him, as though he were one of the brothers. He was solicitous about planting this holy religion everywhere and the widespread fame of his renowned life greatly enlarged the Order in remote places.

The Lord gave him *a learned tongue*,[57] with which he confounded adversaries of truth, refuted *the enemies of the cross of Christ*,[58] brought back to the right way those who had gone astray, made peace with those in discord, and bound together with the bond of charity those who lived in concord. He was a *lamp burning and shining*[59] in the Church of God and a *chosen arrow*[60] prepared *in a seasonable time*.[61] O how often, having put aside his expensive garments and having put on mean ones, and with his feet unshod, he would go about like one of the brothers and ask *the terms of peace*.[62] This he did solicitously *between a man and his neighbor*[63] as often as was necessary and between God and man always. Therefore, a little later God chose him shepherd in his whole holy Church and lifted up his head among the tribes of the people.

100   And that it might be known that this was brought about through the inspiration of God and by the will of Christ Jesus, the blessed father Francis predicted it in words and foretold it by a sign long before it came about. For when the Order and religion of the brothers was beginning to be spread about through the operation of divine grace and was raising its crown of merits to the heavens like a cedar *in the paradise of God*,[64] and, like a *chosen vineyard*[65] was stretching forth its sacred branches to the limits of the world,[66] St. Francis went to the lord Pope Honorius, who was then the head of the Roman Church, and asked him with humble prayer to appoint the lord Hugo, bishop of Ostia, to be the father and lord of himself and all his brothers.[67] The lord pope granted

the prayers of the saint and graciously made over his own authority over the order of brothers to Hugo. And, accepting it reverently and devoutly, he sought in every way to administer the food of eternal life opportunely to those committed to him, like a *faithful and prudent servant*[68] set over the family of the Lord. Therefore the holy father Francis submitted himself to him in all things and revered him with a wonderful and respectful affection.

Francis was led on by the spirit of God with which he was filled, and therefore he saw long before what in the future would be before the eyes of all. For whenever he wished to write to the bishop with regard to some urgent business on behalf of his religious family, or rather because he was constrained by the charity of Christ with which he burned toward him, he never allowed him to be called in his letters *Bishop of Ostia* or *of Velletri*,[69] as others called him in their customary salutations; but, using this formula, he would say: *To the Most Reverend Father, or the Lord Hugo, Bishop of the Whole World*. Often too he would greet him with unusual blessings; and, though he was a son by reason of his devoted submission, at the inspiration of the Holy Spirit, he would at times comfort him with a fatherly colloquy that he might strengthen upon him *the blessings of his fathers, until the desire of the everlasting hills should come*.[70]

101 The lord bishop too was afire with love for the holy man and therefore whatever the blessed man said, whatever he did, pleased the bishop, and he was often deeply affected even by the mere sight of him. He himself testified that he was never so greatly disturbed or upset but that, upon seeing St. Francis or talking with him, every mental cloud would be dispersed and serenity return, melancholy would be put to flight and joy breathed upon him from above. He ministered to the blessed Francis as a servant to

his master; and as often as he saw him, he showed reverence to him as to an apostle of Christ, and bowing down both the inner and the outer man, he would often kiss his hand with his consecrated mouth.

Solicitously and devotedly he sought a way for the blessed father to recover the former health of his eyes, knowing him to be a holy and just man and a man very necessary and very useful to the Church of God. He had compassion on the whole congregation of brothers because of him and he pitied the sons on account of the father. He therefore admonished the holy father to take care of himself and not to discard what was necessary in his infirmity, lest his neglect should be imputed to him as something sinful rather than as something meritorious. St. Francis, however, humbly listened to what was told him by so venerable a lord and so dear a father, and he acted more cautiously thereafter and with less fear regarding things necessary for his cure. But because the disease had already increased so much, for any remedy at all there was required the most skilful advice and the harshest treatment. Thus it happened that his head was cauterized in several places, his veins opened, plasters put on, and eye-salves applied; but he made no progress and seemed only to get constantly worse.

CHAPTER VI

Of the way the brothers who attended St. Francis conducted themselves; and how he disposed himself to live

102   These things St. Francis bore for almost two years with all patience and humility, *giving thanks to God*[71] in all things. But that he might direct his intention more freely to God and, in frequent ecstasy, wander about and enter the workshops of the blessed mansions of heaven and present himself with an

abundance of grace *on high*[72] before the most kind and serene *Lord of all things,*[73] he committed the care of himself to certain brothers who were deservedly very dear to him. For these were men of virtue, devoted to God, pleasing to the saints, acceptable to men, upon whom the blessed father Francis leaned, like a house upon its four columns. Their names, however, I will not mention to spare their modesty, which is a familiar friend to them since they are spiritual men. For modesty is an ornament of all ages, the witness of innocence, the sign of a virtuous mind, *the rod of correction,*[74] the special glory of conscience, the guardian of reputation, and the badge of all uprightness. This virtue adorned all these brothers and made them lovable and kind to men; this grace was common to all of them, but a special virtue adorned each one. One was known for his outstanding discretion,[75] another for his extraordinary patience,[76] the third for his great simplicity,[77] and the last was robust of body and gentle of disposition.[78] These tried with all vigilance, with all zeal, with all their will to foster the peace of mind of their blessed father, and they cared for the infirmity of his body, shunning no distress, no labors, that they might give themselves entirely to serving the saint.

103   But, though the glorious father had been brought to the fulness of grace before God and shone among men of this world by his good works, he nevertheless thought always to begin more perfect works and, like the most skilled soldier in the *camps of God,*[79] the enemy having been challenged, to stir up new wars. He proposed, under *Christ the prince,*[80] to do great things, and, with his limbs failing and his body dying, he hoped for a victory over the enemy in a new struggle. For true virtue knows not a limit of time, since the expectation of a reward is eternal. Therefore he was afire with a very great desire to

return to the first beginnings of humility and, by reason of the immensity of his love, *rejoicing in hope*,[81] he thought to recall his body to its former subjection, even though it had already come to such an extremity. He removed from himself completely the obstacles of all cares, and he fully silenced the clamorings of all anxieties. Though he found it necessary to moderate his early rigor because of his infirmity, he would still say: "Let us begin, brothers, to serve the Lord God, for up to now we have made little or no progress." He did not consider that he had laid hold of his goal as yet,[82] and persevering untiringly in his purpose of attaining holy *newness of life*,[83] he hoped always to make a beginning. He wished to go back again to serving lepers, to be held in contempt, as he once had been. He proposed to shun companionship with men and to retire to the most remote places, so that, having thus put off all cares and laid aside all solicitude for others, only the wall of the flesh would stand between him and God.

104   For he saw many pursuing offices of authority, and despising their rashness, he sought to recall them from this pestilence by his example. He used to say that it was a good and acceptable thing before God to exercise the care of others and that it was becoming that they should undertake the care of souls who would seek in it nothing of themselves but who would attend always to the divine will in all things. Those, namely, who would put nothing ahead of their own salvation and who would pay no heed to the applause of their subjects but only to their advancement; who would seek not display before men, but glory before God; who do not strive after a prelacy, but who fear it; who are not puffed up by such a thing when they have it, but are humbled, and who are not dejected when it is taken away, but are filled with joy. But he said that it was dangerous to

rule, especially at this time when wickedness had grown so greatly and increased so abundantly; and he said that it was better to be ruled. He was filled with sorrow that some had left their *former works*[84] and had forgotten their earlier simplicity after they had found new things. Wherefore he grieved over those who were once intent upon higher things with their whole desire but who had descended to base and vile things, and had left the true joys to roam and wander amid frivolous and inane things in the field of empty freedom. He prayed therefore that God's mercy might free these sons and asked most earnestly that they might be kept in the grace *that had been given to them.*[85]

CHAPTER VII

How Francis came from Siena to Assisi, and of the church of St. Mary of the Portiuncula and of the blessing he gave to the brothers

105   But in the sixth month before the day of his death,[86] while he was at Siena[87] for treatment of the infirmity of his eyes, Francis began to be gravely ill in all the rest of his body; and, with his stomach racked by a long-standing illness and his liver infected, he vomited much blood, so that he appeared to be approaching death. Upon hearing this, Brother Elias hurried to him with great haste from a distant place. Upon his arrival, the holy father recovered so much that, leaving that city, he went with Elias to Le Celle near Cortona.[88] Arriving there, he remained there for some time; and while he was there, his abdomen began to swell, and his legs and feet too, and the ailment of his stomach began to grow worse and worse, so that he could take hardly any food. He then asked Brother Elias to have him brought to Assisi. This good son did what his gracious father asked, and,

when everything had been prepared, he took him to the place he longed for. *All the city rejoiced*[89] at the coming of the blessed father and the mouths of all the people praised God; for *the whole multitude of the people*[90] hoped that the *holy one of God*[91] would die close by, and this was the reason for their great joy.

106   And at the will of God it happened that his holy soul was released from his body and passed to the kingdom of heaven at that place, where, while he was still *in the flesh*,[92] the knowledge of heavenly things was first given to him and the saving unction poured upon him.[93] For though he knew that the kingdom of heaven was set up *in all the habitations of the land*[94] and believed that the grace of God was given to the *elect of God*[95] in every place, he had however experienced that the place of the church of St. Mary of the Portiuncula was endowed with more fruitful graces and visited by heavenly spirits.[96] Therefore he often said to his brothers: "See to it, my sons, that you never abandon this place. If you are driven out from one side, go back in at the other. For this place is truly holy and is the dwelling place of God. Here, when we were but a few, the Most High gave us increase; here he enlightened the hearts of his poor ones by the light of his wisdom; here he set our wills afire with the fire of his love. Here he who prays with a devout heart will obtain what he prays for and he who offends will be punished more severely. Wherefore, my sons, consider this dwelling place of God to be worthy of all honor, and with all your heart, *with the voice of joy and praise*,[97] give glory to God in this place."

107   Meanwhile, as his infirmity increased, all his bodily strength failed and, destitute of all his powers, he could not move himself at all. Still when he was asked by a certain brother what he would prefer to

bear, this lingering and long illness or the suffering of a severe martyrdom at the hands of an executioner, he replied: "My son, that has always been and still is most dear to me and more sweet and more acceptable which pleases the Lord my God most to let happen in me and with me, for I desire always only to be found conformed and obedient to his will in all things. Yet, this infirmity is harder for me to bear even for three days than any martyrdom. I am not speaking of the reward, but only of the intensity of suffering it causes." O martyr and martyr, who smiling and rejoicing most willingly put up with what was most bitter and most difficult to bear! In all truth, not a single member in him remained free of the greatest suffering and, as the natural warmth was gradually lost, he approached nearer to the end each day. The doctors were amazed, the brothers astonished, that his soul could live in flesh so dead, for, the flesh having been consumed, nothing but skin clung to his bones.

108   Now when he saw that his last day was at hand, a fact that had been made known to him by a revelation from God two years earlier,[98] Francis called to him the brothers he wanted and, as it was given to him from above, he blessed each one just as the patriarch Jacob of old had blessed his sons;[99] indeed, like another Moses who, when he was about to ascend the mountain appointed by God, enriched the children of Israel with blessings.[100] Since Brother Elias was sitting at his left side, with the other brothers standing about, Francis, crossing his right hand over his left, placed his right hand upon Elias' head; and, deprived as he was of the light of his bodily eyes and of their use, he said: "On whom am I holding my hand?" "On Brother Elias," they said. "That is what I wish," said Francis; "you, my son, I bless *above all and throughout all*;[101] and, just as the Most High

321

has multiplied my brothers and sons in your hands, so also I bless them all upon you and in you. May God, the King of all, bless you in heaven and upon earth. I bless you as much as I can and more than I can, and what I cannot, may He who can do all things do in you. May the Lord be mindful of your work and of your labor, and may a share be reserved for you in the reward of the just. May you find every blessing you desire, and may whatever you ask worthily be granted to you." "Farewell, all you my sons, *in the fear of God,*[102] and may you remain in him always, for a very great trial will come upon you and a great tribulation is approaching. Happy will they be who will persevere in the things they have begun; from them future scandals will separate some. I am hastening to the Lord and I am confident that I will go to my God *whom I serve* devoutly *in my spirit.*"[103]

At this time he was staying in the palace of the bishop of Assisi,[104] and he therefore asked the brothers to take him as quickly as possible to the place of St. Mary of the Portiuncula. For he wished to give back his soul to God in that place where, as has been said, he first knew the way of truth perfectly.

CHAPTER VIII

What Francis did and said when he died happily

109   The space of twenty years had now passed since Francis' conversion,[105] according to what had been made known to him by the will of God. For when the blessed father and Brother Elias were staying at one time at Foligno, one night when they had given themselves to sleep a certain white-garbed priest of a very great and advanced age and of venerable appearance stood before Brother Elias and said: "Arise, Brother, and say to Brother Francis that eighteen years are now completed since he renounced

the world and gave himself to Christ, and that he will remain in this life for only two more years; then the Lord will call him to himself and he will go the way of all flesh." And thus it happened that the word of the Lord that had been made known long before was fulfilled at the appointed time.

When therefore he had rested for a few days in a place he greatly longed to be in and realized that the time of his death was at hand, he called to him two of his brothers and spiritual sons[106] and commanded them to sing in a loud voice with joy of spirit the Praises of the Lord[107] over his approaching death, or rather, over the life that was so near. He himself, in as far as he was able, broke forth in that psalm of David: *I cried to the Lord with my voice: with my voice I made supplication to the Lord.*[108] A certain brother, however, from among those standing about,[109] whom the saint loved with a great affection, in his anxiety for all the brothers, said to him, when he saw these things and recognized that Francis was approaching his end: "Kind Father, alas, your sons are now without a father and are deprived of the true light of their eyes. Remember therefore your orphan sons whom you are now leaving;[110] forgive them all their faults and give joy to those present and absent with your holy blessing." And the saint said to him: "Behold, my son, I am called by God; I forgive my brothers, both present and absent, all their offenses and faults, and, in as far as I am able, I absolve them; I want you to announce this to them and to bless them all on my behalf."

110   Finally he ordered the book of the Gospels to be brought and commanded that the Gospel according to St. John be read from that place where it begins: *Six days before the Passover, Jesus, knowing that the hour had come for him to pass from this world to the Father.*[111] The minister general[112] had

intended to read this Gospel, even before he had been commanded to do so; this passage had also appeared at the first opening of the book earlier,[113] although the book was the whole and complete Bible in which this Gospel was contained. Francis then commanded that a hair shirt be put upon him and that he be sprinkled with ashes, for he was soon to become dust and ashes. Then, when many brothers had gathered about, whose father and leader he was, and while they were standing reverently at his side awaiting his blessed death and happy end, his most holy soul was freed from his body and received into the abyss of light, and his body *fell asleep*[114] in the Lord. One of his brothers and disciples, a man of some renown, whose name I think I should withhold here because while he lives in the flesh, he prefers not to glory in so great a privilege,[115] saw the soul of the most holy father ascend over many waters directly to heaven. For it was like a star, having in some way the immensity of the moon, but to a certain extent the brightness of the sun, and it was borne upward on a little white cloud.

111   Therefore I cry out concerning him: O how glorious is this saint, whose soul a disciple saw *ascend into heaven,*[116] *fair as the moon, bright as the sun,*[117] and as he ascended upon a white cloud he was shining most gloriously! O truly you are a light of the world, shining in the Church of Christ more splendidly than the sun; behold, you have withdrawn the rays of your light now and, withdrawing into the kingdom of light, you have exchanged company with us miserable ones for company with the angels and saints! O glorious kindness of singular renown, do not put aside the care of your sons though you have now put off your flesh like unto theirs! Know, O know indeed, in what great distress you have left them whose innumerable labors and frequent anxieties merely your presence

always mercifully relieved. O truly merciful and most holy father, you who were always ready to show mercy to your sinning sons and to kindly forgive them! We therefore bless you, worthy father, whom the Most High has blessed, who is *over all things, God blessed forever, amen.*[118]

CHAPTER IX

The sorrowing of the brothers and their joy when they saw Francis bearing the marks of the cross; and of the wings of the seraphim

112   There was therefore a concourse of many people *praising God and saying:*[119] "Praised and blessed be you, our Lord, God, who have entrusted so precious a treasure to us who are unworthy! Praise and glory be to you, ineffable Trinity." The whole city of Assisi rushed in a body and the whole region hastened to see the wonderful things of God which the Lord of Majesty had made manifest in his holy servant. Every one sang a canticle of joy, as their heartfelt gladness prompted them; and all blessed the omnipotence of the Savior for the fulfillment of their desire. However, Francis' sons were filled with sorrow at being deprived of so great a father and they showed the pious affection of their hearts by tears and sighs.

But an unheard of joy tempered their grief and the newness of a miracle threw their minds into great amazement.[120] Their mourning was turned to song and their weeping to jubilation. For they had never heard or read in the Scriptures what was set before their eyes, what they could hardly be persuaded to believe if it had not been proved to them by such evident testimony. For in truth there appeared in him a true image of the cross and of the passion of the *lamb without blemish*[121] who washed away the sins of the world, for he seemed as though he had been recently taken down from the cross, his hands and feet were pierced as though by nails and his side wounded as though by a lance.

They saw his flesh, which before had been dark, now gleaming with a dazzling whiteness and giving promise of the rewards of the blessed resurrection by reason of its beauty. They saw, finally, that his face was like the face of an angel, as though he were living and not dead; and the rest of his members had taken on the softness and pliability of an innocent child's members. His sinews were not contracted, as they generally are in the dead; his skin had not become hard; his members were not rigid, but they could be turned this way and that, however one wished.

113   And because he glowed with such wondrous beauty before all who looked upon him and his flesh had become even more white, it was wonderful to see in the middle of his hands and feet, not indeed the holes made by the nails, but the nails themselves formed out of his flesh and retaining the blackness of iron, and his right side was red with blood. These signs of martyrdom did not arouse horror in the minds of those who looked upon them, but they gave his body much beauty and grace, just as little black stones do when they are set in a white pavement.

His brothers and sons came hurriedly, and weeping, they kissed the hands and feet of their beloved father who was leaving them, and also his right side, in the wound of which was presented a remarkable memorial of him who in pouring forth both *blood and water*[122] from that same place reconciled the world to his Father. Not only those who were permitted to kiss the sacred stigmata of Jesus Christ which St. Francis bore on his body, but even those who were permitted only to see them, thought they had been granted a very great gift. For who, seeing this thing, would give himself to weeping rather than to joy? Or if he wept, would he not do so rather from joy than from sorrow? Whose breast is so much like iron that it would not be moved to sighs? Whose heart so much like stone that it would not be broken to compunction, that it would not be fired to love of God, that it would not be strengthened to good will? Who is so dull, so unfeeling, that he would not realize in truth that as this saint was honored upon earth with so singular a gift, so would he also be magnified in heaven by an ineffable glory?

114 Singular gift and mark of special love, that a soldier should be adorned with the same arms of glory that were suitable for the son of the King by reason of their most excellent dignity! O miracle worthy of everlasting memory, and memorable sacrament worthy of admirable and unceasing reverence, which represents to the eyes of faith that mystery in which the blood of the *lamb without blemish*[123] flowed from five outlets to wash away the sins of the world! O sublime splendor of the living cross that gives life to the dead, the burden of which presses so gently and pricks so delicately that by it dead flesh is made to live and the weak spirit is made strong! He loved you much, whom you adorned so very gloriously. Glory and blessing be *to the only wise God*[124] who renews *signs* and works *new miracles*[125] that he might console the minds of the weak with new revelations and that by means of a wonderful work in things visible their hearts might be caught up to a love of things invisible. O wonderful and lovable disposition of God, which, that no suspicion might arise concerning this new miracle, first mercifully displayed in him who *descended from heaven*[126] what a little later was to be wonderfully wrought in him who dwelt upon earth! And indeed the true Father of mercies[127] wanted to show how great a reward he is worthy of who tried to love him with all his heart, namely, to be placed in the highest order of celestial spirits and indeed in the order nearest to himself.[128]

We can without a doubt attain this reward, if, after the manner of the seraphim,[129] we extend two wings above our head, that is, if we have, after the example of the blessed Francis, a pure intention in all our works and if our actions are upright, and if, directing these to God, we strive tirelessly to please him alone in all our works. These two wings must be joined together to cover the head, because the Father of lights will by no means accept either the uprightness of a work without purity of intention or vice versa, for he says: *If thy eye be sound, thy whole body will be full of light. But if thy eye be evil, thy whole body will be full of darkness.*[130] The eye is not sound if it does not see what is to be seen, lacking the knowledge of truth, or if it looks upon what it should not see, not having a pure intention. In the first case, simple reasoning will show that the eye is not sound, but blind; in the second, that it is evil. The feathers of these wings are love of the Father, who saves us in his mercy, and fear of the Lord, who judges us terribly. These feathers must raise the souls of the elect from earthly things by repressing evil impulses and properly ordering chaste affections. With two wings for flying one is to extend a twofold charity to one's neighbor, namely, by refreshing his soul with the word of God and by sustaining his body with earthly help. These two wings, however, are rarely joined together, for both can hardly be fulfilled by anyone. The feathers of these wings are the various works which must be shown to one's neighbor to advise and help him. Lastly, with two wings the body that is bare of merits must be covered, and this is properly done when as often as sin has intervened it is again clothed with innocence through contrition and confession. The feathers of these wings are the many various affections which are born of hatred for sin and hunger for justice.

115 These things the most blessed father Francis fulfilled most perfectly; he bore the image and form of a seraph and, persevering upon the cross, merited to rise to the ranks of the heavenly spirits. For he was always on the cross, fleeing no labor or suffering, if only he could fulfill the will of the Lord in himself and concerning himself.

The brothers, moreover, who lived with him knew how his daily and continuous talk was of Jesus and how sweet and tender his conversation was, how kind and filled with love his talk with them. His mouth spoke *out of the abundance of* his *heart*,[131] and the fountain of enlightened love that filled his whole being bubbled forth outwardly. Indeed, he was always occupied with Jesus; Jesus he bore in his heart, Jesus in his mouth, Jesus in his ears, Jesus in his eyes, Jesus in his hands, Jesus in the rest of his members. O how often, when he sat down to eat, hearing or speaking or thinking of Jesus, he forgot bodily food, as we read of the holy one: "Seeing, he did not see, and hearing he did not hear."[132] Indeed, many times, as he went along the way meditating on and singing of Jesus, he would forget his journey and invite all the elements to praise Jesus.[133] And because he always bore and preserved *Christ Jesus and him crucified*[134] in his heart with a wonderful love, he was marked in a most glorious way above all others with the seal of him whom in a rapture of mind he contemplated sitting in inexpressible and incomprehensible glory at the right hand of the Father, with whom he, the co-equal and most high Son of the Most High, lives and reigns, conquers and governs in union with the Holy Spirit, God eternally glorious through all ages forever. Amen.

CHAPTER X
Concerning the grief of the ladies at St. Damian's; and how St. Francis was buried with praise and glory

116   Francis' brothers and sons, therefore, who gathered together with a great multitude of people from the cities nearby and rejoiced to be present at such great solemnities, spent the whole night in which the holy father had died singing the praises of God, so much so that, because of the charm of the jubilation and the brightness of the lights, it seemed to be a wake of the angels. But when morning had come, a great multitude from the city of Assisi assembled with all the clergy, and, taking the sacred body from the place where Francis had died,[135] they carried it amid great honor to the city, with hymns and praises and sounding trumpets. They all took up branches of olive trees and of other trees, and, carrying out the obsequies with solemnity, they discharged the duties of praise with many lights and with loud voices. When, with the sons carrying their father, and the flock following their shepherd who was hastening to meet the Shepherd of all, they came to the place where he had himself first planted the religion and order of holy virgins and poor ladies,[136] they placed him in the church of St. Damian, where these same daughters whom he had won for the Lord dwelt; there they paused and the little window through which the handmaids of Christ were accustomed to receive at the appointed time the sacrament of the body of the Lord was opened. The coffin was opened, in which lay hidden the treasure of supercelestial virtues and in which he was being borne by a few who was accustomed to bear many.[137] And behold, the Lady Clare, who was truly illustrious[138] by the holiness of her merits and was the first mother of the

rest since she was the very first plant of this holy Order, came with the rest of her daughters to see their father who would no longer speak to them or return to them but was hastening elsewhere.

117   And redoubling their sighs and looking upon him with great sorrow of heart and many tears, they *began to proclaim*[139] in a restrained voice: "Father, Father, what shall we do? Why do you forsake us in our misery, or to whom do you leave us who are so desolate? Why did you not send us rejoicing ahead of you to the place where you are going, us whom you leave here in sorrow? What do you bid us do, shut up in this prison, us whom you will never again visit as you used to? All our consolation departs with you and no solace like it remains to us buried to the world. Who will comfort us in our great poverty no less of merit than of goods? O Father of the poor, lover of poverty! Who will strengthen us in temptation, O you who experienced innumerable temptations and who knew how to overcome them? Who will console us in our trials, O you who were our *helper in troubles which found us exceedingly?*[140] O most bitter separation, O unfriendly leave-taking! O most dreadful death, that slays thousands of sons and daughters bereft of so great a father, by hastening to remove beyond recall him through whom mainly our efforts, such as they were, were made to flourish!" But their virginal modesty restrained their great weeping; and it was not fitting to mourn too much for him at whose passing a host of the army of angels had come together *and the citizens with the saints and members of God's household* rejoiced.[141] And so, divided between sorrow and joy, they kissed his most radiant hands, adorned with the most precious gems and shining pearls; and, when he had been taken away, the door was closed to them which will hardly again be opened for such great sorrow. O how great

was the sorrow of all over the woeful and pitiable outcry of these poor ladies! How great in particular were the lamentations of his grieving sons! Their special grief was shared by all, so much so that hardly anyone could refrain from weeping when the angels of peace wept so bitterly.[142]

118   Finally, when all had come to the city, they placed the most holy body, amid great rejoicing and exultation, in a sacred place,[143] a place that was to be even more scared in the future; there, to the glory of the supreme Almighty God, he illumines the world by a multiplicity of new miracles, just as up to then he had enlightened it in a wonderful way by the teachings of his holy preaching. Thanks be to God. Amen.

Behold, most holy and blessed Father, I have attended you with praises that are your due and of which you are worthy, though indeed they are insufficient, and I have to some extent set down your deeds in narrative form. Grant me, therefore, miserable as I am, that I may follow you so worthily in the present life that I may mercifully merit to be with you in the future life. Remember, O gracious Father, your poor sons, to whom there remains hardly any comfort after you, their only and one solace. For, though you, their best and first portion, are now joined with the choirs of angels and placed with the apostles on a throne of glory, they, however, still lie in the *mire of dregs*,[144] shut up in a dark prison, crying thus sadly to you: "Present, Father, to Jesus Christ, the Son of the most high Father, his sacred stigmata, and let him see the marks of the cross in your side, feet, and hands, that he may mercifully deign to show his own wounds to the Father, who because of them will indeed be ever gracious to us miserable ones. Amen." So be it. So be it.

HERE ENDS THE SECOND BOOK

BOOK THREE

HERE BEGINS THE THIRD BOOK, CONCERNING THE CANONIZATION OF OUR BLESSED FATHER FRANCIS AND CONCERNING HIS MIRACLES

CHAPTER I

The canonization of our blessed father Francis

119   Therefore the most glorious father Francis, adding an even more happy end to a happy beginning, most happily commended his spirit to heaven in the twentieth year of his conversion, and there, *crowned with glory and honor*[1] and having attained a place *in the midst of the stones of fire,*[2] he stands at the throne of God and devotes himself to furthering effectually the concerns of those he left behind upon earth. What indeed can be denied to him in the imprint of whose stigmata appears the form of him who, being equal to the Father, *has taken his seat at the right hand of the majesty on high, the brightness of his glory and the image of his substance,* and *has effected man's purgation from sin?*[3] What else should there be but that he be heard who has been made comformable unto the death of Christ Jesus in *the fellowship of his sufferings*[4] which the sacred wounds in his hands and feet and side show forth?

Actually, he is already giving joy to the whole world that has been gladdened by a new joy, and he is offering to all the advantages of true salvation. He is brightening the world with the very bright light of his miracles and illuminating the whole world with the brilliance of a new star. Once the world was saddened when it was deprived of his presence, and it saw itself overwhelmed in a pit of darkness, as it were, at his setting. But now, lighted up as the noonday with more refulgent beams by the rising of this new light, it feels that it has lost this universal darkness. All its complaining, *blessed be God,*[5] has now ceased, since every day and everywhere it is filled most abundantly through him with new rejoicing over the abundance of his virtues. *From the east and from the west,*[6] from the south and from the north those come who have been helped through his intercession; thus these things are proved by the testimony of truth. Indeed, while he lived in the flesh, that extraordinary lover of heavenly things accepted nothing of ownership in the world so that he might possess more fully and more joyfully the universal good. It therefore came about that he received in its entirety what he had declined in part, and he exchanged eternity for time. Everywhere he is helping everyone; everywhere he is at the behest of everyone; and, truly a lover of unity, he knows no loss because of such division.[7]

120   While he was still living among sinners, Francis went about through the whole world preaching; reigning now with the angels in heaven, he flies more swiftly than thought as the messenger of the most high King and bestows generous gifts upon all. Therefore all the world honors him, venerates, glorifies, and praises him. In truth, all share in the common good. Who can tell what great miracles and who can tell what kind of miracles God deigns to work everywhere through him? What great miracles is not Francis working in France alone, where the king and queen[8] and all the great ones run to kiss and venerate[9] the pillow Francis used in his sickness? Where also the wise and most learned men of the world, of whom Paris[10] is accustomed to produce a greater abundance than the rest of the world, humbly and most devoutly venerate, admire, and honor Francis, an unlettered man and the friend of true simplicity and complete sincerity. Truly Francis had a free[11]

and noble heart. Those who have experienced his magnanimity know how free, how liberal he was in all things; how confident and fearless he was in all things; with what great virtue, with what great fervor he trampled under foot all wordly things. What indeed shall I say of the other parts of the world, where, by means of his clothing, diseases depart, illnesses leave, and crowds of both sexes are delivered from their troubles by merely invoking his name?

121   At his tomb, too, new miracles are constantly occurring, and, the number of petitions greatly increasing, great benefits for body and for soul are sought at that same place. Sight is given to the blind, hearing is restored to the deaf, the ability to walk is given to the lame, the mute speak, he who has the gout leaps, the leper is healed, he who suffers from a swelling has it reduced, and those who suffer diverse and various infirmities obtain health, so that his dead body heals living bodies just as his living body had raised up dead souls.

The Roman pontiff, the highest of all bishops, the leader of the Christians, the lord of the world, the pastor of the Church, the anointed of the Lord, the vicar of Christ, heard and understood all this. He rejoiced and was happy, he danced with joy and was glad, when he saw the Church of God renewed in his own day by new mysteries but ancient wonders, and that in his own son, whom he bore in his holy womb, cherished in his bosom, nursed with his words, and nourished with the food of salvation. The rest of the guardians of the Church too heard it, the shepherds of the flock, the defenders of the faith, *the friends of the bridegroom*,[12] those who are at his side, the hinges of the world,[13] the venerable cardinals. They congratulated the Church, they rejoiced with the pope, they glorified the Savior, who with the highest and ineffable wisdom, the highest and incomprehensible grace, the highest and immeasurable goodness chooses the foolish and base things of this world[14] that he might thus draw the strong things to himself.[15] The whole world heard and applauded, and the entire realm that was subject to the Catholic faith superabounded in joy and overflowed with holy consolation.

122   But there was a sudden change in things and new dangers arose meanwhile in the world. Suddenly the joy of peace was disturbed and the torch of envy was lighted and the Church was torn by domestic and civil war. The Romans, a rebellious and ferocious race of men, raged against their neighbors, as was their custom, and, being rash, they stretched *forth their hands against* the *holy places.*[16] The distinguished Pope Gregory tried to curb their growing wickedness, to repress their savagery, to temper their violence; and, like a tower of great strength, he protected the Church of Christ. Many dangers assailed her, destruction became more frequent, and in the rest of the world *the necks of sinners*[17] were raised against God. What then? Measuring the future by his very great experience and weighing the present circumstances, he abandoned the city to the rebels,[18] so that he might free the world from rebellions and defend it. He came therefore to the city of Rieti,[19] where he was received with honor, as was befitting. From there he went to Spoleto where he was honored with great respect by all. He remained there a few days, and, after the affairs of the Church had been provided for, he kindly visited, in the company of the venerable cardinals, the Poor Ladies of Christ, who were dead and buried to the world.[20] The holy life of these Poor Ladies, their highest poverty, and their glorious way of life moved him and the others to tears, stirred them to contempt of the world, and kindled in them a desire for the life of retirement. O lovable humility,

nurse of all graces! The prince of the world, the successor of the prince of the apostles, visits these poor women, comes to them lowly and humble in their seclusion; and, though this humility is worthy of just approbation, it was nevertheless an unusual example and one that had not been seen for many ages past.

123   Then he hastened on, hastened to Assisi,[21] where a glorious treasure awaited him, that through it the universal suffering and imminent tribulation might be extinguished. At his approach, the whole region rejoiced, the city was filled with exultation, the great throng of people celebrated their happiness, and the already bright day was further illuminated by brighter lights. Every one went out to meet him and solemn watches were kept by all. The pious fraternity of Poor Brothers went out to meet him, and they all sang sweet songs to Christ the Lord. The vicar of Christ arrived at the place and going first to the grave of St. Francis, he greeted it reverently and eagerly. He sighed deeply, struck his breast, shed tears, and bowed his venerable head with great devotion. While he was there a solemn discussion was held concerning the canonization of the holy man, and the noble assembly of cardinals met often concerning this business. From all sides many came together who had been freed from their illnesses through the holy man of God, and from every side a very great number of miracles gave forth their luster: these were approved, verified, heard, accepted. Meanwhile, the urgency of the affairs of his office pressed upon the pope, a new emergency threatened, and the holy father went to Perugia[22] that by a superabounding and singular grace he might return again to Assisi in the interests of this very great business. Then they met again at Perugia, and a sacred assembly of cardinals was held concerning this matter in the room of the lord pope. They were all in

agreement and they spoke unanimously; they read the miracles and regarded them with great reverence, and they commended the life and conduct of the blessed father with the highest praises.

124   "The most holy life of this most holy man," they said, "needs no attestation of miracles; *what we have seen with our eyes, what our hands have hand-led,*[23] we have proved with the light of truth." They were all transported with joy, they rejoiced, they wept, and indeed in those tears there was a great blessing. They immediately appointed the happy day on which they would fill the whole world with saving happiness. The solemn day came, a day to be held in reverence by every age, a day that shed its sublime rapture not only upon the earth but even upon the heavenly mansions. Bishops came together, abbots arrived, prelates of the Church were present from even the most remote parts of the world; a king too was present,[24] and a noble multitude of counts and princes. They then escorted the lord of all the world and entered the city of Assisi with him amid great pomp. He reached the place prepared for so solemn an event[25] and the whole multitude of glorious cardinals, bishops, and abbots gathered around the blessed pope. A most distinguished gathering of priests and clerics was there; a happy and sacred company of religious men was there; the more bashful habit of the sacred veil was there too; a great crowd of all the people was there and an almost innumerable multitude of both sexes. They hurried there from all sides, and every age came to the concourse of people with the greatest eagerness. *The small and great were there,*[26] the servant and they who were free of a master.

125   The supreme pontiff was there, the spouse of the Church of Christ, surrounded by a variety of his great children and with a crown of glory on his head,

an ornament of honor.[27] He stood there adorned with the pontifical robes and clad in holy vestments ornamented with *jewels set in gold and graven by the work of a lapidary.*[28] The anointed of the Lord stood there, resplendent in *magnificence and glory*[29] *in gilded clothing;*[30] and covered with engraven jewels sparkling with the radiance of spring, he caught the attention of all. Cardinals and bishops stood around him; decked with splendid necklaces and clad in garments as white as snow they showed forth the image of super-celestial beauties and displayed the joy of the glorified. All the people stood in expectation of *the voice of mirth, the voice of gladness,*[31] a new voice, a voice full of all sweetness, a voice of praise, a voice of constant blessing. First Pope Gregory preached to all the people, and with a sweetly flowing and sonorous voice he spoke the praises of God. He also praised the holy father Francis in a noble eulogy, and recalling and speaking of the purity of his life, he was bathed in tears. His sermon had this text: *He shone in his days as the morning star in the midst of a cloud, and as the moon at the full. And as the sun when it shineth, so did he shine in the temple of God.*[32] When the *faithful saying and worthy of all acceptation*[33] was completed, one of the lord pope's subdeacons, Octavian by name,[34] read the miracles of the saint before all in a very loud voice, and the lord Raynerius, a cardinal deacon,[35] a man of penetrating intellect and renowned for his piety and life, spoke about them with holy words and with an abundance of tears. The Shepherd of the Church was carried away with joy, and sighing from the very depths of his being and sobbing, he shed torrents of tears. So too the other prelates of the Church poured out floods of tears, and their sacred vestments were moistened with their abundance. All the people too wept, and with the suspense of their longing expectation, they became wearied.

126   Then the happy pope spoke with a loud voice, and extending his hands to heaven, he said: "To the praise and glory of Almighty God, the Father, Son, and Holy Spirit, and of the glorious Virgin Mary and of the blessed apostles Peter and Paul, and to the honor of the glorious Roman Church, at the advice of our brothers and of the other prelates, we decree that the most blessed father Francis, whom the Lord has glorified in heaven and whom we venerate on earth, shall be enrolled in the catalogue of saints and that his feast shall be celebrated on the day of his death."[36] At this decree, the venerable cardinals began to sing in a loud voice along with the pope the *Te Deum Laudamus*. Then there was raised a clamor among the many people praising God; the earth resounded with their mighty voices, the air was filled with their rejoicings, and the ground was moistened with their tears. New songs were sung,[37] and the servants of God gave expression to their joy in melody of spirit. Sweet sounding organs were heard there and spiritual hymns were sung with well modulated voices. There a very sweet odor was breathed, and a more joyous melody that stirred the emotions resounded there. The day was bright and colored with more splendid rays than usual. There were green olive branches there and fresh branches of other trees. Brightly glittering festive attire adorned all the people, and the blessing of peace filled the minds of those who had come there with joy. Then the happy Pope Gregory descended from his lofty throne, and going by way of the lower steps, he entered the sanctuary to offer *the vows and voluntary oblations*;[38] he kissed with his happy lips the tomb that contained the body that was sacred and consecrated to God. He offered and multiplied his prayers and celebrated the sacred mysteries.[39] A *ring of his brethren*[40] stood

about him, praising, adoring, and blessing Almighty God who had done *great things in all the earth.*[41] All the people increased the praises of God and they paid due thanksgiving to St. Francis in honor of the most holy Trinity. Amen.

These things took place in the city of Assisi in the second year[42] of the pontificate of the lord pope Gregory on the seventeenth day of the calends of the month of August.[43]

CHAPTER II

The Miracles of St. Francis

IN THE NAME OF CHRIST, HERE BEGINS THE ACCOUNT OF THE MIRACLES OF OUR MOST HOLY FATHER FRANCIS

127   Humbly imploring the grace of our Lord Jesus Christ, we will set down briefly, but accurately, under the guidance of Christ, certain miracles, which, as was said, were read before the lord pope Gregory and announced to the people, to excite and promote the devotion of the people now alive and to strengthen the faith of those who are to come.

THE HEALING OF THE CRIPPLED

On the very day on which the sacred and holy body of the most blessed father Francis was laid away like a most precious treasure, anointed with heavenly spices rather than with earthly ointments, a certain girl was brought to the grave; for a year already her neck had been monstrously bent and her head had grown down to her shoulders so that she could look up only sideways. When however she had placed her head for a little while upon the tomb in which lay the precious body of the saint, immediately she raised up her neck through the merits of this most holy man and her head was restored to its proper position, so that the girl was greatly dumbfounded at the sudden change in herself and she began to run away and weep. For now a kind of pit appeared in her shoulder where her head had touched it before, caused by the position which the long illness had brought about.[44]

128 In the region of Narni there was a certain boy whose leg was so bent back that he could not walk at all without the help of two sticks. He was a beggar, and burdened with this infirmity for several years, he did not know his own father and mother. But by the merits of our most blessed father Francis he was freed from this difficulty to the extent that he could walk about freely wherever he wished without the help of the sticks, praising and blessing the Lord and his holy one.[45]

129 A certain Nicholas, a citizen of Foligno, had a crippled left leg and suffered very great pain; he spent such great sums on physicians in an attempt to recover his former health that he incurred indebtedness beyond his wishes and beyond what he could afford. At last, when their help had done him no good at all and his suffering was so great that his cries kept his neighbors from sleeping at night, he vowed himself to God and St. Francis and had himself brought to the tomb of the saint. After he had spent a whole night in prayer before the tomb of the saint, his leg was stretched out and he returned home with great joy without a cane.[46]

130 A boy, too, who had his leg so bent that his knee clung to his chest and his heel to his hips, came to the tomb of St. Francis. His father wore a cilice next to his flesh and his mother mortified herself severely for the sake of the child. The boy was suddenly cured so completely that he was able to run about the streets full of health and happiness, giving thanks to God and St. Francis.[47]

131   In the city of Fano[48] there was a certain crippled man whose legs were full of sores and clung to his hips; they gave off such a stench that those in charge of the hospital would not receive him in the hospital or keep him there. But by the merits of the most blessed father Francis, whose mercy he implored, he was soon made happy in being cured.[49]

132   A certain girl from Gubbio had hands so crippled that she had lost the use of all her members for a year already. Her nurse carried her with a waxen image to the tomb of the most blessed father Francis to obtain the grace of health. After she had been there for about eight days, one day all her limbs were restored to their proper use, so that she was considered fit again for her former tasks.[50]

133   Another boy, too, from Montenero,[51] lay for several days before the doors of the church where the body of St. Francis lies at rest.[52] He was unable to walk or sit down, for from the waist down he was deprived of all his powers and of the use of his limbs. But one day he entered the church, and upon touching the tomb of the most blessed father Francis he came out completely healthy and sound. The little boy himself used to say that while he lay at the tomb of the glorious saint, a certain young man stood before him above the tomb clothed in the habit of the brothers and carrying some pears in his hands. The young man called to him and offered him one of the pears and encouraged him to rise. He took the pear from his hand and said: "See, I am crippled and cannot rise." But then he ate the pear that had been given him and he began to extend his hand for another pear that was offered him by the same young man. The latter urged him again to rise, but feeling the weight of his infirmity upon him, he did not get up. But as he was reaching out his hand toward the pear, the young man, after giving him the pear, took his hand and led him out. He then disappeared from his sight. But seeing that he was made well and whole again, the boy began to call out in a loud voice, showing everyone what had happened to him.[53]

134 A certain woman from the city called Coccorano[54] was brought to the tomb of the glorious father on a stretcher; she could not use any of her members except her tongue. But after remaining a little while at the tomb of this most holy man, she arose completely cured. Another citizen of Gubbio who had brought his crippled son to the tomb of the holy father received him back healthy and wholly restored. He had been so crippled up that his legs clung to his hips and were almost completely withered.[55]

135 Bartholomew, of the city of Narni, was an extremely poor and needy man. He fell asleep once under the shade of a certain walnut tree, and when he awoke, he found himself so crippled up that he could not walk. The infirmity gradually increased and his leg and foot became emaciated, crooked, and withered, so that he could not feel an incision made by a knife nor did he fear a burning with fire. But that true lover of the poor and the father of all needy people, the most holy Francis, showed himself one night in a dream to this man, commanding him to go to a certain bath, where he, moved by great compassion for him, wished to free him from his illness. But when the man awoke and did not know what to do, he told the dream, as it had happened, to the bishop of the city. The bishop, however, exhorted him to go to the bath as he had been told to do, and he made the sign of the cross over him and blessed him. The man then began to drag himself to the place as best he could with the aid of a cane. While he was going along his way in sorrow and with great effort, he heard a voice saying to him: "Go with the peace of the Lord; I am he to whom you vowed yourself." Then, as he approached the bath, he missed the way, for it was night; and again he heard the voice saying to him that he was not walking along the right way, and it directed him to the bath. And when he had come to the place and had entered the bath, he felt one hand placed upon his foot and another on his leg, gently stretching it out. Immediately he was cured, and he jumped from the bath praising and blessing the omnipotence of the Creator and blessed Francis, his servant, who had shown him such favor and power. For the man had been crippled and had been a beggar for the space of six years, and he was advanced in age.[56]

OF THE BLIND WHO RECEIVED THEIR SIGHT

136   A certain woman named Sibyl, who had suffered for many years from blindness, was brought sorrowing to the grave of the man of God. But after she had recovered her sight, she returned home rejoicing and full of gladness.[57] A certain blind man from Spello[58] recovered his sight that had been lost for a long time at the tomb of that sacred body.[59] Another woman from Camerino[60] had lost entirely the sight of her right eye. Her parents laid a piece of cloth that the blessed Francis had touched upon that eye, and after they had made a vow, they gave thanks to the Lord God and to St. Francis for the recovery of the sight of that eye.[61] A similar thing happened to a certain woman from Gubbio, who, after she had made a vow, was able to rejoice in the recovery of the sight she had once had.[62] A certain citizen of Assisi too had lost the light of his eyes for five years. Now since, while the blessed Francis was still alive, this man had been very friendly with him, he always

recalled that friendship when he prayed to the blessed man, and, upon touching the tomb of the saint,
he was healed.[63] A certain Albertino of Narni had
completely lost the light of his eyes for about a year
so that his eyelids hung down to his cheeks. He made
a vow to blessed Francis, and immediately upon recovering his sight, he prepared to visit the glorious
tomb of Francis and he went there.[64]

OF THOSE POSSESSED BY DEMONS

137   There was a man in the city of Foligno, Peter
by name, who, when he was once on his way to visit
the shrine of Blessed Michael the Archangel,[65] either
because of a vow or because of a penance imposed upon him for his sins, came to a certain spring.
Because he was thirsty after the tiresomeness of the
journey, he tasted the water of the spring. But it
seemed to him that he drank devils. And so, obsessed
by them for three years, he did some most wicked
things, horrible to see and horrible to speak of. But
coming to the tomb of the most holy father, with
the devils raging and torturing him cruelly, he was
wonderfully freed from them by a clear and manifest
miracle when he touched the sepulcher.[66]

138   There was a certain woman in the city of
Narni who was subject to a terrible frenzy, and having lost her mind, she did horrible things and spoke
unseemly words. But the blessed Francis appeared to
her in a vision, saying: "Make the sign of the cross."
And she said: "I cannot." Then the saint himself
made the sign of the cross upon her and drove out
all her madness and every deceit of the devil.[67] In
the same way, many men and women who were tormented in various ways by the designs of the devils
and deluded by their deceits were snatched away from
their power through the great merits of the holy and
glorious father. But because such people are often the

victims of delusions, we will go on to more important
things with just a mention of these things.

139   A certain boy, Matthew by name, from the
city of Todi,[68] lay in his bed for eight days as though
dead; his mouth was closed tight and the light of his
eyes was gone; the skin of his face and hands and
feet had turned black as a pot, and all despaired of
his life. But at his mother's vow he recovered with
remarkable speed. He discharged foul blood from
his mouth and it was thought that he was vomiting
up his intestines too. Immediately his mother fell to
her knees and humbly called upon the name of St.
Francis; and as she arose from prayer, the boy began
to open his eyes, to see light, and to suck the breasts.
A little while later the black skin fell off and the
flesh became as it had been at first. He got well and
recovered his strength. As soon as he began to get
well, his mother asked him, saying: "Who delivered
you, son?" And lisping, he answered: "Ciccu,
Ciccu."[69] Again he was asked "Whose servant are
you?" And he answered again: "Ciccu, Ciccu." He
could not speak plainly because he was an infant, and
therefore he shortened the name of blessed Francis
in this way.[70]

140   A certain young man who was on a certain
very high place fell down from that place and lost
his speech and the use of all his limbs. And not eating for three days, nor drinking anything, nor giving
any signs of life, he was thought to be dead. His
mother, however, did not seek the aid of doctors, but
she begged health for him from blessed Francis. And
so, after she had made a vow, she received him back
alive and whole; and she began to praise the omnipo-

tence of the Savior.[71] Another boy named Mancinus was sick unto death and all despaired of any cure for him. But he invoked the name of blessed Francis and recovered instantly. Another boy from Arezzo, Walter by name, who was suffering from a continuous fever and was tormented by a double abscess, was given up by all the doctors; but when the parents made a vow to blessed Francis, he was restored to the health he desired.[72] Another one who was near death made a waxen image, and even before it was finished, he was freed from all his sufferings.

141   A certain woman who had been confined to a sickbed for several years and could neither turn nor move made a vow to God and to blessed Francis and was freed from her sickness completely, and she carried out the necessary duties of her life.[73] In the city of Narni there was a certain woman who for eight years had a hand that was so withered that she could do nothing with it. Finally the most blessed father Francis appeared to her in a vision and stretching her hand made it just as useful as the other.[74] In the same city there was a certain young man who had been afflicted for ten years with a most severe illness; he had become so swollen that no medicine could do him any good at all. But after his mother had made a vow, he immediately recovered his health through the merits of blessed Francis.[75] In the city of Fano there was a certain man afflicted with dropsy. His limbs were swollen horribly. He merited to be freed completely from his illness through the instrumentality of blessed Francis.[76] A certain inhabitant of Todi suffered so much from arthritis in his joints that he could not sit or rest at all. The intensity of his suffering gave him such chills that he seemed reduced to nothing. He called in doctors, used more and more baths, took many medicines, but he could be helped by none of these remedies. One day, however, he

made a vow in the presence of a priest in the hope that St. Francis would give him back his health. And so, after praying to the saint, he soon saw himself restored to his former health.[77]

142   A certain woman who lay paralyzed in the city of Gubbio was freed from her infirmity and made well after calling upon the name of blessed Francis three times.[78] A certain man named Bontadosus suffered such severe pain in his feet and hands that he could not move or turn in any direction. When he could no longer eat or sleep, a certain woman came to him one day urging and suggesting that, if he wanted to be freed very quickly from his infirmity, he should vow himself very devoutly to blessed Francis. Amid great pain that man replied: "I do not believe that he is a saint." But the woman continued persistently in her suggestion, and at last the man vowed himself in this way: "I vow myself," he said, "to St. Francis and I will believe him to be a saint, if he will free me from this illness within three days." By the merits of God's saint he was soon delivered, and he walked, ate, and rested, giving glory to Almighty God.[79]

143   There was a man who had been wounded severely in the head with an iron arrow; the arrow had entered through the socket of his eye and remained in his head, and he could not be helped by the skill of the doctors. Then he vowed himself with humble devotion to Francis, the saint of God, hoping that he could be healed through his intercession. While he was resting and sleeping a little, he was told in a dream by St. Francis that he should have the arrow drawn out through the back of his head. And this was done the next day, just as he saw it in his dream, and he was delivered without any great difficulty.[80]

144 A certain man of Spello, named Imperator, suffered such a severe rupture for two years that all his intestines were descending outwardly through his lower parts. For a long time he had not been able to put them back inside or keep them in place, so that he had to have a truss to keep them inside. He went to doctors over and over, begging them to give him some relief; but they demanded from him a price that he could not pay since he did not have the means or even food for a single day; and so he despaired completely of their help. Finally he turned to God for help and began humbly to call upon the merits of blessed Francis along the way, in the house, or wherever he might be. And thus it came about that within a short space of time he was restored to complete health through God's grace and the merits of blessed Francis.[81]

145 A certain brother who was living under the obedience of our order in the Marches of Ancona was suffering from a very serious infection in the lumbar region or in the region of the ribs, so much so that he had already been given up by the doctors because of the severity of his disease. He then begged the minister provincial under whose obedience he was living to grant him permission to go visit the place where the body of our most blessed father is buried, trusting that he would obtain the grace of a cure through the merits of the saint. But his minister forbade him to go, fearing that he would suffer greater harm from the fatigue of the journey on account of the snow and rain at that time. But while the brother felt a little disturbed over the refusal of permission, one night the holy father Francis stood at his side, saying: "Son, be not disturbed any more about this, but take off the fur coat you are wearing and throw away the plaster and the bandage that is over the plaster and observe your Rule, and you will be delivered." Rising in the morning, he did everything according to Francis' command, and he gave thanks to God for a sudden deliverance.[82]

OF THE CLEANSING OF LEPERS

146 At San Severino in the Marches of Ancona a certain young man named Acto, who was covered all over with leprosy, was considered a leper by all in accordance with the verdict of the doctors. All his limbs were swollen and enlarged, and because of the distention and puffed up condition of his veins he saw everything awry. He could not walk, but lying as he did continuously in his sickbed, he caused his parents sorrow and grief. His father, tortured daily as he was with his son's suffering, did not know what to do about him. At length it came into his heart to commend his son by all means to blessed Francis, and he said to his son: "Son, do you wish to vow yourself to St. Francis, who everywhere is renowned for his miracles, that it might please him to free you from your illness?" He replied: "I want to, father." The father immediately had paper brought and, after he had measured his son's stature in height and girth, he said: "Raise yourself up, son, and vow yourself to blessed Francis, and after he has cured you, you shall bring him a candle as tall as you are every year as long as you live." At the command of his father he rose up as well as he could, and joining his hands, he began humbly to invoke blessed Francis' compassion. Accordingly, after he had taken up the paper measure and completed his prayer, he was immediately cured of his leprosy; and getting up and giving glory to God and to blessed Francis, he began to walk with joy.[83] In the city of Fano, a certain young man named Bonushomo, who was considered paralyzed and leprous by all the doctors, was devoutly offered to blessed Francis by his parents. He was cleansed from the leprosy and cured of his paralysis and made completely well.[84]

OF THE CURING OF THE DUMB AND THE DEAF

147 At Città della Pieve there was a very poor beggar boy who was completely dumb and deaf from his birth. He had a tongue that was very short and mutilated, so much so that it seemed to those who had examined it many times that it had been cut off. One evening he came to the house of a certain man of the city who was called Mark, and by means of signs, as is customary with the mute, he begged shelter from him. He leaned his head sideways, his jaw against his hand, so that it could be understood that he wanted to be sheltered with him for the night. But the man took him into his house with great happiness and willingly kept him with him, for the boy knew how to be a competent servant. He was an ingenious young man, for, though he had been deaf and dumb from the cradle, he understood by signs what was commanded him. One night when the man was at supper with his wife and the boy was waiting on them, the man said to his wife: "I would consider it the greatest miracle if the blessed Francis would give hearing and speech to this boy."

148 And he added: "I vow to the Lord God that if the blessed Francis should deign to work this miracle, I will, for love of him, hold this boy most dear and provide for him as long as he lives." Wonderful indeed! When the vow had been made, the boy immediately spoke and said: "St. Francis lives." And then looking about, he again said: "I see St. Francis standing on high and he is coming to give me speech." And the boy added: "What therefore shall I say to the people?" Then that man arose, rejoicing and exulting greatly, and he made known to all the people what had happened. All those who had seen the boy

before when he could not speak came running, and, filled with admiration and wonder, they humbly gave praise to God and to blessed Francis. The boy's tongue grew and became adapted for speech, and he began to utter properly formed words as though he had always been speaking.[85]

149 Another boy, by the name of Villa, could not speak or walk. His mother made a waxen image in fulfillment of a vow and took it with reverence to the place where the blessed father Francis is buried. When she returned home, she found her son walking and speaking.[86] A certain man, in the diocese of Perugia, had lost completely the faculty of speech. He always kept his mouth open, gaping horribly and in great distress, for his throat was much swollen and puffed up. When he had come to the place where the most holy body is buried and wished to go up the steps to the tomb, he vomited much blood, and completely relieved, he began to speak and to close and open his mouth as was necessary.[87]

150 A certain woman suffered such great pain in her throat that from the excessive burning her tongue clung dried to her palate. She could not speak, nor eat, nor drink. Plasters were applied and medicines used, but she felt no relief from her infirmity with all these things. Finally, she vowed herself in her heart to St. Francis, for she could not speak, and suddenly her flesh broke open and there came from her throat a small round stone which she took in her hand and showed to everyone nearby, and she was soon completely healed.[88] In the city of Greccio there was a certain young man who had lost his hearing, his memory, and his speech, and he could not understand or perceive anything. But his parents, who had great faith in St. Francis, vowed the young man to him with humble devotion; when the vow had been fulfilled, he was most abundantly endowed with the senses he had lacked through the favor of the most holy and glorious father Francis.

To the praise, glory, and honor
of Jesus Christ our Lord,
whose kingdom and empire endure
firm and immoveable forever and ever
Amen

EPILOGUE

151   We have said a few things about the miracles of our most blessed father Francis and have omitted many more things, leaving to those who wish to follow in his footsteps the task of seeking out the grace of a new blessing so that he who has most gloriously renewed the whole world by his word and example, his life and teaching, may always deign to water with new showers of super-celestial gifts the minds of those who love the name of the Lord. I beg, for the love of the poor crucified one and through his sacred wounds, which the blessed father Francis bore in his body, that all who read these things, who see and hear them, may be mindful of me, a sinner, before God. Amen.

> *Benediction and honor*[89] and all praise be *to the only wise God*[90] who always works most wisely *all things in all*[91] unto his glory. Amen. Amen. Amen.[92]

PART II

The Second Life of St. Francis
by
Thomas of Celano

THE SECOND LIFE OF ST. FRANCIS

PROLOGUE

In the Name of our Lord Jesus Christ. Amen

To the Minister General of
the Order of Friars Minor

HERE BEGINS THE PROLOGUE

1   It has pleased the entire holy assembly of the
past general chapter[1] and you, Most Reverend
Father,[2] not without the dispensation of divine wisdom, to enjoin upon our littleness that we set down
in writing for the consolation of those living and for
a remembrance for those to come the deeds and also
the words of our glorious father Francis, in as much
as they were better known to us than to the rest because of our close association with him and our
mutual intimacy.[3] We hasten therefore to obey with
humble devotion the holy injunctions which we may
not pass by; but we are struck with just fear when
we consider more seriously the weakness of our abilities, lest so worthy a matter, in not being treated by
us as it deserves, may derive from us what may be
displeasing to the rest. For we fear that things that
are worthy of all sweetness of taste may be rendered
insipid by the unworthiness of those who dispense
them, and so our efforts will be attributed to our presumption rather than to obedience. For if the examination of the result of our great labor pertained
only to your good pleasure, blessed father, and it
were not opportune for it to be made public, we
would very gratefully accept instruction from your
correction or happiness from your confirmation. For
who, amid such diversity of words and actions, would
be able to so weigh everything on the scales of a pre-

cise examination that all who hear them would be *of one mind*[4] concerning the single points? But since we are seeking with a single heart the benefit of all and of each one, we suggest that they who read these things interpret them kindly and bear with the simplicity of the narration or properly direct it so that reverence for him about whom these things tell may be preserved intact. Our memory, dulled as it is by length of time, like that of untrained men, cannot reach the flights of his subtle words and the wonders of his deeds, for the agility of a practiced mind could hardly comprehend these things if it were confronted with them. Therefore, let the authority of him who has repeatedly commanded us excuse before all the faults of our lack of skill.

2   This little work contains in the first place certain wonderful facts about the conversion of St. Francis that were not included in the legends that were composed some time earlier because they had not come to the notice of the author. Then we intend to portray and to declare with careful zeal what was *the good and acceptable and perfect will*[5] of Francis both for himself and for his followers in every practice of heavenly discipline and in zeal for the highest perfection which he ever had toward God in his sacred affections, and toward men in his examples. Certain miracles are inserted, as occasion for inserting them presents itself. We describe in a plain and simple way the things that occur to us, wishing to accommodate ourselves to the slower ones and also to please the more learned, if we can.[6]

We beg, therefore, kindest father, that you will not despise the small gift of this work which we have put together with no little effort,[7] but will deign to consecrate it by your blessing, correcting what is in error and removing what is superfluous, so that the things that are approved as well said by your learned judgment may indeed grow together with your name *Crescentius* and be multiplied in Christ. Amen.

THUS ENDS THE PROLOGUE

BOOK ONE

HERE BEGINS THE "REMEMBRANCE
IN THE DESIRE OF THE SOUL" OF
THE DEEDS AND WORDS OF OUR
MOST HOLY FATHER FRANCIS[1]

OF FRANCIS' CONVERSION

CHAPTER I

*How he was first called John and afterwards Francis;
how his mother prophecied concerning him, and he
himself also foretold what would come to pass in his
regard; and of his patience in imprisonment*

3   Francis, the servant and friend of the Most
High, to whom divine providence gave this name so
that by means of this singular and unusual name[2]
the knowledge of his ministry might become known
to the whole world, was called John by his mother,
when, being *born again of water and the Holy Spirit,*[3]
he was made a child of grace from a child of wrath.[4]

This woman, a friend of all goodness, bore about
her a certain image in her conduct of the virtue of
that holy Elizabeth, enjoying as she did a certain
privilege of resemblance to her both in the giving of
a name to her son[5] and in her spirit of prophecy.[6]
For while her neighbors were wondering at the nobility of soul and the modesty of Francis, she would say,
as though prompted by divine guidance: "What do
you think this my son will turn out to be? Know that
he will be a son of God by the grace of his merits."

This indeed was the opinion of not a few whom the
youthful Francis pleased by reason of his good inclinations. He always put away from himself everything
that could be regarded as evil by anyone and in his
youth his manners were so refined that it seemed
that he was not born of the parents from whom he

was said to have been born. The name *John* referred to the work of the ministry which he would undertake;[7] the name *Francis* referred to the spread of his fame, which, after he had been fully converted to God, quickly spread everywhere. He considered the feast of John the Baptist to be more illustrious than the feasts of all the other saints,[8] for the dignity of his name left a mark of mystic virtue upon him. *Among those born of women there has not arisen a greater than John;*[9] among the founders of religious orders there has not arisen a more perfect one than Francis. This is an observation that is worthy to be heralded about.

4   John prophecied enclosed within the hidden places of his mother's womb;[10] Francis prophecied future events enclosed within the prison of this world while he was still ignorant of the divine counsel. Indeed, once when there was a bloody battle between the citizens of Perugia and those of Assisi, Francis was made captive with several others and endured the squalors of a prison.[11] His fellow captives were consumed with sorrow, bemoaning miserably their imprisonment; Francis rejoiced in the Lord, laughed at his chains and despised them. His grieving companions resented his happiness and considered him insane and mad. Francis replied prophetically: "Why do you think I rejoice? There is another consideration, for I will yet be venerated as a saint throughout the whole world." And so it has truly come about; everything he said has been fulfilled.

There was at that time among his fellow prisoners a certain proud and completely unbearable knight whom the rest were determined to shun, but Francis' patience was not disturbed. He put up with the unbearable knight and brought the others to peace with him. Capable of every grace, a chosen vessel of virtues, he poured out his gifts on all sides.

CHAPTER II

Of a poor knight whom Francis clothed; and of the vision of his call which he had while he was in the world

5 Freed from his chains a short time later, he became more kindly toward the needy. He now resolved not to turn his face away from any poor man,[12] who in begging asked for the love of God.[13] One day he met a knight who was poor and well nigh naked; moved by pity he gave him for Christ's sake the costly garments he was wearing. How did he conduct himself any differently from the way the most holy Martin conducted himself,[14] except that, while both had the same purpose and both did the same deed, they differed in the way they acted. Francis first gave his garments before the rest of his things; Martin first gave up the rest of his things and then finally his garments. Both lived poor and feeble[15] in this world; both entered heaven rich.[16] The latter, a knight, but poor, cut his garment in two to clothe a poor man; the former, not a knight, but rich, clothed a poor knight with his whole garment. Both, having fulfilled the command of Christ,[17] merited to be visited by Christ in a vision; one was praised for his perfection, the other was graciously invited to fulfill what was yet lacking.

6 Now Francis was soon shown in a vision a splendid palace in which he saw various military apparatus and a most beautiful bride.[18] In the dream Francis was called by name and enticed by the promise of all these things. He attempted, therefore, to go to Apulia to win knighthood; and after he had made the necessary preparations in a lavish manner, he hurried on to gain that degree of military honors. A carnal spirit prompted him to make a carnal interpretation of the dream he had had, while a far

more glorious interpretation lay hidden in the treasures of God's wisdom.

Accordingly, while he was sleeping one night, someone addressed him a second time in a vision and questioned him solicitously as to whether he intended to go. When he had told his purpose to him who was asking and said that he was going to Apulia[19] to fight, he was asked earnestly who could do better for him, the servant or the Lord. And Francis said: "The Lord." The other answered: "Why then are you seeking the servant in place of the Lord?" And Francis said: "Lord, what do you want me to do?" And the Lord said to him: "Go back to the place of your birth for through me your vision will have a spiritual fulfillment." He went back without delay, for he had already become a model of obedience and, giving up his own will, he became a Paul in place of a Saul. Saul is thrown to the ground and heavy blows beget sweet words. Francis, however, changes his carnal weapons into spiritual ones and in place of military glory he receives the knighthood of God. Therefore to the many who were astounded at his unusual happiness he said that he was going to be a great prince.[20]

CHAPTER III

How a band of youths made him their leader, so that he might feed them; and of the change that came over him

7   Francis began to be changed into a perfect man and to become other than his former self. After he had returned home, *the sons of Babylon*[21] followed him and dragged him unwilling to other pursuits than those he intended to follow. For a band of young people of Assisi, who had formerly considered him their leader in their vain pursuits,[22] came

to him now to invite him to their social banquets which always served their wantonness and buffoonery. He was chosen by them to be their leader, for, since they had often experienced his liberality, they knew without a doubt that he would pay the expenses for them all. They gave him obedience so that they might fill their bellies and they endured being subject so that they might be filled. He did not spurn the honor, lest he be thought avaricious, and amid his holy meditations he was mindful of the obligations of courtesy. He prepared a sumptuous banquet, doubled the dainty foods; filled to vomiting with these things, they defiled the streets of the city with drunken singing. Francis followed them, carrying a *staff in his hands*[23] as the master of revels; but little by little he withdrew himself bodily from them, for he was already totally deaf to all these things and was singing in his heart to the Lord.

He was then filled with such divine sweetness, as he himself said, that he became speechless and was totally unable to move from the place. Then a certain spiritual affection took hold of him and carried him away to things invisible, by virtue of which he judged all earthly things to be of no importance but entirely worthless. Stupendous indeed is the condescension of Christ, which gives the greatest gifts to those who are doing the least and *in a flood of many waters*[24] preserves and advances the things that are his. For Christ fed the multitudes with bread and fishes,[25] neither did he repel sinners from his banquet. When they sought him to make him king, he took to flight and *went up to the mountain to pray.*[26] These were the mysteries of God Francis was learning; and ignorant as he was he was being led unto perfect knowledge.

CHAPTER IV

How Francis, clad in a poor man's garments, ate with the poor at St. Peter's; and of his offering there

8   But already he was the chief lover of the poor, already his holy beginnings gave indication of what he was to be perfectly. Accordingly, frequently stripping himself, he clothed the poor, like unto whom he was striving with his whole heart to become, though as yet he had not put his desire into execution.

When he was on a pilgrimage to Rome, he put off his fine garments out of love of poverty, clothed himself with the garments of a certain poor man, and joyfully sat among the poor in the vestibule before the church of St. Peter, where there were many poor, and considering himself one of them, he ate eagerly with them. Many times he would have done a similar thing had he not been held back by shame before those who knew him. Astounded when he came to the altar of the prince of the apostles that the offerings of those who came there were so meager, he threw down a handful of coins at that place, thus indicating that he whom God honored above the rest should be honored by all in a special way.

Several times he also gave poor priests church ornaments, and he showed due honor to all clerics even down to the lowest grade. For, as one about to take upon himself the apostolic mission[27] and one wholly and entirely Catholic, he was filled from the beginning with reverence toward the ministers and the ministry of God.[28]

CHAPTER V

How, while Francis was praying, the devil showed him a woman; and of the answer God gave him and of his treatment of the lepers

9   Thus already beneath his secular garb he wore a religious spirit and, withdrawing from public to solitary places, he was often admonished by a visitation of the Holy Spirit.[29] For he was carried away and enticed by that perfect sweetness which poured over him with such abundance from the very beginning that it never departed from him as long as he lived.

But while he frequented hidden places as more suitable to prayer, the devil tried to drive him away from such places by an evil suggestion. He put into his mind a certain woman who was monstrously hunchbacked, an inhabitant of his city, and who was a hideous sight to all. He threatened to make him like her if he did not leave off what he had begun. But *strengthened in the Lord,*[30] he rejoiced to hear a reply of salvation and grace: "Francis," God said to him in spirit, "what you have loved carnally and vainly you should now exchange for spiritual things, and taking the *bitter for sweet,*[31] despise yourself, if you wish to acknowledge me; for you will have a taste for what I speak of even if the order is reversed." Immediately he was compelled to obey the divine command and was led to actual experience.[32]

For among all the unhappy spectacles of the world Francis naturally abhorred lepers; but one day he met a leper while he was riding near Assisi. Though the leper caused him no small disgust and horror, nevertheless, lest like a transgressor of a commandment he should break his given word, he got off the horse and prepared to kiss the leper. But when the leper put out his hand as though to receive something, he received money along with a kiss. And immediately mounting his horse, Francis looked here and there about him; but though the plain lay open and clear on all sides, and there were no obstacles about, he could not see the leper anywhere.

Filled with wonder and joy as a result, after a few days he took care to do the same thing again. He went to the dwelling places of the lepers, and after he had given each leper some money, he kissed his hand and his mouth. Thus he exchanged the bitter for the sweet, and manfully prepared himself to carry out the rest.

CHAPTER VI

Of the image of the crucified that spoke to him, and of the honor he paid it

10   Changed now perfectly in heart and soon to be changed in body too, he was walking one day near the church of St. Damian, which had nearly fallen to ruin and was abandoned by everyone. Led by the Spirit, he went in and fell down before the crucifix in devout and humble supplication; and smitten by unusual visitations, he found himself other than he had been when he entered. While he was thus affected, something unheard of before happened to him: the painted image of Christ[33] crucified moved its lips and spoke. Calling him by name it said: "Francis, go, repair my house, which, as you see, is falling completely to ruin." Trembling, Francis was not a little amazed and became almost deranged by these words. He prepared himself to obey and gave himself completely to the fulfillment of this command. But since he felt that the change he had undergone was beyond expression, it is becoming that we should be silent about what he could not express. From then on compassion for the crucified was rooted in

his holy soul, and, as it can be piously supposed, the stigmata of the venerable passion were deeply imprinted in his heart, though not as yet upon his flesh.

11   What a wonderful thing and a thing unheard of in our times! Who is not astonished at these things? Who has ever heard like things? Who would doubt that Francis, returning now to his native city,[34] appeared crucified, when, though he had not yet outwardly completely renounced the world, Christ had spoken to him from the wood of the cross in a new and unheard of miracle? From that hour on, his *soul was melted* when his beloved *spoke* to him.[35] A little later,[36] the love of his heart made itself manifest by the wounds of his body. And from then on he could never keep himself from weeping, even bewailing in a loud voice the passion of Christ which was always, as it were, before his mind. He filled the ways with his sighs. He permitted himself no consolation, remembering the wounds of Christ. He met a certain intimate friend, to whom he made known the cause of his grief, and immediately his friend was moved to tears.

Indeed, he never forgot to be concerned about that holy image, and he never passed over its command with negligence. Right away he gave a certain priest some money that he might buy a lamp and oil, lest the sacred image should be deprived of the due honor of a light even for a moment. Then he diligently hastened to do the rest and devoted his untiring efforts toward repairing that church. For, though the divine command concerned itself with the church that Christ had *purchased with his own blood,*[37] Francis would not suddenly become perfect, but he was to pass gradually from the flesh to the spirit.

CHAPTER VII

Of his father's persecution and of that of his brother according to the flesh

12   But now that Francis was giving himself to works of piety, his carnally minded father[38] persecuted him and judging his service of Christ to be madness, he hurled curses at him everywhere. Therefore the servant of God called to his aid a certain low-born and quite simple man, and putting him in the place of his father, he begged him that when his father hurled curses at him he should on the contrary bless him. In truth he turned the word of the prophet to action and showed by deeds what was the meaning of that saying: *They will curse and thou wilt bless.*[39]

At the urging of the bishop of the city, a very pious man, who informed him that it was not lawful to spend anything for sacred uses that had been gotten unlawfully, the man of God gave up to his father the money he had wanted to spend for restoring the church mentioned above.[40] In the hearing of many who had come together, he said: "From now on I can freely say *Our Father who art in heaven,* not *father Peter Bernardone,*[41] to whom, behold, I give up not only the money, but all my clothes too. I will therefore go naked to the Lord." O generous spirit, to whom Christ alone is sufficient! The man of God was then found to be wearing a hair shirt beneath his clothing, rejoicing in the reality of virtues rather than in mere appearances.

His brother according to the flesh,[42] after the manner of his father, pursued him with venomous words. On a certain morning in winter time, that perverse man saw Francis at prayer clothed in poor garments and shivering with the cold; and he said to a certain fellow townsman: "Tell Francis to sell you a pennysworth of sweat." But hearing this, the man of God was filled with gladness and answered smiling: "Indeed, I will sell my sweat more dearly to my Lord." There is nothing more true, for he received not only a hundredfold but even more than a thousandfold in this life, and he won not only for himself but for many others too eternal life hereafter.

CHAPTER VIII

Of the bashfulness Francis conquered and of his prophecy concerning the Poor Virgins

13   Francis strove then to change completely his former delicate way of living and to bring his body, used to luxury, back to the goodness of nature. One day the man of God went through Assisi to beg oil to light up the lamps of the church of St. Damian which he was repairing at that time. And seeing a large group of men playing before the house he wanted to enter, he was filled with bashfulness and retraced his steps. But after he had directed his noble spirit to heaven, he rebuked himself for cowardice and passed judgment upon himself. Immediately he returned to the house and freely explained the cause of his bashfulness; and, in a kind of spiritual intoxication, he begged in French for oil and got it. Most fervently he stirred up everyone for the work of that church and speaking in a loud voice in French, he prophecied before all that there would be a monastery there of holy virgins of Christ. For always when he was filled with the ardor of the Holy Spirit, he burst forth in French to speak his ardent words, foreknowing that he would be especially honored by that people and venerated with a special reverence by them.[43]

CHAPTER IX

How Francis begged food from door to door

14   From the time when he began to serve the common Lord of all, Francis always loved to do common things, shunning in all things singularity, which is soiled with the foulness of all vices. For, while he was pouring out his sweat in the work at that church concerning which he had received a command from Christ, and when he had been changed from a person of extreme delicacy to a lowly and patient laborer, the priest to whose care the church pertained, seeing that Francis was worn down by constant labor and moved to pity, began to give him daily some special food, though it was not dainty since he was poor. Commending the discretion of the priest and welcoming his kindness, Francis nevertheless said to himself: "You will not find a priest everywhere to provide these things always for you. This is not the life of a man who professes poverty. It is not proper for you to get accustomed to such things; gradually you will return to the things you have despised, and you will run again after delicacies. Arise now without delay, and beg from door to door for foods of mixed kinds." He therefore begged for prepared foods from door to door throughout Assisi, and when he saw his bowl full of all kinds of scraps, he was struck with horror; but mindful of God and conquering himself, he ate the food with joy of spirit. Love softens all things[44] and makes every bitter thing sweet.

CHAPTER X

Of Brother Bernard's renunciation of his goods

15   A certain Bernard of the city of Assisi, who was afterwards a son of perfection,[45] since he was

planning to perfectly despise the world after the example of the man of God, humbly sought his advice. He therefore consulted him, saying: "If some one, father, possessed for a long time the goods of some lord and did not want to keep them any longer, what would be the more perfect thing to do with them?" The man of God answered that all of them should be given back to the lord from whom he had received them. And Bernard said to him: "Everything I have, I recognize as having been given me by God, and at your advice I stand ready to give them back to him." "If you wish to prove what you say by deeds," the holy man said, "let us go early in the morning to the church and taking the book of the Gospel, let us seek counsel from Christ."[46] They therefore entered the church early in the morning, and after offering up a prayer, they opened the book of the Gospel, proposing to follow what counsel should first appear. They opened the book and Christ showed them his counsel in it: *If thou wilt be perfect, go, sell what thou hast, and give to the poor.*[47] A second time they did this and *Take nothing for your journey* occurred.[48] They did the same thing a third time and they found: *If anyone wishes to come after me, let him deny himself.*[49] Without delay Bernard fulfilled all these things and he did not transgress any of this advice, not even a single iota of it.

In a short time many others were converted from the corroding cares of the world and returned *into their country*[50] under the guidance of Francis, unto infinite good. It would be long to tell of each one how they all attained *the prize* of their *heavenly call.*[51]

CHAPTER XI

Of the parable Francis spoke before the pope

16   At the time when Francis presented himself
along with his followers before Pope Innocent to
ask for a rule of life,[52] the pope, a man endowed
with the greatest discretion, seeing that his proposed
way of life was beyond his powers, said to him:
"Pray, son, to Christ, that he may show us his will
through you, so that, knowing his will, we may
more securely give assent to your pious desires." The
holy man agreed to the command of the supreme
shepherd and hastened confidently to Christ; he
prayed earnestly and devoutly exhorted his companions to pray to God. But why should we speak at
length? He obtained an answer by prayer and reported the news of salvation to his sons. The familiar talk of Christ is made known in parables. "Francis," he said, "speak thus to the pope. A certain
woman who was poor but very beautiful lived in a
certain desert. A certain king loved her because of
her very great beauty; he gladly married her and
begot very handsome sons by her. When they had
grown to adulthood and been brought up nobly,
their mother said to them: 'Do not be ashamed, my
loved ones, in that you are poor, for you are all sons
of that king. Go gladly to his court and ask him for
whatever you need.' Hearing this they were in admiration and rejoiced, and buoyed up by the assurance
of their royal origin, they regarded want as riches,
knowing that they would be heirs. They boldly presented themselves to the king and they did not fear
the face of him whose likeness they bore. Recognizing his own likeness in them, the king wondered
and asked whose sons they were. When they said
they were the sons of that poor woman living in the
desert, the king embraced them and said: 'You are

my sons and heirs; fear not. For if strangers are fed at my table, it is all the more just that I see to it that those be fed to whom my entire heritage is reserved by right.' The king then ordered the woman to send all the sons he had begotten to the court to be provided for." The saint was made happy and glad by the parable and reported the holy message to the pope.

17   This woman was Francis, because he was fruitful in many sons, not because of any softness in his actions. The desert was the world, untilled and barren at that time in the teaching of virtues.[53] The handsome and numerous progeny of sons was the great multitude of brothers adorned with every virtue. The king was the Son of God, to whom they bore a resemblance by their holy poverty. And they received nourishment at the table of the king, despising all shame over their meanness; for, content with imitating Christ and living by alms, they knew they would be happy amid the reproaches of the world.

The lord pope wondered at the parable proposed to him and recognized without doubting that Christ had spoken in man. He recalled a certain vision he had had a few days before, which, he affirmed, under the guidance of the Holy Spirit, would be fulfilled in this man. He had seen in his sleep the Lateran basilica about to fall to ruin, when a certain religious, small and despised, propped it up by putting his own back under it lest it fall. "Surely," he said, "this is that man who, by his works and by the teaching of Christ, will give support to the Church." For this reason the lord pope readily gave in to the petition of Francis. Therefore, filled with love of God he always showed a special love toward the servant of Christ. And therefore he quickly granted what had been asked, and he promised to grant even greater things than these.[54] Francis, therefore, by reason of the authority granted him,[55] began to scatter the seeds of virtue, going about *the towns and villages*[56] preaching fervently.

CHAPTER XII

Of Francis' love for the Portiuncula, of the life of the brothers there, and of the love of the Blessed Mother for it

18   The servant of God Francis, a person small in stature, humble in mind, a *minor* by profession, while yet in the world chose out of the world for himself and his followers a *little portion,* in as much as he could not serve Christ without having something of the world. For it was not without the foreknowledge of a divine disposition that from ancient times that place was called the *Portiuncula*[57] which was to fall to the lot of those who wished to have nothing whatsoever of the world. For there had also been built in that place a church of the virgin mother who merited by her singular humility to be, after her son, the head of all the saints. In this church the Order of Friars Minor had its beginning;[58] there, as on a firm foundation, when their number had grown, the noble fabric of the order arose.[59] The holy man loved this place above all others; this place he commanded his brothers to venerate with a special reverence;[60] this place he willed to be preserved as a model of humility and highest poverty for their order, reserving the ownership of it to others, and keeping only the use of it for himself and his brothers.[61]

19   The most rigid discipline was observed there in all things, both as to silence and work and as to

the other ordinances of the rule.⁶² To no one was admittance there granted except to specially appointed brothers who, coming from all parts of the world, the holy man wanted to be devoted to God and perfect in every way. So too admittance was prohibited to every secular person. He did not want the brothers dwelling there, who were restricted severely as to number, to have *itching ears*⁶³ for news of worldly things, lest, with their meditation on heavenly things interrupted, they should be drawn to the business of inferior things through those who spread rumors. It was not permitted to anyone there to utter idle words or repeat those uttered by others. If anyone at any time did this, he was taught through punishment to be careful not to let it happen again. Those who dwelt in this place were occupied with the divine praises without interruption day and night, and fragrant with a wonderful odor, they led an angelic life.

This was as it should be. For, according to what the old inhabitants use to say, the place was also called St. Mary of the Angels. The happy father used to say that it had been revealed to him by God that the Blessed Mother loved this church, among all the other churches built in her honor throughout the world, with a special love; for this reason the holy man loved it above all others.

CHAPTER XIII

Of a certain vision

20   A certain brother, given to God, had a certain vision before his conversion about this church which is worth mentioning. He saw a whole host of men in his vision who had been struck blind kneeling about in this church, their faces turned toward heaven. They were all stretching their hands upwards and

crying with tearful voices to God, asking for mercy and light. And behold, a great splendor from heaven approached and spread itself over them all, giving light to each one and the healing they sought.

CHAPTER XIV

Of the rigor of discipline

21   The zealous knight of Christ never spared his body, but exposed it to every hurt both in deed and in word, as though it were something separate from himself. If someone were to count the things this man suffered, he would find that they exceed what is told in that passage of the Apostle where the sufferings of the holy ones are recounted.[64] But that whole first school so subjected themselves to every inconvenience that it was thought an evil thing if someone refreshed himself in anything except in the consolation of the Holy Spirit. For since they girded themselves and clothed themselves with iron hoops and corslets and tried themselves with many vigils and fasts, they would very often have succumbed had they not relaxed the rigor of such abstinence at the earnest advice of their kind shepherd.[65]

CHAPTER XV

Of the discretion of St. Francis

22   One night one of the sheep cried out while the rest were sleeping: "I am dying, brothers, I am dying of hunger." Immediately the good shepherd got up and hastened to give the ailing sheep the proper remedy. He commanded the table to be set, though it was filled with poor things, and, as is often the case, where wine was lacking water took its place.

First he himself began to eat, and then he invited the rest of the brothers to share this duty of charity, lest that brother should waste away from shame. When they had eaten the food with fear of the Lord, the father wove a long parable for his sons about the virtue of discretion, lest something should be lacking in the offices of charity. He commanded them always to give to the Lord a sacrifice seasoned with salt, and carefully admonished each one to consider his own strength in the service of God. He said that to deprive the body indiscreetly of what it needs was a sin just the same as it is a sin to give it superfluous things at the prompting of gluttony. And he added: "Know, dearest brothers, that what I have done in eating, I have done by dispensation, not by desire, because fraternal charity commanded it. Let this charity be an example to you, not the food, for the latter ministers to gluttony, the former to the spirit."

CHAPTER XVI

How Francis foresaw the future and how he committed his order to the Church of Rome; and of a certain vision

23   The holy father, making progress continually in the merits of life and in virtue, while the tree of his order was everywhere spreading by a multiplying of its members and was stretching its branches laden wonderfully with fruits to the ends of the earth, began to meditate alone more often how that new plant might be preserved and how it might increase, bound together by the bond of unity. He then saw many raging savagely against his little flock, like wolves, and men *grown old in evil days*[66] taking occasion from its mere youthfulness to cause it harm.[67] He foresaw that even among his own sons

certain things contrary to holy peace and unity would occur and he did not doubt that, as often happens among the elect, some would rebel, *puffed up by* their *mere human mind*[68] and in spirit would be prepared for quarrelling and prone to scandals.

24 While the man of God revolved these and similar things in his mind more often, one night while he was asleep he saw this vision. He saw a little black hen, much like a tame dove, whose legs and feet were covered with feathers. She had innumerable chicks which pressed close around her, but they could not all get under her wings. The man of God, *arising from sleep*,[69] took to heart what he had meditated on, and became his own interpreter of his vision. "The hen," he said, "is I, small as I am in stature and naturally dark, who ought to be attended through innocence of life by dove-like simplicity, which easily wings its way to heaven, as is most rare in this world. The chicks are my brothers, multiplied in number and in grace,[70] whom Francis' strength does not suffice to defend from the disturbances of men and from *the contradiction of tongues*.[71]

"I will go, therefore, and I will commend them to the holy Roman church, by the rod of whose power those of ill-will will be struck down and the children of God will enjoy full freedom everywhere unto the increase of eternal salvation. From this the sons will acknowledge the kind gifts of their mother and always embrace her venerable footsteps with special devotion. Under her protection, no evil will befall the order, nor will the *son of Belial*[72] pass with impunity over the vineyard of the Lord. Our holy mother herself will emulate the glory of our poverty and will not permit the fame of our humility to be clouded over by the mist of pride. She will keep unbroken in us the bonds of charity and peace, striking the dissenters with her strictest censure. The holy observance of Gospel purity will constantly flourish in her sight, and she will not permit the fragrance of their life to vanish even for an hour." This was the whole intention of the holy man of God in commending himself to the Church; these were the most holy testimonies to the foresight of the man of God in commending himself against the time to come.

CHAPTER XVII

How he asked for the Lord of Ostia as his pope

25   Coming therefore to Rome, the man of God was received with great devotedness by the lord pope Honorius[73] and all the cardinals. For what had been reported of him shone forth in his life and resounded on his tongue; under such conditions there is no room for disrespect. He preached before the pope and the cardinals with ready and fervent foresight, speaking without restraint whatever the spirit suggested. The mountains[74] were moved at his word, and great sighs rose from their innermost depths and bathed the inner man with tears.

When the sermon was finished and a few words spoken familiarly with the lord pope, Francis presented his petition thus: "As you know, my lord, access to such majesty as yours is not easily given to poor and despised men. You indeed hold the world in your hands and business of great importance does not permit you to attend to little afairs. Therefore I beg of the kindness of your holiness that you give me the lord of Ostia[75] as my pope, so that, saving always the dignity of your pre-eminence, the brothers may go to him in the time of need and obtain from him the benefits of his protection and rule."[76] Such a holy petition found favor in the eyes of the pope and soon he appointed the lord Hugo, bishop of Ostia at the time, over the order, as the man of God had asked. That holy cardinal accepted the flock committed to him, became its diligent guardian, its shepherd and its foster-child until his happy death.[77] To this special subjection is due the prerogative of love and care which the holy Roman Church has never ceased to show to the Order of Friars Minor.[78]

THUS ENDS THE FIRST PART

BOOK TWO

26   To preserve the record of the outstanding accomplishments of our forefathers for the memory of their children is a mark of honor to the former and of love for the latter. For truly, those who have not seen the bodily presence of their forefathers are spurred on to good at least by their deeds and moved to better things when their memorable deeds bring back to mind their fathers separated from them by the passing of time. But the first and not the least fruit we derive therefrom is a knowledge of our own littleness, seeing how great was the abundance of their merits and how great the lack of our own. But I think Blessed Francis was a most holy mirror of the sanctity of the Lord and an image of his perfection.[1] All his words, I say, as well as his deeds are redolent of the divine, and if they be diligently examined by a humble disciple, they will imbue him with a wholesome discipline and make him docile to that highest philosophy.[2] Therefore, now that I have set down in humble style[3] and, as it were in passing, some things concerning him, I think it not superfluous to add a few things from the many whereby the saint may be commended and our slumbering affections stirred anew.[4]

OF FRANCIS' SPIRIT OF PROPHECY

CHAPTER I

27   The blessed father, borne up as he was above the things of this world by a certain exaltation, brought whatever is in the world into subjection by a wondrous power, for, always directing the eye of his intellect to the Supreme Light, he not only knew by divine revelation what was to be done, but he also foretold many things *in the spirit of prophecy,*[5] peered into the secrets of hearts, knew things from which he was absent, foresaw and foretold things that were yet to happen. Examples give proof of what we say.[6]

CHAPTER II

How Francis knew that one who was reputed holy was a fraud

28   There was a certain brother of extraordinary sanctity, as far as could be seen outwardly, outstanding in his life, yet quite singular. He spent all his time in prayer and he observed silence with such strictness that he was accustomed to confess not with words but with signs. He derived great ardor from the words of Scripture, and, after hearing them, he relished them with wonderful sweetness. Why should we give many details? He was considered thrice holy by all. The blessed father happened to come to that place and happened to see that brother and hear him called a saint. But when all were commending him and praising him, the father replied: "Leave off, brothers, and do not praise the things the

devil has fashioned in him. Know in truth that it is a temptation of the devil and a fraudulent deception. I am convinced of this and the greatest proof of it is that he does not want to confess." The brothers took this ill, especially the vicar of the saint.[7] "And how could it be true," they inquired, "that the workings of fraud could be concealed under so many signs of perfection?" The father said to them: "Let him be admonished to confess twice or once a week; if he does not do this, you will know that what I have said is true." The vicar took him aside and first joked familiarly with him, then commanded him to confess. He refused, and putting his finger into his ear and shaking his head, he indicated that he would not by any means confess. The brothers were silent, fearing the scandal of a false saint. After not many days, he left religion of his own accord, went back to the world, returned *to his vomit.*[8] Finally, redoubling his crimes, he was deprived at the same time of repentance and of life. Singularity is always to be avoided, for it is nothing else but a lovely precipice. Many singular persons have learned by experience that from singularity *they mount up to heaven, and they go down to the depths.*[9] Attend, on the other hand, to the power of devout confession, which not only makes a person holy, but also manifests his holiness.

CHAPTER III

A similar case in another brother. Against singularity

29   Something similar happened to another brother, Thomas of Spoleto by name. The opinion and firm conviction of all concerning him was that he was a saint. But his apostasy eventually proved the soundness of the judgment of the holy father about

him, namely, that he was a wicked man. He did not persevere long, for virtue sought by fraud does not last long. He left religion and died outside of it, and now he knows what he did.

CHAPTER IV

How Francis foretold the defeat of the Christians at Damietta

30 At the time when the Christian army was besieging Damietta[10] the holy man of God was present with some companions,[11] for they had crossed the sea in a desire for martyrdom. When therefore our soldiers were preparing to go into the fight on the day of the battle, hearing about it, the saint was deeply grieved. He said to his companion: "The Lord has showed me that if the battle takes place on such a day, it will not go well with the Christians. But if I tell them this, I will be considered a fool; if I am silent, I will not escape my conscience. What therefore seems best to you?" His companion answered, saying: "Consider it as nothing to be judged by men, for it is not only now that you will begin to be thought a fool.[12] Keep your conscience free from blame and fear God rather than men." The holy man therefore arose and approached the Christians with salutary warnings, forbidding the war, denouncing the reason for it. But truth was turned to ridicule, and they hardened their hearts and refused to be guided. They went, they joined battle, they fought, and our army was pressed hard by the enemy. In the very time of the battle, the holy man, in great suspense, made his companion go and watch the battle; and when he saw nothing the first or second time, he made him look a third time. And behold, the whole Christian army was turned to flight, and the battle ended in shame, not triumph.

So great was the number of soldiers lost in the disaster that six thousand were among the dead and captured. Compassion pressed upon the holy man over them, nor were they less regretful over the deed. But he mourned especially over the Spaniards, when he saw that their greater impetuosity in the battle had left but a few of them remaining.[13] Let the princes of the world know these things and let them know that *it is not easy to fight against God,*[14] that is, against the will of the Lord. Rashness generally ends in disaster, for since it relies on its own powers, it does not deserve help from heaven. But if victory is to be hoped for from on high, battles must be entrusted to the Spirit of God.

CHAPTER V

Of a brother whose secrets of heart Francis knew

31   At that time when the holy Francis returned from beyond the sea with Brother Leonard of Assisi as his companion, it happened that, weary and fatigued from the journey, he was riding on a donkey for a while. But his companion was following behind him, and not a little tired, he began to say within himself, giving way to a bit of humanness: "This man's parents and mine were not accustomed to play together as equals. Yet he is riding and I on foot am leading the donkey." While he was thinking this, the holy man got down from the donkey and said: "Brother, it is not right that I should ride, and you go on foot, for you were more noble and more powerful than I in the world." That brother was astounded at this and, filled with shame, he knew that he had been found out by the holy man. He cast himself at his feet and, bathed in tears, he made known his thought to him and begged his pardon.

CHAPTER VI

Of the brother over whom Francis saw a devil, and against those who withdraw themselves from the community

32   There was another brother who was quite celebrated before man and even more celebrated through grace before God. The father of all envy envied this man because of his virtues and plotted to cut down this tree that had already reached the heavens and to snatch away the crown from his hands; he went about, overturned, battered, and sifted what belonged to the brother to see if he could put some suitable obstacle before him. And so he put into his mind a desire for solitude, under the appearance of greater perfection, so that he might in the end rush upon him when he was alone and make him fall more quickly, and that, falling alone, he would have no one to lift him up.[15] Why add more details? The brother separated himself from the religion of his brothers and wandered about the world as a stranger and pilgrim. From the tunic of his habit he made a small tunic, with the capuch not sewed to the tunic, and went about thus throughout the region, despising himself in all things. But it happened that when he was going about in this way God's consolation was withdrawn from him and he was assailed with a storm of temptations. *The waters* came *in even unto* his *soul*[16] and both the inner and the outer man were made desolate, and he went about like *a bird* that makes *haste to the snare.*[17] And now he was brought close to the abyss and was being borne along to a precipice, as it were, when the eye of a fatherly providence, pitying the wretched man, *looked upon him for good.*[18] Thus he recovered his understanding through affliction, and returning to himself, he said: "Return, miserable

one, to religion, for there is your salvation." He did not wait, but immediately arose and hurried back to the bosom of his mother.

33   But when that brother came to Siena to the place of the brothers, St. Francis was there. Astonishing to say, as soon as the saint saw him, he fled from him and hurriedly shut himself up in his cell. The brothers, excited, inquired the reason for his flight. He said to them: "Why do you wonder at my flight, paying no attention to the cause? I fled to the protection of prayer to deliver the erring one. I saw in my son what rightly displeased me; but behold, now, by the grace of my Christ, all delusion has departed." The brother knelt down and admitted his guilt with shame. The holy man said to him: "May the Lord forgive you, Brother. But beware for the future that you do not separate yourself from your order and from your brothers under the plea of holiness." That brother then became a friend of the congregation and of the community, being especially attached to those communities where regular observance was more in evidence. O how great are the works of the Lord *in the council of the just and in the congregation!*[19] Indeed, in it those who are troubled are restrained, the crushed lifted up, the tepid spurred on; in it *iron sharpeneth iron,*[20] and *a brother that is helped by his brother* is set up *like a strong city;*[21] and, though you cannot see Jesus because of the worldly throng, the throng of heavenly spirits does not in any way hinder you. Only do not flee, and, faithful unto death, you *will receive the crown of life.*[22]

34   Not long thereafter something not dissimilar happened with another brother. One of the brothers would not submit himself to the vicar of St. Francis, but followed another brother as his own particular

superior. But after he had been admonished by the saint, who was present, through an intermediary person, he immediately threw himself at the feet of the vicar and, spurning his first superior, he submitted himself to the one the saint had appointed as his prelate. But the saint sighed deeply and said to his companion whom he had sent as intermediary: "I saw a devil, Brother, on the back of that disobedient brother, clutching him by the neck. Subdued by such a one sitting on his back, he had spurned the curb of obedience and was following the pulling of the reins by his rider. And," he went on, "when I prayed to the Lord for the brother, the devil suddenly left him in confusion." Such was this man's vision that, though his eyes were weak toward bodily things, they were sharp for spiritual things. And what wonder that a man who does not want to bear the Lord of majesty should be weighed down by a shameful burden? There is no middle way, I say: either you will bear a light burden, which, rather, bears you, or wickedness will sit upon you like a millstone hung around your neck,[23] heavier than a *talent of lead*.[24]

CHAPTER VII

How Francis freed the people of Greccio from wolves and hail

35   Francis liked to stay at the brothers' place at Greccio, both because he saw that it was rich by reason of its poverty and because he could give himself more freely to heavenly things in a more secluded cell hewn from a projecting rock. Here is that place where he brought back to memory the birthday of the Child of Bethlehem,[25] becoming a child with that Child. It happened, however, that the inhabitants were being annoyed by many evils, for a pack of ravening wolves was devouring not only animals but even men, and every year hail storms were devastating the fields and vineyards. One day, while he was preaching to them, Francis said: "To the honor and glory of Almighty God, hear the truth I announce to you. If every one of you confesses his sins and brings forth *fruits befitting repentance*,[26] I give you my word that every pestilence will depart and the Lord, looking kindly upon you, will grant you an increase of temporal goods. But hear this also: again I announce to you that if you are ungrateful for his gifts and *return to your vomit*,[27] the plague will be renewed, your punishment will be doubled, and even greater wrath will be let loose against you."

36 It happened, therefore, by the merits and prayers of the holy father, that from that hour the destruction ceased, the dangers passed, and neither the wolves nor the hailstorms caused any further damage. Moreover, what is greater still, if any hail came over the fields of their neighbors, it either stopped short when it got near the borders of their lands or turned aside to some other region. Now that they had peace, they were *multiplied exceedingly*[28] and filled beyond measure with temporal goods. But prosperity did what it usually does: their faces were covered with grossness and the fat of temporal things; or rather, they were blinded with dung. In the end, relapsing into even worse things, *they forgot God who saved them*.[29] But not with impunity, for the censure of divine justice punishes those who lapse into sin less severely than those who relapse. The anger of God was aroused against them and the evils that had departed returned, and over and above, there was added the sword of man and a heaven-sent sickness consumed very many of them; eventually the whole town was burned up in avenging flames.[30] Of a truth, it is just that they who turn

their backs upon the benefits they have received come to destruction.

CHAPTER VIII

How in his preaching to the Perugians Francis foretold a sedition that was to come among them; and of the praise of unity

37   After some days, when Francis was coming down once from the cell mentioned earlier,[31] he said in a complaining tone to the brothers who were there: "The men of Perugia have done many evil things to their neighbors[32] and their hearts are lifted up unto ignominy. However, the revenge of the Lord is approaching and his hand is on his sword." After a few days had passed, therefore, he arose in fervor of spirit and turned his steps toward the city of Perugia. The brothers could understand clearly that he had seen some vision in his cell. Coming therefore to Perugia, he began to preach to the people who had gathered about; but when some knights rode up on their horses, as is their custom, and crossing their weapons in a military exercise, interfered with his words, the saint turned toward them and sighing, said: "O miserable folly of wretched men who do not consider nor fear the judgment of God! But listen to what the Lord announces to you through me, poor little one. The Lord," he said, "has exalted you above all others around you; for this reason you should be kinder to your neighbors and you should live in a way more pleasing to God. But, ungrateful for God's grace, you attack your neighbors with arms, kill and plunder them. I say to you: this will not go unpunished; but, for your greater punishment, God will cause you to fall into civil war, so that one will rise against the other in mutual sedition. Wrath will teach you, for kindness has not

taught you." Not many days after this an altercation arose among them, arms were taken up against those close to them, the citizens fought against the knights, and the nobles attacked the ordinary people; the battle was fought with such unrestrained fury and slaughter that the neighbors who had been wronged grieved with them.[33] This judgment is worthy of praise, for since they had withdrawn from the One and Highest Good, it would follow necessarily that unity would not remain in them. There can be no more powerful bond in a state than pious love of God, sincere and unfeigned faith.[34]

CHAPTER IX

Of the woman to whom Francis foretold that her husband would change from bad to good

38   In those days when the man of God was going to Le Celle near Cortona,[25] a certain noble woman of the city called Volusiano[36] heard of it and hastened to him. Fatigued after a long journey, in as much as she was very *tender and delicate,*[37] she at length came to the saint. When the most holy father saw her exhaustion and heavy breathing, he pitied her and said: "What is your pleasure, lady?" But she said: "Father, bless me." And the saint said: "Are you married or unmarried?" She answered, saying: "Father, I have a husband who is very cruel and whom I must put up with as an opponent to my serving Jesus Christ; this is my chief sorrow that I cannot fulfill the good resolve that the Lord inspired in me, because my husband prevents me: therefore, I beg of you, holy man, pray for him that the divine mercy may humble his heart." The father wondered at such a virile spirit in a woman and at the spirit of an older person in a girl; and moved to pity, he said: "Go, blessed daughter, and know that you will soon

have consolation because of your husband." And he added: "Say to him on the part of God and on my own part that now is the time of salvation, and afterwards, of justice." After she had received his blessing, she went home, found her husband, and told him these things. Suddenly the Holy Spirit came upon him and he became a changed man and answered with gentleness: "Lady, let us serve God and save our souls in our home." His wife replied: "It seems to me that continence should be established in the soul as a kind of foundation and that the rest of the virtues should be built upon it." "And this," he said, "pleases me as it pleases you." For many years thereafter they lived a celibate life, and they both departed from this life happily on the same day, one as a *morning holocaust,* the other as an *evening sacrifice.*[38] Happy woman, who thus could soften her lord unto eternal life! In her is fulfilled the words of the Apostle: *The unbelieving husband is sanctified by the believing wife.*[39] But such people, if I may use a popular expression, can be counted on one's fingers today.

CHAPTER X

How Francis knew through the Spirit that one brother had given scandal to another, and how he foretold that the former would quit the order

39 Once two brothers came from the Terra di Lavoro,[40] of whom the older gave much scandal to the younger. He was not, I say, a companion, but he was a tyrant. The younger, however, bore it all with admirable silence out of love for God. But when they had come to Assisi and the younger brother had gone to St. Francis (for he was a friend of the saint), the saint said to him among other things: "How did your companion behave toward you on this journey?" He replied: "Quite well, dearest Father." But the saint said to him: "Beware, Brother, lest under the pretext of humility you should lie. For I know how he conducted himself toward you. But wait a little and you will see." The brother was very much surprised that Francis could have known through the Spirit things that had happened in his absence. After not many days, therefore, the brother who had given scandal to his brother, despising the order, was cast out into the world. Without a doubt, it is a sign of perverseness and an evident proof of a failing spiritual sense not to be of one mind with a good companion when on a journey with him.

CHAPTER XI

Of a young man who came to enter religion, but who the saint knew was not led by the Spirit of God

40 At this same time a certain young man of noble birth from Lucca[41] came to Assisi, wanting to enter the order. When he was presented to St. Francis, he begged him on bended knees and with tears to receive him. But looking upon him, the man of God immediately knew through the Spirit that he was not led by the Spirit. And he said to him: "Wretched and carnal man, why have you had the courage to lie to the Holy Spirit and to me? You weep from a carnal spirit and your heart is not with God. Go, for you have no taste for spiritual things." After he had said these things, he was told that the young man's parents were at the door seeking their son to take him home with them; and going out to them, the young man at length went away of his own will. Then the brothers wondered, praising the Lord in his holy servant.

CHAPTER XII

Of a certain cleric who was healed by Francis and of whom Francis foretold that he would suffer worse things because of his sins

41   At the time when the holy father lay ill in the palace of the bishop of Rieti,[42] a certain canon by the name of Gedeon,[43] a dissolute and worldly man, was taken ill and lay in bed amid many pains. He had himself carried before St. Francis and begged with tears to be blessed with the sign of the cross by him. The saint said to him: "Since you lived in the past according to the desires of the flesh, not according to the judgments of God, why should I sign you with the sign of the cross?" But he went on: "I sign you in the name of Christ; but know that you will suffer worse things if after you are delivered, you return to your vomit." And he added: "Because of the sin of ingratitude worse things than the first are inflicted." Therefore, after he had made the sign of the cross over him, the man who had lain there crippled arose healthy, and breaking forth in praise, he said: "I am freed." The bones of his loins, however, made a noise that many heard, as though sticks of dry wood were broken with the hand. But after a short time had elapsed, forgetful of God, he gave his body again to impurity. One evening after he had dined in the home of another of his fellow canons and was sleeping there that night, suddenly the roof of the house fell upon all of them. But the rest escaped death and only that wretched man was cut off and perished. No wonder, that, as the saint said, worse evils than the first followed, for one should be grateful over the forgiveness he has received, and a crime that is repeated displeases doubly.

CHAPTER XIII

Of a certain brother who was tempted

42   While the saint was staying at that same place, a certain spiritual brother from the custody of Marsica[44] who was troubled grievously with temptations said in his heart: "Oh, if I but had something that belonged to St. Francis with me, if only some bits of his fingernails, I believe indeed that this whole storm of temptations would disperse and peace would return, God willing." Therefore, after he had obtained permission, he went to that place and explained the situation to one of the holy father's companions. The brother answered him: "I think it would not be possible for me to give you any of his nails, because, though we cut them for him at times, he orders that they be thrown away and forbids us to keep them." But immediately the brother was called and ordered to go to the saint who was asking for him. Francis said to him: "Find a scissors for me, son, so you may cut my nails." He gave him the iron instrument which he had already taken into his hands for that purpose, and getting the parings, he brought them to the brother who had asked for them; and he, receiving them devoutly, kept them more devoutly, and he was immediately freed from every assault.

CHAPTER XIV

Of a man who offered cloth of the kind the saint had asked for before

43   In that same place the father of the poor, clad in an old tunic, said once to one of his companions whom he had appointed his guardian:[45] "I would like, Brother, that, if you can, you would find some cloth for me for a tunic." The brother, upon hearing this, thought it over in his mind how he might obtain the cloth that was so necessary and so humbly asked for. The next morning early he went to the door intending to go to the village for the cloth; and behold, a certain man was sitting at the door, wanting to speak to him. He said to the brother: "For the love of God, accept this cloth from me for six tunics; and, keeping one for yourself, distribute the rest as it pleases you for the good of my soul." Filled with joy the brother returned to Brother Francis and made known to him the gift from heaven. The father said to him: "Accept the tunics, for the man was sent for this purpose that he might help me in this way in my necessity. Thanks be to Him," he added, "who alone seems to be solicitous for us."

CHAPTER XV

How Francis invited his doctor to dinner at a time when the brothers had nothing to eat; and how the Lord suddenly supplied them abundantly; and of God's providence with regard to his own

44   When Francis was staying in a certain hermitage near Rieti, a doctor[46] visited him daily to take care of his eyes. But one day the saint said to the brothers: "Invite the doctor and give him something very good to eat." The guardian answered him, saying: "Father, we blush to say that we are ashamed to invite him, because we are now so poor." The saint replied, saying: "Do you want me to tell you again?" The doctor, who was standing by, said: "Dearest brothers, I will consider your poverty a real delicacy." The brothers hurried and placed upon the table all they had in their storeroom, namely, a little bread, not much wine, and, that they might eat a bit more sumptuously, the kitchen provided

some vegetables. Meanwhile the table of the Lord had compassion on the table of his servants. There was a knock at the door and it was answered quickly. Behold, a certain woman offered them a basket full of fine bread, fishes and lobster pies, honey and grapes. The table of the poor brothers rejoiced at the sight of these things, and keeping the common things for the next day, they ate the better things that day. With a sigh the doctor spoke, saying: "Brothers, neither you nor we of the world know this man's sanctity as we should." At length they were satisfied, but the miracle gave them greater satisfaction than the banquet. Thus the eye of the Father never despises his children, but rather, the more poor they are, the more richly does providence provide for them. The poor man is provided with a more abundant table than the tyrant, in as much as God is more generous in his gifts than man.

How Francis freed Brother Riccerio from a temptation[47]

44a A certain brother, Riccerio by name, a noble both in his conduct and by his birth, thought so much of the merits of the blessed Francis that he believed that anyone would merit divine grace if he enjoyed the favor of the saint, and that if he lacked it, he would merit the anger of God. And while he aspired so vehemently to obtain the favor of his friendship, he feared greatly lest the saint would see some hidden vice in him on account of which it would happen that he would not show him his favor. Therefore, while this fear daily weighed heavily upon him and he did not reveal his thoughts to anyone, it happened that he came one day, disturbed as usual, to the cell where the blessed Francis was praying. The man of God knew both of his coming and of his disposition, and calling the brother to him, he spoke thus: "Let no fear disturb you in the future, let no temptation upset you, son; for you are very dear to me, and among those who are especially dear to me I love you with a special affection. Come to me with confidence whenever it suits you, and feel free to leave me whenever it suits you." That brother was astonished not a little at this and he rejoiced over the words of the holy father; and thereafter he felt sure of his affection, and he grew, as he had believed, in the grace of the Savior.

CHAPTER XVI

Of the two brothers whom Francis came out of his cell to bless, knowing their wish through the Spirit

45   St. Francis had the custom of spending the whole day alone in his cell, and he did not come among the brothers unless the need for food forced him to come. But he did not come out to eat at the fixed times, for a greater hunger for contemplation more often claimed him. It happened once that two brothers who were leading lives pleasing to God came from afar to the place at Greccio. Their whole reason for coming was to see the saint and to receive from him a blessing they had long desired. Therefore when they came and did not find him because he had already withdrawn and gone to his cell, they were very greatly saddened; and because the uncertainty concerning his return would cause them a long delay, they left, attributing the whole thing to their lack of worthiness. But Francis' companions followed them and consoled them in their desolation. When they had advanced about a stone's throw from the place, the saint suddenly called after them and said to one of his companions: "Tell my brothers who came here to look back at me." Now when

these brothers turned their faces to him, he signed them with the sign of the cross and blessed them with the greatest affection. They then went on their way, praising and blessing the Lord, for they were made more joyful the more they realized that they had gotten what they wanted and had very usefully obtained a miracle.

CHAPTER XVII

How Francis brought water out of a rock by his prayer and gave it to a thirsty peasant

46   Once when the blessed Francis wanted to go to a certain hermitage that he might devote himself more freely to contemplation there, he obtained an ass from a certain poor man to ride on, because he was not a little weak. Since it was summer, the peasant, following the man of God up the mountain, became fatigued from the difficulty and the length of the trip; and before they had reached the place, he collapsed exhausted by a burning thirst. He called after the saint and begged him to have pity on him; he said he would die unless he would be refreshed by some drink. The holy man of God, who always had compassion on those who were suffering, got down without delay from the ass and kneeling upon the ground, he stretched his hands toward heaven; and he did not let up in his prayers until he felt he had been heard. "Hurry," he said to the peasant, "and you will find living water over there, which Christ has just now mercifully brought from the rock for you to drink." O how astounding is the condescension of God which readily inclines him to help his servants! The peasant drank the water that came from the rock by the power of him who had prayed, and he drew drink from the hardest rock. There had never been a flow of water there before,

and, as diligent search has proved, none could be found there afterwards. Why should we wonder that a man who is full of the Holy Spirit should show forth in himself the wonderful deeds of all the just? For, for a man who is joined with Christ by the gift of a special grace it is not something great if he does things similar to the things that have been done by other saints.

CHAPTER XVIII

Of the birds Francis fed, and how one of them perished through greed

47   One day the blessed Francis was sitting at the table with his brothers. Two little birds, one male, the other female, came up, and, solicitous about the bringing up of their newly born little ones, they took the crumbs from the table of the saint as they pleased and as they had been doing day by day. The holy man rejoiced in creatures like these and he coaxed them, as was his custom, and offered them grain solicitously. One day the father and the mother offered their little ones to the brothers, as having been reared at their expense, and after they had given their little ones to the brothers, they did not appear in that place again. The little birds grew tame among the brothers and they perched on their hands, not indeed as guests, but as belonging to that house. They avoided the sight of secular people and professed themselves foster children only of the brothers. The saint observed this and was astonished, and he invited the brothers to rejoice. "See," he said, "what our brothers with the red breasts do, as though they were endowed with reason. For they have said: 'Behold, brothers, we present to you our little ones who have been nourished with your crumbs. Do with them what you wish. We are going

to another home." They became completely tame among the brothers and took their food together with them. But greed broke up the peace, in that the greed of the larger bird persecuted the smaller ones. For when the bigger one had had his fill as he wished, he drove the rest away from the food. "See," said the father, "see what this greedy one is doing. Even though he is full and satisfied, he envies his hungry brothers. He will come to a bad end yet." The revenge followed quickly upon the words of the saint. The disturber of his brothers got up on a vessel of water to drink and immediately fell into the water and suffocating, died. No cat was found nor any beast that would touch the bird that had been cursed by the saint. Greed in men is surely a horrible evil if it is punished in such a way in birds. The words of the saints too are to be feared if punishment follows upon them with such ease.

CHAPTER XIX

How all Francis' predictions about Brother Bernard were fulfilled

48   Another time Francis spoke prophetically in the following way about Brother Bernard who had been the second brother in the order:[48] "I tell you that the most subtle demons and the worst among all the other spirits have been assigned to Brother Bernard to try him; but though they are constantly on watch to make this star fall from heaven, there will be a different end to the affair. He will indeed be troubled, tormented, afflicted; but in the end he will come out of all these things triumphant." And he added: "About the time of his death, all the disturbances will be removed, every temptation will have been overcome, and he will enjoy a wonderful tranquillity and peace; and having run his course, he will go happily to Christ." Of a truth it happened this way; his death was made bright by miracles and what the man of God had predicted was fulfilled to the letter. For which reason the brothers said at his death: "Truly, this brother was not known while he lived." But we leave to others the singing of the praises of this Bernard.

CHAPTER XX

Of a brother who was tempted and who wanted to have something written in the saint's own hand

49 While the saint was living on Mount Alverna alone in a cell, one of his companions[49] longed with a great desire to have something encouraging from the words of the Lord noted down briefly in the hand of St. Francis. For he believed he would escape by this means a serious temptation that troubled him, not indeed of the flesh but of the spirit, or at least that he would be able to resist it more easily. Languishing with such a desire, he nevertheless was afraid to make known the matter to the most holy father. But what man did not tell Francis, the Spirit revealed to him. One day Blessed Francis called this brother and said: "Bring me some paper and ink, for I want to write down the words of the Lord and his praises which I have meditated upon in my heart." After these things he had asked for were quickly brought to him, he wrote down with his own hand the *Praises of God* and the words he wanted, and lastly a blessing for that brother, saying: "Take this paper and guard it carefully till the day of your death." Immediately every temptation was put to flight, and the writing was kept and afterwards it worked wonderful things.[50]

CHAPTER XXI

Of that same brother whose desire Francis fulfilled by giving him his tunic

50 For that same brother another remarkable thing was done by the holy father. For at the time when Francis lay ill in the palace at Assisi,[51] the aforementioned brother thought to himself, saying: "See, the father is approaching death and my soul would be greatly comforted if I could have the tunic of my father after his death." As though the desire of his heart had been a petition by word of mouth, the blessed Francis called him after a little while, saying: "I give you this tunic; take it that it may be yours for the future. Though I wear it while I am alive, it will be yours at my death." Astounded at such great insight on the part of his father, the brother was comforted at length in receiving the tunic, and holy devotion afterwards carried it into France.[52]

CHAPTER XXII

Of the parsley that was found at night among the wild herbs at Francis' command

51 One night during his last illness Francis wanted to eat some parsley and he humbly asked for it. But when the cook had been called to bring some, he replied that he could not gather any in the garden at that time, saying: "I have picked parsley every day and I have cut so much of it that I can hardly distinguish any even in the daylight; how would I be able to tell it from the other herbs in the dark?" The saint said to him: "Go, Brother, and do not worry, but bring back the first herbs you lay your hands on." The brother went into the garden and picked the wild herbs which he first happened on though he could not see them, and he brought them into the house. The brothers looked at the wild herbs, turned them about carefully, and found among them some leafy and tender parsley. The saint ate a little of it and was much comforted. The father said to his brothers: "My brothers, obey a command at the very first word, and do not wait for what has been said to be repeated. Do not say that something is impossible, for, if I should command something that is beyond your strength, obedience would not lack strength." To this extent did the Spirit entrust to him the privilege of the spirit of prophecy.

CHAPTER XXIII

Of the famine Francis foretold would come after his death

52   At times holy men are impelled by an impulse of the Holy Spirit to speak certain wonderful things about themselves, when, for example, either the glory of God demands that they reveal something or the law of charity demands it for the edification of their neighbor. Hence it was that one day the blessed father made known to a certain brother whom he loved a great deal this word which he brought from the secret chamber of the Divine Majesty to which he was admitted familiarly: "Today," he said, "there is upon earth a servant of God for whose sake, as long as he lives, the Lord will not permit famine to rage among men." There was no vanity about this, but it was a holy recital which that holy charity that *is not self-seeking*[53] uttered unto our edification in holy and modest words; nor is that privilege of such wonderful love on the part of Christ toward his servant to be passed over in useless silence. For all of us who saw it know what quiet

and peaceful times passed while the servant of Christ lived and how they were filled with such an abundance of all good things. For there was no *famine of the word of God,*[54] since the words of preachers were greatly filled with power and the hearts of all the hearers were so approved before God. Examples of holiness shone forth in religious life; the hypocrisy of *whited sepulchres*[55] had not yet infected so many holy men, nor had the learning of those *disguising themselves*[56] brought in such curiosity. Deservedly, therefore, did temporal goods abound, since eternal things were so truly loved by all.

53   But after he had been taken away, the order of things was completely reversed and everything was changed; for *wars and insurrections*[57] prevailed everywhere, and a carnage of many deaths suddenly passed through several kingdoms.[58] The horror of famine too spread far and wide, and the cruelty of it, which exceeds the bitterness of everything else, consumed very many.[59] Necessity then turned everything into food and compelled human teeth to chew things that were not even customarily eaten by animals. Bread was made from the shells of nuts and the bark of trees; and, to put it mildly, paternal piety, under the compulsion of famine, did not mourn the death of a child, as became clear from the confession of a certain man.[60] But that it might be made clearly manifest who that faithful servant was, for the love of whom the divine chastisement suspended the hand of its vengeance, the blessed father Francis, just a few days after his death, clearly revealed to that brother to whom he had predicted while he was alive the destruction to come that he himself was that servant of God. For one night, while that brother slept, he called to him in a clear voice, saying: "Brother, a famine is coming which, while I was alive, the Lord did not permit to come upon the earth." The brother awoke at the sound of the voice and later related everything in order as it had happened. On the third night after this the saint appeared again to him and spoke like words.

CHAPTER XXIV

Of the saint's splendor and of our ignorance

54 It should not appear strange to anyone that the prophet of our time should stand forth with such privileges; in fact, freed from the darkness of earthly things and having brought into subjection the pleasures of the flesh, his mind was free to fly to the greatest heights and pure enough to enter into the light. Thus, illumined by the rays of eternal light, he drew from the Word what resounded in his words. Indeed, how different we are today, we who are wrapped in darkness and do not know the necessary things! What do you think is the reason, except that we, being friends of the flesh, are bogged down in the dust of worldliness? For, if *we lift up our hearts with our hands*[61] to heaven, if we would choose to be inclined to eternal things, we would perhaps know what we are ignorant of, namely, God and ourselves. Bogged down in the mire, we can only see the mire; but with our eyes fixed on heaven, we cannot possibly not see heavenly things.

OF POVERTY

CHAPTER XXV

Of the praise of poverty

55 While he was in this valley of tears, that blessed father considered the common wealth of the sons of men as trifles, and, ambitious for higher things, he longed for poverty with all his heart. Looking upon poverty as especially dear to the Son of God, though it was spurned throughout the whole world, he sought to espouse it in perpetual charity. Therefore, after he had become a lover of her beauty, he not only left his father and mother, but even put aside all things, that he might cling to her more closely as his spouse and that *they might be two in one* spirit.[62] Therefore he gathered her to himself with chaste embraces and not even for an hour did he allow himself not to be her husband. This, he would tell his sons, is the way to perfection, this the pledge and earnest of eternal riches.[63] There was no one so desirous of gold as he was desirous of poverty, and no one so solicitous in guarding his treasure as he was solicitous in guarding this pearl of the Gospel. In this, above all, would his sight be offended, if he saw anything contrary to poverty in his brothers either at home or away from home. Indeed, from the very beginning of his religious life unto his death he was rich in having only a tunic, a cord, and drawers, and he had nothing else.[64] His poor habit showed where he was laying up his riches. With this he went his way happy, secure, and confident; he rejoiced to exchange a perishable treasure for the hundredfold.[65]

OF THE POVERTY OF HOUSES

CHAPTER XXVI

56   He taught his brothers to make poor dwellings, of wood, not of stone, and to erect small places according to a humble plan. Often, indeed, speaking of poverty, he would propose to his brothers this saying of the Gospel: *The foxes have dens and the birds of the air have nests; but the Son of Man has nowhere to lay his head.*[66]

CHAPTER XXVII

Of the house at the Portiuncula which he started to destroy

57   Once when a chapter had to be held at St. Mary of the Portiuncula and the time was already at hand, the people of Assisi, seeing that there was no house there, very quickly built a house for the chapter, without the knowledge and in the absence of the man of God. Upon his return, the father looked at the house and took it ill and bewailed it in no gentle tones. Then he himself went up first to destroy the house; he got up on the roof and with strong hands tore off the slates and tiles. He also commanded the brothers to come up and to tear down completely this monstrous thing contrary to poverty. For he used to say that whatever might have the appearance of arrogance in that place would quickly spread throughout the order and be accepted as a model by all. He therefore would have destroyed the house to its very foundations, except that a knight who was standing by cooled the ardor of his spirit when he said that the house belonged to the commune and not to the brothers.

CHAPTER XXVIII

Of the house at Bologna from which Francis drove out even the sick

58   Once when he was returning from Verona and wanted to pass through Bologna, Francis heard that a house had been built there recently. In as much as it was said that it was "the brothers' house," he turned aside and not going on to Bologna, he went another way. But he ordered the brothers to leave that house with haste. Wherefore they abandoned the house and not even the sick remained but

were cast out with the others. Neither was permission given to go back in, until the lord Hugo, who was at that time bishop of Ostia[67] and legate in Lombardy,[68] proclaimed publicly that the house belonged to him. He who at that time was turned out of the house sick gives testimony and writes it down.[69]

CHAPTER XXIX

How Francis refused to enter a cell to which his name had been attached

59   Francis did not want his brothers to live in any place unless there was a definite patron to whom the ownership pertained. For he always wanted the laws for strangers to be observed by his sons, namely, to be gathered under a roof that belongs to another, to go about peaceably, to thirst after their fatherland. Now in the hermitage at Sarteano,[70] when a brother was asked by another brother where he was coming from, he said that he was coming from the cell of Brother Francis. Upon hearing this, the saint said: "Since you have attached my name to a cell, appropriating it thereby to me, look for another one for me to live in, for I will not stay in it any more. The Lord," he said, "when he was in the desert[71] where he prayed and fasted for forty days, did not set up a cell for himself there, nor any house, but he lived beneath the rock of the mountain. We can do without ownership according to the form prescribed,[72] even though we cannot live without the use of houses."

OF THE POVERTY OF FURNITURE

CHAPTER XXX

60   This man not only despised arrogance with

regard to houses, but he also had a great horror of many and exquisite furnishings in the houses. He wanted nothing on the table, nothing in the utensils, that would bring back memories of the world. Everything should show forth our state as pilgrims, everything bespeak our exile.

CHAPTER XXXI

An instance where the table at Greccio was prepared on Easter day, and of how Francis showed himself a pilgrim after the example of Christ

61 It happened one Easter that the brothers at the hermitage of Greccio prepared the table more carefully than they usually did with white linens and glassware. Coming down from his cell, the father came to the table and saw that it was placed high and decorated extravagantly. But he did not smile at the smiling table. Stealthily and little by little he retraced his steps, put on the hat of a poor man who was there, and taking a staff in his hand, he went outside. He waited outside at the door until the brothers began to eat; for they were in the habit of not waiting for him when he did not come at the signal. When they had begun to eat, this truly poor man cried out at the door: "For the love of the Lord God," he said, "give an alms to this poor, sick wanderer." The brothers answered: "Come in, man, for love of him whom you have invoked." He immediately entered and appeared before them as they were eating. But what astonishment, do you think, the beggar caused these inhabitants? The beggar was given a dish, and sitting alone, he put the dish in the ashes. "Now I am sitting as a Friar Minor should sit," he said. And to the brothers he said: "We should be moved by the examples of poverty of the Son of God more than other religious. I saw the table prepared and decorated, and I knew it was not the table of poor men who beg from door to door."

This series of actions proves that he was like that other pilgrim who was alone in Jerusalem that day.[73] But he made the hearts of the disciples burn when he spoke to them.[74]

CHAPTER XXXII

Against curiosity of books

62 Francis taught that the testimony of God should be sought in books, not something precious; edification, not beauty. However, he wanted only a few to be had, such as would be suited to the needs of poor brothers. Wherefore, when a certain minister asked that some magnificent and very valuable books be kept with his permission, he heard this from him: "I do not want to lose the book of the Gospel, which we have promised, for your books. You may do as you please, but my permission will not be made a trap."

ON POVERTY IN BEDS

CHAPTER XXXIII

An instance concerning the lord of Ostia, and praise of him

63 Finally in couches and beds such abundant poverty reigned that he who had a few half-torn rags over some straw considered that he had a wedding bed. Whence it happened at the time a chapter was being held at St. Mary of the Porticuncula, that the lord of Ostia,[75] together with a crowd of knights and clerics, came to visit the brothers. Seeing how the brothers lay upon the ground and noticing that their beds might be taken for the lairs of wild beasts, he wept bitterly and said before all present: "See, here the brothers sleep." And he added: "What will become of us, miserable as we are, who make use of such superfluity?" All who were present were moved to tears and departed greatly edified. This was that lord of Ostia who after he was eventually made the greatest door in the Church resisted always her foes until he returned his blessed soul to heaven as a sacred victim.[76] O pious breast, O bowels of mercy! Placed on high, he grieved that he had no high merits, when, as a matter of fact, he was higher in virtue than in position.[77]

CHAPTER XXXIV

What happened to St. Francis one night when he used a feather pillow

64 Since we have made mention of beds, something else occurred that might be useful to tell. From the time this saint was converted to Christ, he forgot the things of the world and he would not lie on a mattress nor would he have a feather pillow under his head. Neither sickness nor hospitality from outsiders lifted this restriction. But it happened at the hermitage at Greccio, when he was suffering more than usual with the infirmity of his eyes, that he was forced against his will to use a little pillow. On the first night, at an early morning hour, the saint called his companion and said to him: "I have not been able to sleep tonight, Brother, nor could I remain erect at prayer. My head shakes, my knees grow weak and my whole body is shaking as though I had eaten bread made out of darnel.[78] I believe," he said, "that the devil dwells in this pillow that I have under my head. Take it away, because I do not want the devil at my head any longer." The brother sympathized with the complaint of his father and caught the pillow as it was thrown to him to take it away. Therefore going out, he suddenly lost his speech and was oppressed and bound up with such horror that he could neither move his feet from the place nor move his arms in any way. After a while, he was called by the saint, who knew these things, and he was set free and came back and narrated what he had suffered. The saint said to him: "In the evening, while I was saying Compline, I knew clearly that the devil was coming to my cell." And again: "Our enemy is very clever and deeply subtle; when he cannot do us harm inwardly in our soul, he gives the body at least something to murmur about." Let those hear who everywhere are preparing little pillows, so that, wherever they may fall, they may be caught on something soft. The devil willingly follows wealth of things; he likes to stand at expensive beds, especially where necessity does not demand such and profession forbids such. No less does the ancient serpent flee the man who is naked, either because he despises association with the poor, or because he fears the heights of poverty. If a brother gives heed to this that the devil lurks in feathers, his head will be satisfied with straw.

INSTANCES AGAINST MONEY

CHAPTER XXXV

A sharp correction of a brother who touched money with his hand

65   That friend of God despised very greatly all the things of this world, but he cursed money more than all other things. Consequently, from the beginning of his conversion he held it in special contempt and always said it was to be shunned as the devil himself. This saying was given by him to his followers that they should value dung and money at the same price of love.[79] It happened, therefore, one day that a certain secular person entered the church of St. Mary of the Portiuncula to pray, and he left some money near the cross as an offering. When he had gone, one of the brothers simply touched it with his hand and threw it on the window sill. The saint heard what the brother had done, and the brother, seeing that he was found out, hurried to ask pardon, and casting himself upon the ground, he offered himself to stripes. The saint rebuked him and upbraided him most severely because he had touched the money. He commanded him to lift the money from the window sill with his mouth and to place it with his mouth on the asses' dung outside the walls of the place. While that brother gladly fulfilled the command, fear filled the hearts of all who heard of it. All held in greater contempt for the future what was put on the level of dung and they were spurred on daily to contempt by fresh examples.

CHAPTER XXXVI

The punishment of a brother who picked up money

66   Two brothers were once going along the way together and they drew near to the hospital of the lepers. They found a coin on the road and they stopped and discussed between them what was to be done with the dung. One of them, laughing at the conscience of the other brother, tried to take the coin to offer it to the lepers greedy for money.[80] His companion forbade him, lest he be deceived by false piety, and quoted to the rash brother the words of the rule from which it is very clear that a coin that is found is to be trampled on as though it were dust.[81] But he hardened his mind against the admonitions, for by custom he was always a stiff-necked person. He spurned the rule, bent down and took the coin. But he did not escape divine judgment. Immediately he lost his speech; he ground his teeth, but he could not speak. Thus does punishment show up the empty headed; thus does punishment teach the proud to obey the commands of our father. Finally, after he had thrown the foul stuff away, he washed his besoiled lips with the waters of repen-

418

tance and they were loosed to offer praise. There is an old proverb that says: *Correct the fool and he will be your friend.*[82]

CHAPTER XXXVII

The rebuke of a brother who wanted to keep money on the plea of necessity

67   At one time the vicar of the holy father, Peter of Catania,[83] seeing that St. Mary of the Portiuncula was visited by a great number of brothers from afar and that there were not sufficient alms to provide for their needs, said to St. Francis: "Brother, I do not know what I will do, for with these brothers who have come here in such masses from all over, I do not have enough to provide for them properly. May it please you, I beg of you, that some of the goods of the entering novices be kept aside so that we might have recourse to them at the opportune time." The saint answered: "Away with kindness of this kind, dearest Brother, that would act wrongly against the rule for anyone's sake."[84] And the former said: "What then shall I do?" Francis said: "Strip the altar of the Blessed Virgin and take away its many ornaments, since you cannot otherwise come to the help of the needy. Believe me, she would be more pleased to have the Gospel of her son kept and her altar stripped than that the altar should be ornamented and her son despised. The Lord will send someone who will give back to our mother the ornaments he has lent to us."

CHAPTER XXXVIII

Of money that was turned into a snake

68   Once when the man of God was passing through Apulia near Bari, he found a large purse in

the road, full of money, such as is called in the
vocabulary of merchants a money belt.[85] The saint
was admonished by his companion and urgently persuaded that the purse should be taken from the
ground and the money given to the poor. His pity
for the poor was aroused and the mercy that could
be shown to the poor men by giving the money to
them was praised. The saint refused absolutely to
do this and he said it was a trick of the devil. "It is
not lawful, son," he said, "to take something that
belongs to another; and to give away what belongs
to another merits the punishment of sin, not the
glory of merit." They withdrew from the place and
hastened to complete the journey they had begun.
But the brother was not yet satisfied, deluded as he
was by empty pity; he continued to suggest trans-
gression. The saint consented to return to the place,
not to fulfill the brother's wish, but to demonstrate
to a fool the divine mystery. He called a certain
young man, who was sitting on a well along the way,
so that *in the mouth of two or three witnesses*[86] the
mystery of the Trinity might be made clear. When
the three had come to the purse, they saw it filled
with money. The saint forbade any of them to go
near, so that the deceit of the devil might be made
known by the power of prayer. Withdrawing to the
distance *of about a stone's throw,*[87] he gave himself to
holy prayer. Coming back from his prayer, he commanded the brother to lift the purse, which, as he had
prayed, contained a snake instead of the money.
The brother shook all over and was astounded, and
I know not what he was expecting; something unusual was in his mind. Driving away the hesitation
in his heart by his fear of obedience, he took the
purse in his hands. And behold, a not very small
serpent jumped out of the purse and showed the
brother the deception of the devil. The saint said

to him: "Money to God's servants, Brother, is nothing else but a devil and a poisonous snake."

OF POVERTY OF GARMENTS

CHAPTER XXXIX

How the saint rebuked those clothed in soft and fine garments by his word and example

69   This man, endowed with 'power from on high, was warmed inwardly by a divine fire much more than outwardly by bodily clothing. He cursed those in the order who were clothed with three garments or who, without necessity, used soft garments. Such a necessity, however, that was created by pleasure rather than by reason he would say was a sign of an extinguished spirit. "When the spirit becomes tepid," he said, "and gradually grows cold toward grace, flesh and blood necessarily *seek their own interests.*[88] For what remains," he said, "if the soul does not find its delight, but that the flesh should turn to its delights? And then the animal appetite satisfies the craving of necessity, then carnal feeling forms the conscience." And he would add: "Suppose a real necessity comes upon my brother, or some want takes hold of him; if he is quick to satisfy it and thereby to put it a long way away from him, what reward will he receive? He had indeed an opportunity of gaining merit, but he deliberately proved that it did not please him." With these and like words he would strike through to those unfamiliar with necessities, since not to put up with necessities patiently is nothing more than to turn back to Egypt.[89]

Finally, under no circumstances did he want the brothers to have more than two tunics,[90] which, however, he granted might have patches sewn to them.[91] He commanded them to despise fine clothing and those who did not do so he rebuked very sharply before all; and that such might be confounded by his own example, he sewed some rough sackcloth over his own tunic. He asked too that at his death the tunic he would be buried in be covered with sackcloth.[92]

But he permitted the brothers who were forced by sickness or other necessity to have a soft tunic against the skin, in such a way, however, that outwardly the roughness and poorness of the habit be preserved. For he would say: "So much yet will rigor be relaxed and lukewarmness hold sway that the sons of the poor father will not even be ashamed to wear scarlet garments, the color alone being changed." For this reason, we *your children that are strayed*,[93] do not lie to you, father; much more our *iniquity hath lied to itself*.[94] For see, it is now clearer than the light and it grows with each day.

CHAPTER XL

Francis said that those who depart from Poverty must be brought back by experiencing need

70   At times the saint would repeat: "In as far as the brothers depart from poverty, in so much will the world depart from them, and they will seek," he said, "and not find. But if they embrace my Lady Poverty, the world will provide for them, because they have been given to the world unto its salvation." And again: "There is a contract between the world and the brothers: the brothers must give the world a good example, the world must provide for their needs. When they break faith and withdraw their good example, the world will withdraw its hand in a just censure."

The man of God feared a multitude in his solicitude for poverty, for a multitude has the appearance of wealth, if indeed it is not in fact wealth. Hence he used to say: "Oh, if it were possible, my wish would be that the world would see the Friars Minor but rarely and be filled with wonder at the smallness of their number!" Therefore, bound to the Lady Poverty by an indissoluble bond, he looked for her dowry not in the present life, but in the future. He used to chant with more fervent affections and greater rejoicing those psalms that speak of poverty, for instance: *The patience of the poor shall not perish forever,*[95] and *Let the poor see and rejoice.*[96]

OF THE SEEKING OF ALMS

CHAPTER XLI

How Francis praised the seeking of alms

71   The holy father made use of alms begged from door to door[97] much more willingly than those offered spontaneously. He would say that shame in begging is the enemy of salvation, and he affirmed that that kind of shame in begging which does not withdraw the foot is holy. He praised the blush that mounts the modest forehead, but not one who allows himself to be confused by shame. At times exhorting his brothers to go begging for alms, he would use these words: "Go," he said, "for at this last hour the Friars Minor have been lent to the world, that the elect might fulfill in them what will be commended by the Judge: Because *as long as you did it for one of these, the least of my brethren, you did it for me.*"[98] Wherefore he said that the order had been privileged by the Great Prophet,[99] who spoke its name so plainly.[100] Therefore he wanted his brothers to live not only in the cities, but also in

hermitages where all might be given the opportunity to gain merit and the veil of excuse might be stripped from wicked ones.[101]

CHAPTER XLII

Francis' example in begging alms

72   So that he might not offend even once that holy spouse,[102] the servant of the Most High used to do this: if he was invited by lords and was to be honored with a more lavish table, he would first beg some scraps of bread from the houses of neighbors, and thus enriched by want, he would hasten to the table. Asked now and then why he did this, he would say that he would not give up a permanent inheritance for a fief loaned to him for an hour.[103] "It is poverty," he said, "that makes us heirs and kings of the kingdom of heaven, not your false riches."[104]

CHAPTER XLIII

The example Francis gave in the court of the lord of Ostia

73   Once when St. Francis visited Pope Gregory of happy memory, when the latter was still placed in a lower station, and the hour of dinner was at hand, he went out for alms, and returning, placed some of the scraps of black bread on the bishop's table. When the bishop saw this, he was somewhat ashamed, above all because of the newly invited guests. The father, however, with a joyous countenance distributed the alms he had received to the knights and the chaplains gathered about the table; all of them accepted the alms with wonderful devotion, and some of them ate them, others kept them out of reverence. When the dinner was finished, the bishop arose and taking the man of God to

an inner room, he raised his arms and embraced him. "My Brother," he said, "why did you bring shame on me in the house that is yours and your brothers by going out for alms?" The saint said to him: "Rather I have shown you honor, for I have honored a greater lord. For the Lord is well pleased with poverty, and above all with that poverty that is voluntary. For I have a royal dignity and a special nobility, namely, to follow the Lord who, *being rich, became poor for us.*"[105] And he added: "I get more delight from a poor table that is furnished with small alms than from great tables on which dainty foods are placed almost without number." Then, greatly edified, the bishop said to the saint: "Son, do what seems good in your eyes, for the Lord is with you."

CHAPTER XLIV

Francis' exhortation by example and by precept to seek alms

74   In the beginning Francis would at times go out alone for alms to discipline himself and to spare the bashfulness of his brothers. But when he saw that some were not attending to their vocation as they should, he once said: "Dearest brothers, the Son of God was more noble than we and he made himself poor for us in this world. We have chosen the way of poverty out of love for him; we should not be ashamed to go out to beg for alms. It is not right for the heirs of the kingdom to be ashamed of their heavenly inheritance. I say to you, there will be many noble and wise men who will join our order and who will consider it an honor to beg for alms. You, therefore, who are the first fruits among them, should rejoice and be glad and not refuse to do what you are handing down for these holy men to do."

CHAPTER XLV

How Francis rebuked a brother who refused to beg

75   The blessed Francis frequently said that a true Friar Minor should not be long without going out to beg alms. "And the more noble my son is," he said, "the more ready should he be to go, for in this way will merits be heaped up for him." There was a certain brother in a certain place who never went out for alms but always ate more than several together at table. When the saint observed that he was a friend of the belly, one who shared the fruits without sharing the labor, he once said to him: "Go your way, brother fly, for you want to eat the sweat of your brothers and to do nothing in God's work. You are like brother drone who wants to be first to eat the honey, though he does not do the work of the bees." When that carnal man saw that his gluttony was discovered, he went back to the world that he had not as yet given up. For he left the order, and he who was a nothing at begging is no longer a brother; and he who ate more than several together has become a devil in many different ways.

CHAPTER XLVI

How Francis met a brother carrying alms and kissed his shoulder

76   Another time, at the Portiuncula, when a certain brother returned from Assisi with an alms, he began to break forth in song as he neared the place and to praise the Lord in a loud voice. Upon hearing this, the saint jumped up quickly and ran out and kissed the shoulder of the brother; he then put the sack on his own shoulder. "Blessed be my brother," he said, "who goes out readily, begs humbly, and returns rejoicing."

CHAPTER XLVII

How Francis persuaded some knights to seek alms

77   When the blessed Francis was full of infirmities and already approaching his end, he was at the place at Nocera.[106] The people of Assisi sent messengers there and demanded to get him back, lest they give their glory in the body of the man of God to another. As the knights were bringing him reverently on horseback, they came to a certain very poor village, Satriano by name.[107] Here, since hunger and the hour demanded food, they went out, but found nothing for sale; coming back to the blessed Francis, they said: "You must give us something from your alms, for we could find nothing to buy." The saint replied and said: "You find nothing because you trust more in your flies than in God." For he called money flies. "Go back," he said, "to the houses which you visited and offering God's love in place of money, beg humbly for an alms. Do not be ashamed, for all things have been given to us as an alms after sin, and that great Almsgiver bestows his gifts with loving kindness to the worthy and the unworthy." The knights put aside their shame and asking for an alms with readiness, they bought more with the love of God than with money. All gave gladly, and hunger had no power where abundant poverty prevailed.

CHAPTER XLVIII

How a piece of capon was changed into a fish at Alessandria

78   In giving alms Francis was concerned with the profit of souls rather than with aid to the body, and he made himself an example to the rest no less in giving than in receiving. For when he came to Ales-

sandria in Lombardy to preach the word of God and was given hospitality by a certain God-fearing man of praiseworthy reputation, he was asked by him for the sake of observing the holy Gospel to eat of everything put before him.[108] Overcome by the devotion of his host, Francis graciously consented to do so. The host went in haste and carefully prepared a capon seven years old for the man of God to eat. While the patriarch of the poor was sitting at the table and the family was rejoicing, suddenly there appeared at the door *a son of Belial*,[109] poor in all grace, pretending poverty in all necessary things. He proposed craftily the love of God in his asking for alms and in a tearful voice demanded that he be helped for God's sake. The saint held that name blessed above all things and sweeter than honey. Very agreeably he took up a piece of the bird that had been set before him and putting it on some bread, he gave it to the beggar. Why add more? That unhappy man kept the gift to bring reproach upon the saint.

79   The next day, the saint preached the word of God to the gathered people, as was his custom. Suddenly that wicked man began to grumble and tried to show that piece of capon to all the people. "Behold," he cried out, "what kind of man this Francis is who preaches and whom you honor as a saint. Look at the meat he gave me yesterday evening while he was eating." All the people cried out against that wicked man and they reproached him as being possessed by the devil. As a matter of fact, what he trying to tell them was a piece of capon appeared to the people to be a fish. The wretched man himself, astounded by the miracle, was forced to admit what the rest were saying. That unhappy man finally blushed with shame and washed away the exposed crime by his penitence. Before all the

people he begged pardon from the saint, making known to him his evil intention. The meat was changed back to its proper species again after that deceitful man had returned to his right mind.

CHAPTER XLIX

An instance of one whom the saint rebuked for giving away his property to his relatives and not to the poor

80   The saint instructed those who came to the order that first they should give a *notice of dismissal*[110] to the world by offering first their outward possessions to God and then themselves inwardly. Only those who had given away all their goods and retained absolutely nothing did he admit to the order, both on account of the word of the holy Gospel[111] and in order that no scandal would arise over any treasures kept back.

81   It happened in the Marches of Ancona that after Francis had preached there a certain man came humbly asking to be admitted into the order. The saint said to him: "If you wish to be joined with the poor, first distribute your possessions to the poor of the world." When he heard this, the man left, and, impelled by a carnal love, he distributed his goods to his relatives and gave nothing to the poor. It happened that when he came back and told the saint of his generous liberality, the father laughed at him and said: "Go on your way, brother fly, for you have not yet left your home and your relatives. You gave your goods to your relatives and you have defrauded the poor; you are not worthy to be numbered among the holy poor. You have begun with the flesh, you have laid an unsound foundation on

which to build a spiritual structure." That carnal man returned to his own and got back his goods which he did not want to give to the poor and for that reason he abandoned very quickly his virtuous purpose. That same kind of pitiful distribution deceives many today who seek a blessed life with a worldly beginning. For no one consecrates himself to God for the purpose of making his relatives rich, but to acquire life by the fruit of his good works, redeeming his sins with the price of compassion.

For Francis often taught that if the brothers were in want they should rather have recourse to others than to those who are entering the order, first of all for the sake of example, then to avoid all appearance of base advantage.

OF A VISION FRANCIS HAD ABOUT POVERTY

CHAPTER L

82   It pleases me to tell here of a vision the saint had that is worthy to be remembered. One night, after he had prayed for a long time, sleep gradually overtook him. That holy soul was taken into *the sanctuary of God*[112] and he saw *in a dream*,[113] among other things, a certain woman that looked like this: her head seemed to be of gold, her bosom and arms of silver, her abdomen of crystal, and the rest from there on down of iron. She was tall of stature, delicately and symmetrically framed. But this woman of such beautiful form was covered over with a soiled mantle. Getting up in the morning, the blessed father told the vision to that holy man Brother Pacificus,[114] but he did not explain what it meant.

Although many have interpreted this vision as they saw fit, I believe it would not be amiss to hold to the interpretation of Brother Pacificus, which the Holy Spirit suggested to him while he listened. "This beautiful woman," he said, "is the beautiful soul of St. Francis. The golden head is his contemplation and his wisdom regarding eternal things. The bosom and arms of silver are the *words of the Lord*,[115] which he meditated on in his heart and fulfilled in his actions. The crystal, because of its rigidity, signifies sobriety, and because of its brightness, chastity. Iron is the greatest perseverance. But take the soiled mantle to be his despised little body with which his precious soul is covered."

Many, however, having the spirit of God, understand this woman to represent poverty, the spouse of our father. "The reward of glory," they say, "made her golden; the praise of her fame made her silver; the profession of poverty both outward and inward and without treasures made her crystal; final perseverance, iron. But the judgment of carnal men wove a sordid mantle for this renowned woman."

Many adapt this vision to the order, following Daniel's succession of periods of time.[116] But that the vision refers to our father is apparent especially from this fact that, avoiding any arrogance, he refused absolutely to interpret it. Indeed, if it had pertained to the order, he would not have passed over it with complete silence.

OF ST. FRANCIS' COMPASSION FOR THE POOR

CHAPTER LI

Of his compassion for the poor and how he envied those poorer than himself

83 What tongue can tell how great was this man's compassion toward the poor? Truly, he had an inborn kindness which was doubled by a kindness given him from on high. Therefore the soul of Francis melted toward the poor, and to those to whom he could not extend a helping hand, he at least showed his affection. Whatever he saw in anyone of want, whatever of penury, he transferred in his mind, by a quick change, to Christ. Thus in all the poor he saw the Son of the poor lady,[117] and he bore naked in his heart him whom she bore naked in her hands. But though he had laid aside all envy, he could not be without envy of poverty. If indeed he saw someone poorer than himself, he was immediately envious, and in the struggle for complete poverty he feared to be outdone by another.

84   It happened one day when the man of God was going about preaching that he met a certain poor man along the way. When he saw his nakedness, he was struck with compunction, and he turned to his companion, saying: "This man's want brings great shame to us and rebukes our poverty severely." His companion replied: "For what reason, Brother?" And the saint replied with a sad voice: "For my wealth, for my spouse, I chose poverty; but see, poverty shines forth more brightly in this man. Are you ignorant of the fact that the word has gone about the world that we are the poorest of men for Christ's sake? But this poor man proves that the fact is otherwise." O enviable envy! O emulation to be emulated by his sons! This is not that envy that is grieved over the goods of others; it is not that envy that is darkened by the rays of the sun; not that envy that is opposed to kindness; not that envy that is tortured by spite. Do you think that evangelical poverty has nothing about it to be envied? It has Christ and through him it has *all things in all.*[118] Why do you pant after revenues, modern cleric? Tomorrow you will know that Francis was rich, when you will find in your hand the revenues of torments.

CHAPTER LII

How Francis corrected a brother who spoke ill of a poor man

85   Another day when Francis was preaching, a certain poor and infirm man came to the place. Pitying his double affliction, namely, his want and his feebleness, Francis began to speak with his companion about poverty. And when, suffering with the sufferer, Francis' heart had become deeply afflicted, the companion of the saint said to him: "Brother, it is true that this man is poor, but it may also be true that nowhere in the whole province is there a man who is richer in his desires." Immediately the saint rebuked him and said to him when he admitted his guilt: "Hurry quickly and take off your tunic and cast yourself down at the feet of this poor man and acknowledge your guilt. And do not only ask for forgiveness, but ask him also to pray for you." He obeyed and went to make satisfaction and he came back. The saint said to him: "When you see a poor man, Brother, an image is placed before you of the Lord and his poor mother. So too in the sick consider the infirmities which the Lord took upon himself for us." Indeed, there was always *a bundle of myrrh* with Francis;[119] he always looked *on the face* of his *Christ,*[120] always touched *the man of sorrows* who was *acquainted with infirmity.*[121]

CHAPTER LIII

Of the mantle that was given to an old woman at Celano

86   It happened in the winter at Celano[122] that St. Francis was wearing a cloth folded after the manner of a mantle which a certain man from Tivoli,[123] a friend of the brothers, had lent him.

And when he was in the palace of the bishop of the diocese of Marsica,[124] an old woman came up to him begging an alms. Immediately he loosened the cloth from his neck, and though it belonged to someone else, he gave it to the poor woman, saying: "Go, make yourself a dress, for you are greatly in need of one." The old woman smiled, and rather overcome, I know not whether with fear or with joy, she took the cloth from his hands. Quickly she ran away, and lest a delay should bring on the danger of its being asked back again, she cut it with her scissors. But when she found that the cut cloth would not be enough for a dress, encouraged by her first success, she returned to the saint, indicating to him that there was not enough cloth. The saint turned his eyes to his companion, who had the same kind of cloth on his back. "Did you hear, Brother," he said, "what this poor woman said? Let us put up with the cold for the love of God and give the cloth to the old woman so that she may complete her dress." As Francis had given his mantle, so too did his companion give his, and both remained naked so that the old woman might be clothed.

CHAPTER LIV

Of another poor man to whom Francis gave his mantle

87   Another time, when Francis was returning from Siena, he met a certain poor man and said to his companion: "Brother, we must return this mantle to that poor man to whom it belongs. We borrowed it from him until we should meet someone poorer than ourselves." His companion, thinking about his father's need, obstinately refused, lest Francis provide for another by neglecting himself. The saint said to him: " I do not want to be a thief;

for it would be considered a theft in us if we did not give to someone who is in greater need than we." The other gave in, and Francis gave over his mantle.

CHAPTER LV

How he did the same thing for another poor man

88 Something similar occurred at Le Celle near Cortona. Blessed Francis was wearing a new mantle which the brothers had solicitously sought for him. A poor man came to the place loudly bemoaning his dead wife and his family that had been left desolate. The saint said to him: "I give you this mantle for the love of God with this understanding that you do not give it to anyone else unless he pays you well for it." The brothers ran immediately to take back the mantle and prevent the gift of it. But taking courage at the look of the holy father, the poor man hung on to the mantle with both hands and defended it as his own. Finally the brothers redeemed the mantle and the poor man, after receiving the price of it, went away.

CHAPTER LVI

How Francis gave his mantle to a certain man so that he would not hate his lord

89 Once at Collestrada,[125] near Perugia, St. Francis found a certain poor man whom he had known earlier in the world. And he said to him: "Brother, how does it go with you?" But he began with ill will to heap curses upon his lord who had taken all his goods away from him. "Thanks to my lord," he said, "whom I pray the Almighty Lord to curse, I am in a bad way." The blessed Francis, pitying his soul more than his body, since he was persisting in such hatred, said to him: "Brother, forgive your lord out of love for God, so that you may free your soul, and it could be that he will give back what he has taken away from you. Otherwise, you will lose both your possessions and your soul." And he said: "I cannot forgive him completely unless he first give back what he has taken." Blessed Francis, since he had a mantle on his back, said to him: "Behold, I give you this mantle, and I beg you to forgive your lord out of love for the Lord God." Softened and moved by this kindness, he took the gift and forgave the wrongs that had been done him.

CHAPTER LVII

How Francis gave a poor man a part of his tunic

90   Once when Francis was asked by a poor man for something and he had nothing at hand, he unsewed the border of his tunic[126] and gave it to the poor man. At times, too, in similar circumstances, he gave away his trousers. Such was his compassion toward the poor and such the sincerity with which he followed in the footsteps of the poor Christ.

CHAPTER LVIII

How Francis caused the first New Testament in the order to be given to the poor mother of two of the brothers

91   Once the mother of two of the brothers came to the saint confidently asking an alms. The holy father had pity on her and said to his vicar, Brother Peter of Catania:[127] "Can we give some alms to our mother?" Francis was accustomed to call the mother of any brother his mother and the mother of all the brothers. Brother Peter answered him: "There is nothing left in the house that could be given her." And he added: "We have one New Testament from

which we read the lessons at Matins since we do not have a breviary." Blessed Francis said to him: "Give the New Testament to our mother that she might sell it to take care of her needs, since we are admonished by it to help the poor.[128] I believe indeed that the gift of it will be more pleasing to God than our reading from it." The book, therefore, was given to the woman, and thus the first Testament that was in the order was given away through this holy kindness.

CHAPTER LIX

How Francis gave his mantle to a poor woman suffering from an eye disease

92   When St. Francis was living in the palace of the bishop of Rieti trying to get a cure for the infirmity of his eyes,[129] a certain poor woman from Machilone,[130] who had an infirmity similar to that of the saint, came to the doctor. The saint, therefore, addressing his guardian familiarly, said something like this: "Brother guardian, we must give back what belongs to another." He replied: "Let it be given back, Father, if there is such a thing here." "This mantle," he said, "which we borrowed from that poor woman; let us give it back to her, for she has nothing in her purse to take care of her expenses." The guardian answered: "Brother, this mantle is mine and it was not lent to me by anyone. But use it as long as it pleases you; when you no longer want to use it, give it back to me." Actually, the guardian had bought it a little earlier for St. Francis' need. The saint said to him: "Brother guardian, you have always been courteous to me, and I beg of you to show me the same courtesy now." The guardian replied: "Do as you wish, Father, whatever the Spirit suggests to you." Therefore calling a certain secular

person, a very devout man, he said to him: "Take this mantle and twelve loaves of bread and go and say to that poor woman: 'The poor man to whom you lent this mantle thanks you for its loan; but now take back what belongs to you.'" The man went and spoke what he had heard. The woman, thinking she was being mocked, said to him with shame: "Let me alone with your mantle; I don't know what you are talking about." The man insisted and placed the mantle in her hands. When she saw that she was not being deceived and fearing that what she had gotten so easily might be taken away from her, she got up during the night and, not caring about a cure for her eyes, returned home with the mantle.

CHAPTER LX

How three women appeared to Francis along the road and then disappeared again after giving him a new greeting

93   I will narrate in a few words something that is of doubtful interpretation but most certain as regards the fact. When the poor man of Christ, Francis, was hurrying from Rieti to Siena[131] to find a remedy for his eye trouble, he crossed a plain near the town of Campiglia[132] in the company of a certain doctor deeply attached to the order. And behold, three poor women appeared beside the road when Francis was passing. They were all so similar in stature, age, and appearance that you might think that a threefold matter had been perfected by a single form. When Francis approached, they reverently bowed their heads and praised him with this new greeting: "Welcome," they said, "Lady Poverty."[133] Immediately the saint was filled with exquisite joy, in as much as there was nothing in him that he would rather have men salute than what

438

these women had chosen. And at first Francis thought they were really poor women and he turned to the doctor who accompanied him and said: " I ask you, for God's sake, give me something that I might give it to these poor women." Very quickly the doctor got out some money and leaping from his horse, he gave some to each of the women. They, therefore, proceeded a little farther along their way, and when the brothers and the doctor looked around immediately, they saw that the plain was completely empty of any women. They were greatly surprised and they then considered the happening among the miracles of the Lord, knowing that these were not women who had flown away more quickly than birds.

ST. FRANCIS' ZEAL IN PRAYER

CHAPTER LXI

Of the time and place of Francis' prayers and of his disposition in prayer

94   Although the man of God, Francis, was *exiled from the Lord* while *in the body*,[134] he strove constantly to have his spirit present in heaven and thus he was already a *citizen with* the angels[135] and only a wall of flesh separated him from them.[136] His whole soul thirsted after Christ, and he dedicated not only his whole heart, but his whole body as well, to him.

We give here a few of the great things about his prayers that may be imitated by those who come after him, in so far as we have seen them with our own eyes and in so far as it is possible to convey them to human ears.[137] He made his whole time a holy leisure in which to inscribe wisdom in his heart, lest he would be seen to fall back if he did not constantly advance. When visits of secular persons or any other business disturbed him, he would interrupt his prayers rather than end them and return to them again in his innermost being.[138] The world was tasteless to him who was fed with heavenly sweetness, and the delights he found in God made him too delicate for the gross concerns of men.

He always sought a hidden place where he could adapt not only his soul but also all his members to God. When he suddenly felt himself visited by the Lord in public, lest he be without a cell he made a cell of his mantle. At times, when he did not have a mantle, he would cover his face with his sleeve so that he would not disclose the *hidden manna*.[139] Always he put something between himself and the bystanders, lest they should become aware of the bridegroom's touch. Thus he could pray unseen even among many people in the narrow confines of a ship.[140] Finally, when he could not do any of these things, he would make a temple of his breast. Because he was forgetful of himself, there were no sobs or sighs; because he was absorbed in God, there was no hard breathing or external movement.

95 Thus was it at home. But when he prayed in the woods and in solitary places, he would fill the woods with sighs, water the places with his tears, strike his breast with his hand; and discovering there a kind of secret hiding place, he would often speak with his Lord with words. There he would give answer to his judge; there he would offer his petitions to his father; there he would talk to his friend; there he would rejoice with the bridegroom. Indeed, that he might make his whole being a holocaust in many ways, he would set before his eyes in many ways him who is simple to the greatest degree. Often, without moving his lips, he would meditate within himself and drawing external things within himself, he would lift his spirit to higher things. All his attention and affection he directed with his whole being to the one thing which he was asking of the Lord, not so much praying as becoming himself a prayer. With what sweetness of heart do you think he was pervaded when he became accustomed to such things? He knows, but I can only wonder. To him who has experienced it knowledge is given, not to him who has not experienced it. Thus, filled with a glowing fervor of spirit and his whole appearance and his whole soul melted, he dwelt already in the highest realms of the heavenly kingdom.

The blessed father was accustomed not to pass over any visitation of the Spirit with negligence. When indeed such was offered, he followed it, and as long as the Lord would permit, he would enjoy the sweetness thus offered him. When, therefore, while he was pressed by some business or was intent upon a journey, he felt little by little certain touches of grace, he would taste the sweetest manna in frequent snatches. For also along the way, with his companions going on ahead, he would stand still, and turning the new inspiration to fruitfulness, he would not *receive the grace in vain.*[141]

CHAPTER LXII

How Francis devoutly recited the canonical hours

96   Francis recited the canonical hours no less reverently than devoutly. For, though he suffered from infirmity of the eyes, stomach, spleen, and liver,[142] he did not want to lean against a wall or a partition when he chanted, but he always said the hours standing erect and without a capuche,[143] without letting his eyes roam about and without interruption.

When he went through the world on foot, he always stopped to say the hours; when he was on horseback, he got down upon the ground. Wherefore, when he was returning one day from Rome and it was raining steadily, he got down from his horse, and standing there a long time, he was completely soaked with the rain. For he used to say at times: "If the body takes its food in quiet, which, along with itself, will become the food of worms, with what great peace and tranquillity should not the soul take its food, which is God himself."

CHAPTER LXIII

How Francis drove away the imaginings of the heart at prayer

97   Francis thought he had seriously offended, if, when he was at prayer, he would be disturbed by vain imaginings. If something of the kind happened, he did not spare himself the confession of the fault, so that he could atone for it completely. Thus he turned his zeal to immediate use so that but very rarely did he suffer flies of this kind.

One Lent he had made a little vase, using just the little time he had to spare, so that he would not be completely taken up with it. One day, while he was devoutly saying Tierce, his eyes turned to look at the vessel, and he felt that the interior man was thereby impeded in its fervor. Sorrowful therefore that the voice of his heart had been interrupted in its speaking to the ears of God, when Tierce was finished he said before the listening brothers: "Alas, what a worthless work that has such power over me that it can twist my mind to itself! I will sacrifice it to the Lord, whose sacrifice it has impeded." When he said these words, he took the little vase and threw it into the fire to be burned. "Let us be ashamed," he said, "to be caught up by worthless imaginings, for at the time of prayer we speak to the *great King*."[144]

CHAPTER LXIV

Of Francis' Contemplation

98   Francis was often suspended in such sweetness of contemplation that, caught up out of himself, he could not reveal what he had experienced because it went beyond all human comprehension. Through one instance that once became known, it is clear to us how frequently he was absorbed in heavenly sweetness. Once he was riding on an ass when he had to pass through Borgo San Sepolcro.[145] And since he wanted to rest at a certain house of lepers, many found out that the man of God was to pass by. From all sides men and women came to see him, wanting to touch him out of devotion to him. What then? They touched him and pulled him about and cut off little pieces of his tunic to keep. The man seemed insensible to all these things, and paid no attention to the things that happened, as though he were a lifeless corpse. At length they came to the place and, though they had long left the city behind, that contemplator of heavenly things, as though returning to himself from some other place, solicitously inquired when they would come to the city.

CHAPTER LXV

Francis' behavior after prayer

99   When Francis returned from his private prayers, through which he was changed almost into another man, he tried with all his strength to conform himself to others, lest, if the inner fire were apparent to others, he should lose what he had gained under the glow of human favor. Often too he spoke things like these to his familiar friends: "When a servant of God is praying and is visited by a new consolation from the Lord, he should, before he comes away from his prayer, raise his eyes to heaven and with hands joined say to the Lord: 'This consolation and sweetness you have sent from heaven, Lord, to me, an unworthy sinner, and I return it to you so you may keep it for me, for I am a robber of your treasure.' And again: 'Lord, take your good things away from me in this world and keep them for me in the life to come.' Thus," he said, "he ought to speak. And when he comes away from prayer, he should show himself to others as poor and as a sinner, as though he had attained no new grace." For he would say: "It happens that a person loses something precious for the sake of some trifling reward and easily provokes him, who gives, not to give again."

Finally, it was his habit to rise so furtively and so gently to pray that none of his companions would notice him getting up or praying. But when he went to bed late at night, he would make a noise, and even a great noise, so that his going to rest might be noticed by all.

CHAPTER LXVI

How a bishop was deprived of his speech when he came upon Francis at prayer

100   When St. Francis was praying at the place of the Portiuncula, it happened that the bishop of Assisi came to him on a friendly visit, as was his custom.[146] As soon as he entered the place, he went unceremoniously to Francis' cell without being called, and after knocking at the door, was about to enter. But behold, when he put his head in and saw the saint praying, a trembling took hold of him suddenly and his limbs became rigid, and he also lost his speech. Suddenly, by the will of God, he was driven out by force and pushed backward some distance. I believe that he was either unworthy to look upon

this secret thing or that the saint was worthy to keep his secret longer. The astonished bishop returned to the brothers, and with the first word he uttered in confessing his fault, he recovered his speech.

CHAPTER LXVII

How an abbot felt the power of St. Francis' prayer

101   Another time it happened that the abbot of the monastery of St. Justin, in the diocese of Perugia, met Francis.[147] The abbot got down quickly from his horse, exchanged a few words with St. Francis about the welfare of his soul, and then, as he was leaving, he humbly asked St. Francis to pray for him. St. Francis answered him: "I will willingly pray, my lord." When the abbot had gone a little way from St. Francis, the saint said to his companion: "Wait a bit, Brother, because I want to discharge the debt I incurred by my promise." For it was always his custom that, when he had been asked for prayers, he would not postpone the matter, but would quickly fulfill a promise of this kind. Therefore, while the saint was praying to God, the abbot suddenly felt in his soul an unusual warmth and sweetness, such as he had never experienced before in his soul, so much so that he seemed to be completely carried out of himself in ecstasy. He paused for a moment and when he came to himself, he recognized the power of St. Francis' prayer. Thereafter he always burned with a greater love for the order and related the happening to many as a miracle. It is becoming that servants of God bestow upon one another little gifts like this; and it is fitting that there be a *partnership* between them *in the matter of giving and receiving*.[148] That holy love, which is at times called spiritual, is content with the fruit of prayer; charity makes little earthly gifts. To help and to be helped in the

spiritual conflict, to commend and to be commended
before the tribunal of Christ,[149] this I think is the
mark of holy love. But to what great heights in prayer do you think he rose who could thus raise up another by his merits?

ST. FRANCIS' UNDERSTANDING OF HOLY SCRIPTURE
AND THE POWER OF HIS WORDS

CHAPTER LXVIII

The knowledge and the memory of St. Francis

102   Although this blessed man had been educated in none of the branches of learning,[150] still, grasping the wisdom that is of God from above and enlightened by the rays of eternal light, he had a deep
understanding of the Scriptures. For his genius, free
from all stain, penetrated the hidden things of mysteries, and where the knowledge of the masters is
something external, the affection of one who loves
enters within the thing itself. At times he would
read the sacred books and what he put into his mind
once he wrote indelibly in his heart. His memory
substituted for books, for he did not hear a thing
once in vain, for his love meditated on it with constant devotion. This he would say was a fruitful way
of learning and reading, not by wandering about
through thousands of treatises. Him he considered a
true philosopher who put nothing before his desire
for eternal life. But he often said that that man
would easily move from knowledge of himself to a
knowledge of God who would set himself to study
the Scriptures humbly, not presumptuously. He
often explained doubtful questions word for word,
and though he was unskilled in words, he set forth
the sense and meaning admirably.

CHAPTER LXIX

Of the prophetic word Francis expounded at the prayers of a Friar Preacher

103   While Francis was staying at Siena, it happened that a certain friar of the Order of Preachers came there; he was a spiritual man and a doctor of Sacred Theology. Since he had come to visit the blessed Francis, that learned man and the saint enjoyed a long and pleasant conversation about the words of God. The aforesaid master[151] questioned Francis about that saying of Ezechiel: *If thou proclaim not to the wicked man his wickedness, I will require his soul at thy hand.*[152] For he said: "Good Father, I know many who, to the best of my knowledge, are in the state of mortal sin, but I do not always proclaim their wickedness. Will the souls of such men be required at my hand?" The blessed Francis said that he was unlettered and therefore it would be more fitting for him to be taught by that master than for him to interpret the meaning of Scripture. And the humble master said: "Brother, though I have heard these words interpreted by learned men, I would be glad to hear your understanding of the passage." The blessed Francis said to him: "If the passage is to be understood in a general meaning, I would take it that the servant of God should be so aflame in his life and his holiness that he would reprove all wicked men by the light of his example and by the words of his conversation. So, I say, the splendor of his life and the renown of his fame will proclaim to all their wickedness." That man, therefore, went away much edified, and he said to the companions of the blessed Francis: "My brothers, the theology of this man, based upon purity of life and contemplation, is a soaring eagle; but our learning crawls on its belly on the ground.

CHAPTER LXX

Of the things Francis made clear when he was questioned by a cardinal

104   Another time when Francis was in Rome at the home of a certain cardinal, he was asked about some obscure words and brought such profound things to light that you would think he had always dwelt among the Scriptures. The lord cardinal said to him: "I do not ask you as a learned man, but as a man having the Spirit of God, and I therefore willingly accept the word of your reply, for I know it has proceeded from God alone."

CHAPTER LXXI

How Francis answered a brother who urged him to apply himself to reading

105   When Francis was ill and filled throughout with pains, his companion once said: "Father, you have always sought refuge in the Scriptures, and they have always given you remedies for your pains. I pray you to have something read to you now from the prophets; perhaps your spirit will rejoice in the Lord." The saint said to him: "It is good to read the testimonies of Scripture; it is good to seek the Lord our God in them. As for me, however, I have already made so much of Scripture my own that I have more than enough to meditate on and revolve in my mind. I need no more, son; I know Christ, the poor crucified one."

CHAPTER LXXII

Of the swords that Brother Pacificus saw glittering in the mouth of the saint[153]

106   In the Marches of Ancona there was a certain

448

secular person who, forgetful of himself and not knowing God, gave himself completely to vanity. He was called *The King of Verses,* because he was the most outstanding of those who sang impure songs and he was a composer of worldly songs. To put it briefly, so high had worldly glory raised him that he had been crowned with the greatest pomp by the emperor.[154] While he was thus walking in darkness and drawing *iniquity with cords of vanity,*[155] the merciful kindness of God thought to call him back *that he that is cast off should not altogether perish.*[156] By the providence of God the blessed Francis and this man met each other at a certain monastery of cloistered poor nuns.[157] The blessed father had come there with his companions to visit his daughters; that other man had come there with many of his companions to visit a certain relative of his.

The hand of the Lord was laid upon him and he saw with his bodily eyes St. Francis signed in the manner of a cross with two greatly glittering swords, one of which went from his head to his feet, the other from one hand to the other across his breast. He did not know the blessed Francis; but when Francis had been shown to him in so great a miracle, he soon recognized him. But astonished at the vision, he began to resolve to do better things, though only for some future time. But the blessed father, after he had first preached to all in common, turned the sword of God's word upon this man. For, taking him aside, he gently admonished him concerning the vanity of the world and concerning contempt of the world, and then he touched his heart deeply by threatening him with God's judgments. Immediately that man answered: "What need is there for more words? Let us come to deeds. Take me from among men and give me back to the great Emperor." The next day the saint invested him and gave him the

name Pacificus, in as much as he had been brought
back to the peace of God. The conversion of this
man was so much the more edifying to many in that
the circle of his vain companions had been so large.

Rejoicing in the company of the blessed father,
Brother Pacificus began to experience favors that he
had not known before. For he was permitted to see
a second time what was hidden from others. Not
long afterwards, he saw the great sign *Tau* on the
forehead of the blessed Francis, which gave off from
many-colored circles the beauty of a peacock.[158]

CHAPTER LXXIII

*Of the efficacy of Francis' sermons and a certain
doctor's tesimony about it*

107   Although the evangelist Francis preached to
the unlearned people through visible and simple
things, in as much as he knew that virtue is more
necessary than words, nevertheless among spiritual
men and men of greater capacity he spoke enlivening
and profound words. He would suggest in a few
words what was beyond expression, and using fervent gestures and nods, he would transport his hearers wholly to heavenly things.[159] He did not make use
of the keys of philosophical distinctions; he did not
put order to his sermons, for he did not compose
them ahead of time. Christ, the true Power and Wisdom, gave *to his voice the voice of power*.[160] A certain doctor,[161] a learned and eloquent man, once
said: "While I can retain the preaching of others
word for word, only the things that St. Francis speaks
elude me. If I commit any of them to memory, they
do not seem to be the same that dropped from his
lips before."

CHAPTER LXXIV

How by the power of his words he drove out devils from Arezzo through the instrumentality of Brother Sylvester

108 Not only were Francis' words effective when he was present in person, but at times when they were transmitted through others they did *not return to him void*.[162] It happened once that he came to the city of Arezzo, when behold, the whole city was shaken by civil war to the extent that destruction seemed very close. The man of God therefore lodged in a town outside the city and he saw devils rejoicing over that place and stirring up the citizens to each other's destruction. But calling a brother, Sylvester by name, a man of God of worthy simplicity,[163] he commanded him saying: "Go before the gate of the city, and on the part of Almighty God command the devils to leave the city as quickly as they can." Pious simplicity hastened to carry out the command and speaking psalms of praise before the face of the Lord, he cried out loudly before the gate: "On the part of Almighty God and at the command of our father Francis, depart from here, all you devils." Soon thereafter the city returned to peace and the people preserved their civic rights in great tranquility. Wherefore afterwards blessed Francis, when preaching to them, said at the beginning of his sermon: "I speak to you as men who were once subjected to the devil and in the bonds of the devils, but I know that you have been set free by the prayers of a certain poor man."

CHAPTER LXXV

*Of the conversion of that same Brother Sylvester and
of a vision he had*

109   I think it would not be amiss to join to the
present narration the conversion of the aforementioned Sylvester, how the Spirit moved him to
enter the order. Sylvester had been a secular priest
in the city of Assisi,[164] from whom the man of God
had at one time bought stones for the repairing of a
church.[165] When this priest once saw Brother Bernard, who was the first little plant in the order of
Friars Minor after the saint of God, making a perfect renunciation of his goods and giving them to
the poor, he was moved to ravenous avarice and complained to the man of God over the stones he had
sold him, that a fair price had not been given him
for them. Francis smiled, seeing that the priest's soul
was infected with the passion of avarice. But wishing
to give some refreshment to that cursed burning, he
filled the hands of the priest with money without
counting it. The priest Sylvester rejoiced over what
he had been given, but even more did he wonder
at the liberality of the giver. He went home and
often thought about what had happened. He complained with a blessed murmuring that though he
was already growing old, he still loved the world,
and he was astonished that that young man despised
all things. Finally, after he had been filled with a
fragrant odor, Christ opened to him the bosom of
his mercy.

He showed him in a vision the works of Francis,
what great worth they had, with what great luster
they gleamed in his sight, and how they so magnifi-
cently filled the whole structure of the world. For
he saw in his sleep a golden cross coming forth from
the mouth of Francis; its top touched the heavens

and its extended arms encircled both parts of the world in their embrace. Filled with compunction at the sight, the priest shook off harmful delay, left the world, and became a perfect imitator of the man of God. He began to live perfectly in the order and, by the grace of God, he brought his life to a perfect close.[166] But what is there to wonder at if Francis appeared crucified, since all his concern was with the cross? With the cross thus wonderfully rooted in him interiorly, why should it be such a surprising thing if, coming from good ground, it should bring forth such conspicuous flowers, leaves, and fruit? Nothing else could spring up in that soil, since from the first that wonderful cross claimed it for its own. But now I must return to the subject.

CHAPTER LXXVI

Of a certain brother freed from the assaults of the devil

110   It happened that a certain brother was assaulted for a long time by a temptation of the spirit, which is more subtle and much worse than the enticement of the flesh. Finally he came to St. Francis and humbly prostrated himself at his feet; shedding an abundance of bitter tears he could say nothing, prevented as he was by deep sobs. The kindness of the father went out to him and recognizing the fact that he was troubled by evil spirits, he said: "I command you, devils, by the power of God, not to assault my brother any more in the way you have presumed to do up until now." Soon the *blackness of darkness*[167] was dispelled and the brother arose freed; neither did he feel any more vexation, just as though he had never had any.

CHAPTER LXXVII

Of the wicked sow that ate a lamb

111   The fact that Francis' words had a wonderful effect on brutes too appears sufficiently clear elsewhere.[168] I will just touch on one instance that I have at hand. One night when the servant of the Most High was lodging at the monastery of St. Verecundus in the diocese of Gubbio,[169] a certain sheep brought forth a little lamb that night. There was also a very mean sow there that did not spare the life of the innocent lamb but killed it with its cruel jaws. Upon rising the next morning, the men found the lamb dead and they knew that the sow was guilty of the evil deed. When the kind father heard this, he was moved to wonderful compassion, and, remembering another Lamb,[170] he grieved over the dead lamb, saying before all: "Alas, brother lamb, innocent animal, you represent what is useful to all mankind! Cursed be that evil beast that killed you; let no man eat of it, or any beast either." Wonderful to say, that wicked sow immediately began to be ill, and after suffering torments of punishment for three days, it at last suffered avenging death. It was cast out into the monastery ditch, where it lay for a long time dried up like a board, and it did not furnish food for any hungry creature.

AGAINST FAMILIARITY WITH WOMEN

CHAPTER LXXVIII

Of avoiding familiarity with women, and how Francis talked with them

112   That honeyed poison, namely, familiarities with women, which lead astray even holy men, Francis commanded should be entirely avoided.[171] For he feared that from such things the weak spirit would be quickly broken and the strong spirit often weakened. Avoiding contagion from association with them, unless it were a question of a most proven man, Francis said, in accordance with Scripture, was as easy as walking in a fire without having the soles of one's feet burned.[172] And that he might speak from deeds, he always showed *himself an example of all virtue.*[173] Indeed, a woman was so unwelcome to him that you would think that his caution was not a warning or an example but rather a dread or a horror. When their importunate loquaciousness caused him difficulty in speaking with them, he would ask for silence with a humble and *speedy word*[174] and with his face cast down. Sometimes, though, *he looked up to heaven*[175] and seemed to draw from there the answers he gave to those who were muttering *out of the ground.*[176]

But those women in whose minds an urgency of holy devotion had set up the abode of wisdom, he taught by wonderful yet brief words. When he talked with a woman, he spoke what was to be said in a loud voice so that he could be heard by everybody. He said once to a companion: "I tell you the truth, dearest Brother, I would not recognize any woman if I looked into her face, except two. The face of the one and of the other is known to me, but I know no other." Rightly so, Father, for looking upon them makes no one holy. Rightly so, I say, for they provide no profit but only great loss, at least of time. They are an impediment to those who would walk the difficult way and who want to look up to the *face* that *is full of graces.*[177]

CHAPTER LXXIX

A parable against looking at women

113   Francis was accustomed to combat unclean

eyes with the following parable: "A very powerful king sent two messengers to the queen one after the other. The first came back and reported only her words in exact words. For *the eyes of a wise man are in his head*,[178] and he did not let them roam about. The other returned and after a few short words about her message, he recounted a long story of the lady's beauty. 'Truly, lord,' he said, 'I have seen a most beautiful woman. Happy he that enjoys her.' But the king said: 'Wicked servant, you have cast impure eyes upon my wife? It is evident that you wished to purchase what you looked upon so sharply.' He commanded that the first messenger be called back and said to him: 'What do you think of the queen?' And he said: 'I think very well of her, for she listened silently and replied wisely.' 'And there is no beauty in her?' the king said. 'It is for you, my lord,' he said, 'to look upon that; my business was only to deliver a message.' Then this sentence was pronounced by the king: 'You,' he said, 'are chaste of eye, and being even more chaste of body, you shall be my chamberlain. But let this other man depart from my house lest he defile my marriage bed.'"

But the blessed father would say: "Too much confidence makes one guard too little against the enemy. If the devil can get but one hair from a man, he will soon make it grow into a beam. Even if after many years he still has not made him fall whom he has tempted, he is not put out over the delay, as long as he catches him in the end. For this is his business, and he is busy about nothing else by day or by night."

CHAPTER LXXX

An example the saint gave against too great intimacy

114   Once it happened, when St. Francis was go-

ing to Bevagna,[179] that he was not able to reach the town because of his weakness from fasting. His companion, however, sending a messenger to a certain spiritual woman, humbly begged bread and wine for the saint. When she heard this, she ran to the saint along with her daughter, a virgin vowed to God, carrying what was necessary. But after the saint had been refreshed and somewhat strengthened, he in turn refreshed the mother and her daughter with the word of God. But while he preached to them, he did not look either of them in the face. When they departed his companion said to Francis: "Why, Brother, did you not look at the holy virgin who came with such great devotion?" The father answered: "Who must not fear to look upon the bride of Christ? But when a sermon is preached with the eyes and the face she looks at me, but not I at her."

Many times when Francis spoke of this matter he said that all talk with women is frivolous except only for confession, or, in so far as custom demands, a very short admonition. For he said: "What business should a Friar Minor have to transact with a woman, except when she piously asks for holy penance or for advice concerning a better life?"[180]

CONCERNING THE TEMPTATIONS FRANCIS SUFFERED

CHAPTER LXXXI

Of the saint's temptations and how he overcame temptation

115   As the merits of St. Francis increased, so too did his struggle with the ancient serpent. For the greater the gifts bestowed upon him, the more subtle were the temptations and the more serious the assaults hurled against him. Though the devil had often proved him to be a *man of war*[181] and a strenu-

ous battler and one who did not let up in the struggle for even an hour, nevertheless he always tried to attack his always victorious foe. At one time there was sent to the holy father a most serious temptation of the spirit, of course for the increase of his crown. He was in anguish as a result; and filled with sorrows, he tormented and tortured his body, he prayed and he wept bitterly. After being thus assailed for several years, he was praying one day at St. Mary of the Portiuncula when he heard a voice within his spirit saying: "Francis, *if you have faith like a mustard seed, you will say to this mountain, 'Remove from here and it will remove.'* "[182] The saint replied: "Lord, what mountain do you want me to remove?" And again he heard: "The mountain is your temptation." And weeping, Francis said: "Let it be unto me, Lord, as you have said." Immediately all the temptation was driven out, and he was made free and put completely at peace within himself.

CHAPTER LXXXII

How the devil, calling to Francis, tempted him with lust, and how the saint overcame the temptation

116 At the hermitage of the brothers at Sartiano,[183] he who is always envious of the children of God, presumed to do the following against the saint. For seeing the saint continuing to increase in holiness and not neglecting today's profit for yesterday's, he called to Francis at prayer one night in his cell, saying three times: "Francis, Francis, Francis." He answered, saying: "What do you want?" And the other: "There is no sinner in the world whom the Lord will not forgive if he is converted; but whoever destroys himself by harsh penance will not find mercy forever." Immediately the saint recognized the cleverness of his enemy by a revelation, how he was trying to bring him back to lukewarmness. What then? The enemy did not stop short of inflicting upon him another struggle. For seeing that he could not thus conceal his snare, he prepared another snare, namely, the enticement of the flesh. But in vain, for he who had seen through the craftiness of the spirit could not be tricked by the flesh. The devil therefore tempted him with a most severe temptation of lust. But the blessed father, as soon as he noticed it, took off his clothing and beat himself very severely with his cord, saying: "See, brother ass, thus is it becoming for you to remain, thus is it becoming for you to bear the whip. The tunic belongs to the order; stealing is not allowed. If you want to go your way, go."

117   But when he saw that the temptation did not leave him in spite of the scourging, even though all his members were marked with welts, he opened his cell and went out into the garden and cast himself naked into a deep pile of snow. Then gathering handfuls of snow, he made from it seven lumps like balls. And setting them before him, he began to speak to his body: "Behold," he said, "this larger one is your wife; these four are your two sons and your two daughters; the other two are your servant and your maid whom you must have to serve you. Hurry," he said, "and clothe them all, for they are dying of cold. But if caring for them in so many ways troubles you, be solicitous for serving God alone." The devil then departed quickly in confusion, and the saint returned to his cell glorifying God. A certain spiritual brother, who was praying at the time, saw the whole thing by the light of the moon. But when the saint found out later that this brother had seen him that night, he was greatly distressed and commanded him to tell the thing to no one as long as he lived in this world.

CHAPTER LXXXIII

How Francis freed a certain brother from a temptation, and concerning the good that comes from temptation

118   On a certain occasion when one brother who was undergoing temptations was sitting alone with the saint, he said to Francis: "Pray for me, kind Father, for I am sure that I will be immediately freed from my temptations if you will be kind enough to pray for me. For I am afflicted above my strength and I know that this is no secret to you." St. Francis said to him: "Believe me, son, for I think you are for that reason more truly a servant of God; and know that the more you are tempted, the more will you be loved by me." And he added: "I tell you in all truth, no one must consider himself a servant of God until he has undergone temptations and tribulations. Temptation overcome," he said, "is in a way a ring with which the Lord espouses the soul of his servant to himself. There are many who flatter themselves over their long-standing merits and are happy because they have had to undergo no temptations. But because fright itself would crush them even before the struggle, they should know that their weakness has been taken into consideration by the Lord. For difficult struggles are hardly ever put in the way of anyone, except where virtue has been perfected."

HOW DEVILS BEAT FRANCIS

CHAPTER LXXXIV

How devils beat Francis, and how courts are to be shunned

119   Not only was this man attacked by satan with

temptations, but he even carried on a hand to hand battle with satan. Once when he had been asked by the lord cardinal Leo of the Holy Cross[184] to stay with him for a little while in Rome, he chose a certain secluded tower that was divided by nine arched vaults into what looked like small cells for hermits. The first night, therefore, when he wanted to rest after he had poured out his prayers to God, the devils came and made preparations for a hostile struggle with the saint of God. They beat him for a long time very severely and in the end left him as though half dead. After they had gone and he had recovered his breath, the saint called his companion who was sleeping under one of the other arched vaults and said to him when he came: "Brother, I would like for you to stay near me, because I am afraid to be alone. For the devils beat me a little while ago." The saint was trembling and shaking in his members like a person suffering a severe fever.

120 The whole night, therefore, they remained awake, and St. Francis said to his companion: "The devils are the officers[185] of our Lord whom he sends to punish our excesses. But it is a sign of greater grace if nothing is left unpunished in his servant while he is living in this world. Indeed, I do not recall any offense that I have not washed away by satisfaction, through the mercy of God; for he has always so acted with me through his fatherly condescension, that he showed me when I prayed or meditated what was pleasing and displeasing to him. But it could be that he has permitted his officers to rise against me because my staying in the court of important persons does not give a good example to others. My brothers who live in poor places, hearing that I am staying with cardinals, will perhaps suspect that I am enjoying many comforts. Therefore, Brother, I think it better for him who is set as an example for others to

461

shun courts and to make strong those who, putting up with hardships, are bearing the same things." The next morning, therefore, they went to the cardinal and after telling him everything, they bade him farewell. Let the brothers who are court chaplains[186] take note of this and let them know that they have been drawn before their time from the womb of their mother. I do not condemn obedience, but I do condemn ambition, laziness, luxury. Lastly, I propose Francis as a model especially where it is a question of obedience. But let what is displeasing to God be tolerated, since such is pleasing to men.[187]

CHAPTER LXXXV

An example of what was said in the preceding paragraph

121   One thing happened that I think should not be passed over. A certain brother, seeing some brothers living at a certain court and attracted by what desire for glory I know not, wanted to become a court chaplain with them. And while he was curious about the court, he one night saw in his sleep such brothers placed outside of the place of the brothers and separated from their companionship. He also saw them eating from a very foul and unclean pigs' trough, from which they were eating peas mixed with human dung. Seeing this, the brother was greatly astonished and getting up long before daybreak he had no more desire for the court.

CHAPTER LXXXVI

Of the assaults Francis bore in a certain solitary place; a brother's vision

122   Once the saint came with a companion to a certain church situated a long way from any habita-

tion, and wanting to offer a prayer in solitude, he sent his companion away, saying: "Brother, I would like to remain here tonight alone. Go to the hospital and come back to me at dawn." Therefore, after he had remained alone and poured out long and very devout prayers to the Lord, he at length looked about for a place where he might lay his head to sleep. But suddenly, *troubled in spirit*,[188] he began *to feel dread and to be exceedingly troubled*,[189] while his body trembled in every part. He knew clearly that the devils were rising against him and that whole troops of them were rushing with much noise over the roof of the house. He therefore immediately arose and went outside and made the sign of the cross upon his forehead and said: "On the part of Almighty God, I say to you, devils, do with my body whatever is granted you to do with it. I will bear it willingly, for since I have no greater enemy than my body, you will take vengeance for me upon my adversary when you wreak vengeance upon it in my place." Therefore, when they who had come together to frighten his spirit saw that his spirit was ready even though his flesh was weak,[190] they quickly departed confused and in shame.

123   When morning had come, his companion returned to him, and finding the saint prostrate before the altar, he waited for him outside the choir and prayed fervently himself meanwhile before the cross. And behold, he went into ecstasy and saw among the many thrones in heaven one that was more honorable than the rest, ornamented with precious stones, and radiant with all glory. He wondered within himself at this noble throne and considered silently whose it might be. And while he was considering these things, he heard a voice saying to him: "This throne belonged to one of the fallen angels, but now it is reserved for the humble Francis." At length,

coming back to himself, the brother saw the blessed
Francis coming from his prayers, and quickly pros-
trating himself at Francis' feet in the form of a cross,
he said to him, not as to one living in this world,
but as to one already reigning in heaven: "Pray for
me to the Son of God, Father, that he will not impute
to me my sins." The man of God *stretched forth his
hand*[191] and *raised him up,*[192] realizing that something had been shown to him in his prayers. Finally,
as they were leaving that place, the brother asked
the blessed Francis, saying: "What, Father, is your
opinion of yourself?" He replied: "It seems to me
that I am the greatest of sinners, for if God had
treated any criminal with such great mercy, he would
have been ten times more spiritual than I." At these
words the Holy Spirit immediately said in the heart
of the brother: "Know that the vision you saw was
indeed true, for humility will raise this most humble
man to the throne that was lost through pride."[193]

CHAPTER LXXXVII

Of a certain brother who was freed from a temptation

124   A certain spiritual brother, long in religion,
was afflicted with a great temptation of the flesh and
he seemed almost to be sunk into the depths of despair. Every day his suffering was doubled, for his
conscience, more tender than discreet, forced him
to confess about nothing. Indeed, such great zeal
should not be shown in confessing to have had a
temptation but rather in confessing to have given in
to a temptation. But he had such great shame that
he was afraid to make known the whole thing to one
priest, though it amounted to nothing, and so he
divided up his thoughts and told different parts to
different priests. One day, however, when he was
walking with blessed Francis, the saint said to him:

"Brother, I tell you that you need confess your trouble to no one in the future. And do not be afraid, because what is going on in you beyond your responsibility will be unto your glory and not unto your guilt. But as often as you are tempted say with my permission seven *Pater Noster*." Astonished that the saint knew these things, and filled with very great joy, the brother very shortly escaped from all his trouble.

TRUE JOY OF SPIRIT

CHAPTER LXXXVIII

Praise of spiritual joy; the evil of dejection

125   St. Francis maintained that the safest remedy against the thousand snares and wiles of the enemy is spiritual joy. For he would say: "Then the devil rejoices most when he can snatch away spiritual joy from a servant of God. He carries dust so that he can throw it into even the tiniest chinks of conscience and soil the candor of mind and purity of life. But when spiritual joy fills hearts," he said, "the serpent throws off his deadly poison in vain. The devils cannot harm the servant of Christ when they see he is filled with holy joy. When, however, the soul is wretched, desolate, and filled with sorrow, it is easily everwhelmed by its sorrow or else it turns to vain enjoyments."

The saint, therefore, made it a point to keep himself in joy of heart and to preserve the unction of the Spirit and the *oil of gladness*.[194] He avoided with the greatest care the miserable illness of dejection, so that if he felt it creeping over his mind even a little, he would have recourse very quickly to prayer. For he would say: "If the servant of God, as may happen, is disturbed in any way, he should rise immediately to pray and he should remain in the presence of the heavenly Father until he *restores unto him the joy of salvation*.[195] For if he *remains stupified* in sadness,[196] the Babylonian stuff will increase, so that, unless it be at length driven out by tears, it will generate an abiding rust in the heart.[197]

CHAPTER LXXXIX

Of the angelic lute that Francis heard

126   During the days when Francis was staying at Rieti[198] to have his eyes cared for, he called one of his companions who had been a lute player in the world, saying: "Brother, the children of this world do not understand the hidden things of God. For musical instruments that were once destined for the praises of God[199] lust has changed into a means of pleasure for the ears. Therefore, Brother, I would like for you to borrow a lute secretly and bring it here so that with it you may give some wholesome comfort to brother body that is so full of pains." The brother replied: "I am not a little ashamed to do so, Father, because I am afraid men may suspect that I am being tempted to frivolity." The saint said: "Let us then forget about it, Brother. It is good to give up many things so that the opinion of others may not be harmed." The next night, when the saint was watching and meditating about God, suddenly there came the sound of a lute of wonderful harmony and very sweet melody. No one was seen, but the volume of the sound marked the going and coming of the lute player as he moved back and forth. Finally, with his spirit fixed on God, the holy father enjoyed so much the sweetness in that melodious song that he thought he had been transported to another world. When he got up in the morning he called the aforementioned brother and telling him everything just as it had

happened, he added: "The Lord who consoles the afflicted has never left me without consolation. For behold, I who could not hear the lutes of men have heard a far sweeter lute."

CHAPTER XC

How Francis would sing in French when he was cheerful in spirit

127 Sometimes Francis would act in the following way. When the sweetest melody of spirit would bubble up in him, he would give exterior expression to it in French, and the breath of the divine whisper which his ear perceived in secret would burst forth in French in a song of joy. At times, as we saw with our own eyes,[200] he would pick up a stick from the ground and putting it over his left arm, would draw across it, as across a violin, a little bow bent by means of a string; and going through the motions of playing, he would sing in French about his Lord. This whole ecstasy of joy would often end in tears and his song of gladness would be dissolved in compassion for the passion of Christ. Then this saint would bring forth continual sighs, and amid deep groanings, he would be raised up to heaven, forgetful of the lower things he held in his hand.

CHAPTER XCI

How Francis rebuked a brother who was sad and admonished him how to behave

128 Francis once saw a certain companion of his with a peevish and sad face, and not taking this lightly, he said to him: "It is not becoming for a servant of God to show himself sad or upset before men, but always he should show himself honorable. Examine your offenses in your room and weep and groan before your God. When you return to your brothers, put off your sorrow and conform yourself to the rest."[201] And after a few more things he said: "They who are jealous of the salvation of men envy me greatly; they are always trying to disturb in my companions what they cannot disturb in me." So much, however, did he love a man who was full of spiritual joy that he had these words written down as an admonition to all at a certain general chapter: "Let the brothers beware lest they show themselves outwardly gloomy and sad hypocrites; but let them show themselves joyful in the Lord, cheerful and suitably gracious."[202]

CHAPTER XCII

*How the body should be treated so that it will
not murmur*

129   The saint also said once: "Brother body should be provided for with discretion, so that a tempest of bad temper be not raised by it. So that it will not be wearied with watching and that it may persevere with reverence in prayer, take away from it every occasion for murmuring. For it might say: 'I am weak with hunger, I cannot bear the burden of your exercise.' But if after it has eaten sufficient food it should mutter such things, know that a lazy beast needs the spur and a sluggish ass must expect the goad."

Only in this teaching did the most holy father's actions differ from his words.[203] For he subjected his own innocent body to scourgings and want, multiplying its *wounds without cause.*[204] For the warmth of his spirit had already so spiritualized his body, that with his soul thirsting after God, his most holy flesh also thirsted, *O how many ways.*[205]

OF FOOLISH JOY

CHAPTER XCIII

Against vainglory and hypocrisy

130   Welcoming true spiritual joy, Francis studiously avoided vainglory, because he knew that what contributes toward advancement should be loved fervently, while that which is harmful should be no less carefully shunned. He tried to crush vainglory in the seed, not permitting what might offend the eyes of God to endure even for a moment. For very often, when he was being offered much public commendation, weeping and sighing he would immediately change the feeling of his heart to sadness.

During winter, when his small, holy body was covered only with a single tunic, patched quite fully with poor pieces of cloth,[206] his guardian, who was also his companion, obtained a skin of a fox and giving it to him, said: "Father, you are suffering from an infirmity of the spleen and stomach;[207] I pray you, in your love for the Lord, let this skin be sewn beneath your tunic. If the whole skin does not please you, then at least let a part of it be put over your stomach." St. Francis replied to him: "If you want me to permit this under my tunic, then have a piece of the same size attached to the outside, which, sewn on the outside, will show men that there is a skin hidden inside too." The brother heard this, but did not approve; Francis insisted, but did not ask anything else. Finally, the guardian gave his consent and one piece was sewn over the other, so that Francis would not appear outwardly different from what he was inwardly. O you who were the same in word and in life, the same outwardly and inwardly, the same when you were a subject and when you were a superior! You, who gloried always in the Lord, loved nothing of outward glory, nothing of personal glory!

But I pray that I may not offend those who wear skins if I speak of one skin being added above the other; for we know that they who were despoiled of their innocence needed skins.[208]

CHAPTER XCIV

How Francis made a confession concerning hypocrisy

131   One time at the hermitage of Poggio[209] about Christmas time, when a large crowd of people had been called together for a sermon, Francis began with this prologue: "You believe me to be a holy man and for that reason you have devoutly come together. But I tell you," he said, "that during this whole period of fast[210] I have eaten food prepared with lard." In this way he often ascribed to pleasure what had been granted to him because of his infirmity.

CHAPTER XCV

How Francis made a confession of vainglory

132   With like fervor, when at times his spirit was moved to vainglory, he would immediately make it known by an open confession before all. Once when he was going through the city of Assisi, a certain old woman met him and asked an alms of him. Since, however, he had nothing but his mantle, he gave her that with speedy generosity. But feeling an impulse to vain complacency, he immediately confessed before all that he had had this feeling of vainglory.

CHAPTER XCVI

Francis' words against those who praised him

133   He tried to hide the good gifts of his Lord in the secret recesses of his heart, not wanting to let these become an object of praise, for they could then

be the cause of his ruin. For often when he was praised by many, he would answer with words like these: "I can still have sons and daughters; do not praise me as being secure. No one should be praised whose end is yet uncertain. If ever he who has lent these things to me would wish to take back what he has given me, only the body and soul would remain, and these even the unbeliever possesses." Such things he spoke to those who praised him. But to himself he said: "If the Most High had given such great things to a robber, he would have been more grateful than you, Francis."

CHAPTER XCVII

Francis' words against those who praised themselves

134 Francis would often say to his brothers: "No one should flatter himself with evil praise over what a sinner can do. A sinner," he said, "can fast, pray, weep, mortify his flesh. This, however, he cannot do, namely, be faithful to his Lord. Therefore in this should we glory, that we give glory to God, that we serve him faithfully, that we ascribe to him whatever he has given us. The greatest enemy of man is his flesh; it does not know how to recall anything to grieve over it; it does not know how to foresee things to fear them; its only aim is to misuse the present time. But what is worse," he said, "it claims as its own, it transfers to its own glory what was not given to it but to the soul. It seeks for praise for its virtues and the external favor of men for its watchings and prayers. It leaves nothing to the soul, but seeks a reward even for its tears."

CHAPTER XCVIII

How Francis replied to those who asked about his wounds and with what care he hid them

135   It would not be right to pass over in silence those marks of the Crucified that must be venerated even by the highest spirits, how Francis covered them over with a veil, with what great care he hid them.[211] From the very first when true love for Christ had transformed this lover into the very image of Christ, Francis began to conceal and hide his treasure with such great care that for a long time even his closest friends were unaware of it. But divine providence did not want it to be always hidden and not come to the eyes of his loved ones. Indeed, even the exposed location of his members did not permit it to remain concealed. Once when one of his companions saw the stigmata in his feet, he said to Francis: "What is this, good Brother?" But Francis replied: "Take care of your own business."

136   Another time the same brother asked for Francis' tunic to clean it. Seeing that there was blood on it, he said to the saint when he brought it back: "Whose blood is this on your tunic?" But the saint, putting his finger to his eye, said to him: "Ask what this is if you do not know that it is an eye." Rarely, therefore, did he wash his entire hands, but only his fingers, so that his secret should not be betrayed to those standing by. His feet he washed but very rarely, and not less secretly than rarely. When he was asked by anyone to let him kiss his hand, he would give him only half of it, extending only his fingers to be kissed; at times, in place of his hand, he extended his sleeve. He covered his feet with woolen socks, lest the wounds be seen, putting a skin above the wounds to ease the roughness of the wool. But though the holy father could not hide the stigmata in his hands and feet entirely from his companions, he nevertheless took it ill if anyone looked at them. Wherefore his companions, filled with prudence of spirit, averted their eyes when he uncovered either his hands or his feet out of necessity.

CHAPTER XCIX

How a certain brother saw the stigmata by a pious deception

137   While the man of God was living at Siena, it happened that a certain brother came there from Brescia;[212] he wanted very much to see the stigmata of the holy father and insistently demanded of Brothere Pacificus that he be allowed to do so. But the latter said: "When I am about to leave this place, I will ask to kiss his hands; when he gives them to me, I will wink with my eyes at you and you will see them." So, prepared to leave, they both came to the saint, and kneeling down, Brother Pacificus said to St. Francis: "Bless us, dearest Mother, and give me your hand to kiss."[213] He kissed the hand that was not willingly extended and made a sign to the other brother to look. And asking for the other hand, he kissed it and showed it to the other brother. As they were leaving, the father suspected there had been some pious deception there, as indeed there had been. And judging such pious curiosity to be impious, he immediately called Brother Pacificus back and said to him: "May the Lord forgive you, Brother, for sometimes you cause me a lot of distress." Pacificus immediately fell at his feet and humbly asked him, saying: "What distress did I cause you, dearest Mother?" But Francis said nothing, and the incident was closed with silence.

CHAPTER C

How a certain brother got to see the wound in his side

138   While the uncovered location of these members made the wounds in his hands and feet visible to some, no one was worthy to see the wound in his side while Francis was yet alive, with the exception of one person and then only once.[214] For whenever Francis had his tunic cleaned, he would cover the wound in his side with his right hand. At times, however, he covered the wound by putting his left hand over the pierced side. But when one of his companions was rubbing him, his other hand slipped down upon the wound and caused Francis great pain.[215] A certain other brother,[216] seeking out of prying curiosity to see what was hidden to others, said to the holy father one day: "Would it please you, Father, if we cleaned your tunic?" The saint replied: "May the Lord reward you, Brother, I do need it." Therefore, while Francis was taking off his tunic, that brother looked carefully and saw clearly the wound in his side. He was the only one who saw it while Francis was alive; none of the others saw it until he was dead.[217]

CHAPTER CI

How virtues are to be kept hidden

139   In this way this man renounced all glory that did not savor of Christ; in this way he placed an eternal anathema upon the favors of men. He knew that the price of fame diminishes the solitude of the conscience, and that it is by far more harmful to abuse virtues than not to have them at all. He knew that it was not less a virtue to protect what was acquired than to acquire it.[218] Alas, vanity moves us to more things than does charity, and the favor of the world prevails over love for Christ. We do not fix our eyes on our afflictions, we do not *test the spirits*,[219] and when vainglory compels us to act, we think we have been moved by charity. Moreover, if we have done even a little good, we cannot bear its weight, but ridding ourselves of it while we live, we lose it at the shore of eternity. We bear patiently our not being good. We cannot bear at all not to seem good, not to be thought good. And thus we live completely amid the praise of men, because we are nothing else but men.

CHAPTER CII

Of Francis' humility in dress, in opinion, in acts; against maintaining one's own opinion

140 Humility is the guardian and the ornament of all virtues. If the spiritual building does not rest upon it, it will fall to ruin, though it seems to be growing. This virtue filled Francis in a more copious abundance, so that nothing should be wanting to a man adorned with so many gifts. In his own opinion, he was nothing but a sinner, despite the fact that he was the ornament and splendor of all sanctity. He tried to build himself up upon this virtue, so that he would lay the foundation he had learned from Christ.[220] Forgetting the things he had gained, he set before his eyes only his failings in the conviction that he lacked more than he had gained. There was no covetousness in him except the desire to become better, and not content with what he had, he sought to add new virtues.

He was humble in dress, more humble in conviction, most humble in reputation. This prince of God was not known as anyone's superior except by this brightest jewel alone, namely, that among the lesser he was the least. This virtue, this title, this mark indicated that he was the minister general.[221] All lofty speaking was absent from his mouth, all pomp from his gestures, all ostentation from his actions.

In many things he had learned his opinion from a revelation; yet, conferring about it, he would set the opinions of others ahead of his own. He considered the advice of his companions safer, and the view of another seemed better than his own. He used to say that a brother had not given up all things for the Lord if he kept the purse of his own opinion. He preferred to hear blame spoken of himself rather than praise, for the former would lead one to amend his life, the latter to a fall.

CHAPTER CIII

Francis' humility toward the bishop of Terni and toward a certain peasant

141   Once when Francis preached to the people of Terni,[222] the bishop of that city praised him before all at the end of the sermon and said to them: "In this latest hour God has glorified his church in this poor and despised, simple and unlettered man; for this reason we are bound always to praise the Lord, knowing that *he has not done thus for any other nation.*"[223] When the saint heard these things, he accepted it with wonderful kindliness that the bishop had judged him to be contemptible in such express words. And when they were entering the church, he fell at the feet of the bishop, saying: "In truth, lord Bishop, you have done me a great favor, for you alone kept the things that are mine unharmed, whereas others take them away from me. Like a discerning man, you have separated, I say, the pre-

cious from the worthless, giving praise to God and ascribing to me my worthlessness."

142   Not only did the man of God show himself humble before his superiors; but also among his equals and those beneath him he was more ready to be admonished and corrected than to give admonitions. Wherefore when one day he was riding on an ass, because weak and infirm as he was he could not go by foot, he passed through the field of a peasant who happened to be working there just then; the peasant ran over to him and asked solicitously if he were Brother Francis. When the man of God humbly replied that he was the man he was asking about, the peasant said: "Try to be as good as you are said to be by all men, for many put their trust in you. Therefore I admonish you never to be other than you are expected to be." But when the man of God Francis heard this, he got down from the ass and threw himself before the peasant and humbly kissed his feet, thanking him for being kind enough to give him this admonition. Since, therefore, he was so famous as to be thought a saint by many, he considered himself lowly before God and men, neither did he feel any pride over his widespread fame or over his sanctity, not even over the many brothers and sons given him as a first reward for his merits.

CHAPTER CIV

How Francis resigned his office in a chapter, and about a certain prayer

143   A few years after his conversion, Francis, to preserve the virtue of holy humility, resigned the office of superior of the order in a certain chapter[224] before all the brothers, saying: "From now on I am dead to you. But see, here is Brother Peter of Catania, whom I and all of you shall obey." And bowing

down before him, he promised him obedience and reverence. The brothers, therefore, wept, and their sorrow brought forth deep sighs, when they saw themselves, in a certain way, to be orphaned from such a father. But Francis, rising and with his hands joined and his eyes raised to heaven, said: "Lord, I commend to you the family that you heretofore have entrusted to me. But now, because of my infirmities, as you know, most sweet Lord, I am unable to care for it and so I entrust it to the ministers. Let them be obliged to render an account before you, Lord, on judgment day, if any brother of them perishes because of their negligence, or example, or harsh correction." He remained thereafter until his death a subject, conducting himself more humbly than anyone else.

CHAPTER CV

How Francis gave up having any special companions

144   Another time Francis gave over all his companions to his vicar, saying: "I do not wish to appear singular because of a privilege, but let brothers go with me from place to place only as the Lord will inspire them." And he added: "I once saw a blind man with a little dog as his guide along the way." This therefore was his glory that, every vestige of singularity and ostentation having been put aside, *the strength of Christ* was dwelling in him.[225]

CHAPTER CVI

Francis' words against those who desired an office; his description of a Friar Minor

145   But Francis, seeing that some brothers were longing to hold offices, though, besides other things, their very ambition to be placed over others made them unworthy of office, said that such were not Friars Minor, but that, *forgetful of the calling with which* they *were called,*[226] *they had fallen away from that glory.*[227] Some, however, who took it ill when they were removed from office, in as much as it was not the burden they sought, but the honor, he would silence by many words.

Once he said to his companion: "I would not seem to myself to be a Friar Minor unless I were in the state I will describe to you." And he said: "Suppose I, being a prelate among the brothers, should go to the chapter and preach and admonish the brothers, and at the end this should be said against me: 'An unlettered and contemptible person is not suitable for us; therefore we do not want you to rule over us, because you have no eloquence, you are simple and unlettered.' At length I am thrown out with reproaches and despised by all. I say to you, unless I listen to these words with the same face, with the same joy, with the same purpose of sanctity, I am in no way a Friar Minor." And he added: "In an office is found an occasion for a fall; in praise, an occasion for complete destruction; in the humility of being a subject, an occasion for profit for the soul. Why then do we pay more attention to the dangers than to the profit, when we have time to gain profit?"

CHAPTER CVII

How and why Francis wanted the brothers to be subject to the clergy

146 But, though Francis wanted his sons to *be at peace with all men*[228] and to conduct themselves as little ones among all, he taught by his words and showed by his example that they were to be especially humble toward clerics. For he used to say: "We have been sent to help the clergy[229] toward the salvation of souls so that what might be found insufficient in them might be supplied by us. Everyone will receive his reward, not according to the authority he exercises, but according to the labor he does. Know, brothers," he said, "the fruit of souls is most pleasing to God, and it can be better obtained by peace with clerics than by disagreements with them. If they hinder the salvation of people, the revenge pertains to God and he will *repay them in due time*.[230] Therefore, be subject to prelates, so that, in so far as you can help it, no jealousy will spring up. If you will be sons of peace, you will win the clergy and the people for the Lord, and the Lord judges this more acceptable than to win the people but scandalize the clergy. Hide their lapses, supply for their many defects; and when you have done this, be even more humble."

CHAPTER CVIII

Of the respect Francis showed the bishop of Imola

147 Once when St. Francis came to Imola,[231] a city of Romagna,[232] he presented himself to the bishop of the region,[233] asking his permission to preach. The bishop said to him: "It is enough, Brother, that I preach to my people." Bowing his head, St. Francis humbly went outside, and after a short time, he came back in. The bishop said to him: "What do you want, Brother? What are you seeking now?" And the blessed Francis said: "Lord, if a father drives his son out of one door, he must come back in by another." Subdued by this humility, the bishop embraced him with a happy countenance and said: "You and all your brothers may preach in my diocese in the future with my general permission, for your holy humility has merited this."

CHAPTER CIX

*Of the humility and charity of St. Francis and
St. Dominic toward one another*

148   Those two bright lights of the world, St.
Dominic and St. Francis, were together in Rome
once with the lord of Ostia,[234] who later became the
supreme pontiff. And after they had spoken affectionate words in turn about the Lord, the bishop finally
said to them: "In the primitive church the pastors
of the church were poor and were men of charity,
not men of greed. Why," he said, "do we not in the
future make bishops and prelates from among your
brothers who excel all others by their learning and
example? A dispute followed between the saints as
to which one should answer; they both strove not to
anticipate each other but to give way to each other;
what is more, each was urging the other to make the
reply. Each one gave preference to the other, for
each one was devoted to the other. But in the end,
humility conquered Francis, lest he put himself forward; and humility conquered Dominic, so that he
would humbly obey and answer first. Therefore,
replying, the blessed Dominic said to the bishop:
"Lord, my brothers have been raised to a high station, if they only knew it; and even if I wanted to,
I could not permit them to acquire any other dignity." After he had replied thus briefly, the blessed
Francis bowed before the bishop and said: "Lord,
my brothers are called *minors* so that they will not
presume to become greater. Their vocation teaches
them to remain in a lowly station and to follow the
footsteps of the humble Christ, so that in the end
they may be exalted above the rest in the sight of the
saints. If," he said, "you want them to bear fruit for
the church of God, hold them and preserve them in
the station to which they have been called, and bring

them back to a lowly station, even if they are unwilling. I pray you, therefore, Father, that you by no means permit them to rise to any prelacy, lest they become prouder rather than poorer and grow arrogant toward the rest." Such were the answers of these blessed men.

149 What then do you say, O sons of the saints? Jealousy and envy prove you are degenerate, and no less, ambition proves you are illegitimate sons. *You bite and devour one another,*[235] and your conflicts and strifes arise only from your concupiscences. Your wrestling is against the hosts of darkness;[236] your battle is against the armies of devils, and you turn the points of your swords against each other; your fathers, filled with wisdom and *their face being turned toward the propitiatory,*[237] looked familiarly upon one another, while their sons, filled with envy, are *grievous even to behold.*[238] What will the body accomplish, if it has a divided heart? Certainly, the teaching of piety would progress more fruitfully throughout the world, if the bond of charity joined the ministers of the word of God together more firmly. For what we speak or what we teach is rendered greatly suspect, because a certain leaven of hatred is made manifest in us today by evident signs. I know that the good on either side are not at fault, but the bad, who, I think, should be rooted out lest they infect the holy. What then shall I say of those who set their minds *on high things?*[239] The fathers came to the kingdom by the way of humility, not by the way of loftiness; the sons, walking about in the circle of their ambition, do not ask *the way of a city for their habitation.*[240] What is left, that we who do not follow their way should not attain glory? *Far be it from us, Lord!*[241] Make the disciples humble under the wings of their humble master; make kindred spirits kind; *and mayst thou see thy children's chil-*

dren, peace upon Israel.[242]

CHAPTER CX

How each commended himself to the other

150   When the answers of the servants of God had been given, as was narrated above,[243] the lord of Ostia was much edified by the words of both and gave great thanks to God. But as they left, the blessed Dominic asked St. Francis to kindly give him the cord he wore about his waist. St. Francis was reluctant to do this, moved by the same humility to refuse as the other was moved to ask. Finally, however, the blessed devotion of the petitioner won out and Dominic very devoutly put the cord that was given him about himself beneath his inner tunic. Then the two joined hands and commended themselves to one another with great kindliness. The one said to the other: "Blessed Francis, I wish that your order and mine might be made one and that we might live in the church according to the same rule." When at last they left one another, St. Dominic said to several who were there at the time: "In truth, I say to you, all other religious ought to follow this holy man Francis, so great is the perfection of his sanctity."

OF OBEDIENCE

CHAPTER CXI

How Francis always had a guardian for the sake of true obedience

151   In order that this most prudent merchant might profit in many ways and consume the entire present time in gaining merit, he wanted to be driven under the reins of obedience and to submit himself to the direction of another. For this reason he

not only resigned the office of general,[244] but for the sake of the greater good of obedience, he requested a special guardian for himself whom he would cherish as his superior. For he said to Brother Peter of Catania, to whom he had earlier promised holy obedience:[245] "I ask you, for love of God, to give me one of my companions to take your place for me, so that I may devoutly obey him as I would obey you. I know," he said, "the fruit of obedience and that no time passes without profit for him *who submits* his *neck to the yoke* of another."[246] Therefore, after his earnest request had been granted, he remained everywhere subject until his death, always reverently obeying his personal guardian.

But once he said to his companion: "Among the other things the kindness of God has generously granted me, it has granted me this grace that I would obey a novice of one hour, if he were given me as my guardian, as carefully as I would obey the oldest and most discreet person. A subject," he said, "should not consider the man in his superior, but Him for whose sake he is a subject. But the more contemptible is he who rules, so much the more does the humility of him who obeys please."

CHAPTER CXII

How Francis described the truly obedient man, and of three kinds of obedience

152   Another time, sitting with his companions, the blessed Francis spoke something like this with a deep sigh: "There is hardly a religious in the whole world who obeys his superior perfectly." Greatly moved, his companions said to him: "Tell us, Father, what is the perfect and highest obedience." And he replied, describing the truly obedient man under the figure of a dead body: "Take a lifeless body and

place it where you will. You will see that it does not resist being moved, it does not murmur about its position, it does not cry out if it is allowed to lie there. If it is placed on a chair, it will not look up but down; if it is clothed in purple, it looks twice as pale. This," he said, "is a truly obedient man; he does not ask why he is moved, he cares not where he is placed, he does not insist on being changed elsewhere. Raised to an office, he retains his accustomed humility; the more he is honored, the more unworthy does he consider himself." Another time, speaking of these same things, he said that things that are granted after a request are more properly permissions; but if they are enjoined and not asked for, they are sacred obediences.[247] He said that both are good, but that the latter are safer. But that obedience he thought was the highest and was without anything of flesh and blood by which one goes by divine inspiration among the infidels,[248] either for the sake of profit for one's neighbors or out of a desire for martyrdom. To ask for this obedience he thought was highly acceptable to God.

CHAPTER CXIII

That a command under obedience is not to be lightly given

153 Francis therefore thought that a command should but rarely be given under obedience, that that weapon should not be hurled first which should be the last recourse. "The hand must not be quickly laid to the sword," he said. But he thought that he who does not hasten to obey a command of obedience does not fear God or respect men. Nothing is more true than this. For, in a rash superior what is the power to command but a sword in the hand of a madman? And what is more hopeless than a religious who spurns obedience?

CHAPTER CXIV

Of the brother whose capuche Francis threw into the fire because he came without an obedience, though he was drawn by devotion

154   On one occasion Francis took away the capuche from a brother who had come alone and without an obedience[249] and he ordered it to be thrown into a great fire. But when no one withdrew the capuche, for they were frightened whenever the face of their father was even somewhat disturbed, the saint commanded it to be withdrawn from the flames; and it had not been harmed. Although the merits of the saint could bring this about, perhaps merit was not entirely lacking on the part of that brother. For the desire to see the most holy father had spurred him on, though discretion, the charioteer of virtues, was not in him.

OF THOSE WHO GIVE A GOOD OR A BAD EXAMPLE

CHAPTER CXV

Of the example of a certain good brother and of the behavior of the older brothers

155   Francis used to say that the Friars Minor had been sent by the Lord in these latest times[250] to give examples of light[251] to those wrapped in the darkness of sins. He would say that he was filled *with the most sweet savour*[252] and anointed with the strength *of precious ointment,*[253] when he heard of the wonderful works of his holy brothers in distant parts of the world. It happened that a certain brother named Barbaro once hurled an abusive word against another brother in the presence of a certain nobleman from

the island of Cyprus. When he saw that brother somewhat hurt by the conflict of words, he took some asses' dung and put it into his mouth to be eaten as vengeance upon himself; and he said: "Let the tongue that poured out the poison of anger upon my brother eat dung." Seeing this, the knight was struck with astonishment and departed greatly edified; and from that time on he generously placed himself and his goods at the will of the brothers.

All the brothers observed this unfailingly as a custom that if any of them at any time spoke a disturbing word to another, he would immediately cast himself upon the ground and impress kisses upon the other's foot even if the other were unwilling. The saint rejoiced in such things, whenever he heard his sons bring forth from themselves examples of holiness; and he heaped blessings most *worthy of entire acceptance*[254] upon those brothers who by word or deed led sinners to the love of Christ. He wanted his sons to have in themselves the same zeal for souls that filled himself.

CHAPTER CXVI

Of certain ones who gave bad example, and of the saint's curse upon them, and how seriously he took these things

156   Thus also those who brought dishonor upon religious life by their evil deeds or example incurred the heaviest sentence of his curse. For when one day it was told him that the bishop of Fondi[255] had said to two brothers who had come before him and who pretended great contempt for themselves by letting their beards grow rather long: "Beware, lest the beauty of religion be stained by novelties of this kind," the saint arose immediately and *stretching forth* his *hands to heaven*[256] and shedding many tears,

he burst out in words of prayer, or rather of imprecation, after this fashion: "Lord Jesus Christ, who chose your apostles to the number of twelve; though one of this number fell, the rest clung to thee and preached the holy Gospel, filled with one spirit; you, Lord, *in this last hour*,[257] mindful of your ancient mercy, planted the order of brothers as a support of your faith and that the mystery of your Gospel might be fulfilled through them. Who, therefore, will make satisfaction for them before you, if, though they are sent for this, they not only fail to display examples of light to all, but rather show forth the *works of darkness?*[258] By you, most holy Lord, and by the whole celestial court, and by me your little one, may they be cursed who by their bad example tear down and bring to ruin what you have built up in the past through holy brothers of this order and do not cease to build up." Where are they who say they are happy in his blessing and boast that they have gained familiarity with him as much as they have desired? If, which God forbid, they be found to have shown forth the *works of darkness*[259] to the peril of others without repentance, woe to them, woe because of eternal damnation!

157   "The best brothers are put to confusion by the works of the bad brothers," Francis used to say, "and where they themselves have not sinned, they must bear judgment because of the example of the wicked. They therefore transfix me with a sharp sword and plunge it through my bowels *all the day long*."[260] Mainly on this account did Francis withdraw himself from the company of the brothers, lest it happen that he hear anything evil of anyone unto the renewal of his grief.

And he would say: "The time is coming when the order beloved of God will be spoken ill of because of bad examples, so much so that it will be ashamed to show itself in public. But those who will come to enter the order at that time will be led only by the operation of the Holy Spirit, and flesh and blood will put no stain upon them and they will indeed be blessed by the Lord. Although meritorious works may not be found in them, with that charity growing cold that makes saints work fervently, the greatest possible temptations will come upon them, and they who will be found just at that time will be better than those who have gone before them. But woe to those who applaud themselves for the mere appearance of the religious life; they will grow numb with sloth and they will not be able to resist steadfastly the temptations permitted as a trial for the elect; for only those who *have been tried will receive the crown of life,*[261] those whom meanwhile the malice of the wicked has put to the test."

CHAPTER CXVII

Of the revelation made by God to Francis concerning the state of the order and that the order would never fail

158 But Francis was greatly consoled by the visitations of God, by which he was made to feel sure that the foundations of his order would always remain unshaken. It was also promised to him that without a doubt the number of those who would fall away would be replaced by the substitution of elect. For once when he was disturbed over bad examples and, thus distressed, gave himself over to prayer, he brought back this rebuke from the Lord: "Why are you disturbed, little man?[262] Did I not place you over my order as its shepherd, and now you do not know that I am its chief protector? I chose you, a simple man, for this task, that what I would do in you to be imitated by the rest they might follow who wished to follow. I have called, I will preserve and feed, and I will choose others to repair the falling away of others, so that if a substitute is not born, I will make him to be born. Do not be disturbed, therefore, but *work out your salvation*,[263] for though the order were reduced to the number of three, it will by my grace remain unshaken." From then on Francis would say that the very great multitude of imperfect brothers would be overcome by the virtues of one saint, for the deepest darkness is dispersed by even a single ray of light.

AGAINST IDLENESS AND THE IDLE

CHAPTER CXVIII

A revelation made to Francis as to when one is a servant of God, when not

159 From the time that this man began to cling to the Lord, having put aside all transitory things, he allowed hardly a moment of time to pass unused. Indeed, though he had already laid up an abundance of merits in the *treasure house* of the Lord,[264] he was always ready, always zealous for spiritual exercises. Not to do something good he considered a grave offense; not to advance he judged to be a falling back. Once when he was staying in a cell at Siena, he called his sleeping companions one night, saying: "I have asked the Lord, brothers, to deign to show me when I am his servant. And the most kind Lord just now deigned to give me this reply: 'Know that you are then truly my servant when you think, speak, and do holy things.' Therefore have I called you, brothers, because I wish to be filled with shame before you if at any time I do nothing of these three things."

CHAPTER CXIX

The penance for idle words at the Portiuncula

160 Another time, at St. Mary of the Portiuncula, the man of God, considering how much profit from prayer flows away because of idle words after prayer, ordained this remedy against the fault of idle words, saying: "If any of the brothers utters an idle or useless word, he shall be bound immediately to admit his guilt and to say a *Pater Noster* for each idle word. But thus I want it, that if he himself is first to admit the guilt of his fault, he shall say a *Pater Noster* for his own soul; if he is accused of his fault first by another, he shall offer the prayer for the soul of that other."

CHAPTER CXX

How Francis, working himself, despised the idle

161 Francis used to say that the lukewarm who did not make themselves acquainted familiarly with work would be quickly vomited forth from the mouth of the Lord.[265] No one could appear idle before him without being corrected by him with a sharp rebuke. For he himself worked and labored with his hands as an example of all perfection, allowing nothing of that greatest gift of time to escape. But he said once: "I want all my brothers to work and to be employed, and those who do not know how should learn some crafts."[266] And he gave this reason: "That we may be less burdensome to men," he said, "and that the heart or tongue may not wander to unlawful things in idleness." But the profit or the reward of labor he did not commit to the free disposition of the laborer but to the disposition of the guardian or of the family.

CHAPTER CXXI

A lament over idle and gluttonous brothers addressed to St. Francis

162   Holy Father, permit us who are called your sons to raise on high today a lament. The exercise of virtue is odious to many who, wanting to rest before they have labored,[267] prove themselves to be sons of Lucifer rather than sons of Francis. We have a greater abundance of weaklings than of warriors, although they ought to consider this life a warfare, since they have been born to labor.[268] It does not please them to make progress through action; and they cannot do so through contemplation. When they have disturbed all by their singularity, working more with their jaws than with their hands, they hate *him that rebuketh them in the gate,*[269] and they do not permit themselves to be touched even by the tips of the fingers. But I wonder still more at the impudence of those who, according to the word of the blessed Francis, could not have lived at home except by their sweat, and now, without working, feed on the sweat of the poor. Wonderful prudence! Though they do nothing, they consider themselves always occupied. They know the hours of the meals, and if hunger takes hold of them, they complain that the sun has gone to sleep. Shall I believe, good Father, that these monsters of men are worthy of your glory? Not even of the habit! You always taught that we should seek in this wanton and fleeting time the riches of merits, lest it happen that we go begging in the future. These, though, have no part in their fatherland, and they will have to go into exile hereafter. This disease is rampant among subjects because superiors act as though it were not possible to merit a share in the punishment of those whose vices they are tolerating.

OF THOSE WHO MINISTER THE WORD OF GOD

CHAPTER CXXII

What a preacher should be

163   Francis wanted such men to be ministers of *the word of God*[270] who give themselves to the study of spiritual things and are not hindered by other duties. For these, he used to say, have been chosen by a certain great king to deliver to the people the edicts that proceed from his mouth. But he said: "The preacher must first draw from secret prayers what he will later pour out in holy sermons; he must first grow hot within before he speaks words that are in themselves cold." He said that this is an office to be revered and that those who administer it should be reverenced by all. "These," he said, "are the life of the body; they are the attackers of the devils; they are the *light of the world*."[271]

But he considered doctors of sacred theology to be worthy of even greater honors. For he once had it written down for all: "All theologians and those who minister to us the words of God we must honor and venerate as those who minister to us spirit and life."[272] And when he wrote once to Blessed Anthony, he had this salutation placed at the beginning of the letter: "To Brother Anthony, my bishop."[273]

CHAPTER CXXIII

Against those who seek vain praise and an exposition of a word of prophecy

164   But Francis said that preachers who often sell what they do for the price of empty praise are to be pitied. The abnormal growth of such men he at times cured with such an antidote as this: "Why do you glory over men who have been converted when it was my simple brothers who converted them by their prayers?" Finally these words, *So that the barren have borne many,*[274] he explained in the following way. "The *barren,*" he said, "is my poor little brother who does not have the duty of bringing forth children for the Church. This one will *bring forth many* at the judgment, because those he is now converting by his private prayers the Judge will give to him unto glory. *She that had many children is weakened*[275] suggests that the preacher who rejoices over many as though he had brought them forth by his own power will learn that he had nothing to do with them personally." But those who want to be praised rather as rhetoricians than as preachers, speaking as they do with elegance rather than with sincerity, Francis did not greatly love. These, he said, divide wickedly who spend all their time at preaching and none at devotion. But he praised the preacher, certainly, but only one who thinks of himself at the proper time and provides wisely for himself.

OF THE CONTEMPLATION OF THE CREATOR IN HIS CREATURES

CHAPTER CXXIV

The love of the saint toward sensible and insensible creatures

165   Hurrying to leave this world in as much as it is the place of exile of our pilgrimage, this blessed traveler was yet helped not a little by the things that are in the world. With respect to the *world-rulers of this darkness,*[276] he used it as a field of battle; with respect to God, he used it as a very bright *image of his goodness.*[277] In every work of the artist he praised the Artist; whatever he found in the things made he referred to the Maker. He rejoiced in all the works of the hands of the Lord and saw behind things pleasant to behold their life-giving reason and cause.[278] In beautiful things he saw Beauty itself; all things were to him good. "He who made us is the best," they cried out to him. Through his footprints impressed upon things he followed the Beloved everywhere; he made for himself from all things a ladder by which *to come even to his throne*.[279]

He embraced all things with a rapture of unheard of devotion, speaking to them of the Lord and admonishing them to praise him.[280] He spared lights, lamps, and candles,[281] not wishing to extinguish their brightness with his hand, for he regarded them as a symbol of Eternal Light. He walked reverently upon stones, because of him who was called the Rock.[282] When he used this versicle: *Thou hast exalted me on a rock,*[283] he would say for the sake of greater reverence: *Thou hast exalted me at the foot of a rock.*

He forbade the brothers to cut down the whole tree when they cut wood, so that it might have hope of sprouting again. He commanded the gardener to leave the border around the garden undug, so that in their proper times the greenness of the grass and the beauty of flowers might announce the beauty of the Father of all things. He commanded that a little place be set aside in the garden for sweet-smelling and flowering plants, so that they would bring those who look upon them to the memory of the Eternal Sweetness.[284]

He removed from the road little worms, lest they be crushed under foot; and he ordered that honey and the best wines be set out for the bees, lest they perish from want in the cold of winter.[285] He called all animals by the name *brother,*[286] though among all the kinds of animals he preferred the gentle.[287] Who could possibly narrate everything? For that original goodness that will be one day *all things in all* already shown forth in this saint *all things in all*.[288]

CHAPTER CXXV

How the creatures themselves returned his love, and of the fire that did not give him pain

166 All creatures, therefore, tried to give their love in return to the saint and to reply by their own gratitude according as he deserved; they were glad when he caressed them, they agreed when he requested anything, they obeyed when he commanded anything. May the narration of a few instances please the reader. At the time when Francis suffered the infirmity of his eyes and was persuaded to permit treatment of them,[289] a doctor was called to the place. When he came, he brought an iron for cauterizing and ordered it to be put into the fire until it should be red-hot. But the blessed father, strengthening his body now struck with horror, spoke thus to the fire: "My brother fire, that surpasses all other things in beauty, the Most High created you strong, beautiful, and useful. Be kind to me in this hour, be courteous. For I have loved you in the past in the Lord. I beseech the great Lord who made you that he temper your heat now so that I may bear it when you burn me gently." When his prayer was ended, he made the sign of the cross over the fire and then remained fearless. The doctor took the glowing and hot iron in his hands; all the brothers, overcome by human weakness, fled; and the saint offered himself joyfully and eagerly to the iron. The iron was plunged into the tender flesh with a hiss, and it was gradually drawn from the ear to the eyebrow in its cauterizing. How much pain that fire caused, the words of the saint himself, who knows best, testify. For when the brothers who had fled returned, the father said, smiling: "O fainthearted and weak of heart, why did you flee? *In truth I say to you,*[290] I did not feel either the heat of the fire or any pain in my flesh." And

496

turning to the doctor, he said: "If my flesh is not sufficiently burned, burn it again." The doctor, knowing that in similar cases the experience was much different, proclaimed it a miracle from God, saying: "I say to you, brothers, I *have seen wonderful things today.*"[291] I believe that he had returned to primitive innocence, for whom, when he wished it, cruel things were made gentle.

CHAPTER CXXVI

Of the bird that rested in Francis' hands

167   When the blessed Francis was going across the lake of Rieti to the hermitage of Greccio, he was sitting in a certain little boat.[292] A certain fisherman offered him a waterfowl, that he might rejoice over it in the Lord. The blessed father accepted it joyfully, and opening his hands, he gently told it that it was free to fly away. But when it did not wish to leave, but wanted to rest there in his hands as in a nest, the saint raised his eyes and remained in prayer. And returning to himself as from another place after a long while, he gently commanded the bird to go back to its former freedom. So, upon receiving this permission along with a blessing, the bird flew away, showing its joy by a certain movement of the body.

CHAPTER CXXVII

Of the falcon

168   When the blessed Francis was staying in a certain hermitage, shunning in his usual way the sight and conversation of men, a falcon that was making its nest in the place attached itself to him in a great bond of friendship. For always during the night it announced with its song and noise the hour at which the saint was accustomed to rise for worship of God. This was very pleasing to the saint of God, in that, by reason of the great solicitude of the bird for him, any delay on his part because of laziness was driven away. But when the saint was afflicted more than usual by illness, the falcon would spare him and not give the signal for the time of the watches. Indeed, as if instructed by God, it would very gently sound the bell of its voice about dawn. Little wonder if all other creatures too venerated this eminent love of the Creator.

CHAPTER CXXVIII

Of the bees

169 On a certain mountain a cell was once constructed in which the servant of God performed penance most strictly for forty days. When this space of time was completed, he left the place and the cell remained without another inhabitant after him, placed as it was in a lonely spot. An earthen vessel, from which the saint used to drink, was also abandoned there. Once, however, when some men went to that place out of reverence for the saint, they found that vessel filled with bees. They had built little cells in the vessel with wonderful skill, signifying, surely, the sweetness of contemplation that the saint had experienced there.

CHAPTER CXXIX

Of the pheasant

170 A certain nobleman from the commune of Siena sent a pheasant to the blessed Francis while the latter was sick. He accepted it with alacrity, not with the desire of eating it, but, in the way he always rejoiced over such things, out of love for the Creator. And he said to the pheasant: "May our Creator be praised, brother pheasant!" And to the brothers he said: "Let us see now if brother pheasant will stay with us, or if it will go back to its usual and more suitable haunts." One of the brothers took it, at the command of the saint, and placed it at a distance in the vineyard. Immediately, however, it came directly back to the father's cell. Again Francis ordered it placed even farther away; but it came back with the greatest speed to the door of his cell and entered almost by force under the habits of the brothers who were standing at the door. The saint then ordered it to be fed diligently, embracing it and caressing it with soft words. When a certain physician who was quite devoted to the saint of God saw this, he begged the pheasant from the brothers, not wanting to eat it, but to raise it out of reverence for the saint. What more? He took it home with him; but the pheasant, as though it had suffered an injury in being separated from the saint, refused absolutely to eat as long as it was away from Francis' presence. The physician was astonished, and immediately taking the pheasant back to the saint, he told him everything just as it had happened. As soon as the pheasant was put upon the ground, it saw its father, and putting off all grief, it began to eat with joy.

CHAPTER CXXX

Of the tree cricket

171   Near the cell of the saint of God at the Portiuncula there was a tree cricket that used to perch on a fig tree and frequently sing sweetly. At times the blessed father would extend his hand to it and kindly call it to himself, saying: "My sister cricket, come to me." As though endowed with reason, it immediately got up on his hand. And Francis said to it: "Sing, my sister cricket, and praise your Creator

with a joyful song." Obeying without delay, it began to sing, and it did not cease to sing until the man of God, mingling his own praises with its songs, commanded it to go back to its usual haunt. It remained there for eight days in a row, as if bound there. But when the saint would come down from his cell, he would always touch it with his hands and command it to sing, and it was always ready to obey his commands. And the saint said to his companions: "Let us give our sister cricket leave to go now, for it has made us sufficiently happy now; we do not want our flesh to glory vainly over things of this kind." And immediately with permission from Francis, it left, and it did not ever show up there again. Seeing all these things, the brothers were greatly astonished.

OF CHARITY

CHAPTER CXXXI

Of Francis' charity and how he set himself as an example of perfection for the salvation of souls

172   Since the strength of Francis' love made him a brother to all other creatures, it is not surprising that the charity of Christ made him more than a brother to those who are stamped with the image of their Creator. For he used to say that nothing is more important than the salvation of souls, and he often offered as proof the fact that the Only-begotten of God deigned to hang on the cross for souls. This accounts for his struggles at prayer, his tirelessness at preaching, his excess in giving examples.[293] He did not consider himself a friend of Christ unless he loved the souls that Christ loved. And this was the main reason why he reverenced doctors so much,[294] namely, because, as Christ's helpers, they exercised one office with him. He loved his brothers beyond

measure with an affection that rose from his inner-most being, because they were of the same *household of faith*[295] and united by participation in *an eternal inheritance according to the promise.*[296]

173 As often as the severity of his life was re-proved, he would reply that he had been given to the order as an example, that as an eagle he might en-courage his young ones to fly.[297] Wherefore, though his innocent flesh that always subjected itself of its own accord to the spirit did not need any scourging for its offenses, nevertheless, for the sake of example, he heaped punishments upon it, keeping *hard ways*[298] solely because of others. Indeed, rightly, for more respect is paid to the actions than to the words of superiors. By actions, Father, you spoke more sweet-ly, you persuaded more easily, and you showed the way more certainly. Though superiors *speak with the tongues of men and of angels,*[299] but do not show examples of charity, it profits me little, and them not at all. Indeed, where the one who reproves is in no way feared and will takes the place of reason,[300] will seals suffice for salvation?[301] However, we must do what they tell us, that the little streams may flow through narrow channels to the small garden beds.[302] Meanwhile, let a rose be gathered from thorns,[303] so that the *elder* may *serve the younger.*[304]

CHAPTER CXXXII

Of Francis' concern for his subjects

174 Who indeed is clothed with Francis' concern for his subjects? He was always raising his hands to heaven for the true Israelites,[305] and forgetful of himself at times, his first concern was for the salva-tion of his brothers. He prostrated himself at the feet of the Majesty, he offered a sacrifice of the spirit for his sons,[306] he compelled God to grant his graces to them. With love and fear, he had compassion on the little flock he drew after himself, lest after they had lost the world they should lose also heaven. He believed that he would be without future glory unless he made those entrusted to him glorious with him, those whom his spirit brought forth with greater labor than a mother's labor in giving birth to her children.

CHAPTER CXXXIII

Francis' compassion for the sick

175   Francis had great compassion for the sick, great concern for their needs.[307] When the kindness of secular people sent him choice foods, even though he needed them more than others, he gave them to the rest of the sick. He transferred to himself the afflictions of all who were sick, offering them words of sympathy when he could not give them help. On days of fast he himself would eat, lest the sick should be ashamed to eat; and he was not ashamed to beg meat through the public places of the towns for a sick brother. But he admonished the ill to bear their troubles patiently and not to give scandal when all their wishes were not satisfied. Wherefore in one of his rules[308] he had these words set down: "I beg all my sick brothers that they do not become angry in their infirmities or disturbed either against God or against their brothers. Let them not be too solicitous in asking for medicines, nor too desirous that the flesh which is soon to die and which is the enemy of the soul be delivered. Let them *give thanks in all things*,[309] so that they may desire to be as God wants them to be. For whom God has *destined for eternal life*,[310] he instructs by the goads of scourgings and sicknesses, as he himself said: 'Those whom I love, I correct and chastise.' "[311]

176   Francis once took a certain sick brother, who he knew had a longing for grapes, into the vineyard and sitting down under the vine, he first ate to give the other courage to eat.[312]

CHAPTER CXXXIV

Of Francis' compassion toward those who were ill in spirit and of those who act contrary to what he said

177   But Francis cherished with greater kindness and supported with greater patience those sick who he knew were tossed about and bothered by temptations and were fainting in spirit. Therefore, avoiding sharp corrections where he saw there was no danger, he spared the rod to spare the soul. To forestall the occasion of failing and not to let him slip whom it would be difficut to raise up if he fell,[313] this Francis said is the duty of a superior who is a father and not a tyrant.[314] Alas for the pitiable madness of our time! Those who are liable to fall we not only do not raise up or support, but at times we even push them to make them fall. We think nothing of taking away from that Great Shepherd one little sheep for whom he offered on the cross a *loud cry and tears.*[315] You, holy Father, on the other hand, want the erring to amend rather than perish. But we know that the sickness of self-will is more deeply rooted in some and for these cauterizing is needed, not ointment. It is evident that for many it is more wholesome to be ruled *with a rod of iron*[316] than to be stroked with the hand. But *oil and wine,*[317] the *rod and the staff,*[318] harshness and pity, burning and anointing, the prison and kindness, all these *have their season.*[319] All of them the *God of revenge*[320] and the *Father of mercies*[321] needs, but he desires mercy rather than sacrifice.[322]

CHAPTER CXXXV

Of the Spanish brothers

178 Sometimes this most holy man was *out of his mind for God*[323] in a wonderful manner and he rejoiced in spirit as often as a *fragrance*[324] came to him about his brothers. It happened that a certain Spaniard, a cleric devoted to God, enjoyed the sight of and conversation with Francis. This man made Francis happy with this account, among other things, of the brothers who were in Spain. "Your brothers," he said, "live in our country in a certain poor hermitage and they have so established their way of living that half of them take care of domestic needs and the other half spend their time in contemplation. In this way each week those who lead the active life exchange with those who lead the contemplative life and the quiet of those giving themselves to contemplation is changed for the business of work.[325] One day when the table had been set and the absent summoned by the signal, all but one of the contemplatives came together. After a short wait they went to his cell to call him to the table; but he was being refreshed at the more abundant table of the Lord. For he was found prostrate upon his face on the ground, stretched out in the form of a cross; and there was no sign that he was alive either from breathing or from movement. Two candles were burning at his head and at his feet, and they lighted up the cell in a wonderful way with a bright light. He was left in peace, lest they disturb his rapture, lest they *make the beloved to awake,* before *she pleased.*[326] Then the brothers peeped through the chinks of the cell, *standing behind the wall and looking through the lattices.*[327] What more? While the friends were hearkening to her that dwelleth in the gardens,[328] suddenly the light was gone and the brother came to himself again. Immediately he arose and coming to the table, he confessed the fault of his tardiness. Thus," that Spaniard said, "does it happen in our land." St. Francis could not contain himself for joy, sprinkled as he was with such fragrance of his sons. Suddenly he arose to give praise, and, as if his only glory were to hear good things of his brothers, he cried out, moved to his innermost depths: "I give you thanks, Lord, sanctifier and director of the poor, who have given me such joy in hearing such things of my brothers. Bless those brothers, I pray, with your most generous blessing, and sanctify by a special gift all who through their good example cause their profession to give off a fragrant odor."

CHAPTER CXXXVI

Against those who live evilly in hermitages and how he wanted all things to be common to all

179   Though we therefore know the charity of the saint which led him to rejoice in the successses of his beloved brothers, still we believe that he rebuked with no small severity those who lived in a different manner in the hermitages. For many change the place of contemplation into a place of idleness and change the eremitical way of life, which was devised for the perfecting of souls, into a cesspool of pleasure. The norm for such hermits of the present time is to live as each one pleases. But this is not applicable to all, for we know some are living in a hermitage like saints in the flesh in accordance with the very best regulations. We know also that those fathers who were their predecessors bloomed as solitary flowers. Would that the hermits of our time would not fall away from that primitive beauty, the praise of the righteousness of which remains forever.

180   St. Francis, exhorting all moreover to charity,

admonished them to show to one another affability
and the friendliness of family life. "I wish," he said,
"that my brothers would show themselves to be children of the same mother and that if anyone asks for
a tunic or a cord or anything else, the other should
give it to him with generosity. Let them share their
books and anything else that is agreeable, so much
so that one would even force the other to take it."
And lest in this matter he should speak anything of
those things that Christ was not working through
him, he was the first to do all these things.

CHAPTER CXXXVII

*Of the two French brothers to whom he gave his
tunic*

181   It happened that two French brothers of
great sanctity met St. Francis. Rejoicing with an unheard of joy over him, they felt a double joy in that
they had wanted for a long time to see him. After
kind greetings and heart to heart conversation, their
ardent devotion led them to beg St. Francis for his
tunic. Immediately he took his tunic off and standing there naked, he gave it to them with great devotion; then accepting the one brother's tunic that was
poorer, he put it on. He was prepared not only to
give away things like that, but he was ready to spend
himself[329] and he gladly gave whatever was asked
of him.[330]

OF DETRACTION

CHAPTER CXXXVIII

How Francis wanted detractors to be punished[331]

182   Finally, since the soul that is filled with charity hates what is hateful to God, this virtue flourish-

ed in St. Francis. Hating detractors deeply and more than any other kind of wicked men, he said that they carried poison on their tongues and infected others with their poison. Gossipers, therefore, those biting fleas, he avoided when they were speaking, and he averted his ears, as we ourselves have seen, lest they be defiled by hearing such things. For once, when Francis heard a certain brother blacken the reputation of another, he turned to Brother Peter of Catania, his vicar, and spoke this terrible sentence: "Disaster confronts the order, unless these slanderers are checked. Quickly the sweetest savor of the many begins to take on a horrible stench, unless the mouths of the stinking are closed. Arise, arise, examine diligently, and if you find any accused brother innocent, make the accuser known to all by a severe correction. Hand him over to the Florentine pugilist,"[332] he said, "if you yourself cannot punish him." (He used to call Brother John of Florence the pugilist; he was a man of great stature and great strength). "I want you to use the greatest care," he said, "you and all the ministers, lest this horrible disease spread further." But at times he decreed that he who had taken away the good name of a brother should have his tunic taken away and that he should not raise his eyes to God until he first restored what he had taken away. This is why the brothers of that time renounced this vice in a special way and firmly agreed among themselves that whatever would detract from the honor of others or smacked of evil talk should be strictly avoided. Rightly and excellently done! What then is a detractor but the gall of humanity, the leaven of wickedness, the disgrace of the world? What then is a double-tongued man but the scandal of religion, the poison of the cloister, the destroyer of harmony? Alas, the face of the earth is filled with poisonous animals, and no one can escape the teeth of envious rivals. Rewards are offered to those who inform, and when innocence has been destroyed, the palm is at times given to falsehood. Behold, where a person cannot live by his honesty, he may gain food and clothing by tearing down the good name of others.

183   St. Francis therefore often said: "This is what the detractor says: 'Perfection of life is not in me; I have no great knowledge or special grace; as a consequence I find no place either with God or with men. *I know what I will do*:[333] *On the elect I will lay a blot*,[334] and I will play up to those in authority. I know my superior is only a man and that he at times acts in the same way as I do; when therefore the cedars are cut down, only the bramble will be seen in the woods.'[335] Alas, wretched one, feed on human flesh; and since you cannot live otherwise, gnaw on the entrails of your brothers. Such men try to appear good, not to become good; and they accuse others of vices, but do not put off their own vices. They praise only those by whose authority they wish to be cherished; they withhold praise when they think their praise will not be reported to the one they praise. They sell the pallor of the face of fasting for ruinous praises, that they may appear to be spiritual men[336] who judge all things but do not themselves want to be judged by anyone. They rejoice in the reputation of sanctity, not in the fact of it; in the name of angel, but not in virtue."[337]

DESCRIPTION OF THE MINISTER GENERAL
AND OF OTHER MINISTERS

CHAPTER CXXXIX

How the ministers should conduct themselves toward their companions

184   Near the end of Francis' vocation in the

Lord,[338] a certain brother who was always solicitous for the things of God and filled with love for the order, made this request of Francis: "Father, you will pass away and the family that has followed you will be left abandoned in this valley of tears. Point out someone, if you know of anyone in the order, upon whom your spirit may rest and upon whom the burden of minister general may be safely placed." St. Francis answered, accompanying all his words with sighs: "I see no one, son, who would be capable of being the leader of an army of so many different men and the shepherd of so large a flock. But I would like to describe one for you and fashion one, as the saying goes, with my hand, one in whom it may be clearly seen what kind of man the father of this family must be.

185   "He must be a man of most serious life," he said, "of great discretion, of praiseworthy reputation. A man who has no private loves, lest while he shows favor to the one, he beget scandal in the whole group. A man to whom zeal for prayer is a close friend; a man who sets aside certain hours for his soul and certain hours for the flock committed to him. For the first thing in the morning he must begin with the holy sacrifice of the Mass and commend himself and his flock to the divine protection in a prolonged devotion. After his prayers," he said, "he should make himself available to be stormed by all, to give answers to all, to provide for all with kindness. He must be a man who will not commit the foul sin of showing favoritism, a man in whom the care of the lowly and the simple is no less pronounced than his care for the wise and the greater. A man who, though it be his gift to excel in learning, bears the image of pious simplicity in his actions and fosters virtue. A man who detests money as the chief cause of the corruption of our profession and perfection; one who,

as the head of a poor order, should show himself an example for imitation to the rest, does not make wrong use of the pocketbook. For himself a habit and a little book should suffice, and for his brothers it is enough if he has a box of pens and a seal. He should not be a collector of books, nor given to much reading, lest he be taking from his office what he gives to study. He should be a man who consoles the afflicted, since he is the last recourse for the troubled; and if they can find no healing remedies from him, there is danger that the illness of despair may prevail over the sick. He should bend stormy characters to meekness; he should debase himself and relax something of what is his right to gain a soul for Christ. Toward those who take flight from the order let him not shut up the bowels of his mercy, as if they were sheep who had perished, knowing that the temptations that bring a man to such a pass are overpowering temptations.

186   "I would want him to be honored by all as taking the place of Christ and to be provided with everything that is necessary in all charity. However, he must not take pleasure in honors, nor be pleased by favors more than by injuries. If some time he should need more abundant food because he has grown weak or is exhausted, he should take it not in private but in public, so that others may be spared shame in providing for the weaknesses of their bodies. Above all else it pertains to him to examine the secrets of consciences, to bring out the truth from hidden places, but not to listen to the talkative. He must be, finally, a man who in no way will bring down the strong fabric of justice by his eagerness for retaining honors, but who will consider so great an office a burden rather than a dignity. However, he should not let apathy grow out of excessive kindness, nor a letdown in discipline out of lax indulgence, so

that while he is loved by all, he will be none the less feared by those *that work evil*.[339] I would wish, however, that he have companions endowed with goodness of life who will show themselves, just as he does, *in all things an example of good works*:[340] men who are staunch against pleasures, strong against hardships, and so becomingly affable that all who come to them may be received with holy cheerfulness. Behold," he said, "this is what the minister general of the order must be."

CHAPTER CXL

Of the ministers provincial

187 The blessed father required all these same qualities in the ministers provincial too, though in the minister general the single ones had to stand out conspicuously. He wished them to be affable to those in lesser stations, and serene with such great kindness that those who had failed in some way might not be afraid to entrust themselves to their good will. He wanted them to be moderate in giving commands and generous in forgiving offenses; he wanted them to be more ready to bear injuries than to return them; he wanted them to be enemies of vices, but healers of the wicked. Finally, he wanted them to be such that their life would be a mirror of discipline to all the rest. Still he wanted them to be treated with all honor and to be loved, because they bear the burden of cares and labors. He said that they are deserving before God of the highest rewards who govern the souls entrusted to them according to such a norm and such a law.

CHAPTER CXLI

Francis' answer when he was asked about the ministers

188   Once when Francis was asked by a certain brother why he had renounced the care of all his brothers and given them over to strange hands, as though they did not in any way pertain to him, he answered: "Son, I love the brothers as much as I can; but if they would follow my footsteps, I would certainly love them even more and I would not make myself a stranger to them. For there are some among the number of superiors who draw them to other things, proposing to them the example of the ancients,[341] and putting little value upon my admonitions. But what they are doing will be seen in the end." And a little afterwards, when he was afflicted with grave infirmity, he raised himself upon his couch and said in vehemence of spirit: "Who are these who have snatched my order and that of my brothers out of my hands? If I go to the general chapter, I will show them what my will is." And that brother said: "Would you not also change those ministers provincial who have abused their freedom for so long a time?" And sighing deeply, the father spoke this terrible word: "Let them live as it suits them, for the damnation of a few is a lesser loss than the damnation of many!" He did not say this because of all the ministers, but because of some who seemed to claim their prelacy by a hereditary right since they had held office for so long a time. In every kind of regular prelates this he praised most of all, that they do not change their conduct except for the better, that they do not seek popularity, that they do not insist on their power, but fulfill their office.

CHAPTER CXLII

What true simplicity is

189 The saint was zealous with more than usual care to show forth in himself, and he loved in others, holy simplicity, the daughter of grace, the sister of wisdom, the mother of justice. Not all simplicity, however, was approved by him, but only that simplicity which, being content with its God, considers everything else as of little value. This is that simplicity that *glories in the fear of God*,[342] that knows not how to do or to speak evil. This is that simplicity that, examining itself, condemns no one by its judgment; that, surrendering due authority to a better, seeks no authority for itself. This is that simplicity that, not considering *Grecian glories for the best*,[343] chooses rather to act than to learn or to teach. This is that simplicity that, in all the divine laws, leaves wordy circumlocutions, ornaments, and embellishments, vain displays and curiosities, to those who are marked for a fall, and seeks not the bark but the pith, not the shell but the kernel, not the many things, but the much, the greatest and the lasting good. The most holy father demanded this virtue in both the learned and the lay brothers, not considering it contrary to wisdom, but true wisdom's sister, though he thought it easier to be gotten as a habit and more ready to be used by those who are poor as regards learning. Therefore in the *Praises of the Virtues*[344] he composed, he says this: "Hail, Queen Wisdom! The Lord save you, with your sister, pure, holy simplicity."

CHAPTER CXLIII

About John the Simple

190 When St. Francis was passing near a certain village[345] in the neighborhood of Assisi, a certain John, a very simple man, who was ploughing in a field, came to him and said: "I would like for you to make me a brother, for I have long wanted to serve God." The saint rejoiced, and when he had considered the simplicity of the man, he replied to his wish: "If, brother, you want to become our companion, give to the poor whatever you may have, and I will receive you after you have given everything away." Immediately he unhitched the oxen, and he offered one to St. Francis. "Let us give this ox to the poor," he said; "I deserve to receive that much at least of my father's goods." The saint smiled, but approved his disposition of simplicity not a little. When his parents and small brothers heard this, they came running in tears, unhappy, however, about losing the ox rather than about losing the man. The saint said to them: "Be of easy mind! Behold, I give you the ox and take your brother." He therefore took the man with him, and giving him the habit of religion, he made him his special companion because of his grace of simplicity.

When St. Francis would stand in any place to meditate, whatever gestures or movements he would make the simple John would himself repeat and copy. For if Francis spat, he spat; if Francis coughed, he coughed. He joined his sighs to Francis' sighs; and he accompanied Francis' weeping with his own weeping. When the saint raised his hands to heaven, John raised his too, diligently watching him as his model and copying everything he did. The saint noticed this, and once asked him why he did these things. He answered: "I have promised to do everything you do; it is dangerous for me to omit anything." The saint rejoiced because of the brother's simplicity, but gently forbade him to act like that in the future. Not long afterwards this simple brother went to the Lord in that purity of life. The saint often proposed his life for imitation, and with great joy he called him, not *Brother* John, but *Saint* John. Notice that it is a mark of pious simplicity to live according to the laws of one's superiors and to follow always the examples and the precepts of the saint. O that it were given to the *wisdom of men*[346] to follow him reigning in heaven with the great zeal with which simplicity conformed itself to him on earth! What then? Simplicity followed him in life, simplicity went before him to life.

CHAPTER CXLIV

How Francis fostered unity among his sons, and how he spoke of it figuratively

191   It was always Francis' anxious wish and careful watchfulness to preserve among his sons the bond of unity, so that those whom the same spirit drew together and the same father brought forth might be nurtured peacefully in the bosom of one mother. He wanted the greater to be joined to the lesser, the wise to be united with the simple by brotherly affection, the distant to be bound to the distant by the binding force of love. He once set before them this moral similitude that contains no little instruction. "Suppose that one general chapter should be held," he said, "of all the religious in the Church! Because, therefore, there are present the lettered and those without the knowledge of letters, the learned and those who know how to please God without learning, one of the learned and one of the simple are appointed to preach. The wise one, because he is wise, delib-

erates thus within himself: 'There is no place here for display of learning, where there are men perfect in learning; nor would it be becoming for me to make myself conspicuous for my strangeness by uttering subtleties among those most subtle men. To speak simply would probably be the most fruitful thing.' The appointed day dawns, the congregations of the saints are come together, and they are anxious to hear the sermon. The wise man goes forth clothed in sackcloth and his head sprinkled with ashes. And to the astonishment of all, preaching mostly by actions, he shortens his words. 'Great things,' he says, 'have we promised, still greater are promised to us; let us keep the former, let us strive after the latter. Pleasure is short, punishment eternal; suffering is small, glory without measure. Many are called, few are chosen, to all shall retribution be made.' The hearts of the listeners are touched and they break out into tears and indeed they venerate the wise man as a saint. But the simple man says in his heart: 'The wise man has stolen from me everything I was going to do and say. But I know what I will do. I know certain verses of the Psalms; I will play the part of a wise man, after that wise man has played the part of a simple one.' The next day's session comes, the simple man rises and proposes a psalm as his theme. Inspired by the Holy Spirit, he preaches so fervently, so subtly, so sweetly because of this inspired gift from God, that all are filled with amazement and say: 'God's *communication is with the simple.'*"[347]

192   This moral similitude, which he thus proposed, the man of God explained in this way. "Our order," he said, "is a very great company, a kind of general assembly, which has come together from every part of the world to live under one form of life. In it the wise turn to their own advantage what is characteristic of the simple, when they see the illiter-

ate seeking heavenly things with burning zeal and those who have not been taught by men learning to savor spiritual things through the Holy Spirit. In it also the simple turn to their own benefit the things that are proper to the wise, when they see renowned men who could live in glory everywhere in the world humbled in the same way as they themselves. This," he said, "is what makes the beauty of this family shine forth, whose many different ornaments please the father of the family not a little."

CHAPTER CXLV

How the saint wanted to be shaved

193   When St. Francis was shaved, he often said to the one who shaved him: "Be careful that you do not give me a large corona.[348] For I want my simple brothers to have a share in my head." He wished finally that the order should be for the poor and unlearned, not only for the rich and wise. "*With God*," he said, "there is *no respect of persons*,[349] and the minister general of the order, the Holy Spirit, rests equally upon the poor and the simple." He wanted this thought inserted into his rule, but since it was already approved by papal bull, this could not be done.[350]

CHAPTER CXLVI

How Francis wanted great clerics coming to the order to renounce all their possessions

194   Francis once said that a great cleric must in some way give up even his learning when he comes to the order, so that having renounced such a possession, he may offer himself naked to the arms of the Crucified. "Learning takes from many people their docility," he said, "and does not permit them to

bend to humble practices. Wherefore I want the learned first to make this petition to me: 'Behold, Brother, I have lived in the world a long time and I did not truly know my God. I beg of you, give me a place that is removed from the noise of the world where I can think over my years in sorrow, where, recollecting my distracted heart, I can bring my soul to better things.' What kind of man," he said, "do you think he will become who starts out in this way? Surely he would go forth unto all things strong as an unchained lion, and the blessed moisture he has tasted at the beginning will increase constantly in him. He may be assigned confidently to the true ministry of the word, for he will pour out what is bubbling up within him." This is truly a pious teaching. For what is so necessary for a man coming back from such a different world as to eliminate and cleanse away through humble exercises his long standing and deeply imprinted worldly attachments? Quickly they reach perfection who enter the school of perfection.

CHAPTER CXLVII

How Francis wanted the brothers to learn, and how he appeared to a companion who was devoting himself to preaching

195 Francis was sad if learning was sought to the neglect of virtue, especially if each did not *remain in the calling in which he was called*[351] from the beginning. "My brothers," he said, "who are being led by curious craving after learning will find their hand empty on the day of retribution. I want them rather to be made strong in virtues, so that when the times of tribulation come, they will have the Lord with them in their distress. For tribulation will come," he said, "such that books, useful for nothing, will be thrown out of windows and into cubby-holes." He did not say this because Scripture studies displeased him, but in order that he might withdraw all the brothers from a vain desire for learning and because he wanted them to be good in charity rather than superficially learned through curiosity.

He also sensed that times would not be long in coming when he knew that knowledge would be an occasion of ruin, but the striving after spiritual things would be a bulwark of safety to the spirit. To a lay brother who wanted to have a psalter and asked him permission for it he offered ashes in place of the psalter.[352] Appearing in a vision after death to one of his companions who was once giving much time to preaching, Francis forbade him to do this and commanded him to walk in the way of simplicity. *God is my witness*,[353] that after this vision he felt sweetness to the extent that for several days the dew-laden words of his father seemed still to ring in his ears.

OF THE SPECIAL DEVOTIONS OF THE SAINT

CHAPTER CXLVIII

How Francis was moved at the mention of the love of God

196   To touch briefly upon the special devotions of St. Francis will perhaps be neither unprofitable nor unfitting. For, though this man was devout in all things, as one who enjoyed the anointing of the Spirit, nevertheless he was moved toward certain special things with a special love. Among other words used in ordinary conversation, he could never hear *the love of God* without a kind of transformation within himself. For immediately upon hearing *the love of God,* he would become excited, stirred, and inflamed, as though an inner chord of his heart had been plucked by the plectrum[354] of the outward voice of the speaker. He said that to offer the love of God to get an alms was a noble prodigality, and those who valued it less than money were most foolish men.[355] He himself kept unfailingly to his death the resolution he had made while he was still enmeshed in worldly things, namely, that he would never turn away a poor man who asked an alms for the love of God.[356] For on one occasion when a poor man asked an alms for the love of God and he had nothing, he took a scissors and was going to quickly cut up his tunic. He would have done this too, but he was detected by his brothers, and instead he saw to it that the poor man was provided for by some other means.[357] "The love of him," he said, "who loved us much is much to be loved."

CHAPTER CXLIX

Of Francis' devotion to the angels, and what he did out of love for St. Michael

197 Francis venerated with a very great affection the angels who are with us in our struggle and who walk *in the midst of the shadow of death* with us.[358] Such companions who were everywhere with us, he used to say, are to be venerated, such are to be invoked as our guardians. He used to teach that their presence must not be offended, and that we must not presume to do before them what we would not do before men. Because in choir we sing *in the sight of the angels,*[359] he wanted all who could do so to come together in the oratory and there *sing wisely.*[360] He often said that the blessed Michael should be honored more especially than the rest in as much as he has the office of presenting souls to God.[361] He also kept most devoutly a fast of forty days in honor of St. Michael between the feast of the Assumption and his feast.[362] For he said: "Everyone should offer to God, to honor so great a prince, some praise or some special gift."

CHAPTER CL

Of Francis' devotion to our Lady, to whom in particular he entrusted his order

198   Toward the Mother of Jesus he was filled with an inexpressible love, because it was she who made the Lord of Majesty our brother. He sang special *Praises* to her, poured out prayers to her, offered her his affections, so many and so great that the tongue of man cannot recount them.[363] But what delights us most, he made her the advocate of the order and placed under her wings the sons he was about to leave that she might cherish them and protect them to the end. — Hail, advocate of the poor! Fulfill toward us your office of protectress *until the time set by the Father.*[364]

CHAPTER CLI

Of Francis' devotion at Christmas and how he wanted all things to be treated on that feast

199   The birthday of the Child Jesus Francis observed with inexpressible eagerness over all other feasts, saying that it was the feast of feasts, on which God, having become a tiny infant, clung to human breasts. Pictures of those infant members he kissed with thoughts filled with yearning, and his compassion for the Child flooded his heart and made him stammer words of sweetness after the manner of infants. His name was like honey and the honeycomb in Francis' mouth. When the question arose about eating meat that day, since that Christmas day was a Friday,[365] he replied, saying to Brother Morico: "You sin, Brother, calling the day on which the Child was born to us[366] a day of fast. It is my wish," he said, "that even the walls should eat meat on such a day, and if they cannot, they should be smeared with meat on the outside."

200   On this day Francis wanted the poor and the hungry to be filled by the rich, and more than the usual amount of grain and hay given to the oxen and asses. "If I could speak to the emperor," he said, "I would ask that a general law be made that all who can should scatter corn and grain along the roads so that the birds might have an abundance of food on the day of such great solemnity, especially our sisters the larks." He would recall, not without tears, what great want surrounded the poor Virgin on that day.[367] Once when he was sitting at dinner, a certain brother talked about the poverty of the Blessed Virgin and recalled the want of Christ, her Son. Francis immediately arose from the table and, with great sighs and many tears, ate the rest of the meal on the bare ground. For this reason he used to say that this virtue that shone forth so eminently in the King and Queen was a royal virtue. And when the brothers were discussing at a gathering which virtue does more to make one a close friend of Christ, Francis, as though making known to them a secret of his heart, answered: "Know, my sons, that poverty is the special way to salvation; its fruit is manifold, but it is really well known only to a few."

CHAPTER CLII

Of Francis' devotion to the Body of the Lord

201   Francis burned with a love that came from his whole being for the sacrament of the Lord's body, and he was carried away with wonder at the loving condescension and the most condescending love

shown there. Not to hear at least one Mass each day, if he could be there, he considered no small contempt. He frequently received Holy Communion, and he did so with such devotion that he made others also devout. Showing toward that sacrament deserving of all reverence all the reverence he could, he offered a sacrifice of all his members; and receiving the Lamb that was offered,[368] he immolated his own spirit with the fire that burned always upon the altar of his heart. He loved France as a friend of the Body of the Lord,[369] and he longed to die there because of its reverence for sacred things. He wished at one time to send his brothers through the world with precious pyxes, so that wherever they should see the price of our redemption kept in an unbecoming manner, they should place it in the very best place.[370] He wanted great reverence shown to the hands of priests, for to these has been given authority from God over the consecrated bread and wine. Often he would say: "If it should happen that I would meet at the same time some saint from heaven and any poor priest, I would first show honor to the priest and quickly go to kiss his hands. And I would say to the other: 'Wait, St. Lawrence,[371] for the hands of this one touch the *Word of Life,*[372] and have something about them that is more than human.'"

CHAPTER CLIII

Of Francis' devotion to the relics of saints

202   This man, beloved of God, showed himself most devoted to divine worship and he left nothing pertaining to God dishonored because of neglect. When he was at Monte Casale, in the province of Massa,[373] he commanded his brothers to bring the holy relics from a church that had been abandoned by all to the place of the brothers in a most reverent

manner. He was deeply grieved that they had been deprived of the devotion due them already for a long time. But when for some reason his sons had to go to some other place, they forgot the command of their father and neglected the merit of obedience. But one day, when the brothers wanted to celebrate Mass, they removed the cloth from the altar, as is customary, and there they found some very beautiful and fragrant bones. Quite astonished, they were looking at what they had never seen before. When the saint of God returned a little later, he diligently inquired if what he had commanded about the relics had been carried out. Humbly confessing the guilt of their neglected obedience, the brothers merited pardon along with punishment. And the saint said: "Blessed be the Lord my God, who himself carried out what you were to do." Consider diligently the devotion of Francis, notice the *good pleasure of God*[374] concerning our dust, and *magnify with praise* holy obedience.[375] For God obeyed the prayers of him whose voice man did not obey.

CHAPTER CLIV

Of Francis' devotion to the cross and of a certain hidden mystery

203 Finally, who can express, who can understand how far Francis was from glorying in anything *save in the cross of our Lord?*[376] To him alone is it given to know to whom alone it is given to experience it. For, though in some sense we should perceive these things in ourselves, words would in no way suffice to express such wonderful things, defiled as words are by everyday and common things. And perhaps it had therefore to appear in the flesh, because it could not be explained in words. Therefore let silence speak where words are wanting, for the thing itself

cries out where the word fails.[377] Let this alone be made known to human ears that it is not yet fully clear why that mystery appeared in the saint; for, as far as it has been revealed by him, it must get its explanation and reason in the future. He will be found true and trustworthy unto whom nature, the law, and grace will be witnesses.[378]

OF THE POOR LADIES

CHAPTER CLV

How Francis wanted his brothers to deal with the Poor Ladies[379]

204 It would not be proper to pass over the memory of the spiritual edifice, a much nobler edifice than that earthly building, which the blessed Francis founded in that place, under the guidance of the Holy Spirit, after he had repaired that material building.[380] It is not to be thought that it was to repair a church that would perish and was falling down that Christ spoke to him from the wood of the cross in a manner so stupendous that it filled those who heard of it with fear and sorrow. But, as the Holy Spirit had once foretold,[381] the Order of Holy Virgins was to be established there, which, like a polished mass of *living stones*,[382] was one day to be brought there unto the restoration of the heavenly house. Indeed, after the virgins of Christ began to come together in that place, gathered together there from various parts of the world, they professed the greatest perfection in observing the highest poverty and in adorning themselves with all virtues. Though their father gradually withdrew his bodily presence from them, he nevertheless gave them his affection in the Holy Spirit by caring for them. For when the saint recognized by many signs of highest perfection that they had been proved and were ready to make every sacrifice for Christ and endure every difficulty without ever wanting to depart from Christ's holy commandments, he firmly promised them and others who would profess poverty in a similar way of life that he would always give them his help and counsel and the help and counsel of his brothers. This he always diligently carried out as long as he lived, and when he was close to death, he emphatically commanded that it should be always so, saying that *one and the same spirit*[383] had led the brothers and the poor ladies out of the world.

205   At times the brothers wondered that Francis did not visit the holy servants of Christ with his corporal presence more often, and he would say: "Do not believe, dearest brothers, that I do not love them perfectly. For if it were a fault to cherish them in Christ, would it not have been a greater fault to have united them to Christ? Indeed, not to have called them would not have been a wrong; not to care for them once they have been called would be the greatest unkindness. But I give *you an example, that as I have done to you, so you also should do.*[384] I do not want anyone to offer himself of his own accord to visit them, but I command that unwilling and most reluctant brothers be appointed to take care of them, provided they be spiritual men, proved by a worthy and long religious life."

CHAPTER CLVI

How Francis reprimanded certain ones who went of their own accord to the monasteries[385]

206   Once when a certain brother who had two daughters of perfect life in a certain monastery said he would willingly take some poor little gift to that place for the saint, Francis rebuked him very severe-

ly, saying things that should not now be repeated. So he sent the little gift by another brother who had refused to go, but had not persisted obstinately in his refusal. Another brother went in the winter to a certain monastery on an errand of sympathy, not knowing the saint's strong will about not going on such visits. After the fact had become known to the saint, he made the brother walk several miles naked in the cold and deep snow.[386]

CHAPTER CLVII

Of the sermon Francis preached more by example than by words

207   Repeatedly asked by his vicar to preach the word of God to his daughters when he stopped off for a short time at St. Damian's, Francis was finally overcome by his insistence and consented. But when the nuns had come together, according to their custom, to hear the word of God, though no less also to see their father, Francis raised his eyes to heaven, where his heart always was, and began to pray to Christ. He then commanded ashes to be brought to him and he made a circle with them around himself on the pavement and sprinkled the rest of them on his head. But when they waited for him to begin and the blessed father remained standing in the circle in silence, no small astonishment arose in their hearts. The saint then suddenly rose and to the amazement of the nuns recited the *Miserere mei Deus*[387] in place of a sermon. When he had finished, he quickly left. The servants of God were so filled with contrition because of the power of this symbolic sermon that their tears flowed in abundance and they could scarcely restrain their hands from inflicting punishment on themselves. By his actions he taught them that they should regard themselves as ashes and that there was noth-

ing in his heart concerning them but what was fitting
this consideration. This was the way he acted toward
these holy women; his visits to them were very useful, but they were forced upon him and rare. And
this was his will for all his brothers: he wanted them
to serve these women in such a way for Christ, whom
they serve, that like *them that have wings* they would
always guard against the snare laid out for them.[388]

HOW FRANCIS COMMENDED THE RULE OF THE BROTHERS

CHAPTER CLVIII
*How the blessed Francis commended the rule, and of
a brother who carried it about with him*

208   Francis glowed most ardently for the common
profession and the rule, and he blessed with a very
special blessing those who would be zealous about it.
For he called the rule the *book of life*,[389] the *hope of
salvation*,[390] the marrow of the Gospel,[391] the way of
perfection, the key to paradise, the agreement of a
perpetual covenant.[392] He wanted it to be had by all,
to be known by all,[393] and he wanted it to speak everywhere to the interior man unto his comfort in weari-
ness and unto a remembrance of the vows he had
made.[394] He taught them to keep it ever before their
eyes as a reminder of the life they were to live, and,
what is more, that they should die with it.

A certain brother, not unmindful of this direction,
who, we believe, is to be venerated among the number of martyrs, gained the palm of a glorious victory.
For when he was brought to martyrdom by the Saracens, holding the rule in his hands and kneeling
humbly, he said to his companion: "I confess my guilt
before the eyes of God's majesty and before you,
most dear Brother, concerning everything I have done
against this holy rule." The sword followed this brief
confession and brought his life to its end by martyr-

dom; afterwards he became famous for *miracles and wonders*.[395] This brother had entered the order so young that he could hardly bear the fast of the rule, and yet, though a young man, he wore an iron corslet next to his skin. Happy young man, who began happily so that he might finish even more happily.[396]

CHAPTER CLIX

A vision that commended the rule

209 The most holy father once saw a vision, wrought by a heavenly wonder, concerning the rule. At the time when there was a discussion among the brothers about the confirmation of the rule,[397] the following things were shown to Francis, who was greatly anxious about the matter, in his sleep. It seemed to him that he had to gather the finest crumbs of bread from the ground and to distribute them to the many hungry brothers who were standing around him. But while he was afraid to distribute such small crumbs lest such minute particles of dust should fall from his hands, a voice spoke to him from above: "Francis, make one host out of all these crumbs and give it to those who want to eat of it." When he did this, those who did not receive devoutly, or who despised the gift they had received, were soon seen to be greatly infected with leprosy. The saint told all these things to his companions in the morning, regretting that he did not understand the mystery of the vision. But after a little while, while he continued to keep watch in prayer, this *voice came down to him*[398] from heaven: "Francis," it said, "the crumbs of last night are the words of the Gospel, the host is the rule, the leprosy is wickedness." This fidelity to the rule that they had sworn, the brothers of those times, who were eager to go beyond what was required, did not consider difficult or harsh. Neither was there any place for laziness or idleness where the stimulus of love urged them on to ever greater things.

CHAPTER CLX

How Francis discussed with a certain brother about the care of his body

210   Francis, the herald of God, walked in the footsteps of Christ through innumerable labors and severe illnesses, and he did not draw back his foot until he had brought what he had perfectly begun to an even more perfect end. For though he was enfeebled and completely broken in body, he never halted his pursuit of perfection, he never suffered· himself to relax the rigor of discipline. For even when his body was exhausted he could not give it even a little relief without his conscience murmuring. Therefore, when it became necessary, even though he was unwilling, to ease with some soothing remedies the inconveniences of his body, which were beyond his strength, he one day spoke kindly to a certain brother who he knew would give him suitable counsel. "What do you think, my dearest son, of the fact that my conscience murmurs so frequently about the care of my body? It is afraid that I will indulge it too much in its illness and be anxious to come to its aid by means of delicacies carefully sought after. Not that it can take delight any more in anything after it has been worn down so long by illness and after all urge to satisfy taste has left it."

211   The son, acknowledging that the words of his answer were given to him by the Lord, replied faithfully to the father: "Tell me, if you will, Father, with how much diligence did your body obey your commands when it could?" He answered: *"I bear*

530

witness concerning[399] it, son, that it was obedient in all things; it spared itself in nothing, but rushed almost headlong to obey all my commands. It shirked no labor, it refused no discomfort, so long as it could do what was commanded. In this I and it agreed perfectly that we would *serve the Lord Christ*[400] without any reluctance." And the brother said: "Where then, Father, is your generosity, where are your kindness and discretion? Is this a worthy way to repay faithful friends, to accept a kindness willingly, but when the giver is in need not to repay him as he deserves? What could you have done up till now in the service of Christ your Lord without the help of your body? Has it not, as you said, exposed itself to every danger on this account?" "I confess, son," said the father, "this is very true." And that son said: "Is this reasonable then that you abandon so faithful a friend in such great need, a friend who has exposed himself and all that is his for you even unto death? *Far be it from you,*[401] Father, help and staff of the afflicted; *far be from* you *this sin against the Lord.*"[402] "May you be blessed, son," he said, "who propose wisely such salutary remedies for my uncertainties." And he began to speak joyfully to his body: "Rejoice, brother body, and forgive me, for, behold, I now gladly fulfill your desires, I hasten to give heed to your complaints." But how could his exhausted body rejoice now? What could support what had collapsed in every part? Francis was now dead to the world, but Christ was living in him.[403] All the pleasures of the world were a cross to him, because he carried the cross of Christ rooted in his heart. And therefore the stigmata shone forth exteriorly in his flesh, because interiorly that deeply set root was sprouting forth from his mind.

CHAPTER CLXI

What was promised Francis by the Lord for his infirmities

212   Since Francis was thus worn out in every part by sufferings, it is surprising that his strength was sufficient to bear them. But he looked upon these trials not under the name of sufferings but of *sisters*. That they proceeded from many causes is beyond doubt. Indeed, that Francis might be more renowned because of his triumphs, the Most High not only entrusted difficult things to him when he was as yet inexperienced, but now too when he was a veteran in the battle there was given to him the opportunity of triumphing. His followers had in this also an example, for he did not act more slowly because of age nor more indulgently because of illness. Nor was it for no reason that his purgation was completed in this valley of tears, for thus he might give an account even to the last penny, if anything that could be burned clung to him; and thus cleansed most perfectly he might at length take his flight to heaven without delay. I think the best way to understand his suffering is this, that, as he said of others, in bearing them *there is a great reward.*[404]

213   For one night, when he was exhausted more than usual because of the many severe pains of his infirmities, Francis began to pity himself in the depths of his heart. But lest that ready spirit yield carnally to the flesh in anything even for an hour, he kept the shield of patience unshaken by praying to Christ. At length, as he prayed thus in agony, he was given a promise of eternal life by the Lord under this simile: "If the whole *bulk of the earth*[405] and the whole universe were precious gold without price, and if there were given to you as a reward for these severe sufferings you are enduring, after all the pain had been removed, a treasure of such great glory, in comparison with which that aforementioned gold would be nothing or not even worthy of mention, would you not be happy and would you not willingly bear what you are bearing at the moment?" "I would indeed be happy," the saint said, "and I would rejoice *beyond all measure*."[406] "Rejoice, therefore," the Lord said to him, "for your sickness is an earnest of my kingdom; and await the inheritance of that kingdom, steadfast and assured, because of the merit of your patience." But with what great exultation do you think that man rejoiced, blessed as he was by such a happy promise? And not only with what great patience, but also with what great love do you believe he embraced the sufferings of his body? He now knows perfectly, but he was not then able to give expression to what he felt. But he did tell his companions some few things, as much as he could. It was at this time that he composed the *Praises of Creatures*[407] and inflamed them as much as he could to praise their Creator.

OF THE DEATH OF THE HOLY FATHER

CHAPTER CLXII

How Francis exhorted his brothers and blessed them at the end

214   The Wise Man says: *In the end of man is the disclosing of his works.*[408] We see this gloriously fulfilled in this saint. Running *the way of God's commandments*[409] with alacrity of mind, he reached the summit by means of the steps of all the virtues; and like a *beaten work*,[410] he was brought to perfection by the hammer of many kinds of tribulation, and he saw *an end of all perfection.*[411] For it was then that his wonderful works shone forth; and that the way he lived was from God was shown by a judgment of truth, for after he had trampled upon all the allurements of mortal life, he went free to heaven. For to live for the world he considered a disgrace; he *loved his own to the end,*[412] and he accepted death singing. When he was approaching his last days, and the eternal light was taking the place of the temporal light that was being withdrawn, he showed by an example of virtue that he had nothing in common with the world. For, worn down by his serious illness that was being brought to an end with every suffering, he had himself placed naked upon the naked ground, so that in that final hour when the enemy could still rage against him, he might wrestle naked with a naked enemy.[413] He waited without fear for his triumph, and with his hands clasped he was grasping a *crown of justice.*[414] Placed thus upon the ground, with his garment of sackcloth laid aside, he raised his face to heaven as was his custom, and giving his whole attention to that glory, he covered the wound in his right side with his left hand lest it be seen. And he said to his brothers: "I have done what was mine to do; may Christ teach you what you are to do."

215   Seeing these things his sons shed streams of tears and sighing deeply from their innermost being, they were overwhelmed by grief in their compassion. Meanwhile, when their sighs were somewhat quieted, Francis' guardian, who knew the saint's wish more exactly by reason of divine inspiration, hurriedly arose and taking a tunic and trousers and a little cap of sackcloth, he said to their father: "Know that this tunic and trousers and cap have been lent to you by me, by command of holy obedience. But, that you may know that you have no ownership with regard to them, I take away from you all authority to give them to anyone." The saint rejoiced and was glad out of the gladness of his heart, for he saw that he

had kept faith with Lady Poverty to the end.[415] For he had done all these things out of zeal for poverty, so that he would not have at the end even a habit that was his own, but, as it were, lent to him by another. The little cap of sackcloth, however, he wore on his head to cover the wounds he had received when he sought health for his eyes, for which purpose a soft cap of finer wool was rather necessary.

216   After these things, the saint raised his hands to heaven and praised his Christ, because, freed now of all things, he was going to him free. Indeed, that he might show himself to be a true imitator of Christ his God in all things, he *loved to the end*[416] his brothers and sons whom he had loved from the beginning. He had all the brothers present there called to him and soothing them with comforting words in view of his death, he exhorted them with paternal affection to love God. He spoke a long time about practicing patience and poverty, setting the counsels of the holy Gospel ahead of all other prescriptions. Then, with all the brothers sitting about, he extended his right hand over them and beginning with his vicar, he placed it upon the head of each one. "Farewell," he said, "all you my sons, *in the fear of the Lord*,[417] and may you remain in him always! And because a future temptation and tribulation is approaching, happy will they be who will persevere in the things they have begun. I am hastening to the Lord, to whose grace I commend you all."[418] And he blessed in those who were present also all his brothers in the world and all who would come after them unto the end of the world. Let no one claim this blessing for himself which Francis spoke for the absent upon those who were present. As it is set forth elsewhere,[419] the blessing had a special significance, but mainly with regard to the exercise of an office.[420]

CHAPTER CLXIII

Of Francis' death and what he did before he died

217   While therefore the brothers were weeping very bitterly and grieving inconsolably, the holy father commanded that bread be brought to him. He *blessed and broke it*[421] and gave a small piece of it to each one to eat. Commanding also that a book of the Gospels be brought, he asked that the Gospel according to St. John be read to him from the place that begins: *Before the feast of the Passover.*[422] He was recalling that most holy supper which the Lord celebrated as his last supper with his disciples.[423] He did all of this in reverent memory of that supper, showing thereby the deep love he had for his brothers.

Then he spent the few days that remained before his death in praise, teaching his companions whom he loved so much to praise Christ with him. He himself, in as far as he was able, broke forth in this psalm: *I cried to the Lord with my voice: with my voice I made supplication to the Lord.*[424] He also invited all creatures to praise God, and by means of the words he had composed earlier,[425] he exhorted them to love God. He exhorted death itself, terrible and hateful to all, to give praise, and going joyfully to meet it, he invited it to make its lodging with him. "Welcome," he said, "my sister death."[426] To the doctor he said: "Tell me bravely, brother doctor, that death, which is the gateway of life, is at hand." Then to the brothers: "When you see that I am brought to my last moments, place me naked upon the ground just as you saw me the day before yesterday;[427] and let me lie there after I am dead for the length of time it takes one to walk a mile unhurriedly." The hour therefore came, and all the mysteries of Christ being fulfilled in him, he winged his way happily to God.

How a certain brother saw the soul of the holy father at his death[428]

217a   One of Francis's brothers, a man of some renown, saw the soul of the most holy father, like a star, but with the immensity of the moon and the brightness of the sun, ascending over many waters and borne aloft on a little white cloud, going directly to heaven.[429] There was therefore a great concourse of people there, praising and glorifying the name of the Lord. The whole city of Assisi rushed in a body and the whole region hastened to see the wonderful things of God that the Lord had made manifest in his servant. Francis' sons were filled with sorrow at being deprived of so great a father and they showed the pious affection of their hearts by their tears and sighs. However, a new miracle turned their laments to joy and their weeping to jubilation.[430] They saw the body of their blessed father adorned with the stigmata of Christ, in the middle, namely, of his hands and feet; not indeed the holes made by nails, but the nails themselves formed out of his flesh, indeed imbedded in that same flesh, and retaining the blackness of iron; and his right side was red with blood.[431] His flesh, naturally dark before, but now gleaming with a dazzling whiteness, gave promise of the rewards of the future life. His members, finally, had become pliable and soft, not rigid as they generally are in the dead; and they were changed into the likeness of the members of a little child.[432]

CHAPTER CLXIV

Of the vision Brother Augustine saw when he was dying

218   The minister of the brothers in the Terra di Lavoro[433] was Brother Augustine. When he was brought to his last hour, he suddenly cried out in the hearing of those who were standing about, even though he had lost his faculty of speech long before this: "Wait for me, Father, wait for me! Behold, I am coming with you." When the brothers asked in astonishment to whom he was speaking thus, he boldly replied: "Do you not see our father Francis going to heaven?" And immediately that brother's soul, released from his flesh, followed the most holy father.

CHAPTER CLXV

How the holy father appeared after his death to a certain brother

219 The glorious father, clad in a purple dalmatic,[434] appeared on the night and at the hour of his death to another brother of praiseworthy life who was absorbed in prayer at the time; he was accompanied by a great multitude of men. From this multitude of men several separated themselves and said to the brother: "Is not this Christ, Brother?" And he said: "It is he." But the others asked again: "Is not this St. Francis?" The brother answered again in the same way that it was he. Indeed, it seemed to the brother and all that great multitude that Christ and Blessed Francis were one and the same person. This does not seem to understanding people to be in any way a rash judgment, for he who cleaves to God is made one spirit with him,[435] and God will work *all things in all*.[436] The blessed father came at length with that astonishing multitude to a very pleasant place, which, watered with crystal clear waters, gave growth to the fairest plants and was covered with beautiful flowers and filled with every delightful kind of trees. There was a palace there of wonderful size and outstanding beauty, and the new inhabitant of heaven entered it eagerly, for he found in it very many brothers; and he began to eat happily with them at a table prepared most splendidly and filled with many delicious foods.

CHAPTER CLXVI

The vision the bishop of Assisi had about the death of the holy father

220   The bishop of Assisi[437] had gone at that time to the church of St. Michael[438] on a pilgrimage. The blessed father Francis appeared to him in a vision on the night of his death when the bishop was coming back to Benevento where he was staying. Francis said to him: "Behold, Father, I am leaving the world and I go to Christ." Rising in the morning, the bishop told his companions what he had seen, and sending for a notary, he recorded the day and the hour of Francis' death. He was made very sad because of these things, and shedding many tears, he grieved over the loss of his distinguished father. So, when he had gone back to his see, he made known everything in order and gave boundless thanks to the Lord because of his gifts.

Of the Canonization and Translation of St. Francis[439]

220a   *In the name of* the *Lord Jesus.*[440] Amen. In the year of our Lord's incarnation 1226, on October 4, the day he had foretold, twenty years after he had given himself perfectly to Christ and followed the life and footsteps of the Apostles,[441] the apostolic man Francis was freed from the shackles of this mortal life and went happily to Christ;[442] and after he had been buried in the city of Assisi, he began to shine forth with so many and such great and varied miracles, that in a short time he had brought a great part of the world to the admiration of a new age.[443] Because now he was becoming renowned around the various parts of the world by reason of the light of his miracles and everywhere those were coming together who rejoiced over being freed through him from their ailments, the lord pope Gregory, when he was at Perugia with all the cardinals and other prelates of churches, began to have discussions concerning his canonization.[444] All agreed and all said the same thing. They read and approved the miracles that the Lord had worked through his servant and they commended the life and conduct of the blessed father with the highest praises. The princes of the land were first called together for the great solemnity, and the whole assembly of prelates, with an infinite multitude of people, entered the city of Assisi on the appointed day with the blessed pope,[445] to celebrate his canonization there, because of the greater reverence for the saint in that place. When they had all come to the place that had been prepared for so solemn a gathering, Pope Gregory first preached[446] to the whole gathering and with sweet affection announced *the glorious works of God*.[447] He also praised our father Francis in that most noble sermon and when he spoke of the purity of his life, he was bathed in tears. Therefore, when the sermon was finished, Pope Gregory, extending his hands to heaven, proclaimed in a loud voice:[448] "To the praise and glory of Almighty God, the Father, Son, and Holy Spirit, and of the glorious Virgin Mary and of the blessed apostles Peter and Paul, and to the honor of the glorious Roman Church, at the advice of our brothers and of the other prelates, we decree that the most blessed father Francis, whom the Lord has glorified in heaven and whom we venerate on earth, shall be enrolled in the catalogue of saints and that his feast shall be celebrated on the day of his death."[449]

THE PRAYER OF FRANCIS' COMPANIONS
TO HIM[450]

221   Behold, you our blessed Father, the efforts of our simplicity have sought to praise in some measure your magnificent deeds and to recount in part for your glory some few of the many virtues of your sanctity. We know that our words have detracted much from the splendor of your outstanding virtues, for they are unequal to the task of recording the very great deeds of such great perfection. We beg of you and of our readers to consider our love as against our effort, and to rejoice that human pens are really overpowered by the greatness of your wonderful life. For who, great one among the saints, could either frame within himself or impress upon others the ardor of your spirit? Who would be able to conceive of those ineffable affections that flowed uninterruptedly from you to God? But we have written these things out of happiness over your sweet memory, about which, while we live, we will try to tell others, if only in a stammering way. You who were once famishing, are now fed *with the fat of wheat;*[451] you, who up till now were thirsting, drink *of the torrent of pleasure.*[452] But we do not believe that you are so *inebriated with the plenty*[453] of the house of God that you have forgotten your sons, for even he whom you drink is *mindful of us.*[454] Draw us therefore to yourself, worthy Father, that we may run *after thee to the odor of thy ointments,*[455] we who you see are lukewarm because of our sloth, languid because of our

541

idleness, half-living because of our negligence. The little flock is following you with hesitant steps; our weakened eyes cannot bear the dazzling rays of your perfection. *Renew our days as from the beginning,*[456] O mirror and model of the perfect, and do not suffer us who are like you in our profession to be unlike you in our life.

222   Behold, we now lay before the clemency of the Eternal Majesty our humble prayers for the servant of Christ, our minister, the successor of your holy humility and the imitator of your true poverty, who is exercising solicitous care for your sheep with tender affection *from love of* your *Christ.*[457] We beg of you, O holy one, so to stand by him and encompass him that, always following your footsteps, he may obtain forever the praise and glory you have attained.

223   We beseech you also, with all the affection of our hearts, most kind Father, for this your son who now and earlier has devotedly written your praises.[458] He, together with us, offers and dedicates this little work; though it is not done in a way that is worthy of what you deserve, it is done lovingly to the best of our ability.[459] Deign to preserve and deliver him from every evil; increase in him his holy merits; and by your prayers join him forever with the fellowship of the saints.

224   Remember all your sons, Father, who, surrounded by inextricable dangers, follow your footsteps, though from how great a distance, you, most holy Father, know perfectly. Give them strength that they may resist; purify them that they may gleam forth; rejoice them that they may be happy. Pray that *the spirit of grace and of prayers*[460] be poured upon them; that they may have the true humility you had;

that they may observe the poverty you observed; that they may be filled with the charity with which you always loved Christ crucified. Who with the Father and the Holy Spirit lives and reigns world without end. Amen.

PART III

Treatise on the Miracles of Blessed Francis
by Thomas of Celano

Treatise on the Miracles of Blessed Francis
by Thomas of Celano

SELECTIONS

TREATISE ON THE MIRACLES OF THE BLESSED FRANCIS[1]

CHAPTER III

Of Francis' controls over insensible creatures and especially over fire[2]

18   In the province of Rieti a very serious pestilence broke out that so cruelly took the lives of the oxen that there was hardly an ox left there. It was made known at night in a vision to a certain God-fearing man that he should hurry to the hermitage of the brothers and get the water in which the blessed Francis, who was living there at the time, had washed his hands and feet, and sprinkle it upon all the oxen. Rising early in the morning, that man, anxious about his own needs, went to that place and, not knowing the saint, he took the water secretly but with the help of other brothers and he sprinkled it upon all the oxen in accordance with the command that had been given him. From that hour, by the grace of God, the pestilence ceased and did not rage again in that region.

CHAPTER IV

Of Francis' control over sensible creatures[3]

31   Once, when the man of God was traveling from Siena to the Spoleto valley, he came to a certain field on which a rather large flock of sheep was grazing.[4] When he greeted them kindly, as was his custom, they all ran to him, raising their heads and returning his greeting with loud bleating. Francis' vicar noted with very careful attention of his eyes what the sheep did and said to the other companions who were following along behind more slowly: "Did you see what the sheep did to the holy father? Truly he is a great man whom the brutes venerate as their father and, though they lack reason, recognize as the friend of their Creator."

32   The larks[5] are birds that love the noonday light and shun the darkness of twilight. But on the night that St. Francis went to Christ, they came to the roof of the house, though already the twilight of the night to follow had fallen, and they flew about the house for a long time amid a great clamor, whether to show their joy or their sadness in their own way by their singing, we do not know. Tearful rejoicing and joyful sorrow made up their song, either to bemoan the fact that they were orphaned children, or to announce that their father was going to his eternal glory. The city watchmen who guarded the place with great care, were filled with astonishment and called the others to witness the wonder.

CHAPTER V

How the divine clemency responded immediately to Francis' desires[6]

34   When St. Francis was returning from Spain, because he could not go to Morocco as he had wished, he fell into a very grave illness.[7] For, after suffering privation and weakness and having been driven from a lodging place by the incivility of the host, he lost his speech for three days. But after he had somewhat recovered his strength, he said to Brother Bernard[8] while they were going along the way that he would eat a bird if he had one. And behold, a certain horseman came riding across the field, carrying a very

fine bird; he said to the blessed Francis: "Servant of God, kindly accept what the goodness of God sends you." He took the gift with joy, and seeing how Christ was taking care of him, he blessed him for all his gifts.

CHAPTER VI

Of the Lady Jacoba of Settesoli[9]

37   Jacoba of Settesoli,[10] equally renowned for her nobility and her sanctity in the city of Rome, had merited the privilege of a special love from St. Francis. It is not necessary for me to repeat unto her praise her illustrious origin, the dignity of her family, her great wealth, nor finally the wonderful perfection of her virtues, or her long continence as a widow. When therefore the saint lay in that illness that was to end all his suffering and bring to a most happy conclusion the happy course of his life, a few days before his death he wanted to send word to Rome for the Lady Jacoba, that if she wanted to see him whom she loved so ardently in this land of exile before he would go home to his fatherland, she should come with the greatest speed. A letter was written, a swift messenger was sought, and when one was found, he was gotten ready for the journey. Suddenly there was heard at the door the sound of horses, the noise of soldiers, and the crowd of a company of men. One of the companions, the one who had instructed the messenger, went to the door and found her there whom they had wanted to summon from afar. He was completely astonished, ran very quickly to the saint, and not being able to contain himself for joy, said: "I have something good to tell you, Father." And the saint immediately said in quick reply: "Blessed be God, who has guided the Lady Jacoba, our brother, to us. Open the door and bring her in, for

our Brother Jacoba does not have to observe the decree against women."[11]

38   There was a great rejoicing among the noble guests, and amid the rejoicing of spirit there was also a flowing of tears. And that nothing should be lacking to the miracle, the woman was found to have brought what the letter that had been previously written had contained about what should be brought for the father's burial. For God had seen to it that she brought the ashen-colored cloth with which to cover his dying body, also many candles, the cloth for his face, the little pillow for his head, a certain sweetmeat the saint had wanted to eat,[12] and everything the spirit of this man had wanted. I want to tell the outcome of this true pilgrimage, lest I dismiss that noble pilgrim without consolation. A great multitude of nobles, especially the many devout people of the city, awaited the approaching birthday in death of the saint. But the saint was made stronger by the coming of these devout people from Rome, and it seemed for a little while that he would live a little longer. Wherefore that Lady ordered the rest of the company to leave, and only she herself with her children and a few attendants would remain. The saint said to her: "No, for I will depart on Saturday; on Sunday you may leave with all who have come with you." And so it happened. At the time he had foretold, he who had fought so hard in the church militant entered the church triumphant. I will pass over[13] the concourse of people, the cries of rejoicing, the solemn ringing of the bells, the streams of tears; I will pass over the weeping of his sons, the sighs of those dear to him, the lamenting of his companions. I want only to speak of those things that that pilgrim, deprived of the consolation of her father, did to be consoled.

39   She was led quietly, streaming with tears, to Francis, and his body was placed in her arms. "See," said the vicar, "he whom you loved in life you shall hold in your arms in death." She wept hot tears over his body, wept aloud, and sighed deeply; and holding him in her arms and kissing him, she loosened the veil so that she could see him unhindered. Why should we add more? She looked upon that precious body in which also a precious treasure lay hidden, ornamented as it was with five pearls.[14] She saw that work that only the hand of the Almighty had wrought to the astonishment of the whole world, and filled with unaccustomed joy, she drew new life from her deceased friend. On the spot, she gave the advice that the unheard of miracle should not be hidden or covered over in any way, but that with prudent foresight it should be unveiled before the eyes of all. They then all eagerly ran to see the miracle and they found in truth what God had *not done in like manner to every nation,*[15] and they wondered in astonishment. I break off my description, for I do not want to stammer over what I cannot explain. John Frigia Pennates,[16] who at that time was a young man and afterwards a proconsul of the Romans and a count of the papal palace, admitted to the doubts he had had about it, but swore willingly to what at that time he and his mother had seen with their eyes and touched with their hands. Let the pilgrim now return to her fatherland,[17] consoled with such unusual graces, and let us pass on to other things that happened after the death of Francis.

CHAPTER VII

Of the dead who were brought to life through the merits of Blessed Francis[18]

41   To show that all men should love with all

their hearts the wonderful gift of God of confession and to worthily make known that this saint was always close to Christ, it must certainly be told what he did in so wonderful a way while he was living in this world and what his Christ did for him even more wonderfully after his death. For when the blessed father Francis was approaching Celano to preach there, a certain knight invited him with humble devotion, but with great insistence, to dine with him. Francis excused himself and begged off, but in the end he was overcome by the importunate persuasion of the knight. The mealtime came and the table was splendidly prepared. The devoted host was happy and the whole family rejoiced at the coming of the poor guests. Blessed Francis stood, his eyes raised to heaven, and he spoke to the host who had invited him. "Behold," he said, "brother host, I have come to your house to eat, conquered by your prayers. Listen quickly to my admonitions, for you are not going to eat here but elsewhere. Confess your sins with devout contrition, and let nothing remain in you that you do not make known by a true confession. The Lord will repay you today, because you have received his poor ones with such great devotion." The man immediately consented to the holy words, and when the companion of Francis who was a priest was called, he revealed all his sins to him in a good confession. He put his house in order and expected the word of the saint to be surely fulfilled. At length they went in to the table, and when all had begun to eat, that man, after making the sign of the cross upon his breast, extended his hand fearfully toward the bread. But before he drew his extended hand back, he bowed his head and breathed forth his spirit. O how much is not the confession of sins to be loved! Behold, a dead man is brought back to life so that he can make his confession;[19] and that a living person might not perish forever, he is freed from his sins by the gift of an opportunity to confess them.

CHAPTER XIV

Of the blind, deaf, and dumb[20]

124 Bevagna, a noble city, is located in the Spoleto valley. In that city there lived a certain holy woman with an even more holy daughter and a granddaughter who was very devoted to Christ. St. Francis had honored their hospitality by visiting them a number of times. For that woman had a son in the order, a man of accomplished perfection. But one of these people, the granddaughter, was deprived of the light of her external eyes, though her interior eyes, through which God was seen, were endowed with wonderful sight. Asked once to show mercy to her, St. Francis took into consideration their work; he marked the eyes of the blind girl with his spittle three times in the name of the Trinity and restored to her the sight she desired.

CHAPTER XVII

Of the lame and the invalids[21]

174 Many miracles of this kind Francis worked while he was still living in the flesh. Once when he was passing through the diocese of Rieti, he came to a certain village where a woman, bathed in tears, brought an eight year old son in her arms and placed him before Francis. Already for four years the boy had lived enormously swollen, so that he could not even see his legs. The saint picked him up kindly and placed his most holy hands upon the boy's abdomen. At his touch, the swelling went down. He was immediately made whole again, and he gave abundant thanks to God and to his saint along with his mother who was happy again.

178 Once Francis came to the city of Orte to take up lodging there. A boy, James by name, who had lain for a long time twisted up, came with his parents and begged for health from the saint. As a result of his long illness the boy's head was bent down to his knees and some of his bones were broken. After he had received the sign of a blessing from St. Francis, he began in that moment to stand straight again, and he became perfectly straight and was completely cured.

179 Another citizen of that city had a tumor between his shoulders the size of a large loaf of bread. After he was blessed by St. Francis, he was suddenly so completely healed that no trace of the tumor remained.

NOTES

INTRODUCTION

1. Celano lies about eighty miles southeast of Assisi in the region of Abruzzi and the province of Aquila, near the bed of what was once Lake Fucino. In the past there was some discussion about Thomas' place of origin, but it is now generally accepted that it was Celano. Writing in the *Archivum Franciscanum Historicum* (II, 517) in 1909, Fr. Atanasio Masci O.F.M. said: It is absolutely certain that Brother Thomas, the first biographer of St. Francis, was from Celano in the diocese of Marsica in Abruzzi.
2. The *First Life of St. Francis,* no. 56.
3. *Ibid.,* no. 57.
4. Thomas says it took place *sexto namque conversionis suae anno,* the sixth year of his conversion. *Ibid.,* no. 55.
5. *Tempore non multo post. Ibid.,* no. 57.
6. English translation in *XIIIth Century Chronicles,* Placid Hermann O.F.M., Franciscan Herald Press, 1961.
7. Brother Jordan tells us that ninety brothers volunteered and that "twelve clerics and thirteen lay brothers" were chosen to go. See his *Chronicle,* no. 19.
8. An earlier attempt to establish the order in Germany had met with failure, mainly because the brothers did not know the German language. *Ibid.,* no. 5.
9. *Ibid.,* no. 30.
10. *Ibid.,* no. 31.
11. *Ibid.,* no. 33.
12. Brother Mark was appointed custos of Franconia; Brother Angelus of Worms, custos of Bavaria and Swabia; Brother James, custos of Alsace; and Brother John of Pian di Carpine, custos of Saxony. The places over which Brother Thomas had been custos, Mainz, Worms, Cologne, and Speyer, were absorbed into the new custodies of Franconia and Alsace.
13. With the one exception mentioned just below when he gave the relics to Brother Jordan to take back to Germany.
14. In the *First Life,* no. 88, Brother Thomas says: We will now add to this work briefly the rest of the things he [Francis] did from the second last year of his life on, in so far as we have been able to get proper knowledge of them.
15. Brother John Parenti (1227-1232).
16. Brother Otto.
17. See Brother Jordan's *Chronicle,* no. 58-59. Glassberger *(Chronica fratris Nicolai Glassberger, Ordinis Minorum*

observantium, Analecta Franciscana, II, 54) says the relics were of his hair and clothing.

18. May 25, 1230. The new basilica was being built under the direction of Brother Elias and by authorization of Pope Gregory IX. Only the lower church was finished by this date.

19. Minister general from 1244-1247.

20. See the discussions below concerning the various works of Brother Thomas.

21. Minister general from 1247-1257.

22. Pope from 1254-1261.

23. The letters S.F.D. are interpreted to mean *Sancti Francisci Discipulus.* The final *R* in *Cronicar* and in *Mortuor* has a stroke through it, signifying the genitive plural. The inscription therefore commemorates Celano's writing of the two lives of St. Francis and of the sequence of the Requiem Mass, the *Dies Irae.*

24. The Bull *Recolentes, Bullarii Franciscani Epitome,* Sbaralea-Eubel, I, 43.

25. Prologue of the *First Life.* Because this life was so commissioned by Pope Gregory IX, it is often known as the *Legenda Gregoriana.*

26. At Perugia the blessed lord pope Gregory IX, on February 25, in the second year of his glorious pontificate, received, confirmed, and judged this legend worthy to be accepted. The text is quoted here from the *Analecta Franciscana,* X, p. 115.

27. See the section below concerning the literary character of the works of Celano.

28. To my knowledge, no one has actually proposed, with any real conviction, that Brother Thomas was the author of that allegory, though the possibility was suggested by the Quaracchi editors of that little work. The work is ascribed to one of several authors by various writers, but Thomas is not among them. However, the thought and in some parts the expression of the *Sacrum Commercium* bear a striking similarity to the thoughts and expression especially in Brother Thomas' *First Life.*

29. Prologue, no. 1.

30. In the Prologue Brother Thomas says: I have tried ... to set forth ... at least those things that I have heard from his own mouth or that I have gathered from faithful and trustworthy witnesses.

31. The theory that the *Legenda Trium Sociorum,* or at least part of it, was in existence already before Brother Thomas wrote his *First Life* can in no way be substantiated. Nor is it likely that Celano used some written sources embodying an older tradition that is more faithfully represented in the *Legenda Trium Sociorum.* Michael Bihl O.F.M. refuted this latter theory of J. R. H. Moorman *(The*

Sources for the Life of St. Francis, Manchester University Press, 1940, p. 68-75) in the *Archivum Franciscanum Historicum* XXXIX, 1946.

32. *Chronica XXIV Generalium,* in the *Analecta Franciscana,* III, 262: *In quo capitulo [anno 1244] idem Generalis [Crescentius] praecepit universis fratribus quod sibi in scriptis dirigerent, quidquid de vita, signis et prodigiis beati Francisci scire veraciter possent.*

33. This compliment is paid, no doubt, to Brother Thomas' *First Life* and also to that of Julian of Speyer, based upon Celano's *First Life* and written between 1232-1235.

34. In the Latin: *Graecii, 3 idus augusti an. Dom. MCCXLVI.*

35. In the Parma edition, p. 60; in the Holder-Egger edition, p. 176.

36. It seems obvious that Brother Thomas is not merely referring to the order to send in whatever material could be gathered about St. Francis but also to the order he received personally to write the life. He is of course speaking, as it were, in the name of the several companions who had supplied the material, but even Celano by this time could be considered one of those to whom these things were better known, not only because he had already written a legend, but also because, to the new generation of friars, he would seem to have been a rather close companion of St. Francis.

37. The first part of the prayer contains a kind of apology for the work and a word of praise of St. Francis. The second part is a prayer for the minister general. The third part is a prayer for the author himself "who now and earlier has devotedly written your praises." The fourth part is for all the sons of St. Francis.

38. No. 2.

39. No. 94, 98, 198. In these places it seems that the author is using the phrasing of the original material.

40. For instance, no. 26, 34, 68, 82, 100, 101, 111, 121.

41. Prologue, no. 2.

42. *Loc. cit.*

43. See no. 220 of the *Second Life.*

44. *Chronica XXIV Generalium, Analecta Franciscana,* III, p. 269.

45. It is possible, as the Quaracchi editors think, that Crescentius gave his approbation of the *Second Life* in advance of the general chapter and then sent it on to the chapter. *Analecta Franciscana,* X, xxvi.

46. The date given in the manuscript was 1557. Melchiorri's work was entitled: *Leggenda di San Francesco d'Assisi scritta dalli suoi compagni che tut'hora conversavano con lui,* Recanati, 1856.

47. Latin text published by the Bollandists in the *Acta Sanctorum,* and Rinaldi's edition of 1806.

48. *Vie de S. Francois d'Assise,* Paris, 1894.
49. St. Bonaventure's *Legenda Major* was completed about 1262. Bernard of Bessa's work about 1285 or shortly thereafter.
50. Little or no attention is paid anymore to the theory that the *Legenda Trium Sociorum* is the lost *Legenda* written, on the testimony of Bernard of Bessa, by John Ceperano, beginning *Quasi Stella Matutina.*
51. Manuscript found by S. Minocchi in the convent of All Saints at Florence. The error in the date was one that could easily occur. The copyist wrote MCCXXVIII for MCCCXVIII.
52. *Documenta Antiqua,* Quaracchi, I, p. 10, no. 3, and II.
53. The treatment of these much discussed points is necessarily brief here. We hope, however, that it will suffice as an introduction to so complicated yet important a subject, and that it may serve as an incentive for the reader to pursue the subject further.
54. There are four paragraphs toward the end of the *Second Life* (217a-220) that narrate the appearances of St. Francis to certain persons after his death.
55. Arnald of Sarrant O.F.M., the author of the *Chronica XXIV Generalium* (written 1369-1379), speaks of the *Second Life* of Brother Thomas as the *legenda antiqua* in relation to the *Legenda Major* of St. Bonaventure, which was more recent.
56. The *First Life* of Brother Thomas was unknown to Arnald of Sarrant; therefore he speaks of the *Second Life* as the first treatise.
57. *Hic Generalis praecepit multiplicatis litteris Fr. Thomae de Celano, ut* Vitam B. Francisci, *quae* Antiqua Legenda *dicitur, perficeret, quia solum de ejus conversatione et verbis in primo* Tractatu, *de mandato Fr. Crescentii Generalis compilato, omissis miraculis, fecerat mentionem. Analecta Franciscana,* III, 276.
58. Judging from the fact that John of Parma had to write to Brother Thomas repeatedly to get him to carry out the command to write a new treatise, we may conclude that it was not finished before 1250. In addition, in relating the story of the visit of Lady Jacoba of Settesoli to Francis shortly before Francis' death, Celano makes mention of her son, John, as a witness of the things that had occurred on that visit and that he had obtained his information from John. John was therefore living at the time of the writing. It is known however, that John died before 1254, and probably already the first part of 1253, since his two children died after his death and they too were dead by 1254. Hence it is safe to say that the *Treatise on the Miracles* was written between 1250-1253. See *Analecta Franciscana,* X, xxxvii-xxxviii.

59. *Et sic secundum* Tractatum *qui de ejusdem . . . agit miraculis, compilavit, quem cum* Epistola *quae incipit*: Religiosa vestra sollicitudo, *misit eidem Generali. Analecta Franciscana*, III, p. 276.

60. Of the 198 paragraphs, 54 are taken from the *First Life,* 10 from the *Second Life,* and one from the *Legenda ad usum chori* — 65 in all.

61. She left home on Palm Sunday, March 18 or 19.

62. 1243-1254.

63. From December 1254 to May 1261.

64. See the English translation, *Legend and Writings of Saint Clare of Assisi,* The Franciscan Institute, St. Bonaventure, N. Y., 1953, p. 17.

65. *Ibid.,* p. 18.

66. *Analecta Franciscana*, X, p. 119.

67. *Ibid.,* p. xx.

68. This *Legenda* can be conveniently found in the *Analecta Franciscana,* p. 119 to 126.

69. According to the reckoning of that time the day extended from nightfall to nightfall. October 4 therefore began at nightfall of Saturday, the 3.

70. Paragraph 13 of the legend. *Analecta Franciscana*, X, p. 124.

71. *Dictionary of Hymnology,* John Julian, D.D., Dover Publications, Inc., New York, new edition 1957, p. 295-301.

72. *Analecta Franciscana*, X, p. L. Fr. Luke Wadding, however, ascribed both of them to Thomas of Celano.

73. *First Life,* no. 64.

74. Just as examples, see: the *First Life*: 63, 116, 120, 121. There are many others, for instance, the *Second Life,* 76.

75. See, for instance, the *Second Life*: 5, 6.

76. In quoting Holy Scripture in this English volume we have used the Challoner-Douay version for the Old Testament because this version gives more exactly the idea the author of the lives had in mind in using the quotation. For the New Testament we have generally used the new version of the Confraternity of Christian Doctrine.

77. Seneca, Cicero, Sallust, Quintillian, Virgil, Ovid, Juvenal.

78. Sulpicius Severus, St. Gregory the Great, St. Augustine, St. Bernard.

79. The *cursus* or end-pattern is based of course on the last two accents together with the unaccented syllables that accompany them.

80. Among these were E. Lempp, S. Minocchi, L. de Kerval, and others of lesser importance.

81. General chapters were held of course while Brother Elias was vicar. While he was minister general, 1232-1239, apparently no general chapters were held, and this was one point that led up to his deposition. But this was later than the *First Life.*

82. Related opinions hold that Elias told Brother Thomas what to write and Thomas naively accepted for true whatever he was told and consequently that he was completely ignorant of the true state of affairs (e.g. E. Lempp).

83. E. Lempp again, among others.

84. Paragraphs 69, 95, 98, 105, 108, 109.

85. No. 105.

86. *Loc. cit.*

87. In no. 28 he is called "the vicar of the saint." In no. 216 he is referred to as "his vicar."

88. In no. 156 where Francis utters a threat of damnation.

89. In no. 138. We know that the reference is to Elias since the story is told briefly in the *First Life* and Elias is mentioned by name.

90. No. 95.

91. See also the letter Brother Elias wrote to announce to the friars the death of their father.

92. See the *Chronicle of Brother Jordan,* no. 61: But Brother Elias, having been elected minister general, wishing to complete the building he had begun at Assisi in honor of St. Francis, ordered levies upon the whole Order to complete the work.

93. Minister general 1232-1239.

94. At Assisi and at Le Celle near Cortona.

95. He died, however, repentant and absolved in 1253.

96. This is a Scriptural passage, Eph. 4, 6.

97. *First Life,* no. 108.

98. Ecclus. 9, 22.

99. Rom. 1, 9. The passage is from the *First Life* again, no. 108.

100. *Ibid.,* no. 109.

101. Ecclus. 9, 22.

102. The *Second Life,* no. 216.

103. The added details of the placing of the hand upon each one's head and of the blessing of the bread are in no way essential changes. They may simply be details that escaped him in the *First Life* or that came to his attention later.

104. Bonaventure became minister general in 1257 and remained in office until his death in 1274.

105. *Analecta Franciscana,* X, no. 3, p. 558.

106. *Loc. cit.*

107. It soon came to be called the *Legenda Major S. Francisci* to distinguish it from the *Minor Vita B. Francisci* that Bonaventure prepared almost immediately for use in choir.

108. *Analecta Franciscana,* X, lxxii.

109. Brothers Leo and Illuminato were still living at that time.

110. *Archivum Franciscanum Historicum,* VII, 678.

111. Much has been made of this decree, especially by those

who see in it the shadow of the growing dispute between the Spirituals and the Community over poverty in particular. Perhaps something of these troubles did enter in. Bonaventure was a moderate, in his good sense, and perhaps he did try to restore unity among his brethren by his *legenda*.

112. The Assisi and Marseille manuscripts.
113. In the Marseille manuscript.

FIRST LIFE

PROLOGUE

1. Acts 1, 1: In the former book, O Theophilus, I spoke of all that Jesus did and taught,...
2. Gregory IX became pope March 19, 1227. Before this he was known as Hugolino. In 1198 he was created cardinal and in 1206 he was made cardinal-bishop of Ostia. He became a close friend of St. Francis and the first cardinal protector of the Franciscan Order in 1220 or 1221. He died at Rome August 22, 1241.
3. Purity here implies the renunciation of self and of all earthly goods for the sake of living entirely for God.
4. Philip. 1, 22 and 1 Pet. 4, 2. The first book has 30 chapters arranged into 87 paragraphs so numbered by early editors. The historical or chronological order is not, however, followed strictly.
5. The second book has 10 chapters, with the paragraphs numbered from 88 through 118.
6. St. Francis was canonized July 16, 1228. The third book has two parts, in the reverse order of how they are mentioned here. The first part treats of the canonization of St. Francis (paragraphs 119-126); the second part narrates some of the miracles attributed to St. Francis (paragraphs 127-150). The whole is brought to a close with a short epilogue.

BOOK ONE

1. The Spoleto valley lies in central Italy, northeast of Rome.
2. Job. 1, 1. The early biographers do not give the year in which Francis was born. Most modern writers are agreed that he was born either late in 1181 or early in 1182. See the *Second Life*, number 3, for the naming of Francis.
3. The poet is Seneca and the quotation alluded to seems to be from his *Epistulae Morales*, LX: "*Jam non admiror, si omnia nos a prima puerita mala secuntur; inter execrationes parentum crevimus.*" (It is no surprise to me, that

nothing but evil attends us from our early youth; for we have grown up amid the curses invoked by our parents). The Loeb Classical Library, *Seneca Epistulae Morales* I, p. 422-423.

4. Rom. 11, 16 and Mt. 7, 17.

5. Rom. 6, 19, Jn. 8, 34, and Rom. 6, 13.

6. "Up to the twenty-fifth year" could mean the beginning of his twenty-fifth year or "until he was nearly twenty-five." The date of his birth would be either late in 1181 or early in 1182, since his perfect conversion took place in 1206 (or 1207).

7. 2 Mach. 4, 1-2.

8. Gal. 1, 14.

9. St. Augustine, *Confessions*: "Behold with what companions I walked the streets of Babylon, and I wallowed myself in the mire of it,..." The Loeb Classical Library, English translation by William Watts, Vol. I, p. 75.

10. Ps. 32, 13.

11. Is. 48, 9.

12. Ezech. 1, 3.

13. Celano speaks of Francis' youth with severe words. He does so, speaking in hyperbole, after the fashion of biographers of his day, to set up a strong contrast between what Francis was before his conversion and what he became afterwards. Francis did take an active part in the amusements and frivolities of his day, but undoubtedly the *Legenda Trium Sociorum* is correct in its estimate of Francis as a cheerful and generous person by nature, a kind and courteous person who spoke no injurious words and would listen to nothing impure; people who knew him thought surely he was marked for great things (Cap. I). See also no. 83 below.

14. Osee 2, 6.

15. Is. 5, 18.

16. An allusion to Gen. 27, 40: the time shall come, when thou shalt shake off and loose his yoke from thy neck.

17. Cicero, in his *De finibus bonorum,* says: *Quin etiam ipsi voluptarii deverticula quaerunt et virtutes habent in ore totos dies voluptatemque dumtaxat primo expeti dicunt, deinde consuetudine quasi alteram quandam naturam effici, qua impulsi multa faciant nullam quaerentes voluptatem.* English: Even the votaries of pleasure take refuge in evasions: the name of virtue is on their lips all the time, and they declare that pleasure is only at first the object of desire, and that later habit produces a sort of second nature, which supplies a motive for many actions not aiming at pleasure at all. The Loeb Classical Library, translation by H. Rackham, M.A., Book V, xxv, 74.

18. 1 Cor. 7, 34.

19. Wis. 9, 13: For who among men is he that can know the

counsel of God?

20. The nobleman, according to the *Legenda Trium Sociorum,* was a certain count, Gentile by name (Chapter 2). In Apulia Walter of Brienne, famed in the songs of the troubadours, had been fighting since 1202. After Henry VI of Germany had died in 1197, his widow entrusted their son, Frederick II, to the tutelage of Pope Innocent III. This angered the German princes and they joined Markwald, lieutenant under Henry VI, against the Holy Father. In 1202 Walter joined the forces of Innocent III and won victory after victory. Francis, like so many others of his day, dreamed of knighthood and wanted to join Walter of Brienne. He had fought earlier in the war between Assisi and Perugia but had been taken prisoner in 1202 at the bridge of San Giovanni. He had been released the following year (cf. *II Cel.* 4 and *Legenda Trium Sociorum,* chapter 2). The journey to Apulia took place in 1205 and early in the year for Walter was killed in June of that year. Apulia lay some 200 miles southeast of Assisi.

21. Mk. 9, 5.

22. 1 Kg. 17, 26: What shall be given to the man that shall kill this Philistine, and shall take away the reproach from Israel?

23. 1 Kg. 17, 45.

24. An allusion to Eph. 3, 16: and to have Christ dwelling through faith in your hearts.

25. An allusion to Mt. 13, 44: The kingdom of heaven is like a treasure hidden in a field; he who finds it hides it, and in his joy goes and sells all that he has and buys that field.

26. Who this person was is not known.

27. Is. 3, 8.

28. 1 Cor. 13, 12.

29. A city southeast of Assisi, some ten miles or so distant.

30. St. Damian's was about a half mile outside of Assisi.

31. Lk. 2, 44.

32. An allusion to Prov. 16, 16: Get wisdom because it is better than gold: and purchase prudence, for it is more precious than silver.

33. Francis' father was Pietro Bernardone, a rich cloth merchant of Assisi, but not of noble origin. His mother was Lady Pica. Though some authors have attempted to give her a French origin, this cannot be confirmed. There were at least two other children in the family besides Francis, according to the *Legenda Trium Sociorum,* (IX). One of these, Angelo, had two sons of his own, Piccardo and Giovanni. Angelo's descendants, according to Wadding, were reduced to begging in the streets of Assisi. Francis was first called John, when his mother had him baptised

while his father was away. But the father seems to have given him the name Francis upon his return. (See *II Cel.,* 3 and the *Legenda Trium Sociorum,* I).

34. Gen. 6, 6.
35. Ps. 6, 4.
36. Rom. 12, 19: Do not avenge yourselves, beloved, but give place to wrath, for it is written, "Vengeance is mine. I will repay, says the Lord."
37. An allusion to Ps. 108, 31: Because he hath stood at the right hand of the poor, to save my soul from persecutors.
38. Joel 2, 12.
39. Ps. 54, 23.
40. Dan. 2, 22.
41. The reference is not clear, but perhaps the author is referring to Seneca: *Habet enim hoc optimum in se generosus animus, quod concitatur ad honesta.* English: for this is the most excellent quality that the noble soul has within itself, that it can be roused to honorable things. *Epistulae Morales,* translated by Richard M. Gummere, Ph.D., The Loeb Classical Library, XXXIX, p. 260-261.
42. Mt. 4, 10-12: Blessed are you when men reproach you and persecute you, and, speaking falsely, say all manner of evil against you, for my sake. Rejoice and exult, ...
43. Ps. 31, 6.
44. Prov. 14, 26.
45. The Latin *pater carnalis* might signify *father according to the flesh* or, most probably, the idea used here of a contrast between the father's concern over earthly things of the flesh and Francis' sole concern over the things of the spirit.
46. Guido II, bishop of Assisi from about 1204 until his death July 30, 1228.
47. See St. Gregory, *Hom. in Evan.,* 32, as contained in the Roman breviary, IX lesson for the feast of the Stigmatization of St. Francis: *Nihil autem maligni spiritus in hoc mundo proprium possident: nudi cum nudo luctari debemus.*
48. 1 Cor. 7, 34.
49. Seneca, *Epistulae Morales,* XIV, 9, The Loeb Classical Library, p. 88.
50. Probably the Benedictine abbey of St. Verecundus, about six miles south of Gubbio.
51. About twenty miles north of Assisi.
52. Count Spadalunga of Gubbio. See *Archivum Franciscanum Historicum,* Vol. I, p. 144-147.
53. II Paral. 26, 8.
54. In *The Words of Saint Francis,* James Meyer O.F.M., Franciscan Herald Press, 1952, p. 243.
55. Mt. 5, 42.
56. 1 Cor. 3, 11.

57. St. Clare was born in Assisi most probably in 1194 of the noble family of the Offreducci di Coccorano. Her father's name was Faverone; her mother's Ortolana. In 1212 she ran away from home and was received by Francis at the Portiuncula and given a habit similar to his own. Several others followed her, including her sister, Agnes. Francis soon wrote a short rule for them, consisting mainly of Scripture passages. Clare and her sisters lived at St. Damian's. Innocent III granted her the privilege of the highest poverty 1215-1216. In 1218-1219 Cardinal Hugolino (later Gregory IX) prepared a rule for them that did not include strict poverty as she desired it. In 1245 Innocent IV confirmed this rule for all the monasteries of the Poor Clares, but in 1247 he gave them a new rule permitting common property. Clare did not accept it, however, and in 1250 Innocent IV declared that no sister could be forced to accept it, thus nullifying it. Clare wrote a new rule in 1253 which Innocent IV approved orally for her while visiting her on her deathbed. He later approved it by bull. This rule was in accord with Clare's original plan of complete poverty. She died August 11 (12), 1253 and was canonized August 15, 1255. (See: *Legend and Writings of St. Clare of Assisi,* Franciscan Institute, 1953.)

58. The name *Clare* is from the Latin *clara,* meaning bright or clear.

59. Rom. 2, 29.

60. An allusion to Sallust: *nam idem velle atque idem nolle, ea demum firma amicitia est* (for agreement in likes and dislikes—this, and this only, is what constitutes true friendship). The Loeb Classical Library, *Bellum Catilinarium,* XX, 4, p. 34-35.

61. An allusion to James 1, 17: Every good gift and every perfect gift is from above.

62. 1 Cor. 5, 13.

63. See footnote 57 above.

64. Thomas of Celano later wrote a life of St. Clare at the order of Pope Alexander IV, in 1256.

65. St. Bonaventure tells us the church was that of St. Peter, "rather distant from Assisi." *Legenda Major,* II, 7. Most probably it was the church of St. Pietro della Spina, about two miles southeast of Assisi. It no longer exists.

66. The Portiuncula lay deep in the woods about a mile southwest of Assisi. Today this little church is enclosed within the basilica of St. Mary of the Angels. The little church had belonged to the Benedictines of Mount Subasio, but was at that time no longer in use. St. Francis always regarded it as the cradle of his Order.

67. It was the feast of St. Matthias, February 24, probably 1208.

68. Mt. 10, 9. Lk. 10, 4. Mk. 6, 8. Lk. 9, 3.
69. Lk. 9, 2. Mk. 6, 12. Penance is a central point of Franciscan spirituality, meaning a complete turning of the heart to God *(metanoia)*, a complete resignation to the will of God and to his commandments, renunciation of self, complete abandonment to God. This is the sense in which St. Francis used the term (see his *Testament*) and in which Celano uses it. See *The Changing Heart,* Chrysostom Dukker O.F.M., Franciscan Herald Press, 1959.
70. Francis' perfect conversion (the renunciation at the court of the bishop of Assisi) took place in 1206. The "third year of his conversion" would therefore start early in 1208.
71. 2 Cor. 7, 4.
72. An allusion to Gal. 5, 24: And they who belong to Christ have crucified their flesh with its passions and desires.
73. Ecclus. 23, 22.
74. The church of St. George. He was at first buried there, but his remains were translated to the basilica in 1230.
75. See the *Testament* of St. Francis: "The Lord revealed to me this salutation that we should say: The Lord give you peace."
76. Not even the name of this one is known. He is not generally counted among the first followers of Francis, since he is otherwise unknown. Evidently he soon left again.
77. Bernard of Quintavalle. He belonged to a noble and wealthy family of Assisi. He died between 1241 and 1246. The story of his conversion is told at greater length in the *Legenda Trium Sociorum* (VIII). A life of Bernard is given in the *Analecta Franciscana,* III, p. 35-45.
78. Lk. 14, 32: Or else, whilst the other is yet at a distance, he sends a delegation and asks the terms of peace.
79. Mt. 13, 44.
80. The phrases *conceived* and *bring forth* are used several times in Scripture in a similar way: Job 15, 35; Is. 59, 4; Ps. 7, 15.
81. Mt. 19, 21.
82. See no. 30 below.
83. This last sentence occurs at the beginning of the next paragraph in various manuscripts, but it is placed here where it obviously belongs.
84. This seems to have been Peter of Catania. His epitaph attached to the wall of the church of St. Mary of the Angels reads: *Anno Domini MCCXXI, VI° id. martii . . . migravit ad Dominum.* Peter went to the Orient with Francis in 1219 (see the Chronicle of Brother Jordan of Giano, 11) and returned with Francis to be present at the general chapter at Pentecost of 1220, where it seems he was made vicar for Francis. He died March 10, 1221.

85. Job 1, 8.
86. Tit. 2, 12.
87. He was received on the feast of St. George (April 23), two years after the conversion of St. Francis. Therefore in 1208. He died April 22, 1262.
88. Philip the Long was especially zealous for the Poor Clares. According to the *Legenda Trium Sociorum*, Sabbatino and Morico were received before Philip. See footnote 110 below.
89. Is. 6, 6.
90. Jn. 7, 15: How does this man come by learning, since he has not studied?
91. That is, the apostles. Acts 4, 13: Now seeing the boldness of Peter and John, and finding that they were uneducated and ordinary men, they began to marvel, and to recognize them as having been with Jesus.
92. Tob. 13, 6.
93. Zach. 4, 14.
94. Is. 38, 15.
95. Lk. 18, 13.
96. Eph. 6, 10. Phil. 3, 1.
97. Gen. 12, 2.
98. Lk. 5, 6.
99. Mt. 13, 47-48: Again the kingdom of heaven is like a net cast into the sea that gathered in fish of every kind. When it was filled, they hauled it out, and sitting down on the beach, they gathered the good fish into vessels, but threw away the bad.

100. In number 25 above it was said that with the coming of Philip the number of brothers was brought to seven. Apparently Francis was included in that number, for from what is said here in number 29, it is apparent that the number is eight in all with the admission of this last brother. His name is uncertain since we do not know for sure from any of the sources the precise order in which the brothers were admitted. See footnote 110 below.
101. Mk. 1, 4.
102. Rom. 12, 12.
103. See Mt., Chapter 5. The *Legenda Trium Sociorum* (IX) tells of what seems to have been an earlier trip. Immediately after Giles had joined the group Francis went with him to the Marches of Ancona; the other two (Bernard and Peter) went "to another region." They then returned to the Portiuncula, where Sabbatino, Morico, and John of Capella were admitted. Chapter XI tells of four more being admitted but without giving

names. That brought the number to eleven besides St. Francis. See footnote 110.

104. 1 Mach. 5, 54.

105. This is cited from the Roman psalter. The Vulgate reads: "Cast thy care upon the Lord, and he shall sustain thee."

106. St. James Compostella in the province of Galicia in northwest Spain. Next to Jerusalem it was the most popular place of pilgrimage in the Middle Ages.

107. Ps. 146, 2.

108. An allusion to Lk. 17, 10: Even so you also, when you have done everything that was commanded you, say, "We are unprofitable servants; we have done what it was our duty to do."

109. This last sentence is generally found at the head of the next paragraph, but it belongs more logically at the end of this paragraph.

110. This brought the number to twelve, including St. Francis. The names of the first twelve are generally given as: Francis, Bernard of Quintavalle, Peter of Catania, Giles, Sabbatino, Morico, John of Capella, Philip the Long, John of St. Constantia, Barbaro, Bernard Viridante, Angelo Tancredi. The *Legenda Trium Sociorum* (IX) tells the story of Sylvester's conversion just after it tells how Bernard disposed of his money, with Sylvester receiving generous hands full. But it indicates that Sylvester was received a little later. In the same way *The Little Flowers of St. Francis (Actus B. Francisci)* puts the reception of Sylvester a little later. The *Chronica XXIV Generalium* lists them as above. See footnotes 100 and 103 above.

111. Acts 2, 47: And day by day the Lord added to their company such as were to be saved.

112. In his *Testament* Francis said: And after the Lord gave me some brothers, there was nobody to show me what to do; but the Most High himself revealed to me that I was to live according to the form of the Holy Gospel. And I caused it to be written down simply and in a few words, and the Lord Pope approved it for me. *(The Words of St. Francis,* Meyer, p. 245.) This was the very first or primitive rule, which is no longer extant. A reconstruction of it can be found in *Via Seraphica,* Placid Hermann O.F.M. Franciscan Herald Press, 1959, p. 11.

113. John Lothar, count of Segni, elected pope January 8, 1198, died at Perugia July 16, 1216. He was the greatest pope of the middle ages. During his pontificate the two great mendicant Orders were founded, the Dominicans and the Franciscans.

114. The same into whose hands Francis made his complete renunciation in 1206.

115. Cardinal John of St. Paul died in 1215.

116. That is, he persuaded him to join one of the already existing orders.

117. The date was April 16, 1209. There has been considerable discussion in the past as to whether the year was 1209 or 1210. For a discussion of the year 1209 see Fr. Paschal Robinson O.F.M., Vol. II of the *Archivum Franciscanum Historicum*, p. 181-196. For a discussion of the year 1210 see Fr. Dominic Mandic O.F.M., *De Legislatione Antiqua O.F.M.* 1210-1221, Mostar, 1924. More recently the year 1209 was accepted by the Order of Friars Minor in their celebration of the 750th anniversary, 1959. In that year the minister general, the Most Reverend Augustinus Sepinski O.F.M., wrote in his encyclical letter, dated February 11, 1959: *"Vobis sane compertum est in hunc eundem MCMLIX annum, anniversarium DCCL memoriam incidere primae religiosae Professionis, cum nempe seraphicus Conditor a Summo Pontifice Innocentio PP. III, una cum primis Sociis, sanctae Regulae approbationem vivae vocis oraculo obtinuit."* Englsih: "You are indeed aware that in this same year 1959 falls the 750th anniversary of the first religious profession, for the seraphic Founder, with his first companions, obtained from the Supreme Pontiff Pope Innocent III oral approbation of his holy Rule."

118. Job 5, 11.

119. An allusion to Mt. 14, 15: Now when it was evening, his disciples came to him, saying: "This is a desert place and the hour is already late; send the crowds away, so that they may go into the villages and buy themselves food."

120. About forty miles north of Rome.

121. Acts 24, 3.

122. Is. 30, 29.

123. This last sentence is generally found with the next paragraph but it belongs logically here.

124. 2 Cor. 5, 15.

125. Mt. 9, 35.

126. 1 Cor. 2, 4.

127. Acts 9, 28.

128. Prov. 7, 9.

129. Joel 2, 2.

130. Ecclus. 24, 23.

131. Is. 51, 3.

132. This whole section has a strong resemblance to the Bull of Canonization, dated July 19, 1228.

133. An allusion to the three orders St. Francis founded; the first order of Friars Minor; the second of Poor Clares; the third for those living in the world.

134. The Latin equivalent of "lesser brothers" is *minores;* hence, the Order of Friars Minor. The reference here is to the so-called First Rule of 1221, where we read: "And let them be lesser brothers and subject to all who are in the same house." *Opuscula Sancti Patris Francisci Assisiensis,* Quaracchi, 1904, p. 33.

135. Mt. 6, 22: If thy eye be single, thy whole body shall be lightsome (Douay version).

136. Prov. 15, 4: A peaceable tongue is a tree of life; but that which is immoderate, shall crush the spirit.

137. Prov. 15, 1: A mild answer breaketh wrath.

138. *Testament* of St. Francis: And they were content with one tunic patched within and without.

139. Seneca, *Epistulae Morales,* XII, 9: *Ille beatissimus est et securus sui possessor, qui crastinum sine solicitudine expectat* (That man is happiest, and is secure in his own possession of himself, who can await the morrow without apprehension). The Loeb Classical Library, p. 71.

140. First Rule, Chapter 7: And the brothers who know how to work, should work,... Second Rule, Chapter 5: Those brothers to whom the Lord has given the grace of working, should work,...

141. First Rule, Chapter 7: nor are they to accept any position that may cause scandal.

142. Heb. 12, 14.

143. 1 Jn. 3, 18.

144. The twisted river. The place was called thus from the twisting river that flowed down from the heights of Mount Subasio on which Assisi was located. Rivo Torto was a mile or so south of the Portiuncula.

145. This saying was attributed by Peter Cantor (died 1197) to "a certain hermit." *Analecta Franciscana,* Vol. X, p. 33, footnote 5.

146. These words are based on the hymn *Sanctorum meritis* of the Vespers from the common of several martyrs: *Non murmur resonat, non querimonia, / Sed corde impavido, mens bene conscia / Conservat patientiam.*

147. There is some doubt about Celano's statement here that the emperor passed close to Rivo Torto enroute to Rome for his coronation. Most authors think that this was not the case, but that he passed close by on his return from Rome. Those who have made a careful study of the question say that Otto proceeded along the old Via Aemilia from Faenza to Rimini. From Rimini he went along the Via Flaminia through Fano, Cagli, Nocera, Spoleto (at the end of September), and on to Rome, where he was crowned by Innocent III on October 4, 1209. Between October and December 1209, Otto visited in Tuscany. On December 3 he was in Florence. From Decem-

ber 12-14 he was in Foligno. On December 20, in Terni.
From January 5-8, 1210, he was again in Foligno. On
November 4, 1210, he was in Assisi. Apparently he was
in Assisi also much earlier than this, namely between
early December 1209 and early January 1210. The Via
Flaminia passed through Nocera and Spoleto on its way
to Rome. Hence, the emperor would have passed within
20 to 25 miles of Assisi on his way to Rome and within a
little less than this of Rivo Torto. This is not a great
distance, yet it is questionable if it fits Celano's description of a "road close to the hovel" at Rivo Torto. Still,
there is no particular reason why St. Francis could not
have sent one of the brothers that comparatively short
distance to cry out to the emperor as he passed by, while
he himself and his other brothers did "not go out to
watch." Such an unusual occurrence as the emperor passing so close to Rivo Torto might very easily have made
the brothers look upon it as really close by. However,
most authors think Celano is in error in saying that the
emperor passed by on his way to Rome and regard it as
more probable that he passed close by on his return from
Rome when he was most probably in Assisi itself.

148. Otto was excommunicated October 18, 1210, because he
did not carry out his promise to safeguard the rights of
the Church. He thereafter lost the support of the Hohen-
staufen party and eventually suffered a crushing defeat
in 1214. He made some further effort to secure his throne
in 1217 and 1218, but had little success. He died May 19,
1218, reconciled to the Church.

149. See numbers 33 and 36 above.

150. A biblical phrase. Gen. 32, 9 and 12: Return to thy land
and to the place of thy birth, and I will do well for thee.

151. Is. 5, 8: Woe to you that join house to house and lay
field to field.

152. Number 21 above.

153. Prov. 20, 7.

154. The Divine Office.

155. Lk. 11, 2.

156. This prayer Francis inserted also in his *Testament*.

157. Similar thoughts were expressed by Francis in his
Admonitions, III, *De perfecta et imperfecta obedientia*.
See *Opuscula*, p. 6-7.

158. Literally the Latin should be rendered "with both men,"
but the meaning evidently is, with the spiritual and bodily
man, or body and soul.

159. In his *Testament*, Francis said later: I do not wish to
consider sin in them [that is, priests] because I see in
in them the Son of God, and they are my masters.

160. In the Rule of 1221 we read: "And though they be called

hypocrites, let them not quit their good life, nor let them look for expensive clothes in this world, so that they can have their robe in the kingdom of Heaven." *The Words of St. Francis,* p. 252.

161. St. Bonaventure places the apparition narrated here among the things that happened at Rivo Torto. *Legenda Major,* IV, 4.

162. John Bonelli of Florence. St. Bonaventure, *Legenda Major,* IV, 10, and the *Chronica XXIV Generalium, Analecta Franciscana,* III, p. 230, also record this incident.

163. The province of Provence was established as early as 1219 by John Bonelli, sent there by St. Francis.

164. The chapter was held at Arles in 1224. See St. Bonaventure, *loc. cit.*

165. Col. 4, 3: Praying withal for us also, that God may open unto us a door of speech to speak the mystery of Christ (Douay version).

166. Monaldo died at Arles, it is thought.

167. St. Anthony of Padua (Fernando de Bulhoes) was born in Lisbon, Portugal, though his name is inseparably connected with the Italian city of Padua. The year of his birth is not certain, but it may have been as early as 1190. He joined the Order of Canons Regular of St. Augustine in Spain some time not long after 1206. But after the five Franciscan missionaries had been martyred in Morocco in 1220 and their bodies brought to Spain, Anthony felt a great desire to enter the Franciscan Order. This he did shortly after. There is some doubt as to whether he had been ordained before his entry or whether he was ordained as a Franciscan. He was a great theologian and was appointed by St. Francis to be the first lector of theology in the Order (at Bologna). He died June 13, 1231 and was canonized within a year thereafter by Pope Gregory IX. In 1946 he was declared a Doctor of the Church by Pope Pius XII.

168. An allusion to Lk. 24, 45: Then he opened their minds that they might understand the Scriptures.

169. Ps. 18, 11.

170. Jn. 19, 19.

171. Acts 9, 31.

172. Riccerio of Muccia in Piceno. He died in 1236 and was later venerated as a saint. He is mentioned in the Franciscan martyrology on February 7.

173. 2 Cor. 6, 13: Now as having a recompense in kind — I speak as to my children — be you also open wide to us.

174. See Celano's *Second Life,* number 60.

175. Rom. 1, 1; 1 Thess. 2, 9.

176. Lk. 10, 8: Eat what is set before you. II Rule: And ac-

cording to the holy Gospel it is lawful to eat of whatever food is placed before you (chapter III).

177. Acts. 2, 37.

178. Ps. 30, 13.

179. Lk. 4, 15.

180. In the Latin the form is *filium Petri de Bernardone*. The implication seems to be this: Francis is the son, Peter the father, Bernardone the grandfather. Apparently the grandfather was poor, while the father was wealthy. Hence, Francis, thinking of his grandfather, recalls his humble origin.

181. In the second half of the year 1212.

182. Slavonia, on the coast of Dalmatia, on the Adriatic Sea.

183. Ancona, a seaport on the Adriatic, in east-central Italy.

184. Jn. 15, 2: Every branch in me that bears no fruit he will take away; and every branch that bears fruit he will cleanse, that it may bear more fruit.

185. The name is Latinized from Emir-el-mumenin, meaning "head of the believers." He was the sultan of Morocco. The year of this trip was 1213.

186. Gal. 2, 11.

187. Francis returned from Spain in 1214 and was back at the Portiuncula at the end of 1214 or early in 1215. It is possible that Thomas of Celano entered the order at this time; perhaps he was one of the educated and noble men who entered at this time. Some, however, think he entered as early as 1213.

188. Several years are passed over here. This next trip to Syria, "in the thirteenth year of his conversion," took place in 1219. Francis had been present at the Pentecost chapter of that year at the Portiuncula (May 26). He left not long thereafter for the Orient and arrived at Damietta in Egypt on August 29.

189. His companion was Brother Illuminato, as St. Bonaventure tells us in his *Legenda Major,* IX, 8. See the *Second Life* where several companions seem to have been with him. No. 30.

190. The sultan was Melek-el-Khamil, 1217-1238. The crusaders had been fighting from May 9, 1218 at Damietta. After the battle of August 29, 1219, the Christians and Saracens tried to arrange a peace. But war broke out anew on September 26. During this interval of peace Francis spent several days with the sultan.

191. Celano is referring to the stigmata which Francis was to receive in 1224. While Francis was away in Syria, the two vicars Francis had left behind to conduct the affairs of the order (Matthew of Narni and Gregory of Naples) held a chapter and enacted certain constitutions at variance with the Rule. A certain Brother Stephen brought

word of this to Francis and Peter of Catania in Syria. They, together with Elias, provincial of Syria, and Caesar of Speyer, immediately returned to Italy, and Francis went directly to Pope Honorius (who was staying at Orvieto, at the time) and requested a cardinal protector for his Order (Hugolino). This was probably in 1220. See the English translation of Brother Jordan of Giano's *Chronicle* in *XIIIth Century Chronicles,* Placid Hermann O.F.M., Franciscan Herald Press, 1961, numbers 10-14.

192. In ancient times it was known as Mevania. The incident took place at a place called Pian d'Arca, midway between Bevagna and Cannara, about three miles or so south of Assisi.

193. The Latin form is *monadae,* though some codices have *monedula.* The modern Italian form is *mulacchia,* a crow-like bird or daw.

194. Mt. 6, 12 and Lk. 12, 24.

195. Lk. 4, 30.

196. About thirty miles southwest of Assisi.

197. Jud. 13, 16.

198. Lk. 24, 53.

199. About forty-five miles south of Assisi.

200. Literally, a hare. But rabbit sounds better in the complete setting, and much better than the technical lagomorph. A little farther on, the literal meaning is rabbit.

201. Lake Trasimene, about twenty-five miles west of Assisi.

202. This sentence is generally in the preceding paragraph 60, but it seems to belong more logically here.

203. The city of Rieti is about thirty-seven miles northeast of Rome. The lake is about three and a half miles northwest of the city.

204. *Tinca* is the popular Italian name for it. It was probably a tench, belonging to the carp family.

205. About six miles northeast of Narni in Umbria.

206. Mt. 8, 27: What manner of man is this, that even the winds and the sea obey him?

207. See number 58 above.

208. In the Marches of Ancona. Today it is called Ascoli-Piceno.

209. An old Etruscan city, Arezzo lies about thirty-five miles southeast of Florence.

210. About seventeen miles northwest of Orvieto, or some thirty-seven miles west southwest of Assisi.

211. Acts 10, 21.

212. About eleven miles west of Viterbo.

213. Lk. 8, 11 ssq. The parable of the sower and the seed.

214. On the river Nera, some six miles southwest of Terni, not too far from Rieti.

215. Narni.

216. About thirty miles south of Assisi.
217. Mt. 15, 2.
218. Esther 13, 13.
219. Osee 13, 14.
220. About twenty-five miles north of Perugia.
221. 1 Cor. 13, 5: Charity ... seeketh not her own.
222. Phil. 1, 23.
223. Cant. 2, 14.
224. The Latin is *caelibes mansiones,* perhaps an allusion to Quintillian's: *ingenioseque visus est Gavius* caelibes *dicere veluti* caelites, ... That is: And Gavius thought himself a perfect genius when he identified *caelibes,* "bachelors," with *caelites,* "gods," ... The meaning may be: places where there were no women. Cf. Acts 14, 4. See *Institutio Oratoria* of Quintillian in *The Loeb Classical Library,* I, 6, 36.
225. Honorius III became pope July 18, 1216. He died March 18, 1227. It was Honorius who gave the final approbation to St. Francis' rule of life in 1223, the so-called *Regula Bullata.*
226. Hugo is the form used here, though generally Hugolino is used.
227. Acts 2, 37.
228. Hugolino became the first cardinal protector of the Order in 1220 or 1221. See footnote 1 above and footnote 232 below.
229. Jer. 2, 21.
230. Is. 22, 2.
231. Acts 5, 36.
232. Cardinal Hugolino was legate for the first time in Lombardy and Tuscany from January 23, 1217 until September 14, 1219. His second term began with March 14, 1221. Francis met him in the summer of 1217 at Florence, according to various authors. See *Archivum Franciscanum Historicum,* Vol. 19, 1926, p. 530-558.
233. An allusion to Lk. 12, 14: I have come to cast fire upon the earth, and what will I but that it be kindled?
234. Acts 10, 25.
235. See the *Second Life,* number 25.
236. See the *Second Life,* numbers 5 and 90.
237. See also the *Second Life,* numbers 86 and 87.
238. For example, Is. 16, 1; 53, 7; Acts 8, 32, and many others.
239. The Marches of Ancona are northeast of Assisi, on the coast that faces the Adriatic Sea. The city of Ancona is on the coast itself, a good sixty-five miles from Assisi.
240. Osimo is about eight miles or so south of Ancona.
241. The Marches of Ancona formed a province in the Order some years before the death of St. Francis.
242. Gen. 6, 6.
243. This was the monastery of Poor Clares, S. Salvatore in

Colpersito, close to San Severino. San Severi.o lay about thirty-one miles southwest of Ancona. This monastery was founded in 1223, but it is today a Capuchin friary.

244. Literally the Latin means "of both men," but the meaning is given better as "of the inner and outer man," or "of his soul and body." See also footnote 158.

245. Ps. 21, 7.

246. See Dan., chapter 3.

247. Celano, no doubt, has in mind St. Francis' *The Canticle of Brother Sun,* which Francis composed during a long illness in 1225, while he was staying at San Damiano. For an Italian version of this canticle see *Via Seraphica,* Placid Hermann O.F.M., Franciscan Herald Press, 1959, p. 32.

248. See the *Second Life,* number 165.

249. Is. 11, 1.

250. Ecclus. 50, 8.

251. Rom. 8, 21.

252. The Latin reads: *scriptum aliquid, sive divinum sive humanum.* It could be rendered "whether the word of God or of man," or as here, "whether about God or about man." The idea is the same, the name of God can be made from all letters.

253. Jud. 13, 6.

254. Mt. 6, 22: If thy eye be sound, thy whole body will be full of light (Confraternity of Christian Doctrine version).

255. Prov. 15, 4: A peaceable tongue is a tree of life.

256. Tit. 3, 2.

257. These words are from the so-called First Rule (1221) of St. Francis. In the Second Rule *(Regula Bullata,* 1223), it is stated: The rule and life of the Friars Minor is this, namely, to observe the holy Gospel of our Lord Jesus Christ, by living in obedience, without property, and in chastity.

258. Some forty-five miles south of Assisi.

259. Therefore on December 25, 1223.

260. Jn. 8, 56.

261. This is a close imitation of the words used above in number 83.

262. See Ps. 35, 8.

263. 3 Kings 8, 63.

264. 1 Pet. 1, 19.

265. 1 Cor. 1, 10.

BOOK TWO

1. The title of this chapter is missing in certain manuscripts.
2. In number 55 of this first life of St. Francis Celano spoke of the sixth year of Francis' conversion *(sexto namque conversionis suae anno)*, which was 1212; and in number 57 he spoke of the thirteenth year of his conversion *(tertio decimo anno conversionis)*, which was 1219. So here the eighteenth year is 1224. According to Celano's reckoning, the "second last year of his life" *(paenultimo vitae suae anno)* would run from September 14, 1224, to September of 1225, and the last year from that time to Francis' death, October 4, 1226.
3. The indiction was a recurring cycle of 15 years, called in full *the cycle of indiction.* The number attached to the indiction indicated the specific year within the cycle, as here, the fourteenth year within the indiction is meant. Celano is using the Roman or Papal indiction. According to this system the indiction is found by adding 3 to the year in question; thus, 1226 plus 3. The sum is then divided by 15. Hence, the number of the indiction was 82. And within the 82nd cycle, it was the fourteenth year.
4. According to the reckoning of the time (and still used at the present time in some regions of Italy, e.g., Umbria, Tuscany), the day ran from evening to evening (not from midnight to midnight, as we know it). St. Francis died, according to our reckoning, on a Saturday evening, about an hour after dark, October 3. But, according to the reckoning of that time, Sunday, October 4, had already begun with sunset. Hence, as Brother Elias put it in his letter announcing the death of Francis: *Quarto nonas Octobris, die dominica, prima hora noctis praecedentis, pater et frater noster Franciscus migravit ad Christum.* For the entire letter see *Analecta Franciscana*, Vol. X, p. 525-528. Celano too in his *Legenda ad Usum Chori* gives the date very precisely in these words: *Anno Dominicae Incarnationis 1226, quarto nonas Octobris sanctus Franciscus, expletis viginti annis, ex quo perfectissime Christo adhaesit, vitae mortalis compedibus absolutus, die sabbati in sero feliciter migravit ad Deum, sepultus in die dominico. Analecta Franciscana*, X, p. 125-126.
5. Rom. 6, 7.
6. Ps. 76, 11.
7. Lk. 1, 35.
8. Jn. 5, 33.
9. 1 Cor. 1, 20.
10. 1 Cor. 1, 21.
11. 1 Pet. 1, 5.
12. James 5, 17.

13. Ps. 118, 96.
14. 1 Cor. 12, 31.
15. Eph. 5, 32.
16. An adaptation of Lk. 10, 11: Even the dust from your town that cleaves to us we shake off against you.
17. Ps. 30, 21.
18. Ps. 33, 9: O taste and see that the Lord is sweet.
19. Ps. 72, 1.
20. Wis. 1, 1.
21. 1 Cor. 7, 40.
22. 2 Cor. 1, 3.
23. St. Augustine says he did the same thing (*Confessions* VIII, 12); so too St. Gregory of Tours and others.
24. Dan. 3, 39: That we may find thy mercy: nevertheless in a contrite heart and humble spirit let us be accepted.
25. The exact part is not clear but all the evangelists speak of the passion to come and all narrate the passion.
26. Acts 14, 21.
27. Lk. 19, 17.
28. Mt. 25, 21.
29. Alverna is a mountain in Tuscany, in the province and diocese of Arezzo near the middle of the Apennines. This mountain was given to Francis by Count Orlando of Chiusi in Casentino. The count's sons later gave the friars a document confirming the gift. This document stated that the original gift had been made on September 8, 1213. See Johannes Joergensen, *St. Francis of Assisi*, 1913, Longmans, Green, and Co., p. 162.
31. Is. 6, 2: Upon it stood the seraphims: the one had six wings, and the other had six wings: with two they covered his face, and with two they covered his feet, and with two they flew.
32. Brother Elias of Assisi or of Cortona. Not much is known of his early life. He must have been a man of rather exceptional qualities since he merited to be esteemed so highly by St. Francis. Francis appointed him his vicar, that is, after the death of Peter of Catania. He served in this capacity until after the death of St. Francis. In 1227 he was not elected minister general, but was engaged by Pope Gregory IX to superintend the building of a basilica to honor St. Francis. However, he was elected minister general in 1232, an office he held until he was deposed in 1239 because he was abusing the office entrusted to him. He was later excommunicated, but he died penitent and absolved on April 22, 1253.
33. Rufino was a cousin of St. Clare of Assisi. He died in 1270. A life of Rufino is found in the *Chronica XXIV Generalium, Analecta Franciscana*, III, 46-54.
34. Ecclus. 3, 19: My son, do thy works in meekness, and thou shalt be beloved above the glory of men.

35. Ps. 118, 11.
36. 1 Cor. 9, 27: But I chastise my body and bring it into subjection.
37. See number 88 above.
38. Mt. 26, 41: the spirit indeed is willing.
39. Lk. 8, 11: the seed is the word of God.
40. Mk. 6, 6.
41. Lk. 8, 1.
42. Ps. 62, 2.
43. See footnote 17 in Book One.
44. 2 Cor. 4, 16: Wherefore we do not lose heart. On the contrary, even though our outer man is decaying, yet our inner man is being renewed day by day.
45. Ecclus. 18, 6.
46. Mt. 26, 41: The spirit indeed is willing, but the flesh is weak.
47. Phil. 1, 23.
48. Col. 1, 24.
49. Gal. 6, 17.
50. Ps. 35, 8: O how hast thou multiplied thy mercy, O God!
51. The reference is to the appointment of Elias as Francis' vicar, after the death of Peter of Catania. See footnote 32 of Book Two.
52. 1 Jn. 5, 13.
53. Ecclus. 38, 4.
54. The curia was in Rieti from June 23, 1225 to January 31, 1226, as quoted in the *Analecta Franciscana,* X, 76, from Potthast, *Regesta Pontificium Romanorum,* Berolini, 1874, I, n. 7434-7526.
55. Honorius III.
56. See the *Chronicle of Brother Jordan of Giano,* English version in *XIIIth Century Chronicles,* numbers 16-18.
57. Is. 50, 4.
58. Phil. 3, 18.
59. Jn. 5, 35.
60. Is. 49, 2.
61. Ps. 31, 6.
62. Lk. 14, 32.
63. Jerem. 7, 5.
64. Ezech. 31, 8.
65. Jerem. 2, 21.
66. Ps. 79, 12: It stretched forth its branches to the sea and its boughs unto the river.
67. This of course took place earlier, not during the last two years of Francis' life. Francis asked Hugo (or Hugolino) as early as 1216 probably to act in some such capacity and this was later confirmed by Honorius III, probably in 1220 or 1221.
68. Mt. 24, 45.

69. He was bishop of both places. Ostia is at the mouth of the Tiber river, Velletri inland, some thirty miles east.
70. Gen. 49, 26.
71. Tob. 2, 14.
72. Ephes. 1, 3.
73. 2 Mach. 14, 35.
74. Prov. 22, 15.
75. Not enough information is given in any of these instances to determine definitely just who is meant. But most authors think that Brother Angelo Tancredi is meant here. He died in 1258.
76. Brother Rufino is probably meant here. See number 95 above.
77. This is probably Brother Leo, the father confessor of St. Francis, his secretary, and his trusted friend. Leo died in 1271. For a sketch of his life see *Analecta Franciscana*, III, 65-74.
78. This is probably Brother John de Laudibus (of Lodi). Brother Bernard of Bessa wrote of him in his *Liber de Laudibus S. Franciscis*. While Francis was still in the flesh, he merited to touch the wound of the stigmata in his side. *Analecta Franciscana*, III, 668. He died about 1250. Some think, however, that Brother Masseo may be meant. He died in 1280.
79. Gen. 32, 2.
80. Dan. 9, 25.
81. Rom. 12, 12.
82. Phil. 3, 13: Brethren, I do not consider that I have laid hold of it already.
83. Rom. 6, 4.
84. Apoc. 2, 5.
85. Rom. 12, 3.
86. April, 1226.
87. Siena is some seventy miles northwest of Assisi.
88. Le Celle was one of the first places of the friars. It was about two miles north of Cortona. Cortona itself lies about thirty-seven miles northwest of Assisi.
89. Esther 8, 15.
90. Lk. 1, 10.
91. Mk. 1, 24.
92. Phil. 1, 24.
93. See numbers 21 and 22 above.
94. Ezech. 34, 13.
95. Rom. 8, 33.
96. See the *Second Life*, number 19.
97. Ps. 41, 5.
98. This revelation is given more fully in number 109 below.
99. Gen. 49, 1-27.
100. Gen. 33, 1 ssq.

101. Ephes. 4, 6.
102. Ecclus. 9, 22.
103. Rom. 1, 9.
104. See the *Second Life,* number 216.
105. See number 88 above.
106. These two were Brother Angelo Tancredi and Brother Leo, according to the *Speculum Perfectionis,* chapter 10 of the first redaction (Fr. Leonard Lemmens O.F.M., in *Documenta Antiqua Franciscana,* Vol. II), chapter 123 in the Sabatier redaction.
107. That is, Francis' *The Canticle of Brother Sun.*
108. Ps. 141, 28.
109. This is Brother Elias, as is evident from what follows.
110. See the Letter of Brother Elias to all the friars announcing the death of St. Francis, *Analacta Franciscana,* Vol. X.
111. The text, Jn. 13, 1, actually begins: Before the feast of the Passover. The opening words as given here, Six days before the Passover, are the opening words of the preceding chapter, 12, 1.
112. The Latin text has simply *minister,* which could also mean the minister provincial of that province, or even just one who waited on Francis. Minister general, however, seems to be meant, since Brother Elias, the vicar of Francis, was present. The early writers use the terms *minister general* and *vicar* of Francis synonomously for those early years.
113. See number 92 above.
114. Acts 7, 60.
115. Bernard of Besse *(Liber de Laudibus S. Francisci)* says it was Brother James of Assisi. See *Analecta Franciscana,* III, 668.
116. Acts 2, 34.
117. Cant. 6, 9.
118. Rom. 9, 5.
119. Lk. 2, 13.
120. The whole description that follows here and in the next paragraph is evidently based upon the encyclical letter of Brother Elias announcing the death of Francis.
121. 1 Pet. 1, 19.
122. Jn. 19, 34.
123. 1 Pet. 1, 19.
124. Rom. 16, 27.
125. Ecclus. 36, 6: Renew thy signs, and work new miracles.
126. Jn. 3, 13.
127. 2 Cor. 1, 3.
128. That is, the order of seraphim.
129. Celano here explains in allegorical fashion the vision in Is. 6, 1-3 and Ezech. 1, 5-14, 22-25.
130. Mt. 6, 22-23.

131. Mt. 12, 34.
132. St. Bernard of Clairvaux wrote this of him. (See Migne, P. L., 185, 238).
133. An allusion to Francis' *The Canticle of Brother Sun.*
134. 1 Cor. 2, 2.
135. The Portiuncula.
136. See number 18 above.
137. Is. 46, 4: Even to your old age I am the same, and to your gray hairs I will carry you: I have made you, and I will bear you: I will carry and will save.
138. A play on words: *Clara*, by name; and *clara erat.*
139. Josue 3, 3.
140. Ps. 45, 2.
141. Ephes. 2, 19.
142. Is. 33, 7: Behold they that see shall cry without, and the angels of peace shall weep bitterly.
143. Francis was first buried in the church of St. George. In 1230 his remains were translated to the new basilica erected in his honor.
144. Ps. 39, 3.

BOOK THREE

1. Ps. 8, 6.
2. Ezech. 28, 14.
3. Heb. 1, 3. The phrases are arranged a little differently here.
4. Phil. 3, 10.
5. Ps. 65, 20.
6. Mt. 8, 11.
7. In the Holy Saturday canticle *Exultet* the deacon sings: *Qui licet divisus in partes, mutuati tamen luminis detrimenta non novit.* English: And though the fire was spread to kindle other flames, such sharing does not lessen the force of its light.
8. The king was Louis IX who was later canonized. He was born in 1214 and while he was a minor his kingdom was ruled by his mother Blanche. Louis married Margaret, the daughter of Raymond Berengarius, in 1234.
9. The Latin is *adorandum,* but obviously the word is used in its improper sense.
10. Here is meant the university of Paris.
11. There is a bit of a play on words here in the Latin: *Franciscus,* qui super omnes cor *francum* et nobile gessit.
12. Jn. 3, 29.
13. Celano speaks here of the cardinals as *collaterales papae,* using the same phrase St. Bernard used for them *(De*

Consideratione ad Eugenium III, IV, 4, 9). There is also a play on words here in the *cardines mundi* for the *cardinales.*

14. An allusion to 1 Cor. 1, 27-28: But the foolish things of the world has God chosen to put shame the "wise," and the weak things of the world has God chosen to put to shame the strong, and the base things of the world and the depised has God chosen, and the things that are not, to bring to naught the things that are.

15. An allusion to Jn. 12, 32: And I, if I be lifted up from the earth, will draw all things to myself.

16. 1 Mach. 14, 31. On March 27, 1228, the party of Frederick II rebelled against the pope.

17. Ps. 128, 4.

18. Gregory IX left Rome on April 20 or 21, 1228.

19. The Roman curia was at Rieti from April 25 to May 10, 1228.

20. This was the Poor Clare monastery of St. Paul near Spoleto.

21. He was in Assisi from May 26 to June 12, 1228.

22. The pope was in Perugia from June 13 to July 13, 1228.

23. 1 Jn. 1, 1.

24. This was John of Brienne. Born in 1148, he was crowned king of Jerusalem on October 3, 1210. On March 9, 1225 his daughter married the emperor Frederick II who usurped all the rights of the king of Jerusalem. John was crowned emperor of Constantinople in 1228. He later entered the Franciscan Order, but died shortly thereafter, March 23, 1237. His remains were later translated to the church of St. Francis.

25. The church of St. George, then just outside the walls of Assisi; now Santa Chiara, enclosed by a mid-thirteenth century outer wall.

26. Job. 3, 19.

27. Ecclus. 45, 14.

28. Ecclus. 45, 13.

29. Is. 4, 2.

30. Ps. 44, 10.

31. Jer. 25, 10.

32. Ecclus. 1, 6-7.

33. 1 Tim. 1, 15.

34. Octavian Ubaldini de Mugello. He was made a cardinal by Pope Innocent IV (1243-1254) on May 28, 1244.

35. Raynerius Capocci de Viterbo, O. Cist. He had been made a cardinal by Pope Innocent III (1198-1216) in 1216. He was the author of the hymn *Plaude turba paupercula* of the Lauds for the feast of St. Francis and of the antiphon *Coelorum candor splenduit.* He was present at the chapter of 1221, according to the chronicle of Brother Jordan of

Giano (no. 16). He died in 1250.

36. The complete Bull of canonization can be conveniently found in *Via Seraphica*, Placid Hermann O.F.M., Franciscan Herald Press, 1959.

37. It may be that already then one or the other of the hymns in honor of St. Francis had been composed. Pope Gregory IX himself wrote several, like the hymn *Proles de caelo*, and the responsory of the office of St. Francis, *De paupertatis horreo*. The *Sancte Francisce propera* and the *Plange turba paupercula* are also attributed to him.

38. Num. 29, 39.

39. The holy sacrifice of the Mass.

40. Ecclus. 50, 13.

41. Ecclus. 50, 24.

42. In the reckoning of the time this would be the year from March 21, 1228 to March 20, 1229.

43. July 16, 1228, the ninth Sunday after Pentecost. It is apparent from the whole narrative that Brother Thomas of Celano was an eyewitness to the whole ceremony of canonization.

44. This miracle is repeated in Celano's *Tractatus de Miraculis*, no. 160.

45. This is told in shortened form in the *Tractatus de Miraculis*, no. 161.

46. *Ibid.*, no. 162.

47. *Ibid.*, no. 163.

48. Fano lies on the Adriatic Sea, about thirty miles northeast of Ancona.

49. This is told again in the *Tractatus de Miraculis*, no. 164.

50. *Ibid.*, no. 165.

51. There were two cities in Umbria by this name: one was near Perugia, the other near Todi. There was another city by the same name in the region of Sabina, near Rieti.

52. Francis' body lay in the church of St. George at this time.

53. This is told also in the *Tractatus de Miraculis*, no. 166.

54. Coccorano lies about seven miles north of Assisi.

55. This is told also in the *Tractatus de Miraculis*, no. 167.

56. This is told in a greatly condensed version in the *Tractatus de Miraculis*, no. 173.

57. *Ibid.*, no. 130.

58. About five miles southeast of Assisi.

59. This is also told in the *Tractatus de Miraculis*, no. 143.

60. About twenty-three miles east of Assisi.

61. This is told again in the *Tractatus de Miraculis*, no. 136.

62. *Ibid.*, no. 137.

63. *Ibid.*, no. 138.

64. *Ibid.*, no. 139.

65. The shrine at Monte Gargano in Apulia was famous.

66. This is told also in the *Tractatus de Miraculis*, no. 150.

67. *Ibid.*, no. 151.
68. In Umbria, about twenty-three miles south of Perugia.
69. Even today this is a popular nickname for Francis, under the form *Cecco*.
70. This is repeated more briefly in the *Tractatus de Miraculis*, no. 67.
71. *Ibid.*, no. 68.
72. *Ibid.*, no. 69.
73. *Ibid.*, no. 78.
74. *Ibid.*, no. 80.
75. *Ibid.*, no. 79.
76. *Ibid.*, no. 70.
77. *Ibid.*, no. 76.
78. *Ibid.*, no. 71.
79. *Ibid.*, no. 77.
80. *Ibid.*, no. 197.
81. *Ibid.*, no. 113.
82. *Ibid.*, no. 196, in a condensed version.
83. *Ibid.*, 146, in a condensed version.
84. *Ibid.*, 147.
85. *Ibid.*, no. 125, in a condensed version.
86. *Ibid.*, no. 140.
87. *Ibid.*, 141.
88. *Ibid.*, 142.
89. Apoc. 5, 13.
90. Rom. 16, 27.
91. 1 Cor. 12, 6.
92. Mss. 3817, National Library, Paris, adds this note: *Apud Perusium felix dominus Papa Gregorius nonus, secundo gloriosi Pontificatus sui anno, quinto kalendas Marcii, Legendam hanc recepit, confirmavit et censuit fore tenendam. Gratias omnipotenti Deo et Salvatori nostro super omnia dona sua nunc et per omne saeculum. Amen.* English: At Perugia the happy lord pope Gregory the ninth, in the second year of his glorious pontificate, on the fifth day of the calends of March, received and confirmed this legend and decreed it was to be held fast. Thanks be to Almighty God and our Savior for all his gifts now and forever. Amen. — The date was February 25, 1229. Gregory IX was indeed at Perugia at this time with the Roman curia.

SECOND LIFE

PROLOGUE

1. This was the general chapter held at Genoa in 1244.
2. The minister general was Fr. Crescentius of Jesi.
3. From the way this is put here it would seem that Thomas of Celano is writing not in his own name alone but in the name of Francis' closest companions. See the introduction to the *Lives* in this volume.
4. 2 Mach. 14, 20.
5. Rom. 12, 2.
6. The first part or *opus* of this *Second Life* contains 25 numbered paragraphs distributed among 17 chapters. It is a chronological account of the early life of St. Francis and of the early days of his order up to the naming of Cardinal Hugolino to be the protector of the order. In general, however, it is supplementary only to what was said in the *First Life*. The second part or *opus* consists of paragraphs numbered from 26 to 224, distributed over 167 chapters. It covers a wide range of subjects and ends with the canonization and translation of Francis and a prayer to him.
7. It is evident from this that Celano is writing not only from what he knows personally but also from what he has been able to gather from others; and the latter part of the prologue seems to be written in his own name, unlike the first part of the prologue.

BOOK ONE

1. Is. 26, 8: *nomen tuum et memoriale tuum in desiderio animae.* English: thy name and thy remembrance are the desire of the soul.
2. Though the name was not used too often at that time, it became common after St. Francis' day.
3. Jn. 3, 5.
4. Eph. 2, 3: and were by nature children of wrath even as the rest.
5. Lk. 1, 60: And his mother answered and said, "Not so, but he shall be called John."
6. Lk. 1, 45: Elizabeth's words to Mary when Mary visited her cousin after the annunciation.
7. See the *First Life,* no. 16. When Francis was asked by the robbers who he was, he answered: "I am the herald of the great King."
8. In his *First Rule* (1221), chapter 23, he placed John the Baptist immediately after the archangels and angels in his

final prayer.

9. Mt. 11, 11.
10. Lk. 1, 44: The babe in my womb leapt for joy (at the coming of Mary and the unborn child Jesus).
11. Francis was taken prisoner at the bridge of San Giovanni during the battle between the Perugians and the citizens of Assisi in 1202. He was released about a year later, 1203.
12. Tob. 4, 7: And turn not away thy face from any poor man.
13. See the *First Life* where these things are given more at length, no. 4.
14. St. Martin, bishop and confessor, whose feast is celebrated on November 11. The incident referred to here is recounted in the lessons of the second nocturn.
15. Is. 16, 14: *parvus et modicus,* small and feeble.
16. Sulpicius Severus, Epistola III, no. 21: *Martinus hic pauper et modicus caelum dives ingreditur.*
17. Mt. 5, 42: To him who asks of thee give; and from him who would borrow of thee, do not turn away.
18. See the *First Life,* no. 5.
19. About two hundred miles southeast of Assisi.
20. See the *First Life,* no. 7 and 4.
21. Ezech. 23, 17.
22. See the *First Life,* no. 2.
23. Gen. 38, 18.
24. Ps. 31, 6.
25. An allusion to the stories of the multiplication of the loaves and fishes in the Gospel.
26. Mt. 14, 23.
27. See the *First Life,* no. 33, 36, 43.
28. *Ibid.,* no. 46, 62.
29. *Ibid.,* no. 6
30. Eph. 6, 10.
31. Prov. 27, 7.
32. In the opening words of his *Testament* Francis said: And when I came away from them [i.e., lepers], what seemed bitter to me was changed to sweetness of spirit and body for me.
33. Painted in Byzantine style, it is still preserved in the church of St. Clare where it was placed in 1260.
34. The church of St. Damian was about a half mile outside of Assisi.
35. Cant. 5, 6.
36. Actually, it was about eighteen years later.
37. Acts 20, 28.
38. See no. 13 of the *First Life* (and footnote 45 under it). We choose here also to render *pater carnalis* as *carnally minded* rather than as *according to the flesh* because it seems that Celano wishes to emphasize the contrast between the spiritually minded Francis and his father.

39. Ps. 108, 28.
40. The bishop was Bishop Guido. See the *First Life,* no. 14-15.
41. Mt. 6, 9. See the *First Life,* no. 53.
42. Here *according to the flesh* is to be preferred, since that is the emphasis Celano seems to intend.
43. See the *First Life,* no. 120.
44. Probably an allusion to Virgil: *"Omnia vincit amor."* Eclogue X, 69.
45. Bernard of Quintavalle. See the *First Life,* no. 24.
46. *Ibid.,* no. 92.
47. Mt. 19, 21. See also the *First Life,* no. 24.
48. Lk. 9, 3. See also the *First Life,* no. 22.
49. Lk. 9, 23.
50. Gen. 30, 25: And when Joseph was born, Jacob said to his father in law: Send me away that I may return into my country, and to my lord.
51. Phil. 3, 14: I press on towards the goal, to the prize of God's heavenly call in Christ Jesus.
52. In 1209. See the *First Life,* 32-33.
53. See the *First Life,* no. 36-37.
54. *Ibid.,* no. 33.
55. *Ibid.,* no. 36.
56. Mt. 9, 35.
57. Fortini quotes a document from the year 1160 that calls this place "S. Maria de Porzuncula"; *Nova Vita di S. Francesco d'Assisi,* p. 385, (Milan, 1926).
58. See the *First Life,* no. 22, 106.
59. *Ibid.,* 24-30, 44, 57, 106.
60. *Ibid.,* 106.
61. *Ibid.,* 44. See also the *Speculum Perfectionis* (Lemmens, chapter 27; Sabatier, chapter 55). Also below, no. 57 and 59.
62. See the *First Life,* no. 39-41, 41, 51. Also below, no. 160.
63. 2 Tim. 4, 3.
64. Heb. 11, 35-38.
65. See the *First Life,* no. 40.
66. Dan. 13, 52.
67. See the *First Life,* no. 74.
68. Col. 2, 18.
69. Mt. 1, 24.
70. See the *First Life,* no. 33.
71. Ps. 30, 21.
72. Deut. 13, 13.
73. See the *First Life,* no. 73.
74. That is, the cardinals.
75. Hugolino, cardinal bishop of Ostia, later Gregory IX. Hugolino became cardinal protector of the order in 1220 or 1221.

76. Chapter 12 of the *Regula Bullata* (1223) says: I enjoin on the ministers by obedience that they ask of the Lord Pope one of the cardinals of the holy Roman Church to be governor, protector, and corrector of this brotherhood: so that submissive and subject always at the feet of the same holy Church, grounded in the Catholic faith, we may, as we have firmly promised, observe the poverty and the humility and the Holy Gospel of our Lord Jesus Christ. (apud *The Words of St. Francis,* James Meyer O.F.M., Franciscan Herald Press, 1952, p. 294).

77. He died August 22, 1241. The same story of Francis' asking for a cardinal to act as his pope is told in Brother Jordan of Giano's *Chronicle,* no. 14. See the English version: *XIIIth Century Chronicles,* Placid Hermann O.F.M., Franciscan Herald Press, 1961.

78. See the *First Life,* no. 90.

BOOK TWO

1. In Wis. 7, 26, wisdom is called: "the unspotted mirror of God's majesty, and the image of his goodness."

2. See the *First Life,* no. 91.

3. *Ibid.,* prologue, no. 1.

4. *Ibid.,* prologue, no. 2.

5. Apoc. 19, 10. See also the *First Life,* no. 26-27.

6. See also the *First Life,* no. 30, 47-50.

7. Most likely Brother Elias is meant here. By the time the second life was written by Brother Thomas, Elias had been deposed from the office of general (1239) and excommunicated. Celano does not mention him any more by name.

8. Prov. 26, 11: As a dog that returneth to his vomit, so is the fool that repeateth his folly.

9. Ps. 106, 26.

10. Damietta had been besieged for a year by the crusaders. This battle mentioned here took place on August 29, 1219. Though the crusaders suffered a great setback in the battle, they (under John of Brienne) ultimately took Damietta, Nov. 5, 1219, after they had been reinforced by Cardinal Pelagio. But of the original 70,000 inhabitants, only about 3,000 survived.

11. Among his companions were Brothers Illuminato, Peter of Catania, Elias, Caesar of Speyer. See also the *Chronicle* of Brother Jordan of Giano, no. 11, 12, 14.

12. See the *First Life,* no. 11.

13. The fact that there were many Spaniards along on this crusade is confirmed by a document of Pope Honorius III

(March 15, 1219) quoted by Fr. Ferdinand M. Delorme O.F.M. See the *Archivum Franciscanum Historicum,* Vol. XVI (1923), p. 245-246.

14. Ecclus. 46, 8.
15. Eccles. 4, 10: If one fall he shall be supported by the other: woe to him that is alone, for when he falleth, he hath none to lift him up.
16. Ps. 68, 2.
17. Prov. 7, 23: as if a bird should make haste to the snare, and knoweth not that his life is in danger.
18. Ecclus. 11, 13: Yet the eye of God hath looked upon him for good.
19. Ps. 110, 1-2.
20. Prov. 27, 17.
21. *Ibid.* 18, 19.
22. Jam. 1, 12.
23. Mt. 18, 6: it were better for him [he who gives scandal] to have a great millstone hung around his neck, and to be drowned in the depths of the sea.
24. Zach. 5, 7: And behold a talent of lead was carried, and behold a woman sitting in the midst of the vessel.
25. See the *First Life,* no. 84-87.
26. Lk. 3, 8.
27. Prov. 26, 11.
28. Ps. 106, 38.
29. *Ibid.* 105, 21.
30. In 1242 Emperor Frederick II besieged Rieti. Greccio is only a short distance from that city and it may be that it was burned at this time. See *Analecta Franciscana,* Vol. X, p. 152, footnote 20.
31. No. 35 just above.
32. See the *Second Life,* no. 4.
33. The Quaracchi editors of Celano *(Analecta Franciscana,* X, p. 153-154) say that this civil war between the nobles of Perugia and the people began in 1214 and was settled by Pope Innocent III that same year, but that it was renewed in 1217 and again in 1223. They conjecture that Francis' sermon was in 1213 (or 1217).
34. 1 Tim. 1, 5: Now the purpose of this charge is charity, from a pure heart and a good conscience and faith unfeigned.
35. See the *First Life,* no. 105.
36. This city canot be identified. The Quaracchi editors suggest several possibilities: Lisciano Niccone, Reschio, Lusignano, Lucignano. *(Analecta Franciscana,* X, p. 154, footnote 3.)
37. Gen. 28, 56.
38. 4 Kings, 16, 15.
39. 1 Cor. 7, 14.

40. A region just below central Italy, on the western coast. This was one of the early Franciscan provinces.

41. Lucca is about ten miles northeast of Pisa.

42. See the *First Life*, no. 99.

43. According to the Quaracchi editors this man was bursar of the cathedral at Rieti from 1213-1216. He died some time between 1236 and 1246, but the precise date is unknown.

44. In the extreme south of the region of Abruzzi, in the diocese of Marsica.

45. See no. 144 below.

46. Who the doctor was is not known for certain. A certain "magister Nicolaus medicus" is mentioned in documents at Rieti between 1203 and 1233. This may have been Francis' doctor. See *Analecta Franciscana*, X, p. 158, footnote 1.

47. The following paragraph, marked 44a, is omitted in several of the manuscripts. It repeats, to some extent even in the wording, the story told in the *First Life*, no. 49-50.

48. St. Francis is considered the first. See the *First Life*, no. 24, for Bernard's reception into the order.

49. This companion was Brother Leo, a priest and confessor of St. Francis.

50. The original is preserved yet today in the basilica of St. Francis of Assisi. The words of both the Praises of God and of the blessing can be found in the *Opuscula*, p. 124-125, 198-200. Brother Leo added a note to the original in which he said that the paper was given him in the month of September 1224, just after Francis had received the stigmata.

51. That is, the palace of the bishop of Assisi. See the *First Life*, no. 108.

52. See the *First Life*, no. 120. Also no. 181 below. In the latter number is told of another habit taken to England by Brother Lawrence of Beauvais.

53. 1 Cor. 13, 5.

54. Amos 8, 11.

55. Mt. 23, 27: Woe to you, Scribes and Pharisees, hypocrites! because you are like whited sepulchres.

56. 2 Cor. 11, 13: For they are false apostles, deceitful workers, disguising themselves as apostles of Christ.

57. Lk. 21, 9.

58. Celano, no doubt, is exaggerating somewhat, but the rebellion of the Romans against the pope occurred in 1228 (see the *First Life*, no. 122). Frederick II had been excommunicated by Gregory IX in 1227 because he had delayed too long the crusade to Palestine. He went, however, in June 1228. While he was gone, some of his soldiers in Italy attacked the Marches of Ancona and the duchy of Spoleto and later Naples. Thus the war was rather widespread.

59. Several contemporary sources speak of a famine in 1227. Brother Salimbene mentions it in his *Chronicle.* So too the *Chronicum Parmense, 1138-1338* and others. See the *Analecta Franciscana,* X, p. 163-164, footnote 16.

60. The veiled implication here seems to be that the dead child was eaten.

61. Lam. 3, 41.

62. Gen. 2, 24.

63. This whole passage, as well as other similar passages in the *Lives,* is so reminiscent of the *Sacrum Commercium S. Francisci cum Domina Paupertate* that it suggests the thought that perhaps Celano was the author of that work too

64. See St. Francis' *Testament:* And those who came to take up this life, gave all they would possess to the poor, and they were content with one tunic patched inside and out if they wished, besides a cincture and drawers. And we wished to have nothing else. Apud *The Words of St. Francis,* English by James Meyer O.F.M., Franciscan Herald Press, 1952, p. 245.

65. Mt. 19, 29: And everyone who has left house, or brothers, or sisters, or father, or mother, or wife, or children, or lands, for my name's sake, shall receive a hundredfold, and shall possess life everlasting.

66. Mt. 8, 20. In quoting the Gospel passage Celano uses *Son of God* and the past tense *had,* in the latter half of the sentence.

67. See number 25 above.

68. See the *First Life,* no. 74. Apparently, from the context, the legate was not in Bologna itself, but must have been somewhere close by. This incident may have happened in 1219, but more probably it took place in 1221, after Francis' return from the Orient.

69. This, however, is probably not Celano, but the brother who supplied the story at the request of the minister general. This story apparently was amplified by later writers who wanted to use it to show that Francis was opposed to studies in the order. Angelo of Clareno, one of the *Spirituals,* added the detail that the house was a house of studies founded by Peter of Stacia and that Francis drove out the brothers because it was devoted to studies. He also added that Francis cursed Peter and would not retract his curse even after Peter became ill and was dying. At the end of the 14th century an additional chapter was inserted into the *Actus B. Francisci (Little Flowers of St. Francis)* in which the story was repeated from Angelo and this detail added that when Peter was dying, a blob of burning sulphur fell upon him and he burned to death and "the devil came and carried away his soul." It should be emphasized that Celano (and the *Speculum*

Perfectionis) gives the reason for Francis' action precisely as that the people considered the house as being owned by the friars. The whole thing is a good example of how an anecdote grows to suit the purposes of the narrators.

70. In the province of Siena, northwest of Assisi.

71. The Latin word is *carcer,* which here means desert.

72. That is, in the Rule (Second Rule, 1223): The brothers are to take nothing as their own, neither a house, nor place, nor anything, and as pilgrims and strangers in this world, ... let them go confidently in quest of alms (Chapter 6).

73. Lk. 24, 18: Art thou the only stranger in Jerusalem who does not know the things that have happened there in these days?

74. *Ibid.,* 32: Was not our heart burning within us while he was speaking on the road and explaining the Scriptures?

75. Hugolino. See no. 58 above.

76. There is a strong play on words in this sentence: *Ostiensis* (of Ostia), *ostium* (door), *hostibus* (foes), *hostiam* (victim).

77. See the *First Life,* no. 99-101 where Celano praises Hugolino at some length.

78. A wild grass often found growing amid grain.

79. Chapter 8 of the *First Rule* (1221) speaks of money like this: "...because we ought to have no greater use and regard for money and coin than for stones ... And should we find coins anywhere, let us not bother about them any more than the dust we tread under foot." The *Second Rule* (1223) says (chapter 4): "I firmly command all the brothers that they must not in any way accept coins or money, either themselves or through an intermediary person."

80. The Latin is *leprosis pecuniae famulis offerendum.* Lepers were supported by alms, but they always needed money. It is not surprising that some of them became *servants of money* or *greedy for money.* This seems to be a good way to translate the phrase.

81. See footnote 79 just above.

82. This is very similar to Prov. 28, 23: He that rebuketh a man, shall afterward find favor with him.

83. He became vicar probably in 1220, though some have argued that he functioned as vicar, especially in the absence of Francis, even earlier than this. However, the only mention of vicars before this occurs in Brother Jordan of Giano's *Chronicle,* no. 11, at the time of Francis' going to the Orient when he appointed two vicars to act in his place. See also the *First Life,* no. 25, footnote 84.

84. Both the First and the Second Rule bid those entering the order to give their things to the poor, by which is understood, not to the order. And the brothers are forbidden to

meddle in their affairs.

85. The Latin is *funda* (Italian *fonda*), literally a sling; perhaps it is best translated as a money belt.
86. Mt. 18, 16.
87. Lk. 22, 41.
88. Phil. 2, 21.
89. Num. 14, 2-4: And all the children of Israel murmured against Moses and Aaron, saying: Would God that we had died in Egypt:... and they said one to another: Let us appoint a captain, and let us return into Egypt.
90. Thereafter let them give them the clothes of probation, to wit, two tunics without a capuche, a cincture, drawers, and a caperon reaching to the cincture,... And those who have promised obedience, shall have one tunic with a capuche and, such as wish, another without a capuche. *Rule* (1223), chapter 2.
91. And all the brothers shall dress in garments of low value and they may patch them with sacking and other patches with the blessing of God. *Ibid.*
92. See the *First Life*, no. 110. Also below, 225-226.
93. Ps. 17, 46.
94. Ps. 26, 12.
95. Ps. 9, 19.
96. Ps. 68, 33.
97. Both the *First* and the *Second Rule* speak of the obligation of seeking alms. The *Testament* says: And should the wages of our work not be given to us, let us take recourse to the table of the Lord by seeking alms from door to door.
98. Mt. 25, 40.
99. That is, Christ.
100. That is, the *least* brothers.
101. Francis wanted not more than three or four to live in hermitages. Two were to live like Martha, the other one or two like Mary. See his little work *De Religiosa Habitatione in Eremo, Opuscula,* p. 83.
102. That is, Lady Poverty.
103. A fief, Latin *feudum,* in the terminology of the Middle Ages, meant some immovable goods given over by a prince to his trusted servants for a time, during which they might enjoy the usufruct of it.
104. Mt. 5, 3: Blessed are the poor in spirit, for theirs is the Kingdom of heaven.
105. 2 Cor., 8, 9.
106. The present Nocera Umbra, about fourteen miles east of Assisi.
107. The Satriano that lies between Nocera Umbra and Assisi. The incident mentioned here took place probably in September 1226.
108. Lk. 10, 8: And whatever town you enter, and they receive

you, eat what is set before you,... See the *Second Rule,* chapter 3: Into whatever house they enter, let them first say, Peace to this house. And according to the holy Gospel, they shall be free to eat of whatever foods are put before them.

109. 1 Kings 25, 17. He was probably a member of a heretical sect, like the Cathari.
110. Mt. 5, 31.
111. *Ibid.,* 19, 21: If thou wilt be perfect, go, sell what thou hast, and give it to the poor,...
112. Ps. 72, 17.
113. Gen. 20, 3.
114. See no. 106 below.
115. Ps. 11, 7.
116. The reference is to Dan. 2, 36-45; that is, Daniel's interpretation of Nabuchodonosor's dream of the great statue; the succession of the four kingdoms (golden, silver, brass, iron).
117. That is, the Blessed Virign Mary.
118. 1 Cor. 12, 6.
119. Cant. 1, 12.
120. Ps. 83, 10.
121. Is. 53, 3. Celano touched frequently on this subject in the *First Life,* e.g., no. 84, 91, 92, 102, 103.
122. The author's birthplace.
123. About fifteen miles east of Rome. Apparently, therefore, Francis came to Celano on the old Via Valeria.
124. The diocese of Marsica is not named after a city but rather after a stretch of land that was the home of the ancient Marsi. The cathedral church was in the little city called S. Benedetto dei Marsi. After 1580 the episcopal see was located at Pescina, just about seven miles southeast of Celano. Today it is at Avezzano. See *Franziskanische Studien,* 22 (1935), p. 133 ssq.
125. Collestrada was an ancient village about three miles southeast of Perugia, near the bridge of San Giovanni. It marked the boundary between Perguia and Assisi.
126. The Latin text used the popular word *gaida,* meaning the edge or border or part of a garment.
127. See the *First Life,* no. 25. Also no. 67 of the *Second Life.*
128. For example, Lk. 12, 33: See what you have and give alms.
129. See above, no. 41.
130. It was probably a town near Rieti, but it no longer exists.
131. This was in April 1226. See the *First Life,* no. 105, and below, no. 137.
132. There were several towns named Campiglia in that general neighborhood. Going from Rieti to Siena, Francis could have gone along a route that would have taken

him through Campiglia d'Orcia, not too far away from Siena. Or he could have taken another route that would have taken him past Campiglia di Val d'Ombrone. There is no way of knowing which town is meant here.

133. See no. 82 above. Celano is speaking with philosophical terms here in the single form perfecting a threefold matter.

134. 2 Cor. 5, 6: Always full of courage, then, and knowing that while we are in the body we are exiled from the Lord . . . .

135. Eph. 2, 19: Therefore, you are now no longer strangers and foreigners, but you are citizens with the saints and members of God's household.

136. Eph. 2, 14: For he himself is our peace, he it is who has made both one, and has broken down the intervening wall of the enclosure, the enmity, in his flesh.

137. Celano may be speaking here in the name of those who supplied the information.

138. See the *First Life,* no. 96.

139. Apoc. 2, 17: To him who overcomes, I will give the hidden manna.

140. It is not clear whether or not Celano is referring to a particular trip by boat by Francis.

141. 2 Cor. 6, 1: Yes, working together with him we entreat you not to receive the grace of God in vain.

142. See the *First Life,* no. 105, 130.

143. That is, without putting the capuche over his head.

144. Ps. 94, 3: For the Lord is a great God, and a great King above all gods.

145. A town about twenty-two miles northeast of Arezzo.

146. The bishop was Guido. He was bishop of Assisi from about 1204 until his death on July 30, 1228.

147. This was the Benedictine abbey of St. Giustino, about twelve miles northeast of Perugia. See *L'Umbria Francesana,* Nicholas Cavanna O.F.M., Perugia, Unione Tip. Cooperativa, 1910, p. 183.

148. Phil. 4, 15.

149. 2 Cor. 5, 10.

150. See the *First Life,* no. 23.

151. The degree of master, the equivalent of doctor, was the highest academic degree conferred by the universities of the Middle Ages.

152. This is a free quotation of Ezech. 3, 18: If, when I say to the wicked, Thou shalt surely die: thou declarest not to him, nor speak to him, that he may be converted from his wicked way, and live: the same wicked man shall die in his iniquity, but I will require his blood at thy hand.

153. From the following account, however, it does not appear that the swords proceeded from his mouth but were across the body. See the vision of Brother Sylvester,

below in no. 109.

154. Frederick II.

155. Is. 5, 18.

156. 2 Kings, 14, 14.

157. The reference is probably to the same convent of nuns mentioned in the *First Life,* no. 78, and it was probably at this time yet a monastery of Benedictine nuns. Only in 1223 did it become a Poor Clare monastery, and Brother Pacificus entered the order perhaps in 1212, as some say, or in 1215 or 1216, according to others.

158. The *Tau* is a letter of the Greek alphabet. Ezech. 9, 4: And the Lord said to him: Go through the midst of Jersualem: and mark Thau upon the forehead of the men that sigh.

159. See the *First Life,* no. 73, and above no. 25.

160. Ps. 67, 34.

161. The Latin *physicus* meant in the Middle Ages a medical doctor.

162. Is. 55, 11: So shall my word be, which shall go forth from my mouth: it shall not return to me void.

163. See the next paragraph for Sylvester's conversion.

164. It appears from a document quoted by Arnaldo Fortini that Sylvester had been a canon of the church of St. Rufino, but little else is known about him. See Fortini's *Nova Vita di San Francesco d'Assisi,* Milan 1926, p. 178, note 17, and p. 406-408.

165. Most probably St. Damian's. See the *First Life,* no. 18. It could, however, also be the church of St. Mary of the Angels at the Portiuncula. *Ibid.,* no. 21.

166. It is clear that he was already dead at the writing, 1246.

167. 2 Peter 2, 17.

168. See below, no. 167-171 and also the *First Life,* no. 56-61.

169. A Benedictine abbey. See the *First Life,* no. 16.

170. That is, Christ. Jn. 2, 29: Behold, the Lamb of God, who takes away the sin of the world.

171. The Rule of 1223 says in chapter 11: I strictly command all the brothers not to have suspicious associations or conversations with women.

172. Prov. 6, 28: Or can he walk upon hot coals and his feet not be burnt?

173. Ruth 4, 11.

174. Rom. 9, 28.

175. Acts 7, 55.

176. Is. 29, 14: and out of the ground thy speech shall mutter.

177. Esther 15, 17: For thou, my lord, art very admirable, and thy face is full of graces.

178. Eccles. 2, 14.

179. See the *First Life,* no. 58.

180. In the First Rule (1221), chapter 12: The brothers all,

wherever they are or go, shall be on their guard against evil looks and associations with women, and none shall confer alone with them. Let the priests speak respectfully with them in administering Penance or any spiritual advice.

181. Is. 3, 2.
182. Mt. 17, 19.
183. See no. 59 above.
184. Leo Brancaleo was made a cardinal deacon in 1200 and a cardinal priest in 1202. His titular church was that of the Holy Cross in Jerusalem. He died about 1230.
185. The Latin is *castaldus* or *gastaldus*. It has the meaning, in the dialect of the Lombards, of a kind of prefect with the power to punish and coerce people. See *Analecta Franciscana*, X, p. 201, note 3.
186. The Latin is *palatinus*. Brothers were sometimes requested by nobles to serve as a kind of court chaplain. Some were assigned to the task by obedience.
187. Celano evidently does not approve of the friars being at the courts and thinks such a practice was displeasing to God.
188. Jn. 13, 21.
189. Mk. 14, 33.
190. Mt. 26, 41: The spirit indeed is willing, but the flesh is weak.
191. Mt. 14, 31.
192. Acts 3, 7.
193. In his *Sermo de S. Francisco (Opera Omnia,* IX, 577) St. Bonaventure attributes this vision to Brother Pacificus (see above, no. 82, 106) and explains that it was the throne of Lucifer that was reserved for Francis. The *Speculum Perfectionis* too (first redaction, chapter 33; the second redaction, chapters 59-60) attributes the vision to Brother Pacificus. A later tradition attributes it to Brother Amasseo of Marignano (e.g., Ubertino da Casale in the *Arbor vitae crucifixae jesu*).
194. Ps. 44, 8.
195. Ps. 50, 14.
196. Hab. 2, 3.
197. Celano used a similar expression in the *First Life,* where he said that Francis walked about the streets of Babylon with evil companions. Here he is using it for dejection. See no. 2 of the *First Life.*
198. See above, no. 92.
199. See, for instance, Ps. 70, 22; 91, 4; 97, 5. The latter passage reads: Sing praise to the Lord with the harp, with the harp and melodious song.
200. It could be that Celano is using here the words of those who supplied the material, but it seems more likely that he is speaking for himself.

201. See no. 99 above.
202. We read in the First Rule: And let the brothers take heed not to appear sad exteriorly and be gloomy hypocrites, but let them prove to be joyful in the Lord, and merry and becomingly courteous (chapter 7).
203. See below, no. 210-211.
204. Ps. 23, 29.
205. An allusion to Ps. 62, 2: For thee my soul hath thirsted; for thee my flesh, O how many ways.
206. See above, no. 69.
207. See above, no. 69.
208. The reference seems to be to our first parents after their fall in paradise. Gen. 3, 21.
209. Most probably this is Poggio Bustone, about seven miles north of Rieti.
210. The fast from the feast of All Saints until Christmas which was prescribed by the third chapter of the Rule.
211. See the *First Life,* no. 95-96.
212. A city in northern Italy.
213. Since it is Brother Pacificus speaking here, the King of Verses, it is not surprising to see him use the term *mother.*
214. Celano then goes on to explain this, but see the next few notes.
215. This was Brother Rufino. See the *First Life,* no. 95.
216. This is understood to be Brother Elias. *First Life,* no. 95.
217. In the *First Life,* no. 95, Celano expresses his wonder that so few were permitted to see the wound in Francis' side while the saint was yet alive. He then goes on to tell that Brother Elias merited to see it and that Brother Rufino touched it. In no. 102 he then tells how Francis entrusted the care of his person to certain brothers, four in number, but the names are withheld. Their identity can be surmised from the description of each: Angelo Tancredi, Rufino, Leo, John of Lodi. Of the latter Bernard of Bessa *(Liber de Laudibus S. Francisci)* says that he too touched the wound *(Analecta Franciscana,* III, 668). In the *Second Life* here the incident of Brother Rufino is repeated briefly, and also the trickery of Brother Elias is explained. But the statement in the paragraph that only one brother and only once saw the wound is hard to understand. In other sources Rufino is said to have placed his hand into the wound (his life in *Analecta Franciscana,* III, and in the Fourth Consideration on the Stigmata in the *Little Flowers of St. Francis),* and this seems to be implied here. Are we to picture it that Rufino, in his rubbing of St. Francis (presumably his back; the Latin *scalpere* is difficult to render), stood behind him and only touched the wound without seeing it? Incidentally, the *Tractatus de Miraculis* says that many saw the wounds while Francis lived (no. 5), but here

Celano is speaking of the stigmata in general.

218. There is an allusion here to Ovid, *The Art of Love*, II, 13: *Nec minor est virtus, quam quaerere, parta tueri. The Loeb Classical Library.*

219. 1 Jn. 4, 1.

220. Mt. 11, 29: learn of me, for I am meek and humble of heart.

221. That is, the servant of all. In the second Rule, chapter 8, we read: All the brothers shall be bound always to have one of the brothers of this order as the minister general and servant of the whole brotherhood and shall be strictly bound to obey him.

222. A city about fifteen miles northwest of Rieti.

223. Ps. 147, 20.

224. It seems that this was the general chapter of 1220. The expression "a few years after his conversion" cannot be taken too strictly. Some, however, argue that Peter acted as the vicar of Francis prior to this time.

225. 2 Cor. 12, 9. Francis said in his *Testament* that he had always wanted "to have a cleric to do the Office" with him.

226. Eph. 4, 1.

227. Gal. 5, 4.

228. Ps. 12, 18.

229. Francis seems to have been mindful of the decree of the Lateran Council (1215) that there be in cathedral and other churches suitable men to assist the bishop and the clergy in caring for souls. See the *Analecta Franciscana*, X, p. 214, note 8.

230. Deut. 32, 35.

231. A city along the ancient Via Aemilia about twenty miles southeast of Bologna.

232. A region between the Adriatic Sea, the Po River, and the Apennines Mountains.

233. A certain Meinardinus Aldigerii (1207-1249). See note 2, p. 215 of the *Analecta Franciscana*, X.

234. Hugolino was the bishop of Ostia and later Pope Gregory IX. The meeting of these three probably took place after the summer of 1217 and before August 6, 1221, the date of St. Dominic's death. The papal court was at Rome from October 2, 1217 to June 1, 1219; again from December 30, 1219 to January 3, 1220; again from October 21, 1220 to February 21, 1222. In between it was at various other places, especially Rieti and Viterbo. Francis was in the Orient during the summer and early fall of 1219. And Dominic apparently was in Rome early in 1218, late in 1219, early in 1220 and again late in 1220 and the first part of 1221. Most probably the meeting of the three took place in 1220. That seems to be the conclusion of some more recent authors. Others put it back a bit.

Incidentally, Pope Gregory IX canonized both St. Francis (July 16, 1228) and St. Dominic (July 3, 1234). See *Analecta Franciscana*, X, p. 215.

235. Gal. 5, 15.

236. Eph. 6, 12: For our wrestling is not against flesh and blood, but against the Principalities and the Powers, against the world-rulers of this darkness, . . .

237. Exod. 25, 20.

238. Wis. 2, 15.

239. Rom. 12, 16: Do not set your minds on high things.

240. Ps. 106, 4.

241. Acts 10, 14.

242. Ps. 127, 6.

243. See no. 148, above.

244. See above, no. 143.

245. *Loc. cit.*

246. Ecclus. 51, 34.

247. See the *First Life*, no. 45.

248. The Rule (1223), chapter 12: Whoever of the brothers may wish on divine inspiration to go among the Saracens and other non-believers should ask leave for it from their provincial ministers.

249. An obedience is the command of the superior of the province (or of the order), especially of transfer from one place to another, usually a written or printed document.

250. See the *First Life*, no. 36, 37, 89.

251. The expression *exempla lucis* is probably taken from St. Gregory the Great, as found in the homily of the III Nocturn of Matins of the *Commune Confessoris non Pontificis: cum, per bona opera, proximis nostris lucis exempla monstramus.*

252. Exod. 29, 18.

253. Mt. 26, 7.

254. Tim. 1, 15.

255. In the province of Gaeti. Robert, a Cistercian, was at the head of the diocese from 1210 to 1227.

256. 2 Mach. 14, 34.

257. 1 John 2, 18.

258. Rom. 13, 12.

259. *Loc. cit.* There seems to be a rather veiled reference in these lines to Brother Elias who received a special blessing from Francis. See the *First Life*, no. 108.

260. Ps. 43, 9.

261. Jam. 1, 12.

262. The Latin is the diminutive *homuncio,* a word that was used already by such ancient writers as Cicero and Juvenal.

263. Phil. 2, 12.

264. Dan. 1, 2.
265. Apoc. 3, 16: But because thou art lukewarm, and neither cold nor hot, I am about to vomit thee out of my mouth.
266. Francis' *Testament*: And I worked with my hands, and I wish to work; and I wish earnestly to have all the rest of the brothers work at employment such as conforms with propriety. Those who know none, should learn, ...
267. An allusion to what is said in Gen. 2, 2 about God resting on the seventh day after the work he had done.
268. Job 5, 7: Man is born to labor and the bird to fly.
269. Amos 5, 10.
270. Acts 6, 4. Chapter 17 of the First Rule speaks at length of preachers and Chapter 9 of the Second Rule. But Celano is not quoting here from either place.
271. Mt. 5, 14.
272. The *Testament* of St. Francis.
273. St. Anthony of Padua. See no. 48 of the *First Life*. The letter seems to have been written when St. Anthony was appointed to teach the young students of the Order at Bologna. It is now generally accepted as authentic. See the *Chronica XXIV Generalium (Analecta Franciscana,* III, 132) and *Franziskanische Studien,* 31, 1949, p. 135 ssq.; 36, 1954, p. 244-249. Also, *AFH,* 45, 1952, p. 474-492.
274. 1 Kings 2, 5.
275. *Loc. cit.*
276. Eph. 6, 12.
277. Wis. 7, 26.
278. See the *First Life,* no. 80-81.
279. Job. 23, 3.
280. *First Life,* no. 58-61, 77-79.
281. *Ibid.,* no. 80.
282. 1 Cor. 10, 4: And all ate the same spiritual food, and all drank the same spiritual drink (for they drank from the spiritual rock which followed them, and the rock was Christ).
283. Ps. 60, 3.
284. See the *First Life,* no. 81.
285. *Ibid.,* no. 80.
286. *Ibid.,* no. 81. See also above, no. 47, 75, and the following paragraphs here.
287. See the *First Life,* no. 77-79.
288. 1 Cor. 12, 6.
289. See the *First Life,* no. 98-101.
290. Lk. 4, 25.
291. *Ibid.,* 5, 26.
292. See the *First Life,* no. 61.
293. See the *First Life,* no. 90, 97.
294. See no. 163 above.
295. Gal. 6, 10.
296. Heb. 9, 15.

297. Deut. 32, 11: As the eagle enticing her young to fly.
298. Ps. 16, 4: for the sake of the words of thy lips, I have kept hard ways.
299. 1 Cor. 13, 1-3.
300. An allusion to Juvenal, *Satires,* VI, 223: *Sic volo, sic jubeo, sit pro ratione voluntas* (this I wish, this I command, let my will stand in the place of reason). *The Loeb Classical Library.*
301. The use of the seal pertains to superiors. The idea is that mere authority will not do any good under such circumstances.
302. The expression seems to have been prompted by Cant. 6, 1: My beloved is gone down into his garden, to the bed of aromatical spices, . . .
303. Perhaps with Mt. 7, 16 in mind (Do men gather grapes of thorns) Celano switches to "rose be gathered from thorns."
304. Gen. 304. The general idea seems to be that no matter how difficult obedience may be it is still profitable for eternity at least.
305. That is, the good brothers. Jesus said of Nathanael that he was "a true Israelite," Jn. 1, 47.
306. Ps. 50, 19: A sacrifice to God is an afflicted spirit.
307. The *Second Rule,* chapter 6: And if anyone of them fall into illness, the rest of the brothers must wait on him as they themselves would want to be waited on.
308. The *First Rule,* chapter 10, but the wording is slightly changed.
309. 1 Thess. 5, 18: In all things give thanks.
310. Acts 13, 48.
311. Apoc. 3, 19: As for me, those whom I love I rebuke and chastise.
312. See no. 22 above.
313. An allusion to Ps. 144, 14: The Lord lifteth up all that fall.
314. Francis set down in his rule how superiors were to act toward their subjects and he asked mainly for kindness.
315. Heb. 5, 7.
316. Ps. 2, 9.
317. Lk. 10, 34.
318. Ps. 22, 4.
319. Eccles. 3, 1.
320. Ps. 93, 1.
321. 2 Cor. 1, 3.
322. Osee 6, 6: For I desired mercy and not sacrifice.
323. 2 Cor. 5, 13: For if we were out of our mind, it was for God.
324. *Ibid.,* 2, 15: For we are the fragrance of Christ for God.
325. This is what Francis wanted, though he did not suggest the weekly changeover. See his *De religiosa habitatione*

in eremo, Opuscula, 83-84.

326. Cant. 2, 7.

327. *Ibid.,* 2, 9.

328. *Ibid.,* 8, 13: Thou that dwellest in the garden, the friends hearken.

329. 2 Cor. 12, 15: But I will most gladly spend and be spent myself for your souls.

330. We read in Thomas of Eccleston's *De Adventu Fratrum Minorum in Angliam (XIIIth Century Chronicles,* Placid Hermann O.F.M., p. 96) that Brother Lawrence of Beauvais was given a tunic by St. Francis and took it back to England. He had been among the first brothers to go to England in 1224. Most likely he went back to see Francis not too long thereafter and probably received the habit from him in 1226. At the time Brother Thomas of Eccleston was writing, Brother Lawrence was desperately ill; this would be about 1258 or 1259. The "one brother" whose tunic here was poorer would very likely be this Brother Lawrence of Beauvais. See also above in no. 50 for the story of the habit taken to France.

331. Detraction, in its more technical meaning, means revealing a hidden fault of someone, while calumny or slander means the false report of some evil in another. Celano, however, seems to be using the Latin term *detractio* in a broader sense of slander, or perhaps both detraction and slander.

332. The Florentine pugilist or Brother John of Florence is probably the same as John de Laudibus or of Lauds or of Lodi. He is praised in the *Speculum Perfectionis* (second redaction) as a man of "bodily and spiritual courage," "who in his time had been physically stronger than all men." See the English translation, *St. Francis of Assisi,* translated by Leo Sherley-Price, Harper & Brothers, 1959, p. 106.

333. Lk. 16, 4.

334. Ecclus. 11, 33.

335. The idea is somewhat lost behind the metaphorical language here. There is an obvious allusion to Joatham's parable in Judg. 9, 7, ssq, especially verse 15: And it [the bramble to the trees] answered them: If indeed you mean to make me king, come ye and rest under my shadow; but if you mean it not, let fire come out from the bramble, and devour the cedars of Libanus. The meaning of the words here that Francis is putting into the mouth of the slanderer may possibly be this: the slanderer, wanting to slander the good, cuts down the cedars, so that he himself will then stand out, the bramble.

336. Mt. 6, 16: And when you fast, do not look gloomy like the hypocrites, who disfigure their faces in order to appear to men as fasting. Amen I say to you, they have

received their reward.

337. It may be that the last four sentences of this paragraph are Celano's own words rather than a continuation of the words of St. Francis.

338. That is, not long before Francis' death.

339. Prov. 10, 29.

340. Tit. 2, 7.

341. That is, the founders of the older monastic orders.

342. Ecclus. 9, 22.

343. 2 Mach. 4, 15.

344. Also called *Salute to the Virtues*. See *The Words of St. Francis,* James Meyer O.F.M., Franciscan Herald Press, 1952, p. 73.

345. Probably Nottiano, about five miles east of Assisi.

346. 1 Cor. 2, 4.

347. Prov. 3, 32.

348. Or tonsure. Among Franciscans it is frequently called the corona. The meaning of the next sentence is not too clear, but the idea seems to be that Francis did not want the distinction between clerics and lay brothers to be emphasized by too great a difference in the size of the tonsure.

349. Rom. 2, 11.

350. The final rule was approved by Honorius III, November 29, 1223.

351. 1 Cor. 7, 20.

352. Even though it was said in the *First Rule,* chapter 3, that lay brothers might have a psalter if they knew how to read it. The *Speculum Perfectionis* (second redaction, chapter 4) says that this lay brother was a novice.

353. Rom. 1, 9.

354. A plectrum is a tiny piece of ivory, or metal, used in playing a lyre or other such stringed instrument.

355. See above, no. 77.

356. See the *First Life,* no. 17, 115; also above, no. 5.

357. See above, no. 90.

358. Ps. 22, 4.

359. Ps. 137, 1.

360. Ps. 46, 8.

361. The same thought is expressed, for instance, in the Offertory of the Requiem Mass: *Signifer S. Michael repraesentet eas in lucem sanctam.*

362. September 29.

363. See the *Salute to the Blessed Virgin,* composed by Francis, in *The Words of St. Francis,* James Meyer O.F.M., Franciscan Herald Press, 1952, p. 197.

364. Gal. 4, 2.

365. According to the rule Friday is a day of fast, as well as abstinence. Chapter 3.

366. An allusion to the Introit of the III Mass on Christmas: *Puer natus est nobis.*

367. Lk. 2, 7: And she brought forth her firstborn son, and wrapped him in swaddling clothes, and laid him in a manger because there was no room for them in the inn.

368. 1 Pet. 1, 18-19: You know that you were redeemed from the vain manner of life handed down from your fathers, not with perishable things, with silver or gold, but with the precious blood of Christ, as of a lamb without blemish and without spot.

369. The Blessed Eucharist was especially venerated in the region which is now modern Belgium. See *Analecta Franciscana*, X, p. 245, note 6.

370. Francis frequently spoke on this subject; for instance, in his letter to all clerics, *Opuscula*, p. 22-23, and in his *Testament*. In the latter he said: And I want these most holy mysteries above all else to be honored and venerated and kept in choice places.

371. He chose St. Lawrence as an example because, like himself, he was a deacon.

372. 1 Jn. 1, 1.

373. Massa is a mountainous region between Perugia and Arezzo. Monte Casale is only a mile or so from Borgo San Sepolcro.

374. Ps. 68, 14.

375. *Ibid.*, 31.

376. Gal. 6, 14.

377. Celano uses technical terms here from philosophy: *signaculum* or the thing signed or the thing itself, and *signum* or the sign or the word.

378. Celano is speaking of the stigmata in a rather enigmatic way. Writing about 1258, Thomas of Eccleston wrote: But Brother Leo, the companion of St. Francis, told Brother Peter, the minister of England, that the apparition of the Seraph came to St. Francis while he was rapt up in contemplation and more clearly even than was written in his life [i.e. Celano's *legenda*]; and that many things were revealed to him at that time that he did not communicate to any living person. But he did tell Brother Rufino, his companion, that when he saw the angel from afar, he was greatly afraid, and that the angel treated him harshly; and he told him that his Order would continue to the end of the world, that no one of evil will would remain long in the Order, that no one who hated the Order would live long, and that no one who truly loved the Order would come to a bad end. But St. Francis commanded Brother Rufino to wash and anoint with oil the stone on which the angel had stood; this he did. These things Brother Warin of Sedenefeld wrote down from the lips of Brother Leo.

See *XIIIth Century Chronicles,* Placid Hermann O.F.M., Franciscan Herald Press, 1961, p. 161-162.

379. That is, the Poor Clares.
380. St. Damian's church.
381. See above no. 13, where the prophecy is given.
382. 1 Pet. 2, 5.
383. 1 Cor. 12, 11.
384. Jn. 13, 15.
385. The term monastery at that time meant simply a dwelling place of nuns.
386. See above, no. 85.
387. That is, Ps. 50.
388. Prov. 1, 17: But a net is spread in vain before the eyes of them that have wings.
389. Apoc. 3, 5.
390. 1 Thess. 5, 8.
391. No. 32 of the *First Life* explains this.
392. Gen. 17, 13.
393. In this *First Rule,* chapter 23, we read: In the name of the Lord I beseech all the brothers to learn the text and sense of what is written down in this rule of life for the salvation of our soul, and often to call it to mind. *The Words of St. Francis,* p. 283.
394. That is, religious profession.
395. 2 Cor. 12, 12.
396. This was Brother Electus, killed certainly before 1246 and perhaps while Francis was still alive.
397. This was between 1221 and 1223 before the final rule was approved.
398. 2 Pet. 1, 17-18.
399. Jn. 5, 31.
400. Col. 3, 24.
401. Gen. 18, 25.
402. 1 Kings 12, 23.
403. Gal. 2, 20: It is now no longer I that live, but Christ lives in me.
404. Ps. 18, 12.
405. Is. 40, 12.
406. 2 Cor. 4, 17.
407. Otherwise called *The Canticle of Brother Sun.* It was probably composed while Francis was staying at the Poor Clares place at St. Damian's. The verse concerning pardon and peace was added later at the time of a quarrel between the religious and civil authorities of Assisi. The verse about Sister Death was added after the doctor had told him he would surely die. The poem is one of the first in the common language of the people. See one version of it in *Via Seraphica,* Placid Hermann O.F.M.

408. Ecclus. 11, 29.
409. Ps. 118, 32.
410. Exod. 25, 31.
411. Ps. 118, 96. See the *First Life,* no. 90.
412. Jn. 13, 1.
413. The same quotation from St. Gregory, used in the *First Life,* no. 15.
414. 2 Tim. 4, 8.
415. See above, no. 70.
416. Jn. 13, 1.
417. Acts 9, 12.
418. The wording here is very similar to the wording of the blessing in the *First Life,* no. 108.
419. *Ibid.,* no. 108.
420. The idea here is that the blessing should not be considered a personal thing, in so far as Elias is concerned, but as pertaining to his office of vicar. In the *First Life* the very special blessing given to Elias is given in detail. When Celano was writing this *Second Life* Elias had been deposed as general (1239) and was excommunicated by Gregory IX and again by Innocent IV. In referring to the blessing of the *First Life* Celano is implying that Elias had made himself unworthy of it.
421. Mt. 14, 19.
422. Jn. 13, 1. In the *First Life,* no. 110, Celano had misquoted these opening words; here he corrects himself.
423. Mt. 26, 20-29; Mk. 14, 17-25, Lk. 22, 14-38.
424. Ps. 141. See the *First Life,* no. 109.
425. See above, 213 and the *First Life,* no. 109. The reference is to *The Canticle of Brother Sun.*
426. From the *Canticle of Brother Sun.*
427. See above, no. 214.
428. The paragraph that follows here, numbered 217a, is missing in codex A; it is supplied for the most part from the *First Life,* no. 110.
429. These first lines are from the *First Life,* no. 110.
430. The preceding section is found for the most part in the same life, no. 112.
431. *Ibid.,* no. 113.
432. *Ibid.,* no. 112.
433. A region just below central Italy on the western coast.
434. The vestment proper to the deacon.
435. 1 Cor. 6, 17: But he who cleaves to the Lord is one spirit with him.
436. *Ibid.,* 12, 6.
437. Bishop Guido, the same before whom Francis renounced the world.
438. At Monte Gargano, north of Foggia, in Apulia.
439. The following paragraph, numbered 220a, is also missing in codex A. It is made up of passages from various

places of the *First Life*.
440. 1 Cor. 6, 11.
441. See the *First Life*, no. 23.
442. *Ibid.*, no. 88. The *Legenda ad usum chori* adds that it was *late Saturday night* when Francis died. *Analecta Franciscana*, Vol. X, p. 126.
443. *First Life*, no. 119-120.
444. *Ibid.*, 120-124.
445. Most of the preceding is from the *First Life*, no. 123.
446. *Ibid.*, 125.
447. Ecclus. 18, 5.
448. Here the manuscripts break off and the latter part of the proclamation and the translation are missing. We complete the proclamation here from the *First Life*, 126.
449. These words are really from the Bull of Canonization, the text of which can be found in the *Via Seraphica*, Placid Hermann O.F.M. The *Legenda ad usum chori* of Celano adds (no. 13) this little notation: Francis' body remained in the church of St. George "until the wonderful church had been built in his honor and named after him, in which afterwards his sacred body was translated by the brothers of the general chapter." This was May 25, 1230. See *Analecta Franciscana*, Vol. X, p. 124.
450. This final prayer has really four parts to it: a) a part specially directed to St. Francis; b) a prayer for the minister general; c) a prayer for "this your son who now and earlier has devotedly written your praises"; d) a prayer for all the sons of Francis. At first Celano speaks in the name of the several companions who supplied the material; then in his own name.
451. Ps. 80, 17.
452. Ps. 35, 8-9.
453. *Loc. cit.*
454. Ps. 113, 12.
455. Cant. 1, 3.
456. Lam. 5, 21.
457. Rom. 8, 35. The minister general was Crescentius of Jesi.
458. Celano of course is speaking of himself in this elaborate literary apostrophe and prayer.
459. In a sense, the *Life* is considered by Celano the work of himself and of the companions of Francis who supplied the material. But there is no question but what Celano himself wrote the entire work.
460. Zach. 12, 10.

TREATISE ON THE MIRACLES

1. The *Treatise on the Miracles* contains in all 198 paragraphs distributed over 19 chapters. Of these 198 paragraphs 41 pertain to things that happened while Francis was yet alive and therefore have some reference to his biography. However, of these 41, all but 13 are already contained in the two *Lives*. We include in this Appendix only these last 13.

2. Of the six paragraphs in this chapter, four have reference to things that happened while Francis was still alive. However, only paragraph 18 contains material not already contained in the *Lives*.

3. Twelve of the thirteen paragraphs of this chapter pertain to things that happened while Francis was yet alive, but only the two paragraphs given here contain material not already included in the *Lives*.

4. For other stories of sheep see the *First Life*, no. 77-79.

5. See the *Second Life*, no. 200.

6. All of the paragraphs of this chapter (4) refer to things that happened while Francis was alive, but only paragraph 34 contains material not already included in the *Lives*.

7. See the *First Life*, no. 56. But what follows is new.

8. *Ibid.*, no. 24.

9. This whole chapter is new and is given here.

10. Jacoba Giacoma of Settesoli, the widow of Graziano Frangipani. After St. Francis' death she moved to Assisi where she died in 1239. She was buried in the lower church of the basilica of St. Francis.

11. See the *Second Life*, no. 19.

12. The *Speculum Perfectionis* (2nd redaction), no. 112, says: "This is the sweatmeat the people of Rome call *mostaciolli*, and is made of almonds, sugar, and other ingredients."

13. Since they were given in the *First Life*, no. 112-113, 116-118.

14. That is, the five wounds.

15. Ps. 147, 20.

16. The oldest son of Lady Jacoba. The name as it is given here is another form of Frangipani.

17. That is, back to her home in Rome.

18. Of the nine paragraphs of this chapter only paragraph 41 pertains to what happened during Francis' life and is new.

19. An example of this was given in the preceding paragraph 40.

20. Of the thirty paragraphs of this chapter only three pertain to things that happened during Francis' life, and of these three only paragraph 124 is new material not con-

tained in the *Lives*.

21. Of the twenty-five paragraphs of this chapter only four pertain to things that happened during Francis' life, and of these four only paragraphs 174, 178, and 179 contain new material.

MAJOR AND MINOR
LIFE OF ST. FRANCIS
with excerpts from other works
by St. Bonaventure

Translated from the Latin by Benen Fahy
O.F.M., with Introduction by Damien
Vorreux O.F.M. (translated from the
French by Paul Oligny O.F.M.)

This English version of St. Bonaventure's two biographies of St. Francis and excerpts from other works, made by Fr. Benen Fahy, is published for the first time in this volume.

614

INTRODUCTION

"Likewise, we order that a good 'Legend of St. Francis' be written, based on all those already in existence." Such was the directive issued by the General Chapter of the Friars Minor which was held at Narbonne in 1260.[1] The work was entrusted to the minister general himself, St. Bonaventure. His text was approved in 1263. In 1266 it was prescribed as the only canonical, definitive, and exclusive text, with the order that all earlier biographies be burned. . . . If we are to understand why such measures were taken, we have to know the circumstances that warranted them.

Circumstances

The religious fermentation of the forty years that followed the death of St. Francis made a general reorganization of the Order necessary and even urgent.

First of all, in the field of literature, for the Franciscan epic had given rise to a considerable literary production: its character of Messianic renewal lent itself to infinite developments; the extension of the feast of St. Francis to the entire Church actually required that every friary or chapter compose a rather imposing[2] "choral legend"; and certain polemics favored the diffusion of more or less tendentious manifestos. The person and ideal of St. Francis emerged with great difficulty from a mounting flood of writings, libels, and poems in which duly attested facts ran the risk of being lost while puerile imaginings or borrowings from a doubtful source survived. Both the religious and the faithful expected a rather succinct but complete work, of high caliber but yet easy to understand, an "unchanging" portrait of St. Francis. Their expectations were more than answered by this *Life of St. Francis,* which was soon followed by a much shorter, second one that was compiled for liturgical use.

Secondly, in the field of history, the point that gave rise to the quarrel between the "Spirituals" and the "Friars of the Community"[3] needed to be cleared up. The only Rule that the first friars had was the teachings of the gospel and they felt no need of anything else: "There were few of them; they were saints of exceptional quality; they were an élite. Humanly speaking, it was impossible for the thousands of friars who had become members of the Franciscan family to maintain themselves at such a peak."[4] The organization of an internal hierarchy transforming the primitive "fraternity" into an order, the organization of studies, the organization of their rapport with the ecclesiastical hierarchy, and their economic organization: to all these things the founder had to give his consent even in his own lifetime. Under the pressure of circumstances, outstanding men, imbued though they were with the spirit of the gospel, for example, St. Anthony and the Minister General Haymo of Faversham, proceeded with the adaptation of the Order; St. Bonaventure belonged to the lineage of these organizers. He definitely took up his position on the level of spirituality: some had been so rash as to attempt to define the Franciscan ideal by the word "poverty" which, according to Francis himself, is the gospel and is nothing but the gospel. The gospel cannot be summed up in one word, not even in the word "poverty," without being mutilated. It was even more rash to attempt to specify the characteristics of this poverty, although the casuistry of some and the idle fancies of others had indulged in such matters to their heart's content. St. Francis wanted to be an example; the Spirituals wanted to be a reproach to others. St. Bonaventure understood that unity had to have as its basis, not total uniformity of the practical conditions of life, but communion of one and the same ideal in the love of the one and only Father; he agreed to write his "Legend" with this objective in mind.

And finally, in the domain of the relationships between the religious and the parochial and university clergy, a conflict had to be quelled whose stake was important. What was at stake was the value and the very existence of the Order. The hostility[5] itself was followed by the discussion of principles: the clergy regarded complete poverty as evil, the falsification of the gospel, and a deviation from tradition;[6] the right of the Mendicants to hear confessions and to preach was contested; it was denied that St. Francis ever bore the stigmata; his Testament was maliciously interpreted and certain of his recommendations were mercilessly misrepresented. St. Bonaventure had already distinguished himself in the battle by his treatise on "Gospel Perfection," which he wrote in response to the lampoon of William of Saint-Amour.[7] The General Chapter felt that it could not find a better champion of poverty nor a better advocate for the holy founder. For this background we are again indebted to the "Legend." Even if Bonaventure had been left to himself, he would have undertaken it.[8]

Historian

It has been said that St. Bonaventure contributed nothing new to the history of Francis and that he may as well not have written it.

We must admit that his work is not a biography-for-future-historians. Chronology was not his primary concern.[9] The anecdotes succeed each other or are introduced by vague formulas: "One day he said . . . ," "At another time . . . ," "One night when . . ." "A short time elapsed and then. . . ." Nor did the literary form he chose lend itself to contributing anything new. It is a compilation, or as we would say today "a digest," a plagiarism of basic documents which he reworked, rethought, regrouped, and presented in a different form.

And yet, in addition to the fact that St. Bonaventure is the only one who provides us with certain details and episodes,[10] he also gives us new insights. We should not reduce the purpose of the history of Francis to simple "events." Bonaventure wanted to go back to the very beginnings, but he was more interested in the "souls" of the past. And St. Bonaventure is an irreplaceable and unequalled master in helping us in our search for that element on which the authenticity of our Franciscan life depends.

He is a witness who deserves our trust. Before entering the Order, he had already known Francis through the lectures and examples of his teachers, all of them Franciscans: Alexander of Hales, Eudes Rigaud, and John of Parma.

He knew Francis by his own personal observance of the Franciscan Rule and the fraternal life from 1243 to 1263: one does not completely subject oneself for twenty years to no avail to a regime of life that is the expression of the ideal of a saint. To live in the Franciscan atmosphere and to recreate it in oneself is to know Francis.

He knew Francis by travelling through Umbria, by staying in the hermitages, by witnessing the prayer life of the brothers and sisters who had known Francis, by encouraging them to recount their personal experiences and dealings with Francis, and by letting himself be molded by Umbria whose charm impregnates his work just as it impregnated the mind of Francis.

Lastly, Bonaventure collected and examined all available documents with a minuteness that only a "synopsis" of the sources would enable us to appreciate: "liturgical"[11] documents, oral[12] documents, written[13] documents. Our biography of St. Francis is the fruit of this laborious "pilgrimage to the sources." Previously, all that existed was a vast stratum whose tangled veins defied the best minds: if we can now quarry them, the reason is partly because Bonaventure's biography opened up a key-avenue without which the entire mass would have remained a discouraging labyrinth.

Pacifier

Like Christ, Francis was a "scandal" and a "subject of contradiction." St. Bonaventure, who liked to compare the beginnings of the Order with those of the Church,[14] modeled his style of writing on that of the evangelists, especially on St. Luke whose position at the epicenter of the Judeo-Christian quarrels was so delicate.

His primary concern was to present in a very forceful way the pacifying activity of Francis, restoring peace to communities (8, 4) or to cities (6, 9), adopting as his formula of greeting: "May the Lord give you his peace" (3, 2).[15] From that time on, it became manifestly illogical for a Franciscan to carry on quarrels in the name of an ideal that excluded all quarrels.

But once this spiritual position was solidly assured, he still had to use diplomacy to appease the unrest that followed in the aftermath. His *Legend,* without being tendentious, as has been too often said,[16] nevertheless bears witness to a certain flexibility. To begin with, despite all the grievances that he could have nurtured against the somewhat restless "movement" of the Spirituals, St. Bonaventure kept his admiration for "persons." He explicitly recognized the sanctity of the first companions and their value as witnesses; he indirectly pleased them by his unsparing praise of St. Clare, their oracle since the death of their Father. If he avoided calling them by name when he made use of their recollections, he did so in order not to upset their enemies. Nor did he mention by name the unfortunate champion of the "Conventuals," Brother Elias, who appears only under the name of "Vicar of the Saint"[17] in order to avoid once again useless acrimony. Lastly, he attenuated certain of Francis' spectacular exaggerations which ran the risk of scandalizing the over-scrupulous and omitted details that could have added fresh fuel to the controversies. In brief, "where we accuse him of having tried to suppress historical documents, *he* had in mind the suppression of errors of the moral and religious order."[18]

As for the seculars, their pacification required other methods. They took exception to the sanctity and even to the possibility of the Franciscan ideal; they were shown that the founder had lived it, that it had been approved by Christ, for the approbation of the Church had not removed all their doubts. The entire argumentation rested on the fact of the stigmata. The first thing was to "prove" this fact historically; numerous testimonies were collected and closely examined. The most solid and the most precise ones were retained.[19] It was especially a question "of interpreting" the miracle exegetically and spiritually for the consumption of an audience fed on good scholastic philosophy which demanded, before a fact was admitted, that it know its meaning. The interpretation adopted was that of the spiritual conformity of Francis with Christ, since Christ had granted him bodily conformity. The basic Scriptural text was the passage from the Apocalypse (chap. 7) where we see the second "angel rising where the sun rises,"[20] carrying the seal of the living God."[21]

The conflicts drifted from "mysticism" toward "politics." It is to St. Bonaventure that credit is due for having purified the "politics" by putting it back in its one and only viable climate: mysticism. A strong man would have ended up drowning the Order in the quarrels and in provoking schisms and scandals. A new "cunctator," St. Bonaventure believed in the healing value of time and constantly re-injected more religious spirit into the veins of the Order, leaving to circulation the task of nourishing the weakened cells and eliminating those that had already become decomposed.

Writer

St. Bonaventure possessed a marvelous talent and a dignified style; and yet our first contacts run the risk of proving unfavorable to him. After reading the first five or six chapters, we become aware that he abuses clichés: all the churches are "deserted"; one always prays "with great fervor and devotion"; his research is always carried on "most diligently"; if St. Francis possesses a virtue, he is its "perfect model"; if he asks for the slightest thing, he does so with "great humility." In the end one grows tired of present participles, superlatives, and certain repetitions that are difficult to tolerate.

Let us grant that "in a country where a chapel is called a 'basilica,' a shanty a 'palace,' where one greets a seminarian with the title 'your reverence,' the words do not have the same value this side of the Alps."[22] It is none the less true that an assiduous reading uncovers an abundance of unexpected riches, in the full sense of the word. The same thing holds for this biography as for the *opuscula* of St. Francis, or for that matter for every great work: effort must be expended to make oneself worthy of a great mind and a great soul, but once we come to know them through familiarity with them, what enchantment and what profit we deprive if we let ourselves be molded by them!

A work of quality, the *Legenda major* is carefully written even in its details: a choice vocabulary, sure articulations, a broad and dilating rhythm. The hand of the master is everywhere recognizable: even the interpolated clauses textually borrowed from Celano are fused into periodic sentences and espouse their movement. It was written to be read out loud, and only in this way can this "scoring" be effectively brought out, in which a consummate art directs the arrangement of the pauses, the sonorities, and the accents.[23]

The literary genre is not simple: the personal love of the author for the two protagonists of his work, Christ and Francis and the subject itself, Francis' love for Christ, make this biography a lyric poem. Every chapter is garnished with allusions to the *Song of Songs,* the poem of God's betrothal with his people. We know that mysticism has always borrowed its language from human love. It is up to us not to close our mind but to open it. "If you want to understand St. Paul," St. Bonaventure wrote elsewhere, "you must put on the heart of Paul." The same holds for the reader of this biography: if he is one of those "lovers of poverty" to whom the first sentence dedicates the poem, he will comprehend, respond, and, going beyond the two great souls of Bonaventure and Francis, he will cling to Christ.

For, in the last analysis, such is indeed the true interest and the profound value of this work, the reason why the Friars Minor have always been captivated by it and have aligned their ideal with it: the transparence of the gaze that an authentic saint cast on a saint whom he loved gives us a new insight into the soul of Francis as it gave itself to Christ and as Christ fashioned it. The serenity of Bonaventure's work is admitted even by those who judge it to be "apparent."[24] We know where it comes from: it is simply the reflection, through him whose portrait it illumines, of the very peace that reigns within the Blessed Trinity.

The *Legenda major* (several manuscript rubrics point this out) was divided into a prologue and fifteen chapters with a view to its being read in the refectory during the octave of the feast of St. Francis. Another, shorter text, divided into seven chapters of nine paragraphs, was needed for the readings of the divine office in the course of the same octave: this was the *Legenda minor* by the same St. Bonaventure, a text of a remarkable density in which spiritual theology and history are closely fused. It is difficult to condense into fewer lines so many facts and so much ascetical and mystical knowledge. Because of its exceptional success in the domain of hagiographic literature, a translation of the *Legenda minor* will follow that of the *Legenda major*.

—Fr. Damien Vorreux O.F.M.

NOTES

1. *AFH,* 3 (1910), p. 76, no. 75.
   The word *Legend* and especially the adjective legendary conjure up the marvelous and unauthentic nature of certain persons and events, in contradistinction to the historical and real character of duly verified facts. But this misunderstanding must be cleared up. *Legend* here, as for the entire Middle Ages, is not the antithesis of history; it is an historical account having this twofold characteristic: (1) it is meant to be read publicly, as is evident from the etymology of the word; and (2) it is controlled by and subject to the laws of literary composition, in contradistinction to the *florilegia* which are content with grouping anecdotes together. The *Fioretti* would be a typical example of this.

2. Matins consisted of 12 lessons, 9 of which were historical, and the feast was celebrated throughout the octave: 72 lessons in all had to be composed. The scribes had no scruples in plagiarizing Gregory of Tours or Sulpice Sévère in retelling the life of St. Francis. St. Bonaventure had been conducting a campaign since 1257 against this sort of literary extravagance in the Clunian and Cistercian lectionaries.

3. It is to be understood that these words which have been used since 1274 to designate the *branches* of the Order simply describe tendencies. We should not overestimate the importance of the conflict: if there are numerous documents that run the risk of warping the perspectives, the reason is the fact that the Roman Curia and the University of Paris became involved in an affair which geographically was restricted to a few provinces of the Order. And finally we should not forget that just as the Spirituals counted saints and turbulent friars among their sons so the *Community* included saints and pharisees.

4. Valentin M. Breton, *Saint Bonaventure*, Collection: *Les Maîtres de la Spiritualité chrétienne* (Paris: Aubier, 1943), p. 18.
5. Cf. Salimbene, *Chronique*, MGH SS, 32, pp. 420-425.
6. A witness of tradition: Venerable Bede, *Expositio in Lucam*, IV, (Homily 2° loco, of the Common of a Confessor not a bishop): "The gospel does not wish to command Christians not to keep anything."
7. *De periculis*, which was condemned Oct. 5, 1256.
8. It is stimulating to note that, in the defense of poverty, an appeal was made to one of those masters who were themselves attacked in the Order on the grounds of poverty: "Paris is destroying Assisi!" Brother Giles had said.
9. "The story does not always follow the chronological order. Instead, in order to avoid confusion, I chose to be more systematic and group together events which happened at different times . . . " he confesses in his Prologue (no. 4).
10. For example:
   The man from Assisi who spread his mantle under Francis' feet; 1, 1.
   Brother Giles' entrance into the Order; the praises that are bestowed on him (and yet St. Bonaventure had suffered from the caustic, unsparing ironies of Brother Giles); 3, 4.
   The cure of Brother Morico and his entrance into the Order; 4, 8.
   The cult of Francis for the sign Tau; 4, 9.
   The Rule lost by Elias and reinstated in its integral sameness; 4, 11.
   The answer to the doctor who forbade him to cry; 5, 8.
   The trip by night and the miraculous light; 5, 12.
   The miracle in behalf of his doctor: the cracked house; 7, 11.
   The preaching of a theologian; 11, 7.
   His doubts regarding his contemplative or active orientation; 12, 1 and 2.
   Numerous details regarding the stigmata; 13.
11. Especially the Office composed by Julian of Speyer, and the *Legend*, composed by the same author, from whom he borrowed certain words, turns of phrases, and particularly happy cadences.
12. Prologue, no. 4: "There I was able to speak with some of his close friends who were still alive and to interview them carefully." For the journey to Egypt and the stigmata, the main source of information was Brother Illuminato (cf. *The Itinerary of the Soul to God*, chap. VII, No. 3, *Opera Omnia*, V, p. 312).
13. The compilation properly so-called was probably done in the friary of Nantes which St. Bonaventure preferred and where St. Thomas of Aquinas, finding him absorbed in his work and contemplation, said as he withdrew: "Let us leave a saint work for a saint" (cf. Wadding, *Annales*, t. II, 1260, no. 18).

14. *Epist. de* III *quaest.* no. 11, *Opera,* VIII, p. 335.
15. We find the same preoccupation in *The Itinerary of the Soul to God,* Prologue, no. 1: "The peace announced and given to us by our Lord Jesus Christ, our father Francis made the theme of his own preaching. For he proclaimed peace at the beginning and at the end of every sermon; he offered his wish of peace in every greeting; he longed for ecstatic peace in every contemplation, as a dweller of that Jerusalem of which the Man of Peace says — he who was peaceable with those who hated peace: Pray for the peace of Jerusalem" (*The Works of Bonaventure,* I Mystical Opuscula, trans. J. de Vinck (Paterson, N. J. 1960), p. 5). In the *Legenda minor,* the dying Francis bequeathed poverty and *peace* to his sons.
16. Sabatier especially. But not all Franciscans agree with the Franciscanists. Sabatier's principle for the study of St. Francis was: first, the writings of St. Francis; next, the biographies. We can apply this principle to the study of St. Bonaventure: no biography of St. Bonaventure existed before the fourteenth century; the best source is his writings; now, these, especially his letters as minister general, picture him as a calm, level-headed man, an enemy of rigorism in principles that in the end would tyrannize consciences. Certain "historical" omissions that have been too hastily qualified as tendentious must be attributed to this character trait and not to an alleged cunning trick. The *Analecta Franciscana* reduce the affair to more just proportions (t. X, pp. lxix and lxx).
17. In 4, 11, for example, where St. Bonaventure places the blame for the responsibility of the loss of the Rule on Brother Elias with much more bitterness than the other biographies.
18. Gilson, *The Philosophy of St. Bonaventure,* trans. I. Trethowan and F. J. Sheed (New York, 1938), p. 23.
19. From Chapter XIII on, one notices the tedious insistence of St. Bonaventure on the conclusive value of the procession of his witnesses.
20. Dante (*Paradiso,* c. xi) borrows his famous development: "Nacque al mondo un Sole . . . " (Assisi should be called no longer Assisi but the Orient), from this Biblical text no less than his own poetical inspiration.
21. Bartholomew of Pisa relates that while St. Bonaventure was meditating on this text, he heard a voice from heaven saying: "Brother Bonaventure, these words apply literally to Francis" (Wadding, *Annals,* t. IV, p. 290). We should note, however, that in his book: *An Introduction to the Eternal Gospel,* Friar Gerard of Borgo San Donnino had already applied the prophecy of Joachim of Fiore to the stigmatized Francis: "The eternal gospel will be announced by the angel of the sixth seal, carrying

625

Bonaventure, Introduction

the sign of the living God" (cf. Et. Bihel O.F.M., "Sanctus Franciscus fuitne Angelus sexti sigilli," *Antonianum*, 2 (1927), 59-90).

22. Sabatier, *Vie de saint Francois* (Paris, 1931), p. xxvi.
23. The translator has tried to preserve the fullness of the periods so that the English reader may, in so far as possible, enjoy the euphoria of a happy style.
24. Sabatier, *Histoire religieuse et littéraire du Moyen Age*, p. xix: "The serenity of the Franciscan legends is more apparent than real."

Note on the History of the Text

The first copies of the *Legenda major*, 34 in number, one for each province, were published in Paris under the supervision of St. Bonaventure so that they could be given to the provincials assembled for the Chapter of Pisa in 1263.

The Chapter of Paris in 1266 demanded that each friary have its own copy; now, in the second half of the fourteenth century the number of friaries had reached a total of 1,530, and there were about 400 Poor Clare monasteries. We still have around 400 copies dating from the thirteenth and fourteenth centuries.

The first edition was published in Florence in 1509: the *Aurea Legenda major B. Francisci*; the second at Rome in 1596: the *Legenda B. Francisci*, in volume VII of the Vatican edition of the Works of St. Bonaventure; the Bollandists published the *Legenda major* in the *Acta Sanctorum* at Anvers in 1768 (Oct. t. II), pp. 742-798.

All these editions were surpassed by the critical edition published in 1898 by the fathers of the Franciscan College of Quaracchi in the *Opera Omnia* of St. Bonaventure (t. VIII, pp. 504-564). The *Legenda major* was further improved by Fr. Michel Bihel O.F.M., thanks to four manuscripts that had been discovered subsequently. His text is contained in *Analecta Franciscana*, Vol. X, pp. 557-626.

626

MAJOR LIFE OF ST. FRANCIS
by St. Bonaventure

CHAPTER TITLES

[PART II]

Some of the Miracles Which Took Place after St. Francis' Death

630

PREFACE

1   In these last times the grace of God our Savior has dawned in his servant Francis on all who are truly humble and love poverty. In him we can contemplate the excess of God's mercy and his example urges us to forego completely irreverent thoughts and worldly appetites and live like Christ, looking forward eagerly to the happiness that is our hope. He was despised and humbled, but the Most High looked upon him with such condescension and kindness that he was not content merely to raise him from the dust and choose him out from the world, but he inspired him to profess the life of Gospel perfection and made him a leader and an apostle. He was to be a light for those who believe that, by bearing witness of the light, he might prepare a way for the Lord to the hearts of his faithful, a way of light and peace. By the glorious splendor of his life and teaching Francis shone like the day-star amid the clouds, and by the brilliance which radiated from him he guided those who live in darkness, in the shadow of death, to the light. Like the rainbow that lights up the clouds with sudden glory (Sir 50, 8), he bore in his own body the pledge of God's covenant, bringing the good news of peace and salvation to men, like a true Angel of peace. Like St. John the Baptist, he was appointed by God to prepare a way in the desert — that is, by the complete renunciation involved in perfect poverty — and preach repentance by word and example.

God forestalled him by the gift of his divine grace, so that he won the praise of heroic virtue. Then he was filled with the spirit of prophecy and charged with the ministry of Angels, as he burned with the flames of a love worthy of the Seraphim. Like a man who has joined the ranks of the Angels, he was taken up in a chariot of fire, so that there can be no doubt whatever that he came "in the spirit and power of an Elias" (Lk 1, 17), as we shall see in the course of his life. Therefore there is every reason to believe that it is he who is referred to under the image of an Angel coming up from the east, with the seal of the living God, in the prophecy made by another friend of Christ the Bridegroom, St. John the Apostle and Evangelist. When the sixth seal was broken, St. John tells us in the Apocalypse, "I saw a second Angel coming up from the east, with the seal of the living God" (Ap 7, 12).

2   If we consider the perfection of his extraordinary sanctity, we can see beyond all shadow of doubt that this messenger of God was his servant Francis who was found worthy to be loved by Christ, imitated by us, and admired by the whole world. Even while he lived on earth among human beings, he shared the sinlessness of the Angels, so that he became an example to those who followed Christ perfectly. We have plenty of reason to be firmly convinced of this. First of all, there is the mission which he had received "to summon all men to mourn and lament, to shave their heads and wear sackcloth" (Is 22, 12) "and mark the brows of those that weep and wail with a cross" (Ez 9, 4), signing them with the cross of penance and clothing them in his own habit which was shaped like a cross. But besides that, we have an unimpeachable testimony, the seal of truth itself which was impressed on his body and which made him like the living God, Christ crucified. This was not the work of nature's powers or of any human agent, it was accomplished by the miraculous power of the Spirit of the living God alone.

3   I know that I am unworthy and incapable of writing the life of a man so deserving of our imitation and all our veneration, and I would never have attempted it, were it not for the eager desire of the friars and the unanimous request of the general chapter. Besides, I am under an obligation to him and so I felt compelled to do it. When I was a young boy, as I can still remember clearly, I was at death's door and I was saved only by his intercession. If I refused to sing his praises now, I might be accused of being ungrateful. I realize that God saved my life through him and I have felt the power of his intercession in my own case, and so the principal reason why I have written his life now was in order to gather together the different accounts of his virtues and of all that he said and did which were scattered about and partly forgotten. Otherwise they would all be lost, when the friars who lived with him are dead.

4   I wanted to be perfectly sure of the truth about his life and have a clear grasp of it before setting it down for posterity, and so I went to his birthplace and visited the country where he lived and died. There I was able to speak with some of his close friends who were still alive and to interview them carefully, especially those who had first-hand experience of his holiness and had tried to imitate it themselves. The honesty of these witnesses and the obvious fact that they are telling the truth means that we can trust their testimony implicitly. In recording what God in his goodness accomplished by means of his servant, I decided deliberately to avoid using a literary style. A straightforward account will do the reader more good than any attempt at any elaborate literary style. The story does not always follow chronological order. Instead, in order to avoid confusion, I chose to be more systematic and group together events which happened at different times but concerned

633

similar subjects while separating others which occurred at the same time but concerned different subjects.

5   Francis' life from beginning to end is described in the following fifteen chapters which treat of: his life in the world — his complete self-surrender to God and his work on the three churches — the foundation of the Order and the approval of the Rule — the progress of the Order under his guidance, and the confirmation of the Rule — the austerity of his life and the comfort which creatures gave him — his humility and obedience, and God's condescension to his slightest wish — his love for poverty and the miraculous fulfilment of his needs — his loving compassion and the love which creatures had for him — his passionate love and longing for martyrdom — his devotion to prayer — his grasp of Sacred Scripture and his spirit of prophecy — the efficacy of his preaching and his power of healing — the stigmata — his patient endurance and his death — his canonization and the transferal of his remains.

The last section describes the miracles which took place after his death.

[PART I]

CHAPTER I

Saint Francis' Life in the World

1   There lived in the town of Assisi a man whose name was Francis and on his memory a blessing rests because God in his goodness and mercy met him on his way with the abundance of his grace and saved him from the dangers of this life, showering his heavenly favors upon him. As a young boy Francis lived among worldly people and he was brought up like them. Once he had got a slight knowledge of reading and writing, he was given a job in a lucrative trading business. Yet with the help of God's grace, even when he was with his gay companions, although always ready to enjoy himself, he never followed the lure of his passions. The people he lived with were hard-headed business-people and he himself was quite anxious to make money, but he put no trust in his store of riches.

Even as a young man Francis had an open-handed sympathy for the poor which God had inspired in his heart. This bore him company as he grew up and filled his heart with such generosity that he refused to turn a deaf ear to the Gospel and resolved to give alms to everyone who approached him, especially if it was for the love of God. One time he was caught in a rush of business and, contrary to his custom, he sent away a beggar who had begged an alms for love of God without giving him anything. Then he realized what he had done and he ran after him immediately and gave him a generous alms. There and then he promised God that he would never again refuse anyone who asked for love of him, as long as he had anything to give. He kept this resolution with unwearying fidelity until the day he died and he was rewarded with a wonderful increase of grace and love for God. Afterwards when he had put on the person of Christ Jesus to perfection, he used to say that even when he was in the world, he could scarcely ever hear anyone mention the love of God without being deeply affected.

His good life, his gentleness and patience, his almost superhuman readiness to oblige, together with his generosity which exceeded his means, and his pleasant manner were so many indications which marked him out as a young man. They seemed to be almost a foretaste of things to come, indicating that the abundance of God's blessings would be heaped upon him more plentifully than ever in the future. Indeed, one citizen of the town, a very simple man who appears to have been inspired by God, took off his cloak when he met Francis in Assisi one day and spread it under his feet, saying that he deserved the respect of everybody because he would do great things and be honored by the whole Church.

2   As yet, however, Francis had no idea of God's plan for him. He was completely taken up with the affairs of his father's business and his mind was intent on the things of earth because of the corruption of human nature, so that he had never learned to raise his mind to heaven, or acquired a taste for the things of God. Adversity is one of the best means of sharpening a person's spiritual perception and so "the power of the Lord reached out to him and the Most High relented in His dealings with him" (Ez 1, 3; Ps 76, 11). God brought him low with a prolonged illness, in order to prepare his soul to receive the Holy Spirit. When he recovered and was going about dressed as usual

in keeping with his position, he met a knight who was of noble birth but very poor, so that he was not properly clad. Francis felt sorry for him and immediately took off his own clothes and gave them to him. At one and the same time he fulfilled the twofold duty of relieving the poverty of the poor and saving a nobleman from embarrassment.

3   That night as he lay asleep, God in his goodness showed him a vision of a magnificent palace full of armor, bearing Christ's cross as its coat-of-arms. He would let him see that the kindness he had done a poor knight for love of the supreme King would be repaid with an incomparable reward. And so when Francis asked to whom all this belonged, he was told from heaven that it was all for him and his knights. He had no experience of interpreting God's secret revelations and he could not penetrate beyond the appearance of what he saw to the truth which he could not see, and so when he awoke in the morning, he took his extraordinary vision to mean that he was going to achieve great success. He was still ignorant of God's plan for him and he prepared to enlist with a high-ranking knight in Apulia, in the hope of acquiring distinction as a soldier in his service, as his vision seemed to indicate.

He set out shortly afterwards but when he reached the next town, he heard God calling him by his first name as he lay asleep, and saying, "Francis, who can do more for you, a lord or his servant, a rich man or a beggar?" When he replied that a lord or a rich man could do more, he was asked, "Then why are you abandoning the Lord to devote yourself to a servant? Why are you choosing a beggar instead of God who is infinitely rich?" "Lord," replied Francis, "what will you have me do?" And God told him, "Go back to your own town. The vision which you saw foretold a spiritual achievement which will be accomplished in you by God's will, not man's." In the morning Francis went back to Assisi without delay. He was overjoyed and had no care for the future; he was already a model of obedience and he waited patiently on God's will.

4 He withdrew from the busy life of his trade and begged God in his goodness to show him what he should do. He prayed constantly until he was consumed with a passionate longing for God and was ready to give up the whole world in his desire for his heavenly home and think nothing of it. He realized that he had discovered the treasure hidden in the field and like the wise trader in the Gospel he could think of nothing but how he might sell all that he had and buy the pearl he had found. He still did not know how to go about it, but at the same time he was forced to conclude that a spiritual venture could only begin by rejecting the world and that victory over himself would mark the beginning of his service of Christ.

5 One day as he was riding on the plain below Assisi, he met a leper. The encounter was completely without warning and Francis felt sick at the sight of him. Then he remembered his resolve to be perfect and the need to overcome himself first, if he wanted to be a knight of Christ. He immediately dismounted and ran up to kiss the poor man. The leper stretched out his hand, hoping to get something, and Francis put some money in it and kissed it. Then he mounted his horse and looked this way and that about the plain with a clear view in all directions, but there was no sign of the leper. He was thunderstruck but his heart was filled with joy and he sang God's praises in a loud voice, resolving to do even more in the future.

After that he began to frequent secluded spots where he could mourn for his sins, and there as he poured out his whole soul with groans beyond all utterance, he was eventually found worthy to be heard by God, after long and importunate prayer. One day as he prayed in one of his usual haunts, he became completely absorbed in God in the excess of his fervor. Then Jesus Christ appeared to him, hanging on his cross. His soul melted at the sight and the memory of Christ's passion was impressed on the depths of his heart so vividly that whenever he thought of it, he could scarcely restrain his sighs and tears, as he afterwards confessed towards the end of his life. He realized immediately that the words of the Gospel were addressed to him, "If you have a mind to come my way, renounce yourself, and take up your cross and follow me" (cf. Mt 16, 24).

6   Francis now developed a spirit of poverty, with a deep sense of humility, and an attitude of profound compassion. He had never been able to stand the sight of lepers, even at a distance, and he always avoided meeting them, but now in order to arrive at perfect self-contempt he served them devotedly with all humility and kindness, because the prophet Isaias tells us that Christ crucified was regarded as a leper and despised. He visited their houses frequently and distributed alms among them generously, kissing their hands and lips with deep compassion.

When he was approached by beggars, he was not content merely to give what he had — he wanted to give his whole self to them. At times he took off his clothes and gave them away, or ripped or tore pieces from them, if he had nothing else at hand. He came to the aid of priests who were in need, respectfully and devoutly, especially when it concerned the upkeep of the altar. In this way he earned a share in the homage offered to God, while relieving the needs of those who pay homage to him. During this period, too, he made a pilgrimage to the tomb of St. Peter. When he saw the crowds of beggars gathered in front of the church, he was moved partly by the attraction he felt in his devotion and partly by love of poverty to give his clothes to one of the poorest among them. Then he dressed in the beggar's rags and spent the whole day among the crowd there, filled with an unaccustomed joy of spirit. In this way he would learn to make light of what the world esteems and arrive gradually at the perfect observance of the Gospel. He paid great attention to external mortification, so that his whole life might be ruled by the cross of Christ which was imprinted on his heart.

All this took place when Francis still lived and dressed as a layman in the world.

CHAPTER II

*Francis Gives Himself Completely to God
and Rebuilds Three Churches*

1   Christ himself was Francis' only guide during all this time and now in his goodness he intervened once more with the sweet influence of his grace. Francis left the town one day to meditate out-of-doors and as he was passing by the church of San Damiano which was threatening to collapse with age, he felt urged to go in and pray. There as he knelt in prayer before a painted image of the Crucified, he felt greatly comforted in spirit and his eyes were full of tears as he gazed at the cross. Then, all of a sudden, he heard a voice coming from the cross and telling him three times, "Francis, go and repair my house. You see it is all falling down." Francis was alone in the church and he was terrified at the sound of the voice, but the power of its message penetrated his heart and he went into an ecstasy. Eventually, he came back to himself and prepared to obey the command he had received. He was quite willing to devote himself entirely to repairing the ruined church of San Damiano, although the message really referred to the universal Church which Christ "won for himself at the price of is own blood" (Acts 20, 28), as the Holy Spirit afterwards made him realize and he himself explained to the friars.

Making the sign of the cross, he laid his plans immediately. He took some bales of cloth for the market and went straight to Foligno where he sold them, together with the horse he was riding. Then he made his way back to Assisi and went into the church he had been told to repair. There he met the poor priest who was in charge and greeted him respectfully, offering his money for the repairs to the church and for the poor, and begging him humbly to let him live with him for a little while. The priest agreed to let him stay, but for fear of his parents he refused to take the money. In his dislike of money in any form, Francis threw it on the window-sill, and had no more interest in it than if it were dust.

2   When his father heard that Francis was living with the priest, he was very upset and he hurried to the church without delay. When he heard the threats of those who were looking for him and realized that they were drawing near, Francis hid in a secret cave; he was new to the service of Christ and he wished to avoid his father's anger. He remained in hiding for a number of days, imploring God continuously in a flood of tears to deliver him from the hands of his persecutors and enable him, in his goodness, to fulfill the desires he himself had inspired. Eventually he was filled with overflowing joy and fell to reproaching himself as a coward, lacking in determination. At that, he laid aside his fear and left his hiding place, taking the road towards Assisi. When the townspeople saw his haggard looks and the change which had come over him, they thought that he had gone mad, and they threw stones and mud from the streets at him, shouting insults after him as if he were a lunatic. But Francis was deaf to it all and no insult could break or change him. When his father heard the uproar, he immediately rushed after him, determined to crush him, not to protect him. Throwing compassion to

the winds, he dragged him home where he tried to persuade him first with words and then with blows, before he finally put him in chains. But that only made Francis more eager and determined than ever to carry out his plans, as he realized the words of the Gospel, "Blessed are those who suffer persecution in the cause of right; the kingdom of heaven is theirs" (Mt 5, 10).

3   Shortly afterwards his father had to go away and his mother, who had never approved of her husband's action, loosed Francis' bonds and let him go free. She saw that there was no hope of breaking his inflexible determination. Francis gave thanks to God and went back where he had been before. When his father came home and failed to find him, he heaped abuse on his wife and then went after Francis in a storm of rage; if he could not bring him home, at least he could drive him from the country. But God gave Francis courage and he went out to meet his father on his own accord and told him plainly that he was not afraid of ill-treatment or imprisonment, adding that for Christ's sake he would gladly endure any sufering. When his father realized that he could not hope to make him turn back, he concentrated on trying to recover his money, and when he eventually found it on the window-sill, his greed was satisfied and he calmed down a little.

4   Now that he had recovered his money, he arranged to have Francis brought before the bishop of the diocese, where he should renounce all his claims and return everything he had. In his genuine love for poverty, Francis was more than ready to comply and he willingly appeared before the bishop. There he made no delay — without hesitation, without hearing or saying a word — he immediately took off his clothes and gave them back to his father. Then it was discovered that he wore a hair-shirt under his fine clothes next to his skin. He even took off his trousers in

his fervor and enthusiasm and stood there naked before them all. Then he said to his father, "Until now I called you my father, but from now on I can say without reserve, 'Our Father who art in heaven.' He is all my wealth and I place all my confidence in him." When the bishop heard this, he was amazed at his passionate fervor. He jumped to his feet and took Francis into his embrace, covering him with the cloak he was wearing, like the good man that he was. Then he told his servants to bring some clothes for him and they gave him an old tunic which belonged to one of the bishop's farmhands. Francis took it gratefully and drew a cross on it with his own hand with a piece of chalk, making it a worthy garment for a man who was crucified and a beggar. And so the servant of the most high King was left stripped of all that belonged to him, that he might follow the Lord whom he loved, who hung naked on the cross. He was armed with the cross, the means of salvation which would enable him to escape from a shipwrecked world.

5   Now that he was free from the bonds of all earthly desires in his disregard for the world, Francis left the town and sought out a place where he could be alone, without a care in the world. There in solitude and silence he would be able to hear God's secret revelations.

Then as he was walking through the forest joyfully singing in French and praising God, he was suddenly set upon by robbers. They threatened him and asked him who he was but he replied intrepidly with the prophetic words, "I am the herald of the great King." Then they beat him and threw him into a ditch full of snow, telling him, "Lie there, rustic herald of God." With that they made off and Francis jumped from the ditch, full of joy, and made the woods re-echo with his praise to the Creator of all.

6   Eventually he reached a neighboring monastery where he begged an alms and received it without anyone recogniz-

ing him or paying any attention to him. Then he went on to Gubbio where he was recognized by an old friend and made welcome and there he got an old coat, which he accepted like one of Christ's poor. After that, in his love for true humility, he devoted himself to the lepers and lived with them, waiting on them all, for love of God. He washed their feet and bound up their sores, drawing off the puss and wiping them clean. He was extraordinarily devoted to them and he kissed their wounds, he who was soon to play a part worthy of the Good Samaritan in the Gospel. As a reward, God endowed him with such power to heal that his influence over ills of soul or body was miraculous. For example — to mention only one of the many instances which occurred as his name became better known — there was a man from the neighborhood of Spoleto who suffered from a disease which had eaten away his lips and his cheek. The doctors could do nothing for him and he made a pilgrimage to Rome to invoke the intercession of the apostles. As he was on his way home, he met St. Francis. He wanted to kiss the saint's footsteps in his devotion, but Francis would not allow that and he kissed him on the mouth. In his compassion he touched the horrible sore with his lips and immediately the disease disappeared and the sick man was restored to health. It is hard to say which we should admire most, his wonderful condescension in making such a gesture, or his exceptional power in performing this miracle.

7   Now that he was firmly established in the lowliness of Christ, Francis remembered the command he had received from the cross to repair the church of San Damiano. He was a true son of obedience and he returned to Assisi in order to obey the divine command, at least by begging the necessary materials. For love of Christ poor and crucified he overcame his embarrassment and begged from those

who had known him as a wealthy young man, loading himself with stones, although he was weak and worn out with fasting. With God's help and the cooperation of the townspeople he eventually finished the work at San Damiano. Then, in order to avoid becoming lazy, he set about repairing another church dedicated to St. Peter, which was situated farther away from the town. In his pure and unalloyed faith Francis always had a great devotion to the Prince of the Apostles.

8   When he had finished there, he came to a place called the Portiuncula where there was an old church dedicated to the Virgin Mother of God which was now abandoned with no one to look after it. Francis had great devotion to the Queen of the world and when he saw that the church was deserted, he began to live there constantly in order to repair it. He heard that the angels often visited it, so that it used to be called St. Mary of the Angels, and he decided to stay there permanently out of reverence for the angels and love for the Mother of Christ. He loved this spot more than any other in the world. It was here that he began his religious life in a very small way; it was here that he made such extraordinary progress, and it was here that he came to a happy end. When he was dying, he commended this spot above all others to the friars, because it was most dear to the Blessed Virgin.

Before entering the Order, one of the friars had a vision about the Portiuncula. He saw a huge crowd of blind folk kneeling in a circle about the church and looking up to heaven. With tearful voices and outstretched hands, they cried out to God, begging him to have pity on them and give them sight. Then a brilliant light descended from heaven and enveloped them all, giving them back their sight and the health they longed for.

This was the place where St. Francis founded the Order

of Friars Minor by divine inspiration and it was Divine Providence which led him to repair three churches before he founded the Order and began to preach the Gospel. This meant that he progressed from material things to more spiritual achievements, from lesser to greater, in due order, and it gave a prophetic indication of what he would accomplish later. Like the three buildings he repaired, Christ's church was to be renewed in three different ways under Francis' guidance and according to his Rule and teaching, and the three-fold army of those who are to be saved was to win victory. We can now see that this prophecy has come true.

CHAPTER III

The Foundation of the Order — the Rule is Approved

1   As he was living there by the church of our Lady, Francis prayed to her who had conceived the Word, full of grace and truth, begging her insistently and with tears to become his Advocate. Then he was granted the true spirit of the Gospel by the intercession of the Mother of Mercy and he brought it to fruition. He was at Mass one day on the feast of one of the apostles and the passage of the Gospel where our Lord sends out his disciples to preach and tells them how they are to live according to the Gospel was read. When Francis heard that they were not to provide gold or silver or copper to fill their purses, that they were not to have a wallet for the journey or a second coat, no shoes or staff, he was overjoyed. He grasped the meaning of the passage immediately in his love for apostolic poverty and committed it to memory. "This is what I want," he exclaimed. "This is what I long for with all my heart." There and then he took off his shoes and laid aside his staff. He conceived a horror of money or wealth of any kind and

he wore only one tunic, changing his leather belt for a rope. The whole desire of his heart was to put what he had heard into practice and conform to the rule of life given to the Apostles in everything.

2   By divine inspiration he now began to strive after Gospel perfection, inviting others also to lead a life of penance. His words were full of the power of the Holy Spirit, never empty or ridiculous, and they went straight to the heart, so that his hearers were amazed. In all his sermons he began by wishing his hearers peace, saying to them, "God give you peace," a form of greeting which he had learned by a revelation, as he afterwards asserted. He was moved by the spirit of the prophets and he proclaimed peace and salvation. By his salutary warnings he united in the bond of true peace great numbers of people who had been at enmity with Christ and far from salvation.

3   As the force of his teaching and the sincerity of his life became known, others were moved by his example to live a life of penance. They renounced everything they had and came to share his life and dress. First among them was Bernard, a worthy man who was called by God and became Francis' first son, both in time and holiness. When he had discovered Francis' holiness for himself, he decided to renounce the world completely after his example, and he asked his advice about the best way to do it. Francis was filled with the encouragement of the Holy Spirit, when he realized he was being joined by his first follower, and he said, "We shall have to ask God's advice about this." In the morning they went to the church of St. Nicholas where they spent some time in prayer. Then Francis opened the Gospel book three times in honor of the Blessed Trinity, asking God to approve Bernard's plan with a three-fold testimony. The book opened the first time at the words, "If you have a mind to be perfect, go home and sell all

that belongs to you, and give it to the poor" (Mt 19, 21).
The second time they found the phrase, "Take nothing with
you to use on your journey" (Lk 9, 3), and the third time
the words of our Lord caught their eyes, "If any man has
a mind to come my way, let him renounce self, and take
up his cross, and follow me" (Mt 16, 24). "This is our
life and our rule," said Francis, "and everyone who comes
to join our company must be prepared to do this. And so,
if you have a mind to be perfect, go home and do as you
have heard."

4   Within a short while afterwards five others felt the
call of the same spirit and the number of Francis' followers
grew to six. Third among those to join him was Brother
Giles, a man who was full of God and in every way worthy
of the great name he left behind him. He was a very ordinary, uneducated person, but he distinguished himself by
the practice of heroic virtue, as St. Francis had prophesied,
and he was raised to sublime contemplation. For years he
never ceased to raise his heart continually to God and he
used to be so often rapt in ecstasy that he seemed to live
a life worthy of the Angels even when he was on earth, as
I have seen with my own eyes.

5   At this time, too, Father Silvester, a priest from
Assisi and a good man, saw a vision which we cannot pass
over in silence. At first when he saw the way Francis and
his friars were behaving, he looked on it in a purely human
fashion and he was disgusted, but then God visited him
with his grace in order to save him from his rash temerity.
He had a dream in which he saw the whole of Assisi caught
in the coils of a huge serpent, which threatened to devastate
the entire area by its sheer size. Then he saw a cross of gold
coming from Francis' mouth; the top of it reached up to
heaven and its arms stretched far and wide and seemed to
embrace the whole earth. The serpent was completely van-

quished at the sight of it. Father Silvester realized that the vision was a revelation from God; and after he had seen it for the third time, he told St. Francis and his friars all about it. A short time afterwards he left the world and followed in the footsteps of Christ with such perseverance that his life in the Order only served to confirm the vision which he had seen while in the world.

6   St. Francis refused to be carried away with worldly pride when he heard about the vision. He acknowledged God's goodness in the gifts he bestows and became more eager than ever to put the enemy of the human race to flight with all his cunning, and proclaim the glory of Christ's cross. One day when he was in a lonely place by himself, weeping for his misspent years in the bitterness of his heart, the joy of the Holy Spirit was infused into him and he was assured that all his sins had been forgiven. He was rapt in ecstasy and completely absorbed in a wonderful light, so that the depths of his soul were enlightened and he saw what the future held in store for himself and his sons. Then he returned to the friars once again and told them, "Have courage, my dearly beloved, and rejoice in God. There is no need to be upset because there are only a few of us, nor any need to be afraid because we have no experience. God has shown me beyond all shadow of doubt that he will make us grow into a great multitude and that the Order will spread far and wide, by the favor of his blessing."

7   Another good man came to the Order about this time, bringing the number of Francis' sons to seven. Then like a good father he gathered all his sons about him and spoke to them at length about the kingdom of God and the need to disregard the world and do penance, renouncing one's own will. Finally, he told them that he had decided to send them all over the country. Although his spirit was one of poverty and lowliness, free from all pretense and devoid of

649

life-giving powers, Francis had already attracted seven followers and he was anxious to invite the whole world to repent and give it new life in Christ. So he told his companions, "Go and bring to all men a message of peace and penance, that their sins may be forgiven. Be patient in trials, watchful in prayer, and never cease working. Be considerate in your speech, well-ordered in your actions, and grateful to your benefactors. Remember that for all this an eternal kingdom is being made ready for you." The friars humbly cast themselves on the ground before him and welcomed the command of obedience with true spiritual joy. Then he addressed each one of them individually, telling them, "Cast the burden of your cares upon the Lord, and he will sustain you" (Ps 54, 23). This was what he always used to say to any friar on whom he imposed a command in virtue of obedience.

Francis knew that it was up to him to set an example for the friars and he was anxious to practice what he preached; and so, when he had sent the other six in different directions in the form of a cross, he took one of his companions and set out himself in a fourth direction. After a short while, however, he was anxious to see them all again and, as he had no means of summoning them himself, he prayed to God "who called the banished sons of Israel home" (cf. Ps 146, 2). So it was that by God's gracious providence they all met unexpectedly shortly afterwards without being summoned by any human means, much to their surprise. Another four worthy men now came to join them and this brought their number to twelve.

8   When he saw that the number of friars was slowly increasing, Francis wrote a short, simple, rule of life for himself and his companions. This was based on an unshakeable foundation, the following of the Gospel, and to this he added a limited number of other prescriptions, such as

seemed necessary for their life in common. He was anxious to have what he had written approved by the pope, and so, placing all his trust in God's guidance, he decided to present himself with his companions before the Apostolic See. God looked with favor upon his desire and comforted the friars who were frightened at the thought of their inexperience by showing Francis the following vision. It seemed to him that he was walking along a road beside which grew a tall tree and as he drew near he stopped to admire its height. All of a sudden, he felt himself lifted up into the air by God's power, so that he was able to grasp the top of the tree and bend it down to the ground without the slightest difficulty. Full of God as he was, Francis immediately realized that the vision was a prophecy of the way the pope would condescend to his will and he was overjoyed. He spoke to the friars encouragingly and then set out with them on the journey.

9   When they had arrived at the papal court, Francis was brought before the pope. The Vicar of Christ was in the Lateran palace at the time; and when Francis was announced, he was walking in a hall known as the Mirror Hall, lost in deep thought. He knew nothing about the saint, and so he sent him away indignantly. Francis took his leave with all humility, and the following night God showed the pope a vision in which he saw a palm-tree sprouting between his feet and growing until it was a fine tree. As he wondered what the vision meant, the divine light made it clear to him that the palm-tree was the beggar he had turned away the previous day. The next morning he gave his servants orders to search the city for Francis; and when they found him in St. Anthony's hospice, he told them to bring him before him without delay. When he appeared before the Supreme Pontiff, Francis told him of his plans, imploring him humbly and insistently to approve the rule

for him. The pope, Innocent III, was famous for his learning; and when he saw Francis' wonderful purity of heart, together with his determination, and the fiery eagerness of his will, he felt inclined to give his approval. However, the whole idea seemed so new to some of the cardinals, who thought that the rule was too difficult for any human being, that he hesitated to do what Francis asked. One of the cardinals was His Eminence John of St. Paul, Bishop of Santa Sabina, a man who loved holiness and was dedicated to Christ's poor. Inspired by the Holy Spirit, he addressed the pope and his confreres saying, "We must be careful. If we refuse this beggarman's request because it is new or too difficult, we may be sinning against Christ's Gospel, because he is only asking us to approve a form of Gospel life. Anyone who says that a vow to live according to the perfection of the Gospel contains something new or unreasonable or too difficult to be observed, is guilty of blasphemy against Christ, the Author of the Gospel." At that, the successor of St. Peter turned to St. Francis and told him, "My son, pray to Christ that he may show us his will through you. When we are sure of that, we can grant your request without fear."

10   Francis immediately gave himself up completely to prayer; and as a reward for his fervor it was made known to him what he should say, and simultaneously it was revealed to the pope what he should think. Francis told the pope a story which he had learned from God about a wealthy monarch who voluntarily married a poor but very beautiful woman and a had a number of children by her. These resembled him closely, so that they had the right to eat at his table. Then Francis added, by way of explanation, "There is no danger that the sons and heirs of the immortal King will die of hunger. They have been born of a poor mother by the power of the Holy Spirit in the image of

Christ the King and they will be followed by others who will be brought to birth in our Order by the spirit of poverty. If the King of heaven promises his followers an eternal kingdom, he certainly will not let them go short of the material goods he bestows on good and bad without distinction." When the pope heard this story and its explanation, he was amazed and he realized without the slightest doubt that Christ had spoken through Francis. Only a short time before, he had seen a vision from heaven and by divine inspiration he now testified that it would be fulfilled in Francis. As he himself described it, he had a dream in which he saw the Lateran basilica which was threatening to fall being held up by a poor beggarman who put his back to it. "This is certainly the man," he added. "By his work and teaching, he will uphold Christ's Church." As a result of his vision the pope was filled with reverence for Francis and granted his request unconditionally. He always had a special regard for him and, while granting what he asked, he promised to give the friars greater powers in the future. He approved the rule and gave them a mission to preach repentance, conferring the clerical tonsure on the laymen among Francis' companions, so that they could preach the word of God without interference.

CHAPTER IV

The Progress of the Order under Francis' Guidance and the Confirmation of the Rule

1   With God's grace and the pope's approval to support him Francis now felt completely confident and he took the road towards the valley of Spoleto, where he determined to preach Christ's Gospel and live according to it. As he made the journey with his companions, they fell to discussing how they might keep the rule they had been given with all sincerity and live before God in holiness and with ap-

proval in his sight. They debated, too, how they might better themselves and give others good example, so that it was already late while they continued their long conversation. They were tired with all they had done and began to feel hungry, so that they eventually halted on a lonely stretch of the road. There seemed to be no hope of getting anything to eat, but God provided for them unexpectedly; a man came on the scene unannounced, carrying some bread which he gave to them and then immediately disappeared, leaving them with no idea whence he came or where he went. For all their poverty, the friars realized that in Francis' company they could be sure of God's help and the thought of his generosity did more to strength them than the food which they ate. They were filled with spiritual encouragement and they made a firm resolution never to go back on the promise which they had made to Holy Poverty, no matter how much privation or suffering they had to endure.

2   Eventually, they arrived at the valley of Spoleto, still full of these good dispositions, and there they fell to debating whether they should live among the people or seek refuge in solitude. Francis, who was a true servant of Christ, refused to trust in his own opinion or in the suggestions of his companions; instead, he sought to discover God's will by persevering prayer. Then, enlightened by a revelation from heaven, he realized that he was sent by God to win for Christ the souls which the Devil was trying to snatch away. And so he chose to live for the benefit of his fellow men, rather than for himself alone, after the example of Him who was so good as to die for all men.

3   With his companions Francis now went to live in an abandoned hut near Assisi, where they lived from hand to mouth according to the rule of poverty, in toil and penury, drawing their strength rather from tears of compunction

than from any bodily food. They spent the time praying continuously, devoting themselves especially to fervent mental prayer; they had not yet got any of the liturgical books, so that they could not chant the divine office. Christ's cross was their book and they studied it day and night, at the exhortation and after the example of their father who never stopped talking to them about the cross. When the friars asked him to teach them how to pray, he said, "When you pray, say the Our Father, and We adore you, O Christ, in all your churches in the whole world and we thank you, because by your holy cross you redeemed the world."

He also taught them to join with all creation and praise God in his creatures, while venerating priests with special reverence and holding fast to the true faith which is professed and taught by the Catholic Church. This they were to believe firmly and profess with all simplicity. The friars obeyed his teaching to perfection, and whenever they saw a church or a crucifix, even from a distance, they knelt down humbly and prayed the way he had taught them.

4   While they were still living in the hut already mentioned, St. Francis went into Assisi one Saturday because he was to preach as usual in the cathedral the following morning. There he spent the night praying in a shelter in the garden belonging to the canons of the cathedral, as was his custom. In person he was separated from the friars, but then about midnight, as some of them were praying and others slept, a fiery chariot of extraordinary brilliance came in the door of the hut and turned here and there three times about the room. It was surmounted by a globe of light which looked like the sun and lit up the darkness. Those who were awake were dumbfounded, while the others woke up terrified; they could feel the light penetrating their hearts just as it lit up the room, and their consciences were laid bare to one another by force of its brightness. As they read

one another's hearts, they all realized simultaneously that their father who was absent from them in person was present with them in spirit under the appearance of this vision. They were sure God had shown him to them in this glorious chariot of fire, radiant with the splendor of heaven and inflamed with burning ardor, so that they might follow him as loyal disciples. Like a second Elias, God had made him a "chariot and charioteer" (cf. 4 Kgs 2, 12) for all spiritual people. Certainly, it seems that God opened the eyes of these ordinary men at the request of St. Francis, so that they might contemplate his divine power, just as he had once opened the eyes of the servant of the prophet Eliseus, so that he could see "the whole mountainside beset with flaming horses and chariots there about Eliseus" (cf. 4 Kg 6, 17).

When Francis rejoined his companions, he began to probe the depths of their consciences, exhorting them to take courage from the wonderful vision they had seen. He made a number of predictions about the future growth of the Order and, as he continued to reveal secrets beyond the grasp of human understanding, the friars realized that the Spirit of God dwelt in his servant Francis so abundantly that they need have no hesitation in following his life and teaching.

5   After this, at God's prompting, Francis brought his little flock of twelve friars to St. Mary of the Portiuncula. It was there that the Order of Friars Minor had been founded by the merits of the Mother of God, and it was there, too, that it would grow to maturity by her intercession.

From the Portiuncula, Francis set out as a herald of the Gospel to preach the kingdom of God in the towns and villages in the vicinity, "not in such words as human wisdom teaches, but in words taught him by the Spirit" (1 Cor 2, 13). To those who saw him he seemed like a man from another world as, with his gaze fixed on heaven where his heart always dwelt, he tried to lift their thoughts on high. As a result of his efforts the supernatural vineyard of Christ began to put forth shoots which gave out a pleasing fragrance before God and produced fruit in abundance, lush and rich.

6   Carried away by the force of his preaching, great numbers of people adopted the new rule of penance according to the form instituted by St. Francis which he called the "Order of the Brothers of Penance." The way of penance is common to all those who are on the road to heaven and so this way of life includes members of both sexes, clerics and lay-folk, married or single. How meritorious it is in the eyes of God is clear from the numerous miracles worked by some of those who followed it. Unmarried women were inspired to profess a life of perpetual virginity, among whom St. Clare was especially dear to God. She was the first flower in Francis' garden, and she shone like a radiant star, fragrant as a flower blossoming white and pure in springtime. She was his daughter in Christ and foundress of the Poor Clares. Now she has been glorified in heaven and on earth the church pays her the honor which is her due.

7   It was not just that the masses were stirred by the fervor of the moment; great numbers were seized with the desire to imitate the perfection of Christ and these followed Francis' footsteps, making light of the fleeting attractions of the world. Their number grew daily, so that the Order was spread all over the world in a very short time. Poverty, which was all they had to meet their expenses, made them ready to undertake any task, while giving them strength for any kind of toil and leaving them free to travel without difficulty. They possessed nothing that belonged to this world; they loved nothing, and so they feared to lose nothing. They were free from care, with no anxiety to disturb them or worry to distract them. Their hearts were at peace as

they lived from day to day, looking forward to the morrow without a thought as to where they would find shelter for the night. In those parts of the world where they were unknown and despised they were often insulted, but they were so meek in their devotion to Christ's Gospel that they preferred to remain where they had to endure physical persecution, rather than return where their holiness was recognized and they might become proud of the honor shown them. Their very poverty seemed to them overflowing abundance as, in the words of the prophet, they "made much of the little they had" (cf. Sir 29, 30).

A Moslem took pity on some of the friars who had arrived in a pagan country and offered them money for the food they needed, but they refused to accept it. He was amazed, because he could see they were destitute. Then he realized that it was for love of God that they had become beggars and refused to take money, and he felt so attracted to them that he offered to supply all their needs, as long as he had anything left. What a priceless treasure poverty is! Its extraordinary charm could move even the savage heart of a barbarian to pity and kindness. And what a crime, what an unspeakable crime, that any Christian should trample underfoot the Gospel pearl for which a pagan showed such reverence.

8   At this time, too, a religious of the Order of the *Crucigeri* who was called Moricus was lying ill in a hospital near Assisi. It was a long drawn-out illness and his condition was so bad that the doctors had given up all hope, but then he appealed to St. Francis and sent a message to him, entreating him of his goodness to pray to God for him. Francis agreed immediately and said a prayer for him; then he took some bread-crumbs and dipped them in oil taken from the lamp which burned before our Lady's altar, making a sort of pill out of them. This he sent with one of the

friars to the sick man saying, "Take this medicine to our brother Moricus. By means of it Christ's power will restore him to perfect health and when he is strong and ready for the fray once more, he will bring him into our company for the rest of his life." The moment the sick man took the medicine which had been prepared under the inspiration of the Holy Spirit, he immediately recovered and was able to get up. God gave him such strength of body and soul that he joined Francis' company a short time afterwards and was able to keep the rule which allows only a single tunic. Under this he wore a hair-shirt next to his skin for years and never ate cooked food, contenting himself with herbs, vegetables, and fruit. For years, too, he never ate bread or drank wine and yet he remained strong and in perfect health.

9   As Christ's servants increased in merit and virtue, the high esteem in which they were held became known all over the country, so that people came to see St. Francis from all parts of the world. Among them was a successful song-writer who had been crowned by the emperor and was known as the King of Verse. He made up his mind to approach Francis who was known for his disregard of all that belongs to the world and when he met him in a mon-astery at San Severino where the saint had come to preach, the power of God came upon him. There he saw Francis, the Apostle of Christ's Cross, signed with the sign of the Cross in the form of two swords of fire, one of which reached from his head to his feet, while the other crossed his chest from hand to hand. He did not know Francis by sight but he realized that the person pointed out to him by such a miracle could be no other. He was dumbfounded at the vision and immediately began to make good resolutions for the future; the saint's words moved him to compunction, as if a spiritual sword coming from his mouth had pierced

him. There and then he said good-bye to popular renown and joined Francis by professing his rule. When Francis saw that he had abandoned the world with its troubles and chosen Christ's peace, he called him brother Pacificus. Pacificus afterwards became very holy; and before he left for France, where he was the first provincial minister, he was found worthy to have a vision of a great cross which appeared in different colors on St. Francis' forehead and lit up his whole face with a beautiful radiance. Francis always had great reverence for this particular sign, and he often recommended others to use it. He used to put it at the end of all his letters, as if his only desire was "to mark the brows of the true disciples of Jesus Christ who weep and wail with this sign of the cross," as we read in the prophet Ezechiel (Ez 9, 4).

10   As the number of friars increased with the passing of the years, Francis used to summon them all like a good shepherd to a general chapter at St. Mary of the Portiuncula. There, according to the measure of God's judgment, he would assign to each one the mission given him by obedience in this life of poverty. At these meetings no provision whatever was made for what they needed, and sometimes more than five thousand friars turned up. God cared for them in his providence, so that they had enough to eat and enjoyed good health, while they overflowed with spiritual contentment.

Francis could not preside personally at the chapter of the different provinces, but by his unremitting prayer and the power of his blessing he was always there in spirit in his anxious care for his subjects. On one occasion he even appeared visibly at such a chapter by God's power. It was at the chapter of Arles and the famous preacher whom we now honor as St. Anthony was preaching to the friars on the proclamation Pilate wrote on the Cross, "Jesus of Nazareth, the king of the Jews." One of the friars a, holy man named Monaldus, felt a sudden inspiration to look towards the door of the chapter hall; there with his own eyes, he saw St. Francis standing in mid-air with his arms stretched out in the form of a cross, blessing the friars. The friars who were present felt such wonderful consolation in their hearts that they were assured by the Holy Spirit that their father had really been there. It was only afterwards that they heard he had been seen and the saint himself remarked that he had been there, so that they had external proof for what they already believed. It seems that almighty God who had enabled St. Ambrose, bishop of Milan, to be present at the burial of St. Martin and pay his respects to that holy prelate, permitted Francis to assist at the sermon given by his preacher St. Anthony. In this way he would attest the truth of Francis' words, especially those concerning Christ's Cross which he bore as his servant.

11   When the Order was already well established and Francis was thinking of having the rule which had been approved by Pope Innocent confirmed for all time by his successor Pope Honorius, God granted him the following vision. He saw himself picking up some tiny crumbs of bread from the ground, with which he had to feed a large number of friars who were standing about. The crumbs were so small that he was afraid to distribute them lest they slip through his fingers. Then he heard a voice from heaven telling him, "Francis, make one piece out of all those crumbs and give it to those who are willing to eat it." He did so, and the friars who failed to accept it with due reverence, or despised it when they had taken it, were soon seen to be suffering from leprosy. In the morning Francis told his companions all about it. He was upset because he could not understand the meaning of his vision; but the following day, while he was watching in prayer, he heard a voice

telling him, "Francis, those crumbs, the other night, are the words of the Gospel. The single piece is the rule and the leprosy is wickedness."

And so Francis decided to shorten the rule which he wanted to have confirmed, because it had become too long by the addition of numerous texts from the Gospel, as his vision indicated. Then he was led by the Holy Spirit into the mountains with two companions, where he fasted on bread and water; and there he dictated the rule as the Holy Spirit inspired him in his prayer. When he came down from the mountain, he gave the rule to the vicar of the Order; but a few days later the vicar claimed that he had accidentally mislaid it, and so the saint went into solitude once more and rewrote the rule just as before, as if he heard the words from God's own lips. Afterwards he obtained papal confirmation for it from his holiness Pope Honorius, who was then in the eighth year of his pontificate.

Francis used to exhort the friars fervently to be faithful to the rule, saying that he had dictated everything as it was revealed to him by God and that nothing he had prescribed came from himself. This was proved by God's own testimony only a short time afterwards when Francis received the stigmata of our Lord Jesus Christ. This was the seal of Christ, the supreme High Priest, with which he gave the rule and its author his divine approval, as we shall explain later when we have finished describing Francis' virtues.

CHAPTER V

The Austerity of Francis' Life and the Comfort Which Creatures Gave Him

1   When Francis saw that great numbers of lay people were being inspired by his example to embrace Christ's Cross fervently, he took heart and like a brave leader in Christ's army he determined to carry off the prize of victory by prac-

ticing virtue to a heroic degree. Recalling the words of St. Paul, "those who belong to Christ have crucified nature, with all its passions, all its impulses" (Gal 5, 24), he mortified his lower appetites so strictly that he scarcely took enough food or drink to stay alive. In this way he would cloth himself with the armor of the Cross. He used to say that it was hard to satisfy one's material needs without giving in to the inclinations of sensuality. As long as he enjoyed good health, he scarcely ever ate cooked food. When he did, he mixed it with ashes or destroyed its taste, usually by adding water. He never drank enough water, even when he was burning with thirst — not to mention taking wine — and he devised ways of practicing even greater self-denial, becoming better at it day by day. He was already perfect in every way, but still he was always beginning afresh, just as if he were only starting, and he castigated his natural desires by punishing his body.

However, on his missionary journeys, in preaching the Gospel, he always took whatever food was put before him by those who gave him hospitality. But when he returned home, he kept strictly to the rule of fasting. He was hard on himself but accommodating towards his neighbor. In this way he obeyed Christ's Gospel in everything and did people as much good by eating as by fasting. More often than not, his weary body had only the bare earth for a bed and he usually slept in an upright position with a piece of wood or a stone at his head. He was content with one worn habit, as he served God in cold and nakedness.

2   Someone asked him once how he could protect himself from the piercing cold of winter with such poor clothing and he replied with a fervent spirit, "If we are on fire with longing for our heavenly home in our hearts, we will have no difficulty in enduring this exterior cold." He had a horror of expensive clothes and used to be delighted with

coarse garments, adding that John the Baptist was praised by our Lord for being roughly clad. If the habit he was given felt too soft, he used to sew pieces of cord on the inside because, as he used to say, it is in the palaces of the rich that we must look for men who go clad in soft garments, not in the hovels of the poor. He knew from his own experience that the devils were afraid when they saw a person wearing rough clothes, whereas soft or luxurious garments gave them courage to attack more fiercely.

One night he used a pillow of feathers, contrary to his custom, because he had a headache and was suffering from pain in his eyes; but a devil got into it and gave him no rest until morning. He prevented him from devoting himself to prayer, until finally he called his companion and told him to take the pillow out of his cell. The moment he left the cell with the pillow, the friar lost the use of his limbs. Then Francis, who knew in spirit what was happening, called out to him and immediately all his strength of soul and body was completely restored to him.

3   Francis watched over himself with rigid self-discipline and was especially careful to preserve perfect purity of soul and body. In the early years of his religious life he often jumped into a snow-filled ditch in wintertime, in order to preserve the white robe of purity from the flames of passion and subdue completely the enemy which was part of his own nature. He used to say that a religious should infinitely prefer to have his body suffer biting cold rather than allow the slightest taint of evil desire to enter his heart.

4   One night when he was praying in his cell at the hermitage of Sarteano, the Devil called him three times, "Francis, Francis, Francis." When Francis replied, asking him what he wanted, the Devil went on, "There is not a sinner in the whole world whom God will not forgive, if

he repents. But if a man kills himself by doing too much penance, he will never find forgiveness." By God's inspiration the saint saw his treachery at once and realized that Satan was trying to reduce him to half-heartedness. This was proved by what followed, because he immediately felt a grave temptation of the flesh, provoked by him whose "very breath will set coals aflame" (Jb 41, 12). The moment he felt it coming, Francis tore off his habit in his love for chastity and began to scourge himself with a cord. "There, brother ass," he exclaimed, "that is your place, to be scourged like that. The habit is a sign of the religious state and an indication of a good life; a lustful person has no right to it. If you want to go another road, off with you!" Then in an excess of fervor he opened the door and went out into garden where he rolled naked in the deep snow. After that he gathered up some of it with both hands and made seven heaps with it and stood before them, saying to his body, "Look, the big one here is your wife and those four are your children, two boys and two girls. The other two are the servants you need to look after them, a man and a woman. And now hurry up and find clothes for them — they are dying of cold. But if all the trouble it takes to look after them is too much for you, then keep your services for God alone." At that the tempter took his leave defeated, and the saint returned triumphantly to his cell. The cold had pierced him to the bone but the flame of passion within him had been utterly quenched, so that he never felt anything like it again. A friar who had been busy praying at the time saw what happened in the clear moonlight. When Francis discovered that he had been seen, he told him all about the temptation which he had felt and commanded him never to tell anyone what he had seen during his lifetime.

5   Besides teaching the friars to mortify the passions of

the flesh with its impulses, Francis insisted that they should watch over their exterior senses by which death enters the soul with the greatest vigilance. He warned them to beware of the sight of women and avoid close friendships or conversation with them which can often lead to a fall. Indiscretion in this matter, he affirmed, could crush the weak and weaken the strong, adding that it was as hard for anyone who had much to do with them to avoid being ensnared as it was to "walk on hot coals without burning one's feet" (cf. Prv 6, 27). He avoided the sight of women so carefully himself that he scarcely knew any woman by sight, as he once confessed to his companion. He was convinced that it was dangerous to allow any representation of them to enter one's mind because the flames of passion could easily be rekindled or the purity of a clean heart be stained. He often remarked that any conversation with women was pointless except on the occasion of confession or a brief instruction. Such contact could be of benefit to their spiritual progress and did not exceed the limits of religious behavior. "What," he asked, "has a religious got to do with women anyway, unless they are looking for confession or ask for spiritual direction? When a man is too sure of himself, he becomes less wary of the enemy, and if the Devil can call his own even one hair of a man's head, he will lose no time in making a rope of it."

6   He taught the friars especially to avoid idleness, the root of all evil desires, and he set them an example by curbing his lower nature, when it was given to revolt or laziness, by practicing continual self-discipline or devoting himself to useful work. He used to call his body "Brother Ass," as if it were fit for nothing more than hard labor and frequent ill-treatment with a whip, while having only the poorest type of food to live on. If he saw that a friar was given to standing about idle, waiting to be fed by the labor

of others, he called him "Brother Fly," because he detracted from the good done by others and did no good himself, so that he lost the respect and esteem of all. With reference to such friars, the saint once remarked, "I want my friars to work and to be kept busy. If they are idle, their hearts or their tongues will soon be occupied with unlawful subjects." He was anxious to see the friars observe the silence which is recommended in the Gospel, being careful at all times to avoid every thoughtless word for which they might be brought to account on the day of judgment (cf. Mt 12, 36). He used to be quite sharp in correcting any friar who indulged habitually in gossip, declaring that a prudent reserve helped to maintain purity of heart and was an important virtue. Sacred Scripture tells us, "Of life and death, tongue holds the keys" (Prv 18, 21), more because of its power of speech than because it can taste.

7   Francis did his utmost to encourage the friars to lead austere lives, but he had no time for exaggerated self-denial which excluded tender compassion or was not tempered with discretion. One night a friar who had fasted too long was tormented with hunger and could get no rest. Like a good shepherd, Francis realized how badly he was faring and called him. Then he put some bread before him and advised him gently to eat it, and began to eat himself first, to avoid embarrassing him. The friar overcame his embarrassment and began to eat; he was overjoyed at seeing the saint's exquisite tact which enabled him to relieve his material needs and gave him such a wonderful example. In the morning Francis called the whole community together and told them what had happened, taking the opportunity to tell them, "You should take an example from the charity involved, not from the fact that we indulged in food." He also taught them to practice prudence, not the prudence

recommended by our fallen nature, but that practiced by Christ whose life is the model of all perfection.

8   In his present state of weakness man is incapable of imitating the crucified Lamb of God perfectly and avoiding all the stains of sin. And so Francis taught his friars by his own example that those who are trying to be perfect must cleanse themselves daily with tears of contrition. He had attained extraordinary purity of soul and body, yet he never ceased from purifying his spiritual vision with floods of tears and thought nothing of the fact that it was costing him his sight. As a result of his continual weeping, he developed serious eye-trouble, but when the doctor advised him to restrain his tears if he wanted to avoid losing his sight, he replied, "Brother doctor, we share this world's light in common with the flies; we must not refuse to enjoy the presence of everlasting light merely to save it. Our bodies were given the power of sight for the sake of our souls; the sight which our souls enjoy was not given us for the sake of our bodies." He preferred rather to lose his sight than to check the fervor of his spirit and restrain the tears which sharpened his spiritual vision and enabled him to see God.

9   On one occasion the doctors were anxious to perform a cauterization and the friars insisted that he should have it done. Francis agreed humbly because he realized it would be good for him, as well as being extremely painful. They sent for a surgeon and when he came, he put a searing-iron in the fire in preparation for the operation. Francis trembled with fear, but then he began to encourage his body, addressing the fire like a friend, "My brother fire, your splendor is the envy of all creation. The Most High made you strong, beautiful, and useful. Be gentle to me now, be kind. I beg the great God who created you to temper your heat, so that you will burn gently and I may endure it." When he had finished his prayer, he made the sign of the cross over the

red-hot instrument and waited unafraid. The sizzling iron was plunged into the soft flesh and drawn from his ear to his eye-brow. We can gather how much pain the burn caused him from his own words, as he told his friars, "Give thanks to the Most High, for I can say truthfully that I never felt the slightest burn or any pain." Then he turned to the doctor and added, "If that was not enough, you can do it again." When the doctor saw the extraordinary strength of his spirit which was revealed in his frail body, he hailed it as a miracle, telling the friars, "My brothers, I assure you I have seen a miracle with my own eyes." Such was his pure love of God that Francis had arrived at a point where his body was in perfect harmony with his spirit, and his spirit with God. As a reward, God disposed that all creation, which must spend itself in the service of its Maker, should be subject to his will and obey his command.

10   Another time when he was very ill at the hermitage of Sant' Urbano, Francis felt the need of something to give him strength and he asked for a glass of wine. They told him there was not a drop in the place they could give him, so he told them to bring some water. When it was brought, he blessed it with the sign of the cross and immediately it was changed into excellent wine. The poverty of a lonely friary had been unable to provide it, and so his sanctity procured it. At the taste of the wine, he immediately felt much better, so that it was clear that both the liquid and the one who drank it were supernaturally renewed. The changing of the water and the improvement in his health were so many indications of the extent to which he was "quit of the old self, and clothed in the new self" (cf. Col 3, 9-10).

11   Not only did all creation obey his slightest wish; by his providence God himself condescended to his will. On one occasion he was afflicted with a number of different ailments simultaneously and he longed to hear some music

to keep up his spirits. The fear of giving scandal made it impossible to get anyone to play for him, but then an angel came in answer to his prayer. One night as he lay awake thinking about God, he suddenly heard the sound of a lyre playing a melody of incredible beauty. He could see no one, but the rise and fall of the music showed that the musician was walking back and forth. With his spirit all intent on God, Francis felt such pleasure at the wonderful melody that he thought he had left this world and the friars who were closest to him were well aware that something had happened. They knew from various indications that he was often visited by God who comforted him beyond measure, so that he could not hide it from them completely.

12   At another time when he was walking near Padua with a companion, while on a missionary journey from Lombardy to the Marches of Treviso, they were overtaken by nightfall and enveloped in pitch darkness. The road was dangerous in the dark because of the river and the marshes and his companion said to him, "Father, pray that we may be kept safe from all danger." The saint replied confidently, "God has power to banish the darkness and give us light, if it pleases him in his kindness." The words were scarcely out of his mouth when a brilliant light shone about them with a heavenly radiance and they could see their way clearly and for quite a distance around, although it was dark everywhere else. By its guidance they found their way and were comforted in spirit. They still had a long way to go until they arrived where they were to spend the night, but they finished their journey safely, singing hymns of praise to God.

We should try to realize the purity of conscience and the degree of virtue which Francis had attained. Fire lost its burn and water its taste at his wish; an angel came to cheer him by his light, showing that the whole of creation waited upon his material needs, so holy had he become.

CHAPTER VI

Francis' Humility and Obedience — God's Condescension to His Slightest Wish

1   Francis had humility in abundance, the guardian and the crowning glory of all virtue. He was a mirror and a shining example of Christian perfection but in his own eyes he was only a sinner, and it was on this that he based his spiritual progress, laying the foundation he had learned from Christ, as a careful architect should (cf. 1 Cor 3, 10). The Son of God, he used to say, descended from the sublimity of the Father's bosom to share our misery and become our Lord and Teacher, in order to teach us humility by word and example. Therefore, as Christ's true disciple, he was careful to preserve a low opinion of himself and appear worthless in the eyes of others, keeping in mind the words of the supreme Teacher, "What is highly esteemed among men is an abomination in God's sight" (Lk 16, 15). He often used to remark, "What a man is before God, that he is and no more." Consequently he was convinced that it was foolish to be elated when people showed him marks of respect; he was upset by praise, but overjoyed when he was insulted. He liked to have people scorn him — that spurred him on to do better — and hated to be praised, which could lead to a fall. When people praised the height of his sanctity, he used to command one of the friars to do the opposite and heap insults upon him. Then, as the friar obeyed reluctantly and called him a boor and a time-server, worthless and good for nothing, he would listen cheerfully and say with a smile, "God bless you, my son. What you say is true. That is the kind of thing the son of Peter Bernardone should have to listen to."

2   He would not hesitate to confess his faults even when preaching in public, in order to appear contemptible in the eyes of others. One time when he was very ill, he departed from the rigor of his usual abstinence and took a little meat to regain his strength. Then, when he had only barely recovered, he felt urged to humiliate himself for his weakness in genuine self-contempt. "It is not right," he declared, "that everyone should think that I never eat meat, when I really did eat it unknown to them." Inspired with a true spirit of humility, he set out there and then and made his way to the town square in Assisi, where he assembled the whole population. After that he entered the principal church in procession with the friars whom he had brought with him, and there he took off his habit and put a rope around his neck. Then he told one of the friars to lead him to the stone where criminals were punished, in full view of all the people. He mounted the stone and preached vigorously, although it was bitterly cold and he was still weak and feverish. He told them all that they should not regard him as a spiritual man, but as a sinner and a glutton, worthy only of contempt. The onlookers were amazed at the extraordinary spectacle. They knew how austere a life he led and they were deeply moved, but they made no secret of the fact that they thought his humility was rather to be admired than imitated. His action certainly seems to have been intended rather as an omen reminiscent of the prophet Isaias (cf. Is 20, 3) than as an example. However, it is a lesson in true humility and shows the true follower of Christ that he is bound to disregard all earthly praise and subdue the displays of bloated pride, while renouncing all lying pretense.

3   Francis often behaved like this, so that others might regard him as something worthless, fit only to be cast aside, and he might preserve true holiness of heart. He was care-

ful to conceal the gifts which God showered upon him as closely guarded secrets and refused to expose them to the praise of others, which might lead to a fall. When he was acclaimed as a saint by the crowds, he would say, "I might have sons and daughters yet. Don't praise me as if I were safe. You should never praise anyone until you see how he turned out in the end." That was what he said to others and then, addressing himself, he would add, "If almighty God had done so much for a criminal, he would be more thankful than you, Francis." He used to often tell the friars, "No one should flatter himself for anything a sinner is capable of doing. A sinner can fast, pray, weep, and do physical penance. The one thing he cannot do is to remain faithful to God. Anyone who gives back to God the praise which belongs to him really has something to boast about, if he serves him faithfully and attributes to him the gifts he bestows."

4   Like the wise trader in the Gospel, Francis was anxious to profit by every possible occasion and use all his time to gain merit, and so he wished to live in obedience to another rather than be a superior, and obey rather than command. He resigned his position as general of the Order and asked for a guardian whom he could obey constantly. He was convinced that the fruits of obedience are so abundant that anyone who submits to it can never spend a moment without drawing some profit from it. He always used to promise to obey the friar who happened to be with him on his journeys, and he once remarked to his companions, "Among the many graces which God has given me in his goodness is this: I would obey a novice only one hour in the Order, if he were made my guardian, just as willingly as if he were the oldest and most experienced friar in the Order. A subject should never look upon his superior as a man; he should remember God for love of

whom he is subject. The more contemptible the superior, the more valuable is the humility of him who obeys."

He was asked on one occasion who was a truly obedient person and he gave the example of a dead body. "Take a corpse," he said, "and put it wherever you like. You will see that it does not object to being transferred, does not complain about where it is put, and does not protest when cast aside. If you set it on a throne, it will look down, not up; if you dress it in royal robes, it will only seem paler than ever. A person like that is truly obedient; he does not mind where he is put, and he makes no effort to be sent elsewhere. If he is promoted to office, he preserves his humility, and the more he is honored, the more unworthy he thinks himself."

5   Another time he told his companion, "I should not regard myself as a Friar Minor unless I were prepared to behave like this. Suppose I were a superior and I went to a chapter where I addressed the friars and gave them some advice. But then, when I have finished, they all say, 'You are not the right superior for us. You have no education and you are not a good speaker. Besides, you are illiterate and inexperienced.' Then I am thrown out ignominiously and despised by them all. I tell you, if I were not prepared to take all that without being disturbed or without losing my peace of mind, with a firm determination to use it all for my own sanctification, I should not be a Friar Minor." And he continued, "The office of superior may lead to a fall, and praise is a dangerous precipice, but the lowly position of a subject contains great benefit for the soul. Why are we more anxious to run risks than to gain merit? Time has been given us only so that we can gain merit."

It was for this reason that Francis who was a model of humility wanted his followers to be known as Friars Minor and their superiors as ministers. In this way he kept to the language of the Gospel (cf. Mt 25, 45) which he had promised to observe, and impressed upon his friars that it was to learn humility that they had come to the school of Christ. Christ the teacher of humility instructed his disciples in perfect humility by telling them, "Whoever would be a great man among you, must be your servant, and whoever has a mind to be first among you, must be your slave" (Mt 20, 26-7).

When the bishop of Ostia, the protector and foremost champion of the Order, who was afterwards to become pope with the name of Gregory IX as Francis prophesied, asked him if he would allow his friars to be promoted to various offices in the Church, the saint replied, "My lord, my friars are called Minors so that they will never think of becoming superiors. If you want them to bear fruit in the Church, keep them strictly to their vocation and never let them take, any office in the Church."

6   Because Francis preferred humility in himself and in his friars to any earthly honor, God who loves the humble judged him worthy of the highest honor. This was revealed to one of the friars, a virtuous and holy man, in a vision which he had from heaven. He was travelling with St. Francis when they went into an abandoned church, where they prayed fervently. There this friar was in an ecstasy and saw a vision of a multitude of thrones in heaven, one of which was radiant with glory and adorned with precious stones and ranked higher than the rest. He marvelled at its splendor and fell to wondering whose it was going to be. Then he heard a voice telling him, "That throne belonged to one of the fallen angels. Now it is being kept for the humble Francis." When the friar came back to himself, he followed the saint out of the church as usual. As they continued on their journey conversing together about

God, the friar remembered his vision and discreetly asked the saint what he thought of himself. "It seems to me," Francis replied, "that I must be the greatest of all sinners." When his companion reproached him, declaring that he could not possibly say that with a good conscience, or really believe it, Francis continued, "If Christ had shown such mercy towards the greatest criminal in the world, I am convinced that he would be much more grateful to God than I am." At the sight of such extraordinary humility, his companion was convinced of the truth of his vision; he knew from the testimony of the Gospel that the truly humble person is exalted to the height of glory from which the proud man is excluded.

7   On another occasion, while he was praying in an abandoned church near Monte Casale in the province of Massa Trabaria, it was revealed to saint Francis that a number of sacred relics had been left there. He was sorry to see them deprived of the honor due to them for so long and he told the friars to take them to the friary. However, he had to leave immediately afterwards and the friars forgot to do what he had told them, neglecting the merit of obedience. But then one day when they were preparing for Mass and the cover was taken off the altar, they found there a number of glistening clean bones which gave off a beautiful perfume. They were astonished, as they saw before their eyes the relics which had been brought there by God's power, not by any human agency. A short time afterwards St. Francis returned and he asked whether they had done what he told them to do with the relics. The friars confessed humbly that they had been negligent in obeying his command and Francis forgave them, imposing a penance on them. Then he added, "Blessed be my Lord and God; he did himself what you should have done."

We should never let ourselves forget the care which God

in his providence has even for our mortal remains; and the regard which he has for Francis' incomparable holiness. When human beings failed to carry out his command, God himself condescended to do his wish.

8   One day St. Francis arrived at Imola where he went to the bishop and humbly asked him for permission to summon the people and preach to them. "It is enough, brother, that I should preach to my own flock," the bishop replied abruptly. Francis bowed his head in genuine humility and took his leave. Less than an hour later, however, he returned once more. The bishop was annoyed and he asked him what he was looking for this time. Then Francis replied respectfully and without the slightest arrogance, "My lord, when a father throws his son out one door, he must come in by another." The bishop was disarmed by his humility; he smiled and put his arm around him and said, "Henceforth you and all your friars have general permission to preach in my diocese. Holy humility deserves that."

9   On another occasion St. Francis arrived at Arezzo when the whole town was being torn with faction fights and threatened with destruction. There he was given hospitality in a village near the town and he could see the devils rejoicing over it and urging the people on to mutual slaughter. He was anxious to put the malicious powers of evil to flight and so he sent brother Silvester, who was a man of dove-like simplicity, telling him to approach the town like a herald. "Go up to the town gate," he said, "and in the name of almighty God command the devils in virtue of obedience to go away immediately." Silvester was a genuinely obedient man and he immediately did what he was told. He approached the town gate, singing a hymn of praise to God, and there he cried aloud, "In the name of almighty God and by the command of his servant Francis, away with you, all you devils!" There and then the town

was restored to peace and the townspeople set about re-
forming the laws governing their mutual rights peacefully.
Once the malignant and presumptuous influence of the
demons which encompassed the town like a besieging army
had been counteracted, it needed only the wisdom of a beggar, that is, Francis' humility, to restore peace and save the
day. By the heroic practice of humble obedience Francis had
gained complete authority over the rebellious spirits, so
that he could crush their frantic efforts and put an end
to the violence they attempted.

10   In their pride the demons take flight at the sight
of the sublime virtue practiced by those who are truly
humble. However, God in his goodness occasionally allows
them to distress us, as St. Paul tells us of himself (cf. 2
Cor 12, 7) and St. Francis learned by his own experience.
He had been invited by his Eminence Cardinal Leo, titular
of the church of Santa Croce, to visit him in Rome and
he accepted the invitation out of respect for the Cardinal
who was a close friend of his. The very first night he was
there, when he had finished praying and was trying to get
some rest, he was surrounded by devils who attacked him
brutally. They beat him severely for a long time and then
went off, leaving him half-dead. As they left, St. Francis
called his companion and told him what had happened.
Then he added, "The devils can only do what God in his
providence allows them and I am convinced they attacked
me now because it does not look well that I should be living
in a palace like this. When the friars who live in poor
friaries hear that I am staying with a cardinal, they may
think that I am getting mixed up in worldly affairs, or being
showered with honors and having a good time. Anyone
who is intended to be an example for others should avoid
palaces and be content to live a humble life among ordinary friars in ordinary friaries. In that way he will

678

share the poverty of others and give courage to those who have to bear similar privation." In the morning, then, they went to the cardinal and said good-bye and took their leave.

11   The saint had a horror of pride, which is the cause of all evil, and of disobedience, which is its worst offspring. On the other hand, he always had a warm welcome for humble repentance. A friar was brought before him one time who had sinned against obedience and merited just punishment. Looking at him, Francis could see sure signs that he was genuinely sorry and he was so pleased with his humble contrition that he decided to be easy on him. At the same time, he was anxious to avoid encouraging others to revolt by letting him off too lightly and so he ordered his capuche to be taken off and thrown into the fire. That would show all the friars the kind of punishment which disobedience deserved. Then, when the capuche had been in the flames for a while, Francis ordered it to be taken out and given back to the penitent. It was taken out and there was not the slightest trace of a burn on it. With one and the same miracle God approved Francis' holiness and the humble contrition of the delinquent.

Francis' humility, therefore, is worth imitating; it was honored even on earth, so that God inclined to his slightest wish and the citizens of Arezzo underwent a change of heart. He repulsed the presumptuous attacks of the devils by his command and tempered the heat of a fire at will. This is the humility which exalts those who possess it and is respectful towards all; and consequently it is found worthy to be revered by all.

CHAPTER VII

Francis' Love for Poverty — His Needs
Are Supplied Miraculously

1   Among the supernatural gifts which Francis received
from God, the Generous Giver, his love for absolute poverty
constituted a special privilege which enabled him to grow
rich in spiritual wealth. He saw that it had been the constant companion of the Son of God, but that now it was
scorned by the whole world, and so he espoused it in undying love. For poverty's sake he abandoned his father and
mother and divested himself of everything he had. No
one was so greedy for gold as he was for poverty; no
treasure was guarded as jealously as he guarded this Gospel
pearl. He used to be particularly offended if ever he saw
anything contrary to poverty among the friars. From the
first moment of his religious life until his death, his sole
wealth consisted in a habit, a cord, and a pair of trousers,
and he was content with that.

The memory of the poverty felt by Christ and his Mother
often reduced him to tears and he called poverty the Queen
of the Virtues because it was so evident in the life of the
King of Kings and of the Queen, his Mother. When the
friars asked him privately what virtue made one dearest
to Christ, he replied as if revealing his closest secret, "Believe me, my brothers, poverty is the special way of salvation. It is the source of humility and the root of all perfection and its fruit is manifold, though unseen. This is
the treasure hidden in the field in the Gospel to buy which
we must sell all — and anything that cannot be sold should
be abandoned for love of it."

2   "Anyone who wants to practice perfect poverty," he
said, "must renounce all worldly wisdom and even secular
learning, to a certain extent. Divested of these possessions,

he will be able to make the great acts of God his theme (cf. Ps 73, 15-16) and offer himself naked to the embrace of the Crucified. Anyone who clings to his own opinions in the depths of his heart has not renounced the world perfectly."

When speaking about poverty to the friars, Francis often quoted the words of the Gospel, "Foxes have holes, and the birds of the air their resting-places; the Son of Man has nowhere to lay his head" (Mt 8, 20), and he gave orders that the houses they built should be small, like those of the poor. There the friars should live not as if the house belonged to them, but as strangers and pilgrims in a house which was not their own. It was part of a pilgrim's life, he said, to shelter under another's roof and pass on peacefully, longing for home. On a number of occasions, he ordered the friars to leave a house, or even had it pulled down, if he thought that it offended against Gospel poverty, either because the friars claimed the building as their own or because it was too sumptuous. He used to say that poverty was the basis of the whole Order; the whole structure of their life was founded on it, so that if it were solid, the Order would stand firm, but that if it were undermined, the whole fabric would be completely demolished.

3   He had been taught by a revelation that anyone entering the Order should begin by fulfilling the precept of the Gospel, "If you have a mind to be perfect, go home and sell all that belongs to you, and give it to the poor" (Mt 19, 21). In obedience to the Gospel and in order to avoid scandal, such as might arise if a friar retained his property, he never received anyone into the Order unless he had renounced everything and kept nothing for himself. When a man asked to be received to the Order in the Marches of Ancona, he told him, "If you want to join Christ's poor, give what you have to the poor in the world."

681

At that the candidate went off, but he was influenced by human affection to give his belongings to his relatives, not to the poor. When he came back and told the saint what he had done, Francis reproached him bitterly and said, "On your way, Brother Fly. You never left your home or your family. You gave what you had to your relatives and cheated the poor. You are not worthy of Christ's poor. You tried to begin your religious life by yielding to an earthly attachment and laid a worthless foundation for a spiritual building." The poor fellow immediately returned to his family and demanded his property; he had refused to give it to the poor and so he quickly abandoned the idea of embracing the religious life.

4   At another time the community at St. Mary of the Portiuncula was so much in need that they had nothing to offer the friars who came there visiting. Francis' vicar approached him and told him how badly off they were and asked him to allow them to keep some of the property which those entering the Order brought with them; then the friars could fall back on this when the need arose. Francis, who was not without his own share of divine guidance, replied, "My dear brother, God forbid that we should sin against the rule for anyone. I should prefer to see you strip our Lady's altar bare rather than have you commit the slightest sin against our vow of poverty or the observance of the Gospel. The Blessed Virgin will be better pleased to see her altar laid bare and the Gospel counsel observed perfectly, rather than to have the altar properly decorated and her Son's counsel violated, which we have promised to observe."

5   When the saint was journeying with a companion near Bari in Apulia, they came across a large purse on the road, which seemed to be bursting with money. His companion appealed to him and tried to persuade him to pick

it up and give the money to the poor, but Francis refused. The whole thing was a trick of the Devil, he added, pointing out that what his companion wanted him to do — to take what belonged to another and make a present of it — was sinful, not meritorious. They continued on, in a hurry to finish their journey. But the friar would not give in; he was deceived by a spirit of false generosity and he pestered the saint, saying that he had no interest in relieving the needs of the poor. Eventually Francis patiently agreed to return, in order to unmask the Devil's trickery, not to do what his companion wanted. They made their way back to the purse, together with a young man whom they met on the road. There the saint prayed for a little while and then he told his companion to pick up the wallet. The friar was dumbfounded and afraid; he could feel there was some evil influence at work. However, in obedience to the saint's command, he overcame his reluctance and stretched out his hand. Immediately a huge snake jumped out of the purse and disappeared with it, so that the friar was convinced beyond all shadow of doubt that it was the Devil who was there. The enemy's treacherous cunning was unmasked and Francis remarked to his companion, "For those who serve God, my brother, money is a Devil, a poisonous snake."

6   Some time afterwards St. Francis had an unusual experience while on his way to Siena on business. On the long, level, stretch between Campiglia and San Quirico he was met by three poor women who were exactly alike in height, age, and appearance. They greeted him with a new salutation, saying, "Welcome, Lady Poverty."

Francis was overcome with joy at the words in his love for true poverty. There was nothing he was more pleased to see people acclaim in him than the virtue they had singled out for praise. The three women disappeared from view all at once and the friars who accompanied the saint, when they reflected on their extraordinary similarity, their strange greeting, and their sudden disappearance, could only conclude that the whole episode held some mystical significance for the saint.

It seems that the three poor women, who were so alike and greeted him so strangely and disappeared so suddenly, represented the crowning beauty of Gospel perfection. Their sudden appearance indicated that Francis observed Gospel perfection equally in his poverty, chastity, and obedience, although he had chosen the privilege of poverty for his special boast, calling it his mother, his bride, and his lady fair. It was in poverty that he chose to surpass others, because it had shown him how to regard himself as the last of all. Whenever he saw anyone who was more poorly dressed than he, he immediately reproached himself and roused himself to imitate him. He was jealous of his poverty and he was afraid of being outdone, as he fought to deserve it. One day he met a beggar on the road and when he saw how poorly dressed he was, his heart was touched and he exclaimed sorrowfully to his companion, "His poverty puts us to shame. We have chosen poverty as our wealth and look, it is more resplendent in him."

7   For love of poverty Francis much preferred to use alms which had been begged from door to door, rather than those which had been given spontaneously. Whenever he was invited to a banquet in his honor by the nobility, he would always beg some bread at the neighboring houses first. Then he would take his place at the table, rich in his poverty. He did this once when he was the guest of the bishop of Ostia, who was a great friend of his, and when the bishop complained that he had dishonored him by going for alms when he was to eat at his table, he replied, "My lord, I have done you a great honor because I honored

684

a greater Lord. God is pleased with poverty, especially that poverty which involves voluntary begging for Christ's sake. This is the royal dignity which our Lord Jesus assumed when he became poor for our sake, so that he might make us rich by his poverty. It was his will to make us heirs and kings of the kingdom of heaven, if we are willing to become truly poor in spirit, and I refuse to relinquish this dignity for the sake of the deceptive wealth which has only been given you on loan for a short time."

8   When he encouraged the friars to quest for alms, Francis used to say, "Go, because in these last days the Friars Minor have been given to the world for its benefit, so that the elect may behave towards them in such a way as to deserve the praise of the Judge on the day of judgment and hear the words, 'When you did it to one of the least of my brethren here, you did it to me'" (Mt 25, 40). Therefore, he said that it was wonderful to be able to beg with the title of Friar Minor because our Lord himself had used it so clearly in the Gospel, when describing the reward given to the elect. Whenever he had the opportunity, he went begging on the principal feasts of the year; as he remarked, the words of the Psalmist, "Man should eat the food of angels" (Ps 77, 25) are fulfilled in God's poor, because the bread of angels is that which has been begged for love of God and given at the inspiration of the angels, and gathered from door to door by holy poverty.

9   One Easter Sunday he was staying at a hermitage which was so far from the nearest house that he could not go begging. Then he remembered our Lord who had appeared to the two disciples on the road to Emmaus that very day in the guise of a pilgrim, and he begged an alms from the friars themselves, like a pilgrim or a beggar. When he had received it humbly, he spoke to them, telling them how they should pass through this world like strangers and

685

pilgrims and celebrate the Lord's Pasch continually in poverty of spirit, like the Hebrews in the desert, the Pasch that is his passage from this world to the Father.

When Francis went for alms, he was moved by true liberty of spirit, not by greed, and so God the Father of the poor had special care for him.

10   St. Francis became very ill at Nocera one time and he was brought back to Assisi by an escort sent out by the townspeople. As they accompanied the saint on the way, they came to a little village called Satriano where they stopped for food because it was late and they were hungry. They tried a number of different houses but could find nothing to buy and had to return empty-handed. Then the saint told them, "You got nothing because you put more trust in your flies than in God." "Flies" was the term he used for money. "Go back to the houses you have tried already and ask the people in all humility to give you an alms, offering God's love as the only price. Do not imagine that it would be shameful or beneath your dignity. After the fall of Adam everything in the world has been given as an alms to the worthy and the unworthy by God, the great Almsgiver, in his generosity and kindness." The knights overcame their embarrassment and went begging for alms and got more for love of God than they had been able to buy. The villagers who were poor themselves were deeply moved by God's grace and they generously offered their services as well as anything else they had to give. Francis' wealthy poverty supplied the need which money had not been able to satisfy.

11   When he was lying ill at a hermitage near Rieti, Francis was attended by a doctor who did what he could for him. The saint had no means of recompensing him in his poverty, but God repaid his devoted efforts, so that he would not be without a reward here in this life. The doctor

had just spent all his money building a new house, when one of the walls cracked from top to bottom, so that the whole building threatened to collapse and it seemed humanly impossible to do anything about it. However, he placed all his trust in St. Francis and with complete faith he asked the friars to give him something which the saint had touched. After repeated requests he eventually got a small amount of hair and he put this in the crack one evening. When he got up in the morning, he found the opening closed so tightly that there was no trace of the crack and he could not pull out the hairs. He had ministered conscientiously to the failing body of God's saint and so he escaped the danger of having his home collapse.

12   Another time, while travelling to a hermitage where he planned to devote himself to prayer, St. Francis rode an ass belonging to a poor laborer because he was weak. It was summertime and, as the owner of the animal followed the saint into the mountains, he was exhausted by the long and gruelling journey. Fainting with thirst, he suddenly cried out after the saint. "I'll die of thirst, if I don't get a drink immediately." Francis dismounted there and then and knelt on the ground with his hands stretched out to heaven, and there he prayed until he knew that he had been heard. When he had finished, he told his benefactor, "Go to that rock and you will find running water. Christ in his mercy has made it flow there for you just now." By God's wonderful condescension which bows so easily to his servants a thirsty human being was able to drink from a rock, quenching his thirst from solid stone, by the power of one man's prayer. Water had never been found at that spot before and none could ever be found there afterwards, although a careful search was made.

13   In a later chapter we shall describe how Christ mul-

tiplied the food on board ship at the intercession of his servant Francis. Here it is sufficient to say that for a number of days the saint saved the whole crew from the danger of starvation with the small quantity of food he had received as alms. Just as he drew water from a rock in imitation of Moses, on this occasion he imitated Eliseus by multiplying their provisions.

Christ's poor, therefore, have nothing to fear. Francis' poverty was so well supplied that it provided miraculously for the needs of those who came to his aid, procuring food and drink and a house, when money or any other means could not be found. Poverty such as that will certainly never be left short of the necessities which God gives to everybody in the ordinary course of divine providence. If a solid rock gave drink in plenty to a poor man who was thirsty at the request of a beggar, nothing in the whole world will refuse its service to those who have left all for the Creator of all.

CHAPTER VIII

Francis' Loving Compassion and the Love Which Creatures Had for Him

1   Compassion, as St. Paul tells us, is all-availing and it filled the heart of Francis and penetrated its depths to such an extent that his whole life seemed to be governed by it. It was loving compassion which united him to God in prayer and caused his transformation into Christ by sharing his sufferings. It was this which led him to devote himself humbly to his neighbor and enabled him to return to the state of primeval innocence by restoring man's harmony with the whole of creation.

Loving compassion made him regard everything with affection but especially the souls which Jesus Christ redeemed with his precious blood. If he saw one of them being stained with sin, he grieved with such heartfelt pity that he seemed to be in travail over them continually, like a mother in Christ. This was the principal reason why he had such respect for those who preach God's word — by their labor and zeal for the conversion of sinners and their pastoral anxiety they beget children in the name of Christ, our dear Brother who was crucified for sinners. He was convinced that such a work of mercy was more acceptable to the merciful Father than any sacrifice, particularly if it was done in a spirit of perfect charity, more by example than by preaching, more by fervent prayer than by long-winded sermons.

2   St. Francis used to say that we should feel sorry for a preacher who sought his own glory in his work and not the good of his listeners, or who destroyed by the example of his bad life what he had accomplished by his teaching. Such a man was devoid of any true religious spirit. He maintained that an ordinary friar with no claim to eloquence was in a better position because he encouraged others to do good by his good example. He explained the phrase, "The barren womb bears many" (1 Kgs 2, 5) in this way, "The barren woman is my poor friar who is not appointed to bring forth children in the Church. But at the last judgment he will bring forth many, because then the Judge will set down to his glory all those whom he is now converting to Christ by his secret prayers. 'The fruitful mother is left to languish' (*ibid.*) means that the vain and loquacious preacher who now prides himself on those whom he imagines he has begotten by his own powers will see then that he had nothing to do with their salvation."

3   Francis was ablaze with fervid eagernesse and he longed for the salvation of souls with heartfelt compassion.

He used to say that it was like a sweet-smelling perfume to him or a soothing balm, when he heard that people were being converted to the way of truth as a result of the good name holy friars had won for themselves all over the world. When he was told of such incidents, he was overjoyed and he heaped his most welcome blessings on the friars who were responsible for bringing sinners to Christ's love.

On the other hand, those who harmed the Order by their evil deeds incurred the frightful penalty of his curse, as he said, "May God and all the saints of heaven curse those who obstruct and bring to ruin by their bad example what he has achieved in the past and continues to achieve by the holy friars of this Order, as I, too, curse them."

He was so upset when he saw inexperienced members of the Order being given scandal that he felt it would have been too much for him, if God had not upheld him in his mercy. As he prayed anxiously for his sons to God, the merciful Father, after he had been disturbed at the sight of some bad example, he heard the following answer, "Poor fellow, what are you worried about? When I made you shepherd of my Order, do you think that I ceased to be its principal protector myself? The very reason I chose you was because you had nothing to boast of, and so what I did in you would be attributed to divine grace, not to human effort. It is I who have called the friars; I will keep them and be their Shepherd. If some fall by the wayside, I will raise up others in their place. If they are not born, I will have them born. No matter how badly this Order is shaken, it will remain steadfast, through my gift."

4   In Francis' eyes the vice of detraction in particular seemed to be the antithesis of the religious spirit and an enemy of grace. He had a horror of it, like a snake-bite or a deadly pest, and he declared that it was an abomination in God's sight because the detractor feeds on the blood

of the souls which he kills with his tongue. Once when he heard a friar taking away another's good name, he turned to his vicar saying, "Quick, quick! Look into it carefully. If the friar accused is innocent, make an example of his accuser for all the others by correcting him severely." He sometimes sentenced a friar guilty of hurting another's good name to be deprived of his habit, adding that he should not raise his eyes to God until he had done his best to restore what he had taken. "A detractor," he used to say, "is guilty of greater wickedness than a robber, because Christ's law which reaches its perfection in love obliges us to desire the good of our neighbor's soul more than of his body."

5   Francis sympathized lovingly and compassionately with those stricken with any physical affliction and he immediately referred to Christ the poverty or deprivation he saw in anyone. He was kind and gentle by nature and the love of Christ merely intensified this. His soul melted at the sight of the poor or infirm and where he could not offer material assistance he lavished his affection. A friar once brusquely refused a beggar who had asked for an alms at an awkward moment. When Francis heard about it, he made the friar take off his habit in his love for the poor, and cast himself at the feet of the beggar, confessing his fault and begging his prayers and forgiveness. The friar obeyed humbly and Francis remarked gently, "My dear brother, when you see a beggar, you are looking at an image of our Lord and his poor Mother. When you see a sick person, remember the infirmities he bore for us." Francis saw Christ's image in every poor person he met and he was prepared to give them everything he had, even if he himself had urgent need of it. He even believed that they had a right to such alms, as if they belonged to them. When he was returning from Siena on one occasion, he met a beggar at a time when he himself was wearing a short cloak

over his habit because he was not well. At the sight of the poor man's destitution, Francis said to his companion, "We'll have to give this cloak back to that poor beggar, because it belongs to him. We only got it on loan until we found someone in greater need of it." His companion, however, knew well that the saint himself needed the cloak badly and he was reluctant to see him neglect himself while providing for someone else. "But," protested the saint, "God the great Almsgiver will regard it as a theft on my part, if I do not give what I have to someone who needs it more." Whenever he received anything for his needs from a benefactor, he always used to ask permission to give the article away, if he met someone poorer than himself. He spared absolutely nothing — cloaks, habits, books, or altarcloths — as long as he was in a position to do so, he gave them all to the poor, in order to obey the commandment of love; and when he met beggars carrying heavy loads on the road, he often took the weight on his own weak shoulders.

6   The realization that everything comes from the same source filled Francis with greater affection than ever and he called even the most insignificant creatures his brothers and sisters, because he knew they had the same origin as himself. However, he reserved his most tender compassion for those creatures which are a natural reflection of Christ's gentleness and are used in Sacred Scripture as figures of him. He often rescued lambs, which were being led off to be slaughtered, in memory of the Lamb of God who willed to be put to death to save sinners.

While he was staying at the monastery of San Verecundo in the diocese of Gubbio one time, a lamb was born there during the night. It was attacked immediately by a vicious sow which had no mercy on the innocent creature and killed it with one hungry bite. When he heard about it, the saint was deeply moved as he remembered the immaculate Lamb of God and he mourned for the death of the lamb before them all saying, "Brother lamb, innocent creature, you represented Christ in the eyes of men. A curse on the wicked beast which killed you. May no human being or any animal ever eat of it." There and then the vicious sow fell sick and after suffering for three days it evenutally expiated its crime by death. The carcass was thrown into the monastery moat where it lay for a long time and became as hard as a board, so that even the hungriest animal refused to eat it.

If cruelty in an animal led to such a terrible end, what will be the lot of evil men when the time of punishment comes eventually. In this incident the faithful, too, can see the power of Francis' tender love and how abundantly it filled him, so that it was acclaimed in their own way even by the animals.

7   When he was travelling near Siena, St. Francis came upon a large flock of sheep grazing in a field. He greeted them lovingly, as usual, and immediately they stopped grazing and ran to him, standing there with their heads erect and their eyes fastened on him. They showed their appreciation of him so clearly that the shepherds and the other friars were amazed to see the shearlings and even the rams jumping excitedly about him.

Another time he was offered a present of a sheep at the Portiuncula and he accepted it gladly in his love of innocence and simplicity, two virtues which the image of a sheep naturally recalls. He exhorted the animal to give God praise and avoid offending the friars, and the sheep was careful to follow his instructions, just as if it realized the affection he had for it. If it was entering the church and heard the friars singing in the choir, it would go down on one knee spontaneously and bleat before the altar of our Lady, the Mother of the Lamb, as if it were trying to greet her. At the elevation during Mass, it would bow profoundly on bended knees and reproach those who were not so devout by its very reverence, while giving the faithful an example of respect for the Blessed Sacrament.

On another occasion while in Rome, St. Francis had a lamb with him which he kept out of reverence for the Lamb of God; and when he was leaving, he gave it to Lady Jacoba di Settesoli to keep. The lamb accompanied its mistress to church and stayed there with her, refusing to leave until she left, just as if the saint had trained it in its spiritual exercises. When she was late getting up in the morning, the lamb nudged her with its horns and roused her with its bleats, urging her to hurry and get to church. She was amazed and became very fond of the animal which had been a disciple of St. Francis and was now a master of the religious life.

8   Another time St. Francis was offered a live hare at Greccio. He put it on the ground and left it free to go where it pleased, but the moment he called it, it jumped into his arms. He held it affectionately and seemed to pity it like a mother. Then, warning it gently not to let itself be caught again, he allowed it to go free. But every time he put it on the ground to let it off, the hare immediately jumped into his arms, as if in some mysterious way it realized the love he had for it. Eventually Francis had the friars bring it off to a safer place in the woods.

In the same way a rabbit which was caught on an island in Lake Trasimene was afraid of everyone else, but entrusted itself to Francis' embrace as if that were its home. When he was crossing Lake Piediluco on his way to Greccio, a fisherman offered him a water-bird. Francis took it gladly and then opened his arms to let it off but it would not go. The saint stood there praying with his eyes raised to heaven, and after a long time he came back to himself and once more encouraged the bird to fly away and praise

God. When he had given it his blessing, the bird showed its joy by the movements of its body and then it flew off. On the same lake he was offered a live fish which he addressed as brother, as usual, and put it back in the water beside the boat. The fish played about there in front of him, as if it were attracted by his affection, and would not go away until he gave it his permission with a blessing.

9   One time when Francis was walking with another friar in the Venetian marshes, they came upon a huge flock of birds, singing among the reeds. When he saw them, the saint said to his companion, "Our sisters the birds are praising their Creator. We will go in among them and sing God's praise, chanting the divine office." They went in among the birds which remained where they were, so that the friars could not hear themselves saying the office, they were making so much noise. Eventually the saint turned to them and said, "My sisters, stop singing until we have given God the praise to which he has a right." The birds were silent immediately and remained that way until Francis gave them permission to sing again, after they had taken plenty of time to say the office and had finished their praises. Then the birds began again, as usual.

A cicada used to perch on a fig-tree beside St. Francis' cell at the Portiuncula and sing there, inspiring the saint to praise God for its song, because he could admire the glory of the Creator in the most insignificant creature. Then one day he called it and when it hopped on to his hand as if it had been taught by God, he told it, "Sing, my sister cicada. Sing a song of praise to God your Creator." Immediately the cicada started to chirp and never stopped until the saint told it to go back to its usual perch. There it remained for a whole week and it came and went every day, singing at his command. Finally the saint remarked to his companions, "We must give our sister cicada permission

to go away. She has given us enough pleasure by her singing and inspired us to praise God for a whole week." Immediately he gave it leave, the cicada disappeared and was
never seen there again, as if it did not dare transgress his
command in the slightest way.

10   When Francis was ill at Siena, a pheasant which
had just been caught alive was sent to him by a nobleman.
The moment it saw the saint and heard his voice, the bird
stayed with him so affectionately that it refused to be
separated from him. They took it outside the friary to the
vineyard a number of times, to let it off, but it always ran
back to the saint, as if it had lived with him all its life.
Eventually they gave it to a man who often used to come to
see the saint, but immediately the bird stopped eating its
food, as if it did not like to be out of Francis' sight. When
they brought it back, it began to eat as soon as it saw Francis and gave every sign of being delighted.

When Francis arrived at the hermitage on Mount La
Verna to keep the fast in honor of St. Michael the Archangel, a flock of birds of all kinds wheeled about his cell,
singing and showing their joy at his arrival. They seemed
to be inviting their father to stay with them. When he saw
them, Francis remarked to his companion, "I see that it is
God's will we should stay here, our sisters the birds are so
glad to see us." During his stay there, a falcon which was
nesting at that spot became a great friend of his and woke
him every night with its song just at the time he used to
rise to say the office. The saint was delighted; by its anxious
care for him the bird allowed him no time for laziness. But
when he needed a longer rest than usual, the falcon had
pity on him and did not wake him up so early; as if it had
been instructed by God, it would then call him about dawn
with its bell-like song.

The joy shown by the varied flock of birds and the falcon's song certainly seem to have been a divine portent, indicating that Francis who was dedicated to the praise and worship of God was about to be praised aloft on the wings of contemplation and honored with the vision of the Seraph.

11   When St. Francis was living in the hermitage at Greccio one time, the local people were in a very bad way because of a series of disasters which had struck them. Ravenous packs of wolves had been known to attack human beings as well as livestock in the area and every year the corn and the vineyards were laid waste by hailstones. In the course of a sermon which he preached to them, the saint told them, "For the honor and glory of almighty God, I promise you that all these calamities will come to an end and God will shower his blessing on you, if you trust me and show that you want mercy for yourselves by making a good confession and bringing forth worthy fruits of repentance. But I promise you this too, if you are ungrateful and go back to your old ways, your afflictions will be renewed and be worse than ever, and God's anger will be redoubled." The townspeople did penance on his advice and from that time their troubles were at an end. The danger passed and the wolves and the hail did no more harm. In fact, hailstorms which devastated neighboring areas and were approaching their lands either stopped or changed course. The hail and the wolves kept the pact St. Francis had made, and as long as the people observed God's law as had been agreed they made no attempt to molest them, now that they were living good lives.

We should have the greatest reverence, therefore, for St. Francis' loving compassion which had such wonderful charm that it could bring savage animals into subjection and tame the beasts of the forest, training those which were tame already and claiming obedience from those which had rebelled against fallen mankind. This is that virtue which subjects all creation to itself and "is all-availing, since it promises well both for this life and for the next" (1 Tm 4,8).

CHAPTER IX

Francis' Passionate Love — His Longing for Martyrdom

1 No human tongue could describe the passionate love with which Francis burned for Christ, his Spouse; he seemed to be completely absorbed by the fire of divine love like a glowing coal. The moment he heard the love of God being mentioned, he was aroused immediately and so deeply moved and inflamed that it seemed as if the deepest chord in his heart had been plucked by the words. He used to say that to offer the love of God in exchange for alms was generosity worthy of a nobleman and that anyone who thought less of it than money was a fool. The incalculable worth of divine love was the only thing that could win the kingdom of heaven. He used to say, "Greatly to be loved is His love, who loved us so greatly."

Francis sought occasion to love God in everything. He delighted in all the works of God's hands and from the vision of joy on earth his mind soared aloft to the life-giving source and cause of all. In everything beautiful, he saw him who is beauty itself, and he followed his Beloved everywhere by his likeness imprinted on creation; of all creation he made a ladder by which he might mount up and embrace Him who is all-desirable. By the power of his extraordinary faith he tasted the Goodness which is the source of all in each and every created thing, as in so many rivulets. He seemed to perceive a divine harmony in the interplay of powers and faculties given by God to his creatures and like the prophet David he exhorted them all to praise God.

2   The memory of Christ Jesus crucified was ever present in the depths of his heart like a bundle of myrrh, and he longed to be wholly transformed into him by the fire of love. In his extraordinary devotion to Christ, he fasted every year for forty days, beginning at the Epiphany, the time when Christ himself lived in the desert. Then he would go to some lonely place and remain there shut up in his cell, taking as little food and drink as possible, as he spent all his time praying and praising God. He loved Christ so fervently and Christ returned his love so intimately that he seemed to have his Savior before his eyes continually, as he once privately admitted to his companions. He burned with love for the Sacrament of our Lord's Body with all his heart, and was lost in wonder at the thought of such condescending love, such loving condescension. He received Holy Communion often and so devoutly that he roused others to devotion too. The presence of the Immaculate Lamb used to take him out of himself, so that he was often lost in ecstasy.

3   He embraced the Mother of our Lord Jesus with indescribable love because, as he said, it was she who made the Lord of majesty our brother, and through her we found mercy. After Christ, he put all his trust in her and took her as his patroness for himself and his friars. In her honor he fasted every year from the feast of Saints Peter and Paul until the Assumption. He had an unshakeable love for the Angels who burn with a marvellous fire, so that they are taken out of themselves to God and long to inflame the souls of the elect. Each year he fasted and prayed in their honor for forty days from the feast of the Assumption. In his ardent zeal for the salvation of souls he was particularly devoted to St. Michael the Archangel because it is his task to bring souls before God.

The mercy of all the saints, who are like blazing coals in

God's temple, enkindled in Francis a divine fire, so that he embraced all the Apostles with the greatest affection, and especially Saints Peter and Paul because of their passionate love of Christ. In his reverence and love for them, he used to keep a special forty-day fast in their honor. Christ's beggar, Francis had only two mites of which he could dispose in generous charity, his body and his soul. But in his love for Christ he spent them so uninterruptedly that he seemed to be always immolating his body by rigorous fasting or his soul by its ardent desire. In this way he offered a visible holocaust like the priests in the court of the temple, while burning sweet-smelling herbs on the altar of his heart.

4   The fervor of Francis' love united him so closely to God that his heartfelt compassion was enlarged so as to embrace all those who shared the same gifts of nature and of grace as he. His tender love made him the brother of all creatures, and so it is no wonder that the love of Christ should unite him even more closely with those who bear the image of their Maker and are redeemed by the blood of their Creator. He would not think himself Christ's lover, if he did not compassionate the souls whom he redeemed. He used to say that nothing should take precedence over the salvation of souls, because it was for souls that the only-begotten Son of God hung upon the Cross. It was for souls that he wrestled in prayer, for souls that he was so active in preaching, and it was for them that he went beyond all limits in giving good example. When he was reproached for his excessive austerity, he would reply that he was intended to be an example for others; his innocent body, which had voluntarily become subject to the spirit, needed no punishment for sin, yet for the sake of good example, he inflicted frequent penances on it. It was solely for the sake of others that "he kept to the paths that

are hard to follow" (Ps 16, 4). He used to say, "I may speak with every tongue that men and angels use; yet, if I lack charity (1 Cor 13, 1-3) and fail to set others an example of virtue, I am of little use to them and none to myself."

5   In the fervor of his love he felt inspired to imitate the glorious victory of the martyrs in whom the fire of love could not be extinguished or their courage broken. Inflamed with that perfect love "which drives out fear" (1 Jn 4, 18), he longed to offer himself as a living victim to God by the sword of martyrdom; in this way he would repay Christ for his love in dying for us and inspire others to love God. In the sixth year of his religious life he decided to go to Syria to preach repentance and belief in Christ to the Moslems. He boarded a ship for the voyage, but they were driven to Dalmatia by contrary winds. There he stayed for some time, but he could not find a vessel to continue his journey and so, feeling that his desire had been frustrated, he approached a ship's crew who were leaving for Ancona and asked them to take him with them, for love of God. They refused because he had not the money for the fare, but Francis put his trust in God and stowed away on the ship with his companion. Then a man came along who seems to have been inspired by God, bringing the food they needed. He approached one of the sailors, a religious man, and told him, "Keep this safe for the friars who are hiding on board, and give it to them when the time comes." So it was that when the crew had run out of provisions because the gale-force winds prevented them from making progress for a number of days, the only food they had left was the alms which had been given to Francis. This was not very much but God multiplied it so that there was enough for everyone until they reached Ancona, although the storm continued and kept them at sea for many

days. When the crew realized that they had been saved from the danger of death on all sides by St. Francis, they gave thanks to God who shows how loveable and wonderful he is in his friends and servants. They were men who knew the dangers of the ocean and now they acknowledged the miracle God had worked for them.

6   When he left the coast, Francis went on a missionary journey about the countryside, sowing everywhere the seed of salvation and reaping an abundant harvest. However, the prize of martyrdom still attracted him so strongly that the thought of dying for Christ meant more to him than any merit he might earn by the practice of virtue. Therefore, he took the road towards Morocco with the intention of preaching the Gospel of Christ to the sultan and his subjects, hoping to win the palm of victory in this way. His desire bore him along so swiftly that even though he was physically weak he used to leave his companion behind and hurry ahead, as if he was enraptured in his anxiety to achieve his purpose. When he had travelled as far as Spain, however, he fell sick by God's design, because he had other plans in store for him. Prevented by his illness from gaining martyrdom, Francis realized that his life was still necessary for the family he had founded, even though he was convinced that death was a prize to be won, and so he returned to tend the flock which had been committed to his care.

7   Still his passionate love urged him on, and a third time he set out to preach faith in the Trinity among the pagans by shedding his blood. In the thirteenth year of his religious life he made his way to Syria where he courageously surmounted all dangers in order to reach the presence of the sultan of Egypt. At that time fierce fighting was taking place between the Christians and the Moslems and the two armies were drawn up opposite each other at

702

close quarters in the field, so that there was no means of passing safely from one to the other. The sultan had decreed that anyone who brought him the head of a Christian should be rewarded with a Byzantine gold piece. However Francis, the knight of Christ, was undaunted and had high hopes that he would soon realize his ambition. The thought of death attracted him, instead of frightening him, and so he decided to make the journey. He prayed and was strengthened by God, as he chanted the words of the Psalmist, "What though I walk with the shadow of death all around me? Hurt I feel none, while you are with me" (Ps 22, 4).

8   He took with him as his companion a friar named Illuminatus who was an enlightened man of great virtue, and as they set out on their way they met two lambs. The saint was overjoyed at the sight of them and he told his companion, "Place all your trust in God, because the words of the Gospel will be fulfilled in us, 'Remember, I am sending you out to be like sheep among wolves' (Mt 10, 16)." When they had gone farther, they were met by men of the sultan's army who fell upon them like wolves upon sheep and seized them fiercely. They ill-treated them savagely and insulted them, beating them and putting them in chains. Then, exhausted as they were by the ill-treatment they had received, they were dragged before the sultan by God's providence, just as Francis wished. The sultan asked them by whom and why and in what capacity they had been sent, and how they got there; but Francis replied intrepidly that they had been sent by God, not by man, to show him and his subjects the way of salvation and proclaim the truth of the Gospel message. He proclaimed the triune God and Jesus Christ, the Savior of all, with such steadfastness, with such courage and spirit, that it was clear the promise of the Gospel had been fulfilled in him, "I will give you such

eloquence and such wisdom as all your adversaries shall not be able to withstand, or to confute" (Lk 21, 15).

When the sultan saw his enthusiasm and courage, he listened to him willingly and pressed him to stay with him. Francis, however, was inspired by God to reply, "If you are willing to become converts to Christ, you and your people, I shall be only too glad to stay with you for love of him. But if you are afraid to abandon the law of Mahomet for Christ's sake, then light a big fire and I will go into it with your priests. That will show you which faith is more sure and more holy." To that the sultan replied, "I do not think that any of my priests would be willing to expose himself to the flames just to defend his faith, or suffer any kind of torture" (he had just caught a glimpse of one of his priests, an old and highly esteemed man, who slipped away the moment he heard Francis' proposal). Then Francis continued, "If you are prepared to promise me that you and your people will embrace the Christian religion, if I come out of the fire unharmed, I will enter it alone. But if I am burned, you must attribute it to my sins; on the other hand, if God saves me by his power, you must acknowledge 'Christ the power of God, Christ the wisdom of God' (cf. 1 Cor 1, 24) as true God, the Lord and Savior of all." The sultan replied that he would not dare to accept a choice like that, for fear of a revolt among his people.

Then he offered Francis a number of valuable presents, but the saint was anxious only for the salvation of souls; he had no interest in the things of this earth and so he scorned them all as if they were so much dust. The sultan was lost in admiration at the sight of such perfect disregard for worldly wealth and he felt greater respect than ever for the saint. He refused, or perhaps did not dare, to become a Christian, but at the same time he implored the saint to take the gifts and give them to the Christian poor or to churches, for his salvation. Francis, however, did not want to be bothered with money and besides he could see no sign of a genuinely religious spirit in the sultan, and so he absolutely refused to agree.

9   Francis now realized that there was no hope of converting the Moslems and that he could not win the crown of martyrdom, and so by divine inspiration he made his way back to the Christian camp. So it was that by the disposition of God's merciful providence and by the merits of his holiness, Christ's lover longed to die for him with all his heart, but never succeeded; he was saved from death to be afterwards decorated with an extraordinary privilege, and yet he had the merit of martyrdom for which he longed. The fire of divine love burned the more perfectly in his heart for all that it only became clearly visible in his flesh later on in his life. It was well for him — his body never fell by the tyrant's sword, yet it was marked with the likeness of the Lamb that was slain; he was doubly happy — "he did not lose his life in persecution, but he was not deprived of the martyr's palm" (cf. Breviary, Office of St. Martin of Tours, ant. at *Vespers*).

CHAPTER X

Francis' Devotion to Prayer

1   Saint Francis realized that he was an exile from the Lord's presence as long as he was at home in the body (cf. 2 Cor 5, 6, 8), and his love of Christ had left him with no desire for the things of this earth. Therefore, he tried to keep his spirit always in the presenc of God, by praying to him without intermission, so that he might not be without some comfort from his Beloved. Prayer was his chief comfort in this life of contemplation in which he became a fellow-citizen of the angels, as he penetrated the dwelling places of heaven in his eager search for his Beloved,

from whom he was separated only by a partition of flesh. Prayer was his sure refuge in everything he did; he never relied on his own efforts, but put his trust in God's loving providence and cast the burden of his cares on him in insistent prayer. He was convinced that the grace of prayer was something a religious should long for above all else. No one, he declared, could make progress in God's service without it, and he used every means he could to make the friars concentrate on it. Whether he was walking or sitting, at home or abroad, whether he was working or resting, he was so fervently devoted to prayer that he seemed to have dedicated to it not only his heart and his soul, but all his efforts and all his time.

2   Francis would never let any call of the Spirit go un- answered; when he experienced it, he would make the most of it and enjoy the consolation afforded him in this way for as long as God permitted it. If he was on a journey, and felt the near approach of God's Spirit, he would stop and let his companions go on, while he drank in the joy of this new inspiration; he refused to offer God's grace an ineffectual welcome (cf. 2 Cor 6, 1). He was often taken right out of himself in a rapture of contemplation, so that he was lost in ecstasy and had no idea what was going on about him, while he experienced things which were beyond all human understanding.

As he was passing through the crowded village of Borgo San Sepolcro on one occasion, the crowds rushed out to meet him in their excitement. He was riding an ass because he was not well and they pulled him and dragged him this way and that and crowded all about him, pushing against him on every side, but he seemed insensible to it all and, like a dead body, noticing nothing that was going on. Long after they had passed the village and left the crowds behind, they came to a leper hospital and then, as if coming back from far away, he inquired anxiously when they would be near Borgo San Sepolcro. His mind was fixed on the glory of heaven and so he had lost all track of changes of place or time or people. His companions knew from their own experience that this often happened to him.

3   Francis learned in his prayer that the presence of the Holy Spirit for which he longed was granted more intimately, when he was far from the rush of worldly affairs. Therefore, he used to seek out lonely places in the wilderness and go into abandoned churches to pray at night. There he often had to endure frightful attacks from the Devil who fought hand-to-hand with him and tried to withdraw him from prayer. But Francis was armed with supernatural weapons and the more violently they attacked him, the more courageous he was in practicing virtue and the more fervent in prayer. Then he would say with all confidence to Christ, "Hide me under the shelter of your wings, safe from the evildoers who wrong me' '(Ps 16, 8), and to the demons, "Do what you can to me, wicked and deceitful spirits. You can do nothing beyond what God allows you and I will be more than happy to suffer everything that God has decided I should endure." The devils in their pride could not stand such steadfast courage, and they retreated in confusion.

4   Then when he was alone and at peace, Francis would make the groves re-echo with his sighs and bedew the ground with his tears, as he beat his breast and conversed intimately with his Lord in hidden secrecy. Here he defended himself before his Judge; here he spoke with his Lover. Here, too, the friars who were watching occasionally heard him cry aloud, imploring God's mercy for sinners, and weeping for the passion of Christ, as if he saw it before his eyes.

He was occasionally seen raised up from the ground and surrounded with a shining cloud, as he prayed at night with his hands stretched out in the form of a cross. The brilliance which enveloped his body was a sign of the miraculous light which flooded his soul. There is good proof, too, that on such occasions the hidden depths of God's wisdom were revealed to him, although he never said anything about it except when love of Christ or the good of his neighbor demanded it. He was accustomed to say, "It often happens that an invaluable treasure is lost for the sake of a worthless reward, and God who bestowed his gift once will not be prevailed upon to give again so easily."

When he rejoined the friars after spending some time praying alone during which he was almost completely transformed, he used to be more careful than ever to appear just like the rest; any progress he had made interiorly might be robbed of its reward by the marks of esteem he would receive if it were visible. If he was among others when he was suddenly visited by his Lord, he would always try to hide it from them, so that no one might perceive the near approach of his Spouse. If he was praying with the friars, he completely avoided all deep breathing and sighing, or any outward display, either because he loved to keep things to himself or because he had descended into the depths of his heart and was lost in God. He often said to his companions, "If a religious is visited by God in his prayer, he should say, 'Lord, you have sent this comfort from heaven even though I am a sinner and unworthy, and I entrust it to your keeping because I know that I only steal your treasures.' When he leaves his prayer, such a person should seem as much a sinner and worthy of contempt as if he had received no new favor."

5   One time when Francis was praying at the Portiuncula, the bishop of Assisi came to visit him, as was his custom. As soon as he entered the enclosure, he went straight to the cell where the saint was praying. A little pre-

sumptuously, he knocked on the door and made as if to enter. But the moment he put his head in and saw the saint at his prayers, he was seized with a fit of trembling, while his limbs became rigid and he lost his speech. Then he was forcibly ejected and thrown back quite a distance the way he had come. He was dumbfounded and he went immediately to the other friars and, as God restored his speech, he immediately confessed his fault.

On another occasion the abbot of the monastery of San Giustino in the diocese of Perugia met the saint and immediately dismounted to pay him his respects and discuss his spiritual life with him. When they had conversed pleasantly for some time, the abbot took his leave and humbly asked Francis to pray for him. "I shall be glad to pray for you," the saint replied. After the abbot had gone a little way, Francis turned to his companion and said, "Wait a little while, brother. I want to keep the promise I have made." Then, as St. Francis prayed, the abbot suddently felt a warmth and joy of spirit he had never experienced before, so that he was lost in ecstasy and completely rapt out of himself in God. He remained like that for a short while and then, coming back to himself, he recognized the power of Francis' prayer. Ever afterwards he had greater love for the Order than before and he told the story to many people as a miracle.

6   St. Francis was accustomed to recite the divine office with great reverence and devotion. Although he suffered in his eyes, his stomach, his spleen, and his liver, he never leaned against the wall or partition for support while saying the psalms; he stood upright with his head uncovered and his eyes closely guarded, as he said the hours without shortening them. If he was travelling, he would stop, and he never abandoned this practice if it happened to be raining. He was want to say, "If our bodies must take their

food in peace — our bodies which will one day be the food of worms, just like the food we eat — what peace and quiet should not our souls enjoy to receive their food, which is the food of life?"

He regarded it as a serious fault if his mind wandered or was full of empty imaginings, when he was trying to pray. Whenever it happened, he confessed it without delay and atoned for his fault immediately. This careful attention had become a habit with him, so that he very seldom suffered troublesome distractions of this kind.

During Lent one year he carved out a dish to occupy his spare moments and prevent them from being completely lost. Then when he was reciting Tierce, it came into his mind and distracted him a little. At that he was seized with fervor and he threw the dish into the fire, saying, "I will make a sacrifice of it to God, because it interfered with his sacrifice." He said the psalms with as much attention and fervor as if he could see God there before his eyes and when God's name occurred in them he seemed to lick his lips, it gave him such pleasure.

He was anxious to honor God's name with special reverence, whether it merely came into his mind, or he saw it written down or heard it pronounced. He once told the friars that they should pick up any pieces of paper they found lying around and put them aside carefully, for fear that God's holy name might be trodden underfoot, if it happened to be written on them. When he pronounced the word "Jesus" or heard someone say it, he was filled with joy and he seemed to be completely transformed, as if he had suddenly tasted something marvellous or caught the strain of a beautfiul harmony.

7 Three years before he died St. Francis decided to celebrate the memory of the birth of the Child Jesus at Greccio, with the greatest possible solemnity. He asked and

obtained the permission of the pope for the ceremony, so that he could not be accused of being an innovator, and then he had a crib prepared, with hay and an ox and an ass. The friars were all invited and the people came in crowds. The forest re-echoed with their voices and the night was lit up with a multitude of bright lights, while the beautiful music of God's praises added to the solemnity. The saint stood before the crib and his heart overflowed with tender compassion; he was bathed in tears but overcome with joy. The Mass was sung there and Francis, who was a deacon, sang the Gospel. Then he preached to the people about the birth of the poor King, whom he called the Babe of Bethlehem in his tender love.

A knight called John from Greccio, a pious and truthful man who had abandoned his profession in the world for love of Christ and was a great friend of St. Francis, claimed that he saw a beautiful child asleep in the crib, and that St. Francis took it in his arms and seemed to wake it up.

The integrity of this witness and the miracles which afterwards took place, as well as the truth indicated by the vision itself, all go to prove its reality. The example which Francis put before the world was calculated to rouse the hearts of those who are weak in the faith, and the hay from the crib, which was kept by the people, afterwards cured sick animals and drove off various pestilences. Thus God wished to give glory to his servant Francis and prove the efficacy of his prayer by clear signs.

CHAPTER XI

Francis' Grasp of Sacred Scripture and His Spirit of Prophecy

1   St. Francis had never studied Sacred Scripture, but unwearied application to prayer and the continual practice of virtue had purified his spiritual vision, so that his keen

intellect was bathed in the radiance of eternal light and penetrated its depths. Free from every stain, his genius pierced to the heart of its mysteries and by affective love he entered where theologians with their science stand outside. Once he had read something in the sacred books and understood its meaning, he impressed it indelibly on his memory; anything he had once grasped carefully, he meditated upon continually.

When the friars asked him if he would allow the learned men who were entering the Order to continue the study of Sacred Scripture, he replied, "I do not mind, provided that they do not neglect prayer, after the example of Christ of whom we are told that he prayed more than he studied. They should not study merely in order to have something to say; they should study so as to practice what they have learned and then encourage others to do likewise. I want my friars to be true disciples of the Gospel and to progress in knowledge of truth in such a way as to grow in simplicity, without separating the simplicity of the dove from the cunning of the serpent, because our Lord himself joined them in one phrase."

2   St. Francis was consulted at Siena by a religious who was a doctor of theology about a number of difficult questions, and he expounded the secrets of divine wisdom so clearly that the theologian was amazed and exclaimed, "His theology soars aloft on the wings of purity and contemplation, like an eagle in full flight, while our learning crawls along the ground."

Francis was not an experienced teacher, but he had no lack of knowledge, so that he was able to resolve doubtful questions and bring all their implications to light. There is nothing strange in the fact that he should have been enlightened by God to understand the Scriptures; by his perfect conformity with Christ he practiced the truths which are contained in them and carried their Author in his heart by the abundant infusion of the Holy Spirit.

3   St. Francis possessed the spirit of prophecy to such a degree that he could foretell the future and read the secrets of men's hearts; he saw what went on in his absence as if it were present, and he often appeared to those who were far away. He was present when the Christian army was besieging Damietta, bearing the armor of faith, not that of war; and when he heard that they were preparing to attack, he was very upset and told his companion, "If they go into action today, God has revealed to me that it will be bad for the Christians. But if I say that, they will say I am a fool. And if I do not say it, my conscience will give me no rest. What do you think I should do?" His companion replied, "Brother, do not worry about being criticized. This will not be the first time you were called a fool. Obey your conscience and have more regard for God than for human beings." When he heard that, the saint jumped to his feet and brought his advice to the Christian army, telling them that they should not go into battle and that they would lose. True as his prophecy was, they made a joke of it and obstinately refused to turn back. They advanced and engaged in combat with the enemy, but the entire Christian army was routed, so that the action ended in disgrace, not in victory. Such havoc was wreaked on the Christian ranks that about six thousand men were killed or taken prisoners, and it was clear that the wisdom of a beggar was not to be scorned. As we read in Sacred Scripture, "There are times when a man of piety sees truth more clearly than seven sentinels high in a watch-tower" (Sir 37, 18)

4   Another time, after his return from overseas, St. Francis went to preach at Celano and a knight begged him to come and have dinner with him. So he came to the house and the whole family was there to celebrate his arrival

with his companions. However, before they sat down St. Francis offered praise to God, as was his custom, and stood there praying, with his eyes raised to heaven. When he had finished, he beckoned his generous host aside and told him, "Brother host, you persuaded me to come and dine with you, and I came. But now do what I tell you immediately, because you are going to eat in another world, not here on this earth. Confess all your sins with genuine sorrow and leave nothing untold. God means to reward you today for having given his poor such a warm welcome." The knight took his advice and confessed all his sins to Francis' companion, and put his affairs in order, doing everything he could to prepare for death. Eventually they took their places at table and just as they were beginning to eat, their host suddenly dropped dead, as the saint had foretold. So it was that as a reward for his kindness in showing hospitality, he received the reward given to prophets, because he had given a prophet the welcome due to a prophet, as we read in the Gospel (cf. Mt 10, 41). Warned by the saint's prophecy, the knight had prepared for immediate death and clad in the armor of repentance he escaped eternal damnation and was received into the eternal dwelling-places.

5   When the saint was lying sick at Rieti, a loose-living and worldly cleric named Gedeon fell seriously ill and took to his bed. He had himself brought before the saint and, together with those who were present, he begged him tearfully to bless him with the sign of the cross. But the saint replied, "How could I make the sign of the cross over you. You have indulged your passions for years without a thought for God's judgment. However, I shall make the sign of the cross over you, in the name of God, because your friends are pleading with me. But remember that you will have worse to suffer in future, if you go back to your

old ways once you have been cured. The sin of ingratitude always leaves people worse off than ever." The moment he made the sign of the cross, the sick man recovered and got up from his bed, praising God with the words, "I am saved." The bystanders heard his bones cracking like dry weed being broken. A short time afterwards, however he forgot God once more and gave his body over to impurity again. Then one night after he had dined in the house of a fellow canon and had gone to bed, the roof of the house fell in on them all. The others escaped, but he was trapped and killed, so that the last state of that man was worse than the first, by God's just retribution. He had shown himself ungrateful and turned his back on God when he should have been thankful for being forgiven. A crime which is repeated is doubly offensive.

6   A noble lady who was a very religious person, once came to St. Francis to tell him her troubles and ask for help. She had a husband who behaved cruelly towards her and tried to prevent her from serving Christ, and she begged the saint to pray for him that God in his goodness might touch his heart. When Francis heard her story, he told her, "Go in peace and you can be sure your husband will be a comfort to you in the near future." And he added, "Tell him from God and from me that this is the time of mercy, but that the day of retribution must follow." He gave her his blessing and the woman went off and gave her husband the message. There and then the Holy Spirit came upon him and he became a new man, so that he answered gently, "Let us serve God together and save our souls." At his wife's suggestion they lived a life of continence for years and they both died the same day.

St. Francis' supernatural gifts were certainly extraordinary; they enabled him to give back life to aging limbs and move stubborn hearts to repentance, while the amazing ciarity of his spirit allowed him to see into the future and read the secrets of consciences. Like a second Eliseus, he had received a double share of the spirit of the prophet Elias.

7   St. Francis once told a friend of his in Siena what would become of him eventually and the theologian who had asked him to explain the Scriptures for him heard about it. He went to the saint and asked if he had really said what this man claimed. Francis not only admitted that he had said it but, as the theologian was so anxious to know what was going to happen to someone else, he foretold what would become of him in the end. And, to convince him all the more, he mentioned a scruple which he had on his conscience and which he had never revealed to anyone and cured him of it with sound advice. To prove the truth of Francis' prophecy, the religious in question eventually died the way he had foretold.

8   When St. Francis was on his way home from overseas, he was accompanied by Brother Leonard of Assisi. He was tired and worn out and he rode on an ass for part of the journey, while his companion walked. Brother Leonard, too, was very tired and, yielding to human weakness, he began to complain to himself, "My family was better off than his and now I have to walk and lead his ass, while he gets a ride." When this thought came to his mind, the saint suddenly jumped off the ass and exclaimed, "Brother, it is not right that I should ride while you have to walk. You were of higher birth and position in the world than I." Brother Leonard was dumbfounded and overcome with embarrassment; he realized that he had been caught and he fell at Francis' feet and tearfully confessed his fault, begging his forgiveness.

9   Another friar who was a good religious and very

716

devoted to St. Francis had the idea that anyone who enjoyed the saint's intimate affection would enjoy God's favor and that the person to whom he refused his friendship would be rejected by God. He was obsessed with this idea and it disturbed him; he longed to be on close terms with the saint, but he never told his secret to anyone. Then one day Francis invited him to come to him with every sign of affection and told him, "Do not let these ideas disturb you, my son. You are most dear to me, among all my special friends, and I am only too glad to show you all the love and friendship I can." The friar was amazed and he became more attached to the saint than ever. As he grew in the love of Francis, he was showered with still greater gifts by the grace of the Holy Spirit.

When St. Francis was living in his cell on Mount La Verna, one of his companions wanted to have some short phrases of the Bible in the saint's own hand-writing; he was being assailed by a violent temptation of the spirit and he was sure it would put an end to it, or at least make it easier to bear. He was all on edge and he was worn out with longing, but he was so shy that he was afraid to tell the saint what he wanted. However, Francis learned from the Holy Spirit what his companion was afraid to tell him, and he asked him to bring a pen and paper. Then he wrote a number of phrases in praise of God with his own hand and added a blessing for the friar saying, "Take this piece of paper and keep it carefully as long as you live." The friar took the gift he wanted so badly and his temptation vanished immediately. The page of writing was afterwards preserved and worked miracles, testifying to St. Francis' wonderful power.

10   There was another friar who was a very holy man to all appearances and lived an exemplary life, though he was a law unto himself in many ways. He spent all his time

praying and he observed silence so carefully that he always made his confession by signs, not by words. St. Francis happened to come to the friary one time and he saw this friar and spoke to the others about him. They had nothing but praise for him, but the saint told them, "My dear brothers, please do not praise him like that. It is a trick of the Devil. You will soon see for sure that it is a temptation of Satan, a devilish trick." The friars did not take his words seriously; they were convinced that so many clear indications of holiness could never mask a treacherous fraud. A few days later, however, the friar abandoned the Order and the penetrating insight which the saint had into the secrets of his heart became clear.

In the same way Francis often foretold accurately the fall of those who seemed to stand firm, and the conversion of others who seemed confirmed in evil. He seemed to have had access to the source of eternal light, in the miraculous splendor of which he saw what went on at a distance, as if it were before his eyes.

11   St. Francis was praying in his cell and interceding before God for the friars one day, when his vicar was presiding at a Chapter. There one of the friars, under some pretext or other, refused to submit to obedience and Francis became aware of it in spirit. He called a member of the community and told him, "Brother, I saw the Devil on that friar's back, holding him tightly by the neck. With a wicked spirit like that in control, it is no wonder that he refused to be guided by obedience and gave rein to his own inclination. But the moment I prayed to God for him, the Devil went off in confusion. Now go and tell that friar to submit to obedience immediately." When the friar heard the message, he repented immediately and humbly cast himself at the vicar's feet.

12   Another time two friars made a long journey to

Greccio to see the saint and get his blessing, which they had wanted for years. When they arrived, he could not be found; he had already left the friary and gone off to his private cell. They were very disappointed, as they took their leave; but then as they went down the path, the saint came out of his cell unexpectedly and called after them. He could not possibly have heard of their arrival or departure by any human means, but he blessed them in Christ's name with the sign of the cross, just as they desired.

13   Two friars from the Terra di Lavoro once came to see St. Francis. The elder of the two had given his companion a bad example; and when they met the saint, he asked the younger friar how his companion had behaved on the way. The friar replied saying that he had behaved, "well enough," but Francis told him, "Be careful, brother, not to tell lies under the pretext of obedience. I know well enough how he behaved, but just wait and see." The friar was amazed that he should know in spirit what went on at such a distance. A few days later the friar who had misbehaved abandoned the Order and left; he neglected to ask the saint's forgiveness and refused to submit to correction. This single incident demonstrated two things clearly: the justice of God's judgments, and the penetrating power of the spirit of prophecy.

14   That Francis appeared in person, by God's power, to those who were absent, is proved beyond all doubt from what we have written in an earlier chapter; it is sufficient to recall how he appeared to the friars in a chariot of fire, and to the Chapter of Arles in the form of a cross. There can be no doubt that this was due to a special disposition of Divine Providence; his miraculous appearance in person was intended to show how close and rseponsive his spirit was to the light of eternal wisdom. As we read

719

in the Book of Wisdom, "There is nothing so agile that it can match wisdom for agility; age after age, she finds her way into holy men's hearts, turning them into friends and spokesmen of God" (Wis. 7, 24 and 27). God, the supreme Teacher, usually reveals his mysteries to the simple, to those who are poor and despised. We can see this first of all in the case of David, the greatest of the prophets, and then in St. Peter, the Prince of the Apostles, and now we see it once more in the case of Francis, Christ's poor beggar. They were simple men with no claim to learning, but they won renown under the guidance of the Holy Spirit; David was a shepherd and he was chosen to become a leader of the Synagogue, to lead the flock God saved from Egypt; Peter was a fisherman and he was chosen to fill a net, which is the Church, with a multitude of faithful. Francis, however, was a trader and he was appointed to buy the pearl which is the Gospel life, selling everything he had for Christ's sake.

CHAPTER XII

The Efficacy of Francis' Preaching — His Powers of Healing

1   Francis, Christ's faithful servant and minister, was anxious to behave always with perfect loyalty to him, and so he concentrated especially on practicing those virtues in which, by the inspiration of the Holy Spirit, he knew God took the greatest pleasure.

On one occasion he fell victim to a serious doubt; and some time afterwards, when he returned from where he had been praying, he put it before the friars who were closest to him, to have it resolved. "What do you think of this, Brothers?" he said. "Which do you think is better? That I should devote all my time to prayer, or that I should go about preaching. I am a poor and worthless religious. I have no education and I am inexperienced in speaking; I have received the gift of prayer rather than that of preaching. Besides, prayer earns merit and a multitude of special favors, while preaching seems to be only a way of sharing the gifts which have been received from heaven. Prayer helps to purify the desires of the heart and unites a person to the one, true, and supreme Good, while giving an increase of virtue. The labor of preaching allows dust to enter into the soul and involves a lot of distraction and relaxation of religious discipline. In prayer we talk to God and listen to him and live a life worthy of the angels, with the angels for our companions. When preaching, we have to descend to the level of human beings and live among them as one of them, thinking and seeing and hearing and speaking about human affairs. But, on the other hand, there is one argument which seems to count more than all the rest in God's eyes and it is this: the only-begotten Son of God, who is Wisdom itself, came down from the Father's embrace to save souls. He wanted to teach the world by his own example and bring a message of salvation to the men whom he had redeemed at the price of his Precious Blood, washing them clean in it and upholding them by its taste. He kept nothing for himself, but generously surrendered all for our salvation. We are bound to act always according to the model which has been set before us in him as on some high mountain, and so it seems that it is more in accordance with God's will that I should renounce the peace of contemplation and go out to work." He discussed this problem with the friars over a number of days, but he could not make up his mind which course of action he should choose as being more pleasing to Christ. The spirit of prophecy had enabled him to penetrate the deepest secrets, but he was unable to solve his own difficulty satisfactorily. That was the way God wanted it, so that Francis might remain humble and the value of preaching might be proved by a revelation from heaven.

2   Francis had learned deep secrets from the Teacher of all, but he was a true Friar Minor and he was not ashamed to ask advice from those who were not as advanced as he. He was always anxious to discover how or in what way he could serve God more perfectly according to his will. As long as he lived this was his greatest desire, the sum total of his philosophy, to inquire from everybody, learned or unlearned, perfect or imperfect, young or old, what was the most heroic way to reach the summit of perfection.

He now chose two of the friars and sent them to Brother Silvester. Silvester was the man who had seen a cross coming from his mouth, and he spent all his time in prayer on the mountain above Assisi. They were to tell him to ask God to solve his doubts and send him the answer in God's name. He sent the same message to St. Clare, telling her to pray with her sisters and find out God's will by means of the holiest and most simple of the sisters who lived under her. By the inspiration of the Holy Spirit Brothers Silvester and St. Clare both came to the same conclusion. It was God's will that Francis should go out to preach as a herald of Christ.

When the friars returned and told the saint God's will as they had learned it, he refused to delay and set out immediately. He left with such eagerness to obey God's command and he travelled so quickly that the hand of God seemed to be upon him, giving him new strength from heaven.

3   When he was near Bevagna, he came to a spot where there was a huge flock of birds of various kinds. The moment he saw them, he ran to them and greeted them as if they understood, and they all turned towards him and waited for him. Those that had perched on the bushes bent their heads, when he came near, and looked at him in an extraordinary way. He went straight up to them and ap-

pealed to them all to hear the word of God saying, "My brothers, you have a great obligation to praise your Creator. He clothed you with feathers and gave you wings to fly, appointing the clear air as your home, and he looks after you without any effort on your part." As he continued speaking to them like this, the birds showed their pleasure in a wonderful fashion; they stretched out their necks and flapped their wings, gazing at him with their beaks open. In his spiritual enthusiasm Francis walked among them, brushing them with his habit, and not one of them moved until he made the sign of the cross and gave them permission to go. Then they all flew away together with his blessing. His companions who were waiting on the road saw everything and when the saint rejoined them, in the purity and simplicity of his heart, he began to reproach himself for his negligence in never preaching to the birds before.

4   Continuing his journey, Francis preached in the neighboring villages, and eventually he came to Alviano. Here he summoned the whole population and called for silence, but he could scarcely be heard above the cries of the swallows which were nesting there and making a lot of noise. He spoke to them, while the whole crowd listened, and said, "My sisters, it is my turn to speak now. You have said enough already. Listen to God's word and be quiet until the sermon is over." Immediately they all became silent, just as if they understood, and they never moved until the whole sermon was finished. The onlookers were amazed and gave glory to God. The story of this miracle was told far and wide, so that people had great reverence for the saint and were moved to greater faith.

5   In Parma, for example, a dedicated student who was studying diligently with a number of others was annoyed by the screeching of a swallow and he remarked to his companions, "This must be one of the birds that disturbed St.

Francis when he was preaching, until he told them to be quiet." Then he turned to the swallow and commanded it confidently, "In the name of God's servant Francis, I command you to come to me and keep quiet." The moment it heard Francis' name, the bird became quiet, as if it had learned its lesson from him, and gave itself into the student's hands, as if they were a safe refuge. The student was dumbfounded and immediately let the bird go; he never heard it screeching again.

6   Another time when St. Francis was preaching on the seashore at Gaeta, the crowds pressed in on him in order to touch him. He had a horror of such popular enthusiasm and he jumped into a small boat which was drawn up on the beach. There and then the boat moved out from the shore without the help of oars, as if it were guided by some intelligent power, while the whole multitude looked on in amazement. When it reached a certain distance out, it stopped and stayed there without moving, while the saint preached to the people on the shore. When he was finished and the crowd left after seeing the miracle and getting his blessing, and could no longer bother him, the boat returned to land of its own accord.

A person would certainly have to be really perverse and obstinate to refuse to listen to St. Francis' preaching. Even dumb creatures submitted to his miraculous powers and inanimate objects came to his aid when he preached, as if they had life.

7   Christ, the power of God, Christ the wisdom of God (1 Cor 1, 24), whom the Spirit of God had anointed, was with his servant Francis in everything he did, lending him eloquence in preaching sound doctrine and glorifying him by the extraordinary power of his miracles. Francis' words were like a blazing fire which penetrated the depths of the heart and filled the minds of his hearers with wonder. They

had no claim to any literary style, but gave every sign of being the result of divine inspiration.

He was due to preach before the pope and the cardinals on one occasion and at the suggestion of the bishop of Ostia he learned a carefully prepared sermon by heart. But when he stood before them all to deliver his edifying message, his mind went blank and he could not remember a word. He told them what had happened quite humbly and invoked the aid of the Holy Spirit. Then his tongue was suddenly unloosed and he spoke so eloquently that he moved the hearts of his exalted listeners to true sorrow, and it was clear that it was the Spirit of God who spoke, not he.

8   Francis had first convinced himself of the truth of what he preached to others by practicing it in his own life and so he proclaimed the truth confidently, without fear of reproof. He denounced evil wherever he found it, and made no effort to palliate it; from him a life of sin met with outspoken rebuke, not support. He spoke with equal candor to great and small and he was just as happy addressing a handful of listeners as a large gathering. Men and women of every age flocked to see and hear this new preacher who had been given to the world by God, as Francis moved from place to place preaching fervently, "the Lord aiding him, and attesting his word by the miracles that went with him" (Mk 16, 20). Francis, the herald of truth, cast out devils by the power of God's name and healed the sick. By the efficacy of his preaching he moved hearts which had become hardened to repentance — which is greater still — and restored health to bodies and souls. We can see this from some of the miracles which he worked and which we shall now describe by way of illustration.

9   In Tuscany the saint was welcomed warmly by a knight who gave him hospitality and then pleaded with

him urgently for his only son who had been crippled since birth. Francis raised his hand over him in blessing and cured him instantly, so that strength came to his whole body even as they looked at him. The boy was completely cured and got back his strength; he got up there and then, "walking, and leaping, and giving praise to God" (Acts 3, 8).

At the request of the Bishop of Narni, Francis made the sign of the cross from his head to his feet over a paralytic who had lost the use of his limbs, and restored him to perfect health.

In the diocese of Rieti there was a boy who was so bloated that he had not been able to see his feet for four years. His mother brought him tearfully to St. Francis and the moment he laid his hands upon him, the boy was cured.

At Orte there was a boy who was crippled, so that his head was bent down to his feet and some of his bones were broken. When Francis made the sign of the cross over him at his parents' request, he was cured instantly and was able to stand upright.

10   A woman in Gubbio whose hands were withered and bent, so that she could do nothing with them, was cured instantly when Francis made the sign of the cross over her in God's name. There and then she returned home and prepared some food for him and for the poor with her own hands, like St. Peter's mother-in-law in the Gospel.

In the village of Bevagna a girl who was blind recovered her sight, when he anointed her eyes three times with spittle, in the name of the Blessed Trinity.

A woman in Narni recovered her sight, when he made the sign of the cross over her.

There was a boy in Bologna who had one eye covered with a malignant growth, so that he could see nothing with it and nothing could be done for him. When St. Francis made the sign of the cross over him from his head to his feet, he recovered his sight so completely that when he afterwards joined the Order of Friars Minor, he used to say that he could see much better with the eye which had been cured than with the one which had always been sound.

At San Gemini St. Francis was given hospitality by a man whose wife was troubled by an evil spirit. The saint prayed and then commanded the Devil in virtue of obedience to go out of her. By God's power he was driven out so quickly that it proved beyond all doubt that the Devil's obstinate pride cannot resist the power of obedience.

In Città di Castello an evil spirit which had taken violent possession of a woman went off in a rage, when he had been commanded under obedience by St. Francis, and left the woman who had been possessed free in body and soul.

11   One of the friars was suffering from such a terrible affliction that many were convinced it was a case of diabolical possession, not a physical disorder. It often seized him with such force that he rolled about, foaming at the mouth, while his limbs contracted or stretched out and were twisted and turned, or sometimes rigid and inflexible. At times he was stretched at full length and raised from the ground until his feet were on a level with his head. Then he would suddenly fall to the earth again. Francis was full of pity for him in his incurable affliction and he sent him a mouthful of the bread he was eating. The sick friar improved so much at the taste of it that he never suffered from his affliction again.

In the territory of Arezzo a woman had been in labor for a number of days and was at death's door, so that there was no hope for her and only God could save her. Francis happened to pass by that way, riding on horseback because he was ill, and when the animal was being returned to

727

its owner, it was brought through the village where the woman was. When the local people learned this was the horse St. Francis had used, they took the reins and laid them on the dying woman. The moment they touched her, the danger passed and she gave birth in perfect safety.

A man from Città della Pieve who was a good and sincere person had a cord which St. Francis had worn. There were some people suffering from various illnesses in the town, and he visited their homes and gave the patients a drink of water in which he had dipped the cord. Many were cured in this way.

Sick people who ate bread which Francis had touched often made a quick recovery, by God's power.

12   Because of the extraordinary miracles which highlighted his preaching, the people listened to St. Francis' words as if an angel from God were speaking. The extraordinary degree of virtue he had attained, and his spirit of prophecy; the power of his miracles, together with his divine appointment to preach, and the obedience irrational creatures paid him; the profound change of heart in those who heard him, and the fact that he had been taught by the Holy Spirit without the aid of man, and commissioned to preach by the Supreme Pontiff as the result of a revelation, in addition to the rule in which the approach to preaching is laid down, and which was approved by Christ's Vicar, together with the mark of the Great King which was impressed on his body like a seal — these were all so many testimonies which proclaimed before the whole world that Christ's Francis deserved to be respected because of his office, to be believed because of his teaching, and to be admired for his sanctity, and that therefore he preached Christ's Gospel as a spokesman from God himself.

CHAPTER XIII

The Stigmata of St. Francis

1   St. Francis never failed to keep himself occupied doing good; like the angels Jacob saw on the ladder (cf Gn 28, 12), he was always busy, either raising his heart to God in prayer, or descending to his neighbor. He had learned how to distribute the time in which he could gain merit wisely, devoting part of it to his neighbor by doing good, and part to the restful ecstasy of contemplation. According to the demands of time or circumstances he would devote himself wholly to the salvation of his neighbor, but when he was finished, he would escape from the distracting crowds and go into solitude in search of peace. There he was free to attend exclusively to God and he would cleanse any stain he had contracted while living in the midst of the world.

Two years before his death, after a period of intense activity, he was led by Divine Providence to a high mountain called La Verna, where he could be alone. There he began a forty-day fast in honor of St. Michael the Archangel, as was his custom, and he soon experienced an extraordinary in-pouring of divine contemplation. He was all on fire with heavenly desires and he realized that the gifts of divine grace were being poured out over him in greater abundance than ever. He was borne aloft not as one who would search curiously into the divine majesty and be crushed by its glory (cf. Prv 25, 27), but as a faithful and wise servant anxious only to discover God's will, which he wanted to obey with all his heart and soul.

2   By divine inspiration he learned that if he opened the Gospels, Christ would reveal to him what was God's will for him and what God wished to see realized in him. And so Francis prayed fervently and took the Gospel book from

the altar, telling his companion, a devout and holy friar, to open it in the name of the Blessed Trinity. He opened the Gospel three times, and each time it opened at the passion, and so Francis understood that he must become like Christ in the distress and the agony of his passion before he left the world, just as he had been like him in all that he did during his life. His body had already been weakened by the austerity of his past life and the fact that he had carried our Lord's Cross without interruption, but he was not afraid and he felt more eager than ever to endure any martyrdom. The unquenchable fire of love for Jesus in his goodness had become a blazing light of flame, so that his charity could not succumb even before the flood-waters of affliction (cf. Ct 8, 6-7).

3   The fervor of his seraphic longing raised Francis up to God and, in an ecstasy of compassion, made him like Christ who allowed himself to be crucified in the excess of his love. Then one morning about the feast of the Exaltation of the Holy Cross, while he was praying on the mountainside, Francis saw a Seraph with six fiery wings coming down from the highest point in the heavens. The vision descended swiftly and came to rest in the air near him. Then he saw the image of a Man crucified in the midst of the wings, with his hands and feet stretched out and nailed to a cross. Two of the wings were raised above his head and two were stretched out in flight, while the remaining two shielded his body. Francis was dumbfounded at the sight and his heart was flooded with a mixture of joy and sorrow. He was overjoyed at the way Christ regarded him so graciously under the appearance of a Seraph, but the fact that he was nailed to a cross pierced his soul with a sword of compassionate sorrow.

He was lost in wonder at the sight of this mysterious vision; he knew that the agony of Christ's passion was not in keeping with the state of a seraphic spirit which is immortal. Eventually he realized by divine inspiration that God had shown him this vision in his providence, in order to let him see that, as Christ's lover, he would resemble Christ crucified perfectly not by physical martyrdom, but by the fervor of his spirit. As the vision disappeared, it left his heart ablaze with eagerness and impressed upon his body a miraculous likeness. There and then the marks of nails began to appear in his hands and feet, just as he had seen them in his vision of the Man nailed to the Cross. His hands and feet appeared pierced through the center with nails, the heads of which were in the palms of his hands and on the instep of each foot, while the points stuck out on the opposite side. The heads were black and round, but the points were long and bent back, as if they had been struck with a hammer; they rose above the surrounding flesh and stood out from it. His right side seemed as if it had been pierecd with a lance and was marked with a livid scar which often bled, so that his habit and trousers were stained.

4   When he realized that he could not conceal the stigmata which had been imprinted so plainly on his body from his intimate companions, he was thrown into an agony of doubt; he was afraid to make God's secret publicly known, and he did not know whether he should say what he had seen, or keep it quiet. He called some of the friars and asked them in general terms what he should do. One of them, who was called Illuminatus, was enlightened by God and he realized that some miracle had taken place because the saint was still completely dazed. He said to him, "Brother, remember that when God reveals his secrets to you, it is not for yourself alone; they are intended for others too. If you hide something which was intended to do good to many others, then you have every reason to fear that you

will be condemned for burying the talent given to you."
Francis often said, "It is for me to keep my secret to
myself," but when he heard these words, he described the
vision he had just seen apprehensively, adding that the Person who had appeared to him had told him a number of
secrets which he would never reveal to anyone as long as
he lived.

We can only conclude from this that the message given
him by the Seraph who appeared to him on the Cross was
so secret that it could not be communicated to any human
being.

5   True love of Christ had now transformed his lover
into his image, and when the forty days which he had intended spending in solitude were over and the feast of St.
Michael had come, St. Francis came down from the mountain. With him he bore a representation of Christ crucified
which was not the work of an artist in wood or stone, but
had been reproduced in the members of his body by the
hand of the living God. "Kings have their counsel that
must be kept secret" (Tob 12, 7), and so Francis who realized that he shared a royal secret did his best to conceal the
sacred stigmata. However, it is for God ·to reveal his wonders for his own glory; he had impressed the stigmata on
St. Francis in secret, but he publicly worked a number of
miracles by them, so that their miraculous, though hidden,
power might become clearly known.

6   In the province of Rieti a fatal disease had attacked
cattle and sheep and carried great numbers of them off so
quickly that nothing could be done for them. Then a devout man was told in a vision at night to go immediately to
the friars' hermitage where St. Francis was staying and
get the water with which he had washed his hands and
feet and sprinkle it over the live-stock. He got up in the
morning and went to the hermitage and got the water se-

cretly from the saint's companions. Then he sprinkled the sick cattle and sheep. The animals were lying on the ground exhausted, but the moment that a mere drop of the water touched them, they immediately recovered their normal strength and stood up and hurried off to pasture, as if there had never been anything wrong with them. The miraculous power of water which had touched the stigmata banished the disease and saved the live-stock from the fatal sickness.

7   Before St. Francis went to stay on La Verna it often happened that clouds would form over the mountain and violent hailstorms would devastate the crops. After his vision, however, the hail stopped, much to the amazement of the local people. The unusually clear skies proclaimed the extraordinary nature of his vision and the power of the stigmata which he received there.

One winter-time, because he was weak and the road was bad, the saint was riding an ass belonging to a poor man. It was snowing and the approach of darkness made it impossible for them to reach shelter, so that they had to spend the night under the lee of an overhanging cliff. Francis heard his benefactor grumbling to himself and turning this way and that; he was wearing only a few clothes and he could not fall asleep in the biting cold. He himself was ablaze with the fervor of divine love and he stretched out his hand and touched him. At the touch of his hand, which was warm with the heat of the coal used to purify the lips of the prophet Isaias, the cold disappeared and the man felt as warm as if he had been hit with a blast of hot air from an oven. He immediately felt better in body and soul and he slept more soundly in the rocks and the blizzard until morning than he had ever slept in his own bed, as he used to say afterwards.

It is certain, therefore, that the stigmata were impressed

upon St. Francis by God's power, because it is God who purifies, illuminates, and inflames by the intervention of the Seraphim. These sacred wounds purified animals of disease and granted clear skies, as well as physical warmth. This was proved more clearly than ever after Francis' death by the miracles which we shall describe in their own place.

8   Francis was very careful to try and hide the treasure he had found in the field (cf. Mt 13, 44), but he could not prevent everybody from seeing the stigmata in his hands and feet, although he always kept his hands covered and wore shoes. A number of the friars saw them during his lifetime, and to put the matter beyond all doubt they testified to this under oath, although they were good religious and deserved to be believed. Some of the cardinals who were close friends of the saint also saw them and celebrated their praise in various hymns and antiphons which they composed in his honor, thus bearing witness to the truth in their words and writings. In a sermon which he preached in public and at which I was present with a number of other friars, His Holiness Pope Alexander asserted that he had seen the stigmata with his own eyes during the saint's lifetime. More than fifty friars with St. Clare and her nuns and innumerable lay people saw them after his death. Many of them kissed the stigmata and felt them with their own hands, to prove the truth, as we shall describe later.

However, Francis succeeded in covering the wound in his side so carefully that no one could get more than a glimpse of it during his lifetime. A friar who used to wait on him carefully gently prevailed upon him to take off his habit and have it shaken out, and as he watched closely he saw the wound. He put three of his fingers on it immediately, so that he was able to feel as well as see how big it was. The friar who was Francis' vicar at that time managed to see the wound by a similar subterfuge. Another of his companions, a man of extraordinary simplicity, put his hand in under his capuche to massage his chest because he was not feeling well, and accidentally touched the wound, causing the saint great pain. As a result, Francis always wore trousers which reached up to his arm-pits, in order to cover the scar on his side. The friars who washed his trousers or shook out his habit found them stained with blood. This clear proof left them with no doubt of the existence of the wound which they afterwards contemplated and venerated with others on his death.

9   O valiant knight of Christ! You are armed with the weapons of your invulnerable Leader. They will mark you out and enable you to overcome all your enemies. It is for you to bear aloft the standard of the High King, at the sight of which the rank and file of God's army take heart. And you bear, nonetheless, the seal of the supreme High Priest Christ, so that your words and example must be regarded by everyone as genuine and sound beyond all cavil. You bear the scars of the Lord Jesus in your body, so that no one should dare oppose you. On the contrary, all Christ's disciples are bound to hold you in devout affection. God's witness in your favor is beyond all doubt; the sacred stigmata were witnessed not just by two or three, which would have been enough, but by a whole multitude, which is more than enough, and they leave those who are unbelieving without excuse. The faithful, on the other hand, are confirmed in their faith and raised up by confident hope and inflamed with the fire of divine love.

10   The very first vision you saw has now been fulfilled; it was revealed to you then that you were to be a captain in Christ's army and that you should bear arms which were emblazoned with the sign of the cross. At the beginning of your religious life the sight of the Crucified pierced your soul with a sword of compassionate sorrow. There can be

no doubt that you heard Christ's voice from the cross, which seemed to come from his throne in his sanctuary on high, because we have your own word for it. Later on, Brother Silvester saw two swords piercing you in the form of a cross. When St. Anthony was preaching on the proclamation fixed to the Cross, Monaldus saw you raised up in the air with your arms outstretched in the form of a cross, and we know now beyond all shadow of doubt that these were not imaginary visions, but revelations from heaven.

Finally, towards the end of your life, you had a sublime vision of a Seraph, in which you saw the lowly form of the Crucified. This inflamed your heart and marked your body, so that you bear the seal of the living God, like the "second" angel coming up from the east" mentioned by St. John in the Apocalypse (Ap 7, 2). This confirms our belief in the visions just mentioned, for which we have reliable testimonies.

Seven visions of Christ's Cross were miraculously seen in you or concerning you, and these appeared like so many portents at different stages in your life. The first six led like so many steps to the seventh which you have now attained and in which all is finally consummated. At the outset of your religious life Christ's Cross was put before you and you took it up and carried it always by living blamelessly, giving others an example to follow. The Cross proves so clearly that you attained the height of Gospel perfection that no sincere person could spurn the example of Christian holiness which you gave in your poor person. No true Christian could oppose it, and no one with any humility could make little of it, because it comes from God and deserves to be welcomed.

CHAPTER XIV

Francis' Patient Endurance and His Death

1   Francis now hung, body and soul, upon the Cross with Christ; he burned with love for God worthy of a seraph and, like Christ, he thirsted for the salvation of the greatest possible number of human beings. He could no longer walk because of the nails protruding from his feet, and so he had himself carried, half-dead as he was, through the towns and villages, to encourage others to bear Christ's Cross. To the friars he used to say, "My brothers, we must begin to serve our Lord and God. Until now we have done very little." He longed with all his heart to return to the humble beginning he had made at first and to nurse the lepers once more, as he had done before, making his body which was already worn out with toil serve him once again as it had served him before. With Christ for his leader, he proposed to achieve great victories and, even as his limbs bordered on collapse, he hoped to triumph over his enemy the Devil once again, because he was fervent and courageous in spirit. The goad of love never ceases to urge a person on to greater efforts and leaves no room for discouragement or sloth. In Francis, however, spirit and flesh were so much in harmony and so prompt to obey that, as his spirit strained after the height of sanctity, his body — far from being an obstacle — tried to surpass its desires.

2   Merit, as we know, is crowned by patient endurance, and so Francis began to suffer all kinds of illnesses, so that his treasure might be augmented. There was scarcely a single part of his body which did not have some pain to suffer. The prolonged agony he endured eventually reduced him to a state where he had no flesh left and his skin clung to his bones. He was hemmed in with agonizing pain, but he called his trials his sisters, not his pains.

When he was suffering greater than usual one time, a

friar who was a very simple man said to him, "Brother, you should pray to God and ask him to be easier on you. He seems to be treating you too roughly." The saint groaned aloud at the words and exclaimed, "If I did not know your complete simplicity, I would never let you come near me again, because you dared to find fault with God for the way he is treating me." Then he threw himself on the ground, shaking every bone in his body with the fall, although he was worn out from his long illness, and kissing the earth, he added, "I thank you, my Lord and God, for all the pains I suffer and I beg you to make them a hundred times worse, if you want to. Nothing would make me more happy than to have you afflict me with pain and not spare me. Doing your will is consolation enough, and more than enough, for me." To the friars he seemed like a second Job; the vigor of his mind increased as his body became weaker. He knew the day of his death a long time beforehand and, as it approached, he told the friars that he must soon fold his tent (cf. 2 Pt 1, 14), as Christ had revealed to him.

3   For two years after he had received the stigmata — that is twenty years after the beginning of his religious life — Francis endured the purifying blows of various illnesses which formed him like a stone ready to be fitted into the heavenly Jerusalem and raised him to the height of perfection, like ductile metal under the blows of a hammer. Then he asked to be brought to St. Mary of the Portiuncula, so that he might yield up his spirit where he had first received the spirit of grace. When he arrived there, he was anxious to show that he had no longer anything in common with the world, after the example of Eternal Truth. In his last serious illness, wich was destined to put an end to all his suffering, he had himself laid naked on the bare earth, so that with all the fervor of his spirit he might strug-

gle naked with his naked enemy in that last hour which is given him to vent his wrath. As he lay there on the ground, stripped of his poor habit, he raised his eyes to heaven, as his custom was, and was lost in the contemplation of its glory. He covered the wound in his right side with his left hand, to prevent it being seen, and he said to the friars, "I have done what was mine to do. May Christ teach you what is yours."

4   His companions were overcome with sorrow and wept bitterly; one of them whom the saint called his guardian was inspired by God and took a habit with a cord and trousers, and offered them to Christ's beggar, as he realized this was what he wanted. "I am giving you the loan of these," he said, "as a beggar, and you are to take them in virtue of obedience." The saint was delighted and his heart overflowed with happiness; this proved that he had kept his faith with Lady Poverty to the end. Raising his hands to heaven, he gave praise to Christ for freeing him from all his burdens and allowing him to go freely to meet him. He had acted as he did in his anxiety for poverty, and he was unwilling even to keep a habit unless it was on loan. Christ hung upon his Cross, poor and naked and in great pain, and Francis wanted to be like him in everything. That was why at the beginning of his religious life he stood naked before the bishop, and at the end he wished to leave the world naked. In obedience and love he begged the friars who were standing by him to let him lie naked on the ground, when they saw he was dead, for as long as it takes to walk a mile unhurriedly.

Surely he was the most Christ-like of men! His only desire was to be like Christ and imitate him perfectly, and he was found worthy to be adorned with the marks of his likeness; in his life he imitated the life of Christ and in his death he imitated his death, and he wished to be like him still when he was dead.

5   As the moment of his death drew near, the saint had all the friars who were there called to his side; he spoke to them gently with fatherly affection, consoling them for his death and exhorting them to love God. He mentioned especially poverty and patient endurance and the necessity of holding to the faith of the holy Roman Church, and gave the Gospel preeminence over any other rule of life. The friars were grouped about him and he stretched out his arms over them in the form of a cross, because he loved that sign, and blessed all the friars, both present and absent, in the power and in the name of the Crucified. Then he added, "I bid you good-bye, all you my sons, in the fear of God. Remain in him always. There will be trials and temptations in the future, and it is well for those who persevere in the life they have undertaken. I am on my way to God, and I commend you all to his favor."

When he had finished his inspiring admonition, he told them to bring a book of the Gospels and asked to have the passage of St. John read which begins, "Before the paschal feast began" (Jn. 13, 1). Then, as best he could, he intoned the psalm, "Loud is my cry to the Lord, the prayer I utter for the Lord's mercy," and recited it all down to the last verse, "Too long have honest hearts waited to see you grant me redress" (Ps 141, 1-8).

6   At last, when all God's mysteries had been accomplished in him, his holy soul was freed from his body and assumed into the abyss of God's glory, and Francis fell asleep in God. One of the friars, a disciple of his, saw his soul being borne on a white cloud over many waters to heaven, under the appearance of a radiant star. It shone with the brightness of sublime sanctity, full of the abundance of divine wisdom and grace which had earned for

him the right to enter the home of light and peace, where he rests with Christ for ever.

The provincial minister of the friars in the Terra di Lavoro, Brother Augustine, a holy and upright man, was at death's door at that time. He had been unable to speak for some time, but now those who were with him suddenly heard him crying out, "Wait for me, father. Wait! I am coming with you." The friars were amazed and asked him to whom he was speaking. He replied, "Can't you see our father Francis. He is going to heaven." There and then his holy soul left his body and followed his father.

The bishop of Assisi was on a pilgrimage to the shrine of St. Michael on Monte Gargano at that time, and St. Francis appeared to him on the night of his death, saying, "See, I am leaving the world and going to heaven." When he got up in the morning, the bishop told his companions what had happened. On his return to Assisi, he investigated the matter carefully and came to the conclusion that St. Francis left the world at the time he appeared to him in his vision.

At the time of St. Francis' death, when it was already dusk, a great flock of larks gathered over the building, although they normally prefer the light of day and avoid the shades of night. There they remained, flying about and singing with unusual joy, clearly testifying by the sweetness of their song to the glory of the saint who had so often called upon them to praise God.

CHAPTER XV

*The Canonization of St. Francis and the Solemn
Transferal of His Remains*

1   From the time when he was first influenced by grace and took the earliest steps in his spiritual ascent, Francis the servant and friend of the Most High, the founder and

leader of the Order of Friars Minor, made steady progress and eventually he attained the height of sanctity. He was a model of penance, a herald of truth, a mirror of holiness, and an example of Gospel perfection, but poverty was his profession. He was rich in his poverty and exalted in his lowliness; he was full of life in the midst of mortification, and his simplicity led him to supernatural prudence, so that he was marked out by the practice of all the virtues. God had brought him renown in a wonderful fashion during his life, but he made him more renowned than ever in death. As he left the world and his holy soul entered the dwelling places of eternity, where it was glorified by a full draught from the fountain of life, there remained on his body the clear signs of future glory. His flesh, which had been crucified along with its passions and had become a new creature, bore the image of Christ's passion by a singular privilege and gave some inkling of the resurrection to come by this unheard-of miracle.

2   In his holy hands and feet could be seen the nails which had been miraculously formed out of his flesh by God; they were so much part of his flesh that, when they were pressed on one side, they immediately jutted out further on the other side, as if they were made of solid material which reached right through. The wound in his side which was not the result of any human action could be seen clearly, just like the wound in our Savior's side, which gave birth to the mystery of redemption and human rebirth. The nails were black like iron, but the side wound was red, and the flesh was contracted into a sort of circle, so that it looked like a beautiful rose. The rest of his skin which was naturally inclined to be dark and had become more so in his illness, became shining white, giving us some idea of the beauty which will belong to the bodies of the saints in heaven.

3   His limbs were relaxed, and soft to touch; they seemed to have regained the tenderness of childhood, bearing clear marks of his childlike innocence. The nails showed up black against his shining skin and the wound in his side looked like a rose in full flower, so that it is no wonder the onlookers were amazed and overjoyed at the varied beauty of the miracle. His sons mourned the loss of such a loving father, but they were filled with gladness when they kissed the marks of the supreme King in his body. The extraordinary miracle turned their sorrow to joy and the realization of what it meant turned their curiosity into amazement. The sight was so unusual and so sublime that those who saw it were confirmed in their faith and inspired to greater love, while those who heard about it were lost in amazement and longed to see for themselves.

4   When the townspeople heard that the saint was dead and learned about the stigmata, they came in crowds to the place, all anxious to see with their own eyes; that would banish all doubt from their minds and add joy to the affection they felt for the saint. A large number of people from Assisi were admitted to see the stigmata and kiss them.

One of those who was allowed to see the body of St. Francis was a knight called Jerome who was an educated and prudent man. He was a very well known person, but he was unbelieving like the Apostle St. Thomas and he doubted the reality of the stigmata. In his eagerness he did not hesitate to move the nails in full sight of the friars and all the people, and he felt the saint's hands and feet and side with his fingers. As he felt the marks of Christ's wounds under his touch, the doubt vanished from his heart and from the hearts of others. As a result he and many others afterwards bore witness to the truth which he had verified so carefully, and swore to it on the Gospel.

5   Francis' friars and sons who had been summoned to his deathbed spent the night on which he died singing God's praises with all the people, so that it seemed as if angels were keeping watch and no one would think obsequies were being celebrated for the dead. In the morning the crowd which had gathered took branches from the trees and brought his body to Assisi, singing hymns and canticles and carrying a multitude of lights. As they passed the church of San Damiano where the noble Virgin Clare who is now in glory in heaven lived with her sisters, they made a short stop and let them see and kiss his body with its heavenly jewels. Eventually they reached the town with great rejoicing and reverently laid the precious treasure they were carrying in the church of San Giorgio. It was there that he had gone to school as a little body, and it was there that he afterwards preached for the first time; there, too, he found his first resting-place.

6   Our holy father left this world on Saturday evening, October 3, in the year of our Lord 1226, and he was buried the following day. He immediately became famous for the numerous and extraordinary miracles which were worked through his intercession, because God looked with favor upon him. In his lifetime his sublime holiness was made known to the world in order to show people how they should live by the example of his perfect uprightness. Now that he was reigning with Christ, his sanctity was to be proclaimed from heaven through the miracles worked by God's power, to strengthen the faith of the whole world. All over the world the glorious miracles and the wonderful favors which were obtained through his intercession inspired countless numbers to serve Christ faithfully and venerate his saint. Word of what was taking place, as well as the facts themselves, came to the ears of the pope, Gregory IX,

744

so that he was aware of the miracles God was working through his servant Francis.

7   The pope was fully convinced of his extraordinary sanctity, not only by the miracles which he heard about after his death, but also by what he knew from his own experience during the saint's lifetime, what he had seen with his own eyes and touched with his own hands. He had no doubt whatever that Francis had already been glorified by God in heaven and in his anxiety to act in harmony with Christ whose Vicar he was, he was disposed to glorify him on earth, as being worthy of all veneration. He had the various miracles worked by the saint recorded in writing and approved by witnesses, in order to convince the whole world that Francis had been glorified in heaven. Then he submitted them to be examined by the cardinals who seemed to be least favorable to the process and when they had checked them carefully and agreed unanimously, he decreed that Francis should be canonized, with the advice and consent of the cardinals and of all the prelates who were then in the papal court. On Sunday, July 16, in the year of our Lord 1228, the pope himself came to Assisi and canonized St. Francis in a long ceremony which it would be tedious to describe.

8   In 1230 a general chapter of the Order which was attended by great numbers of the friars was held at Assisi and on May 25 St. Francis' body was transferred to the basilica which had been built in his honor. As his remains, marked with the seal of the supreme King, were being borne through the town a number of miracles were worked by the power of Christ whose image they bore; thus his lifegiving influence might move the hearts of the faithful to follow Christ. In his lifetime he had been pleasing to God and beloved by him, and so God raised him up to heaven by the grace of contemplation like Henoch (cf. Gn 5, 24), and

bore him away in a fiery chariot of burning love, like Elias (cf. 4 Kgs 2, 11). It was only right, then that as he enjoyed eternal spring among the flowers of paradise, his remains should be fragrant with the fame of the wonderful effects which they caused on earth.

9   St. Francis had been famous during his life for the miracles which he worked, and from the time of his death until the present day, he has been glorified all over the world by the extraordinary prodigies which God performs in his honor. The blind, the deaf, the dumb, and the crippled; those suffering from dropsy or paralysis; the possessed and the lepers, the castaways and the captives, — all have found help through his merits. For every disease, every need and danger, there is a remedy. And the dead who were raised to life through his intercession proclaimed the power of the Most High before all the faithful, as God glorified his saint, he to whom be honor and glory through endless ages. Amen.

PART II

SOME OF THE MIRACLES WHICH
TOOK PLACE AFTER ST. FRANCIS' DEATH

I *The Power of the Stigmata*

1   As I set out to describe some of the authentic miracles of St. Francis, for the honor of almighty God and the glory of the saint who has already been raised to the glory of heaven, I have decided to start with the miracle in which the power of Christ's Cross is especially clear and its glory renewed. When Francis put on his new self, he was marked out by a new and unheard-of miracle; by an extraordinary privilege which had never before been granted to a human being in the course of history. He was emblazoned with the sacred stigmata, so that even his body which was destined to die was made like the body of the Crucified. No human tongue can suffice to praise such a miracle. All Francis' efforts, whether they were known to others or made in secret, were directed towards the Cross of our Lord. The seal of the Cross had been impressed upon his heart from the beginning of his religious life and he was anxious to carry it in his body too. So he clothed himself with the Cross and put on the habit of penance which was in the form of the Cross. He had put on the person of Christ crucified in his heart, and now his body was clothed with the armor of the Cross; God had routed the powers of evil in the sign of the Cross and now his army would do battle for him under the same standard.

From the moment when Francis first began his active

service in the army of the Crucified, a number of the mysteries of the Cross were seen in his life, as must be clear to anyone who studies his biography. In the seven visions which he had of our Lord's Cross, he was transformed into the likeness of the Crucified in thought and desire and deed by ecstatic love of him. It was only right, therefore, that the supreme King who in his loving kindness condescends beyond all human expectation to those who love him should emblazon his body with the standard of the Cross. It was love of the Cross which had seized him from the beginning and it was the honor of bearing the Cross which was to make him a cause of admiration for the world.

2   To prove the reality of the stigmata beyond all doubt, besides the testimony of those who examined them and touched them, which is above all suspicion, we have a number of extraordinary visions and miracles which took place after the saint's death; and these help to banish all hesitation from our hearts.

His Holiness Pope Gregory IX of happy memory, of whom St. Francis had foretold that he would be pope, was inclined to doubt the wound in Francis' side, before the canonization of the saint. Then one night, as the pope himself used to relate with tears, St. Francis appeared to him in a dream. His face seemed a little hard and he reproached him for his doubts. Then he raised his right arm and showed him the wound and told him to get a glass and catch the blood which was streaming from his side. The pope got the glass in his vision and it seemed to fill up to the brim with blood. After that, he was so devoted to the stigmata and so eager in his conviction that he could never allow anyone to call these wonderful signs into doubt by attacking them in their pride, and he corrected such people severely.

3   A friar of the Order who was a preacher and well known for his virtuous life was convinced of the truth of the stigmata. However, he began to wonder in a purely human fashion how such a miracle could be possible, with the result that doubt crept into his heart. The struggle went on in his mind for a long time and his inquisitive nature began to get the better of him. Then St. Francis appared to him in his sleep one night. His feet were covered with mud and he seemed at once humble and reproachful, patient and angry. "What is all this struggle about in your mind?" he asked. "What doubt has defiled you? Look at my hands and my feet." The friar could see the stigmata on his hands, but he could not see them on his mud-covered feet. "Wipe off the mud from my feet," said the saint, "and you will see where the nails are." The friar took his feet devoutly and seemed to wipe off the mud and feel the wounds with his hands. The moment he woke up, he burst into tears and purified the ideas he had entertained by publicly confessing his doubts with a flood of tears.

4   There was a married woman in Rome who was known for her good life and her noble ancestry who had chosen St. Francis as her advocate and kept a painting of him in her room where she prayed to God in secret. One day when she was praying, she looked closely at the picture: there was no sign of the stigmata, and she was surprised and upset. In reality there was nothing to be surprised at — the artist had left them out. For a number of days she thought hard what the reason for the omission might be. Then one day the stigmata suddenly appeared in the painting, just as they can be seen in other paintings of the saint. The woman was frightened and she immediately called her daughter who was also a very religious person, and asked her if the stigmata had really been missing from the picture previously. Her daughter replied that they had;

and she swore that the stigmata had been omitted and that now they were there. However, it often happens that the human heart lays a trap for itself and calls the truth into doubt, and so the woman began to doubt once more, thinking that perhaps the stigmata had been there from the first. In order to prevent the miracle which had been performed from being treated lightly, God in his omnipotence now worked another; the marks immediately disappeared and the picture was left shorn of its privileges so that this second miracle proved the first one.

5   At Lerida in Catalonia a man called John who was very devoted to St. Francis was walking along a road one evening where an ambush had been laid with intent to kill. John himself had no enemies, but the attack was intended for his companion who bore a close resemblance to him. One of the assailants sprang from his hiding place and, thinking John was his enemy, he attacked him so fiercely with his sword that there was no hope for his recovery. The very first blow he received severed his shoulder and arm almost completely from his body and another thrust pierced his chest, making such a gash that the escaping breath would have blown out half a dozen candles.

The doctors were convinced that he could not be saved; his wounds were festering and the smell was so bad that even his wife could hardly stand it. No human remedy could do anything for him and so he had recourse to St. Francis, begging his intercession as fervently as he could. Even while he was being attacked, he had commended himself to him and to the Blessed Virgin. As he lay there alone on his bed of pain, fully conscious and repeating the name Francis continually, a man dressed in the habit of the Friars Minor entered by the window and stood beside him, as it seemed to him. He addressed him by name and said, "You had confidence in me, and so God will save you." When

750

the dying man asked him who he was, he replied that he was St. Francis and immediately bent over him and unwound his bandages. Then he seemed to anoint all his wounds with ointment. The moment John felt the touch of those holy hands which drew their power of healing from our Savior's stigmata, his flesh was renewed and the puss disappeared, so that his wounds closed up and he was completely restored to health. Then the saint disappeared. Realizing that he had been cured, John called his wife and broke out joyfully praising God and St. Francis. She came running and when she saw her husband, whom she thought she would have to bury the following day, standing on his feet, she was terrified and she filled the whole neighborhood with her screams. When the rest of the family arrived, they tried to get John back to bed, thinking that he had gone mad, but he would not hear of it and tried to show them that he was healed. They were all so astonished that they seemed to be beside themselves and thought they were imagining things. It was only a few short hours since they had seen him covered with ghastly injuries and putrefying flesh, and now here he was in the best of health and delighted with himself. "Do not be afraid," he told them. "Do not think you are imagining things. St. Francis has just left me a moment ago and it was he who healed all my wounds with the touch of his holy hands." As news of the miracle went round, the whole population came to see for themselves, and when they saw the miracle which the stigmata of St. Francis had worked, they were full of joy and admiration, and acclaimed Christ's cross-bearer with loud praise.

Francis bore the stigmata of Christ who died for us in his goodness and rose again miraculously from the dead and by the power of his wounds healed the human race which had been wounded and left half-dead; and so it was only right that he who was dead to this world and lived with Christ should cure an injured man by appearing to him miraculously and touching him with his hands.

6   At Potenza in Apulia there was a cleric called Roger who was an honorable man and a canon of the principal church. He was stricken with illness and one day he went into a church to pray. There was a painting of St. Francis there which showed the stigmata and he began to have doubts about this sublime miracle, because it was so unusual and seemed impossible. As the wound of doubt pierced his heart and his thoughts were taken up with all kinds of baseless ideas, he suddenly felt a heavy blow on his left hand beneath his glove. At the same time he heard a noise like the sound of a javelin being thrown from a catapult. He was dumbfounded at the sound and he felt pain in his hand. He pulled off his glove in order to see with his eyes what he had perceived by his hearing and touch. There had been no trace of an injury on his hand before, but there in the middle of his palm he saw a wound which looked as if it had been inflicted by an arrow. The pain was so great that he thought he would faint. Strange to relate, there was no trace of the wound in the glove; the pain of a wound which was inflicted without any sign was the penalty for the hidden wound of doubt in his heart. Goaded by the terrible pain, he went about for two days screaming and telling everybody how he had been unbelieving. He affirmed his belief in the stigmata of St. Francis and swore that every shadow of doubt had disappeared. He humbly begged the saint to help him by his stigmata and he lent weight to the prayers of his heart with a flow of tears. Once he renounced his incredulity and his heart was healed, his hand was healed too. The pain disappeared, so that he did not feel its burn any more and there was no trace of the blow. By God's loving providence the hidden illness in his soul was cured by visibly cauterizing his flesh, and once his

soul was healed, his body was healed too. He became humble and earnest in his religious duties and he was a good friend of the Order and St. Francis. This public miracle was certified under oath and we learned of it in a letter sealed with the bishop's seal.

There can be no doubt, therefore, about the stigmata, and there should be no sour looks because God is good, as if a gift of this kind were not in harmony with his goodness. Many members of Christ's body adhere to their Head with the same seraphic love as Francis, so that they are found worthy to wear the same armor in battle and will be raised to the same glory in heaven. No one in his right mind would claim that this was for anything but the glory of Christ.

II *The Dead Who Were Raised to Life*

1   At Monte Marano near Benevento a woman died who had been particularly devoted to St. Francis. That night a number of priests came to celebrate the obsequies and sing the office of the dead, and there, in full sight of them all, the woman sat up in bed and called one of them who was her uncle. "I want to go to confession, father," she told him. "Hear my sin. I was dead and I was condemned to a cruel prison because I had never confessed the sin which I shall reveal to you. But St. Francis prayed for me because I had always served him devotedly when I was alive, and so I was allowed to come back to my body. When I have confessed this sin, I shall enjoy eternal life. The moment I have revealed it, you will see that I am going to my promised reward." Then she confessed fearfully to the terrified priest and received absolution, after which she composed herself in the bed and died happily.

2   At Pomarico in the mountains of Apulia there was a mother and father who had one daughter who was very young and to whom they were completely devoted. She

fell seriously ill and died and her parents, who had no hope of having another child, thought they would die with her. Their friends and relatives gathered for the tragic funeral, but her mother only lay there, overcome with indescribable sorrow and utterly lost in her anguish, so that she had no idea what was going on. Then St. Francis came to visit the grief-stricken woman, accompanied by another friar. He knew that she was devoted to him and he spoke to her gently. "Do not weep," he said. "The light of your life for whom you mourn is going to be restored to you by my intercession." The woman rose to her feet immediately and told them all what the saint had said. She refused to allow the body to be removed; instead she invoked the name of St. Francis with complete faith and took her dead daughter by the hand. To the amazement of them all, she raised her up alive and well.

3   The friars in Nocera Umbra asked a man named Peter for the loan of a cart which they needed for a little while, but he refused foolishly. He insulted them and uttered a blasphemy against the name of St. Francis, because they had asked for an alms in his honor. But then he regretted his stupidity because he was afraid God would avenge the saint, as happened there and then. His eldest son fell ill and died after a short time. The poor man threw himself on the ground, calling on St. Francis tearfully, "It was I who sinned," he said. "It was I who spoke maliciously. You should have punished me in my own person. Holy saint, give me back my son in my repentance, as you took him when I blasphemed. I give myself to you — I will always be at your service. I will offer a sacrifice of praise to Christ in honor of your name." At these words, the boy arose and told him to stop mourning. He explained that when he left his body, St. Francis took charge of him and eventually brought him back again.

4   The seven-year-old son of a notary in Rome wanted to follow his mother, as she was going to visit St. Mark's church, but she made him stay at home. So the child jumped from a window of the palace and suffered multiple injuries and was killed instantly. His mother had not gone very far and when she heard the noise, she suspected what had happened. She came running back and when she found her son had been taken from her in such tragic circumstances, she immediately turned upon herself and moved the whole neighborhood to sorrow with her screams. A friar called Raho, of the Order of Friars Minor, was on his way to the church to preach and he went up to the boy and asked his father confidently, "Do you believe that St. Francis can raise your child from the dead because of the love he had for Christ who gave back life to men by his crucifixion?" The child's father replied that he did believe and was prepared to profess it faithfully, adding that he would serve the saint for the rest of his life, if he were found worthy to receive such a favor from God through his intercession. Then the friar prostrated himself in prayer with his companion and called on the bystanders to join them. At that, the boy began to yawn. Then he opened his eyes and raised his arms and got up. He was able to walk immediately in full view of them all, so that he was restored at once to life and health by the saint's wonderful power.

5   In Capua a boy who was playing with a number of others on the banks of the Volturno accidentally fell into the water. The current dragged him under immediately and buried him beneath the sand at the bottom. The children who were playing with him began shouting and a crowd gathered round. Humbly and devoutly they invoked the intercession of St. Francis, that he might look with favor upon the faith of the child's parents who were devoted to him and save their son from death. Then a man who had

been swimming some distance away heard the commotion and came up to the crowd and asked where the boy had disappeared. He called on the name of St. Francis and eventually found the spot where the mud had formed a sort of tomb around the boy's body. He pulled him out and took him from the water, but to his sorrow he saw that he was already dead. They could all see that he was dead, but they still kept crying and shouting, "St. Francis, give the child back to his father." Even a number of Jews who were there were moved with pity and repeated, "St. Francis, give the child back to his father." Without warning, the boy stood up, to their joy and amazement. He asked them to bring him to the church of St. Francis, so that he could thank him by whose power he knew he had been miraculously restored to life.

6   At Suessa Aurunca a house in the street called Alle Colonne collapsed and buried a young man who was killed instantly. The people who had heard the noise came running from all sides and lifted up the beams and stones and gave the dead man back to his mother. She was overcome with bitter sobbing and cried out as best she could, "St. Francis, St. Francis, give me back my son!" The bystanders joined with her, begging St. Francis' aid, but the victim never opened his mouth or gave any sign of life, and so they laid the remains on a bed and prepared to bury him the following day. However, his mother put her trust in God and the merits of his saint and she vowed that she would cover St. Francis' altar with a new cloth, if he restored her son to life. Then about midnight, the young man began to yawn and, as his body became warm, he got up alive and well and began to praise God. He gave the clergy and all the people reason to praise God and thank him and St. Francis joyfully.

7   A young boy named Gerlandino from Ragusa went

out to the vineyard at vintage-time. He wanted to fill some flasks of wine from the vat and he bent down under the wine-press. Suddenly the wooden supports gave way and the heavy stones crashed down upon him, crushing his head fatally. His father immediately came running, but he had no hope and made no move to help him; instead he left him where he had fallen under the weight. The vine-dressers heard his cries of anguish; they shared his sorrow and pulled his son from the wreckage, but he was already dead. His father cast himself at Jesus' feet and begged him humbly to give him back his son, through the merits of St. Francis whose feastday was near. He redoubled his prayers and vowed a number of good works, promising that he would visit the tomb of St. Francis with his son, if he were raised from the dead. Immediately the boy whose whole body had been crushed was restored to life and perfect health. He stood up before them all, rejoicing, and reproached them for mourning, saying that he had been restored to life by the prayers of St. Francis.

8   St. Francis also raised another man to life in Germany, as Pope Gregory stated in an apostolic letter addressed to the friars who had convened for a chapter at the time the saint's body was transferred. I have not included an account of this miracle because I have no knowledge of it and I trust that the pope's testimony will be worth more than any written description.

III   *Those Whom St. Francis Saved*
from the Danger of Death

1   Near Rome a nobleman named Radulfo and his wife who was a very devout woman gave hospitality to some of the friars out of reverence and love for St. Francis. That night one of the sentries fell asleep at the top of a tower where he was resting on a bundle of wood which

had been left in a niche in the wall. Suddenly the bundle went to pieces and the sentry fell on the roof of the palace and from there to the ground. The whole household was roused at the sound of the crash and when they realized that the sentry had fallen, the owner of the castle and his wife came running with the friars. The man who had fallen was so fast asleep that he did not wake up even at his second fall or when they all gathered round him shouting. Eventually he woke up, as they tried to drag him along, and he complained that he had lost some sleep, because he had been resting peacefully in St. Francis' embrace. When they told him how he had fallen and he realized that he was on the ground, not where he had been resting at the top of the tower, he was dumbfounded. He had no recollection of anything having happened, yet he could not deny it. Then he made a promise before them all to do penance out of reverence for God and St. Francis.

2   At Pofi in Campania a priest whose name was Thomas went out to fix the mill which belonged to his church. As he walked by the canal, where there was a strong current and the water was deep, he fell in accidentally and was caught in the water-wheel. He lay there face upwards, imprisoned by the timbers, with the water streaming over his mouth. He could not say a word, but he invoked St. Francis mournfully with all his heart. He was there for a long time and his companions had given up hope for him, when they managed to force the mill backwards, so that he was thrown clear and floundered about in the water, beating his arms. Then a Friar Minor dressed in a white habit, tied with a cord, gently took him by the arm and led him out of the water, telling him, "I am St. Francis, to whom you appealed." The priest was stupefied at his escape and he tried to kiss the saint's footprints. He ran about anxiously, asking his companions,

"Where is he? Where did the saint go? Which way?" They were all terrified and fell to the ground, acclaiming God's glorious deeds and the merits of his lowly servant.

3   A number of young boys from Celano went out to gather herbs in a field where there was an abandoned well with about twelve feet of water which was surrounded by a thick growth of herbs at the top. The boys separated and were running about the field, when without warning one of them stumbled into the well. As he fell into the depths, he had recourse to St. Francis in his heart, calling to him with complete confidence, "St. Francis, help me." The others looked all over the place for him and ran about shouting and crying in search of him. When they discovered that he had fallen into the well, they ran back to the town for help and explained what had happened. They returned with a crowd of people and one of the men went down the well on a rope; there he found the boy quite unharmed, resting on the surface of the water. When they pulled him out, he told them all, "When I fell in, I invoked the protection of St. Francis and he was there immediately to help me. He put out his hands and caught me gently and never left me until he brought me out of the well, with your help."

4   When the bishop of Ostia, who was afterwards Pope Alexander IV, was preaching before the Roman Curia in the church of St. Francis at Assisi, a huge stone which had been left carelessly on a high stone cornice rolled over under its own weight and fell down, hitting a woman on the head. They were all sure that her head was crushed and that she had been killed outright, and so they covered her with the cloak she was wearing and prepared to take her outside for the funeral, when the sermon was over. But she had been laid before the altar of St. Francis and she commended herself confidently to him. When the sermon was over, she stood up safe and sound before them all and there was no

trace of any injury to be seen on her. For years she had suffered from almost constant headaches, but from that moment she was completely free from them, as she afterwards testified.

5   At Tarquinia a number of men had gathered at the friary to cast a bell and an eight-year-old boy called Bartholomew brought some food to the friars for the workmen. Just then a strong gust of wind struck the house and knocked out a big heavy door, throwing it violently on top of the boy, so that they were sure he must have been crushed to death by the weight. He was completely covered by the fallen door and nothing could be seen of him. Everyone there rushed to the spot, calling upon St. Francis' powerful intercession. His father was rooted to the ground and could not move in his grief, but he commended his son to St. Francis with his prayers and supplications. They lifted the weight from the boy and far from being dead, he seemed quite happy, just as if he had been roused from sleep. There was no sign of any injury on him. When he was fourteen years of age, he became a friar and was afterwards a learned man and a well-known preacher.

6   A number of men from Lentini had cut a huge stone in a quarry which was intended for the altar of a church in honor of St. Francis which was to be consecrated within a short time. Almost forty men were trying to maneuver it on to a cart, but after repeated efforts the stone fell on one of them and covered him as if he were in a tomb. The others were thrown into confusion and did not know what to do and most of them went off in despair. The ten who remained turned to St. Francis, begging him tearfully not to let a man die so horribly in his service. Then they took heart and moved the stone so easily that there was no doubt St. Francis' hand was there. The man stood up, safe and sound. His sight had been bad before the accident, but now he

recovered it perfectly, to prove to everyone how powerful St. Francis' intercession is in desperate cases.

7   A similar incident occurred at San Severino in the Marches of Ancona. A huge stone which had been brought from Constantinople for the basilica of St. Francis was being pulled along by a large number of men, when it suddenly fell on one of them. They were sure that he was not only dead, but completely crushed. But St. Francis came to his aid and raised the stone, so that he escaped safe and sound without injury and jumped up, pushing the stone aside.

8   A man from Gaeta called Bartholomew had spent a lot of energy on the construction of a church in honor of St. Francis, when a beam which had been badly placed fell and struck him on the neck, injuring him seriously. He realized that he was at death's door and being a devout religious man he asked a friar for Viaticum. The friar was sure that he would die immediately and that he would not have time to get the Blessed Sacrament, and so he told him in the words of St. Augustine, "Only believe, and you have received Him." The following night St. Francis appeared to him, accompanied by eleven friars and carrying a lamb in his arms. He approached his bed and called him by name saying, "Bartholomew, do not be afraid. The Devil wanted to prevent you from serving me, but he will not triumph over you. This is the Lamb for whom you asked and whom you received by your sincere desire. By his power you will be restored to full health of body and soul." Then the saint drew his hands over the dying man's injuries and told him to go back to the work he had begun. Bartholomew got up early the following morning and showed himself happy and well to those who had last seen him half-dead. They were lost in amazement, but he inspired them with reverence and love for the saint both by

761

his own example and by the miracle the saint had performed.

9   One day a man named Nicholas from Ceprano fell into the hands of his enemies. They attacked him savagely and heaped injury upon injury until they were sure he was dead or at the point of death. But at the first blow Nicholas cried out, "St. Francis, help me. St. Francis, come to my aid." A number of people heard him from a distance, but they could do nothing to help him. Eventually he was carried home, bathed in his own blood, and confidently asserting that he would not die from his wounds. He added that he felt no pain even then, because St. Francis had come to his aid and had persuaded God to give him time for repentance. Events proved that he was right; as soon as the blood was washed away, he was perfectly healed, contrary to all human expectations.

10   The son of a nobleman from Castel San Gimignano was seriously ill, so that there was no hope for his recovery and he was at his last breath. A stream of blood flowed from his eyes, just like the flow from a vein cut in a person's arm, and various other signs of approaching death could be seen in his body. They were sure that he was practically dead; his breathing was very feeble and all his strength was gone, so that he could not move and had lost the use of his senses. He seemed to be quite dead. The friends and relatives of his parents came to mourn with them as usual and could think of nothing but the funeral. However, the boy's father put his trust in God and ran to the church of St. Francis in the village where he tied a rope round his neck and cast himself humbly on the ground. He redoubled his prayers and his vows and by his signs and tears he was found worthy to have St. Francis as his advocate before Christ. He went home and found his son restored to health, so that his grief was changed to joy.

11   God worked a similar miracle through the intercession of St. Francis for a girl in a town called Thamarite in Catalonia, and for another in Ancona. Both of them were seriously ill and at the point of death, but when their parents confidently invoked St. Francis, he restored them immediately to perfect health.

12   A cleric called Matthew from Vicalvi had taken poison and was so sick that he could not speak; there seemed to be nothing to do but wait for the end. A priest tried to make him confess to him but he could not get a word out of him. However, Matthew prayed to Christ in his heart and begged him by the intercession of St. Francis to rescue him from the power of death. God gave him strength and the moment he pronounced the saint's name devoutly before those who were present, he threw up the poison and gave thanks to his rescuer.

IV   *Those Rescued from Shipwreck*

1   The crew of a ship which was in distress ten miles off Barletta had almost lost hope and, as the storm worsened, they put out anchors. However, the ropes parted as the sea rose higher in the gale-force winds and the anchors were lost, so that they were tossed about at the mercy of the waves. Eventually, by God's providence, the storm passed and the sailors prepared to do everything they could to recover their anchors; the broken ropes were still floating on the surface of the water. They found that they could achieve nothing by their own efforts and they called on all the saints in turn, but they could not even recover one the whole day, though they were bathed with perspiration. There was one of the crew whose name was Perfectus, although he was far from perfect in his life, and he said jeeringly to his companions, "Well, you have called on all the saints in turn and not one of them has come to help us.

Let's try this Francis. He is new to their company. Maybe he will dive into the sea and get us our anchors." The others took him up seriously, not as a joke, and made a spontaneous pact with the saint, reproaching Perfectus for his insulting language. There and then the anchors suddenly appeared floating alone on the surface, as if the iron had become as light as wood.

2   A pilgrim who was returning from abroad by ship was worn out by severe attacks of fever. He had great devotion to St. Francis and had chosen him as his patron in the court of heaven; he was not perfectly recovered from his illness and he was tormented by burning thirst. There was no water left on board, but he began to cry out in a loud voice, "Go and get me a drink. Do not hesitate. St. Francis has filled my gourd with water." Sure enough, they found his gourd full of water, although it had been thrown aside empty a short while before. Another day a storm arose, so that the waves broke over the ship and it was being battered by the gale and they were afraid that they would be shipwrecked. Then the sick man began shouting all over the vessel, "Get up! Come to meet St. Francis. He is coming to us. He is here to help us." Then he fell prostrate with a great cry and a flood of tears. At the sight of the saint, he recovered his health immediately and the sea became calm.

3   Brother James of Rieti was crossing a river in a small boat with a number of other friars and they stepped out on to the bank first. Then, just as he was preparing to leave the boat, it capsized accidentally. The boatman was able to swim, but the friar sank immediately. The friars who were on dry land implored St. Francis, begging him tearfully to come and help his son. In the depths of the river Brother James could not open his mouth to speak, but he entreated St. Francis' help with all his heart. And St. Francis was there to help him, so that he walked along

the bottom of the stream as if it were dry land and picked up the sunken boat and brought it to the shore. His clothes were perfectly dry and not a drop of water had touched his habit.

4   A friar called Bonaventure was crossing a lake with two other men, when a timber in the boat gave way under the force of the water and it went down and they with it. From the waters of the lake they begged St. Francis confidently to have pity on them and the boat suddenly rose to the surface, full of water, and brought them safely to land under the saint's guidance.

A friar from Ascoli who was lost in a river was saved by St. Francis in a similar fashion.

A party of men and women who were in the same danger on Lake Piediluco were rescued from their peril when they called upon the name of St. Francis.

5   A number of seamen from Ancona were being tossed about in a violent storm and in imminent danger of sinking. They had no hope and they begged St. Francis to help them. Then a great light appeared over their boat and the sea miraculously became calm, as if the saint could command the winds and the sea by his extraordinary power.

I am convinced it would be impossible to give a complete description of all the miracles which brought glory to St. Francis among seafarers and still bring him glory, and of all the times that he came to the aid of those who had given up all hope. Even when he was on earth, the whole of creation waited upon him, as it was originally intended to, and so it is no wonder that now he is in heaven he should enjoy authority over the waves.

V   Prisoners Who Were Set Free

1   In Greece a man-servant was wrongfully accused of theft before his master. His master had him loaded with

chains and kept in close captivity, but the woman of the house had pity on him; she was convinced that he was innocent of the charge laid against him and she pleaded with her husband to set him free. However, he was obdurate and refused to agree, so that his wife had recourse to St. Francis and recommended the innocent man to his intercession. Francis, the protector of the poor, responded immediately and came to visit the prisoner. He loosed his bonds and forced open his cell. Then, taking him by the hand, he led him out, telling him, "I am St. Francis. Your mistress entrusted you to me." The prisoner was terrified and he wandered about the top of a cliff, trying to find a way down, when he suddenly found himself on level ground, thanks to the power of his rescuer. He went back to his employer's wife and told her all about the miracle, so that she became more fervent than ever in her love for Christ and her devotion to St. Francis.

2   A poor man from Massa Trabaria owed a knight a sum of money. In his poverty he had no means of paying him and so he was arrested by his creditor who wanted the money. He implored him to have pity on him and give him another chance, for love of St. Francis. But the nobleman proudly scorned his entreaties and made light of the saint and his love, as if it were worth nothing. "I will lock you up where neither St. Francis nor anyone else will be of any use to you," he exclaimed. He tried to do just that, and prepared a dungeon where he bound his prisoner with chains and threw him in. Shortly afterwards St. Francis came there and broke open the cell; then he loosed the prisoner's bonds and led him home unharmed. His power prevailed over the proud nobleman and rescued the prisoner who had committed himself to him; and he changed the knight's self-assertiveness into gentleness by the miracle.

3   A man called Albert from Arezzo was thrown into prison for debts which he had never contracted and he commended himself to St. Francis in his innocence with all humility; he was very attached to the Order and he had a special veneration for St. Francis above all the other saints. His creditor declared blasphemously that neither God nor St. Francis would be able to free him from his hands. However, on the vigil of the saint's feast Albert kept a strict fast and gave his ration of food to a poor beggar for love of St. Francis. That night, as he lay awake, St. Francis appeared to him. As he entered the cell, the chains fell from the prisoner's hands and feet and the door opened of its own accord, while a number of flagstones came tumbling down from the roof. Albert went home a free man. Ever afterwards he continued his devotion to St. Francis and fasted on the vigil of his feastday. Each year he offered a candle in his honor and every year he added an extra ounce to it, as a sign of his increasing devotion.

4   When Gregory IX was pope, a man called Peter from Alife was accused of heresy and taken prisoner at Rome, where the pope gave him over to the bishop of Tivoli for safe-keeping. The bishop took him with his diocese as the forfeit, and put him in chains, throwing him into a dark dungeon from which there was no escape. There the prisoner was given a ration of food and drink. Then, hearing that it was the vigil of the feast of St. Francis, he entreated him with prayers and tears to have pity on him; he had now purified his faith and renounced all heresy and become a devout client of St. Francis who was one of Christ's most loyal servants. As a result, he was found worthy to be heard by God, through the merits of St. Francis. At twilight on the evening of his feastday, St. Francis took pity on him and came into his prison. He called him by name and told him to stand up. Peter was terrified and

asked who it was. He was told that it was St. Francis. There and then he saw the chains on his feet broken by the power of the saint's presence. At the same time, some of the iron bolts fell from the stone walls of the cell, so that the walls opened and left the way free for him to escape. He was free but he was so overcome that he could not make his escape; instead he rushed to the door of the cell and frigthened the guards with his cries. They told the bishop how he had been freed from his bonds and when he had heard the whole story, he visited the prison himself. There he realized clearly that the power of God had been at work and he fell down to worship him. The chains were shown to the pope and the cardinals and when they saw what had happened, they were amazed and gave thanks to God.

5   Guidolotto from Castel San Gimignano was falsely accused of poisoning a man and of plotting to kill his son and the rest of his family in the same way. He was arrested by the city magistrate, loaded with chains, and locked up in a tower. However, he put his trust in God and committed his cause to the patronage of St. Francis, leaving it to him to prove his innocence. While the magistrate was busy thinking how he could force his prisoner to confess his crime by torture, and how he would put him to death, St. Francis came to Guidolotto the night before the man was to be tortured. The prisoner spent the whole night surrounded with a bright light; he was overjoyed and full of confidence and he was sure that he would be safe. In the morning the torturers came and led him out and put him on the rack, where they heaped iron weights on top of him. They took him down a number of times and put him up again, hoping to make him confess more quickly by the repetition of the agony. However, the prisoner seemed to enjoy it all and his innocence was clear from his face. As he gave

no sign of suffering, they lit a huge fire under him, but not a hair of his was harmed, although he was hanging head-downwards. Then they poured boiling oil over him, but he overcame it all by the power of the protector to whom he had committed himself. Eventually they let him go and he went off safe and sound.

VI *Those Saved in Childbirth*

1   There was a countess in Dalmatia who was a very good women, besides being renowned for her noble birth; she had great devotion to St. Francis and was always very kind to the friars. When her time came to give birth to a child, she was in agony and felt such pain that it seemed the birth of the child must be the death of the mother. There seemed to be no hope that the child could be born without her dying; her labor seemed destined to end in her death, not in the birth of her child. Then she remembered St. Francis and his power and glory; her faith was roused and her devotion enkindled. She turned to him as a source of efficacious help, a loyal friend, the comforter of the devout, and the refuge of the afflicted. "Holy St. Francis," she prayed, "I beg you with all my heart to have pity on me. I offer my vows to you mentally — I cannot put them in words." The saint lost no time in showing pity; the words were scarcely out of her mouth, when all her pain was at an end. Her labor was over and she gave birth to her child; her distress was relieved and she brought forth her child in complete safety. She did not forget the promises which she had made or go back on her resolution; she had a beautiful church built and gave it to the friars in honor of the saint, when it was finished.

2   A woman named Beatrice who lived near Rome had only a few days left before the expected birth of a child, but now the child had been dead four days. The poor woman

was in agony and the pangs of death seemed to be upon her; the dead fetus was bringing its mother to the grave; without even seeing the light of day, it was bringing its mother into deadly peril. She had recourse to various doctors, but there was no human remedy for her. The unhappy woman had inherited more than her share of the curse placed upon our first parents; she was to be the tomb of her own off-spring and could look forward only to the grave for herself as well. Eventually she recommended herself to the Friars Minor through an intermediary and begged them for some relic of the saint. By Divine Providence, they happened to find a small piece of a cord which he had once worn and as soon as it was laid on her, the pain left her and the fetus which threatened her with death was delivered, so that she was restored to perfect health.

3   Juliana, the wife of a nobleman from Calvi dell' Umbria, spent years mourning for the death of her babies. She was constantly lamenting her misfortune; a short time after their birth, she had buried every child she bore with such difficulty. She was now four months with child and her past experience made her worry more about its death than its birth, but she prayed confidently to St. Francis asking that her unborn child would live. Then one night as she was asleep, a women appeared to her in a dream, carry-ing a beautiful baby which she offered to her. Juliana was afraid to take it; she was sure she must soon lose it, but the woman insisted, "Take it and do not be afraid. St. Francis has had pity on your sorrow and it is he who is sending it to you. This baby will live and enjoy perfect health." At that Juliana woke up. The vision she had seen made her realize that she had the support of St. Francis and she was overjoyed. From then on she redoubled her prayers and promised a number of votive offerings for the life of her child. Eventually the time came for her child-bearing and

she bore a son. He was a fine, strong, baby, as if he had received an increase of vitality through the intercession of St. Francis, and he gave his parents cause to be more devoted than ever to Christ and his saint.

St. Francis worked a similar miracle in Tivoli. There a woman had had a number of girls and was worn out longing for a boy, so she brought her prayers and votive offerings to St. Francis. Through his intercession, she conceived and gave birth to twin boys, although she had only asked for one.

4   A woman in Viterbo whose time had come seemed to be at the point of death; she was in an agony of pain and suffered all the distress of womankind. Her physical resources were gradually waning and nothing could be done for her. Then she appealed to St. Francis and was saved and gave birth in complete safety. Now that she had received the favor she desired, she forgot the kindness which had been shown her and neglected to attribute it to the honor of St. Francis. She even engaged in servile work on his feastday, but the moment she stretched out her right arm to work, it became rigid and withered. When she tried to bend it back with her other hand, that too suffered a similar fate and became withered. The fear of God seized her and she renewed her promises and recovered the use of her limbs which she had lost by her ingratitude and contempt. This happened through the intercession of the humble and merciful St. Francis to whom she once more entrusted herself.

5   A woman from Arezzo had been in labor for a week and her life was in danger. Her skin had turned black and they had all given up hope for her, but she made a votive offering to St. Francis and began to impore his help even as she lay dying. The moment she made the promise, she fell asleep and saw St. Francis speaking to her

in a dream. He asked her if she recognized him and if she could say the "Hail, holy Queen" in honor of our Lady. She told him that she could recognize him and that she knew the prayer. "Then," said the saint, "start it, and before you are finished, you will give birth to your child safely." At these words the woman woke up and began to say fearfully, "Hail, holy Queen." When she said the words, "thine eyes of mercy" and mentioned the Fruit of our Lady's virginal womb, she was immediately delivered from her suffering and gave birth to a beautiful child. She gave thanks to the Queen of mercy who had been so good as to have pity on her, through the intercession of St. Francis.

VII   *The Blind Who Recovered Their Sight*

1   In the friary at Naples there was a friar named Robert who had been blind for years; the flesh had grown over his eyes, so that he could not move his eyelids. A lot of strange friars were passing through there on their way to various parts of the world and St. Francis, the mirror of obedience, was anxious to encourage them on their journey by a miracle, and so he cured Robert in the following way. One night he was lying in bed, so sick that he was ready to die, and the prayers for the dying had already been recited. Then St. Francis appeared to him with three other friars who were noted for their sanctity, St. Anthony, Brother Augustine, and Brother James of Assisi. They had followed him perfectly in their lifetime and now they were overjoyed to accompany him after his death. St. Francis took a knife and cut away the superfluous growth, giving Robert back his sight and rescuing him from the point of death. "Robert my son," he told him, "the favor I have done you is a sign for the friars who are going to distant lands. I will go before them and guide their steps. They should go joyfully and carry out the command given them with all eagerness."

2   At Thebes in Greece a blind woman fasted on bread
and water on the vigil of the feast of St. Francis, and early
on the morning of the feast her husband brought her to the
friars' church. During Mass she opened her eyes at the elevation of Christ's Body; she saw it clearly and adored It
devoutly. Even as she adored, she cried out and said to all
those who had turned round when she shouted, "Thanks be
to God and his saint! I can see Christ's Body." When Mass
was over, she went home in joy of spirit having recovered her
sight. She was happy not merely because she had recovered
the sight of her eyes, but because through the merits of St.
Francis and her own faith she had caught her first glimpse
of the adorable Sacrament, which is the light of souls,
living and true.

3   A fourteen-year-old boy from Pofi in Campania was
attacked by a sudden illness and lost his left eye completely.
Agonizing pain forced the eye from its socket, so that it
hung down along his cheek by a sinew the full length
of a finger; it remained like that for a whole week and became completely dried up. The only thing left was to cut it
off; the doctors had no hope. Then his father implored the
help of St. Francis with all his heart. The saint never wearies
of helping those in trouble and he was quick to come to the
aid of his supplicant. He restored the eye to its proper position and its former health, giving back to the boy the
sight he longed for.

4   At Castro dei Volsci in the same district a heavy pile
of timber fell from a height and struck a priest on the head,
blinding his left eye. It was St. Francis' vigil and as he lay
on the ground, he appealed to him mournfully in a loud
voice, saying, "Help me, holy father, so that I can go to
your feast, as I promised your friars." There and then he
stood up, perfectly healed, and he broke out into a hymn
of joy and praise, so that the onlookers who were sympathiz-

773

ing with him were amazed and delighted. He went to the feast, telling everybody how he had experienced the saint's mercy and power.

5   A man from Monte Gargano was chopping down some timber in his vineyard, when he struck his own eye and split it in two, so that half of it hung outside the socket. He was sure no human being could help him in his terrible misfortune and he promised that he would fast on the feast of St. Francis, if he helped him. The saint immediately restored his eye to its proper position and rejoined it, giving him back his sight, so that no trace of the injury remained.

6   The son of a nobleman who was blind from birth received sight through the intercession of St. Francis. As a result, he was called Illuminatus. Afterwards when he came of age, he joined the Order, refusing to be ungrateful for the benefit he had received. He made such progress in the life of grace and virtue that he seemed to be a true child of the light. Eventually he brought a life of holiness to a holy end, by the merits of St. Francis.

7   At Zancato near Anagni a knight called Gerard had gone completely blind. Two Friars Minor who were coming from abroad happened to come to his house for hospitality and they were warmly welcomed by the whole household, out of reverence for St. Francis. They were well looked after and they continued the journey to a neighboring friary, after thanking God and their host. Then one night St. Francis appeared to one of them in a dream and told him, "Get up and go back with your companion to your benefactor's house. It was Christ and myself that he welcomed in you and I want to repay him for his kindness. He was struck with blindness as a result of his sins which he has never tried to expiate in confession." Then he disappeared. The friar

got up immediately in obedience to his command and together with his companion he came to the house, where they told their benefactor all that had happened. He was amazed and told them that what they said was true. He was moved to tears and went to confession willingly; he promised to make amends and once he had put his soul in order, he immediately recovered his sight. The story of the miracle was told everywhere and it moved great numbers of people to venerate St. Francis and confess their sins humbly and practice hospitality.

7a   A man who had been falsely charged with stealing was condemned by Ottaviani the magistrate of Assisi to lose his eyes; the sentence was carried out by the knight Otto and the public officials. His eyes were forced out and the nerves cut with a knife. Then the poor man was brought to the altar of St. Francis where he implored the saint's pity. He claimed that he was innocent and by the intercession of the saint he received new eyes within three days. They were smaller, but his sight was just as good as it had ever been. The knight Otto bore witness to this extraordinary miracle under oath before James, the lord abbot of San Clemente, who was investigating it on the authority of Bishop James of Tivoli. Another witness was Brother William of Rome who was commanded to tell the truth under pain of excommunication by the minister general of the Order of Friars Minor, Brother Jerome. He bore testimony under oath before a number of provincial ministers and other important members of the Order, saying that when he was still a layman, he saw the person in question and that he then had both eyes. Afterwards he witnessed his torture, when his eyes were put out, and asserted that he personally examined the eyes as they lay on the ground and turned them over with a stick. Afterwards he saw the man after he had recovered his eyes by God's power and could see clearly.

VIII *Those Who Were Cured of Various Diseases*

1   At Citta della Pieve there was a boy who was a beggar and had been deaf and dumb since his birth. His tongue was so short and slender that those who had examined it were inclined to think that it had been almost completely cut out. A man named Mark took him into his home for love of God; and when he realized that he had found a benefactor, the boy often stayed with him. One evening when Mark was having supper with his wife and the boy was there, he remarked to his wife, "I think it would be a great miracle if St. Francis gave him back his hearing and his speech." And he continued, "I promise God solemnly that if St. Francis is so good as to do that, I will pay this boy's expenses as long as he lives." There and then the boy's tongue grew and he spoke saying, "Glory be to God and St. Francis. He has given me back my speech and my hearing."

2   Brother James of Iseo suffered a bad hernia while he was still a boy living in his father's house. Notwithstanding his youth and his infirmity, he was inspired by the Holy Spirit to join the Order of St. Francis, but he never told anyone about his injury. When the body of St. Francis was being transferred to the church where his remains are now kept like a precious treasure, Brother James took part in the celebration, paying due honor to the sacred relics of the saint who had been glorified in heaven. There he approached the tomb and embraced it devoutly. Immediately all his organs were restored to their proper position and he felt that he was healed. He laid aside the truss he had been wearing and never felt any pain after that.

Brother Bartholomew of Gubbio, Brother Angelus of

Todi, Father Nicholas of Ceccano, John of Sora, a man from Pisa, and another from Cisterna, Peter from Sicily, and a man from Spello near Assisi, together with many others, were miraculously cured of similar ailments by the mercy of God and the intercession of St. Francis.

3 A woman from the Marittima who had suffered from mental illness for five years had lost her sight and hearing. She used to tear her clothes with her teeth and had not the slightest fear of fire or water; to crown it all she eventually developed epilepsy. Then God took pity on her and one night she was miraculously enlightened by his saving light and saw St. Francis sitting on a high throne. She threw herself on the ground before him and begged him to cure her. As he gave no sign of granting her petition, she made a vow, promising that as long as she could she would never refuse an alms to anyone who asked her for love of God or his saint. St. Francis immediately remembered the pact he himself had made with God so long ago, and he blessed her with the sign of the cross, restoring her to perfect health.

It has also been stated that a girl from Norcia, as well as the son of a nobleman and a number of others, were delivered from a similar affliction by the saint.

4 A man named Peter from Foligno was making a pilgrimage to the shrine of St. Michael, when he committed an offense against the reverence expected of a pilgrim and drank at a well. There and then a number of devils entered into him. For three years afterwards he was possessed, and he tore at his own body, while speaking and behaving frightfully. However, he occasionally had lucid intervals and he heard of the efficacy of St. Francis' power in putting demons to flight. He implored his intercession with all humility and went to his tomb. The moment he touched it, he

was miraculously delivered from the devils who tormented him.

St. Francis also had pity on a woman from Narni who was possessed, and on many others, but it would take too long to describe their sufferings and how they were cured.

5   A leper called Bonomo from Fano who was paralyzed was brought to the church of St. Francis by his parents and completely cured of both diseases.

A young man by the name of Atto from San Severino who was covered with leprosy was cured by the merits of St. Francis, when he made a vow and had himself brought to the saint's tomb.

The saint excelled in curing this disease because in his love of humility and kindness he had devoted himself to the service of the lepers.

6   A noble woman called Rogata in the diocese of Sora had suffered from a flow of blood for twenty-three years and had endured all kinds of treatment from various doctors. Her condition was so serious that she often seemed on the point of dying, but if the flow was stopped, her whole body swelled up. Then she heard a young man singing in the local tongue about the miracles which God had worked through St. Francis. She was overcome with sorrow and burst into tears. Then her faith was roused and she exclaimed, "O blessed father Francis! You are famous for such great miracles! If only you would be so good as to cure me of my illness, then you would enjoy greater glory than ever, because you have not performed a miracle like that yet." No sooner had she uttered her prayer than she felt that she had been cured by the saint's intercession.

St. Francis also healed her son Marius whose arm was paralyzed, when they made a vow in his honor. A woman from Sicily who had suffered from a flow of blood for seven years was also healed by the saint.

7   There was a woman called Prassede in Rome who was well known for her religious fervor; she had lived for almost forty years in a tiny cell for love of her Eternal Bridegroom and she received a special favor from St. Francis. One day she went up on the roof of her cell to get something she needed. There she was struck by dizziness and fell off, breaking her leg and one foot, and dislocating her shoulder. Then St. Francis appeared to her, clad in robes of glory, and spoke to her gently. "Get up," he said. "Get up, do not be afraid." He took her by the hand and raised her up; then he disappeared. She looked this way and that about the cell, convinced that she was seeing a vision. Her screams brought help and when a light was struck, she realized that she had been completely healed by St. Francis and she related everything as it had happened.

IX   *Those Who Refused to Honor the Saint by Not Keeping His Feastday*

1   In the town of Le Simon near Poitiers a priest called Reginald who had great devotion to St. Francis told his parishioners that the saint's feastday should be celebrated solemnly. However, one of the parishioners knew nothing about the saint's power and he paid no attention to the order. He went to cut some wood on his land and as he prepared to start, he heard a voice saying three times, "This is a holyday. It is wrong to work." But he was stubborn and neither the priest's authority nor the miraculous voice could stop him. Then God worked another miracle of his power, in honor of his saint and to punish the offender. The man was holding a fork in one hand and when he raised the axe with his other hand to start working, both his hands became firmly stuck to the implements by God's power, so that he could not loose his fingers to let them go. He was dumbfounded and did not know what to do. He raced off to the church and crowds of people came from

all sides to see the miracle. A number of priests had gathered
there to celebrate the feast and one of them advised him to
make an act of sorrow before the altar. He committed himself with all humility to St. Francis, and as he had heard the
voice three times, he made three vows, one that he would
keep St. Francis' feastday, the second that he would visit the
church on that day, and the third that he would make a pilgrimage to the saint's tomb. When he had taken the first
vow, one of his fingers became free, and after the second another was freed. When he made his third vow, a third finger
was released, and after it his whole hand. There was a huge
crowd there and eventually his other hand was freed, as they
prayed to the saint for mercy. So he was restored to complete
freedom and he put aside his implements, while they all
praised God and the miraculous power of his saint which had
stricken him and cured him so wonderfully. The implements
still hang there in front of the altar of St. Francis in memory
of the incident.

A number of other miracles which took place there and in
neighboring districts show what an exalted position St.
Francis enjoys in heaven and how reverently his feast should
be celebrated on earth.

2   A woman in Le Mans put her hand to the distaff and
took up the spindle on St. Francis' feastday; immediately
her hands became paralyzed and her fingers ached with
burning pain. The punishment brought her to her senses
and she recognized the saint's power; she was sincerely
sorry and she ran off to the friars. They begged St. Francis
to have pity on her and she was immediately restored to
health. No trace of injury remained on her hands but her
fingers retained the marks of burns, as a reminder of what
had happened.

Three other women, from Campania, from Olite in Spain,
and from Piglio, were miraculously punished for their

obstinacy in refusing to observe the saint's feastday, and miraculously delivered by the saint's intercession, when they repented.

3   A knight from Borgo San Sepolcro in the province of Massa Trabaria spoke lightly of St. Francis' miracles; he insulted pilgrims who came to his tomb and slandered the friars, making fun of them in public. On one occasion, when he attacked the saint's renown, he committed the additional crime of blasphemy. "If it is true," he said, "that this Francis is a saint, may I fall by the sword today. If it is not true, then may I go safe." God's anger made no delay in punishing him as he deserved, because even his prayer was sinful. A short while afterwards, he wronged his nephew and the young man took a sword and ran it through his body. He died that very day in his crimes, a slave of the Devil and a child of darkness, so that others might learn to praise St. Francis' miracles devoutly and not attack them blasphemously.

4   A judge called Alexander did everything he could with his poisoned tongue to prevent people from honoring St. Francis. As a result, he was deprived of his tongue by the divine judgment and remained dumb for six years. As he suffered in the very organ by which he had sinned, he was reduced to heartfelt contrition and he was sorry that he had talked so loudly against the saint's miracles. St. Francis had pity on him and his indignation died away; he received the penitent back into his favor, as he appealed to him humbly, and restored his speech. From that time on, the man devoted his blasphemous tongue to praising the saint, so that the punishment he had endured served at once to reform him and make him devout.

X *Various Other Miracles*

1   At Gagliano-Alterno in the diocese of Sulmona a woman named Mary who was very devoted to our Lord and St. Francis went out one summer's day to get something to eat. It was very warm and she became faint with thirst, but there was anothing to drink; she was alone on the barren mountainside. She lay down on the ground, almost unconscious, and began to pray devoutly to St. Francis. As she continued praying humbly and lovingly, she was overcome by the heat and the thirst, together with the hard work, and she fell asleep. Then St. Francis came to her and called her by name. "Get up," he said. "Drink the water which God is giving to you and many others." The woman awoke at the words and felt stronger. She grasped a fern which was growing beside her and pulled it out by the roots. Then she dug about with a piece of wood and discovered running water. At first it was only a drop, but it suddenly developed into a spring, by God's power. She drank and had enough. Then she washed her eyes; her eyes had been bad as a result of a long illness, but now she felt that she had received new sight. She hurried home and told everyone about the extraordinary miracle, to the glory of St. Francis. People came from far and near when they heard the story, and experience proved the power of the water; many people were cured of various diseases after they had been to confession and used the water. There is a spring there to this day and an oratory has been built in honor of St. Francis.

2   A cherry-tree belonging to a man at Sahagun in Spain miraculously revived and produced leaves, flowers, and fruit, contrary to all expectations. The inhabitants of the countryside around Villa Silos were delivered from a plague of insects which attacked the vines, by the miraculous intercession of St. Francis. A priest from Palencia put a barn

belonging to him under the protection of St. Francis and the saint freed it from wheat-worms which used to invade it every year. A local land-owner from Petramala in Apulia entrusted his land to the care of St. Francis and the saint kept it free of locusts, although everything in the neighborhood was destroyed by them.

3   A man whose name was Martin drove his cows a long way out of the village to pasture, when one of them broke its leg so badly that there was nothing he could do for it. The only thing left was to save the hide, and as he had nothing with which to remove it he went home, leaving St. Francis to look after the cow. He entrusted the animal to his protection, to save it from the wolves until he returned. Early next morning he came back to the cow he had left in the woods; he found it grazing and restored to perfect health, so that the could not tell the leg which had been broken from the others. He gave thanks to the good shepherd who had taken such good care of his cow and healed it.

In his humility St. Francis knew how to come to the aid of all who called upon him and he did not make light even of the lowliest human needs.

He restored a mule to a man from Amiterno from whom it had been stolen, and he repaired a bowl which had been shattered for a woman from Antrodoco. He restored a plowshare which had been broken into smithereens for a man at Monte dell'Olmo.

4   In the diocese of Sabina there was an eighty-year-old woman whose daughter died and left an infant who had not yet been weaned. The poor old woman was destitute and she had no milk and there was no one else to give the baby even a drop, so that she did not know where to turn. The baby grew weaker and then one night the old woman turned to St. Francis and implored his help, destitute as

she was of all human aid. As she prayed in tears, St. Francis came to her, in his love of innocent children, and told her, "I am Francis whom you have invoked so tearfully. Give the baby your breast and God will give you plenty of milk." She did as he told her and immediately her breasts gave plenty of milk. The miraculous gift Francis had given her became known to everybody and a crowd of men and women flocked to see it. They could not deny the evidence of their own eyes, and so they were all moved to praise God in the miraculous powers and the loving kindness of his saint.

5   A man and his wife at Scoppito had an only son for whom they mourned every day because of his pitiful condition. His arms were joined to his neck and his knees drawn up against his chest, so that his heels pressed against his buttocks. He looked more like a monster of some kind than the offspring of human parents. His mother was overcome with sorrow and she implored Christ, invoking the aid of St. Francis, to have pity on her in her misery and disgrace. One night she fell into a troubled sleep in her grief and St. Francis appeared to her. He spoke to her gently and asked her to bring the child to a neighboring friary which was dedicated to him, and pour some water from the well there over him, in the name of God; this would restore him to health. She neglected to obey the saint's command and he came a second and a third time; and this time he walked before them and brought the child and his mother to the gate of the friary. A number of noble women were visiting the friary out of devotion and when the woman told them all about her vision, they brought the child in to the friars. Then they drew water from the well and the highest ranking of them all washed the child with her own hands. He was cured instantly and all his limbs were re-

stored to their proper position; they were overcome with amazement at the miracle.

5a   A young man called Ubertino from Rivarolo Canavese near Susa joined the Order of Friars Minor, and during his novitiate he had a frightening experience as a result of which he went mad and his right side was completely paralyzed, so that he could not hear or speak. He was unable to move and could feel nothing. After he had been confined to bed for some time, to the sincere sorrow of the friars, the fast of St. Francis came along, and on the vigil he enjoyed a period of lucidity. He appealed to the saint as best he could with a heart full of faith, although his voice was distorted. The following morning, when all the friars were busy singing prayers in the church, St. Francis, wearing the habit of the Order, appeared to the novice in the infirmary, and a great light shone there. He stretched out his hand and felt the novice's right side. Then he drew his hand gently down along his body from his head to his feet and put his fingers in his ears, making a mark of some kind on his shoulder. "This is a sign," he said, "that God will restore you to perfect health through me, because it was after my example that you entered the Order." Then he put a cord about him because he was not wearing one and told him, "Get up and go into the church and give God the praise which is his due, along with the other friars." The boy reached out to touch him with his hands and kiss his footprints in gratitude, but the saint disappeared. The young novice recovered his physical health perfectly and the use of his reason, together with the full use of his faculties. He entered the church, to the amazement of the friars and the congregation who were present and had seen him paralyzed and out of his mind. He joined in their prayers and told them all about his miraculous cure, so that they were moved to greater devotion towards Christ and St. Francis.

6   At Cori in the diocese of Ostia, a man lost the use of his leg, so that he could neither walk nor move about. He was in frightful agony and had given up hope of any human remedy. Then one night he began to complain to St. Francis, as if he saw him present there before him, saying, "St. Francis, help me. Remember the way I served you and the loyalty I showed you. I supplied an ass for you and I kissed your hands and feet. I always had great devotion to you, and I was your benefactor. Now look at me dying with the pain of this torment." St. Francis was moved by his complaints and he remembered the services which he had done him. In gratitude for his devotion he appeared to the man together with another friar in a vision. He told him that he had come in answer to his appeal and that he had a cure for him. He touched the place where the pain was with a small stick shaped like a cross. At that the abscess burst and the man was completely cured. And, what is more wonderful still, the mark of the cross remained impressed on the spot where the ulcer had been cured, to remind the man of the miracle. This was the mark with which Francis sealed his letters, whenever charity demanded that he should write to someone.

7   Our hearts have been absorbed in describing the various miracles of St. Francis, but now by the intervention of the glorious standard-bearer of the Cross, they return once more to the Cross, by divine guidance. This is to remind us that, just as the Cross marks the highest point of all that Francis had done to win salvation while fighting in the army of Christ, so it has become the hallmark of all that brings him honor, now that he is sharing Christ's triumph.

8   The deep and wonderful mystery of the Cross in

which the gifts of grace and the reward of virtue — all the treasures of wisdom and knowledge — are hidden so sublimely that it is unknown to the wise and prudent of this world, was fully revealed to Christ's beggar; his whole life followed the way of the Cross; it held no attraction except that of the Cross; it proclaimed nothing but the glory of the Cross. At the beginning of his religious life, Francis could truly say with St. Paul, "God forbid that I should make a display of anything, except the cross of my Lord Jesus Christ" (Gal 6, 14). At all times during his life, he could say with equal truth, "Peace and pardon to all those who follow this rule" (Ibid. 16). But at the end of his life he could say with greater truth than ever, "I bear the scars of the Lord Jesus printed on my body" (Ibid. 17). And we long to hear nothing more from him every day than the words, "Brethren, the grace of our Lord Jesus Christ be with your spirit. Amen" (Ibid. 18).

9   You can make your boast in the glory of the Cross without fear now, O glorious standard-bearer of the Cross. It was from the Cross you began, and according to the rule of the Cross that you made progress, and it was in the Cross that you brought your life to its final consummation. Now, by the witness of the Cross, all the faithful see the glory you enjoy in heaven. Those who abandon the Egypt of this world can follow you with complete confidence; the Cross of Christ will part the waters of the sea like Moses' rod, and they shall traverse the desert to the promised land of the living, where they shall enter by the miraculous power of the Cross, having crossed the Jordan of our human mortality.

May Christ Jesus crucified, the true leader and savior of his people, lead us there by the merits of his servant Francis, to the glory of the triune God, who lives and reigns for ever and ever. Amen.

MINOR LIFE OF ST. FRANCIS
by St. Bonaventure

CHAPTER TITLES

791

CHAPTER I

The Beginning of St. Francis' Religious Life

1   *First lesson:* The grace of God our Savior has dawned in our times in his servant Francis; our merciful Father, the source of all that gives light, came to meet him on his way with a plentiful share of his choicest blessings. We see in the course of Francis' life that God was not. content merely to lead him from the obscurity of the world into the light, bringing him renown by his gifts of exalted virtue and merit; he did more — he proved Francis' claim to fame by the mysteries of the Cross which he accomplished in him so strikingly.

Francis came from the town of Assisi in the valley of Spoleto; he was called John by his mother, but his father changed his name to Francis. He retained the name his father gave him without forfeiting the privilege indicated by the one his mother chose. As a boy he was brought up among worldly companions and in a worldly atmosphere; when he had some idea how to read and write, he was given a job in a profitable trading business. However, with the help of God's grace, he never indulged his passions, like his loose-living companions, or put his trust in his store of riches, like his greedy business friends.

2   *Second lesson:* Even as a young man, Francis' spirit was one of gentle kindliness and generous compassion for the poor. This seemed to have been implanted in the depths

of his being by God and it remained with him all his life, so that his heart overflowed with goodness. He would not turn a deaf ear to the Gospel and he made a resolution never to refuse anyone who asked him for an alms, especially if it was for love of God. When he was at the very peak of his youthful career, he solemnly promised God that he would never turn away from anyone who begged an alms from him for love of God, as long as he had anything to give. He kept this generous resolution all his life and it led him to an ever higher degree of grace and love for God. This fire of divine love was never extinguished in his heart, but as a young man he was taken up with the cares of this world and could not grasp the hidden message contained in God's words. Then the hand of God came upon him; he suffered a prolonged and distressing illness, while his heart was enlightened by the infusion of the Holy Spirit.

3   *Third lesson:* After he had recovered his strength to a certain extent and undergone a change of heart, he happened to meet a knight who was of noble birth, but completely destitute. He was reminded of Christ, the generous King who became so poor, and he felt such pity for the man that he took off the new clothes he had just got for himself and clothed him with them, keeping nothing for himself.

The following night, as he slept, Christ for love of whom he had come to the aid of the poor knight showed him a vision in his goodness; he saw a beautiful palace, full of armor, all emblazoned with the Cross. And he promised him that everything he saw would belong to him and to his knights, if he took up the standard of the Cross and bore it faithfully. After that, Francis began to withdraw from the rush of business; instead, he sought out lonely places where he could mourn for his sins. There he gave himself over unceasingly to groans beyond all utterance, imploring God to show him the way to perfection, and after prolonged and insistent prayer, he was found worthy to have his request granted.

4   *Fourth lesson:* One day as he was praying in solitude, Jesus Christ appeared to him, hanging on his Cross. He made Francis realize so vividly the force of the Gospel words, "If any man has a mind to come my way, let him renounce self, and take up his cross, and follow me" (Mt 16, 24) that his heart was filled with compassion and burned within him with the fire of love. His soul melted at the sight of the vision, and the memory of Christ's passion was impressed so intimately on the depths of his heart that the wounds of his crucified Lord seemed to be always before his mind's eye, and he could scarcely restrain his sighs and tears. Now that he no longer had any regard for all that he owned in the world, and thought nothing of it for love of Jesus Christ, Francis felt that he had found the hidden treasure, the brilliant pearl of great price, mentioned in the Gospel. He was eager to make it his own and he decided to give up everything he had; in a business deal worthy of a saint, he would renounce his position as an earthly trader and become like the trader in the Gospel.

5   *Fifth lesson:* He left the town one day to meditate out of doors and, as he was passing by the church of San Damiano, which was threatening to collapse with age, he was inspired by the Holy Spirit to go in and pray. He knelt there before an image of our Lord on his Cross and he felt great pleasure and consolation in his prayers, so that his eyes were full of tears as he gazed at the Cross. Then, with his own ears, he heard a miraculous voice coming to him from the Cross, saying three times, "Francis, go and repair my house. You see, it is all falling down." At first

he was terrified at the divine command expressed in these extraordinary words; but then he was filled with joy and wonder, and he stood up immediately, prepared to put his whole heart into obeying the command and repairing the material building. However, the message really referred to the universal Church which Christ bought with the price of his Precious Blood, as the Holy Spirit afterwards made him realize, and he himself explained to his close companions.

6   *Sixth lesson:* For love of Christ Francis disposed of everything he had there and then, to the best of his ability, and offered the money to the poor priest who was attached to the church, that he might use it to repair the building and give alms to the poor. He also entreated him earnestly to let him stay with him for a while. The priest agreed to let him stay, but for fear of his parents, he refused to take the money; in his sincere disregard for worldly wealth, Francis threw the crude metal on a window-sill, and had no more regard for it than if it were dust.

When he heard that his father's rage had been aroused against him by what he had done, he tried to avoid his anger, and he hid in an obscure cave for a number of days, where he fasted with prayers and tears. Eventually, however, he was clothed with power from on high and his heart overflowed with spiritual joy; he came out bravely into the open and went into the town, without the slightest fear. When the children saw his haggard looks, they thought that he was out of his mind and had gone mad. They threw mud from the streets at him, as if he were a half-wit, and shouted after him insultingly; but no insults could break or change him, and he passed through it all as if he could not hear a thing.

7   *Seventh lesson:* His father was beside himself with rage and he behaved as if he had become a stranger to all

human pity. He dragged his son home and beat him, putting him in chains, in the hope that by wearing him down with physical punishment, he could turn his heart to the attractions of the world. However, the only result of his efforts was to make it clear beyond all doubt that Francis was more than willing to endure any torture for Christ. When he realized that he could not change his mind, he insisted vehemently that Francis should go before the bishop of the diocese with him and renounce into his hands his right of succession to the family property. Francis was only too glad to obey and as soon as he reached the bishop's presence, he made no delay, he never hesitated for a moment, or said or listened to a word from anyone; instead, he tore off all his clothes, including even his trousers, and stood there naked before them all. He seemed to be beside himself in his fervor, and he was not ashamed to be stripped naked for love of Christ who hung naked for us on the Cross.

8   *Eighth lesson:* Now that he was free from the bonds of all earthly desires in his disregard for the world, Francis left the town; he was free and without a care in the world and he made the forest resound, as he sang God's praises in French. As the herald of the great King, he refused to be terrified when he met a band of thieves, and he continued to praise God. He was a pilgrim, half-naked and penniless, and he was glad to suffer tribulation, like the apostles.

In his love of utter humility, he now dedicated himself to the service of the lepers; by devoting himself to the care of such pitiful outcasts, he would learn to disregard the world and his own self, before attempting to teach such self-contempt to others. He had always had a horror of lepers, above any other class of human beings; but now grace was infused into him in greater measure, and he devoted himself to waiting on their needs with such humility of heart that he washed their feet and bound their sores, drawing out the pus and wiping away the corrupt matter. In the excess of his indescribable fervor, he did not even hesitate to kiss their ulcerous sores, kissing the dust with his mouth (cf. Lam 3, 29). He would expose himself to every kind of indignity, that he might bring his rebellious lower nature into subjection to the rule of the spirit; so he would gain complete control of himself and be at peace, once he had subdued the enemy that was part of his own nature.

9   *Ninth lesson:* Now that he was firmly established in the lowliness of Christ and had become rich in his poverty, Francis set about repairing the church in obedience to the command he had received from the Cross. He had absolutely nothing to start with, but he devoted himself to the task wholeheartedly, loading his own back with stones, although he was worn out with fasting. He begged help in the form of alms from those among whom he had lived as a wealthy young man, and he was not ashamed. People eventually came to help him in their devotion to him, because they could see already that his was no ordinary holiness. With their cooperation he repaired the church of San Damiano and another dedicated to the Prince of the Apostles, followed by a third dedicated to the Blessed Virgin, all of which were abandoned and in ruins. In this way the work which God afterwards planned to accomplish through him on a spiritual plane was mysteriously foreshadowed in a visible, material fashion. Like the three churches he repaired, the universal Church of Christ was to be renewed in three different ways under his guidance and according to his directions, his rule and teaching. The voice which he heard from the Cross, which repeated the command to repair God's house three times, was a prophetic sign which we now see fulfilled in the three Orders which he founded.

798

CHAPTER II

The Foundation of the Order — the Power of Francis' Preaching

1   *First lesson:* When he had finished the work on the three churches, Francis went to live at the one dedicated to the Blessed Virgin. There by the merits and intercession of the Mother of God who gave birth to the Price of our redemption, he was found worthy to be taught the way to perfection, by the spirit of Gospel truth which was infused into him from above. One day at Mass the passage of the Gospel was read which recounts how our Lord sent his disciples out to preach and laid down the form of the Gospel life for them, telling them that they were not to have gold or silver or money to fill their purses, nor a wallet for their journey, no second coat, no spare shoes or staff (cf. Mt 10, 9). The moment Francis heard these words, the Spirit of Christ came upon him and clothed him with such power that he adopted the way of life described, not only in mind and heart, but also in his daily life and dress. He took off his shoes there and then, threw away his staff, and discarded the purse with his money. He kept only one tunic to wear, and exchanged his leather belt for a rope. His only anxiety of mind now was to discover how he might practice what he had heard and conform perfectly to the rule given to the apostles for their guidance.

2   *Second lesson:* Like a second Elias, Francis now began to take up the defense of truth, all inflamed as he was with the fiery ardor of the Spirit of Christ. He invited others to join him in the pursuit of perfect holiness, urging them to lead a life of penance. His words were full of the power of the Holy Spirit, never empty or ridiculous, and they went straight to the depths of the heart, so that his hearers were astonished beyond measure and hardened sinners were

moved by their penetrating power. As his high and holy ideals became more widely known by the force of his sincerity and his straightforward teaching, together with his personal life, a number of others were encouraged to follow his example and lead a life of penance. They left all behind and came to join him, sharing his way of life and dress. In his humility, Francis decided that they should be known as Friars Minor.

3   *Third lesson:* By God's calling the number of friars soon grew to six and, like a devoted father and shepherd, Francis sought out a lonely place where he could weep over the misspent years of his youth, which had not been free from sin, in the bitterness of his heart. There he implored mercy and grace for himself and his sons the friars, whose father he had become in Christ. Then his whole being was bathed in an excess of joy and he was given the assurance that all his sins were completely forgiven to the last farthing. He was rapt in ecstasy and completely absorbed in a sort of light which seemed to give life, so that he could see clearly what the future held in store for himself and his friars, as he afterwards told them confidentially, in order to encourage his little flock. Then he foretold the future growth of the Order and how it would expand, by God's providence.

After a brief delay, they were joined by a number of newcomers, so that their number grew to twelve, and Francis decided to present his inexperienced band of followers to the Apostolic See. He had set down briefly in writing the way of life which God had shown him in all humility, and he was anxious to have it approved by the Holy See with the fulness of the Apostolic authority.

4   *Fourth lesson:* As Francis was on his way with his companions, determined to carry out his plan and gain an audience with the Supreme Pontiff, Innocent III, Christ,

the power of God, Christ the wisdom of God, in his merciful condescension, came to meet him on his way. By means of a vision he instructed his Vicar on earth to give a peaceful hearing to this poor beggarman and grant his petition with good grace. In his vision the pope saw the Lateran basilica threatening to collapse and being held up by a poor, wretched-looking individual of slight stature who put his back to it, to prevent it from falling. When Francis appeared before him, the learned pontiff was struck by the purity of his heart and his disregard for the world, and he was deeply impressed by his love for poverty and his determination to be perfect, as well as his zeal for souls and the burning fervor of his will. "Beyond doubt," he exclaimed, "this is the man who will uphold Christ's Church by his work and teaching." From that moment, he became completely devoted to the saint and he bowed graciously to his request. He approved the rule and gave the saint and his companions a mission to preach repentance, granting all their petitions there and then and promising generously to make even further concessions in the future.

5   *Fifth lesson:* With God's grace and the authority of the Supreme Pontiff to support him, Francis now felt completely confident and he took the road towards the valley of Spoleto. He had conceived true Gospel perfection in his heart and professed it solemnly by his vows, and now he was eager to practice it in his own life and teach it to others by his preaching. Together with his companions, he discussed the question whether they should go out among the people or live in solitude, and he begged God in persevering prayer to make known his will in this matter. Then he was enlightened by a revelation and he realized that he had been sent by God to win for Christ the souls which the Devil was trying to snatch away. And so he concluded that he should choose to live for others, rather than for himself

alone. Thereupon, he went to live in an abandoned hut near Assisi, where he could share a life of poverty and strict religious discipline with his friars, and preach the word of God to the people, whenever he had the opportunity. He became a herald of the Gospel and he went about the towns and villages, preaching the kingdom of God "not in such words as human wisdom teaches, but in words taught him by the Spirit" (1 Cor 2, 13). And God guided him in his speech by his revelations, and "attested his words by the miracles that went with them" (Mk 16, 20).

6   *Sixth lesson:* Francis was spending the night in prayer on one occasion, as was his custom, and he withdrew from the company of the friars. Then about midnight, as some of the friars slept and others prayed, a brilliant chariot of fire came through the door of the hut. It was surmounted by a ball of light which shone like the sun, and it turned here and there three times about the room. The friars who were awake were dumbfounded at the sight of the miraculous splendor, while those who were asleep woke up terrified. The shining light seemed to illuminate their hearts, just as it lit up their surroundings, and their consciences were laid bare to one another by its extraordinary powers of penetration. As they looked into one another's hearts, they all realized at once that it was their father Francis whom they had seen under the appearance of this vision. God had revealed him to them as one who came "in the spirit and power of an Elias" (Lk 1, 17), and had been made a leader of his spiritual army, "a chariot and a charioteer" (cf. 4 Kgs 2, 12) for his chosen people. When the saint rejoined the friars, he took occasion from the vision they had been shown from heaven to encourage them. He probed the depths of their consciences and foretold the future; his miracles brought him such renown that it was clear that the twofold spirit of Elias rested upon him in

abundance. There could be no doubt that it was perfectly safe for anyone to follow his life and teaching.

7   *Seventh lesson:* At this time a religious of the Order of the *Crucigeri* who was called Moricus was lying ill in a hospital near Assisi. It was a long drawn-out illness and he was faring so badly that they thought he was at the point of death. Then he recommended himself to St. Francis by means of an intermediary and begged him to be so good as to pray to God for him. In his compassion the saint agreed willingly; he gave himself to prayer and then he took some bread-crumbs and mixed them with oil from the lamp which burned before our Lady's altar, making a sort of pill out of them. This he sent by the friars to the sick man saying, "Take this medicine to our brother Moricus. In his power, Christ will restore him to perfect health by means of it, and when he is ready for the fray, he will bring him into our company for the rest of his life." The moment the sick man took the prescription which had been made up under the inspiration of the Holy Spirit, he stood up, completely cured. God gave him such strength of body and soul that he joined St. Francis' Order a short time afterwards. For years he wore a hair-shirt next to his skin and never ate cooked food, refusing to drink wine or touch anything that had been boiled.

8   *Eighth lesson:* At this time, too, a priest from Assisi, Father Silvester, a man of good life and dove-like simplicity, had a vision. He saw the whole countryside being swallowed up in the embrace of a huge serpent which seemed to threaten the various regions of the world with destruction, it looked so horrible and disgusting. Then he saw a shining cross of gold coming from St. Francis' mouth. The top of it reached up to heaven and its arms stretched far and wide and seemed to reach to the ends of the earth, and the mere sight of it in all its glory was enough to put the terrible

serpent to flight. Father Silvester was a religious-minded man and after he had seen this vision for the third time, he realized that St. Francis had been chosen by God to take up the standard of the Cross and crush the wicked serpent's power. This he would do by enlightening the hearts of the faithful by the glorious witness of his life and teaching. He told the saint and his friars what he had seen and a short time afterwards he left the world; after Francis' example, he followed in Christ's footsteps with such perseverance that his life in the Order only served to confirm the vision he had seen while he was still in the world.

9   *Ninth lesson:* Another friar called Pacificus, when he was still a layman, met St. Francis at San Severino, where he was giving a sermon in a monastery. There the power of God came upon him and he saw the saint signed with the sign of the Cross in the form of two swords of fire, one of which reached from his head to his feet, while the other crossed his chest from hand to hand. He did not know St. Francis by sight, but he realized that the person pointed out to him by such a miracle could be no other. He was overcome with amazement; the power of the saint's words moved him to sorrow for his sins and left him terrified, as if he had been transfixed with a spiritual sword coming from his mouth. He said goodbye to worldly popularity and joined the saint by professing his rule.

He afterwards made great progress in religious perfection and became provincial in France, where he was the first to hold that office. Before he left to take up his post, he was found worthy to have a vision of a great Cross which appeared in different colors on St. Francis' forehead and lit up his whole face with a beautiful radiance. Francis always had great reverence and affection for this particular sign and he often spoke in its praise; he made it before starting to do anything and the letters charity demanded he should write he signed with it in his own hand. His only desire seemed to be to mark the brows of those who weep and wail and are truly converted to Jesus Christ with this sign of the Cross, as we read in the prophet Ezechiel (Ez 9, 4).

CHAPTER III

St. Francis' Outstanding Virtues

1   *First lesson:* As a loyal follower of Jesus crucified, St. Francis crucified his lower nature with all its passions, from the very beginning of his religious life, by practicing strict self-discipline; he restrained the impulses of sensuality with such rigid self-control that he scarcely took enough food or drink to keep himself alive. As long as he was in good health, he scarcely ever ate cooked food; when he did, he occasionally mixed ashes with it, so that he got no pleasure out of eating it. As a rule, however, he was content to destroy the taste by adding water. He was particularly strict when it was a question of having anything to drink; he refused to let his fallen nature enjoy the use of wine, so that his spirit might be occupied with the light of wisdom. It should help us to realize this all the more clearly when we remember that he would scarcely drink enough ordinary water, even when he was almost dying with thirst. More often than not, the bare earth was the only bed his tired body had to lie on, and his pillow was a stone or a piece of wood. His clothes were simplicity itself — nothing more than a coarse, rough covering to protect him. He knew for certain from his own experience that poor, uncouth dress put his wicked enemies to flight, while soft or expensive clothes only gave them courage to attack all the more fiercely.

2   *Second lesson:* While keeping watchful guard over himself with rigid self-discipline, St. Francis was especially careful in his efforts to protect the inestimable treasure of chastity, which we carry in a shell of perishable earthenware. By practicing the most perfect interior and exterior purity, he did everything he could to preserve it as something holy and held in honor. In the early years of his religious life, in the courage and fervor of his spirit he often threw himself into a ditch full of ice or snow in the depths of winter. He did this to gain complete control over the enemy which was part of his own nature and to preserve the white robe of purity from the heat of passion. As a result of such strenuous efforts his lower nature was completely subject to him and his attractive purity was so evident in his use of all his bodily senses that he seemed like "a man that had bound his eyes over by covenant" (Jb 31, 1). He was not content merely to avoid looking about him in a way which would pander to his lower nature; he studiously renounced the slightest glance which could only satisfy idle curiosity.

3   *Third lesson:* St. Francis had attained perfect purity of heart and soul, and the height of sanctity was within his grasp. However, in his great longing for the unstained brilliance of heavenly light, he never ceased trying to sharpen his spiritual vision with floods of tears, and he made no account of the fact that it was costing him his eyesight. As a result of his continual weeping, he developed serious eyetrouble, but when the doctor advised him to restrain his tears, if he wanted to avoid losing his sight, he refused to obey. He would prefer, he asserted, to lose the sight of his eyes than to restrain his devotion and stop the tears which cleansed his spiritual vision and enabled him to see God.

Francis was at peace in his utter loyalty to God and he

felt a heavenly joy in his heart which showed in his face, even in the midst of his tears. In the purity of his blameless conscience, he experienced such an infusion of happiness, that his spirit was continually lost in God, and he rejoiced without interruption in the works of his hands.

4   *Fourth lesson:* St. Francis was completely imbued with profound humility, the guardian and the crowning glory of all virtue. By the range of virtues which shone forth in his life, he stood head and shoulders above all others, but humility seems to have reached the highest degree of all in him, and he was the least of all. In his own opinion, he was the greatest of sinners, and he believed that he was nothing more than a frail and worthless creature; yet, in reality, he was an example of holiness, chosen by God and shining by his manifold gifts of grace and virtue, and con-secrated by the sanctity of his life. He did everything he possibly could to appear worthless in his own eyes and before others; he would confess his secret faults publicly and hide God's gifts in the depths of his heart; he refused to expose himself to human praise, for fear it might be an occasion of falling. In his eagerness to practice humility perfectly, not only was he submissive to his superiors — he even obeyed his inferiors as well; he used to bind himself to obey his companion in his travels, no matter how ordinary a friar he was. St. Francis had no desire to wield authority like a superior; in his humility he preferred to obey those who were subject to him, as their minister and servant.

5   *Fifth lesson:* Sublime poverty is the companion of humility and so, as a perfect follower of Christ, St. Francis espoused it in undying love. For poverty's sake he left his father and mother and abandoned everything he had. No one was so greedy for gold as he was for poverty; no one ever guarded a treasure more carefully than he guarded this

Gospel pearl. From the first moment of his religious life until his death, his sole wealth consisted in a habit, a cord, and a pair of trousers. Destitution seemed to be the only thing in which he took any pride, penury his only source of joy.

If he saw anyone who seemed to be more poorly dressed than he, he immediately fell to reproaching himself and roused himself to imitate him. He was jealous of his poverty and it seemed as if his noble spirit was afraid of being surpassed in his efforts to practice it. He had chosen poverty as the pledge of his eternal inheritance and preferred it to every temporal thing; he thought nothing of the deceitful riches of this world which are only loaned to us for a brief interval, and he loved poverty above any form of wealth. He was anxious to outdo everyone in the practice of poverty; and it was poverty that had taught him to regard himself as the last of all.

6   *Sixth lesson:* St. Francis' love of absolute poverty won for him a share in the wealth to which true, spiritual simplicity is the key. In the whole world he had nothing he could call his own; yet everything in the world seemed to belong to him in God, the Creator of the world. His attitude towards creation was simple and direct, as simple as the gaze of a dove; as he considered the universe, in his pure, spiritual, vision, he referred every created thing to the Creator of all. He saw God in everything, and loved and praised him in all creation. By God's generosity and goodness, he possessed God in everything, and everything in God. The realization that everything comes from the same source made him call all created things — no matter how insignificant — his brothers and sisters, because they had the same origin as he. However, he reserved his most tender compassion for those which are a natural reflection of Christ's gentleness and are used as figures of him in Sacred Scripture. So it

was that by God's divine power the brute beasts felt drawn towards him and inanimate creation obeyed his will. It seemed as if he had returned to the state of primeval innocence, he was so good, so holy.

7   *Seventh lesson:* St. Francis was filled with such a spirit of gentle compassion, which came to him from the Source of Mercy itself, that he seemed to have a mother's tenderness in caring for the sufferings of those in misery. He was kind by nature and the love of Christ merely intensified this. His whole soul went out to the sick and the poor, and where he could not offer material assistance he lavished his affection; the poverty or deprivation he saw in anyone he immediately referred to Christ in his heartfelt compassion. In every poor person he met, he saw the image of Christ and he insisted on giving them anything which had been given to him, even if he had urgent need of it; indeed, he believed that he was bound to give it to them, just as if it belonged to them. He spared nothing — cloaks, habits, books, or altarcloths — as long as he was in a position to do so, he gave them all to the poor. He wanted nothing more than to spend and be spent himself, in order to fulfill the duty of being compassionate towards others.

8   *Eighth lesson:* Like a sharp sword all on fire, zeal for the salvation of others piereced the depths of Francis' heart in his burning love; wounded by the grief of his compassion, he seemed to be on fire with eagerness, and it penetrated his whole being. If he saw a soul redeemed with the Precious Blood of Jesus Christ being stained with sin, he would be overcome with sorrow, and weep so compassionately that he seemed to be in travail over them continually, like a mother in Christ. This was the reason why he was so energetic in prayer, so active in preaching; this was why he went beyond all limits in giving good example — he would not think himself Christ's lover if he did not

compassionate the souls whom he redeemed. His innocent body which had voluntarily become subject to the spirit needed no punishment for sin; yet, for the sake of good example, he inflicted frequent penances and burdens on it. It was for the sake of others that "he kept to the paths that are hard to follow" (Ps 16, 4). Christ gave himself up to death for the salvation of others, and Francis desired to follow in his footsteps to the last.

9   *Ninth lesson:* We can appreciate the fiery strength of the perfect love by which Francis was borne towards God, in his love for Christ his Bridegroom, when we remember that he longed to offer himself to God as a living sacrifice by the sword of martyrdom. Three times he took the road towards pagan lands with this end in view, but on two occasions Divine Providence stood in his way. The third time, with God's help, he succeeded in gaining an audience with the sultan of Babylon, but only after he had been insulted, beaten, put in chains, and had endured severe ill-treatment. There he preached Jesus Christ with such convincing proof of spiritual power that the sultan was lost in admiration; by God's will he became gentle and gave the saint a kind hearing. When he saw his spiritual fervor and his courage, together with his disregard for this earthly life, and the power of his divine words, he became completely devoted to him. He treated him with great honor and offered him valuable presents, begging him to stay with him a little while. However, in his genuine self-contempt and disregard for the world, Francis scorned the gifts as if they were so much dust. When he saw that he could not achieve his goal, despite the fact that he had done everything he possibly could, he made his way back to Christian territory, after receiving a warning from God. So it was that Christ's lover longed to die for him with all his heart, but never succeeded. In this way, his life was preserved,

so that he might later be decorated with a unique privilege, without losing the merit of the martyr's death for which he longed.

CHAPTER IV

Francis' Devotion to Prayer — His Spirit of Prophecy

1 *First lesson:* St. Francis felt like an exile, as long as he remained in this earthly life separated from God and, at the same time, his love of Christ had left him insensible to all earthly desires. Therefore, he tried to keep his spirit in the presence of God, by praying to him without intermission, so that he might not be without some comfort from his Beloved. Whether he was walking or sitting, at home or abroad, whether he was working or resting, he was so wholeheartedly intent on prayer that he seemed to have dedicated to it not only his heart and his soul, but all his efforts and all his time. He was often taken right out of himself in such an excess of devotion that he was lost in ecstasy. Then he experienced things which were beyond all human understanding, and he would be completely oblivious of all that went on about him.

2 *Second lesson:* In order to prepare for the infusion of spiritual comfort in greater peace, he would seek out some lonely spot or an abandoned church where he could go to pray at night. There he often had to endure frightful attacks from the devils who fought with him hand-to-hand and tried to withdraw him from prayer. However, he always succeeded in putting them to flight by the unfailing power of his fervent prayers; that he would be left alone and at peace, and he would make the groves re-echo with his sighs and bedew the ground with his tears, as he beat his breast in sorrow. Here, in hidden secrecy, he defended himself before his Judge; here he pleaded with his Father;

here he enjoyed the company of his divine Bridegroom; here he spoke with his Lover. Here, too, he was seen raised up from the ground and surrounded with a shining cloud, as he prayed at night with his arms stretched out in the form of a cross. The raising of his body from the ground, with the miraculous light which accompanied it, was a sign of the marvelous elevation and enlightenment which took place in his soul.

3   *Third lesson:* By the supernatural power of his striving after God, the secrets of divine wisdom were made known to him; there is clear proof of this, although he never revealed it unless the salvation of others demanded it, or he was commanded to do so by divine revelation. He had never studied Sacred Scripture under any human teacher, but unwearied application to prayer and the continual practice of virtue had purified his spiritual vision, so that his intellect was bathed in the radiance of eternal light and could penetrate its depths with its pure gaze. The spirit of the prophets rested upon him, in all its different forms, with an overflowing abundance of grace. By its miraculous power the saint often appeared to those who were far away and knew what went on at a distance; he could read the secrets of men's hearts and foretell what the future was to bring. There are many examples which prove this beyond doubt and I shall now describe a few of them.

4   *Fourth lesson:* In a provincial chapter at Arles St. Anthony, who was then a famous preacher and is now one of Christ's saints, preached an eloquent sermon to the friars on the proclamation Pilate wrote on the Cross, "Jesus of Nazareth, the King of the Jews." There St. Francis, who was then living far away, appeared at the door of the chapter hall; he was standing in mid-air with his arms stretched out in the form of a cross, blessing the friars. He brought

them all such spiritual comfort that their own interior witness was enough to convince them that his miraculous appearance was endowed with heavenly power. The saint himself was not unaware of this, so that it is clear that his spirit was penetrated with the light of that eternal Wisdom of which we read, "Nothing is so agile that it can match wisdom for agility; nothing can penetrate this way and that, ethereal as she; she finds her way into holy men's hearts, turning them into friends and spokesmen of God" (Wis 7, 24, 27).

5   *Fifth lesson:* When the friars were assembled in chapter as usual one day at St. Mary of the Portiuncula, one of them, under some pretext or other, refused to submit to obedience. St. Francis was praying in his cell at the time, interceding before God for the friars, and he became aware in spirit of what was happening. He had one of the friars summoned to him and told him, "Brother, I saw the Devil on that disobedient friar's back, holding him tightly by the neck. With a wicked spirit like that in control, he refused to be guided by obedience and gave rein to the Devil's suggestions. Go and tell that friar to submit to obedience immediately. The person who sends him this message is the person whose prayers made the Devil take flight in confusion." When he heard the message, the friar was seized with remorse; he was enlightened by the light of truth and he cast himself on the ground before the saint's vicar. He acknowledged his guilt and begged forgiveness, accepting the penance which was imposed upon him and performing it willingly, so that he always obeyed humbly after that.

6   *Sixth lesson:* When St. Francis was living in his cell on Mount La Verna, one of his companions had a great desire to have some short phrases of the Bible in the saint's own hand-writing. He was being assailed by a violent temp-

tation of the spirit and he was sure the writing would put an end to it, or at least make it easier to bear. He was worn out with longing and he was all on edge; but he was so humble, so self-effacing and unassuming, that he was overcome with shyness and did not dare to tell St. Francis about it. However, Francis learned from the Holy Spirit what his companion was afraid to tell him. He told the friar to bring him a pen and paper and then he wrote out some verses in praise of God with his own hand, as the friar wished, and added his blessing at the end. He gave the friar what he had written and immediately his temptation vanished. The sheet of paper was afterwards preserved and it restored innumerable people to health, showing the whole world how high a place the saint who wrote it held in God's eyes, that he should be able to give such efficacious power to a written message.

7   *Seventh lesson:* Another time a noble lady who was a very religious person came to St. Francis, confidently asking his help. Her husband treated her cruelly and tried to prevent her from serving Christ, and she begged the saint to pray to God for him, that he would soften his hard heart by his grace. When Francis heard what she wanted, he spoke to her and encouraged her in her good desires. He promised her that she would soon enjoy the consolation she longer for, and he told her to tell her husband from him and from God that this was the time of mercy, afterwards of justice. The woman put her trust in the words which the saint spoke to her and when she had received his blessing, she returned home without delay. There she met her husband and told him what the saint had said, expecting her wish to be granted without hesitation, as she had been promised. The moment her husband heard the words, the spirit of grace came upon him; his heart was touched, so that he allowed his wife to serve God freely and offered to

serve him with her. At his wife's suggestion, they lived a life of continence for many years, and they died the same day, she in the morning, "a morning sacrifice," he in the evening, "an evening offering" (cf. Nm 28, 8, 23).

8 *Eighth lesson:* When the saint was lying sick at Rieti, a looseliving and worldly cleric named Gedeon became seriously ill. He was brought to St. Francis, lying on a stretcher, and together with those who were present he begged him tearfully to bless him with the sign of the cross. But the saint replied, "You have lived a life of sinful indulgence, without a thought for God's judgment. I shall make the sign of the cross over you, not for your own sake, but because of the sincere petition of those who are pleading for you. But I tell you here and now that if you go back to your old ways, after you have been cured, you will infallibly have worse to suffer." Then he made the sign of the cross over him from his head to his feet and they all heard his bones cracking like dry wood being broken. The sick man stood up there and then, completely cured, and he gave praise to God saying, "I have been saved." After a short time, however, he forgot God once more and gave his body over to impurity. Then one evening he had supper at the house of one of the canons and spent the night there. That night the roof of the house collapsed on them all without warning; the others escaped death, but he was killed. So it was that this one event revealed the severity of God's justice for those who are ungrateful, and the accuracy and truth of the spirit of prophecy which filled St. Francis.

9 *Ninth lesson:* When St. Francis went to preach at Celano after his return from overseas, a knight begged him insistently to come to dinner. Francis was reluctant, but his host almost forced him to come, in his devotion to him. Before they sat down to eat, the saint offered praise and prayers to God as usual, like the truly spiritual man

he was. There he learned in spirit that his host must die in the very near future, and he remained standing with his mind fixed on God and his eyes raised up to heaven. When he had finished praying, he drew his host aside and told him that he was going to die soon, advising him to go to confession and encouraging him to do what good he could. The knight took his advice and confessed all his sins to the saint's companion. He put his affairs in order and entrusted himself to God's mercy, doing everything he could to prepare for death. They were all beginning their meal when the knight, who seemed quite strong and well, suddenly passed away, as the saint had foretold. He was carried off by a sudden death, but he was clad in the armor of repentance, thanks to St. Francis' spirit of prophecy. So he escaped eternal damnation and entered the dwelling-places of heaven, as our Lord promised in the Gospel.

CHAPTER V

Creatures Obey St. Francis — God's
Condescension towards Him

1   *First lesson:* The Spirit of God who had anointed him, together with "Christ the power of God, Christ the wisdom of God" (1 Cor 1, 24), was always with St. Francis. By his grace and power, hidden secrets were revealed to the saint and the elements were made subject to him. On one occasion, he was advised by his doctors to allow a cauterization in the hope of curing his eye-trouble. The friars begged him to agree and the saint humbly gave his consent. He knew that it would be an opportunity to practice virtue, as well as a remedy for his bodily ills. However, he recoiled instinctively at the sight of the searing-iron which was red hot; then he addressed the burning fire, calling it his brother, and commanded it in the name of God the Creator and by his power to temper its heat and

burn gently, so that he could bear it. The sizzling iron was plunged into the soft flesh and drawn from his ear to his eyebrow. Full of God as he was, Francis was overjoyed in spirit, "Give praise to the Most High!" he told the friars. "I can truthfully say that the heat of the fire did not harm me and I felt no pain."

2   *Second lesson:* St. Francis was seriously ill one time at the hermitage of Sant' Urbano and he felt the need of something to build up his strength. He asked for a glass of wine, but they told him there was none to give him. Then he told them to bring some water, and when it was brought, he made the sign of the cross over it and blessed it. Immediately, what had been ordinary water became excellent wine; Francis' holiness procured what the poverty of a lonely friary had not been able to provide. At the taste of the wine, he improved rapidly and it was clear beyond all doubt that God, the generous Giver, had enabled him to enjoy the drink he longed for, not because the taste appealed to him, but because it would restore him to health.

3   *Third lesson:* Another time, while traveling to a hermitage where he planned to devote himself to prayer, St. Francis rode an ass belonging to a poor laborer, because he was weak. It was summertime and, as the owner of the animal followed the saint into the mountains, he was exhausted by the long and grueling journey. Fainting with thirst, he began to cry out insistently, saying that he would die immediately, if he did not get something to drink. Francis dismounted there and then and knelt on the ground with his hands stretched out to heaven, and there he prayed until he knew that he had been heard. When he had finished, he said to his benefactor, "Go to that rock and there you will find running water. In his goodness Christ has made it flow from the solid stone just now for you to drink." The man ran to the spot Francis pointed out

and he had his fill of water which had been produced from a rock by the power of one man's prayer, a drink which God offered him from solid stone.

4   *Fourth lesson:* When St. Francis was preaching on the seashore at Gaeta on one occasion, the multitude crowded about him in their eagerness. He was anxious to avoid their demonstrations of enthusiasm and he stepped into a small boat which was close by the shore. While the crowd looked on in amazement, the boat moved out from the land without the aid of oars, as if it were being guided by some intelligent power. When it had gone a short distance out to sea, the boat stopped and remained there in the same position, despite the waves, while the saint preached to the people standing on the beach. When he was finished, he gave his blessing to the crowd who had seen the miracle, and pleaded with them to disperse. Then the boat moved in to land once more under the impulse of a divine command. Creation, which obeys its Author so well, was completely submissive to Francis who worshipped the Creator perfectly, and obeyed him without hesitation.

5   *Fifth lesson:* When St. Francis was staying in the hermitage at Greccio one time, the local people were in a very bad way because of a series of disasters which had struck them. Every year the corn and the vineyards were laid waste by hailstorms and ravenous packs of wolves had been known to attack human beings as well as livestock. St. Francis had pity on them in their misfortune, and he promised them in a sermon that all their troubles would be at an end, if they went to confession and were genuinely sorry for their sins, adding that he would guarantee it himself. They repented as a result of his exhortation and the moment they did so, the danger passed and they suffered no more calamities; neither the wolves nor the hailstorms did any further damage. In fact, hailstorms which

swept over neighboring areas and were approaching their territory either died away or changed course.

6 *Sixth lesson:* On another occasion, St. Francis was journeying about the valley of Spoleto preaching, when he came to a place near Bevagna in which a huge flock of birds of various kinds had gathered. The moment he saw them, the Spirit of God came upon him and he hurried to them. He greeted them cheerfully and told them to be quiet and listen to the word of God attentively. He spoke to them at length about the benefits God bestows on his creatures and the praise which they owe him. The birds showed their pleasure in a wonderful manner; they stretched out their necks and flapped their wings, opening their beaks and looking at him closely. They seemed to be trying to feel the marvelous power of his words. It was only right that St. Francis, who was so full of God, should have felt such tender affection for these irrational creatures; in their turn, they were so attracted towards him that they listened as he taught them and obeyed when he commanded them. They flocked about him quite tamely, when he came to them, and they stayed with him without any encouragement when he wanted them to listen to him.

7 *Seventh lesson:* When St. Francis tried to go overseas in search of the prize of martyrdom, he was prevented from achieving his goal by bad weather at sea. There the Ruler of all came to his aid and provided for him in his goodness; he worked a miracle for him when he was at sea, so that he was saved from the danger of death, together with a number of others. Francis was trying to make his way back from Dalmatia to Italy and he boarded a ship without any provisions whatsoever. Even as he stepped on the vessel, a man was sent by God bringing the food which Christ's beggar would need. He called a member of the crew who was a religious man and gave it to him, telling him to give

819

it to the friars who had nothing, when the time came. The ship was unable to make any headway because of the gale-force winds and they ran out of supplies, so that only a small portion of the alms St. Francis received from heaven was left. By his merits and prayers this small supply increased so much with God's help that it provided for all their needs, as the storm continued for several days before they reached Ancona, the port which was their destination.

8   *Eighth lesson:* On another occasion St. Francis was on a missionary journey with a companion and, as they were travelling from Lombardy to the Marches of Treviso, they were overtaken by night. It was a dangerous journey in the dark because of the river and the marshes, and his companion implored him to ask God to help them in their necessity. Francis replied with complete confidence, "God has power to banish the darkness and grant us the gift of his light, if it pleases him in his goodness." The words were scarcely out of his mouth when they were surrounded with such a brilliant light that, by God's power, they could see their way clearly; they could even see a large part of the country on the other side of the river, although it was dark everywhere else.

9   *Ninth lesson:* It was only right that a brilliant light from heaven should go before Francis in the darkness; this of itself would be enough to prove that those who follow in the footsteps of the light of life can never be engulfed in the darkness of death. Although they still had a long way to go, the light guided their steps miraculously with its brightness and gave them spiritual comfort, so that they arrived safely at the place where they were to stay, singing hymns of praise to God.

What a wonderful, what an outstanding person St. Francis was! Fire lost its burn, and water its taste, at his command; a rock produced water in abundance and inanimate creatures waited upon him; savage animals became tame and brute beasts listened to him eagerly. God himself, the Lord of all, bowed to his wish in his goodness; he supplied him generously with food and guided his steps with his light. Francis was a man of indescribable holiness and so all creation was subject to him, and the Creator of all condescended to him.

CHAPTER VI

The Stigmata of St. Francis

1   *First lesson:* St. Francis was a faithful and devoted servant of Christ and two years before he died he observed a forty-day fast in honor of St. Michael the Archangel on a mountain called La Verna, where he lived in complete solitude. There he experienced an extraordinary infusion of divine contemplation; he was all on fire with heavenly desires and he realized that the gifts of divine grace were being poured out over him in greater abundance than ever. The fervor of his seraphic longing raised him up to God and, in its compassionate tenderness, made him like Christ who chose to hang upon the Cross in the excess of his love. Then one morning about the feast of the Exaltation of the Holy Cross, as he was praying on the mountainside, Francis saw a Seraph with six fiery wings coming down from the highest point in heaven. The vision descended swiftly and came to rest in mid-air quite near him; then he saw that the Seraph was nailed to a cross although he had wings. His hands and feet were stretched out and nailed to the Cross, while the wings were arranged about him wonderfully; two of them were raised above his head and two were stretched out in flight, while the remaining two were joined to his body and covered it.

2   *Second lesson:* Francis was dumbfounded at the sight

and his heart was flooded with a mixture of joy and sorrow. He was overjoyed to see how graciously Christ regarded him, as he appeared to him so intimately in this miraculous vision. But the sight of the cruel way he was nailed to the Cross pierced his soul with a sword of compassionate sorrow. Then Christ who appeared to him visibly, granted him spiritual enlightenment and Francis realized that, although the agony of the passion was not in keeping with the state of a seraphic spirit which is immortal, his vision had a deep meaning for him. It was set before his eyes that, as Christ's lover, he might know he was to resemble Christ crucified perfectly, not by physical martyrdom, but by the fervor of his spirit. As the vision disappeared, after they had conversed mysteriously in great intimacy, it left his heart ablaze with seraphic eagerness and marked his body with the visible likeness of the Crucified. It was as if the fire of love had first penetrated his whole being, so that the likeness of Christ might be impressed upon it like a seal.

3   *Third lesson:* There and then the marks of nails began to appear in his hands and feet, the heads of which were in the palms of his hands and on the instep of each foot, while the points protruded on the opposite side. The heads appeared black and round in his hands and feet, but the points were long and bent back; they rose above the surrounding flesh and jutted out above it. The curved portion of the nails on the soles of his feet was so big and stood out so far that he could not put his foot firmly on the ground; a man could put his finger through the loop without difficulty, as I have been told by people who saw the stigmata with their own eyes. His right side was marked with a livid scar which often bled, and it looked as if it had been pierced with a lance. His habit and trousers used to be soaked with blood, so that the friars who washed them

knew at once that Christ's servant bore the likeness of the Crucified in his side, just as he bore it in his hands and feet.

4   *Fourth lesson:* Full of God as he was, Francis realized that he could not possibly conceal from his intimate companions, the stigmata which had been imprinted so plainly on his body. At the same time, he was afraid to make God's secret publicly known and he was thrown into an agony of doubt — should he reveal what he had seen, or keep silent about it. His conscience was pricking him and he eventually gave a full account of the vision, although very hesitantly, to the friars who were closest to him. He told them, too, that Christ had revealed a number of secrets to him, at the time of the apparition, which he would never communicate to any human being, as long as he lived. True love of Christ had now transformed his lover into his image, and when the forty days which he had intended spending in solitude on the mountain were over and the feast of St. Michael the Archangel had come, St. Francis came down from the mountain. With him he bore a representation of Christ crucified which was not the work of an artist in wood or stone; it had been inscribed on the members of his body by the hand of the living God.

5   *Fifth lesson:* In his humility and genuine sanctity, Francis did his best and took the greatest care to hide the sacred marks, but it was God's good pleasure to work a number of public miracles by means of them, for his own glory. This he did in order that Francis might shine like a brilliant star in the midst of the thick darkness, as the hidden power of the stigmata became publicly known through these miracles. Before St. Francis went to stay on La Verna, it often happened that dark clouds would form over the mountain and violent hailstorms would devastate the crops. After his vision, with its happy consequences, the hail stopped, much to the joy and amazement of the local

people. The unusually clear skies were to proclaim the extraordinary nature of his vision and the power of the stigmata which he received there.

6   *Sixth lesson:* Another time there was a serious outbreak of disease in the province of Rieti which affected sheep and cattle to such an extent that there seemed to be no remedy. Then a devout man was told in a vision at night to go immediately to the friars' hermitage where St. Francis was staying; there he was to obtain some of the water with which the saint washed his hands and feet and sprinkle the sick animals with it, which would put an end to the disease. The man did exactly as he was told and God granted miraculous power to the water which had touched the sacred wounds. The moment the affected animals felt even the slightest drop of it, their deadly illness was completely cured and they recovered their usual strength, so that they trotted off to pasture, as if there had never been anything wrong with them.

7   *Seventh lesson:* After he had received the stigmata, St. Francis' hands enjoyed such extraordinary power that their saving touch restored the sick to perfect health, and gave back life to limbs which had been paralyzed and withered. What is more, they even restored to life people who had been fatally injured. By way of anticipation, I shall mention two of the many miracles he worked and describe them briefly. At Lerida a man named John, who had great devotion to St. Francis, was wounded so badly one night that no one could believe he would survive the night. Then St. Francis appeared to him in a vision and touched his wounds with his sacred hands. There and then he restored him to perfect health, so that the whole countryside was loud in its praise of the standard-bearer of the Cross, saying that he was worthy of everyone's veneration. Who would not be surprised to see an acquaintance of his cruelly injured

and then enjoying perfect health, at almost one and the same time? Who could remember that, without being moved to give thanks? Certainly, no one could recall such a miracle of power and goodness in a spirit of faith, without feeling some increase of devotion.

8   *Eighth lesson:* At Potenza in Apulia there was a cleric named Roger who entertained frivolous thoughts about St. Francis' stigmata. Then without warning, he suffered a wound in his left hand, beneath his glove, as if he had been hit by an arrow from a crossbow; the glove itself, however, was completely untouched. For three days he was tormented by agonizing pain, so that he was heartily sorry for what he had done, and he appealed to St. Francis, pleading with him to help him by his glorious stigmata. He was cured so completely that all his pain disappeared and no trace of the injury remained. This is a clear indication that the stigmata were impressed on Francis by the power of Christ and shared his virtue, because it is he who punishes by inflicting injury, and cures by applying remedies, crushing the rebellious and restoring the brokenhearted (Lk 4, 18).

9   *Ninth lesson:* It was only right that St. Francis should be decorated with this extraordinary privilege; all his efforts, whether they were known to others or made in secret, were directed towards our Lord's Cross. What was his extreme gentleness, his austerity, his deep humility, his ready obedience, his absolute poverty, his perfect chastity; what were his bitter contrition, his gift of tears, his heartfelt compassion, his ardent zeal, his longing for martyrdom, his unlimited charity; what were all the outstanding virtues which made him so like Christ, if not the signs of an ever-increasing likeness to him and a preparation for the reception of his stigmata? The whole course of his life from the very beginning was marked with the glorious

mysteries of Christ's Cross. Eventually, at the sight of the majestic Seraph and of the abjection of Christ crucified, he was completely changed into the likeness of what he saw by a transforming fire of divine origin. For this we have the testimony of those who saw the stigmata and felt and kissed them; they took an oath that this was true, asserting that they had seen them with their own eyes and so made their testimony more certain.

CHAPTER VII

St. Francis' Death

1   *First lesson:* Francis now hung body and soul upon the Cross with Christ; the fervor of his seraphic love raised him up to God and he was consumed with zeal for souls, so that he shared his Lord's thirst for their salvation. He could no longer walk because of the nails protruding from his feet, and so he had himself carried, half-dead as he was, about the towns and villages. Like "the second angel coming up from the east" (Ap 7, 2) of whom St. John speaks in the Apocalypse, he enkindled the hearts of God's servants with a divine fire, and set their feet on the way of peace, marking their brows with the seal of the living God. He longed with all his heart to return to the humble beginning he had made at first, and to nurse the lepers once more, as he had done before, making his body which was already worn out with toil, serve him once again, as it had served him before.

2   *Second lesson:* With Christ for his leader, he proposed to achieve great victories, and even as his limbs bordered on collapse, he hoped to triumph over his enemy the Devil once again, because he was fervent and courageous in spirit. Merit, as we know, is crowned by patient endurance, and so, as Christ's poor, worthless servant, Francis

began to suffer from a variety of illnesses, that his treasure of glory might be increased. His suffering was so great that there was not a single part of him which did not have its share of agony; he had no flesh left and his skin seemed to cling to his bones. He was hemmed in with agonizing pain, but he called his cruel sufferings his sisters, not his pains. He bore them joyfully and praised God, thanking him for everything; the humble and happy way he could rejoice in his sufferings reminded the friars who were looking after him of St. Paul, while the courage of his steadfast spirit made him seem like a second Job.

3   *Third lesson:* St. Francis knew the day of his death a long time beforehand and, as it approached, he told the friars that he must soon fold his tent (cf. 2 Pt 1, 14), as Christ had revealed to him. Two years after the reception of the sacred stigamata — that is twenty years after the beginning of his religious life — he asked to be brought to St. Mary of the Portiuncula; it was there that he had first received the spirit of holiness and grace, through the Virgin Mother of God, and it was there that he would pay the price of his mortality and so win the prize, an eternal reward. When he arrived there, he was anxious to show that he had no longer anything in common with the world, after the example of Eternal Truth. In his last serious illness, which was destined to put an end to all his suffering, he had himself laid naked on the bare earth; he wished to struggle naked with his naked enemy, in that last hour which is given him to vent his wrath. As he lay there in the dust on the ground, like an athlete stripped for the arena, he covered the wound in his right side with his left hand, to prevent it being seen, and fixed his clear gaze on heaven. He was lost in the contemplation of its glory and he praised God for enabling him to go to him freely, stripped of everything in this world.

4   *Fourth lesson:* As the moment of his death drew near, the saint had all the friars who were there called to his side; he spoke to them gently with fatherly affection, consoling them for his death and exhorting them to love God. He bequeathed to them poverty and peace, a possession which was theirs by right of inheritance, entreating them earnestly to aim at an eternal goal and be on their guard against the dangers arising from the world. And with all the eloquence he could command, he implored them to follow in the footsteps of Jesus crucified. He was the father of the poor, and the friars sat grouped about him, as he lay there, his eyes already dim from weeping, not from old age. He was half blind and at the point of death, and he stretched out his arms over them in the form of the Cross, the sign he loved so well, and blessed all the friars both present and absent, in the power and in the name of Christ crucified.

5   *Fifth lesson:* Then he asked them to read the passage of St. John's Gospel which begins, "Before the paschal feast began" (Jn 13, 1); only a partition of flesh now separated him from his Beloved and he would listen to the beat of his voice in the Gospel phrases. All God's mysteries had been finally accomplished in him and he died quietly, praying and singing a psalm. His holy soul was freed from his body and absorbed in the abyss of eternal glory.

That very moment one of the friars, a disciple of the saint who was well known for his sanctity, saw his soul being borne on a white cloud over many waters straight to heaven, under the appearance of a radiant star. It shone with the beauty of a pure conscience, clad in the glory of his outstanding merits; the abundance of grace he had received and the Christ-like virtues he had practiced bore it aloft so surely that nothing could delay its entry into the vision of eternal light and glory.

6   *Sixth lesson:* The provincial minister of the friars in the Terra id Lavoro, Brother Augustine, a man who was very close to God, was at death's door at that time. He had been unable to speak for a long time, but now those who were with him suddenly heard him cry out, "Wait for me, father. Wait! I am coming with you." The friars were amazed and asked him to whom he was speaking. He told them he could see St. Francis going to heaven, and the moment he said it, he died peacefully.

The bishop of Assisi was on a pilgrimage to the shrine of St. Michael on Monte Gargano at the time, and St. Francis appeared to him at the moment of his death. He seemed happy and told the bishop that he was overjoyed to be leaving the world and going to heaven. When he got up in the morning, the bishop told his fellow pilgrims what had happened. On his return to Assisi, he investigated the matter carefully and discovered beyond all shadow of doubt that St. Francis had left the world the very moment he appeared to him in his vision.

7   *Seventh lesson:* In his infinite goodness God showed what St. Francis had been when he lived on earth by the prodigies and miracles which took place after his death. By his merits and intercession, God restored sight to the blind, hearing to the deaf, speech to the dumb; he made the lame walk and enabled the paralyzed to feel and move about; he cured those who had withered or crippled limbs, or were suffering from hernia; he rescued prisoners from captivity and brought those in danger of shipwreck to port and safety; he granted a safe delivery to women who were in childbirth, and cast out the Devil from those who were possessed; he cured those suffering from a hemorrhage and cleansed the lepers, healed people who had received fatal

injuries; he even restored the dead to life, which is the greatest miracle of all.

8   *Eighth lesson:* All over the world God's gifts are still being bestowed in abundance, through Francis' intercession; I who have written this life know this from my own experience. When I was still only a child, I became seriously ill and my mother made a vow to St. Francis, so that I was snatched from the jaws of death and restored to perfect health and strength. I remember it well and I put it on record now, for fear that I might be condemned for ingratitude, if I failed to mention such a favor.

Holy father, receive my poor thanks, such as they are, so unequal to what you deserve and the gifts you have given me. Receive our offering and forgive us our shortcomings. Pray for those who are devoted and loyal to you, that you may save them from the dangers of the present life and lead them to eternal happiness.

9   *Ninth lesson:* Nothing remains now but to say a few words by way of conclusion to all that we have written. The person who has read the whole story up to these words should meditate on one last point, which is this: St. Francis' wonderful life from the very beginning, his efficacy in preaching, and his outstanding virtues; his spirit of prophecy and his grasp of Sacred Scripture, together with the obedience shown him by irrational creatures; the reception of the stigmata and his marvelous passage from this life to heaven, are so many testimonies — seven in all — which proclaim him before the whole world as the glorious herald of Christ, bearing in his own body the seal of the living God (Ap 7, 2). They prove that he is worthy of all veneration by reason of his office, that his teaching is true, and that his holiness should arouse our admiration.

Those who abandon the Egypt of this world can follow Francis with complete confidence; the Cross of Christ will part the waters of the sea for them like Moses' rod, and they will traverse the desert to the promised land of the living, where they will enter by the miraculous power of the Cross, having crossed the Jordan of our human mortality.

May our Savior and Leader, Jesus, bring us there, through the intercession of St. Francis. To him be all praise and honor and glory, with the Father and the Holy Spirit in perfect Trinity, for ever and ever. Amen.

EXCERPTS FROM OTHER WORKS
WORKS
by St. Bonaventure

INTRODUCTION

The information on St. Francis which St. Bonaventure gathered to write a long and a short life served him in good stead also in his other writings, especially in the five sermons on St. Francis which are counted among his authentic works. Of the many references to the Seraphic Saint that are found in the nine big volumes of the Seraphic Doctor's *Opera Omnia,* we have selected eleven excerpts from the sermons and seventeen others which relate or refer to events in the life of St. Francis.

Some of these are even more striking and informative than the corresponding parts of the biographies. St. Bonaventure makes it clear that he is not just telling pious stories but narrating real happenings for which he had reliable testimonies. "His Holiness Pope Alexander told me. . . . The man who told me the story saw the whole thing with his own eyes. . . . A friar who stayed with St. Francis tells the story. . . ."

Especially noteworthy are St. Bonaventure's detailed account, description, and proofs of the stigmata of St. Francis. "Many lay folk saw the wounds with their own eyes. . . . Over a hundred clerics bore witness . . . under oath . . . that they had seen the stigmata with their own eyes and had touched them with their hands." And he recalls his own visit to Mt. La Verna thirty-three years after the death of St. Francis (i.e. in 1259), "the very mountain where I meditated on what I am writing . . . and one of his companions who was there at the time told me this himself (i.e., about the stigmata) and many others also."

The twenty-eight excerpts which follow, in our opinion, deserve a place among the sources for the life of St. Francis. They were translated from the Latin into English by Fr. Benen Fahy O.F.M.

— M. A. H.

1   God calls Job his servant because of his humility. . . .
Seven sons he had and three daughters (Jb 1, 2). The
name Job means "sufferer" and he is a good figure of St.
Francis, because his life was full of suffering. St. Francis
never ceased weeping, either for his own sins or those of
others. And if we look at the first generation of friars, we
see that he too had seven sons, and that he himself was the
eighth. Then at God's command he divided them into groups
and sent them two by two to the four corners of the
earth. Eventually God brought them all together again, at
his prayer.

St. Francis also had three daughters. At the beginning
of his religious life he repaired three churches, one in honor
of Sts. Cosmas and Damian, one in honor of St. Peter, and
a third in honor of our Lady. It was in the third church
that God revealed to him the kind of life he was to lead.

Moreover, he founded three orders. The first was the
Order of Friars Minor, and the second the Order of the
Sisters of St. Clare (at first they were known as the Poor
Ladies of Sts. Cosmas and Damian, but now that St.
Clare has been canonized, they are called the Sisters of
St. Clare). He also founded a Third Order, which is called
the Order of Penitents or the Brothers of Penance. St. Fran-
cis founded these three institutions and they were like three
daughters to him. They exist only for the service of God.
And so St. Francis was a humble servant, like Job, and
gave due honor to God (Sermon II on St. Francis, *Opera
Omnia,* IX, 576).

2   St. Francis was like unalloyed gold, purified in the furnace of poverty. . . . A friar who stayed at Montepulciano near Siena with St. Francis tells the story that one day they had nothing to eat except some dry bread, and they ate it in the open space in front of the church where there was a fountain. Then they went into the church and St. Francis was overcome with joy. He stayed there for a full hour and the friar was tired. Afterwards he asked the saint how he was feeling, and Francis replied that from the beginning of his religious life he had never felt such pleasure. God is pleased with poverty, the poverty that is accompanied by frugality, purity, humility, simplicity, kindness. Then Francis made a pilgrimage to St. Peter's in Rome, asking the Prince of the Apostles to be his patron, and he never betrayed the pledge he had made to poverty (Sermon II on St. Francis, *Opera Omnia*, IX, 579).

3   By his zeal for the Faith, St. Francis became God's chosen instrument. He went all over the world to spread the Faith. Three times he tried to go overseas, but was prevented by shipwreck. He went to the sultan in Spain, and to Morocco, where some of our friars afterwards died as martyrs. The third time he reached the sultan and proclaimed the Christian Faith, hoping that he would be torn limb from limb for it. But the sultan said: "We will call our philosophers and discuss our faith and yours." To this the saint replied, "Our faith is greater than human reason. Reason is of no use unless a person believes. I cannot argue from Sacred Scripture either, because they do not believe in it. Instead, make a big fire with wood, and I will go into it with your philosophers. When we see who is burned, we shall know whose religion is wrong." There and then the sultan's philosophers slipped away without waiting, and the sultan smiled saying: "I do not think I could find anyone to go into the fire with you." "Then I will go in on my own," said

St. Francis. "If I am burned, it is because of my sins. If not, then you should welcome our Christian Faith." But the ruler replied, "I could never do that. My people would stone me. But I believe that your Faith is good and that your religion is the true religion." From that moment faith in Christ was infused into his heart (Sermon II on St. Francis, *Opera Omnia,* IX, 579).

4   St. Francis had great devotion to the Incarnation and the Cross of Christ. In his love for our Lord and in his life, he was changed into Christ crucified, as the Seraph with six wings appeared to him. He had huge nails in his hands and feet, and they were bent double where they stuck out from the soles of his feet; there was also a wound in his side. He could say with all truth, in the words of the bride, "You have wounded me." He was dark-skinned by nature and because of his rigid penance; but his skin appeared gleaming white and red at his death, and he asked to be left lying naked for as long as it takes to walk a mile. With St. Paul he could say, "With Christ I hang upon the Cross. God forbid that I should make a display of anything except the Cross of our Lord Jesus Christ" (Gal 2, 19; 6, 14) (Sermon II on St. Francis, *Opera Omnia,* IX, 580).

5   Brother Pacificus had a vision in which he saw St. Francis marked with the sign of the Cross in the form of two gleaming swords, one of which reached from his head to his feet and the other from hand to hand across his chest.

It was also because of his zeal that he (Francis) was rapt in ecstasy the time that he went to preach in the cathedral. The friars had remained in the hut where they were living and he was about a mile away from them — which would be a mile and a half the way they calculate distance there — and he appeared to them in a fiery chariot. Their hearts were bathed in its radiance, so that they could see one another's consciences. He was taken away like Elias and found favor with God, so that he pleased God by his zeal for holiness. No one seems to worry nowadays about the harm which the Devil is doing, but St. Francis used to shed tears every day for his own sins and those of others (Sermon II on St. Francis, *Opera Omnia,* IX, 581).

6   When St. Francis was due to preach before Pope Honorius, he had his sermon all prepared on the advice of Pope Gregory; but when he began to speak, he could not remember a word. Then he told them, "Someone wrote a sermon for me (that is, Pope Gregory IX), and it was a profound sermon which I was to preach to you. But now I have forgotten all of it. If you will wait a little while, I shall pray to God and he will give me something to say." Then he gave himself to prayer, and he preached a marvelous sermon. More learning had he than his elders (cf. Ps 118, 100). He was a great saint. Creation in all its complexity as well as the divine simplicity of the uncreated was an open book to him. His spiritual powers enjoyed perfect freedom, and there was no darkness in him. He penetrated hidden secrets, and he appeared to those who were far away. He enjoyed God's illuminating spirit to the full. If we too have a mind to share the light of wisdom, we must avoid being occupied with material things (Sermon III on St. Francis, *Opera Omnia,* IX, 581-582).

7   St. Francis resembled the Father's power of creation by the numerous miracles which he worked. He cleansed lepers, raised the dead, and healed the sick; he restored speech to the dumb. He also enjoyed the power of command; not only were other human beings subject to him; he also had command over the fishes in the sea and all that flies through the air and the cattle (Gn 1, 26).

For example, we read that as he was travelling between two towns on one occasion he passed through a woods where the deer took to flight as he approached with his companion. But he called after one of them and told it, "Stop! Why are you running away?" The deer stood still immediately at his command, and he approached it and put his hands on its shoulders. "Go, now," he told it, "and give praise to God."

The birds of the air were subject to him in the same way. We are told that he came upon a huge flock of birds singing in a field one time, as he was on a journey. They were making a lot of noise with their singing, but he told them to be quiet and immediately they were silent. Afterwards he commanded them to sing once more, and they started off again (Sermon III on St. Francis, *Opera Omnia,* IX, 583).

8   St. Francis had knowledge of what was hidden; he knew many secrets and could foretell the future. His Holiness Pope Alexander told me that St. Francis foretold the death of Pope Honorius and the election of Gregory IX, who was then Cardinal Bishop of Ostia. He also prophesied that an earthquake would take place on a certain day and hour, and it happened just as he had foretold (Sermon III on St. Francis, *Opera Omnia,* IX, 583).

9   St. Francis practiced true humility and it was love of humility that made him call his Order the Order of Friars Minor, which means exactly what it says. He was the least of all, or at least he believed that he was the least of all. The first provincial minister he appointed, whose name was Pacificus, was a companion of his; and one day he had a dream in which he seemed to be carried away into paradise. There he saw a great number of thrones, all of them occupied, and one higher than all the others which was vacant. He asked to whom this belonged, and he was told that it belonged to St. Francis.

As a result of his dream, Pacificus asked the saint one day what he thought of himself. "I think that I am the greatest sinner in the world," the saint replied. "That is the way I feel and I have no doubt about it." "How can you say that?" asked Pacificus. "Look at all the thieves there are in the world, all the fornicators and murderers." St. Francis replied, "There is no one in the whole world who would not be more grateful than I, if God had given him as many extraordinary gifts as he has given me. That is why I think I am the greatest sinner in the world" (Sermon IV on St. Francis, *Opera Omnia,* IX, 588).

10   Some people are surprised that a Seraph should have been sent to St. Francis, when he was about to receive the stigmata of Christ's passion. They ask, "Was a Seraph crucified?" Certainly not. A Seraph is a spirit who is so called because of his fervent love, and the fact that a Seraph was sent to St. Francis means that he was on fire with the ardor of love. That is what the appearance of the spirit meant; the marks of the Cross which were imprinted on his body were a sign of the love which he felt for Christ crucified. He was completely transformed into Christ by the fervor of his love for him.

In proof of the stigmata we have the miracle which took place in a certain district where all the livestock fell sick. They ceased to take their food and died in a short time. No one knew what to do to save them; and one of the local people went to a holy man for advice, telling him how his stock was dying off. This holy person told him to get the water in which St. Francis had washed his hands and feet and sprinkle it over the animals and they would be cured. He did so and the animals immediately went back to their food. The man who told me the story saw the whole thing with his own eyes. St. Francis, therefore, resembled heaven by reason of his all-embracing love; but the Cross is the sign of perfect love, and so it had to be seen in him (Sermon IV on St. Francis, *Opera Omnia,* IX, 589).

11   God miraculously imprinted the sacred stigmata on his (Francis') body, as we can see from the number of witnesses, from their authority, and from their holiness. The number of witnesses alone is a sufficient guarantee; a large number of trustworthy lay folk who saw the wounds with their own eyes and over a hundred clerics bore witness to them. If any matter can be certified by the voice of two or three witnesses (Mt 18, 16), as we read in the Gospel, surely a hundred witnesses is more than enough.

However, the authority of the witnesses makes the miracle absolutely certain. It has been confirmed and authenticated by the Roman Curia which has supreme authority on this earth; and those who preach against the stigmata are excluded from the communion of the faithful by the same authority because they reject the truth.

Finally, the eminent sanctity of the witnesses banishes all doubt. St. Francis' companions were men of great holiness; their virtuous lives and their holiness were clear to all. And they were not content merely to affirm the truth of the stigmata in an off-hand way, but they swore to it under oath, declaring that they had seen the wounds with their own eyes and touched them with their hands. . . .

These marks were most unusual. They were quite contrary to all the laws of nature, and they far exceeded anything a human agent could do. They were unusual: it has never been heard that these precious jewels were seen in anyone else. They were contrary to the laws of nature, because Francis' side was pierced, so that it bled; and yet he never wore a bandage, although he worked hard and continuously for a long time afterwards. They were beyond the power of a human agent: it was not just that his hands were wounded or pierced through — that could have been done with a piece of wood or iron — the nails actually grew out of his flesh, with the head on one side and the point bent back on the other. They jutted out from the flesh and were

843

separated from it in his hands and feet. It was so extraordinary that no Christian could have any doubt that these marks had been given to him by a wonderful miracle (Sermon V on St. Francis, *Opera Omnia*, IX, 593).

12   Last of all, St. Francis speaks of the obedience in which his whole Order is to be subject to the head of the ecclesiastical hierarchy, when he says, "Brother Francis promises obedience to His Holiness Pope Honorius . . ." (Rule of 1223, c. 1). The name Francis was only given to the saint on second thought; at his baptism, his mother gave him the name John (Expositio super Regulam Fratrum Minorum, c. 1, n. 11., *Opera Omnia*, VIII, 396).

13   We also have the example of St. Francis to show that living on alms from day to day is quite in harmony with Christian perfection. St. Francis went begging and exhorted his friars to beg and, in addition, he proved the value of begging by the miracles which he performed. We see this in the case of the ship's crew whom he fed with what was left of the alms which had been given him, and whom he afterwards saved from all danger. Moreover, he got the pope to confirm his rule in which he says, "The friars are to serve God in poverty and humility, and beg alms trustingly" (Rule of 1223, c. 6) (De perfectione evangelica, quaest. 2, a. 2, fund. 23, *Opera Omnia*, V, 138a-139b).

14   Our Lord Jesus Christ brought us the good news of that peace which surpasses all our thinking (Phil 4, 7), and St. Francis only repeated his message. He spoke of peace at the beginning and end of all his sermons, and peace was the greeting which he had for everyone. In his prayer he aimed at ecstatic peace, like a citizen of the heavenly Jerusalem of which the Psalmist says, "Among the enemies of peace, for peace I labor; pray for all who bring Jerusalem peace" (Ps 119, 7; 121, 6). Francis knew

that Solomon's throne of heavenly wisdom could be attained only in peace; there, in the city of peace, he makes hiᴜ abode, dwells in Sion (Ps 75, 3).

For all my sins, I too thirsted for this heavenly peace with an aching heart, like St. Francis, I who am the seventh to succeed him as minister general of the Order, although I am unworthy in every way. About the time of his feastday, thirty-three years after his death, I went to mount La Verna, by God's providence, in search of peace of soul. While I was there, I devoted myself to contemplating subjects which would raise my heart to God, and I thought of the miracle which had happened to St. Francis in that very spot, the vision he had of a Seraph with six wings which looked like Christ crucified. The moment it came into my mind, I realized that this vision showed how St. Francis was lost in ecstasy in his prayer, and how a person can arrive at this.

The six wings can be taken to mean the six degrees of enlightenment by which the soul is prepared, step by step, stage by stage, until it arrives at peace, through the ecstatic rapture of Christian contemplation. However, there is only one way to achieve this, burning love of Christ crucified. This love carried St. Paul up into the third heaven (2 Cor 12, 2) and made him so like Christ that he could say, "With Christ I hang upon the cross, and yet I am alive; or rather, not I; it is Christ who lives in me" (Gal 2, 19 seq.). It completely absorbed the heart of St. Francis, so that it became visible in his flesh and he bore the stigmata of Christ's passion in his body for two years before he died (Itinerarium, prol. 1-3, *Opera Omnia,* V, 295ab).

15   Remember St. Francis' sermons before the sultan! The sultan suggested that the saint should hold a disputation with his priests, but Francis replied that the Christian Faith could never be discussed from a purely rationalistic

standpoint, because it transcends reason, and it was no use discussing it on the basis of Sacred Scripture, because his opponents did not accept it. Then he asked the sultan to have a fire lit and offered to go into it with his priests. We can see from this that we should be careful not to mix so much of the water of philosophy with the wine of theology that we are left with water instead of wine. That would certainly be a perverted miracle; we read that Christ changed water into wine, not vice versa (Collationes in Hexaemeron, c. 19, n. 14, *Opera Omnia*, V, 422b).

16   "Humility," says St. Bernard, "is the virtue which enables a man to know himself perfectly, so that he becomes worthless in his own eyes" (De gradibus hum., c. 1, n. 2, PL 182, 943). St. Francis had humility like this, with the result that he thought he was a worthless sinner. This was his heart's true love, his heart's true quest (Wis 8, 2) from the beginning of his religious life until his death; it was for this that he left the world, and had himself led through the town stripped of his habit. It was for this that he served the lepers, and confessed his faults publicly in his sermons, commanding one of his companions to shower him with insults (De perfectione ad sorores, c. 2, n. 1, *Opera Omnia*, VIII, 110a).

17   Like Christ, we should never give ourselves up to rejoicing to such an extent as to forget fear. St. Francis gives us the same example; when he was showered with marks of respect, he told his companion that they earned no merit in such company. It was when they were insulted that they made their greatest gains (Hexaemeron, c. 18, n. 11, *Opera Omnia*, V, 416a).

18   In order to encourage them to practice poverty in the use of clothing, our Lord told his disciples, "You are not to have more than one coat apiece" (Lk 9, 3). In this

the teaching of the Master was in harmony with that of his Precursor, who told the crowds, "The man who has two coats must share with the man who has none" (Lk 3, 11). Interpreted in a spiritual sense, these words of our Lord condemn all forms of pretense and hypocrisy. In other words, his disciples were not to appear one way in private and another in public; they were not to be like the people he condemned in the words, "They come to you in sheep's clothing, but are ravenous wolves within" (Mt 7, 15). St. Francis was always careful to avoid this pitfall; when he was sick, he refused to allow a piece of fur to be sewn on the inside of his habit until a similar piece was sewn on the outside (Comment in Evang. Lucae, c. 9, n. 7, *Opera Omnia*, VII, 218-219).

19   Our Lord showed his disciples that they should live poorly, telling them, "Take nothing with you to use on your journey" (Lk. 9, 3). In other words, they were to have no temporal means of support; by their example they were to proclaim the truth of St. Paul's words, "Empty-handed we came into the world, and empty-handed, beyond question, we must leave it" (1 Tm 6, 7). To make this perfectly clear, our Lord descended to details and said, "No staff, for support, or wallet to keep anything, or bread to eat, or money to buy provisions." He excluded any human means of support, to show that those who preach the Gospel should rely on God alone in their great trust in him, according to the words of St. Peter, "Throw back on God the burden of all your anxiety; he is concerned for you" (1 Pt 5, 7). And so, when St. Francis sent the friars out to preach, he used to say to them in the words of the Psalm, "Cast the burden of your cares upon the Lord" (Ps 54, 23). However, this does not mean that our Lord forbids prudent provision for the future; he merely forbids us to worry or be anxious, as he says himself, "Do not fret over

tomorrow; for today, today's troubles are enough" (Mt 6, 34) (Comment. in Evang. Lucae, c. 9, n. 5, *Opera Omnia*, VII, 218a).

20   Our author tells us that he was speaking to Brother Giles one time and he remarked that we were not prudent traders, like St. Francis. We waste everything we have, whereas we should be prepared to pay a man well for striking us. We have not even got the prudence of an ass; when an ass is carrying a load, he carries it all the better the more he is beaten and abused. In the same way, a truly obedient man must never cease doing good; indeed he should do it all the better when he has to suffer for it. Otherwise he can never attain contemplation (Hexaemeron, c. 23, n. 26, *Opera Omnia*, V, 448b-449a).

21   One of the friars tells the story that a woman was possessed by a devil who said that St. Francis did them a lot of harm and that five thousand of them had come together to try to overthrow him. The friar who heard this from the devil told St. Francis, but he only stood up and said that this made him stronger than ever (*Ibid.*, c. 18, n. 23, *Opera Omnia*, V, 418a).

22   If anyone reads the book of Wisdom, it will make him love God fervently. St. Francis often read it, for all his poverty, and his heart was ablaze with love. And that was perfectly obvious; he bore the stigmata of Christ crucified in his hands and feet and side (Sérmon II in Parasceve, *Opera Omnia*, IX, 265b).

23   The passion of Christ was impressed so vividly on St. Francis' memory that it seemed to him he could see Christ on his Cross (5 Sermo de angelis, *Opera Omnia*, IX, 626ab).

24   My dearly beloved, the angels are always remind-

ing us of all that God has done for us. Who created us? Who redeemed us? What have we done? Whom have we offended? If we would only remember this, we would realize that we have no excuse but to weep. Such heartfelt contrition was the gall with which St. Paul bathed his eyes, and St. Peter, too, went out and wept bitterly (Lk 22, 62). This was the gall which bathed the eyes of Mary Magdalen, because she also wept bitterly, and St. Francis wept so bitterly that he lost his sight. In our turn, we also should bathe our eyes in this bath, that we may have sight (*Ibid.,* 625-626a).

25   St. Francis wept so much that his doctors told him that he would have to stop, if he did not want to go blind. Eventually he actually did go blind, as a result of his constant weeping (1 Sermo de S. Maria Magdalena, *Opera Omnia,* IX, 557a).

26   If you ask what is the virtue which makes a person love creatures, because they come from God and exist for him, I reply that it is compassion and a sort of natural affection. For example, we see that even now a person can be very fond of a dog because it obeys him faithfully. In the same way, man in his original state had a natural inclination to love animals and even irrational creatures. Therefore, the greater the progress a man makes and the nearer he approaches to the state of innocence the more docile these creatures become towards him, and the greater the affection he feels for them. We see this in the case of St. Francis; he overflowed with tender compassion even for animals, because to some extent he had returned to the state of innocence. This was made clear by the way irrational creatures obeyed him (3 Sent., d. 28, q. 1, concl., *Opera Omnia,* III, 622b).

27   If a person turns his eyes wholeheartedly towards

this throne of grace and fixes his gaze on Christ hanging on his Cross, in a spirit of faith, hope, and charity, in devout admiration, exultation, appreciation, praise, and jubilation, then he celebrates the Pasch, that is, the passover, with him. With the cross for a staff, such a person will leave Egypt and pass through the Red Sea to the desert. There he will taste hidden manna and rest with Christ in his tomb, dead to the whole world. Yet, as far as it is possible in this land of exile, he will realize the meaning of the words Christ spoke to the Good Thief, "This day you shall be with me in Paradise" (Lk 23, 43).

This was also revealed to St. Francis on the very mountain where I meditated on what I am writing here. There, in a rapture of contemplation, a Seraph with six wings appeared to him, nailed to a Cross. One of his companions who was there at the time told me this himself and many others also. The saint was completely lost in God in ecstasy; he was made an example of perfect contemplation, just as he had already become an example of perfect action. Like a second Jacob, he was now to become Israel (cf. Gn 35, 10). More by his example than by his teaching God would invite all truly spiritual persons, through him, to go out of themselves in ecstasy and seek their refuge in God alone (Itinerarium, c. 7, n. 2 seq., *Opera Omnia,* V, 312b).

28   If any man has a mind to come my way, let him renounce self (Lk 9, 23). . . . But that is not enough, and so our Lord adds, "And take up his cross daily," by the constant practice of mortification, so that he can say in the words of St. Paul, "With Christ I hang upon the Cross" (Gal 2, 19); "we carry about continually in our bodies the dying state of Jesus" (2 Cor 4, 10), because "those who belong to Christ have crucified nature, with all its passions, all its impulses" (Gal 5, 24).

Note that our Lord says that his follower must take up his

cross daily; a man must take up the cross of penance anew every day, so that he can say, "Now I resolve to begin afresh" (Ps 76, 11). This was what St. Francis did; when he lay dying, he said that he was only beginning then to do something. "My brothers," he said to the friars, "we must begin now to do something. Up to now we have done very little." Christ's Cross has the power to give a person new life; "though the outward part of our nature is being worn down, our inner life is refreshed from day to day" (2 Cor 4, 16) (Comment. in Evang. Lucae, c. 9, n. 37, *Opera Omnia,* VII, 228ab).

LEGEND OF THE
THREE COMPANIONS

Translated from the Latin and Italian by
Nesta de Robeck, with Introduction by
Théophile Desbonnets O.F.M. (translated
from the French by Paul Oligny O.F.M.).

Nesta de Robeck's English version of *The Legend of the Three Companions* was first published in *St. Francis of Assisi: His Holy Life and Love of Poverty* (Franciscan Herald Press, Chicago, 1964, pp. 1-124), Library of Congress Catalog Card Number: 64-17584; SBN: 8199-0100-8.

INTRODUCTION

In 1244, at the Chapter of Genoa, Crescentius Grizi of Jesi was elected minister general. Before the close of the chapter, the new general "directed that all the friars make known to him in writing all that they might know with certitude concerning the life and miracles of St. Francis. In answer to this order, Brothers Leo, Angelus, and Rufinus who had been Francis' companions committed to writing in the form of a "legend" many facts that they had witnessed or that they had heard of from brothers worthy of credence.[1]

This information, furnished by Arnald of Sarrant in the *Chronicle of the Twenty-Four Generals*, constitutes in some way the birth of the *Legend of the Three Companions*. This legend enjoyed a peaceful status among Franciscan sources for almost six centuries. In 1768, the Bollandists, who took exception to the *Fioretti*, incorporated the *Legend* without discussion into the *Acta Sanctorum* along with the *Vita I* of Celano and the *Legenda major* of St. Bonaventure.

Around 1894, Paul Sabatier, subjecting "the documents we have on St. Francis of Assisi to a serious examination in order to establish the relative value of each of them," noted, in the wake of others, the gap that seems to exist between nos. 67 and 68-73 in the *Legend of the Three Companions*. To explain this gap, he formulated the hypothesis that the traditional text had been mutilated. It, therefore, did not represent the original legend in its entirety.

It was only a working hypothesis and an especially fruitful one since it ended in resurrecting the *Speculum Perfectionis*. But the success of a working hypothesis is not enough to substantiate its claims: one often ends up finding something quite different from what one set out to find.[2]

This was undoubtedly the opinion of Father Van Ortroy who, in a famous article in the *Analecta Bollandiana*,[3] subjects the *Legend of the Three Companions* to such a severe criticism that he demolishes it: the *Legend* was no more than a bad parody of official legends dating from the last part of the thirteenth century, and even from the first quarter of the fourteenth.

Paul Sabatier answered Fr. Van Ortroy with an article entitled "The Authenticity of the Legend of St. Francis by the so-called Three Companions."[4] This was the birth of the "Franciscan Question." It is still not resolved, even though its bibliography would fill several pages. Since the *Legend of the Three Companions* is one crux in this question, we will have to examine in some detail the problem it raises.

I. The Manuscripts

We are now in possession of some twenty manuscripts of the *Legend of the Three Companions*. We see no value in giving a complete list of them.[5] We shall simply point out those that deserve special mention.

1. Brussels. Royal Library, cod. 7771-2.[6] This manuscript, which the Bollandists call 'noster" (ours) is a copy they made of a manuscript (which today is lost), dating from 1454 and which had belonged to the friary of the Friars Minor of Louvain.

2. Rome. Vatic. Library, cod. 7339.[7] This is a manuscript of the fourteenth century. Its text is rather mediocre and contains several interpolations not found in the other manuscripts: a prologue "Praefulgidus ut lucifer"; the episode of the mysterious pilgrim who wanted to see the new-born child; a comparison between Samson and Francis; and interpolations that come perhaps from *De Cognatione B. Francisci*.

3. Foligno. Capuchin Friary.[8] This manuscript dates from the fifteenth century. It had previously been in the friary of Spello, hence the name of the manuscript, Spello-Foligno, which is sometimes given to it.

4. Rome. Friary of St. Isidore, cod. 1/25.[9] This manuscript dates from the first half of the fourteenth century. It belongs

to the same family as the preceding one and like it has an interesting peculiarity.[10]

5. Sarnano. Common Library, cod E n 60.[11] This manuscript, which dates from the beginning of the fourteenth century, has unfortunately been mutilated (it begins with no. 6 and ends in the middle of no. 63). It was discovered in 1939 by Fr. G. Abate. The text is obviously the same as that of the other manuscripts but in general it seems to be closer to the sources used by the compiler.

6. Paris. Mazarine Library, cod. 989.[12] This manuscript is dated 1460. The text is practically the same as the one published by the Bollandists in the *Acta Sanctorum.*

7. Verdun. Municipal Library, cod. 76.[13] This fifteenth-century manuscript contains a translation of the *Legend* in Picardian dialect.

8. The sole reason for mentioning the preceding manuscript is because it contains what is probably the oldest French translation of the *Legend of the Three Companions.* Others are Italian translations; only one deserves our attention.

In 1577, an Oratorian Muzio Achillei copied an Italian translation of the *Three Companions* of an older manuscript. This translation omitted the last two chapters of the original Latin, but on the other hand contained numerous other chapters.

In 1856, Fr. Stanilaus Melchiorri received the Muzio manuscript and published it. In the preface of this edition he noted that the Italian text was for all practical purposes a faithful translation of the traditional text of the *Three Companions,* but that the translator had "like a busy bee examined a goodly number of other documents," especially Celano, Bartholomew of Pisa, and the *Speculum Vitae* and that abundant extracts from these latter rounded out his work.

Forty years later, Father Marcellino da Civezza and Teofilo Domenichelli who, like Sabatier and a few others, were convinced that the text of the *Three Companions* was incomplete, believed that they had found in this Italian translation a witness to the existence of a more complete state of the *Legend.* With the help of the Italian text they therefore began their search for the original Latin text. In 1899 they published the result of this reconstruction under the title "La Leggenda di San Francesco, scritta da tre suoi Compagni, pubblicata per la prima volta nella vera sua integrità."

This endeavor had its hour of fame: approved by certain ones, like Sabatier, contended by others, such as Van Ortroy, it no longer enjoys any repute at present. In fact, the (relative) ease with which these authors were able to reconstruct the text by reinstating the short extracts from Celano and the *Speculum Perfectionis* in the correct place which can be suspected under the tangled texture of the Italian translation,"[14] should have warned them that their undertaking rested on a true begging of the question.

We would not have mentioned this manuscript were there not various translations still available to which we will call attention further on.

II. Editions

In 1926, on the fly-leaf of the edition of his *Vie de saint François d'Assise,* Paul Sabatier announced: "To appear later . . . Vol. X, *Legenda trium Sociorum,* Critical Edition." In 1936, the Fathers of Quaracchi, in offering the prospectus of Vol. X of the *Analecta* in the process of preparation, announced in their turn: D-3, *Trium Sociorum, quae fertur, Legenda S. Francisci.*

In view of the number of known manuscripts and their substantial identity, one might have thought that a critical edition of the *Legend of the Three Companions* should not have encountered insurmountable obstacles and that, consequently, at least one of these projects would see the light of day. Nothing of the sort happened, and no critical edition of this text exists to date. Fr. G. Abate is the only one who began one and gave, by way of a note in his edition of the manuscript of Sarnano, the variants of the Vatican and Foligno manuscripts.

Before making an inventory of the various editions of the *Legend,* may we express the hope that someone in the near future will bring this work to a successful conclusion.

Manuscript editions.

1. *Appendix inedita ad "Vitam primam," auctoribus tribus ipsius sancti Francisci sociis, . . . Acta Sanctorum* Octobris t. II, 732-742. This is the edition published in 1769 based on the Brussels manuscript (the "our" manuscript).

2. *Vita sancti Francisci de Assisio a Leone, Rufino, Angelo ejus sociis scripta, dictaque Legenda trium sociorum* ex cod. Bibl. Vatic. 7339. Pisauri (typ. Nobili) 1831. Editor anonymous (Rinaldi), pp. iv-62.

3. *Leggenda di S. Francesco d'Assisi scritta dalli suoi Compagni che tutt'hora conversavano con Lui, edita ed illustrate dal Padre Stanislao Melchiorri,* Recanati (typ. Morici e Badaloni) 1856, pp. vi-254. This is the edition of the manuscript of Muzio Achillei. Only a few copies were printed and it became so rare that, according to Fr. M. da Civezza and T. Domenichelli, neither Sabatier nor Msgr. Faloci-Pulignani ever saw a copy of it.[15]

4. *Legenda S. Francisci Assisien. a BB. Leone . . . ex cod. membr. Bibl. Vatic. num. 7339. Leggenda di S. Francesco . . . edita e corretta per cura del canonico Leopoldo Amoni.* Rome (typ. Monaldi) 1880, pp. 182. This edition has the Latin text of the *Three Companions* on the left page and the corresponding translation of the Muzio text on the right page. The author himself translated chapters 17 and 18 which are missing in the Muzio manuscript. The other chapters of the Muzio manuscript are placed in the appendix. Frs. M. da Civezza and T. Domenichelli point out that the Latin text manifestly comes from the Rinaldi edition and that it was not checked against the manuscript as the title would seem to lead us to believe.[16]

5. *Legenda trium sociorum, ex cod. Fulginatensi.* Edited by M. Faloci-Pulignani in *MF* 7 (1898), pp. 81-107. This is the edition of the Foligno manuscript but, according to Sabatier, with "regrettable errors of transcription."

6. *Legenda S. Francisci Ass. tribus ipsius sociis hucusque adscripta, Redactio antiquior juxta cod. Sarnanensem.* Edited by Fr. G. Abate in *MF* 39 (1939), pp. 375-432. This is the edition of the Sarnano manuscript: the variants of the Vatican

and Foligno manuscripts which are combined with it make it the first attempt at a critical edition.

7. *La Leggenda di S. Francesco . . . pubblicata per la prima volta nella vera sua integrità dai Padri Marcellino da Civezza e Teofilo Domenichelli . . .* Rome, 1899, pp. cxxxvi-270. We spoke of this edition above. On the right-hand side of the page it has the text of the Muzio manuscript and on the left-hand side the Latin text as reconstructed by the authors.

French translations.

Of the French translations which have been made, we might mention:

1. *Légende de saint François d'Assise par ses trois compagnons, manuscript du XIIIe siècle, publié pour la première fois par M. l'abbé Symon de Latreiche.* Paris (2nd edition), 1865, pp. 298. This is the French translation of the Muzio manuscript according to the edition of Fr. S. Melchiorri. We should note that Muzio Achillei states that he copied an older manuscript (vetustiori), in 1577; under the pen of Fr. Melchiorri it had become very old (antichissime). This is how it became a thirteenth century manuscript.

2. *La vie de saint François d'Assise racontée par les frères Léon . . . , traduite pour la première fois du latin . . . par M. l'abbé Huvelin,* Paris, 1891, pp. xx-158. The author himself tells us that he followed the Vatican manuscript.

3. Arvède Barine. *Saint François d'Assise et la légende des trois Compagnons.* Paris (2nd edition), 1901, pp. x-254. The translation forms the second part of this work. The author does not inform us which manuscript he used, but from the episode of the "mysterious pilgrim" we may deduce that it was the Vatican manuscript, probably known through the Amoni edition.

4. *La légende de saint François d'assise, écrite par trois de ses compagnons, publiée dans son intégrité par les PP. Marcellin de Civezza et Théophile Domenichelli . . . Traduction française du texte latin* (par L. de Kerval). Rome, Vannes, 1902.

5. *Légende de saint François d'assise, écrite par trois de*

ses compagnons, publiée pour la première fois dans sa véritable intégrité par les RR. PP. Marcellin de Civezza et Théophile Dominichelli. O.M. Traduction, introduction et notes d'Arnold Goffin, Bruxelles, 1902, pp. 309.

The title of editions 4 and 5 adequately indicates the text they follow. All the above observations regarding the original retain their value in regard to these two translations.

6. *La légende des trois Compagnons . . . traduite du latin par l'abbé Louis Pichard,* Paris, 1926, pp. 236. This is the translation of the text of the manuscript 989 of the Mazarine Library, which is obviously identical with the edition in the *Acta Sanctorum.*

III. The Problems Posed by the Legend of the Three Companions

Since the appearance of Fr. Van Ortroy's article and Paul Sabatier's answer, the criticism of the *Legend of the Three Companions* presents itself for all practical purposes in the form of the following four questions:

(a) Is the *Legend* authentic?

(b) Is it complete?

(c) Is the introductory letter authentic?

(d) Is the introductory letter part of the *Legend*?

There are numerous ways of combining the answers to these four questions. It can be said that all possible hypotheses have been upheld. In Fr. Abate's study[17] we will find the list of the outstanding names of the critics along with the position they have taken on this problem: it comprises 26 names and fills three entire pages.

It is not our intention here to study all the solutions proposed and to examine their merits. Let us simply call attention to the following extreme solutions:

(a) The *Legend* is authentic and contains elements prior to I *Celano* (Moorman).[18]

(b) The *Legend* is only a belated, unauthentic imitation that dates from the last part of the thirteenth or the beginning of the fourteenth century (Van Ortroy).[19]

We shall first examine the question of the integrity of the

861

Legend, then the problems posed by the introductory letter, and finally the most important problem, that of the authenticity of the *Legend.*

IV. Is the Legend of the Three Companions Complete?

Chapter 16 of the *Legend* ends with the evocation of events that date from 1221; after a brief reminder of the stigmata, it jumps from these events directly to the death of St. Francis in 1226. Many things happened between these two dates, and the quick evolution of the Order had even provoked a veritable conscience-crisis in St. Francis. How can we admit that Leo, Angelus, and Rufinus, ever faithful companions, could have passed over so important a period?

Is the gap between chapters 16 and 17 an indication of a deliberate or accidental mutilation? Or, despite this gap — which would then have to be explained — is the text we have the integral text of the *Legend?* This is how the question of the integrity of the *Legend of the Three Companions* is posed.

Paul Sabatier thinks that the lacuna points to a mutilation and in fact everything inclined him to state that the *Legend* is *incomplete*: this hypothesis was helpful since it led him to resurrecting the *Speculum Perfectionis.* It served the thesis he sustained in a marvelous way; namely that the ideal of St. Francis was distorted by the party of the Community symbolized by Crescent of Jesus; and that his hypothesis seems to be confirmed by the existence of an apparently more complete form of the legend, the one which was published in 1856 by Fr. S. Melchiorri.[20]

Van Ortroy, on the contrary, believes that the *Legend* is complete: the lacuna only underscores the clumsiness of the imitation and especially it has the manuscript tradition in its favor.

On this point, it does seem that Van Ortroy is right, or to put it more precisely, that on this point his conclusion does not exceed the premises in our possession. He notes: "For example, the examination of the manuscripts — and they are rather numerous — bears witness to a text that is invaribly the same. In order to maintain nevertheless that the traditional

862

text underwent mutilations, we should need to prove that all the known copies come from one and the same original which already had lacunae. But this is pure conjecture that has no solid basis whatsoever." [21]

We therefore admit that the traditional text of the *Legend of the Three Companions* is complete.[22] The lacunae toward the end of the text remain, for the time being, unexplained.[23]

V. *The Introductory Letter*

Dated from Greccio in 1246, a dedicatory letter to the Minister General Crescentius of Jesi precedes the *Legend.* Two passages in this letter give rise to difficulties.

First, the authors say that they did not write this introductory letter in the form of a legend (quae tamen per modum legendae non scribimus); now, it is clear that the text that follows is presented as a legend and observes its formal rules.[24]

Further on, they add: "if the venerable biographers (that is to say, Thomas of Celano and Julian of Speyer) had been acquainted with our accounts, they would not have passed them over in silence." Now, one third of the *Legend* is composed of textual extracts from I Celano and from Julian of Speyer. Consequently, it was not new facts that were passed over in silence.[25]

Is the contradiction between the text of the *Legend* and the statements of the introductory letter real or only apparent? Such basically is the question that is posed.

The partisans of the authenticity of the *Legend* evidently admit the authenticity of the introductory letter and its connection with the text.

Conversely, most of those who regard the *Legend* as apocryphal are however partisans of the authenticity of the letter, but the letter would then belong to another document that is lost today. Such a position is, to say the least, surprising, for if the *Legend* is not authentic, what advantage, what reasons are there for reserving a special fate for the introductory letter?

A primary reason would be to transfer the guarantee of authenticity to another document adduced by the letter. Such documents do exist, but is there truly any objective reason to assign the letter as a preface to them? It is not enough that their contents do not contradict them.

Another reason, a "sentimental one," is that this letter is a very beautiful composition that stands up well when compared to the most beautiful compositions of French literature and one would not condemn this "charming prairie" to the hell of the apocrypha, for in it the companions admit they have culled "certain flowers which to them were the most beautiful."

But here it seems that those who wish to dissociate the introductory letter from the *Legend* are mistaken. In transposing the argumentation of Van Ortroy regarding the integrity of the *Legend,* we could say: for example, the examination of the manuscripts — and they are rather numerous — bears witness to a connection between the introductory letter and the text of the *Legend.* In order to prove that the introductory letter belongs to another document, there would have to be other manuscripts in which the *Legend* would not be preceded by the letter, or many manuscripts in which the letter would be the preamble of another document. But this is pure conjecture that has no solid foundation.

We admit then that in the present state of our knowledge of manuscript tradition, the introductory letter must not be dissociated from the *Legend* and that it must follow the same fate as the *Legend.*

For the time being, this leaves the relative contradiction between the text of the letter and the contents of the *Legend* unexplained.

VI. The Authenticity of the Legend

It is extremely difficult to approach the study of the authenticity without preconceived ideas. All the writings that have appeared on this subject are proof of this. As objectively as possible, we shall attempt a description of the data of the problem without taking a stand on the questions that are still controverted.

1. The data of external criticism.

In his work, the *Conformities,* written between 1385 to

1399, Bartholomew of Pisa frequently quotes the *Legend of the Three Companions,* thus proving that at that time it was considered a universally admitted source for the biography of St. Francis.[26]

The first known mention of the *Legend* is found in *Chronicle of the Twenty-Four Generals,* a work of Arnald of Sarrant, and dated from the second half of the fourteenth century. For the author of this chronicle the *Legend* dates from 1246; and it is only later that Celano would have composed his *Vita II.* But Arnald of Sarrant wrote more than a century after the facts and does not indicate the source of his information.

Before the *Chronicle of the Twenty-Four Generals* there is no mention of the *Legend* written by Brother Leo and his companions. This observation would have little value if we found even an implicit citation of it in a prior work: but there is none. This silence, which would be surprising on the part of Bernard of Besse or of Salimbene, becomes especially impressive on the part of the Spirituals who were living at the end of the thirteenth century or the beginning of the fourteenth. It was in their interest to neglect nothing that could come from the entourage of Brother Leo. Now, neither Ubertino da Casale nor Clareno mention or cite the *Legend of the Three Companions,* whereas they do cite the *Speculum Perfectionis* and other writings attributed to Brother Leo.

The number of manuscripts that are known — some twenty, coming in great part from Franciscan milieus — is surprising. The *Legend of the Three Companions* has never been an official legend that benefited from all the solicitudes of professional copyists and, on the other hand, it likewise must have been a victim of the decree of the Chapter of Paris in 1266 which ordered the destruction of the legends prior to the *Legenda major.* Let us recall, by way of comparison, that we have only two manuscripts of *2 Celano* and only one of the *Treatise of miracles* and that practically all the manuscripts of *1 Celano* come from Cistercian milieus.

Of all the manuscripts of the *Legend,* the oldest is that of Sarnano, discovered and published by Fr. G. Abate. It would date from the beginning of the fourteenth century and would consequently constitute the oldest witness of the existence of the *Legend*.

External criticism enables us to state that the *Legend of the Three Companions* surely existed around 1320-1330. On the contrary, the silence of the Spirituals and to a lesser degree the abundance of the manuscripts seem to forbid assigning it a definite older date.

2. The data of internal criticism.

The first man who tackles a problem exercises a strong influence upon it by his own approach to it. And so it is with the internal criticism of the *Legend of the Three Companions* which will always depend for its form on Van Ortroy. Whether we follow his footsteps, like Fr. Abate, or whether, like Fr. Clasen, we oppose him, it is always within the framework that he set up in his article in the *Analecta Bollandiana.*

In this article the text of the *Three Companions* occupies the left column of each page. In the right column, entitled *Sources,* there are parallel passages taken from other works treating of the same subject and whose date of composition is known. Van Ortroy drew the conclusion that the *Legend* was posterior to the most recent of these texts, in this case the *Liber de Laudibus* of Bernard of Besse.

Moreover, Van Ortroy thought he could discover in the text of the *Three Companions* four anachronisms which could only be the work of a later editor. As early as 1901, Paul Sabatier did justice to the alleged anachronisms;[27] in 1964, Fr. Clasen again examined the question[28] and reached the same conclusion: there are no real anachronisms in the *Three Companions;* there is only a difference of perspective between the editor who relates history-in-the-process-of-its-making and ourselves who look at history-already-made. It is therefore useless to examine this question in detail.

The method Fr. Van Ortroy inaugurated was excellent; it was even ahead of its time. In those days it was almost believed that all these questions would be solved once new manuscripts were found, manuscripts that until then had been forgotten and were in the nooks of some library. The abundant

866

harvest of manuscripts that were exhumed during the first quarter of the twentieth century amply justified this belief, thereby explaining, for example, Fr. Bihl's position who in numerous places in his writings denied that the literary method by itself could solve the problems of criticism.[29]

But since 1922, the date of the discovery of the manuscript 1046 of Perugia by Fr. Delorme, only the manuscript of Sarnano discovered by Fr. Abate has been added to the collection. The hunt for manuscripts seems to be over; we must therefore be satisfied with the ones we have and apply to them the only method that remains available: the literary method. Fr. Abate had already been applying it, and it enabled him to reach several important conclusions. S. Cavallin proposes the same method in an article whose title well defines the method that should henceforth be used: "The Franciscan Question as a philological problem."

Certainly Fr. Van Ortroy was correct in those early days of research in taking a census of the texts parallel to the *Legend*. The fact that he used this as a complementary proof of a hypothesis of which he was convinced, without subjecting them to a thorough analysis, is regrettable; for, it is clear that all these parallel passages do not have the same meaning.

The form of the text. To be convinced of this, it is not enough to consider them as a whole nor is it enough to read the commentary of the critics. We must examine the parallel texts step by step, word by word. A good way to do this consists in underlining the words and expressions common to the text of the *Three Companions* and the text of the alleged source.

We will then note that when the *Three Companions* parallel *1 Celano* and Julian of Speyer on the one hand and to a slight degree the manuscript called *Anonymous of Perugia*[30] on the other, the parallel continues for entire sentences and practically without transpositions. In this case the *Legend* does not, so to speak, have a word that is proper to it, and we get the impression that the editor simply strove to compose a cursory summary of a text he had before him.

The case is especially striking, for example, with regard to nos. 16-18 which are almost exclusively made up of expressions and sentences from *1 Celano* 8-13, and nos. 25-27 are composed of expressions and sentences from Julian of Speyer 15-17.

On the contrary, when the parallel exists with *2 Celano* it is evident only for isolated words, short expressions, and with frequent transpositions.

The difference is particularly noticeable in the events of the life of St. Francis which Celano had already related in his *Vita I* but which he treats again in his *Vita II,* as, for example, the "kissing of the leper," which was studied by Cavallin,[31] or the "dream of arms."[32] There we find a very close parallel with the texts of *1 Celano* and an extremely hazy parallel with *2 Celano.* We get the impression that the author of *3 Celano* thought he had something new to say but that mistrusting his qualities as a writer he preferred to follow the source before him (*1 Celano*) closely and to inject what he had to say here and there.

We must therefore admit that *1 Celano* and *2 Celano* are not in the same situation with respect to the *Three Companions*; otherwise, as Cavallin notes, "it would become impossible to explain why the compiler of the *Legend* took up the sentences of *1 Celano* in the same chapter scarcely without modifying them, but very much modified those of *2 Celano.*"[33]

Fr. Van Ortroy had also found parallels between the *Legend of the Three Companions* and the *Legenda major* of St. Bonaventure, parallels that we must now examine.

There are not many of them and as a whole they are of little significance, for they consist of short, rather banal, sentences, so much so that there is a non-negligible probability of seeing them spring spontaneously from writers totally independent of each other, but who are treating the same subject.[34]

There is, however, a parallel with the *Legenda major* that poses a real problem. We are referring to nos. 69-70 with chapter 13 of the *Legenda major* regarding the imprinting of the stigmata. It is indeed difficult to imagine under the pen of the compiler of the *Three Companions* a phrase of a "cursus" as elegant as the sentence "Cum enim seraphicis desideriorium ardoribus . . . "; it is also difficult to imagine on his part the highly technical use of such a philosophical expression as "sursum agere." Here the *Three Companions,* clearly depend on the *Legenda major.*

Is this lone parallel enough to overthrow the conclusions we have reached? And shall we have to admit that, although not dependent on *2 Celano,* the *Three Companions* do depend on the *Legenda major* which was written 12 years later?

Let us note, however, that in no. 69 there is an ablative absolute "qua visione disparente" precisely where St. Bonaventure had written "disparens igitur visio," and that the compiler did not accustom us to such a concern for latinity. Does this mean that a different writer wrote no. 69? This would bring us to the hypothesis of Sabatier in a modified form: a *Legend of the Three Companions,* not mutilated by order of Crescent, but completed at a later date by someone else.[35]

Fr. Van Ortroy had also found parallels with the *Liber de Laudibus* of Bernard of Besse and the *Vita beati Aegidii.* But these parallels are truly by far too few and too insignificant to compel us to modify a conclusion which the ensemble of the other parallels imposes. At best we can admit that each of them poses a clearly defined problem and is susceptible to an equally delimited solution, all the more so since the attentive examination of these passages shows that, in reality, Bernard of Besse and the author of the *Vita Aegidii* depend on *Anonymous of Perugia.*

The study of the text, therefore, clearly suggests that if the author of the *Three Companions* depends on *1 Celano* and Julian of Speyer, he surely does not depend on *2 Celano,* nor probably, with perhaps one exception, on the *Legenda major.*

After a very searching examination of Fr. Van Ortroy's position, Fr. Clasen reached the same conclusions. He notes that Van Ortroy's theory obliges us to presuppose that the authors of the *Three Companions* would have worked in the following way: "Jot down, first of all, one by one, the sentence models and scraps of phrases on different cards, and then transcribe them as such in the order in which these cards are arranged."[36]

869

The contents. After having closely studied the text of the *Three Companions* in its relationship with the parallel texts which could have been its sources, we can also subject it to other proofs, this time not in regard to its form but as to its contents.

The first of these proofs consists in what Paul Sabatier calls the quantity of the marvelous. "Reduced to its simplest terms, it might be expressed in the following proposition: the role of the marvelous in a document is in direct proportion to the age of the document. A document contemporary to the facts it reports contains scarcely more than the seeds of the marvelous. This latter naturally tends to develop and, if we have ten different documents on one and the same fact bearing no date, we can classify them chronologically almost without any chance of error, simply by observing the place occupied by the marvelous."[37]

Even a superficial examination of the parallels between the *Three Companions* and *2 Celano* clearly shows that there is more of the marvelous in Celano. For example, in 3 S 2, Francis' mother simply answers her neighbors; in 2 C 3, she speaks "under the inspiration, as it were, of a divine oracle." In 3 S 4, while a prisoner in Perugia, Francis answers his companions with the assurance of a young man full of life; in 2 C 4 his answer becomes a prophecy. In 3 S 12, Francis meets a leper and embraces him; but in 2 C 9, the leper disappears miraculously, implying that he was Christ.

A second proof consists in observing whether certain preoccupations that appeared at a very determined period do not underlie the redaction of the text. Now, as Fr. Clasen notes, there is no discussion in the *Three Companions* regarding the observance of poverty, neither by way of allusion to the battles between the seculars and the Mendicants which took place at the University of Paris from 1252 to 1272 nor by way of an allusion to the struggles that made the Spirituals opponents of the party of the Community from the end of the thirteenth century up to the Council of Vienne in 1311 and even beyond that date.[38]

The argument "a silentio" is obviously always a delicate one to handle; but, as Fr. Clasen remarks, preoccupations relative to the observance of poverty under one or the other form that we have evoked, are just as evident in the *Speculum Perfectionis* and in the *Acts* as they are in the *Legenda major* and the *Liber de Laudibus.*

We shall conclude this presentation of the data of internal criticism with the final remark of Fr. Clasen: there are a certain number of terms and statements in the *Legend* that can only have come from the Companions, for otherwise they would evince an affectation of archaism which a later compiler could not have kept up to the very end of his work without imperfections.

To sum up, apart from the smallest of details, all the arguments of internal criticism lead us to assign the composition of the *Legend of the Three Companions* to a late date. More specifically, this date falls between Julian of Speyer and *2 Celano,* and under these conditions, why not 1246, the date mentioned by the introductory letter.

3. *Solutions.*

Having arrived at this point of our research, it must have become evident to the reader that there are only two possible solutions.

First solution. The arguments of external criticism carry the day and impose a late date for the composition of the *Legend of the Three Companions,* that is to say, the beginning of the fourteenth century.[39]

But this solution does not answer the question posed by internal criticism: why did the compiler follow *1 Celano* and Julian of Speyer step by step and deviate so much from *2 Celano*?

A psychological explanation is impossible, whatever expedient we use. Sabatier, Cavallin, and Clasen have all noted this.

Perhaps we might advance a hypothesis by seeking to determine, not the documents that the compiler had before him, but those he might have actually consulted. There is no difficulty in this for the *Legenda major.* Almost every friary must have had a copy of it. For Bernard of Besse, there is no problem either. But for Celano? Let us not forget that in 1266 the Chapter of Paris ordered that all earlier legends be destroyed.

The question boils down to knowing under what form and in what state the compiler could have knowledge of these legends at the beginning of the fourteenth century. Without prejudging the results that such a study may contribute, a study which to our knowledge has not been undertaken, we nonetheless believe that there is more chance of it ending in the contrary result, that is to say, in showing that a compiler, working at the beginning of the fourteenth century in a Franciscan friary could not have even found a copy of *1 Celano*.

Second solution. We might consider that the arguments of internal criticism carry the day and demand an earlier date, more specifically 1246, the date of the introductory letter.

But this solution does not answer the question asked by external criticism: why does it seem that the *Legend of the Three Companions* appeared only at the beginning of the fourteenth century?

Here, we can only propose a hypothesis, a door of research. Following the Chapter of Genoa in 1244, documents were sent to Crescent to be transmitted to Celano. They came from Brother Leo and his companions, but also from other friars. At this stage, there were but a very few copies of these documents, perhaps only one copy.

Once used by Celano for the redaction of his *Vita II*, they had fulfilled their mission; they may have disappeared, and that is what happened to some of them;[40] at best, they were stacked in a corner and forgotten. They were forgotten even if they escaped the destruction ordered by the Chapter of Paris (an order that did not perhaps affect them: they were not legends but documents).

Then, at a much later date, in a fervent milieu, a rummager, not completely satisfied with the official legend of St. Bonaventure, found the forgotten document in the bottom of a closet or on some library shelf. He transcribed it "for his edification." The renown of the supposed authors, the quality of the text did the rest: the legend became famous.

VII. The Style, the Author, and his Sources

Paradoxical as it may seem to speak of the style of a work that so closely follows certain sources that antedate it, we can speak of the style of the *Legend of the Three Companions.*

Fr. Abate and S. Cavallin have made very pertinent observations on this subject, thereby opening up a way that we must now systematically explore.

The Style. Fr. Abate notes a very decided tendency to transform what is given in direct discourse into indirect discourse and the systematic replacement of the word *Lord* by *God.*[41]

Cavallin notes "in Celano an obvious tendency to place the verb after its objects according to the usage of classical language, whereas the *Legend of the Three Companions* presents a more Roman (modern) order of words." He notes also that "Celano uses the ablative absolute, the gerund, and the infinitive skillfully where the *Legend* has personal tenses or present participles."[42]

Whatever may be said of this analysis of style, all critics agree in admitting the literary skill of the redactor, both in the way he uses and transforms earlier sources and in the way in which he composes what is proper to him.

The author. Who then is the author of the *Legend*?

Surely it is not Brother Leo. We are well acquainted with his style in documents which undoubtedly must be attributed to him, and this style is not that of the *Legend.*

The identification of the author is bound up with the date attributed to the *Legend*. It was in this way that various names[43] have been proposed by those who reject the·date 1246 for the *Legend* and the authorship of the Companions.

At least by way of hypothesis, we propose the name of one of the three signers of the letter: Brother Angelus. In *De Cognatione S. Francisci,* Arnald of Sarrant, comparing each of the first twelve companions to the twelve Apostles of Christ, compares Brother Angelus to St. Matthew and writes: "Just as St. Matthew wrote the Gospel of Christ, Angelus wrote the life of St. Francis."

It is objected that Arnald of Sarrant let himself become

involved by the following schema: among the four evangelists, St. Matthew is represented by an angel; it is therefore Brother Angelus who corresponds to him and, so that the correspondence might be complete, Brother Angelus had to write a life of St. Francis. But, a few pages farther on, Thomas of Celano is compared to St. Matthew with the reminder of the figure of the angel. Likewise, Brother Leo is first compared to St. John represented by the eagle and Arnald of Sarrant reminds us that he wrote a life of St. Francis in which the celebrated formula "nos qui cum illo fuimus" is the counterpart of "et qui vidit testimonium perhibuit" of St. John. But a few pages farther on, St. Bonaventure is the one who is compared to St. Matthew with the reminder of the figure of the eagle, whereas Brother Leo is compared this time to St. Mark.[44]

The incoherence that reigns in these comparisons is perhaps the sign that the author does not attach very great importance to it. Under these conditions we could admit that he did not allow himself to become involved in exhausting the parallelisms at any cost and that, consequently, what he says of Brother Angelus might be the witness of an earlier tradition attributing to him a special role in the redaction of the *Legend*.

One might also object that Arnald of Sarrant was content with transcribing the date of the introductory letter. But in that case, he should have likewise attributed the redaction of a life of St. Francis to Rufinus, which he did not do. And in this case likewise, he would not have characterized the work of Leo as he did, since the formula "nos qui cum illo fuimus" is not found in the *Legend*.

The sources. We have already pointed out that a minute examination shows on the one hand a very close parallel between the text of the *Legend* and, on the other hand, the *Vita I* of Celano, the *Vita S. Francisci* of Julian of Speyer, and *Anonymous* of Perugia. This parallel proves that these three works are the sources from which the author of the *Legend* drew.

Concerning the *Vita I* of Celano composed in 1228 and the *Vita S. Francisci* of Julian of Speyer composed between 1232

874

and 1235, there is nothing to say: their date of composition does not conflict with the use made of them.

Anonymous of Perugia, on the contrary, demands a more detailed examination: the date that we can attribute to the *Legend* depends in part on the period when it was written.

Anonymous of Perugia (not to be confounded with the *Legend of Perugia*) got its name from the fact that its author is unknown and from the fact that the only known manuscript of it was preserved at Perugia for a long time. This manuscript disappeared in the course of the nineteenth century, but there are two copies of it. The first was printed in 1671 at the request of the Bollandist D. Papebroch;[45] the second by Fr. Ubaldo Tebaldi, librarian and archivist of the *Sacro Convento* of Assisi, in the course of the eighteenth century on the occasion of a correspondence with another Bollandist, C. Suyskens.[46]

This manuscript contained first of all a *Vita beati Aegidii* somewhat different from the one found in the *Chronicle of the Twenty-four Generals.* This was the life that the *Acta Sanctorum* reproduced for April 23, and it was in order to get the text that Papebroch had asked for a transcript of the manuscript. But the manuscript also included *Anonymous of Perugia,* whose text was not used by Suyskens until a century later.

Among other information, Fr. Tebaldi made it known to Suyskens that the manuscript did not date back farther than the fifteenth century.

The only question that arises here is the date of this work. In the prologue the author presents himself as a "disciple of the Companions of Francis." Fr. Abate concludes from this that he belonged to the second Franciscan generation, that he was therefore a contemporary of St. Bonaventure, and that he could not have written his account before 1250-1260.[47] It seems that this conclusion is not a convincing one: if we admit — and this is unlikely — that the expression "disciple of the Three Companions" excludes the fact that the author knew St. Francis,[48] he need only have entered the Order in 1227 in order to belong to the second generation. He would then have had ample time to assemble witnesses and write his work before 1245.

But one can object to this on the ground that in no. 14, where it is related that Brother Giles had just been accepted among the very first companions, we read: "homo devotissimus et fidelissimus, cui Dominus gratiam multam dedit." Fr. Abate concludes that this eulogy and use of the past tense signifies that the author wrote after the death of Giles which occurred in 1261. Here again, the conclusion is not a convincing one: the sentence in question is very simply translated: "a very devoted and faithful man to whom God gave great favor"[49] and so we need not consider it as a posthumous eulogy.

But, even if we should have to understand this sentence as a posthumous eulogy, Fr. Abate's deduction is not conclusive: the sentence could be an interpolation. Regarding the same Brother Giles, we read in *1 Celano* 25: "throughout all of his long life, he practiced holiness, righteousness, piety, leaving us examples . . . " In 1228, Celano could not have spoken of Giles' long life, and yet no one draws the conclusion from this remark that the *Vita I* antedates Giles' death.

This leads us to a more general observation. We have a work — the *Legend of the Three Companions* — well attested to by numerous manuscripts; the minute study of its text proves that its author depends on *1 Celano* and on Julian of Speyer and does not depend on *2 Celano,* all works that are perfectly dated. But to reject the conclusion called for by this study, a work is quoted, as a witness, whose date is unknown, a work that exists only in the form of two copies of a later manuscript and whose smallest details are accepted with criticism.

Rather than establish the date of the *Legend of the Three Companions* on the basis of the hypothetical date of *Anonymous of Perugia,* logic demands that we establish the date of *Anonymous* on the basis of the *Legend.*

VIII. Conclusion

Up to this point we have tried to describe the data of the problem as objectively as possible without reaching a decision.

Since, as is evident, neither solution has conclusive evidence to support it, we had no intention of seeking the assent of the reader.

We cannot, however, indefinitely maintain our position as an impartial spectator, and the moment now comes when a choice must be made. We shall do it, well aware ·of the several probable but not yet verified hypotheses that such a choice presupposes. Anyone who makes a different choice should also take into account the hypotheses that are implied.

The two questions which remain to be answered are: what is the date of the *Legend of the Three Companions;* and by whom was it written?

The answer to the first, according to our way of thinking, is that the *Legend of the Three Companions* dates from 1246, that at first it was probably only a document which disappeared temporarily, after having been used by Celano, and which appeared again only at the beginning of the fourteenth century.

In answer to the second question, which is of far less importance, we express it as our opinion that its redaction can be attributed to Brother Angelus.

Having made this choice, we shall now try to answer a few other questions that we have left in abeyance.

We have already said that the oppositions that exist between the introductory letter and the text of the *Legend* should not be exaggerated.

The promise made in the Letter is carried out as long as there is something new in the *Legend*. It so happens that a new element is presented in the form of further clarifications which are added to the earlier legends. These were then transcribed. A superficial reading might lead us to believe that the *Legend* contains nothing more than a repetition of things already known. But actually there are new things, since the parallels with *2 Celano* prove that the text of the *Legend* does not depend on it and that, on the contrary, there is nothing to prevent it from being a source for *2 Celano.* Finally, there are a few facts we would not otherwise know were it not for the *Legend of the Three Companions.*

The statement "we did not formulate our accounts in the manner of a legend" need not be taken literally. Perhaps it is just a manner of expression: a formula of false modesty by an author who declares that he does not want to compete with his predecessors, whereas he indeed intends to show that basically he is not so inferior to them after all.

There remains the question of the lacuna that exists between chapters 16 and 17. It is a real problem and becomes a greater one — we admit this — if one considers the last two chapters a subsequent appendix. To attempt an explanation, we will have to leave the strict framework of the *Legend of the Three Companions.*

Let us forget for a few moments the near-sighted view of the man who assembles details in order to compare them and let us imagine in broad outlines how things could have happened.

The Companions decided to answer the invitation of Crescentius. The documents they sent him came in the form of a package (we deliberately use the word) and contained the following items: the text of what we call the *Legend of the Three Companions* up to chapter 16; the recollections of Brother Leo, approximately as manuscript 1046 has preserved them for us; and perhaps one other item.

This package was preceded by the introductory letter which no longer offers any contradictions; two-thirds of the introduction actually were not edited in the form of a legend; the proportion of new things noticeably increased; properly speaking there was no lacuna.

Celano used these documents and incorporated their substance into his *Vita II.* Once used, interest in the fate of this dossier dwindled and it was left forgotten in some closet.

Brother Leo, however, continued to write his recollections. He perhaps found his introductory letter or reconstructed it from memory, unless he had kept a duplicate of it. These recollections of Brother Leo were preserved: certain passages, such as the "Intentio Regulae," were even frequently copied.

St. Bonaventure wrote the *Legenda major* and the Chapter

of Paris ordered the destruction of all earlier legends, and the years rolled by.

At the close of the thirteenth century or the beginning of the fourteenth, some friars who were not satisfied with the official legend, attempted to gather together whatever was still in existence of the earlier tradition.

The recollections of Brother Leo (died in 1271), which were undoubtedly never completely forgotten, reappeared first. Then Celano was rediscovered. From the amalgam of these two, the *Speculum Perfectionis* was born.

Later, the package sent by Crescentius was found, or at least its first part. The letter then appeared as a preface to the sixteen chapters of the *Legend* and was to remain attached to it. Someone finally completed these sixteen chapters and drew their inspiration for them from the *Legenda major*.

Some may object that the description just drawn up is a pure figment of the imagination. We would prefer to say that just as a paleontologist reconstructs a prehistoric animal with the help of a few fossilized bones, so have we attempted to reconstruct the development by utilizing all the elements we know of. That such a reconstruction requires imagination is evident; that it is unsound, we are not so sure.

This reconstruction especially safeguards all the scraps of truth contained in each of the positions taken by the critics.

Thus, when Sabatier affirms that the *Legend of the Three Companions* is incomplete, he is mistaken if we consider only the traditional text; for, in that case, the missing part which, it is claimed, have been found should have the same stylistic characteristics as the part that has been preserved; but he is correct if his statement means that the traditional text does not represent all that was sent by the three Companions.

Frs. M. da Civezza and T. Domenichelli are wrong when they state that in order to find the *Legend* in its entirety we have but to reconstruct the Latin text and that the Muzio manuscript is a translation of this; but they are probably right if they are of the opinion that this tradition could in a certain measure be a witness of a primitive form of the *Legend*.

The Interest of the Legend

The long critical study which we have just made has perhaps sown doubt in the mind of the reader. What confidence can one put in a work that is so bitterly disputed?

The reader should be reassured, for — and this is not the least paradox of the *Legend* — it poses no basic problem. The facts it reports are not contradicted by the other biographies and the polemic does not deform its intentions.[50]

Provided that we know that this rather short work does not say everything, we can enjoy all its charm without any mental reservations. The sincerity and simplicity that comes through have something about them that fascinates us. To some extent it seems as though we were reading Celano who would be neither pompous nor a moralizer, or Brother Leo whose language is less rough.

The portrait of St. Francis in the *Legend of the Three Companions* is just as true as that drawn by Celano or St. Bonaventure. The author does not take the same point of view, and the change in perspective that results, if it obscures certain details, brings out others which without it would have remained forgotten.[51]

To know St. Francis well, we must not neglect any testimony worthy of credence; the *Legend of the Three Companions* is one of them; it should therefore be read.

— Fr. Theophile Desbonnets O.F.M.

I Fiori dei Tre Compagni (The Flowers of the Three Companions), Italian version by Nello Vian, with Introduction and Notes by Fr. Jacques Cambell O.F.M., xxxii-452 pp. (Milan, 1967), is an attempt to restore the original *Legend of the Three Companions.* But Fr. Heribert Roggen O.F.M. tells us that Fr. Cambell "is mistaken when he thinks he has reconstructed the *Legenda Antiqua de Perugia* or even the *Legenda Trium Sociorum*" (Letter of Nov. 21, 1968).

The English translation of *The Legend of the Three Companions* which follows was made by Nesta de Robeck from the Latin text found in the library of Sarnano by Fr. Giuseppe Abate and published by him in the *Miscellanea Francescana*, vol. 39 (1939), pp. 375-432; also from the Italian edition by Fr. Zefferino Lazzeri O.F.M. (Florence, 1923) and that by Ezio Franceschini (Milan, 1957). — M. A. H.

NOTES

1. *Chronicle of the Twenty-Four Generals, AF* III, p. 262.
2. Sabatier himself did not think otherwise. "There was nothing arbitrary about the reconstruction of the 118 chapters. To tell the truth, I was very much tempted to look upon them as the part that was suppressed by the Three Companions, but several considerations prevented me from formulating this thesis as absolute and definitive" (*Spec. Perf.,* p. xxiii). "If a document did not correspond with my research, did that make it any less a good document" (*Etudes inédites,* p. 374).
3. "La Légende de S. François d'Assise dite 'Legenda trium sociorum," *AB* 19, (1900), pp. 119-197.
4. P. Sabatier, "De l'authenticité de la Légende de saint François dite 'des trois compagnons,'" *Revue historique* 75 (1901).
5. The date will be found in the article of Fr. Van Ortroy, "La Légende," pp. 121-122 which needs but very few additions.
6. Description in *AFH* 1 (1908), 307.
7. Description in M. da Civezza e T. Domenicelli, *La Leggenda di S Francesco* . . . (Rome, 1899). p. lxi.
8. Description in *OCH* 1, p. 359.
9. Description in *OCH* 1, p. 366.
10. In no. 5 where all the other manuscripts have: *in quoddam speciosum* (or *spatiosum*) *et amoenum palatium* — in other words, where there is no allusion to the presence of a wife in this vision—, the manuscript of Foligno has the reading: *in quodam speciosae sponsae et amoenum palatium* and the manuscript of St. Isidore's has the strange wording: *in quodam speciose spose amoenum,* where *spose* is evidently a double of *speciose.* S. Cavallin, who made this observation, notes that "the strangeness does not lie in the dittography of *speciosum,* which in itself is rather banal, but rather that the same error appears in *2 Celano* where it has no paleographic reason whatsoever." And he concludes: "In the concurrence for priority, the *Legenda trium sociorum* must be considered up to now as having a clear advantage over *2 Celano.*" Cf. Sam. Cavallin, "La question franciscaine comme problème philologique," in *Eranos* 52 (1954), 239-270: here 268.
11. Description in G. Abate, "Nuovi studi sulla Leggenda di S. Francesco detta die 'tre compagni'" in *MF* 39, (1939), 645.
12. Description in P. Sabatier, *Speculum,* p. clxvi.
13. Description in *EF* 30, (1913), 638.
14. Fr. Van Ortroy, in *AB* 19, (1900), 458.

15. M. da Civezza e T. Domenichelli, *La Leggenda,* p. xix.
16. *Ibid.,* p. lxi.
17. G. Abate, "Nuovi studi," p. 27.
18. J.R.H. Moorman, *The Sources for the Life of St. Francis,* (Manchester, 1940). See on this subject, P.M. Bihl, "Contra duas novas hypotheses prolatas a Joh. R.H. Moorman," in *AFH* 39 (1946-48), pp. 3-37.
19. Fr. Van Ortroy, *La Légende,* p. 120.
20. Cf. *supra,* II. Editions, no. 3.
21. Fr. Van Ortroy, *La Légende,* p. 124.
22. Or to put it more accurately: nothing at the present time justifies the assertion that the text is incomplete.
23. Further on, we shall attempt to propose a few explanatory hypotheses.
24. For example: the narrative follows a plan whose broad outlines respect chronology; the editing respects the laws of the "cursus."
25. This is one of the points that was strongly stressed by Fr. Van Ortroy. His argumentation may be summed up as follows: If Crescentius requested that they transmit to him what was known about St. Francis, it was not that a copy of the official legends be sent to him; moreover. the letter promises something new, and the Legend does not do this. There is therefore a discrepancy between the promises of the letter and the contents of the Legend. This discrepancy proves that the letter and likewise the Legend is a forgery or that the letter has no reference to the *Legend.* We shall see further on that this contradiction should not be exaggerated. The companions did not claim that their contribution was new. For the promises of the letter to be kept, it suffices that there be something new in the *Legend* and, despite what Fr. Van Ortroy thinks, it does contribute something new.
26. Quoting no. 67, he writes (*AF* V, 162): "as we find almost at the end of the *Legend of the Three Companions.*" From this we may conclude that at the end of the fourteenth century and probably before that time, the *Legend* existed as we know it.
27. The four alleged anachronisms have to do with: the date of approbation of a first rule by Innocent III (no. 51); the date of approbation of a second rule (no. 24); the date of approbation of the rule by Honorius III (no. 62); the date of the approbation of the Third Order (no. 60). This last case is rather revealing of Fr. Van Ortroy's way of reasoning. The *Legend* says: "each of these Orders was confirmed in its time by the Sovereign Pontiff." Fr. Van Ortroy says: the definitive confirmation of the Third Order dates from 1289, therefore the *Legend* is later than 1289. But, as Paul Sabatier noted, how can we forget the numerous bulls by which Honorius III and Gregory IX defended the Third Order and accorded privileges to it, and how can we not think that

each of these bulls was the equivalent of a confirmation for those who received them and who were not doctors of canon law.

28. S. Clasen, "Zur Kritik Van Ortroys an der 'Legenda trium sociorum,'" in *Miscellanea Melchior de Pobladura,* (Rome, 1964) t. 1, pp. 61-65.

29. M. Bihl, "Disquisitiones Celanenses," in *AFH* 20 (1927), 457. Later, Fr. Bihl qualified his position, especially in his article "Zur Kritik des *Speculum Perfectionis* gelegentlich der Neuausgabe desselben von P. Sabatier," in *FS* 22 (1935), 113-148.

30. Cf. *infra.,* VII, Sources.

31. No. 11 and 12 of the *Legend.* Cf. S. Cavallin, *La question,* pp. 254-261.

32. Nos. 5 and 6 of the *Legend* which we have examined in detail in a study still unedited.

33. S. Cavallin, *La question,* p. 263.

34. Fr. Abate ("Nuovi Studi," p. 256) thought that he could enlarge upon one of these parallels, thus making it more significant. The reference is to a passage that.St. Bonaventure (*Legenda major* 3, 3) borrowed from Julian of Speyer (no. 17) and which is found in the *Three Companions* in no. 27. But the expression *beati Francisci* used by Julian is found as such in the *Three Companions,* whereas St. Bonaventure, following a fully proven way of acting, transforms it into *viri Dei.* The *Three Companions* here depend on Julian of Speyer and not on St. Bonaventure. — For the question of the fortuitous encounters between independent writers, see, R. Marichal, "La Critique des texts," in *Histoire et ses méthodes,* (Paris, 1961), 1315.

35. The Italian version by Fr. S. Melchiorri according to the Muzio manuscript does not have the last two chapters. We might consider this as a witness of a primitive form of the *Legend,* and in this way justify the hypothesis of a *Legend* that was completed at a later date.

36. S. Clasen, "Zur Kritik," p. 59.

37. P. Sabatier, *De l'authenticité,* p. 5.

38. S. Clasen, "Zur Kritik," p. 65.

39. More specifically, between 1310 and 1325. This would explain why Ubertino da Casale had not known of it since he wrote in 1305 and why Clareno, who wrote in 1330, could not have been affected by the diffusion of this legend.

40. "Once the materials collected by the *Three Companions* had been reworked and went into the making of *2 Celano,* there was no reason to preserve them. It is not surprising, therefore, if no traces of them remained." A. Fierens, "Les problèmes de la Legenda trium sociorum," *Rapport sur les travaux du séminaire historique de l'Université de Louvain* (Louvain, 1908), 306. — Some of them were perhaps not forgotten and could have been used by St. Bonaventure. The detailed study of the alterations he made in the

paragraphs of Celano which he transcribed would tend to prove this.

41. This systematic change of *Dominus* into *Deus*, or vice versa is a real mannerism with certain copyists: the observation by Fr. Abate does not perhaps have the importance he attributes to it; it is possible that this change is due solely to the copyist of the manuscript of Sarnano.

42. S. Cavallin, *La question*, p. 262.

43. Fr. Gratien proposed John of Celano (*EF* 15 1906, 144); Fr. Delorme, Arnald of Sarrant (*La Legenda antiqua . . .* (Paris, 1926) p. xix.

44. *De cognatione sancti Francisci,* published by Fr. Delorme: "Pages inédites sur saint Francois, "*MF* 42, (1942), 103-131; cf. p. 118, 120, and 125.

45. This is the text of the copy, whose elements had been scattered by Suyskens throughout the "Commentarius praevius" of the *Acta Sanctorum*, t. 2, Oct.), and which Fr. Van Ortroy published, "La leggenda latina di S. Francesco secondo l'Anonimo Perugina," *MF* 9 (1902), 33-48.

46. Cf. Fr. G. Abate, "Nuovi studi," p. 233.

47. *Ibid.,* p. 231.

48. The text of the prologue is not strictly identical in the two copies. The text published by Fr. Van Ortroy, interpreted in a certain way, would not militate against the fact that the author knew St. Francis; but to make sure we have chosen the most unfavorable hypothesis.

49. This favor could be his entrance into the Order, the fact that he was a close friend of St. Francis, or some noteworthy spiritual favor. St. Bonaventure (*Opera omnia,* IX, p. 269) tells us that Giles merited the grace of ecstacies for thirty years. We can speak of all these things as having happened in the past, even before the death of the person concerned. To make the argument conclusive, the text would have to read *dederat,* not *dedit.*

50. The most rabid detractor of the *Legend,* Fr. Van Ortroy, himself admits that "nothing is more peaceful nor more soothing than the *Legend of the Three Companions*" (*La Légende,* p. 120).

51. Here are a few details that impress us: many times he left the table, having hardly eaten, in order to rejoin his companions at play (no. 9); in the absence of his father, he piled the table with food to give it to the poor (no. 9); although he did not speak French well (no. 10), he liked to use it (no. 10, 24; etc.).

CHAPTER TITLES

885

LETTER

To the Reverend Father in Christ, Brother Crescentius, by the grace of God Minister General. To him Brother Leo, Brother Rufino, and Brother Angelo, unworthy companions of our blessed father Francis, offer their dutiful and devout reverence in our Lord.

1. The command of the last general chapter is also that of Your Reverence, and it orders all the friars to communicate to Your Paternity any signs and wonders of our blessed father Francis which they either know personally or can truthfully vouch for. Therefore it has seemed to us who, though unworthy, conversed at length with him, that we ought truthfully to recount to Your Paternity some of the many facts of which we either were eye witnesses, or heard from holy friars, especially from Brother Philip, Visitor of the Poor Ladies, Brother Illuminato of Rieti, Brother Masseo of Marignano, and Brother John who was the companion of the venerable Brother Giles, and heard many of these facts either from Brother Giles himself, or from Brother Bernard of holy memory, the first companion of blessed Francis.

We do not intend merely to report miracles which are not the cause of sanctity although they prove it; we wish to relate some notable facts of his holy life to the praise and glory of the most high God, and of our holy father, and which may be of edification to those who desire to follow in his footsteps. We shall not recount these things in the form of a legend, since other legends have been written of his life and of the miracles which God has deigned to work through him. Using our own judgment, we wish rather to gather the most beautiful of the many flowers blooming in a pleasant field: we do not propose to follow an historical sequence, and are studiously omitting those things which have already been told in the aforesaid legends with words as accurate as they are polished.

If you should consider it advisable, the few things we shall here tell might be inserted in other legends, and we are convinced that had venerable men who wrote those legends been acquainted with the things we recount they would on no account have omitted them: rather they would have embellished them with their own eloquent words and thus have transmitted them to posterity.

May Your Paternity live wholly in our Lord Jesus Christ and in him we, your dutiful sons commend ourselves humbly and devoutly.

Written at Greccio on the 11th day of August, 1246.

PROLOGUE TO THE LEGEND OF
OUR BLESSED FATHER FRANCIS

Resplendent as the dawn and as the morning star,[1] or even as the rising sun, setting the world alight, cleansing it, and giving it fertility, Francis was seen to rise as a kind of new light.

Like the sun he shone by his words and works upon a world lying torpid amid wintry cold, darkness, and sterility, lighting it up with radiant sparks, illuminating it with the rays of truth, and setting it afire with charity, renewing and embellishing it with the abundant fruit of his merits, and enriching it wonderfully with various fruit-bearing trees in the three orders he founded. Thus did he bring the world to a kind of season of spring.

---

1. The opening words of the prologue, *Praefulgidus ut lucifer, et sicut stella matutina*, particularly the second phrase, led some authors to think that this legend was the legend *Quasi stella matutina* of John of Ceperano, mentioned by Bernard of Bessa in his *Liber de Laudibus Beati Francisci, Analecta Franciscana*, III, p. 666, but which is not extant. This opinion, however, is not regarded seriously by anyone today.

CHAPTER I

*Of Francis' birth, of his vanity, eccentricity,
and prodigality; and how he came to be
liberal and charitable to the poor*

2. The father of the blessed and evangelical man Francis was
named Peter, the son of the merchant Bernardone; and he
was absorbed in making money. On the other hand, Francis'
mother Pica was an excellent woman; and like another Elizabeth, she gave birth to her blessed son in the absence of
his father who had gone to France on business.[1]

She wished the child to be called John, and on the very
day of his baptism a pilgrim stopped to beg at the door.
Having received alms from the serving maid the stranger
said to her: "I beg you to show me the child born today
for I greatly wish to see him."

The maid answered that this was impossible, but the
pilgrim insisted that he would never go away unless his wish
were granted. The maid was annoyed and went back into
the house leaving the pilgrim outside; but, when the Lady
Pica heard what had happened, she was amazed and told
the maid to show the child to the stranger. When this was

---

1. Pietro Bernardone, Francis' father, was not of noble origin, but he
was a rather wealthy cloth merchant. Some have thought that Lady
Pica, Francis' mother, was of French origin, but this cannot be confirmed.

done the pilgrim took the baby into his arms with great devotion and joy, as Simeon had once taken the infant Jesus,[2] and he said: "Today two children have been born in this city; this one will be among the best of mankind, and the other among the worst."

The whole world has seen what was verified in Francis. In regard to the other, many people are convinced of the truth of the prophecy.

When Peter returned from France, he insisted that his son should be called Francis after the country he had recently left.

Francis grew up quick and clever, and he followed in his father's footsteps by becoming a merchant. In business, however, he was very different from Peter, being far more high-spirited and open-handed. He was also intent on games and songs; and day and night he roamed about the city of Assisi with companions of his own age. He was a spendthrift, and all that he earned went into eating and carousing with his friends. For this his parents often remonstrated with him, saying that in squandering such large sums on himself and others, his style of living made him appear not so much their son as the son of some great prince. However, being rich and loving him tenderly, they allowed him free rein in order to avoid displeasing him. When the Lady Pica heard the neighbors commenting on her son's extravagance, she answered: "What do you think my son will be? Through grace he will become a son of God."

In all things Francis was lavish, and he spent much more on his clothes than was warranted by his social position. He would use only the finest materials; but sometimes his vanity took an eccentric turn, and then he would insist on the richest cloth and the commonest being sewn together in the same garment.

3. He was naturally courteous in manner and speech. The words came spontaneously from his heart, and he determined

---

2. Lk. 2, 28.

never to say a rude or unseemly word to anyone. Although a gregarious and worldly youth he would not answer if anyone addressed him with bad language. This caused his fame to spread throughout the entire province, and many who knew him said he would do great things. Grace, working through these natural virtues, brought him to the point of being able to say to himself: "Since you are courteous and generous to men from whom you only receive vain and transitory favors, it is only fair that you should be equally so to those in need, since the Lord God is magnanimous in repaying whatever is given to his poor." From that time on Francis welcomed the poor and gave them abundant alms.

Although a merchant, he squandered his wealth, never counting the cost. One day when he was in the shop selling cloth, a beggar came in and asked for alms for the love of God; but Francis was so intent on the business of making money that he gave nothing to the poor man. Then, enlightened by divine grace, he accused himself harshly, saying: "If that beggar had made his request in the name of some great prince, you would surely have given him what he asked; how much more so you should have done it when he begged in the name of the King of kings and Lord of all!" Taught by this experience, he resolved in his heart never again to refuse anything that might be asked of him in the name of God.

CHAPTER II

*How Francis was taken a prisoner to Peru-
gia; and of two visions which came to
him when he had the intention of being
knighted.*

4.During a year of war between Perugia and Assisi Francis
was captured together with many of his fellow citizens and
was taken to prison in Perugia.[1] Because of his distinguished
bearing, he was put among the nobles. One day his companions were especially downhearted, but Francis, who was
naturally cheerful, far from appearing sad, seemed almost to
be enjoying himself. One of his fellow prisoners reproached
him as a fool for looking happy at being in prison. Francis
answered: "Is that what you think of me?" The day will
come when I shall be honored by the whole world." Among
his companions there was one who had injured a fellow
prisoner, for which reason all the others wished to cold-
shoulder him; but Francis alone refused and urged them to
follow his example. After a year, on the conclusion of peace,
he, with the other prisoners, returned to Assisi.

5. A few years later an Assisian nobleman was planning to
start for Apulia on a military expedition which he hoped
would bring him money and honors. Hearing of this, Francis
was fired with the wish to accompany him and to get knighted

---

1. The battle took place in 1202. Francis remained a prisoner for about
a year and was released probably early in 1203.

by a certain Count Gentile.[2] He prepared magnificent equipment; and, though his fellow citizen was a nobleman, Francis was by far the more extravagant of the two. He was absorbed in this plan and keen to set out, when one night he was visited by the Lord, who, seeing him so bent on honor and glory, drew him to himself by means of a vision. While Francis was asleep, a man appeared who called him by name and led him into a vast and pleasant palace in which the walls were hung with glittering coats of mail, shining bucklers, and all the weapons and armor of warriors. Francis was delighted, and reflecting on what could be the meaning of all this, he asked for whom the splendid arms and beautiful palace were intended; and he received the answer that they were for him and his knights.

On awaking, Francis rose gleefully, thinking, after the manner of worldlings (for he had not yet tasted the spirit of God) that he was destined to become a magnificent prince and that the vision was prophetic of great prosperity. What he had seen spurred him on to start for Apulia and to get himself knighted in the following of Count Gentile. His glee was such that people, in surprise, asked the reason of his delight and received the answer: "I know that I shall become a great prince."

6. One day immediately preceding this vision Francis had shown sure signs of nobility and chivalry, for he had given all his own fine accoutrements and clothes to a poor, needy knight. And we think that this magnanimity played no small part in bringing about the vision.

Now it happened that, after the start for Apulia, Francis felt unwell on arriving at Spoleto; and thinking with apprehension about the journey, he went to bed; but, half asleep,

---

2. Walter of Brienne was devoting himself to the defense of the cause of the pope against the German princes who were angered because the widow of Henry VI had entrusted their son to the tutelage of Innocent III. Francis set out with this knight to join Walter early in 1205, but he soon returned to Assisi.

he heard a voice calling and asking him whither he was bound. He replied, telling of his plan. Then he, who had previously appeared to him in sleep, spoke these words:

"Who do you think can best reward you, the Master or the servant?"

"The Master," answered Francis.

"Then why do you leave the Master for the servant, the rich Lord for the poor man?"

Francis replied: "O Lord, what do you wish me to do?"

"Return to your own place," he was bidden, "and you will be told what to do. You must interpret your vision in a different sense. The arms and palace you saw are intended for other knights than those you had in mind; and your principality too will be of another order."

Francis awoke and began to turn all this over in his mind. After the first vision he had been in a transport of delight, filled with desires for worldly prosperity; but this one left him puzzled and perplexed. He thought about it so intensely that he slept no more that night. Immediately at daybreak he started back towards Assisi in glad expectation that God, who had shown him the vision, would soon reveal his will for the future. Francis now waited to be guided by him for the salvation of his soul. His mind was changed and he gave up all thought of going to Apulia.

CHAPTER III

How the Lord came into his heart with
marvelous sweetness and in the strength
of this he began to derive great benefit in
despising himself, and through prayer,
almsgiving, and love of poverty.

7. Soon after Francis had returned to Assisi, his companions
elected him king of the revels, and gave him a free hand
to spend what he liked in the preparation of a sumptuous
banquet as he had often done on other occasions. After the
feast they left the house and started off singing through the
streets. Francis' companions were leading the way; and he,
holding his wand of office, followed them at a little distance.
Instead of singing, he was listening very attentively. All of
a sudden the Lord touched his heart, filling it with such sur-
passing sweetness that he could neither speak nor move. He
could only feel and hear this overwhelming sweetness which
detached him so completely from all other physical sensations
that, as he said later, had he been cut to pieces on the spot
he could not have moved.

When his companions looked around, they saw him in
the distance and turned back. To their amazement they saw
that he was transformed into another man, and they asked
asked him: "What were you thinking of? Why didn't you
follow us? Were you thinking of getting married?"

Francis answered in a clear voice: "You are right: I was
thinking of wooing the noblest, richest, and most beautiful
bride ever seen." His friends laughed at him saying he was

a fool and did not know what he was saying; in reality he had spoken by a divine inspiration. The bride was none other than that form of true religion which he embraced; and which, above any other is noble, rich, and beautiful in its poverty.

8. From that hour he began to consider himself as naught and to despise all those things he had formerly cherished; but he still did so imperfectly, not being as yet entirely detached from worldly vanities. He gradually withdrew from the tumult of earthly things and applied himself secretly to receive Jesus Christ into his soul with that pearl of great price which he so desired as to be willing to sell all he possessed in order to gain it. To this end he often hid himself from the eyes of deceitful men and withdrew to pray in secret, incited to do so by the same sweetness in his heart which took possession of him with increasing frequency, drawing him apart to pray far from all public meeting places.

He was already a benefactor of the poor, but from this time onwards he resolved never to refuse alms to anyone who begged in God's name; but rather to give more willingly and abundantly than ever before. If a poor person begged of him when he was far from home, he would always give him money, if possible; when he had none he would give his belt or buckle; or, if he had not even these, he would find a hiding place and, taking off his shirt, give it to the beggar for love of God. In addition to this, he was most liberal in buying vases and other objects pertaining to the service and adornment of churches and he sent them secretly to poor priests.

9. Sometimes it happened that Francis remained in the house alone with his mother while his father was away on business; on these occasions he would heap the table with loaves, both for dinner and supper, as though for the whole family. One day his mother asked him why he prepared so much bread, and he replied that he wished to distribute the loaves to those in need because he had promised always to give alms

to anyone who begged from him in God's name. His mother loved him more than her other children,[1] and therefore she let him have his way in these things; but she observed all he did, and often secretly marveled at it.

In former years he had so enjoyed the company of his friends that he was always ready to join them; they only had to call and Francis would leave the table and be off, having barely tasted his food, and leaving his parents greatly distressed at such untimely haste. Now, however, his whole heart was entirely bent on seeing, hearing, and attending to the poor; and he gave them generous alms in the name of God.

10. He was still living in the world though already greatly changed by divine grace; and sometimes the longing seized him for a place where, as an unknown stranger, he could give his own clothes to some beggar, taking the beggar's miserable rags in exchange and setting out himself to beg for love of God.

At this time he happened to go to Rome on pilgrimage, and in the church of Saint Peter he noticed that many people left what seemed to him very inadequate offerings. He said to himself: "Surely, the greatest honor is due to the Prince of the Apostles; how then can some folk leave such meagre alms in the church where his body rests?" Full of fervor he took a handful of money from his purse and threw it in through a grating in the altar; the coins made such a clatter that those present heard it and were greatly astonished at such munificence.

Francis then left the church, and on the steps before the entrance a number of beggars were asking for money from those who came and went. Francis quietly borrowed the

---

1. There were two other sons besides Francis. One, we know, ridiculed Francis' choice of life (Chapter VII, below). The other, apparently, was Angelo, who later had two sons, Piccardo and Giovanni. It is said that they were ultimately reduced to begging on the streets of Assisi.

clothes of one of these beggars, changing into them from his own; and, dressed in rags, he stood on the steps with the others, asking for alms in French, a language he delighted to speak, though he did not know it very well.

After a while he changed back into his own garments and returned to Assisi, devoutly praying that the Lord would show him the right path. At home he told no one of his secret, and turned to God who alone was his never failing guide; neither did he ask advice of anyone except sometimes of the Bishop of Assisi. He looked in vain in those around him for that real poverty which he desired above all earthly things and in which he wanted to live and die.

CHAPTER IV

*Among the lepers Francis begins to con-
quer himself, and to find sweetness in what
formerly had been distasteful to him.*

11. One day while Francis was praying fervently to God, he received an answer. "O Francis, if you want to know my will, you must hate and despise all that which hitherto your body has loved and desired to possess. Once you begin to do this, all that formerly seemed sweet and pleasant to you will become bitter and unbearable; and instead, the things that formerly made you shudder will bring you great sweetness and content." Francis was divinely comforted and greatly encouraged by these words. Then one day, as he was riding near Assisi, he met a leper. He had always felt an overpowering horror of these sufferers; but making a great effort, he conquered his aversion, dismounted, and, in giving the leper a coin, kissed his hand. The leper then gave him the kiss of peace, after which Francis remounted his horse and rode on his way. From that day onwards he mortified himself increasingly until, through God's grace, he won a complete victory.

Some days later he took a large sum of money to the leper hospital, and gathering all the inmates together, he gave them alms, kissing each of their hands. Formerly he could neither touch or even look at lepers, but when he left them on that day, what had been so repugnant to him had really and truly been turned into something pleasant. Indeed, his previous aversion to lepers had been so strong, that, besides being incapable of looking at them, he would not even approach the places where they lived. And if by chance he happened to pass anywhere near their dwellings or to see one of the lepers, even though he was moved to give them an alms through some intermediate person, he would nevertheless turn his face away and hold his nose. But, strengthened by God's grace, he was enabled to obey the command and to love what he had hated and to abhor what he had hitherto wrongfully loved. In consequence of this he became such a friend to the lepers that, as he himself declared in his *Testament*, he lived with them and served them with loving eagerness.

12. After his visits to the lepers Francis changed for the better. Taking with him a favorite Assisian companion of his own age,[1] he used to seek out remote and solitary spots, telling his friend that he had found a great treasure. This pleased the other young man, who followed Francis gladly whenever he called. They went frequently to a cave near Assisi, and while the friend, on the lookout for treasure, remained outside, Francis went in alone, and, with his heart full of a new, unaccustomed fervor, he prayed to God his Father. He wished that none should know what he did in the cave but God alone, to whom he prayed assiduously to show him how to find the heavenly treasure.

When the Devil saw Francis' good beginning, he tried ingeniously to turn him from it by suggestions of fright or disgust. In Assisi there was a humpbacked and deformed woman; and the Devil recalled her to Francis' mind with the threat that, unless he turned from the good he had embarked on, he would free her from her deformity and cast it upon him. Francis, however, was strong in the Lord and, heedless of the Devil's threats, he prayed devoutly in the cave that

---

1. The companion's name is not known.

God would direct his steps into the right way. He endured great mental anguish and could find no rest for he was searching how he could put into practice what was in his heart. Importunate ideas came and went and greatly worried and distressed him. His heart was aglow with divine fire, and even outwardly he could not hide the new ardor which was taking possession of him and filling him with repentance for his past grave sins. He found no satisfaction in evil whether past or present; but he also lacked confidence in his own capacity for avoiding evil in the future. When he emerged from the cave and rejoined his friend, this inner struggle had so changed him as to make him appear a different man.

CHAPTER V

*How the Crucifix spoke to him for the first
time; and how he henceforth carried the
passion of Christ in his heart until his death.*

13.One day while Francis was fervently imploring God's mercy,
the Lord revealed to him that he would shortly be taught
what he was to do. From that moment he was so full of joy
that, beside himself for gladness, he would let fall occasional
words of his secret for men to hear. This happened in spite
of his habitual caution; for he did not speak openly and
merely declared that he no longer wished to go to Apulia
but would do great things in his own land. His companions
noticed how changed he was; and indeed his heart was
already far from them, even though occasionally he accepted
their company. They tried to probe into his mind and again
asked whether he was thinking of marrying, and as before
he answered in a figure of speech: "I shall bring home a bride,
more beautiful, richer, and nobler than any you have ever
seen."

A few days after this, while he was walking near the
church of San Damiano, an inner voice bade him go in and
pray. He obeyed, and kneeling before an image of the crucified Savior, he began to pray most devoutly. A tender,
compassionate voice then spoke to him: "Francis, do you not
see that my house is falling into ruin? Go, and repair it for
me." Trembling and amazed Francis replied: "Gladly I will

do so, O Lord." He had understood that the Lord was speaking of that very church which, on account of its age, was indeed falling into ruin.

These words filled him with the greatest joy and inner light because in spirit he knew that it was indeed Jesus Christ who had spoken to him. On leaving the church he found the priest who had charge of it sitting outside, and taking a handful of money from his purse, he said: "I beg you, Sir, to buy oil and keep the lamp before this image of Christ constantly alight. When this is spent I will give you as much as you need."

14. From that hour his heart was stricken and wounded with melting love and compassion for the passion of Christ; and for the rest of his life he carried in it the wounds of the Lord Jesus. This was clearly proved later when the stigmata of those same wounds were miraculously impressed upon his own holy body for all to see.[1] Henceforth he continually mortified his body most harshly, not only when he was well, but also when he was ill. Seldom indeed did he relax this severity; so much so, that on his deathbed he confessed to having sinned grievously against Brother Body.

One day he was roaming about alone near the church of Saint Mary of the Angels, weeping and lamenting aloud. A certain God-fearing man heard him and, thinking he must be ill, asked pityingly the reason for his distress. Francis replied: "I weep for the passion of my Lord Jesus Christ; and I should not be ashamed to go weeping through the whole world for his sake." Then the other man fell to crying and lamenting with him.

Often when he rose from prayer we saw that his eyes were inflamed and red from his bitter weeping. Besides shedding these abundant tears, Francis also abstained in memory **15.**of our Lord's passion from eating and drinking. When he happened to be at table with people of the world and food

---

1. In 1224. See Chapter XVII concerning the stigmata.

pleasant to the taste was offered to him, he ate very little, making some excuse in order not to appear to be fasting. Alone with the friars, he would sprinkle ashes on his food, trying to hide his penance by saying that Brother Ash was chaste. Once during a meal a certain brother remarked that the Blessed Virgin was so poor that she had hardly anything to set before her Son our Lord. On hearing this, Francis sighed, deeply moved, and leaving the table, he ate his bread sitting on the floor.

Often, having sat down to a meal, he had hardly begun when he would stop eating and drinking and become absorbed in meditation on heavenly things. When this happened he did not wish to be interrupted by talk, and he would sigh deeply. He bade the friars when they heard him sighing in this way to praise God and to pray faithfully for him.

We have recounted these incidents of his weeping and abstinence to show that after the vision and the words spoken by the Crucifix, Francis until his death was always conformed to the passion of Christ.

CHAPTER VI

*How he escaped from the persecution of
his father and relatives by living with the
priest of Saint Damian's.*

16. Filled with joy at the vision and words of Christ crucified, Francis took various pieces of cloth of different colors for sale in the city of Foligno, and he sold not only the wares, but also the horse he was riding. He then returned to the church of Saint Damian, found the poor priest, and humbly kissing his hands, told him of what he proposed to do.

The priest was astounded at Francis' sudden conversion and at first he did not believe in it. Thinking Francis to be joking, he refused the proffered money, and this was due to the fact that not long before he had seen Francis having a good time with his relatives and friends.

Francis insisted more urgently and begged the priest to receive him as a guest for love of God. Finally the priest consented to his staying on, but, for fear of Francis' relatives, he would on no account accept the money; whereupon Francis threw the coins in through the window, so truly had he come to despise all gain.

While Francis was staying in the priest's house, his father went round inquiring for news of his son. When he heard what had happened and where Francis was, calling together his friends and neighbors, he hurried off to find him.

Francis was still a recent recruit to the service of Christ; and when he heard of the threats of his pursuers, foreseeing their arrival, he hid from his father's anger by creeping into a secret cave which he had prepared as a refuge. There he stayed for a whole month; and only one person in his father's house knew of his hiding place. He ate the food brought to him secretly and prayed continually with many tears that the Lord would deliver him from such persecution and grant him the fulfilment of his desire.

17. He prayed unceasingly with tears and fasting, not relying on his own industry or virtue, but placing all his trust in God; and although he was still in the darkness of the world the Lord filled his soul with ineffable joy and a wonderful light. Glowing with this inner radiance he left the cave, ready to face the insults and blows of his persecutors, and light-heartedly he took the road to Assisi. Trusting in Christ, his heart divinely aflame, Francis now reproached himself for his sloth and vain fears.

When his friends and relatives saw him, they covered him with insults, calling him a fool and a madman, and hurling stones and mud at him. Seeing him so changed, they thought he must be out of his mind.

But God's servant paid no heed to all this; unmoved by insults, he thanked almighty God for everything.

Finally, the news reached his father; and, hearing of Francis' reception at the hands of his fellow citizens, he hurried out to find him, not indeed to set him free, but to chastise him. Throwing moderation and discretion to the winds, he sprang on his son like a wolf on a lamb; and, his face furious, his eyes glaring, he seized him with many blows and dragged him home. Francis was then shut up in a dark cellar, and for many days his father used threats and blows to bend his son's will, to drag him back from the path of good he had chosen, and to force him to return to the vanities of the world.

18. All this strengthened Francis in alacrity to carry through his resolution, and he patiently endured the blows and hard words. When his father had to leave home on urgent business, his mother, who disapproved of her husband's action, reasoned gently with her son. But when she saw that his mind was irrevocably made up and that nothing would move him from his good resolution, she was filled with tender pity, and, breaking his bonds, she set him free.

Giving thanks to almighty God, Francis went back to his former refuge; but he now enjoyed the greater liberty of one who had been tried and strengthened through having suffered trials and temptations.

In the meanwhile Peter Bernardone returned home; and, on finding his son gone, he added sin to sin by abusing his **19.** wife. He then went to the palace of the commune and denounced Francis to the civil authorities, demanding the restitution of the money of which he said he had been robbed by his son.

When the authorities saw how enraged Peter was, they sent a messenger to summon Francis. But he answered that, since by divine grace he had obtained freedom, he was the servant only of God and therefore no longer owed obedience to the civil authorities but was outside their jurisdiction. The city counselors did not wish to force the issue, and answered Peter that as Francis had entered the service of almighty God he was no longer their subject.

Peter then realized that no satisfaction was to be had from the civil authorities, so he repeated his accusation before the Bishop of Assisi. The Bishop, a wise and prudent man, sent word to Francis that he must appear and answer his father's indictment; and he replied to the messenger: "I will willingly appear before the Lord Bishop who is the father and lord of souls."

He, therefore, went to the Bishop who received him gladly saying: "Your father is highly incensed and greatly scandalized by your conduct. If therefore you wish to serve God, you must first of all return him his money, which indeed may have been dishonestly acquired. God would not wish you to use it for restoring the church through sin on the part of your father, whose anger will abate when he gets the money back. Trust in the Lord, my son, and act manfully, fearing nothing, for he will help you and provide you with all that is necessary for repairing the church."

20. Thereupon the servant of God rose joyfully, comforted by the Bishop's words and holding out the money, he said: "My Lord Bishop, not only will I gladly give back the money which is my father's, but also my clothes." Going into the Bishop's room he stripped himself of his garments and placing the money on them he stood naked before the eyes of the Bishop, his father, and all present and said: "Listen all of you and mark my words. Hitherto I have called Peter Bernardone my father; but because I am resolved to serve God I return to him the money on account of which he was so perturbed, and also the clothes I wore which are his; and from now on I will say 'Our Father who art in heaven,' and not Father Peter Bernardone." On that occasion it was seen that the servant of God wore a hair shirt under his colored clothes.[1]

His father rose up burning with grief and anger and he gathered up the garments and money and carried them home. Those present at this scene took the side of Francis because Peter had left him without any clothing, and moved with pity, they started to weep over him.

---

1. Celano says that Francis died after he had completed twenty years from his conversion (I Cel., 88, 109; also Celano's *Legenda ad usum chori*). This would place the date of his conversion in 1206, since he died in October, 1226. Some, however, still place the date of his conversion in 1207, but the former date is preferred. The bishop of Assisi was Bishop Guido.

The Bishop, seeing Francis' fortitude of spirit, was in admiration of his fervor and constancy and gathered him into his arms, covering him with his own cloak. He had clearly understood that the servant of God had acted on a divine inspiration, and he realized that a great mystery lay behind the scene he had witnessed; therefore, from that hour he helped and comforted Francis, loving him with tender charity.

CHAPTER VII

Of the trouble involved in restoring the church of Saint Damian; and how Francis began to conquer himself by begging.

21. Francis the servant of God was now stripped of all worldly things and free to serve the divine justice. He held his life of no account and dedicated himself to the service of God in every possible way. He returned to Saint Damian, gay and full of fervor, clothed in a hermit's garment; and he re-assured the priest of the church with the same words that the Bishop had addressed to him. Then he started back to the city where he began to praise God loudly in the streets and public places; and when he had finished his song of praise, he set to begging for stones with which to restore the church. He called to the passers-by: "Whoever gives me one stone will have one reward; two stones, two rewards; three stones, a treble reward." Many other simple words fell from his lips and he spoke from the fervor of his heart for he had been chosen by God to be simple and unlearned, using none of the erudite words of human wisdom; and in all things he bore himself with simplicity. Many people mocked him as a madman, but others were moved to tears when they saw how quickly he had passed from worldly pampering and vanity to loving God. He paid no heed to ridicule and gave thanks to God in great fervor of spirit.

It would be difficult to specify all the hard work that had

to be done to restore the church. At home Francis had been coddled, whereas now he carried a load of stones on his own shoulders and endured many hardships for love of God. The priest who watched his labors saw how fervently he gave himself to the service of God laboring even beyond his strength; and though the priest himself was a poor man, he procured special food for Francis because he knew how delicately he had been brought up, and how in his father's house he had eaten only what was excellent. Francis himself confessed that he would not touch anything he did not like.

22.　　One day, however, when he noticed that the priest was providing him with special food, he reflected: "Wherever you may happen to go, do you suppose that you will find another such priest who will treat you so kindly? This is not the life of the poor such as you wished to choose: rather you should go, bowl in hand, from door to door, and driven by hunger, collect the various morsels you may be given. It is only thus that you can live voluntarily for love of Him who was born poor, lived poor in this world, and remained naked and poor on the cross."

So, one day, with great fervor he took a bowl and went through the streets of the city begging for alms from door to door just as he had described the begging of the poor. People dropped a variety of scraps into the bowl; and knowing what his former life had been, many were exceedingly astonished at such self-degradation and at seeing him so completely changed.

When it came to eating the contents of the bowl, Francis' stomach turned, for he had never seen such a mess, let alone tried to eat it. At last, making a great effort, he started to gulp it down, and it seemed to him the most delicious food in the world. His heart leaped with joy and he thanked God, for he realized that, though weak and afflicted in body, he was able to endure anything, however hard, for love of the Lord. He praised and thanked God who had changed what was bitter into sweetness and had comforted him in so many ways. He also asked the priest, from then onwards, not to procure or prepare any more food for him.

23. When his father saw him in this pitiful plight, he was filled with sorrow, for he had loved him very dearly; he was both grieved and ashamed to see his son half dead from penance and hardships, and whenever they met, he cursed Francis. When the servant of God heard his father's curses, he took as his father a poor and despised outcast and said to him: "Come with me and I will give you the alms I receive; and when I hear my father cursing me, I shall turn to you saying: 'Bless me, Father'; and then you will sign me with the cross and bless me in his place." And when this happened, the beggar did indeed bless him; and Francis turned to his father, saying: "Do you not realize that God can give me a father whose blessing will counter your curses?" Many people, seeing his patience in suffering scorn, were amazed and upheld him admiringly.

One winter's day, miserably clothed, Francis was praying when his own brother passed by and said ironically to a companion: "Ask Francis to sell you a few cents worth of sweat." The servant of God heard the words and replied gaily in French: "I will sell my sweat at a higher price to my God."

24. In the meanwhile he was working steadily at restoring the church, and, because he wished that the light should be kept burning, he went through the city begging for oil. On approaching one house he saw a number of men busy playing and gambling; and overcome by shyness he turned away being ashamed to go in and beg from them. But then he thought better of it, and accusing himself of sin, he hurried back to the place, went in, and confessed his fault to all the company, how he had been ashamed to ask them for alms. He entered the house in fervor of spirit for love of God, and begged in French for oil for the church of Saint Damian.

While working there with other men, he called out loudly and joyfully in French to the passers-by: "Come and help us do this work for the church of Saint Damian which will become a monastery of women whose life and fame will cause our heavenly Father to be universally glorified."

In these words filled with the spirit of prophecy, he foretold the future, for this is the holy place in which the excellent order of the Poor Ladies and holy virgins was to flourish. This came about some six years after the conversion of blessed Francis, and their excellent manner of life and glorious institution was duly approved by the Lord Pope Gregory IX of blessed memory, at that time Bishop of Ostia; and his decision was confirmed by the authority of the Apostolic See.[1]

---

1. Saint Clare left the world six years after Francis' conversion (I Cel., 18); therefore in 1212. Her way of life was approved by Innocent III, who granted her the privilege of the "highest poverty" in 1215 or 1216. Her final rule, which she prepared herself, was approved by Innocent IV by papal bull on August 9, 1253, just before her death.

CHAPTER VIII

How Francis was so imbued with Christ's counsels of evangelical perfection that he changed his outward garment, and took as his own the exterior and inner counsels of perfection.

25. Until the work of restoring the church of Saint Damian was completed, blessed Francis still wore the garments of a hermit with a strap to serve as a belt, and he carried a staff and had sandals on his feet. Then, one day during the celebration of Mass he heard the words in which Christ bade his disciples go out and preach, carrying neither gold nor silver, nor haversack for the journey, without staff, bread, or shoes, and having no second garment. After listening to the priest's explanation of these words of the Gospel, full of unspeakable joy, he exclaimed: "This is what my whole heart desires to accomplish."

He learned these words by heart, meditating on what he had heard; and joyfully he started to put them into practice. He discarded his second garment, and from that day onwards he used no staff, shoes, or haversack; he kept one miserable tunic, and instead of the strap took a length of cord as a belt. He set his whole heart and mind on how he could best carry out the words of grace that he had heard, and, divinely inspired, he began to speak in public very simply of penitence and the life of evangelical perfection. His words were not greeted with ridicule, neither were they spoken in vain; for they possessed the strength of the Holy Spirit and went straight to the hearts of the listeners rousing them to vehement astonishment.

26. In later years Francis declared that it was our Lord who taught him to greet people with the words: "The Lord give you peace!" Therefore, when beginning to preach, he always gave this greeting of peace to all present. It was certainly remarkable, if not miraculous, that, before Francis' conversion these same words had been proclaimed in Assisi by a forerunner, who often greeted the folk he met in the streets with "Pax et Bonum," — Peace and All Good! This man vanished after Francis had been converted;[1] and one may suppose that, as John the Baptist heralded Christ, so this stranger did for Francis. He indeed was filled with the spirit of prophecy; and taking up the words of his predecessor, by his own preaching and salutary counsels he was able to unite in peace many who had formerly hated each other and were living in sin.

27. The truth of his teaching was brought home to people by the simplicity of his way of life, and two years after his own conversion several men were drawn to follow his example of penitence, and they left everything in order to join him. The first of these was Brother Bernard[2] of holy memory. He well knew how luxuriously Francis had lived in the world; therefore, when he saw how he labored to restore ruined churches and what a harsh life he led, Bernard too resolved to sell his possessions and give all to the poor. It seemed to him the will of God that he should follow Francis in clothing and his whole manner of life. With this in mind he went one day secretly to see God's servant and opened his heart to him, also inviting him to come that evening and lodge in his house.

Francis joyfully gave thanks to God, because so far he had had no companions and Master Bernard was a virtuous

---

1. There is no record of who he may have been.
2. Bernard of Quintavalle was the son of a noble Assisi family. He died between 1241 and 1246.

28. and godly man. Therefore, as arranged, he went to Bernard's house and remained there all night in great joy of heart. Bernard put a question to him: "If a man receives from God few or many possessions and, having enjoyed them for a number of years, now no longer wishes to retain them, what would be the best thing for him to do?" Blessed Francis answered that in that case it were better for the man to give back to God what he had received; to which Master Bernard rejoined: "Then, Brother, I will give all my worldly goods to the poor for love of God who gave them to me, according as you may think best." And blessed Francis said to him: "Tomorrow early we will go to church; and as the Lord taught his disciples, we will learn from the book of the Gospel what to do."

Therefore, they rose early; and with another man named Peter,[3] who also wished to join them, they went to the church of Saint Nicholas near the chief square of the city. They went in to pray, but, being simple men, they did not know how to find the passage in the Gospel telling of the renunciation of the world. Therefore, they besought God that he would show them his will the first time they opened the book.

29. When their prayer was ended, blessed Francis, kneeling before the altar, took the closed book, opened it and saw written: "If you wish to be perfect, go, sell what you have, and give to the poor, and you shall have treasure in heaven" (Mt. 19, 21). At this blessed Francis gave thanks to God with great joy; but because of his devotion to the blessed Trinity, he desired a threefold confirmation of the words and opened the book of the Gospel a second and a third time. At the second opening he read: "Take nothing for your journey" (Lk. 9, 3), and at the third: "If any man will come after me, let him deny himself" (Mt. 16, 24). Each time he opened the book blessed Francis gave thanks to God for this threefold

---

3. Peter of Catania. He became vicar for Francis in 1220 and died March 10, 1221.

confirmation of the resolution and desire which he had long held in his heart; and he said to the aforementioned Bernard and Peter: "O Brothers, this is our life and rule and the life and rule of all those who may wish to join us. Go, therefore, and act on what you have heard."

So Master Bernard, who was very rich, sold all his possessions, and distributed a great deal of money to the poor of the city. Peter too, according to his means, followed our Lord's counsel. Having sold everything, these two both took the habit of poverty which blessed Francis had already adopted when he abandoned the life of a hermit; and from then on, he and they lived according to the precept of the holy Gospel as the Lord had shown them. Because of this blessed Francis said in his *Testament*: "The Lord himself showed me that I should live according to the holy Gospel."

CHAPTER IX

*Of the vocation of Brother Sylvester, and of
his vision before he entered the fraternity.*

30. On the occasion when, as we have said, Master Bernard
gave all his goods to the poor, Francis was there, helping
him. A priest named Sylvester was also present from whom
Francis had bought some stones when he was repairing the
church of Saint Damian and was still alone without any
companions. Seeing so much money being scattered broad-
cast on Francis' advice, Sylvester was moved by envy and
approached the servant of God, saying: "You did not fully
pay for those stones you bought from me."

Francis scorned avarice and greed, and when he heard
this unjust complaint, he went up to Bernard, and putting
his hand into the pocket of Bernard's cloak which contained
the money, he drew out a handful of coins, and in great
fervor of spirit gave them to the dissatisfied priest, saying:
"Are you fully paid now, Master Priest?" Sylvester replied,
"Yes, Brother," and went home, well pleased with what he
had received.

31. But a few days later, by divine inspiration, this same priest
began to reflect on Francis' action, and said to himself: "Am
I not a miserable man, old as I am, to be avid for temporal
goods, when this young man despises and hates them for
love of God?" During the following night in a dream he

saw an immense cross reaching to the sky, and its foot was planted in the mouth of Francis, while the arms spread from one end of the world to the other. On awaking, the priest realized and was convinced that blessed Francis was indeed the friend and servant of Jesus Christ and that the form of religion he was introducing would spread over the entire earth. Thus Sylvester was brought to fear God, and he began to do penance while still living in his own house. Before long, however, he entered the fraternity in which he lived perfectly and died gloriously.

32. In the meanwhile, as we have said, Francis and his two companions had no fixed dwelling; so they went to a poor, derelict church called Saint Mary of the Angels, or the Portiuncula, that is, the Little Portion, where they built a hut to serve as a shelter. Not many days later a man of Assisi named Giles came to them,[1] and kneeling down with great reverence and devotion, he begged the servant of God to receive him as a companion. Seeing him so faithful and devout, Francis admitted him most willingly; and he realized that God would grant them many graces through Giles; this also came true.

These four brothers were united in immense spiritual joy and gladness; but in order to advance their work, they sepa-**33.**rated. Blessed Francis, taking with him Brother Giles, went into the Marches of Ancona, while the others took another direction. As they were journeying through the Marches, they rejoiced greatly in the Lord, and Francis in a loud, clear voice sang the praise of God in French, glorifying and blessing the goodness of the Almighty. Their hearts indeed overflowed with joy, as though they had found the greatest treasure in the evangelical field of holy poverty; and for her sake they gladly and freely considered all temporal things as dung.

Then the saint said to Brother Giles: "Our fraternity will

---

1. Giles was received on the feast of Saint George, April 23, 1208. He died April 22, 1262.

little else than reproaches at having left their own possessions in order to eat at the expense of others. This caused them much suffering and great want. They were persecuted by their friends and relatives and by the citizens generally, both rich and poor, of all ranks, who derided them as madmen and fools, because at that time no one spontaneously left his own goods to beg from door to door.

The brothers often asked the advice of the Bishop, who received Francis with kindness, but said: "It seems to me that it is very hard and difficult to possess nothing in the world." To this blessed Francis replied: "My Lord, if we had any possessions we should also be forced to have arms to protect them, since possessions are a cause of disputes and strife, and in many ways we should be hindered from loving God and our neighbor. Therefore in this life we wish to have no temporal possessions."

The Bishop was greatly pleased by these words of God's servant; and indeed Francis despised all passing things, especially money, so much that he laid the greatest stress on holy poverty and insisted that the brothers should be most careful to avoid money. He made and tried several rules before the last one which he left to his brothers;[2] and in one of these he expressed the scorn in which money should be held: "Let us beware that, having left all things, we do not forfeit eternal life for so worthless and mean a thing; and if somewhere we

---

2. Francis first wrote a very short rule which was approved orally by Pope Innocent III in 1209. This is the so-called Primitive Rule, which, however, is not extant. The so-called First Rule was prepared by Francis in 1221. It was not submitted for formal approbation, in part because it was just the Primitive Rule with the addition of some prescriptions that had been approved by papal delegates present at the various general chapters, and in part at least because it was too long and was not cast in sufficiently legal terminology to prove satisfactory. The Second or final rule, the so-called *Regula Bullata*, was approved November 29, 1223 by Pope Honorius III. A first draft of this final rule seems to have been lost or destroyed.

be like a fisherman who throws his net into the sea and draws out a great number of fishes, and he leaves the small ones in the water and keeps the large ones in a jar." Thus he prophecied the increase of the order, and this greatly astonished Brother Giles, considering how few the brothers then were.

As yet Francis did not preach sermons to the people they met; nevertheless in passing through towns and castles he exhorted all men and women to fear God and to do penance for their sins, while Brother Giles exhorted them to believe and to follow the excellent counsels of Francis.

34. When the people heard them, they said: "Who are these men, and why do they speak like this?" They made this comment because at that time the fear and love of God had died out in the country and no one spoke of penance which indeed was considered as folly. This attitude was caused by the temptations of the flesh, the cupidity of the world, and the pride of life; the whole of mankind seemed engulfed in these three evil forces.

Opinions varied about these men who were so obviously set on following the Gospel: some people declared that they were fools or drunk, but others maintained that such words were not those of folly. One listener said: "Either these men are following the Lord in great perfection, or they must be demented, since their way of life appears desperate, with little food and going about barefoot and clad in the poorest garments." For the moment the brothers' manner of holy life frightened those who saw them, and as yet no one was ready to join them. Indeed, the young women fled when they saw them approaching from afar for fear of their being madmen. Having journeyed through the province, Francis and Giles returned to the Portiuncula.

35. A few days later they were joined by three other men of Assisi, Sabbatino, Morico, and John of Capella; and they humbly prayed blessed Francis to receive them as brothers. When they begged for alms in the city they received very little else than reproaches at having left their own possessions in order to eat at the expense of others. This caused them much suffering and great want. They were persecuted by their friends and relatives and by the citizens generally, both rich and poor, of all ranks, who derided them as madmen and fools, because at that time no one spontaneously left his own goods to beg from door to door.

The brothers often asked the advice of the Bishop, who received Francis with kindness, but said: "It seems to me that it is very hard and difficult to possess nothing in the world." To this blessed Francis replied: "My Lord, if we had any possessions we should also be forced to have arms to protect them, since possessions are a cause of disputes and strife, and in many ways we should be hindered from loving God and our neighbor. Therefore in this life we wish to have no temporal possessions."

The Bishop was greatly pleased by these words of God's servant; and indeed Francis despised all passing things, especially money, so much that he laid the greatest stress on holy poverty and insisted that the brothers should be most careful to avoid money. He made and tried several rules before the last one which he left to his brothers;[2] and in one of these he expressed the scorn in which money should be held: "Let us beware that, having left all things, we do not forfeit eternal life for so worthless and mean a thing; and if somewhere we

---

2. Francis first wrote a very short rule which was approved orally by Pope Innocent III in 1209. This is the so-called Primitive Rule, which, however, is not extant. The so-called First Rule was prepared by Francis in 1221. It was not submitted for formal approbation, in part because it was just the Primitive Rule with the addition of some prescriptions that had been approved by papal delegates present at the various general chapters, and in part at least because it was too long and was not cast in sufficiently legal terminology to prove satisfactory. The Second or final rule, the so-called *Regula Bullata*, was approved November 29, 1223 by Pope Honorius III. A first draft of this final rule seems to have been lost or destroyed.

should happen to find money, let us treat it as the dust under our feet."

One day a man of the world placed some money by the crucifix in the church of the Portiuncula; and a simple-minded brother took it in his hands and put it on the window sill. When Francis heard from the brother what had happened and how he had touched the money, he ordered him to take it in his mouth, carry it out of the church, and drop it on the nearest dung heap he could find.

CHAPTER X

How blessed Francis foretold to his six companions all that would happen to them on their journeys through the world, and exhorted them to patience.

36. Saint Francis being already full of the grace of the Holy Spirit called the six brothers together in the wood surrounding Saint Mary of the Angels where they often gathered tr pray; and there he foretold many future things. "Dear Brothers, let us consider our vocation, and how God, in his great mercy, called us not only for our salvation but for that of many; and to this end we are to go through the world exhorting all men and women by our example as well as by our words to do penance for their sins, and to live keeping in mind the commandments of God." And he added: "Do not be afraid to preach penance even though we appear ignorant and of no account. Put your trust in God who overcame the world; hope steadfastly in him who, by the Holy Spirit, speaks through you to exhort all to be converted to him and to observe his commandments. You will find some men to be faithful and kind and they will receive you gladly; but you will also find many who are unfaithful, proud, and blasphemous, and they will insult and injure you and your words. Therefore prepare your hearts to suffer everything humbly and patiently."

When the brothers heard these words they began to be afraid, but the saint said to them: "Do not fear; before long many noble and wise men will join us, kings and princes too, with numbers of men, and very many people will be converted to the Lord and he will multiply and increase this his family in the whole world."

37. After these words the saint blessed them; and thus fortified, those godly men started out faithfully following Francis' directions. Whenever they came on a wayside cross or church, they bowed in prayer, saying: "We adore you, O Lord Christ, and bless you in all the churches in the world because by your holy cross you have redeemed the world."

The people they met were extremely surprised because in dress and manner of life they were so different from all others, and appeared almost like wild men of the woods. Whenever they came to a town or village or castle or house, they spoke the words of peace, comforting all, and exhorting men and women to love and fear the Creator of heaven and earth, and to observe his commands.

Some people listened gladly; but others only mocked them as fools and humbugs, and refused them admittance into their houses for fear they might be thieves and make off with something. Thus in many places they suffered innumerable trials and insults, and, finding no hospitality, they were driven to take shelter under the porticoes of the churches or houses. Many people asked where they came from, and to what order they belonged; and though it was wearisome to answer such numerous questions, they replied simply that they were penitents from Assisi; and indeed their community was not yet organized as a religious order.

38. At that time two of them arrived in Florence, and in begging through the city, they could find no house ready to take them in. They came to one which had a portico containing a baking oven, so they said to each other: "Here we might spend the night." They asked the mistress of the house whether, for love of God, she would give them hospitality. But when she refused to admit them into the house, they humbly begged to be allowed to sleep near the oven under the portico; but she was joined by her husband who, seeing the brothers in the portico, called and said: "Why did you allow those good-for-nothings to stay in the portico?" She replied that she had refused to let them into the house but had consented to their lying outside in the portico where there was nothing to steal but some wood. Her husband would not even allow her to lend the strangers any blankets in which to wrap themselves, though it was very cold; and this because he thought they were thieves and vagabonds. They spent a very frugal night near the oven, warmed only by the glow of divine love, and covered with the blankets of Lady Poverty; and then, very early, they went to the chief church for Matins.

39. After daybreak the mistress of the house went to the same church, and when she saw the brothers kneeling devoutly in prayer, she said to herself: "If these men had been vagabonds and scoundrels as my husband thought, they would not be praying with such reverence." She was still absorbed in these thoughts when a man named Guido began to give alms to all who were in the church, and when he came to the brothers he would also have given them money, but they refused. Then he said: "Why will you not accept money like the other poor?" Brother Bernard answered: "It is true we are poor, but to us poverty is not the burden it is to others for we have become poor voluntarily by the grace of God, and we wish to follow his precepts." The man Guido then asked whether they had ever possessed worldly goods; and from them he learned that indeed they had been rich but had sold everything and given all to the poor for love of God. And he who answered thus was Brother Bernard, the first son of Saint Francis; and today we believe him to have been indeed a saint, since on earth he was the first to embrace peace and penitence and to follow Francis by selling all he had and giving it to the poor, according to the Gospel counsel of perfection. And he persevered to the end in holy poverty and purity.

When the woman saw how the brothers refused money, she went up to them saying that, if they were willing, she would gladly receive them into her house as guests for love of God. They answered humbly: "God reward you for your good will." However, when Guido heard that the brothers had found no lodging, he took them home with him, saying: "This is the lodging prepared for you by the Lord; stay here as long as you will."

Giving thanks to God they stayed with him some time, edifying him greatly by their words and example in the fear of the Lord so that he generously gave many things to the poor.

40. As we have said before, the brothers suffered many things both from grown-up people and from children, and sometimes even their wretched garments were filched from them. When this happened, the servants of God remained naked, since, in accordance with the Gospel, they wore only a tunic; they did not even claim the return of the stolen garments; only if someone, moved by pity, chose to give them back, the brothers accepted them gladly. Sometimes they were pelted with mud; sometimes jesters put dice into their hands inviting them to play; others pulled at them from behind, dragging them along by their cowls. These and other similar pranks were played on them by people who considered them of no account and tormented them as they pleased. The brothers suffered all this, hunger, thirst, cold, nakedness, and many immense tribulations, firmly and patiently, as Saint Francis had bidden them. They were not dejected, they never cursed their tormentors; but like men whose faces are set to a great reward they exulted in tribulations and joyfully prayed to God for their persecutors.

CHAPTER XI

The acceptance of four other brothers; and the ardent mutual charity of the first brothers, and of their eagerness to work and pray, and of their perfect obedience.

41. People now saw how the brothers rejoiced in the midst of trials and tribulation; how zealous they were in prayer; and how they did not accept money like other people, nor keep it when it was given them; and how they really loved one another. Seeing all this, many became convinced that the brothers were true disciples of Jesus Christ; and with remorse in their hearts they came to ask the brothers pardon for having previously injured and insulted them. The brothers forgave them gladly, saying: "The Lord forgive you," and gently admonished them concerning their salvation. Some men asked to be received as companions,[1] and because the brothers were few, Francis had authorized all six of them to accept new recruits; and with these they all returned to Saint Mary of the Angels. When they were all together, joy filled their hearts, and they no longer remembered past injuries.

They were constant in prayer and in working with their

---

1. After the reception of Sabbatino, Morico, and John of Capella, came Philip the Long, John of Saint Constantia, Barbaro, Bernard Viridante, and Angelo Tancredi. Though the reception of Sylvester is usually given early in these sources, he seems to have been received after these first eleven brothers.

hands; this they did in order to banish idleness, the enemy of the soul. They rose at midnight and prayed with many sighs; and each deeply loved the other and cared for him as a mother cares for a cherished only child. Charity burned so ardently in their hearts that it was easy to risk life itself, not only for love of Jesus Christ, but also for the soul and body of any one of the brothers.

42. One day two of the brothers came upon a madman who started throwing stones at them; and when one saw a stone aimed at the other he intercepted it, wishing rather to receive the blow himself. Indeed, each was ready to give his life for the other. This and similar things were possible because they were so deeply rooted in mutual love: each one humbly reverenced his brother as a father or mother; and those brothers who held some office, or were distinguished by some special gift appeared the most humble and unpretentious of all. The brothers were bound by absolute obedience to the one who had authority over them: they did not question whether an order were just or unjust because they were convinced that whatever they might be bidden to do would be the will of God. Therefore obedience was easy to them. They abstained from carnal desires, each one judging himself and being attentive not to offend his brothers in any way.

43. If by any chance a brother let fall some word that might perturb another, his conscience pricked him so sharply that he could not rest until, prostrate on the ground, he had confessed his fault, asking that his brother's foot should be placed on his mouth. If the offender chanced to be a prelate, he ordered the other to obey, and thus they banished all rancor from their midst and kept themselves in perfect charity.

Once in Rimisius, a city of Cyprus, in the presence of a noble of the place, it happened that a brother named Barbaro said something that perturbed another brother; seeing this Barbaro took up some asses' dung from the road and started to eat it, saying: "Let the mouth which said a hurtful word to a brother submit to this shameful punishment." On seeing this the noble was so edified that he offered himself and all his goods to the friars to be used as they thought best.

Each brother studied to oppose any vice with the opposite virtue, helped and guided by the grace of our Lord Jesus Christ. Nothing was considered as private property; any book given to one brother was used by all according to the rule observed and handed down by the Apostles; because the brothers lived in true poverty they were correspondingly generous and openhanded with everything given them for love of God. For love of him they gladly gave to all who asked something of them, and especially they handed on to the poor any alms they received.

44. When they were walking along the roads and some poor person begged from them for love of God, if they had nothing else, they would give some garment of their own, however shabby it might be. Sometimes a brother would give his cowl, detaching it from his habit; sometimes a sleeve; or they would rip open a seam and give part of their habit in order to observe the Gospel injunction: "Give to whoever may ask."

One day a poor man came to Saint Mary of the Angels where the brothers lived and asked for alms. A cloak was hanging there which had belonged to a brother when he was still in the world. Saint Francis bade him give it to the beggar, and he did so promptly and willingly. And because of the reverence and devotion with which he made the gift that brother seemed to see it rising up to heaven and new joy flooded his soul.

45. When people who were rich in worldly goods came to the brothers, the latter received them gladly and kindly and sought to draw them away from sin and to bring them to penance. Often the brothers would beg their superior not to send them to their native places, for they wished to avoid familiarity and intercourse with their own relatives and to observe the words of the prophet: "I am become a stranger unto my brethren and an alien to my mother's children."

The brothers were able to rejoice so truly in poverty because they did not desire riches and despised all passing things such as are pursued by those who love this world. Especially money they trampled underfoot; and following the teaching and example of Saint Francis, they considered gold as having the same weight and worth as the dung of an ass. They rejoiced continually in the Lord because, in themselves, and between each other, there existed nothing to disturb them. The more they were separated from the world, the closer became their union with God. They followed the narrow way of the cross and the path of righteousness; and they cleared away all obstacles from the way of penitence and the observance of the Gospel in order to make the path smooth and safe for those who were to come after them.

CHAPTER XII

How Saint Francis with his eleven companions went to the papal court to present his project to the Pope and to obtain from him the confirmation of his rule.

46. Saint Francis saw that his brothers were increasing in number and in merits, and already they were twelve men,[1] all steadfastly set on one purpose. Therefore he, being the twelfth, said to the others: "I see, Brothers, that God in his mercy means to increase our company: let us therefore go to our holy Mother the Roman Church and lay before the Supreme Pontiff what our Lord has begun to work through us; so that with his consent and direction we may continue what we have undertaken."

All the brothers agreed to this proposal, and they set out with Francis for Rome; and he said to them: "Let us take one among us as our guide and consider him the vicar of Jesus Christ, following wherever he leads, and leaving him to choose our lodging." They elected Brother Bernard, Francis' first companion, for this office, and gladly followed the suggestion of their father.

While they journeyed along they talked joyfully of the words of God; indeed they spoke only of his honor and glory and of the salvation of their souls, and they often stopped to pray. And the Lord always prepared a place where they

---

1. Francis, plus the eleven mentioned in the preceding chapters and footnotes.

were met with hospitality and their needs provided for.

47. When they arrived in Rome they found there the Bishop of Assisi who welcomed them most gladly because he honored Francis and the brothers with a special love. At first, not knowing the reason for their coming, the Bishop was apprehensive, fearing that they might be planning to leave their native place where the Lord had begun to work wonderful things through them. He was happy to have men in his diocese whose life and behavior gave him great satisfaction. However, when he heard the reason for their coming and what they had in mind, he rejoiced and promised them his advice and help.

The Bishop was a friend of the Cardinal of Sabina, known as the Lord John of Saint Paul, a man full of divine grace who loved all servants of God. When he heard from the Bishop of Francis' life and sanctity, he desired to see him and some of the brothers. He therefore sent for them, and received **48.** them with honor and devotion. They spent several days with him and he was edified by their words and example and saw that their works corresponded to what he had heard; and he commended himself to their prayers, and, as a special favor, requested that they would consider him as one of themselves. Finally, he asked Francis the reason for their coming to Rome, and on hearing what was in their minds, he offered to plead their cause at the papal court.

He then went to the Curia and spoke to Pope Innocent III: "I have found a most excellent man who desires to live according to the form of the Gospel and in everything to observe evangelical perfection. I am convinced that through this man our Lord wills to renew the faith of Holy Church in the whole world." The Pope was very astonished at these words and bade the Cardinal to bring blessed Francis to him.

49. The folowing day the Cardinal presented the servant of God to the Pontiff to whom he opened his heart disclosing all his holy intention. Being gifted with great wisdom and discretion, the Pope approved Francis' desire and exhorted him and the brothers at length, and blessed them, saying: "Go, Brothers, with the Lord; and according to how he may inspire you, preach penitence to all. Then, when he multiplies your numbers and increases his grace in you, come and report all to Us, and We will then concede more to you, and entrust you with greater tasks."

The Pope earnestly desired to make sure that the concessions he had already given to the brothers, and those he might make in the future, were indeed according to the will of God; therefore, before the saint left his presence, he said to him and the brothers: "My sons, your plan of life seems too hard and rough. We are convinced of your fervor, but We have to consider those who will follow you in the future, and who may find that this path is too harsh." When however the Pope saw the brothers' constancy of faith, and how their hope was entirely anchored in Jesus Christ, and their unshakeable fervor, he said to blessed Francis: "My son, go and pray to God that he may reveal whether what you ask proceeds indeed from his most holy will; and this in order that We may be assured that in granting your desire We shall be following the will of God."

50. While the saint was praying according to the bidding of the Lord Pope, God spoke to him in spirit by a parable: "A poor and beautiful maiden lived in a desert, and a king, seeing her beauty, took her as his bride since he was sure she would bear him splendid sons. The marriage contract was drawn up and the marriage consummated, and many sons were born. When they grew up, their mother said to them: 'My children, do not be fearful and diffident, for your father is a king. Go, therefore, to his court, and he will give you all you need.' When the king saw these children, he marveled at their beauty, and recognizing their likeness to himself, he said: 'Whose sons are you?' They answered that they were the children of a poor woman who lived in the desert; upon which the king embraced them joyfully, saying: 'Fear nothing, for you are my children: and seeing how many

strangers eat at my table, you who are my lawful sons will do so with far greater right.' He embraced them joyfully and decreed that all his children by the woman of the desert should be summoned to his court, and there be provided for." This vision was shown to blessed Francis while he prayed, and he understood that the poor woman was himself.

51. After this prayer and vision, blessed Francis presented himself again to the Pope and repeated to him the parable which the Lord had shown him, and he concluded: "I am that poor woman whom God in his mercy has loved and honored, and through whom he has begotten legitimate children. The King of kings himself has told me that he will provide for all the sons he wills to raise up through me; because if he cares for strangers, he will also do so for his own children. Since God, in his loving providence towards all mankind, gives so many good things of the earth to the unworthy and to sinners, in far greater measure will he provide for evangelical men who deserve his favor."

On hearing this the Pope was greatly amazed, also because, before Francis appeared, he had had a vision that the church of Saint John Lateran was only saved from falling by being upheld on the shoulder of a small, insignificant man. He had awakened depressed and surprised, and, being wise and discreet, he had pondered long on the meaning of the vision. A few days later blessed Francis and the brothers came to him, and, as we have already explained, he learned the reason of their visit; and blessed Francis appealed to him for the confirmation of the rule, which he had written in brief and simple words, taken for the most part from the Gospel texts, and which he and his brothers strove with all their strength to put perfectly into practice. Then, when the Pope looked at Francis and saw him fervent in the love and service of God, in his own mind he compared his vision of the Lateran with that related by Francis and he began to say to himself: "This is surely a holy and religious man by whom the church of God will be supported and upheld.' Then he embraced

Francis and approved the rule he had written, and gave him permission to preach penance to all; and this permission was extended to all the brothers who had the approval of Francis.

52. Having obtained these favors, blessed Francis thanked God, and kneeling on the ground, promised obedience and reverence to the Lord Pope. According to the injunction of the same Lord Pope, in like manner the other brothers promised obedience and reverence to blessed Francis.

After receiving the blessing of the Supreme Pontiff and having visited the church of the Apostles, blessed Francis received the tonsure with the other eleven brothers, as had been arranged by the aforesaid Cardinal who wished them all to have the clerical tonsure.[2]

53. On leaving Rome the servant of God went out into the world amazed that his desire should have been satisfied so quickly; and he increased in hope and trust in the Savior who in holy revelations had shown him things still in the future. Before these things could be verified, one night, after he had lain down to sleep, he seemed to be walking along a certain path, near to which was a great tree, tall, beautiful, strong, and large. On approaching, he stood beneath it and he was amazed at its height and splendor. Suddenly he was lifted up so that his hand touched the top, and at that touch, the tree gently subsided to the level of the ground. This indeed had already happened, since the Lord Pope is the highest and most beautiful of all earthly trees, and at the petition of blessed Francis he had bent down with great benignity.

---

2. After the approbation of the first short rule in 1209, Francis and the brothers made their profession and were raised to the status of clerics by the pope.

CHAPTER XIII

The efficacious preaching of blessed Francis. The first place where he dwelt with the brothers and how they left it.

54. From this time onward Saint Francis wandered through cities, villages, and hamlets, and began to preach with increasing perfection, not using learned words of human wisdom, but through the doctrine and virtue of the Holy Spirit most confidently proclaiming the kingdom of God. He was a genuine preacher confirmed by apostolic authority; therefore he spoke no honeyed words of flattery or blandishment; what he preached to others he had already put into practice himself and his teaching of the truth was full of assurance. The power and truth of what he said did not come from any human source; and his words impressed many learned and cultured men who hastened to see and hear him as though he were a being from another century. Many of the people, nobles and commoners alike, were touched by divine inspiration and began to imitate Francis' way of life, and to follow in his steps. They abandoned the cares and pomps of the world, desiring to live under his direction, guidance, and discipline.[1]

---

1. The location in the text of what is said here, just as in I Cel., 36-37, supports the opinion that the Third Order was founded very soon after the approbation of the Primitive Rule, perhaps already in 1209 or 1210.

55. The blessed father was then living with his sons in an abandoned and derelict hut at Rivotorto, near Assisi. The place was so cramped that they could hardly sit or lie down to sleep; and very often for lack of bread their only food was turnips, for which, in their poverty, they begged here and there.

Blessed Francis wrote the brothers' names on the beams of the hut so that each one, when he wished to sit or pray, should know his own place, and that no unnecessary noise due to the close quarters should disturb the brothers quiet of mind.

One day while they were still living in this place, a peasant came along driving his donkey with the intention of taking possession of the hut. Fearing that the brothers might protest, he drove the donkey straight in, saying: "In with you, in with you; this place will just do for us." When the blessed Father heard the words and realized the peasant's intention, he was considerably annoyed, especially because the commotion caused by the man and his donkey had disturbed the brothers intent upon silent prayer. So he turned to them: "Dear Brothers, I know that God has not called me to entertain a donkey and live in the company of men, but to show men the way of salvation by preaching and wise counsel. We must, therefore, above all, make sure of being able to pray and give thanks for the graces we receive."

So they left the hut which later was used by poor lepers, and they moved to Saint Mary of the Angels, the Portiuncula; nearby was a little dwelling in which they lived before they
56. received the church itself. The abbot of the monastery of Saint Benedict on Mount Subasio was divinely inspired to offer this sanctuary to Francis; and Francis accepted it very humbly, and openly and affectionately commended it to the minister general of the order and all the brothers, insisting that, of all the shrines and churches dedicated to the Blessed Virgin throughout the world, this was the one nearest to her heart. The brothers' love and veneration for this place was

further increased by the vision of a certain friar, greatly beloved by blessed Francis, who treated him as an intimate, familiar friend. This man while still in the world earnestly desired to serve God faithfully, as indeed he subsequently did on entering the order; and he had a vision of a multitude of people, all blind; they were kneeling on the ground round Saint Mary of the Angels with joined hands and upturned eyes and they cried pitiably to God, praying that, in his mercy, he would give them sight. While they were praying, a great light came from heaven and rested above them, shedding its healing radiance. On awaking, the man promised his faithful service to God; and a few days later he left the passing vanities of the world and entered the order, where he served God humbly and devoutly.

CHAPTER XIV

The chapter of the fraternity which was held twice a year at Saint Mary of the Angels.

57. After blessed Francis had been given the sanctuary of Saint Mary of the Angels, the Portiuncula, by the abbot of Saint Benedict, he decided that twice in the year, at Pentecost, and at the feast of Saint Michael in September, all the brothers should gather there and hold a chapter.

At the Pentecost meeting the brothers discussed how to observe the rule more perfectly; and some of them were appointed as preachers and others were assigned to different posts in the various provinces.[1] In this chapter Saint Francis exhorted the brothers, reprimanding what was blameworthy, and directing them as he was inspired by the Spirit of God. In all he said he spoke lovingly, and carried out what he preached in his own actions. He held the prelates and priests of Holy Church in veneration; he honored the old, and those who were of noble birth and wealthy, but above all he loved the poor, and his heart went out to them in compassion. He deferred to everyone very humbly, and though he was the first among the brothers, standing high above them all, he appointed one as his guardian and supe-

---

1. The Franciscan order was divided into provinces or regional territories as early as 1217.

rior; and he obeyed him devoutly with great humility, thus routing any occasion for pride. He abased himself before all men so that one day he might deserve to be raised up among the saints and elect in the presence of God.

He admonished the brothers faithfully to observe the holy Gospel and the rule to which they had bound themselves; to bear themselves reverently and devoutly towards the services of the Church and all ecclesiastical observances; to hear Mass and adore the Body of the Lord with devotion and worship. He also taught the brothers to honor with special respect all priests who were ministers of the sacraments; and wherever they might happen to meet such a priest they should bow before him, and not only kiss his hands, but, if he were riding, even the hooves of his horse, out of reverence for his priestly authority.

58. Blessed Francis also warned his brothers never to judge or criticize those who live in luxury, eat fastidiously, and indulge in superfluous and splendid clothes; God, he said, is their Lord and ours; he has the power to call them to himself and to justify them. He insisted that the friars should reverence such men as their brothers and masters, and they are indeed brothers since they are children of the same Creator; while they are our masters since they help the good to do penance by giving them what is necessary to the body. To this blessed Francis added: "The general behavior of the friars among people must be such that all who see or hear them may be drawn to glorify our heavenly Father and to praise him devoutly." His great desire was that he and his brothers should abound in the good works for which men give glory and praise to God.

He also said to the brothers: "Since you speak of peace, all the more so must you have it in your hearts. Let none be provoked to anger or scandal by you, but rather may they be drawn to peace and good will, to benignity and concord through your gentleness. We have been called to heal wounds, to unite what has fallen apart, and to bring home those who have lost their way. Many who may seem to us to be children of the Devil will still become Christ's disciples."

59. Besides insisting on these things, the kind father reproved his brothers when they were too harsh on themselves, wearing out their strength in excessive vigils, fasts, and corporal penance. Some of them mortified their bodies so severely in order to repress all the natural human impulses that they appeared to be hating themselves. Francis being filled with the wisdom and grace of our Savior, reproached the brothers gently for all this and, using rational arguments, he forbade such excesses, binding up their wounds with the bandages of sane precepts and directions.

None of the friars assembled at the chapter ever dared to recount any worldly events: they spoke together of the lives of the holy fathers of old, and how they might best live in God's grace. If by chance anyone among those present was troubled or tempted, the very sight of blessed Francis and his fervent and gentle exhortations were sufficient to drive away all temptation and trouble. He spoke indeed not as judge but as a tender father to his children, as a kind doctor to his patients; he suffered with the sick, and grieved with those in tribulation. Nevertheless he knew how to reprove evil doers and to impose discipline on the obstinate and rebellious.

At the end of the chapter he blessed all the friars and assigned to each his province; he gave permission to preach to anyone who had the spirit of God and the necessary eloquence, whether cleric or brother. When all present had received his blessing, in great joy of spirit they started on their way through the world as pilgrims and strangers, taking nothing with them for the journey except their office book.

Whenever they came on a priest, rich or poor, good or bad, they bowed humbly before him; and when it was time to seek shelter for the night they preferred to lodge with **60.** priests sooner than with layfolk. If, however, the priest could not offer them hospitality, they sought out the houses of God-fearing, spiritual men. In every village and place they came to, the Lord inspired some good person to receive them until houses could be built and set aside for their use.

God gave them his Spirit and the manner of speech necessary to satisfy the needs of the time so that their words penetrated into many hearts; especially into those of the young rather than of the old. Thus many youths left father and mother and all they possessed to follow the friars and to be clothed in their habit. In this way the blade of separation worked actively in the world when many young people turned to religion, leaving their families in the morass of sin. When the friars received anyone into the fraternity, they brought him to Saint Francis so that the novice might humbly and devoutly receive the habit from his hands.

Not only men, but also women and unmarried virgins were fired by the brothers' preaching, and, on their advice, entered the prescribed convents to do penance; and one of the brothers was appointed as their visitor and guide. Married men and women, being bound by the marriage vow, were advised by the friars to dedicate themselves to a life of penance in their own houses.[2]

Thus through blessed Francis' perfect devotion to the Blessed Trinity the Church of Christ was renewed by three new orders;[3] and this had been prefigured through his previous reparation of three churches.[4] His three distinct orders were each in due time approved and confirmed by the sovereign pontiff.

---

2. This again is a reference to the Third Order. See footnote 1 in Chapter 13.
3. The First Order for men; the Second Order, or Poor Clares, for women; the Third Order for men and women who cannot leave the world but wish to live according to the ideals of Saint Francis.
4. Francis first repaired the church of Saint Damian, then that of Saint Peter, then the little church of Our Lady of Angels or the Portiuncula.

CHAPTER XV

Of the death of the Lord Cardinal John, first protector of the friars; and how the Lord Cardinal Ugolino, Bishop of Ostia, took his place as father and protector of the order.

61. The venerable father, the Lord Cardinal John of Saint Paul, often helped and advised blessed Francis; and he praised his life and works and those of his friars to all the other cardinals. Thus they too were moved to love the servant of God and his brothers so warmly that each one wished to have several brothers in his household; not for any special service, but for the devotion and affection he felt towards them.

On the death of the Cardinal John of Saint Paul, another cardinal, Ugolino by name, then bishop of Ostia, was divinely inspired with a particular love of blessed Francis, and he took to his heart also all the friars and protected them and cared for them together with blessed Francis.[1] He behaved towards them all as a tender father; indeed, he showed himself even more than an earthly father whose love includes all his children. The Cardinal's heart was warmed with such spiritual

---

1. Cardinal Ugolino, the Bishop of Ostia, seems to have undertaken the function of cardinal protector unofficially already about 1217. In 1220 or 1221 he was appointed officially to this office. He was an intimate friend of Saint Francis and helped him in many ways, particularly in the writing of his final rule. Ugolino became Pope Gregory IX in 1227.

fervor that he was drawn by a special preference in God for his servant Francis and all the brothers. When blessed Francis heard of this cardinal's fame — and indeed he was pre-eminent among the other cardinals — he went to him with his friars. The Cardinal received them with great joy and said: "I offer you myself, and am ready to help, advise, and protect you as you may wish; and I ask that, for love of God, you will remember me in your prayers."

Then blessed Francis gave thanks that God had deigned to inspire the Cardinal to take him and the friars under his protection, and he said to the Cardinal: "Willingly, my Lord, I take you as father and protector of our order; and it is my wish that the brothers should always pray for you." He then requested the Cardinal to be present at the chapter of the brothers to be held at Pentecost; and in his kindness the Cardinal accepted and was present each year at the friars' gathering. As he was riding towards Saint Mary of the Angels, the friars came to meet him, and he dismounted, and for the love he bore them he went with them on foot to the church where he preached and celebrated Mass in which Francis, the servant of God, sang the Gospel.[2]

---

2. This was probably the so-called Chapter of Mats in 1221 (or, according to some, 1222). See the account of this chapter in Brother Jordan of Giano's *Chronicle*, no. 16-18; in English translation, *XIIIth Century Chronicles*, Placid Hermann O.F.M., Franciscan Herald Press, 1961.

CHAPTER XVI

The election of the first ministers; and how
they were sent out into the world.

62.Eleven years had passed since the beginning of the fraternity, and the friars had increased in numbers and merits.
The time had come for the election of ministers who, with
some of the brothers, might be sent out to all the provinces in
every country where the Catholic faith is cultivated, observed,
and venerated.[1]

In some provinces the friars were indeed received, but
were not allowed to build or set up houses in which to dwell;
they were driven out of other provinces or not even allowed
to enter because the inhabitants feared they might be heretics.
This happened because, when Pope Innocent III approved
the order and rule of the friars, he had not confirmed it in
writing; and through this omission the friars suffered many

---

1. The province of Provence was established already in 1219 by Brother
   John Bonelli, sent there by Francis. About the same time, the friars
   went to Germany, but, as is indicated in the next paragraph, they
   were forced to leave because of their deficiency in the language and
   the difficulties that arose as a result. In 1221, however, they were
   successful in setting up a flourishing province there. In 1224 the
   friars went to England. Brother Jordan's *Chronicle* gives an interesting account of the mission in Germany. Thomas of Eccleston, *The
   Coming of the Friars Minor to England*, gives an interesting account
   of the mission to England. See *XIIIth Century Chronicles* for both.

tribulations at the hands of both the clergy and the laity. This was also the reason why they had to fly from various provinces. Harried and distressed, they were set upon by thieves who stripped and robbed and beat them; and they returned to blessed Francis very embittered. They suffered such treatment in various countries north of the Alps, in Germany and Hungary, and also in others.[2]

When this came to the ears of the Cardinal Bishop of Ostia, he summoned blessed Francis and went with him to the Lord Pope Honorius, since by this time Pope Innocent was dead.[3] At the Cardinal's instance the Pope solemnly confirmed and sealed another rule, inspired by Christ, which blessed Francis composed, and which, in substance, was the same as the one which had already been approved by Pope Innocent. In this rule the time to elapse between the chapter meetings was lengthened to a year, in order to avoid the excessive strain and fatigue on the brothers living in the more distant provinces.[4]

63. Blessed Francis also petitioned the Lord Pope Honorius for a cardinal of the Holy Roman Church, that is, the Lord Bishop of Ostia, who would be a father to the order, and that the brothers could turn to him in all questions relating to their life.[5] Blessed Francis made this request because of a vision in which he had seen a small, black hen with hairy legs, and feet like those of a domestic pigeon; and this hen had so many chickens that she could not possibly shelter them under her wings and they ran about beyond her. When blessed Francis awoke and thought over this vision in the

---

2. See Brother Jordan's account, no 5-7.
3. Pope Innocent III died in 1216.
4. The First Rule of 1221 prescribed that the ministers ''beyond the sea and beyond the mountains'' should come to the general chapter only every three years because of the distance. The rest were to assemble every year at Pentecost. Chapter 18.
5. This was in 1220 or 1221. See the account in II Cel., 26. It might be noted that a strict chronological order is not being followed, especially in this section.

light of the Holy Spirit, he realized that he was the hen, and he said: "I am that hen, by nature small and black, whereas I should be simple as a dove, flying up to heaven on the wings of love and virtue. The Lord, in his mercy, gives and will give me many children whom I cannot protect by my own strength; therefore, I must put them under the care of our holy Mother the Church, and she will protect and nourish them under the shadow of her wings."

64. A few years after this vision he came to Rome, and went to see the Lord Bishop of Ostia; and he commanded Francis to go with him the following morning to the Curia because he wished that Francis should speak to the Lord Pope and the assembled cardinals, and, with loving devotion, should commend his order to them. Blessed Francis demurred saying that he was simple and unlearned; nevertheless he had to accompany the Lord Bishop to the Curia. On seeing him, the Lord Pope and the Cardinals were filled with joy; and standing there before them, blessed Francis spoke as he had been taught and prepared to do by the Holy Spirit. When he had finished, he commended his order to the Lord Pope and to all the cardinals, who were greatly edified by his preaching; and their hearts were moved to love both him and his brothers.

65. Then blessed Francis said to the Sovereign Pontiff: "My Lord and Master, I am filled with compassion and concern for your continual and indispensable labor in watching over God's Church; and I am ashamed that you should spend so much care on us Friars Minor. We know that many nobles and rich men who are also very religious cannot come into your presence, and it puts us to shame, and alarms us that we, who are the poorest and most despised of religious, not only have access to you, but dare to stand at your door and knock at this sanctuary of Christian virtues. For this reason I humbly beseech Your Holiness to give us as our father this Lord Bishop of Ostia so that, when necessity arises, the

949

brothers can appeal to him, always saving your pre-eminent dignity."

The Pope was pleased with this petition of blessed Francis, and granted it by appointing the Lord Bishop of Ostia as protector of his order.

66. On receiving this nomination from the Lord Pope, the Lord Bishop of Ostia acted as a true protector of the friars, and wrote to a number of prelates who had persecuted the brothers, urging that such opposition should cease. It would be far better, continued the Bishop, if the friars were invited to dwell and preach in the different provinces; and that those in authority should help and advise them, and treat them as good and holy religious working with the formal approbation of the Holy See. The Cardinal Protector sent similar letters to a number of other cardinals.

At the next chapter blessed Francis gave permission to the ministers to receive new brothers into the order, and he sent them back to those provinces where they had encountered opposition, bearing letters of the Cardinal and the rule duly approved and sealed by the Holy See. This official support reassured the prelates who formerly had been antagonistic to the friars, and they gave them ample permission to edify all men and to live and preach in their provinces. When people saw the humble and saintly lives of the friars and heard their words of peace and compassion, many spirits were inflamed with love of God and were drawn to do penance, so that with fervor and humility they took the holy habit of the order.

67. When blessed Francis saw the faith and love of the Lord Bishop of Ostia for the friars, he was drawn still closer to him in the bond of affection. By a divine revelation blessed Francis knew that the Bishop would become Pope, and in his letters he always addressed him: "To the venerable Bishop in Christ, the father of the whole world." This prophecy was verified shortly afterwards, for on the death of Pope

Honorius III, the Lord Bishop of Ostia was elected Sovereign Pontiff under the name of Gregory IX. From that day on he was the great benefactor and defender of the friars and of other religious, and above all of Christ's poor, for which reason he is believed to be a saint.

CHAPTER XVII

*The holy death of blessed Francis and
how, two years previously, he had received
the stigmata of our Lord Jesus Christ.*

68. For twenty years blessed Francis was perfectly conformed
to Christ having followed in the steps of the Apostles; and
then on October 4, 1226 he passed joyfully to God.[1] Through
many labors he had come to the possession of eternal rest
and had merited to appear before the presence of the Lord.
A friar, famous for sanctity, saw the soul of blessed Francis,
like a star, large as the moon, and radiant as the sun, raised
up above great waters and borne by a shining cloud straight
up to heaven. This saint indeed had labored assiduously in
the Lord's vineyard, untiringly fervent in prayer, fasting,
vigils, and preaching; he had walked in paths leading to
salvation, caring attentively for his fellow men in watchful
compassion and in humble disregard for himself. All this he
had done from the beginning of his conversion until he departed to Christ whom he had loved with his whole heart,

1. Francis' death occurred about one hour after nightfall on Saturday
night and he was buried the next day. According to the reckoning of
the day at that time (and still in use in some places), October 4 began with nightfall the day before, since each day was reckoned from
nightfall to nightfall, and not from midnight to midnight as we
reckon it. According to our reckoning, then, it was still Saturday
night, October 3, when Francis died. But according to the reckoning
of the time, it was already October 4.

with whom his mind was always filled, whom he praised continually with his voice and glorified in his works. He loved God so fervently that it sufficed for Francis to hear him named to be so fired with love that his whole person glowed and he broke into the words: "At the name of God the heavens and earth should bow down."

69. It was the Lord's will that the entire world should know of the love of blessed Francis and how his heart was filled with the thought of Christ's passion. Therefore while he was still alive, God conferred on him the wonderful prerogative of a most singular privilege. Wrapt in divine contemplation, blessed Francis was absorbed in seraphic love and desire; and through the tenderness of his compassion he was transformed into a living crucifix. Thus the inmost desire of his burning love was fulfilled. One morning two years before his death, about the feast of the Exaltation of the Cross, while he was praying on the side of a mountain named La Verna, there appeared to him a seraph in the beautiful figure of a crucified man, having his hands and feet extended as though on a cross, and clearly showing the face of Jesus Christ. Two wings met above his head, two covered the rest of his body to the feet, and two were spread as in flight.

When the vision passed, the soul of Francis was afire with love; and on his body there appeared the wonderful impression of the wounds of our Lord Jesus Christ. Blessed Francis did all in his power to hide these wounds, not wishing that God's gift should be seen by men; but he could not hide this gift entirely, and it became known to his intimate companions.

70. After his death, however, all the brothers who were present saw clearly that his body bore the wounds of Christ in hands and feet. In those wounds there appeared to be nails, but these were formed by Francis' own flesh which had taken on the shape and color of iron nails. The right side over the ribs looked as though it had been pierced by a lance with a plain and obvious wound, covered with a red scar with crimson edges, and during blessed Francis' lifetime blood often flowed from this wound.

The undeniable truth of these wounds was apparent during blessed Francis' life, and when he died they could be clearly seen and touched. After his death the Lord made the truth of them still more manifest through miracles which occurred in different parts of the world. These miracles touched the hearts of many persons who had not rightly judged and appreciated the servant of God during his life time, and had doubted about the stigmata. Their doubt was changed into such faith and certainty that many who had formerly decried the servant of God were moved through the Lord to accept the truth and they became fervent in praising him and in spreading his fame and teaching.

CHAPTER XVIII

The canonization of blessed Francis, and the translation of his body.

71. Francis the servant of God already shone in different parts of the world through the new light of miracles; and from far and near people who had received great and singular graces through his merits came to revere his holy body. Therefore Pope Gregory, after consultation with the cardinals and many other prelates and after they had read and approved the miracles which God had performed through his servant, inscribed his name in the list of the saints, ordering that his feast should be celebrated on the day of his death.

The celebrations in the city of Assisi were attended by a number of prelates, princes and barons and innumerable crowds from all parts of the world, invited especially by the Lord Pope to be present at the solemnity which took place 72. in 1228, the second year of his pontificate.[1] The Sovereign Pontiff had deeply loved the saint during his lifetime; and having canonized him with great magnificence, he also laid the first stone of the church to be built in his honor, which also he enriched with many sacred gifts and precious ornaments.

Two years after his canonization the saint's holy body was honorably translated to this new church from the place where

---

1. Francis was canonized two years after his death, July 16, 1228.

it had been temporarily buried.[2] The Sovereign Pontiff gave to the new church a cross adorned with precious stones and containing a relic of the cross of our Lord; he also sent various ornaments and a number of vessels for the service of the altar together with many beautiful vestments. He exempted this church from any inferior jurisdiction and by his apostolic authority declared it to be the mother church of the whole order of the Friars Minor; and this is clearly shown in the public privilege which was signed and sealed by all the cardinals.

73. These official exterior honors would have counted for little, but the saint, dead in body, was alive in spirit and glory, and through him the Lord converted and healed numbers of people, both men and women. Besides this, after the saint's death and through his merits, many men of noble birth, together with their sons, took the Franciscan habit; and many ladies, with their daughters, entered the convents of the Poor Ladies. Men of learning and scholars, some of them laymen, others holding church offices and dignities, showed their contempt for all worldly allurements by renouncing them completely and entering the order of the Friars Minor. Thus they accepted and in all things conformed to the poverty and example of our Lord Jesus Christ and his blessed servant Francis, each according to the measure of divine grace.

Of Saint Francis it could be said, as of Samson,[3] that he killed many more by his death than he had when alive. It is a certain fact that our holy father Saint Francis is alive in the life of glory. May we be brought to this same life of glory through his merits who lives for all eternity. Amen.

---

2. His remains were transferred from the church of Saint George to the new basilica May 25, 1230.
3. Judges 16, 30.

LEGEND OF PERUGIA

Translated by Paul Oligny from the annotated French version by Damien Vorreux, with an Introduction by Théophile Desbonnets.

This English translation of the Legend of Perugia, made by Paul Oligny from *Saint François d'Assise: Documents, Écrits et Premières Biographies* (T. Desbonnets & D. Vorreux, eds., Paris, 1968), pp. 859-989, is published for the first time in this volume.

INTRODUCTION

In order to write his *Vita II*, Thomas of Celano made use of the oral and written recollections of the companions of St. Francis. The research and identification of the documents that have preserved these memories for us constitutes, as we have already said, one part of the Franciscan Question.

Brother Leo was a privileged witness of the life of Francis, especially in his latter days. He was his secretary,[1] his infirmarian, and his confessor: we may then be assured, a priori, that his contribution must have been important. And indeed Angelus Clareno and Arnald of Sarrant rate him as a biographer of St. Francis on the same footing as Celano, St. Bonaventure, and Julian of Speyer. Many alluded to the writings attributed to him.

We must now set out on our search for the writings of Brother Leo.

The writings of Brother Leo

The witnesses of Peter Olivi, of Ubertino da Casale, and of Angelus Clareno tell us that a part of the writings of Brother Leo were written in the form of scrolls (*rotuli*), and Ubertino da Casale likewise points out "that one book is in the closet of the friars of Assisi," from which Ubertino took several texts "written by the hand of Brother Leo," for his argumentation.

Joergensen, in a very evocative style, seems to us to have perfectly imagined the genesis of these scrolls. "And when the young men had departed and Brother Leo was again alone in his poor little cell, whose whitewashed walls always seemed to him to be shining with bright sunlight, then the old Franciscan sat down at his work-table and began to write just as in the old days when St. Francis dictated. Memory after memory came upon him, one sheet of parchment was written full after another in his beautiful clear handwriting, and when twilight came and the clouds grew gold in the evening over Perugia's distant towers, then Brother Leo rolled up his parchments and carried them down the road which under the olive trees passes along Assisi's wall out to St. Clara's convent."

These scrolls, which unfortunately we no longer possess, have had a lively history. In 1305 Ubertino da Casale, who quotes them probably from memory[3] in his *Arbor Vitae,* tells us: "It was with great sorrow that I learned that these scrolls have been misplaced and are perhaps even lost."[4] But in 1311, in the *Declaratio* which he presented during the proceedings that made him an opponent of the party of the Community, he pointed out that the facts he brought out could be found "in the scrolls written by Brother Leo, which I have before me."[5] Had the lost scrolls been found? Or was the rumor of their being lost devoid of truth? It matters not. But what must be noted, as Paul Sabatier stressed,[6] is that in these proceedings Ubertino's adversaries never challenged the statement that these writings were attributed to Brother Leo. This means that for them, as well as for him, Brother Leo was indeed their author.

The "Intentio Regulae" and the "Verba"

By gathering together all the texts quoted by Ubertino da Casale, then by selecting certain ones and completing them with quotations or allusions from other authors, such as Peter Olivi, Francis of Fabriano, and Angelus Clareno, we can reconstruct two rather well structured fragments which consequently form a solid point of departure in our search for the writings of Brother Leo.

In 1901, Father Lemmens found these fragments in

the manuscript 1/73 of St. Isidore and published them in Volume I of his *Documenta Antiqua Franciscana.*

The manuscript entitled the first of these fragments: *S.P.N. Francisci Intentio Regulae.*[7] The text that followed tallied exactly with a long quotation given by Ubertino da Casale in his *Arbor Vitae,* with this slight difference that Ubertino da Casale sometimes abridged or summarized the text and warned the reader that he was doing so.

The manuscript entitled the second fragment: *Verba S.P. Francisci.*[9] This time the text tallied with a long quotation made by Clareno in his *Expositio Regulae,*[10] except for two differences: manuscript 1/73 contained a paragraph (no. 3) which Clareno had not quoted, and the quotation made by Clareno ended with a paragraph that is missing in the manuscript. In his edition, Father Lemmens thought it opportune to complete the text of the manuscript by adding the last paragraph as it is found in Clareno. Father Delorme took Father Lemmens to task for doing this.[11] But this rather justified censure in no way lessened the primary result that could be considered as established: the *Intentio Regulae* and the *Verba* constituted, both as to their content and form (that is to say, essentially for the ordering of their paragraphs), two fragments from the work of Brother Leo.

Should these fragments then be considered, as Fr. Lemmens thought, as two *opuscula,* that is, as works forming a whole and having their own existence?

Two observations, at least, seem to be opposed to this view. Manuscript 1/73 obviously appears as a collection of extracts that have come from many places; it was one of those notebooks, and there were many of them, in which the scribe made notes for his personal use of the thoughts he met in the course of his reading. This character is particularly evident in the part that Fr. Lemmens published under the title *Extractiones de Legenda antiqua*[12] and which contains small traces of *2 Celano.* It therefore seems reasonable to think that the *Intentio* and the *Verba* are also extracts from more important works.

On the other hand, the *Verba* begins with an "Item dicebat . . ." which surely indicates that the quotation continues another text.

The problem now is to discover the work from which these two extracts were taken. Among the documents we have, only the manuscript of Perugia contains the text of the *Intentio* and the *Verba* in the order attested to by Ubertino da Casale, Angelus Clareno, and manuscript 1/73.

The manuscript 1046 of Perugia

Though this manuscript had already been known, Fr. Delorme in 1922 was the first to draw attention to a text it contained and which up until then had remained unnoticed by the research scholars. A very detailed study along with the edition of certain fragments then appeared in the *Archivum Franciscanum Historicum.*[13]

From this study we learn first of all that although the manuscript was mutilated and is from the fourteenth century, a very searching discussion of its constituent elements enables us to fix its date with great probability at 1311.[14]

Description of the manuscript

On the first folio of the manuscript there is a summary. The writing, although old, is not that of the copyist but rather that of one of the successive owners of the manuscript. This summary cannot be dated.

As for the part that interests us, we find: "Legenda major et antiqua sancti Francisci." Unfortunately with the disappearance of notebooks XI, XII, and XV of the manuscript, the *Legenda major* is minus its beginning and end and lacks the beginning of the text that interests us.

The absence of notebook XV is very regrettable for, as a result, we will never know if the redactor of the summary really transcribed the title written by the copyist himself at the beginning of the work or whether he took it upon himself to entitle it *Legenda antiqua*. Fr. Delorme inclined toward the first hypothesis and made this manuscript the oldest witness to use the term *Legenda antinqua*. In view of the great variety of different texts that the authors of the fourteenth century grouped under the unvarying appellation of *Legenda antiqua,* it seems preferable to be more prudent. For this reason from now on we will designate this text by the term *Compilation of Perugia* and the part of which a translation is presented herewith by the term *Legend of Perugia.*[15]

The contents of the manuscript

The copyist had underscored the existence of three sections in the text that he was transcribing by illuminated initials. The largest of the initials of the entire manuscript marks the beginning of the third section: the copyist certainly wished to point out that what was to follow constituted an especially important section. To facilitate his study, Fr. Delorme in turn subdivided this third section into three parts.

The text of the manuscript of Perugia is thus divided into five parts.

A — comprising 21 numbers, composed of four paragraphs of *2 Celano,* the *Verba S. Francisci,* and texts already published by Fr. Lemmens in the *Documenta Antiqua Franciscana.*[16]

B — comprising 20 numbers, entirely borrowed from *2 Celano.*

C — (beginning with the large initial), comprising 17 numbers, 15 of which had already.been published by Fr. Lemmens.

D — comprising 33 numbers, practically unpublished.

E — comprising 24 numbers, composed of the *Intentio Regulae* and texts already published by Fr. Lemmens.

When Fr. Lemmens published the text of the *Compila-*

tion of Perugia in 1926,[17] he thought it useless to reproduce section B which only contained texts from Celano; furthermore, he headed his edition with section CDE which formed a whole and completed it with section A from which he took out the 4 numbers of Celano. The numbering of this edition does not therefore correspond with the one he had first adopted in the study that had appeared in the *Archivum Franciscanum*. The references given by the authors who wrote before 1926 become incomprehensible if we forget this detail.[18] The translation offered in this volume bears the numbering of the edition of 1926; and all references are to this edition.

The manuscript of Perugia gives us a compilation, as Fr. Delorme had rightly judged, and that is what justifies the way in which he presented his edition.

The presence of the illuminated initials, as we have already noted, divides this compilation into three distinct parts; or more precisely it shows us that the copyist juxtaposed three autonomous units. This observation is corroborated by the fact that in other manuscripts that have preserved fragments of this compilation for us the sections are ordered differently.[19]

It is therefore necessary to examine each of these units separately, exactly as if each one of them had come from a different manuscript.[20]

Analysis of the sections

Section B — We shall examine section B first. It contains only extracts from *2 Celano*. Despite the reticence of Fr. Bihl,[21] we must admit with Fr. Delorme that this section provides proof of the care with which the copyist transcribed the texts before him and this all the more so since the transcribed chapters were evidently extracts.

Fr. Delorme thought that the origin of these extracts had to be sought in one of those collections that pious friars had compiled for their personal devotion at a time prior to the decree of 1266; their private nature enabled them to escape the proscription.[22]

In reality the reconstruction of the genealogy of the various manuscripts of *2 Celano* shows that these extracts were selected with a precise purpose in mind around 1310 and from a complete manuscript of *2 Celano*.[23]

Section CDE. If we now study section CDE, we will note first of all that here we find the *Intentio Regulae* complete and in the order attested to by Ubertino da Casale and manuscript 1/73 of St. Isidore. It begins with number 66 of our text, but this number is joined to the preceding one in the following way: 64 — "At the time when blessed Francis was sick in the bishop's residence at Assisi. . . ." 65 — "A doctor came to the residence to see him. . . ." 66 — "One day Brother Riccerio came to the same residence. . . ." As Fr. Delorme remarks: "these three chapters are so related to each other that they follow each other without interruption. What happened in the *Intentio Regulae*? Since the passage had a special pungency, copies of it were made and these were circulated in preference to other passages. In the extract, the beginning of the account was neither more nor less adapted by the transposition of the *jaceret infirmus in palatio episcopatus Assisii* of no. 64 instead of and in the place of the *in eodem palatio* of no. 66. In that way the bond that connected these pages to the preceding ones was broken, a bond that the manuscript of Perugia reestablished."[24]

This observation enables us to confirm the fact, already pointed out,[25] that the *Intentio* must not be considered as an *opusculum* properly so-called.

On the other hand, since the examination of section B has proved to us that the copyist was faithful, we can certainly attribute the authorship of nos. 64-67 to Brother Leo, and by considering the unity of style, extend this authorship to the entire section CDE. Fr. James Cambell notes: "Everything here speaks in favor of Brother Leo: the imperfection of the language . . ., the continuous use of *and,* the 44 *maxime quia,* the 22 *multotiens,* the 17 *nos qui cum eo fuimus,* etc."[26]

In 1311, in his *Declaratio,* Ubertino da Casale concluded a quotation of the *Intentio Regulae* with this sentence: "All this is found, written by the hand of Brother Leo, in the book in Assisi." By that he meant the book that was then at the Sacro Convento of Assisi. The great number of bulls placed at the beginning of the manuscript of Perugia proves with sufficient probability that it too was transcribed at the Sacro Convento: we are therefore led to wonder whether the unit of sections CDE, which the copyist set off so well by beginning them with a large initial, is not the transcription of the book written by the very hand of Brother Leo and which was at that time in the closet of the friars of Assisi. The hypothesis is tempting but there is little probability that we will ever be able to confirm it.

Moreover we may wonder whether the text that has come down to us in this manuscript is complete. Fr. Delorme doubted it. He pointed out that "the blank columns at the end of the manuscript, clarified by the context of the last chapter, indicated that the scribe had not completed his work."[27]

There is also an evident lacuna at the end of no. 10 and at the beginning of no. 12. In his edition Fr. Delorme was induced to restore the end of no. 10 by the text corresponding to chapter 3 of the *Tractatus de indulgentia S. Mariae de Portiuncula de François Bartholi*[28] and to restore no. 11 and the beginning of no. 12 according to the Little manuscript.[29] No. 58 was also clearly truncated.

Lastly, the discussion of the place-data that one can read in no. 5 tends to show either that this number is not in its proper place or that an episode is missing before no. 1.

Whatever the case may be, one point seems assured: all of this section is the work of Brother Leo and consequently predates 1271, the date of his death. But perhaps it is possible to determine the time when these pages were written with greater preciseness.

From a certain number of clues, Fr. Delorme thought that he could conclude that these texts were anterior to the *Vita II* of Celano. We could then, with sufficient probability, date them from 1246 and consider them as a part of what the Companions sent to Crescentius. The detailed examination of the parallels that exist between the manuscript of Perugia and the *Vita II* bolster this conclusion and show that these texts are a direct source of the *Vita II*. This was not the opinion of Fr. Bihl who in his *Disquisitiones Celanenses* reexamined each of the clues proposed by Fr. Delorme and reduced them to ashes.[30]

The erudition of Fr. Bihl was truly prodigious and still arouses admiration. We would not be lacking in respect for his memory if we were to say that his whole argumentation is built on the *a priori* idea that the texts furnished by the manuscript of Perugia could not antedate the *Vita II*.

On the other hand, it is very evident that of the clues proposed by Fr. Delorme — as is always the case regarding clues — none was solid enough to withstand the heavy artillery of erudition, but their convergence was nevertheless significant enough to make the conclusion he claimed to draw from them probable.

Section A — Section A, which we are now going to examine, is much less homogenous and it is difficult to draw safe conclusions from it. Let us first recall that as a result of the disappearance of one of the notebooks of the manuscript we do not have the beginning. We can evaluate the extent of what is missing — 5 or 6 columns — but it is difficult to imagine their contents.[31]

The four numbers of *2 Celano* which we find there lead to the same conclusion as those of section B. Their examination proves the faithfulness of the scribe, and the detailed study of the variants shows that these extracts come from the same manuscript as do those of section B. We may then wonder whether their true place is not in this section and whether this displacement in section A is not due uniquely to the copyist of the manuscript of Perugia.[32]

No. 116, which recounts a vision of Brother Leo, must have come from a *Life* of Brother Leo and must be dated for the end of the thirteenth century.

Nos. 111-115 correspond to the *Verba S. Francisci* as they are found in the *Expositio Regulae* of Clareno, but with the insertion between nos. 114 and 115 of a paragraph from Celano[33] which Fr. Delorme did not publish. The comparison of this group of paragraphs with manuscript 1/73 of St. Isidore and with the quotation of Clareno shows that tradition varied as to the contents of the *Verba* and that, contrary to what Fr. Lemmens thought, there is no reason to consider them as an *opusculum* having its own existence. Regarding them Fr. Delorme wrote: "With due regard for the formal attribution that Ubertino da Casale and Angelus Clareno makes of them, for me they constitute a fragment or a stray piece of the famous *Rotuli* of Brother Leo, the last thing he perhaps wrote."[34]

This remark is probably true, but we cannot neglect the role Conrad of Offida[35] and other members of the party of the Spirituals could have played in the transmission and amplification of these texts. No. 113 (paragraph 4 of the *Verba*) especially bears the trace of their intervention: St. Francis, plagued by the ministers who did not want another rule, appealed to Christ and "immediately the voice of Christ was heard in the air answering. . . ." If, by way of example, we compare this text with No. 43 where St. Francis also appeals to Christ and where "he heard in spirit a voice say to him . . ." we will readily grasp this intrusion of the supernatural which transforms the inner inspiration into an external revelation.[36]

The *Verba S. Francisci,* at least in the form in which we know them, are therefore of a later date and rightly considered as suspect.[37]

As for the other numbers (98, 110, and 117), they are on an equal footing with those of section CDE and we can with sufficient probability draw analogous conclusions from them.

Was Brother Leo also their author? It is possible, although two considerations may make us doubt it: the language and the style are relatively more supple than in the part we can attribute to him; and, on the other hand, he is named here along with Brother Angelus.[38]

But, whoever the author is, the detailed comparison of the two texts proves that these paragraphs also were a source of *2 Celano*: they date therefore from the same epoch as those of section CDE.

A source of the Vita II of Celano

The texts which the *Legend of Perugia* has preserved for us give at least a partial answer to the "Franciscan Question" inasmuch as they indicate the sources of the *Vita II*. It is therefore possible to begin to pass judgment on the use that Thomas of Celano made of them. The unbiased comparison[39] of the texts shows that Celano made good use of his sources. If he happened to summarize certain events[40] and even to make a choice among certain others, we cannot accuse him of having omitted some truly important ones. Partially renouncing his own style, however, he extended respect for his sources to the point of borrowing sentences and expressions that he did correct, one might say, only when the roughness of Brother Leo's Latin became unbearable to his scholarly ears.[41]

The interest of the Legend of Perugia

Besides supplying us with one of the sources of Celano, the *Legend of Perugia* gives us an especially moving portrait of St. Francis. There is nothing conventional about this portrait such as an official hagiographer might paint. There is not even any testimony that would have to be transferred to the dossier of the confrontation that the times provoked between the conservatives and the progressives. It is simply the evocation of the memory of a friend and that is why it moves us so much.

This portrait has all the qualities of a memoir. Its tone is simple; there is no labored style nor tendency to moralize that betrays the professional writer who is thinking of his public like Celano or St. Bonaventure. The accuracy of the details,[42] precious for the historian, shows us that the narrator remade in spirit the journeys that he had previously made in the company of Francis, and that he relived the events in which he had participated. Lastly, the everyday blends with the sublime as in every human life, and Francis looms not as a stained-glass saint but as one who is very close to us.[43]

The *Legend of Perugia* also has all the defects of a memoir. First of all, there is great disorder: there is no plan; the evocations are joined to each other without concern for chronology and arise from associations that are not always evident. Furthermore, a very definite tendency to digress is evident — an habitual fault with old people. And lastly — another fault of old people — there is a longing for times past. One expression keeps recurring: *tunc temporis,* at that time . . .; and this, not only to designate in a vague way a former era, but especially to contrast it with the period during which the narrator is writing. "At that time, a certain thing was done . . .; and the brethren of those days were not like those of today . . ."; etc.

This reassessment of the recollections of "the good old days" sheds much light on the person of Brother Leo as being fearful of the present and having his eyes turned toward the past; it also enlightens us as to the evolution of the Order between the time of the death of Francis and that when the narrator wrote. This evolution had already begun during the lifetime of Francis. There are many proofs of this. We cannot however accept all that the *Legend of Perugia* has to say about it indiscriminately; obviously Brother Leo sometimes projected on the lips of Francis his own reactions to a situation that occurred much later than the events he reports.

With all its faults and deficiencies, however, the *Legend of Perugia* is one of the most authentic eye-witness accounts and the most vivid we have of St. Francis. Here we find the freshness of the *Fioretti* plus the guarantee of an authentic eye-witness, and that is why reading it enthralls the modern reader.

— Fr. Theophile Desbonnets O.F.M.

While our omnibus was in preparation, a critical edition of the *Legend of Perugia,* with an English translation on facing pages, was published by Oxford University Press in its series of Medieval Texts: Rosalind B. Brooke, ed.-trans., *Scripta Leonis, Rufini et Angeli Sociorum S. Francisci* (Oxford: At the Clarendon Press, 1970). As the title indicates, the *Legend of Perugia* is regarded as being a redaction of the original *Legend of the Three Companions.* The volume also contains the *Vita Beati Fratris Egidii* (critical edition of Latin text with English translation), pp. 304-349. — In the translation which follows, the captions are those which were added by Fr. Desbonnets. — M.A.H.

NOTES

1. We even have some very precious autographs of his: his annotations on the text of the blessing that St. Francis had written for him; a breviary he copied for St. Clare.

2. J. Joergensen, *Saint Francis of Assisi: A Biography*, trans. from the Danish by T. O'Conor Sloane (Longmans, Green and Co., New York, 1928), p. 383.

3. The fact that they are quoted "from memory" does not exclude the possibility of a quasi-literal fidelity to the text. The men of the Middle Ages had a very developed memory: for example, if the book which was being read in the refectory was not within reach, the lector often recited from memory. Cf. R. Aigrain, *L'Hagiographie* (Paris, 1953), p. 244.

4. Ubertino da Casale, *Arbor Vitae*, Bk. V, chap. V.

5. Ubertino da Casale, "Declaratio," *ALKG* 3 (1887), 168.

6. P. Sabatier, *Vie de saint François,* (1st ed.), p. lxiv. Cf. *Speculum Perfectionis* (Paris, 1898), p. cxlvii.

7. Published in *DAF*, vol. 1, pp. 83-99.

8. *Arbor Vitae,* Bk. V, chap. III.

9. Published in *DAF,* vol. 1, pp. 100-106.

10. Angelus Clareno, *Expositio Regulae*, published by Fr. L. Oliger, Quaracchi, 1912, pp. 126-130.

11. Fr. Ferdinand M. Delorme, the *Legenda antiqua S. Francisci* (Paris, 1926). p. xviii.

12. Published in *DAF,* vol. 3, 25-49.

13. Fr. Ferdinand M. Delorme, the "Legenda antiqua S. Francisci du ms. 1046 de la bibliothèque de Pérouse," *AFH* 15 (1922), pp. 23-70 and 278-332.

14. *Ibid.,* 30.

15. Strictly speaking, the term is inaccurate. This text does not follow the formal rules for writing "legends" as they were conceived in the Middle Ages. We shall use it, however, in view of the difficulty of finding another that is satisfactory and does not lead to confusion.

16. Either in vol. 1 for the *Intentio Regulae* and the *Verba,* or in vol. 2 (*Speculum Perfectionis, redactio prima*) for the other texts.

17. Fr. Ferdinand M. Delorme, the *Legenda antiqua S. Francisci, text of the ms.* 1046 (M 69) of *Perugia,* (Paris 1926), pp. xxxii-70. The title of this edition is exactly the same as that of the study that appeared in AFH. When there is a possibility of

972

confusion, we shall designate it by the phrase "Paris edition."

18. This twofold numbering is very awkward in itself, but to complicate the situation even more, the French translation of this text, which was published under the title *Saint François raconté par ses premiers compagnons* (Paris, 1927 and 1946), is divided by the translator Abbé M.J. Fagot into chapters which have no relationship whatsoever with the two numberings. Lastly, Fr. J. Cambell who has reedited this text under the title *I Fiori dei tre compagni* (Milan, 1967), felt that on the basis of certain criteria he too had to change the order of the text. We are therefore faced with four different ways of making references.

19. Manuscript C 9.2878 of the National Library of Florence and manuscript C4 of the Library of the University of Uppsala suggest the order CDE-B, the place of section A being left undecided.

20. Failure to admit this necessity is the reason why certain critics have felt that they could catch Fr. Delorme in the act of a contradiction. Cf. for example, M. Beaufreton, *Saint François d'Assise* (Paris, 1925), p. 313.

21. M. Bihl, "Disquisitiones Celanenses," *AFH*, 20 (1927), 468ff.

22. Fr. F. M. Delorme, the "Legenda," *AFH*, 15 (1922), 44.

23. Cf. Th. Desbonnets, "Recherches sur la généologie des biographies primitives de saint François," *AFH*, 60 (1967), 273-316.

24. Fr. F. M. Delorme, the "Legenda," *AFH*, 15 (1922), 69.

25. Cf. *supra*, "Intentio Regulae."

26. J. Cambell, "La vita di S. Francesco . . . ," *Doctor Seraphicus*, 12 (1965), 10.

27. Fr. F. M. Delorme, the "Legenda," *AFH*, 15 (1922), 320.

28. Published by P. Sabatier, (Paris, 1900), pp. 7-12.

29. Cf. A. G. Little, "Un nouveau manuscript franciscain. . . ." *OCH*, 3 (1914-1919), 1-110. This manuscript contains the chapters that are found in the manuscript of Perugia; it also contains others which, although not found there, evidently come from the same origin and cannot be neglected in an inventory of the sources of *2 Celano*.

30. M. Bihl, "Disquisitiones Celanenses," *AFH*, 20 (1927), 488-496.

31. We can however show that the two paragraphs that precede no. 1 ought to be two paragraphs of *2 Celano*: cf. Th. Desbonnets, "Recherches," *AFH*, 60 (1967), 300.

32. This remark could perhaps clarify, if it were confirmed, certain relationships that exist among the Compilation of Perugia, the Compilation of Avignon, and the *Speculum Perfectionis*.

33. *2 Celano* 146 came, as we have said, from the same manuscript as all the other nos. of Celano and was perhaps inserted here by the copyist of the manuscript of Perugia because of the similarity of them with no. 115.

34. Fr. F. M. Delorme, the "Legenda," *AFH*, 15 (1922), 328.
35. Cf. *Speculum Perfectionis*, interpolation: "Verba fr. Conradi," *OCH*, 1 (1903), 370-392 and "Ricordi di S. Francesco . . . ," *MF*, 7 (1898), 131-136.
36. Cf. *supra*.
37. Fr. J. Cambell deleted them from his edition. Cf. *supra*, n. 18.
38. No. 100.
39. The concordance tables found at the end of this volume facilitate this comparison.
40. For example, the story of the lay brother who wanted a psalter (no. 70, 72-74) is reduced to three lines (2 C. 195).
41. Celano takes the upper hand and concludes with a moralizing consideration.
42. For example, Francis' cell at the Portiuncula is the last cell near the hedge of the garden located behind the house, the one in which Brother Rainier the gardener later lived (no. 84); at Greccio, it is the cell near the large hall (no. 94); at Rieti, where St. Francis went to be treated for his eyes, his host is called Tabald and the podestà ordered a curfew (no. 24); the road leading to Celle de Cortona runs along the foot of Lisciano (no. 27); etc.
43. For example, his desire when sick to eat some pike (no. 29) or to hear some music (no. 24).

CHAPTER TITLES

THE LEGEND OF PERUGIA

PENANCE AND THE VIRTUE OF DISCRETION

1   In the early days of the Order, that is to say, at the time when Francis began to group a few brothers around him, he lived with them at Rivo Torto.[1] One night around midnight, when all were sleeping on their poor straw mattresses, one of the brothers began to cry out: "I am dying! I am dying!" Blessed Francis got up and said: "Get up, Brothers; bring a light!" A torch was lit and blessed Francis asked: "Who cried out: I am dying?"

One brother said, "I did."

And blessed Francis said to him: "What ails you, Brother?. What are you dying from?"

"I am dying of hunger," he answered.

Blessed Francis, a man full of charity and discretion, did not want the brother to blush from eating alone. He had a meal prepared then and there and everyone partook of it. It must be said that this brother and the others with him were recently converted and inflicted excessive penances on their bodies.

After the meal, blessed Francis said to the other brothers: "My brothers, I say to you, let everyone of you take his constitution into consideration. If one of you can do with less food than another, it is not my wish that he who needs to eat more should try to imitate the first. Let each one take his own constitution into account and give his body what it needs. If, in the matter of eating and drinking we are obliged to deny ourselves those superfluous things which are harmful to the body and the soul, we must forego even more so excessive mortification, for God desires loving kindness and

977

not sacrifice."[2] He added: "My dear brothers, it was my wish that out of love for my brother all of us should partake of his meal so that he would not blush: we did so out of love and because he greatly needed it. I warn you, I will not do this again, for it would be neither religious nor upright. Rather it is my desire and command that each and everyone, while respecting our poverty, give his body what it needs."[3]

2   The first brothers and, for a long time, those who still came after them mortified their bodies not only by excessive abstinence from drink and food but even by vigils, the cold, and manual work. They even wore cinctures made of iron and cuirasses if they could obtain them and also the roughest hairshirts they could find. That is why the saintly Father, considering that the brothers could become sick from this practice — which is what did happen in a short time to many of them — forbade, in a chapter, any brother from wearing anything on his flesh except his tunic.[4]

We who lived with him can testify to this about him: from the time he had brothers and throughout all his life, he practiced the virtue of discretion for them (keeping always intact our Order's required poverty and virtue, which are traditional among the senior brothers); as for himself, at the beginning of his conversion before he had brothers, and then during all his life, he treated his body harshly. And yet, as a young man, he was by nature delicate and frail; in the world he could live only surrounded with attention.[5] One day, when the brothers were beginning to transgress poverty and to be intemperate in the matter of food and other things they used,[6] he preached a sermon to all the brothers in the course of which he said having certain ones in mind: "My brothers, does it not seem that my health requires a special diet?[7] And yet, because I must be a model and example to all the brothers, I wish to be satisfied with very poor food and coarse appointment."[8]

THE PRAISE OF MENDICANCY

3   As soon as blessed Francis had gathered a few brothers about him, he greatly rejoiced over their conversion
and their amiable companionship which the Lord had given
him. He had so much affection and respect for them that
he did not send them out to beg: they would blush, he
thought, if they were to go out and beg alms. To spare them
this shame, he went begging every day by himself.

But this was too exhausting for his body. Even when he
was in the world, he was by nature delicate and frail; since
he himself had withdrawn from the world, he had grown
even weaker due to excessive abstinence and the mortifications he imposed upon himself. In view of the fact that
he himself could not withstand such fatigue, and since the
brothers had chosen this vocation and should have been
faithful to it despite their repugnance and their lack of experience, and since they still lacked the necessary discernment
to be the first to say to him: "We wish to go begging," he
spoke to them as follows: "My dear brothers and sons, do
not be ashamed to go begging for alms, for God became
poor for our sake in this world.[9] That is why we have
chosen the road of genuine poverty in imitation of his
example and that of his most holy Mother: this is the inheritance that our Lord Jesus Christ has acquired and left
us, to us and to those who, following him, have chosen to
live in holy poverty."[10] Then he added: "In truth I say to
you, many nobles and scholars of this world will enter our
Order and will consider themselves highly honored to
beg for alms. Go therefore and beg with confidence, with
a joyful heart, and with the blessing of the Lord God. You
ought to ask for alms with more cheerfulness and joy than
a man who would offer[11] a hundred pennies for one: in
exchange for the alms that you solicit, you will offer the
love of God, since you will say: 'Give us an alms for the

love of God!' and heaven and earth are nothing when compared to this love."

Since they were still few in number, he could not send them out two by two; he therefore sent them singly through the towns and villages. On their return, each one showed blessed Francis the alms he had collected, and they said to one another: "I brought back more than you did." Blessed Francis rejoiced to see them gay and happy. From that time on, each one eagerly sought permission to go on the quest.

4   At this time, when blessed Francis was living with the brothers whom he had then, his soul was of an admirable purity: from the moment that the Lord had revealed to him that he and his followers were to live according to the holy gospel,[12] he resolved to live it to the letter and strove to apply it to his life at all times. For example, when the brother cook wanted to serve them vegetables, he forbade him to soak them in hot water the night before, as is the custom, in order to implement the gospel saying: "Do not worry about tomorrow."[13] And the brother waited until the end of Matins to begin soaking his vegetables in water. That is the reason why many of the brothers for a long time asked for and accepted only whatever alms they needed for one day in the places where they lived, and especially in the cities.

TACTFULNESS TOWARD A SICK PERSON

5   At a certain time when St. Francis was staying in the same friary,[14] there was a brother, a man of deep spiritual life and already old in the Order, who was very weak and sick. Looking at him, blessed Francis was moved to pity. But at that time the brothers, whether sick or healthy, joyfully and patiently welcomed poverty which took the place of abundance. If they were sick, they refused medication; in fact they contrived to do what was injurious to their health. Blessed Francis, therefore, said to himself:

"If this brother were to eat some grapes early in the morning, I think they would do him some good." One day he got up without making any noise, awakened this brother and brought him into a vineyard near the church. He chose a vinestock that had beautiful and good bunches of grapes. Sitting down near the vineyard with this brother, he began to eat some grapes so that the brother would not be ashamed to eat them alone. While eating them, the brother praised the Lord God. As long as he lived, he often mentioned to his brothers with great emotion and devotion the Father's tactfulness in his behalf.

THE POWER OF HIS PRAYER

6   At a certain time, when blessed Francis was in this same friary,[15] he stayed to pray in a cell behind the house. One day while he was there, the bishop of Assisi[16] came to see him. He entered the house and knocked on the door of the cell that led to where Francis was. When the door was opened,[17] he immediately entered the cell; it had been furnished with mats and a small nook where blessed Francis stayed. Since he knew that the holy Father had shown him signs of close friendship and tokens of love, he entered without embarrassment and lifted up the mat to see him. But hardly had he passed his head through the small nook when, willy-nilly, he was violently thrust outside by the will of the Lord because he was not worthy to see the saint. He left the cell immediately, walking out backwards, trembling and stunned. He confessed his fault to the brothers and his sorrow for having entered the cell that day.

7   There was a brother, a man of deep spiritual life and already very old in the Order,[18] who was a close friend of blessed Francis. It so happened at one time that he was a prey for many days to most serious and cruel diabolical suggestions. And so he fell into the deepest despair. He suffered from them every day, and all the more so since he

was ashamed to go and confess them each time. He mortified himself in an excessive way by fasting, vigils, tears, and the discipline. He had been tormented daily for a long time when, by a divine disposition, blessed Francis came to that place. One day when Francis was walking around the friary with a brother and with the one who was tormented in this way, the blessed Father withdrew himself a little from the first brother, approached the one who was tempted and said to him: "My dear brother, I wish and order that from this moment on you need not confess those suggestions and temptations of the Devil to anyone. Fear not: they have done no injury to your soul whatsoever. But every time you are troubled by these suggestions, I give you permission to recite the *Our Father* seven times."

The brother rejoiced at these words and over the fact that he was not bound to confess these temptations, especially since he was ashamed to confess them every day, which aggravated his torment. He admired the holiness of his Father who had come to know of his temptations through the Holy Spirit. In fact, he had opened himself only to priests and he had changed priests often because he was ashamed to tell the extent of his weakness and his temptations to one priest alone. As soon as blessed Francis had spoken to him, he was freed of that great interior and external trial from which he had suffered so long. Through the grace of God and the merits of blessed Francis, he lived in great peace and tranquility of soul and body.

THE PORTIUNCULA, THE MIRROR OF THE ORDER

8   Seeing that God wanted to multiply the number of the brothers, one day blessed Francis said to them:

"My dear brothers and sons, I see that the Lord wishes us to increase in number. In my opinion, it would be well and in conformity with religion to ask our bishop or the canons of St. Rufino, or the abbot of the monastery of St. Benedict[19] for a small and poor church where the brothers may recite their Hours and, next to it, a small and poor house built of earth and wood where the brothers can sleep and go about their work. The place we are using[20] is no longer suitable and the house too small, since it pleases the Lord to multiply us. Above all, we have no church where the brothers may recite their Hours; and were someone to die, it would not be fitting to bury him here in the church of the secular clerics." All the brothers agreed with him.

He then went and presented his request to the bishop. The latter answered: "Brother, I have no church to give you."

He then went to the canons of St. Rufino and made the same request to them; they answered as the bishop did.

Next, he went to the monastery of St. Benedict of Mount Subasio and made the same speech to the abbot as he did to the bishop and the canons, and told him the answer he had already received from the bishop and the canons. The abbot, moved with pity, took counsel with his brothers. God having so decided, they gave blessed Francis and his brothers the church of St. Mary of the Portiuncula, the poorest church they owned. No poorer church could be found in the whole territory of the city of Assisi. This was what blessed Francis had long desired. The abbot said to blessed Francis: "Brother, we have granted your request. But it is our wish that, if the Lord multiplies your Order, this friary will be the head[21] of all those that you will found." These words were approved by blessed Francis and by all the brothers.

The saint was very happy that this place had been given to the brothers because the church bore the name of the Mother of Christ, because it was very poor, and also because of its name of Portiuncula. The fact that it was called the church of the Portiuncula was indeed a presage that it would become the mother and head of the Order of the poor lesser brothers. The church had been given the name Portiuncula because the aforesaid place where the church had been built had already been called Portiuncula for a very long time.

Blessed Francis said: "It was the Lord's will that no other church[22] be given to the brothers nor did he allow the first brothers to build one or possess another because this one was, as it were, a prophecy that is now fulfilled by the arrival of the lesser brothers." Although it was very poor and almost in ruins for a long time, the inhabitants of the aforementioned place and those of the city of Assisi always had a great devotion for this church, a devotion that has continued to grow even to this day.

As soon as the brothers arrived in this place to take up their residence, the Lord increased their number almost daily. The news of the brothers as well as their renown spread throughout all the valley of Spoleto.

Many years ago, before the people of the country had named St. Mary of the Portiuncula, this church had nevertheless been called St. Mary of the Angels; moreover, even after the brothers had begun to repair it, the men and women of that region still said: "Let us go to St. Mary of the Angels."

The abbot and his monks had given this church to blessed Francis and his brothers without any restriction: they had demanded no payment or yearly rent. Nevertheless, blessed Francis as a good and prudent master, wanted to build his house on solid rock[23] and his Order on true poverty. And so, every year he sent a basket full of small fish, called loaches, to the monks. He did this as a sign of very great humility and poverty so that the brothers would not own any place as their own, or dwell in any place that was not the property of someone else, and so that they would not have the right either to sell or to alienate a property in any way whatsoever. And so each year the brothers brought their small fishes to the monks. Because of the humility of blessed Francis who did this because he wished them well, the monks in return offered him and his brothers the gift of a vessel full of oil.

9   We who lived with blessed Francis bear witness that he said with great insistence: "Of all the churches in the world that the blessed Virgin loves, she bears the greatest love for this one." He spoke in this way because of the numerous prerogatives given by God to this friary and because this had been revealed to him in that very place. That is why during all his life, he bore a great devotion and a great respect for this place. And so that the memory of it would remain engraved in the hearts of the brothers, he wished, as his death was drawing near, to have it written down in his testament that the brothers should do likewise. In fact when he was near death, he said before the minister general and the other brothers:

"I wish to make arrangements regarding the friary of the Portiuncula and leave them as a testament to my brothers[24] so that this place will always be treated by them with great reverence and devotion.

"Let them do as the old brothers did. This was already a holy place; they preserved its holiness by praying there continually night and day and by observing silence there constantly. And if they sometimes spoke after the time determined for the beginning of silence it was always to converse about the glory of God and the salvation of souls with much uplifting fervor. If it so happened — and this was rare — that a brother engaged in a futile or inopportune conversation, he was immediately chided by another.

"They afflicted their bodies not only by fasting but also by frequent vigils, cold, insufficient clothing, and manual work. Very often, in fact, in order not to remain idle, they went and helped the poor in their fields; and these latter sometimes gave them bread in return for the love of God. By these virtues and others as well, they sanctified themselves and sanctified this place. Those who succeeded them did likewise for a long time thereafter, but never with equal intensity.

"But then the number of the brothers and the faithful who joined together in this place exceeded the number that was customarily received there, mainly because it was the meeting place of all the brothers of the Order[25] and the welcoming center of all those who wished to enter it. Furthermore, the brothers today are less fervent in prayer and other good works, more inclining to useless conversation and even to communicating the news of the world. This is why this place is no longer treated by the brothers who live there and by the others with the respect and devotion befitting it and which I would like to see reign there.

10   "It is my wish therefore that this place be always under the direct authority of the minister general so that he may watch over it with great care and especially that he may gather a good and holy family of religious there. Let the clerics chosen be among the holiest and most upright, and also from among those who, in the whole Order, know best how to sing the divine office, so that not only the brothers but also the other faithful may listen to them gladly and with much devotion. And let holy, discreet, and virtuous brothers and lay people be chosen to serve them.

"It is also my wish that no brother nor anyone else enter this friary, except the minister general and those who serve the brothers. Let the brothers of this friary speak to no one, except to those who serve them and the minister general when he visits them. It is also my wish that the lay people who serve them bring them no word or news of the world that is not beneficial to their souls.[26] If it is my wish that no one enter this friary, I do so in order to make it easier for the brothers to keep their purity and holiness; if no useless or harmful word to the soul is uttered there, this place will remain pure and holy to the sound of hymns and the praises of the Lord.

"When one of the brothers of this friary dies,[27] the minister general will call another holy brother to replace the deceased, in whatever friary he may be found. Why do I make these arrangements? Because, if the brothers and the friaries where they reside stray some day from the purity of life and holiness that are befitting, I wish that at least this community be a beautiful mirror of the Order, a candelabra before the throne of God and the blessed Virgin. May the Lord, thanks to it, have mercy on the sins and failings of the brothers; may God always guard and protect our Order and its little nursery!"

11   What follows took place at the time of the chapter, for at that time it was held every year at St. Mary of the Portiuncula.[28] By the grace of God, the brothers had multiplied and were multiplying every day. Now, all they had for the general gathering was a poor small hut covered with straw and a wall made of branches and mud, such as the brothers had built when they settled in that place. The inhabitants of Assisi noticed this and organized a group to come to their aid. In a few days and with much haste and fervor they built a large house made of stones cemented together, but without the consent of blessed Francis and in his absence.

When he returned for the chapter from the province where he was and saw the house they had built in that place, he was very astonished. Then he said to himself that this house would serve as an excuse for the brothers in the friaries where they lived or would live to erect or have erected large buildings. Since he desired that this friary should always be the model and the very pattern of all the fraternities, one day before the end of the chapter he got up, climbed on the roof of this house and ordered several brothers to climb up with him. With their help, he began to throw the tile with which the house was covered down to the ground, having decided to demolish it.

987

Some knights and other inhabitants of Assisi happened to be there. The commune had provided for a surveillance corps to protect the place against the lay people and outsiders who, having come from all over to see the chapter of the brothers, were massed near the friary. Seeing that blessed Francis and the other brothers wanted to destroy the house, they came closer and said to blessed Francis: "Brother, this house belongs to the commune of Assisi, and we are here to represent the commune; that is why we are telling you not to destroy this house." Blessed Francis answered them: "Well, if this house belongs to you, I do not want to touch it." He came down immediately, and so did the brothers who were with him.

That is why the people of Assisi for a long time decided that each year the podestà, whoever he was, would be obliged to see to it that the house had a roof and that the necessary repairs be made.

12   At another time, the minister general[29] wanted to have two small houses built there for the brothers of this friary to provide lodging and a place for the singing of the divine office. At that time all the brothers of the Order and all the postulants came flocking to this place: likewise all the brothers who resided there were disturbed almost every day. Because of the great numbers who flocked there, they had no place to sleep nor to recite their Hours since they had to give the cells they occupied to others. This was a constant disturbance to them, for after their work it was practically impossible for them to provide for the needs of physical health and their spiritual life.

This house was almost entirely completed when blessed Francis returned to this place. One morning from the cell in which he had spent the night he heard the noice that the brothers were making at their work. He wondered with astonishment what this could be and asked his companion.

"What is that noise? What are the brothers doing?" His companion told him the whole story.

Francis sent for the minister general and said to him: "Brother, this friary is the model and mirror of our Order. So that the brothers of the entire Order who come here may take back to their friaries the good example of poverty, I wish that the brothers of this friary bear with inconvenience and disturbance for the love of the Lord God rather than experience tranquility and consolations. Otherwise, the other brothers of the Order will cite this example for building their friaries and will say: 'At the friary of the Portiuncula, the first friary of the brothers, they built on a great and grand scale; we may therefore build well in our friaries since we are poorly housed.' "

CONSTRUCTION ORDERS

13   A brother, a man of deep interior life, to whom blessed Francis showed great friendship, lived in a hermitage.[30] Realizing that if Francis came to that place, he would not have a suitable place to stay, he had a cell built in a solitary corner near the friary of the brothers where blessed Francis might pray when he came to that place.

In fact a few days later blessed Francis did arrive. As the brother was leading him to this cell, blessed Francis said to him: "This cell is too beautiful for my liking. If you want me to spend a few days there, have it lined inside and out with gravel and branches. Now, this cell was not cemented but built of wood; since the wood was smooth and had been worked with an ax and an adze, it seemed too beautiful to blessed Francis. So the brother had it arranged as the saint had requested. In truth, the smaller and the more conformable to the religious state the cells and the houses of the brothers were, the more the saint delighted in seeing them and staying in them.

After he had lived and prayed in that cell for some time,

one day when he had gone out and was near the friary of the brothers, one of them came up to him. "Where do you come from?" blessed Francis asked. "From your cell," the brother answered. Blessed Francis immediately responded: "Since you have called it my cell, someone else will occupy it from now on, not I!"

We who lived with him often heard him repeat this saying of the gospel: "Foxes have holes and the birds of the air have nests, but the Son of Man has nowhere to lay his head."[31]

And he said: "When the Lord withdrew into solitude to pray and fast for forty days and nights, he did not have a cell or a house built for himself but he took shelter under a rock of the mountain." That is why, following his example, he refused to have either a house or a cell on this earth and forbade that they be built for him. Moreover, if he inadvertently said to the brothers: "Have a cell prepared for me," he no longer wanted to live in it afterwards because of the saying of the gospel: "Do not be anxious for your life."[32]

As death approached, he insisted that it be written in his Testament that all the cells and houses of the brothers were to be constructed solely of earth and wood in order better to safeguard poverty and humility.[33]

14   While he was at Siena for treatment of his eyes, he lived in a cell where an oratory was built after his death out of veneration for him. Lord Bonaventure, who had given the brothers the land on which their friary was erected, said to blessed Francis one day: "What do you think of this friary?" The blessed Father answered: "Do you want me to tell you how the friaries of the brothers should be built." "Why certainly," he answered. The saint said to him:

"When the brothers arrive in a city where they do not yet have a residence, and they find someone who wants to give them a piece of land to build a friary with a garden and the necessary space, they must first of all decide that the area is adequate, and not exceed it; they must never lose sight of the holy poverty that we have promised to observe nor of the good example that we are bound to give to others."

The holy Father spoke in this wise because he wanted to remove from the brothers any pretext to violate the rule of poverty in the houses, churches, gardens, and other things which they used. He also did not want them to own any friary, but always to live in them as pilgrims and strangers.[34] And if he wanted only a few of them in each house the reason was because it seemed to him difficult for a large community to observe poverty. Now, from the beginning of his conversion, his constant wish was that holy poverty be observed perfectly.

15 Next, they must go and find the bishop of the city and say to him: "Lord, a certain person has decided for the love of God and the salvation of his soul to give us the land necessary to build a friary. The first thing we are doing is coming to you, since you are the father and master of the souls of all the flock entrusted to you, and therefore of ours and of those of our brothers who will live in this place. With the blessing of the Lord and yours, we wish to found a house there."

The saint spoke in this fashion because the good of souls, which the brothers wish to achieve among the people, will be greater if, living in peace with prelates and clerics, they win the people and the clergy over to God rather than if they were to convert only the people to the scandal of the clergy. And he said: "The Lord has called us to re-awaken the faith and to assist the prelates and clerics of our holy Mother the Church. Likewise we are bound, to the extent possible, to love them always, to honor and venerate them. The brothers, as a matter of fact, are called 'lesser' because they must remain very humble with regard to all the men of this world, humble in all their behavior and by their example, as well as by their name. When, at the beginning of my conversion, I withdrew from the world and from my father according to the flesh, the Lord put his words in the mouth of the bishop of Assisi to give me counsel and courage in the service of Christ. For that reason and for so many other eminent qualities that I perceive in prelates, I wish to love, venerate, and consider not only bishops but even humble priests as my lords."[35]

16   "After having received the blessing of the bishop, let them go and dig a large ditch around the property they received to build a friary; there let them plant a good hedge in place of a wall as a sign of holy poverty and humility. Then, let them have poor and small houses built of earth and wood and a few cells where the brothers may sometimes pray and work more at ease and especially safe from useless chatter. Let them also have churches built. But the friars may not erect large churches under pretext of preaching to the people nor under any other pretext. Their humility will indeed be greater and their example that much more forceful if the brothers go and preach in other churches, thereby observing holy poverty, humility, and good traditions; and should it happen that prelates or clerics, whether religious or secular, come and visit the brothers, the houses, cells, and churches of those who live there will by their poverty be a true preaching and a source of edification."

He added: "Too often the brothers have large buildings erected; by doing this they violate our holy poverty, give rise to murmurings and give bad example to their neighbors. Then, under pretext of looking for a better and holier friary, they abandon this place and its buildings. Then the benefactors who gave them alms, and even others, are greatly scandalized and disturbed at this news or at this spectacle. Let the brothers therefore have small and poor buildings, and in that way remain faithful to their religious profession and to their duty to give good example. That is better than giving bad example while doing good, which would run counter to their profession. And should it happen that the brothers wish to abandon this small residence and its poor buildings for a more decent friary, the example would be less pernicious and the scandal less great."

LAST TESTAMENT AND WILL

17   At that time and in the same cell where blessed Francis had thus spoken to Lord Bonaventure, he had an attack of vomiting one night due to his stomach illness. The strain was so violent that he began to spit blood, and this continued throughout the night and into the morning. His companions, seeing his weakness and the pains caused by his sickness, thought that he was going to die. Wtih great chagrin they said to him with tears in their eyes: "Father, what will happen to us? Bless us as well as all the other brothers. Leave your children the expression of your last will and testament so that if the Lord wishes to take you from this world, the brothers may remember them and say: 'Here are the words that our Father left his sons and his brothers as he was dying.' " The blessed Father said to them: "Call Brother Benedict of Pioraco[36] for me." This brother was a priest, a discriminating man, a saint, and one of the early members of the Order. It was he who sometimes celebrated Mass for blessed Francis in that very cell. As a matter of fact, although Francis was sick, he always wanted with all his heart and soul to hear Mass whenever he could. And when this brother was near him, blessed Francis said to him: "Write that I bless all my brothers, those who are in the Order and those who will enter it until the end of the world."

When the brothers were assembled at the close of the chapter, it was his custom to bless and absolve all the brothers, that is, all who were present, those of the entire Order, and even those who were to enter it later on. In fact, he blessed all the brothers, those who were in the Order and those who were to come to it not only on the occasion of a chapter but very frequently.

Blessed Francis then said to them: "Since my weakness and my sufferings prevent me from speaking, I shall summarize my will for my brothers in a few words: in memory of my blessing and of my testament, let them love one another and respect each other; let them love and always respect my Lady Holy Poverty; let them always be faithful and submissive to prelates and to all the clerics of our holy Mother the Church." He then admonished the brothers to fear and avoid bad example. Finally, he cursed those who by their baleful bad example would cause men to speak evil of the Order and of the life of the brothers, even of the good and holy brothers who would then suffer much shame and sorrow.[37]

SWEEPING CHURCHES, BROTHER JOHN THE SIMPLE

18   When blessed Francis was living at St. Mary of the Portiuncula and as yet had but a few brothers, he sometimes traveled through the hamlets and visited the churches in the vicinity of Assisi, proclaiming and preaching repentance to men. He brought along a broom to clean the churches. He suffered a great deal, in fact, when he entered a church and saw it dirty. And so, when he finished preaching to the people, he gathered together all the priests who were there and took them aside so that the laity could not hear. He then spoke to them of the salvation of souls[38] and especially reminded them of the solicitude they were to exercise in keeping churches, altars, and everything that is used in the celebration of the divine mysteries clean.

19   One day blessed Francis entered the church of a

village situated in the region of Assisi and began to sweep it. The news immediately spread to the village, for the inhabitants always enjoyed seeing and listening to him.

A certain John, a man of admirable simplicity who was tilling his field next to the church, notified of his arrival, went to find him while he was sweeping. He said to him: "Brother, I want to help you; give me your broom." He took the broom and finished the task. Then they sat down and this man said to blessed Francis: "For a long time I have been wanting to serve God, especially since I heard about you and your brothers; but I did not know how to go about finding you. Since the Lord has graciously arranged this encounter, I want to do everything you want me to do." On seeing such fervor, blessed Francis rejoiced in the Lord, especially since there were as yet few brothers; and this man with his pure simplicity,[39] it seemed to him, ought to make a good religious. He said to him: "Brother, if you wish to share our life and join us, you must divest yourself of everything you have acquired honestly and give it to the poor according to the counsel of the holy gospel. This is also what those of my brothers who were able to have already done." Immediately the man ran to the field where he had left his oxen, unharnessed them, and brought one of them to blessed Francis. "Brother," he said, "I have been serving my father and all those in the house for many years. This ox is but a small part of the inheritance that is mine. I want you to take it and give it to the poor in whatever way seems best to you according to God."

Seeing that he was preparing to leave them, the man's brothers, who were still very young, and all those of the household began to cry bitterly and to groan out loud. At this spectacle, blessed Francis was moved to pity, all the more so since they were a numerous family and without resources. He said to them: "Prepare a meal: we shall eat together; and do not cry, for I am going to restore your joy to you." Everyone immediately busied himself, and the

995

meal took place in general joy. When it was over, blessed Francis said to them: "Your son wishes to serve God; you should not grieve over this but rather rejoice. This is an honor for you not only in the eyes of God but also in the eyes of the world. Both your souls and bodies will profit by it; God will be honored by someone from your midst; and all our brothers will henceforth be your sons and your brothers. Because one of God's creatures wants to serve the Creator and since to be a servant of God is to be a king,[40] I do not wish and must not give your child back to you. But in order that you may receive and preserve some consolation from him and since you are poor, I want him to divest himself of this ox in your favor, although according to the holy gospel, he should rather give it to other poor people." All were much at ease at these words and, since they were poor, they especially rejoiced over the fact that the ox was returned to them.

Blessed Francis, who always loved untainted and holy purity in himself and in others, took a liking to John; he gave him the habit and immediately made him his companion. This brother was so simple that he felt bound to do everything that blessed Francis did. When Francis was in a church, the brother wanted to see him and observe him so that he might conform himself to him in all his attitudes; if he genuflected or raised his joined hands in prayer, if he spat or coughed, the brother did the same. Blessed Francis was very amused at this simplicity. Nevertheless, he began to reprimand him. But the other answered: "Father, I promised to do all that you would do; therefore I want to do all that you do." And blessed Francis was in admiration and joy at seeing such purity and simplicity. This brother made such progress in all the virtues and in sanctity that Francis and the other brothers were amazed at such perfection. He died shortly afterwards, without deviating from this holy perfection. That is why blessed Francis related the story of his life with great interior and external joy to the brothers and why he called him not "Brother John" but "St. John."

THE REJECTED POSTULANT

20   At that time, blessed Francis was traveling and preaching in the province of the Marches. One day when he was preaching to the inhabitants of a small market-town, a man came up to him: "Brother," he said, "I wish to leave the world and enter your religious family." The saint answered him: "Brother, if you wish to enter our fraternity, you must, according to the counsel of perfection given in the holy gospel, first distribute all your goods to the poor and then completely renounce your own will." At these words the man quickly went and distributed his goods to his family; he was led by the flesh and not by the spirit. Returning to blessed Francis he said to him: "Brother, I have done what you told me to do; I divested myself of all of my possessions." Francis said to him: "What did you do?" "Brother," he replied, "I gave all my goods to certain members of my family who needed them." Blessed Francis, informed by the Holy Spirit that he was a carnal man, answered: "Go your way, Brother Fly: after having given your goods to your family, do you expect to live among your brothers on alms?" The man immediately went away, obstinate, and refused to give his goods to other poor people.

REGAINED SERENITY

21   At that same time, while staying at the Portiuncula, Francis was a prey to a very serious spiritual temptation for the good of his soul. He was greatly disturbed by it both within and without, in his soul and in his body. Sometimes he even shunned the company of his brothers because he could not by reason of this temptation offer them his usual smile. He mortified himself by doing without food and by abstaining from talk. He often withdrew to the forest near the church in order to pray: there

he could give free rein to his grief and pour out abundant tears in the Lord's presence, so that the Master who can do all things might condescend to send him a remedy from heaven for so great a disturbance. He was plagued by this temptation for more than two years, night and day.

Now, one day while he was at prayer in the church of St. Mary, in spirit he heard this word of the gospel: "If your faith were the size of a mustard seed you could say to this mountain, 'Move from here to there,' and it would move."[41] Blessed Francis asked: "What is this mountain?" "The mountain is your temptation." "Then, Lord, may it be done to me according to your word." And immediately he was freed of it, so much so that it seemed to him that he had never been troubled by that temptation.

THE MEAL WITH A LEPER

22 One day when blessed Francis had returned to the church of St. Mary of the Portiuncula, he found Brother James the Simple in the company of a leper covered with ulcers. That day the leper had come as far as the church. The holy Father had earnestly recommended this leper and those who were disfigured by leprosy to Brother James. In those days the brothers lived in leper-hospitals.[42] Brother James was, so to speak, the doctor of those who were the worst cases, and he wiped, cleaned, and dressed their sores with a generous heart.

Blessed Francis reproached Brother James: "You should not take our Christian brothers out, for that is neither good for you nor for them." — Christian brothers was the name he gave to the lepers. — He made this remark, despite his joy at seeing the brother help them and serve them, first of all because he did not want him to take those who were the worst cases out of the hospital; secondly, because the brother was very simple and sometimes brought several lepers to the church of St. Mary; and lastly, because men usually abhor these unfortunates covered with sores.

No sooner had blessed Francis pronounced these words when he regretted them. He immediately went and confessed his sin to Brother Peter of Catanii who at that time was the minister general, for he thought that in reprimanding Brother James he had despised and saddened the leper; that is why he confessed his sin with the intention of making reparation for it before God and the leper.

He therefore said to Brother Peter: "I ask you to approve of and especially not to refuse me the penance that I wish to perform." Peter answered: "As you wish, Brother." He had so much veneration, fear, and submission in regard to blessed Francis that he never wanted to countermand his orders; and yet in this circumstance, as in many others, he was inwardly and outwardly afflicted. The saint said to him: "My penance will be to eat with my Christian brother and from the same dish." When he sat down for the meal with the leper and the other brothers, a bowl was put between them. Now the leper was completely covered with sores and ulcers. His fingers, which he used to eat with, were eaten away and tinged with blood, so much so that when he put them into the bowl, blood dripped from them. Brother Peter and the other brothers were greatly saddened at this sight, but they dared say nothing for fear of the Father.

He who writes these lines saw this scene and bears witness to them.

BROTHER PACIFICUS; THE THRONE OF LUCIFER; THE ANGEL WITH THE ZITHER

23   One day blessed Francis was going through the valley of Spoleto; he was accompanied by Brother Pacificus, a native of the March of Ancona, who formerly in the world had been dubbed "the king of poets." Pacificus was a master of noble and courtly song. They were given hospitality in the leprosarium of Trevi. Blessed Francis said to Brother Pacificus: "Let us go to Bovara, to the church of St. Peter, for I want to spend the night there." This church, situated

not far from the leprosarium, had no resident priest, for at that time Trevi was in ruins and had only a few inhabitants.[43]

On the way, Francis said to Brother Pacificus: "Go back to the leprosarium: I want to be alone tonight; return tomorrow before daylight." When he was alone, Francis recited Compline and other prayers, and then wanted to rest and sleep. But he could not, for his mind was beset with fear and disturbed by suggestions from the Devil. He got up immediately, went outside of the church and made the sign of the cross, saying: "Devils! I command you on behalf of God almighty, use all the power given you by the Lord Jesus Christ to make my body suffer. I am ready to endure everything, for I have no greater enemy than my body; in this way you will avenge me on this adversary and enemy."[44] The suggestions ceased immediately. Returning to the place where he wanted to spend the night, he fell asleep and rested peacefully.

In the morning Brother Pacificus joined him. Blessed Francis was standing before the altar inside the choir, praying. Pacificus waited for him outside the sanctuary before the crucifix praying to the Lord. Hardly had he begun his prayer when he was caught up in ecstasy, whether in the body or outside it, God alone knows.[45] He saw a host of thrones in the sky; one, higher than all the others, was radiant with the glory and brilliance of all kinds of precious stones. Admiring its splendor, he wondered what this throne was and for whom it was prepared.[46] Suddenly he heard a voice say to him: "This was Lucifer's throne. Blessed Francis will occupy it in his stead."

When Pacificus had regained his senses, Francis left the choir and approached him. The brother immediately threw himself at the feet of blessed Francis, his arms in the form of a cross; for, in view of his vision, he already considered him as an inhabitant of heaven. He said to him:

"Father, forgive me my sins and pray the Lord to pardon me and have pity on me." Blessed Francis extended his hand, raised him up and saw that he had seen a vision during his prayer; he seemed to be completely transformed and spoke to Francis not as a man living here on earth but as one of the elect already reigning in heaven. Pretending that nothing had happened, for he did not want to reveal his vision, he asked blessed Francis: "Brother, what do you think of yourself?" "I think," he answered, "that I am the greatest of sinners." Immediately Brother Pacificus heard the voice in his heart saying to him: "By this sign you will recognize the truth of your vision: just as Lucifer was hurled from his throne because of his pride, so will blessed Francis deserve to be exalted because of his humility and take his place."[47]

24   At the time when blessed Francis was living at Rieti, he occupied a room in the house of Teobaldo Saraceni[48] for a few days; he was undergoing treatment for his eyes there. One day he said to one of his companions who had learned to play the zither when he was in the world: "Brother, *the children of this world*[49] have no understanding of the things of God. Formerly, the saints used such musical instruments as the zither, psalteries, and others to praise God and console their soul;[50] now these instruments promote vanity and sin, contrary to the will of the Lord. I wish you would secretly procure a zither from a respectable man and play me some beautiful music; afterwards, we will put words and the "Praises of the Lord" to it. My body is afflicted with many severe pains; I would like in this way to change the physical suffering into joy and spiritual consolation." It should be said that during his sickness blessed Francis had composed the "Praises of the Lord."[51] Sometimes he had the brothers sing them for the glory of God, the consolation of his soul, and the edification of their neighbors. The brother answered him:

"Father, I would be ashamed to go and procure that instrument for myself: the people of this city know that when I was a layman, I learned how to play the zither,[52] and I fear that they will fancy that I am tempted to play it again."
"In that case," said the saint, "Let's not talk about it any more."

The next night, around midnight, unable to sleep, he heard a zither near the house where he was staying. Its song was the most exquisite and the sweetest that he had ever heard in his life. The musician withdrew but could still be heard. Then, he returned and played without interruption for a good hour. Blessed Francis, considering that the hand of God and not the hand of man was at work in this, was filled with utmost joy. In the joy of his heart he fervently praised the Lord who had condescended to grant him so great and so rare a consolation. In the morning on rising, he said to his companion: "Brother, I asked you but you did not grant my request, but the Lord who consoles his friends in their tribulations[53] deigned this night to console me." And he told him what had happened. The brothers were in admiration, believing that this was a great miracle. They were sure that God himself had intervened for the consolation of blessed Francis, for by a decree of the podestà no one could go about in the city, not only in the middle of the night but even as early as the third ringing of the bells. Moreover, as the saint himself declared, the zither came and went in silence, without words or any vocal noise for one hour for the consolation of his soul.

THE VINEYARD OF RIETI

25   Around the same time blessed Francis was staying near the church of St. Fabian to have his eyes attended to. This church was near the gates of this city[54] and was in the care of a poor secular priest. As it so happened, the Lord Pope Honorius was residing at that time in this city

with the cardinals.[55] A number of the cardinals, accompanied by clerics, almost daily visited the saint out of respect and devotion. The church had a small vineyard near the house where Father Francis was staying. Since this house had but one door, all those who came to see him passed through the vineyard. The grapes were ripe, and the pleasant spot tempted one to take a siesta there: the vineyard was almost completely pillaged; certain ones picked the grapes and either ate them right on the spot or took them home, while others trampled them under foot. The priest was scandalized and disturbed: "This year," he said, "my vintage is lost. The vineyard is small but every year I harvest enough grapes for my needs."

Informed of this, blessed Francis summoned the priest to him and said: "Stop being disturbed and scandalized: nothing can be done about it. Place your trust in the Lord, because through me, his poor servant, he can repair the damage. Tell me: how many loads of wine does your vineyard produce every year?" "Thirteen," the priest answered. "Cease despairing," replied blessed Francis; "don't burden anyone with your wrongs; don't trouble anyone any more with your complaints. Have confidence in the Lord and in my words: if you harvest less than twenty loads, I promise to make up the difference." The priest agreed and kept still.

Now it so happened, thanks to God's goodness, that he did not harvest less than twenty loads, according to the saint's promise. This priest was full of admiration, as were those who were informed about it; they considered the incident a great miracle due to the merits of blessed Francis. The vineyard was, as a matter of fact, pillaged; and even if it had been laden with grapes, it seemed impossible for the priest and the others to get twenty loads of wine from it. We who lived with Francis bear testimony that when he had said: "So it is," or "So it shall be," his word was al-

1003

ways fulfilled. We have seen many of his promises fulfilled in this way, both during his life and after his death.[56]

THE MEAL OFFERED TO THE DOCTOR

26   At that time, blessed Francis was staying at the hermitage of the brothers of Fonte Colombo, near Rieti for treatment of his eyes. One day the eye doctor came to visit him and talked with him, as usual, for an hour: he was preparing to leave when the saint said to one of his companions: "Go and have a good meal served to our doctor." His companions answered him: "Father, we blushingly admit that our food supply is so low at this moment that we are ashamed to invite him and offer him anything to eat." Blessed Francis answered: "O men of little faith,[57] do not make me repeat myself." The doctor said to blessed Francis and his companions: "Brother, it is precisely because the brothers are so poor that it would be a pleasure to eat with them." This doctor was very rich and, although the saint and his companions had often invited him, he never wanted to share a meal with them. The brothers went and prepared the table and blushingly placed on it the little bread and wine they had as well as a few vegetables that they had prepared for themselves. All sat down at table.

Hardly had the meal begun when someone knocked on the door of the hermitage: a brother got up to answer it: it was a woman who was bringing a large basket full of white bread, fish, lobster-pie,[58] some honey, and some grapes that seemed to have been freshly picked. All this was sent to blessed Francis by the lady of a castle about seven miles from the hermitage. Whereupon the brothers and the doctor were in great admiration as they pondered the sanctity of the Father. The doctor said to the brothers: "My brothers, neither you nor I appreciate as we should the sanctity of this man."

THE PREDICTION OF A CONVERSION

27   One day blessed Francis went to Le Celle di Cortona and followed the road that passed at the foot of a fortified town called Lisciano. He was near the friary of the brothers of Preggio, when a noble lady of this town ran up to him to speak to him. One of the saint's companions had turned around and saw this very tired lady advancing in great haste. He ran to blessed Francis and said to him: "Father, for the love of God, let us wait for the lady who is following us and who is making such an effort to have a talk with you."

Blessed Francis, being a generous man and full of piety, waited for her. When he saw this completely exhausted lady approach him with great fervor and devotion, he said to her: "Are you married or single?" "Father," she said, "for a long time the Lord has given me the unwavering desire to serve him. I had and still have a strong desire to save my soul; but my husband is so cruel toward me and toward himself that he is an obstacle to my serving Christ; sorrow and anguish also afflict my soul to the point of death." The saint, considering her fervor, her youth, and her frailty, was moved to pity for her. He blessed her saying: "Go; you will find your husband at your house; you will tell him for me that I beg both of you to save your souls in your house for the love of our Lord who, in order to save us, suffered the passion of the Cross."

She left, entered her house, and found her husband there, as the saint had told her. "Where have you been?" he asked. "I have just been to see blesesd Francis," she answered. "He blessed me and his words have gladdened and consoled my soul in the Lord. Moreover, he ordered me to tell you in his behalf: 'I beg you, save your souls by continuing to live in your house.'" At these words, the grace of God descended on him immediately through the merits of blessed Francis. He answered with much kindness and gentleness, completely and suddenly transformed by

1005

the Lord: "Lady, as of today, let us serve Christ according to his desires, and let us save our souls as the saint said." His wife said to him: "Lord, it seems to me that it would be good if we lived in chastity, for it is a very pleasing virtue to God and one that procures a great recompense." Her husband answered: "Since that is what you wish, so do I, for in that matter as in every good work, I wish to conform my will to yours."

From that day on and for many a year, they lived in chastity, giving much alms to the brothers and to the other poor. Many people, not only the laity but religious as well, were astounded to see the sanctity of this man who had changed so quickly from being a worldly man into a spiritual man. Both husband and wife persevered to the end in these good works and other similar ones. They died within a few days of each other. They were greatly mourned because of the radiance of their lives and the good example they had given in praising and blessing the Lord who had given them the grace, among others, of serving him in perfect union of heart. Even today those who knew them remember them and pray to them as to two saints.

ANOTHER POSTULANT REJECTED

28   In the days when no one was allowed to come and share the life of the brothers without the permission of blessed Francis,[59] the son of a resident of Lucques, who was a noble in the eyes of the world,[60] came in search of him along with other companions who wanted to enter the Order. The saint, who was then sick, was living in the palace of the bishop of Assisi. As the brothers presented the newcomers to blessed Francis, the young noble bowed before him and began to weep bitterly imploring him to accept him.

Blessed Francis looked at him and said: "You miserable and carnal man! Why do you lie to the Holy Spirit and to me?[61] It is the flesh that makes you cry, not the spirit." Hardly had he said these words when the young man's parents arrived on horseback at the door of the palace to take him back and lead him away. Hearing the horses, the young man looked out the window and saw his parents. He immediately got up, rejoined them, and returned to the world with them, just as the Holy Spirit made it known to blessed Francis. The brothers and all the bystanders were in admiration, exalting and praising God in his saint.

THE MIRACLE OF THE PIKE

29   In those days, since he was very sick in the palace of the bishop of Assisi, his brothers begged him earnestly to take some nourishment. But he answered them: "No, brothers, I have no desire to eat; however, if I had some pike,[62] perhaps I would eat some" Hardly had he finished the sentence when someone brought a basket containing three well-cooked pike and a quantity of lobster. The holy Father gladly ate some of it. All of this had been sent to him by Brother Gerard, the minister at Rieti.[63] The brothers were in great admiration as they considered the sanctity of blessed Francis. They praised the Lord who obtained for his servant what men could not give him, for it was winter and the country could not furnish what had just been brought.

INSIGHT INTO CONSCIENCES

30   One day blessed Francis was traveling with a brother from Assisi, a man of interior life, the descendant of a noble and rich family.[64] The saint, who was weak and sick, was riding on a donkey. The brother, travel worn, began to ruminate and say to himself: "His family could not be compared to mine, and now he is in the saddle and I, although very tired, am walking and goading his beast." He had reached this point in his thoughts when suddenly

blessed Francis got off his donkey and said to him: "Brother, it is neither just nor proper that I should ride while you walk, for in the world you were nobler and richer than I." The brother, filled with amazement and shame, threw himself at his feet in tears, confessed his secret thoughts and admitted his sin. He greatly admired the sanctity that had immediately seen through his thought. And so, when the brothers at Assisi begged the Lord Pope Gregory and the cardinals to canonize blessed Francis, this brother testified before them to the authenticity of this episode.

31   A brother,[65] a spiritual man and a friend of God, was living in the friary of the brothers of Rieti. One beautiful day he got up and, desiring to see Francis and to receive his blessing, made his way with great devotion to the hermitage of the brothers of Greccio where the blessed Francis was then residing. The saint had already eaten his meal and returned to the cell that had been put at his disposal for prayer and rest. It was Lent, and the blessed one left his cell only to take a little nourishment and return immediately. The brother did not therefore find him. He was very grieved, especially since he was supposed to return to his friary that same night and since he attributed this misfortune to his sins. The saint's companions consoled him and the brother started to return.

He had not gone more than a stone's throw when, by the will of the Lord, blessed Francis came out of his cell; he called one of his companions (the one who was accompanying the brother the short distance to the fountain of the lake) and asked him: "Tell that brother to turn toward me!" The brother turned toward the saint and he blessed him with a sign of the cross. Full of inner and outer joy, he praised the Lord who had heard his desire. His consolation was all the greater because, to his way of thinking, he had received this blessing without having requested it and without any human intervention by the will of God. The saint's companions and the other brothers of the friary were full of admiration. They considered it a miracle, for no one had told blessed Francis of the brother's arrival. Furthermore, neither his companions nor the other brothers would have dared approach the saint if he had not called them. Wherever he stayed on to pray, in the other friaries as in this one, he wanted to remain alone, forbidding anyone to disturb him without being summoned.

THE LESSON OF POVERTY AT GRECCIO

32   Once, in this same friary of Greccio, a minister of the brothers came in search of blessed Francis in order to celebrate the feast of the Nativity with him.[66] Because of the feast and the visit of the minister, the brothers had prepared a beautiful table, draped with beautiful white linen that they had bought, and adorned with drinking glasses. When blessed Francis came down from his cell to eat and saw the table arranged and adorned with refinement, he went out without being seen and borrowed the hat and staff of a poor man who was spending the day at the friary. He called one of his companions in a low voice and with him entered the door of the hermitage unbeknown to all. Meanwhile, the brothers sat down at table without him: it was his wish that they should not wait for him if he did not arrive on time for meals.

His companion closed the door and remained inside close to it. The saint knocked on the door and the brother opened it for him immediately. He entered, his hat on his back and staff in hand, like a pilgrim. When he reached the door of the house where the brothers were eating, he cried out as the beggars do: "For the love of the Lord God, give an alms to this poor and sick pilgrim." The minister, as well as the other brothers, immediately recognized him and said to him: "Brother, we too are poor, and since we are numerous we need the alms that we eat. But, for the love of God whom you have invoked, come in and we will give you a share of the alms that the Lord has procured for us." He entered and remained standing near the table. The minister handed him the bowl from which he was eating and a piece of his bread. He took them and sat down on the ground near the fire in front of the brothers who had taken their place at table. Then he said sighing: "When I saw this sumptuous and refined table, I did not consider it to be the table of poor religious who go from door to door every day. We must follow the example of humility and poverty more than the other religious because that is what we have been called to do and have promised before God and man. Now, it seems to me that I am sitting as a brother ought to." All were filled with confusion, for they realized that he spoke the truth. Some burst into tears seeing him seated on the ground and considering with what sanctity and appropriateness he had taught them the lesson.

CARDINAL HUGOLINO VISITS THE PORTIUNCULA

33   Blessed Francis used to say that the brothers should have modest and reasonable furniture that would edify the people of the world; that if a poor man was invited by the brothers, he should be able to sit down next to them and not on the ground, while they themselves would be sitting on chairs. One day when the Lord Pope Gregory was bishop of Ostia, he came to the friary of St. Mary of the Portiuncula. He entered the house of the brothers and wanted to see their dormitory which was in the same building. He was accompanied by a large retinue of knights, monks, and clerics. Seeing that the brothers slept on the ground on poor and miserable pallets covered with a little straw, with no pillows, and with a few remnants of frayed blankets, he began to weep bitterly in the presence of all and cried out: "See where the brothers sleep! And we, miserable creatures, who concede so much superfluous comfort to ourselves, what will happen to us?" He was greatly

edified and so were those with him. He saw no table, for the brothers ate on the ground.

Although this friary from its very beginning had many more visitors than any other friary in the Order — all who entered the Order took the habit there — the brothers of this friary always ate on the ground, whether numerous or only a few. And as long as the holy Father lived, the brothers of this friary sat on the ground to eat, thereby conforming themselves to his example and will.

THE MIRACLE OF THE WOLVES AND THE HAIL AT GRECCIO

34   The brothers of the friary at Greccio were virtuous and poor, and the inhabitants of the country, despite their poverty and simplicity, were more pleasing to blessed Francis than those of the rest of the province. Consequently, he often went there to relax or tarry. There was an especially small, poor, and very solitary cell here to which holy Francis liked to withdraw. His example, his preaching, and that of his brothers were the reason, together with the grace of God, why many of the inhabitants entered the Order.[67] Many women took the vow of virginity and adopted a religious habit; each one had her own house, but they led a common life; they practiced virtue, mortification, fasting and prayer; one got the impression that they were living apart from the world and their relatives; despite their youthful age and their great simplicity, they seemed to have been formed by holy religious women who had been in the service of Christ for a long time. That is why blessed Francis often said to the brothers, in speaking of the men and women of this town: "There is no large city where so many have been converted to penance; and still, Greccio is only a small town."

The brothers at Greccio, as was the custom of the brothers at that time in many of the friaries, sang the praises of the Lord in the evening. Then, men and women, great and small, would come out of their homes, stand on the road before the town, and alternate with the brothers, repeating in a loud voice: "Blessed be the Lord God." Even the little children who hardly knew how to talk praised God according to their ability.

Now, in those days, these people had been suffering from calamities for many years. Enormous wolves were devouring the men, and every year hail devastated their vineyards and fields. One day when he was preaching, Francis said to them: "This is what I announce to you for the honor and glory of God. If each one of you turns from his sins and returns to God with all his heart and with the firm resolve and will to persevere, I have confidence that our Lord Jesus Christ in his mercy will deliver you from the scourge of the wolves and the hail from which you have been suffering for so long a time. He will increase and multiply spiritual and temporal blessings on you. But I warn you, if you return to your vomit[68] — please God, this will not happen — this chastisement and scourge will return, and even worse catastrophes along with them." Through the power of Divine Providence and the merits of the holy Father, these calamities ceased at once. And what was even more extraordinary and more of an astonishing miracle, when the hail came and devastated the fields of their neighbors, it stopped, without causing any damage, at their boundaries.

And so they were showered with spiritual and temporal blessings for sixteen to twenty years. But wealth bred pride and hatred: they even engaged in battles with swords and did not hesitate to murder; they killed animals in an underhanded way, pillaged and robbed at night, and committed many other heinous crimes. When the Lord saw that their works were evil, that they were not observing the conditions laid down by his servant, his wrath flared up against them; he stayed the action of his goodness, and the scourge of the hail and the wolves reappeared,[69] as holy Francis had warned them, and they were harassed with more serious evils than at first. The town was entirely burned; they lost all their possessions and came off with only their lives.[70] The brothers and those who had heard blessed Francis predict prosperity and adversity to these people admired his sanctity as they saw all his words being fulfilled to the letter.

THE CURSE OF PERUGIA

35   One day[71] when blessed Francis was preaching in the public square of Perugia before a huge gathering of people, some knights began to gallop there in full armor, for the sport of it, so much so that they interfered with the sermon. The men and women who were listening attentively to the sermon protested, but to no avail; the knights continued. Turning toward them, blessed Francis said to them with all the ardor of his soul: "Listen and retain well what the Lord announces to you through the mouth of his servant. And do not say: Nonsense, he's a man from Assisi! (Blessed Francis spoke that way because a great hatred divided[72] the people of Assisi from those of Perugia). — The Lord has glorified you above all your neighbors: you should therefore be very grateful to your Creator and humble yourself not only before the Almighty but even before your neighbors. And yet your heart is puffed up with arrogance, audacity, and pride. You pillage your neighbors and kill many of them. I also say to you, if you do not mend your ways very soon and if you do not make reparation for the damage you have caused, the Lord, who does not allow any injustice to be done without chastisement, is preparing a terrible vengeance, punishment, and humiliation for you. He will set you one against the other; discord and civil war will break out, and they will cause you worse calamities than those that could come to you from your neighbors."

As a matter of fact, when blessed Francis preached, he did not conceal the vices of the people when they publicly offended God or neighbor. But the Lord gave him such great grace that all those who heard or saw him had only fear and veneration for him because of the riches of the gifts he had received from God. Likewise, even when he reprimanded them, they were ashamed, but they were also edified; sometimes this was even a motive for him to pray to God for them with greater fervor, and they were converted to the Lord.

It so happened a few days later that, with the permission of God, fighting broke out between the nobles and the people. The people pursued the knights who, for their part, sacked many fields, trees, and vineyards with the help of the Church and did the greatest harm possible to the people. They, in turn, devastated the fields, trees, and vineyards of the knights. In this way the inhabitants of Perugia were punished and suffered much more than the neighbors they had molested. Blessed Francis' prediction was being fulfilled to the letter.

THE EFFICACY OF PRAYER

36   In the course of one of his journeys, blessed Francis met the abbot of a monastery who had much affection and veneration for him.[73] The abbot dismounted from his horse and talked with him for an hour about the salvation of his soul; before leaving, he asked him with great devotion to pray for him. "Gladly," he said. When the abbot was some distance away, blessed Francis said to his companion: "Brother, wait a few minutes: I want to pray for that abbot as I promised I would." And he began to pray. If someone out of devotion asked him to pray for the salvation of his soul, it was Francis' custom to say the prayer as soon as possible, lest he should forget it afterwards.

The abbot, however, continued on his way; he had not

gone very far when suddenly he received a visit of the Lord in his heart. A sweet warmth came to his face and he was wrapped in ecstacy for a brief moment. When he came to himself, he knew that blessed Francis had prayed for him. From that time on, he had even greater devotion for the saint, for he himself had experienced the excellence of his sanctity. As long as he lived, he considered the event a great miracle and often told what happened to him to the brothers and others.

MEDITATION ON THE PASSION AND HUMILITY OF CHRIST

37   Blessed Francis suffered for a long time from his liver, spleen, and stomach, right up to the time of his death. In addition to that, in the course of the voyage to preach to the Sultan of Babylonia and of Egypt, he had contracted a very serious disease of the eyes caused by fatigue and especially by the excessive heat he had to endure both in going and in returning. But the love that filled his soul since his conversion to Christ was so ardent that, despite the prayers of his brothers and of many other men moved by compassion and pity, he did not trouble himself about taking care of his sicknesses.

Every day he meditated on the humility and example of the Son of God; he experienced much compassion and much sweetness from this, and in the end, what was bitter to his body, was changed into sweetness.[74] The sufferings and bitterness which Christ endured for us were a constant subject of affliction to him and a cause for interior and external mortification; consequently, he was totally unconcerned with his own sufferings.

One day, just a few years after his conversion, he was following the road that passes near St. Mary of the Portiuncula and, as he was walking by himself, he was lamenting and weeping out loud. A spiritual man, whom we know well and who reported it to us, met him at that time. This

man had been very kind to the saint and had consoled him
before he even had one brother and continued to do so.
He said to him: "What is the matter, brother?" He thought
that he was suffering from some infirmity. Blessed Francis
answered: "I ought to travel through the whole world,
crying and moaning without any false shame over the passion of my Lord!" The man began to cry with him and
wept bitterly.

38   During his eye sickness, he endured such sufferings
that one day a minister said to him: "Brother, why don't
you have your companions read some passage from the
prophets or some other chapters from the Scriptures to
you? Your soul would exult in the Lord and would thereby
receive an immense consolation." He knew that blessed
Francis experienced much joy in the Lord when the Sacred
Scriptures were read to him. But he answered: "Brother,
every day I find such sweetness and consolation in recalling to mind and meditating on the humility the Son of
God manifested while he was on earth that I could live
until the end of the world without hearing or meditating on
any other passages from the Scriptures." He often repeated
to himself and repeated to the brothers this verse of David:
"My soul refused to be consoled."[75] That is why, wanting
to be, as he frequently said, the example and model of all
the brothers, he not only refused medication but even the
food that he needed in his sicknesses. He was harsh to
his body, both when he was well (even though he was always frail and weak) and in the course of his sicknesses that
he might remain faithful to this program.

STRICTNESS WITH HIMSELF DURING HIS SICKNESS

39   At that time, when he was recovering from a very
serious sickness, it seemed to him, as he examined his conscience, that he had become somewhat lax. Yet he had eaten
very little, for due to his numerous, diverse, and long in-

firmities, he could barely tolerate any nourishment. One day he got up, still suffering from a quartan and had all the people assemble in the square for a sermon. At its conclusion he asked all of them to remain until he returned. Going into the church of San Rufino, he went down to the Confession with Brother Peter Catanii, the first minister general whom he himself had chosen, and with a few other brothers. He ordered Brother Peter to obey and not oppose what he wanted to say and do, and Peter answered him: "I can and ought not to desire anything but your wish in what concerns both of us."

Blessed Francis took off his tunic and ordered Brother Peter to lead him in this fashion before the people with a cord around his neck. He ordered another brother to take a bowl full of ashes, to mount the place where he had preached from and to sprinkle them on his head; but this brother, moved by pity and compassion, did not want to obey. Brother Peter led blessed Francis as he had been ordered to do, both he and the other brothers moaning out loud.

When he stood before the people on the square where he had preached, the saint spoke in these terms: "You think I am a holy man, as do those who, on the basis of my example, leave the world and enter the Order and lead the life of the brothers. Well, I confess to God and to you that during my illness I ate meat and ate some stew." All the people dissolved into tears out of pity and compassion; since it was winter, it was very cold and he was not yet over the quartan. They struck their breasts, accusing themselves and said: "This holy man accuses himself with deep humility of having taken care of his health when he so clearly needed it. We who know his life so well, we know that it is because of his excessive abstinence and austerity since his conversion that we see him live in a body that is almost dead. What shall we do, wretched that we are, we who all our life have lived and wish to live according to the pleasure and desires of the flesh."

40   In the days when he was spending the Lent of St. Martin in a hermitage,[77] the brothers seasoned the food with pork fat, for oil greatly distressed him. At the end of the Lent, as he was preaching to a large crowd assembled not far from the hermitage, he began with the words: "You come to me with great devotion and you think I am a holy man: but I confess to God and to you that during the Lent I spent at this hermitage, I ate some vegetables cooked with pork fat."

It sometimes happened, when he ate with the brothers or with friends of the brothers that he somewhat relaxed his corporal mortifications because of his ailments, but immediately inside the house or outside it, he proclaimed before the brothers and even before the laity who were ignorant of this detail: "I ate this or that." For he did not want to hide from men what was known to God. If in the company of religious or lay people he was disturbed by thoughts of vainglory, pride, or another vice, he immediately confessed it to them in a simple way and without concealing anything. One day he said to his companions: "Near God, in the hermitages or in the other friaries where I stay, I want to live as if men were watching me. Since they take me for a saint, I would be a hypocrite if I did not live the life befitting a saint."

Once, during winter, as a remedy for his sick spleen and the cold in his stomach, one of his companions, who acted as his guardian, obtained a fox skin and asked him for permission to sew it under his tunic in the area of his spleen and stomach. At the time it was severely cold. Now, from the time he began to serve Christ, blessed Francis would not agree to wear anything more than one tunic regardless of the weather — and this he continued to do until his death — not to speak of sewing on a piece for the purpose of lining it.[78] The saint answered: "If you want me to wear that skin under my tunic, sew a piece of it on the outside so that people will know that I am wearing a fur under my habit." And so it was done. But blessed Francis did not wear it long, although he needed it because of his infirmities.

41   On another occasion, he was passing through Assisi and many people were following him. A little poor lady asked him for an alms for the love of God. He then and there took the mantle off his shoulders and gave it to her. But he immediately confessed before everyone that his action had aroused a feeling of vainglory in him.

He gave many other similar examples. We, who lived with him, saw them and heard them; but it would take too long to record them in writing. His main and paramount concern always was not to be a hypocrite in the eyes of God. His sickness made some discretion necessary for his body, but he considered himself obligated to give good example to the brothers and to other men in order to remove any and all occasion for murmuring and scandal. He preferred to endure patiently the demands of his body — which he did up to the day of his death —rather than gratify it, although he could have done so without failing God or the duty to give good example.

42   Seeing that the saint continued, as he had always done, treating his body harshly and refusing to have his eyes treated, and in view of the fact that he was beginning to lose his eyesight, the bishop of Ostia, who later became pope, admonished him with much love and compassion: "Brother, it is not good to refuse to have your eyes treated, for your health and your life are very useful, both to yourself and to others. You who have always sympathized with the ills of your brothers, should not have such cruelty toward yourself, for this sickness is serious and you are

1019

in a great and evident need. That is why I command you to get relief and submit to treatment."

Two years before his death, already very sick and suffereing especially from his eyes, he was living in a cell made of mats near San Damiano. The minister general,[79] seeing that his case was serious, ordered him to accept help and care. Moreover, he told him that he wanted to be present when the doctor began the treatment in order to see to it that he received the proper care and to comfort him, for he was suffering greatly. But at that time it was very cold and the weather was not propitious to begin the treatment.

THE CANTICLE OF THE SUN

43   During his stay in this friary, for fifty days and more, blessed Francis could not bear the light of the sun during the day or the light of the fire at night. He constantly remained in darkness inside the house in his cell. His eyes caused him so much pain that he could neither lie down nor sleep, so to speak, which was very bad for his eyes and for his health. A few times he was on the point of resting and sleeping, but in the house and in the cell made of mats, that had been made ready for him, there were so many mice running around here and there, around him and even on him, that they prevented him from taking a rest; they even hindered him greatly in his prayer. They annoyed him not only at night but also during the day. When he ate, they climbed up on the table, so much so that he and his companions were of the opinion that it was a diabolical intervention, which it was.

One night, as he was thinking of all the tribulations he was enduring, he felt sorry for himself and said interiorly: "Lord, help me in my infirmities so that I may have the strength to bear them patiently!" And suddenly he heard a voice in spirit: "Tell me, Brother: if, in compensation for your sufferings and tribulations you were given an immense and precious treasure: the whole mass of the earth changed into pure gold, pebbles into precious stones, and the water of the rivers into perfume, would you not regard the pebbles and the waters as nothing compared to such a treasure? Would you not rejoice?" Blessed Francis answered: "Lord, it would be a very great, very precious, and inestimable treasure beyond all that one can love and desire!" "Well, Brother," the voice said, "be glad and joyful in the midst of your infirmities and tribulations: as of now, live in peace as if you were already sharing my kingdom."

The next morning on rising, he said to his companions: "If the emperor gave a kingdom[80] to one of his servants, how joyful the servant would be! But if he gave him the whole empire, would he not rejoice all the more? I should, therefore, be full of joy in my infirmities and tribulations, seek my consolation in the Lord, and give thanks to God the Father, to his only Son our Lord Jesus Christ, and to the Holy Spirit. In fact, God has given me such a grace and blessing that he has condescended in his mercy to assure me, his poor and unworthy servant, still living on this earth, that I would share his kingdom. Therefore, for his glory, for my consolation, and the edification of my neighbor, I wish to compose a new "Praises of the Lord,"[81] for his creatures. These creatures minister to our needs every day; without them we could not live; and through them the human race greatly offends the Creator. Every day we fail to appreciate so great a blessing by not praising as we should the Creator and dispenser of all these gifts." He sat down, concentrated a minute, then cried out: "Most high, all-powerful, and good Lord. . . ." And he composed a melody to these words which he taught his companions.

His heart was then full of so much sweetness and consolation that he wanted Brother Pacificus, who in the world had been the king of poets and the most courtly master of song, to go through the world with a few pious and spiritual friars to preach and sing the praises of God. The best preacher would first deliver the sermon; then all would sing the "Praises of the Lord," as true jongleurs of God. At the end of the song, the preacher would say to the people: "We are the jongleurs of God, and the only reward we want is to see you lead a truly penitent life." Then he added: "Who are, indeed, God's servants if not jongleurs who strive to move men's hearts in order to lead them to the joys of the spirit?"[52] When he spoke in this way of "the servants of God," he especially had in mind the Friars Minor who had been given to the world to save it.

He called these "Praises of the Lord," which opened with the words: "Most high, all-powerful, and good Lord," the "Canticle of the Sun." The sun was the most beautiful of all the creatures, the one which, better than all the others, could be compared to God. He said: "At sunrise, every man ought to praise God for having created this heavenly body which gives light to our eyes during the day; at evening, when night falls, every man ought to praise God for that other creature, our brother fire, which enables our eyes to see clearly in the darkness. We are all like blind people, and it is through these two creatures that God gives us light. Therefore, for these two creatures and for the others that serve us each day, we ought to praise their glorious Creator in a very special way." He himself did so with all his heart, whether sick or well, and he gladly invited the others to sing the glory of the Lord. When he was laid low by sickness, he often intoned this canticle and had his companions take it up; in that way he forgot the intensity of his sufferings and pains by considering the glory of the Lord. He did this until the day of his death.

44   At the time when he was very sick — the "Praises of the Lord" had already been composed — the bishop of Assisi excommunicated the podestà. In return, the po-

destà had it announced to the sound of the trumpet in the streets of the city that every citizen was forbidden to buy from or sell anything whatsoever to the bishop or to transact any business with him. There was a savage hatred between them. Blessed Francis, who was very sick at that time, pitied them. It pained him to see that no one, religious or lay, intervened to reestablish peace and concord between them. So he said to his companions: "It is a great shame for us, the servants of God,[83] that at a time when the podestà and the bishop so hate each other no one can be found to reestablish peace and concord between them!" On this occasion he added the following strophe to his canticle:

All praise be yours, my Lord,
Through those who grant pardon for love of you;
Through those who endure sickness and trial.
Happy those who endure in peace;
By you, Most High, they will be crowned.

He then called one of his companions and said to him: "Go and find the podestà and tell him for me that he should go to the bishop's palace with the notables of the commune and with all those he can assemble." When the brother had left, he said to the others: "Go, and in the presence of the bishop, of the podestà, and of the entire gathering, sing the Canticle of Brother Sun. I have confidence that the Lord will put humility and peace in their hearts and that they will return to their former friendship and affection."

When everyone had gathered at the place of the cloister of the bishop's palace, the two brothers stood up, and one of them was the spokesman: "Despite his sufferings, blessed Francis," he said, "has composed the 'Praises of the Lord' for all his creatures, to the praise of God and for the edification of his neighbor; he asks you to listen with great devotion."

With that, they began to sing. The podestà stood up and joined his hands as for the gospel of the Lord, and he listened with great recollection and attention; soon tears flowed from his eyes, for he had a great deal of confidence in blessed Francis and devotion for him. At the end of the canticle, the podestà cried out before the entire gathering: "In truth I say to you, not only do I forgive the lord bishop whom I ought to recognize as my master, but I would even pardon my brother's and my own son's murderer!" He than threw himself at the feet of the lord bishop and said to him: "For the love of our Lord Jesus Christ and of blessed Francis, his servant, I am ready to make any atonement you wish." The bishop stood up and said to him: "My office demands humility of me, but by nature I am quick to anger; you must forgive me!" With much tenderness and affection, both locked arms and embraced each other.

The brothers were in admiration to see that the sanctity of blessed Francis had fulfilled to the letter what he had said of the peace and concord to be restored between these two men. All who witnessed the scene ascribed the grace so promptly given to the two adversaries to a miracle due to the merits of the saint. These two men, forgetting all past offensive words and after a very great scandal, returned to a very great concord. We who lived with blessed Francis attest that if he said: "Such and such a thing is taking place" or "will happen," his words were fulfilled to the letter. We have seen with our own eyes many examples which it would take too long to write down and to recount.[84]

THE CANTICLE AND EXHORTATION FOR THE POOR LADIES

45   At the same time and in the same friary, blessed Francis, after having composed the "Praises of the Lord for his creatures," dictated a canticle, words and music, for the consolation of the Poor Ladies of the monastery

of San Damiano. He was well aware of the fact that his sickness greatly grieved them. Since he could not go in person to visit and console them, he had his companions bring them what he had composed for them.

He briefly told them what his will was in regard to them for the present and the future, and how mutual charity should reign in their hearts and behavior. The fact is, it was due to his preaching and to his example that they had become converted to Christ at the time when there were but few brothers.[85] Like a nursery that had been planted by the brothers, they were the joy and edification not only of the Order of the brothers, but of the entire Church. When he thought of them, his spirit was always moved to pity because he knew that from the beginning of their conversion they had led and were still leading an austere and poor life by free choice and out of necessity. Since the Lord had assembled them from everywhere to be joined in a life of holy charity, poverty, and obedience, Francis sent a message begging them to live and die in that state. He especially asked them to treat their bodies with discernment and discretion, and to use the alms God would send them with joy and thanksgiving. He recommended that the healthy sisters bear patiently with the fatigue brought on by their care of the sick, and that the latter endure their sicknesses and their needs with patience.

SICKNESS

46   When the preferable season for eye-treatment was approaching,[86] blessed Francis left this friary although his sickness caused him much suffering. His head was covered with a large hood that the brothers had made for him. Since he could not bear daylight, he wore a woolen and linen band over his eyes sewed to his hood. His companions led him by horseback, to the hermitage of Fonte Colombo, near Rieti, to consult a physician of that city, an eye specialist.

This man came to examine blessed Francis and told him that he would have to cauterize the cheek up to the eyebrow in order to relieve the most affected eye. But the saint did not want to begin the treatment before the arrival of Brother Elias.[87] He was expected but did not arrive, because he was detained by all kinds of hindrances. The saint hesitated to let himself be treated. In the end he was obliged to give in, but he did so especially out of obedience to the lord bishop of Ostia and to the minister general. He found it bitterly repugnant to be so concerned about himself; that is why he wanted the decision to come from his minister.

47   One night when the pain prevented him from sleeping, he had pity and compassion on himself and said to his companions: "My dearest brothers and my little children, bear with joy the pain and fatigue that my infirmity causes you. The Lord will take the place of his poor servant to recompense you both in this world and in the next; he will credit you with the good works that you have to neglect in order to take care of me. You will obtain an even greater recompense than those who serve the whole Order. You should say to me: 'We are making a loan to you, and the Lord will pay your debts to us.' " The holy Father spoke in this fashion to encourage and sustain the weak and scrupulous who might have thought: "We can no longer pray, and this additional fatigue is beyond our strength." He also wanted to forewarn them against sadness and discouragement, lest they lose the merit of their fatigues.

48   One day the doctor arrived with his cautery to treat his eyes. He had a fire lighted and put the instrument in it so that it would become red-hot. Blessed Francis, to comfort his soul and calm his anxiety, said to the fire: "Brother Fire, the Lord created you as something noble and useful among all creatures. Be courteous to me in this hour, for I have always loved you and will continue to do so for

the love of the Lord who created you. I pray our common Creator to temper your heat that I may be able to endure it." After saying this prayer, he made the sign of the cross over the fire. All of us who were with him had to leave because we were overcome by emotion and piety; only the doctor remained with him.

After the operation, we returned and he said to us: "Cowards! Men of little faith! Why did you run away? In truth I say to you, I felt no pain whatsoever, not even the heat of the fire. If it is not burnt enough, then start all over again and burn it even more!"[88] The doctor, noting that he did not even give a twitch, considered this a great miracle. He said to the brothers: "And yet he is a frail and sick man. I would hesitate to make a similar burn on men with a robust and healthy body, for fear that they could not bear it, as I have experienced more than once." The burn was a long one; it extended from the ear to the eyebrow. For years a fluid accumulated night and day in the eyes; and that is why with the doctor thought it well to treat the veins from the ear to the eyebrow. Other doctors who were opposed to this procedure considered the operation inadvisable; and this proved to be correct, for it brought him no relief. Another pierced both ears to no avail.

RESPECT FOR ALL CREATURES

49   It is not surprising that fire and other creatures sometimes showed respect for him. In fact, we who lived with him were witnesses of his affection and respect for them and of the pleasure they gave him. He had so much love and sympathy for them that he was disturbed when they were treated without respect. He spoke to them with a great inner and exterior joy, as if they had been endowed by God with feeling, intelligence, and speech.[89] Very often it was for him the occasion to become enraptured in God.

One day when he was seated near the hearth, his linen

drawers caught fire the whole length of his leg without his being aware of it. He felt the heat, but when one of his companions saw that his clothes were burning and hurried to extinguish them, he said to him: "No, my dearest brother, don't harm our Brother Fire." He did not let him put it out. The brother ran to find blessed Francis' brother guardian and led him to the place. They extinguished the fire but against Francis' will. He did not even want them to extinguish a candle, a lamp, or fire, as one does when it is no longer needed, so great was his tenderness and pity for that creature. He also forbade the brother to throw embers or half-burned logs to the winds, as is customarily done: he wanted them to be placed gently on the ground out of respect for Him who had created them.

50　　During one Lent at Mount La Verna, it so happened that one day at mealtime his companion lit a fire in the cell where he ate. After starting the fire, he went and found the saint in the cell where he was praying and resting in order to read to him, as usual, the gospel of that day's Mass. When blessed Francis could not hear Mass, he wanted the gospel of the day read to him before eating. When he arrived to eat in the cell where the fire had been lit, the flames had already reached the roof and it was beginning to burn. His companion tried to put it out as best he could but, being all alone, he was unsuccessful. Blessed Francis did not want to help him; but he carried away a pelt with which he covered himself when he went into the forest at night. The brothers of the friary, which was situated at some distance from the cell built apart from it, hurried as soon as they saw the fire and extinguished it. Blessed Francis returned to eat. After the meal he said to his companion: "I will never use that pelt again to cover myself, for I sinned through avarice by not wanting my Brother Fire to consume it."

51   When he washed his hands, he chose a place where the rinse water would not be trampled under foot. When he had to walk on stones, he did so with fear and respect for love of Him who is called "the Rock."[90] When he recited the passage from the psalm: "He set me high on a rock," he changed it to: "Under the feet of the rock you have exalted me."[91] He recommended to the brother who went out to cut fire wood not to cut down the entire tree, but to leave a part of it; he gave the same order to a brother in the friary where he was staying. Likewise he told the brother gardener not to plant vegetables everywhere, but to leave a part of the ground for hardy plants which in time would produce our sisters the flowers. He even said that the brother gardener ought to reserve a place in a corner for a beautiful small garden where he would put all kinds of aromatic herbs and flowering plants so that in their season they might invite all men who looked at them to praise God; for every creature says and proclaims: "God has created me for you, O man!"

We who lived with him saw him find great cause for interior and external joy in all creatures; he caressed and contemplated them with delight, so much so that his spirit seemed to live in heaven and not on earth. That is so true that in recognition for the numerous consolations he had received and was receiving from God's creatures, he composed "The Praises of the Lord for His Creatures" a short time before his demise. It was his way of inciting the hearts of those who would hear this canticle to give glory to God so that the Creator would be praised by all for all his creatures.[92]

DETACHMENT AND GENEROSITY

52   At that time a poor woman from Machilone came to Rieti to have her eyes treated. One day the doctor came to visit blessed Francis and said to him: "A woman with

eye trouble came to see me; but she is so poor that I am obliged to help her and pay her expenses." Blessed Francis, moved to pity for the woman, immediately called one of his companions who was his guardian and said to him: "Brother Guardian, we must return our neighbor's property." "What neighbor's property, brother?" "The mantle we received as a loan from that poor woman with eye trouble; we must give it back to her." "Brother, do what you think best."

Crying with joy, blessed Francis called one of his close friends, a spiritual man, and said to him: "Take this mantle and a dozen loaves of bread. Tell the poor woman whom the doctor will point out to you: A poor man to whom you loaned this mantle thanks you for the loan you made him; accept what belongs to you."

The brother left and communicated blessed Francis' words to the woman. Thinking that he was making fun of her, she replied, fearful and embarrassed: "Leave me in peace, I don't know what you mean." But the brother put the mantle and the dozen loaves of bread in her hands; she then saw that he had spoken the truth and accepted everything, overwhelmed but very happy. Then, fearful lest they would come and take the gift away from her, she quickly got up at night and joyfully returned to her house. Blessed Francis had also told his guardian to pay the poor woman's expenses every day for the love of God for as long as she would live there.

We who lived with him bear testimony that whether sick or well, he displayed a great deal of charity and pity not only toward his brothers but also toward the poor, the sick, and the healthy. He deprived himself of necessary things, which the brothers procured for him with great difficulty but most willingly; and after having cajoled us not to be angry, he gave away with great interior and external joy what he had denied his own body. That is why the minister general and his guardian[93] forbade him to give his tunic to any brother without their permission. Some brothers, in fact, sometimes would ask him for it out of devotion, and he would immediately give it to them. It also sometimes happened that when he saw a sick or poorly clad brother, he would cut his habit in half and give him one part and keep the other for himself, for he had and wanted to have only one tunic.

53   Once when he was traveling through a province preaching, two brothers from France met him; and the meeting gave them much consolation. At its conclusion, they asked him for his tunic for the love of God and out of devotion to him. As soon as he heard the love of God invoked, he took off his tunic and remained scantily dressed for a moment. (When someone said to him: Give me your tunic or your cord or some other thing for the love of God, it was his custom to give it to them at once out of respect for the Lord who is called "Love."[94] But he was greatly displeased, and, in fact, he often reproved the brothers if they invoked the love of God for a mere trifle. He said: "The love of God is so great and noble a thing that we should say the word only rarely, in case of necessity and with profound respect.") Then one of the French brothers took off his tunic and gave it to him.

He very often found himself in great need and in a very embarrassing situation when he had given away a piece of his tunic or the entire tunic in that way. He could not find another one so quickly or have another one made; for, he always wanted it to be very poor and made of pieces, and even sometimes lined with patches inside and out.[95] It was a rare or almost unheard of thing for him to agree to wear a tunic made of new cloth; he tried to procure a tunic that a brother had worn a long time. He even sometimes received part of a tunic from one brother and the rest from another. Because of his numerous infirmities and his sensitivity to cold, he would add a piece of new cloth on the inside. He observed this practice of poverty in his habits until the year he returned to the Lord. It was only a short time before his death, when he was suffering from dropsy, almost completely dehydrated and overcome with infirmities, that the brothers prepared several tunics for him so that he could change night and day when he needed it.

54   One day a poor man dressed in rags came to one of the hermitages of the brothers and asked them for a small piece of cloth for the love of God. Blessed Francis begged the brother to try and find a piece or a patch of cloth to give him. The brother searched the whole house and returned saying that he could find nothing.

Lest the poor man would have to leave empty-handed, blessed Francis, fearing that his guardian would stop him, went quietly away, took a knife, sat down where he was not seen, and cut away a piece that was sewn inside his tunic in order to give it secretly to the poor man. But the guardian who had immediately understood what he wanted to do, overtook him and forbade him to give the poor man anything. At that very time it was very cold, and the saint was sick and trembling. Blessed Francis then said to him: "If you don't want me to give him this piece, then you will have to find one to give our poor brother." And so the brothers, because of blessed Francis, gave the poor man a piece of their own clothing.

Sometimes the brothers of a friary where he stopped would loan him a mantle when he traveled through the country, either on foot or astride a donkey, to preach. (In fact, when he was sick, he could no longer go on foot and sometimes had to use a donkey; he consented to use a horse only in urgent circumstances and in cases of absolute necessity. Such was the case until shortly before his death, when he became seriously sick.) But he agreed to accept the mantle they offered him only on condition that he could give it to a poor man he might meet or who would approach him, provided he was convinced that this unfortunate man really needed the garment.

55   In the early days of the Order when blessed Francis was living at Rivo Torto with the only two brothers who were then with him,[96] a man, who must have been the third brother, left the world to share their life. He had been living there a few days wearing the clothes he had brought with him, when a poor man presented himself to ask for an alms from blessed Francis. The saint said to the one who was to be the third brother: "Give the poor brother your coat." He immediately and joyfully took it off and gave it to the poor man. And it was very evident that in this incident the Lord had put a new grace in his heart, because he had given his coat joyfully.

56   Another time, when he was staying at St. Mary of the Portiuncula, a poor old woman whose two sons were in the Order came to the friary to ask blessed Francis for an alms; for, that year she had nothing to live on. Blessed Francis said to Brother Peter Catanii who at the time was minister general: "Can we find something for our mother?" (For he said that the mother of a brother was his mother and the mother of all the brothers of the Order.) Brother Peter answered: "We have nothing in the house we can give her, especially in view of the fact that we would have to give her a rather sizeable alms to carry her through. However, there is a New Testament in the church from which we read the lessons at Matins." In those days, the brothers had no breviaries and only a few psalters. Blessed Francis answered: "Give our mother the New Testament; she will sell it to take care of her needs. I firmly believe that we will give greater pleasure to the Lord and to the Blessed Virgin his Mother by giving it to her than by reading it." And so they gave it to her.

It can be said and written of blessed Francis what is

said and read of Job: "Have I ever seen a wretch in need of clothing, or a beggar going naked?"[97] For those of us who lived with him, it would take too long to write and recount not only what we learned from others about his charity and goodness toward the poor but also what we saw with our own eyes.

MIRACULOUS CURES

57   At that time, when blessed Francis was living at the hermitage of St. Francis [sic], at Fonte Colombo, the cattle-plague, from which no beast ordinarily escapes, broke out among the herds of the village of St. Eli, located near the hermitage. All the oxen were stricken, and death began to take its toll. One night, an inhabitant of the village, a spiritual man, had a vision and heard a voice say to him: "Go to the hermitage where blessed Francis is living. Get some of the water in which he has washed his hands and feet and sprinkle some of it on all your oxen; they will be cured at once."

The man got up before daybreak, went to the hermitage and told everything to the saint's companions. At meal time, they took the water from a receptacle in which he had washed his hands. That night they asked him permission to wash his feet without telling him why. They gave this water to the man who took it with him and, just as one would sprinkle holy water, he sprinkled it on the oxen that were lying almost dead and on all the others with them. Immediately by the grace of God and the merits of blessed Francis they were all cured. At that time, blessed Francis was already bearing the wounds in his hands, in his feet, and in his side.

58   In the days when blessed Francis, suffering from his eyes, was spending a few days in the palace of the bishop of Rieti, a cleric of the diocese, named Gedeon,[98] a very worldly man, was stricken with a very serious sickness

1034

that had confined him to bed for a long time; he was suffering especially from his kidneys. It was impossible for him to move or to turn over in bed without help; he could get up and walk only with the aid of several others. When they supported him in this way, he walked with a stoop; and he was bent over because the pains in his back prevented him from standing upright.

One day he had himself carried before blessed Francis, cast himself at his feet,[99] and asked him with copious tears to make the sign of the cross over him. Blessed Francis answered: "How shall I sign you with the sign of the cross, you who have lived according to your desires of the flesh, without meditating on the judgments of God or fearing them?" But Francis was so grieved at the sight of his infirmities and suffering that, moved to pity, he said: "I sign you in the name of the Lord. If it pleases God to cure you, beware of returning to your vomit.[100] For, in truth I say to you, if you return to your vomit, evils worse than the first[101] will be heaped upon you, and you will incur a terrible chastisement by reason of your sins, your ingratitude, and your contempt of God's goodness." He made the sign of the cross over the cleric. Immediately he straightened up, and stood up, freed of his infirmities; and when he straightened up one could hear the bones in his back crack like dry wood that snaps in one's hands.

But a few years later he returned to his vomit, in defiance of the recommendations that the Lord had made to him through his servant Francis. . . .[102]

THE PRAISE OF BEGGING

59   After his stay at Siena and at Le Celle di Cortona, blessed Francis returned to St. Mary of the Portiuncula and then went to stay at Bagnara, north of Nocera, where they had just built a house for the brothers; and he lived there for a certain time. But because his feet and legs had begun to swell due to his dropsy, his condition worsened. The

people of Assisi were informed of this and immediately sent a few knights to this friary to bring him back to Assisi.[103] They were in fact afraid to let him die there and in that case be forced to relinquish the possession of his holy body to others. The knights, therefore, brought the sick man back to Assisi.

During the trip, they stopped at a small market-town in the region of Assisi[104] to eat. Blessed Francis stopped at the house of a man in that locality who received him with joy and charity. The knights went through the entire village to buy provisions: they found nothing. Returning to blessed Francis, they said to him, jokingly as it were: "Brother, you will have to give us some of your alms, for we found nothing to buy." Blessed Francis answered with great spiritual fervor: "If you found nothing it is because you placed your confidence in your flies, that is to say, in your pennies, and not in God. Go back to the houses you went to without shame; and instead of asking for merchandise to buy, ask alms for the love of God. The Holy Spirit will act in you, and you will find an abundance of everything."

They went and asked for alms as the holy Father had recommended to them. Men and women gave them of what they had generously and joyfully. Overjoyed, they came back to find blessed Francis and told him what had happened. They considered the thing miraculous, for everything had transpired as he had predicted.

60   Blessed Francis believed that asking for alms for the love of God was an act of the greatest nobility, dignity, and courtesy before God and even before the world. As a matter of fact, all that the heavenly Father has created for man's use, since sin has entered the world he has continued to give man gratuitously and by way of alms, to the worthy and unworthy, because of his love for his well-beloved Son. Consequently, blessed Francis used to say that the servant

of Christ who goes and asks for alms for the love of God should do it more confidently and more joyfully than a man who, wanting to buy something, would say in proof of his courtesy and generosity:[105] "For something worth a penny, I offer a hundred silver marks!"[106] The servant of God offers a thousand times more; in exchange for an alms, he offers the love of God in comparison with which all the things of earth and even of heaven are nothing.

Before the brothers became numerous and when blessed Francis was traveling extensively and preaching, there were as yet no friaries in the cities and towns where he went to preach, and he often received invitations to eat and lodge with some noble and rich person who wanted to prove to him his devotion. He knew very well that, for the love of God, his host had made lavish preparations for all that his body needed; nevertheless, at meal time he went begging in order to give good example to the brothers and because of the nobility and dignity of Lady Poverty. Sometimes he said to his host: "I will never renounce my royal dignity, my heritage,[107] my vocation, my profession which is that of a Friar Minor and to go and ask for alms. Even if I were to bring back only three scraps, I would go, because that is my duty and I wish to exercise it." And he begged from door to door contrary to the will of his host. It sometimes happened that his host accompanied him. Then, appropriating for himself the alms collected by blessed Francis, he would keep them as relics out of devotion for him. The writer has seen this happen many times and bears witness to it.

61   One day when blessed Francis was visiting the lord bishop of Ostia — who later became pope — he stole away at meal time to go and ask for alms, but almost stealthily because of the lord bishop. When Francis returned, the bishop was at table and had begun to eat, for he had invited a few knights who were relatives of his.

Blessed Francis placed his alms on the bishop's table, and then sat down next to him; for, that was the place the lord bishop reserved for him when he received the saint. The bishop was somewhat embarrassed by the fact that blessed Francis had gone begging, but said nothing because of the guests. When blessed Francis had eaten, he took his alms and distributed them in the name of God to the knights and to the bishop's chaplains. All accepted them with great respect. Some ate them, while the others kept them out of devotion for the saint. In accepting them, they even removed their caps as a sign of veneration for him. The lord bishop greatly rejoiced at this devotion, especially in view of the fact that the alms were not white bread.

At the conclusion of the meal, the bishop brought blessed Francis into his room and embraced him with utmost joy, as he said: "O my most simple brother, why did you slight me by going out and begging? My house is also the house of the brothers." Blessed Francis answered: "On the contrary, I paid you a great honor, lord. As a matter of fact, when an inferior fulfills his responsibility well and obeys his lord, he gives homage both to the Lord and to his prelate." Then he added: "I must be the example and model of your poor.[108] I know that in the Order there are and will be brothers, true Friars Minor in name and conduct. For the love of the Lord God and by the grace of the Holy Spirit, who instructs them and will instruct them in all things, they will demean themselves in all humility and submission to serve their brothers. But there are also some and will be some who, held back by shame and coerced by the usages of the world, disdain and will disdain to humble themselves and to demean themselves to beg and perform servile work. That is why I must by my comportment instruct those who have entered and will enter the Order so that they may have no excuse before God in this world and in the next. And so, when I am at your house, you who are our master and our pope, or at the houses of the mighty and rich of this world who offer me and even impose on me their hospitality for the love of God, I do not want to be ashamed to go begging. Furthermore, it is a title of nobility for me, a royal dignity, and an honor which the sovereign King confers on me. He, the Master of all things, willed to make himself the servant of all for us. Rich and glorious in his majesty, he came, poor and despised, in our humanity. It is my wish, therefore, that the present brothers and those to come know that I experience more interior and external consolation in sitting down at the poor table of the brothers, on which I see the miserable alms gathered from door to door for the love of God, than in sitting down at your table or at the table of other lords, laden with all kinds of dishes, although you offer me this profusion out of devotion for me. The bread of alms is, in fact, a sacred bread, sanctified by the praise and love of God, since the brother who goes begging must begin by saying: "Praised and blessed be the Lord God!" Then he must say: "Give us an alms for the love of the Lord God!"

The lord bishop, very edified by this conversation with the holy Father, then said to him: "My son, do as you think best, for the Lord is with you and you with him."

62   Blessed Francis often said that no brother should spend a long time without going out to beg. The more noble and great a brother was in the world the more the holy father was delighted and edified to see him go on the quest and perform servile work to give good example.

That is what was done formerly. In the early days of the Order, when the brothers lived at Rivo Torto, there was a brother who prayed little and did no work, who never went begging, for he was ashamed, but he ate well. Considering his behavior, blessed Francis was warned by the Holy Spirit that this brother was a sensual man. One day he said to him: "Go your way, Brother Fly, for you wish to eat the fruit of the labor of your brothers, while you remain idle in the vineyard of God. You resemble Brother Drone who gathers nothing, does no work, but eats the fruit of the activity of the working bees." He left without even asking forgiveness, for he was a sensual man.

63   During one of blessed Francis' sojourns at St. Mary of the Portiuncula, a brother, a spiritual man, was returning from Assisi where he had gone to beg. Having arrived near the church, he began to praise God out loud and with much joy. Blessed Francis heard him and went out along the road to meet him. Full of joy, he kissed the shoulder that was carrying the double sack full of alms. Then he put it on his own shoulders and carried it into the house of the brothers. There he publicly announced before all: "This is the way I want to see my brother go on the quest and return: happy and joyful."

SERENITY AND JOY AT THE APPROACH OF DEATH

64   At the time when blessed Francis returned from the friary of Bagnara,[109] he was very sick and confined to bed in the episcopal palace of Assisi. The inhabitants feared that he might die during the night without their knowledge and that the brothers would secretly take his body away and bury it in another city. So they decided to keep a sharp lookout every night near the palace. At that time blessed Francis was very weak. To comfort his soul and ward off discouragement in the midst of his grave and serious infirmities, he often had the brothers sing for him the "Praises of the Lord" which he had previously composed during his sickness. He also had the Praises sung at night for the edification of those who were on guard because of him near the palace.

Brother Elias, seeing that in this way blessed Francis derived joy and courage in the Lord in the midst of such great suffering, said to him one day: "My dearest brother, I am very consoled and edified to see the joy that you experience and manifest to your companions in such affliction and sickness. Surely the men of this city venerate you as a saint in life and in death; but since they firmly believe that your serious and incurable sickness will soon lead to your death, they could think and say to themselves as they hear the 'Praises of the Lord' sung: How can he display such great joy when he is going to die? Would it not be better to think of death?"

Blessed Francis answered him: "Do you remember the vision at Foligno where you told me a voice warned you that I would not live beyond two years?[110] Before you had your vision, thanks to the Holy Spirit who puts every good thought in the heart and every good work on the lips of his faithful, I often thought of death, day and night. Since your vision, I have been even more zealous in thinking of the hour of my death every day." Then he added with emotion: "Brother, let me rejoice in the Lord and sing his praises in the midst of my infirmities: by the grace of the Holy Spirit I am so closely united to my Lord, that, through his goodness, I can indeed rejoice in the Most High himself."

65   In those days a doctor from Arezzo, named Buongiovanni (Good John), a friend and favorite of blessed Francis, came to the palace to see him. The saint questioned the doctor about his sickness and said to him: "What do you think, Brother John,[111] of my dropsy?" (Blessed Francis did not want to call those whose name was "Good" by their name out of respect for the Lord who said: "No one is good but God alone."[112] Likewise in his letters he called no one *father* or *master* out of respect for the Lord who said: "You must call no one on earth your father, . . . nor must you allow yourselves to be called teachers.")[113]

The doctor answered him: "Brother, with the grace of

God, all will be well." He did not want to tell him that
he was going to die soon. Blessed Francis replied: "Brother,
tell me the truth, what is your prognosis? Do not be
afraid; for, thanks to God, I am not a coward who fears
death. The Lord, by his grace and in his goodness, has so
closely united me to himself that I am as happy to live as I
am to die." The doctor answered him: "Father, according
to our medical science, your disease is incurable, and you
will die either at the end of September or the fourth day of
the nones of October." Then blessed Francis who was lying
on his bed in an extremely weakened condition, extended his
arms and raisd his hands toward the Lord with great devotion and respect, crying out, his body and soul permeated
with joy: "Welcome, Sister Death!"

BROTHER ROGER AND HIS BOOKS

66   Brother Roger[114] of the March of Ancona, a noblemen by birth and more noble by his holiness, was dearly
loved by blessed Francis. One day Brother Roger came to the
palace to visit him. In the course of their conversation,
which was about the Order and the observance of the rule,
the brother asked him: "Father, tell me what your intentions
were when you began to have brothers, what they are today
and which of them you think you will keep until the day
you die? I would like to be sure of your intentions and
your first and last will so that we, the cleric brothers,
who have books, may keep them, recognizing, of course,
that they belong to the Order?" Blessed Francis answered
him: "Brother, my first and final intentions and desires
are as follows: if my brothers had been willing to listen
to me, none of them would have had anything else but
the habit granted to them by the rule, with a cord and
drawers."

THE NAME: FRIARS MINOR

67   One day blessed Francis said to the brothers: "The Order of Friars Minor is a little flock that the Son of God in these latter times has asked of his Father, saying to him: 'Father, it is my wish that you raise up and give to me a new and humble people who, in this hour, will distinguish themselves by their humility and poverty from all those who have preceded them and who will be content to possess me alone as their sole riches.' And the Father said to his well-beloved Son: 'My Son, your request is fulfilled.' That is why," blessed Francis added, "the Lord has willed that the brothers be called 'lesser' because they are this people whom the Son of God asked of his Father and of whom he said in the gospel: 'There is no need to be afraid, little flock, for it has pleased your Father to give you the kingdom,'[115] and again: 'In so far as you did this to one of the least (minor) of these brothers of mine, you did it to me.' "[116]

Without a doubt the Lord was speaking in these texts of all those who have the spirit of poverty, but he was also referring to the creation in his Church of the Order of Friars Minor. Since it had been revealed to blessed Francis that he was to call his followers "Friars Minor," he had this name inserted in the rule[117] that he brought to the Lord Pope Innocent III, who approved it and did so before promulgating it officially in the Council.[118]

Christ also revealed to blessed Francis the greeting which the brothers were to use and which he recorded in his Testament: "God revealed a form of greeting to me, telling me that we should say, 'May the Lord give you peace.' "[119]

In the early days of the Order, when blessed Francis was travelling about in the company of a brother who was one of the first twelve, the latter greeted men and women on the roads and in the fields by saying to them: "May the Lord give you peace!" The people were completely astonished, for they had never heard any other religious greet them that way. Moreover, a few men asked in an offensive tone of voice: "What is the meaning of that kind of greeting?" The brother was ashamed and said to blessed Francis: "Brother, allow me to use a different greeting." Blessed Francis answered: "Let them talk; they do not have a sense of the things of God. Don't be ashamed, because nobles and princes of this world will show respect to you and to the other brothers because of this greeting." And he added: "Is it not wonderful that the Lord has willed a humble people different from those who have preceded them, people who are content to possess him alone, the Most High and most glorious Lord, as their riches?"

RESISTANCE OF THE BROTHERS

68   If some brother were to ask those of us who lived with him why blessed Francis did not have the strict poverty he spoke about to Brother Roger observed, we would answer them with the very words we heard from his mouth. What he said to Brother Roger he also said to other brothers, on the subject of poverty, as well as many other regulations which he included in the rule: he had asked the Lord in assiduous prayer and meditation to reveal them to him for the benefit of the Order, and he declared that they were entirely in conformity with the will of God. But later when he explained these regulations to the brothers, they found them difficult and unbearable; for, they did not know what was going to take place in the Order after Francis' death. He did not wish to have a conflict with the brothers, so greatly did he fear scandal for himself and for the others; and hence he complied with their request, against his own will. He later apologized for it before the Lord. But so that the word which the Lord had put in his mouth for the good of the brothers would not return to the Lord empty,[120] he wanted to fulfill it in himself so that he might

1044

obtain recompense for it from the Lord. And so his spirit found comfort and peace in practicing poverty.

A MINISTER AND HIS BOOKS

69   At the time when he returned from overseas, a minister had a conversation with him one day regarding the chapter on poverty and wanted to know his will and mind on this subject. He particularly asked for clarifications on the passage in the rule which quotes the prohibitions of the gospel: "Take nothing for the journey."[121] Blessed Francis answered him: "My thinking is that the brothers should have nothing but their habit, a cord, and drawers, as the rule says, and shoes in case of necessity."

The minister replied: "What then shall I do, I who possess so many books worth more than fifty pounds?" He said this so that he could keep them with a safe conscience; for, he had qualms of conscience about possessing these books, knowing that blessed Francis interpreted the chapter on poverty very strictly. Blessed Francis answered him: "Brother, I can not and must not go against my conscience and against the observance of the holy gospel which we have professed." These words filled the minister with sadness. When Francis saw how disturbed he was, he said to him with deep emotion, addressing all the friars through him: "You want to pass in the eyes of men as Friars Minor and be called faithful observers of the holy gospel, but in practice what you want is to keep your treasures."[122]

The ministers knew very well that according to the rule, the brothers were bound to observe the holy gospel. Yet they had the passage in the rule that reads "Take nothing for the journey" suppressed, since they thought they were not obliged to observe the perfection of the holy gospel. That is why blessed Francis, warned by the Holy Spirit of this mutilation, cried out in the presence of a few brothers: "Do the ministers think that they are making light of God and of me? Well, so that all the brothers may know and be forewarned that they are bound to observe the perfection of the gospel, I wish it to be written in the beginning and at the end of the rule: the brothers are bound to observe the holy gospel of our Lord Jesus Christ. And so, that the brothers may always be inexcusable[123] before God, I wish with God's help to put into practice and always observe the prescriptions which God has placed in my mouth for the salvation and usefulness of my soul and the soul of my brothers." Thus he observed the holy gospel to the letter from the day he began to have brothers until the hour of his death.

A NOVICE AND THE PSALTER

70 Once there was a brother novice[124] who could read the Psalter, but not very well. Since he very much liked to read it, he asked the minister general for permission to have a Psalter. The minister consented to it. However, the brother did not want to avail himself of it until he had obtained the permission of blessed Francis.

He had heard it said that the holy father did not want to see his brothers eager for learning and for books, but that he preferred to see them — as he preached it — eager for pure and holy simplicity,[125] for prayer, and for Lady Poverty. That is the way the first brothers were trained. These first brothers were saints and believed that such was the surest way to salvation.

Not that Francis ever despised or regarded sacred learning with disfavor: on the contrary, he showed a fond respect for the scholars of the Order and for all scholars, as he himself says in his Testament: "We should honor and venerate theologians, too, and the ministers of God's word, because it is they who give us spirit and life."[126]

But, foreseeing the future, he knew through the Holy Spirit and often repeated that many of the brothers, under pretext of edifying others, would abandon their vocation, that is to say, pure and holy simplicity, prayer and Lady Poverty; they would consider themselves more fervent and more on fire with the love of God because of their knowledge of the Scriptures, whereas precisely because of it they would inwardly remain empty and cold; and they would not be able to return to their former vocation since they had let the time given them to live in this holy vocation slip by. "And I strongly fear," he concluded, "that what they seem to have will be taken away from them,[127] because they have abandoned their vocation."

ELOQUENCE AND PRAYER

71   He also said: "There are many brothers who day and night put all their energy and all their attention into the pursuit of knowledge, thereby abandoning prayer and their holy vocation. And when they have preached to a few men or to the people, and learn that certain ones were edified or converted to penance through their discourse, they are puffed up and pride themselves on the results and work of others. For, those whom they think they edified or converted to penance by their discourse were actually edified or converted by God through the prayers of the holy brothers who are completely ignorant of it; God wishes it this way for fear it should be grounds for pride for them. Behold my Knights of the Round Table: the brothers who hide in abandoned and secluded places to devote themselves with more fervor to prayer and meditation, to weep over their sins and those of others. Their holiness is known to God, but most often unknown to the brothers and to men. When their souls will be presented to the Lord by the angels, the Lord will reveal the effect and reward of their labors, that is to say, the host of souls saved by their prayers. And he will say to them: 'My sons, see the souls saved by your prayers; since you were faithful in small things, I will trust you with greater.' "[128]

Blessed Francis explained the text: "The barren woman bears sevenfold, but the mother of many is desolate,"[129] as follows. "The barren woman," he said, "is the good religious who by his holy actions and virtues, sanctifies himself and edifies the others." He often repeated this saying in his conversations with the brothers[130] and often, at the chapter of St. Mary of the Portiuncula, before the ministers and the other brothers. In this way he instructed the ministers and the preachers in the exercise of their responsibilities. He told them that the exercise of their office of minister or their duty as preachers and the anxieties these entail should not make them abandon prayer; that they ought to beg and do manual work like the other brothers in order to give good example and for the good of their souls and the souls of others. He added: "The brothers who are subjects will be very edified to see their ministers and their preachers devote themselves readily to prayer, and demean and humble themselves." A faithful disciple of Christ, Francis himself practiced what he preached to others as long as he enjoyed good health.

THE NOVICE AND THE PSALTER AGAIN

72   One day when blessed Francis had come to the hermitage where the above-mentioned novice was living, this brother came and said to him: "Father, it would be a great consolation to me to have a Psalter; but although the minister general has given me permission to have one, I do not wish to keep it without your consent."

This was blessed Francis' answer: "The Emperor Charles, Roland, and Oliver, all paladins and valiant knights who were mighty in battle, pursued the infidels even to death, sparing neither toil nor fatigue, and gained a memorable victory for themselves; and by way of conclusion, these holy martyrs died fighting for the Faith of Christ. We see many today who would like to attribute honor and glory to themselves by being content with singing about the exploits of others." We find the explanation of these words in the Admonitions[131] where he wrote: "The saints endured all of this (i.e., trials, persecutions, ignominy, etc.), but we who are servants of God try to win honor and glory by recounting and making known what they have done." He was saying in different words: "Knowledge produces self-importance; love makes the building grow."[132]

73   Another time when blessed Francis was seated near a fire and was warming himself, this brother came and badgered him with the problem of his Psalter. The saint answered him: "And when you have a Psalter, you will want a breviary; and when you have a breviary, you will install yourself in a chair like a great prelate, and you will order your brother: Bring me my breviary!" As he said this he was carried away with deep emotion, took some ashes from the hearth, sprinkled them on his head and rubbed some on himself, repeating :"That's the breviary!" The brother was completely dumbfounded and ashamed.

Blessed Francis then said to him: "I, too, Brother, was tempted to have books; but that I might know God's will on this point, I took the book of the gospels and I asked the Lord to make it known to me on the first page where I opened the book what he wanted of me. When my prayer was over, I opened the book and my eyes fell on this verse: 'The secret of the kingdom of God is given to you, but to those who are outside everything comes in parables.'"[133] And he added: "Many are they who desire to exalt themselves to the heights of knowledge, but blessed is he who prefers to renounce knowledge for love of the Lord God!"

74   A few months later, while blessed Francis was staying at St. Mary of the Portiuncula, he was near his cell on the road that goes behind the house, when this brother came to him again and spoke to him about his Psalter. The saint said: "Go and do what your minister tells you to do." Whereupon, the brother returned by the same road he had

come. Blessed Francis had remained on the road reflecting on what he had said to the brother. All of a sudden he cried out: "Wait a minute, Brother, wait!" He rejoined him and said: "Come back with me and show me the place where I told you to do what your minister would tell you to do regarding your Psalter." They returned to the spot. Blessed Francis knelt down before the brother and said to him: *"Mea culpa,* Brother, *mea culpa*: whoever wishes to be a Friar Minor must possess only the tunic granted him by the rule,[134] the cord and drawers, and in addition shoes if necessity or sickness demands it."

Every time a brother came and asked him for advice of this kind, he always gave the same answer. He said: "The worth of knowledge is proportionate to the actions it produces; there is no better sermon than the practice of the virtues."

This was the equivalent of saying: "Every tree can be told by its own fruit."[135]

TOLERANCE OF CERTAIN ABUSES

75 During the time when blessed Francis was living in the palace of the bishop of Assisi, one of his companions said to him one day: "Father, forgive me, but many others have already commented on what I wish to say to you. You know how formerly, through the grace of God, the whole Order bloomed in the purity of perfection, how the brothers zealously and fervently observed holy poverty in all things: houses, furniture, and clothing. In this, as in all their external comportment, they were of one mind, solicitous to remain completely faithful to our profession and our vocation, and to give good example by being of one mind in the love of God and of neighbor. Now, for some time this purity and perfection are beginning to change for the worse, and the brothers excuse themselves by saying that numbers run counter to observance; many even believe that the people are more edified by this new way of life and that it is more fitting to conduct oneself in this way. They despise the way of simplicity and of poverty which, nevertheless, was the source and basis of our Order. In view of these abuses, we believe that you cannot be in agreement with them, but we are surprised, if such is the case, that you put up with them and do not correct them."

76   Blessed Francis answered: "Brother, may the Lord forgive you for wanting to set yourself against me in this way and involve me in questions that no longer fall within my province. As long as I was in charge of the brothers and they remained faithful to their vocation and profession, my examples and my exhortations were enough for them; and yet I was very frail at the beginning of my conversion. But when I saw that the Lord each day multiplied the number of the brothers, and that through lukewarmness and lack of generosity they began to deviate from the straight and sure way which they had followed until then and take, as you say, a wider road without respecting either their profession, their vocation, or good example; and when I realized that neither my advice nor my example could make them abandon the road on which they had embarked, I put the Order back in the hands of God and of the ministers. I relinquished my post and resigned, excusing myself at the general chapter because my sickness would not allow me to care for the brothers. And yet, if the brothers had walked and were still walking according to my will, I would prefer that they have no other minister but myself until the day of my death. In fact, when subjects are good and faithful, when they know and fulfill the will of their superior, then the superior has scarcely any anxiety concerning them. What is more, I would experience such joy seeing the quality of the brothers and such comfort at the thought of our progress that I would let them have their own way and I would feel no added burden, even if I were nailed to a bed through sickness.

"My duty, my mandate as superior of the brothers is of a spiritual order because I must repress vices and correct them. But if through my exhortations and my example I can neither suppress nor correct them, I do not wish to become an executioner who punishes and flogs, as the secular arm does. I have confidence in the Lord that they will be punished by invisible enemies (those valets of the Lord in charge of punishing in this world and in the next those who transgress God's commandments); they will be punished and corrected by the men of this world to their great shame and confusion, and in that way they will return to their profession and vocation.

"Nevertheless, until the day of my death, I will continue to teach my brothers by my example and my life how to walk the road that the Lord showed me and which I in turn showed them, so that they may have no excuse before the Lord and so that later I may not have to give an account before God for them or for myself."

77　　Blessed Francis caused it to be written down in his Testament that all the houses of the brothers were to be made of clay and wood as a sign of holy poverty and humility and that the churches built for them were to be small. On this specific point of building with wood and mud, it was his wish that St. Mary of the Portiuncula the first friary where the Lord began to multiply the brothers, be taken as an example. He wanted this friary always to be a model and a reminder to the present and future brothers.

Nevertheless certain ones told him that in their opinion it was not good to build with wood and mud, because in certain countries and provinces wood was more expensive than stone. Blessed Francis did not want to discuss the matter with them because at that time he was very sick and even on the threshold of death and he died shortly afterwards. But he caused it to be written in his Testament: "The friars must be very careful not to accept churches or poor dwellings for themselves, or anything else built for them, unless they are in harmony with the poverty which we have promised in the rule; and they should occupy these places only as strangers and pilgrims."

We who were with him when he composed the rule and practically all of his writings testify that he had prescriptions included in it to which certain brothers, especially superiors, were opposed. These brought him the opposition of his brothers during his lifetime; now that he is dead, they would be very helpful to the entire Order. But since he feared scandal, he yielded against his will to the wishes of the brothers. Yet he often said: "Woe to those brothers who are opposed to what I know to be the will of God for the greatest good of the Order, even if I do bow to their will against my own." And he often repeated to his companions: "What pains and grieves me is to see the opposition of certain brothers to the instructions I receive from the goodness of God through prayer and meditation for the present and future good of the entire Order and which are — God assures me — in conformity with his will. But some friars, on their own authority and with the sole light of their knowledge, suppress them and oppose me by saying: "These prescriptions are to be kept and observed; these others are not." Nevertheless, he so greatly feared scandal, as we have already said, that he refrained from interfering in many things and bowed before the will of the brothers, though much against his own will.

AGAINST IDLE TALK

78   When our most holy Father Francis was staying at St. Mary of the Portiuncula it was his daily custom, after the meal, to devote himself together with the brothers to some manual work to combat laziness. He, in fact, considered it harmful for himself and for the brothers to lose the benefit of prayer, which had been obtained through grace, by indulging in useless conversation after praying.

In order to avoid this, he made the following regulation which all the brothers were to observe:

"If a brother, either while travelling or working with others engages in some useless talk, he will be obliged to recite the *Our Father* together with the Praises of God at the beginning and end of prayer.[137] If the guilty one accuses himself of it, as soon as he becomes aware of this lapse, he will say the *Our Father* and the Praises of the Lord for himself: if he is chided by a brother before he accuses himself, he will say the *Our Father* in the way indicated for this brother. If he is reproved by a brother, is refractory, and does not want to recite the *Our Father,* he will say two for the one who admonished him, provided another brother joins the first to testify that the idle word was indeed spoken. He shall recite these Praises of the Lord at the beginning and at the end of prayer, loud enough and clear enough for all brothers present to hear and understand; during that time, they must be quiet and listen. A brother who is present at idle talk without stopping it will be obliged to recite the *Our Father* and the Praises of the Lord for the guilty one. Every brother who meets one or more brothers in a cell, a house, or elsewhere will always be solicitous to praise and bless God."

The most holy Father had the habit of reciting these Praises of the Lord; his great desire and his wish was to see the brothers and even other men inject a great deal of zeal and devotion into their recitation.

DEVOTION TO THE EUCHARIST

79   After the chapter of St. Mary of the Portiuncula, in which for the first time brothers were sent to overseas countries,[138] blessed Francis, who had stayed in this friary with a few brothers, said to them: "My dearest brothers, I ought to be a model and example to all. If I, therefore, have sent my brothers into distant countries where they will undergo fatigue, humiliations, hunger, and all kinds of trials, it is fair and good, it seems to me, that I also leave for a distant country so that my brothers will suffer their trials and privations with patience, knowing that I, too, am enduring as much." And he added: "Go and pray to the Lord that he may lead me to choose the country where I shall best work for his glory, for the advancement and salvation of souls, and for the good example of the Order."

When he was about to go and preach in a distant country or even in a neighboring province, it was the most holy father's custom to pray and have others pray that the Lord might inspire him to go where God preferred him to go.

The brothers, therefore, withdrew to pray and, when they were finished, they returned to blessed Francis, who said to them: "In the name of our Lord Jesus Christ, of the glorious Virgin, his Mother, and of all the saints, I choose the country of France. It is a Catholic nation, and, more than all the other Catholic nations of the holy Church, it bears witness to the greatest respect for the Body of our Lord Jesus Christ,[139] and nothing would please me more than to go among these people."

80   Blessed Francis had a great deal of respect and devotion for the Body of Christ. He wanted it written in the rule that in the provinces where they lived, the brothers were also to devote much care and regard for It, to exhort and encourage clerics and priests to reserve the Body of Christ in a decent and fitting place and, if the clerics did not do so, to attend to it themselves.[140] He even resolved one day to send brothers into all the provinces with ciboria in which they would place the Body of Christ should they find it here or there in an unbecoming place. Out of respect for the most holy Body and Blood of our Lord Jesus Christ, he wanted to include in the rule that if the brothers found writings with the name of the Lord on them or words of the ritual of the most holy Sacrament carelessly abandoned in an unsuitable place, they were to

collect them and put them aside, thereby honoring the Lord in the words he has spoken. Many objects, in fact, become sacred through the words of God, and the Sacrament of the altar is confected by virtue of the words of Christ. He did not write this regulation in the rule because the ministers did not judge it opportune to make it obligatory, but he decided to leave the expression of his will in this regard in his Testament and in his other writings. He likewise decided to send brothers into all the provinces with beautiful and good bread irons.

He selected the brothers he wanted to bring with him and said to them: "In the name of the Lord, go out two by two with becoming dignity; in the morning, observe silence until after tierce[141] by praying to God in your heart. Let there be no useless conversation, for although you are travelling, your conduct must be as upright as if you were in a hermitage or in your cell. Wherever we are, wherever we go, we bring our cell with us. Our brother body is our cell and our soul is the hermit living in that cell in order to pray to God and meditate. If our soul does not live in peace and solitude within its cell, of what avail is it to live in a man-made cell?"

PEACE RESTORED TO AREZZO

81   When they arrived at Arezzo, they found the entire city a prey to a dreadful scandal and to a war that was raging night and day. There were two factions in the city, and they had been mortal enemies for a long time. Blessed Francis was staying in a hospital in the suburbs of the city. As he heard the din and shrieks night and day, it seemed to him that the demons were exulting and egging on the inhabitants to destroy their city by fire and other scourges. Moved by pity for this city, he called Brother Sylvester. He was a priest of admirable simplicity and purity, a man of God of solid faith, esteemed by blessed Francis as a saint.

He said to him: "Go to the gate of the city and, as loud as you can, order all the devils to leave that city."

Brother Sylvester got up, went to the city gate and cried out with all his might: "Praised and blessed be the Lord Jesus Christ. On behalf of God almighty and in virtue of the obedience due to our Father Francis, I order all the devils to leave this city!" Thanks to the goodness of God and the prayer of blessed Francis, it so happened that peace and concord were restored between the inhabitants without any other kind of sermon.

Blessed Francis was not able to preach to them on this occasion. But much later he said to them in the course of a sermon: "I speak to you as people who formerly were enchained by demons. You were bound hand and foot and sold like animals; you had handed yourselves over to the power of the demons by subjecting yourselves to the will of those who have destroyed themselves, who continue to destroy themselves, and wish your own ruin and the ruin of your entire city. You are wretched and ignorant people, for you do not recognize God's blessings. Some among you do not know it, but some time ago, God freed your city through the merits of a most holy brother named Sylvester."

A TRIP TO FRANCE INTERRUPTED

82 On his arrival in Florence, blessed Francis met Lord Hugolino, the bishop of Ostia, who later became pope. He had received from Pope Honorius the legation of the duchy of Spoleto, Tuscany, Lombardy, and the Marches of Treviso as far as Venice. The lord bishop greatly rejoiced at the arrival of blessed Francis.

But when he learned that Francis wanted to go to France, he opposed the plan: "Brother, I do not want you to cross the mountains, for there are a number of prelates and others in the Roman Curia who would like to interfere with the interests of your Order. The other cardinals and I, who love your Order, will protect it and help it much more effectively

if you remain within the frontiers of this province." Blessed
Francis answered: "Lord, I would be greatly ashamed of
myself if I stayed here and sent my brothers to far distant
provinces."

The lord bishop answered him with a tone of reproach
in his voice: "Why did you send your brothers to undergo
so many trials so far away and die of hunger?" Blessed
Francis answered in a great prophetic outburst: "Lord, do
you think and believe that the Lord has sent the brothers for
this province alone? Verily I say to you: God has chosen
and sent the brothers for the good and salvation of all men
in the entire world; they will be received not only in believing countries but also among the infidels. Let them observe what they have promised God and God will give
them, both among the infidels and the believing nations, all
that they will need."

The lord bishop admired this statement and admitted
that the saint was right. Though he did not allow blessed
Francis to leave for France, Francis could at least send
Brother Pacificus and other brothers to that country.[142] As
for himself, Francis returned to the valley of Spoleto.

PORTRAIT OF A TRUE FRIAR MINOR

83   As the time for convoking the chapter at St. Mary
of the Portiuncula was approaching, blessed Francis said
to his companion: "I would not consider myself a Friar
Minor if I did not have the disposition that I am going to
describe to you: With great devotion and veneration, the
brothers come and find me and invite me to the chapter;
touched by their affectionate insistence, I go with them.
When all have gathered, they beg me to proclaim the word
of God before that assembly. I rise and preach as the Holy
Spirit inspires me.

"Let us suppose that after the sermon they reflect and
rise up against me and say: 'We no longer want you to rule
over us.[143] You have no eloquence whatsoever; you are too

simple and we are ashamed to have a boor and an illiterate for a superior; from now on, no longer lay claim to call yourself our superior.' They boo me and expel me. . . . Well, I would not consider myself a Friar Minor if I were not as joyful when they speak disparagingly of me, shamefully reject me, and take away my office as when they honor and respect me, provided that in both cases the advantage be the same for them. For, if I rejoice at their gain and their devotion when they exalt and honor me (which might be dangerous for my soul), how much more ought I to rejoice over the gain and salvation of my soul when they speak disparagingly of me by rejecting me shamefully, because that is a true gain for me!"

SISTER CRICKET

84   It was summer. Blessed Francis was then living at the friary of St. Mary of the Portiuncula in the last cell near the hedge of the garden behind the house where Brother Rayner the gardener lived after Francis' death. One day, as he was coming out of his cell, he saw a cricket within reach of his hand perched on the branch of a fig tree that was growing near the cell. He stretched out his hand and said: "Come, Sister Cricket." It immediately climbed along his fingers. Meanwhile the saint caressed it with the other hand, saying to it: "Sing, Sister Cricket." It obeyed him at once and began to sing. This was a great consolation for the saint and he praised the Lord. He kept it in his hand that way for an hour. Then, he put it back on the branch from which he had taken it.

For eight days, each time the saint came out of his cell he found it in the same place, took it in his hands, and as soon as he told it to sing, it did. At the end of eight days, he said to his companions: "Let us now allow our sister cricket to go where she wants to. She has sufficiently delighted us and our flesh could find in her a reason for vainglory." Given permission to leave, the cricket then and there went away and was no longer seen. The companions admired her gentleness and obedience toward the saint. Blessed Francis found so much joy in creatures for love of the Creator that the Lord tamed the wild beasts to console the body and soul of his servant.

AN EXAMPLE FOR ALL THE BROTHERS

85   In those days, Blessed Francis was living at the hermitage of St. Eleutherius, not far from Contigliano, in the district of Rieti. Since he was wearing but one tunic and it was extremely cold, he was obliged to line the inside of it; so did his companion. His body felt some relief from this. A short time after, as he had just finished his prayer, overjoyed, he said to his companion: "I must be a model and an example to all the brothers. Therefore, although my body needs a lined tunic, I must think of my brothers who are experiencing the same need and who do not have or cannot procure for themselves a like tunic. I must therefore put myself in their place and share their privations, so that they may endure them patiently because they see the way I live."

We who lived with him cannot say how many numerous and urgent needs he refused his body, both in food and in clothing, in order to give good example to the brothers and thereby help them to bear their poverty more patiently. At all times, but especially when the brothers had multiplied and when he had resigned from his post as superior, blessed Francis' main concern was to teach the brothers, more by his actions than by words, what they ought to do and what they ought to avoid.

86   One day, noticing and learning that certain ones were giving a bad example in the Order and that the brothers were not maintaining themselves on the heights of their profession, Francis was painfully moved to the depths

of his heart and said to the Lord in his prayer: "Lord, I give you back the family you gave me."

The Lord answered him: "Tell me, why are you so sad when a brother leaves the Order or when others do not walk in the way I have shown you? Tell me, who planted the Order of the brothers? Who converts men and urges them to enter it to do penance? Who gives them the strength to persevere? Is it not I?" And the inner voice said to him: "In you I did not choose a scholar nor an orator to govern my religious family, but I wanted a simple man so that you and the others may know that I am the one who watches over my flock. I placed you in their midst as a sign,[144] so that they may see the works that I accomplish in you and so that they in turn may accomplish them. Those who follow my way possess me and will possess me even more fully, but those who wish to deviate from it will be despoiled of what they seem to have.[145] That is why I tell you not to be saddened about this; do what you have to do and do it well; apply yourself to your work, for I have planted the Order of the brothers in an everlasting charity. Know that I have so much love for this Order that, should one of the brothers return to his vomit and die outside the Order, I shall send another one to receive the crown destined for him; if he is not born yet, I shall see to it that he is. To convince you that I cherish the life and Order of the brothers with all my heart, I say to you that even if there were only three members, I would never abandon it."

87   These words greatly comforted blessed Francis, for he was extremely disconsolate when he learned that the brothers were giving a bad example. Although he could not help being saddened when he heard of some sin, he nevertheless recalled these comforting words of the Lord to mind and talked with his companions about them. In the chapters and even in his usual spiritual conferences[146] he

also said: "I resolved and swore to observe the rule; the brothers are also pledged to do so. Since I resigned my post as superior because of my sickness, for the greatest good of my soul and of my brothers, my only obligation to them is to give them good example. In fact, I learned from the Lord and know in an unquestionable way that, even if the sickness had not been a sufficient reason to retire, the greatest service I can render the Order is to pray to the Lord to govern, preserve, protect, and defend it.[147] I pledged myself to this before God and before the brothers: and I surely expect that I shall have to give an account to the Lord for every brother who is lost by my bad example."

When a brother came and told him that he, Francis, should be somehow involved in governing the Order, he answered: "The brothers have the rule which they swore to observe.[148] That they may have no excuse, I also swore before them, since the time it pleased the Lord to make me their superior, to observe it myself, and I wish to continue to do so until the end of my life. And so, since my brothers know what they have to do and to avoid, there remains for me only to preach to them by example, for that is why I was given to them during my lifetime and after my death."

RESPECT FOR THE POOR

88   As he was travelling one day through a province preaching, Francis met a poor man. Seeing this poor man's distress, he said to his companions: "This man's poverty puts us to shame and takes us to task for our poverty." His companions answered: "How is that, Brother?" "I am greatly ashamed," he said, "when I meet someone poorer than myself. I chose holy poverty and made her my Lady, my delight, my spiritual and temporal treasure. God and all mankind know that I profess poverty. I ought to blush for shame when I meet someone poorer than myself."

89   Once blessed Francis had gone to the hermitage of

the brothers near Roccabrizia[149] to preach to the people of that region. Now, on the day of the sermon, a poor, miserable and sick man came in search of him. Blessed Francis was moved by his distress and spoke to his companion of his poverty and sickness. His companion answered him: "Brother, it is true, he is very poor, but perhaps there is no other man richer in desire in all province than he." The saint chided him for having spoken so uncharitably, and the brother admitted his sin. Blessed Francis then said to him: "Are you willing to perform the penance I shall give you?" "Gladly," he said. "Well, take off your tunic and go and throw yourself half clothed at the feet of that poor man; tell him how you have sinned against him by disdaining him, and ask him to pray that God may forgive you." The brother went and did what blessed Francis had prescribed; then he got up, put his tunic back on and returned.

Blessed Francis said to him: "Do you want to know in what way you sinned against this poor man, or better still, against Christ himself? When you see a poor man, you must consider the one in whose name he comes, namely, Christ, who took upon himself our poverty and weakness. The poverty and sickness of this man are, therefore, a mirror in which we ought to contemplate lovingly the poverty and weakness which our Lord Jesus Christ suffered in his body to save the human race."

THE CONVERTED ROBBERS

90   In a hermitage of the brothers located north of Borgo San Sepolcro, robbers came periodically to ask the brothers for some bread; usually they hid in the tall forest which covers the region and sometimes they came out of it to rob travellers in the open country or on the highways. Certain brothers said: "It is wrong to give them alms, for they are robbers who inflict all sorts of evils on people." Others, seeing that they begged with humility and that neces-

sity drove them to this, gave them alms at times always encouraging them to be converted to penance.

Meanwhile, blessed Francis came to the hermitage. When the brothers asked him whether they should or should not give the robbers bread, he answered: "If you do what I am about to tell you, I have confidence in the Lord that you will win over their souls. Go and obtain some good bread and some good wine; bring them to the place where you know these men stay, and cry out: "Come out, brother robbers! We are brothers and we have brought you some good bread and some good wine." They will immediately come to you. Then, spread out a table cloth on the ground,[150] put the bread and wine on it, and serve them with humility and good humor. During and after the meal, you will propose the words of the Lord to them. Then make this first request of them for the love of God: make them promise you not to strike any man and not to harm anyone. That is only the beginning. Do not ask everything all at once; they would not listen to you. The robbers will promise you this because of the humility and the charity you have shown them. Another day, in gratitude for the good promise they have made to you, bring them in addition to bread and wine, some eggs and cheese, and serve them as you did the first time. After the meal, say to them: 'Why do you stay here all day long dying of hunger, suffering so much, doing so much evil in thought and in act? You will lose your souls if you are not converted to the Lord. It would be much better for you to serve God who will give you what you need for your bodies in this world and who in the end will save your souls.' And the Lord in his goodness will inspire them to be converted because of the humility and charity that you have shown them."

The brothers got up and did all that blessed Francis had counselled them to do. Through the mercy and grace of God, the robbers listened and fulfilled the brothers' requests one by one. Touched by their charity and affability, they even carried wood on their backs to the hermitage. By the mercy of God and thanks to the charity and goodness to which the brothers had given witness, some entered the Order, while others were converted to penance[151] and promised while holding the hands of the brothers, never to do evil in the future but to live by the work of their hands. The brothers of the hermitage and those who heard the good news were full of admiration as they considered the holiness of blessed Francis and the quick conversion of these faithless and lawless men, as foretold by him.

IMPOSTURE OF A BROTHER WHO PASSED FOR A SAINT

91   Once there was a brother who led a holy and exemplary life: he gave himself over to prayer night and day and observed silence so strictly that when he went to confession to a brother priest, he did so by signs, without saying a word. To all appearances he was full of piety and fervent love of God. For example, when he was with the brothers, even though he did not talk, he displayed such external and internal joy on hearing some pious conversation that he incited the brothers and all those who saw him to devotion. All were inclined to look upon him as a saint.

He had been living that way for several years when blessed Francis came to the friary where this brother was living. When Francis learned of his way of acting, he said to the brothers: "You may be sure that if he does not want to confess his sins, this is a temptation and a trick of the Devil." In the meantime, the minister general came to the friary to visit blessed Francis and he began to praise this brother. Blessed Francis said to him: "Believe me, Brother, this man is led and seduced by the evil spirit." The minister general answered: "I find it astonishing and almost unbelievable that a man who shows so many signs and proofs of holiness can be what you say he is." "Test him then," Francis replied, "by asking him to confess his sins twice or at least once a week. If he refuses, you will see that I am telling you the truth."

One day when the minister general was speaking to this brother, he said to him: "Brother it is my strict wish that you go to confession twice a week, or at least once a week." The other put a finger to his lips and shook his head, showing by gestures that he would do nothing of the kind. The minister did not insist for fear of scandalizing him. A few days later this brother left the Order of his own free will, returned to the world, and donned secular clothing.

One day, two of blessed Francis' companions met this man on the highway. He was walking all alone like a very poor pilgrim. With compassion they said to him: "Unfortunate man, where is the upright and holy life that you were leading? You did not want to show yourself nor speak to your brothers; the only thing you liked was the life of a solitary. And now you go through the world like a man who no longer wants to know either God or his servants." He answered them, but in doing so swore many times by the faith, like impious people do. The brothers said to him: "Unfortunate man, why do you swear by the faith that way, like impious men do, you who when you were in the Order not only abstained from useless words but even from upright conversation!" He answered them: "Things were bound to turn out this way."[152] They parted. A few days later, the man died. The brothers and the others were in admiration, considering the holiness of blessed Francis who had predicted his fall at a time when he was considered a saint by the brothers and by other men.

CONSOLATIONS AFTER DIABOLICAL PERSECUTIONS

92   Blessed Francis once went to Rome to pay a visit to the Lord Hugolino, bishop of Ostia, who later became pope. After a few days with him, he took leave of him and went to visit Lord Leo, cardinal of Holy Cross. This cardinal was very affable and courteous. He liked to meet blessed

Francis whom he greatly esteemed. With great devotion he begged him to spend a few days with him, for it was winter, the cold was very penetrating, and almost every day the wind and rain raged, as often happens during that season. "Brother," he said to him, "travelling is impossible in this weather. It is my wish, if it so pleases you, that you remain with me until the weather becomes favorable. Since I feed a certain number of poor people every day in my house, you will be treated as one of them." The lord cardinal spoke in this fashion because he knew that blessed Francis wanted to be received as a poor man wherever hospitality was offered him.[153] And yet his holiness was so outstanding that the lord pope, the cardinals, and the mighty of this world who knew him, respected him as a saint. The cardinal added: "I will give you a good, secluded lodging where you will be able to eat or pray as you wish."

Angelo Tancredi,[154] one of the first twelve brothers, was standing near the cardinal. He said to blessed Francis: "There is a beautiful, high, and spacious tower, not far from here, on the city wall, that has nine rooms. There you can isolate yourself as if you were in a hermitage." "Let us go and see it," the saint replied. It pleased him and, returning to the lord cardinal, he said to him: "Lord, I shall stay near you perhaps for a few days." The cardinal was very pleased. Brother Angelo had the tower prepared so that the saint could live there with his companion night and day, for he did not want to come down either during the day or during the night, for as long as he would be the cardinal's guest. Brother Angelo himself offered to bring them their meals which he would deposit outside, for neither he nor anyone else was supposed to enter. Blessed Francis went and took up his abode in the tower together with his companion.

Now, the first night, as he was getting ready to sleep, the devils came and trounced him soundly. He immediately called to his companion who was occupying a room some distance away. The brother jumped up and came to him. Blessed Francis said to him: "The devils, brother, have beaten me severely. I wish you would keep me company because I am afraid to stay alone." The brother remained close to him all night. Every bone in Francis' body was trembling. He was like a man victimized by a fever. Both of them remained awake until morning.

During all this time, blessed Francis talked with his companion and said to him: "Why did the devils beat me? Why did they receive permission from the Lord to hurt me?" And he continued his reflection in this manner: "The devils are our Lord's policemen. Just as the podestà sends his policemen to punish a guilty man, so too does the Lord correct and chastise those he loves through his policemen, that is, the devils whom he permits to do this work. It often happens that a religious, even the 'perfect'[155] religious sins through ignorance.[156] Since he is ignorant of his sin, he is chastised by the devil, so that this chastisement may serve as a lesson to him, and he may understand and attentively consider within himself how he has sinned. For to those whom the Lord tenderly loves here on earth, nothing remains unpunished.

"As for me, by the grace and goodness of God, I see no infraction from which I have not been purified by confession and satisfaction. In his goodness the Lord has revealed to me in prayer all that can please him or displease him. But it is possible, it seems to me, that the Lord had me chastised by his policemen for the following reason: Surely, the cardinal was spontaneously very generous in my behalf: undoubtedly, my body needs some consideration and I can accept it without remorse. And yet, my brothers who are going through the world, suffering hunger and all kinds of tribulations, living in small humble houses and in hermitages, on learning that I am the guest of the lord cardinal, could find in this a pretext to complain against me. They could say: 'While we are enduring all sorts of privations, he is enjoying every kind of comfort!' Now, I am always bound to give a good example; that is the reason why I was given to them. The brothers are more edified when I live with them in poor friaries; they bear their tribulations with more patience when they learn and know that I am eduring as much as they are."

The holy father had always been weak. Even in the world he had a frail and weak constitution, and his sickness worsened until the day of his death; but he always wanted to give a good example to the brothers and remove from them every pretext to complain and say: "He grants himself all that he needs, but we have nothing." Therefore, whether sick or well, he suffered so many privations until the day of his death that if all the brothers knew them, as we do who lived with him for a certain period of time until the end of his life, they would not be able to recall them to mind without shedding tears, and they would bear trials and privations with more patience.

Before daylight, blessed Francis came down from the tower, went and found the lord cardinal, told him all that had transpired and all that he had said to his companion. He added: "The people have great confidence in me and regard me as a saint; now, as you see the devils have thrown me out of my prison!" He wanted to remain in retreat in this tower as in a prison without speaking to anyone except his companion. The lord cardinal was exceedingly happy to see him again; but, because he regarded and respected him as a saint, he acquiesced to his will not to stay there any longer. Blessed Francis therefore took leave of him and went back to the hermitage of "St. Francis,"[157] at Fonte Colombo, near Rieti.

93   One day blessed Francis went to the hermitage of Mount La Verna. He liked its isolation so much that he wanted to keep a Lent there in honor of St. Michael. He had climbed the mountain before the feast of the Assumption of

the glorious Virgin Mary. He counted the days between this feast and that of St. Michael: there were forty. Then he said: "In honor of God, of the blessed Virgin Mary, his Mother and of blessed Michael, the prince of the angels and of souls,[158] I wish to observe a Lent here." He went into the cell he wanted to occupy during all that time; and during the first night, he prayed to God to show him by a sign if it was God's will that he live there. As a matter of fact, when blessed Francis stopped in a place to pray or when he was traveling through the world to preach, he was always concerned about knowing the will of God so that he might conform himself to it and please the Lord. He sometimes feared that, under pretext of withdrawing into solitude to pray, his body was in reality seeking only to escape from the fatigues of preaching throughout the world, this world for which Christ did not hesitate to come from heaven on earth. He also asked prayers of those who to him seemed to be friends of God, so that the Lord would make it known to him whether, to fulfill his will, he ought to go and preach to the people or withdraw himself to this solitary place to pray.[159]

He was still praying when dawn was breaking, and suddenly birds of all kinds came and perched on the cell in which he was staying. But they did not all come at the same time: first one came and sang his melodious song and withdrew; then another came, sang, and he, too, went away; and so on. For blessed Francis this was a cause of great admiration and consolation. As he was wondering what this meant, the Lord answered him interiorly: "It is a sign that God will give you many graces and consolations in this cell." And so it truly came to pass. In fact, among many other hidden or known graces which the Lord bestowed upon him, there is the vision of the seraph that filled his soul with consolation and united him closely to God for the remainder of his life. When his companions brought him his meal that day he told him what had happened.

He knew nothing but consolations in that cell, though he suffered from devils during the night and from many tribulations, as he himself related to his companion. One day he said to him: "If the brothers knew all that the devils make me endure, not one of them would refuse me his pity and compassion." These persecutions sometimes made it impossible for him to be completely at the disposal of the brothers and to show them his deep affection for them as often as he would have liked to.

94   In those days, blessed Francis was living at the hermitage of Greccio. He remained in the rear cell, behind the large room, praying day and night. Now, one night, shortly after he had retired to sleep, he called to the companion who was occupying the large and oldest room. He got up and went into the corridor at the entrance of the cell where blessed Francis was sleeping. The saint said to him: "Brother, tonight I can neither sleep nor stand up to pray,[160] for my head is swimming and my legs are shaking so much that one would say that I ate some wheat bread." His companion answered him with a few kind and soothing words.

Blessed Francis said to him: "I think the Devil is hiding in the pillow under my head." In fact, the day before, Lord John of Greccio, whom the saint loved very much and to whom he showed a great affection throughout his whole life, had bought a feather pillow for him. Now, ever since he had left the world, Francis wanted neither a mattress nor a feather pillow, even when he was sick or because of any other pretense. But this time, the brothers had compelled him to accept it against his will because of his very serious eye-sickness. He therefore threw the pillow at his companion.

The latter picked it up, put it on his left shoulder, held it there with his right hand, and left the corridor. He immediately lost his speech and could not take one step; he could move neither his arms nor hands, not even enough to get rid of the pillow. There he stood, like a man bereft of feeling, unconscious of what was taking place inside himself and about him. This lasted for well over an hour, when, thanks to God, blessed Francis called him. Immediately he came to himself, threw the pillow behind him and rejoined blessed Francis. When he had recounted his adventure, the holy Father said: "Tonight, while reciting compline I sensed that the Devil entered my cell." He was now certain that it was indeed the Devil who had prevented him from sleeping and from standing up to pray. He then said: "The Devil is full of craftiness and of wiles. Seeing that by the goodness and grace of God he cannot harm my soul, he attacks my body in order to prevent me from sleeping and from standing up to pray. He wants to stifle the fervor and joy in my heart, so that I will complain about my sickness."

REVERENT RECITATION OF THE OFFICE

95   Blessed Francis suffered a great deal for many years in his stomach, spleen, liver, and eyes. But he had so much fervor and prayed with so much reverence that he refused to lean against the wall or the partition while praying; he stood most of the time, with his capuche lowered. Sometimes, however, he did kneel. Thus he spent a great part of the day and night in prayer. And when he traveled on foot from place to place, he always stopped to recite the hours. If he was riding on horseback because of his continual infirmities, he dismounted to say his office.

When he left Rome, after the few days he spent with Lord Leo,[161] it began to rain as he was leaving the city and continued to do so all that day. Because of his weakness he went on horseback but, to recite his hours, he dismounted and stood on the road despite the rain which drenched him. He said: "If the body wishes to be at ease and relaxed when it takes nourishment that will become the prey of worms along with it, in what peace and serenity should not the soul takes its nourishment, God himself!"

BROTHER BODY

96   He further said: "The Devil exults when he can extinguish or impede the devotion and joy brought about by pure prayer or other good works in the heart of God's servant. If the Devil takes hold of a servant of God, and if the latter is not wise enough to eliminate this bond as soon as possible by confession, contrition, and satisfaction, it would be very easy for the Devil to take the slightest thing and turn it into an ever heavier burden."

He added: "In taking food, sleep, and the other necessities of the body, the servant of God must act with discretion so that Brother Body has no excuse to complain: 'I can neither stand up, remain a long time in prayer, nor preserve joy in my tribulations, nor perform other good works, for you do not give me what I need.' If, on the contrary, the servant of God provides for the necessities of his body with discretion by observing the golden mean, and if Brother Body is then lazy, negligent, or sleepy during prayer, vigils, and other good spiritual works, then it must be chastised like a bad-tempered and lazy beast of burden that wants to eat but refuses to work and carry its burden.

"And if destitution and poverty do not enable us to give Brother Body, whether sick or well, what it needs or what it has uprightly and humbly requested of its brother or superior for the love of God, then let Brother Body patiently bear its privations for the love of the Lord; the Lord will weigh them and will impute them to it as martyrdom. And since the brother did what depended on him, by explaining his situation, we cannot hold him responsible, even if the body would have to suffer grave consequences."

THE VIRTUE OF JOY

97   From the beginning of his conversion to the day of his death, blessed Francis had always been hard on his body. But his primary and main concern was always to

possess and preserve spiritual joy within and without. He declared that if the servant of God strove to possess and preserve interior and external spiritual joy, which proceeds from purity of heart, the devils could do him no harm, but would be forced to admit: "Since this servant of God preserves his joy in tribulation as well as in prosperity, we can find no way to harm his soul."

One day he reproved one of his companions who looked sad and downcast: "Why do you display the sadness and sorrow that you feel for your sins that way? It is a matter between you and God. Pray to him that in his goodness he give you the joy of salvation.[162] In my presence and in the presence of others, try to be always joyful, for it is not fitting that a servant of God appear before the brothers or other men with a sad and glum face."[163]

He also said: "I know that the devils envy me because of all the graces I have received from the goodness of the Lord. Since they cannot harm me directly, they try to do it in my companions. If they cannot strike either me or my companions, they withdraw full of confusion. Conversely, if I happen to be tempted and downcast,[164] I need only contemplate the joy of a companion and I go from the temptation and despondency to interior joy."[165]

THE BLESSING OF THE CITY OF ASSISI

98   One day when blessed Francis was confined to his bed by sickness in the episcopal palace of Assisi, a brother, a spiritual and holy man, said to him sportingly and jokingly: "For how much would you sell your old clothes to the Lord? Soon canopies and precious silks will cover this body now clothed in rags." At the time, because of his sickness, he was wearing a fur vest covered with rough homespun and a coarse tunic. Blessed Francis, or rather the Holy Spirit speaking by his mouth, answered in a great outburst of joy: "What you say is true; that's the way it will be."

99   While he was living in that palace, seeing that his sickness grew worse from day to day, he had himself carried on a stretcher to St. Mary of the Portiuncula. He could not have endured going on horseback, because it would have aggravated his very painful illness. Since those who were carrying him took the road that went past the hospital,[166] he told them to put the stretcher on the ground so that he would be facing Assisi. For all practical purposes he could no longer see by reason of his long and serious eye-sickness. Then he raised himself a little and blessed the city of Assisi saying:

"Lord, I believe that this city was formerly the refuge and abode of wicked and unjust men of evil repute throughout the country; but I also see that, by your superabundant goodness, at a time chosen by you, you have shown this city the riches of your love. It has become the abode and residence of those who know you as they should, who give glory to your name and diffuse the sweet fragrance of a pure life, a solid faith, and a good reputation among all Christian people. I therefore beg you, Lord Jesus Christ, Father of mercies,[167] do not look upon our ingratitude, but recall to mind the infinite love that you have shown to this city. May it always remain the abode and residence of those who will know and glorify your blessed and glorious name in the ages to come. Amen."

His prayer finished, they bore him to St. Mary of the Portiuncula.

OUR SISTER DEATH

100   From the day of his conversion to that of his death, blessed Francis, whether sick or well, was always solicitous to know and do the will of the Lord. One day one of the brothers said to him: "Father, your life and conduct have been and still are a torch and a mirror not only for your brothers but for the entire Church. It will be the same with your death. It will cause much sorrow and sadness to the

brothers and to countless others, but it will be an immense consolation and an infinite joy to you. You will, indeed, go from great labor to great repose, from an ocean of suffering and of temptations to eternal happiness. The strict poverty which you have always loved and voluntarily practiced from your conversion until the last day will be replaced by infinite riches, and temporal death by eternal life where you will see constantly and face to face the Lord your God, whom you have contemplated in this world with so much fervor, desire, and love."

He added without any dissimulation: "Father, know in truth that, if the Lord does not send from the height of heaven a remedy for your body, your sickness is incurable and, according to the doctors, you do not have much longer to live. I am warning you of this to comfort your spirit, so that you may constantly rejoice in God, inwardly and outwardly, and so that your brothers and those who are coming to visit you may find you joyful in the Lord. They know for certain that you are going to die soon, and your death, for those who witness it or will hear it described, must constitute a memory and an example, as your life and conduct have already been."

Then blessed Francis, despite the overpowering burden of his sickness, praised the Lord in a great joyful outburst of body and soul, saying to his companion: "Since I must soon die, have Brother Angelo and Brother Leo come and praise our Sister Death for me." Both arrived and, forcing back their tears, sang the Canticle of Brother Sun and of the other creatures, which the saint had composed during his sickness for the glory of God and for the consolation of his soul and of that of the others. Before the last strophe,[168] they added a few verses on our Sister Death to this canticle:

> All praise be yours, my Lord, through Sister Death,
>   From whose embrace no mortal can escape.
> Woe to those who die in mortal sin!

Happy those She finds doing your will!
The second death[169] can do no harm to them.

THE LAST VISIT OF "BROTHER JACOBA"

101   One day blessed Francis called his companions and
said to them: "You know how much Lady Jacoba di Settesoli has always been and still is attached to our Order.[170]
I believe that if you were to inform her of my condition
it would be a great kindness to her and a great consolation.
Write her to send you some of that grey-colored monastic
material for a tunic, like the one the Cistercians manufacture
in overseas countries. Have her also send some of that cake
that she prepared for me many times when I was in Rome."
The Romans called this cake made of almonds, sugar, or
honey and other ingredients *mostacciuolo*. The lady was a
very pious widow, related to the noblest and richest families
of Rome. Through the merits and preaching of blessed
Francis, she had received the gift of tears and fervor from
God, to the extent that she seemed to be another Mary Magdalen.

The letter had just been written, as the saint had requested, and they were about to appoint a brother to deliver it, when suddenly there was a knock at the door. A
brother went to open it, and there he found Lady Jacoba
who had hastened from Rome to visit blessed Francis, The
brother immediately returned to warn blessed Francis that
Lady Jacoba had arrived to see him, accompanied by her
son and several other persons. He said to Francis: "What
shall we do, Father? Shall we allow her to enter and come
to your bedside? As a matter of fact, by the will of the
saint, it had long been prescribed that for the honor and
dignity of this friary no woman was to enter the cloister.
Blessed Francis answered: "That rule is not applicable to
this lady whose great faith and devotion brought her from
so great a distance." Ushered into the room, she began to

weep profoundly. And marvel of marvels, she had brought a grey-colored shroud cloth with which to make a tunic, as well as everything she had been asked to bring in the letter. The brothers regarded with the keenest admiration the holiness of blessed Francis.

Lady Jacoba said to the brothers: "My brothers, I was about to begin to pray and in spirit I heard a voice say to me: Go and visit your father, blessed Francis. But hurry; do not lose a moment, for if you delay, you will not find him alive. You will bring the required quantity of cloth to make him a tunic, and the ingredients for a particular cake. In addition, take a large quantity of wax for light and some incense also."

Now, blessed Francis had not mentioned incense in the letter. But the Lord had inspired this lady to bring it to recompense her and console her soul and also that we might better know the great sanctity of this poor man whom the Lord wished to surround with so many honors at the moment of his death. He who had inspired the Magi to bring presents to honor the Infant, his well-beloved Son, at the time of his birth and poverty, also inspired this noble lady who lived so far away to come with presents to venerate and honor the body of his servant saint who cherished and loved the poverty of his well-beloved Son in life and in death with such love and fervor.

The lady made the cake the father had desired. But he hardly touched it, for with each day his strength waned, and he was nearing his end. She also had a great many candles made. These were to burn before the holy body after his death. With the material she brought, the brothers made for blessed Francis a tunic which served as a shroud. He himself ordered the brothers to sew sackcloth over it as a sign of most holy humility and poverty. And it so happened by the will of God that blessed Francis went to the Lord during the week Lady Jacoba had come.

HUMILITY AND OBEDIENCE

102   From the beginning of his conversion, blessed Francis, wise that he was, decided with the help of the Lord to build not only his own life but his house, that is, his Order, called the Order of the Friars Minor, firmly on a solid rock, namely, on the most exalted humility and poverty of the Son of God.

He built it on deep humility. That is why, from the very beginning, when the brothers began to multiply, he made it clear that they were to live in lazarets to serve the lepers. At that time, when postulants presented themselves, whether nobles or commoners, they were forewarned that among other things they would have to serve the lepers and live in their hospitals.[171]

He built the Order on most exalted poverty. We read in the rule[172] that the brothers must live in their houses "as pilgrims and strangers, and that they must desire nothing under heaven," except holy poverty; and for this the Lord will feed them in this world with bodily nourishment and virtues, and it will assure them heaven, their inheritance in the next life.

He also chose this foundation of perfect humility and poverty for himself. Even though he was an exalted person in the Church of God, of his own free will he wanted to be regarded as being on the lowest rung not only in the Church but even among his brothers.

103   One day when he was preaching to the people of Terni in the town square in front of the bishop's palace, the bishop of the city, a discerning and spiritual man, listened to the sermon. When it was over, he rose and among other words of exhortation said: "From the time he planted and built his Church, the Lord has always endowed her with holy persons to make her grow by word and example. And in these latter days, he has shed luster on her through this poor, humble, and unlettered man. (As he said this, he

1079

pointed his finger toward Francis). That is why you are bound to love and honor the Lord and to keep yourselves from all sin, for he has not bestowed such great favor on all nations."[173]

Then the bishop came down from the place where he had spoken to the people and entered his cathedral with blessed Francis. Then blessed Francis bowed before the lord bishop, threw himself at his feet and said to him: "In truth, lord bishop, I say to you: no man in this world has ever paid me the honor you have today. Other men say: He is a saint! Thereby they attributed glory and holiness to a creature and not to the Creator. You, on the contrary, as a discerning man, have made a distinction between what is base and what is precious."

104   When honors were lavished upon him and his sanctity was trumpeted, blessed Francis often replied: "I have no guarantee that I will never have sons or daughters." And he added: "If, at a certain moment, the Lord wanted to take away the treasure he has confided to me,[174] what would I have left? A body and a soul; the infidels have just as much. And I must even believe that if a robber or an infidel had received as many graces from the Lord as I have, he would be more faithful to God than I am."

He also said: "An artist who paints our Lord or the Blessed Virgin honors them and recalls them to our mind; nevertheless, the painting claims no other merit than what it is, a creation made of wood and color. God's servant is like a painting: a creature of God, through whom God is honored because of his blessings. He must not lay claim to any more merit than the wood and color do. Honor and glory must be given to God alone. The only thing we must retain for ourselves, as long as we live, is shame and confusion, for as long as we live, our flesh is always hostile to the grace of God."[175]

105   Blessed Francis wanted to remain humble among his brothers. In order to preserve the greatest humility, he resigned his post as superior a few years after his conversion on the occasion of a chapter held at St. Mary of the Portiuncula.[176] In the presence of all the brothers, he spoke as follows: "As of today and as far as you are concerned, I am dead. But here is Brother Peter Catanii whom all of us will obey." Then, all the brothers began to weep out loud and to shed abundant tears. Next, blessed Francis bowed before Brother Peter and promised to show him respect and obedience. From that time on, he was subject to him until his death, just as any one of the brothers.

106   Being subject to the minister general, he also wanted to be subject to the provincial ministers; in each of the provinces where he stayed or traveled to preach, he obeyed the minister of that province. And for even greater perfection and humility, he said one day, long before his death, to the minister general: "I wish always to have at my side one of my companions who will represent your authority for me and whom I shall obey as if I were obeying you. For the sake of good example and for love of the virtue of obedience, I wish that during my life and at the hour of my death you will in this way always be near me." From that time on and until his death, he always had one of his companions as his guardian[177] whom he obeyed as the minister general.

One day he said to his companions: "Among other graces, the Most High has given me the grace to obey a one-day-old novice, were he my guardian, as willingly as the foremost and oldest religious of the Order. The subject should, in fact, see in his superior not the man but God, for love of whom he subjects himself." He also said: "There is no superior in the whole world who would be afraid of his subjects and of his brothers as much as I, if God so willed it. But the Most High has given me the grace to accommodate myself to all, even to the humblest brother in the Order."

And we who lived with him often saw with our own eyes that frequently, as he himself bore witness, if some brother did not give him what he needed or spoke a harsh word to him, he immediately withdrew to pray. When he returned he did not want to remember anything and did not say: "Brother so-and-so neglected to take care of me or said such-and-such a thing to me." The closer he came to death, the more attentive he was in studying the best way of living and dying with utmost perfection, in absolute humility and poverty.

THE LAST BLESSING FOR BROTHER BERNARD

107   The day on which Lady Jacoba prepared the cake for blessed Francis, he remembered Brother Bernard and said to his companions: "That cake would please Brother Bernard." And speaking to one of them, he said: "Go and tell Brother Bernard to come here immediately." The brother left at once and brought Brother Bernard to him. He sat down at the foot of his bed and said: "Father, I beg you to bless me and to give me some evidence of your affection. If you manifest it to me with a fatherly tenderness, I believe that the other brothers of the Order and God himself will love me more for it."[178]

Blessed Francis could no longer see, for he had long lost his sight. He stretched out his hand and laid it on the head of Brother Giles, the third brother, who at the moment was close to Brother Bernard. Francis thought he was placing his hand on Brother Bernard's head. But in feeling, as the blind do, Brother Giles' head, he recognized his mistake through the power of the Holy Spirit and said: "That is not Brother Bernard." The latter drew closer to blessed Francis and he put his hand on his head and blessed him. Then he said to one of his companions: "Write what I am going to say. Brother Bernard was the first brother the Lord gave me.

He was the first one who put into practice and fulfilled the perfection of the gospel to the letter by distributing all his goods to the poor. For that and for many other merits, I am obliged to love him more than any other brother of the Order. I therefore wish and order, to the extent that lies in my power, that the minister general, whoever he is, cherish him and honor him as myself, that the ministers provincial and the brothers of the whole Order look upon him as taking my place." These words were a cause of great consolation to Brother Bernard and for all those who were present.

108   One day, blessed Francis, considering the very exalted perfection of Brother Bernard, prophesied regarding him in these words in the presence of a few brothers: "I say to you: the strongest and most subtle devils have been sent to Brother Bernard to test him. He will be harassed by them with countless torments and temptations. But the Lord, who is good, will deliver him, as death approaches, from all temptations and every interior and external trial. He shall establish his soul and body in such peace, serenity, and consolation that all the brothers who will witness this or will hear of it, will find a cause of great admiration in it and will consider it miraculous. It is in this peace and interior and external consolation that he will leave this world to go to the Lord."

For all those who had heard them, these words were a great cause of admiration, for all that blessed Francis had foretold under the inspiration of the Holy Spirit was fulfilled to the letter and point for point. As he approached death, Brother Bernard's spirit was so peaceful and tranquil that he did not want to stay in bed. If he agreed to do so, he remained almost seated, for he feared that the slightest vapor would go to his head and cause him to wander or dream, thereby diverting his thoughts from God. Sometimes when this did happen, he immediately got up and struck himself saying: "What happened? Why did I think of that?" To bring him around, they made him inhale rose water, as is customary. But being near death, he no longer wanted any, for he was constantly plunged in the meditation of God, and if anyone offered him some he said: "Do not disturb me!" Likewise, wishing to die relaxed, peaceful, and serene, he abandoned all attention to his body to a brother who was a physician and who was taking care of him. He said to him: "I do not want to concern myself any longer with drinking and eating; I entrust that care to you. If you give me something, I'll take it; if you do not, I will not bother."

From the day he fell sick, he wanted a brother priest at his side until the hour of his death. And when a thought came into his mind for which his conscience reproached him, he immediately confessed it and acknowledged his sin. After his death, his flesh became white and soft, and he seemed to smile. He appeared to be more handsome than in life, and those who looked at him found more pleasure in looking at him dead than they did when he was alive; for, he seemed to them to be a saint with a smiling face.

A PREDICTION FOR SISTER CLARE

109   During the week in which blessed Francis died, Lady Clare, the first little plant of the Order of Sisters, abbess of the Poor Ladies of San Damiano of Assisi, emulator of St. Francis in the continual observance of the poverty of the Son of God, was also very sick and was fearful of dying before blessed Francis. She wept bitterly and could not console herself at the thought of not seeing him again before his death, her only father next to God, her interior and external comfort, he who was the first one to establish her solidly in the grace of the Lord. She made this known to the saint through the intermediary of a brother.

On hearing this, Frarncis was moved with compassion; for he loved Clare and her sisters with a paternal affection for the saintly life they were leading and because it was he who with the grace of God had converted her by his advice, shortly after the arrival of the first brothers. Her conversion greatly edified not only the Order of the brothers but the whole Church. Since Francis could not grant her desire to see him again, because both of them were sick, he sent her in writing, for her consolation, his blessings and absolution from all the infractions of his orders and desires, and of the orders and desires of the Son of God. Furthermore, to rid her of all sadness and console her in the Lord, he said to the brother she had sent, or rather the Holy Spirit said it through his mouth: "Go and bring this letter to Lady Clare. You will tell her to banish the sorrow and sadness she experiences at the thought of never seeing me again. Let her know, in truth, that before she dies she and all her sisters will see me again and will receive great consolation from me."

A short while later, blessed Francis died during the night. In the morning, the people of Assisi, men and women and all the clergy, came in search of his body in the friary. To the chant of hymns and canticles, holding green palms in their hands, they bore him by the will of God to San Damiano, so that the word the Lord had spoken by the mouth of his saint might be fulfilled and that his daughters and servants might be consoled. The iron grill of the window through which the sisters received Holy Communion and heard the word of God was pulled back; the brothers lifted up the body of blessed Francis from the stretcher and held it in their arms before the opening for at least a minute. Lady Clare and her sisters experienced a very great consolation from this. Nevertheless they wept bitterly and felt great pain; for, next to God, the holy Father was their one and only consolation in this world.

THE LARKS

110   Saturday night after Vespers, before nightfall,

when blessed Francis went to God, a flock of larks assembled above the roof of the house where he was lying in bed. They were flying rather low and turned in circles as they sang. We who lived with blessed Francis and who have written these memoirs bear witness that many times we heard him say:

"If I could talk to the emperor, I would beg him, for the love of God, to grant my prayer and to publish an edict forbidding anyone from trapping our sisters the larks or from inflicting any harm on them. Furthermore, all the podestàs of the cities, all the lords of castles and of villages ought to oblige their subjects every year on the day of the Nativity of the Lord to throw wheat or other grain on the roads outside the cities and towns so that on this great solemnity the birds and especially our sisters the larks would have food. I would also like, out of respect for the Son of God, that on this great night the [statue of the] blessed Virgin Mary would be placed at the manger between the ox and the ass, and that everyone be obliged to give our brothers the oxen and the asses a generous amount of feed. On Christmas day, finally, all the poor ought to be invited by the rich to a lavish meal."

As a matter of fact, blessed Francis had a greater respect for the solemnity of Christmas than for the other feasts of the Lord. Our salvation is effected in the other feasts but, he said, from the day our Savior was born it became certain that we would be saved! And so on this day he wanted every Christian to exult in the Lord, and, for love of him who gave us the gift of himself, joyfully to give handsome presents not only to the poor but also to the domestic animals and birds.

He said of the lark: "Our Sister Lark wears a capuche like a religious. It is a humble bird that goes freely along the roads in search of a little grain. Even if she finds some in horse-dung, she pecks at them and eats them. As she flies, she praises the Lord, like those good religious who despise earthly things and whose life is in heaven.[179] In addition, her raiment, that is, her plumage, is earth-colored. In this way she gives good example to religious who ought not to wear garish and choice garments, but dark colored like the ground." For all these reasons, blessed Francis dearly loved and freely contemplated our sisters the larks.[180]

THE RULE AND POVERTY

111   Blessed Francis often repeated the words: "I was never a robber: by that I mean that for the alms which are the inheritance of the poor, I have always accepted less than I needed so that I would not defraud the other poor. To act otherwise would be to steal."

112   Since the ministers general urged blessed Francis to grant the right of ownership, at least in common, so that such a large number of brothers would have a reserve in case of need, the saint appealed to Christ in his prayer and consulted him on this point. The Lord immediately responded that the community as well as the individual members must be completely poor; for, the brothers compose its family and, no matter how numerous it is, he would take care of it as long as it had confidence in him.

113   Since blessed Francis had withdrawn to a mountain with Brother Leo of Assisi and Brother Bonizzo of Bologna to write the rule (the first one, dictated by Christ, had been lost), many ministers assembled around Brother Elias, the saint's vicar, and said to him: "We have learned that this brother Francis is composing a new rule. We are afraid that he will make it so difficult that we will not be able to observe it. You will go and find him and tell him that we refuse to be obligated to this rule. He may write it for himself, but not for us." Brother Elias told them that he would not go because he feared the reproaches of Francis. But since they insisted, he told them that in any case he would not go without them. And they all left together.

When Brother Elias, escorted by the ministers, arrived near the retreat of blessed Francis, he called to him. Francis answered and, noticing the ministers, asked: "What do these brothers want?" Elias answered: "They are ministers who have learned that you were writing a new rule and, fearing that it will be too difficult, say and solemnly declare that they do not want to be bound by it; you may write a rule for yourself, but not for them."

Blessed Francis turned his face heavenward and, addressing Christ, said: "Lord, did I not tell you that they would not have confidence in you?" The voice of Christ was immediately heard in the air: "Francis, nothing in the rule comes from you; everything in it comes from me. I wish this rule to be observed to the letter, to the letter, to the letter, without gloss, without gloss, without gloss." And the voice added: "I am aware of human weakness, but I also know the help I wish to give it. Let those who do not want to observe the rule leave the Order!"

Blessed Francis turned toward the brothers and said: "Did you hear? Do you want me to have it repeated?" And the ministers withdrew totally ashamed and striking their breasts.

114   Since blessed Francis was at the general chapter of St. Mary of the Portiuncula, called the Chapter of Mats, attended by five thousand brothers, several among them, wise and learned men, approached the lord cardinal, the future Pope Gregory, who was present.[181] They asked him to persuade blessed Francis to follow the advice of the learned brothers and to let himself be directed by them. And they appealed to the rules and teachings of St. Benedict, St. Augustine, and St. Bernard.

Blessed Francis listened to the admonition of the cardinal on this subject, then took him by the hand, led him before the assembled chapter and spoke to the brothers in these terms: "My brothers, my brothers, God called me to walk in the way of humility and showed me the way of simplicity. I do not want to hear any mention of the rule of St. Augustine, of St. Bernard, or of St. Benedict. The Lord has told me that he wanted to make a new fool[182] of me in the world, and God does not want to lead us by any other knowledge than that. God will use your personal knowledge and your wisdom to confound you; he has policemen to punish you, and I put my trust in him. Then to your shame you will return to your first state, whether you like it or not!" The cardinal, dumbfounded, kept silence, and all the brothers were gripped by fear.

115   One day, certain brothers said to blessed Francis: "Father, do you not see that the bishops sometimes refuse us permission to preach and thereby oblige us to remain several days doing nothing in a region before we can speak to the people? It would be desirable to obtain a privilege from the lord pope for the friars for the salvation of souls."

He answered them vehemently: "You, Friars Minor, do not know the will of God and you do not let me convert the whole world as God wishes. You must first convert the prelates by your humility and your respectful obedience. When they see the holy life that you lead and the respect that you show them, they themselves will ask you to preach and convert the people; they will bring you your audience better than the privileges for which you clamor and which will lead you into pride. If you are despoiled of all cupidity, if you lead their people to respect the rights of their churches, the bishops will ask you to hear the confessions of their people. Furthermore, this concern should not be yours, because if sinners are converted, they will find many confessors. For myself, the privilege I ask of the Lord is never to be indebted to any man but to be subject to all and to convert the entire world in conformity with the holy rule more by example than by word."

116   One day, our Lord Jesus Christ said to Brother Leo, a companion of blessed Francis: "I have regrets regarding the brothers."

"Why, Lord?"

"For three reasons. First, because they are not grateful for the blessings that I give them generously every day by procuring their nourishment without their having to sow or reap. Secondly, because they complain all day long and do nothing. Thirdly, because they provoke each other to anger, do not return to charity, and do not forgive the injuries they have received."

THE PARALITURGY OF THE LAST SUPPER AND DEATH

117   One night, blessed Francis was so weighed down with sickness and pain that it was almost impossible for him to lie down and sleep. In the morning, since the pains had lessened somewhat, he had all the brothers of the friary summoned. When they were assembled before him, he considered them as representing the brothers of the whole Order. Then, beginning with one brother,[183] he blessed them all by putting his right hand on the head of each one. He also blessed all those who were living in the Order or who were to enter it until the end of the world. He seemed to have compassion for himself because he could not see his sons and brothers before dying.

Then, he had breads brought in and he blessed them. Since he was too weak to break them himself, he had them broken by a brother, took the pieces and gave one to each of the brothers, recommending that they eat all of it and not keep any of it. Following the example of the Lord who on Holy Thursday wanted to eat with his apostles before dying, blessed Francis, it seems, not only wanted to bless all the brothers present and in their person the whole Order, but also to eat this blessed bread with them as if they were eating it in the company of all the brothers. We may well believe that such was his intention for, although it was not a Thursday, blessed Francis had said to the brothers that he thought it was Thursday.

One of the brothers kept one of the pieces of bread and after blessed Francis' death all those who ate some of it were immediately cured of their sicknesses.

NOTES

1. The exact location of Rivo Torto has not yet been established. It is quite probable that it was situated on the road to Foligno, about one mile from the Portiuncula.
2. Mt. 9, 13 and 12, 7. Citation from Os. 6, 6.
3. Francis also obliged Brother Albert of Pisa to eat twice as much (Eccleston, *De Adventu*, 14; cf. P. Hermann, *XIIIth Century Chronicles*, p. 117).
4. Perhaps at the Chapter of Mats; 3 S 59; Fior 18.
5. A statement that will be repeated in the next number and which confirms 1 C 3.
6. Even if there is no allusion here to the Easter meal at Greccio (2 C 61), this episode sheds light on the comportment of the brothers and Francis' reaction as described here by his companions.
7. *Pitantia,* a word from the monastic vocabulary; literally, it means extra food, an overfeeding; then, a special diet in general. The English word "pittance," meaning a small portion, is derived from it.
8. A statement repeated several times by St. Francis; cf. *infra,* n. 92.
9. Cf. 2 Kgs. 6, 3.
10. Cf. Kgs. 9, 6, 10.
11. Despite the Biblical allusion: Mk. 4, 8 (which undoubtedly influenced the copyist of LP) we nevertheless prefer to read *offeret* rather than *afferet*: the logic of the reasoning is better expressed and the text becomes more conformable to Sp 18 and to the *Leg. Vetus* (DFA, II, 94).
12. Test. 14.
13. Mt. 6, 34.
14. The order of the paragraphs must have been disrupted. The reference here cannot be to Rivo Torto: first of all, the incident took place near a church, and secondly, the brother is already "old in the Order." Celano (2 C 176) and St. Bonaventure (LM 10, 5) say the incident took place at the Portiuncula. Cf. Sp 28.
15. At the Portiuncula (cf. preceding number).
16. Guido II, the same one who presided at St. Francis' total renunciation: 1 C 14.
17. By the special companion whom Francis had at his "hermitage."

18. The same formula as in no. 5. Is it the same brother? Could it be Brother Bernard (no. 108 below) or even the scrupulous Leo?

19. Concerning the abbey San Benedetto of Mt. Subasio, cf. *Ombrie franciscaine*, pp. 5 and 99-100.

20. Here we are back in the period of Rivo Torto.

21. Today we would say "motherhouse." The abbot perhaps remembered that Francis had repaired this chapel. 1 C 21.

22. Allusion to the failure of the previous requests in which Francis discerned the direct action and will of God, and not the avarice of men.

23. Cf. Mt. 7, 24.

24. Nothing of the kind is found in the Testament of St. Francis.

25. Every year for the chapter of Pentecost (see the following no.).

26. Cf. Herm 3 and also the Rule of St. Benedict (67, PL 66, 914).

27. Beginning with this word there is a lacuna in the ms.; the reconstruction is according to Bartholi, *Tractatus de indulgentia,* chap. 3. Likewise all of paragraphs 11 and 12 up to "the noise that the brothers were making at their work" is a restoration according to the Little ms.

28. For the periodicity, cf. J. de Vitry, *Letter* of October 1216 (ed. R.B.C. Huygens, Leiden, 1960, p. 75); for the place. cf. 1 Kgs. 18, 2. (Its final redaction dates from 1221.)

29. By comparing this with Sp 8, we can conjecture that the reference is to Brother Elias.

30. Celano is more specific: the hermitage of Sarteano (2 C 59).

31. Mt. 8, 20; cf. 2 C 56.

32. Lk. 22, 22.

33. Cf. Test 24. — This last paragraph which closes no. 13 in the AFH edition is the first of no. 14 in the Paris edition.

34. Cf. Test 24 and '2 Kgs. 6, 2.

35. Compare with Adm 26, 1 Let 33, etc.

36. This is the only testimony we have on the existence and activity of this brother (moreover his origin is diversely pointed out in the parallels: Prato, Piratro . . .). Brother Leo, secretary, confessor, and the usual chaplain, was probably absent. — Brother Pacificus was present at the scene: cf. 2 C 137.

37. He blessed . . . he recommended . . . he cursed . . . : the blessing, exhortation and curse of St. Francis in some friaries follows the reading of the rule in the refectory and at the chapter.

38. We might also translate this as: the salvation of their soul.

39. The expression is taken up again a little farther on. For St. Francis this virtue is the sister of "Queen Wisdom"; cf. SV 1.

40. Pontifical; admonition of the bishop to the future subdeacons, before taking the "step." — Missal, Postcommunion of the

Notes, Legend of Perugia

Mass for Peace. — *Glossa interlin.,* ad Rm. 1, 1 in Nicholas of Lyra, *Biblia sacra,* T. 6, Venice, 1588, fol. 3 v. The expression is also found in a letter attributed to St. Leo: *Ad Demetriadem,* PL 55, 165.

41. Mt. 17, 20.

42. This information takes us back to a very early date and would justify Fr. Delorme's hypothesis that "Peter Catanii was minister general of the friars earlier than is commonly believed" (Sept. 29, 1220, until March 10, 1221, the date of his death).

43. Trevi was destroyed by Diebold of Sweinspeunt, duke of Spoleto in Sept. 1213. Ceded to Foligno in 1215, it was then rebuilt. Pacificus' vision took place therefore in 1214 (AFH XX, 483). Cf. J. Cambell, *I Fiori,* 404.

44. Cf. Adm. 10, 2.

45. Cf. 2 Cor. 12, 2.

46. Regarding this "Perilous Throne," we should remember that "the Italians read the story of the Grail directly from the French text before reading it in the Italian version." A. Viscardi, "La Quête du Saint-Graal dans les romans du m. â. italien," *Lumière du Grall* (Cahiers du Sud, Paris, 1951), p. 277.

47. Michael's battle against Lucifer. Ap. 20, 2-4, and Jude 9. Here we also have the frequent theme of "decimus ordo" called to fill the places left empty by the fallen angels: cf. Y. Congar, "Aspects ecclésiologiques de la querelle entre Mendiants et Séculiers, *AHDLMA* 28, 1961, 129 (Paris, Vrin, 1962). And patristic references in Y. Lefèvre, *Elucidarium et les lucidaires,* (Paris, 1953), pp. 114, 118.

48. Who was perhaps a physician and of distant Arab origin; but he was a canon of Rieti and probably lived in the episcopal palace: cf. Fortini, *Nuova Vita,* 1 b., pp. 304-306.

49. Cf. Lk. 16, 8.

50. For the praise of God: Ps. 150; for consolation and peace of soul: 1 Kgs. 16, 23.

51. The "Lauds of God" for Brother Leo, or the "Lauds of the Lord" that follow the *Our Father,* or more likely the Canticle of the Creatures (cf. *infra,* no. 43). SP 121 says that during his last two years he often had these "Praises of the Lord" sung to him to the great scandal of Brother Elias.

52. This does not necessarily mean that this brother musician was a native of Rieti. Brother Pacificus' renown was so well known that it could have reached that city. The fact that this paragraph follows the episode of the vision of the throne led to the thought that the reference is indeed to the "king of poets" (Fr. Cambell detaches this paragraph and adds it to paragraph 85).

53. 2 Cor. 1, 4.

54. Three miles to the north of Rieti.

55. "He remained there from June 23, 1225, to Jan. 31, 1226." A. Potthast, *Regesta Romanorum pontificum,* nos. 7434-7526. Cardinal Hugolino was one of the members of the Curia (1 C 99).
56. The same statement at the end of no. 44.
57. Cf. Mt. 14, 31.
58. A translation of the restoration proposed by Cambell: *pastillis cammarorum* instead of *mastillis gymarorum* in the text.
59. This very likely takes us back to the days when St. Francis was still minister general.
60. Fr. Cambell interprets *De Luca* as the name of a family (rather than the name of the city) and points out that the first Franciscan tertiary (who died the same day as his wife, like the hero of the preceding paragraph) was called Lucensis or Luchesio.
61. Cf. Acts 5, 3.
62. It is perhaps not without interest to point out here the remark of a contemporary gastronomic reporter, Salimbene: "A large, live pike was offered to the King (St. Louis). In *France,* pike enjoys the reputation of a very fine fish of great value." *Chronique,* MGH SS, 32, and P. Hermann, *XIIIth Century Chronicles,* p. 238.
63. The reference here is perhaps to Gerard of Modena. The same Salimbene gives us some precious information regarding him. *Chronique,* MGH SS, 32, 75.
64. Probably Brother Leonard of Assisi: 2 C 31.
65. Probably Brother Riccerio. There are similar episodes in 2 C 44bis and 45.
66. In 2 C 61 and LM 7, 9, it was the feast of Easter.
67. The sentence that follows presents a confusion of ideas and syntactical blunders that makes the translation difficult. Yet it is important for the history of the Third Order to which no. 27 already alluded. We note here a few traits that are in common with the "Beguine convents."
68. Cf. 2 P 2, 22.
69. What is in brackets is taken from the Cambell edition and not from Delorme.
70. Cf. 2 C 36, n. 5.
71. 2 C 37 points out that on leaving his cell at Greccio (of which mention has just been made) Francis went to Perugia.
72. "And still divides," according to Sp 105.
73. The abbot of St. Justin of the diocese of Perugia, according to 2 C 101.
74. Cf. Test. 3.
75. Ps. 77, 3.
76. The crypt where the relics of the saints are preserved and venerated.

77. At Poggio Bustone and around Christmas, according to 2 C 131.
78. Cf. 1 Kgs. 2, 14; 2 Kgs. 2, 16; Test. 16.
79. Brother Elias: 1 C 98.
80. Do we have here an additional reminder of epic literature and of the sharing of lands conquered by the knights or does the comparison refer simply to the reigning emperor?
81. The text here is in the singular; the entire paragraph goes on to speak of the "Praises of the Lord" in the plural, as the title of the Canticle of the Creatures. The adjective *new* suggests that this was a literary genre cultivated several times by St. Francis (cf. *supra*, no. 24); but the only text we have in the vernacular is the one in question here.
82. Cf. Adm 21, 2.
83. This is a turn of phrase habitual with St. Francis. Cf. for example, Adm 6, 3.
84. The same statement was made above: the end of no. 25.
85. Another obscure sentence with muddled statements. We do not know whether the fact of their conversion in the early days of the Order is: the reason why Francis desired to send them his last will and testament; an additional motive for them to live in charity; or a reason for the brothers to be joyful and edified. . . . Nothing, however, prevents us from interpreting the sentence as applying not to the sisters among themselves but to the relationship between the two Orders: a recalling to mind of the old bonds and the permanent duties of service and charity.
86. Springtime. Cf. no. 42.
87. Who wished to be present for the operation; cf. *supra*, no. 42.
88. A recollection of the playful humor of St. Lawrence as he was burning on the grill: "The meal is done, turn and eat." St. Ambrose has transmitted it to us (*De off.* 1, 41); Prudentius put it in verse in his *Peristephanon*; it found its way into the divine office (Antiphon of the Magnificat); and it can be found in all the sermons and in all the Passions of St. Lawrence. Cf. E.R. Curtius, *La Littérature européenne et le m. â. latin* (Paris, 1956), Excursus, IV-4, p. 525.
89. This could also be translated as follows: as if they could hear what he said to them about God, understand him, and answer him.
90. 1 Cor. 10, 4.
91. Ps. 27, 5.
92. *Deus ab omnibus laudaretur.* Here as in Sp 118, we have an authorized interpretation of the Canticle of the Creatures; the passive *Laudato Si* indicates that men (understood) give praise to God and not the creature whose name is introduced at each strophe by the preposition *through*.

93. Probably Brother Elias and Brother Angelo.
94. 1 Jn. 4, 8 and 16.
95. Cf. *supra,* no. 40.
96. Bernard and Peter. The third, who will be mentioned next, was Giles. And he is perhaps the source, if not the redactor of no. 55. (The reader will find an amplification in the *Life of Blessed Giles,* chap. 1, in which the author — Brother Leo? — has also put in the mouth of Francis a parable of the emperor and of his servant that resembles the vision of no. 43).
97. Jb. 31, 18.
98. A canon, according to 2 C 41.
99. Difficult to interpret literally in view of the state of the sick man as described above. This is a typical cliché, using an external and corporal gesture to express an inner attitude.
100. 2 Pt. 2, 22.
101. Mt. 12, 45.
102. The conclusion of the narrative, which is missing in the Perugian ms., is found in 2 C 41: "One evening after he had dined in the home of another of his fellow canons and was sleeping there that night, suddenly the roof of the house fell upon all of them. But the rest escaped death and only that wretched man was cut off and perished."
103. About twenty miles.
104. Satriano, according to 2 C 77.
105. Raoul of Houdenc (1170-1230 c.), in his *Roman des Ailes,* which is, as it were, a catechism of chivalry, teaches that no one will excel if his prowess does not possess these two wings: to the right, the wing of largesse, and to the left the wing of courtesy. This notion and doctrine were current at the time: A. Micha, "Une source latine du Roman des Ailes," *RMAL* 1 (1945), 305-309.
106. The same parable as in no. 3, but for an object worth a penny one would offer a hundred times its value. The repetition of the theme and the variety of the constituent parts proves that this was a comparison dear to Francis.
107. Cf. 2 Kgs. 6, 4.
108. *Your poor:* the Order had been entrusted to Cardinal Hugolino who was "the governor, master, protector, and corrector of the whole fraternity": 2 Kgs. 12, 3, and Test. 33. — To Francis' way of thinking, he took the place of the "pope": this is the meaning of the expression *apostolicus noster* which he uses a little farther on.
109. Cf. *supra,* no. 59.
110. Cf. 1 C 109.
111. In the Delorme edition: Finiato; — in different mss.: Welcome.
112. Lk. 18, 19. — The chronicler Salimbene, whose original name was Ognibene: All-well, recounts that he, too, and for the

same reason, was renamed by the last brother to whom St. Francis had given the habit of the Order. *Chronica,* MGH SS, 32, p. 38.

113. Mt. 23, 9-10.
114. Paragraphs 66-77 form the *Intentio Regulae.* — Rizzerio (Riccieri, Roger), born at Mussia not far from Camerino, died in 1236. He was one of the two students converted at Bologna by a sermon of St. Francis (was it in 1213 or in 1218 or perhaps in 1222, in the course of a famous sermon witnessed by Thomas of Spalato? Cf. Test. Min.). On Rizzerio, read the Fior. 27.
115. Lk. 12, 32.
116. Mt. 25, 40, 45.
117. 1 Kgs. 6, 3.
118. Perhaps at the Lateran Council in 1215. Unless *in concilio* is to be taken to mean: according to his counsel, since certain mss. do have the reading *in consistorio.*
119. Test. 23. — Certain paragraphs of the Legend of Perugia, such as this one, seem to have been composed according to the same laws as the Razos, borrowing from the works of the troubadours a few autobiographical elements that were then presented in a historical fashion in the redaction of a coherent biography. Cf. J. Boutière and A.H. Schutz, *Biographies des Troubadours* (Toulouse-Paris, 1950).
120. Cf. Is. 55, 11.
121. Lk. 9, 3.
122. *Loculos,* with all that the word implies, in the mind of St. Francis, of badly acquired wealth and of appropriation of all sorts of goods, the spirit of independence, of egoistic knowledge, and of self-will.
123. Compare with Rom. 1, 21.
124. The anecdote is thus delimited in time: the novitiate was instituted on Sept. 22, 1220, by the Bull *Cum secundum consilium* of Honorius III. — The minister general was probably Brother Elias.
125. SV 1.
126. Test. 13.
127. Cf. Mt. 13, 12.
128. Mt. 25, 23.
129. 1 Kgs. 2, 5; Is. 54, 1.
130. Literally, his collations. It is the traditional word for spiritual reading in common, at local chapters, either in ancient monasticism (cf. the *Collations* of Cassian) or among the Friars Minor where they left written traces in the Admonitions of St. Francis.
131. Adm 6, 3.
132. 1 Cor. 8, 1.

133. Mk. 4, 11.
134. 2 Kgs. 2, 14-15.
135. Lk. 6, 44 and cf. Adm 7.
136. Verse 24. But wood and mud are not mentioned there. Cf. *supra,* nos. 13-16.
137. At the beginning and at the end of which prayer? Of the *Our Father* itself which has just been mentioned? Or of silent prayer in common? Or of the canonical hours and of the Office of the Blessed Virgin, which St. Francis himself said if we are to believe the rubric of these same praises of God, mentioned at the end of no. 78.
138. Another reading: across the mountains.
139. This reputation of Francis is sometimes tied in with the Eucharistic movement of Liège. Its protagonist was St. Julian of Mont-Cornillon (1191-1258). But in addition to the fact that Liège belonged at the time to the Empire, it was only around 1230 that the recluse made his revelations known and in 1246 that the feast of Corpus Christi was instituted.

    If we want a few precise facts to explain St. Francis' statement, we can, if the worst comes to the worst, point out: (1) that the saint was present at the death of Innocent III in 1216 (Eccleston, *De Adventu,* 15) and (2) there met Cardinal Jacques de Vitry, the fervent biographer of St. Mary of Oignies (+1213), a promoter of Eucharistic worship. (Cf. O. Van Rieden, *Das Leiden Christi im Leben des hl. Fr.,* Rome, 1960, who believes that the epistolary campaign of St. Francis in behalf of the Eucharist can be dated from that time.

    But there is also a current of "French" thought and a group of "French" facts:

    Liturgical: the use of the sanctuary lamp which became general around the end of the twelfth century; the showing and elevation of the Host confirmed by the synodal decrees of Eudes of Sully, the bishop of Paris from 1197 to 1208.

    Literary: either in Latin: a truly extraordinary flowering of treatises on the Body and Blood of Christ. J. de Ghellinck, art. "Eucharistie au XII siècle en Occident," DTC; — or in French: cf. D.C. Hontoir, ocr, *"La Queste del Saint Graal," Studia Eucharistica,* (Anvers, 1946), 132-55.

    Lastly, miraculous (and these perhaps had the greatest influence): from the time of the miracle of St. Yves de Braine in the diocese of Soissons (in 1153) which caused considerable stir, we know of numerous Eucharistic miracles: cf. E. Dumoutet, *Corpus Domini* (Paris, 1942), pp. 117-25. St. Thomas even devoted an article to them in his *Summa* (IIIa, q. 76, art. 8).

    On this question, see *Dict. Spirit,* art. *France,* col. 873, and

A. Callebout, "Autour de la rencontre à Florence de s. Fr. et du card. Hugolin," *AFH* 19 (1926), pp. 530-40.

140. 2 Let 4-5 and 11; Test 11-13.
141. Cf. Herm 4.
142. Brother Pacificus came, therefore, to Francis in 1217; he founded the first Franciscan friary of France at Vézelay, known by the name of La Cordelle.
143. Cf. Lk. 19, 14.
144. Ct. 8, 6 and Ag. 2, 23.
145. Mt. 13, 12 and Lk. 8, 18-26.
146. Cf. *supra*, no. 71.
147. Missal: the oration for the *Asperges.*
148. Compare with Lk. 16, 29; "They have Moses and the prophets."
149. Cf. Sp 37, n. 1.
150. A luxury that St. Francis had begrudged his brothers one Easter or Christmas: nos. 32-33.
151. Is this the formula indicating entrance into the "Third Order"?
152. This could also be translated: "I cannot help swearing."
153. Cf. *supra*, no. 61.
154. Possibly Brother Angelo of Rieti. He may have been one of the redactors of a few other paragraphs of the Legend of Perugia, if not of this one.
155. The spiritual life was often presented as comprising three stages: beginners, those making progress, and the "perfect."
156. This was another current theory. There were three ways of sinning: through weakness, ignorance, and malice. Each species was related to one of the Persons of the Trinity according to Mt. 12, 32. Cf. *Liber de modo bene vivendi*, chap. 26, *De Peccato*, PL. 184, 1246.
157. Sic, as *supra*, no. 57.
158. A twofold statement based on Scripture and the liturgy, as St. Francis often did: prince of the angels, Dn. 10, 13; leader of the heavenly army, Apoc. 12, 7; prince of the souls he leads into paradise: Offertory of the Mass of the Dead.
159. Other examples: *supra*, no. 79, and especially LM 12, 2.
160. Standing: see the beginning of no. 95. — For the symptoms of the sickness, cf. 2 C 64.
161. Cf. *supra*, no. 92.
162. Ps. 51, 14.
163. Father Delorme says in a note regarding this last word: "I very much question the reading *turbulentum* of 2 C 128." Yet it probably is a quotation from Is. 42, 4.
164. *Acidiosus*: spiritual laziness or disgust of good and of God was considered at that time as one of the capital sins.
165. "Since the scribe left the remainder of fol. 124 blank, the integral text of the LP given in section III by the ms. of Perugia ends here. For its range and importance it deserved to

receive primary importance. Of sections I (a mixture of non-homogeneous narratives) and II (pure extracts from 2 C), all that remains in nos. 98-117. We have kept them last, but apart from and without the directly Celanine chapters" (Delorme).

166. Holy Savior Hospital, run by the Crozier Fathers. A few traces of it remain, embedded in the walls of Casa Gualdi.

167. 2 Cor. 1, 3, which applies this expression to "the Father of our Lord Jesus Christ."

168. Probably before the repetition of the second refrain.

169. Apoc. 2, 11 and 20, 6.

170. Cf. 3 C 37-39.

171. 1 Kgs. 9, 3. — Cf. Fior. 25, n. 1.

172. 2 Kgs. 6, 2, 6.

173. Ps. 147, 20.

174. Allusion to the parable of the talents: Mt. 25, 15.

175. A doctrine forcefully stated in Admonitions 5 and 10.

176. "Probably Sept. 29, 1220" (Cambell).

177. The word "guardian" here designates therefore a *personal* authority; later it was to take on the local meaning of president and superior of a fraternity.

178. This request of Bernard is not the attempt of an overgrown child wishing to be preferred. It is an attitude of faith combining the desire for greater holiness with the conviction that a blessing is an efficacious sign of a growth in grace; the scene is set against the background of the solemn blessings of the patriarchs of their children. Francis' blindness makes the parallel with the dying Jacob, explicitly mentioned in 1 C 108, all the more striking.

179. Phil. 3, 20.

180. After nos. 111 to 115, which constitute the "Verba S. Francisci," one gets the impression that these are additional paragraphs, grouped somewhat at random without regard to the chronology, and retained lest any fragment capable of bringing water to the windmill of the Spirituals be lost.

181. Cf. 2 C 63 and especially 188.

182. Fool: *paccus*: another Italianism (pazzo). Its use can be taken as a guarantee of the authenticity of the discourse. — The sequel reminds us of 1 Cor. 1, 20 ff.

183. To be compared not only with no. 107 but also with 2 C 216.

MIRROR OF PERFECTION

Translated by Leo Sherley-Price,
with an Introduction by
Theophile Desbonnets O.F.M.

This English version of the Mirror of Perfection by Leo Sherley-Price was first published in 1959 by Harper Brothers, New York, in *St. Francis of Assisi: His Life and Writings as recorded by his contemporaries*; Library of Congress Catalog Card Number: 60-8137. T. Desbonnets' Introduction was translated from the French by Paul Oligny.

INTRODUCTION

In 1959, Alexander Masseron began a chapter in his book devoted to the writings of Brother Leo and to the *Mirror of Perfection* as follows: *"Speculum Perfectionis seu S. Francisci Assisiensis legenda antiquissima auctore fratre Leone nunc primum edidit Paul Sabatier.* That occurred in 1898. The title sounded like a battle fanfare calling all Franciscanists to the austere joys of combat."[1]

The echoes of this battle have now died down; the principal figures[2] have all disappeared one after the other: the importance of their work and of their discoveries testify that they were passionate research scholars and gives them a right to the gratitude of all those who love St. Francis. It is nonetheless difficult for us to imagine that the resurrection of the *Mirror of Perfection* by Paul Sabatier could have stimulated such discussions. Only the history of criticism[3] can explain why such importance was attached to this text for so long a time. The only conceivable reason is that at a time when manuscript 1046 of Perugia was not yet known, the *Speculum Perfectionis* was the sole text that contained the recollections of Brother Leo and gave us, although in a distorted way, one of the sources Thomas of Celano had used.

We see no value in describing the phases of the battle Alexander Masseron alludes to, since the greater number of the problems posed by the *Speculum Perfectionis* are now resolved.[4]

The first edition

Enough has already been said regarding the evolution of

the research[5] that led Paul Sabatier toward the *Speculum Perfectionis.*

Paul Sabatier published his discovery in 1898.[6] The volume contains a very valuable introduction divided into two parts.

In the first, by way of recalling to mind the life of Brother Leo and the history of the early days of the Order, the author states the thesis that he was to uphold constantly: the portrait that Celano and St. Bonaventure painted of St. Francis for us is inaccurate because it was knowingly distorted in the name of authority and under the influence of preoccupations that were perhaps respectable but foreign to the concern for truth. For the true portrait of St. Francis we must go to Brother Leo, the author of the *Speculum Perfectionis.*

While the reading of this first part is captivating,[7] especially in view of the talent of the author, it is the most debatable part of the work. Subsequent studies have shown that Brother Leo was not, at least not directly, the author of the *Speculum Perfectionis.* They have also shown that if there were divergencies regarding the interpretation of the ideal Franciscan, these differences had not, at least up to the time of St. Bonaventure's generalate, stood in the way of manifesting the truth. The existence of the *Vita II* is proof of this and, whatever Paul Sabatier may have thought, it clears Crescentius of Iesi of the suspicions that he raised about him.

The second part consists of descriptions of manuscripts, an especially ungrateful work which the author continued in the other volumes of the Collection of documents and the Opuscula of historical criticism. Despite a few errors in identifying the described fragments,[8] these pages, which the average reader skips, have lost none of their value. When we think of the amount of patient research and strenuous work they represent, the reader will understand that we are not sparing in our admiration for the man who wrote them.

Following the Introduction, we have the text of the *Speculum Perfectionis*. Although the variants are pointed out, it is not a genuine critical edition. The abundant notes that accompany the text must be read with a great deal of circumspection since a good part of their contents is now useless.

The publication of this text and especially the theses defended by Paul Sabatier gave rise to a vigorous movement of criticism and research. New manuscripts or new documents were discovered and Paul Sabatier thought it necessary to reedit the *Speculum Perfectionis*. He presented his work to the British Society of Franciscan Studies in 1923 and the first texts were sent to the printer in 1925. Due to Sabatier's illness, the publication was postponed. When he died on March 4, 1928, the printing of the text was almost completed but Sabatier had not finished the introduction. His heirs sent his notes to Professor A.G. Little who saw the edition through. It comprised two volumes.[9]

Only a few changes were made in the text published in the first volume and these had to do with minor points.

Unlike the 1898 edition, this is a true critical edition, as the abundance of variants given shows.

The critical study which is taken up in the second volume is quite different from the one in the 1898 edition. It does not do away with the need to refer to that edition, which is more complete on certain points; but since Sabatier did not substantially modify his original thesis, the arguments he advances must be discussed one by one.

The manuscripts

In order to establish the text of his second edition, Paul Sabatier examined 45 manuscripts,[10] 11 of which truly served to determine the text. Among these 11 manuscripts we can distinguish two groups.

The first group, called "The Portiuncula Collection,"[11] includes 5 copies that have a certain number of common traits: they are moderate in size, written by non-professional copyists (which results in a relatively large divergence among the texts), and they all come from friaries of the strict observance.

The second group or "the Northern Collection,"[12] on the contrary, consists of manuscripts of large size, carefully produced by professional copyists; those whose origin is known come from Crozier monasteries.

Sabatier thought that the manuscripts of the first group were passed around more or less secretly, whereas the second, which were later, were copied by various religious who wanted to understand St. Francis in a country where his prestige in the fifteenth century was immense. They were made for libraries.

The explicit and the date of composition

Two manuscripts of the northern group and one of the Portiuncula[13] group give a hint as to the date when the *Speculum* was written.

The manuscript of the friary of Ognissanti at Florence states that the work was concluded on "the fifth of Ides, May, 1318," that is to say, on May 11, 1318. The two northern manuscripts have "the fifth of the Ides of May, 1228," which in our computation would be the equivalent of May 11, 1227.[14]

Since the Mazarin manuscript had been discovered first, Paul Sabatier had accepted the 1227 date without question. Furthermore it served as a brilliant confirmation of his thesis. But both of the two northern manuscripts — the examination of their variants proves this — come from the same ancestor: they represent only one single witness which is contrary to the witness of the manuscript of Ognissanti.

Many details of the text are at variance with the date

1227 and a strange addition to the subject (an allusion to a local saint of Utrecht, St. Kunera) makes the *explicit* of the northern manuscript unreliable, proving that the copyist was distracted. If one of the manuscripts is faulty, it is the northern one in which the copyist transformed MCCCXVIII into MCCXXVIII by transcribing the third C by an X. The date 1227 is therefore erroneous and that of 1318, without being absolutely certain — only one manuscript gives it — is very probable.

The incipit and the literary form

All the manuscripts begin the text with the following remark: "This work has been compiled in the form of a legend[15] based on what the companions of blessed Francis had formerly written or caused to be written."

This remark embarrassed Paul Sabatier very much, for it ruined a great part of his thesis and contradicted the date 1227 which he attributed to the *Speculum*. He therefore tried to minimize its importance by attempting to show that it was a later interpolation, but his demonstration, despite its art and subtlety, is not absolutely convincing.

The analysis we are about to make of the text shows, on the contrary, that this remark describes very accurately what the *Speculum* is:[16] a compilation of extracts taken from already existing writings and, for the most part, well dated ones.

The sources of the Speculum Perfectionis

The *Speculum Perfectionis* comprises 124 chapters.[17] Hardly had it been published when numerous critics[18] called attention to the fact that one could discover different sources in it. What made their identification difficult was the very fact that it bore such a resemblance to the *Vita II*, whereas the *Speculum* depends on a document that Thomas of Celano had used: one could have concluded hastily that the

Speculum was based directly on the *Vita II*. Only the discovery in 1922 of the 1046 manuscript of Perugia, which acquainted us with a document used by Thomas of Celano and, independently, by the compiler of the *Speculum,* enabled us to determine, for each of the chapters, the source it comes from.

For example, we find: one chapter[19] that comes from the *Vita I* of Celano; 29 chapters[20] that come from the *Vita II*; 90 chapters[21] that are taken from a collection of recollections of the first companions, of which the manuscript of Perugia gives a rather good picture; 2 chapters that have a parallel elsewhere;[22] and finally 2 apparently original chapters: chapter 84 which is a poem in Leonine hexameter to the glory of the Portiuncula, and chapter 85 which paints the picture of the perfect Friar Minor.

Critics generally agree that all these materials were regrouped but not reworked by the compiler of the *Speculum.*

There is an evident regrouping: the *Speculum* does not aim to be a biography that follows the chronological order, at least partially, but rather a character study of St. Francis, divided into 12 parts. Such already had been the aim of the second part of the *Vita II* and of the *Legenda major,* and it is likely that they played their part in influencing the compiler in the choice of his plan.

But material was not reworked: by that we mean that the profound meaning of the documents was not changed. The author nevertheless injected a great number of modifications into the texts before him. B. Terracini[23] made a study of the variants of the text of *2 Celano* and his conclusions can be applied to all the documents that were used. With him we may note that the syntactical inversions which are repugnant to the Italianizing style of the *Speculum* are in general resolved; that the ellipses, often obscure, are clarified by repetitions and a generous supply of pronouns, adjectives, and superadded verbs; that the tenses of the verbs are changed, and lastly that there is an evident tendency to dilute the text by additions, a great number of which take on the appearance of glosses.

In short, we can say that if, by the choice of the texts that he transcribed, by the plan he pursued to incorporate them, and by the few glosses he added to them, the editor of the *Speculum classifies* himself as a "Spiritual," the examination of the variants that he supplies shows nevertheless that he was prompted much more by stylistic or exegetical preoccupations than he was by polemic ones. He used the texts as he found them, and if some of them have polemic overtones, the reason lies in the fact that he found them to be such.

The origin of the Speculum Perfectionis

The circumstances in which the *Speculum Perfectionis* saw the light of day have not yet been completely clarified. In the present state of our knowledge, it seems nevertheless that we may propose the following hypothesis.

At the end of the thirteenth and the beginning of the fourteenth century, the other biographies having been destroyed by order of the Chapter of Paris (in 1266), the life of St. Francis was known only through the *Legenda major* which was far from satisfactory to everyone. The *Vita II* and the recollections of Brother Leo and of the first companions having been found, a friar drew from them a collection of facts passed over in silence by St. Bonaventure:[24] manuscript 1046 of Perugia is a copy of this collection. Then, this same friar, or another, undertook to produce with the help of this collection a work systematically built on the plan inspired by that of the *Legenda major*: the result was the *Speculum Perfectionis*. It is probable that the work was not written all at once and that copies of it were taken before it was completed: the short version[25] which is found in the manuscripts of the Compilation of Avignon is probably the witness of the first form of its redaction.[26] The work quickly enjoyed great popularity both within and outside the Order, and at the end of the fifteenth century — Bartholomew of Pisa is our witness — it was one of the classical sources of the biography of St. Francis.

Interest in the Speculum Perfectionis

The *Speculum Perfectionis* has received the attention of critics for three-quarters of a century and as a consequence it is known quite well. Is it a work of great importance?

If we have in mind only the knowledge of St. Francis that it gives us, then the answer is no. The *Speculum* tells us nothing we did not already know from other sources. Its reading even leaves us with a rather distressing impression of an exacerbated polemic. This is surprising since, as we have already pointed out, the changes it makes in the text it transcribes are purely stylistic or exegetical.

How does it happen that the texts here take on a polemic tone that they do not seem to have to the same degree in the document from which they come? The plan according to which these documents are utilized has something to do with it, but more so the choice of the first chapter which takes on the aspect of a preface and sets the tone for the whole work.

Because of its polemical quality and its supernatural element,[27] the first chapter embarrassed Paul Sabatier; it was incompatible with the date 1227 which he wanted to keep. The solution, as in analogous cases, was to decide that this first chapter was a later interpolation which disfigured the work. In reality all the manuscripts prove that this chapter is indeed the first chapter as willed by the author; and its presence confirms, if need be, the late date of the *Speculum Perfectionis*.

Conversely, if we bear in mind the history of the Order and the spiritual movements that spread through the Order at the beginning of the fourteenth century, the study of the *Speculum* and especially the history of its composition is replete with interest, even if at the present time it poses more questions than it answers.

The *Speculum,* in its attempts to complete the official portrait of the *Legenda major,* remains a witness to the filial devotion of the Franciscans of the fourteenth century and the expression of their love of St. Francis: as such it interests us and touches us. To that must be added that it is the only work that has preserved for us the portrait of the ideal Franciscan (Chap. 85) — the man in whom the qualities of the existing friars was recapitulated — and that without it we would not have this magnificent page, worthy of an anthology.

— Fr. Théophile Desbonnets O.F.M.

NOTES

1. A. Masseron, *Oeuvres de saint François d'Assise*, (Paris, 1959), p. 183. — The two explosives in the title were: *S. Francisci Assisiensis legenda antiquissima*, the oldest legend of St. Francis of Assisi, and: *auctore fratre Leone*, written by Brother Leo.
2. The leading figures were: Paul Sabatier, died in 1928; Msgr. M. Faloci-Pulignani, died in 1940; Fr. Leonhard Lemmens, died in 1929; Fr. Michael Bihl, died in 1950; Fr. Ferdinand Delorme, died in 1952. But there were many others who went into the arena also.
3. This history has yet to be written. It should take into consideration the unexpected discoveries to which we have already alluded, and likewise the men involved — who can weigh what effect Paul Sabatier's being a Protestant had on the discussion — and even their temperament.
4. All those at least that have to do with the place the *Speculum* has in the sources of the life of St. Francis. Those that still remain to be solved have to do with the history of the formation of the text.
5. Cf. P. Sabatier, *Vie de saint François* (1894).
6. P. Sabatier, *Speculum Perfectionis seu S. Francisci Assisiensis legenda antiquissima*, (Paris: Fischbacher, 1899), pp. ccxiv-376.
7. We must moreover guard against becoming captivated by Sabatier's bewitching style.
8. He often attributes texts to the *Speculum* that in reality belong to the document used and reworked by the compiler.
9. P. Sabatier, *Le Speculum Perfectionis ou Mémoires de frère Léon* (Manchester: University Press, 1928-1931) 2 vols., pp. xxxii-350 and xxxvi-276.
10. In the first edition he examined only 16.
11. We owe this appellation to H. Boehmer who had studied these documents for his own edition of the writings of St. Francis. As a matter of fact, we do not know where they were written.
12. The Northern or Netherlands Collection because of the place of origin of these manuscripts.
13. North: Mazarin, 1743; Liège Seminary, 6 F 12. Portiuncula: Florence, monastery of Ognissanti.
14. The difference is due to the fact that the year then did not begin with January 1.
15. Which precisely means: to be read in public.

16. This conclusion would still be true, even if we were to prove that the remark is truly an interpolation.
17. One passage must be added to these, with no rubric in the manuscripts. Sabatier considered it an interpolation, which is very questionable.
18. One of the first to make this remark was A. Fierens, "Les origines du Speculum Perfectionis," *Rapport sur les travaux du séminaire historique de l'Université de Louvain,* (Louvain, 1907), 344-378.
19. Chapter 83.
20. Chapters: 5, 6, 14, 15, 29-32, 47-49, 51, 53, 54, 69, 70, 74-78, 80, 86, 93.
21. Chapters: 1-4, 7-13, 16-28, 33-38, 44-46, 50, 52, 55-68, 71-73, 81, 82, 87-92, 94-119, 121-124.
22. Chapter 79 has a parallel in Eccleston 13; chap. 120, which contains the text of the *Canticle of Brother Sun.*
23. Benvenuto A. Terracini, "Il 'cursus' e la questione dello Speculum Perfectionis," *Studi Medievali,* 4 (1912-1913), 65-109.
24. This does not mean that he recounts *all* the happenings which St. Bonaventure had not mentioned nor that he sometimes did not transcribe some to which St. Bonaventure had alluded.
25. This short version ends with chapter 97; it follows the tradiional order of the chapters but omits certain ones.
26. On the contrary, the *Speculum Perfectionis* published by Fr. Lemmens (DAF, t. II) according to manuscript 1/73 of the friary of St. Isidore and to which its editor imprudently assigned the note *redactio prima,* first redaction, cannot in any way be considered as the first form of the *Speculum Perfectionis* published by Sabatier. His text has no stylistic alterations that are characterisic of the compiler, and his plan is not even a rough draft of the plan we know.
27. The reference is to no. 4 of the *Verba S. Francisci.*

CHAPTER TITLES

1117

Mirror of Perfection

1122

1

PROLOGUE

S. Francis's reply to the Ministers who were unwilling to obey the Rule.

AFTER the second Rule written by blessed Francis had been lost, he went up a mountain (*Monte Colombo, near Rieti*) with Brother Leo of Assisi and Brother Bonizo of Bologna, to draw up another, and under the guidance of Christ he had it written down. But many Ministers came in a body to Brother Elias, the Vicar of blessed Francis, and said, 'We hear that Brother Francis is drawing up a new Rule, and we fear that he will make it so harsh that it will be impossible for us to keep it. So we would like you to go and tell him that we are not willing to be bound by this Rule. Let him make it for himself, and not for us.' But Brother Elias feared a rebuke from the holy Father, and refused to go. And when they all pressed him, he said that he would not go without them, so they all went together.

When Brother Elias approached the place where blessed Francis was standing, he called to him. And when he had answered and saw the Ministers, he asked, 'What do these Brothers want?' Brother Elias said, 'They are Ministers, who hear that you are drawing up a new Rule, and they fear that you intend to make it too harsh. They refuse to be bound by it, and ask you to make it for yourself, and not for them.'

At this blessed Francis raised his face to heaven and spoke to Christ, saying, 'Lord, was I not right when I said that they would not believe me?' And all present heard the voice of Christ answer from heaven, 'Francis, nothing in this Rule is yours; for all is Mine. I wish the Rule to be obeyed to the letter, to the letter, without a gloss, without a gloss. I know what the frailty of man can achieve, and I know how much I intend to help them. So let those who are not willing to obey the Rule leave the Order.'

Then blessed Francis turned to the friars and said, 'You have heard! You have heard! Do you want this to be repeated?' And the Ministers confessed their fault and went away confused and terrified.

ON THE PERFECTION OF POVERTY

2

Firstly, how blessed Francis made known his will and intention (which he maintained from beginning to end) with regard to the observance of poverty.

FRIAR Richard of the March was a man of noble birth, but even more noble in his holiness, and blessed Francis loved him dearly. One day he visited blessed Francis in the palace of the Bishop of Assisi, and among other matters that they discussed relating to the Order and the observance of the Rule, he asked him particularly on the following, saying, 'Tell me, Father, what was your original intention when you began to have brethren? And what is it to-day? And do you intend to maintain it to the day of your death? If I know this, I shall be able to testify to your intention and will from first to last. For example, may we friars who are clergy and possess many books keep them, provided that we regard them as the property of the Order?'

Blessed Francis said to him, 'I assure you, brother, that it has been and remains my first and last intention and desire—had the brethren only believed me—that no friar should possess anything but a habit, a cord, and an undergarment, as our Rule allows.'

But if any friar should be inclined to ask, 'Why did not blessed Francis insist that poverty was observed by the friars in his own day, as he told Brother Richard? And why did he not enforce its observance?', we who were with him can answer this question as we have heard it from his own mouth, for he himself spoke to the friars on this and on many other matters. For the guidance of the Order he also caused many things which he had learned from God by constant prayer and meditation, to be written in the Rule, declaring them to be in accordance with God's will. But after he had revealed these things to the friars, they thought them harsh and unbearable, for they did not know what was to happen in the Order after his death.

And because he feared dissension between himself and the friars, he was not willing to argue with them, but reluctantly yielded to their wishes, and asked pardon of God. But in order that the words which the Lord had put into his mouth for the guidance of the friars should not pass unheeded, he resolved to observe them himself, and by so doing to obtain his reward from God. At length he found contentment in this, and his soul received comfort.

3

Saint Francis's reply to a Minister who asked his permission to have books; and how the Ministers removed the chapter containing the Gospel prohibitions from the Rule without his knowledge.

ONCE, when blessed Francis had returned from overseas, one of the Ministers was discussing the chapter on poverty with him, wishing in particular to learn his own will and interpretation of it; especially since at that time the Rule contained a chapter on the prohibitions of the Gospel, namely, *Take nothing with you on the journey,* etc.

And blessed Francis answered him, 'My intention is that the friars should possess nothing but a habit, with a cord and undergarment, as the Rule requires. And anyone who is compelled by necessity may wear sandals.'

The Minister said, 'What shall I do, for I have books worth more than fifty pounds?' He said this because he wished to have them with a clear conscience, and knowing how strictly blessed Francis interpreted the chapter on poverty, it troubled him to possess so many books.

Blessed Francis said to him, 'I will not, should not, and cannot go against my own conscience and the perfection of the holy Gospel which we have vowed to observe.' Hearing this, the Minister was grieved; but seeing him so disturbed, blessed Francis said to him with great fervour of spirit in the presence of all the friars, 'You wish people to recognize you as Friars Minor, and to regard you as men who observe the holy Gospel; yet you want to have chests for your books!'

But although the Ministers knew that the friars were obliged to observe the holy Gospel according to the Rule, they removed from the Rule the chapter where it is said, *Take nothing for your journey*, and thought that by so doing they would not be bound to observe the perfection of the Gospel. This was revealed to blessed Francis by the Holy Spirit, and he said in the presence of certain friars, 'The Friar Ministers think they can deceive God and me. On the contrary, in order that all friars shall know themselves bound to observe the perfection of the Gospel, I wish it to be written at the beginning and at the end of the Rule that friars are bound to the strict observance of the Holy Gospel of our Lord Jesus Christ. And in order that the brethren may never have any excuse to set aside the things that I have proclaimed and still proclaim, which the Lord has placed in my mouth for their salvation and my own, I intend to demonstrate these things before God by my own actions, and by His help, I will observe them for ever.'

So, from the early days when he began to have brethren to the day of his death, blessed Francis observed the whole of the Gospel to the letter.

4

On the novice who sought his permission to own a psalter.

AT another time a friar novice who knew how to recite the psalter, although not fluently, obtained leave from the Minister

General to have his own copy. But having heard that blessed Francis did not wish his friars to hanker after learning and books, he was not happy about having it without his permission. So when blessed Francis was visiting the friary to which this novice belonged, the novice said to him, 'Father, it would give me great pleasure to have a psalter. But although the Minister General has granted permission, I would like to have it with your approval.' To which blessed Francis replied, 'The Emperor Charles, Roland, Oliver, and all the paladins and men of valour were mighty in battle, fought the Infidels until death with great sweat and toil, and they gained a famous victory. And the holy martyrs themselves gave their lives in battle for the Faith of Christ. But in these days there are many who wish to win honour and praise from men by merely telling of their deeds. In the same way, there are many among us who want to win honour and praise by merely proclaiming and reciting the deeds of the Saints.' As though to say, 'Our concern is not with books and learning, but with holy deeds; for learning brings pride, but charity edifies.'

Some days later, as blessed Francis was sitting by the fire, the novice spoke to him again about the psalter. And blessed Francis said to him, 'Once you have a psalter, you will want a breviary. And when you have a breviary, you will sit in a high chair like a great prelate, and say to your brother, "Bring me my breviary!"' As he spoke, blessed Francis in great fervour of spirit took up a handful of ashes and placed them on his head, and rubbing his hand around his head as though he was washing it, he exclaimed, 'I, a breviary! I, a breviary!' And he repeated this many times, passing his hand over his head. And the friar was amazed and ashamed.

Later, blessed Francis said to him, 'Brother, I was tempted in the same way to have books, but in order to learn the will of our Lord in this matter, I took the Gospels and prayed the Lord to reveal His will to me at the first opening of the book. And when my prayer was ended, at the first opening of the book

I came upon the words of the holy Gospel, *It is granted to you to understand the secret of God's kingdom; the rest must learn of it by parables.*' And he said, 'There are so many who are eager to acquire learning, that blessed is the man who is content to be without it for love of the Lord God.'

Many months later, when blessed Francis was at S. Mary of the Porziuncula, this friar spoke to him yet again about the psalter as he stood on the road near his cell beyond the house. And blessed Francis told him, 'Go and do as your Minister says on this matter.' When he heard this, the friar turned back along the road, while blessed Francis stood thinking over what he had said to the friar. Suddenly he called after him, saying, 'Wait for me, brother, wait for me!' Overtaking him, he said, 'Come back and show me the place where I told you to do as your Minister directs about the psalter.' So when they had arrived at the place, blessed Francis knelt down before the friar and said, '*Mea culpa*, brother, *mea culpa*; for whoever wishes to be a Friar Minor should possess nothing but a habit with a cord and undergarment, as the Rule allows him. And those whom need obliges to do so may have sandals.' And whenever friars came to him to ask his advice on this matter, he used to give them the same reply. He often used to say, 'A man's knowledge is revealed by his actions, and the words of a Religious must be supported by his own deeds; for *the test of the tree is in its fruit.*'

5

On observing poverty in books and beds, buildings and appointments.

THE most blessed Father used to teach the friars to value books for their witness to God and not for their costliness, for their edification and not their elegance. He wished books to be few and held in common, and suitable to the needs of penniless friars. They were so badly provided with beds and blankets that whoever had some threadbare rags spread over straw regarded it as a fine bed.

He also told the friars to build their houses small and their cells of wood, not of stone, and he wanted them built in a humble style. He abhorred pretentious buildings, and disliked superfluous or elaborate appointments. He wished nothing about their tables or appointments to appear worldly or to remind them of the world, so that everything should proclaim their poverty and remind them that they were pilgrims and exiles.

6

How Saint Francis compelled all the friars to leave a house which had been called 'the house of the friars.'

WHILE he was passing through Bologna, he heard that a house had recently been built there for the friars. Directly he learned that it was known as 'the house of the friars,' he turned on his heel and left the city, giving strict orders that all the friars were to leave it at once and live in it no longer.

So they all abandoned it, and even the sick were not allowed to remain, but were turned out with the rest, until the Lord Ugolino, Bishop of Ostia and Legate in Lombardy, publicly proclaimed that the house belonged to him. One of these friars, who was sick and obliged to leave the house, is still living to-day, and has written this account.

7

How Saint Francis wished to destroy a house which the people of Assisi had built at S. Mary of the Porziuncula.

AT this period the friars had only a single poor cell thatched with straw, with walls of wattle and daub. So when the time drew near for the General Chapter, which was held each year at

S. Mary of the Porziuncula, the people of Assisi, realizing that the friars were increasing in number daily, and that all of them assembled there each year, held a meeting. And within a few days, with great haste and zeal, they erected a large building of stone and mortar while blessed Francis was absent and knew nothing of it.

When he returned from one of the Provinces and arrived for the Chapter, he was astonished at the house built there. And he was afraid that the sight of this house might make other friars build similar large houses in the places where they lived or were to live, and he desired this place to remain the example and pattern for all other houses of the Order. So before the Chapter ended he climbed onto the roof of the house and told other friars to climb up with him. And with their help he began to throw to the ground the tiles with which the house was roofed, intending to destroy it to the very foundations. But some men-at-arms of Assisi were present to protect the place from the great crowd of sightseers who had gathered to watch the Chapter of the Friars. And when they saw that blessed Francis and other friars intended to destroy the house, they went up to him at once and said, 'Brother, this house belongs to the Commune of Assisi, and we are here to represent the Commune. We forbid you to destroy our house.' When he heard this, blessed Francis said to them, 'If the house is yours, I will not touch it.' And forthwith he and the other friars came down.

As a result of this incident, the people of the City of Assisi decreed that thenceforward whoever held the office of Mayor should be responsible for the repair of the house. And each year for a long time this decree was carried out.

8

How he rebuked his Vicar because he was having a small house built for the recitation of the Office.

ON another occasion the Vicar of blessed Francis began to have a small house built at S. Mary's, where the friars could be quiet and recite the Hours, because so many friars visited the place that they had nowhere in which to say the Office. For all the friars of the Order used to come there, because no one was received into the Order except in S. Mary's.

When the building was nearly completed, blessed Francis returned to the friary, and while in his cell he heard the noise made by the workmen. Calling his companion, he inquired what the friars were doing, and his companion told him all that was happening.

Blessed Francis immediately sent for his Vicar, and said to him, 'Brother, this place is the example and pattern of the whole Order. I would rather have the friars living here put up with trouble and discomfort for love of the Lord God, so that other friars who come here carry away to their own houses a good example of poverty, rather than that they should enjoy every convenience and that these others should carry back to their own houses an example of building, saying, "At the friary of Saint Mary of the Porziuncula, which is the chief house of the Order, there are such and such great buildings, so we may rightly build in our own places as well." '

9

How he was not willing to remain in a well-built cell, or one that was called his own.

ONE of the friars, a deeply spiritual man, who was very intimate with blessed Francis, had a cell built standing a little distance from the hermitage where he lived, so that blessed Francis could remain at prayer there whenever he visited the place. So when blessed Francis came there, this friar conducted him to the cell; but although it was built only of wood, rough-hewn with axe and hatchet, the Father said, 'This cell is too fine. If you wish me to stay here, have a cell made with branches and ferns as its only covering inside and out.' For the poorer and smaller the house or cell, the readier he was to live in it. And when the friar had done this, blessed Francis remained there for some days.

One day, however, when he had left the cell, one of the friars went to look at it, and afterwards came to the place where blessed Francis was. Seeing him, the holy Father said to him, 'Where have you come from, brother?' 'I have come from your cell,' he replied. Then blessed Francis said, 'Because you have called it mine, some one else shall use it henceforward, and not I.' For we who were with him have often heard him quote the saying, *Foxes have holes, and the birds of the air their resting-places; the Son of Man has nowhere to lay His head*. He also used to say, 'When the Lord remained in the desert, where He prayed and fasted forty days and forty nights, He did not have a cell or house built for Him there, but sheltered beneath the rocks in the mountains.' So, after His example, he would not have any house or cell that could be called his own, nor did he ever have one built. Indeed, if ever he chanced to say to the friars, 'Go and make that cell ready,' he would not afterwards live in it, because of that saying in the holy Gospel, *Be not anxious, etc.* For even at the time of his death he had it written in his Testament that all cells and houses of the friars were to be built only of wood and clay, the better to safeguard poverty and humility.

1135

The Saint's purpose and method of choosing building sites in towns.

ONCE when blessed Francis was in Siena for treatment of his disease of the eyes, Master Bonaventura (*not the Saint*), who had given the friars the land on which the friary was built, said to him, 'Father, how do you like this place?' And blessed Francis said to him, 'Do you wish me to explain how the houses of the friars should be built?' 'Please do, Father,' he replied. And blessed Francis said, 'When the friars come to any city where they have no house, and meet anyone there who is willing to give them sufficient land to build a house, have a garden, and all that is necessary, they should first reckon how much land is sufficient for them, always bearing in mind holy poverty and the good example that we are obliged to show in all things.'

This he said because he did not want the friars to transgress against poverty in any way, either in their houses, churches, gardens, or anything else that they used. He did not wish them to possess places by right of ownership, but to live in them *as strangers and exiles*. This was why he did not wish the friars to live together in large numbers in their houses, because he thought it difficult to observe poverty in a large community. And from the beginning of his conversion until his death it was his intention that absolute poverty should be observed in all things.

'When the friars have examined the land necessary for a house,' he said, 'they should go to the Bishop of that city and say to him, "My Lord, so-and-so is willing to give us so much land for the love of God and for the salvation of his soul, so that we may build a house there. We are therefore coming to you first of all, because you are the father and lord of the souls of all the flock entrusted to you, as well as of ourselves and of all the brethren who will dwell in this place. So, with God's blessing and your own, we would like to build there." '

He spoke thus because the harvest of souls which the friars desire to gather is more readily obtained by working in harmony with the clergy, thereby helping both them and the people, than by antagonizing them, even though they may win the people. And he said, 'The Lord has called us to maintain His Faith, and support the Bishops and clergy of Holy Church. So we are bound always to love, honour and respect them to the best of our ability. For, as their name implies, the Friars are called Minors because they ought to be more humble than all other men in this world, both in example and in action. At the beginning of my conversion the Lord put His word into the mouth of the Bishop of Assisi so that he might counsel me rightly and strengthen me in the service of Christ; because of this and many other excellent virtues that I see in prelates, I wish to love and respect not only the Bishops but the poor priests as well, and to regard them as my masters.

'When the friars have received the blessing of the Bishop, let them go and mark out the boundaries of the land which they have accepted for their house, and as a sign of holy poverty and humility, let them plant a hedge instead of building a wall. Afterwards let them erect simple little huts of clay and wood, and a number of cells where the friars can pray or work from time to time in order to increase their merit and avoid idleness. Their churches are to be small; they are not to build great churches in order to preach to the people, or for any other reason, for they show greater humility and a better example when they visit other churches to preach. And should prelates or clergy, whether Religious or secular, visit their houses, their humble little dwellings, cells, and tiny churches will speak for themselves, and these things will edify them more than any words.'

He said also, 'Friars often raise large buildings, and violate our holy poverty, and by so doing provoke criticism and set a bad example. And sometimes, in order to obtain a better or holier place, or a larger congregation, they abandon their own

1137

houses out of covetousness and greed; or they pull them down and build others that are large and pretentious. Consequently those who have contributed to their cost, and others who see it, are greatly offended and distressed. So it is better for friars to erect humble little buildings, remaining loyal to their profession and setting a good example to their neighbours, rather than to act contrary to their profession and set a bad example to others. But should the friars ever leave a poor little house for one in a more suitable place, the offence caused would be less.'

11

How friars, especially those who had been prelates and scholars, opposed Saint Francis's desire to erect humble friaries and buildings.

As a sign of holy poverty, and humility blessed Francis decreed that the churches of the friars were to be small and their houses built only of wood and clay. For he wanted the friary of Saint Mary of the Porziuncula to be a pattern especially for buildings constructed of wood and clay, so that it might be a permanent memorial for all friars, present and to come, since it was the first and chief house of the whole Order. But some of the friars opposed him in this matter, saying that in some Provinces timber was more costly than stone, so that it did not seem sensible to them that their houses should be built of wood and clay.

But blessed Francis refused to argue with them, especially since he was nearing death and seriously ill. So he caused it to be written in his Testament: *Friars are to beware of accepting churches, houses, and all other places built for them unless they conform to holy poverty; and they are always to lodge in them as strangers and pilgrims.*

But we, who were with him when he wrote the Rule and most of his other writings, testify that he had many things written in the Rule and in his other writings to which many friars were opposed, especially the prelates and scholars among us; and to-day these things would have been very beneficial and valuable to the whole Order. But he had a great fear of scandal, and yielded, although with reluctance, to the wishes of the brethren. But he often said: 'Woe to those friars who oppose me in this matter, which I am firmly convinced to be the will of God for the greater usefulness and needs of the whole Order, although I unwillingly submit to their wish.' So he often used to say to his companions, 'It causes me great grief and distress that in these matters, which I learn from God with great effort in prayer and meditation, and which I know to be in accordance with His will, certain brethren who rely on their own experience and false prudence, oppose me and render them ineffective, saying, "These things are to be held and observed, and not those." '

12

How he regarded it as theft to obtain alms beyond one's needs.

BLESSED Francis used to say to his friars, 'I have never been a thief in the matter of alms, and obtained or used more than I needed. I have always accepted less than my needs, lest other poor folk should be cheated of their share; for to act otherwise would be theft.'

13

How Christ told blessed Francis that He did not wish friars to possess anything, either in common or individually.

WHEN the Friar Ministers urged him to allow the friars to possess something, at least, in common, so that so great a company might have some resources, blessed Francis called upon Christ in prayer, and took counsel with Him on the matter. And Christ at once answered him, saying, 'It is My will to withhold all things from them, both in general and in particular. I will always be ready to provide for this family, however great it may become, and I will always cherish it so long as it shall trust in Me.'

14

Saint Francis's hatred of money, and how he punished a friar who touched money.

FRANCIS, the true friend and imitator of Christ, utterly despised all things belonging to this world, and hated money above all else. He always urged his brethren both by word and example to avoid it as they would the devil. And he told the friars to have as little love and use for money as for dung.

One day, a layman happened to enter Saint Mary of the Porziuncula to pray, and laid some money near the cross as an offering. When he had left, one of the friars unthinkingly picked it up and placed it on a window ledge. But when this was reported to blessed Francis, this friar, realizing himself detected, at once hastened to ask forgiveness; and, falling to the ground, offered himself for punishment.

The holy Father reproved him, and took him severely to task for touching the money; and he ordered him to take the money from the window in his mouth, carry it outside the friary, and lay it on a heap of ass's dung.

When this friar readily obeyed this order, all who saw or heard were filled with the greatest fear, and thenceforward despised money as ass's dung. And further examples moved them to despise it altogether.

15

On avoiding luxury and many changes of clothing; and on being patient in privations.

BLESSED Francis, endowed with virtue from on high, was warmed by divine fire within rather than by outward clothing. He strongly disapproved of those in the Order who wore three garments and used finer clothing than necessary. He used to say that any need revealed by a love of pleasure and not by reason was the sign of a dead spirit, for 'when the spirit becomes lukewarm and inward grace grows cold, it follows that flesh and blood seek their own pleasures.' He also used to say, 'When the soul lacks any desire for spiritual joys, the flesh is bound to turn to its own. Then the lower desires plead the excuse of necessity, and the desires of the flesh influence the conscience. But if a genuine need besets any Brother and he immediately hastens to satisfy it, what reward can he expect? For an opportunity has arisen to win merit, but he has already shown clearly that he has no desire for it. For to refuse to endure these wants patiently is nothing but a return to Egypt' (*Exod.* xvi. 2).

Lastly, he desired that friars should on no account possess more than two habits, although he allowed these to be lined with patches stitched together. He used to say that choice materials were abhorrent, and sharply rebuked those who acted contrary to this; and in order to shame such people by his own example, he always repaired his own habit with rough sacking. For this reason, even in death he directed that his burial habit was to be covered with sacking. But if any friars were troubled by sickness, or had other needs, he would allow them another soft garment next the skin, provided that austerity and roughness was always maintained in their outer garment. For he used to say with the greatest sorrow, 'Henceforward strictness will be so greatly relaxed and lukewarmness rule, that the sons of a poor Father will not be ashamed to wear scarlet cloth, only the colour being changed.'

16

How he refused to comfort his own body with things that he thought other friars might lack.

WHILE blessed Francis was staying in the hermitage of Saint Eleutherius near Rieti, he lined his own habit and those of his companions with some pieces of cloth because of the intense cold—for, as was his custom, he had only one habit—and as a result his body began to derive a little comfort. A short while afterwards, when he returned from prayer, he said with great joy to his companion, 'It is my duty to be the pattern and example to all the brethren; so although it is necessary for my body to have a lined habit, I must consider my other brethren who have the same needs, and who perhaps do not and cannot possess it. I must therefore have sympathy with them in this matter, and endure the same privations as they, so that when they see me doing so, they may have the strength to bear theirs patiently.'

But we who were with him cannot express either in words or writing how many great necessities he denied his body in order to give a good example to the friars, and help them to bear their poverty patiently. For once the friars began to increase in numbers, he made it his chief and particular concern to teach the brethren what they should do or avoid by his own actions rather than by words.

17

How he was ashamed to see anyone poorer than himself.

ONCE, when he had met a poor man and considered his poverty, he said to his companion, 'This man's poverty brings great shame on us, and is a stern rebuke to our own. For since I have chosen holy poverty as my lady, my delight, and my spiritual and bodily treasure, I feel the greatest shame when I find someone poorer than myself. And the story has gone round the whole world that I am vowed to poverty before God and men.'

18

How, when the first friars were ashamed, he encouraged and taught them to go out and seek alms.

WHEN blessed Francis began to have friars he was full of joy at their conversion, and that God had given him a goodly company. And he had such love and respect for them that he did not insist that they went out for alms, because it was clear to him that they were ashamed to go. So, in order to spare them the shame, he used to go out every day to collect alms alone. But he had been accustomed to comfort in the world, was frail by nature, and was further weakened by overmuch fasting and hardship. And when he became exhausted by his efforts, he realized that he could not continue this work single-handed. He knew, also, that his brethren were called to the same way of life, although they were ashamed to follow it; for as yet they did not fully realize this, nor were they discerning enough to say, 'We also will go out for alms.'

So he said to them, 'My dearest brothers, little children, do not be ashamed to go out for alms, for our Lord made Himself poor in this world for our sakes, and we have chosen to follow His example on the road of true poverty. This is our heritage, which our Lord Jesus Christ has won and bequeathed to us and to all who desire to live after His example in most holy poverty. I solemnly assure you that many of the noblest and wisest men of this age will join our company and regard it as a great honour to go out begging. So go out for alms confidently and gladly with the blessing of God. You should be more willing and happy to go for alms than a man who brings back an hundred coins in exchange for one, because you are offering the love of God to those from whom you ask alms when you say, "Give us alms for the love of the Lord God," for in comparison with Him heaven and earth are as nothing.'

But because the friars were as yet few in number, he could not send them out two by two, but he sent them singly through the towns and villages. So when they returned with the alms they had obtained, each of them showed blessed Francis the alms that he had received. And one would say to another, 'I have received more alms than you.' And blessed Francis was glad when he saw them so happy and cheerful. And thenceforward each of them readily asked permission to go out begging.

19

How he did not wish the friars to be provident and anxious for to-morrow.

WHILE blessed Francis was with the first friars, he lived with them in such poverty that they observed the holy Gospel to the letter in all things and through all things, from the very day when our Lord revealed to him that he and his friars were to live according to the pattern of the holy Gospel. He therefore forbade the friar who cooked for the brethren to put dried beans into warm water in the evening, as is usual, when he intended to give them to the friars to eat on the following day. This was in order to observe the saying of the holy Gospel, *Do not fret over to-morrow*. So the friar delayed putting them to soften until after Matins on the day when they were to be eaten. Many friars, especially in towns, continued to observe this custom for a long time, and would not seek or accept more alms than were necessary to support them for a single day.

How by word and example he reproved friars who had prepared a lavish meal on Christmas Day because a Minister was present.

WHEN one of the Friar-Ministers had visited blessed Francis in order to keep the Feast of Christmas with him in the friary at Rieti, the friars prepared the tables rather elaborately and carefully on Christmas Day in honour of the Minister, putting on fair white linen and glass vessels. But when the Father came down from his cell to eat, and saw the tables raised up from the ground and prepared with such great care, he went back secretly and took the hat and staff of a poor beggar who had arrived that day. And calling in a low voice to one of his companions, he went out of the door of the friary unseen by the brethren in the house, while his companion remained inside near the door. Meanwhile the friars came in to dine, for blessed Francis had ordered that, whenever he did not come at once at mealtime, the friars were not to wait for him.

When he had stood outside for a while, he knocked on the door, and his companion immediately opened to him. And entering with his hat on his back and his staff in his hand, he came like a stranger or beggar to the door of the room where the friars were eating, and called out, 'For the love of God, give alms to this poor sick stranger!' But the Minister and the other friars recognized him at once. And the Minister replied, 'Brother, we are poor as well, and because we are so many, the alms that we have only meet our needs. But for the love of God which you have invoked, come in and we will share with you the alms which the Lord has given us.'

When he had entered and stood before the friars' table, the Minister handed to him the plate from which he was eating, and also some bread. And taking it, he humbly sat down on the floor beside the fire in the sight of the friars sitting at table. Then he sighed and said to the brethren, 'When I saw the table elaborately and carefully laid, I felt that this was not the table of poor religious who go around for alms from door to door each day. Dearest brothers, we are under a greater obligation than other Religious to follow the example of Christ's humility and poverty, for it is to this end that we have been called and professed before God and men. So it seems to me that I am sitting like a Friar Minor, because the feasts of our Lord and the Saints are better honoured in the want and poverty by which these Saints won heaven than in the luxury and excess by which a soul is estranged from heaven.'

The friars were ashamed at his words, realizing that he was speaking no more than the truth. And seeing him seated on the ground, wishing to correct and teach them in such a holy and simple way, some of them began to weep aloud. For he warned the brethren to eat humbly and simply, so as to edify lay folk. And if any poor man should visit them or be invited by the friars, he was to sit with them as an equal, and not the poor man on the floor and the friars on high.

21

How the Lord Bishop of Ostia wept and was edified by the poverty of the friars at the time of the Chapter.

WHEN the Lord Bishop of Ostia, who later became Pope Gregory (IX), attended the Chapter of the friars at Saint Mary of the Porziuncula, he entered the house with many knights and clergy to see the friars' dormitory. And seeing how the friars lay on the ground and had nothing beneath them but a little straw, and a few poor broken-down pallets, and no pillows, he began to weep freely before them all, saying, 'Look how the friars sleep here! But we, wretched creatures, enjoy so many luxuries! What will become of us?' So he and all the others were much edified. He did not even find a table in the place, because the friars used to eat on the ground; for as long as blessed Francis lived, all the friars in that house used to eat on the ground.

22

How, at blessed Francis's advice, the soldiers obtained their needs by asking alms from door to door.

WHEN blessed Francis was in the friary at Bagni near the city of Nocera, his feet began to swell badly because of the disease of dropsy, and he became seriously ill. When the people of Assisi heard of this, they hurriedly sent soldiers to the friary to escort him to Assisi, fearing that if he remained there, others would obtain his most holy body. But while they were bringing him, they stopped in a fortress-town belonging to the Commune of Assisi in order to eat; and blessed Francis rested in the house of a poor man who welcomed him willingly and gladly. Meanwhile the soldiers went through the town to buy themselves what they needed, and found nothing. So they came back to the holy Father and told him jokingly, 'Brother, you will have to let us share your alms, for we cannot buy anything to eat!' Then blessed Francis said to them with great fervour, 'You have not found anything because you trusted in your flies (*meaning, your money*), and not in God. Go back to the houses where you went trying to buy food; put aside your shame, and ask alms for the love of the Lord God. The Holy Spirit will move them to give generously.' So they went away and asked alms as blessed Francis had told them; and those from whom they asked alms gave them whatever they had with great gladness and generosity. And recognizing that a miracle had happened to them, they returned to blessed Francis praising God with great joy.

The holy Father used to regard it as an act of great nobility and dignity before God and the world to ask alms for love of the Lord God, for all things which our heavenly Father has created for the use of men are granted freely despite their sin both to the worthy and to the unworthy through the love of His beloved Son. He used to say that the servant of God ought to ask alms for the love of God more willingly and gladly than one who, out of his own generosity and sympathy, might go and say, 'If anyone will give me a penny, I will give him a thousand pieces of gold.' For, by asking alms, the servant of God offers the love of God to those of whom he begs, and in comparison with this all things in heaven and earth are nothing.

So before the friars increased in numbers, and even after they became numerous, whenever a friar went through the world preaching, and was invited by anyone, however noble or wealthy, to eat and lodge with him, he would always go for alms at meal-time before he came to his host's house, in order to uphold the good example of the friars and the dignity of Lady Poverty. Blessed Francis often used to say to his host, 'I will not resign my royal dignity and heritage, and my profession and that of my brethren (that is, to beg bread from door to door).' And sometimes his host would go with him and carry the alms which blessed Francis had collected, and preserve them like relics out of devotion to him.

The writer has seen this happen many times, and testifies to these things.

23

How he went out for alms before he would go in to the Cardinal's table.

ONCE when blessed Francis was visiting the Lord Bishop of Ostia, who later became Pope Gregory (IX), he went out unobserved at dinner-time in order to ask alms from door to door. And when he returned, the Lord of Ostia had already gone in to table with many knights and nobles. But when the holy Father entered, he laid the alms that he had collected on the

1148

table before the Cardinal, and sat down beside him, for the Cardinal always wished that blessed Francis should sit next him at table. The Cardinal was somewhat embarrassed to find that blessed Francis had gone out for alms and laid them on the table; but he said nothing at the time because of his guests.

When blessed Francis had eaten a little, he took up his alms and in the name of the Lord God distributed a little to each of the knights and chaplains of the Lord Cardinal. And they all accepted them with great reverence and devotion, reaching out their hoods and sleeves; and some ate the alms, while others kept them out of devotion to him.

After dinner the Cardinal entered his own apartment, taking blessed Francis with him. And stretching out his arms, he embraced him with great joy and gladness, saying, 'My simple brother, why have you shamed me to-day by going out for alms when you visit my house, which is a home for your friars?' 'On the contrary, my lord,' replied blessed Francis, 'I have shown you the greatest honour; for when a servant does his duty and fulfils his obedience to his lord, he does honour to his lord.' And he said, 'It is my duty to be the pattern and example of our poor friars, especially as I know that in this Order of friars there are, and will be, friars who are Minors in name and in deed, who, for love of the Lord God and by the anointing of the Holy Spirit Who will guide them in all things, will be humble and obedient, and the servants of their brethren. There are also, and will be, some among them who are held back by shame or bad custom, and who scorn to humble themselves and stoop to going for alms and doing other servile work. Because of this I must by my own actions teach those who belong, and will belong, to the Order, that they are inexcusable in the eyes of God both in this life and in the life to come. So while I am with you, who are our Lord and Apostolic Protector, or with other great and wealthy men of this world who for love of God not only receive me into your houses but even press me to eat at your table, I will not be ashamed to go out for alms.

1149

Indeed, I intend to regard and retain this practice as the highest nobility and royal dignity, and to do it in honour of Him Who, though He was Lord of all, willed for our sakes to become the servant of all. And when He was rich and glorious in His majesty, He came as one poor and despised in our humility. So I want all present or future friars to know that I regard it as a greater consolation of soul and body to sit at the poor little table of the brethren, and to see in front of me the meagre alms that they beg from door to door for love of the Lord God, than to sit at your table and that of other lords, abundantly provided with different dishes. For the bread of charity is holy bread, hallowed by the praise and love of God, and when a friar goes out for alms he should first say, "Praised and blessed be the Lord God!" And afterwards he should say, "Give us alms for love of the Lord God." '

The Cardinal was much edified by the holy Father's words, and said, 'My son, do whatever seems good to you, for God is with you, and you with Him.' For, as blessed Francis often said, it was his wish that no friar should remain long without going out to beg alms, both because of its great merit, and lest he should become ashamed to go. Indeed, the nobler and greater a friar had been in the world, the more pleased and edified he was when he went for alms and did other humble work as the friars were then accustomed to do.

24

On the friar who neither prayed nor worked, but ate well.

IN the early days of the Order, when the friars were living at Rivo Torto near Assisi, there was one friar among them who prayed little and did no work; he refused to go out for alms, but used to eat heartily. Thinking the matter over, blessed Francis knew by the Holy Spirit that the man was a lover of the flesh, and said to him, 'Be off with you, Brother Fly, since you want to eat up the labours of your brethren, and be idle in the work of God. You are like a barren and idle drone, who gathers nothing and does no work, but consumes the toil and gain of the good bees!'

So he went his way, and because he was a lover of the flesh, he neither asked mercy nor found it.

25

How he went out with fervour to meet a beggar who was walking along with his alms and praising God.

ON another occasion, when blessed Francis was at S. Mary of the Porziuncula, a friar of true spiritual poverty was coming along the street on his way back from Assisi with alms, and as he walked he was cheerfully singing God's praises in a loud voice. As he drew near the church of S. Mary, blessed Francis heard him, and at once went out to meet him with the greatest fervour and joy. He ran up to him in the road, and joyfully kissed the shoulder on which he was carrying a bag with alms. Then he took the bag from his shoulder, laid it on his own shoulder, and thus bore it into the friary. And he told the brethren, 'This is how I want a friar of mine to go out and return with alms, happy, joyful, and praising God.'

26

How the Lord revealed to him that the friars were to be called Minors, and were to proclaim peace and salvation.

ONE day blessed Francis said, 'The Order and life of the Friars Minor is a little flock which the Son of God has asked of His heavenly Father in these latter days, saying, "Father, I would that

Thou shouldest form and give Me a new and humble people in these latter days, who will be unlike all others who have preceded them in humility and poverty, and content to possess Me alone." And the Father said to His beloved Son, "My Son, it is done as Thou hast asked." '

So blessed Francis used to say that God willed and revealed to him that they should be called Friars Minor, because they were to be the poor and humble people whom the Son of God had asked of His Father. Of this people the Son of God Himself speaks in the Gospel: *Do not be afraid, My little flock. Your Father has determined to give you His kingdom.* And again: *Believe Me, when you did it to one of the least of My brethren here, you did it to Me.* And although the Lord was speaking of all poor and spiritual people, He was referring more particularly to the Order of Friars Minor which was to arise in His Church.

Therefore, since it was revealed to blessed Francis that it should be called the Order of Friars Minor, he caused it to be written in his first Rule, which he took before the Lord Pope Innocent III; who approved and granted it, and later proclaimed it publicly in Consistory.

The Lord also revealed to him the greeting which the friars were to use, and he caused this to be written in his Testament, saying: *The Lord revealed to me that I should say as a greeting,* 'The Lord give you peace.'

In the early days of the Order, while he was travelling with a friar who was one of the first twelve, he used to greet men and women along the road and in the fields, saying, 'The Lord give you peace.' And because people had never heard such a greeting from any Religious, they were very startled. Indeed, some said indignantly, 'What do you mean by this greeting of yours?' As a result the friar became embarrassed, and said to blessed Francis, 'Allow me to use some other greeting.' But the holy Father said, 'Let them chatter, for they do not understand the ways of God. Don't feel ashamed because of this, for one day the nobles and princes of this world will respect you and the other friars for this greeting. For it is no marvel if the Lord should desire to have a new little flock, whose speech and way of life are unlike those of all its predecessors, and which is content to possess Him alone, the Most High and most glorious.'

ON CHARITY AND COMPASSION TOWARDS ONE'S NEIGHBOUR

27

Firstly, how blessed Francis made concessions to a friar who was dying of hunger by eating with him, and how he warned the friars to use discretion in their penance.

DURING the period when blessed Francis began to have brethren, and was living with them at Rivo Torto near Assisi, one night while all the brethren were asleep one of the friars cried out, saying, 'I am dying! I am dying!' Startled and frightened, all the friars awoke. Blessed Francis got up and said, 'Rise, brothers, and light a lamp.' And when it was lit, he said, 'Who was it who said, "I am dying"?' The friar answered, 'It is I.' And he said, 'What is the matter, brother? How are you dying?' And he said, 'I am dying of hunger.'

The holy Father at once ordered food to be brought, and having great charity and discretion, he ate with him lest he should be ashamed to eat alone; and, at his wish, all the other friars joined them. For that friar and all the others were newly converted to the Lord, and used to discipline their bodies without restraint. After they had eaten blessed Francis said to the other friars, 'My brothers, everyone must consider his own constitution, for although one of you may be able to sustain his body on less food, I do not want another who needs more food to try and imitate him in this matter. Each brother must consider his own constitution and allow his body its needs, so that it has the strength to serve the spirit. For while we are bound to avoid over-indulgence in food, which injures both body and soul, we must also avoid excessive abstinence, especially as the Lord *desires mercy, and not sacrifice.*' And he added, 'Dearest brothers, necessity and charity for my brother have moved me to act as I have done, and we have eaten with him lest he be ashamed to eat alone. But I do not wish to do so again, for it would be neither regular nor fitting. It is my wish and command that each of you is to satisfy his body as need demands and so far as our poverty allows.'

For the first friars, and those who followed them for a long while, afflicted their bodies beyond measure by abstinence from food and drink, by vigils, by cold, by coarse clothing, and by manual labour. They wore iron bands and breast-plates, and the roughest of hair shirts. So the holy Father, considering that the friars might fall ill as a result of this—as had already happened in a short time—gave orders in Chapter that no friar should wear anything but the habit next his skin.

But we who were with him bear witness that although he was discreet and moderate towards the brethren throughout his life, this was in order that they should never fall away from poverty and the spirit of our Order. Nevertheless, from the beginning of his conversion until the end of his life, the most holy Father was severe towards his own body, although he was frail by nature and while in the world could not have lived without comfort. At one time, therefore, considering that the friars were exceeding the bounds of poverty and sincerity in food and other matters, he said to a number of friars as representing all the brethren, 'Do not let the brethren imagine that any concession is necessary to my own body. For since it is my duty to be a pattern and example to all the friars, I wish to have, and to be content with, scanty and very poor food, and to make use of all other things in the spirit of poverty, and to shun delicate food altogether.'

1155

How he made a concession to a sick friar by eating grapes with him.

ON another occasion, while blessed Francis was living in the same place, one of the friars, who was a spiritual man and an early member of the Order, was ill and very weak. As he looked at him, the holy Father felt great compassion for him. But because at that time the friars, both healthy and sick, were cheerfully regarding their poverty as plenty, and would not use or ask for medicines in sickness, but willingly accepted bodily privations, blessed Francis said to himself, 'If only this brother could eat some ripe grapes first thing in the morning, I think they would do him good.'

And he acted on this idea, for he rose very early one day, and calling the friar to him privately, led him into a vineyard near the friary. Choosing a vine where the grapes were good to eat, he sat down beside the vine with the friar, and began to eat the grapes lest the brother should be ashamed to eat alone. And as they ate the friar was cured, and they praised God together. This friar remembered the compassion and kindness of the most holy Father for the rest of his life, and often used to tell the brethren about it with devotion and tears.

28

How he stripped himself and his companion to provide clothing for a poor old woman.

AT Celano, one winter, blessed Francis had a length of cloth folded to form a cloak, which a friend of the friars had lent him. When an old woman came to him asking alms, he immediately took the cloth from his shoulders, and although it did not belong to him, he gave it to the poor old woman, saying, 'Go and make a garment for yourself, for you need it badly enough!'

The old woman laughed and was astonished—whether from fear or joy I cannot say—and took the cloth from his hands. Fearing that if she delayed he might take it back, she hurried away and cut up the cloth with shears. But when she discovered that the cloth was not sufficient for a garment, she put her trust in the kindness already shown by the holy Father, and told him that the cloth was not sufficient for a garment.

The Saint looked at his companion, who was wearing a similar piece of cloth on his shoulders, and said, 'Do you hear what this poor woman says? Let us put up with the cold for the love of God, and give the cloth to this poor woman so that her garment can be completed.' And at once his companion gave her his own, just as blessed Francis had done. So both of them remained without a cloak in order that the poor woman might be clothed.

30

How he regarded it as robbery not to give a cloak to one who had greater need.

ONCE when he was returning from Siena, he met a poor man on the road, and said to his companion, 'We ought to return this cloak to the poor man, whose it is; for we have accepted it as a loan until we should find someone poorer than ourselves.' But knowing how badly the generous Father needed it, his companion protested strongly that he should not neglect himself to provide for someone else. But the Saint said to him, 'I refuse to be a thief, for we should be guilty of theft if we refused to give it to one more poor than ourselves.' So the kindly Father gave away the cloak to the poor man.

How he gave a cloak to a poor man on a certain condition.

AT Celle di Cortona blessed Francis was wearing a new cloak which the friars had taken great trouble to obtain for him. But when a poor man came to the friary, weeping for his dead wife and poverty-stricken, bereaved family, the compassionate Saint said to him, 'I give you this cloak on condition that you part with it to no one unless he buys it from you and pays a good price.' Hearing this, the friars ran to take the cloak away from the poor man; but taking courage from the face of the holy Father, he clung to it with both hands. And at length the friars bought back the cloak, and paid a fair price for it to the poor man.

32

How, through the alms of blessed Francis, a poor man forgave his injuries and abandoned his hatred for his master.

AT Celle, in the lordship of Perugia, blessed Francis met a poor man whom he had formerly known in the world, and asked him, 'Brother, how are things with you?' But the man began to utter angry curses on his master, saying, 'Thanks to my master—God curse him!—I have had nothing but misfortune, for he has stripped me of all that I possess.'

Seeing him persist in mortal hatred, blessed Francis was filled with pity for his soul, and said, 'Brother, pardon your master for the love of God, and free your own soul; it is possible that he will restore to you whatever he has taken away. Otherwise, you have lost your goods and will lose your soul as well.' And the man said, 'I cannot fully forgive him unless he first restores to me what he has taken away.' Then blessed Francis said to him, 'Look, I will give you this cloak; I beg you to forgive your master for the love of the Lord God.' And at once his heart was melted and touched by this act of kindness, and he forgave his master his wrongs.

33

How he sent a cloak to a poor woman who, like himself, suffered from her eyes.

A POOR woman of Machilone came to Rieti to be treated for a disease of the eyes. And when the doctor visited blessed Francis, he said to him, 'Brother, a woman has come to me with a disease of the eyes, and she is so poor that I have to pay her expenses myself.' As soon as he heard this he was moved with pity for her, and calling one of the friars who was his Guardian, he said to him, 'Brother Guardian, we have to repay a loan.' 'What is this loan?' asked the Guardian. And he said, 'This cloak, which we have borrowed from a poor, sick woman, and which we must return to her.' And the Guardian said, 'Do whatever seems best to you, Brother.'

Then blessed Francis, with great merriment, called a friend of his who was a spiritual man, and told him, 'Take this cloak, and twelve loaves with it, and go to this poor woman with a disease of the eyes whom the doctor will point out to you. And say to her, "The poor man to whom you lent this cloak thanks you for the loan of it; take back what belongs to you."' So he went and said to the woman all that blessed Francis had told him. But thinking that he was making a fool of her, she was nervous and embarrassed, saying, 'Leave me in peace; I don't know what you are talking about.' But he laid the cloak and the twelve loaves in her hands. Then, realizing that he was speaking in earnest, she accepted them with fear and reverence, rejoicing and praising the Lord. And afraid that they might be taken from her, she rose secretly by night and returned home with joy. But blessed Francis had arranged with the Guardian to pay her expenses daily as long as she remained there.

We who lived with him testify to the greatness of his charity and compassion towards sick and healthy alike, both to his own friars and to other poor folk. For after persuading us not to be upset, he used to give away to the poor with great inward and outward joy even his own bodily necessities, which the friars had sometimes obtained with great trouble and difficulty, thus depriving himself even of things that he badly needed. Because of this the Minister General and his Guardian told him not to give away his habit to any friar without their permission. For in their devotion to him the friars used sometimes to ask him for his habit, and at once he would give it; but sometimes he divided it and gave away a portion, retaining part for himself, for he wore only a single habit.

34

How he gave away his habit to friars who asked it for the love of God.

WHEN he was travelling through one of the Provinces preaching, two French friars met him. And having received great consolation from him, they finally begged his habit for the love of God. And as soon as he heard 'for the love of God,' he took off his habit and gave it to them, remaining unclothed for a good while. For when anyone invoked the love of God he would never refuse his cord, or habit, or anything that they asked. But he was very displeased, and often rebuked the friars, when he heard them use the words 'for the love of God' without good cause. For he used to say, 'The love of God is so sublime and precious that it should only be mentioned on rare occasions and in great need, and then with great reverence.'

But one of these friars removed his own habit, and gave it to him in exchange. Whenever he gave away his own habit, or part of it to anyone, he suffered great want and distress, because he could not obtain another or have it made quickly, especially as he always wished to have a shabby habit, patched up with pieces of cloth, sometimes both inside and out. Indeed, he would seldom or never wear a new habit, but obtained an old habit from another friar. And sometimes he would obtain part of his habit from one friar, and part from another. But at times he used to line it inside with new cloth, because of his frequent illnesses and chills of the stomach and spleen. He observed this absolute poverty in clothing up to the very year in which he departed to the Lord. For, a few days before his death, since he was suffering from dropsy and almost dried up by his many ailments, the friars made him several habits, so that his habit could be changed night or day whenever necessary.

35

How he wished to give some cloth to a poor man secretly.

ON another occasion a poor man came to the friary where blessed Francis was staying, and begged a piece of cloth from the friars for the love of God. When he heard of this, the holy Father said to one of the friars, 'Search through the house, and see if you can find any length or piece of cloth, and give it to this poor man.' But having gone around the whole house, the friar told him that he could find nothing.

So in order that the poor man should not go away empty-handed, blessed Francis stole away quietly—lest the Guardian should forbid him—and took a knife. Then he sat down in a remote place and began to cut away part of his habit which was sewed on the inside, intending to give it to the poor man secretly. But the Guardian noticed him, and at once forbade him to give it away, especially as there was a hard frost at the time, and he was very frail and cold. So the holy Father said to him, 'If you do not want me to give the man this piece, you must make sure that some other piece is given to our poor brother.' And at the insistence of blessed Francis, the friars gave the poor man some cloth from their own garments.

Whenever he travelled about the world preaching, if any brother lent him a cloak, he would not accept it unless he was allowed to give it to any poor man whom he met or who came to him, if the voice of his own conscience told him that it was necessary to that person. He always went on foot, and only rode a donkey after he became ill. Only in the most pressing need would he use a horse; normally he refused to ride at all, and only did so a short while before his death.

36

How he told Brother Giles, before he was received into the Order, to give his cloak to a poor man.

AT the beginning of the Order, when he was living at Rivo Torto with only two friars, a man named Giles, who became the third friar, came to him from the world in order to share his way of life. And when he had remained there for some days, still wearing his secular clothes, a poor man came to the place asking alms of blessed Francis. Turning to Giles, blessed Francis said to him, 'Give this poor brother your cloak.' At once Giles gladly removed it from his back and gave it to the poor man. Then it became clear to him that God had imparted a new grace to his heart, since he had given his cloak to the poor man with great cheerfulness. So he was received into the Order by blessed Francis, and constantly advanced in virtue to the greatest perfection.

37

On the penance that he imposed on a friar who had wrongfully criticized a certain poor man.

WHEN blessed Francis had gone to preach at a house of the friars near Rocca Brizzi, it happened that on the day he was due to preach, a poor, sick man came to him. Full of compassion for him, he began to speak about the man's poverty and sickness to his companion. And his companion said to him, 'Brother, it is true that this man seems poor enough, but it may be that no one in the whole Province has a greater desire for riches.' He was at once severely rebuked by blessed Francis, and confessed his fault. Then the Father said to him, 'Are you ready to perform the penance that I give you?' 'I will do it willingly,' he replied. And he said to him, 'Go and remove your habit, and throw yourself naked at the poor man's feet, and tell him how you have sinned in speaking ill of him, and ask him to pray for you.' So the friar went and did all that blessed Francis had told him. Then he rose and resumed his habit, and returned to blessed Francis. And the Father said to him, 'Do you want to know how you sinned against him, and against Christ Himself? Whenever you see a poor man, remember Christ in Whose Name he comes, and how He took upon Himself our poverty and weakness. For this man's poverty serves us as a mirror, in which we should view and consider with pity the weakness and poverty of our Lord Jesus Christ, which He endured in His own body for our salvation.'

38

How he ordered a New Testament to be given to a poor woman, the mother of two friars.

ANOTHER time, while he was staying at S. Mary of the Porziuncula, a poor old woman, who had two sons in the Order, came to the friary asking alms of blessed Francis. He immediately asked Brother Peter Catanii, who was then Minister General, 'Have we anything to give our mother?' For he used to say that the mother of any friar was mother to himself and to all the friars. Brother Peter said to him, 'There is nothing in the house that we can give her, for she wants the kind of alms that can sustain her bodily needs. But in the church we have a single New Testament, from which we read the lessons at Matins.' (For at that time the friars had no breviaries and few psalters.) So blessed Francis said to him, 'Give the New Testament to our mother, so that she can sell it for her needs. I am sure that this will please our Lord and the Blessed Virgin better than if we were to read from it.' So he gave it to her. For it can be said and written of him as is read of blessed Job: *Loving care has borne me company as I grew up from childhood, ever since I left my mother's womb.*

To us who lived with him it would be a long and very difficult task to write or describe not only what we have learned from others about his charity and kindness toward the friars and other poor folk, but what we have seen with our own eyes.

ON THE PERFECTION OF HOLY HUMILITY AND OBEDIENCE IN BLESSED FRANCIS AND HIS FRIARS

39

Firstly, how he resigned his office as head of the Order, and appointed Friar Peter Catanii as Minister General.

IN order to preserve the virtue of holy humility, blessed Francis resigned the chief office before all the friars during a Chapter held a few years after his conversion, saying, 'I am now as though dead to you. Look to Peter Catanii, whom you and I will all obey.' And falling to his knees before him, he promised him obedience and reverence.

At this all the friars wept, and intolerable grief wrung deep groans from them when they saw themselves deprived of so great a Father in this way. But with eyes raised to heaven and hands clasped, the blessed Father rose and said, 'Lord, I commend to Thee the family which hitherto Thou hast entrusted to me. Because of my infirmities which Thou knowest, sweetest Lord, I now entrust it to the Ministers, for I no longer have the strength to care for it. They shall render account to Thee in the Day of Judgement, O Lord, if any friar shall have perished through their negligence, bad example, or harsh correction.'

Thenceforward until his death he remained subject to them, behaving himself more humbly in all things than any others.

40

How he gave up his own companion, not desiring to have any particular companion.

ON another occasion he gave up all his companions to his Vicar, saying, 'I do not wish to appear alone in the privilege of having an especial companion of my own. Let the friars accompany me from place to place as the Lord shall move them.' And he added, 'Recently I saw a blind man who had only a little dog to guide him on his way, and I do not want to seem better than he.'

For it was always his glory to renounce every trace of privilege and ostentation so that the virtue of Christ might dwell in him.

41

How the disloyalty of the Ministers caused him to surrender his office.

ONCE, when asked by one of the friars why he had abandoned his charge of the friars and entrusted them into the hands of others as though they did not belong to him at all, he replied, 'My son, I love the brethren to the utmost of my power, but if they would follow in my footsteps I should love them still more, and would not make myself a stranger to them. For some of the superiors pull them in another direction, holding up to them as patterns the men of long ago, and disregarding my warnings. But what they are doing and the way in which they are now acting will appear more clearly in the end.'

And shortly afterwards, when he was burdened with severe illness, he raised himself in bed, and cried out in vehemence of spirit, 'Who are these who have torn my Order and my friars out of my hands? If I come to the General Chapter I will make my intention clear!'

*How he humbly obtained meat for the sick, and urged them to be
humble and patient.*

BLESSED Francis was not ashamed to obtain meat for a sick friar
in the public places of cities, but he warned those who were ill
to endure want patiently, and not to create a disturbance when
there was not sufficient food for their needs.

So in the first Rule he caused this to be written: *I beg my sick
friars not to grow impatient in their infirmities, nor to complain against
the Lord or the brethren, nor to insist on having medicines, nor to have
an undue desire to liberate this swiftly-perishing body, which is the
enemy of the soul. But let them give thanks for all things, that they
may desire to be men such as God wills them to be; for those whom
the Lord has predestined to eternal life He trains with the spur of
scourges and infirmities. As He Himself says:* 'It is those I love that
I correct and chasten.'

*The humble reply of blessed Francis and blessed Dominic when they
were both asked whether they were willing for their friars to become
prelates in the Church.*

IN the city of Rome, when those two illustrious lights of the
world, blessed Francis and blessed Dominic, were together in
the presence of the Lord Cardinal of Ostia, who later became
Pope, and when each in turn had spoken sweetly of God, my
Lord of Ostia at length said, 'In the primitive Church the
pastors and prelates were poor men, burning with charity, not
with greed. Why should we not choose bishops and prelates
from among your friars, so that they may influence all the others
by their witness and example?'

Then there arose a humble and devout dispute between the

Saints as to which of them was to reply, for neither wished to take precedence, but each deferred to the other, urging him to answer. But at length the humility of Francis prevailed, in that he did not answer first, while Dominic also prevailed, in that by answering first he also humbly obeyed.

So blessed Dominic said, 'My Lord, my friars have already been raised to a noble state if they will only realize it; and in so far as I am able, I will never permit them to obtain any shadow of dignity.' Then blessed Francis, bowing low before the Lord Cardinal, said, 'My Lord, my friars are called Minors so that they may not presume to become greater. Their vocation teaches them to remain in a humble place, and to follow in the footsteps of Christ's humility, so that by this means they may at last be exalted above others in the eyes of the Saints. So if you wish them to bear fruit in the Church of God, hold them to the observance of their vocation. And should they aspire to high place, thrust them down to their proper level, and never allow them to rise to any prelacy.'

Such were the replies of the Saints, and when they had ended, the Lord of Ostia was much edified by the answers of both, and gave profound thanks to God.

As they were both taking leave together, blessed Dominic asked blessed Francis if he would consent to give him the cord which he wore; but although he asked this favour out of love, blessed Francis refused it out of humility. At length Dominic's loving persistence prevailed, and having obtained the cord, he girded it beneath his habit and wore it devoutly from that time on.

Then each placed his hands between the hands of the other and commended himself to him with the most affectionate regard. And blessed Dominic said to blessed Francis, 'Brother Francis, I wish that your Order and mine could become one, and that we could live within the Church under the same Rule.' When at length they had taken leave of one another, blessed Dominic said to those standing by, 'I tell you in all truth that every Religious should imitate this holy man Francis, so great is the perfection of his sanctity.'

44

How, in order to establish humility, he wished all the friars to serve lepers.

FROM the first days of his conversion blessed Francis, like a wise builder, established himself with God's help on the firm rock of the perfect humility and poverty of the Son of God. And because of his own profound humility, he called his Order that of Friars Minor.

So at the commencement of the Order he wished the friars to live in leper-houses to serve them, and by so doing to establish themselves in holy humility. For whenever anyone, whether noble or commoner, entered the Order, among the other instructions given him, he was told that he must humbly serve the lepers and live with them in their houses, as was laid down in the Rule: *Seeking to possess nothing under heaven save holy poverty, in which they will be nourished by the Lord with food for body and soul in this world, and in the life to come will attain the heritage of heaven.*

So he laid foundations both for himself and others on the deepest poverty and humility, for when he might have become a great prelate in the Church of God, he chose and willed to be humble, not only in the Church but among his own friars as well. For in his opinion and desire, this lowliness was to be his highest dignity in the sight of God and men.

45

How he wished the glory and honour of all his good words and deeds to be given to God alone.

WHEN he had been preaching to the people of Terni in the town square, as soon as his sermon had ended, the bishop of the place, who was a discerning and spiritual man, rose and said to the people, 'From the beginning, when our Lord planted and founded His Church, He has always enlightened it through holy men who have fostered it by word and example. But now in these latter days He has enlightened it through this poor, undistinguished and unlearned man Francis. Therefore love and honour our Lord, and beware of sin; *for He has not dealt so with any other nation.*'

When he had ended speaking, the Bishop came down from the place where he had preached and entered the Cathedral. And blessed Francis went up to him, bowed before him, and threw himself at his feet, saying, 'My Lord Bishop, I assure you that no man in this world has ever done me such honour as you have done me this day. For other men say, "This is a holy man," and attribute glory and holiness to me, rather than the Creator. But you are a discerning man, and have distinguished between the precious and the worthless.'

For when blessed Francis was praised and called a saint, he used to answer such comments by saying: 'I am not as yet so secure that I might not have sons and daughters! For if at any time the Lord were to deprive me of the treasure that He has entrusted to me, what would remain to me but a body and a soul, and even unbelievers have this? In fact, I am quite sure that if the Lord had granted a thief or an unbeliever as many great gifts as He has to me, they would have been more faithful to Him than I. For in a picture of our Lord and the Blessed Virgin painted on wood, it is the Lord and the Blessed Virgin who receive honour, while the wood and the painting claim nothing for themselves; in the same way a servant of God is a kind of picture of God, in whom God is honoured for His favour. But he may not claim any credit for himself, for in comparison with God he is less than the wood and the painting; indeed, he is nothing at all. Honour and glory are to be given to God alone; but to a man himself nothing but shame and sorrow as long as he lives amid the miseries of this world.'

1170

How until his death he wished to have one of his companions as his Guardian, and to live under obedience.

WISHING to remain in perfect humility and obedience until death, he said to the Minister General a long while before this, 'I would like you to transfer your own authority over me to one of my companions, whom I will obey in your place; for holy obedience is of such merit that I wish it to remain with me both in life and death.' And thenceforward until his death he had one of his own companions as his Guardian, and obeyed him in the place of the Minister General. He once said to his companions, 'The Lord has granted me this favour among others, that if a novice who had entered the Order this very day were assigned to me as Guardian, I would obey him as gladly as one who is senior and of long standing in the Order. For a man under authority should regard his superior not as a man, but as God, for love of Whom he is subject to him.' Later he said, 'Did I so wish it, the Lord could make me more feared by my friars than any other Superior in the world. But the Lord has granted me the favour of desiring to be content with everything, as one who is of no account in the Order.'

As he himself testifies, we who lived with him have seen with our own eyes how, when some of the friars did not provide for his needs, or spoke to him in a way that usually provokes a man, he at once went away to pray; and when he returned, he would not recall anything, nor did he ever say, 'So-and-so did not please me,' or, 'So-and-so said this to me.'

Persevering in this way of life, the nearer he drew to death, the more careful he was to consider how he could live and die in all humility and poverty, and in the perfecting of all virtues.

On the perfect way of obedience which he taught.

THE most holy Father used to say to his friars, 'Dearest brothers, carry out an order at once, and don't wait for it to be repeated. Don't plead or object that anything in a command is impossible, for if I were to order you to do something beyond your strength, holy obedience would not fail to support you.'

48

How he compared perfect obedience to a dead body.

ONCE, while he was sitting with his companions, he voiced this complaint: 'There is hardly a single Religious in the whole world who obeys his superior well!' His companions at once said to him, 'Tell us, Father, what is the perfect and best form of obedience?' In reply he described true and perfect obedience under the simile of a dead body. 'Take up a dead body,' he said, 'and lay it where you will. You will see that it does not resist being removed, or complain of its position, or ask to be left alone. If it is lifted on to a chair, it does not look up, but down. If it is clothed in purple, it looks paler than ever. In the same way, one who is truly obedient does not question why he is moved, does not mind where he is placed, and does not demand to be transferred. If he is promoted to high office, he remains as humble as before, and the more he is honoured, the more unworthy he considers himself.'

Whenever blessed Francis received direct and simple commands, rather than requests, he regarded them as commands under holy obedience. But he believed that the highest form of obedience, in which flesh and blood plays no part, is to go among the unbelievers under the inspiration of God, either to help one's fellow men or with a desire for martyrdom. He considered that to seek martyrdom was truly acceptable to God.

49

How it is dangerous to give an order under obedience too hastily, or to disobey an order given under obedience.

THE blessed Father considered that an order under obedience should be given but seldom, and that it was a weapon not to be used in the first instance, but in the last resort. He said, 'The hand should not be laid on the sword too hastily.' He used to say that when a man has no pressing reason to delay, then if he does not quickly obey an order given under obedience he neither fears God nor respects man. Neither is anything more true than this, for the authority to command in the hands of a person who uses it rashly is like a sword in the hand of an angry man. And who is more abandoned than a Religious who ignores or despises obedience?

50

How he answered friars who were persuading him to ask permission for them to preach freely.

SOME of the friars said to blessed Francis, 'Father, do you not realize that sometimes the bishops will not allow us to preach, and make us wait around idle in one place for many days before we can preach the word of God? It would be better if you sought some privilege from the Lord Pope in this matter, for it concerns the salvation of souls.'

He answered them with a stern rebuke, saying, 'You Friars Minor don't understand God's will, and won't allow me to convert the whole world in the way God wills. For first of all I want to convert the bishops by our holy humility and respect.

When they come to see our holy way of life and our humble respect for them, they will ask you to preach and convert the people. These things will draw people to your preaching far better than your privileges, which would only lead you into pride.

'And if you are free from all avarice and can persuade the people to restore their rights to the churches, they will themselves ask you to hear the confessions of their people; although you need not concern yourselves on this matter, for once they are converted, they will easily find confessors. For my part, the only favour that I ask of God is that I may never receive any favours from men. I wish to show respect to everyone, and by obedience to the holy Rule, to convert all men by my own example rather than by words.'

51

On the custom by which the friars in those days effected a reconciliation when one friar had offended another.

HE used to say that the Friars Minor had been sent by God in these latest days to set an example to those who were shrouded in the darkness of their sins. He said that whenever he heard about the great achievements of holy friars who were scattered all over the world, he was bathed in the sweetest of perfumes and anointed with the virtue of precious unguents.

On one occasion one of the friars happened to speak harshly to another in the presence of a nobleman of Cyprus. Directly he realized that his brother was somewhat distressed by this, he was angry with himself, and taking up some ass's dung, he put it in his mouth, and ground it with his teeth, saying, 'The tongue that has poured out the poison of anger against my brother shall see what dung tastes like!' The nobleman who saw this was struck with amazement, and went away much edified; and thenceforward he placed himself and all his property at the disposal of the friars.

All the friars observed a custom that whenever any of them said anything hurtful or offensive to another, he would at once throw himself to the ground and kiss the feet of the offended brother, humbly asking his pardon. The holy Father was very happy whenever he heard that his sons were setting examples of holiness of their own accord, and he lavished most acceptable blessings on friars who brought sinners to the love of Christ by word or deed. For he desired that his sons should bear a true resemblance to him in the zeal for souls that filled him so completely.

52

How Christ complained to Brother Leo, the companion of blessed Francis, about the ingratitude and pride of the friars.

THE Lord Jesus Christ once complained to Brother Leo, the companion of blessed Francis: 'Friar Leo, I am grieved with the friars.' And Brother Leo replied, 'Why so, Lord?' And the Lord said, 'For three reasons. Firstly, because they do not recognize My blessings, which, as you know, I pour upon them so freely and abundantly, although they neither sow nor reap. Secondly, because they grumble and are idle all day long. And thirdly, because they often provoke one another to anger and do not return to love, nor do they pardon any injury that they receive.'

53

How he gave a true and humble answer to a Doctor of the Order of Preachers, who questioned him on a passage of Scripture.

WHILE he was staying in Siena he was visited by a Doctor of Theology from the Order of Preachers, a man who was both humble and sincerely spiritual. When he had discussed the words of our Lord with blessed Francis for some while, this Doctor asked him about the passage in Ezekiel: *When I threaten the sinner with doom of death, it is for thee to give him word and warn him.* And he said, 'Good Father, I know many people who are in mortal sin, and do not warn them of their wickedness. Will their souls be required at my hand?' Blessed Francis humbly answered that he was no scholar, so that it would be more profitable for him to receive instruction from his questioner than to offer his own opinion on Scripture. The humble Doctor then added, 'Brother, although I have heard this passage expounded by various learned men, I would be glad to know how you interpret it.' So blessed Francis said, 'If the passage is to be understood in general terms, I take it to mean that a servant of God should burn and shine in such a way by his own life and holiness that he rebukes all wicked people by the light of his example and the devoutness of his conversation; in this way the brightness of his life and the fragrance of his reputation will make all men aware of their own wickedness.'

Greatly edified, the Doctor went away, and said to the companions of blessed Francis, 'My brothers, this man's theology is grounded on purity and contemplation, and resembles a flying eagle; but our knowledge crawls along the ground on its belly.'

54

On preserving humility, and on being at peace with the clergy.

BLESSED Francis wished his sons to be at peace with all men and to behave themselves humbly to everyone, but he showed them by his own words and example to be especially humble to the clergy. For he said, 'We have been sent to help the clergy in the salvation of souls, so that we may supply whatever is lacking in them. But men will not be rewarded according to their office, but their work. Remember, my brothers, that the winning of souls is what pleases God most, and we can do this better by working in harmony with the clergy than in opposition. But if they obstruct the salvation of the people, vengeance belongs to God, and He will punish them in His own time. So obey your superiors, and let there be no wrongful jealousy on your part. If you are sons of peace, you will win both clergy and people, and this will be more pleasing to God than if you were to win the people alone and alienate the clergy. Conceal their mistakes and make up for their many defects; and when you have done this, be even more humble than before.'

55

How he humbly obtained the church of S. Mary of the Angels from the Abbot of S. Benedict at Assisi, and how he wished the friars always to live there and behave with humility.

WHEN blessed Francis saw that the Lord willed to increase the number of the friars, he said to them: 'My dearest brothers and sons, I realize that God wills to add to our numbers. It seems good and godly to me that we should obtain from the Bishop, or from the Canons of S. Ruffino, or from the Abbot of S. Benedict some church where the friars may say their Hours, and have some poor little dwelling near by made of clay and wattle where the brethren may rest and work. For this place is not suitable or adequate for the friars now that the Lord wills to increase our numbers, especially as we have no church here where the friars can say their Hours. And if any friar were to die, it would not be fitting to bury him here or in a church belonging to the secular clergy.' And all the friars supported this suggestion.

So he went to the Bishop of Assisi and put this request to him. But the Bishop said, 'Brother, I have no church to offer you,' and the Canons gave the same answer. Then he went to the Abbot of S. Benedict on Monte Subasio, and made the

1177

same request to him. The Abbot was roused to sympathy, and took counsel with his monks; and guided by the grace and will of God, he granted to blessed Francis and his friars the church of S. Mary of the Porziuncula, which was the smallest and poorest church that they had. And the Abbot said to blessed Francis, 'See, Brother, we have granted your request. But if the Lord causes this congregation of yours to grow, we wish this place to become the chief of all your churches.' His suggestion pleased blessed Francis and his brethren, and he was delighted with this place granted to the friars, especially since the church was named after the Mother of Christ, and was so poor and small. He was also happy that it was called the *Porziuncula*, which foreshadowed that it was destined to become the Mother-House and chief church of the poor Friars Minor, for it had been known by this name from earliest times. So blessed Francis used to say, 'This was why the Lord willed that no other church should be given to the friars, and that the first friars should not build a new church or have any but this'; for in this way an old prophecy was fulfilled by the coming of the Friars Minor. And although it was poor and nearly in ruins, the people of the city of Assisi and the whole district had for a long time held the church in great reverence. To-day their reverence is still greater, and grows day by day.

So the friars at once went to live there, and the Lord added to their numbers almost daily. And the fragrance of their reputation spread marvellously through the Vale of Spoleto and many parts of the land. But in ancient times it had been called S. Mary of the Angels, because it was said that the songs of angels were often heard there.

Although the Abbot and monks had made a free gift of the church to blessed Francis and his friars, he, as a good and experienced master-builder, wished to establish his house—that is, his Order—on a firm foundation of absolute poverty. So each year he sent to the Abbot and monks a basket or jar full of little fish, known as *lasche*. This served as a reminder of their greater poverty and humility, and of the fact that the friars were to possess no place of their own, or live in any place that was not the property of others, so that the friars had no right to buy or sell anything. But when the friars carried the fish to the monks each year, the monks used to give them a jar of oil, in recognition of the humility of blessed Francis who had done this of his own free will.

Those of us who lived with blessed Francis testify that he solemnly affirmed that it had been revealed to him that the Blessed Virgin had a greater love for this church than for any others in the world, because of the many favours that God had granted there. So thenceforward he held it in the greatest reverence and devotion; and in order that the friars should always remember this in their hearts, he had it written in his Testament at his death that all friars should do likewise. For about the time of his death he said in the presence of the Minister General and other friars: 'I wish to entrust and bequeath the friary of S. Mary of the Porziuncula to my brethren by my Testament, in order that it may always be held in the greatest reverence and devotion by the friars. Our earliest brethren always did this, and because this place is holy, beloved, and chosen before all others by Christ and the glorious Virgin, they preserved its sanctity by constant prayer and silence day and night. If they had occasion to speak after the close of the appointed silence, they did so with the greatest devotion and sincerity, and only on matters which concerned the praise of God and the salvation of souls. And if ever anyone began to talk unprofitably or idly—although this seldom occurred—he was at once corrected by another friar.

'These brethren used to discipline their bodies with many fasts and vigils, with cold, nakedness, and manual labour. To avoid idleness they often helped the poor in their fields, and afterwards gave them the bread of the love of God. They hallowed the place with these and other virtues, and kept themselves in sanctity. But since those days, because friars and layfolk visit the place more often than before, and because the friars are less zealous in prayer and good works, and are more undisciplined in engaging in idle conversation and discussing worldly events than they used to be, the place is not held in so great a reverence and devotion as was customary hitherto, and as I would wish it to be.'

Having said this, he ended with great fervour, saying, 'I wish this place always to be under the direct control of the Minister General and servant, so that he may exercise the greatest care and responsibility in providing a good and holy family for it. The clergy are to be chosen from among the better, more holy, and more suitable of the friars, who best know how to recite the Office and who are fully professed in the Order, so that both layfolk and the other friars may see and hear them gladly and with great devotion. The lay-brothers chosen to serve them are to be holy men, discreet, humble and honest. I do not wish anyone else, whether layfolk or friars, to enter the place, except the Minister General and the lay-brothers who serve them. The friars themselves are not to speak to anyone except the brothers who serve them and the Minister General when he visits them. Similarly, the lay-brothers who serve them are never to gossip with them or tell them worldly news, or anything that is not of benefit to their souls. I particularly desire that no one else shall enter this place, so that its purity and holiness may the better be preserved, and that nothing unedifying be done or said there. Let the whole place be kept pure and holy with hymns and praises to God.

'And whenever any of the friars shall pass away to the Lord, I wish the Minister General to send a holy friar from another house to take his place. For even if other friars have at times fallen away from purity and sincerity, I wish this place to be blessed, and to remain for ever as a mirror and holy pattern for the whole Order, and as a lamp burning and shining before the throne of God and of the Blessed Virgin. For the sake of this place may God pardon the defects and faults of all the friars, and protect this Order, His little plant, for ever.'

56

On the humble reverence which he showed by sweeping and cleaning churches.

ONCE while he was staying at S. Mary of the Porziuncula and there were as yet few friars, blessed Francis went through the villages and churches round about the city of Assisi proclaiming and preaching to the people that they should do penance. And he carried a broom to sweep out churches that were dirty, for he was very grieved when he found any church not as clean as he wished.

So when he had ended his sermon, he would always gather all the priests in some private place so that he would not be overheard by layfolk, and speak to them about the salvation of souls, stressing in particular how they should take care to keep the churches and altars clean, as well as everything that concerned the celebration of the Divine Mysteries.

57

On the peasant who found him humbly sweeping a church; how the man was converted, entered the Order, and became a holy friar.

ONCE blessed Francis went to a village church in the neighbourhood of Assisi, and humbly began to sweep and clean it. A report of what he was doing immediately spread through the whole village, for the people were always happy to see him and even more happy to listen to him. But when a peasant named John, a man of wonderful simplicity, heard about it as he was ploughing in his field, he went to him at once and found him humbly and devoutly sweeping the church. And he said to him, 'Brother, give me the broom; I would like to help you.' And taking the broom from his hands, he swept the rest of the church.

While they were sitting down together, he said to blessed Francis, 'Brother, I have longed to serve God for a long time, especially since I have heard accounts of you and your friars, but I did not know how to find you. Now that it has pleased God that I should see you, I would like to do whatever you think best.' Recognizing his fervour, the blessed Father gave thanks to God, for at that time he had few brethren, and it seemed that the man's simplicity and purity would make him a good Religious. So he said to him, 'Brother, if you wish to join our life and society, you will have to strip yourself of all that you possess, so far as is right, and give it to the poor as the holy Gospel teaches. For all my friars who could do so have done the same.'

Hearing this, the peasant at once went back to the field where he had left his oxen and untied them. And he led one of them to blessed Francis, saying, 'Brother, I have served my father and family for many years, and although my part of the inheritance is small, I would like to take this ox as my share, and give it to the poor as you think best.' But when his parents and brothers, who were still small, realized that he intended to leave them, they began to weep aloud, and uttered such pitiful cries of grief that blessed Francis was moved to compassion, for the family was large and they were simple folk. He said: 'Prepare a meal for us all, and let us eat together. And don't weep, because I am going to make you really happy.' So they prepared it at once, and all ate together with great joy.

After the meal blessed Francis said to them, 'This son of yours wishes to serve God, and you ought not to be grieved at this, but very glad. It will bring you great honour and blessing in soul and body, both in the eyes of God and those of the world, for God will be honoured by your own flesh and blood, and all our friars will become your sons and brothers. I cannot and may not return your son to you, for he is God's creature and wishes to serve his Creator, to serve whom is to reign. But in order to console you I want him to give you this ox as he would do to the poor, although he should have given it to other poor folk as the Gospel teaches.' And they were all comforted by the words of blessed Francis, and overjoyed that the ox was restored to them, for they were very poor.

And because blessed Francis took the greatest delight in pure and holy simplicity, whether in himself or others, he immediately clothed Brother John in the religious habit and humbly took him as his own companion. Now John was so simple that he thought himself obliged to copy everything that blessed Francis did. So whenever blessed Francis stood to pray in church or anywhere else, he wanted to watch him so that he could follow his every movement. And if blessed Francis knelt, or raised his hands to heaven, or spat, or sighed, he did the same. When the Father noticed this, he took him to task with great amusement for simplicity of this sort. But he answered, 'Brother, I have promised to do everything that you do, so I must imitate you in all things.' And blessed Francis was amazed and very pleased to find him so pure and simple.

In due course Brother John made such progress in all virtues and good ways that blessed Francis and all the friars marvelled at his perfection. And after a few years he died in this state of holy virtue, and in later days blessed Francis used to tell the friars about his conversion with great joy, and spoke of him, not as Brother John, but as holy John.

58

How he punished himself by eating out of the same dish as a leper, because he had caused him humiliation.

WHEN blessed Francis had returned to the church of S. Mary of the Porziuncula, he found Brother James the Simple there with a leper who was covered with sores. For blessed Francis had entrusted this leper and all the others to his care, because he was like a doctor to them, and gladly handled their wounds, changed the dressings, and looked after them, for at that time the friars used to live in the leper-hospice.

Blessed Francis reproved Brother James, saying, 'You should not take our brothers in Christ about in this way; it is not fitting for you or for them.' For although he wished to serve them, he did not want him to take those who were badly diseased outside the hospice, because people looked on them with such revulsion. But Brother James was so simple that he used to go with them from the hospice as far as the church of S. Mary, as though he was walking with the friars. And blessed Francis himself used to call the lepers 'brothers in Christ.'

As soon as he had uttered these words, blessed Francis reproached himself, feeling that the leper had been put to humiliation by the rebuke given to Brother James. So wishing to make amends to God and the leper, he confessed his fault to Peter Catanii, who was Minister General at the time. And he said, 'I wish you to confirm the penance that I have chosen to do for this fault, and ask you not to oppose me in any way.' 'Do as you wish, Brother,' he replied. For Brother Peter so venerated and feared him that he would not presume to oppose him, although he often had cause to regret it.

Then blessed Francis said, 'This is to be my penance: I am going to eat out of the same dish as my brother in Christ.' So when he sat down at table with the leper, a single dish was placed between blessed Francis and the leper. Now the leper was covered in sores and repulsive, especially as the fingers with which he took pieces of food from the dish were shrivelled and bleeding, so that when he placed them in the dish blood and matter dripped into it. Brother Peter and the other friars were greatly shocked as they watched this, but dared not say anything because of their fear and reverence for the holy Father.

The writer saw these things himself, and testifies to them.

59

How he put devils to flight by humble prayer.

BLESSED Francis once visited the church of S. Peter of Bovara near the castle of Trevi in the Vale of Spoleto, and with him went Brother Pacificus, who in the world had been known as 'The King of Verse,' a nobleman and master of singers at the Court. But the church was deserted, and blessed Francis said to Brother Pacificus, 'Go back to the leper-hospice, for I would like to remain alone here to-night; but come back for me very early to-morrow.'

So he remained there by himself, and when he had said Compline and other prayers, he wished to rest and sleep, but could not do so, for his soul grew afraid, his body trembled, and he began to experience diabolic temptations. So making the sign of the Cross he immediately left the church, saying, 'In the Name of Almighty God, I tell you devils that you may do to my body whatever our Lord Jesus Christ allows, for I am ready to endure anything. My own body is the worst enemy that I have, so that you will be taking vengeance on my own adversary and direst foe.' At once these temptations ceased, and when he had returned to the place where he had been lying, he fell into a peaceful sleep.

60

On the vision seen by Brother Pacificus, and how he heard that the seat of Lucifer was reserved for the humble Francis.

EARLY next morning Brother Pacificus returned and found blessed Francis standing before the altar in prayer. So he waited for him outside the choir, and himself prayed before the crucifix. And as he began to pray, he was caught up into heaven—whether his spirit left his body I cannot tell—and saw many thrones set in heaven. One of these was more exalted and glorious than all others, adorned and glowing with all kinds of precious stones. As he admired its beauty, he began to wonder whose throne it might be; when all at once he heard a voice saying to him, 'This was the throne of Lucifer, and the humble Francis shall sit on it in his place.'

As soon as he returned to himself, blessed Francis came out to him, and immediately Brother Pacificus fell at his feet, folding his arms in the form of a cross. And gazing at him as though he were already seated on that throne in heaven, he said to him, 'Father, hear my petition, and ask God to have mercy on me and forgive my sins.' But blessed Francis stretched out his hand and raised him, knowing inwardly that Brother Pacificus had seen some vision during his prayer, for he seemed quite altered, and spoke to him not as though he were living in the body, but already reigning in heaven. And Brother Pacificus was unwilling to talk about his vision afterwards, but began to speak of other things. Later he said, 'Brother, what do you think of yourself?' And blessed Francis replied, 'I think that I am a greater sinner than anyone in this world.' And at once it came to the mind of Brother Pacificus, 'By this sign you can be sure that the vision that you have seen is true. For as Lucifer was cast down from that throne because of his pride, so blessed Francis will merit to be raised up and take his place on it because of his humility.'

61

How blessed Francis had himself led naked before the people with a rope tied round his neck.

ONCE when he had recovered somewhat from a very grave illness, he felt that he had been rather self-indulgent during it, although in fact he had eaten very little. So although not yet recovered from quartan fever, he got up one day and had the people of the town of Assisi called together in the square for a sermon. But after the sermon he asked the people not to leave the place until he returned. And he went into the Cathedral of S. Ruffino with many of the friars, and with Brother Peter Catanii, who had been a canon of that church and was chosen as the first Minister General by blessed Francis. And he ordered Brother Peter under obedience to do whatever he told him without argument. Brother Peter answered, 'Brother, I neither may or should desire anything or do anything either on your behalf or my own without your permission.'

Then blessed Francis removed his habit, and told Brother Peter to fasten a cord round his neck and lead him naked in front of the people to the place where he had preached to them. He told another friar to take a bowl of ashes, and go up to the place where he had preached; and when they arrived, he was to throw the ashes in his face. This friar did not obey him, because of the deep compassion and pity that he had for him; but Brother Peter, however, took the cord fastened round his neck, and led him along as he had ordered. And as he went he wept aloud, and the other friars with him shed tears of compassion and grief.

When blessed Francis had been led naked before the people to the place where he had preached, he said to them, 'You, and all who have followed me in renouncing the world and entered the Order and life of the Friars, believe me to be a holy man. But I confess before God and you that during my illness I have eaten meat and stew flavoured with meat.' In their great devotion and pity for him, most of the people began to weep, especially as it was winter and bitterly cold, and he had not yet recovered from quartan fever. And they beat their breasts, accusing themselves, and saying, 'We know that this saint leads a holy life, for he has reduced his body to the likeness of a living corpse by his abstinence and austerity ever since his conversion to Christ. And if he accuses himself with such remorse for having taken what was right and necessary for his body, what shall we

1187

wretches do, who have spent our entire lives gratifying the desires of the flesh, and still do so?'

62

How he wanted everyone to know what comforts his body had enjoyed.

ON another occasion, while he was living in a certain hermitage (*Poggio Bustone*) during the Fast of S. Martin (*November* 11 *until the Eve of Christmas*), he had eaten some food cooked in lard, because oil was very bad for him in his weakness. At the end of the fast, as he was preaching to a great crowd of people, the opening words of his sermon were, 'You have come to me with great devotion, supposing me to be a holy man; but I confess before God and you that during this fast I have eaten food cooked in lard.'

Whenever he was eating with layfolk, or when some delicacy had been prepared by the friars because of his weakness, he would usually publish the fact both inside and outside the house in front of any friars and layfolk who did not know about it, saying, 'I have eaten such and such food,' for he did not wish to conceal from man what was known to God. In the same way, in whatever place or company his spirit was tempted to pride, vainglory, or any other sin, he at once confessed it to them openly and without concealment. On one occasion he said to his companions, 'In any hermitage or other place where I stay I wish to live as though everyone could see me; for if they think me a holy man and I do not lead a life becoming to a holy man, I shall be a hypocrite.'

When it was bitterly cold and one of his companions, who was his Guardian, wanted to sew a small piece of fox fur under his habit to protect his weak stomach and spleen, blessed Francis said, 'If you want me to wear fox fur under my habit, I must wear a piece of fur outside, so that everyone may know that I am wearing it underneath as well.' So he had it made in this

1188

way; but although it was very necessary to him, he seldom wore it.

63

How he accused himself of vainglory directly he had given alms.

WHILE he was walking through the town of Assisi, a poor old woman asked alms of him for the love of God, and he immediately gave her the cloak from his back. And forthwith he confessed to those following him that he had felt vainglory in doing so.

We have seen and heard so many other similar instances of his sublime humility that we who knew him well cannot relate them all, either in words or writing. But blessed Francis's chief concern was that he should not be a hypocrite in the eyes of God. And although dispensations were often essential because of his infirmities, he felt that he must always set a good example to the friars and to others; so he patiently endured every privation in order to remove all grounds for criticism.

64

How he described the state of perfect humility in his own case.

WHEN the time of the Chapter was approaching, blessed Francis said to his companion, 'It seems to me that I would not be a true Friar Minor unless I were in the state that I will describe to you. Suppose that the friars invite me to the Chapter with great respect and devotion, and touched by their devotion, I go to the Chapter with them. During the assembly they ask me to proclaim the word of God and preach before them, so I rise and preach to them as the Holy Spirit moves me. Suppose that after my sermon they all cry out against me, saying, "We will not have you ruling over us! You have not the necessary eloquence, and you are too stupid and simple. We are very ashamed to have such a simple and contemptible Superior over us; henceforward do not presume to call yourself our Superior!" So they depose me with abuse and contempt. It seems to me that I would not be a true Friar Minor unless I were just as happy when they abused me and deposed me in disgrace, unwilling that I should remain their Superior, as when they held me in respect and honour, for in either case their welfare and usefulness is my first desire. For if I was happy when they praised and honoured me in their devotion—which may well be a danger to my soul—I ought to rejoice and be far happier at the benefit and health brought to my soul when they abuse me, for this is a sure spiritual gain.'

65

How he humbly desired to visit distant Provinces, as he had sent other friars; and how he instructed the friars to go through the world humbly and devoutly.

AT the end of the Chapter, when many friars were sent to a number of Provinces overseas, blessed Francis remained behind with some of the friars. And he said to them, 'Dearest Brothers, it is my duty to provide a pattern and example to all the friars. So, as I have sent friars to distant lands to endure toil and abuse, hunger and thirst, and other hardships, it is only right, and holy humility requires, that I should likewise go to some distant Province. When the brethren hear that I am undergoing the same trials as they, they will bear their own hardships all the more patiently. So go and pray God that He will guide me to choose the Province where I can best labour to His glory, to the benefit of souls, and be a good example to our Order.'

For whenever the most holy Father intended to go to any Province, he would first pray, and send the friars to ask God that He would guide his heart to go to whatever place was most pleasing to Him. And at once he said to them with joy, 'In the Name of our Lord Jesus Christ, of the glorious Virgin His Mother, and of all the Saints, I choose the Province of France, for it is a Catholic nation, and they show an especial reverence to the Body of Christ above other Catholics. This is a great joy to me, and because of this I will most gladly live among them.'

Blessed Francis had such great reverence and devotion to the Body of Christ that he caused it to be written in the Rule that in every Province where the friars lived, they were to give much thought and care to this matter, and to plead with priests to reserve the Body of Christ in worthy and fitting places; and if they neglected this, the friars were to do it themselves.

He also wished it to be included in the Rule that wherever friars found the Name of our Lord or the words by which the Body of Christ is consecrated lying about in unseemly places, they were to gather them up and lay them in a seemly place, and by so doing honour our Lord in His words. And although he did not write this in the Rule because the Ministers did not think that the friars ought to be compelled to do this, he made his wishes clear to the friars on this matter in his Testament and other writings. Indeed, at one time he wished to send friars through all the Provinces carrying fair clean pyxes, and wherever they found the Lord's Body reserved unworthily, they were to place It in these pyxes with all honour. He also wanted to send friars through all Provinces with good new wafer-irons to make fine pure hosts.

When blessed Francis had chosen the friars he wished to take with him, he said to them, 'Take the road two and two in the Name of the Lord. Be humble and sincere. Keep silence from dawn until after Terce, praying to God in your hearts, and do not indulge in idle and unprofitable conversation. Although you are travelling, let your words be as humble and devout as in a hermitage or cell. For wherever we are, or wherever we go, we always take our cell with us; for Brother Body is our

1191

cell, and our soul is the hermit who lives in it, constantly praying to God and meditating on Him. If the soul cannot remain quiet in its cell, then a cell made with hands is of little value to a Religious.'

When he arrived in Florence, blessed Francis found there the Lord Ugolino, Bishop of Ostia, who later became Pope Gregory. When the Cardinal heard from blessed Francis that he proposed to go to France, he forbade it, saying, 'Brother, I do not want you to cross the Alps, for there are many prelates who would willingly damage the prospects of your Order at the Roman Court. But I and other Cardinals who love your Order will protect and support it all the more willingly if you remain within this Province.'

Blessed Francis answered the Cardinal, 'My Lord, I should be very ashamed if I sent my brothers to distant Provinces, while I remained here without sharing any of the hardships that they have to suffer for God's sake.' As though in reproof, the Lord Cardinal said to him, 'Why have you sent your friars to such distant places to die of hunger and undergo other hardships?' Moved by the spirit of prophecy, blessed Francis replied with deep fervour, 'My Lord, do you imagine that God has raised up the friars solely for the benefit of these Provinces? I solemnly assure you that God has chosen and sent the friars for the benefit and salvation of the souls of all men in this world. They will be welcomed not only in the countries of the faithful, but in those of unbelievers as well, and they will win many souls.'

The Lord Bishop of Ostia wondered at his words, and admitted that he spoke the truth. And because he would not allow him to go to France, blessed Francis sent Brother Pacificus and many other friars, while he himself returned to the Vale of Spoleto.

How he showed the friars how to win the souls of some bandits by humility and charity.

A PARTY of bandits who used to hide in the woods and rob travellers occasionally came for food to a hermitage of the friars situated above Borgo San Sepolcro. Some of the friars said that it was not right to give them alms, while others did so out of compassion, and urged them to repent. Meanwhile blessed Francis came to this friary, and the brothers asked him whether it was right to give them alms. And he said to them, 'If you will do as I tell you, I trust in God that we shall win their souls. So go and bring some good bread and wine, and take it to the woods where they live. And shout to them, saying, "Brother bandits, come to us. We are friars, and are bringing you some good bread and wine!" And they will come at once. Then you must spread a cloth on the ground, place the bread and wine on it, and serve them humbly and gladly until they have eaten. After the meal speak to them of our Lord's words, and end by asking them for the love of God to grant your first request, which is to promise not to strike or injure anyone. For if you ask for everything at once, they will not listen to you; but because you are humble and loving they will promise this immediately. On a later day take them eggs and cheese with the bread and wine to show that you appreciate their promise, and serve them until they have eaten. And after the meal say to them, "Why do you stay here all day to die of hunger, and suffer so much hardship? And why do you do so many evil things, for which you will lose your souls unless you turn to God? It is better to serve God, for He will both supply your bodily needs in this world, and save your souls at the last." Then God will move them to repentance because of the humility and charity that you have shown them.'

So the friars did everything that blessed Francis had told

them, and by the grace and mercy of God the bandits listened to them, and punctiliously observed all that the friars had humbly asked of them. Further, because of the friars' humility and friendship towards them, they themselves humbly began to serve the friars and carried logs up to the hermitage on their shoulders for them. At length some of the bandits entered the Order; the others confessed their crimes and did penance for their sins, laying their hands in those of the friars, and promising that henceforward they would live by their own labour and never do such things again.

67

How he was beaten by devils, and thus knew that God was better pleased when he stayed in poor and humble places than with Cardinals.

BLESSED Francis once went to Rome to visit the Lord Cardinal of Ostia. And when he had stayed with him for some days, he visited the Lord Cardinal Leo, who was greatly attached to him. Because it was winter, and utterly unfit for travelling on foot because of the cold, wind and rain, Cardinal Leo invited him to stay with him for a few days, and to receive his food from him as a beggar at the same time as other beggars who used to eat in his house every day. He said this because he knew that whenever blessed Francis was offered hospitality, he always wished to be treated as a beggar, although the Lord Pope and Cardinals welcomed him with the greatest devotion and reverence, and venerated him as a saint. And he added, 'If you wish, I will give you a good secluded house where you can pray and have your food.' Then Friar Angelo Tancredi, who was one of the first twelve friars and was also staying with the Cardinal, said to blessed Francis, 'Brother, near here is a spacious and secluded tower, where you could live as though in a hermitage.' When blessed Francis had seen it, he was pleased with it, and returning to the Lord Cardinal, he said, 'My Lord, perhaps I will remain with you for some days.' And the Cardinal was delighted. So Brother Angelo went and prepared a place in the tower for blessed Francis and his companion. And because he did not wish to leave the tower during his stay with the Cardinal, Brother Angelo promised to bring up food to him and his companion each day.

During the first night after blessed Francis had gone there with his companion, when he wished to sleep devils came and gave him a violent beating. Calling to his companion, he said, 'Brother, devils have been giving me a violent beating; I would like you to stay with me, for I am afraid to remain alone.' And his companion stayed near him that night, for blessed Francis shook like a man with fever, so that both of them remained awake the whole night. Meanwhile blessed Francis said to his companion, 'Why have the devils beaten me? And why has God given them power to hurt me?' And he went on, 'The devils are God's constables, for just as the authorities send a constable to punish a wrong-doer, so does God correct and punish those whom He loves through the devils who are His constables and act as His servants in this office. Even a perfect Religious often sins in ignorance; consequently, if he does not realize his sin, he is punished by the devil so that he may realize and carefully consider how he may have sinned, whether inwardly or outwardly. For in this life God leaves nothing unpunished in those whom He loves with a tender love. By the mercy and grace of God, I do not know whether I have offended Him in any way for which I have not atoned by confession and satisfaction. Indeed, God in His mercy has granted me the favour to receive in my prayer a clear knowledge of any way in which I please or displease Him. Perhaps He is now punishing me through His constables because, although the Lord Cardinal was glad to do me a kindness, and although rest is necessary to my body, my brethren who go through the world suffering hunger and many hardships, and other brethren who live in squalid little huts, may have grounds for complaint against me when they hear that I am lodging with a cardinal. They may say, "We are enduring many hardships while he is living in luxury!" But I am always obliged to set a good example, and this is why I was given to them. For the friars are more edified when I live among them in their poor little huts than when I live elsewhere; and they bear their own difficulties all the more patiently when they hear that I am bearing the same.'

It was always the chief and constant concern of our Father to set a good example to us all, and to avoid any occasion for complaint from other friars. Because of this, whether in health or sickness, he suffered so greatly that whenever friars who knew him intimately—as did we who were with him until the day of his death—read of or recall these sufferings, they cannot restrain their tears, and they all bear their own troubles and privations with greater patience and joy.

So blessed Francis came down from the tower very early in the morning, and going to the Lord Cardinal, told him all that had happened and what he and his companion had endured. And he said to him, 'People think that I am a holy man, but devils have driven me out of the tower!' And although the Cardinal was delighted to have him, he knew and reverenced him as a Saint, and did not wish to oppose him once he had become unwilling to remain there. So blessed Francis bade him farewell, and returned to the hermitage of Fonte Colombo, near Rieti.

68

How he rebuked friars who wanted to follow the path of prudence and learning and not of humility; and how he foretold the reform and restoration of the Order to its early state.

WHEN blessed Francis was at the Chapter General held at S. Mary of the Porziuncula—known as the Chapter of Mats, because the only shelters there consisted of rush-mats, which were used by five thousand friars—a number of prudent and learned friars went to the Lord Cardinal of Ostia who was present, and said to him, 'My Lord, we wish that you would persuade Brother Francis to follow the advice of the wiser brethren, and allow himself to be guided by them.' And they quoted the Rules of Saint Benedict, Saint Augustine, and Saint Bernard, which lay down the principles of the regular life.

The Cardinal repeated all that they had said to blessed Francis in the form of advice; but without making any answer he took the Cardinal by the hand and led him before the friars assembled in Chapter. And he spoke to the friars in the fervour and power of the Holy Spirit, saying, 'My brothers! my brothers! God has called me by the way of simplicity and humility, and has in truth revealed this way for me and for all who are willing to trust and follow me. So I do not want you to quote any other Rule to me, whether that of Saint Benedict, Saint Augustine, or Saint Bernard, or to recommend any other way or form of life except this way which God in His mercy has revealed and given to me. The Lord told me that He wished me to be a new kind of simpleton in this world, and He does not wish us to live by any other wisdom but this. God will confound you through your own prudence and learning. And I trust in the constables of God, that He will punish you through them. Eventually, whether you wish it or not, you will return with great remorse to your first state.'

The Cardinal was utterly dumbfounded and said nothing; and all the friars were filled with great fear.

69

How he foresaw and predicted that learning would bring disaster on the Order, and how he forbade one of his friars to study the science of preaching.

BLESSED Francis was very grieved whenever he found virtue neglected in favour of the sort of learning that brings pride, especially if anyone was not persevering in the vocation to which he had first been called. He used to say, 'Friars of mine who are seduced by a desire for learning will find their hands empty in the day of trouble. I would rather have them grow stronger in virtue, so that when the time of trial comes, they will have God with them in their struggle. For a troublous time is coming when books will be no good for anything, and will be cast aside in windows and corners.'

He did not say this because the study of Holy Scripture displeased him, but to restrain all the friars from a useless preoccupation with learning. He would rather have them excel in charity than in strange forms of knowledge. He already sensed that before long a time was coming when the corrupting influence of learning would bring disaster. He therefore appeared after his death to one of the friars who was over engrossed in the study of preaching to rebuke and forbid him. And he ordered him to study how to walk in the way of humility and simplicity.

70

How those who were to enter the Order in the coming time of trouble would be blessed, and those who were tested would be better than their predecessors.

BLESSED Francis used to say, 'The time is coming when this Order, so dear to God, will be brought into such disrepute by the bad example of evil friars that its members will be ashamed to appear in public. But those who come to receive the habit of the Order in those days will be guided solely by the workings of the Holy Spirit: flesh and blood will not contaminate them, and they will be truly blessed by God. And although no noble works will be done by them because the love that enables the Saints to labour so fervently will have grown cold, they will be assailed by tremendous temptations. But those who are found worthy in those days will be better friars than their predecessors.

'But woe to those who maintain only an outward show and pretence of the Religious Life, who congratulate themselves, trusting in their own cleverness and knowledge, and are shown to be good for nothing. For they do not devote themselves to good works in the way of the Cross and of penitence, nor in the honest observance of the Gospel which their profession binds them to observe purely and simply. Men like these will not stoutly resist the temptations which God allows to test His chosen; but those who have been tried and approved will receive the crown of life, and the evil lives of the apostates will only spur them to greater efforts.'

71

Saint Francis's answer to a friar who asked why he did not correct the abuses that occurred in the Order in his own time.

ONE of blessed Francis's companions once said to him, 'Father, forgive me, but I would like to speak to you about something that several of us have recently been discussing.' He went on, 'You know how in earlier days, by the grace of God, the whole Order flourished in the purity of perfection; how all the friars were loyal to holy Poverty in all things with great fervour and strictness, in such things as small and humble dwellings and furnishings, and in few and poor books and clothes. Furthermore, they had a common purpose and zeal in all outward things, and carefully observed all the obligations proper to our profession and vocation, and which are intended for the edification of all. So they were united in the love of God and their neighbour, and were truly apostolic and evangelical men.

'But for some while now this purity and perfection has begun to decline, although many offer as an excuse the great number of the friars, saying that this is why they cannot observe this ideal.

Furthermore, many friars have become so blind as to imagine that people will be edified and turned to devotion by their present ways rather than by the former, and they imagine that they are living more sensibly in this way. They despise and disregard the way of holy simplicity and poverty, which is the first principle and foundation of our Order. So we have been considering these things, and are quite certain that they are displeasing to you. But if they displease you, we cannot understand why you tolerate them and do not correct them.'

Blessed Francis answered, 'Brother, God forgive you for wanting to criticize and oppose me, and to involve me in matters which no longer concern my office. As long as I held a position of authority over the friars, and they persevered in their vocation and profession, they were content with my feeble care, example and preaching, although from the beginning of my conversion I had always been a sick man. But later I considered how the Lord had added to the number of the friars, and how, through lukewarmness and lack of zeal, they were beginning to turn aside from the right and sure way by which they had once walked. They entered on the broader way that leads to death, and did not hold to their vocation and profession, nor were they willing to abandon this perilous and deadly road, despite my constant preaching, warning and example. Because of this I surrendered the rule and direction of the Order to God and the Ministers. But when I resigned the office of Superior, I explained to the brethren in General Chapter that my infirmities would no longer allow me to have charge of them. Yet, were they willing to live in accordance with my intentions, I would not wish them to have any other Minister but myself to comfort and help them until the day of my death. For once a good and faithful subject knows and obeys the will of his superior, the latter need have little anxiety about him. Indeed, I would be so happy at the good progress of the brethren—both on their own account and my own—that even if I were lying ill in bed I would not feel ashamed to fulfil this office for them, for the duties of a superior are entirely spiritual; that is, to overcome, correct and amend their faults by spiritual means. But since I am not able to correct and amend these things by my preaching, advice and example, I am not willing to become an executioner, and use punishment and flogging like the authorities of this world. I trust in the Lord that the unseen enemies of the friars, who are God's constables, will punish them in this life and the life to come, until they have taken vengeance on those who transgress His commandments and the vows of their profession. I hope that they will be reproached by the men of this world to their shame and disgrace, and as a result will return to their vocation and profession.

'However, to the day of my death I will not cease to teach the brethren by my own good example and actions to follow the way which God has shown me, and which I have taught to them by word and example. So they will have no excuse to plead before God, and I shall not be summoned to account for them before God.'

Here follows the account which Brother Leo, the companion and confessor of blessed Francis, wrote down for Brother Conrad of Offida at San Damiano near Assisi, saying that he had it from the mouth of Saint Francis himself.

While blessed Francis was standing in prayer behind the pulpit in the church of S. Mary of the Angels with his hands upraised to heaven, he called upon Christ to have mercy on the people in the great troubles which were bound to come. And the Lord said, 'Francis, if you wish Me to have mercy on the Christian people, do this for Me: see that your Order remains in the state in which it was founded, for nothing but this will remain to Me in the whole world. And I promise you that, for love of you and your Order, I will not allow any troubles to come upon the world. But I warn you that the friars will turn back from this way in which I have set them, and will provoke Me to such anger that I shall rise up against them. And I shall summon the devils, and grant them all the power that they have desired; and they will stir up such antagonism between the friars and the world that no friar will be able to wear the habit of your Order except in the woods. And when the world loses its faith, no light will remain save that of your Order, because I have set it as a light to the world.'

And blessed Francis said, 'How will my brethren survive when they live in the woods?' And Christ said, 'I shall feed them as I fed the Children of Israel with manna in the desert, for they will be good like them; and they will return to the original state in which your Order was founded and begun.'

72

How souls are converted by the prayers and tears of the humble and simple brethren, when they seem to be converted by the learning and preaching of others.

THE most holy Father did not wish his friars to hanker after learning and books, but taught them to build their lives on holy humility, to practise pure simplicity and devout prayer, and to love Lady Poverty, on which the Saints and first friars had established themselves. He used to say that this was the only sure road to their own salvation and the edification of others, because Christ, Whom we are called to follow, showed and taught us this way alone by His own teaching and example.

Looking into the future, the blessed Father knew through the Holy Spirit, and often told the friars, that in the hope of edifying others, many would abandon their vocation, which is holy humility, pure simplicity, prayer and devotion, and the love of Lady Poverty. He said, 'Because they will think themselves more gifted, more filled with devotion, fired with love, and enlightened by divine knowledge through their study of the

Scriptures, that they will as a result remain inwardly cold and empty. Consequently, they will be unable to return to their first vocation, because they will have wasted the time when they should have been following this vocation in useless and misguided study. I fear that even the grace that they seemed to possess will be taken away from them, because they have completely neglected the grace that had been given them, which is to hold to and follow their true vocation.'

He also said, 'There are many brethren who devote all their energy and zeal to the acquisition of learning, neglecting their holy vocation, and straying from the way of humility and holy prayer both in mind and body. When they have preached to the people, and learn that some have been helped or moved to penitence, they grow conceited and congratulate themselves as though the others' gain were their own. But they will have preached rather to their own condemnation and hurt, and have really achieved nothing except as the instruments of those through whom God has obtained this result. For those whom they imagined they were edifying and converting through their own learning and preaching have been edified and converted by God Himself through the prayers and tears of holy, poor, humble and simple brethren, although these holy men are not aware of it. For it is the will of God that they should know nothing of it, lest they become proud.

'These friars are my Knights of the Round Table, who remain hidden in deserts and lonely places in order to devote themselves more completely to prayer and meditation, lamenting their own sins and the sins of others, living simply and behaving humbly, whose sanctity is known to God, and at times to other friars, but unknown to the world. When the angels present their souls before God, He will show them the fruit and reward of their labours, namely, the many souls that have been saved by their prayers and tears. And He will say to them, "My dear sons, these souls have been saved by your prayers, tears, and example, and *since you have been faithful over little things, I have great things to commit to your charge*. Other men have preached and laboured with their words of wisdom and learning, but through your merits, I have brought about the fruit of salvation. So receive the reward of your labours and the fruit of your merits, which is an everlasting kingdom gained by your humility and simplicity, and by the power of your prayers and tears." And *bearing their sheaves with them*, that is, the fruit and merit of their holy humility and simplicity, these holy brethren will enter into the joy of the Lord with joy and exultation.

'But those who have cared for nothing except to know and point out the way of salvation to others, and have made no effort to follow it themselves, will stand naked and empty-handed before the judgement-seat of Christ, bearing only the sheaves of confusion, shame, and grief. Then shall truth of holy humility and simplicity, of holy prayer and poverty, which is our vocation, be exalted, glorified, and proclaimed; the truth which those who were swollen with the wind of their learning betrayed by their own lives and by the words of their empty learning, saying that truth was falsehood, and blindly and cruelly persecuting those who walked in the truth. In that day the error and falsity of the opinions in which they lived—which they proclaimed as truth, and by which they have thrust many people into a pit of darkness—will be finally exposed in grief, confusion, and shame. And they themselves, together with their misguided opinions, will be *cast into outer darkness* with the spirits of darkness.'

Commenting on the passage, *See how at last the barren womb bears many, and the fruitful mother is left to languish*, blessed Francis used to say, 'The barren represents the good Religious, simple, humble, poor, and despised, who edifies others at all times by his holy prayers and virtues, and brings forth fruit with groans of sorrow.' He often used to say this to the Ministers and other friars, especially in General Chapter.

How he taught and wished that superiors and preachers should occupy themselves in prayer and in humble tasks.

FRANCIS, the faithful servant and perfect imitator of Christ, feeling himself wholly united to Christ through the virtue of holy humility, desired this humility in his friars before all other virtues. And in order that they might love, desire, acquire, and preserve it, he gave them constant encouragement by his own example and teaching, and particularly impressed this on the Ministers and preachers, urging them to undertake humble tasks.

He used to say that they must not allow the duties of high office or the responsibility of preaching to stand in the way of holy and devout prayer, going out for alms, doing manual labour when required, and carrying out other humble duties like the rest of the brethren, both as a good example and for the good of their own and others' souls. He said, 'The friars under obedience are much edified when their Ministers and preachers gladly devote their time to prayer, and apply themselves to humble and undistinguished tasks. Unless they do this they cannot admonish other friars without embarrassment, injustice, and self-condemnation; for if we follow Christ's example, we must act rather than teach, and our acting and teaching must go together.'

74

How he taught the friars to know when he was God's servant and when he was not.

BLESSED Francis once called together a large number of friars and said to them, 'I have asked God to show me when I am His servant and when I am not; for I have no wish to live except as His servant. And in His mercy the most gracious Lord has given me this answer: "You may know that you are My servant when your thoughts, words, and actions are holy." So I have called you together, my brothers, and disclosed this to you, so that whenever you see me lacking in all or any of these respects I may be put to shame in your eyes.'

75

How he particularly wanted all the friars to do manual labour from time to time.

HE used to say that brethren who were lacking in zeal and unwilling to apply themselves simply and humbly to any work would quickly be spewed out of God's mouth. No idler could appear before him without at once receiving a sharp rebuke, for he, who was the pattern of all perfection, worked humbly with his own hands, and never allowed God's best gift of time to be wasted.

He said, 'I wish all my brethren to work and to occupy themselves humbly in good works, so that we do not become a burden to other men, or allow our hearts and tongues to wander in idleness. So those who do not know a trade are to learn one.'

But he said that the profit and payment for work was not to be received by the workers but by the Guardians, who were to use it at their discretion for the good of the community.

ON HIS ZEAL FOR THE OBSERVANCE OF THE RULE, AND FOR THE ORDER AS A WHOLE

76

Firstly, how he praised those who observed the Rule, and wished the friars to know the Rule, discuss it, and die in it.

BLESSED Francis, who observed the Holy Gospel perfectly and zealously, earnestly desired that all friars should observe the Rule, which itself is nothing other than a perfect observance of the Gospel; and he gave his especial blessing to those who are, and will be, zealous in this.

He used to tell his followers that our profession was the book of life, the hope of salvation, the pledge of glory, the heart of the Gospel, the way of the cross, the state of perfection, the key of paradise, and the compact of the eternal covenant. He wanted the Rule to be understood and accepted by all, and wished the friars to discuss it in their conferences, and meditate on it frequently by themselves, in order to remind them of their guiding vows. He also taught them that the Rule should be always before their eyes, as a reminder of the life they should lead and had bound themselves to follow. And, in addition, he wished and taught the friars that they should die with it before them.

77

On a holy lay-brother who was martyred holding the Rule in his hands.

ONE of the lay-brothers, whom we firmly believe to have been admitted into the choir of Martyrs, did not forget this sacred ordinance and command of our blessed Father. For when he went among the Saracens in his desire for martyrdom, and while he was being led to martyrdom by the unbelievers, he held the Rule in both hands with great fervour. And he knelt down humbly before his companion and said, 'Dearest brother, I confess myself guilty, before the eyes of the Divine Majesty and before you, of all the offences that I have committed against this Rule.'

After this short confession the sword fell and ended his life, and he attained the crown of martyrdom. This man had entered the Order so young that he could hardly bear the fasts imposed by the Rule, but while still a boy he had worn a breastplate next to his body. Happy young man, who began so happily, and ended his life even more happily!

78

How he wished the Order always to remain under the protection and discipline of the Church.

BLESSED Francis said, 'I will go and entrust the Order of Friars Minor to the holy Roman Church. The rod of her authority will daunt and restrain those who wish it ill, and the sons of God will everywhere enjoy full freedom to pursue their eternal salvation. Let her sons acknowledge the kindly blessings of their Mother, and embrace her sacred feet with particular devotion.

'Under her protection no harm will come upon the Order, and the son of Satan will not trample over the vineyard of the Lord with impunity. Our holy Mother will herself imitate the glory of our poverty, and will not permit our observance of humility to be overshadowed by the cloud of pride. She will preserve unimpaired the bonds of love and peace that exist between us, and will impose her gravest censure on the unruly. The sacred observance of evangelical poverty will ever flourish before her, and she will never allow the fragrance of our good name and holy life to be destroyed.'

79

The four privileges granted by God to the Order and revealed to Saint Francis.

BLESSED Francis said that God had granted him four privileges, and made them known to him by an angel. These were: that the Order and profession of Friars Minor would endure until the Day of Judgement; that no one who deliberately persecuted the Order would live long; that no wrong-doers, who intended to live an evil life in the Order, would be able to remain in it for long; and that anyone who sincerely loved the Order, however great a sinner, would obtain mercy at the last.

80

On the qualities required in the Minister General and his colleagues.

So great was his zeal to maintain perfection in the Order, and so vital did he consider the perfect observance of the Rule, that he often wondered who might be suitable to govern the whole community after his death, and with God's help to maintain it in perfection; but he could not think of anyone.

Not long before his death, one of the friars said to him, 'Father, you will soon depart to God, and this family which has followed you will remain in this vale of tears. Give us some indication, therefore, if you know of any member of the Order in whom you have confidence, and on whom the burden of the Minister Generalship might worthily be laid.'

Breaking into frequent sighs as he spoke, blessed Francis replied, 'My son, I do not know of any leader suitable for so great and varied an army, or any shepherd for so vast and scattered a flock. But I will describe the qualities that the leader and shepherd of this family should possess. Such a man should be sober living, very discreet, of excellent reputation, and without personal attachments, so that he does not cause dissension in the Order by showing favour to individuals. He should be a lover of prayer, so that he will divide his time between the needs of his own soul and those of his flock. Early in the morning he should place the most holy Sacrifice of the Mass before all else, and spend much time at his devotions, lovingly commending himself and his flock to the protection of God. But when his prayer is ended, he should place himself at the disposal of the brethren and invite questions, answer their inquiries, and attend to the needs of all with charity, patience, and courtesy.

'He should not be *a respecter of persons*, and should devote as much attention to the simple and ignorant as to the wise and learned. Should he be granted the gift of learning, let him nevertheless show evidence of piety and simplicity, patience and humility in his behaviour. Let him foster these virtues in himself as well as in others, constantly exercising them in practice and inspiring others to do so by example rather than by words. He should loathe money, which is the chief corrupter of our profession and perfection. Being the head and example of the Order, he should be imitated by all, so let him never be engrossed in finances.

'His habit and breviary should be sufficient possessions for him; others can take care of his pen-case, quill, papers and seal. He should not collect books or be absorbed in much study, lest the time given to this detract from his proper duties. He should give devout comfort to those in trouble, for he is the ultimate resort of the distressed; for if they cannot obtain healing remedies from him, the disease of despair will overpower the afflicted. He should show mildness in order to bend the unruly to gentleness, and forego some of his own rights if it will win a soul. He should show pity to those who desert the Order, as to sheep who have perished, and never refuse mercy to them, realizing that temptations that could drive them to such a fall must have been overwhelming, and that were God to permit him to be tested in the same way, he might himself fall into an even deeper pit.

'I would have the Minister General, as Vicar of Christ, to be held in the greatest devotion and reverence by all, and his needs supplied with all goodwill in so far as our humble way of life allows. But he must not delight in honours, or be more pleased to receive favours than injuries; honours must not alter his way of life except for the better. Should he need better or more palatable food on occasion, he is not to take it in private but in public, so that others who are sick or frail may not be embarrassed when they need similar concessions.

'It is his particular duty to examine the secrets of the conscience, and to extract the truth from where it lies hidden. Let him at first regard all accusations as suspect, until truth begins to appear after careful inquiry. He should not pay attention to garrulous people, and when they accuse others he should treat them with particular reserve, and should not believe them too readily. He should be a man who would never betray or relax the proper forms of justice and equity in a desire to retain personal regard. He must at the same time take care that no soul is destroyed by excessive severity, that sloth is not aroused by undue lenience, or discipline undermined by careless indulgence. In this way he will be feared by all, and loved by those who fear him. But he should always remember and feel that his office of authority is a burden to him rather than an honour.

'I would like him to have as colleagues men of recognized honesty, who are firmly opposed to luxury, resolute in difficulty, kind and understanding to offenders, and having an equal affection for all. Men who take no reward for their work but their bare bodily needs, and who seek nothing but the glory of God, the welfare of the Order, the good of their own souls, and the well-being of all the brethren. Men who are agreeable to all whom they meet, and receive all who come to them with

1211

holy joy, demonstrating the ideal and observance of the Gospel and the Rule purely and simply in their own lives.

'This is the kind of man,' he said, 'who should be Minister-General of this Order, and these are the kind of colleagues that he ought to have.'

81

How God spoke to him when he was greatly distressed by friars who were falling away from perfection.

BECAUSE of the boundless zeal that he had at all times for the perfection of the Order, he was naturally distressed whenever he heard of or saw any imperfection in it. And beginning to realize that some of the friars were setting a bad example in the Order, and had begun to decline from the highest ideals of their profession, his heart was moved to the deepest grief, so that he once said to our Lord in prayer, 'Lord, I return to You the family which You have given me!' And at once the Lord answered him, 'Tell Me, O simple and ignorant little man, why are you so distressed when some brother deserts the Order, and when the friars do not follow the way that I have showed you? Tell Me, Who has founded this Order of friars? Who turns men to penitence? Who gives them grace to persevere in it? Is it not I? I have not chosen you to rule My family because you are a learned and eloquent man, for it is not My will that you or those who were true friars and true observants of the Rule should walk by the way of learning and eloquence. I have chosen you, a simple and unlearned man, so that both you and the others may realize that I will watch over My flock. And I have appointed you as a sign to them, in order that the things that I have performed in you may also be performed in them. For those who walk in the way that I have showed you possess Me, and shall possess Me even more fully; but those who walk by another way will be stripped of even what they seemed to possess. I tell you, therefore, do not be too distressed about the others, but continue to do as you are doing, and to work as you are working, for I have established the Order of friars in everlasting love. Rest assured that I have so great a love for the Order that if any brother returns to his own vomit and dies outside the Order, I will send another friar into the Order to win a crown in his place; and if such a friar has not been born, I will cause him to be born. And in order that you may know how sincerely I love the life and Order of the friars, I promise that were there only three friars remaining in the entire Order, it would still be My Order, and I will not abandon it to all eternity.'

And when he had heard these things, his soul was marvellously comforted.

And although, in his constant zeal for the perfection of the Order, he was not entirely able to restrain his vehement grief when he heard of any fault committed by the friars, through which a bad example or scandal might arise, after he had been comforted by the Lord in this way he called to mind the words of the psalm: *Never will I retract my oath to give Thy just commands observance.* He said, 'I have vowed to observe the Rule which the Lord Himself gave to me and to those who desire to follow me. And all these friars have vowed themselves to this as I have done. So now that I have laid down my responsibility for the brethren because of my infirmities and for other weighty reasons, I am not bound to do anything other than pray for the Order and show the friars a good example. For God has shown me, and I know it to be true, that if my infirmities did not excuse me, the greatest assistance that I could give to the Order would be to spend each day in prayer for it to God, Who governs, preserves, and maintains it. For I have bound myself before God and the brethren, that if any friar should perish through my bad example, I should be obliged to render account to God for him.'

These were the words that he used to repeat inwardly to

quieten his heart, and he often expounded them to the friars during addresses and Chapters. So if any friar ever told him that he ought to intervene in the government of the Order, he would reply, 'The friars already have their Rule, and they have vowed to observe it. And after God had been pleased to appoint me as their superior, I vowed before them that I would observe it myself, so that they would not be able to plead any excuse on my account. The friars already know what to do, and what to avoid, so that no duty remains for me except to set them an example by my own actions. This is why I have been given to them, both during my life and after my death.'

82

On the special devotion that he had for S. Mary of the Angels, and the rules that he made against idle conversation there.

As long as he lived he always had an especial zeal and desire to preserve the most perfect life and conversation in the holy house of S. Mary of the Angels above all other houses of the Order, because it was the head and mother of the entire Order. He intended and desired this place to be the very pattern and example of humility, poverty, and evangelical perfection to all other houses, and wished the friars living in it always to be more careful and thoughtful than others, both in avoiding evil and in doing everything which tends to the perfect observance of the Rule.

So in order to avoid idleness—which is the root of all evils, especially in a Religious—he once ordained that each day after their meal the friars should join him in some kind of work, so that they should not wholly or partly lose the benefit gained in time of prayer by useless and idle conversation, to which men are particularly prone after meals.

He also laid down and firmly ordered it to be observed, that if any friar walking with or working among the others uttered any idle remark, he was obliged to recite one *Our Father* and to say the *Praises of God* at the beginning and end of this prayer. Should he realize what he had done and confess his fault, he was to say the *Our Father* and *Praises* for his own soul. But if he were first rebuked by another friar, he was to say them for the soul of the friar who had corrected him. Similarly, if the guilty friar made excuses or refused to say the *Our Father*, he would be required to say it twice for the soul of the friar who had corrected him. But if, on his own evidence and that of another, it was established that he had gossiped, he was required in addition to say the *Praises* at the beginning and end of his prayer in a loud voice, so as to be heard and understood by all the friars near by; and while he was saying it, the other friars were to stand and listen. If any friar heard another passing idle remarks and kept silent without correcting him, he was required to say the *Our Father* and the *Praises* for the soul of the other friar. And any friar who entered a cell or house and found another of the brethren there was at once to praise and bless God devoutly.

The most holy Father was always careful to say these *Praises* himself, and taught them to the other friars with fervent will and desire; and he encouraged them to say the *Praises* reverently and devoutly.

83

How he told the friars never to leave S. Mary of the Angels.

ALTHOUGH blessed Francis was aware that the kingdom of heaven was established in every place on earth, and believed that the grace of God could everywhere be given to the faithful, he had learned from experience that S. Mary of the Angels was filled with richer grace and often visited by celestial spirits. So he often said to the friars, 'My sons, see that you never abandon this place! If you are driven out of one door, re-enter by another, for this place is holy indeed; it is the dwelling-place of Christ and His Virgin Mother. When we were few, it was here that the Most High increased us; it was here that He illumined the souls of His poor ones with the light of His wisdom; it was here that He kindled our desires with the fire of His love. Whosoever prays here with a devout heart shall obtain whatever he asks, while an evil-doer shall receive heavier punishment.

'My sons, regard this place as most worthy of all reverence and honour as the true dwelling-place of God, especially dear to Him and to His Mother. Glorify God the Father, and His Son Jesus Christ our Lord in the unity of the Holy Spirit in this place with all your hearts and with the voice of praise and confession.'

84

The favours granted by God in S. Mary of the Angels.

> HOLY of Holies is this place of places,
> Rightly deemed worthy of the highest honours!
> Happy its surname 'of the holy Angels,'
> Happier its dedication to 'Saint Mary':
> And now the third name of 'The little Portion'
> Foretells the Mother-House of all the Order.
> Here the fair presence of the holy Angels
> Sheds light around it, filling it with splendour;
> Here in the long night-watches of the brethren
> Praises soar upwards, piercing the heavens.
> Once long abandoned, fallen into ruin,
> Francis restored it to its former honour;
> Of the three churches which the holy Father
> Raised with his own hands, this is best and dearest.
> This place our Father chose for his own dwelling,
> Here in stern penance clad his limbs in sack-cloth,
> Subdued his body and its errant passions,
> Made it obedient to the spirit's bidding.
> This holy temple God chose as the birthplace

Of the Friars Minor, humble, poor, and joyful,
While the example of the holy Father
Drew a great army, walking in his footsteps.
Here for the tonsure of her golden tresses
Came the sweet virgin Clare, the spouse of Jesus,
Casting behind her all the pomps and pleasures
Loved by the worldly, and embracing penance.
Here did the Orders of the Friars and Ladies
Spring into being, born of one fair Mother,
Mary most holy, who in her new offspring
Gave to the world new patterns of her First-born.
Here the broad highway of the old world changed
Into the narrow way to life eternal;
And to the faithful, called from every nation,
New grace was given freely by the Father.
Here was the Holy Rule to guide the Order
Written by Francis; Poverty exalted;
Pride was cast headlong, and the Cross upraised
Once more among us for the world's salvation.
Whenever Francis, worn and frail in body,
Weary in spirit, sought for rest and comfort,
In the sweet silence of this sanctuary
Here he found healing, comfort, and refreshment.
And when the Devil doubting and confusion
Sowed in his spirit, here was Truth revealed;
Here, too, was granted to the holy Father
All that he asked for in his intercession.

ON HIS ZEAL FOR THE PERFECTION OF THE FRIARS

85

Firstly, how he described the perfect friar.

THE most blessed Father, having in some degree transformed the friars into saints by the ardour of his love and by the fervent zeal for their perfection which fired him, often pondered on the virtues that ought to adorn a good Friar Minor. He used to say that a good Friar Minor should imitate the lives and possess the merits of these holy friars: the perfect faith and love of poverty of Brother Bernard; the simplicity and purity of Brother Leo, who was a man of most holy purity; the courtesy of Brother Angelo, who was the first nobleman to enter the Order, and was endowed with all courtesy and kindness; the gracious look and natural good sense of Brother Masseo, together with his noble and devout eloquence; the mind upraised to God, possessed in its highest perfection by Brother Giles; the virtuous and constant prayer of Brother Rufino, who prayed without ceasing, and whose mind was ever fixed on God, whether sleeping or working; the patience of Brother Juniper, who attained the state of perfect patience because he kept the truth of his low estate constantly in mind whose supreme desire was to follow Christ on the way of the Cross; the bodily and spiritual courage of Brother John of Lauds, who in his time had been physically stronger than all men; the charity of Brother Roger, whose whole life and conversation was inspired by fervent charity; the caution of Brother Lucidus, who was unwilling to remain in any place longer than a month, for when he began to like a place, he would at once leave it, saying, 'Our home is not here, but in heaven.'

86

Saint Francis tells the friars a parable about pure looks, in order to illustrate chaste conduct.

AFTER the fundamental virtue of holy humility, blessed Francis loved and wished to see pre-eminent in the friars among the other virtues that of fair and pure chastity. Wishing to teach the friars to have chaste eyes, he gave an example of impure looks by the following parable.

A devout and powerful king sent two messengers in succession to his queen. The first returned and simply reported the words of the queen, saying nothing about the queen herself. The other messenger returned, and having briefly delivered his message, gave a lengthy description of the queen's beauty. 'Indeed, Your Majesty,' he said, 'I have seen the most beautiful of women. Happy the man who enjoys her!'

The king said, 'Vile fellow, you have been casting impure looks on my queen! It is evident that you have secretly hoped to possess what you saw.' So he recalled the first messenger and said to him, 'What do you think of the queen?' 'She is an excellent lady,' he wisely replied, 'for she listened to me willingly and with patience.' Then the king asked, 'And do you think her beautiful?' He replied, 'Your Majesty, it is your privilege to look at her and decide this; my duty was only to deliver her message.' The king then made this decree, 'You have pure eyes; be chaste in body as well. You shall serve in my apartments and enjoy my pleasures. But this shameless fellow is to leave my palace lest he defile my bed.'

1219

'Therefore,' said blessed Francis, 'who will not fear to gaze upon the bride of Christ?'

87

The three sayings that he left to the friars to preserve their perfection.

ONCE when he wanted to vomit because of his disease of the stomach, he did so with such violence that he brought up blood all night until morning. When his companions saw him almost dying from extreme exhaustion and pain, they said to him with the deepest grief and many tears, 'Father, what shall we do without you? To whose charge will you leave us orphans? You have always been father and mother to us; you have conceived and brought us forth in Christ. You have been our leader and shepherd, our instructor and corrector, teaching and correcting us by your example rather than by words. Where shall we go, sheep without a shepherd, children without a father, rough and simple men without a leader? Where shall we go to find you, O Glory of Poverty, Praise of Simplicity, and boast of our sinful nature? Who now will show us blind men the way of truth? How shall we hear your mouth speaking to us, and your tongue giving us counsel? Where will be your burning spirit, which guides us along the way of the Cross, and inspires us to evangelical perfection? Where will you be, so that we may run to you, light of our eyes? Where can we seek you, comfort of our souls? O Father, are you dying? You are leaving us abandoned, sad, and full of despair!

'Alas for this day! For a day of tears and bitterness, a day of desolation and grief is coming upon us! And no wonder, for your life has been a constant light to us, and your words have been like burning torches, always lighting us along the way of the Cross to evangelical perfection, and to the love and imitation of our sweet and crucified Lord.

'Father, at least give your blessing to us and to the other

1220

friars, the sons whom you have begotten in Christ, and leave us some memorial of your will which the brethren can always have in remembrance, and say, "Our Father left these words to his friars and sons at his death." '

Then the most loving Father turned his eyes towards his sons, and said, 'Send Brother Benedict of Piratro to me.' For this friar was a holy and wise priest, who sometimes celebrated Mass for blessed Francis when he was lying ill; for however sick he might be, he always wished to hear Mass whenever possible. And when he had come, blessed Francis said, 'Write that I give my blessing to all my brethren in the Order, and to all who will enter it in time to come until the end of the world. And since I cannot speak much because of my weakness and the pain of my disease, I wish briefly to make my will and purpose clear to all the brethren, both present and to come. As a sign that they remember me, my blessing, and my Testament, I wish them always to love one another, as I have loved them. Let them always love and honour our Lady Poverty, and remain faithful and obedient to the bishops and clergy of holy Mother Church.'

At the close of Chapters, our Father always used to bless and absolve all the friars in the Order, both present and to come, and in the fervour of his love he often did so out of Chapter. But he used to warn the brethren that they must beware of setting a bad example, and he cursed all who by their bad example caused people to speak ill of the Order and life of the friars, since the good and holy friars are put to disgrace and great distress by such behaviour.

88

On the love that he showed the friars when nearing death, by giving to each a fragment of bread after the example of Christ.

ONE night blessed Francis was in such distress from the pain of his disease that he could not sleep or rest all night long. But at dawn, when his pain eased somewhat, he sent for all the friars in the house. And making them sit down before him, he looked upon them as representatives of the whole Order. And laying his right hand on the head of each in turn, he blessed them all, both present and absent, as well as those who were to enter the Order until the end of the world. And he seemed to grieve because he was unable to see all his friars and sons before his death.

But wishing to imitate his Lord and Master in his death as he had done so perfectly in his life, he ordered loaves to be brought to him. And having blessed them, he had them broken into many fragments, for his great weakness would not allow him to break them himself. Then he took the bread and gave a piece to each of the friars, asking them to eat all of it.

In this way, as on the Thursday before His death our Lord had desired to eat with His Apostles as a sign of His love, so did His perfect imitator blessed Francis wish to show the same sign of love to his own brethren. It is clear that he wished to do this in imitation of Christ, for he later inquired whether it were Thursday; and when he was told that it was another day, he said that he had thought it was Thursday.

One of the friars preserved a piece of this bread, and after the death of blessed Francis many sick people who tasted it were immediately healed of their diseases.

89

How he feared that the friars might be put to trouble by his illness.

WHILE he was unable to sleep because of his ailments, he realized that the friars were becoming very distracted and tired on his account. And because he had a deeper concern for their souls than for his own body, he began to fear that their constant efforts to serve him might cause them to commit some small offence against God through impatience.

So with great pity and compassion he once said to his companions, 'My dearest brothers and little sons, do not allow your labours for me in my illness be a burden to you, for God will repay you for me, His little servant; He will reward you with all the fruits of your labours, both in this world and the next. You will win more merit for the things that you have had to leave undone in your care for me in my illness, than if you had done them for yourselves; for whoever helps me helps the whole Order and life of the friars. In fact, you can say to me, "We are accumulating credit on your account, and God Himself will be in our debt." '

The holy Father spoke in these terms wishing to encourage and support their faint spirits, and moved by his great zeal for the perfection of their souls. For he was afraid that, because of their work for him, some of them might say, 'We cannot pray because we have so much work to do,' and becoming tired and impatient, they might lose the great reward due for their modest labours.

90

How he counselled the Sisters of Saint Clare.

AFTER blessed Francis had composed *The Praises of the Lord in His Creatures*, he also wrote some holy words with a melody to comfort and edify the Poor Ladies, knowing that they were in great distress over his illness. And being unable to visit them personally, he sent these words to them by his companions. For in these words he wished to make his purpose clear to them, namely, that they were to live and converse humbly, and be of one mind in charity. For he saw that their conversion and holy life was not only a source of glory to the Order of Friars, but of edification to the whole Church.

But knowing that from the beginning of their conversion they had led a life of great confinement and poverty, he always felt the greatest pity and compassion for them. So in these words he asked that as the Lord had gathered them together from many places into one in order to live in holy charity, poverty, and obedience, they must always persevere in them until death. He particularly emphasized that they should make proper provision for their bodily needs out of the alms that the Lord gave them with joy and thankfulness. And he asked above all that the healthy sisters be patient in their labours for the sick, and the sick be patient in their illnesses.

ON HIS CONSTANT FERVOUR OF LOVE AND PITY
FOR THE PASSION OF CHRIST

91

Firstly, how he had no thought for his own infirmities because of his devotion to the Passion of Christ.

So fervent were the love and compassion of blessed Francis for the sorrows and sufferings of Christ, and so deep was his inward and outward grief over the Passion day by day that he had never considered his own infirmities. Consequently, although he suffered from ailments of the stomach, spleen, and liver over a long period until the day of his death, and had endured constant pain in his eyes ever since his return from overseas, he was never willing to undergo any treatment for its cure.

So the Lord Cardinal of Ostia, seeing how harsh he had always been on his own body, and how he was already beginning to lose his sight because he refused to undergo a cure, urged him with great kindness and compassion, saying, 'Brother, you are not doing right in refusing treatment, for your life and health are of great value not only to the friars, but to the layfolk and the whole Church. You have always had a great sympathy for your brethren when they are sick, and have always been kindly and merciful; you must not be cruel to yourself in so great a need. I therefore order you to have yourself cured and helped.' For because the most holy Father took boundless delight in imitating the humility and example of the Son of God, he always regarded anything unpleasant to the body as welcome.

How he was found loudly lamenting the Passion of Christ as he walked along.

A SHORT while after his conversion, as he was walking alone along the road not far from the church of S. Mary of the Porziuncula, he was uttering loud cries and lamentations as he went. And a spiritually-minded man who met him, fearing that he was suffering from some painful ailment, said to him, 'What is your trouble, brother?' But he replied, 'I am not ashamed to travel through the whole world in this way, bewailing the Passion of my Lord.' At this, the man joined him in his grief, and began to weep aloud.

We have known this man and learned of this incident through him. He is one who has shown great kindness and compassion to blessed Francis and to us who were his companions.

93

How his outward signs of joy sometimes gave place to tears and compassion for Christ.

INTOXICATED by love and compassion for Christ, blessed Francis sometimes used to act in ways like these. For the sweetest of spiritual melodies would often well up within him and found expression in French melodies, and the murmurs of God's voice, heard by him alone, would joyfully pour forth in the French tongue.

Sometimes he would pick up a stick from the ground, and laying it on his left arm, he would draw another stick across it with his right hand like a bow, as though he were playing a viol or some other instrument; and he would imitate the movements of a musician and sing in French of our Lord Jesus Christ.

But all this jollity would end in tears, and his joy would melt away in compassion for the sufferings of Christ. And at such times he would break into constant sighs, and in his grief would forget what he was holding in his hands, and be caught up in spirit into heaven.

ON HIS ZEAL FOR PRAYER AND THE DIVINE OFFICE, AND HIS DESIRE TO PRESERVE THE SPIRIT OF JOY IN HIMSELF AND IN OTHERS

94

Firstly, on prayer and the Divine Office.

ALTHOUGH he had been troubled for many years by the infirmities already described, he was so devout and reverent at prayer and the Divine Office that whenever he was at prayer or reciting the Divine Office he would never lean against a wall or support. He always stood upright and bareheaded, although he sometimes knelt. Indeed, he devoted the greater part of the day and night to prayer, and even when he was travelling around on foot, he would always halt when he wished to say the Hours. But if he were riding because of his infirmity, he would always dismount to say the Office.

One day it was raining heavily, and he was riding because of his infirmity and pressing need. And although he was already drenched to the skin, he dismounted from the horse when he wished to say the Hours, and said the Office standing in the road with the rain pouring down on him, as though he had been in a church or cell. And he said to his companion, 'If the body likes to take its food in peace and at ease, although it becomes food for worms, how much greater should be the soul's reverence and devotion when it receives the food which is God Himself.'

How he always loved spiritual joy, both in himself and others.

It was always the supreme and particular desire of blessed Francis to possess an abiding joy of spirit outside times of prayer and Divine Office. This was the virtue that he especially loved to see in his brethren, and he often reproached them when they showed signs of gloom and despondency.

He used to say, 'If the servant of God strives to obtain and preserve both outwardly and inwardly the joyful spirit which springs from purity of heart and is acquired through devout prayer, the devils have no power to hurt him, and say, "We can find no way to get at him or hurt him, because this servant of God preserves his joy both in trouble and in prosperity." But the devils are delighted when they discover means to quench or disturb the devotion and joy which springs from true prayer and other holy practices. For if the devil can obtain a hold over one of God's servants, he will soon transform a single hair into a log to hurl at him unless he is a wise man and takes care to remove and destroy it as quickly as possible by the power of holy prayer, contrition, and satisfaction.

'Therefore, my brothers, since this spiritual joy springs from cleanness of heart and the purity of constant prayer, it must be your first concern to acquire and preserve these two virtues, so as to possess this inward joy that I so greatly desire and love to see both in you and myself, and which edify our neighbour and reproach our enemy. For it is the lot of the Devil and his minions to be sorrowful, but ours always to be happy and rejoice in the Lord.'

How he censured one of his companions for showing a gloomy face.

BLESSED Francis used to say, 'Although I know that the devils envy me the blessings that God has given me, I also know and see that they cannot harm me through myself, so they plan and try to hurt me through my companions. But if they cannot hurt me either through myself or through my companions, they retire in great confusion. Indeed, whenever I am tempted or depressed, if I see my companions joyful, I immediately turn away from my temptation and oppression, and regain my own inward and outward joy.'

So the Father used to censure those who went about with gloomy faces, and once rebuked a friar who appeared with a gloomy face, saying, 'Why are you making an outward display of grief and sorrow for your sin? This sorrow is between God and yourself alone. So pray Him in His mercy to pardon you and restore to your soul the joy of His salvation, of which the guilt of your sins has deprived it. Always do your best to be cheerful when you are with me and the other brethren; it is not right for a servant of God to show a sad and gloomy face to his brother or to anyone else.'

It should not be imagined, however, that our Father, who loved dignified and sensible behaviour, wished this spiritual joy to be shown in levity or empty chatter, for these things are not evidence of spiritual joy, but of emptiness and folly. He greatly disliked laughter and idle gossip in a servant of God; in fact, he preferred him not to laugh, and to avoid giving others any occasion for hilarity. In one of his Counsels he gave an even clearer definition of the nature of spiritual joy in a servant of God, saying, 'Blessed is the Religious who has no pleasure or joy except in the most holy sayings and works of the Lord, and by these inspires men to the love of God in joy and gladness.

And woe to the Religious who takes delight in idle and foolish talk, and by them provokes men to laughter.'

By a joyful face, therefore, he understood fervour, thoughtfulness, and the disposition and preparation of mind and body to a ready undertaking of every good work; for this fervour and readiness often have a greater influence on people than by the good deed itself. Indeed, however good an action may be, if it does not seem to have been done willingly and fervently, it tends to produce distaste rather than edification. So he did not wish to see a gloomy face, which often betrays a sluggish body and a melancholy mind. He always loved to see gravity of face and deportment both in himself and others, and did his best to encourage this by word and example. For experience had taught him that grave and restrained behaviour provided a wall and strong shield against the darts of the devils; he knew that without the protection of this wall and shield the soul resembled an unarmed soldier among powerful and well-armed enemies, ever eager and intent on his death.

97

How he told the friars to satisfy their bodily needs, lest prayer be lost through sickness.

OUR most holy Father, knowing that the body was created to serve the soul, and that bodily actions were to be performed for spiritual ends, used to say, 'In eating, sleeping, and satisfying the other needs of the body, the servant of God should make sensible provision for his Brother Body so that he may not have cause to complain and say, "I cannot stand upright and continue at prayer, nor can I be cheerful in my troubles or do other good things, because you do not provide for my needs." But if the servant of God satisfies his body wisely, adequately, and suitably, and Brother Body wants to be careless, fat, and sleepy in prayer, vigils, and other good works, then he must punish him like a fat and idle beast of burden, because he wants to eat but not to be useful and carry his load. However, if Brother Body cannot have what he needs in health or sickness because of want and poverty, and has humbly and honestly asked it of his brother or superior for the love of God, but has not received it, let him bear it patiently for love of our Lord, Who will comfort him; for Christ Himself endured want, and found no comfort. And if he bears this want patiently, God will credit it to him as his martyrdom. And because he has done whatsoever he could—and humbly asked for his needs—he will be absolved from all blame, even though his body become gravely ill as a result.'

ON CERTAIN TEMPTATIONS WHICH THE LORD
ALLOWED TO ASSAIL HIM

98

Firstly, how the devil entered a pillow under his head.

WHILE blessed Francis was staying in the hermitage of Greccio he was at prayer one night in the last cell beyond the large cell, and during the early hours of the night he called to his companion who was sleeping near him. This friar rose and came to the door of blessed Francis's cell, and the saint said to him, 'Brother, I have not been able to sleep to-night, and I can't stand up to pray because my head shakes and my knees tremble violently. I think I must have eaten some darnel bread.'

When the friar had expressed his sympathy, blessed Francis said, 'I am sure that the devil is in this pillow under my head!' (For ever since he had left the world he had always declined to lie on a feather mattress or use a feather pillow, but the friars had compelled him against his will to have this pillow because of his disease of the eyes.) So he threw it to his companion, who caught it in his right hand and laid it on his left shoulder. But directly he passed through the door of the cell, he lost his speech, and could neither put down the pillow nor move his arms. So he stood there upright, with his senses benumbed and unable to stir from the spot. Having stood like this for some while, by the grace of God blessed Francis called to him; and at once he regained his senses, and let the pillow fall behind his back.

Coming back to blessed Francis, he told him what had happened to him, and the saint said, 'While I was saying Compline late last evening I felt the devil entering the cell. And I know that the devil is very cunning, for when he realized that he could not harm my soul, he wanted to prevent my body receiving its needs, so that I could neither sleep nor stand up to pray. He thought that he would disturb my devotion and joy of heart in this way, and make me complain of my affliction.'

99

On the grave temptation that he endured for more than two years.

WHILE he was living in the friary of S. Mary, a very grave temptation was inflicted on him for the good of his soul. He was so tormented in mind and body by this, that he often withdrew from the company of the friars because he could not show them his usual cheerfulness. Nevertheless, he continued to discipline himself by abstinence from food, drink, and speech; and he prayed more constantly and shed more abundant tears, so that the Lord might be pleased to grant some remedy strong enough for so great a trial.

When he had been troubled in this way for more than two years, he happened to be praying in the church of S. Mary one day, when he heard in spirit the words of the Gospel: *If you have faith, though it be but like a grain of mustard seed, you have only to say to this mountain, Remove from this place to that, and it will remove.* At once blessed Francis asked, 'Lord, what is this mountain?' And the reply came, 'This mountain is your temptation.' 'In that case, Lord,' said blessed Francis, 'let it happen with me as You have said.' And from that moment he was so completely freed that it seemed to him as though he had never had any temptation.

In the same way, at the time when he received the Stigmata of our Lord in his own body on the holy mountain of La Verna, he suffered so many temptations and troubles from the devils that he could not display his former joy. And he told his companion (*Brother Leo*), 'If the brethren knew how many great trials and afflictions the devils bring upon me, there is not one of them who would not be moved to compassion and pity for me.'

100

How he was plagued by mice; and how the Lord comforted him, and assured him of His Kingdom.

Two years before his death, while he was staying at S. Damian in a cell made of rush-mats, he was suffering intensely from his disease of the eyes, and for more than fifty days he could not bear the light of day, or even firelight. And in order to increase both his affliction and his merit, God allowed a horde of mice to infest the walls of his cell, and they ran over and around him day and night, so that he could neither pray nor rest. Even when he was eating, they climbed onto his table and worried him greatly, so that both he and his companions clearly recognized it as a temptation by the devil.

So one night, tormented by so many troubles and feeling sorry for himself, he prayed inwardly, 'Lord, look on me and help me in my troubles, and give me strength to bear them patiently.' And at once he heard a voice within his soul, saying, 'Tell Me, brother; if in recompense for these infirmities and tribulations you were to be given so vast and precious a treasure that, were the whole world pure gold, its stones jewels, and all its waters balsam, you would regard them as nothing in comparison to this vast treasure, would not you be very happy?' And blessed Francis replied, 'Lord, such a treasure would be vast and precious, very lovely and desirable.' And he heard the voice speaking to him once more, 'Then be glad, brother, and rejoice in your troubles and infirmities. As for the rest, trust in Me, as though you were already in My Kingdom.'

Rising early, he said to his companions, 'If an Emperor were to grant a whole kingdom to one of His slaves, ought not that slave to be full of joy? And if he were to bestow his entire empire on that slave, would be not be even happier?' And he continued, 'I should therefore rejoice in my infirmities and troubles, and *be strong in the Lord*, always giving thanks to God the Father, and to His only Son Jesus Christ, and to the Holy Spirit, for the great grace granted me by the Lord, for He has deigned to assure me, His unworthy servant, of His Kingdom while still living in the flesh. So, to His praise, for our own comfort and to edify our neighbours, I want to compose a new *Praise of the Lord in His creatures*; for we daily make use of them, and cannot live without them, and through them the human race greatly offends their Creator. For we are always ungrateful for His many graces and blessings, and do not praise the Lord, the Creator and Giver of all good gifts, as we should.' And sitting down, he began to meditate awhile.

Afterwards he said, *Most High, Almighty, good Lord, etc.*, and he set the words to a melody, and taught his companions to recite and sing it. For his soul was so full of consolation and sweetness at that time that he wished to send for Brother Pacificus, who had been known in the world as 'The King of Verse' and had been master of the choir at a noble court, and he wanted to give him a number of good and spiritual friars, who could go around the world with him, reciting and singing the *Praises of the Lord*. He said that he would like the friar who was the best preacher to speak to the people first, and afterwards they were all to sing the *Praises of the Lord* together as minstrels of God. And when the *Praises* were ended, the preacher was to say to the people, 'We are God's minstrels, and ask you to repay us for our songs by living in true penitence.' 'For what are God's servants but His minstrels,' he said, 'who must inspire the hearts of men and stir them to spiritual joy.' And in so saying, he referred particularly to the Friars Minor, whom God had given to the people for their salvation.

1236

101

Firstly, how he foretold the restoration of peace between the Bishop and Mayor of Assisi through the influence of the Praises of the Creatures which he had composed and ordered his companions to sing before them.

AFTER blessed Francis had composed *The Praises of the Creatures*, which he called *The Song of Brother Sun*, a serious dispute happened to arise between the Bishop of Assisi and the Mayor. As a result, the Bishop excommunicated the Mayor, and the Mayor issued an order forbidding anyone to sell anything to the Bishop, to buy anything from him, or to make any agreement with him.

Although blessed Francis was ill when he heard of this, he was deeply grieved on their account, especially as there was no one to make peace between them. And he said to his companions, 'It brings great disgrace on us when the Bishop and Mayor hate one another in this way, and no one can make peace between them.' So he immediately wrote a verse to be included in the *Praises* for this occasion, and said:

> *Praise to Thee, my Lord, for those who pardon one another*
> *For love of Thee, and endure*
> *Sickness and tribulation;*
>
> *Blessed are they who shall endure it in peace,*
> *For they shall be crowned by Thee,*
> *O Most High.*

Then he called one of his companions and said, 'Go to the Mayor, and ask him from me to go to the Bishop's house with the city councillors and any others he can bring with him.' And when this friar had left, he said to two other companions, 'Go and sing *The Song of Brother Sun* before the Bishop, the Mayor, and those who are with them. I trust that the Lord will at once humble their hearts, and that they will return to their former affection and friendship.'

So when the whole company had assembled in the cloister-garth of the Bishop's house, the two friars rose, and one of them said, 'Blessed Francis in his sickness has composed a *Praise of the Lord in His Creatures*, in order to praise the Lord and edify his fellow men, so he asks you to listen to it with great devotion.' And they began to recite and sing it.

At once the Mayor rose and clasped his hands, listening with the greatest devotion, as though he were hearing the Lord's Gospel; and he wept profusely, for he had great faith in blessed Francis and a great devotion to him. And when the *Praises of the Lord* were ended, the Mayor said before the whole company, 'I solemnly assure you that I forgive the Lord Bishop, and wish to acknowledge him as my lord. And even if some man had slain my brother or my son, I would forgive him.' With these words, he cast himself at the Bishop's feet, and said to him, 'See now, for the love of our Lord Jesus Christ and of His servant blessed Francis I am willing to offer any amends that you please.' But the Bishop took him by the hands and raised him, saying, 'My office requires me to be humble, but I am quick-tempered by nature; I therefore beg you to forgive me.' So they embraced and kissed one another with great kindness and affection.

The friars were astonished and overjoyed when they saw that the reconciliation which blessed Francis had foretold had been thus fulfilled to the letter. And all present regarded it as a great miracle, and attributed it wholly to the merits of blessed Francis, that the Lord had moved them so swiftly, and that without

1238

uttering a word they had turned back from great discord and scandal to complete harmony.

But we who were with blessed Francis testify that whenever he said of anything, 'This is so,' or 'This will be,' it always took place to the letter. And we have seen this happen so often that it would take us a long time to write or describe it.

102

How he foretold the fall of a friar who refused to confess under the pretext of observing silence.

THERE was once a friar who was outwardly a man of sincere and holy life, and seemed to pray constantly day and night. And he observed perpetual silence, so that whenever he confessed to a priest, he did so by signs instead of words. He seemed so devout and fervent in the love of God that when he sometimes sat with the other brethren, although he did not speak, he was filled with inward and outward joy at hearing devout conversation, and thus moved other friars to devotion.

But when he had followed this way of life for several years, blessed Francis happened to visit the place where he was living. And learning of his way of life from the other friars, he told them, 'It is most certainly a temptation of the devil that makes him unwilling to confess.' Meanwhile the Minister General came to visit blessed Francis, and began to praise this friar to him. But blessed Francis said, 'Believe me, Brother, this friar has been led away and deceived by a wicked spirit.' The Minister General replied, 'It seems strange and almost incredible to me that this could be the case when the man shows so many signs of holiness and good works.' But blessed Francis said, 'Test him by telling him to confess at least once or twice a week in Chapter. If he refuses to obey, you will know that what I have said is true.'

So the Minister General said to the friar, 'Brother, I require you to confess twice, or at least once, in Chapter.' But the friar laid his finger on his lips, shaking his head and showing by signs that he was not willing to do so because of his love for silence. And fearing to offend him, the Minister let him go. But not many days later this friar left the Order of his own will, and returned to the world wearing secular clothes.

One day two companions of blessed Francis chanced to be walking along a certain road when they met this man, who was walking alone like a very poor pilgrim. Feeling sorry for him, they said, 'Wretched man, what has happened to your sincere and holy way of life? For once you refused to speak or explain yourself to your brethren, and now you go wandering about the world like a man who knows nothing of God!' And he began to talk to them, often swearing 'By my faith!', which is a common worldly expression. And they said, 'Unhappy man! Why do you swear by your faith like worldly men? Once you used to keep silence, not only from idle words, but even from good words.' So they parted company, and not long afterwards he died. And we were all amazed when we realized how everything that blessed Francis had foretold when the friars had regarded the man as a saint had come true to the letter.

103

On the man who begged Saint Francis with tears to admit him into the Order.

AT the time when no one was admitted into the Order without the approval of blessed Francis, the son of a nobleman of Lucca came with many others who wished to enter the Order to see blessed Francis, who was then lying ill in the palace of the Bishop of Assisi. And when they all presented themselves to blessed Francis, he bowed before him and began to weep aloud, begging him to admit him. But blessed Francis looked at him and said, 'Wretched and worldly man, why are you lying to the Holy Spirit and to me? Your tears are worldly and not spiritual.'

And while he was speaking, the man's relatives arrived outside the palace on horseback, wishing to seize him and carry him back with them. Hearing the clatter of horses, he looked through a window and saw his relatives. And at once he went down to them, and returned to the world with them as blessed Francis had foreseen.

104

On the priest's vineyard, which was stripped of its grapes because of Saint Francis.

BLESSED Francis was once staying with a poor priest at the church of S. Fabian near Rieti because of his disease of the eyes, and the Lord Pope Honorius was visiting the city with his whole court at the same time. And because of their devotion to blessed Francis, many cardinals and other high clergy came to see him almost daily.

Now this church had a small vineyard adjoining the house where blessed Francis was lodged, and nearly all those who visited him passed through the vineyard to the door of the house. And because the grapes were ripe and the place very pleasant, the entire vineyard was stripped and despoiled of its grapes. So the priest began to feel indignant, saying, 'Although it is a small vineyard, I used to make sufficient wine from it for my needs, but this year I have lost the whole crop.'

When blessed Francis heard of this he sent for him, and said, 'Father, do not worry any more, for we cannot do anything about it now. But trust in the Lord, for He is able to repair your loss in full for the sake of me, His little servant. Tell me, how many measures of wine did you obtain when your vineyard was at its best?' 'Thirteen measures, Father,' the priest replied. Blessed Francis said to him, 'Have no more regrets, and say no hard words because of this. Trust in God and my word, and if you obtain less than twenty measures of wine, I will have it made up to you.' So the priest kept silence and said no more; and at the time of vintage he obtained no less than twenty measures of wine. And the priest was amazed, as were all who heard of it, and said that even if the vineyard had been full of grapes, it could not have produced twenty measures of wine.

But we who were with him testify that what he said about this, and everything else that he foretold, was always fulfilled to the letter.

105

How the knights of Perugia obstructed his preaching.

WHILE blessed Francis was preaching in the square at Perugia, some knights of Perugia began to canter around the square on horseback, exercising with their weapons. This greatly hindered his preaching, and although those who were listening protested, they refused to desist. So blessed Francis turned to them, and said in great fervour of spirit: 'Listen, and understand what the Lord proclaims through me, His little servant; and don't say, "This is a fellow from Assisi!"' (He said this because there was, and still is, a long-standing feud between the men of Perugia and Assisi.) And he went on, 'God has elevated you above your neighbours, and because of this you should be all the more ready to acknowledge your Creator by being humble, both towards God and to your neighbours. But your hearts are swollen with pride, and you attack your neighbours and kill many of them. I warn you that unless you speedily turn to God and compensate those whom you have injured, God Who leaves no crime unpunished will cause you to rise up against one another to your greater hurt and disgrace. You will be rent asunder by sedition and civil strife, and suffer far greater damage than your neighbours could ever inflict on you.'

For blessed Francis would never remain silent when he preached on the sins of the people, but rebuked them all openly and boldly. But the Lord had endowed him with such grace that all who heard and saw him, whatever their rank and condition, felt a great fear and reverence for him because he possessed the grace of God in such abundance. So men were always edified by his words, however severely they were rebuked by him, and were either converted to God or pricked in conscience.

A few days later God permitted a dispute to arise between the knights and the citizens, as a result of which the people drove the knights out of the city. And the knights, supported by the Church, devastated their fields, vineyards, and trees, and wrought every possible evil on the people. In retaliation, the people wrecked all the property of the knights, and both people and knights were punished just as blessed Francis had foretold.

106

How he foresaw the secret temptation and trouble of one of the friars.

ONE of the friars, a sincerely spiritual man and a friend of blessed Francis, had for many days been subjected to very severe temptations by the devil, and was almost reduced to despair. Every day he was so tormented by temptation that he was ashamed to confess as often as he should, and because of this he afflicted himself with much fasting, vigils, tears, and scourging.

By the will of God blessed Francis came to this friary, and one day while this brother was walking with him, the Father was enlightened by the Holy Spirit as to his trouble and temptation. Withdrawing a short distance from the friar who was walking with him, he turned to the troubled brother and said, 'Dearest Brother, henceforward I do not wish you to feel obliged to confess these temptations of the devil. And do not be afraid, for they have not harmed your soul. But, with my approval, say seven *Our Fathers* whenever they trouble you.'

The friar was very relieved when blessed Francis told him

that he was not obliged to confess them, for he had been very uneasy in mind on this matter. But he was dumbfounded that blessed Francis knew about this thing, which was known only to the priests to whom he had made his confession. And by the grace of God and the merits of blessed Francis he was immediately delivered from his temptation, and thenceforward continued in the greatest peace and tranquillity. And it was because the Saint had hoped for this that he confidently excused him from confession.

107

On the things that he foretold of Brother Bernard, and how they were all fulfilled.

NOT long before his death, some tasty food was prepared for blessed Francis, whereupon he thought of Brother Bernard, who was the first friar that he had. Saying to his companions, 'This dish is good for Brother Bernard,' he immediately sent for him. When Brother Bernard arrived, he sat down beside the bed where the Saint was lying, and said to him, 'Father, I beg you to bless me and give me some sign of affection, for if you show your paternal love towards me, I am sure that God Himself and the brethren will love me more.'

Blessed Francis could not see him, because he had already lost the sight of his eyes many days before; but he reached out his right hand and laid it on the head of Brother Giles, the third of the friars, thinking that he was laying it on the head of Brother Bernard, who was sitting beside him. Immediately aware of this through the Holy Spirit, he said, 'This is not the head of my Brother Bernard.' Then Brother Bernard came closer, and laying his hand on his head, blessed Francis gave him his blessing. Then he said to one of his companions, 'Write down what I tell you. Brother Bernard was the first friar that the Lord gave me, and he was first to observe the absolute perfection of the

Gospel by giving all his property to the poor. Because of this, and because of his many other merits, I cannot help loving him more than any other friar in the whole Order. As far as I may, I therefore desire and decree that whoever becomes Minister General is to love and honour him as they would myself. Let the Minister and all the friars of the Order regard him as taking my place.' And Brother Bernard and the other friars were greatly comforted by his words.

Knowing the sublime perfection of Brother Bernard, blessed Francis had prophesied before a number of friars, saying, 'Some of the most powerful and cunning devils have been assigned to tempt Brother Bernard, and they will bring many troubles and trials upon him. But as his end is drawing near the Lord in His mercy will take away all his troubles and temptations, and will establish such peace and consolation in his soul that all the brethren who see it will be filled with wonder, and reverence it as a great miracle. And in this peace and consolation of soul and body he will pass away to the Lord.'

To the great wonder of all the friars who heard these things from blessed Francis all his words about Brother Bernard were fulfilled to the letter. For during the illness that led to his death Brother Bernard enjoyed such peace and consolation of spirit that he did not want to lie down. And whenever he did so, he reclined in a sitting position so that no faintness, however slight, might mount to his head and interrupt his contemplation of God, or bring about sleep or delirium. And whenever he felt this happening, he would at once start up and strike himself, saying, 'What was that? Why was I thinking of that?' And he refused to accept any medicine, but said to the friar who offered it, 'Do not disturb me.'

In order to die in greater freedom and peace, Brother Bernard thenceforward entrusted the care of his body to one of the brethren who was a doctor, saying, 'I do not wish to be consulted about what I eat or drink. I leave that to you. If you give it me, I will take it; if you do not, I shall not ask for it.' But when he began to grow weaker he wished to have a priest always with him until the hour of his death; and whenever he remembered anything that burdened his conscience, he confessed it forthwith. After death his flesh became white and soft, and he seemed to smile, so that he became more lovely in his death than in his life. And all were even happier to gaze at him dead than alive, for he seemed 'a smiling saint' indeed.

108

How, shortly before his death, Saint Francis promised blessed Clare that she should see him; and how this came about after his death.

DURING the week in which blessed Francis died, Lady Clare, the first flower of the Poor Sisters of S. Damian in Assisi, feared that she might die before him, for they were both seriously ill at that time. She wept bitterly and could not be comforted, because she thought that she would be unable to see blessed Francis, her only Father after God, before her death, for he had been her comforter and teacher, and had first established her in the grace of God.

So she sent word of her fears by one of the friars, and when he heard of it, the Saint was moved with compassion for her, for he loved her with an especial and paternal affection. But realizing that he could not fulfil her desire to see him, he wrote a letter to comfort her and all the Sisters, and sent her his blessing. And he absolved her from any fault that she might have committed against his counsel and against the commands and teachings of the Son of God. And so that she might put aside all sadness, he was guided by the Holy Spirit to say to the friar whom she had sent, 'Go and tell the Lady Clare to put aside all sorrow and grief, for she cannot see me now. But promise her that before her death both she and her Sisters shall certainly see me, and be greatly comforted because of me.'

Soon afterwards, when blessed Francis had passed away in the night, all the people and clergy of Assisi came very early to take his holy body from the place where he had died, and they all sang hymns and praises and carried branches of trees. And by the will of God they bore him to S. Damian, so that the words that God had spoken through blessed Francis to comfort his daughters should be fulfilled.

And when the iron grille through which the Sisters used to receive Communion and hear the word of God had been removed, the friars lifted the holy body from its bier and raised it in their arms in front of the window for a long while. And Lady Clare and her sisters were comforted by this, although they were filled with grief and wept aloud when they saw themselves deprived of the consolation and counsel of so great a Father.

109

How he foretold that his body would be honoured after his death.

ONE day, while blessed Francis was lying ill in the house of the Bishop of Assisi, a spiritual friar said to him with a smile, as though joking, 'How much would you charge the Lord Bishop for all your sackcloth? One day many canopies and silken palls will cover this little body of yours which is now clothed in sackcloth!' For at that time he had a cowl patched with sacking, and a habit of sacking.

And blessed Francis—speaking not with his own words but with those of the Holy Spirit—replied with great fervour and joy of soul, 'What you say is true, for it will be to the praise and glory of my Lord!'

ON GOD'S PROVIDENCE FOR HIM IN MATERIAL THINGS

110

Firstly, how the Lord provided for the friars who were sharing their frugal meal with a doctor.

ONE day, while blessed Francis was staying in the hermitage of Fonte Colombo near Rieti because of his disease of the eyes, the oculist visited him. When he had stayed some while and was about to take his leave, blessed Francis said to one of his companions, 'Go and give the doctor the best meal that you can.' The friar replied, 'Father, I am ashamed to say that we are so poor at the moment that it would embarrass us to invite him to a meal.' Blessed Francis replied, 'O man of little faith, don't make me repeat my order!' Then the doctor said to blessed Francis, 'Brother, it is because the friars are so poor that it would give me all the more pleasure to eat with them.' For the doctor was a very rich man, and although blessed Francis and his companions had often invited him to a meal, he had not hitherto accepted.

So the brethren went and laid the table, and with great embarrassment they placed on it a little bread and wine, together with a few cabbages that they had prepared for themselves. When they had sat down to their frugal meal and begun to eat, there was a knock at the door of the house. One of the friars rose and opened it, and there stood a woman carrying a large hamper full of fine bread, fish, crayfish patties, honey and fresh grapes, which had been sent to blessed Francis by the lady of a castle about seven miles away.

The friars and the doctor were amazed and delighted when they saw this, and recalling the holiness of blessed Francis, they ascribed it wholly to his merits. Then the doctor said to the friars, 'My brothers, neither you nor we realize the great holiness of this man!'

111

On the fish that he craved during his illness.

On another occasion, when blessed Francis was very ill in the palace of the Bishop of Assisi, the friars begged him to take some nourishment. 'I have no inclination to eat,' he replied, 'but if I could have a little angel-fish I might be able to eat it.'

No sooner had he spoken than a man came in carrying a basket containing three large and well-cooked angel-fish, together with some crayfish delicacies which had been sent him by Brother Gerard, the Minister at Rieti. And the holy Father ate these with pleasure. The friars were amazed at God's providence, and praised the Lord Who had provided these things for His servant, for such food was unobtainable in Assisi during the winter.

112

On the food and cloth that he wanted at his death.

One day at S. Mary of the Angels, during blessed Francis's last illness which was to cause his death, he called his companions together and said, 'You know how the Lady Jacoba of Settesoli has been and is most faithful and devoted to our Order and to me. I am sure that she will regard it as a great favour and consolation if you inform her of my condition. Ask her especially to send me some plain ashen-coloured cloth, and with it some of that sweetmeat that she has often made for me in the City.' (This is the sweetmeat which the people of Rome call *mostaccioli*, and is made of almonds, sugar, and other ingredients.) For the Lady Jacoba was a sincerely spiritual woman, and belonged to one of the noblest and richest families in the whole of Rome. Through the merits and preaching of blessed Francis she had received such grace from God that she seemed like another Magdalene, full of tears and devotion for the love and sweetness of Christ.

So the brethren wrote a letter as the Saint had instructed them, and one of the friars went to find a brother to take the letter to the lady. But suddenly there was a knock at the friary gate, and when one of the friars opened it, there stood the Lady Jacoba, who had come in great haste to visit blessed Francis. Directly he knew this, one of the friars hastened to blessed Francis and told him with much joy how the Lady Jacoba had arrived from Rome with her son and many other people to visit him. 'What shall we do, Father?' he inquired. 'Shall we allow her to enter and come to you?' (He asked this because in order to preserve good order and devotion at S. Mary's, blessed Francis had made a rule that no woman should enter the enclosure.) Blessed Francis replied, 'This rule need not be observed in the case of Lady Jacoba, whose faith and devotion have impelled her to travel here from such a distance.'

So Lady Jacoba came in to blessed Francis, and when she saw him, she wept. Wonderful to relate, she had brought ashen-coloured cloth for a habit, and everything mentioned in the letter as though she had already received it. And she told the friars, 'My brothers, while I was at prayer I was told in spirit, "Go and visit your Father, blessed Francis. Hurry, and do not delay, for you will not find him alive if you wait long. And take with you this cloth for a habit, and such and such things, and make him some of that sweetmeat. Take with you also a large amount of wax for candles, and some incense." ' (All these things, with the exception of the incense, had been mentioned in the letter that was about to be sent.)

So God, Who had guided the kings to go with gifts to honour His Son, also inspired this noble and holy lady to go with gifts to honour His best-beloved servant on the day of his death, which was rather the day of his true birth. Then Lady Jacoba prepared the food that the holy Father had wished to eat, but he could only take a little of it because he was steadily growing weaker and drawing nearer to death. She also had many candles made to burn before his most holy body after death, and from the cloth the friars made him the habit in which he was buried. But he told the friars to sew him in sack-cloth as a sign of holy Humility and of the Lady Poverty. And during the week in which Lady Jacoba arrived, our most holy Father passed away to the Lord.

ON HIS LOVE FOR CREATURES, AND OF
CREATURES FOR HIM

113

Firstly, on his especial love for hooded larks, because to him they were an image of the good Religious.

BEING completely absorbed in the love of God, blessed Francis clearly perceived the goodness of God both within his own soul, already endowed with perfect virtue, and in all created things, so he therefore had an especial and profound love for God's creatures, and especially for those which he thought of as representing some truth about God or religion.

Above all birds he loved the little lark, known in the language of the country as *lodola capellata* (the hooded lark). He used to say of it, 'Sister lark has a hood like a Religious and is a humble bird, for she walks contentedly along the road to find grain, and even if she finds it among rubbish, she pecks it out and eats it. As she flies she praises God very sweetly, like good Religious who despise earthly things, whose *minds are set on the things of heaven,* and whose constant purpose is to praise God. Her plumage resembles the earth, and she sets an example to Religious not to wear fine and gaudy clothing, but cloth of a humble price and colour, just as earth is inferior to the other elements.'

Because he saw these things in them, he always looked on them with great pleasure, so it pleased God that these little birds should give him a sign of affection at the hour of his death. For late that Saturday evening, after Vespers on the night when he passed away to the Lord, a great flight of larks assembled above the roof of the house where he lay. And they circled around it in the form of a wheel, singing sweetly as they flew and seeming to praise God.

114

How he wanted to persuade the Emperor to enact an especial law requiring everyone to provide generously for birds, cattle, asses, and the poor on Christmas Day.

WE who were with blessed Francis and write about these events testify that we have often heard him say, 'If I ever speak to the Emperor, I shall beg him for love of God and myself to enact an especial law, forbidding anyone to kill our sisters the larks or do them any harm. Similarly, all mayors of towns and lords of castles and villages should be obliged each year on the Nativity of our Lord to see that their people scatter wheat and other grain on the roads outside towns and villages, so that our sisters the larks and other birds may have food on such a solemn festival. And in reverence for the Son of God, Who with the most blessed Virgin Mary rested in a manger that night between an ox and an ass, anyone who owns an ox or an ass should be obliged to give them the choicest of fodder on Christmas Eve. And on Christmas Day the rich should give an abundance of good things to all the poor.'

For blessed Francis had a deeper veneration for the Nativity of our Lord than for other festivals, and he said, 'Since our Lord has been born for us, it is for us to accept salvation.' He wanted every Christian to rejoice in the Lord on that day, and for love of Him Who gave Himself for us, he wished everyone to provide generously not only for the poor, but for beasts and birds as well.

*On the love and obedience of fire to blessed Francis when he was
cauterized.*

WHEN blessed Francis came to the hermitage of Fonte Colombo
to undergo a cure for his eyes—which he did under obedience
to the orders of the Lord Cardinal of Ostia and of Brother Elias
the Minister General—the doctor came to visit him one day.
When he had examined him, he told blessed Francis that he
wished to make a cautery from the jaw up to the eyebrow of
the weaker eye. But because Brother Elias had expressed a
desire to be present when the doctor began the operation,
blessed Francis did not wish the treatment to begin until Brother
Elias's arrival. The Father was also much disturbed at being the
object of so much attention, and wanted the Minister General
to be responsible for giving instructions. But Elias had been
delayed by much business, and when they had waited for him
in vain, blessed Francis at length asked the doctor to proceed.

When the iron had been placed in the fire to make the cautery,
blessed Francis was afraid that he might show weakness, and
wishing to strengthen his resolution, spoke to the fire, saying,
'Brother Fire, so noble and useful among other creatures, be
gentle to me in this hour, for I have always loved you and will
always do so for love of Him Who created you. I pray our
Creator, Who made us, to temper your heat so that I can bear
it.' And as he ended this prayer, he blessed the fire with the sign
of the cross. At this moment we who were with him were so
overcome with pity and compassion for him that we all fled,
and left him alone with the doctor. When the cautery was
completed we came back, and he said, 'Faint-hearts! Men of
little faith! Why did you run away? I assure you that I felt no
pain or heat from the fire. Indeed, if this cautery does not
satisfy the doctor, let him do it again.' The doctor was amazed
at his words, and said, 'My brothers, I would be afraid to apply

so drastic a cautery to the strongest man, let alone to one who is so frail and ill. But he did not flinch or betray the least sign of pain.' Although all the veins from the ear to the eyebrow had been seared, this operation did not benefit him, nor did a second, when another doctor pierced both his ears with a red-hot iron.

It is not surprising that fire and other creatures sometimes obeyed and revered him, for we who were with him often saw how much he loved them, and what pleasure he took in them. Indeed, his spirit was stirred by such love and compassion for them that he would not allow them to be treated without respect. He used to speak to them as though they were rational creatures with such inward and outward joy that at times he was rapt in ecstasy.

116

How he would not allow the fire that had burned his under-linen to be extinguished.

AMONG all lesser created things blessed Francis had an especial love for fire, because of its beauty and usefulness, and would not allow it to be denied its natural function. Once while he was sitting close to the fire, his linen underclothes caught fire near the knee without his notice; and although he felt the heat, he was unwilling to put out the flames. Seeing his clothes alight, his companion ran to put out the flame, but blessed Francis would not allow it, saying, 'Dearest brother, do not hurt Brother Fire!' So his companion ran to the friar who was Guardian and brought him to blessed Francis, and against his wishes the Guardian beat out the flames. But so dearly did he love fire that, however pressing the need, he would never put out a flame, whether a lamp or a candle. And he would not allow any friar to throw burning or smouldering wood from one place to another, as is often done; he wished them to lay it properly on the ground out of reverence for God Who created it.

117

How he would never again use a fleece because he had not allowed Brother Fire to burn it.

ONE day, while he was observing Lent on Mount La Verna, his companion laid a fire at dinner time in the cell where he used to eat. When the fire was alight he went to fetch blessed Francis from another cell where he was at prayer, and took a missal with him in order to read him the Gospel for the day; for whenever he had been unable to hear Mass, the Father always wished to hear the Gospel for the day read before his meal.

On returning to the cell where he had lit a fire to cook the meal, the friar found that the flames had already reached the roof and were burning it. He did his best to extinguish the flames, but could not do so single-handed, and blessed Francis was unwilling to help him. His only action was to pick up a fleece that he used as a covering at night, and go away with it into a wood. But when the other friars, who were living some distance away, saw his cell burning down, they ran at once and put out the fire. Some time later blessed Francis returned for a meal, and when he had eaten, he said to his companions, 'I shall not use this fleece over me again, for in my avarice I would not allow Brother Fire to consume it.'

118

On his especial love for water, rocks, wood, and flowers.

NEXT to fire he had an especial love for water, because it symbolizes holy penitence and tribulation, and at Baptism the soul is cleansed from its stains and receives its first purification. So whenever he washed his hands he chose a place where the water would not be trodden underfoot as it fell to the ground. For the same reason, whenever he had to walk over rocks, he trod reverently and fearfully, out of love for Christ Who is called *The Rock*: so whenever he recited the psalm *Thou wilt set me high up on a rock*, he used to say with great reverence and devotion, *Thou hast set me up at the foot of the rock.*

He told the friar who cut and chopped wood for the fire that he must never cut down the whole tree, but remove branches in such a way that part of the tree remained intact, out of love for Christ, Who willed to accomplish our salvation on the wood of the cross.

In the same way he told the friar who cared for the gardens not to cultivate all the ground for vegetables, but to set aside a plot to grow flowers to bloom in their season, out of love for Him Who is called *The Rose on the plain and the Lily on the mountain slopes*. Indeed, he told the brother-gardener that he should always make a pleasant flower-garden, and cultivate every variety of fragrant herb and flowering plant, so that all who saw the herbs and flowers would be moved to praise God. For every creature proclaims, 'God made me for your sake, O man.'

We who were with him have seen him take inward and outward delight in almost every creature, and when he handled or looked at them his spirit seemed to be in heaven rather than on earth. And not long before his death, in gratitude for the many consolations that he had received through creatures, he composed *The Praises of the Lord in His Creatures*, in order to stir the hearts of those who heard them to the praise of God, and to move men to praise the Lord Himself in His creatures.

119

How he praised the sun and fire above all other creatures.

ABOVE all creatures unendowed with reason he had a particular love for the sun and for fire. He used to say, 'At dawn, when the sun rises, all men should praise God, Who created him for our use, and through him gives light to our eyes by day. And at nightfall every man should praise God for Brother Fire, by whom He gives light to our eyes in the darkness. For we are all blind, and by these two brothers of ours God gives light to our eyes, so we should give special praise to our Creator for these and other creatures that serve us day by day.'

Blessed Francis himself always offered this praise until the day of his death, and even when his illness grew more serious he used to sing *The Praises of the Lord in His Creatures* which he had composed. Later he asked his companions to sing them, so that their occupation with the praises of God might make them forget the bitterness of his suffering and disease. And since in Holy Scripture the Lord Himself is called *The Sun of Justice*, and because blessed Francis thought the sun the loveliest of God's creatures and most worthy of comparison with Him, he gave its name to the *Praises of God in His Creatures* which he had written when the Lord had assured him of His Kingdom. And he called them *The Song of Brother Sun*.

120

The Praises that he composed when the Lord assured him of His kingdom.

Most High, Almighty, good Lord,
Thine be the praise, the glory, the honour,
And all blessing.

To Thee alone, Most High, are they due,
And no man is worthy
To speak Thy Name.

Praise to Thee, my Lord, for all Thy creatures,
Above all Brother Sun
Who brings us the day and lends us his light.

1258

Mirror of Perfection

Lovely is he, radiant with great splendour,
And speaks to us of Thee,
O Most High.

Praise to Thee, my Lord, for Sister Moon and the stars
Which Thou hast set in the heavens,
Clear, precious, and fair.

Praise to Thee, my Lord, for Brother Wind,
For air and cloud, for calm and all weather,
By which Thou supportest life in all Thy creatures.

Praise to Thee, my Lord, for Sister Water,
Who is so useful and humble,
Precious and pure.

Praise to Thee, my Lord, for Brother Fire,
By whom Thou lightest the night;
He is lovely and pleasant, mighty and strong.

Praise to Thee, my Lord, for our sister Mother Earth
Who sustains and directs us,
And brings forth varied fruits, and coloured flowers, and plants.

Praise to Thee, my Lord, for those who pardon one another
For love of Thee, and endure
Sickness and tribulation.

Blessed are they who shall endure it in peace,
For they shall be crowned by Thee,
O Most High.

Praise to Thee, my Lord, for our Sister bodily Death
From whom no man living may escape:
Woe to those who die in mortal sin.

1259

Blessed are they who are found in Thy most holy will,
For the second death cannot harm them.

Praise and bless my Lord,
Thank Him and serve Him
With great humility.

ON HIS DEATH, AND THE JOY THAT HE SHOWED WHEN HE KNEW THAT DEATH WAS DRAWING NEAR

121

Firstly, how he answered Brother Elias when the latter reproved him for his obvious joy.

WHEN he was lying ill in the episcopal palace at Assisi, the hand of God appeared to press upon him more heavily than usual, and the people of Assisi feared that if he were to die during the night, the friars might take his holy body and carry it to some other place. So they arranged to post men on guard around the walls of the palace each night.

To comfort his soul and strengthen his resolution during the violent attacks of pain that constantly racked him, blessed Francis often asked his companions to sing him the *Praises of the Lord* during the day, and to do so during the night to edify and console those who were keeping watch outside the palace on his account.

Seeing that blessed Francis was comforted and rejoicing in the Lord in this way despite his great pain, Brother Elias said to him, 'Dearest Brother, the great joy shown by you and your companions gives me great comfort and edification. But the people of this city venerate you as a saint, and are well aware that you will soon die of your incurable disease; so when they hear the *Praises* sung day and night they are likely to say to themselves, "How can this man show so much joy when he is about to die? He ought to be preparing himself for death." '

Blessed Francis said to him, 'Do you remember the vision that you saw at Foligno, when you told me that it had been revealed to you that I had only two years to live? Before you had this vision, by the grace of God Who implants all good things in our hearts and inspires the words of the faithful, I often meditated upon my end both by day and by night. And after you had that vision, I was even more careful to give daily thought to my death.' Then he continued in great fervour of spirit, 'Brother, allow me in my infirmities to *rejoice in the Lord* and in His praises, for by the grace and assistance of the Holy Spirit I am so united and conjoined to my Lord that by His mercy I may rightly rejoice in Him, the Most High.'

122

How he persuaded a doctor to tell him how long he had to live.

AT that time a doctor from Arrezzo named John Buono, a close friend of blessed Francis, came to visit him in the bishop's palace, and blessed Francis asked him, 'Finiate, what do you think about this dropsical disease of mine?' (For he would never call him by his proper name (*Buono–Good*), because he never addressed anyone who was called Good by their name out of reverence for the Lord, Who said, *God is good, and He only*. For the same reason he would never call anyone Father or Master, or use these titles in a letter, out of reverence for our Lord, Who said, *Nor are you to call any man on earth your father. Nor are you to be called teachers.*)

The doctor said to him, 'Brother, God willing, all will be well with you.' Again blessed Francis said to him, 'Tell me the truth. What is your real opinion? Don't be afraid to tell me, for by God's grace I am not such a coward as to fear death. By the grace and help of the Holy Spirit I am so united to my Lord that I am equally content to die or to live.'

Then the doctor told him frankly, 'Father, according to our

medical knowledge your disease is incurable, and it is my belief that you will die either at the end of September or in early October.' Then blessed Francis, lying on his bed, most reverently and devoutly stretched out his hands to God, and with great joy of mind and body, said, 'Welcome, Sister Death.'

123

How, as soon as he heard of his approaching death, he ordered the Praises that he had written to be sung.

AFTER this, one of the friars said to him, 'Father, your life and teaching have been, and remain, a light and mirror not only to your friars but to the whole Church, and your death will be the same. And although your passing will be an occasion of sorrow and grief to your brethren and many others, to you it will bring consolation and infinite joy. For you will pass from great toil to great repose, from many sorrows and temptations to eternal peace, from earthly poverty, which you have always loved and observed perfectly, to true and boundless riches, from death in this world to everlasting life in which you will see the Lord your God face to face, and gaze on Him Whom you have loved with such fervent love and desire in this life.' Then he said frankly, 'Father, you already know for certain that, unless the Lord sends you healing from heaven, your disease is incurable, and the doctors have said that you have only a short while to live. But I have spoken as I have to strengthen your spirit, so that you may continue to rejoice in the Lord both inwardly and outwardly. So the friars and others who visit you will always find you rejoicing in the Lord, and both to those who see it and others who hear of it after your passing not only your life and teaching but your death itself will be an everlasting memorial.'

Although blessed Francis was in greater pain from his diseases than usual, when he heard that Sister Death was fast approaching, he was filled with fresh joy, and praised the Lord in great fervour of spirit, saying, 'If it be my Lord's pleasure that I should die soon, call me Brother Angelo and Brother Leo, and let them sing to me of Sister Death.' And when these two friars, filled with sorrow and grief, had come to him, they sang with many tears the *Song of Brother Sun* and the other creatures which the Saint had written. And before the last verse of the Song, he added these lines on Sister Death:

> Praised be Thou, my Lord, for Sister Bodily Death
> From whom no man living may escape.
>
> Woe to those who die in mortal sin,
> And blessed are those who are found in Thy most holy will,
> For the second death can do them no ill.

124

How he blessed the city of Assisi while he was being carried to die at S. Mary's.

THE most holy Father had now been informed by the Holy Spirit as well as by the doctors that his death was near. Hitherto he had been lodged in the bishop's palace, but when he felt himself growing steadily worse and his bodily powers failing, he asked to be carried on a litter to S. Mary of the Porziuncula, so that his bodily life should draw to its close in the place where his spiritual life and light had come into being.

When the brethren who were carrying him arrived at the hospice standing by the road half-way between Assisi and S. Mary's, he asked the bearers to set the litter on the ground. And although his long-standing and severe disease of the eyes had almost deprived him of sight, he had the litter turned to face the city of Assisi. Raising himself a little, he blessed the city, saying, 'Lord, it is said that in former days this city was the haunt of wicked men. But now it is clear that of Thine infinite mercy and in Thine own time Thou hast been pleased to shower especial and abundant favours upon it. Of Thy goodness alone Thou hast chosen it for Thyself, that it may become the home and dwelling of those who know Thee in truth and glorify Thy holy Name, and spread abroad the fragrance of a good report, of holy life, of true doctrine, and of evangelical perfection to all Christian people. I therefore beseech Thee, O Lord Jesus Christ, Father of mercies, that Thou wilt not remember our ingratitude, but ever be mindful of Thine abundant compassion which Thou hast showed towards it, that it may ever be the home and dwelling-place of those who know Thee in truth and glorify Thy blessed and most glorious Name for ever and ever. Amen.'

When he had ended his prayer, he was carried on to S. Mary's. There, on October the third, 1226, in the fortieth year of his life and after twenty years of perfect penitence, he departed to the Lord Jesus Christ, Whom he had loved with all his heart, with all his mind, with all his soul, and all his strength, with the most ardent desire and with utter devotion, following Him perfectly, hastening swiftly in His footsteps, and at last coming in the greatest glory to Him Who lives and reigns with the Father and the Holy Spirit for ever and ever. *Amen.*

Here ends the Mirror of Perfection,
which tells of the state of the Friar Minor,
and in which the perfection of his vocation and profession
may be seen accurately reflected.

All praise and glory to God the Father, and to the Son, and to the Holy Spirit.
ALLELUIA! ALLELUIA! ALLELUIA!
Honour and exaltation to His most blessed servant Francis.
ALLELUIA!
Amen.

LITTLE FLOWERS
OF ST. FRANCIS

A modern English translation from the
Latin and the Italian with Introduction,
and Notes, by Raphael Brown.

This English version of The Little Flowers of
St. Francis by Raphael Brown was first pub-
lished in 1958 by Hanover House, Garden
City, N. Y., in the book of the same title
(Library of Congress Catalog Card Number:
58-11308), which also contains The Life and
Sayings of Brother Giles and The Life of
Brother Juniper.

INTRODUCTION

For the last hundred years the *Fioretti*, or *The Little Flowers of St. Francis*, has been the most widely read book about the "Poverello," the Little Poor Man of Assisi, who is the most popular figure in the history of Christianity after Jesus Himself and the Blessed Virgin. But the true story of this great classic of world literature and of its author, as revealed by modern Franciscan research, has not yet been told.

We shall therefore briefly survey in the Introduction the life of St. Francis and of the author of this book, the crucial role which it played in the turbulent early history of the Franciscan Order, its historical value, its Latin and Italian versions with their various additional parts, its rise to world-wide popularity in modern times, the special features of this new edition, and lastly the literary and spiritual qualities of the *Fioretti*.

At the outset it may be advisable to dispel a fairly common misconception: *The Little Flowers* was not written by St. Francis himself, but by an Italian Franciscan who lived a hundred years after the Saint died.

St. Francis of Assisi

This extraordinary man whom all the world loves and honors as a faithful mirror of Christ began life as a gay playboy. He was born in Assisi in central Italy in 1182, the son of a wealthy middle-class linen merchant, Pietro di Bernardone. Francis was a gentle, likable, and fun-loving boy. He learned to read and write Latin at St. George's Church school, and his father, who often traded in France, taught him some French.

In his youth he was deeply influenced by the high ethical ideals of medieval chivalry as reflected in the great epic poems which he heard the troubadours sing: selfless devotion to a lofty goal, loyalty to a liege lord, considerate courtesy toward all persons, and generous compassion for the poor and the weak. Young Francis dreamed of winning fame and glory as a valiant knight in armor.

But his military career was brief and disappointing. Captured during a battle between Assisi and Perugia, he spent a frustrating year as a cheerful and popular prisoner of war. After a period of illness he set out to fight for the Pope, but a revelation which he received in nearby Spoleto urged him to serve the Lord rather than man, so he went home and began to turn to Christ in solitary prayer. At this time he was also granted an unforgettable vision of Jesus suffering His Passion on the Cross.

Characteristically, Francis then began to help poor priests and the needy and even to associate with paupers. During a pilgrimage to St. Peter's Tomb in Rome, he spent a day dressed as a beggar. Later near Assisi he embraced a man who had leprosy. While he was praying fervently for divine guidance in the old chapel of San Damiano, Christ in the Crucifix said to him: "Francis, go and repair My Church which, as you see, is falling into ruins."

Soon his greedy father, exasperated by his son's extravagant generosity and strange vocation, summoned him before the Bishop's court in order to recover the money he had spent. But Francis stripped himself naked to symbolize his complete renunciation of the world for God. This climax of his conversion, which occurred in 1206, when he was about twenty-five, marked the beginning of his twenty years of knightly service to his true liege lord, Christ the King.

Dressed in a hermit's robe, he spent over two years nursing victims of leprosy and repairing three small churches near Assisi: San Damiano, San Pietro, and the Portiuncula or St. Mary of the Angels. There on February 24, 1209, the Holy Spirit revealed to him in the Gospel of the Mass (Matt. 10:9 ff.) the specific way of life to which God was calling him. He then began to preach brief, informal sermons in Assisi.

Within a few weeks three companions—Bernard, Peter

Catani, and Giles—joined him. Soon they set out on a first mission journey, Francis and Giles going to the Marches of Ancona while the other two took another direction. After eight more volunteers had taken up the new life, in 1210 they wrote a simple Rule based on the Gospels and traveled to Rome, where Pope Innocent III gave them his verbal approval. Probably at this time Francis was ordained a deacon; out of humility he never became a priest.

On returning to Assisi the twelve Friars Minor lived for a while in extreme destitution in a shed at Rivo Torto and then, as their numbers increased, they moved to the Portiuncula, which was given to them by the Benedictines of Mount Subasio. In that chapel in 1212 Francis gave the religious habit to an aristocratic eighteen-year-old girl of Assisi named Clare, who thereby became the Foundress of the Second Order of cloistered nuns.

St. Francis was the first founder of an Order to include in its Rule a chapter dealing with foreign missions. In 1212 and again a year later he tried in vain to reach the Moslems in North Africa and Spain, with the hope of preaching to them —and of dying as a martyr. While attending the Lateran Council in Rome in 1215, he formed a lasting friendship with St. Dominic. The following year he obtained from Pope Honorius III the Portiuncula Indulgence. In 1217, when the General Chapter organized provinces and missions in European countries and the Holy Land, he volunteered to go to France. But Cardinal Hugolin (later Pope Gregory IX) persuaded him to remain in Italy, where he preached throughout 1218. The next year, however, he left two Vicars to govern the Order and sailed to join the Crusaders at the siege of Damietta in Egypt. There at the risk of his life he preached to the Sultan.

The Saint's return to Italy in 1220, suffering from malaria and glaucoma, marked the beginning of the great spiritual trial in his life when (according to his first biographer) he complained that some of his friars were "piercing me with a hard sword and stabbing it into my heart all day." Within a few months he obtained from the Holy See the appointment of Cardinal Hugolin as Protector of the Order, and then he proceeded to resign as its effective administrator, naming in his place Peter Catani and (after the latter's death in 1221) the famous Brother Elias. Next he wrote the long, eloquent Rule of 1221, but found that he must revise and rewrite it twice before it was formally approved in 1223.

In order to understand the nature of this great trial, this "dark night of the spirit," which the Poverello suffered for over two years, we must have a clear idea of the novel form of the religious life which he introduced into the traditional mold of monastic chastity, poverty, and obedience. In his mind the basic conception of the Order of Friars Minor was quite simple: it was the literal, deliberate imitation of the way of life of Christ and His Apostles as described in the Gospels. In practical application this meant an itinerant life divided almost equally between prayer and preaching and supported by work (if possible manual) or by begging, with the greatest stress laid on voluntary self-denial and renunciation of property—all for the single purpose of enabling oneself and inducing others to live a life of ever closer union with Christ in His Church.

Now an objective study of early Franciscan documents definitely reveals that some friars, represented by the two Vicars of 1219 and later by Brother Elias, failed to grasp or accept this ideal. In its stead they advocated a combination of traditional monastic asceticism and conventual life with a more active and especially a more intellectual apostolate. As a result, St. Francis found an influential group within the Order trying to modify the way of life which he was convinced that God had inspired him to adopt.

In the end, while retaining as much of his original ideal as he could, he humbly submitted to the prudent mediation and guidance of his friend, Cardinal Hugolin, who persuaded him that some degree of adaptation was essential so that the Order might most effectively "repair the Church" by contributing a full measure of co-operation to the educational and missionary apostolates which were so sorely needed at that time. With the Cardinal he also instituted the lay Third Order in 1221.

The Poverello regained his peace of soul when in a crucial revelation he received divine assurance that Christ Himself would always remain the principal head of the Order and that all friars who sincerely wished to follow their Founder would do so. On emerging from this "dark night," the Saint experienced the mystical joy of holding in his arms the Babe of Bethlehem before the realistic crib which he prepared at Greccio on Christmas Eve, 1223. Then at last he was ready for "the final seal" (Dante): the transforming union that God bestowed on him by imprinting the five holy Stigmata on his body on Mount Alverna in September, 1224.

After another two years of increasingly painful illness (eye, stomach, liver, and spleen sickness, with dropsy), during which he composed the beautiful *Canticle of Brother Sun* and wrote an inspiring Testament, St. Francis died peacefully at his beloved Portiuncula on October 3, 1226. His friend Pope Gregory IX canonized him two years later.[1]

Such, in brief outline, was the life of the world's greatest follower of Christ. For one of the most vivid profiles of his personality which has ever been written, we must turn to the *Fioretti*.

The Garden of "The Little Flowers"

The Little Flowers of St. Francis blossomed during the age of Dante in one of the most beautiful gardens on the face of the earth: the Marches (or borderlands) of Ancona and Fermo, a little-known area of central Italy lying between the Apennine Mountains and the Adriatic Sea that has been called a country of unsurpassed, almost terrible beauty . . . the world as a garden—the garden where God walked in the cool of the day."

To this paradise on earth, over a mountain pass, two strangely robed, barefooted young men of Assisi came in the spring of the year 1209. As Francis and Giles strode down the steep winding road in the shadow of rugged, barren peaks, the whole splendor of that gentle, serene, and lovely landscape was spread out before them. Their hearts thrilled as they perceived its waves of long wooded hills extending to the shining curve of the Adriatic seacoast only thirty miles away, its score of small white towns basking in the bright sun on the hilltops —"A city on a hill cannot be hidden"—and its deep warm valleys and sloping meadows rich in wheat and vines.

While the two friars walked through the vast forests of poplar, oak, and beech, and inhaled the soft fragrance of honeysuckle, clover, mountain lilies, and white roses mingling with the fresh sea breezes, it is no wonder that—as an old chronicle noted—"Francis sang aloud in French, praising and blessing the Lord for His goodness. For they felt their hearts overflow with fervent joy, as though they had acquired an immense treasure. And indeed they could rejoice greatly, because they had given up very much." Only a few weeks earlier in Assisi, with Brothers Bernard and Peter, they had begun to live a new life of extreme poverty, for the love of God. Now in return Divine Providence was giving them this treasure, this earthly paradise, as one of the choice fields of their realm-to-be. Francis prophesied then to Giles: "Our Order will be like a fisherman who throws out his net and catches a great mass of fishes. . . ."[2]

For in the garden of the Marches he found a fertile soil in which the seeds of his revolutionary spiritual message were soon destined to bear richer fruit than anywhere else. Psychologically the simple farmers and villagers of the Marches resembled him very much. They too were practical mystics endowed with a rare combination of poetic fancy and shrewd common sense, profound religious insight and sturdy practicality. Abstemious, frank, gay, friendly, warmhearted, loving nature and living close to it in their garden land, they embraced with extraordinary enthusiasm his inspiring message of peace through mystic union with God and good will toward all of God's creatures. In fact, his first biographer reported that when the Saint came to the city of Ascoli on a subsequent journey through the Marches, "in their eagerness to see and hear him they trod on one another. And thirty men (clerics and lay persons) received the holy habit of the Order from him."

Soon the woods and hills of the Marches were dotted with the humble little friaries which the early Franciscans called mere "places" (*loci*). By the year 1282 the small Province of the Marches had the amazing total of eighty-five friaries—twice as many as Tuscany or Umbria; and a century later it had ninety.[3] The majority of those houses were undoubtedly isolated hermitages, for the friars of the Marches were preeminently contemplatives. As evidence of this significant trend, the *Fioretti* contains no less than sixteen passages in which a friar is described as "praying in the woods."

It is therefore obvious that those friars had effectively grasped the essence of the spirituality of St. Francis: the absolute unconditional primacy of the interior life, the life of ceaseless inner union with God, constant humble contemplation of the Savior, and intimate loving communion with Him which the Poverello called "the spirit of prayer." And he repeatedly insisted that the various occupations of his friars should never be allowed to extinguish that holy flame in their hearts. Now it is evident that such a life can be lived in a hermitage in the woods or on a hillside better than anywhere else, as the contemplatives of all ages have found. It is also a little-known but significant fact that St. Francis himself founded and frequently resided in at least twenty-five such hermitages.

However, he also traveled and preached, not only all over Italy but even in France, Spain, Syria, and Egypt. His twenty-year apostolate was a continuous alternation between preaching tours and extended retreats in his beloved hermitages. But in that novel combination of the active with the contemplative life lay the key to the tragic dissension which nearly rent the Order in two during its first hundred years and which directly inspired the writing of *The Little Flowers* by a fervent friar of the Marches about the year 1330.

Owing to a number of factors, such as the extreme loftiness of the Saint's ideal and way of life and the amazingly rapid expansion of the Order—to say nothing of our fallen human nature—three more or less clearly identifiable groups began to evolve among his many followers soon after his death: (1) the moderates who were sincerely convinced that a minimum of adaptation was necessary in order to perform the various apostolic tasks which the Church was increasingly assigning to the friars in towns, universities, and foreign missions; (2) the relaxed who went decidedly too far—in the opinion of such ascetical moderate leaders as St. Bonaventure—and abandoned Franciscan poverty and contemplation in all but name; and (3) opposed to both those groups the so-called *zelanti,* or Spirituals, fanatical Joachimist rigorists and contemplatives who considered the Rule and Testament of St. Francis divinely inspired documents that were equal in rank to the Gospels and were destined to effect in an imminent new age the complete regeneration of the Church and society along lines allegedly foretold in writings of the famous twelfth-century Abbot Joachim of Calabria, who was "gifted with the prophetic spirit" (Dante).

The Author

A brief outline of the bitter century-long conflict between those three groups is necessary in order to understand the historical function, the basic theme, and many of the characters and topical allusions of *The Little Flowers*. But instead of presenting a dry chronicle of events, we shall try to enable the reader to relive those momentous decades as they were experienced by the great writer who is the author of the *Actus* (the Latin original of the *Fioretti*): Brother Ugolino di Monte Santa Maria. Unfortunately very little information about his life and activities is available. Nevertheless, thanks to his book we know a good deal about his close friends and their associates of the preceding generation. Several of them played prominent roles in the history of the Order in the Marches, and their lives and example had a profound influence on his outlook and hence on his writings.

Hitherto unknown documents of 1294 and 1342 which were discovered in local archives in 1957 by Father Giacinto Pagnani, O.F.M.—and generously communicated to me—establish that his surname was Boniscambi (not Brunforte of Sarnano) and that members of that family were then well-to-do citizens of the little town of Monte Santa Maria in Giorgio, now called Montegiorgio, in the Marches. The years of his birth and death are not on record, but since he knew Brother John of Penna who died about 1270, he himself must have entered the Order at least a few years earlier. And we know that he was still living in 1342.[4] His active career therefore spans the crucial period 1270–1340 when the dramatic conflict involving the Spirituals came to a crisis. By 1280 all of the first companions of St. Francis had probably died. Ugolino does not claim to have met any of them, but his intimate friend, a lay brother named James of Massa, had known Brothers Leo, Masseo, Giles, Juniper, and Simon as well as St. Clare. Moreover, Ugolino was acquainted with at least three other friars of the second generation who had known the Saint's companions (see the Chart showing the oral tradition of the *Actus-Fioretti*).

Principally from James of Massa the young Ugolino heard many fascinating and inspiring stories about the Poverello that were not included in the incomplete official biographies by Thomas of Celano and St. Bonaventure. At this time only the latter's *Legenda* was approved by the Order. However, in 1276 a General Chapter issued a call for additional material concerning the lives of St. Francis and his companions. Perhaps it was then that Brother Ugolino began to take notes on the unpublished anecdotes that he heard the older friars tell while sitting around the fire on long winter evenings in a hermitage in the Marches.

A talented writer, he could not fail to notice that these new materials added depth and verve and color to the standard portrait of the Poverello. Moreover, they contributed a considerable number of vivid new sketches of his adventures during the early years of the Order with his favorite companions, particularly Brothers Leo, Masseo, Bernard, Giles, and Rufino. Several delightful stories told by Brother James of Massa illustrated the way of life which the Saint led with the first friars in their little hermitages, such as the Carceri on Mount Subasio above Assisi. Above all, Brother Ugolino imbibed from his several informants—and later transmitted to the world in his book—much of the joy-filled spirit of St. Francis and his faithful followers of the first generation.

The Spirituals

In those evening conversations—or perhaps alone with Brother James in the woods—Ugolino no doubt also learned more about the painful beginnings of dissension among the friars during the Poverello's lifetime. The tribulations of his closest companions after his death were common knowledge.

Brothers Bernard, Masseo, and Riccieri suffered repression. Bernard even had to leave Assisi and did not dare to return until the despotic Brother Elias was deposed as General in 1239 and subsequently excommunicated. While St. Francis was alive, his relations with Elias, according to the earliest documents, were marked by mutual respect and affection. But after the Founder's death, Elias' unmastered pride and ambition apparently became his dominant motives. It was therefore natural that his sensational fall and death-bed repentance resulted in the circulation of all sorts of stories about him, true and false, and that the Spirituals later made him a symbol of their opponents.

It must be emphasized at this point, however, that none of the intimate companions of St. Francis, although they may have sympathized to some extent with the zeal for poverty and self-denial of the Spirituals, was ever accused of the latter's doctrinal errors or rebellious actions. Nevertheless, like the outspoken Blessed Brother Giles, they did not hesitate to manifest their disapproval of the relaxed party in the Order.

Under Elias or his successor some seventy Spirituals in the Marches, including Simon of Assisi, Lucido the Elder, and Matthew of Monte Rubbiano, were severely punished and exiled. But a new Minister General, Blessed John of Parma (1247–57), liberated and pardoned them. Unfortunately, although he was a saintly man, he was apparently tainted with the doctrinal errors of Joachimism, which resulted in his resignation and trial under his successor, St. Bonaventure (1257–74). Only the intervention of a cardinal (later Pope Hadrian V) enabled John to retire to the hermitage of Greccio for the rest of his life. Brother James of Massa's famous Vision of the Tree in Chapter 48 expresses the intense resentment of the Spirituals over the trial of their friend Blessed John of Parma.

Now in 1274—during Ugolino's early years in the Order—a new crisis arose in the Marches. A rumor (later proved unfounded) that the Second Council of Lyons would impose the collective legal ownership of property on all religious orders led the Spirituals to assert that they would never accept such a ruling. Feeling ran high as the friars of the province divided into two factions. Finally the leading Spirituals, including the two later known as Angelo of Clareno and Liberato of Macerata, were condemned by their superiors to life imprisonment for heresy and insubordination.

However, in 1289 a new General visited the province, liberated them, and assigned them to a mission to Armenia. But finding themselves pursued by accusations, they returned to Italy in 1294 and sought the advice of several prominent Spirituals who had remained in the Marches and Umbria: Conrad of Offida, Peter of Montecchio, and the famous Umbrian friar-poet Jacopone da Todi. All agreed that Liberato and Angelo should consult the new Pope Celestine V, a saintly old hermit monk. He gave them permission to live according to the Rule and Testament of St. Francis as a separate Order to be called the Poor Hermits of Pope Celestine.

But within a few months the elderly Pope made what Dante bitterly called "the great refusal": he resigned. When his successor, Boniface VIII, abolished the Poor Hermits, some of them fled to Greece. Henceforth their status with regard to both the Order and the Church was that of rebels. Their followers eventually divided into two groups: the *Clareni,* who were tolerated in some dioceses (e.g., those found later in La Foresta and Sarnano), and who later joined the Observant Franciscans; and the several heretical sects of *Fraticelli.* As Livario Oliger, O.F.M., the leading expert on the Spirituals, has pointed out, their movement failed because its members, despite their idealism, fell into the following grave errors: they stressed the contemplative life at the expense of the mixed life; they equated the Rule with the Gospel; they adopted the divisive Joachimist idea of a carnal Church persecuting a spiritual Church; and above all they erred in thinking that they could withdraw from obedience to the Church in the name of St. Francis who (as even Sabatier admitted)[5] always insisted on humble supernatural submission to the authority of the Church.

Brother Ugolino and the Spirituals

At this crucial turning point in the history of the Order, Brother Ugolino and every other friar who sympathized in any way with the ascetical ideals of the Spirituals, insofar as they represented the spirit of the first friars, faced a soul-searing decision: should they join the Celestine Hermits or remain in the Order? Just at this time, in the fall of 1295, Conrad of Offida, one of the foremost Spirituals in the Marches, received an important letter from his friend, Jean Pierre Olieu (Olivi), a famous Spiritual leader in southern France with whom he had been closely associated in Florence and Mount Alverna in 1285–89, together with the brilliant Italian Spiritual Ubertino da Casale. In this long letter Olieu fervently urged Conrad and the other Spirituals of the Marches not to leave the Order. "For," he wrote, "did the holy Brother Giles or Brother Leo or Brother Masseo or the other companions of St. Francis who were similar to them in holiness ever leave the Order because of such things?"[6] Now Conrad had known Brother Leo well. In fact, before Leo died in 1270, St. Francis is said to have appeared to Conrad in a vision and told him to visit the elderly Leo in order to gather material about the Saint's life from him.

While it cannot be demonstrated that Olieu's letter prevented Conrad from leaving the Order, it is a fact that he and his intimate friend Peter of Montecchio—another prominent Spiritual—remained loyal Franciscans and apparently broke off relations with the separatist Spirituals under Angelo of Clareno and Ubertino da Casale. The influence which their decision had on Brother Ugolino can hardly be overestimated, since he writes of them as heroes and saints whom he venerated.

The wisdom of the stand taken by Conrad, Peter, and Ugolino received further confirmation during the unedifying verbal battles which raged before the world, at the Papal Court in Avignon between 1309 and 1324, when several Popes had to redefine the doctrinal meaning of Christian and Franciscan poverty. This period of political contention between the various factions in the Order culminated in an anti-Spiritual Minister General joining forces with a Prince of Bavaria in electing an anti-Pope!

Now it is of profound significance for our understanding of *The Little Flowers* that at about this time we find the author, Brother Ugolino di Monte Santa Maria, in Naples. For Naples in those years was under the rule of King Robert the Pious and his devout Franciscan Tertiary wife, Queen Sancha, both of whom had a well-known sympathy for the Spirituals, while remaining loyal Catholics enjoying friendly relations with the Popes and the superiors of the Order. We can only surmise that Brother Ugolino went to this favorable center in order to write his book. All we know is that in 1319 he was a witness to a peace pact between two towns in the Marches, and in 1331 he testified briefly in Naples against Andrea da Gagliano, a partisan of the excommunicated Minister General. It is noteworthy that when Brother Ugolino had to take a public stand he sided with the elements in the Order that remained in union with the Church. From a chronological note at the end of the Chapter 41 (found in only two manuscripts), it appears that he wrote that chapter—and hence perhaps most of his book —after 1327.[7] In 1342, according to a recently discovered will, he was back in the Marches. Then he disappears from history, leaving us his masterpiece, the *Actus Beati Francisci et Sociorum Ejus* (*The Deeds of St. Francis and His Companions*), which became in the later Italian condensation, *I Fioretti di San Francesco* (*The Little Flowers of St. Francis*).

By writing this most popular of all books on St. Francis, the fervent and talented friar struck a powerful blow for the true Franciscan ideal which he shared with James of Massa, Conrad of Offida, John of Alverna, and Queen Sancha: the reform of the Order from within by the personal holiness of individual friars living the way of life of St. Francis to the fullest extent of their capacities. Perhaps in his old age, after witnessing the tragic conflicts which had shaken the Order to its foundations during his lifetime, he felt inclined to agree with the good friend of his youth in the Marches, Blessed John of Alverna, who, like all the saints, refusing to judge his brethren, had declared before he died in 1322: "Sons, you did not come to raise yourselves up as judges of others, but to offer your wills to God. . . . When I came into the Order, I received this grace from God, that for all the things I saw in the Order I gave praise and thanks to God. And as a result I always lived in peace."[8]

The effect on Ugolino of this attitude of Blessed John of Alverna, as well as the example of several other saintly friars who were not Spirituals, notably James of Falerone and John of Penna, is the saving element which raises his book far above the level of a sectarian Spiritual tract to that of a masterly treatise on the genuine Franciscan spirit. Their influence also served to infuse into his soul and his writings that humble supernatural submission to the Church and that crucial balance between the active and the contemplative lives, which, with strict poverty, formed the essence of the true Franciscan life as it was conceived and lived by the Founder.

Thanks in large part to the many charming stories of James of Massa about St. Francis and his companions, Brother Ugolino's *Actus* became one of the most popular Franciscan documents of the fourteenth and fifteenth centuries. (Over eighty fifteenth-century manuscripts of the Italian translation are extant.) Most of the *Actus* was incorporated into several fifteenth-century compilations of Franciscan history. Thus with other Spiritual works such as the *Speculum Perfectionis* and the writings of Olieu and Ubertino da Casale, it played a major role (that is only now being fully recognized) in the important Observant reform of the early fifteenth century under the three great Saints, Bernardine of Siena, James of the March, and John of Capistrano. Therefore by giving to the world a broader and more vivid portrait of the Poverello and by glorifying his early companions and his later followers in the Marches who, while remaining loyal members of the Order and the Church, had fought and suffered for the pure Franciscan ideal, Brother Ugolino made a major contribution to the regeneration of his Order.

Historical Value

But the element in his work which is of the greatest value to the world today is the twenty-six incidents (not chapters) dealing with St. Francis which appear first in this book, written perhaps as much as a century after the Poverello's death. The reader has every right to know to what extent this relatively late document is historically reliable. How trustworthy was Brother James of Massa, Ugolino's principal informant? Obviously we should not take literally the statement that all his visions and words were inspired by the Holy Spirit. He was no more infallible than any other chronicler. But it should be recorded to his credit that independent accounts of four of his stories which have come to light in recent decades tend to confirm his reports, at least in their main outlines.[9] True, the alleged meeting of Brother Giles and King Louis was apparently based on a confusion with another Giles. And the tales in the *Actus* concerning the controversial Brother Elias are no doubt highly inaccurate in detail if not in substance, although they were widely accepted at the time. A polemical element is undeniably present, but it is found in only ten of the *Actus*' seventy-five chapters (and several may not have been written by Ugolino).

Nevertheless, even after we admit that the work undoubtedly shows a certain tendency to overstress the marvelous, that a few chapters may border on the legendary, and that some passages betray literary embellishment, the fundamental question remains: what do the foremost modern students of the book have to say regarding the value of its unique additions to our knowledge of St. Francis and his companions? The substance of their verdict is that the *Actus* represents, not folklore, but a direct oral tradition transmitted by several of the Saint's closest friends—Leo, Masseo, and Giles—through a few intermediaries to the author, and that this oral tradition, although occasionally inaccurate in chronology and topography, is in the main reliable, unless disproved by earlier evidence. With all due reservations, the definite historical value of the *Fioretti's* special contribution to our appreciation of St. Francis has been acknowledged by such scholars as Paul Sabatier, the Bollandist François van Ortroy, S.J., Archbishop Paschal Robinson, O.F.M., the Capuchin Father Cuthbert, the Anglican historian John R. H. Moorman, and the great *Fioretti* expert Benvenuto Bughetti, O.F.M., of the Collegio di San Bonaventura at Quaracchi—with Msgr. Michele Faloci-Pulignani, Maurice Beaufreton, and G. M. Bastianini, O.F.M. Conv., dissenting.

How then can we explain the puzzling fact that many of its most interesting stories were not recorded in the first official biographies of the Saint, which were based on the testimony of a number of his companions, including Leo, Angelo, and Rufino? The answer is quite simple. It is really a matter of psychology. The Poverello's best friends would naturally hesitate to mention—and an official biographer would hesitate to describe—a recently canonized Saint of the Church shaking hands with a wolf or eating nothing for forty days or telling his companion to twirl around in a public crossroad or go into a church and preach a sermon while wearing only his breeches. Such delightful human-interest anecdotes are either not reported to the first official biographer or (as the subtitle of the *Actus* specifically states) they are deliberately "omitted," especially in the case of a colorful Saint like the Poverello about whom innumerable little-known anecdotes were only gradually recorded in the century after his death—so many in fact that I have been able to collect well over one hundred in *The St. Francis Nobody Knows* and *Fifty Animal Stories of St. Francis,* which are still unknown today.

The same criterion applies with still greater force to the intimate spiritual experiences which Francis may have revealed to one or two close friends who in turn hesitated to report them for publication until decades had passed.

The "Actus"

Unfortunately the monks and friars who copied medieval manuscripts functioned more nearly like modern newspaper rewrite men than like photoduplicating machines. They did not hesitate to edit the text before them by condensing it or by trying to improve its vocabulary, syntax, and titles. Being only human, they often misread and miscopied. As a rule, they concocted new versions of unfamiliar personal and place names. Most confusing of all, sometimes they freely changed the order of the chapters, and if the codex on which they were writing still had some blank space at the end, they proceeded to fill it with miscellaneous matter, which the next copyist then included in his manuscript.

As a consequence of these faulty methods of transcription, we do not know today exactly how many chapters Brother Ugolino's original *Actus* included, for scholars believe that about six of the seventy-six that appear in Sabatier's edition were perhaps added by scribes. But at least four anecdotes which are not found in any hitherto collated *Actus* codex are ascribed to Ugolino by the Franciscan annalist Luke Wadding (d. 1667). The total, therefore, would still be about seventy-five.

It is quite evident, however, that Ugolino's work comprises two distinct sections, which are in fact separated by subtitles in some manuscripts (and in this edition): (1) a series of chapters dealing with St. Francis and his companions, including contemporaries such as St. Anthony, St. Clare, and Brother Simon of Assisi; and (2) another series dealing with some holy friars who lived in the Province of the Marches two or three generations later, most of whom were contemporaries of the author. However, the strong internal unity of style and theme which links both sections certainly suggests that the *Actus* as a whole was written by one principal author, Ugolino di Monte Santa Maria, who in fact names himself twice and refers to himself twelve times (all but two instances occurring in the second section). There is also one specific reference to a writer or secretary who recorded an anecdote as it was told to him by Ugolino.[10] A few other brief passages may be interpolations.

The "Fioretti" and "The Considerations on the Holy Stigmata"

Between 1370 and 1385, about fifty years after Brother Ugolino had finished writing the *Actus*, a talented friar with a passion for anonymity decided to translate most of that work into Italian. His identity is still completely unknown. According to philologists, he probably came from the southeastern part of Tuscany, close to Umbria. He must have spent much time on Mount Alverna. Although we do not have the particular Latin manuscript which he used, it is evident that, when not condensing, he translated very faithfully. The humble yet elegant simplicity and charm of his style rank him as one of the great writers of medieval Italian literature, a worthy contemporary of Petrarch and Boccaccio.

He selected fifty-three of the most appealing chapters in both sections of the *Actus* and gathered them in a bouquet which he aptly called *Fioretti* (Little Flowers), a title that was then in vogue. Next he proceeded to compile an entirely new treatise entitled *The Considerations on the Holy Stigmata*, in which he skillfully combined another five *Actus* chapters with texts from Thomas of Celano, St. Bonaventure, various fourteenth-century Franciscan writings, and local traditions to form an inspiring new work which, despite its occasional lapses in chronology or topography, has been described as "the most beautiful piece of Franciscan literature that we possess."

Additions

Within a century several important additions were made to the *Fioretti* and *The Considerations on the Holy Stigmata* in some fifteenth-century manuscripts: (1) *The Life of Brother Juniper;* (2) *The Life of Brother Giles;* (3) *The Sayings of Brother Giles;* (4) various *Additional Chapters* taken from the *Actus* and other fourteenth-century Franciscan writings.

The first three additions, although not written by either Brother Ugolino di Monte Santa Maria or the anonymous translator of the *Fioretti*, have an organic affinity with the first section of Ugolino's work, as they record the lives and sayings of two of St. Francis' closest companions.

The Life of Brother Juniper is a striking illustration of a valuable document, the first extant version of which is found over a century after the events which it narrates. Only brief references to the hilarious doings of the unpredictable clowning friar appeared in earlier texts—for quite understandable reasons. Never was there a better example than Brother Juniper of the need for firm spiritual direction. Our edition uses the late fourteenth-century Latin text in *The Chronicle of the Twenty-four Generals* except for Chapter 6, in which we have included a more extensive Italian version containing an unknown incident that reveals the secret of Juniper's almost Slavic cult of the Humiliated Christ.

Two early biographies of Brother Giles are available: a relatively short one written by Brother Leo after Giles' death in 1262, and a longer one in *The Chronicle*. Some early manuscript and printed editions of the *Fioretti* contain excerpts from both. In this edition we have translated the complete Latin text of Brother Leo's work as found in all published versions of the best available manuscripts, adopting chapter headings when necessary from *The Chronicle*.

The incomplete Italian translation of *The Sayings of Brother Giles*, which is found in most modern editions of the *Fioretti* and which has served as the basis for all foreign translations, is extremely free, inaccurate, and unfaithful to the original in style and spirit. Only the starkly simple Latin conveys all the pith and pungency and power of the saintly Franciscan lay brother who had the caustic wit of a Shaw and the love of paradox of a Chesterton. Yet even St. Bonaventure venerated him. We have translated the first twenty-one chapters of the Latin text.

Some medieval and modern editions of the *Fioretti* contain a miscellany of *Additional Chapters* ranging in number from one to twenty, usually including the famous *Canticle of Brother Sun*. Apart from *The Canticle* and two chapters borrowed from the *Actus*, most of them have no direct or indirect connection with Ugolino's work. They are taken from various compilations of anecdotes about the early friars which were made during the fourteenth century and which culminated in the four invaluable Summas of early Franciscan history: *The Conformities* of Bartholomew of Pisa (1399), the *Speculum Vitae* of Fabian of Igal (1440), *La Franceschina* of Giacomo Oddi of Perugia (1470), and the Spanish *Floreto de Sant Francisco* (1492).

The problem of the *Additional Chapters* presents modern editors of *The Little Flowers* with a choice of alternatives: (1) exclude all such materials; (2) include all twenty *Fioretti* additions; (3) include *The Canticle* and the nineteen *Actus* chapters that are not in the *Fioretti* or in *The Considerations on the Holy Stigmata;* or (4) include all thirty-seven additional chapters.

The Italian edition of Benvenuto Bughetti, O.F.M., followed the second course, although he considered the *Additional Chapters* "encumbering." The recent French editions of Alexander Masseron and Omer Englebert were modeled on Bughetti's, but used the ambiguous subtitle "Complete Edition," which a Franciscan critic has stated should rather read "Contaminated Edition." A recent Dutch version adopted the third alternative, i.e., presented a complete translation of the *Actus*. The translator and the publisher of this edition have also decided to follow the third course, thus bringing the complete work of Brother Ugolino to the public for the first time in English.

The "Fioretti" Becomes a World Classic

The first printed edition of the *Fioretti* was published in 1476 in Vicenza, the first of seventeen editions in that century.

Soon, however, St. Francis himself, along with such works as *The Conformities* and *The Little Flowers*, came under the attacks of the Protestant Reformers. Pier Paolo Vergerio (1498–1565) in particular made the *Fioretti* a target of his zeal, denouncing the book as a shocking collection of blasphemous and ridiculous fables, although he felt obliged to admit that it contained some "golden words" and "jewels." Some critics have even asserted without any evidence that the work was once placed on the Index of Forbidden Books, but it was never listed in any edition of the Index. However, owing in part to these attacks, it was published only half a dozen times in the sixteenth century and almost forgotten in the seventeenth. The rationalistic scholars of the following century, including the Bollandists, looked upon it with disdain, despite its rebirth in popularity with the edition of Filippo Buonarroti in 1718.

The history of modern *Fioretti* studies began in 1822 with the important edition of Antonio Cesari, but did not bear significant fruit until Paul Sabatier and other scholars turned their attention to the original Latin text in a useless search for a nonexistent pre-*Actus Floretum* which they thought Wadding had used. A high point was reached in 1902 with Sabatier's preliminary edition of the *Actus*. However, it was based on only a few of the available manuscripts, and they lacked several *Fioretti* chapters; but the Latin text of those chapters was soon found in the valuable so-called Little Manuscript, which was published in 1914. The 1920s witnessed unproductive controversies concerning the region of origin of the *Fioretti* (Tuscany or the Marches) and regarding its historical value. The interest of scholars in its still unsolved problems unfortunately subsided, only to arise again after 1950 with the important studies of Quaglia, Pagnani, Vicinelli, Abate, Terzi, Petrocchi, Fortini, and others (see Bibliography).

Meanwhile the *Fioretti* had become "the breviary of the Italian people" and one of the favorite books of the reading public of all European and American countries. In 1952 a motion picture based on the book was made in Italy, with Franciscan friars playing all but the leading role. In the United States the Great Books Foundation recently added *The Little Flowers of St. Francis* to its reading and discussion program.

A New Look at "The Little Flowers"

No less than seven different translations into English have appeared in the last hundred years (all but two by non-Catholics). However, none of those versions—and very few in any language—include certain features which are essential to give the reader a faithful reproduction and a true understanding of Brother Ugolino's work. In preparing this popular new edition, therefore, the translator and the publisher wished to provide it with several useful features embodying the contributions of modern Franciscan research.

This translation, while following the chapter-structure of the *Fioretti,* is based primarily on the original Latin text of the *Actus* as published not only in Sabatier's preliminary edition but in eight other printed versions. Thus it takes advantage of numerous significant variants (often needed to correct corruptions), and it includes the many important phrases, sentences, or entire paragraphs which were omitted either in the *Fioretti* or in the particular Latin manuscript which the Italian translator used. However, the Italian text has also been followed whenever it adds to the clarity or the beauty of the Latin.

This translation deliberately avoids an artificial Victorian imitation of medieval English in favor of modern colloquial English, which (as Michael Bihl, O.F.M., remarked of a German edition based in part on the Latin) may perhaps be less elegant, but has the compensating advantage of being more faithful to the original.

Again adopting a recommendation of the late Father Bihl, the greatest Franciscan scholar of our times, this edition is equipped with a minimum of brief Notes and References designed to supply: (a) correction or confirmation of historical data, (b) identification of all incidents first recorded in the *Actus,* and (c) compact references to relevant sources, parallel texts, or important topical studies. Unfortunately it is still true, as Paschal Robinson, O.F.M., wrote in 1912, that "no critical exhaustive study exists about the historical value of the single parts of the *Actus-Fioretti.*" In view of the widespread popularity of the book and of its status as a classic of world literature, it would seem that the scholars of the Franciscan

Order owe to the public a thorough scientific study of each of its chapters. While the Notes of this edition are primarily designed for the average reader, the References may also be of some use to researchers who will prepare those long-overdue studies.

Three brief Appendices supply additional significant texts and comments on two of the work's most famous chapters, "The Perfect Joy" (Ch. 8) and "The Wolf of Gubbio" (Ch. 21), and provide a summary of factual and doctrinal information concerning the puzzling "Mystery of the Stigmata."

In addition, condensed Biographical Sketches outline the careers of all principal characters who are mentioned in more than one chapter, while a Chart shows the transmission of the oral tradition of the *Actus* from the companions of St. Francis to the author.

This edition would of course not be complete without a selective Bibliography of general texts and periodicals, important editions of the *Actus* and the *Fioretti*, and outstanding studies, for no such list of references is available.

Interested readers will no doubt also welcome the Map of the *Fioretti* Country which shows all the towns, villages, and hermitages in Umbria and the Marches that are mentioned in this book.

Lastly, a few technical points: scriptural quotations are adapted from the Douay-Rheims translation of the Vulgate (used in the *Actus-Fioretti*); chapter headings have been selected from various Latin or Italian versions (mostly the former), primarily for conciseness; personal and geographic names have been anglicized whenever that form seemed more natural; the term *Frater* (*Frate*) has been translated as "Brother" when used in the vocative or when accompanying a name (even of a priest) and as "friar" when standing alone; for the Latin *locus* referring to an early Franciscan friary, "Place" has been adopted in preference to "place," "friary," "monastery," or "convent."

The translator wishes to express his cordial thanks to the Florentine publishers Adriano Salani and G. C. Sansoni for their kind permission to make use of the editions of the *Fioretti* prepared, respectively, by Benvenuto Bughetti, O.F.M., and Mario Casella, which are now recognized as the best versions of the Italian text. It is unfortunately impracticable to list all the numerous historians and librarians—Franciscan and secular, Italian and American, Catholic and non-Catholic—who have generously contributed advice, facts, articles, or books to this work. However, Mr. Zoltan Haraszti, Keeper of Rare Books at the Boston Public Library, deserves special mention with his staff for their courtesy in facilitating my research in the valuable Paul Sabatier collection, where I found almost fifty important items in the great Protestant scholar's unpublished marginal notes. I can only record here my intense gratitude to all who have assisted me—particularly to my wife who typed the manuscript, and to Mr. John J. Delaney, editor of Image Books, whose patient guidance improved my work—and exculpate them from the errors and imperfections of this edition.

Literary and Spiritual Qualities

The remarkable psychological insight and talent of the author of the *Actus* and the charming simplicity and elegance of the Italian translator's style suffice to explain why the *Fioretti* has long been considered a masterpiece of early Italian literature. But to account for the book's rise in recent times to the status of a classic of world literature, more profound causes must be sought.

Here we touch on the secret of the popularity of St. Francis himself and of all his faithful followers through the ages. Two basic elements, which are not often found together in contemporary writing, probably arouse in modern readers of various nationalities and cultures a lasting affection for *The Little Flowers:* its strikingly natural humanness and its soaring spiritual power.

These charming anecdotes about the Poverello and his companions are rich in those human-interest qualities which all popular entertainment and reading possess: dramatic movement, vivid personalities, and stirring emotion—to say nothing of delightful humor. Moreover, they are narrated with a childlike artlessness that is almost akin to that of the Gospels.

Surely it is primarily the fact that the *Fioretti* so faithfully reflects the magnetic spirituality of St. Francis that has won for it a permanent place in the hearts of mankind. More than any other single book, it has brought St. Francis to the world because it has succeeded so well in capturing and communicating the very essence of his spirit and his message.

Today more than ever before, humanity is suffering because it is trying desperately to live without that spirit and that message, which are after all exactly the same as those of Christ, though transmuted by the magic of the Poverello's personal charm. Our unhappy world needs more than ever to learn from him the great lesson that true joy and peace are found only in loving and knowing and serving God as he did, with complete selflessness and dedication and humility. Today millions of spiritually starved souls rightly sense that Francis' pure, generous love for God and man and all created things is the only hidden source of power that will ever unite all men in the peaceable service of their Creator and of their neighbor.

Yet even in this heartless age of guided missiles for mass destruction it is an impressive and an encouraging fact that no less than one and a half million men and women throughout the world are actually serving their God and their neighbor in the various Franciscan religious and lay families.[11] In addition, there are many others, both in and out of the Catholic Church, who look upon the Little Poor Man of Assisi with love and veneration because his beautiful life is to them the most convincing proof on record that Christianity *can* be radiantly lived in this sad world.

Few books beside the New Testament convey that regenerating message so forcefully and so eloquently as *The Little Flowers,* for the simple reason that in its pages throbs the great vibrant heart of the most faithful follower and perfect imitator of Jesus Christ the world has ever seen.

In conclusion, here is a lovely old Franciscan text which strikingly illustrates that unique distinction of St. Francis of Assisi and which also summarizes one of the basic themes of *The Little Flowers:*

> One night when Blessed Peter Pettinaio of the Third Order was praying in the Cathedral of Siena, he saw Our Lord Jesus Christ enter the church, followed by a great throng of saints. And each time Christ raised His foot, the form of his foot remained imprinted on the ground. And all the saints

tried as hard as they could to place their feet in the traces of His footsteps, but none of them was able to do so perfectly. Then St. Francis came in and set his feet right in the footsteps of Jesus Christ.[12]

IN THE NAME OF OUR CRUCIFIED LORD
JESUS CHRIST
AND OF HIS VIRGIN MOTHER MARY

THIS BOOK CONTAINS
CERTAIN LITTLE FLOWERS, MIRACLES, AND INSPIRING STORIES
OF
THE GLORIOUS LITTLE POOR MAN OF CHRIST
SAINT FRANCIS
AND OF SOME OF HIS HOLY COMPANIONS
AS REVEALED BY THEIR SUCCESSORS
WHICH WERE OMITTED IN HIS BIOGRAPHIES
BUT WHICH ARE ALSO VERY USEFUL AND EDIFYING

TO THE PRAISE AND GLORY OF JESUS CHRIST! AMEN.

CHAPTER TITLES

PART ONE: THE LITTLE FLOWERS OF ST. FRANCIS

I Some Marvelous Deeds of St. Francis
and His First Companions

Little Flowers of St. Francis

Part One

THE LITTLE FLOWERS
OF ST. FRANCIS

I SOME MARVELOUS DEEDS OF ST. FRANCIS
AND HIS FIRST COMPANIONS

1 *About the Twelve First Companions of*
St. Francis

First it should be known that the glorious St. Francis was conformed to Christ in all the acts of his life. For just as the
Blessed Christ, when He began His preaching, chose twelve
Apostles to despise all things of this world and to follow Him
in poverty and in the other virtues, so St. Francis, when he began to found the Order, had twelve chosen companions who
were followers of the most complete poverty.

And just as one of the twelve Apostles of Christ, being rejected by God, in the end hanged himself by the neck, so one
of the twelve companions of St. Francis, whose name was
Brother Giovanni di Capella, left the Order, and in the end
hanged himself by the neck with a rope. To the elect this is a
great lesson and reason for humility and fear when they reflect
that no one is certain of persevering to the end in the grace of
God.

And just as those holy Apostles were for the whole world
marvels of holiness, filled with the Holy Spirit, so these most
holy companions of St. Francis were men of such sanctity that
the world has not had such wonderful and holy men from the
times of the Apostles until now. For one of them was caught
up to the third heaven like St. Paul, and that was Brother Giles.
Another—tall Brother Philip—was touched on the lips by an
angel with burning coal, like Isaias the Prophet. Another—
Brother Silvester, a very pure virginal soul—spoke with God as
one friend with another, as Moses did. Another, by the keenness of his mind, soared up to the light of divine wisdom, like

the eagle (John the Evangelist)—and this was the very humble Brother Bernard, who used to explain Holy Scripture in a most profound way. Another was sanctified by God and canonized in Heaven while he still was living in this world, as though he had been sanctified in his mother's womb—and he was Brother Rufino, a nobleman of Assisi and a man most loyal to Christ.

And thus all of them were favored with evident marks of sanctity, as will be reported hereafter.[1]

2 *About the Perfect Conversion of Brother Bernard*

Among them the first and the first-born, both by priority in time and by privilege of sanctity, was Brother Bernard of Assisi, whose conversion took place in the following way.

St. Francis was still dressed as a layman, although he had already renounced the world, and for a long time he had been going around Assisi looking contemptible and so mortified by penance that many people thought he was simple-minded, and he was laughed at as a lunatic and driven away with many insults and stones and mud by his relatives and by strangers. Yet being nourished by the divine salt and firmly established in peace of soul by the Holy Spirit, he bore all the insults and scorn with great patience and with a joyful expression on his face, as if he were deaf and dumb.

Now the Lord Bernard of Assisi, who was one of the richest and wisest noblemen in the whole city, whose judgment everyone respected, wisely began to think over St. Francis' utter contempt for the world and his great patience when he was insulted and the fact that although he had been scorned and despised by everybody for two years, he always appeared more serene and patient. He began to think and to say to himself: "This Francis certainly must have great graces from God."

So inspired by the Lord, he invited St. Francis to have supper with him one evening. The Saint humbly accepted and ate supper with him that evening.

But the Lord Bernard secretly wished and planned to put St. Francis' holiness to a test, so he invited him to sleep in his house that night. And when St. Francis humbly agreed, the

Lord Bernard had a bed prepared in his own room, in which a lamp was always kept burning at night.

Now St. Francis, as soon as he entered the room, in order to conceal the divine graces which he had, immediately threw himself down on the bed, showing that he wished to sleep. But the Lord Bernard planned to watch him secretly during the night. And he too soon lay down, and he used such cunning that after he had rested in bed a while, he pretended to be sleeping soundly, and he began to snore loudly.

Therefore St. Francis, who faithfully concealed the secrets of God, when he thought that the Lord Bernard was fast asleep, during the first part of the night, got out of bed and began to pray. Looking up to Heaven and raising his hands, he prayed with intense fervor and devotion, saying: "My God and my all!" And he sobbed out those words with so many tears and kept repeating them with such devout persistence that until matins he said nothing but "My God and my all!"[1]

St. Francis said this while contemplating and marveling at the goodness of Almighty God who seemed to take compassion on the imperiled world and was preparing to provide a remedy for its salvation through the little poor man Francis himself. For being enlightened by the spirit of prophecy, when he foresaw the great things which God was to accomplish through his Order, and when under the guidance of that same spirit he considered his own incapacity and small degree of virtue, he called upon the Lord in order that God, without whom human weakness can achieve nothing, should by His compassion and almighty power supply, assist, and accomplish what he himself would not be capable of doing. And that is why he said: "My God and my all!"[2]

Now the Lord Bernard saw the very inspiring actions of St. Francis by the light of the lamp burning there. And while he was attentively meditating on the words which the Saint was saying and carefully observing his devotion, he was touched by the Holy Spirit in the depths of his heart and felt inspired to change his life.

Therefore when morning came, he called St. Francis and said to him: "Brother Francis, I have definitively resolved in my heart to leave the world and to follow you in whatever you order me to do."

1303

When St. Francis heard this, he rejoiced in spirit and said: "Lord Bernard, what you say is so great and difficult an undertaking that we must seek the advice of Our Lord Jesus Christ concerning it, so that He Himself may deign to show us His will regarding it and teach us how we should carry it out. So let us go together to the Bishop's Church where there is a good priest, and we will have him say Mass, and after hearing it, we will pray there until tierce. And in our prayer we will ask the Lord Jesus Christ to deign to show us in three openings of the missal the way which He wants us to choose." And the Lord Bernard replied that this pleased him a great deal.

They therefore went to the Bishop's Church.[3] And after they had heard Mass and had prolonged their prayers until tierce, the above-mentioned priest took up the missal at the request of St. Francis and the Lord Bernard. And having made the Sign of the Cross, he opened it three times in the name of Our Lord Jesus Christ.

At the first opening there appeared the words that Christ said in the Gospel to the young man who asked Him about the way of perfection: "If you wish to be perfect, go, sell all you have, and give to the poor, and come, follow Me."

At the second opening there appeared those words which Christ said to the Apostles, when He sent them out to preach: "Take nothing for your journey, neither staff, nor wallet, nor bread, nor money," wishing thereby to teach them that they should place all their hope for support in God and concentrate entirely on preaching the Holy Gospel.

At the third opening of the missal there appeared those words which Christ said: "If anyone wishes to come after Me, let him deny himself, and take up his cross, and follow Me."

And when they had seen these words, St. Francis said to the Lord Bernard: "That is the counsel which Christ gives us. So go and do perfectly what you have heard. And blessed be Our Lord Jesus Christ who has deigned to show us His Gospel way of life!"

On hearing this, the Lord Bernard immediately went and brought out all his possessions and sold all that he owned—and he was very rich. And with great joy he distributed it all to the poor. Carrying the money in a pocket in his bosom, he gave it out plentifully and generously to widows and orphans and pilgrims and monasteries and hospitals. And in all this St. Francis accompanied him and faithfully assisted him.

Now when a man named Lord Silvester saw St. Francis giving away so much money to the poor and causing it to be given away, he was seized with greed and said to St. Francis: "You did not pay me all you owe me for those stones you bought from me to repair the churches." Then St. Francis, marveling at his greed and not wishing to argue with him, as a true observer of the Gospel—giving to everyone who asked—put his hands in the Lord Bernard's bosom and then placed them, filled with money, in the Lord Silvester's bosom. And he said: "If you ask for more, I will give you still more." But he was satisfied and went home.

Later that evening, when he thought over what he had done during the day, he reproached himself for his greed and reflected on the fervor of the Lord Bernard and the holiness of St. Francis. And on the first and the second and the third night he was given this vision from God: from the mouth of St. Francis came forth a cross of gold, the top of which reached to Heaven, while its arms seemed to extend from east to west, to the end of the world. As a result of this vision he was touched by the Lord, and for God's sake he disposed of all his property and gave it away to the poor. And later he became a Friar Minor, and in the Order he was so holy and filled with grace that he spoke with God as one friend to another, as St. Francis several times experienced and as will be narrated hereafter.

Similarly the Lord Bernard, after he had given all his property away for God, received so much grace from God that he was often rapt in contemplation by the Lord. And St. Francis used to say of him that he was worthy of all reverence, and that it was he who had founded this Order, because he was the first who had begun to live the poverty of the Gospel by distributing all he had to the poor, retaining nothing whatever for himself, but offering himself naked to the arms of the Crucified. May He be blessed by us forever and ever! Amen.[4]

3 *About the Humility and Obedience of*
St. Francis and Brother Bernard

Francis, the very devout servant of Christ Crucified, had become almost blind, so that he could see very little, as a result of his severe penances and continual crying.

One day he left the Place where he was and went to a Place where Brother Bernard was staying, in order to speak about God with him. And when he came to the Place, he found that Bernard was praying in the woods, completely absorbed in holy contemplation and united with God.[1]

Then St. Francis went into the woods and called him, saying: "Come and talk to this blind man!"

But Brother Bernard did not answer St. Francis and did not go to him because, as he was a great contemplative, his consciousness was at that moment suspended and uplifted in God.

Brother Bernard had a remarkable ability to speak about God, as St. Francis had already experienced many times, and that was why he wanted very much to talk to him. So after a while he called him again a second and a third time, repeating the same words: "Come and talk to this blind man." But Brother Bernard did not hear him at all and so he did not answer him or go to him. Therefore St. Francis went away, feeling rather disappointed, wondering and almost complaining within himself that Brother Bernard, though .called by him three times, had not wanted to come to him.

While St. Francis was thinking that way as he returned along the path, he said to his companion when he had gone a short distance: "Wait here for me a moment!" And he went to a solitary spot nearby and began to pray, begging God to reveal to him why Brother Bernard had not answered him. And as he was praying, a Voice came to him from God that said: "And why are you troubled, you poor little man? Should a man leave God because of any creature? Brother Bernard, when you called him, was united with Me, and so he could not go to you or answer you. Therefore do not be surprised if he could not talk to you, because he was so unconscious of his surroundings that he did not hear you at all."

1306

As soon as St. Francis had received this answer from God, he immediately went back toward Brother Bernard in a great hurry, in order humbly to accuse himself of the thoughts he had just had against him.

But the holy Brother Bernard, seeing him coming, ran to meet him and threw himself down at his feet. And the humility of St. Francis and the charity and reverence of Brother Bernard came together. Then St. Francis made him get up and told him very humbly about the thoughts and anxiety which he had regarding him, and how God had reproved him for it. And he ended thus: "Under holy obedience I order you to do whatever I command you."

Brother Bernard was afraid that St. Francis might order something excessive, as he often did, and he wanted to escape from that obedience as best he could. So he replied: "Father, I am ready to obey you, if you also promise me to do what I command you."

St. Francis replied: "I agree."

Then Brother Bernard said: "Say what you want me to do, Father."

And St. Francis said: "In order to punish my presumption and the insolence of my heart, I command you under holy obedience, while I lie on my back on the ground, to put one of your feet on my throat and the other on my mouth, and thus to step over me three times from one side to the other. And while stepping on me that way, you are to insult and mock me, and especially you are to say: 'Lie there, you country lout, son of Pietro di Bernardone!' And you must inflict still greater insults on me, saying: 'How is it that you have so much pride, since you are such an extremely worthless creature?'"

When Brother Bernard heard this, it was hard for him to do it. However, because of holy obedience, he performed as courteously as he could what St. Francis had commanded him to do.[2]

And when it was done, St. Francis said: "Now, Brother Bernard, order me to do what you want me to do, because I have promised to obey you."

Brother Bernard said: "Under holy obedience I command you that whenever we are together you scold and correct me harshly for my faults."

When St. Francis heard this, he was very much surprised, because Brother Bernard was so holy that St. Francis had great reverence for him and did not think that he should be corrected at all.

And henceforth St. Francis avoided staying too long with him, so that on account of that obedience he should not have to speak a word of correction to him whom he knew to be so saintly. But though he longed to see Brother Bernard or to hear him speak of God, he would leave him and go away as soon as he could. And it was wonderful to see how certain conflicts took place in the revered Father and in his first-born son, Brother Bernard, especially how the obedience and charity and the patience and humility of each came into conflict. But it was also very inspiring to see the affection and awe and humility with which St. Francis treated and spoke to Brother Bernard.

To the praise and glory of Christ. Amen.

4   *How St. Francis Went to St. James, and about the Question That the Angel Asked Brother Elias*

In the beginning of the Order, when there were few friars and the Places had not yet been occupied, St. Francis, to satisfy his devotion, went to visit St. James in Galicia, and he took with him some companions, one of whom was Brother Bernard.[1]

And while they were traveling along the road, they found in a certain land a poor sick man for whom St. Francis felt compassion, and he said to Brother Bernard: "Son, I want you to stay here and take care of this sick man."

And Brother Bernard quickly and humbly genuflected and bowed his head, thus accepting the command of the holy Father, and he stayed in that place while St. Francis went on to St. James with his other companions.

When they arrived there and were spending the night in prayer and adoration in the Church of St. James, God revealed to St. Francis in that church that he should found many Places throughout the world, because his Order was destined to spread and grow to a large number of friars. Consequently, as a result of this divine command, he henceforth began to accept Places in various lands.

When he returned along the same road, St. Francis found Brother Bernard. Now the sick man whom he had entrusted to his care had fully recovered. So the following year St. Francis gave Brother Bernard permission to go to St. James. Meanwhile St. Francis went back to the Valley of Spoleto.

And when he was staying in a certain isolated Place[2]—he and Brother Masseo and Brother Elias and several others—one day St. Francis went into the woods to pray. Now his companions had great reverence for him and they were afraid to disturb his prayers in any way because of the great graces which God gave him in prayer.

And it happened that a very handsome young man, dressed as though prepared to go on a journey, came to the gate of the Place and knocked so urgently and loudly and long that the friars were amazed at such an unusual way of knocking. Brother Masseo went to the gate and opened it and said to the young man: "Son, I think you have never yet come to a gate of the friars because you don't know how to knock gently."

The young man answered: "And how should I knock?"

Brother Masseo said to him: "Knock three times, one knock after another. Then wait until the friar has said one Our Father and comes to you. And if he does not come by that time, knock again."

But the young man replied: "I am in a great hurry because I have to make a long journey—that is why I knock so loudly. I have come here to talk to Brother Francis, but he is now in contemplation in the woods, and therefore I don't want to disturb him. So go and send Brother Elias to me, for I have heard that he is very wise, and I want to ask him a question."

Brother Masseo went and told Brother Elias to go to the young man, but as he was proud and irritable he became angry and refused to go. Then Brother Masseo did not know what to do or what to say to the young man, because if he said, "Brother Elias cannot come," he would be lying, but if he said that Brother Elias was angry and did not want to come, he was afraid of giving the young man a bad example.

Meanwhile, as Brother Masseo delayed in coming, the young man knocked again as before. Then the friar went back to the gate and said to the young man: "You did not knock the way I told you to do."

Now the young man was an angel of God, and foreseeing Brother Masseo's answer, he said: "Brother Elias does not want to come to me, so go to Brother Francis and tell him that I have come to speak to him, but as I do not want to disturb him in his prayers, tell him to send Brother Elias to me."

Then Brother Masseo went to Brother Francis, who was praying in the woods with his face turned toward Heaven. And he told him all the young man's message and Brother Elias' answer.

Without moving or lowering his face, St. Francis said: "Go and tell Brother Elias to go to the young man immediately, under obedience."

When Brother Elias heard St. Francis' order, he was so angry that when he went to the gate, he opened it violently, making a great noise and disturbance, and said to the young man: "What do you want?"

And the young man replied: "Take care, Brother, not to be angry, as you appear to be, because anger darkens the mind and prevents it from discerning the truth."

Then Brother Elias said: "Tell me what you want!"

And the young man answered: "I ask you whether it is lawful for observers of the holy Gospel to eat whatever is set before them, as Christ said to His Disciples. And I also ask you whether it is lawful for any man to impose on observers of the holy Gospel anything that is contrary to the liberty of the Gospel?"

Brother Elias replied arrogantly: "I know the answer very well, but I won't tell you. Go on your way."

The young man said: "I know the answer to that question better than you do."

Then Brother Elias angrily slammed the gate shut and went away. And he began to think over the question and to be puzzled, and he could not find the answer. For when he was Vicar of the Order, he had dared to make a regulation, beyond the Gospel and beyond the Rule of St. Francis, that no friar in the Order could eat meat, so that question was aimed directly at him. Not knowing how to solve the problem, and reflecting that the young man was humble and that he had said he could answer that question better than Brother Elias could, he went back to the gate and opened it in order to ask the young man about the question. But when he opened the gate, no one was there, and he could not find the young man, though he searched round about. For that young man was an angel of God, and he had not waited because Brother Elias in his pride was not worthy to speak with an angel.[3]

When this had happened, St. Francis, to whom all had been revealed by God, came back from the woods and strongly scolded Brother Elias in a loud voice, saying: "You do wrong, proud Brother Elias, for you drive away the holy angels who come to visit and instruct us. And I tell you, I strongly fear that your pride will make you end your days outside this Order." And so it happened to him later, as St. Francis had prophesied to him, for he died outside the Order.

On the same day and at the same hour as that angel went away, he appeared in the same form to Brother Bernard, who was returning from St. James and was standing on the bank of a broad river which he could not cross. And he greeted Brother Bernard in his own language, saying: "God give you peace, good Brother."

Brother Bernard marveled at the young man's good looks and the language of his own native land, and also at his peaceful greeting and joyful features, and he asked him: "Where are you from, good young man?"

The angel replied: "I have come from the Place where St. Francis is staying, and I went to speak with him, but I was unable to do so because he was contemplating God in the woods, and I did not want to disturb him. And Brother Masseo and Brother Giles and Brother Elias were staying with him in that Place. And Brother Masseo taught me how to knock at your gate the way the friars do. But Brother Elias, because he did not want to answer the question which I asked him, later regretted it and wanted to hear and see me, but could not do so."

And after saying these words, the angel said to Brother Bernard: "Dear friend, why are you hesitating to cross the river?"

He replied: "Because I am afraid of the deep water I see."

And the angel said: "Let us cross over together—don't be afraid!"

And taking his hand, in an instant he deposited Brother Bernard safely on the other side of the river.

Then Brother Bernard realized that he was one of God's angels, and with great devotion and reverence and joy he said in a loud voice: "O blessed angel of God, tell me your name!"

The angel replied: "Why do you ask my name, which is wonderful?"

And having said that, he disappeared and left Brother Bernard very happy, so that he was filled with joy during all the rest of his journey. And he noted the day and hour when the angel had appeared to him. And when he came to the Place where St. Francis was staying with his above-mentioned companions, he told them the whole story in detail. Therefore, they knew for sure that that same angel had appeared to them and to him on the same day and at the same hour. And they gave thanks to God. Amen.

5 How Brother Bernard Went to Bologna

Because St. Francis and his companions had been called by God and chosen to bear the Cross of Christ in their hearts and in their actions and to preach it by their words, they appeared to be and they were crucified men, both as to their habit and their austere life and their deeds and their actions. Therefore they had a greater desire to receive shame and insults for the love of Christ than the vain honors or respect or praise of the world. On the contrary, they rejoiced in being insulted, and they were made sad by being honored. And so they went through the world as pilgrims and strangers, taking with them nothing but Christ Crucified. And because they were living branches of the True Vine, that is Christ, they produced great and good fruit in the souls that they won for God.

Once in the beginning of the Order it happened that St. Francis sent Brother Bernard to Bologna, in order that he might produce fruit for God according to the grace which God had given him. And Brother Bernard, arming himself with the Cross of Christ and taking holy obedience as his companion, made the Sign of the Cross and left and came to Bologna.[1]

When the children saw him in his unusual and contemptible

habit, they began to make fun of him and insult him, as they would do with a lunatic. But the truly holy Brother Bernard endured all their insults not just patiently but with intense joy, for the love of Christ. Moreover, in order to follow and be truly conformed to Christ, who made Himself "the reproach of men and the outcast of the people," he deliberately went to the public square of the city and sat down there so that people would have a better opportunity to make fun of him. While he was sitting there, many boys and men gathered around him, and some of them pulled him back and others forward, and some threw dust at him and others stones, and some pushed him heavily this way and others that way. At all these insults Brother Bernard remained patient and rejoicing, with a happy expression on his face, and he did not resist or complain at all. Furthermore, he deliberately went back to that same square for several days in order to endure the same mistreatment. And no matter how much they insulted him, his joyful features always showed that his soul was not troubled.

And because patience is a work of perfection and a proof of virtue, a certain learned doctor of laws, seeing and reflecting on Brother Bernard's constancy and virtue in not being at all disturbed by any injury or insult for so many days, said to himself: "That man certainly must be a saint." And going up to Brother Bernard he asked him: "Who are you, and why have you come here?"

As his reply Brother Bernard put his hand in his bosom and brought out the Rule of St. Francis, which he bore in his heart and practiced in his deeds, and gave it to him to read.[2]

And when that judge had read it through, reflecting on its lofty state of perfection, he was utterly amazed, for he was an intelligent man. And turning to his companions, he said with the greatest surprise and admiration: "This certainly is the highest form of religious life I have ever heard of! And therefore this man and his companions are some of the holiest men in the world. So those who insult him are committing a very great sin, for he should be given the highest honors rather than insults, as he is a great and true friend of God!"

And he said to Brother Bernard: "My dear man, if I were to show you a place where you could serve God in a suitable way, and you wished to accept it, I would be very glad to give it to you for the salvation of my soul."

Brother Bernard answered: "Dear Sir, I believe that Our Lord Jesus Christ has inspired you to do this. And so I willingly accept your offer, for the honor of Christ."

Then the judge led Brother Bernard with great joy and affection to his home. And later he showed him the place which he had promised him and gave it to him, and arranged and prepared it all at his own expense. And henceforth he became a father and a special protector to Brother Bernard and his companions.[3]

And Brother Bernard began to be greatly honored by the people because of his holy conversation, to such a point that those who were able to touch or hear or see him considered themselves blessed. But Brother Bernard, like a true and humble disciple of Christ and the humble Francis, fearing that the worldly honor which was being shown him there might interfere with the peace and salvation of his soul, left and went back to St. Francis.

And he said to St. Francis: "Father, the Place has been founded in the city of Bologna, so send some friars to maintain it and stay there, because I am no longer doing any good there. Rather because of the great honor that is shown me, I am afraid of losing more than I would gain there."

Then St. Francis, on hearing in detail all that God had performed through Brother Bernard, rejoiced and exulted and began to praise and thank God, who was thus beginning to spread the poor little followers of the Cross for the salvation of the people. And then he chose some of his companions and sent them to Bologna and Lombardy. And as the devotion of the people toward them increased, they began to accept many Places in various districts.

To the praise and reverence of the good Jesus. Amen.

6 *About the Beautiful Death of Brother Bernard*

Brother Bernard was so holy that St. Francis, as long as he lived, had a very affectionate reverence for him, honored him by often talking with him, and in his absence often praised him highly.

One day while St. Francis was praying devoutly, God revealed to him that Divine Providence was to allow Brother Bernard to endure many fierce attacks by devils. For many days, therefore, St. Francis, having great compassion for Brother Bernard, whom he loved as a son, prayed to God for him and wept, committing him to the Lord Jesus Christ, so that He might give him victory over so many trials of the devil. And while St. Francis was thus praying and watching anxiously and fervently, one day God gave him this answer: "Francis, do not fear, because all the temptations by which Brother Bernard is to be assailed are given to him and permitted by God so that he may practice virtues and earn a crown of merit. And in the end he will win a joy-filled victory over all the enemies that attack him. For this Brother Bernard is one of the great ones of the Kingdom of God."

St. Francis was made exceedingly happy by this answer, and he gave fervent thanks to the Lord Jesus Christ. And henceforth he no longer had any doubts or fears regarding Brother Bernard, but loved him with ever increasing joy and treated him with still greater affection and reverence.[1]

He showed this affection for him not only during his life but also at the hour of his death. For when St. Francis was dying, like the holy Patriarch Jacob, with his devoted sons standing around him, grieving and weeping over the departure of their beloved father, he asked: "Where is my first-born son? Come to me, dear son, so that my soul may bless you before I die."

Then Brother Bernard whispered to Brother Elias, who was at that time the Vicar of the Order: "Father, go to the Saint's right hand, so that he may give you his blessing."

And when Brother Elias had placed himself on the right side, St. Francis, who had lost his sight from too much weeping, put his right hand on Brother Elias' head and said: "This is not the head of my first-born, Brother Bernard."

Then Brother Bernard went to his left hand, and St. Francis crossed his arms, and changing the position of his hands, put his left hand on the head of Brother Elias and his right hand on Brother Bernard's head, and he said to him: "May the Father of my Lord Jesus Christ bless you with every spiritual and heavenly blessing in Christ. And as you were the first one in this holy Order who was chosen to give the example of the Gospel life and to imitate Christ in the poverty of the Gospel —for not only did you generously give up your belongings and distribute them entirely among the poor for the love of Christ, but you also offered yourself up to God as a sweet sacrifice in this Order—so may you be blessed by Our Lord Jesus Christ and by me, His poor little servant, with everlasting blessings, going and coming, watching and sleeping, living and dying. Whoever blesses you shall be filled with blessings, and whoever curses you shall not remain unpunished. Be the head of all your Brothers, and let all the friars obey your orders. You have permission to receive into the Order and to send away from it whomever you wish. And no friar has any power over you. And you are free to go and to stay wherever you wish."[2]

After the death of St. Francis the friars loved and revered Brother Bernard as a venerable father. And when he was dying, many friars came to him from different parts of the world. Among them was that angelic and godlike Brother Giles. When he saw Brother Bernard, he said with great joy: "*Sursum corda,* Brother Bernard, *sursum corda!*"

And the saintly Brother Bernard secretly told one of the friars to prepare for Brother Giles a place suitable for contemplation.

And when Brother Bernard came to the last hour of his life, he had them raise him up, and he said to the friars who were standing around him: "My very dear Brothers, I do not want to say much to you. But you must reflect that I have been in the state in which you are now, and that you will be in the state in which I am now. And I find this in my soul: not for a thousand worlds equal to this one would I want not to have served Our Lord Jesus Christ. And I accuse myself to my Lord and Savior Jesus Christ and to you of all my offenses. My dearest Brothers, I beg you to love one another."

And after he had said those words and given some other good advice, as he lay back on his bed, his features became very radiant and joyful, to the great amazement of all the friars present. And in that same joy his blessed and most holy soul, crowned with glory, passed from this life to the life of the angels and the blessed in the victory which had previously been promised to him.

To the praise and glory of Christ. Amen.

7 About the Wonderful Forty Days' Fast of St. Francis

Because St. Francis, the true servant of Christ, was in certain things like another Christ, given to the world for the salvation of people, God the Father willed to make him in many acts conformed and similar to His Son Jesus Christ, as is shown in the venerable group of the twelve companions, in the wonderful mystery of the holy Stigmata, and in the continuous fast of the holy Lent which he kept in this way.

Once when St. Francis was near the Lake of Perugia on Carnival Day, in the home of a devoted friend with whom he had spent the night, he was inspired by God to go and spend Lent on an island of that lake. St. Francis therefore asked his friend, for the love of Christ, to take him in his little boat to an island in the lake where no one lived, and to do this on the night of Ash Wednesday, so that nobody should perceive it.

And that man, because of the great devotion which he had for St. Francis, thoughtfully carried out his wish. He arose during the night and made his little boat ready and rowed him to that island on Ash Wednesday. And St. Francis took along nothing but two small loaves of bread.

When they reached the island and the friend was leaving to return home, St. Francis earnestly asked him not to reveal to anyone that he was there, and not to come for him before Holy Thursday. And so the man left the island, and St. Francis remained there alone.

As there was no building where he could take shelter, he went into a very dense thicket in which many thorn bushes and small trees had made a sort of little cabin or den. And he began to pray and contemplate heavenly things in that place.

And he stayed there all through Lent without eating and without drinking, except for half of one of those little loaves of bread. His devoted friend came for him on Holy Thursday, as they had agreed. And of the two loaves, he found one whole and half of the other. It is believed that St. Francis ate the other half out of reverence for the fast of the Blessed Christ, who fasted forty days and forty nights without taking any material food. And so with that half loaf he drove from himself the poison of pride, while according to Christ's example he fasted forty days and forty nights.

Later through his merits, God performed many miracles in that place where St. Francis had practiced such marvelous abstinence. From that time men began to build houses on that island and to live there; and in a short while a fine and large walled village was made. And there also is the Place of the Friars Minor which is called the Island. And the men and women of that village still have great reverence and devotion for the place where St. Francis kept that Lent.[1]

To the glory of Christ. Amen.

8 *How St. Francis Taught Brother Leo That Perfect Joy Is Only in the Cross*

One winter day St. Francis was coming to St. Mary of the Angels from Perugia with Brother Leo, and the bitter cold made them suffer keenly. St. Francis called to Brother Leo, who was walking a bit ahead of him,[1] and he said: "Brother Leo, even if the Friars Minor in every country give a great example of holiness and integrity and good edification, nevertheless write down and note carefully that perfect joy is not in that."

And when he had walked on a bit, St. Francis called him again, saying: "Brother Leo, even if a Friar Minor gives sight to the blind, heals the paralyzed, drives out devils, gives hearing back to the deaf, makes the lame walk, and restores speech to the dumb, and what is still more, brings back to life a man who has been dead four days, write that perfect joy is not in that."

And going on a bit, St. Francis cried out again in a strong voice: "Brother Leo, if a Friar Minor knew all languages and all sciences and Scripture, if he also knew how to prophesy and to reveal not only the future but also the secrets of the consciences and minds of others, write down and note carefully that perfect joy is not in that."

And as they walked on, after a while St. Francis called again forcefully: "Brother Leo, Little Lamb of God, even if a Friar Minor could speak with the voice of an angel, and knew the courses of the stars and the powers of herbs, and knew all about the treasures in the earth, and if he knew the qualities of birds and fishes, animals, humans, roots, trees, rocks, and waters, write down and note carefully that true joy is not in that."

And going on a bit farther, St. Francis called again strongly: "Brother Leo, even if a Friar Minor could preach so well that he should convert all infidels to the faith of Christ, write that perfect joy is not there."

Now when he had been talking this way for a distance of two miles, Brother Leo in great amazement asked him: "Father, I beg you in God's name to tell me where perfect joy is."

And St. Francis replied: "When we come to St. Mary of the Angels, soaked by the rain and frozen by the cold, all soiled with mud and suffering from hunger, and we ring at the gate of the Place and the brother porter comes and says angrily: 'Who are you?' And we say: 'We are two of your brothers.' And he contradicts us, saying: 'You are not telling the truth. Rather you are two rascals who go around deceiving people and stealing what they give to the poor. Go away!' And he does not open for us, but makes us stand outside in the snow and rain, cold and hungry, until night falls—then if we endure all those insults and cruel rebuffs patiently, without being troubled and without complaining, and if we reflect humbly and charitably that that porter really knows us and that God makes him speak against us, oh, Brother Leo, write that perfect joy is there!

"And if we continue to knock, and the porter comes out in anger, and drives us away with curses and hard blows like bothersome scoundrels, saying: 'Get away from here, you dirty thieves—go to the hospital! Who do you think you are? You certainly won't eat or sleep here!'—and if we bear it patiently and take the insults with joy and love in our hearts, oh, Brother Leo, write that that is perfect joy!

"And if later, suffering intensely from hunger and the painful cold, with night falling, we still knock and call, and crying loudly beg them to open for us and let us come in for the love of God, and he grows still more angry and says: 'Those fellows are bold and shameless ruffians. I'll give them what they deserve!' And he comes out with a knotty club, and grasping us by the cowl throws us onto the ground, rolling us in the mud and snow, and beats us with that club so much that he covers our bodies with wounds—if we endure all those evils and insults and blows with joy and patience, reflecting that we must accept and bear the sufferings of the Blessed Christ patiently for love of Him, oh, Brother Leo, write: that is perfect joy!

"And now hear the conclusion, Brother Leo. Above all the graces and gifts of the Holy Spirit which Christ gives to His friends is that of conquering oneself and willingly enduring sufferings, insults, humiliations, and hardships for the love of Christ. For we cannot glory in all those other marvelous gifts of God, as they are not ours but God's, as the Apostle says: 'What have you that you have not received?'

"But we can glory in the cross of tribulations and afflictions, because that is ours, and so the Apostle says: 'I will not glory save in the Cross of Our Lord Jesus Christ!'"[2]

To whom be honor and glory forever and ever. Amen.

9 *How God Spoke to St. Francis Through Brother Leo*

Once in the beginning of the Order St. Francis was with Brother Leo in a little Place where they did not have any books to use in saying the Divine Office. One night when they got up to recite matins, St. Francis said to Brother Leo: "Dear Brother, we have no breviary with which to say matins, but so as to spend the time in praising God, I will say something and you must answer what I tell you, and be careful not to change my words. I will say this: 'Oh, Brother Francis, you have done so much evil and sin in the world that you deserve hell'—and you, Brother Leo, shall answer: 'It is true that you deserve the depths of hell.'"

And the very pure-hearted Brother Leo replied with the sim-

1320

plicity of a dove: "All right, Father. Begin in the name of the Lord."

Then St. Francis began to say: "Oh, Brother Francis, you have done so many evil deeds and sins in the world that you deserve hell."

And Brother Leo answered: "God will perform so much good through you that you will go to Paradise."

And St. Francis said: "Don't say that, Brother Leo! But when I say: 'Oh, Brother Francis, you have done so many wicked things against God that you deserve to be cursed by God,' then you answer this way: 'You certainly deserve to be placed among the damned.'"

And Brother Leo replied: "All right, Father."

Then St. Francis said aloud, crying and sighing and beating his breast: "Oh, my Lord God of Heaven and earth, I have committed so many evil deeds and sins against You that I deserve to be utterly damned by You."

And Brother Leo answered: "Oh, Brother Francis, God will make you such that you will be remarkably blessed among the blessed."

St. Francis wondered why Brother Leo always answered just the opposite of what he told him to say, and he scolded him, saying: "Why don't you answer as I tell you, Brother Leo? I command you under holy obedience to answer what I tell you. I will say: 'Oh, wicked little Brother Francis, do you think God will have pity on you, for you have committed too many sins against the Father of mercy and the God of all consolation for you to deserve any mercy?' And you, Brother Leo, Little Lamb, answer: 'You certainly are not worthy of finding mercy.'"

And then Brother Leo answered: "Go ahead, Father, because I will say just what you tell me."

And St. Francis, kneeling down and lifting his hands toward the Lord and looking up to Heaven with a joyful expression, said very sadly: "Oh, Brother Francis, you great sinner—oh, you wicked Brother Francis, do you think God will have mercy on you, for you have committed so many sins?"

But Brother Leo answered: "God the Father, whose mercy is infinitely greater than your sins, will be very merciful to you and moreover will give you many graces."

At this reply St. Francis was gently angry and patiently troubled, and he said to Brother Leo: "Brother, why have you dared to go against obedience and to have already answered so many times the opposite of what I told you?"

And then Brother Leo exclaimed very humbly and reverently: "God knows, dear Father, that each time I have resolved in my heart to answer as you told me, but God makes me speak as pleases Him and not as pleases me."

St. Francis was amazed at this and said to him: "Brother, I beg you to answer me this time as I tell you."

Brother Leo replied: "Go ahead, in God's name, for this time I will answer as you wish."

And St. Francis cried out, weeping: "Oh, wicked little Brother Francis, do you think God will have mercy on you?"

Brother Leo answered: "Yes, Father, God will have mercy on you. Besides, you will receive a great grace from God for your salvation, and He will exalt and glorify you for all eternity, because 'whoever humbles himself shall be exalted'—and I cannot say anything else because God is speaking through my mouth!"

And they stayed up until dawn in this humble contest, with many tears and great spiritual consolations.[1]

To the praise and glory of Our Lord Jesus Christ. Amen.

10 *How Brother Masseo Tested St. Francis' Humility*

Once St. Francis was staying at the Place of Portiuncula with Brother Masseo of Marignano, a man of great holiness and discernment and grace in speaking about God, because of which St. Francis loved him very much.

One day when St. Francis was coming back from the woods, where he had been praying, and was at the edge of the forest, Brother Masseo went to meet him, as he wanted to find out how humble he was, and he said to St. Francis, half jokingly: "Why after you? Why after you? Why after you?"

St. Francis replied: "What do you mean, Brother Masseo?"

"I mean, why does all the world seem to be running after you, and everyone seems to want to see you and hear you and obey you? You are not a handsome man. You do not have great learning or wisdom. You are not a nobleman. So why is all the world running after you?"

On hearing this, St. Francis rejoiced greatly in spirit, and he raised his face toward Heaven and stood for a long time with his mind absorbed in God.

Coming back to himself, he genuflected and praised and gave thanks to God. Then with great fervor of spirit he turned to Brother Masseo and said: "You want to know why after me? You want to know why after me? You really want to know why everyone is running after me? I have this from the all-holy eyes of God that see the good and the evil everywhere. For those blessed and all-holy eyes have not seen among sinners anyone more vile or insufficient than I am. And so in order to do that wonderful work which He intends to do, He did not find on earth a viler creature, and therefore He chose me, for God has chosen the foolish things of the world to put to shame the wise, and God has chosen the base things of the world and the despised, to bring to naught the noble and great and strong, so that all excellence in virtue may be from God and not from the creature, in order that no creature should glory before Him, but 'let him who takes pride, take pride in the Lord,' that honor and glory may be only God's forever."

Then Brother Masseo, at such a humble answer spoken with such fervor, was deeply moved and knew for sure that St. Francis was grounded in true humility, as a true and humble disciple of Christ.[1]

To the glory of Christ. Amen.

11 *How St. Francis Made Brother Masseo Twirl Around*

Once St. Francis was traveling in Tuscany with Brother Masseo, whom he most willingly used to take along as his companion because of his pleasant conversation and unusual discretion and because of the help which he gave him in his raptures by dealing with people and hiding him from them, so that they should not disturb him.

One day they were walking along a road together, with

Brother Masseo going a bit ahead of St. Francis. But when they came to a crossroad where three roads met, where they could go to Siena or Florence or Arezzo, Brother Masseo said: "Father, which road should we take?"

St. Francis replied: "We will take the road ·God wants us to take."

Brother Masseo said: "How will we be able to know God's will?"

St. Francis answered: "By the sign I will show you. Now under the merit of holy obedience I command you to twirl around in this crossroad, right where you are standing, just as children do, and not to stop turning until I tell you."

So Brother Masseo obediently began to turn around, and he twirled around so long that he fell down several times from dizziness in his head, which usually results from such turning. But as St. Francis did not tell him to stop, and he wanted to obey faithfully, he got up again and resumed his gyrations.

Finally, after he had been twirling around bravely for a long time, St. Francis said: "Stand still! Don't move!"

And he stood still. And St. Francis asked him: "What direction are you facing?"

Brother Masseo replied: "Toward Siena."

And St. Francis said: "That is the road God wants us to take."

While they were going along that road, Brother Masseo marveled very much over St. Francis' having made him twirl around in such a childish way before all the lay people who were passing by. However, because of his reverence for the Saint, he did not dare say anything to him about it.

When they drew near to Siena and the people of the city heard that St. Francis was arriving, they came out to meet him. And out of devotion they carried him and his companion under the arms to the Bishop's mansion, so that their feet hardly touched the ground all the way.

Now at that same hour some citizens of Siena were fighting together, and two of them had already been killed. So St. Francis went there and stood up and preached to those men in such a beautiful and holy way that he brought all of them back to peace and great unity and harmony.

And when the Bishop of Siena heard about the wonderful

deed which St. Francis had performed, he invited him into his house and made him welcome that day and also overnight. The next morning the truly humble St. Francis, who sought nothing but the glory of God in his actions, got up early with his companion and left without the Bishop's knowing it.

Brother Masseo murmured at this as they went along the road, saying to himself: "What has this good man done? Yesterday he made me twirl around like a child, and today he did not say one good word or express his thanks to the Bishop who honored him so much!"

And it seemed to Brother Masseo that St. Francis had acted indiscreetly. But then, by an inspiration from God, he came back to his senses and reproached himself severely in his heart: "Brother Masseo, you are too proud, passing judgment on the work of divine grace, and you deserve hell for revolting against God with your indiscreet pride! For yesterday on this journey Brother Francis performed such holy deeds that they would not be more marvelous if an angel had done them. So if he should order you to throw stones, you should obey him. For all that he did on this journey was the work of God, as is shown by the good results that followed. Because if he had not made peace between those men who were fighting, not only would the sword have slain many bodies, as it had already begun to do, but—what is still worse—many souls would have been thrown into hell by the devil. And so you are very stupid and proud for murmuring against what was clearly the will of God."

Now all these things which Brother Masseo was pondering in his heart as he walked along a bit ahead of St. Francis were revealed to the latter by the Holy Spirit, to whom all things are bare and open. And calling Brother Masseo, the Saint came up to him and disclosed the secret thoughts of Masseo's heart by saying to him: "Hold to the thoughts which you are thinking now, for they are good and helpful to you and inspired by God. But the complaining that you did before was blind and evil and proud and was planted in your soul by the devil."

On hearing this, Brother Masseo was astounded, and he clearly realized that St. Francis knew the secrets of his heart, and he understood with certainty that the Spirit of divine wisdom and grace guided St. Francis in all his actions.[1]

To the praise and glory of Our Lord Jesus Christ. Amen.

12 *How St. Francis Tested Brother Masseo's Humility*

St. Francis wished to humble Brother Masseo, in order that pride should not lift him up because of the many gifts and graces which God gave him, but that he should advance from virtue to virtue by means of humility. And one day when he was staying at a solitary Place with those truly saintly first companions of his, among whom was Brother Masseo, he said to him before all the others: "Brother Masseo, all these companions of yours have the grace of prayer and contemplation, but you have the grace of preaching the word of God to satisfy the people who come here. Therefore, so that the friars may give themselves better to prayer and contemplation, I want you to take care of opening the gate, giving out alms, and cooking the meals. And when the friars are eating, you are to eat outside the gate of the Place, so that you may satisfy with a few good devout words the people who come to the Place before they knock at the gate. Thus no one else need go out to them except you. And you are to do this by merit of holy obedience."

Then Brother Masseo immediately bowed his head, lowering his cowl, and humbly accepted and faithfully obeyed this order. For several days he served as gatekeeper, almsgiver, and cook.

But his companions, as men enlightened by God, began to feel intense remorse in their hearts, reflecting that Brother Masseo was a man of great perfection and prayer, like themselves or even more so, and yet the whole burden of the Place was put on him and not on them. Consequently they agreed among themselves, and they went to ask their holy Father that he should kindly distribute the duties among them, because their consciences simply could not bear having Brother Masseo burdened with so much work. Furthermore, they felt that they would be cold in their prayers and troubled in their consciences if Brother Masseo were not relieved of those duties.

On hearing this, St. Francis agreed to their charitable suggestion. And calling Brother Masseo, he said to him: "Brother Masseo, these companions of yours want to share in the duties I gave you, and so I want those duties to be divided among them."

And Brother Masseo said very humbly and patiently: "Whatever you impose on me—either in part or in whole—I consider it done by God."

Then St. Francis, seeing their charity and Brother Masseo's humility, gave them a wonderful sermon on holy humility, teaching them that the greater the gifts and graces which God gives us, the greater is our obligation to be more humble, because without humility no virtue is acceptable to God. And after he had finished preaching, he distributed the duties among them with great affection and gave all of them a blessing by the grace of the Holy Spirit.[1]

To the glory of God. Amen.

13 *How St. Francis Lifted Brother Masseo in the Air, and How St. Peter and St. Paul Appeared to St. Francis*

Just as Christ, according to the Gospels, sent His disciples, two by two, to all the towns and places where He was to go Himself, so St. Francis, the wonderful servant of God and true follower of Christ, in order to conform himself perfectly to Christ in all things, after he had gathered twelve companions, following Christ's example sent them out in groups of two to preach to the world. And to give them an example of true obedience, he himself was the first to go, following the precedent of Christ who first practiced what He taught. Therefore, after he had assigned various other parts of the world to his friars, taking Brother Masseo as his companion, he set out on the road toward the Province of France.

And one day when they came to a village and they were quite hungry, they went begging for bread for the love of God, according to the Rule. And St. Francis went along one street and Brother Masseo along another. But because St. Francis was a very small and insignificant-looking man, and therefore was considered a common little pauper by nearly all who did not know him—for human foolishness judges not what is inside but only externals—he received nothing but a few mouthfuls of food and some small pieces of dry bread. But to Brother Masseo, because he was a tall handsome man, people gave plenty of good large pieces and some whole loaves.

When they had finished begging, the two came together to eat somewhere outside the village. They found nothing but the dry ground to put their begged food on, because that region was quite bare of stones. However, with God's help they came to a spring, and beside it there was a fine broad stone, which made them very happy. And each of them placed on the stone all the pieces of bread he had acquired. And when St. Francis saw that Brother Masseo's pieces of bread were more numerous and better and bigger than his, he was filled with intense joy because of his longing for poverty, and he said: "Oh, Brother Masseo, we do not deserve such a great treasure as this!" And he repeated those words several times, raising his voice each time.

Brother Masseo replied: "Dear Father, how can this be called a treasure when there is such poverty and such a lack of things that are necessary? For here we have no cloth, no knife, no dish, no bowl, no house, no table, no waiter, no waitress."

St. Francis answered: "That is what I consider a great treasure—where nothing has been prepared by human labor. But everything here has been supplied by Divine Providence, as is evident in the begged bread, the fine stone table, and the clear spring. Therefore, I want us to pray to God that He may make us love with all our hearts the very noble treasure of holy poverty, which has God as provider."

And after he had said those words and they had prayed and eaten the pieces of bread and drunk the spring-water, they arose to travel on toward France, rejoicing and praising the Lord in song.

And when they came to a certain church, St. Francis said to his companion: "Let's go in and hear Mass and pray there." And they entered, but as the priest was absent, St. Francis went and hid himself behind the altar to pray. And while he was praying there, he was given a divine vision and visitation

1328

which wholly inflamed his soul with such an intense longing and love for holy poverty that flames of love seemed to issue from his face and mouth.

And going out to his companion, all afire with love, he said forcefully: "Ah! Ah! Ah! Brother Masseo, give yourself to me!"

And he said it three times. And Brother Masseo, greatly amazed at his fervor, threw himself into the holy Father's arms when he said for the third time: "Give yourself to me!"

Then St. Francis, with his mouth wide open and repeating very loudly "Ah! Ah! Ah!", by the power of the Holy Spirit lifted Brother Masseo up in the air with his breath and projected him forward the length of a long spear.

Brother Masseo was completely astounded. And later he told his companions that he had experienced such spiritual consolation and sweetness in being raised up and projected by the breath of St. Francis that he did not recall ever having had such a great consolation in all his life.

Afterward, St. Francis said to Brother Masseo: "My dear companion, let us go to Rome, to St. Peter and St. Paul, and let us pray to them to teach us and help us to possess the infinite treasure of holy poverty."

And St. Francis added: "My dear and beloved Brother, the treasure of blessed poverty is so very precious and divine that we are not worthy to possess it in our vile bodies. For poverty is that heavenly virtue by which all earthly and transitory things are trodden under foot, and by which every obstacle is removed from the soul so that it may freely enter into union with the eternal Lord God. It is also the virtue which makes the soul, while still here on earth, converse with the angels in Heaven. It is she who accompanied Christ on the Cross, was buried with Christ in the Tomb, and with Christ was raised and ascended into Heaven, for even in this life she gives to souls who love her the ability to fly to Heaven, and she alone guards the armor of true humility and charity. So let us pray to the very holy Apostles of Christ, who were perfect lovers of the pearl of the Gospel, that they may procure this grace for us from Our Lord Jesus Christ: that He who was an observer and teacher of holy poverty may by His most holy mercy grant that we may be worthy to be true lovers and observers and humble followers of the most precious and beloved poverty of the Gospel."

When they arrived in Rome, conversing like that, they entered St. Peter's Church. And St. Francis went into one corner of the church and Brother Masseo to another, to pray to God and His holy Apostles that they might instruct and help them to possess the treasure of holy poverty. And they prayed for it a long time with great devotion and many tears. And while they were persisting humbly in prayer, the holy Apostles Peter and Paul appeared in great splendor to St. Francis. And embracing and kissing him, they said: "Brother Francis, because you request and desire to observe what Christ and the holy Apostles observed, Our Lord Jesus Christ Himself has sent us to announce to you that your desire is fulfilled and your prayer is answered, and that the treasure of very holy poverty is perfectly granted to you and your followers. And on behalf of Christ we say to you that whoever by your example perfectly follows this desire shall be assured of the happiness of everlasting life. And you and all your followers shall be blessed by God." And after saying those words they disappeared, leaving St. Francis full of consolation.

Rising from prayer, he went to his companion and asked him whether God had revealed anything to him. And he answered: "No." Then St. Francis told him how the holy Apostles had appeared to him and what they had revealed to him. And both of them were so overwhelmed with joy and happiness that they forgot to go to France, as they had first intended, but they hastened to return to the Valley of Spoleto, where this heavenly and angelical way of life was to begin.[1]

To the glory of Christ. Amen.

14 *How While St. Francis Was Talking about*
God with His Companions, Christ Appeared
among Them

Our very holy Father Francis plunged all his thoughts into the Blessed Christ and directed all his efforts and desire and way of praying and speaking and conversing toward His pleasure, both for himself and his other companions. Once he wanted to talk about God and the salvation of souls when he was with those holy and apostolic companions of his, who had come together in one Place to converse about God, at the beginning of the Order when they were still few. The devout Father was sitting with his very blessed sons, and in fervor of spirit he commanded one of them in the name of the Lord to open his mouth and say about God whatever the Holy Spirit suggested to him.

But after that friar had at once obediently begun and uttered marvelous words under the guidance of the Holy Spirit, St. Francis told him to be quiet. And he ordered another to speak similarly about God according to the grace which the Holy Spirit gave him. And as he obeyed and was speaking very profoundly about the Lord by the grace of God, St. Francis imposed silence on him as he had on the first. And he ordered a third to say something without preparation in praise of Our Lord Jesus Christ. And this third one, following the example of the others and humbly obeying, likewise began to speak so profoundly about the hidden mysteries of the Divinity that there was no doubt the Holy Spirit was speaking through him and the others, and that St. Francis certainly knew it.

And this was also proved by a specific sign, for while those holy simple men were thus, at their Father's command, one after another speaking sweetly about God and spreading the perfume of divine grace, Our Lord Jesus Christ appeared among them in the form of a very handsome young man. And giving His blessing to all of them, He filled them with such sweet grace that St. Francis as well as all the others were rapt out of themselves, and they lay on the ground like dead men, completely unconscious.

Later when they regained consciousness, St. Francis said to them: "My dear Brothers, give thanks to Our Lord Jesus Christ who has deigned to reveal the treasures of divine wisdom through the mouths of simple ones. For God is He who opens the mouths of infants and the dumb, and when He wishes, He makes the tongues of the simple speak very wisely."[1]

To the glory of God. Amen.

15 *How St. Clare Ate a Meal with St. Francis and His Friars*

When St. Francis was staying in Assisi, he often visited St. Clare and consoled her with holy advice. And as she had a very great desire to eat a meal with him once, she asked him several times to give her that consolation. But St. Francis always refused to grant her that favor.

So it happened that his companions, perceiving St. Clare's desire, said to St. Francis: "Father, it seems to us that this strictness is not according to divine charity—that you do not grant the request of Sister Clare, a virgin so holy and dear to God, in such a little thing as eating with you, especially considering that she gave up the riches and pomp of the world as a result of your preaching. So you should not only let her eat a meal with you once, but if she were to ask an even greater favor of you, you should grant it to your little spiritual plant."

St. Francis answered: "So you think I should grant this wish of hers?"

And the companions said: "Yes, Father, for she deserves this favor and consolation."

Then St. Francis replied: "Since it seems so to you, I agree. But in order to give her greater pleasure, I want this meal to be at St. Mary of the Angels, for she has been cloistered at San Damiano for a long time and she will enjoy seeing once more for a while the Place of St. Mary where she was shorn and made a spouse of the Lord Jesus Christ. So we will eat there together, in the name of the Lord."

He therefore set a day when St. Clare would go out of the monastery with one sister companion, escorted also by his companions.

And she came to St. Mary of the Angels. And first she reverently and humbly greeted the Blessed Virgin Mary before her altar, where she had been shorn and received the veil. And then they devoutly showed her around the Place until it was mealtime. Meanwhile St. Francis had the table prepared on the bare ground, as was his custom.

And when it was time to eat, St. Francis and St. Clare sat down together, and one of his companions with St. Clare's companion, and all his other companions were grouped around that humble table. But at the first course St. Francis began to speak about God in such a sweet and holy and profound and divine and marvelous way that he himself and St. Clare and her companion and all the others who were at that poor little table were rapt in God by the overabundance of divine grace that descended upon them.

And while they were sitting there, in a rapture, with their eyes and hands raised to Heaven, it seemed to the men of Assisi and Bettona and the entire district that the Church of St. Mary of the Angels and the whole Place and the forest which was at that time around the Place were all aflame and that an immense fire was burning over all of them. Consequently the men of Assisi ran down there in great haste to save the Place and put out the fire, as they firmly believed that everything was burning up.

But when they reached the Place, they saw that nothing was on fire. Entering the Place, they found St. Francis with St. Clare and all the companions sitting around that very humble table, rapt in God by contemplation and invested with power from on high. Then they knew for sure that it had been a heavenly and not a material fire that God had miraculously shown them to symbolize the fire of divine love which was burning in the souls of those holy friars and nuns. So they withdrew, with great consolation in their hearts and with holy edification.

Later, after a long while, when St. Francis and St. Clare and the others came back to themselves, they felt so refreshed by spiritual food that they paid little or no attention to the material food. And when that blessed meal was over, St. Clare, well accompanied, returned to San Damiano.

The sisters were very glad to see her, for they had feared that St. Francis might send her to direct some other monastery, as he had already sent her holy sister Agnes to be Abbess of the Monastery of Monticelli in Florence. For at that time St. Francis was sending Sisters out to rule other monasteries. And he had once said to St. Clare: "Be prepared, in case I have to send you somewhere else." And she had replied like a truly obedient daughter: "Father, I am always ready to go wherever you send me." And so the sisters rejoiced greatly when they had her back. And henceforth St. Clare was much consoled in the Lord.[1]

To the glory of Christ. Amen.

16 *How God Revealed to St. Clare and Brother Silvester That St. Francis Should Go and Preach*

The humble servant of Christ, St. Francis, at the beginning of his conversion, when he had already gathered many companions and received them in the Order, was placed in a great agony of doubt as to what he should do: whether to give himself only to continual prayer or to preach sometimes. He wanted very much to know which of these would please Our Lord Jesus Christ most. And as the holy humility that was in him did not allow him to trust in himself or in his own prayers, he humbly turned to others in order to know God's will in this matter.

So he called Brother Masseo and said to him: "Dear Brother, go to Sister Clare and tell her on my behalf to pray devoutly to God, with one of her purer and more spiritual companions, that He may deign to show me what is best: either that I preach sometimes or that I devote myself only to prayer. And then go also to Brother Silvester, who is staying on Mount Subasio, and tell him the same thing."

This was that Lord Silvester who had seen a cross of gold issuing from the mouth of St. Francis which extended in length to Heaven and in width to the ends of the world. And this Brother Silvester was so devout and holy that God immediately granted or revealed to him whatever he asked in prayer. The Holy Spirit had made him remarkably deserving of divine communications, and he conversed with God many times. And therefore St. Francis was very devoted to him and had great faith in him. This holy Brother Silvester often stayed alone in the above-mentioned Place.

Brother Masseo went, and as St. Francis had ordered him, gave the message first to St. Clare and then to Brother Silvester. When the latter received it, he immediately set himself to praying. And while praying he quickly had God's answer. And he went out at once to Brother Masseo and said: "The Lord says you are to tell Brother Francis this: that God has not called him to this state only on his own account, but that he may reap a harvest of souls and that many may be saved through him."

After this Brother Masseo went back to St. Clare to know what she had received from God. And she answered that both she and her companion had had the very same answer from God as Brother Silvester.

Brother Masseo therefore returned to St. Francis. And the Saint received him with great charity: he washed his feet and prepared a meal for him. And after he had eaten, St. Francis called Brother Masseo into the woods. And there he knelt down before Brother Masseo, and baring his head and crossing his arms, St. Francis asked him: "What does my Lord Jesus Christ order me to do?"

Brother Masseo replied that Christ had answered both Brother Silvester and Sister Clare and her companion and revealed that "He wants you to go about the world preaching, because God did not call you for yourself alone but also for the salvation of others."

And then the hand of the Lord came over St. Francis. As soon as he heard this answer and thereby knew the will of Christ, he got to his feet, all aflame with divine power, and said to Brother Masseo with great fervor: "So let's go—in the name of the Lord!"[1]

And he took as companions Brother Masseo and Brother Angelo, holy men. And he set out like a bolt of lightning in his spiritual ardor, not paying any attention to the road or path.

They arrived at a village called Cannara. And St. Francis began to preach, first ordering the swallows who were twittering to keep quiet until he had finished preaching. And the swallows obeyed him. He preached there so fervently that all the men and women of that village, as a result of his sermon and of the miracle of the swallows, in their great devotion wanted to follow him and abandon the village. But St. Francis did not let them, saying to them: "Don't be in a hurry and don't leave, for I will arrange what you should do for the salvation of your souls." And from that time he planned to organize the Third Order of the Continent for the salvation of all people everywhere.[2]

And leaving them much consoled and disposed to do penance, he left there and came between Cannara and Bevagna. And while going with the same fervor through that district with his companions, he looked up and saw near the road some trees on which there was such a countless throng of different birds as had never been seen before in that area. And also a very great crowd of birds was in a field near those trees. While he gazed and marveled at the multitude of birds, the Spirit of God came over him and he said to his companions: "Wait for me here on the road. I am going to preach to our sisters, the birds."

And he went into the field toward the birds that were on the ground. And as soon as he began to preach, all the birds that were on the trees came down toward him. And all of them stayed motionless with the others in the field, even though he went among them, touching many of them with his habit. But not a single one of them made the slightest move, and later they did not leave until he had given them his blessing, as Brother James of Massa, a holy man, said, and he had all the above facts from Brother Masseo, who was one of those who were the companions of the holy Father at that time.

The substance of St. Francis' sermon to those birds was this: "My little bird sisters, you owe much to God your Creator, and you must always and everywhere praise Him, because He has given you freedom to fly anywhere—also He has given you a double and triple covering, and your colorful and pretty clothing, and your food is ready without your working for it, and your singing that was taught to you by the Creator, and your numbers that have been multiplied by the blessing of God—and because He preserved your species in Noah's ark so that your race should not disappear from the earth. And you are also indebted to Him for the realm of the air which He assigned to you. Moreover, you neither sow nor reap, yet God nourishes you, and He gives you the rivers and springs to drink from. He gives you high mountains and hills, rocks and crags as refuges, and lofty trees in which to make your nests. And although you do not know how to spin or sew, God gives you and your little ones the clothing which you need. So the Creator loves you very much, since He gives you so many good things. Therefore, my little bird sisters, be careful not to be ungrateful, but strive always to praise God."

Now at these words of St. Francis, all those birds began to open their beaks, stretch out their necks, spread their wings, and reverently bow their heads to the ground, showing by their movements and their songs that the words which St. Francis was saying gave them great pleasure. And when St. Francis noticed this, he likewise rejoiced greatly in spirit with them, and he marveled at such a great throng of birds and at their very beautiful variety and also at their attention and familiarity and affection. And therefore he devoutly praised the wonderful Creator in them and gently urged them to praise the Creator.

Finally, when he had finished preaching to them and urging them to praise God, St. Francis made the Sign of the Cross over all those birds and gave them permission to leave. Then all the birds rose up into the air simultaneously, and in the air they sang a wonderful song. And when they had finished singing, according to the form of the Cross which St. Francis had made over them, they separated in an orderly way and formed four groups. And each group rose high into the air and flew off in a different direction: one toward the east, another toward the west, the third toward the south, and the fourth toward the north. And each group sang marvelously as it flew away.

Thereby they signified that, just as St. Francis—who was to bear the marks of Christ's Cross—had preached to them and made the Sign of the Cross over them, so they had separated in the form of a cross and had flown away, singing, toward the four quarters of the world, thus suggesting that the preaching of the Cross of Christ, which had been renewed by St. Francis, was to be carried throughout the world by him and by his friars, who, like birds, possess nothing of their own in this world and commit themselves entirely to the Providence of God.

And so they were called eagles by Christ when He said, "Wherever the body shall be, there the eagles will gather." For the saints who place their hope in the Lord will take on wings like eagles and will fly up to the Lord and will not die for all eternity.[3]

To the praise of Christ. Amen.

17 *How a Young Friar Fainted When He Saw St. Francis Speaking with Christ*

A young boy who was pure as a dove and innocent as an angel was received into the Order while St. Francis was living. And he stayed in a certain small Place where the Brothers did not have cells and because of poverty slept on the ground without beds.

One day St. Francis came to that little Place. And in the evening, after saying compline, he went to rest somewhat before the others, so that later in the night, while the others were sleeping, he could get up and pray, as he usually did.

That boy decided carefully to observe where St. Francis went, so as to know how holy he was, and especially what he did when he got up during the night. In order that sleep should not prevent him, the boy lay down to sleep beside St. Francis and tied his cord to that of St. Francis, so that he would feel it when the Saint got up. And St. Francis was not aware that he had tied the cords together.

During the first part of the night, when all the friars were fast asleep, St. Francis got up, and finding his cord attached, he untied it so carefully that the boy did not feel anything. And St. Francis went out to a hill near the Place where there was a very beautiful forest in order to pray alone in a small hut that was there.

A little while later the boy awoke and found that his cord was untied and that St. Francis was gone. So he immediately got up in order to observe the holy Father, as he had planned. Finding the gate leading to the forest open, he thought the Saint had gone out that way, and he quickly went after him into the woods and reached the top of the hill where St. Francis had gone to pray.

And when he came to the place where St. Francis was praying, he stopped at a certain distance, for he began to hear a number of persons talking. Going nearer in order to see and hear more clearly what they were saying, he perceived a marvelous light completely surrounding St. Francis, and in that light he saw Christ and the Blessed Virgin Mary and St. John the Baptist and St. John the Evangelist and a great throng of angels, who were talking with St. Francis.

On seeing and hearing all this, the boy began to tremble, and he fainted and fell like a corpse onto the path that led back to the monastery.

Later, when that very wonderful conversation was over and the mystery of that holy apparition was ended, St. Francis, while returning to the Place in the dark of the night, stumbled on the boy lying on the path as though he were dead. And he had compassion on the boy, and taking him up in his arms St. Francis carried him back to his bed, like the good shepherd carrying his little lamb.

And later, hearing from the boy how he had seen that vision, the Saint commanded him not to tell it to anyone during his lifetime.

The boy did indeed keep the secret. He grew up in great grace of God and devotion to St. Francis, and he lived as a worthy member of the Order until he died. And only after the death of St. Francis did he reveal all that vision to the friars.[1]

To the glory of Our Lord Jesus Christ. Amen.

18 *About the Marvelous Chapter That St. Francis Held at St. Mary of the Angels*

Once the most faithful servant of Christ, St. Francis, held a General Chapter on the plain at St. Mary of the Angels, where more than five thousand friars gathered together. And St. Dominic, the head and founder of the Order of Friars Preachers, was also there with seven friars of his Order. He was at that time going from Bologna to Rome, and on hearing about the Chapter which St. Francis was holding on the plain at St. Mary of the Angels, he went to see it.

There was also present at that Chapter the Lord Hugolin, Cardinal of Ostia, who was very devoted to St. Francis and his friars. St. Francis prophesied that he would be Pope, and so it happened: he was later the Pope called Gregory the Ninth. As the Court of the Lord Pope was then in Perugia, that Cardinal deliberately came to Assisi, and he used to come every day to see St. Francis and his friars, and sometimes he sang the Mass, and sometimes he gave a sermon to the friars at the Chapter.

The Cardinal felt the greatest delight and inspiration when he came to visit that holy assembly and saw the friars sitting about on the plain around St. Mary in groups of sixty or a hundred or two or three hundred, all occupied only in talking about God or in praying, weeping, or doing deeds of charity. And they were so quiet and meek that there was no sound or noise. And marveling at such a great crowd organized as an army camp, he would say with tears and great devotion: "Truly this is the camp and the army of the knights of God!"

Indeed in all that throng no one was heard telling stories or jokes, but wherever a group of friars gathered, either they prayed or recited the office, or they wept over their own sins or those of their benefactors, or they talked about the salvation of souls.

And in that camp each group had made tents covered on top and round about with rushes and mats; accordingly this Chapter was called the Chapter of Rushes or Mats. They slept on the bare ground or on some straw, and their pillows were stones or pieces of wood.

As a result, everyone who saw or heard them had such devotion for them, and the fame of their holiness was so great, that many people came to see them from the Pope's Court, which was then nearby at Perugia, and from other parts of the Valley of Spoleto. Many counts and barons and knights and other noblemen and many plain people, and cardinals and bishops and abbots with other members of the clergy, flocked to see this very holy and large and humble gathering of so many saintly men, such as the world has never seen. And they came especially to see the venerable leader and very saintly Father of all that company, who had stolen such beautiful prey from the world and had gathered such a fine and devout flock to follow in the footsteps of the true shepherd Jesus Christ.

When the entire General Chapter had assembled, St. Francis, the holy Father of all and Minister General, stood up and with fervor of spirit explained the word of God and of life to that holy flock, and—in a loud voice, as clear as a bugle, which divine unction gave him—preached to them whatever the Holy Spirit made him utter. And he took these words as the theme of his sermon: "My little sons, we have promised great things, but far greater things have been promised to us by God. Let us keep those promises which we have made, and let us aspire with confidence to those things that have been promised to us. Brief is the world's pleasure, but the punishment that follows it lasts forever. Small is the suffering of this life, but the glory of the next life is infinite." And preaching very devoutly on these words, he consoled and encouraged all the friars to reverence and obedience to Holy Mother Church and to sweet brotherly love, to pray for all the people of God, to have patience in the adversities of the world and temperance in prosperity, to maintain an angelic purity and chastity, to remain in peace and harmony with God and with men and with their own conscience, to humility and meekness toward all, to the contempt of the world and a love and fervent practice of holy poverty, to care and attention in holy prayer and the praise of God, to place all their hope and anxiety for soul and body in the Good Shepherd who nourishes our bodies and souls: Our Blessed Lord Jesus Christ.

And then he said: "In order that you may better observe this, by merit of holy obedience I command all you friars who are gathered here that none of you is to have any care or anxiety concerning anything to eat or drink or the other things necessary for the body, but to concentrate only on praying and praising God. And leave all your worries about your body to Christ, because He takes special care of you."

And all of them received this order with joy in their hearts and on their faces. And when St. Francis ended his sermon, they all ran and gave themselves to prayer.

But St. Dominic, who was present, was greatly surprised at St. Francis' command and thought that he was proceeding in an imprudent way in ordering that not a single friar in such a large gathering should take any thought regarding things that are necessary for the body, and he thought that such a great crowd would suffer as a result. But the Lord Jesus Christ

1341

wanted to show that He takes special care of His sheep and His poor, for by God's Providence it soon happened that He inspired the people of Perugia, Spoleto, Foligno, Spello, Assisi, and all the surrounding country to bring food and drink to that holy assembly. And all of a sudden men came from those places with many donkeys, mules, and wagons loaded with bread and wine, beans and cheese, and all other good things to eat which they thought those blessed poor men of Christ would need and could use. Moreover, they brought large and small pitchers and glasses and tablecloths and other things which such a crowd would need.

And whoever among them could bring the most supplies or serve most thoughtfully considered himself fortunate to provide for the needs of all in that holy gathering. And you could see the knights and noblemen who came to the meeting gladly and humbly and devoutly serving that assembly of saints. You could see members of the clergy faithfully and eagerly running around everywhere like servants. You could see young men serving with so much reverence that it seemed as though they were serving, not the poor friars, but the Apostles of Our Lord Jesus Christ.

Therefore, when St. Dominic saw all this and realized that Divine Providence was acting through them, he humbly reproached himself for having misjudged St. Francis regarding the imprudent order, and he meekly knelt before him and accused himself of his fault, adding: "God is truly taking care of these holy little poor men, and I did not realize it. Therefore I promise henceforth to observe the holy poverty of the Gospel. And in the name of God I lay a curse upon all the friars of my Order who shall presume to have private property."

Thus St. Dominic was greatly edified by St. Francis' faith and the obedience and poverty of such a great and orderly assembly and by Divine Providence and the abundant supply of all good things. For as a truly saintly and wise man he acknowledged in all he said the perfectly faithful Lord who, just as He makes the lilies and plants of the fields grow and He nourishes the birds of the air, also furnishes everything that His devoted poor men need.

During that same Chapter St. Francis was told that many

friars were wearing breastplates and iron rings on their flesh, and as a result some had become ill and some were dying, and others were hindered in praying. So St. Francis as a very wise Father commanded under holy obedience that whoever had a breastplate or an iron ring should take it off and deposit it before him. And they did so. And at least five hundred breastplates and many more iron rings worn on the arm or the torso were found, and they formed a large pile. And St. Francis made the friars leave them there.

Later when the Chapter was over, St. Francis instructed and encouraged all of them to do good, and he taught them how to escape without sin from this evil world. And he sent them all back to their provinces comforted and filled with spiritual joy, with God's blessing and his own.[1]

To the glory of Our Lord Jesus Christ—may He be blessed! Amen.

19 *How God Spoke to St. Francis, and How St. Francis Made the Wine Increase in a Poor Priest's Vineyard*

Once when St. Francis was suffering grievously in his eyes, the Lord Cardinal Hugolin, the Protector of the Order, because he loved him dearly, wrote to him, ordering St. Francis to come to him in Rieti, where there were some very good eye doctors. And when St. Francis received the letter of the Lord Cardinal, he went first to San Damiano, where the very devout spouse of Christ St. Clare was. For he intended to visit her and console her before he left, and then go to Rieti.

And the first night after he went to San Damiano, his eyes became so much worse that he could not see any light. Since he was unable to leave, St. Clare had a little cell made for him out of reeds and straw, in which he might stay in seclusion and get more rest.

And St. Francis stayed there for fifty days with such pain in his eyes and so greatly disturbed by a large number of mice instigated by the devil that he was unable to obtain any rest at all, either by day or night. And after he had been enduring that trial and tribulation for many days, he began to reflect and to realize that it was a punishment from the Lord for his sins. And he began to thank God with all his heart and to praise him, crying in a loud voice: "My Lord, I deserve this and much more." And he prayed to the Lord, saying: "My Lord Jesus Christ, Good Shepherd, who have shown Your very gentle mercy to us unworthy sinners in various physical pains and sufferings, give grace and strength to me, Your little lamb, that in no tribulation or anguish or pain I may turn away from You!"

And when he had uttered this prayer, a Voice came to him from Heaven that said: "Francis, answer Me. If the whole earth were made of gold, and all the oceans and rivers and springs were balsam, and all the mountains and hills and rocks were precious stones, and you found another treasure that was as much more valuable than all those things as gold is than earth, and balsam than water, and gems than mountains and rocks, and if that most valuable treasure were given to you for this illness of yours, should you not be very happy and rejoice greatly?"

St. Francis answered: "Lord, I am not worthy of so precious a treasure."

And the Voice of God said to him: "Rejoice therefore, Brother Francis, because that is the treasure of eternal life which I am keeping for you. And right now I invest you with it. And this illness and affliction are a pledge of that blessed treasure."

Then St. Francis, thrilled with joy by that glorious promise, called his companion and said: "Let's go to Rieti—to the Lord Cardinal!"

And after first consoling St. Clare with holy and honey-sweet words and saying good-by to her humbly, as he usually did, he set out for Rieti.[1]

But when he arrived near Rieti, such a great crowd of people came out to meet him that he therefore did not want to go into the city, but turned aside and went to a certain church that was about two miles away from the town. But the people, knowing that he was staying at that church, flocked out to see him in such throngs that the vineyard of the priest of that church—for it was vintage time—was completely ruined and all the grapes were taken and eaten. When the priest saw the damage, he was bitterly sorry and he regretted that he had allowed St. Francis to go into his church.

The priest's thoughts were revealed to the Saint by the Holy Spirit, and he summoned the priest and said to him: "My dear Father, how many measures of wine does this vineyard produce in a year when it produces well?"

The priest answered: "Twelve."

And St. Francis said: "Then I beg you, Father, to bear patiently my staying here in this church of yours for some days, because of the rest and quiet that I find here. And let everyone take the grapes from this vineyard of yours, for the love of God and my poor little self. And I promise you on behalf of my Lord Jesus Christ that this year you will get twenty measures."

St. Francis did this—staying on there—because of the great good which he saw the Lord was performing in the souls of the people who came there, for he saw that many of them, when they went away, were inebriated with the love of God and converted to heavenly longings, forgetting the world. Therefore it seemed to him better that the material vineyard should be damaged than that the vineyard of the Lord of Hosts should be sterile in heavenly wine.

So the priest trusted in the promise of St. Francis and freely let the people who came there take and eat the grapes. It certainly is a wonderful thing that the vineyard was completely stripped and ruined by them, so that only a few little bunches of grapes remained. But when the vintage came, the priest, trusting in the Saint's promise, gathered those little bunches of grapes and put them in the wine press and pressed them. And as St. Francis had promised, he obtained twenty measures of the very best wine that year.

By that miracle it was clearly shown that, just as through the merits of St. Francis the vineyard with its ruined grapes had produced an abundance of wine, so the Christian people, who were sterile in virtue because of sin, through the merits and teaching of St. Francis frequently brought forth good fruits of penance.[2]

To the glory of Our Lord Jesus Christ. Amen.

20 *How St. Francis Appeared in Glory to a Novice Who Was Tempted to Leave the Order*

A very delicate young man of noble birth entered the Order of St. Francis. A few days after he took the habit, through the instigation of the devil, he began to hate the habit he was wearing so much that he felt as though he was wearing a very coarse sack. The sleeves got on his nerves, he disliked the cowl, and the length and roughness of the habit seemed an unbearable burden to him. And so it happened that as his distaste for the Order increased, he firmly resolved to throw the habit away and return to the world.

Now the novicemaster of this young man, to whom he had been assigned in the beginning, had taught him that when he passed in front of the altar of the friary in which the Blessed Sacrament of the Body of Christ was kept, he should kneel down very reverently and bow very devoutly with his head uncovered and his hands crossed on his chest. And this young man always carefully did so.

And it happened on the night when he had decided to put aside the habit and leave the Order that he had to pass before the altar of the friary, and there, as usual, he knelt and bowed. And all of a sudden he was rapt in spirit and was shown a marvelous vision by God.

For he saw passing before him an almost countless throng of saints, two by two, in procession, and they were dressed in very ornate and precious vestments, and their faces and hands and the visible parts of their bodies were shining more radiantly than the sun. And they marched by, singing hymns, while angels were solemnly and beautifully chanting their joy.

Among those saints there were two who were more splendidly dressed and adorned and who were surrounded by such brilliance that they dazzled anyone who looked at them. And almost at the end of that procession he saw one who was adorned with such glory that he seemed like a new knight being especially honored by the others.

When that young man saw this vision, he was greatly amazed, and he did not know what the procession meant. Yet he did not question those who were passing by—nor could he as he was overwhelmed with bliss. But when the whole procession had passed and he saw only the last ones, he gained courage and ran to them, asking them very timidly: "Dear friends, I beg you to tell me who are those very wonderful persons who are in this venerable procession?"

They turned their radiant faces toward him and answered: "Son, all of us are Friars Minor who have just come from the glory of Paradise."

And he asked again: "Who are those two who shine more brightly than the others?"

And they replied: "Those two who are brighter than the others are St. Francis and St. Anthony. And that last one whom you saw being so honored is a holy friar who recently died. Because he fought valiantly against temptations and persevered in his holy undertaking until the end, we are now conducting him in triumph and glory to the joy of Paradise, with the Saints as companions, while the angels rejoice. And these very beautiful garments which we are wearing were given to us by God in exchange for the rough habits which we wore with patience as religious. And the glorious radiance which you see in us was given to us by God for the humble penance and holy poverty and obedience and pure chastity which we observed to the end with joyful minds and faces. Therefore, son, it should not be hard for you to wear the 'sack' of such a fruitful Order because if, with the 'sack' of St. Francis, for the love of Our Lord Jesus Christ, you despise the world and mortify your body and fight valiantly against the devil, you will likewise have a similar garment and will shine with us in glory."

And when they had said those words, the young man came back to himself. And encouraged by that vision, he rejected all temptation and acknowledged his fault before the guardian and the other friars.

Henceforth, moreover, he longed for the roughness of penance and of the habit as for wealth. And thus converted into a better man, he lived a very holy life and died in the Order.[1]

To the glory of Our Lord Jesus Christ. Amen.

21 *How St. Francis Tamed the Very Fierce Wolf of Gubbio*

At a time when St. Francis was staying in the town of Gubbio, something wonderful and worthy of lasting fame happened.

For there appeared in the territory of that city a fearfully large and fierce wolf which was so rabid with hunger that it devoured not only animals but even human beings. All the people in the town considered it such a great scourge and terror—because it often came near the town—that they took weapons with them when they went into the country, as if they were going to war. But even with their weapons they were not able to escape the sharp teeth and raging hunger of the wolf when they were so unfortunate as to meet it. Consequently everyone in the town was so terrified that hardly anyone dared go outside the city gate.

But God wished to bring the holiness of St. Francis to the attention of those people.

For while the Saint was there at that time, he had pity on the people and decided to go out and meet the wolf. But on hearing this the citizens said to him: "Look out, Brother Francis. Don't go outside the gate, because the wolf which has already devoured many people will certainly attack you and kill you!"

But St. Francis placed his hope in the Lord Jesus Christ who is master of all creatures. Protected not by a shield or a helmet, but arming himself with the Sign of the Cross, he bravely went out of the town with his companion, putting all his faith in the Lord who makes those who believe in Him walk without any injury on an asp and a basilisk and trample not merely on a wolf but even on a lion and a dragon. So with his very great faith St. Francis bravely went out to meet the wolf.

Some peasants accompanied him a little way, but soon they said to him: "We don't want to go any farther because that wolf is very fierce and we might get hurt."

When he heard them say this, St. Francis answered: "Just stay here. But I am going on to where the wolf lives."

Then, in the sight of many people who had come out and

climbed onto places to see this wonderful event, the fierce wolf came running with its mouth open toward St. Francis and his companion.

The Saint made the Sign of the Cross toward it. And the power of God, proceeding as much from himself as from his companion, checked the wolf and made it slow down and close its cruel mouth.

Then, calling to it, St. Francis said: "Come to me, Brother Wolf. In the name of Christ, I order you not to hurt me or anyone."

It is marvelous to relate that as soon as he had made the Sign of the Cross, the wolf closed its terrible jaws and stopped running, and as soon as he gave it that order, it lowered its head and lay down at the Saint's feet, as though it had become a lamb.

And St. Francis said to it as it lay in front of him: "Brother Wolf, you have done great harm in this region, and you have committed horrible crimes by destroying God's creatures without any mercy. You have been destroying not only irrational animals, but you even have the more detestable brazenness to kill and devour human beings made in the image of God. You therefore deserve to be put to death just like the worst robber and murderer. Consequently everyone is right in crying out against you and complaining, and this whole town is your enemy. But, Brother Wolf, I want to make peace between you and them, so that they will not be harmed by you any more, and after they have forgiven you all your past crimes, neither men nor dogs will pursue you any more."

The wolf showed by moving its body and tail and ears and by nodding its head that it willingly accepted what the Saint had said and would observe it.

So St. Francis spoke again: "Brother Wolf, since you are willing to make and keep this peace pact, I promise you that I will have the people of this town give you food every day as long as you live, so that you will never again suffer from hunger, for I know that whatever evil you have been doing was done because of the urge of hunger. But, my Brother Wolf, since I am obtaining such a favor for you, I want you to promise me that you will never hurt any animal or man. Will you promise me that?"

1349

The wolf gave a clear sign, by nodding its head, that it promised to do what the Saint asked.

And St. Francis said: "Brother Wolf, I want you to give me a pledge so that I can confidently believe what you promise."

And as St. Francis held out his hand to receive the pledge, the wolf also raised its front paw and meekly and gently put it in St. Francis' hand as a sign that it was giving its pledge.

Then St. Francis said: "Brother Wolf, I order you, in the name of the Lord Jesus Christ, to come with me now, without fear, into the town to make this peace pact in the name of the Lord."

And the wolf immediately began to walk along beside St. Francis, just like a very gentle lamb. When the people saw this, they were greatly amazed, and the news spread quickly throughout the whole town, so that all of them, men as well as women, great and small, assembled on the market place, because St. Francis was there with the wolf.

So when a very large crowd had gathered, St. Francis gave them a wonderful sermon, saying among other things that such calamities were permitted by God because of their sins, and how the consuming fire of hell by which the damned have to be devoured for all eternity is much more dangerous than the raging of a wolf which can kill nothing but the body, and how much more they should fear to be plunged into hell, since one little animal could keep so great a crowd in such a state of terror and trembling.

"So, dear people," he said, "come back to the Lord, and do fitting penance, and God will free you from the wolf in this world and from the devouring fire of hell in the next world."

And having said that, he added: "Listen, dear people. Brother Wolf, who is standing here before you, has promised me and has given me a pledge that he will make peace with you and will never hurt you if you promise also to feed him every day. And I pledge myself as bondsman for Brother Wolf that he will faithfully keep this peace pact."

Then all the people who were assembled there promised in a loud voice to feed the wolf regularly.

And St. Francis said to the wolf before them all: "And you, Brother Wolf, do you promise to keep this pact, that is, not to hurt any animal or human being?"

The wolf knelt down and bowed its head, and by twisting its body and wagging its tail and ears it clearly showed to everyone that it would keep the pact as it had promised.

And St. Francis said: "Brother Wolf, just as you gave me a pledge of this when we were outside the city gate, I want you to give me a pledge here before all these people that you will keep the pact and will never betray me for having pledged myself as your bondsman."

Then in the presence of all the people the wolf raised its right paw and put it in St. Francis' hand as a pledge.

And the crowd was so filled with amazement and joy, out of devotion for the Saint as well as over the novelty of the miracle and over the peace pact between the wolf and the people, that they all shouted to the sky, praising and blessing the Lord Jesus Christ who had sent St. Francis to them, by whose merits they had been freed from such a fierce wolf and saved from such a terrible scourge and had recovered peace and quiet.

From that day, the wolf and the people kept the pact which St. Francis made. The wolf lived two years more, and it went from door to door for food. It hurt no one, and no one hurt it. The people fed it courteously. And it is a striking fact that not a single dog ever barked at it.

Then the wolf grew old and died. And the people were sorry, because whenever it went through the town, its peaceful kindness and patience reminded them of the virtues and the holiness of St. Francis.[1]

Praised be Our Lord Jesus Christ. Amen.

22 *How St. Francis Freed Some Doves and Made Nests for Them*

A boy of the town of Siena caught a number of turtle doves in a snare, and he was carrying them all alive to the market to sell them.

But St. Francis, who was always very kind and wonderfully compassionate, especially toward gentle animals and little birds, was stirred by love and pity on seeing the doves. And he said to the boy who was carrying the doves: "Good boy, please give me those doves so that such innocent birds, which in Holy Scripture are symbols of pure, humble, and faithful souls, will not fall into the hands of cruel men who will kill them."

The boy was then inspired by God to give all the doves to St. Francis.

When the kind Father had gathered them to his bosom, he began to talk to them in a very gentle way, saying: "My simple, chaste, and innocent Sister Doves, why did you let yourselves be caught? I want to rescue you from death and make nests for you where you can lay your eggs and fulfill the Creator's commandment to multiply."

And St. Francis took them with him and made a nest for all of them.

And the doves settled in the nests made by St. Francis, and laid their eggs and reared their young right among the friars, and they increased in numbers. They were so tame and familiar with St. Francis and the other friars that they seemed to be like chickens that had always been raised by the friars. And they did not leave until St. Francis gave them permission, with his blessing.

The Saint had said to the boy who gave him the doves: "My son, one day you will become a Friar Minor in this Order, and you will serve Our Lord Jesus Christ well."

And it happened as the Saint foretold, because later the boy entered the Order and, through the merits of St. Francis, he led a praiseworthy and very exemplary life until he died.

So St. Francis not only obtained comfort for those little birds in this life but also the joys of eternal life for that youth.[1]

May Our Lord Jesus Christ be praised! Amen.

23   *How St. Francis Saw the Place of the*
       Portiuncula Besieged by Devils

Once at the Place of the Portiuncula, when St. Francis was praying devoutly, as was his custom, by divine revelation he saw the whole Place surrounded and besieged by devils, as by a great army. But not one of them was able to enter into the

Place because the friars were so holy that the devils could find no one to whom they could gain admittance.

However, while they were thus persevering, one of the friars was stirred to anger and impatience against one of his companions, and he thought how he could accuse him and take revenge on him. As a result, the gate of virtue being abandoned and the door of wickedness being open, he gave the devil a way to come in. And immediately, while St. Francis was watching, one of those devils entered into the Place and attacked that brother as a winner attacks a loser, and he crouched on the friar's neck.

When the compassionate Father and shepherd, who always watched over his flock very faithfully, saw that a wolf had entered to devour one of his little lambs, and knew that his sheep were in great danger, he had that friar called to him.

And when the friar obediently came running to his anxious shepherd, St. Francis ordered him to reveal at once the poison of hatred against his neighbor that he had conceived and kept in his heart, as a result of which he had given himself over to the enemy.

And he, seeing that the holy Father had read his thoughts, was afraid and revealed his wound—all his poison and rancor—and acknowledged his fault and humbly asked for forgiveness and a penance. And when he had done that, he was absolved from his sin and received the penance, and all of a sudden St. Francis saw the devil fly away.

And the friar, having thus been freed from the hands of the cruel beast, gave thanks to God and to St. Francis, and he persevered to the end in great holiness of life, through the merits of his shepherd.[1]

To the praise of the Lord Jesus Christ and of the holy Father. Amen.

24 *How St. Francis Converted the Sultan and the Prostitute Who Solicited Him to Sin*

Spurred on by zeal for the faith of Christ and incited by a desire for martyrdom, St. Francis at one time went beyond the seas with twelve of his very holy companions, planning to travel right to the Sultan of Babylonia.

Now when he arrived in a certain country of the Saracens, where such cruel men guarded the roads that no Christian passing through there could escape being killed, by the grace of God they were not killed, but were taken prisoners, beaten in various ways and very roughly bound and then led before the Sultan.

In his presence St. Francis preached under the guidance of the Holy Spirit in such a divine way about the holy Catholic faith that he offered to enter the fire for it. As a result, the Sultan began to feel great devotion for him, both because of the unshakable conviction of his faith and because of his contempt of the world—for though he was utterly poor he would not accept any gifts—and also because of his fervent longing for martyrdom. And thereafter the Sultan willingly listened to him and asked him to come back to see him many times. Moreover, he generously granted permission to him and to his companions to go anywhere and freely preach wherever they wished in all his empire. And he gave them a certain little token so that no one who saw it should harm them.[1]

After receiving that generous permission, St. Francis sent those chosen companions of his, two by two, into various lands of the Saracens to preach the faith of Christ. And with one companion he chose a certain district, and he went into an inn where he had to rest overnight. And there he found a certain woman who was very beautiful in face and body but very foul in mind and soul. That cursed woman solicited St. Francis to commit a most shameful act with her.

St. Francis answered her: "If you wish me to do what you want, you must also do what I want."

"I agree," she said. "So let's go and prepare a bed." And she led him toward a room.

But St. Francis said to her: "Come with me, and I will show you a very beautiful bed." And he led her to a very large fire that was burning in that house at that time. And in fervor of spirit he stripped himself naked and threw himself down on the fire in the fireplace as on a bed. And he called to her, saying: "Undress and come quickly and enjoy this splendid, flowery, and wonderful bed, because you must be here if you wish to obey me!" And he remained there for a long time with a joyful face, resting on the fireplace as though on flowers, but the fire did not burn or singe him.

On seeing such a miracle that woman was terrified and felt remorse in her heart. And she not only repented her sin and evil intention but was also perfectly converted to the faith of Christ, and through the merits of the holy Father she became so holy in grace that she won many souls for the Lord in that region.[2]

At last, seeing that he was unable to gather the fruit which he desired in that country, St. Francis, as a result of a revelation from God, prepared to return to the lands of the faithful with all his companions, and he assembled them together again. Then he went back to the Sultan and told him that he planned to leave.

The Sultan said to him: "Brother Francis, I would willingly be converted to the faith of Christ, but I am afraid to do it now, because these Saracens, if they heard about it, would immediately kill me and you, with all your companions. And since you can still do a great deal of good, and I have to do many important things for the salvation of my soul, I do not want to bring about your premature death and mine. But show me how I can achieve salvation, and I am ready to obey you in everything."

Then St. Francis said to him: "My Lord, I am leaving you now, but after I have returned to my country and at the call of God, gone to Heaven, after my death, through Divine Providence, I will send you two of my friars from whom you will receive the baptism of Christ and you will be saved, as my Lord Jesus Christ has revealed to me. And meanwhile free yourself from all that may hinder you, so that when the grace of Christ comes to you, He may find you well disposed in faith and devotion."

The Sultan gladly agreed and promised to do so, and he faithfully obeyed.

After saying good-by to him, St. Francis went back to the lands of the faithful with that venerable group of his holy companions. And after some years St. Francis gave up his soul to God by the death of the body.

And the Sultan grew ill. But awaiting the fulfillment of the dead Saint's promise, he stationed guards at the gates with orders to bring quickly to him two friars in the habit of St. Francis if they should show up.

At that time St. Francis appeared to two of his friars and ordered them to travel without delay to the Sultan and to obtain for him the salvation which the Saint had promised him. Those friars set out immediately and devoutly to fulfill his command. And after going over the sea, they were led to the Sultan by his guards.

When he saw them, the Sultan was filled with intense joy and he said: "Now I know indeed that the Lord has sent His servants to me for my salvation, as St. Francis promised me through a divine revelation."

And after receiving instructions in the faith of Christ and holy Baptism from those friars, he died reborn in that illness, and his soul was saved through the merits of St. Francis.[3]

To the glory of Christ the Blessed. Amen.

25 *How St. Francis Miraculously Healed a Man with Leprosy in Soul and Body*

That true disciple of Christ, St. Francis, while he was still living in this miserable and pitiable world, being enlightened by the Holy Spirit, always strove with all his strength to follow in the footsteps of Our Lord Jesus Christ, the perfect Master.

Thus as Christ Himself condescended to become a pilgrim, so St. Francis showed himself and his friars as true pilgrims, and he also had it written in the Rule that all his friars should serve the Lord in this world as pilgrims and strangers.

Moreover, as Christ came not only to serve people with leprosy, healing and cleansing them in body, but He also wished to die for them, sanctifying and cleansing them in their soul, so St. Francis, longing to be entirely conformed to Christ, used to serve victims of leprosy with very great affection, giving them food, washing their sore limbs, cleaning and washing their clothes, and, moreover, frequently and fervently giving them kisses. And so it happened many times that God by His power simultaneously healed the soul of one whose body the Saint healed, as we read of Christ.

1356

And therefore St. Francis not only served victims of leprosy willingly, but, in addition, he ordered that the friars of his Order should serve them with care wherever they might be going or staying in the world, for the love of Christ who for our sake wished to be considered like a man with leprosy. And the friars used to do this in many places very gladly, as truly obedient sons.[1]

Now it happened once, in a Place near the one where St. Francis was then living, that the friars were taking care of leprosy patients and sick people in a hospital. And a certain man was there who was so seriously ill with leprosy and so impatient and irritable that everyone was sure he was possessed by an evil spirit—and such was the case. For he not only attacked any of the friars who nursed him with horribly foul language and shot insults at them like arrows, but what was worse, he would also whip and wound them in various ways. Yet the most fearful and worst of all was that he would curse and blaspheme the Blessed Christ and His most holy Mother and the other Saints, so that no one could be found who could or would take care of him.

And although the friars tried to endure the insults and injuries meekly in order to increase the merit of their patience, their consciences could not tolerate his blasphemous insults to Christ and His holy Mother, lest they should seem to be participating in such a great sin. Therefore they decided to abandon that man completely in order not to become blasphemers of God and supporters of an instrument of the devil.

But they did not want to do this until they had duly told the whole story to St. Francis, who was then living in another Place nearby.

After hearing them, St. Francis went to that perverse man with leprosy, and entering, he greeted him: "God give you peace, my dear brother."

The man answered reproachfully: "What peace can I have from God, who has taken from me all peace and everything that is good, and has made me all rotten and stinking?"

And St. Francis said: "My dear son, be patient, because the weaknesses of the body are given to us in this world by God for the salvation of soul. So they are of great merit when they are borne patiently."

And the sick man replied: "How can I bear patiently this constant pain that is afflicting me day and night? For not only am I burned and crucified by my sickness, but I am sorely wronged by the friars whom you gave me to take care of me, because there is not one who serves me the way he should."

Then St. Francis, knowing by the Holy Ghost that he was troubled by an evil spirit, went and began to pray devoutly to God for him.

And having prayed, St. Francis came back to him and said: "Dear son, I want to take care of you, since you are not satisfied with the others."

And the sick man replied: "All right. But what more can you do for me than the others?"

And St. Francis said: "I will do whatever you want."

And the leprosy patient said: "I want you to wash me all over, because I smell so bad that I cannot stand it myself."

Then St. Francis immediately had water boiled with many sweet-scented herbs. Next, he undressed the man with leprosy and began to wash him with his holy hands, while another friar poured the water over him.

And by a divine miracle, wherever St. Francis touched him with his holy hands, the leprosy disappeared, and the flesh remained completely healed.

And as externally the water washed his body and the flesh began to heal and be wholly cleansed from leprosy, so too interiorly his soul began to be healed and cleansed. And when the man with leprosy saw himself being healed externally, he immediately began to have great compunction and remorse for his sins. And he began to cry very bitterly. Just as his body was washed with water and cleansed from leprosy, so his conscience was baptized by tears and contrition and cleansed from all evil and sin.

When he was completely washed and healed physically, he was perfectly anointed and healed spiritually. And he was overcome with such compunction and weeping that he humbly accused himself and cried out in a loud voice: "Woe to me, for I deserve hell for the insults and injuries I have given to the friars and for my impatience and blasphemies against God!"

So for a good fifteen days he kept bitterly lamenting his

sins with a remarkable wailing that burst from the inner depths of his soul. And he constantly sought nothing but the mercy of God. And with that compunction and weeping he confessed all his sins to a priest.

St. Francis, seeing such a clear miracle which God had performed through his hands, gave thanks to God and left there for a distant region, so that when that miracle became known to the people they should not all run to him, because through humility he wanted to flee any worldly glory, and in all that he did, as a faithful and prudent servant, he sought to procure the honor and glory of God and not his own, and to receive humiliation and disgrace among men for himself.

Later, as it pleased God, the man who had had leprosy and whose body and soul had been healed, soon after the fifteen days of his marvelous penance, fell sick with another illness. And well armed with the Sacraments of the Church, he died a holy death.

While St. Francis was praying in a certain remote Place in a forest, the dead man's soul, brighter than the sun, appeared to him in the air going to Paradise, and said to him: "Do you recognize me?"

St. Francis said to him: "Who are you?"

And he answered: "I am the man with leprosy whom the Blessed Christ healed through your merits. And today I am going to Paradise and to eternal life—for which I give thanks to God and to you. Blessed be your soul and your body, and blessed be your words and your deeds, because many souls are being saved and will be saved by you in the world. And know that there is not one day when the holy angels and all the other saints do not give fervent thanks to God for the holy fruits which are produced through you and your Order in different parts of the world. Therefore be comforted, and give thanks to God. And abide with the blessing of God!"

And having said those words, he disappeared on his way to Heaven.

And St. Francis remained much consoled.[2]

Praised be Christ. Amen.

26 How St. Francis Converted Three Murderous Robbers, and How the Pains of Hell and the Glory of Paradise Were Revealed to One of Them

Wishing to lead all men to salvation, the blessed Father Francis traveled through various provinces. And wherever he went, he always acquired a new family for the Lord because he was guided by the Spirit of God. As a vessel chosen by God, it was his mission to spread the balsam of grace. Therefore, he went to Slavonia, the Marches of Trevisi, the Marches of Ancona, Apulia, the Saracen country, and many other provinces, multiplying everywhere the servants of Our Lord Jesus Christ.

Once when St. Francis was going through Monte Casale, a village in the district of Borgo Sansepolcro, he was visited by a young nobleman of that town who was very delicate.

When he came to St. Francis, he said to him: "Father, I would like very much to become one of your friars."

But St. Francis answered him: "Son, you are young, delicate, and noble. Perhaps you could not endure our poverty and our hard life."

But he said: "Father, are you not men, as I am? So since you who are like me endure it, I too, with the help of Christ, will be able to bear it."

This answer pleased St. Francis very much, and he received him into the Order at once and gave him his blessing and named him Brother Angelo.

And that young man's conduct was so good that soon afterward St. Francis appointed him guardian of the Place of Monte Casale.

At this time there were in that area three famous robbers who committed many crimes thereabouts. One day those robbers came to the Place of the friars, and they asked Brother Angelo, the guardian, to give them something to eat. And the guardian answered, scolding them severely: "You robbers and cruel murderers—not only are you not ashamed of stealing from others the fruit of their labor, but in your audacity you even dare to eat up the offerings which have been given to the servants of God! You do not deserve that the earth should bear you up, for you respect no man and you scorn God who created you! So go about your business—and don't you ever come back here!"

They were angry at this, and they went away highly indignant.

That same day St. Francis came back to the Place, carrying a sack of bread and a little jug of wine which he had begged with his companions. And when the guardian told how he had driven the robbers away, St. Francis scolded him severely, saying: "You acted in a cruel way, because sinners are led back to God by holy meekness better than by cruel scolding. For our Master Jesus Christ, whose Gospel we have promised to observe, says that the doctor is not needed by those who are well but by the sick, and 'I have come to call not the just but sinners to penance,' and therefore He often ate with them. So, since you acted against charity and against the example of Jesus Christ, I order you under holy obedience to take right now this sack of bread and jug of wine which I begged. Go and look carefully for those robbers over the mountains and valleys until you find them. And offer them all this bread and this wine for me. And then kneel down before them and humbly accuse yourself of your sin of cruelty. And then ask them in my name not to do those evil things any more, but to fear God, and not to offend their neighbors. And if they do so, I promise them that I will supply them with provisions for their needs and I will give them food and drink all the time. And when you have humbly told them that, come back here."

While the guardian went to carry out St. Francis' order, the Saint began to pray and begged the Lord to soften the hearts of those robbers and convert them to repentance.

The obedient guardian found them and gave them the bread and wine, and did and said what St. Francis had commanded. And it pleased God that while those robbers were eating the gifts which St. Francis had sent them, they began to say to one another: "What terrible tortures are waiting in hell for us who are such miserable and unhappy men! For we go around not merely robbing and beating and wounding our neighbors but also killing them! And yet we feel no fear of God or remorse of conscience over those horrible crimes and murders that we commit. But here is this holy friar who just came to

us because of a few words which he said to us quite rightly
on account of our wickedness, and he very humbly accused
himself of his fault before us. And, besides, he brought us a
very generous promise of the holy Father and charitably gave
us the bread and wine. Those friars really are saints of God,
and they deserve Paradise. But we are sons of eternal damnation who deserve the pains of hell, and every day we increase
the vengeful flames by our horrible crimes. And we do not
know whether we will be able to obtain mercy from God for
the crimes and misdeeds which we have committed so far."

When one of them had said those and similar words, the
other two said: "What you say certainly is the truth. But what
should we do?"

And he said: "Let's go to St. Francis, and if he gives us
hope that we can obtain mercy from God for our great sins,
let's do whatever he commands us, so that we may free our
souls from the punishment of hell."

All three agreed to follow this advice. And so they went in
haste to St. Francis and said to him: "Father, because of our
many great sins we do not believe we can obtain mercy from
God, but if you have confidence that God will have mercy on
us, we are ready to do penance with you and to obey you
in whatever you command us."

Then St. Francis made them welcome with kindness and
holy affection, and he consoled them by telling them many inspiring true stories, and he gave them back assurance that
they would win God's mercy. Moreover he promised them that
he would obtain mercy and grace for them from the Lord
Jesus. He also taught them how the infinite greatness of divine
mercy surpasses all our sins, even if they are boundless, and
how, according to the Gospels and St. Paul the Apostle, Christ
came into this world in order to redeem sinners.

As a result of these wholesome instructions, the three robbers renounced the world and the devil and his works, and
St. Francis received them into the Order, and they remained
faithful to him in mind and deed. And they began to do great
penance.

Two of them lived only a short time after their praiseworthy
conversion and at God's call went from this world to Paradise.[1]

But the third lived on, and thinking over the many great

sins which he had committed, he began to do such penance that for fifteen successive years, except for the regular forty-day fasts which he made as the others did, on three days a week he always ate only a little bread and drank water. And he was satisfied with only one habit, and he always walked around barefoot, and he never slept after matins.

During that fifteen-year period St. Francis passed from this sad world to our home in Heaven.

Now when this friar had persevered in that strict penance for many years, one night after matins such a temptation to fall asleep came over him that he simply could not resist it and stay awake as he usually did. Finally, being unable to overcome his drowsiness or to pray, he yielded to the temptation and went and lay down on his bed to sleep.

The moment he rested his head on the bed, he fell into a rapture and was led in spirit up a very high mountain on which there was a very deep ravine. And on each side there were broken and splintered rocks and uneven ledges jutting out from the rocks, so that this ravine was a frightening thing to look at.

And the angel who was leading the friar held him over and then pushed him down from the top of that ravine. He fell down headlong, striking and bouncing off from rock to rock and ledge to ledge, until he reached the bottom of the ravine, where it seemed to him as though all his bones and limbs were shattered and broken.

And while he was lying wounded on the ground like that, his guide called to him: "Get up, because you still have a long journey to make."

The friar answered: "You seem to me a very unreasonable and cruel man, for although you see me dying from the fall that has broken me to pieces, yet you say to me, 'Get up!' "

And the angel went to him and by touching him instantaneously healed all his limbs and made him perfectly well.

And then the angel showed him a great plain full of sharp and cutting stones and thorns and briars and muddy and watery swamps, and told the friar that he had to walk barefoot across it until he came to the end of that plain, where there was a blazing furnace that could be seen from a distance, which he had to enter.

When the friar had crossed all the plain with great anguish

and pain and had reached the furnace, the angel said to him: "Go into that furnace, because you must."

The friar answered: "Oh, what a cruel guide you are to me! You see me nearly dead because of that frightful plain and so exhausted that I need a real rest—and now as rest you say to me, 'Go into that blazing furnace!'"

And while he looked at the furnace, he saw all around it many devils with red-hot iron pitchforks in their hands, with which they suddenly drove him in as he hesitated to enter.

When he had gone into the fire, he looked and saw a man who had been his godfather and who was all on fire. And he exclaimed: "Oh, unhappy godfather, how did you come here?"

And he replied: "Go a little farther into this fire and you will find my wife, your godmother, who will tell you the reason for our damnation."

When the friar had gone somewhat farther through the fire, the godmother appeared, all on fire, sitting enclosed in a measure of burning corn. And he asked her: "Oh, unfortunate and unhappy godmother, why have you fallen into such a cruel torment?"

And she replied: "Because during the great famine, which St. Francis prophesied would come, when my husband and I sold grain, we falsified the measure, and consequently I am burning in this narrow measure."[2]

After she had said those words and he had stood there for a while, the angel who was leading the friar thrust him out of the furnace, and then said to him: "Get ready to go on, because you still have a horrible peril to go through."

And he said, complaining: "Oh, you very cruel guide—you have no pity on me! You see that I have been nearly burned alive in that furnace—yet you say, 'Come on a dangerous and horrible journey!'"

But then the angel touched him and made him feel perfectly well and strong.

Next the angel led him to a bridge which he could not pass over without great danger because it was very small and narrow and very slippery and without any railing on the side. And underneath it flowed a terrible river filled with serpents and dragons and scorpions and toads, and it gave out a fearful stench. And the angel said to him: "Go across that bridge, because you must."

But he answered: "How can I go across it without falling into that dangerous river?"

The angel said: "Come after me, and put your foot where you see me put mine, and that way you will cross it all right."

The friar walked after the angel, as he had told him, and he safely reached the middle of the bridge.

And when he was there in the middle, the angel flew away, up to a very marvelous mansion on top of a very high mountain, a long way off on the far side of the bridge. And he noticed that the angel had flown away. But when he remained on the bridge without a guide, and he looked down and saw the heads of those horrible beasts rising out of the river with mouths open, ready to devour him if he fell, he was so terrified that he simply did not know what to do or say, because he could not go forward or backward.

So, finding himself in such trouble and danger, and seeing that he had no one to turn to except God, he bowed down and embraced the bridge and began to call on the Lord Jesus Christ with all his heart, sobbing, that He might deign to save him by His most holy mercy. And after he had prayed, it seemed to him that wings were growing on him. And with great joy he waited until they had grown, hoping that he would be able to fly to the far side of the river where the angel had flown.

But after some time, owing to his great desire to cross that bridge and his haste, he began to fly, and because his wings were not yet fully grown, he fell onto the bridge, and all the feathers also fell out. So in his fright he again clung to the bridge and begged with tears for Christ's mercy, as before.

And after he had prayed, again it seemed to him that his wings were growing. But like the first time he hastened to fly without waiting for them to grow perfectly, and again he fell down onto the bridge, and his wings dropped off as before.

Realizing that he fell that way because of the haste he had to fly before he was ready, he began to say to himself: "If the wings grow a third time, I certainly will wait until they are big enough so that I can fly without falling again."

And while he was thinking this, he saw the wings growing

for the third time, and he waited a long time until they were quite large. And it seemed to him that between the first and second and third growth of wings he had to wait for a hundred and fifty years or more. But finally, when he believed that the wings had grown to perfection, for the third time he raised himself in the air with all his strength and flew up to the palace to which the angel had flown.

When he reached the gate of that marvelous palace, he knocked, and the gatekeeper asked him: "Who are you who have come here?"

He answered: "I am a Friar Minor."

The gatekeeper said: "Wait for me, because I am going to bring St. Francis to see whether he acknowledges you."

While he went for St. Francis, the friar began to look at the wonderful walls of that marvelous palace. And those walls seemed so transparent with brightness that he could clearly see all that was going on inside and the choirs of saints who were inside. And while he was gazing at them in amazement, St. Francis and the holy Brother Bernard and Brother Giles appeared, and after St. Francis such a great multitude of men and women saints of God who had followed in his footsteps that they seemed to be countless.

And when St. Francis came to him, he said to the gatekeeper: "Let him come in, because he is one of my friars."

Then St. Francis led him in. As soon as the friar entered, he felt such consolation and sweetness that he forgot all the tribulations he had had before, as if they had never happened.

Then St. Francis showed him many wonderful things there, and later said to him: "Son, you have to go back to the world and stay there for seven days. During that time prepare yourself carefully and with all devotion, as well as you can, because after the seven days I will come for you, and then you will accompany me to this marvelous place of the blessed."

St. Francis was dressed in a wonderful robe adorned with very beautiful stars, and his five Stigmata were like five very bright stars which radiated such brilliance that they lit up the whole palace with their rays. And Brother Bernard had on his head a very beautiful crown of stars. And Brother Giles was radiant with bright light. And he recognized many other holy

Friars Minor in glory with St. Francis whom he had never seen in the world.

Having taken leave of St. Francis, he returned to the world, though quite unwillingly. When he awoke and came back to himself and recovered consciousness, the friars were ringing for prime, so that although it seemed to him like many years, the time in which he had had that vision was not more than from matins until the dawn of the same night.

And the friar told his guardian the vision and also about the period of seven days. And soon he began to have a fever.

And on the seventh day St. Francis came for him with a great throng of glorious saints, as he had promised. And he led to the joys of the blessed in the Kingdom of Eternal Life the soul of that friar that had been purified in the vision under the guidance of the angel.[3]

To the praise and glory of Our Lord Jesus Christ. Amen.

27 How St. Francis Converted Two Students in Bologna

At one time while St. Francis was traveling, he came to the city of Bologna. When the people heard about his arrival, they ran to see him, and there was such a crowd that he could hardly walk. For they all wanted to see him, as a new flower of the world and an angel of the Lord, so that he had a hard time to reach the city square.

And when the entire square was filled with men and women and students, St. Francis stood up on a high place in the center and began to preach what the Holy Spirit dictated to him. And he preached such marvelous and astounding things that he seemed to be not a man but an angel. And his heavenly words seemed like sharp arrows which were shot from the bow of divine wisdom and pierced the hearts of everyone so effectively that by this sermon he converted a very great multitude of men and women from a state of sin to remorse and penance.[1]

Among them were two noble students from the Marches of Ancona. One was called Pellegrino, whose home was in Falerone, and the other's name was Riccieri from Muccia.

Among others whose hearts had been touched interiorly by divine inspiration through the sermon, they came to St. Francis, saying that they had an intense desire to leave the world and receive the habit of his friars.

Then St. Francis, considering their fervor, knew by a revelation of the Holy Spirit that they were sent by God, and moreover he understood what way of life each of them would find most suitable. Therefore he received them with joy, saying to them: "You, Pellegrino, keep to the path of humility in the Order. And you, Riccieri, serve the friars."

And so it happened. For Brother Pellegrino never wanted to become a cleric but remained a lay brother, although he was a very learned scholar and an expert in Roman law. By means of that humility he attained to very great perfection in virtue and especially to the grace of compunction and love for Our Lord Jesus Christ.

For inflamed by the love of Christ and burning with the desire for martyrdom, he went to Jerusalem in order to visit the Holy Places of the Savior, carrying with him the Book of the Gospels. And when he read about the sacred places where the God-man had walked, and he touched them with his feet and saw them with his eyes, he bowed down to pray to God and confidently embraced those very holy spots with his arms and lovingly kissed them with his lips and moistened them with tears of devotion, so that he inspired great devotion in all who saw him.

As Divine Providence ordained, he returned to Italy. And like a true pilgrim and citizen of the heavenly Kingdom, he very rarely visited his noble relatives. He would encourage them to despise the world, and by his serious conversation he would urge them to love God, and then, quickly and hurriedly, he would leave them, saying that Christ Jesus who makes the soul noble is not found among relatives and familiar friends.

Brother Bernard, the first-born son of our very holy Father Francis, used to say something truly wonderful about this Brother Pellegrino, namely, that he was one of the most perfect friars in this world.

And he really was a pilgrim. For the love of Christ, which he always had in his heart, did not allow him to find peace in any creature or to attach his affections to any temporal thing, but he always strove for his heavenly home and looked to his heavenly home, and he climbed from virtue to virtue until he transformed the lover into the loved one. Finally Brother Pellegrino passed, full of virtue, from this life to Christ whom he loved with all his heart, and rested in peace, with many miracles before and after his death.[2]

Brother Riccieri, the companion of Brother Pellegrino on earth and now his fellow citizen in Heaven, led an active life, living in great sanctity and humility, traveling on foot, and devoutly and faithfully serving his neighbors, the friars. And he became very intimate and popular with St. Francis, so that he learned many things from the Saint and under his instruction clearly grasped the truth concerning many doubtful points, and he perceived the will of the Lord in matters with which he had to deal. And as the holy Father prophesied, he served the friars. He was appointed Minister in the Province of the March of Ancona. And owing to the zeal for God which always burned in his heart, he governed the province for a long time in great peace and wisdom, following the example of Christ who preferred action to teaching.

Now after some time, for the good of his soul, Divine Providence permitted a very great temptation to come over him, so that in his intense anxiety and trouble he afflicted himself severely with abstinence and disciplines and tears and prayers day and night. But he could not free himself from that temptation. And many times he was led into intense despair, because owing to the power of the temptation he believed himself abandoned by God.

But while he was plunged into extreme desolation and desperation, he reflected in his heart and said to himself: "I will get up and go to my Father Francis. And if he welcomes me and shows himself friendly to me, as he usually does, I believe that God will still be merciful to me. But if not, it will be a sign that I have been abandoned by God. . . ."

So he set out and went to St. Francis. The Saint was then lying seriously ill in the palace of the Bishop of Assisi. And while he was meditating about God, the whole matter of that friar's temptation and desperation and plan and coming was revealed to him by God.

St. Francis immediately called his companions, Brother

Masseo and Brother Leo, and said to them: "Go out quickly to meet my dear son Riccieri, and embrace and welcome him for me, and tell him that of all the friars who are in the world, I have a special love for him."

Now like obedient sons they went right out to meet Brother Riccieri. And finding him on the road, as St. Francis had said, they embraced him and told him the Father's loving words, which so filled his soul with sweet consolation that he was almost beside himself with joy. How happy he showed himself, and how he expressed his joy, and how he praised and thanked God with all his heart because God had made his journey successful, can hardly be put in words. O good Jesus, You never abandon those who hope in You, but always give us strength with a temptation so that we can sustain it!

He went to the place where that angelic and godlike man Francis was lying. And although St. Francis was gravely sick, he got to his feet and went to meet Brother Riccieri. And embracing him affectionately, he said to him: "My very dear son, Brother Riccieri, among all the friars who are in the world I have a special love for you."

And after saying that, he made the Sign of the Cross on his forehead and lovingly kissed him on the same spot and then said to him: "My beloved son, God gave you that temptation in order that you might gain very great merit. But if you do not want any more of that merit, you will not have it."

It is wonderful to relate that as soon as St. Francis had said those words, all that diabolical temptation suddenly left the friar, as though he had never in his life felt it. And he remained utterly consoled in God.[3]

To the glory of Our Lord Jesus Christ. Amen.

28 About Brother Bernard's Gift of Contemplation

How much grace God often gave to the poor men who followed the Gospel and who voluntarily gave up all things for the love of God was manifested in Brother Bernard of Quintavalle who, after he had taken the habit of St. Francis, was very frequently rapt in God by the contemplation of heavenly things.

Thus one time it happened that while he was attending Mass in a church and his whole mind was on God, he became so absorbed and rapt in contemplation that during the Elevation of the Body of Christ he was not at all aware of it and did not kneel down when the others knelt, and he did not draw his cowl back as did the others who were there, but he stayed motionless, without blinking his eyes, gazing straight ahead, from morning until none.

But after none he came back to himself and went through the Place shouting in a voice filled with wonder: "Oh, Brothers! Oh, Brothers! Oh, Brothers! There is no man in all this country, no matter how great and noble he is, who, if he were promised a very beautiful palace full of gold, would not willingly carry a sack full of the most filthy manure in order to obtain that very noble treasure!"

Now the mind of this Brother Bernard was so uplifted to that heavenly treasure which is promised to those who love God that for fifteen continuous years he always went about with both his mind and his face raised toward Heaven. And during those fifteen years, because his mind was raised to the light of Heaven and his feelings were utterly absorbed by divine graces, he never satisfied his hunger at meals. He used to eat a little of everything that was set before him, for he used to say that to abstain from what a man does not enjoy cannot be called perfect abstinence, because true abstinence is to resist things that taste good.

He also attained to such clarity of understanding that even great scholars of the Church consulted him for solutions of difficult questions, and he unraveled obscure problems in whatever passage of the Bible they requested.

And because his mind was utterly freed and detached from earthly matters, he used to soar to the heights of contemplation as a swallow flies high up into the sky. And sometimes for twenty days, sometimes for thirty days, he used to stay alone on the tops of mountains, contemplating heavenly things. Therefore Brother Giles used to say of him that this gift which was given to Brother Bernard of Quintavalle was not given by

God to everyone, namely, that he should feed while flying, like swallows.[1]

And because of that outstanding grace which had been given him by the Lord, St. Francis used to talk with him willingly and frequently both day and night. So that sometimes they were found to have spent an entire night together rapt in God in the woods, where they had met to talk about Our Lord Jesus Christ, who is blessed forever and ever. Amen.

29 *How St. Francis Freed Brother Rufino from a Temptation of the Devil*

Brother Rufino, one of the great noblemen of Assisi, a companion of St. Francis and a man of great sanctity, was once, while St. Francis was alive, very fiercely attacked and tempted in his soul by the devil on the subject of predestination. For the ancient enemy injected the suggestion into his heart that he was damned and was not among those who were predestined to eternal life, and that whatever he did in the service of the Order was wasted. As a result of this temptation, which lasted many days, he became very sad and depressed, and he was ashamed to tell St. Francis about his conflict. Nevertheless, he did not stop performing his usual prayers and fasts.

Therefore the ancient enemy, wishing to heap sorrow onto sorrow, which sorely wounds the servants of God, also added to his inner struggle an outer one by attacking him outwardly by false apparitions.

So one day he appeared to him in the form of the Crucified One and said to him: "Oh, Brother Rufino, why do you afflict yourself with prayers and penances since you are not among those who are predestined to eternal life? And you should believe me, because I know whom I have chosen and predestined. And do not believe the son of Peter Bernardone if he tells you the contrary. And also do not ask him about this matter, because neither he nor anyone else knows it—no one but I who am the Son of God knows it. Therefore believe me for sure that you are among the damned. And Brother Francis himself, your Father, is also damned. And whoever follows him is deceived."

1372

Brother Rufino on hearing these words became so darkened by the Prince of Darkness that he lost all the faith and love which he had had for St. Francis, and did not want to tell him anything about himself.

But the Holy Spirit revealed what Brother Rufino did not tell the holy Father. Therefore, when St. Francis perceived spiritually the great peril of Brother Rufino, he sent Brother Masseo to him to tell him to come to him. For Brother Rufino and St. Francis and Brother Masseo were staying at the Place of Mount Subasio near Assisi.

Brother Rufino answered sharply: "What have I to do with Brother Francis?"

Then Brother Masseo, who was filled with divine wisdom, clearly recognizing the deceit of the evil enemy, said: "Oh, Brother Rufino, don't you know that Brother Francis is like an angel of God who has brought light to so many souls in the world and from whom we too have so many gifts of God's grace? Therefore, by all means I urge you to come to him, because I clearly see that you are deceived by the devil."

On hearing this, Brother Rufino set out at once and went to St. Francis. And when St. Francis saw him coming in the distance, he began to cry: "Oh, Brother Rufino, you naughty boy, whom have you believed?"

And when Brother Rufino came to him, the Saint told him in detail all about the temptation, exterior and interior, which he had had from the devil. And he showed Brother Rufino clearly that the one who had appeared to him and had suggested the above-mentioned things to him was the devil and not Christ, and therefore he should in no way consent to his suggestions.

"But when the devil says to you again, 'You are damned,'" St. Francis said, "you answer him confidently, 'Open your mouth—and I will [empty my bowels] in it!'[1] And let it be a sign to you that he is the devil that when you say those words, he will immediately go away. You should also have known that he was the devil because he hardened your heart to everything that is good, for that is exactly his job. But the Blessed Christ never hardens the heart of the faithful man but rather softens it, as He says through the Prophet: 'I will take away your heart of stone and will give you a heart of flesh.'"

Then Brother Rufino, seeing that St. Francis had told him in detail all about his interior and exterior temptation, and being moved to remorse by his words, began to weep bitterly and knelt before him and humbly acknowledged his fault in having concealed his temptation from him. And he remained greatly consoled and comforted by the advice of the holy Father and completely changed for the better.

Finally St. Francis said to him: "Go to confession, son. And do not stop devoting yourself to your usual prayers. And know for sure that this temptation will be very helpful and consoling to you, as you will find out in a short while."

So Brother Rufino went back to his cell to pray in the woods. And while he was praying with many tears, the ancient enemy came in the appearance of Christ, as in the previous apparitions, and said to him: "Brother Rufino, didn't I tell you not to believe the son of Peter Bernardone and not to exhaust yourself with weeping and praying, because you are damned? What good does it do you to afflict yourself while you are alive, since when you die you will be damned?"

Brother Rufino quickly answered: "Open your mouth—and I will [empty my bowels] in it!"[2]

Then the devil angrily went away with such a commotion and fall of rocks on Mount Subasio (which was nearby) that a great mass of stones hurtled down for a long while, where the fearful ravine filled with rocks is still to be seen. And the collisions of the falling rocks caused horrible flashes of fire through the ravine of that mountain. The noise of the stones was so frightful that St. Francis and his companions were amazed and came out of the Place in order to see what was happening.

Then Brother Rufino clearly realized that it had been the devil who had deceived him. So he went back to St. Francis and prostrated himself on the ground and accused himself again of his fault.

And St. Francis comforted him once more with kind words and sent him back to his cell deeply consoled.

Later while he was praying in it very devoutly, the Blessed Christ appeared to him and made his whole soul burn with divine love, saying: "Son, you did well to believe Brother Francis, because he who made you depressed was the devil. But

I am Christ, your Master, and to make you perfectly sure of it I give you this sign: as long as you live, you will never again be sad or depressed."

And after saying that, Christ gave Brother Rufino His blessing and left him in such joy and peace of soul and inspiration of mind that he was absorbed in God day and night.

Thereafter he was so confirmed in grace and in the assurance of his eternal salvation that he became completely changed into a new man. And his mind was so concentrated on Heaven and he persevered so much in prayer that he would spend days and nights in praying and in contemplating divine things, if others would let him.

Therefore St. Francis used to say of him that Brother Rufino had been canonized in Heaven by the Lord Jesus Christ while he was still alive and that he would not hesitate to say "St. Rufino" (except in his presence), though he was still living on earth.[3]

To the glory of Our Lord Jesus Christ. Amen.

30 *How St. Francis Sent Brother Rufino to Preach in Assisi without His Habit*

Brother Rufino was so absorbed in God as a result of continual contemplation that he became almost mute and insensible to external things. He used to speak very rarely, and, besides, he had neither the gift nor courage nor ability to preach the word of God.

Nevertheless, one day St. Francis told Brother Rufino to go to Assisi and preach to the people whatever God would inspire him to say.

But Brother Rufino answered: "Reverend Father, please excuse me and don't send me on that assignment because, as you well know, I do not have the grace of preaching, and also I am just a simple ignorant fellow."

Then St. Francis said: "Because you did not obey me at once, I also command you under holy obedience to go to Assisi naked—wearing only your breeches—and to go into some church and preach to the people naked like that!"

At this command Brother Rufino obediently undressed and

went to Assisi naked and entered into a church. And after he had knelt in reverence before the altar, he went up into the pulpit and began to preach.

At this, the children and men began to laugh and to say: "Look—they are doing so much penance they have gone crazy!"

Meanwhile, St. Francis, thinking over the prompt obedience of Brother Rufino, who was one of the foremost gentlemen of Assisi, and the very difficult command he had given him, began to reproach himself very severely, saying: "How can you, the son of Peter Bernardone—you vile little wretch—order Brother Rufino, who is one of the noblest citizens of Assisi, to go naked and preach to the people like a madman? By God, I am going to see to it that you yourself experience what you order others to do!"

And having said that, in the fervor of the Holy Spirit he too immediately took off his habit and went to Assisi naked, accompanied by Brother Leo, who very discreetly carried along the Saint's habit and Brother Rufino's.

And when the people of Assisi saw him naked too, they laughed at him as at a lunatic, thinking that both he and Brother Rufino had gone mad from doing too much penance.

But St. Francis found and entered the church where Brother Rufino had already begun to preach. And he was saying these words devoutly and severely: "Oh, dear people, flee the world. Give up sin. Restore to others what belongs to them if you want to escape hell. But keep God's commandments and love God and your neighbor if you want to go to Heaven. And do penance, because the Kingdom of Heaven is drawing near!"

Then St. Francis went up naked into the pulpit, and he began to preach so marvelously about contempt for the world, holy penance, holy voluntary poverty, the desire for the Kingdom of Heaven, and about the nakedness and humiliations and most holy Passion of Our Lord Jesus Christ Crucified that the whole crowd of men and women who had gathered there for the sermon in great numbers began to weep very bitterly. And with unbelievable devotion and compunction of heart they cried out aloud to God for mercy, so that nearly all of them were converted to a new state of mind.

And not only there, but throughout all Assisi on that day

there was such mourning among the people over the Passion of Our Lord Jesus Christ that so much weeping had never been heard in that town.

And after the people had thus been edified and Christ's sheep had been consoled by the deed of St. Francis and Brother Rufino, and after they had received a blessing in the name of Our Lord Jesus Christ, St. Francis put Brother Rufino's habit on him again, and he himself got dressed with him.

And so wearing their habits once more, they went back to the Place of the Portiuncula, glorifying and praising the Lord for having given them the grace to overcome themselves by self-contempt and for having edified the little sheep of Christ by their good example and for having shown how the world is to be despised.

And on that day the devotion of the people toward them increased so much that those who could touch the hem of their clothes considered themselves blessed.[1]

To the glory of Our Lord Jesus Christ, who is blessed! Amen.

31 *How Brother Rufino Was One of Three Chosen Souls*

Just as Our Lord Jesus Christ says in the Gospel, "I know my sheep, and Mine know Me," so our blessed Father Francis, like a good shepherd, knew by divine revelation all the merits and virtues of his companions. And furthermore he knew their faults and failings. Consequently he knew how to provide the best remedy for all by humbling the proud and exalting the humble and by blaming vices and praising virtues, as we read in the wonderful revelations which he had concerning that first family of his.

For once—to record only one instance among many—St. Francis was sitting in a certain little Place with his companions and he was talking with them about God. But Brother Rufino, a man who was very remarkable for his holiness, was not with them then in that conversation because he had not yet come out of the woods, where he had gone to pray and contemplate. And while St. Francis was continuing his holy exhortations and holy conversation with those companions, Brother

Rufino—a noble citizen of Assisi but a still more noble servant of God, who was of virginal purity and uplifted by the noble grace of divine contemplation and adorned by the sweet-smelling flowers of virtue before God and men—came out of the forest where he had been contemplating heavenly things and passed by not far from St. Francis.

When the Saint perceived him in the distance, he turned to his companions and asked them: "Tell me, dear Brothers, who do you think is the holiest soul that God has in the world now?"

And they humbly answered that they thought he himself was honored with that privilege.

But St. Francis said to them: "I am of myself the most unworthy and the vilest man that God has in the world. But do you see Brother Rufino there coming out of the woods? God has revealed to me that his soul is one of the three holiest souls that God has in this world now. And I frankly tell you that I would not hesitate to call him St. Rufino while he is still living his life in the body, since his soul has been confirmed in grace and sanctified and canonized in Heaven by Our Lord Jesus Christ."

But St. Francis never said those words in the presence of Brother Rufino.

In such incidents it was shown that like a good shepherd, the holy Father knew his sheep in their failings also, as he clearly showed with Brother Elias, whom he scolded several times for his pride; and with Brother Giovanni di Capella, to whom he prophesied that because of his malice he would hang himself by the throat; and with that friar whose throat the devil held fast when he was corrected for disobedience; and with the friars who were coming from Terra di Lavoro, when he reproved one of them for the offense he gave his companion on the way. Moreover, he knew those sheep of his in whom grace abounded, as is evident with Brother Bernard and Brother Rufino and many other friars, whose secret faults and virtues he clearly knew by revelation from the Blessed Christ. Amen.[1]

32 *How Christ Appeared to Brother Masseo*

Those first companions of our blessed Father Francis who were poor in material things but rich in God did not hope or strive to become rich in gold or silver but tried with all their strength to enrich themselves with holy virtues, by which we attain the true everlasting riches of Heaven.

It happened one day that Brother Masseo, one of the holy Father's chosen companions, was with them while they were talking about God. And one of them told this story: "There was a man who was a great friend of God and who had much grace in the active and the contemplative life, and at the same time he had such extreme and profound humility that he considered himself a very great sinner. That humility sanctified and confirmed him in grace and made him constantly grow in virtues and gifts of God, and what is still better, it never let him fall away from God in sin."

When Brother Masseo heard these marvelous things about humility and realized that it was the treasure of salvation and eternal life, he began to be inflamed with such love and desire for that virtue of humility, which was most worthy of divine favor, that, looking up toward Heaven, with great fervor he made a vow and a very powerful resolve never to consent to rejoice in this world until he should feel that most excellent humility perfectly present in his soul.

And after he had made that vow with a holy motive, he remained shut up in his cell almost all the time every day, afflicting himself with fasts, vigils, prayers, and a very bitter weeping before God in order to obtain that virtue without which he considered himself worthy of hell and with which, as he had heard, that friend of God had been so richly endowed.

And while Brother Masseo remained sad in that desire for many days, it happened that he went into the forest one day. And he was going through it in fervor of spirit, uttering mournful cries and tearful sighs, ardently begging the Lord to give him that divine virtue.

And because the Lord heals those who are contrite in heart and willingly hears the prayers of the humble, while Brother Masseo was standing there, a Voice came from Heaven that called him twice: "Brother Masseo! Brother Masseo!"

And he knew by the Holy Spirit that it was the Voice of Christ, and he answered: "My Lord!"

And Christ said to him: "What do you want to give—what do you want to give in order to possess that grace you are asking for?"

And Brother Masseo replied: "Lord, the eyes out of my head!"

And Christ said to him: "But I want you to have your eyes and the grace too."

And after saying that, the Voice vanished. And Brother Masseo remained so filled with the grace of the desired virtue of humility and with the light of God that from then on he rejoiced all the time. And often when he was praying, he would express his joy in a soft constant cooing sound like a gentle dove: "Ooo-Ooo." And he would remain in contemplation that way, with a joyful expression on his face and a happy heart. Moreover, he became extremely humble and considered himself the least of all the men in the world.

Brother James of Falerone, of holy memory, asked him why he never changed tone in his rejoicing. And he replied very joyfully: "Because when we have found all that is good in one thing, it is not necessary to change tone."[1]

To the glory of Our Lord Jesus Christ. Amen.

33 How St. Clare Miraculously Imprinted the Cross on Some Loaves of Bread

St. Clare, a most devout disciple of the Cross of Christ and a noble little plant of St. Francis, was so holy that not only bishops and cardinals but also the Pope strongly desired to see and hear her, and often visited her in person.

At one time among others the Pope went to St. Clare's monastery in order to listen to her heavenly and divine conversation, for she was a shrine of the Holy Spirit. And as both of them conversed for a long time about the salvation of the soul and the praise of God, St. Clare meanwhile ordered loaves of bread to be set out on the tables for all the Sisters, for she wished to keep those loaves after they had been blessed by the Vicar of Christ.

So when their very holy conversation was over, the Saint knelt with great reverence and asked the Supreme Pontiff whether he would deign to bless the loaves of bread which had been placed on the tables.

The Pope answered: "Very faithful Sister Clare, I want you to bless those loaves of bread and to make over them the Sign of the Cross of Christ to whom you have offered yourself completely as a spotless sacrifice."

But St. Clare replied: "Most Holy Father, please excuse me, but I would deserve to be severely blamed if a vile little woman like myself should presume to give such a blessing in the presence of the Vicar of Christ."

And the Pope answered: "So that it should not be attributed to presumption, but that you may also earn merit by doing it, I command you under holy obedience to make the Sign of the Cross over these loaves of bread and to bless them in the name of Our Lord Jesus Christ."

Then St. Clare, as a truly obedient daughter, very devoutly made the Sign of the Cross over those loaves of bread and blessed them. And a marvelous thing happened: all of a sudden a very beautiful and clearly marked cross appeared on all the loaves.

Afterwards some of those loaves were eaten with great devotion, and some were set aside as evidence of the miracle for the future.

And when the Holy Father saw the miraculous cross that had been made by the spouse of Christ, he first gave thanks to God and then, after granting to St. Clare the consolation of his blessing, he took some of the bread and left.

At that time there were living in that monastery Sister Ortolana, St. Clare's mother, and Sister Agnes, her sister, all of whom, with many other holy nuns and spouses of Christ, were full of virtue and of the Holy Spirit. St. Francis used to send many sick persons to them. And by the power of their prayers and of the Cross, which they loved with all their hearts, they would restore to health everyone over whom they made the Sign of the Cross.[1]

To the glory of Christ. Amen.

34 *How St. Louis, the King of France, Visited Brother Giles*

When St. Louis, the King of France, decided to go on a pilgrimage and visit the shrines throughout the world, he heard reliable reports about the wonderful holiness of the saintly Brother Giles, who had been one of the first companions of St. Francis, and he resolved and set his heart on paying him a personal visit. Therefore in that journey he made a detour to Perugia, where he had heard that Brother Giles was staying at that time.

And upon arriving at the gate of the friars' Place as a poor and unknown pilgrim with only a few companions, he asked very earnestly for Brother Giles, without telling the brother porter who it was who was asking for him. So the brother porter went and told Brother Giles that some pilgrim was asking for him at the gate.

Now Brother Giles immediately perceived spiritually that it was the King of France. So in great fervor he came out of his cell and quickly ran to the gate. And without asking any questions, though neither had ever seen the other, both of them hastened to embrace each other, kneeling together very devoutly and exchanging an affectionate kiss, as though they had been intimate friends for a long time. Despite all this, they did not say anything to each other, but remained in that embrace, with those gestures of loving friendship, in silence. And after they had stayed that way for a long time without saying a word, they separated. And St. Louis continued on his journey, and Brother Giles went back to his cell.

But while King Louis was leaving, a friar asked one of his companions who was the man who had hastened to embrace Brother Giles so affectionately, and the other answered that he was King Louis of France who had wanted to see Brother

Giles during his pilgrimage. And after saying this, he and the King's companions rode rapidly away.

Now the friars were very sorry that Brother Giles had not said a single good word to the King, and they complained to him very much, saying: "Oh, Brother Giles, how is it that you were unwilling to say anything to such a great King who came from France in order to see you and hear some good words from you?"

Brother Giles answered: "Dear Brothers, do not be surprised that neither he nor I was able to say anything to each other, because in the moment when we embraced, the light of divine wisdom revealed his heart to me and mine to him. And so by God's grace we looked into each other's hearts, and whatever he thought of saying to me or I to him, we heard without sound made by lips and tongue even better than if we had spoken with our lips—and with greater consolation. For if we had wanted to explain with the help of our voices what we felt in our hearts, because of the defect of human language, which cannot clearly express the secret mysteries of God except by mystic symbols, that conversation would have saddened rather than consoled us. And so you should know for sure that the King departed marvelously consoled."[1]

To the glory of Our Lord Jesus Christ. Amen.

35 *How St. Clare Was Miraculously Carried on Christmas Eve to the Church of St. Francis*

At one time the most devout spouse of Christ, St. Clare, while staying at San Damiano, was seriously ill, so that she was unable to go and say the office in church with the other nuns.

Now the Feast of the Nativity of Our Blessed Lord Jesus Christ came, when the Sisters used to recite matins and devoutly receive Holy Communion at the Mass of the Nativity. While all the others went to matins, St. Clare remained alone in bed, seriously ill and very sad because she could not go with the others to attend such a holy ceremony and have that spiritual consolation.

But Our Lord Jesus Christ wished to give this most faithful spouse of His a consolation, and He miraculously let her attend in spirit both the matins and the Mass as well as the whole celebration of the Feast by the friars in the Church of St. Francis, so that she clearly heard the organ and the friars' chanting to the end of the Mass. Moreover, she received Holy Communion and was fully consoled. Then He had her carried back to bed.

Now when the Sisters had finished the office in San Damiano, they came back to St. Clare and said to her: "Oh, dear Mother, Sister Clare, what great consolations we have had in this holy Feast of the Savior's Nativity—if only you could have been with us!"

But she answered: "My dear little sisters and daughters, I give thanks and praise to God, my Blessed Lord Jesus Christ, because my soul had the consolation of attending all the ceremonies of this most holy night—but still greater and more solemn and beautiful ones than yours. For by the grace of my Lord Jesus Christ and through the intercession of my most blessed Father St. Francis, I was present in the Church of my Father St. Francis, and with my bodily and spiritual ears I heard all the chanting and the organ, and moreover I received Holy Communion there. So rejoice and praise Our Blessed Jesus Christ with all your hearts for such a great grace which He gave me, since while I was lying here sick, as I said, I was present at the whole ceremony in the Church of St. Francis— whether in the body or outside the body, I don't know; my God who took me there to attend His ceremony knows."[1]

To the glory of Our Lord Jesus Christ. Amen.

36 *How St. Francis Explained to Brother Leo a Vision Which He Had Seen*

At a certain time when St. Francis was seriously ill, Brother Leo was taking care of him with great devotion and zeal. And once while Brother Leo was near St. Francis and gave himself to prayer, he was rapt in an ecstasy and was led in spirit to a very great, broad, and rapid river.

And as he was watching those who were crossing it, he saw several friars with loads on their backs go into the river. Suddenly the powerful current swept them away, and the depth of the water sucked them under. Some others went as far as one third of the way across, and others got halfway across, and others almost all the way to the other bank. But all of them, in various ways according to their burdens, were submerged by the rushing waters and finally fell and died a cruel death, without any chance of being saved, because of their heavy burdens which they were carrying on their backs.

And Brother Leo felt very sorry for them when he saw such a tragedy.

Then all of a sudden, while he was standing there, some friars appeared without any load or burden of any kind. Only holy poverty shone forth in them. And they went into the river and crossed over without any trouble. And after he had seen that, Brother Leo came to himself again.

Now St. Francis, sensing in spirit that Brother Leo had seen a vision, called him and said: "Tell me what you saw."

And after he told him everything he had seen, St. Francis said to him: "What you saw is true, for the great river is this world. The friars who were swallowed by the river are those who do not want to follow the teachings of the Gospel and do not keep voluntary poverty. But those who went across without danger are the friars who, having the spirit of God, neither love nor desire nor possess any carnal or earthly thing in this world, but 'having food and sufficient clothing' they are 'content,' following Christ naked on the Cross. And joyfully and willingly they embrace, take up, and carry every day the very light and sweet burden of His Cross and the yoke of His very holy obedience. And consequently they pass easily and without danger—indeed with joy—from this world to God, who is blessed forever and ever. Amen."[1]

37 How St. Francis Was Very Kindly Received in a Home

Late one evening, when the venerable and admirable Father St. Francis arrived at the house of an important and noble gentleman, he and his companion were welcomed and given lodging with so much reverence and courtesy that it seemed as though that nobleman was welcoming angels from Paradise.

Because of this courtesy, St. Francis conceived a great affection for him. For that nobleman received St. Francis when he entered the house with a friendly embrace and the kiss of peace. And after he entered, the nobleman washed and wiped St. Francis' feet and humbly kissed them. And he lit a great fire and prepared the table with an abundance of good food. And while they were eating, he served them with a joyful expression on his face.

After they had eaten, the nobleman said to St. Francis and his companion: "Father, I offer you myself and my belongings. Whenever you need habits and cloaks or anything, buy it and I will pay for it. And know that I am ready to provide for all your needs, because the good Lord has given me an abundance of worldly property, and so for love of Him I willingly give to those who are poor and in need."

Consequently St. Francis, when he saw his great courtesy and affection and when he heard his generous offer, felt such love in his heart for him that later when he was going away with his companion, he said: "That gentleman certainly would make a good member of our Order: he is so grateful to God, so kind to his neighbor, so generous to the poor, and so cheerful and courteous to guests. For, dear Brother, courtesy is one of the qualities of God, who courteously gives His sun and His rain and everything to the just and to the unjust. And courtesy is a sister of charity. It extinguishes hatred and keeps love alive. And because I have observed so much divine virtue in this good man, I would be glad to have him as a companion. Therefore I wish that we go back to him some day, in case God might perhaps touch his heart so that he should want to join us in serving the Almighty. Let us pray the Lord God to infuse that desire into his heart and to give him the grace to put it into effect."

It certainly is wonderful that a few days later, after the Saint had prayed, the Lord granted the desire of his heart and did not deprive him of what he had prayed for. For a few days after he had uttered his prayer, St. Francis said to his companion: "Dear Brother, let's go to the courteous nobleman, because I have a sure confidence in God that with his generosity in temporal things he will give himself to our Order as a companion."

And taking that road they approached the house of the above-mentioned man. But before they came to him, St. Francis said to his companion: "Wait a while for me, as first I want to ask God to make our journey successful, so that Christ may deign, through the merits of His most holy Passion, to grant to us poor little weak ones the noble prey whom we are thinking of snatching from the world."

And after saying that, St. Francis began to pray very fervently in a certain place where he could clearly be seen by that courteous nobleman. And as Christ arranged matters, while that nobleman was looking here and there, he saw St. Francis praying very devoutly and standing before Christ, and the Blessed Christ standing before St. Francis in a very bright light and looking very beautiful. And in that bright light he saw that St. Francis was raised a great distance above the ground in a physical and spiritual uplifting.

When that nobleman clearly perceived all these things, the hand of the saving Lord quickly came over him, and he was so touched at heart by God and inspired to scorn and leave the world that he immediately went out of his mansion and ran in fervor of spirit toward St. Francis. And when he came to him, he found St. Francis standing on the ground, praying very devoutly. So that nobleman likewise began to pray, and he knelt down and very fervently and eagerly begged him to deign to let him do penance and stay with him.

Then St. Francis, seeing and hearing that the nobleman was urgently asking what he himself had wished, and realizing that this very wonderful conversion had been accomplished by the power of the Lord, rose to his feet in joy and fervor of spirit and devoutly embraced and kissed him, thanking and praising God for having added such a knight to his army.

Meanwhile, that man said to St. Francis: "My holy Father, what do you command me to do? At your order I am ready to give everything I have to the poor and to run after Christ with you, unburdened by all temporal things."

And so it came about that through the merits and prayers of St. Francis, and following his advice, he distributed all his property to the poor and became a Friar Minor. And he lived all the rest of his life in great penance and sanctity and purity.[1]

To the glory of Christ. Amen.

38 *How It Was Revealed to St. Francis That Brother Elias Was to Leave the Order*

At one time when St. Francis and Brother Elias were staying together as members of the community in a certain small Place, it was revealed to St. Francis by God that Brother Elias was damned and would leave the Order and finally die outside the Order. Consequently St. Francis conceived such a distaste for him that he did not want to speak to him or converse with him or see him or eat with him. And if it sometimes happened that Brother Elias was coming toward him, St. Francis would turn aside and go in another direction in order not to meet him.

When this had happened several times, Brother Elias began to notice and realize that St. Francis was displeased with him. So wishing to know the reason, one day he went up to St. Francis to speak to him, and when St. Francis tried to avoid him, he respectfully detained him by force and began to beg him earnestly to explain to him the reason why he was avoiding his company and conversation that way.

And St. Francis answered him: "Because it has been revealed to me by God that as a result of your sins you will leave the Order and die outside the Order. Moreover, it has been revealed to me by the Lord that you are damned."

On hearing this, Brother Elias burst into tears and threw himself at St. Francis' feet, saying: "My reverend Father, I beg you by the love of Christ not to avoid me and drive me away from you because of that, but—like a good shepherd who, following the example of Christ, goes to seek the sheep that has wandered—seek and find and accept this sheep that will perish without your help. And I beg you to pray your holy prayers to God for me, your sheep, so that He may, if it be possible, revoke the sentence of my damnation. For it is written that God can remit the sentence if the sinner makes amends for his fault. And I have so much faith in your prayers that if I were lying in the depths of hell and you prayed to God for me, I would feel some relief. So I beg you again to recommend me, a sinner, to God who came to save sinners, that He may not forget me at the end, but that when the end of my life comes, He may deign to have mercy on me."

And Brother Elias said this with great devotion and weeping, so that St. Francis was moved with fatherly pity and promised him that he would pray to God for him. And while he was very fervently praying to God for him, he understood by a revelation that his prayer had been granted by the Lord as to revoking the sentence—that is, that in the end the soul of Brother Elias would not be damned, but that he surely would leave the Order and die outside the Order.

And that is what happened. For when Frederick the King of Sicily revolted against the Church and consequently the Pope excommunicated him with all those who gave him aid and advice, Brother Elias, who was considered one of the wisest men in the world, at the invitation of King Frederick went over to his side and became a rebel against the Church and an apostate from the Order. For that he was excommunicated by the Pope and deprived of the habit of St. Francis.

And while he was thus excommunicated, he became seriously ill. When his own brother—a lay brother who had remained in the Order and a man of good life and pure and praiseworthy conversation—heard about his illness, he went to visit him. And among other things he said to him: "My dear brother, I am very sorry that you are excommunicated and that you will die without a habit outside your Order. But if you can see any way by which I could deliver you from that great danger, I would be glad to go to any trouble for you."

Now Brother Elias answered: "Dear brother, I see no other way but for you to go to the Pope and ask him, for the love of Christ and His servant and standard-bearer St. Francis, through whose teaching I left the world, to absolve me from the excommunication and restore to me the habit of the Order."

The brother replied: "I will gladly labor for your salvation, if I can obtain that grace."

And leaving him, he went to the Pope and very humbly asked him to have mercy on his brother for the love of Christ

1389

and of St. Francis. And through the grace of God and the help of St. Francis' prayers it happened that the Lord Pope granted to the brother that if he went back and found Brother Elias alive, he might absolve him of the excommunication and restore the habit to him.

So the brother joyfully hurried away from the Papal Court and hastened back to Brother Elias in order to bring him that absolution. And by Divine Providence and the prayers of St. Francis, he found Brother Elias alive but very close to death, and he absolved him from the excommunication. And after putting on the habit again and receiving the last Sacraments of the Church, Brother Elias ended his life in peace and went to the Lord. And it is believed that he obtained this grace at the end and that his soul was saved through the merits and prayers of St. Francis, in which Brother Elias had placed so much faith.[1]

To the glory of Christ. Amen.

39 *How St. Anthony Preached and Was Heard by Men of Different Languages*

At one time that wonderful vessel of the Holy Spirit, St. Anthony of Padua, one of the chosen followers and companions of St. Francis, whom St. Francis used to call his bishop,[1] was preaching before the Pope and Cardinals in a consistory where there were men from different countries—Greeks and Latins, French and Germans, Slavs and English—and men of many other different languages and idioms. And being inflamed by the Holy Spirit and inspired with apostolic eloquence, he preached and explained the word of God so effectively, devoutly, subtly, clearly, and understandably that all who were assembled at that consistory, although they spoke different languages, clearly and distinctly heard and understood every one of his words as if he had spoken in each of their languages. Therefore they were all astounded and filled with devotion, for it seemed to them that the former miracle of the Apostles at the time of Pentecost had been renewed, when by the power of the Holy Spirit they spoke in different languages.

And in amazement they said to one another: "Is he not a

Spaniard? How then are we all hearing him in the language of the country where we were born—we Greeks and Latins, French and Germans, Slavs and English, Lombards and foreigners?"

The Pope also was astonished at St. Anthony's profound knowledge of Holy Scripture and said: "He is truly the Ark of the Covenant and the Treasury of Holy Scripture!"

Such then are the soldiers whom our leader St. Francis had —companions who could nourish with the marrow of the Holy Spirit and arm with heavenly weapons against the snares of the enemy not only the flock of Christ but also the Vicar of Christ with his venerable College of Cardinals.[2]

To the glory of Our Lord Jesus Christ, who is blessed forever and ever. Amen.

40 How St. Anthony Converted the Heretics by Preaching to the Fishes

Our Blessed Lord Jesus Christ, wishing to show how holy was His most faithful servant St. Anthony and how devoutly people should listen to his preaching and wholesome teaching, at one time among others rebuked the foolishness of the infidels and the ignorant and the heretics by means of irrational animals—fishes—just as in ancient times in the Old Testament He rebuked the ignorance of Balaam by the mouth of an ass.

For once when St. Anthony was in Rimini, where there was a great number of heretics, wishing to lead them back to the light of the true faith and onto the path of truth, he preached to them for many days and argued about the faith of Christ and about Holy Scripture. But they were stubborn and hardhearted, and not only did they not accept his holy teaching but, moreover, they refused to listen to him.

So one day, by an inspiration from God, St. Anthony went to the mouth of the river near the sea. And standing on the bank between the sea and the river, he began to call the fishes in God's name, as for a sermon, saying: "You fishes of the sea and river, listen to the word of God, since the faithless heretics refuse to hear it!"

And as soon as he said that, all of a sudden such a great

throng of large and small fishes gathered before him near the
bank as had never been seen in that sea or river. And all of
them held their heads a bit out of the water, gazing intently
at St. Anthony's face. There you would have seen the big fishes
staying close to the little ones, while the smaller ones peacefully swam or stayed under the fins of the larger fishes. You
would also have seen the different types of fishes hasten to
group themselves together and range themselves before the
Saint's face like a field painted and adorned with a marvelous
variety of colors. You would have seen schools of big fishes
occupy the distant places in order to hear the sermon, like an
army ranged for battle. You would have seen the middle-sized
fishes take their positions in the center and stay in their places
without any disturbance, as though they were instructed by
God. And you would have seen a great and very dense crowd
of small fishes come in a hurry, like pilgrims going to receive
an indulgence, and approach closer to the holy Father as to
their protector. And so first the smaller fishes near the bank,
secondly the middle-sized, and thirdly the largest fishes, where
the water was deeper, attended this divinely arranged sermon of St. Anthony—all in very great peace and meekness and
order.

Then when all the fishes were in their places in perfect order, St. Anthony solemnly began to preach, saying: "My fish
brothers, you should give as many thanks as you can to your
Creator who has granted you such a noble element as your
dwelling place, so that you have fresh and salt water, just as
you please. Moreover He has given you many refuges to escape from storms. He has also given you a clear and transparent element and ways to travel and food to live on. Your
kind Creator also prepares for you the food that you need
even in the depths of the ocean. When He created you at the
creation of the world, He gave you the command to increase
and multiply, and He gave you His blessing. Later during the
Flood, when all the other animals were perishing, God preserved you alone without loss. He has also given you fins so
that with that additional power you can roam wherever you
wish. It was granted to you, by order of God, to keep alive
Jonas, the Prophet of the Lord, and to cast him onto dry land
safe and sound on the third day. You offered the tribute money

to Our Lord Jesus Christ, when as a poor man He had nothing to pay the tax. You were chosen as food for the Eternal King, Our Blessed Lord Jesus Christ, before His Resurrection and in a mysterious way afterwards. Because of all these things you should praise and bless the Lord, who has given you so many more blessings than to other creatures."

At these and similar words and preaching of St. Anthony, some of the fishes began to open their mouths, and all of them nodded their heads, and by these and other signs of reverence they praised God as much as they could.

Then St. Anthony, seeing how reverent the fishes were toward God the Creator, rejoiced in spirit and cried out in a loud voice: "Blessed be the Eternal God because the fishes of the waters give God more honor than heretical men, and animals lacking reason listen to His word better than faithless men!"

And the longer St. Anthony preached, the more the throng of fishes increased, and not one of them left the place which it had taken.

At this miracle the people of the city, including the abovementioned heretics, came running. And when they saw the marvelous and extraordinary miracle of the fishes listening to St. Anthony, all of them felt remorse in their hearts, and they sat down at his feet so that he should preach a sermon to them.

Then St. Anthony preached so wonderfully about the Catholic religion that he converted and brought back to the true faith of Christ all those heretics who were there, and the faithful he sent home with his blessing, strengthened in their faith and filled with joy.

St. Anthony also dismissed the fishes with God's blessing, and they all swam away to various parts of the sea, rejoicing and expressing their joy and applause in amazing games and gambols.

After this, St. Anthony stayed in Rimini for many days, preaching and reaping much spiritual fruit, both by converting heretics and by stimulating the piety of the clergy.[1]

To the glory of Our Lord Jesus Christ who is blessed forever and ever. Amen.

41   *About Brother Simon of Assisi and
His Marvelous Life*

In the beginning of our Order, when St. Francis was still living, a certain young man of Assisi joined the Order and was
called Brother Simon. The Almighty Lord God gave him such
graces and consolations and raised him to such a degree of
contemplation and elevation of mind that his whole life was a
mirror of holiness, as I heard from those who were with him
for a long time.

He was very rarely seen outside his cell. If he sometimes
went among the friars, he was always eager to talk about God.
He never had any schooling and he nearly always lived in the
woods. And yet he spoke so profoundly and so loftily about
God and the love of Christ that his words seemed supernatural.

Thus one evening when he went into the woods with
Brother James of Massa to talk about God, they spoke so very
sweetly and devoutly about Christ's love that they spent the
whole night in that conversation. And in the morning it seemed
to them that they had been there only a short while, as he who
was with him told me.

This Brother Simon received such consolations from the
Holy Spirit that when he felt a divine illumination and visitation of God's love coming over him, he used to lie down on
his bed as if he wanted to sleep, because the sweet peace of
the Holy Spirit required of him not only mental but also physical rest. And in such divine visitations he was often rapt in
God and became completely insensible to material things.

For one time it happened that while he was thus rapt in
God and seemed to be quite unconscious of the exterior world,
though wholly burning within with divine love and graces, a
friar who wished to prove by an experiment whether he really
was insensible as he appeared, went and took a live coal from
the fire and placed it on his bare foot. But Brother Simon did
not feel the coal at all, and moreover he felt no pain and suffered no wound in his flesh, although that coal stayed on his
foot until it had entirely burned itself out.

When this Brother Simon would sit down for meals with the friars, before he took any food for the body, he would take and give to his companions some food for the soul by speaking of God. Thus it happened one time that while he was speaking very fervently of God with the friars a certain young man of San Severino was converted to the Lord. In the world he had been noble and delicate in constitution and very sensual. But Brother Simon, when he received that young man into the Order and gave him the habit, kept in his charge the secular clothes he had taken off. And the young man stayed with Brother Simon in order to be instructed by him in the religious life.

But our enemy the devil, who strives to hinder every good, rushed upon that young man like a roaring lion, and by his evil breath, which sets coal on fire, enkindled within his flesh such burning torments that the boy lost hope of being able to resist so strong a temptation. Consequently he went to Brother Simon and said to him: "Give me back the clothes I wore in the world, because I can't stand the strain of this sensual temptation any longer!"

But Brother Simon felt great compassion for him and said to him: "Sit down here with me for a moment, my son." And while Brother Simon was pouring some beautiful words about God into the ears of that boy, he extinguished the flames of lust and took his temptation completely away.

Later the temptation returned several times, and the youth again asked for his clothes, but Brother Simon drove it away by talking to him about God.

Finally one night the temptation attacked him so much more violently than usual that he could not resist it for anything in the world, so he went to Brother Simon and said: "You must give me back my clothes now, because I simply cannot stay any longer!"

Then Brother Simon as a devout father had compassion on him and said, as he usually did: "Come, son, and sit beside me a while."

The distraught boy went to Brother Simon and sat down beside him. And while he was talking about God, the boy rested his head on Brother Simon's chest, because of his melancholy and depression. But Brother Simon, feeling very sorry for him, raised his eyes toward Heaven, and while he was praying to God with great devotion and compassion for the young man, he was rapt in an ecstasy, and finally his prayer was granted by God. And when Brother Simon came back to himself, the boy felt that he was completely freed from his temptation, as if he had never experienced it, so that the harmful ardor of the temptation was changed into the fervor of the Holy Spirit. And because he had been close to the live coal—Brother Simon —he became all afire with love for God and for his neighbor.

For one day when a certain criminal was captured and condemned to lose both his eyes, that young man courageously went, moved by compassion, to the governor while the council was in session. And with many tears and prayers he asked that he be given the grace that one of his eyes be extracted so that the criminal should not be deprived of both his eyes. But the governor and the council, seeing the youth's great fervor and burning charity, granted the criminal a complete pardon.

Moreover, one day when Brother Simon was praying in the woods and feeling a very great consolation from the Lord in his soul, a flock of birds, called rooks because of the great noise and clamor they make, began to disturb him with their cries, so he ordered them in the name of Jesus to go away and never to come back there again.[1] And it is wonderful to relate that, although that Place of Brunforte in the Custody of Fermo existed for over fifty years, those birds were never seen or heard again anywhere around the Place or district or entire region. And I, Brother Ugolino di Monte Santa Maria, stayed there for three years, and I observed that wonder in a sure way, and it was known among both the lay people and the friars of the whole Custody.[2]

To the glory of Christ. Amen.

42 About the Wonderful Miracles That God Performed through Some Holy Friars

In former times the Province of the Marches of Ancona was adorned and bright like the sky with brilliant stars that were the holy and exemplary Friars Minor who shone like stars above and below—before God and their neighbor—with radiant virtues, and who illumined the Order of St. Francis and the world by their example and teaching. Their memory is truly a blessing from God.

Among them some were like greater constellations that shone more brightly than others: for instance, first of all, Brother Lucido the Elder, who was indeed resplendent with sanctity and aflame with the love of God, and whose glorious preaching was inspired by the Holy Spirit and reaped marvelous fruit.[1]

Another was Brother Bentivoglia of San Severino, who was seen by Brother Masseo of San Severino raised up into the air at a great height while he was praying in the woods.

As a result of that miracle this Brother Masseo, who was then a pastor, left his pastorate and became a Friar Minor, and he lived such a saintly life that he performed many miracles before and after his death. His body rests in Murro.[2]

The above-mentioned Brother Bentivoglia, when he was once staying alone at Trave Bonanti nursing and taking care of a man suffering from leprosy, received an obedience from his superior to leave there and go to another Place which was fifteen miles away. Not wishing to abandon the sick man, with great fervor of charity he took him up and set him on his own shoulders. And burdened that way he carried him from early dawn until sunrise all that distance of fifteen miles, from the Place of Trave to the Place where he was sent, which was called Monte Sanvicino. If he had been an eagle, he could hardly have flown that distance in such a short time. Everyone in that region who heard about this divine miracle was filled with amazement and admiration.[3]

Another friar was Peter of Montecchio, a real saint, who was seen by Brother Servodeo of Urbino (at that time his guardian in the old Place of Ancona)[4] raised in the air about five or six cubits above the ground, that is, the pavement of the church, up to the feet of the Crucifix before which he was praying.

This Brother Peter, once while he was keeping the Lent of St. Michael with great devotion, on the last day of that Lent was praying in church, and he was heard talking with the most holy Archangel Michael and the Archangel talking with him, by a young friar who had carefully hidden under the high altar in order to observe him. And this is what they were saying.

The Archangel St. Michael said: "Brother Peter, you have labored faithfully for me, and you have afflicted your body in many ways. Now I have come to console you. So ask whatever grace you desire—and I will obtain it for you from the Lord."

Brother Peter answered: "Most holy prince of the heavenly army and most faithful defender of God's honor and most compassionate protector of souls, I ask you for this grace: that you obtain for me from God the forgiveness of all my sins."

The Archangel Michael replied: "Ask for another grace, because I will easily obtain that one for you."

But as Brother Peter did not ask for anything else, the Archangel concluded, saying: "Because of the faith and devotion which you have for me, I will obtain for you that grace which you request and many others."

When their conversation was over—and it lasted a great part of the night—the Archangel St. Michael went away and left Brother Peter intensely consoled.[5]

Brother Conrad of Offida was living in the days of that holy Brother Peter. When they were members of the community at the Place of Forano in the Custody of Ancona, one day Brother Conrad went into the woods to contemplate God, and Brother Peter secretly went after him in order to see what happened.

Now Brother Conrad began to pray very devoutly and with many tears to the Blessed Virgin Mary that she might obtain for him from her Son this grace: that he might be allowed to feel a little of that sweetness which St. Simeon felt on the day of her Purification when he held in his arms the Blessed Savior Jesus.

He earned the granting of his prayer by the most merciful Lady. For the glorious Queen of Heaven appeared with that Blessed little Son of hers in her arms in such dazzling splendor that it not only drove away the shadows but also outshone all lights. And approaching the holy Brother Conrad, she put in his arms that Blessed little Son who is more beautiful than the sons of men.

Brother Conrad took him with very great devotion and pressed his lips to His and clasped Him to his heart. And in these loving embraces and kisses he felt as though his soul were melting away with ineffable consolation.

Now Brother Peter was watching all this in the bright light, and he too felt a great sweetness in his soul. And he remained hidden in the woods. But when the Blessed Virgin Mary and her Son left Brother Conrad, Brother Peter hurried back to the Place, so as not to be seen by him.

Later when Brother Conrad returned, overflowing with joy and happiness, Brother Peter called him and said: "Oh, you heavenly man, you have had a great consolation today!"

Brother Conrad said: "What do you mean, Brother Peter? What do you know about what I have had?"

Brother Peter said: "I know very well—I know very well, you heavenly man, how the Blessed Virgin Mary visited you with her Blessed little Son."

When Brother Conrad heard that, he asked Brother Peter not to tell it to anyone, because as a truly humble man he wanted to keep secret the graces which God gave him. And after this the love between the two of them was so great that they seemed to have one heart and one soul in all things.[6]

Once in the Place of Sirolo this Brother Conrad by his

prayers freed a woman who was obsessed by the devil. And in the morning he immediately fled from that Place so that the mother of the liberated girl should not find him and he should not be acclaimed by a crowd of people. For Brother Conrad had prayed for her all that night, and he had appeared in a vision to her mother while he was liberating her.

To the praise and glory of Our Lord Jesus Christ. Amen.

43 *How Brother Conrad Converted a Young Friar*

The life of this Brother Conrad of Offida, a wonderful follower of Gospel poverty and the Rule of our Father St. Francis, was so saintly and full of merit before God that the Lord Jesus Christ repeatedly honored him with many miracles while he was alive as well as after his death.

Among others, once when he came on a visit to the Place of Offida, the friars asked him, for the love of God and of charity, to give a good talking to a certain young friar in that Place who was acting so childishly and foolishly that he was disturbing both the old and young members of the community very much, and he cared little or nothing for the divine office and the other regular practices of the religious life.

So Brother Conrad felt sorry for that young man and for the other friars whom he was disturbing. And yielding humbly to their request he called the boy aside. And in all charity he said such persuasive and inspired words of reproof to him that suddenly the hand of the Lord came over that youth, and by the power of divine grace he was changed into another man: from a child he became a mature man, so obedient, so thoughtful and kind, so devout, so peaceable and helpful and so eager to practice all virtues that, just as formerly the whole community had been disturbed by him, afterwards they all rejoiced because of his complete conversion to virtue. And they loved him very much, as though he were an angel.

As it pleased God, soon after his conversion that young man fell ill and died, and the friars grieved a great deal. And a few days after his death, while Brother Conrad, who had converted him, was praying devoutly one night before the altar of the friary, the soul of that friar came and greeted Brother Conrad affectionately, as a father. And Brother Conrad asked him: "Who are you?"

He replied: "I am the soul of that young friar who died recently."

And Brother Conrad said: "Oh, my dear son, how are you?"

He replied: "Beloved Father, by the grace of God and your teaching, I am well, because I am not damned. But on account of some of my sins which I did not fully expiate owing to lack of time, I am suffering very much in Purgatory. So I beg you, Father, as by your compassion you helped me when I was alive, to deign to help me now in my sufferings by saying some Our Fathers for me, because your prayers are very acceptable before God."

Brother Conrad willingly agreed and said one Our Father with the *Requiem aeternam*.

After he had said it, the soul said: "Oh, dear Father, what relief I feel now! I beg you to say it again."

And when he had prayed again, the soul said: "Holy Father, when you pray for me, I feel all refreshed, so I beg you not to stop praying for me!"

So Brother Conrad, realizing that the soul was thus helped by his prayers, said one hundred Our Fathers for him.

And when he had finished saying them, the friar said: "Dear Father, on behalf of Our Lord Jesus Christ I thank you for the charity you have shown me. May He give you an eternal reward for this kindness, because through your prayers I have been freed from all suffering! And now I am going to the glory of Paradise."

And after saying that, the soul went away.

Then Brother Conrad, in order to give joy and consolation to the friars, told them all that had happened during that night, and he and they were greatly consoled.

To the glory of Our Lord Jesus Christ. Amen.

44 *How Brother Peter of Montecchio Was Shown Who Suffered Most from the Passion of Christ*

At the time when the above-mentioned Brother Conrad and Brother Peter—two bright stars in the Province of the Marches and two heavenly men—were living together in the Custody of Ancona, at the Place of Forano (which they liked very much), there was so much love and charity between them that both seemed to have one heart and one soul, and they bound themselves together in this agreement: that in charity they must reveal to each other all the consolations which the mercy of God might grant to either one.

One day, after they had made that pact, it happened that Brother Peter was praying and meditating devoutly on the Passion of Christ. And His Most Blessed Mother and John the beloved Disciple were standing before Christ Crucified—and our blessed Father Francis was also there with his Stigmata. And there came to him the holy desire to know which of those three had suffered most from the Passion of Christ: the Mother who had given Him birth or the beloved Disciple who had rested on His breast or St. Francis who was crucified with Christ.

And while he was thinking these devout thoughts, weeping many tears, the Virgin Mary appeared to him with St. John the Evangelist and our blessed Father Francis, dressed in very noble raiment of heavenly glory; but St. Francis seemed to be dressed in a more beautiful garment than St. John.

And as Brother Peter was very frightened by this vision, St. John comforted him and said to him: "Do not be afraid, dear Brother, because we have come to console you and to clear up your doubt. Know therefore that the Mother of Christ and I grieved more than any other creature over the Passion of Christ, but after us St. Francis felt greater sorrow than any other. And that is why you see him in such glory."

And Brother Peter asked him: "Most holy apostle of Christ, why does the clothing of St. Francis seem more glorious than yours?"

St. John replied: "This is the reason: because when he was in the world, for the love of Christ he wore plainer clothes than I."

And having said these words, St. John gave Brother Peter a glorious garment which he was holding in his hand, and said to him: "Take this robe which I have brought to show you."

And when St. John wanted to clothe him in that robe, Brother Peter in amazement began to run and shout (for he was awake, not asleep, when he saw this): "Brother Conrad, dear Brother Conrad, come quick! Come and see something marvelous!" And at those words the holy vision vanished.

Then, when Brother Conrad came, he told him everything in detail. And they gave thanks to God. Amen.

45 *About the Conversion, Life, Miracles, and Death of the Holy Brother John of Penna*

When Brother John of Penna, one of the bright stars of the Province of the Marches, was still a young boy in the world, one night a very beautiful boy appeared to him and called him, saying: "John, go to Santo Stefano where one of My friars is due to preach. And believe his teaching and listen to his words, for I have sent him there. And after you have done that, you will have a long journey to make. And afterward you shall come to Me."

He immediately arose and felt a marvelous change in his soul. And going to Santo Stefano, he found there a great crowd of men and women who had come together from different villages in order to hear the word of God. And he who was to preach was a friar called Brother Philip, who was one of the first friars who came to the Marches of Ancona, when only a few Places had been founded in the Marches.

This Brother Philip rose up and preached with great devotion, not in the learned words of human wisdom, but announcing the Kingdom of God and eternal life by the power of the Spirit of Christ.

Now when the sermon was over, the above-mentioned boy, Brother John, went to Brother Philip and said to him: "Father,

Little Flowers of St. Francis

if you would receive me in the Order, I would be glad to do penance and to serve the Lord Jesus Christ."

The friar, being a holy and enlightened man, perceived the boy's marvelous innocence and ready will to serve God, and he said to him: "Come to see me in the city of Recanati on a certain day, and I will see that you are received." (For a Provincial Chapter was to be held in that Place then.)

In his innocence the boy reflected in his heart: "This will be the long journey that was revealed to me, which I am to make and then go to Heaven." He thought that would happen as soon as he was received in the Order. So he went and was received. But his expectation was not fulfilled then.

And during the Chapter the minister said: "Whoever wants to go to the Province of Provence by merit of holy obedience—I will send him there." Now when Brother John heard this, he felt a great desire to go there, thinking that perhaps that was the long journey he had to make before he went to Paradise. But he was too bashful to speak up. Finally he confided in Brother Philip, who had arranged for him to be received in the Order, and said to him: "Father, I ask you to obtain this grace for me: that I may be able to go and stay in Provence." For in those times the friars used to volunteer to go to foreign provinces so that they might be like pilgrims and strangers in this world and fellow citizens of the saints and servants of God in Heaven.

Brother Philip, seeing his simplicity and holy intention, obtained permission for him to go to that province. And Brother John set out with great joy, feeling sure that when he had finished that journey, he would go to Heaven.

But as it pleased God, he stayed in that province for twenty-five years, living a life of great and exemplary sanctity, but hoping every day that what had been promised to him would be fulfilled. And although he grew in virtue and holiness, and he was loved by both the friars and the lay people in all that province, he nevertheless could not see the least sign of his desire being granted.

One day while he was devoutly praying and weeping and lamenting to God that his exile and pilgrimage in this life were being prolonged too much, the Blessed Lord Jesus Christ appeared to him, at the sight of whom his soul melted with love.

1404

And Christ said to him: "My son, Brother John, ask Me for whatever you want."

And he answered: "My Lord, I don't know what to say, because I want nothing but You. But I ask You only for this: that You forgive me all my sins, and give me the grace to see You again when I need You still more."

The Lord said to him: "Your prayer is granted." And after saying that, He vanished from his sight. And Brother John remained greatly consoled.

At last the friars of the Marches heard about his reputation for sanctity and arranged with the General that a written order be sent to him to return to the Marches. When he saw that order, he gladly set out, saying to himself: "This is the long journey after which I will go to God."

Now when he returned to his own province, he was not recognized by any of his relatives. But from one day to the next he waited and expected that God would have mercy on him and fulfill the promise that had been made to him.

But his life was still further prolonged, for he stayed on a good thirty years after his return to the Marches. And during that time he often served as guardian with great discretion. And the Lord performed many miracles through him.

Among a number of other gifts, he had the spirit of prophecy. For once when he was absent from his Place, one of his novices was attacked by the devil and so strongly tempted to leave the Order that he yielded and decided that he would leave as soon as Brother John came back to the Place.

But by the spirit of prophecy Brother John knew about that temptation and decision. And as soon as he came home, he called that novice and said to him: "Come, son—I want you to confess." And when he came, Brother John added: "First listen to me, son."

And then he told the novice all about his temptation, as God had revealed it to him. And he concluded: "My son, because you waited for me and did not want to leave without my blessing, God has given you this grace: that you will never leave this Order, but that you will die in this Order with the Lord's blessing."

And then that novice was strengthened in his good intention, and he stayed in the Order and became a holy friar.

And Brother John himself told me, Brother Ugolino, all these things.

Now Brother John was always a man with joy and peace of mind. He was silent and rarely spoke. And he was a man of great devotion and prayer, and especially after matins he did not go back to his cell, but stayed praying in church until dawn.

And one night after matins while he was praying fervently, an angel of the Lord appeared and said to him: "Brother John, your journey has come to the end which you have been awaiting so long. Therefore I announce to you on God's behalf that you may ask for whatever grace you desire—and also that you must choose either one entire day in Purgatory or seven days of suffering in this world."

And when Brother John had rather chosen seven days of suffering in this world, he suddenly fell ill with a number of different sicknesses in succession. For he was plagued with strong fevers and pains and gout in hands and feet and convulsions and intestinal troubles and many other sufferings. But what was worse than all the other afflictions was that a devil stood before him holding a large scroll on which were written all his sins and faults and failings of thought and deed, and the devil said to him: "Because of all these things which you thought and said and did, you are damned to the depths of hell!"

And the sick friar forgot all the good things that he had ever done, and that he was or ever had been in the Order. But he thought that he was utterly damned, as the devil was saying. So when he was asked by anyone how he felt, he would answer: "Bad—because I am damned!"

Seeing this, the friars of the Place sent for an old friar named Brother Matthew of Monte Rubbiano who was a very holy man and an intimate friend of Brother John.

Now Brother Matthew came to him on the seventh day of his tribulations and greeted him, saying: "How are you feeling, dear Brother?"

He replied: "Bad—because I am damned!"

Then Brother Matthew said: "How can you say that? Don't you remember that you often confessed to me, and I completely absolved you from all your sins? Don't you also remember that you have served God for many years in this holy Order? Besides, don't you remember that the mercy of God is greater than all the sins in the world, and that Christ Our Blessed Savior paid an infinite price to God our Father in order to redeem us? So you can be perfectly sure that you will be saved and not damned."

And then, when he had said that, as the seven-day period of Brother John's purgation was over, his temptation left him, and a feeling of consolation came over him. And with great joy he said to Brother Matthew: "Because you are tired and it is already time for bed, I want you to go and rest."

Now Brother Matthew did not want to leave him, but Brother John insisted so much that finally he left and went to get some rest.

And while Brother John remained alone with the friar who was taking care of him, Our Blessed Lord Jesus Christ appeared to him in a very bright light and sweet fragrance, just as He had promised to appear to him once more when he would need Him most. And He completely cured him of all his sicknesses.

Then Brother John joined his hands and gave thanks to God for having brought his long journey in this sad life to a happy end, and he was united for all eternity to his Lord Jesus Christ, like a chosen member to the head. And so with great joy and confidence and consolation he commended and gave up his soul to God and passed from this mortal life to eternal life with the Blessed Christ, whom he had desired and awaited for so long a time.

And this Brother John was buried in the Place of Penna San Giovanni.[1]

To the glory of Christ. Amen.

46 *How Brother Pacifico Saw the Soul of His Brother Going to Heaven*

In that Province of the Marches after the death of our Father St. Francis there were two brothers in the Order, Brother Humble and Brother Pacifico, both of whom were men of great sanctity and perfection.[1]

One of them, Brother Humble, lived in the Place of Soffiano and died there. But the other was a member of a community in a Place at some distance from him. And as it pleased God, when Brother Pacifico was staying in that distant Place, one day while he was praying in a solitary and lonely spot, the hand of the Lord came over him. And being rapt in ecstasy, he saw the soul of his brother, Brother Humble, ascend directly up to Heaven without any delay or hindrance.

Many years later it happened that the brother who lived on was made a member of the community at that Place of Soffiano where his brother had died and was buried. Now at that time, at the request of the Lords of Brunforte, the friars gave up the Place of Soffiano for another, so that they transferred the remains of the holy friars who had been buried there.[2] And when they came to the grave of Brother Humble among the others, his brother, Brother Pacifico, took up the bones very devoutly and washed them with excellent wine and then wrapped them in a white napkin, weeping over them and kissing them very reverently.

But the other friars who were present were surprised and shocked at this, because while he had a reputation for great holiness, it seemed to them that he was grieving for his brother out of a natural and worldly affection, and that he was showing greater devotion to those remains than to those of the other friars who had been no less saintly than Brother Humble and were worthy of the same honor as he.

Knowing that the friars were misjudging him, Brother Pacifico humbly explained to them: "My dear Brothers, do not be surprised because I have done something that I did not do to the others, for—blessed be God—it was not a natural affection that motivated me, as you thought. But I acted that way because, when my brother left this world and went to the Lord, I was praying in a solitary place far away from him and I saw his soul ascending straight up to Heaven. So I am certain that these bones of his are holy and are destined to rest some day in God's Paradise. That is why I am doing what you see. And if God had granted me such certainty regarding the other friars, I would have shown the same reverence for their bones."

Consequently, perceiving his good and holy motive, the

friars were greatly edified. And they praised God who performs such great wonders for His holy friars.

To the glory of Christ. Amen.

47 *How the Blessed Virgin Appeared to a Holy Friar When He Was Ill*

In the Marches of Ancona, in a certain solitary Place called Soffiano, there was in former times a certain Friar Minor (whose name I do not remember) of such great holiness and grace that he seemed to be godlike. And he was often rapt in the Lord.

Once when he was in a rapture and his mind was absorbed in God—for he had the grace of contemplation to a remarkable degree—various kinds of birds came to him and very tamely rested on his head and shoulders and arms and hands, and there they sang beautifully. When he came out of his contemplation, he was so overflowing with joy that he seemed rather like an angel, for then his face radiated in a marvelous way his communion with God, to such an extent that it aroused wonder and surprise in those who saw him.

He always remained alone and spoke very rarely, and he was in prayer or contemplation almost continually day and night. But when he was asked a question, he answered so pleasantly and wisely that he seemed more like an angel than a man. And the friars felt great reverence for him. He was pleasant to everyone and his conversation was always spiced with divine salt.

He persevered in this praiseworthy practice of the virtues until the end of his heavenly life. And by disposition of Divine Providence he became so mortally ill that he was unable to take any food. And he did not want to be given any medicine for his body. But he placed all his confidence in the heavenly doctor Jesus Christ and in His Blessed Mother. And he merited the grace of being visited and consoled in a wonderful way by the Blessed Virgin Mary, the Queen of Mercy.

For one day while he was lying alone and was preparing himself for death with all his strength, the Blessed and Glorious Mother of Christ herself appeared to him, accompanied

1409

by a throng of angels and holy virgins, amid a bright light, and she went close to the sick friar's cot. When he saw her, he was filled with inexpressible joy and consolation of both mind and body. And he began to beg her humbly to pray to her beloved Son that He might deign by His merits to lead him out of the dark prison of the flesh. And as with many tears he kept fervently begging her to do so, the Blessed Virgin Mary answered him, calling him by his name and saying: "Do not fear, my son, because your prayer is granted. For I have seen your tears. And I have come to give you a little consolation before you leave this life."

With the Blessed Mother of Christ there were three holy virgins, each of whom carried in her hands a box filled with an electuary that was so sweet in taste and fragrance that words cannot describe it. And as the Blessed Virgin Mary took one of those boxes and opened it, the whole house was filled with the perfume. And taking a spoon in her glorious hands, she gave a bit of the heavenly electuary to that sick friar. When he tasted it, he experienced such grace and sweetness that it seemed to him his soul would quickly leave his body. So he began to say to the glorious Virgin Mary: "No more, oh dear Mother of Jesus Christ and Blessed Lady—no more, oh blessed doctor, for I cannot bear such sweetness!"

But the merciful and kind Mother of God urged him on and consoled him by speaking a great deal to him about the Lord Jesus Christ, and she frequently made him take more of the electuary until that first box was empty.

Then as she took the second box and placed the spoon in it, the sick friar gently complained to her: "Oh Blessed Mother of God, if my soul has nearly melted from the perfume and sweetness of the first box, how can I bear the second? I beg you, oh Blessed above all the saints and holy angels, not to give me any more!"

Our Lady answered: "Son, you must take a little of this second box." And giving him a little of the second electuary, she said to him: "Now, my son, you have had enough. But rejoice, because I shall soon come back to you, and I shall lead you to the Kingdom of my Son which you have always longed for and desired."

And saying good-by to him, she vanished from his sight.

1410

And he remained so comforted and consoled by the sweetness of that electuary, which had been brought from the apothecary of Paradise and administered to him by the hands of the Blessed Virgin Mary, that for several days he did not take any material food, but felt strong in body and mind, for it was not a medicine of this world but of Heaven. And he was given a profound spiritual insight, and his eyes were opened by such a radiant divine light that he clearly saw in the book of eternal life all who would be saved until Judgment Day.

And a few days later, on the last day of his life, while talking with the friars and rejoicing greatly in mind and body, he passed from this unhappy life to the Lord Jesus Christ.[1]

To the glory of Christ. Amen.

48 *How Brother James of Massa Saw in a Vision All the Friars Minor in the World*

Brother James of Massa—to whom God opened the door of His secrets and gave a perfect knowledge and understanding of Holy Scripture and of the future—was so saintly that Brother Giles of Assisi and Brother Mark of Montino used to say that they knew no one in the world who was greater in God's sight. Brother Juniper and Brother Lucido felt the same way. When Brother John, the companion of Brother Giles, was my spiritual director, I wanted very much to see him. For while I was asking Brother John about certain spiritual matters, he said to me: "If you want to be well instructed in the spiritual life, hasten to have some talks with Brother James of Massa, because Brother Giles wanted to be instructed by him. And nothing can be added to or taken away from his words, for his mind has penetrated into the secrets of Heaven, and his words are the words of the Holy Spirit. And there is no man on earth whom I have wanted so much to see."

This Brother James, about the beginning of the ministry of Brother John of Parma, was once rapt in an ecstasy while praying, and he remained unconscious for three days, so that the friars began to wonder whether he was dead. And in that rapture God revealed to him an understanding of Scripture and a knowledge of the future. And therefore, when I heard about it, my desire to see him and talk to him increased.

And when it pleased God that I have an opportunity to speak to him, I questioned him in this way: "If what I have heard about you is true, please do not hide it from me. For I heard that when you remained lying almost dead for three days, God showed you among other things what was going to happen in our Order. Brother Matthew, to whom you revealed it under obedience, said so."

For Brother Matthew, who was then Minister of the Province of the Marches, summoned him after that rapture and ordered him under obedience to tell him what he had seen.

Now Brother Matthew was a man of marvelous gentleness and holiness and simplicity. And he would often tell the friars in his talks to them: "I know a friar to whom God has shown all that will happen in our Order—and also some amazing secrets which, if they were uttered, would hardly be understood or even believed."[1]

Now Brother James revealed to me and told me, among other things, something very astounding, that is, that after many things which were shown to him concerning the condition of the Church Militant, he saw in a vision a certain very beautiful and high tree, and its roots were of gold, and its fruits were men, and all of them were Friars Minor. And the number of its principal branches corresponded to that of the provinces in the Order, and each branch had as many fruits as there were friars in that province. And then he knew the number of all the friars in the whole Order and in each province and also their name and face and age and condition and rank and position and their honors and graces and merits and faults.

And he saw Brother John of Parma standing on the highest part of the central branch of that tree, and on the tops of the branches which were around that central branch stood the ministers of all the provinces. And after this he saw Christ sitting on a very great white throne. And Christ called St. Francis and gave him a chalice full of the spirit of life, and sent him forth, saying to him: "Go and visit your friars. And let them drink from this chalice of the spirit of life, for the spirit of Satan will rise up and attack them, and many of them

1412

will fall and will not rise again." And Christ gave St. Francis two angels to go with him.

Then St. Francis came to offer the chalice of life to his friars as he had been ordered to do. And he began by offering it to Brother John, the Minister General, who accepted the chalice from St. Francis' hand and drank it all quickly and devoutly. And after he had drunk, he suddenly became all luminous and bright like the sun.

And after him St. Francis offered the chalice of the spirit of life to all the others, one after another, but very few of them accepted it with fitting reverence and devotion and drank all of it. Those few who did take it reverently and drank it all suddenly became as bright as the sun. But those who spilled it all or did not take it reverently became dark and black and deformed and horrible to see, like devils. And those who drank part but spilled part became more or less luminous or dark according to the degree of their drinking or spilling.

But shining more brightly than all the others on the tree was the above-mentioned Brother John who, having drunk more fully from the chalice of life, had a profound insight into the depths of God's true light, and in it he perceived that the whirlwind of a great storm was arising against that tree and would shake and tear its branches. Therefore he went down from the top of the branch where he had been standing, past all the branches, and hid himself in the solid part of the tree's trunk.

And while he gave himself to contemplation there, Brother Bonaventure, who had drunk part of the chalice and had spilled part, went up to the branch and place which Brother John had left. And when he was in that place, the nails of his fingers turned to iron and became as sharp and cutting as razors. And leaving his place, he wanted to attack Brother John with rage and fury, to hurt him. But seeing this, Brother John cried for help to Christ, who was sitting on the throne. And at his cry, Christ called St. Francis and gave him a very sharp flintstone and said to him: "Go and with this stone cut the nails of Brother Bonaventure with which he wants to tear Brother John, so that he cannot hurt him!"

Then St. Francis came and cut Brother Bonaventure's nails

as Christ had ordered him to do. And so Brother John stayed in his place, shining brightly.[2]

After this, a violent hurricane arose and struck the tree so strongly that the friars began to fall from it. And those who had completely spilled the chalice of the spirit of life fell first. And those who fell turned dark and were carried away by devils to realms of darkness and pain. But Brother John and those who had completely drunk the chalice were carried by angels to the realm of eternal life, light, and glory.

And he who saw the vision understood clearly and remembered every particular detail that he saw, such as the names and persons and places and ages and states of everyone whom he saw in the realms of light and darkness. And the hurricane and fierce storm lasted, with the permission of God's justice, until the tree was torn up by the roots and crashed to the ground and the wind blew it completely away.

Now as soon as that hurricane and storm stopped, from the root of the tree, which was of gold, came forth another tree that was all of gold and that produced golden fruits and flowers. Regarding that tree's growth, depth, fragrance, beauty, and virtue, it is better to be silent than to speak now.

But I do not want to omit one thing which he who saw this vision used to tell, for it sounded very noteworthy to me. For he said that the way in which the Order would be reformed would be very different from the way in which it was founded, because the working of the Holy Spirit, without there being a leader, will choose uneducated youths and simple, plain persons who are looked down upon. And without their having any example or teacher—even against the teaching and practice of the teachers—the Spirit of Christ will select them and fill them with holy fear and a very pure love of Christ. And when their number has increased in various places, then He will send them an utterly pure and saintly shepherd and leader, wholly conformed to Christ.

To the praise and glory of Christ. Amen.

49 *How Christ Appeared to Brother John of Alverna*

How glorious our blessed Father Francis is in the sight of God appears in the chosen sons whom the Holy Spirit added to his Order, for as Solomon says, the glory of the father is in his wise sons.

Among them shone in a very special way in our times the venerable and saintly Brother John of Fermo, who sparkled in the skies of the Order like a marvelous star owing to the radiance of his grace. (Because of the long time which he spent at the holy Place of Alverna and because he passed from this life there, he was also called Brother John of Alverna.)[1]

For when he was a boy in the world, he had the wise heart of an old man, and he longed with all his soul to take up the life of penance which keeps the mind and body pure. When he was still a little boy, he began to wear a breastplate of mail and an iron band on his flesh, and he used to carry the cross of abstinence every day. And especially while he was staying with the canons at St. Peter in Fermo, who lived in ease, before he received the habit of the holy Father, he used to avoid physical comfort and to practice self-control with amazing strictness, and he enjoyed inflicting the martyrdom of abstinence on his body.

But as his companions were so opposed to his angelic zeal that they took his breastplate away from him and interfered with his abstinence in various ways, inspired by God he thought of abandoning the world with its lovers and of offering up the flower of his angelic purity to the Crucified in the Order of St. Francis, in whom he had heard that the wounds of Christ's Crucifixion had been renewed.

Now after he had received the habit of the Friars Minor while still a boy and he had been committed to the care of a holy novicemaster for spiritual training,[2] he became so fervent and devout that when he heard that master speak of God, his heart would melt like wax near the fire, and interiorly he felt so inflamed with the sweet grace of God's love that he could not stay still exteriorly and endure such consolation, but in his

1415

spiritual intoxication he felt forced to get up and run or walk around the garden or the woods or the church, depending on how the interior fire and stimulus of the spirit impelled him.

Later, with the passing of time, God's grace made this angelic man grow continually in virtue and heavenly gifts and ecstasies and raptures, so that at times his mind was raised to the splendor of the cherubim, at times to the ardor of the seraphim, and at other times to the joys of the angels. And furthermore, sometimes it drew him on to the mystical kisses and intense embraces of Christ's love not only in interior spiritual graces but also in exterior signs, as with an intimate friend.

Thus it happened once that his heart became enkindled with the fire of God's love in an extraordinary way, and that flame lasted in him for three full years, during which he received marvelous consolations and divine visitations and was often rapt in God. In brief, during that time he seemed all on fire and aflame with the love of Christ. (And this was on the holy Mount Alverna.)[3]

But because God takes special care of His sons, giving them at different times either consolations or trials, either prosperity or adversity, depending on what He sees that they need to remain humble or to enkindle their longing for heavenly things still more—after the three years were over, while Brother John was staying in a certain Place—it pleased God in His goodness to withdraw that light and fire of divine love from him and to deprive him of all spiritual consolations, leaving him without love or light and utterly miserable and depressed and mournful. Consequently, when his soul did not feel the presence of his Beloved, in his anguish and torment he went through the woods, running here and there, anxiously seeking and calling aloud with tears and sighs for his dear Friend who had recently abandoned him and hidden, and without whose presence his soul could find no peace or rest. But nowhere and in no way could he find his Blessed Jesus Christ and enjoy as before the sweet spiritual consolations of His loving embraces.

And he endured that trial for many days, mourning and sighing and weeping and praying God in His mercy to give him back the beloved Spouse of his soul.

Finally, when it pleased God to have sufficiently tested his patience and inflamed his longing, one day while Brother

1416

John was walking up and down in the woods where he had made himself a little path to walk on, being tired and unhappy and depressed he sat down there, leaning against a beech tree, and raised his tear-stricken face toward Heaven. And all of a sudden He who heals and lightens the weight of contrite hearts, Our Blessed Lord Jesus Christ, appeared on the path where Brother John had been walking, but He said nothing.

When Brother John saw Him and recognized Him, he immediately threw himself at His feet, and weeping uncontrollably he very humbly begged Him to help him, saying: "Help me, my Lord, because without You, my sweet Savior, I remain in darkness and grief. Without You, most gentle Lamb, I remain in worry and fear. Without You, Son of Almighty God, I remain in confusion and shame. For without You I am deprived of all that is good. Without You I am blind in the dark, because You are Jesus, the true Light of the World. Without You I am lost and damned, because You are the life of souls and the life of lives. Without You I am sterile and dry, because You are the God of Gods and the giver of graces. But in You I find all consolation because You are Jesus, our Redemption, love, and desire, our refreshing bread and wine who give joy to the choirs of angels and the hearts of all the saints. So enlighten me, most kind Master and compassionate Shepherd, because, though unworthy, I am Your little lamb."

But because the longing of holy men increases to greater love and merit when God delays in granting its fulfillment, the Blessed Christ went away from him along the path. Then Brother John, seeing that Christ was leaving without answering his prayer or saying anything to him, arose and ran after Him and again humbly threw himself at His feet, holding Him back with holy eagerness. And with fervent tears he implored Him, saying: "Oh, sweetest Jesus, have pity on me because I am suffering. Grant my prayer by the abundance of Your mercy and the truth of Your salvation. And give me back the joy of Your countenance and Your look, because the whole world is full of Your mercy. Lord, You know how intense my suffering is! I beg You to come quickly to the help of my darkened soul."

Again the Savior went away from him without saying anything to him or giving him any consolation. And it seemed as if He wished to leave as He went along the path. But He was acting like a mother with her baby when she withdraws her breast from him to make him drink the milk more eagerly, and he cries and seeks it, and after he has cried, she hugs and kisses him and lets him enjoy it all the more.

So Brother John followed Christ a third time with greater fervor and desire, weeping, like a baby following its mother or a boy his father or a humble pupil his kind teacher. And when he came up to Him, the Blessed Christ turned toward him and looked at him with a joyful and loving expression on His face, and He held out and opened His holy and merciful arms as the priest does when he turns to the people. And as He opened His arms, Brother John saw marvelous rays of light issuing from the holy breast of Christ that illuminated not only the whole forest but also his own soul and body with divine splendor.

Then the Holy Spirit suddenly revealed to Brother John the humble and reverent act which he should perform toward Christ. For he immediately threw himself down at Christ's feet, and the Savior showed him His blessed feet, over which Brother John wept so much that he seemed like another Magdalen. And he said devoutly: "I beg You, my Lord, not to consider my sins. But by Your most holy Passion and by the shedding of Your Precious Blood, deign to reawaken my soul to the grace of Your love, since it is Your commandment that we love You with all our heart and all our strength—and no one can fulfill that commandment without Your help. So help me, O most lovable Son of God, to love You with all my heart and all my strength!"

Now while Brother John was praying fervently lying at Christ's feet, he received so much grace that he felt completely renewed and pacified and consoled, like Magdalen. And then feeling again within himself the fire of divine love and knowing that the gift of divine love had returned to him, he began to give thanks to God and humbly to kiss the Savior's feet.

Then as he raised his head to look gratefully up at the Savior's face, Christ held out His most holy hands and opened them for him to kiss. And while He opened them, Brother John arose and kissed His hands.

And when he had kissed them, he came closer and leaned against the breast of Christ, and he embraced Jesus and kissed His holy bosom.[4] And Christ likewise embraced and kissed him.

And when Brother John kissed the holy breast of Christ, he perceived so heavenly a fragrance that if all the scents and perfumes in the world were fused together they would seem a putrid stench compared to that divine fragrance. Moreover the above-mentioned rays issued from the Savior's breast, throwing light into his mind interiorly and exteriorly and into everything around him. And in that embrace, fragrance, light, and holy breast of the Lord Jesus Christ, Brother John was rapt in ecstasy and utterly consoled and marvelously enlightened. For henceforth, because he had drunk from the fountain of the Lord's breast, he was filled with the gift of wisdom and the grace of God's word, and he often spoke marvelous supernatural words. And because from his belly flowed streams of living water which he had imbibed from the depths of the breast of Our Lord Jesus Christ, he therefore converted the minds of those who heard him and reaped wonderful spiritual fruit.

Furthermore, that fragrance and light which he had perceived endured within his soul for many months. And what is still more: on that path in the forest where the Savior's blessed feet had walked and at some distance roundabout he perceived that same light and fragrance for a long time, whenever he went there.[5]

When Brother John was coming back to himself after his rapture, the Blessed Christ disappeared. Yet afterward he always remained consoled and enlightened. For then he did not find the Humanity of Christ—as he who heard about it from Brother John told me—but he found his own soul buried in the depths of the Divinity. And this was proved by many clear manifestations.

For he used to utter such inspiring and profound and luminous words before the Roman Curia and before kings and barons and masters of theology and doctors of canon law that he moved all of them to wonder and surprise. Although Brother John was almost an uneducated man, he nevertheless solved and explained in an amazing way the most subtle and abstract problems concerning the Trinity and other deep mysteries of Holy Scripture.[6]

Now that Brother John was, as we have seen, raised up first to the feet of Christ with tears, then to the hands with graces, and third to the blessed breast with a rapture and rays of light—these are great mysteries which cannot be explained in brief words. But let him who wants to understand it read St. Bernard on the Canticle of Canticles, who there describes the successive groups: the beginners at the feet, those progressing at the hands, but the perfect at the kiss and embrace.

And that the Blessed Christ gave such grace to Brother John while saying nothing teaches us that, as the Good Shepherd, He strove more to feed the soul with divine grace than to make exterior sounds ring in the bodily ears, because the Kingdom of God is not in external things but in the innermost ones, as the psalmist says, "All His glory is within."

To the glory of Our Lord Jesus Christ. Amen.

50 *How Brother John of Alverna, While Saying Mass on All Souls' Day, Saw Many Souls Liberated from Purgatory*

Once when Brother John of Alverna was saying Mass on the day after All Saints' Day for all the souls of the dead, as the Church has ordained, he offered with such fervent charity and compassionate pity that most high Sacrament—which the souls of the dead desire more than all the other things we can do for them because of its efficacy—that he seemed to be consumed by the ardor of his devotion and his supernatural brotherly love.

When therefore during that Mass he reverently elevated the most holy Body of Christ and offered It to God the Father, praying to Him that for the love of His Blessed Son Jesus Christ, who had hung on the Cross to save souls, He might mercifully deign to free from the sufferings of Purgatory those souls whom He had created and redeemed, all of a sudden he saw an almost countless number of souls going out of Purgatory like innumerable sparks of fire issuing from a blazing furnace. And he saw them flying up to their heavenly home through the merits of Christ who hung on the Cross for humanity's salvation and who is offered up every day in that most holy Host for the living and the dead. For He is the Blessed God and Man, Light and Life, Redeemer and Judge and everlasting Savior. Amen.

51 *How Brother James of Falerone Appeared After He Died to Brother John of Alverna*

At the time when Brother James of Falerone, a man of great sanctity, was seriously ill in the Place of Mogliano in the Custody of Fermo, Brother John of Alverna, who was then staying in the Place of Massa, on hearing about his illness, began to pray fervently to God for him in mental prayer, with the heartfelt desire that Brother James might recover his health if it were good for his soul, because Brother John loved him as if he were his own father.

And while he was thus praying devoutly, he was rapt in an ecstasy and saw in the air a great throng of many angels and saints above his cell which was in the woods. And they shone with such brightness that they illuminated the whole countryside.

And among those angels he saw that sick Brother James for whom he was praying, standing there radiant with light and dressed in white clothes. He saw among them our blessed Father Francis adorned with the holy Stigmata of Christ and resplendent in great glory. He also saw and recognized the saintly Brother Lucido and Brother Matthew the Elder of Monte Rubbiano and many other friars whom he had never seen or known in this life, with many saints, and all of them were radiant with similar glory and brightness.

And while Brother John was gazing with great delight at that blessed throng of saints, it was revealed to him that the soul of the sick friar would certainly be saved and that he was destined to die from that illness, but that he would not go to Heaven immediately after dying because he had to be purified in Purgatory for a short while.

Now on seeing this, Brother John rejoiced so much over the salvation and glory of that friar that he did not grieve over the death of his body, but with great spiritual consolation he frequently called him, saying within himself: "Brother James, my dear Brother James, faithful servant of Christ and friend of God—Brother James, my beloved Father—Brother James, companion of the angels and of the saints!"

And so being sure of the death of Brother James and rejoicing over the salvation of his soul, he came back to himself and set out at once from the Place of Massa, where he had had this vision.

And he went to visit Brother James at Mogliano, where he found him so weak from his illness that he could hardly speak. And Brother John announced to him that he was going to die but that his soul would be saved and go in joy to the glory of eternal life, according to the certainty which he had been given by divine revelation.

Brother James, being assured of his salvation, was utterly filled with joy both in mind and countenance, and he made Brother John welcome with a beautiful smile and a happy expression on his features, thanking him for the joyful news he brought. And because Brother James loved him like a son, he commended himself fervently to Brother John, telling him that his soul was about to leave his body.

Then Brother John eagerly asked him to agree to come back to him after dying and tell him how he was—which Brother James promised to do if it pleased the Savior to allow him.

And after he had said that, as the moment of his death was approaching, Brother James began to recite with devotion these words of the psalm: "Oh, in peace—Oh, in Him— Oh, I will sleep— Oh, I will rest!" And after saying that verse, with a joyful and happy expression on his face, he left this life and went to the Lord Jesus Christ.

And after he had been buried, Brother John went back to the Place of Massa and waited for Brother James to carry out his promise to return to him on the day when he said he would. And while on that day he was waiting and praying, Christ appeared to him in a bright light with a great throng of angels and saints, but Brother James was not among them. So Brother John in great surprise fervently commended him to Christ.

1422

Later, on the next day, while Brother John was praying in the forest of Massa, Brother James appeared to him, all in glory and joy, accompanied by angels.

And Brother John said to him: "Oh, holy Father, why did you not return and speak to me on the day you promised?"

Brother James answered: "Because I needed a little purifying. But at that same hour when Christ appeared to you, I appeared to the holy lay brother James of Massa while he was serving Mass—and he also saw the Host at the Elevation changed into an indescribably beautiful living Boy. And I spoke to that Brother and said: 'Today I am going to the Kingdom of God with that Boy, for no one can go there except through Him!' And at the same moment when you commended me to Christ, your prayer was heard and I was liberated."

And after saying that he went to the Lord. And Brother John was greatly consoled. Now Brother James of Falerone died on the Vigil of St. James the Apostle in July, and was buried in the Place of Mogliano, where he performs many miracles.[1]

To the glory of God. Amen.

52 *How Brother John Saw All Created Things in a Vision*

Because the above-mentioned Brother John of Alverna had completely renounced all the passing pleasures and consolations of this world and had placed all his affection and all his hope in God, the divine Goodness granted him new consolations and wonderful revelations, especially when the great Feast Days of Our Blessed Lord Jesus Christ came around.

So it happened once that when the Savior's Nativity was approaching, he was eagerly awaiting some consolation from God concerning the sweet Humanity of Christ. The Holy Spirit—who knows how to give Its gifts as It wishes, as to time and place, without regard to "him that wills, or him that runs, but to God who shows mercy"—granted to Brother John, not the consolation that he was awaiting regarding the Humanity of Christ, but such a great and intense and fervent love for the charity of Christ, by which He had humbled Himself to take on our humanity, that it seemed to him as though his soul was drawn out of his body and his soul and heart were burning a hundred times more than if he had been in a furnace. Being unable to endure that burning, he became frightened and panted and shouted out loud, because owing to the excessive intensity of his love he could not restrain himself from shouting.

Now at the hour when he felt that ardent love, so strong and sure a hope of his salvation came over him that if he had died then, he would not have believed at all that he had to pass through Purgatory. And that great love lasted, with interruptions, for half a year. But the fervor lasted more than a year, to such a degree that sometimes for an hour he seemed to be dying.

And after that time he received countless visitations and consolations from God, as I several times observed with my own eyes and as many others frequently observed. For because of his overflowing fervor and love he could not conceal the visitations, and many times I saw him rapt in ecstasy.

Among them, one night he was raised to such a marvelous light in God that he saw in the Creator all created things, both in Heaven and on earth, all disposed in their various realms, for instance how the choirs of blessed spirits are disposed under God—and also the earthly paradise and the Blessed Humanity of Christ. And he likewise perceived the lower realms. And he saw and felt how all created things are related to the Creator, and how God is above and within and without and around all created things.

Afterward God raised him above every creature so that his soul was absorbed and assumed into the abyss of the Divinity and Light, and it was buried in the ocean of God's Eternity and Infinity, to the point where he could not feel anything that was created or formed or finite or conceivable or visible which the human heart could conceive or the tongue could describe. And his soul was so absorbed in that abyss of Divinity and ocean or mass of light that it was like a drop of wine absorbed in a deep sea. And as that drop finds nothing in itself but the sea, so his soul saw nothing but God in all and above all, within all and without all things—yet three Persons in one God and one God in three Persons.

And he felt that eternal infinite love which led the Son of

1424

God to incarnate out of obedience to His Father. And by meditating and pondering and weeping on that path of the Incarnation and Passion of the Son of God, he came to unutterable insights. And he said that there is no other way by which the soul can enter into God and have everlasting life except through Christ, who is the Way, the Truth, and the Life.

In that same vision there was also shown to him everything that was done by Christ from the fall of the first man until the entrance into eternal life of Christ,[1] who is the head and leader of all the elect who have existed since the beginning of the world, who are, and who will be until the end, as has been announced by the holy Prophets.

To the glory of Our Lord Jesus Christ. Amen.

53 *How While Saying Mass Brother John Fell Down As If He Were Dead*

Something wonderful and worthy of lasting fame happened to that Brother John, as the friars who were present have related.

Once when Brother John was staying in the Place of Mogliano of the Custody of Fermo in the Province of the Marches, during the first night after the Octave of St. Lawrence—within the Octave of the Assumption of the Blessed Virgin Mary—he arose before the time for matins. And while the Lord filled his soul with grace, he recited matins with the friars. But after saying matins, he went into the garden, because he felt such sweet consolation from the great graces which he derived from those words of the Lord *Hoc est Corpus Meum* (This is My Body) that he shouted out loud and repeated in his heart "*Hoc est Corpus Meum.*"

He was enlightened by the Holy Spirit regarding those words, and the eyes of his soul being opened, he saw Jesus Christ with the Blessed Virgin and a throng of angels and saints. And he understood that saying of the Apostle that we are all one body in Christ, and each of us is a member one of another, and that with the saints we may grasp what is the breadth, the length, the sublimity, and the depth, and know the love of Christ that surpasses all knowledge, for it is wholly in this Most Holy Sacrament which is brought into being when the words *Hoc est Corpus Meum* are said.

And when dawn came, stirred by divine grace, with those words on his lips, he went into the church in great fervor of spirit. And thinking no one saw or heard him—though a friar was praying in the choir and heard it—he was so troubled by the intensity of the grace that he could not prevent himself from shouting loudly three times.

And he remained in that condition until it was time for the Mass which he was to celebrate. So he went to vest. But when he reached the altar, the grace of fervent devotion increased within him, and the love of Christ also grew in him. And he was given a certain ineffable sense of God's presence which he could not express in words. He was afraid that this feeling and marvelous fervor might increase so much he would have to interrupt the Mass, so that he did not know what to do—whether to proceed or to wait.

However, as he had once had a similar experience, and the Lord had so tempered his emotion that he had not had to interrupt the Mass, he hoped that he might proceed this time. Nevertheless he feared what might happen, because such infusions of divine grace cannot be controlled by human beings.

When he had proceeded as far as the Preface of the Blessed Virgin, the supernatural illumination and sweet consolation of God's love increased so much within him that when he reached the *Qui pridie* he could hardly endure such overwhelming sweetness. Finally, when he came to the Consecration itself and began to pronounce the words of the Consecration over the Host, he kept repeating the first half of the formula—*Hoc est—Hoc est*—very often, and he was unable to go any further. And the reason why he could not go on was that he felt and saw the presence of Christ and of a throng of angels and saints, so that he almost fainted because of their grandeur which he felt in his soul.

Therefore the guardian of the Place anxiously came running to assist him and stood beside him, and a friar stood behind him with a lighted candle, while the other friars were watching in fear with many other men and women, including some of the most prominent persons in the province who were

1426

in the church to hear Mass, and all of them stood around the altar, waiting, and many were weeping, as women do.

But Brother John, almost beside himself with sweet bliss and joy, was standing there without finishing the Consecration because he saw that Christ did not enter into the Host or rather that the Host was not changed into the Body of Christ, until he added the other half of the formula, *Corpus Meum.*

Finally, after a long time, when it pleased God, Brother John, unable to bear the great majesty of Christ the Head, as the paradise of the Mystical Body was revealed to him, exclaimed aloud: *"Corpus Meum!"* The appearance of the bread immediately vanished, and in the host appeared the Lord Jesus Christ, the Blessed Son of God Incarnate and Glorified. And He showed him the humility and love which led Him to take flesh in the Virgin Mary and which makes Him come into the hands of the priest every day when he consecrates the host. And that humility held him in such sweet consolation and ineffable and unutterable wonder that he was not able to complete the remaining words of the Consecration. For as Brother John himself said, that humility and condescension of the Savior toward us is so marvelous that our body cannot endure it or words describe it. And as a result he could not proceed.

Therefore after saying *"Hoc est Corpus Meum,"* he was rapt in an ecstasy and fell backward, but was held up by the guardian who was standing beside him, for otherwise he would have fallen to the ground. And as the other friars and lay people who were in the church ran up, he was carried into the sacristy as if he were dead. For his body had turned cold like a corpse. And his fingers were so stiffly contracted that they could hardly be opened or moved. And he lay there unconscious from morning until terce. This happened during the summer.

Now as I was present and wished very much to know what God's mercy had done in him, almost as soon as he came back to himself I went to him and asked him for the love of God to consent to tell me all about it. And because he used to confide in me a great deal, by the grace of God he told me all about it.

And among other things he told me that before and while he was consecrating, his heart became liquefied like heated wax, and his body seemed to be without bones, so that he could not lift his arms or his hands to make the Sign of the Cross over the host. And he added that before he became a priest, it was revealed to him that he would faint that way during Mass. But as he had already said many Masses and that prophecy had not been fulfilled, he had thought that revelation had not come from God. Nevertheless about fifty days before the Assumption of the Blessed Virgin when this thing happened to him, it was revealed to him that it would happen to him around the Feast of the Assumption. But later he had forgotten that promise.[1]

To the praise and glory of Our Lord Jesus Christ. Amen.

Part Two

THE CONSIDERATIONS ON
THE HOLY STIGMATA

In this part we shall contemplate with devout consideration the glorious, sacred, and holy Stigmata of our blessed Father St. Francis which he received from Christ on the holy Mount Alverna. And because those Stigmata were five, like the five Wounds of Our Lord Jesus Christ, therefore this treatise shall have Five Considerations.

The First will be about the way St. Francis came to the holy Mount Alverna.

The Second will be about the life he lived and the conversation he had with his companions on that holy mountain.

The Third will be about the apparition of the Seraph and the imprinting of the most holy Stigmata.

The Fourth will be about St. Francis' going down from Mount Alverna after he had received the holy Stigmata and about his return to St. Mary of the Angels.

The Fifth will be about certain apparitions and revelations which were given after the death of St. Francis to some holy friars and to other pious persons concerning those glorious Stigmata.

The First Consideration: How Count Orlando
of Chiusi Gave Mount Alverna to St. Francis

Regarding the First Consideration, you should know that St. Francis, some time before he had the Stigmata of the Savior, moved by an inspiration from God, left the Valley of Spoleto to go to the Romagna with his companion Brother Leo.

And on their way they passed by the foot of the castle and walled village of Montefeltro, where at that time a great banquet and festival were being held to celebrate the knighting of one of the Counts of Montefeltro. When St. Francis heard from the villagers about the festivity that was taking place, and that many noblemen had gathered there from various districts, he said to Brother Leo: "Let's go up to that festival, for with God's help we will gather some good spiritual fruit."

Among the noblemen who had come to that meeting was a great and wealthy Count from Tuscany named Orlando of Chiusi in Casentino who, because of the marvelous things he had heard about the holiness and miracles of St. Francis, had a great devotion for him and wanted very much to see him and hear him preach.

St. Francis arrived at that village and entered and went to the square where all those noblemen were assembled. And in fervor of spirit he climbed onto a low wall and began to preach, taking as the theme of his sermon these words in Italian: "So great is the good which I expect that all pain is to me a delight." And under the dictation of the Holy Spirit he preached on this theme so devoutly and so profoundly—proving its truth by the various sufferings and martyrdoms of the holy Apostles and Martyrs, and by the severe penances of the holy Confessors, and by the many tribulations and temptations of the holy Virgins and of the other Saints—that everyone stood there gazing attentively at him, listening to him as though an angel of God were speaking. Among them, Count Orlando was touched to the heart by God through the marvelous preaching of St. Francis, and he decided to have a talk with him after the sermon about the state of his soul.

Therefore, when the sermon was over, he took St. Francis aside and said to him: "Father, I would like to speak to you about the salvation of my soul."

But St. Francis, who was very tactful, answered: "I am glad. But this morning go and honor your friends, since they invited you to the festival, and have dinner with them, and after dinner we will talk together as much as you wish."

Count Orlando therefore went to dine, and after dinner he returned to St. Francis and had a long talk with him about the state and salvation of his soul. And at the end Count Orlando said to St. Francis: "Brother Francis, I have a mountain in Tuscany which is very solitary and wild and perfectly suited for someone who wants to do penance in a place far from people or who wants to live a solitary life. It is called Mount Alverna. If that mountain should please you and your companions, I would gladly give it to you for the salvation of my soul."

Now St. Francis had a most intense desire to find some solitary place where he could conveniently devote himself to contemplation. So when he heard this offer, he first praised God who provides for His little sheep, and then he thanked Count Orlando, saying: "Sire, when you go home, I will send two of my companions to you, and you can show them that mountain. And if it seems suitable for prayer and penance, I very gladly accept your charitable offer."

And after he said that, St. Francis left. And when he had ended his journey, he returned to St. Mary of the Angels.

And likewise Count Orlando, after the knighting festival was over, returned to his castle named Chiusi, which is a mile away from Mount Alverna.[1]

After St. Francis had returned to St. Mary of the Angels, he sent two of his companions to Count Orlando. They searched for him, but because they did not know that part of the country they had great difficulty in finding his castle. When they arrived, he was very glad to see them, and he welcomed them with great joy and kindness, as though they were angels of God.

And wishing to show them Mount Alverna, he sent about fifty armed men with them, perhaps to protect them from wild animals. With this escort the friars climbed up Mount Alverna and explored it for a place where they might set up a house to live in. Finally they came to a part of the mountain where there was a small plateau that was very suitable for prayer and contemplation. And they decided in the name of the Lord to make their dwelling and that of St. Francis in that place.

With the help of the armed men who accompanied them, they cut down some branches with swords and built a little hut with the branches.

And having thus in the name of God accepted and taken possession of Mount Alverna and of the friars' Place on that mountain, with the count's permission, they left and went back to St. Francis.[2]

And when they came to him, they told him that the place was very solitary and suitable for contemplation. And they told him in detail how they had taken possession of it.

On hearing this news St. Francis was very happy. And praising and thanking God, he said to those friars with a joyful expression: "My sons, our Lent of St. Michael the Archangel is approaching. I firmly believe that it is the will of God that we spend that Lent up on Mount Alverna, which has been prepared for us by Divine Providence, so that for the honor and glory of God and the glorious Virgin Mary and the holy angels, we may merit from Christ to consecrate that blessed mountain with penance."

Then, having said that, St. Francis took with him Brother Masseo of Marignano of Assisi, who was a man of great wisdom and eloquence, and Brother Angelo Tancredi of Rieti, who was a man of very noble birth and had been a knight in the world, and Brother Leo, who was a man of the greatest simplicity and purity, because of which St. Francis loved him very much and used to reveal nearly all his secrets to him.

With those three friars St. Francis began to pray. And when their prayer was finished, he commended himself and the above-mentioned friars to the prayers of the friars who were staying behind. And with those three, in the name of Jesus Christ Crucified, he set out for Mount Alverna.

And as they were leaving, St. Francis called one of his three companions—Brother Masseo—and said to him: "Brother Masseo, you are to be our guardian and our superior on this journey. And while traveling and stopping together, we will follow our custom: either we will say the office or we will talk about God or we will keep silence. And we will not take any thought about eating or sleeping, but when the time for overnight rest comes we will beg for a little bread, and we will stop and rest in the place which God will prepare for us."

Then those three companions nodded. And making the Sign of the Cross, they set out.

And the first evening they came to a Place of the friars, and they stayed there overnight.[3]

The second evening, because of bad weather and because

they were tired and were unable to reach any Place of the friars or any village or house, when night came on with bad weather, they sought shelter in an abandoned and uninhabited church. And they lay down to rest there.

While his companions were sleeping, St. Francis began to pray. And he was persevering in prayer when, during the first watch of the night, a great number of the fiercest devils came with very great noise and tumult, and they began to attack and persecute him. One took hold of him here, another there. One pulled him down, another up. One threatened him with one thing, another scolded him for something else. And so they strove to disturb his praying in different ways.

But they were not able to do so because God was with him. And when St. Francis had endured those attacks of the devils for some time, he began to cry out in a loud voice: "You damned spirits, you can do only what the hand of God allows you. And therefore in the name of Almighty God I tell you to do to my body whatever God allows you. I will gladly endure it since I have no enemy worse than my body. And so if you take revenge on my enemy for me, you do me a very great favor."

Then the devils seized him with great violence and fury, and began to drag him around the church and to hurt him and persecute him much more than before.

And then St. Francis cried out and said: "My Lord Jesus Christ, I thank You for the great love and charity which You are showing me, because it is a sign of great love when the Lord punishes His servant well for all his faults in this world, so that he may not be punished for them in the next world. And I am prepared to endure with joy every pain and every adversity which You, my God, wish to send me for my sins."

Then the devils, having been humiliated and defeated by his endurance and patience, went away.

And in fervor of spirit St. Francis came out of the church and entered into a forest that was nearby. And there he gave himself to prayer. And praying and weeping and beating his breast, he sought Jesus Christ, the spouse and delight of his soul. And at last he found Him in the secret depths of his heart. And he spoke to Him reverently as to his Lord. Then he answered Him as his Judge. Next he entreated Him as a father. Then he talked with Him as with a friend.

During that night and in that forest, his companions, after they awoke, stood listening and wondering what he was doing. And they saw and heard him devoutly praying with tears and cries to God to have mercy on sinners. And they also saw and heard him weeping aloud over the Passion of Christ, as if he were seeing it with his own eyes.

That same night they saw him praying with his arms crossed on his chest, raised up above the ground and suspended in the air for a long time, surrounded by a bright cloud.

And so he spent that whole night in holy contemplation without sleeping.[4]

The next morning, as his companions knew that, owing to his exhaustion and lack of sleep during the night, St. Francis was too weak to be able to continue the journey on foot, they went to a poor local peasant and asked him, for the love of God, to lend his donkey for their Father, Brother Francis, who could not travel on foot. Hearing Brother Francis mentioned, the man asked them: "Are you friars of that Brother Francis of Assisi about whom people say so much good?"

The friars answered, "Yes," and that it was really for him that they were asking for the donkey.

Then with great devotion and care this good man saddled the donkey and led it to St. Francis, and with great reverence helped him get into the saddle.

Then they continued their journey, the peasant walking with them behind his donkey. And after they had gone a while, he said to St. Francis: "Tell me, are you Brother Francis of Assisi?"

St. Francis answered that he was.

"Well, then," said the peasant, "try to be as good as everyone thinks you are, because many people have great faith in you. So I urge you: never let there be anything in you different from what they expect of you."

When St. Francis heard these words, he did not mind being admonished by a peasant, and he did not say to himself, as many proud fellows who wear the cowl nowadays would say, "Who is this brute who admonishes me?" But he immediately got off the donkey and threw himself on his knees before the farmer and humbly kissed his feet, thanking him for having deigned to admonish him so charitably.

Then his companions and the peasant very devoutly helped him to his feet and set him on the donkey again. And they traveled on.[5]

When they had climbed about halfway up the mountain, because the summer heat was very great and the path was long and steep, the peasant began to suffer intensely from thirst, and he called ahead to St. Francis: "I am dying of thirst. If I don't have something to drink, I'll suffocate in a minute!"

So St. Francis immediately got off the donkey and began to pray. And he remained kneeling on the ground, raising his hands toward Heaven, until he knew by revelation that God had granted his prayer. Then he said to the peasant: "Run quickly to that rock, and there you will find running water which Christ in His mercy has just caused to flow from the rock."

The man ran to the place which St. Francis had shown him, and found a very fine spring that had been made to flow through the hard rock by the power of St. Francis' prayer. And he drank all he wanted, and felt better.

And it truly seems that that spring was produced by a divine miracle through the prayers of St. Francis, because neither before nor afterward was any spring ever seen there or anywhere nearby.

After he had done this, St. Francis, with his companions and the peasant, gave thanks to God for having shown them this miracle. And then they traveled on.[6]

And as they drew near to the peak that forms Mount Alverna itself, it pleased St. Francis to rest for a while under a certain oak tree standing by the path that is still there now.

While resting under the oak tree St. Francis began to study the location and the scenery. And when he was absorbed in this contemplation, a great number of all kinds of birds came flying down to him with joyful songs, and twittering and fluttering their wings. And they surrounded St. Francis in such a way that some of them settled on his head and others on his shoulders and others on his knees, and still others on his arms and lap and on his hands and around his feet. They all showed great joy by their tuneful singing and happy movements, as if they were rejoicing at his coming and inviting and persuading him to stay there.

Seeing this, his companions and the peasant were greatly surprised. St. Francis rejoiced in spirit and said to them: "My dear Brothers, I believe it is pleasing to Our Lord Jesus Christ that we accept a Place and live a while on this solitary mountain, since our little brothers and sisters the birds show such joy over our coming."

After saying these words, he arose and they journeyed on. And at last they came to the spot which his companions had first selected, where until then there was nothing but a very poor little hut made of tree-branches.[7]

To the glory of God and of His Most Holy Name. Amen.

And this is the end of the First Consideration, namely, how St. Francis came to the holy Mount Alverna.

The Second Consideration: How St. Francis Spent His Time with His Companions on Mount Alverna

The Second Consideration deals with what St. Francis did with his companions on that mountain.

In this connection you should know that when Count Orlando heard that St. Francis had come with three companions to live on Mount Alverna, he was very happy. And the next day he left his castle with many men and came to visit him, bringing bread and other necessities for him and for his companions.

When he arrived up there, he found them praying. And going near, he greeted them.

Then St. Francis stood up and welcomed Count Orlando and his men with great affection and joy. And afterward they began to talk together. And after they had talked and St. Francis had thanked him for the holy mountain which he had given them and for his coming, he asked Count Orlando to have a poor little cell made for him at the foot of a very beautiful beech tree that was about a stone's throw from the friars' Place, because that spot seemed to him very suitable for devout prayer. And Count Orlando had it made without delay.

Afterward, because evening was drawing near and it was time to leave, St. Francis preached a short sermon to them before they left.

Then, after he had preached and given them his blessing, since Count Orlando had to leave, he called St. Francis and his companions aside and said to them: "My dear friars, I do not want you to lack anything which you may need on this wild mountain, because of which you might have to give less attention to spiritual things. So I want you—and I say this once for all—just to send to my house for anything you need. And if you do not do so, I will really be offended."

After he had said this, he left with his men and returned to the castle.[1]

Then St. Francis had his companions sit down, and he gave them instructions regarding the way of life which they and whoever wished to live as religious in hermitages should lead. And among other things he especially stressed to them the observance of holy poverty, saying: "Don't pay so much attention to the charitable offer of Count Orlando that you should in any way offend our Lady Poverty. You can be sure that the more we despise poverty, the more will the world despise us and the greater need will we suffer. But if we embrace holy poverty very closely, the world will come to us and will feed us abundantly. God has called us to this holy Order for the salvation of the world. And He has made this contract between us and the world: that we give the world a good example and that the world provide us with what we need. So let us persevere in holy poverty, because it is the way of perfection and the pledge and guarantee of everlasting riches."

And after many beautiful and inspiring words and instructions on this subject, he concluded: "That is the way of life which I place upon myself and on you. And because I see that I am drawing near to death, I intend to stay alone and recollect myself with God and weep over my sins before Him. And let Brother Leo, whenever it seems right to him, bring me a little bread and a little water. And on no account let any lay persons come to me, but deal with them yourselves."

And after he had said those words, he gave them his blessing and went off to the cell by the beech tree. And his companions stayed in the Place with the firm intention of obeying the orders of St. Francis.[2]

A few days later St. Francis was standing beside that cell, gazing at the form of the mountain and marveling at the great chasms and openings in the massive rocks. And he began to pray, and then it was revealed to him by God that those striking chasms had been made in a miraculous way at the hour of Christ's Passion when, as the Gospel says, "the rocks split." And God wanted this to be manifested in a special way here on Mount Alverna in order to show that the Passion of Christ was to be renewed on that mountain in the soul of St. Francis by love and compassion and in his body by the imprinting of the Stigmata.

As soon as St. Francis had received this revelation, he shut himself up in his cell and recollected himself completely in his soul and prepared himself to meditate on the mystery of that revelation. And from that time, St. Francis, through constant prayer, began to experience more often the sweet consolations of divine contemplation, as a result of which he was many times so rapt in God that he was seen by his companions raised bodily above the ground and absorbed in God.[8]

In these contemplative raptures God revealed to him not only present and future things but also the secret thoughts and desires of the friars, as his companion Brother Leo experienced during those days.

For Brother Leo suffered a very great spiritual (not physical) temptation from the devil, so that there came to him an intense desire to have some inspiring words written by St. Francis' own hand. For he believed that if he had them, the temptation would leave him either entirely or partly. And although he had that desire, through shame or reverence he did not dare tell St. Francis about it. But the Holy Spirit revealed to the Saint what Brother Leo did not tell him. St. Francis therefore called him and had him bring an inkhorn and pen and paper. And with his own hand he wrote a Praise of Christ, just as Leo had wished. And at the end he made the sign of the Tau and gave it to him, saying: "Take this paper, dear Brother, and keep it carefully until you die. May God bless you and protect you from all temptation! Do not be troubled because you have temptations. For I consider you more of a servant and friend of God and I love you more, the more you are attacked by temptations. Truly I tell you that no one should consider himself a perfect friend of God until he has passed through many temptations and tribulations."

Brother Leo accepted that writing with fervent love and faith. And at once all temptation left him.

And going back to the Place, with great joy he told his companions what a grace God had given him in receiving those words written by St. Francis' own hand. He carefully put the paper away and kept it. And later the friars performed many miracles with it.[4]

From that hour Brother Leo, with great innocence and good intention, began carefully to observe and meditate on the life of St. Francis. He quietly tried as much as he could to see what the Saint was doing. And because of his purity he merited time and time again to see St. Francis rapt in God and raised above the ground. He found him outside the cell raised up into the air sometimes as high as three feet, sometimes four, at other times halfway up or at the top of the beech trees—and some of those trees were very high. At other times he found him raised so high in the air and surrounded by such radiance that he could hardly see him. Then Brother Leo would kneel down and prostrate himself completely on the ground on the spot from which the holy Father had been lifted into the air while praying.

When St. Francis was raised so little above the ground that he could reach him and touch his feet, what did that simple friar do? He would go to him quietly and embrace and kiss his feet and say with tears: "God, have mercy on this sinner. And through the merits of this very holy man, let me find Your grace and mercy."

And while Brother Leo was praying and recommending himself to God as before, through the merits of the holy Father, he experienced very great visitations of divine grace. And because of these things which Brother Leo frequently told about the Saint, he had such great devotion for him that very often he watched the hidden doings of St. Francis by night and day with holy ingenuity.

And one time among others, when he was standing there under St. Francis' feet and the latter were raised so high above the ground that Brother Leo could not touch him, he saw a scroll written in letters of gold come down from Heaven and rest on St. Francis' head. And on the scroll these words were written: HERE IS THE GRACE OF GOD. And after he had read it, he saw it return to Heaven.[5]

Through the gift of this grace of God that was in him, St. Francis was not only rapt in God in ecstatic contemplation, but he was also sometimes consoled by visitations of angels. One day while he was thinking about his death and the state of his Order when he was no longer alive, and he was saying, "Lord God, after my death what will happen to Your poor little family which in Your kindness You entrusted to this sinner? Who will console them? Who will correct them? Who will pray to You for them?" and similar words, an angel sent by God appeared to him and consoled him by saying: "I tell you on behalf of God that your Order will last until Judgment Day. And no one, no matter how great a sinner he is, will fail to obtain mercy from God if he has a heartfelt love for your Order. And no one who from malice persecutes your Order will be able to live long. Moreover, no one in your Order who is very evil and who does not amend his life will be able to persevere in the Order. Therefore do not grieve if you see some friars in your Order who are not good and who do not observe the Rule as they should. And do not think then that your Order is declining, because there will always be very many in it who will perfectly observe the Gospel life of Christ and the purity of the Rule. And immediately after their earthly life they will go to eternal life without passing through Purgatory at all. Some will live the life less perfectly, and they will be purified in Purgatory before they go to Paradise, but the period of their purgation will be entrusted to you by God. But do not worry about those who do not keep your Rule at all, says God, because He does not care about them."

And after the angel had said those words, he disappeared, leaving St. Francis greatly comforted and consoled.[6]

The Feast of the Assumption of Our Lady was then approaching, and St. Francis sought a convenient place that was more isolated and remote in which he might spend in greater solitude the Lent of St. Michael the Archangel, which began on the Feast of the Assumption.

Therefore he called Brother Leo and said to him: "Go and stand in the door of the oratory of the friars' Place, and when I call you, come to me."

Brother Leo went and stood in the doorway, and St. Francis walked some distance away and called loudly.

Hearing himself called, Brother Leo went to him. And St. Francis said to him: "Son, let's look for a more remote place, from which you cannot hear me when I call you."

And while they were seeking, they saw on the side of the mountain facing the south a spot that was isolated and perfectly suited to his purpose. But they could not reach it, because in front of it there was a very deep and fearful chasm in the rock. So with great effort they put a log across as a bridge and went over it.

Then St. Francis sent for the other friars and told them that he intended to spend the Lent of St. Michael in that solitary place, where he could pray alone, away from the others. And so he asked them to make a poor little hut for him there, where they could not hear him if he shouted.

And when the hut was made, St. Francis said to them: "Go back to your Place and leave me here alone, because with God's help I intend to spend this Lent here without distraction or disturbance of mind. And so none of you must come to me, and don't let any lay person come to me. But you, Brother Leo, come only once a day with a little bread and water, and once again at night at the hour for matins. And at that hour come silently, and when you reach the end of the bridge, just say: '*Domine, labia mea aperies.*' And if I answer inside, '*Et os meum annuntiabit laudem tuam,*' go across and come to the cell, and we will say matins together. But if I do not reply at once, then go right back."

And St. Francis said this because sometimes he was so rapt in God that he could not talk for a night and day, and he did not hear or feel anything with his bodily senses. Brother Leo very carefully observed this order.

And after he said this, St. Francis gave them his blessing, and they went back to the Place.[7]

Now the Feast of the Assumption came, and St. Francis began the holy fast with great abstinence and severity, mortifying his body and comforting his spirit by means of fervent prayers, watchings, and scourgings.

And while he was doing so he continually increased in virtue. And he prepared his soul to receive divine mysteries and illuminations, and his body to sustain the cruel attacks of the devils, with whom he often fought bodily.

Among other times, one day during this fast St. Francis came out of his cell in fervor of spirit and went to pray in a cavity nearby under a rock, below which there is a horrible and fearful precipice and a great drop to the ground. All of a sudden the devil appeared in a terrifying form, amid a great uproar, and began to beat him in order to throw him down.

Having nowhere to flee and being unable to endure the exceedingly cruel sight of the devil, St. Francis quickly turned around, with his hands and face and his whole body against the rock. And he commended himself to God, while groping with his hands for anything that he could grasp.

But as it pleased God, who never lets His servants be tried more than they can endure, suddenly by a miracle the rock to which he was clinging yielded to the form of his body and received him into itself. And as if he had put his hands and face into some liquid wax, the shape of his face and hands was imprinted on that rock. And thus with the help of God he escaped from the devil.[8]

But what the devil was not able to do to St. Francis at that time, namely, throw him down from there, he did later on, a good while after the death of St. Francis, to one of his dear and devout friars. One day while the friar was fitting in place some pieces of wood so that people could safely go there out of devotion to St. Francis and to the miracle which occurred there, the devil gave him a push while he was carrying a big log on his head that he wanted to place there, and made him fall with that log on his head. But God, who had saved and preserved St. Francis from falling, through his merits saved and preserved that devout friar of his from the danger of the fall. For as he fell, that friar with great fervor commended himself in a loud voice to St. Francis, who immediately appeared to him and set him down on the rocks below without any shock or injury. Now the other friars had heard his cry when he fell and they thought he was dead and dashed to pieces on the sharp rocks, since he had fallen from such a great height. So with great sorrow and weeping they took the stretcher and went down the other side of the mountain to fetch the pieces of his body and bury them. And when they had already come down the mountain, the friar who had fallen met them, carrying on his head the log with which he had fallen, and he was singing the *Te Deum laudamus* in a loud voice. As the friars were greatly amazed, he told them in detail how he had fallen and how St. Francis had saved him from all harm. Then all the friars came back to the Place with him, singing the *Te Deum* and praising and thanking God and St. Francis for the miracle he had performed for his friar.[9]

St. Francis, therefore, persevering in that fast, as we have said, although he endured many attacks from the devil, nevertheless received many consolations from God, not only through the visits of angels but likewise of wild birds. For during the whole of that forty days' fast a falcon that had its nest there near his cell would wake him up every night before matins by singing and beating its wings against the cell. And it would not leave until he arose to say matins. But at times when St. Francis was more tired or weak or ill, the falcon, like a tactful and compassionate human being, would sing somewhat later. And so St. Francis took a great liking for this holy "clock," because the falcon's thoughtfulness helped him to drive away all laziness and stimulated him to pray. Besides, it sometimes kept him company in a tame way during the daytime as well.[10]

Finally, pertaining to this Second Consideration, as St. Francis was greatly weakened in body, partly by his severe abstinence and partly by the attacks of the devils, and he wished to comfort his body with the spiritual food of the soul, he began to think of the limitless glory and joy of those who are blessed with eternal life. And then he began to pray that God might grant him the grace of tasting a little of that joy.

And while he was meditating on that thought, all of a sudden an angel appeared to him in a very bright light, holding a viol in his left hand and a bow in his right hand. And as St. Francis gazed in amazement at the angel, the latter drew the bow once upward across the viol. And immediately such a beautiful melody invaded St. Francis' soul and suspended all his bodily senses that, as he later told his companions, he wondered whether, if the angel had drawn the bow down again, his soul would not have left his body owing to the unbearable loveliness of the music.[11]

And that is all regarding the Second Consideration.

*The Third Consideration: About the Apparition
of the Seraph and the Imprinting of the
Holy Stigmata on St. Francis*

Regarding the Third Consideration, that is, the apparition of the Seraph and the imprinting of the Stigmata, you should know that when the Feast of the Cross in September was approaching, Brother Leo went one night at the usual time to say matins with St. Francis.

And after he had called *"Domine, labia mea aperies"* from the end of the bridge, as he usually did and as he had been ordered to do by the Saint, St. Francis did not answer. Now Brother Leo did not go back, as St. Francis had instructed him, but with a good and holy intention he went across the bridge and quietly entered the Saint's cell. By the bright moonlight shining in through the door, he saw that he was not in the cell. Not finding him, he thought that he might be praying outside somewhere in the woods. So he came out and silently walked among the trees looking for him by the light of the moon.

And at last he heard St. Francis' voice speaking, and he went closer to hear what he was saying. In the moonlight he saw St. Francis on his knees, with his face lifted toward the sky and his hands held out to God, saying these words with fervor of spirit: "Who are You, my dearest God? And what am I, your vilest little worm and useless little servant?" And he repeated those words over and over, and he said nothing else.

Brother Leo marveled greatly at this, and he looked up and gazed at the sky. And while he was looking, he saw come down from the heights of Heaven a torch of flaming fire that was very beautiful and bright and pleasing to the eyes and that descended and rested on St. Francis' head. And he heard a voice come out of that flame and speak with St. Francis, and the Saint answered the speaker.

But seeing this and thinking himself unworthy to be so close to that holy spot where this marvelous apparition was taking place, and also fearing to offend St. Francis or to disturb him in his contemplation of such holy secrets, in case the Saint should hear him, he silently went back so that he could not hear what was said. And he stood at a distance, waiting to see the end.

And watching carefully, he saw St. Francis hold his hand out to the flame three times. And finally, after a long time, he saw the flame return to Heaven.

So Brother Leo went away, feeling reassured and joyful, and began to return quietly to his cell, so that the Saint should not hear him.

But as he was confidently leaving, St. Francis heard the sound of his feet on some twigs and leaves, and he said: "Whoever you are, I command you, in the name of Our Lord Jesus Christ, to stay where you are. Don't move from that spot!"

So Brother Leo obediently stood where he was and waited. And later he told his companions he was so terrified then that he would have preferred that the earth should swallow him up than to wait for St. Francis who, he thought, was angry with him. For Brother Leo took the greatest care not to offend his Father, so that through his fault St. Francis should not deprive him of his companionship. In fact, he felt such faith and love for the Saint that he did not care at all to live without him. And therefore whenever any friars were speaking about the Saints, Brother Leo used to say: "My dear friends, all the Saints are great, but St. Francis is also among the great ones because of the miracles which God performs through him." And he used to speak more willingly about him than about the others. So it is no wonder that he was terrified at his voice.

When St. Francis came up to him, he asked: "Who are you?"

Brother Leo replied, trembling: "I am Brother Leo, Father."

And recognizing him, St. Francis said to him: "Why did you come here, Little Brother Lamb? Did I not tell you many times not to go around watching me? Tell me under holy obedience whether you saw or heard anything?"

Brother Leo answered: "Father, I heard you talking and praying and saying often with great wonder, 'Who are You, my dearest God? And what am I, Your vilest little worm and useless little servant?' And then I saw a flame of fire come down from Heaven and speak with you, and you replied several times and held out your hand to it three times, but I don't know what you said."

Then Brother Leo knelt down before St. Francis and confessed the sin of disobedience which he had committed against his order, and with many tears he begged St. Francis to forgive him.

Then he asked very reverently: "Father, please explain to me the words I heard and also tell me those I did not hear."

Now St. Francis loved Brother Leo very much on account of his purity and meekness, and seeing that God had revealed to him or allowed the humble Brother to see some things, St. Francis consented to disclose and explain to him what he was asking.

And he said to him: "Little Brother Lamb of Jesus Christ, in those things which you saw and heard when I said those words, two lights were shown to my soul: one of the knowledge and understanding of the Creator, and the other of the knowledge of myself. When I said, 'Who are You, my dearest God?' then I was in a light of contemplation in which I saw the depths of the infinite goodness and wisdom and power of God. And when I said, 'What am I?' I was in a light of contemplation in which I saw the grievous depths of my vileness and misery, and therefore I said, 'Who are You, the Lord of infinite wisdom and good and mercy, that You deign to visit me, a most vile and abominable and contemptible worm?' And God was in that flame which you saw, and He spoke to me under the form of that flame, as He had formerly spoken to Moses.

"And among other things which He said to me then, He asked me to give Him three gifts. And I replied: 'My Lord, I am entirely Yours. You know that I have nothing but a habit and cord and breeches, and those three things are likewise Yours. So what can I offer or give to Your majesty? For Heaven and earth, fire and water, and everything in them are Yours, Lord. Who indeed has anything that is not Yours? Therefore when we offer You anything, we give You back what is Yours. So what can I offer to You, the Lord God, King of Heaven and earth and all creation? For what do I have that is not Yours?'

"Then God said to me: 'Put your hand in your bosom and offer me whatever you find there.' I searched and I found there a coin of gold that was so large and bright and beautiful that I had never seen one like it in this world, and then I offered it to God.

"God said to me again: 'Make Me another offering as before.'

"But I said to God: 'Lord, I do not have and do not love and do not want anything but You, and for love of You I have despised gold and all things. So if anything more is found in my breast, You put it there, and I give it back to You, the Ruler of all things.'

"And I did this three times. And after making the third offering, I knelt down and blessed and thanked God, who had given me something to offer. And I was immediately made to understand that those three offerings symbolized the holy golden obedience, the very great poverty, and the very radiant chastity which by His grace God has granted me to observe so perfectly that my conscience reproaches me nothing.

"And just as I put my hand in my bosom and offered and gave those three coins back to God who had placed them there Himself, so God infused into my soul the power always to praise and magnify Him with my voice and heart for all the good things and all the graces which He has granted to me through His very holy goodness.

"So those are the words which you heard when you saw me raise and hold out my hand three times. But be careful, Little Brother Lamb, not to go watching me any more. Now return to your cell with the blessing of God. And take good care of me. For in a few days God will do such astounding and wonderful things on this mountain that the whole world will marvel at them. For He will do something new which He has never done to any other creature in this world."[1]

And after saying those words, he had the Book of the Gospels brought to him, for God had placed in his mind the idea that what God wanted to do with him would be shown to him in opening the Book of the Gospels three times. So when the Book was brought, St. Francis gave himself to prayer. And when he had finished praying, he had Brother Leo open the Book of the Gospels three times in the name of the Holy Trinity. And it pleased Divine Providence that in those three openings the Passion of Christ always appeared before him. Thereby he was given to understand that as he had followed Christ in the acts of his life, so he had to follow Him and be conformed to Him in the afflictions and sufferings of the Passion before he left this world.[2]

And from that time St. Francis began to taste and feel more abundantly the sweetness of divine contemplation and divine visitations.

Among others he had one which immediately preceded and prepared him for the imprinting of the Stigmata, in this way. The day before the Feast of the Cross in September, while St. Francis was praying secretly in his cell, an angel appeared to him and said on God's behalf: "I encourage you and urge you to prepare and dispose yourself humbly to receive with all patience what God wills to do in you."

St. Francis answered: "I am prepared to endure patiently whatever my Lord wants to do to me."

And after he said this, the angel departed.

The next day came, that is, the Feast of the Cross. And St. Francis, sometime before dawn, began to pray outside the entrance of his cell, turning his face toward the east. And he prayed in this way: "My Lord Jesus Christ, I pray You to grant me two graces before I die: the first is that during my life I may feel in my soul and in my body, as much as possible, that pain which You, dear Jesus, sustained in the hour of Your most bitter Passion. The second is that I may feel in my heart, as much as possible, that excessive love with which You, O Son of God, were inflamed in willingly enduring such suffering for us sinners."

And remaining for a long time in that prayer, he understood that God would grant it to him, and that it would soon be conceded to him to feel those things as much as is possible for a mere creature.[3]

Having received this promise, St. Francis began to contemplate with intense devotion the Passion of Christ and His infinite charity. And the fervor of his devotion increased so much within him that he utterly transformed himself into Jesus through love and compassion. And while he was thus inflaming himself in this contemplation, on that same morning he saw coming down from Heaven a Seraph with six resplendent and flaming wings. As the Seraph, flying swiftly, came closer to St. Francis, so that he could perceive Him clearly, he noticed that He had the likeness of a Crucified Man, and His wings were so disposed that two wings extended above His head, two were spread out to fly, and the other two covered His entire body.

On seeing this, St. Francis was very much afraid, and at the same time he was filled with joy and grief and amazement. He felt intense joy from the friendly look of Christ, who appeared to him in a very familiar way and gazed at him very kindly. But on the other hand, seeing Him nailed to the Cross, he felt boundless grief and compassion. Next, he was greatly amazed at such an astounding and extraordinary vision, for he knew well that the affliction of suffering is not in accord with the immortality of the angelic Seraph. And while he was marveling thus, He who was appearing to him revealed to him that this vision was shown to him by Divine Providence in this particular form in order that he should understand that he was to be utterly transformed into the direct likeness of Christ Crucified, not by physical martyrdom, but by enkindling of the mind.[4]

During this marvelous apparition, all of Mount Alverna seemed to be on fire with very bright flames, which shone in the night and illumined the various surrounding mountains and valleys more clearly than if the sun were shining over the earth.

The shepherds who were guarding their flocks in that area witnessed this. And they were gripped by intense fear when they saw the mountain aflame and so much light around it, as they later told the friars, declaring that the fiery light remained above Mount Alverna for an hour or more.

Likewise, because of the brightness of that light, which shone through the windows of the inns in the district, some

muleteers who were going to Romagna got up, thinking that
the sun had risen, and they saddled and loaded their animals.
And while they were on their way, they saw that light cease
and the real sun rise.[5]

Now why those holy Stigmata were imprinted on St. Francis
is not yet entirely clear. But as he himself told his companions,
this great mystery is reserved for the future.

Brother Leo told this account to Brother James of Massa,
and Brother James of Massa told it to Brother Ugolino di
Monte Santa Maria, and Brother Ugolino, a good and trustworthy man, told it to me who am writing.[6]

During that seraphic apparition Christ, who appeared to St.
Francis, spoke to him certain secret and profound things which
the Saint was never willing to reveal to anyone while he was
alive, but after his death he revealed them, as is recorded further on. And these were the words: "Do you know what I
have done?" said Christ. "I have given you the Stigmata which
are the emblems of My Passion, so that you may be My
standard-bearer. And as I descended into Limbo on the day
when I died and took from there by virtue of these Stigmata
of Mine all the souls that I found there, so I grant to you that
every year on the day of your death you may go to Purgatory
and by virtue of your Stigmata you may take from there and
lead to Paradise all the souls of your Three Orders, that is,
the Friars Minor, the Sisters, and the Continent, and also others
who have been very devoted to you, whom you may find there,
so that you may be conformed to Me in death as you are in
life."[7]

Now when, after a long time and a secret conversation, this
wonderful vision disappeared, it left a most intense ardor and
flame of divine love in the heart of St. Francis, and it left a
marvelous image and imprint of the Passion of Christ in his
flesh. For soon there began to appear in the hands and feet of
St. Francis the marks of nails such as he had just seen in the
body of Jesus Crucified, who had appeared to him in the form
of a Seraph. For his hands and feet seemed to be pierced
through the center with nails, the heads of which were in the
palms of his hands and in the upper part of his feet outside
the flesh, and their points extended through the back of the
hands and the soles of the feet so far that they seemed to be

1450

bent and beaten back in such a way that underneath their bent and beaten-back point—all of which stood out from the flesh—it would have been easy to put the finger of one's hand as through a ring. And the heads of the nails were round and black. Likewise in his right side appeared the wound of a blow from a spear, which was open, red, and bloody, and from which blood often issued from the holy breast of St. Francis and stained his habit and breeches.[8]

Consequently his companions, before they knew it from him, nevertheless noticed that he did not uncover his hands or feet and that he could not put the soles of his feet on the ground. Later, finding that his habit and breeches were bloody when they washed them for him, they felt sure that he had the image and likeness of Christ Crucified clearly imprinted in his hands and in his feet and likewise in his side.

And although he tried hard to hide and conceal from them those glorious Stigmata, which had thus been clearly imprinted in his flesh, on the other hand he saw that he could scarcely hide them from his intimate companions. Nevertheless he feared to make public the secrets of God. So he was in an agony of doubt as to whether or not he should reveal the vision of the Seraph and the imprinting of the Stigmata.

Finally, urged on by his conscience, he called to himself some of his more intimate companions, and speaking in general terms, he explained his doubt to them without describing what had happened. And he asked for their advice.

Among those friars there was one called Illuminato who was very holy, and he was truly illumined by the grace of God. Realizing that St. Francis must have seen something marvelous, because he seemed almost stunned, he answered this way: "Brother Francis, you must know that God sometimes shows you His divine mysteries not only for yourself but also for the sake of others. So it would seem that you should rightly be afraid of being judged guilty of hiding your talent if you keep hidden something which God has shown you for the future good of many other persons."

Then St. Francis, being moved by these words—although at other times he used to say, "My secret to me"—with very great awe described the above-mentioned vision in detail, adding that Christ, who appeared to him, had said to him certain things which he would never tell anyone while he lived.[9]

Now although those very holy wounds, inasmuch as they were imprinted on him by Christ, gave him very great joy in his heart, nevertheless they gave unbearable pain to his flesh and physical senses.

Consequently, being forced by necessity, he chose Brother Leo, who was simpler and purer than the others. And he revealed everything to him, and he let him see and touch those holy wounds. And St. Francis entrusted his wounds only to him to be touched and rebound with new bandages between those marvelous nails and the remaining flesh, to relieve the pain and absorb the blood which issued and flowed from the wounds. When he was ill, he let the bandages be changed often, even every day in the week, except from Thursday evening all through Friday until Saturday morning, because he did not want the pain of the Passion of Christ which he bore in his body to be eased at all by any man-made remedy or medicine during the time when our Savior Jesus Christ had for us been arrested and crucified, had died and been buried. For the love for Christ, on that day of the Crucifixion he wished to hang, truly crucified with Christ in the sufferings of the Cross.

Sometimes it happened that when Brother Leo was changing the bandage of the wound in the side, St. Francis, because of the pain which he felt from the loosening of the bloody bandage, would put his hand on Brother Leo's chest over his heart. And from the contact of those holy hands on which were imprinted the venerable Stigmata, Brother Leo would feel such sweetness of devotion in his heart that he nearly fainted and fell to the ground. He would begin to sob and be rapt in a life-giving trance.

Lastly, regarding this Third Consideration, when St. Francis had finished the fast of St. Michael the Archangel, by divine revelation he made ready to return to St. Mary of the Angels. So he called Brother Masseo and Brother Angelo, and after many holy words and instructions, he commended to them as strongly as he could that holy mountain, saying that he had to go back to St. Mary of the Angels with Brother Leo. And after this, he said good-by to them and blessed them in the name of Jesus Crucified. And granting their request, he held out to them his very holy hands adorned with those glorious Stigmata, to see and touch and kiss. And leaving them thus consoled, he departed and went down the holy mountain.[10]

To the glory of Our Lord Jesus Christ. Amen.

The Fourth Consideration: How, After the Imprinting of the Holy Stigmata, St. Francis Left Mount Alverna and Returned to St. Mary of the Angels

Regarding the Fourth Consideration, you should know that after the true love of Christ had perfectly transformed St. Francis into the true likeness of Christ Crucified, having finished the forty days' fast in honor of St. Michael the Archangel on the holy Mount Alverna, the angelic man Francis went down the mountain with Brother Leo and a devout peasant on whose donkey he rode, for owing to the nails in his feet he could not well go on foot.

When he came down from the mountain, the fame of his sanctity had already spread through the region, and the shepherds had reported how they had seen Mount Alverna all aflame and that this was a sign of some great miracle which God had done to St. Francis. So, when the people of the district heard that he was passing by, all of them—men and women, small and great—came out to see him and with devotion and desire tried to touch him and kiss his hands. As he was unable to deny them to the veneration of the people, although he had bandaged the palms, nevertheless to conceal the Stigmata still more, he bound them over again and covered them with his sleeves, and held out only his bare fingers for the people to kiss.

But even though he strove to hide and conceal the mystery of the glorious Stigmata in order to avoid all occasion of worldly glory, it pleased God, who had secretly imprinted those marks, openly to manifest many miracles for His glory by the virtue of those Stigmata, especially during this journey from Alverna to St. Mary of the Angels and later very many in various parts of the world, during the lifetime of St. Francis

and after his glorious death, in order that the hidden and marvelous power of those Stigmata and the exceedingly great
mercy and love of Christ for him to whom God had given them
in a wonderful way might be manifested to the world by clear
and evident miracles, some of which we shall record here.[1]

As St. Francis was drawing near a village on the border of
the County of Arezzo, a woman came to him, weeping loudly
and carrying in her arms her eight-year-old son. For four years
he had had dropsy, and his stomach was so swollen that when
he stood straight he could not see his legs or feet. The woman
put her little boy down before St. Francis and begged him to
pray to God for him. First, St. Francis began to pray. Then
having prayed, he put his holy hands over the boy's stomach.
At their contact all the swelling rapidly disappeared, and the
boy was perfectly cured. Then St. Francis gave him back to
his mother. She received him with intense joy, and took the
child home, giving thanks to God and His Saint. And she
gladly showed her cured son to everyone in the district who
came to her house to see him.[2]

That same day St. Francis passed through Borgo San
Sepolcro. And before he came near the town, crowds from the
city and the farms ran to meet him. And many of them went
before him with olive branches in their hands, crying out
loudly: "Here comes the saint! Here comes the saint!"

And because of the devotion and desire that the people had
to touch him, they pressed and thronged around him. But he
went along with his mind raised and absorbed in contemplating God. Although he was touched or held or pulled, like someone who is unconscious he paid no attention at all to what was
being done or said around him. And he did not even notice
that he was traveling through that town or district.

Now when he had passed Borgo and the crowds had gone
home and he reached a leprosarium a good mile beyond
Borgo, he came back to himself like someone returning from
the other world, and he asked his companions: "When will we
be near Borgo?"

For his mind had been concentrating on and rapt in the
splendors of Heaven and he had actually not perceived the
changes of time and place or the people who met him. His

companions learned by experience that this happened to him several other times.[3]

St. Francis arrived that evening at the friars' Place of Monte Casale, where there was a friar who was so cruelly sick and so horribly tortured by illness that it seemed more like a tribulation and torment of the devil than a natural sickness. For at times he would throw himself on the ground and roll around with a shocking expression, foaming at the mouth and shaking all over. At other times all his limbs were contracted or extended, or they would bend or twist or become stiff and hard. Sometimes when he was all rigid and tense, his heels would touch his head and he would jump up in the air and then suddenly fall flat on his back. When St. Francis, sitting at table, heard the friars tell about the serious and incurable sickness of this friar, he felt compassion for him. And he took a piece of bread which he was eating and made the Sign of the Cross over it with his holy stigmatized hands and sent it to the sick friar. As soon as the latter had eaten the bread, he was perfectly healed and never felt that illness again.[4]

When the next morning came, St. Francis sent two of the friars who were in that Place to stay at Alverna. And he sent back with them the peasant who had accompanied him behind the donkey that he had loaned him, as the Saint wanted him to return to his home with it.

While the friars were going with that peasant and entering the district of Arezzo, some men of that district saw them from a distance and rejoiced greatly, thinking that it was St. Francis, who had passed by there two days before. One of their women, who had been in labor for three days and could not be delivered, was dying, and they thought she would be safe and sound again if St. Francis laid his holy hands on her. But when the friars came near and the men realized that it was not St. Francis, they were very sorry. Yet though the Saint was not there in person, his power was not lacking, because their faith was not lacking. Then a wonderful thing happened! The woman was dying—she already showed the signs of death. But the men asked the friars whether they had anything which had been touched by the very holy hands of St. Francis. The friars reflected and searched carefully, and finally found nothing that St. Francis had touched with his hands except the halter of the donkey which he had ridden. With great reverence and devotion they took that halter and placed it on the body of the pregnant woman, devoutly calling on the name of St. Francis and faithfully commending her to him. And what more is there to say? The minute the woman had that halter on her body she felt freed from all danger, and she gave birth in joy and safety, without any difficulty.[5]

After St. Francis had been in that Place for some days, he left and went to Città di Castello. Then many of the citizens brought before him a woman who had been possessed by a devil for a long time, and they humbly asked him to free her because she was disturbing the whole neighborhood with mournful howling and piercing shrieks and barking like a dog. So St. Francis, having first prayed and made the Sign of the Cross over her, commanded the devil to leave her. And it immediately departed, leaving her sound in body and mind.[6]

And as the news of this miracle spread among the people, another woman with great faith brought to him a little boy of hers who was seriously ill with a cruel ulcer. And she reverently asked him to consent to make the Sign of the Cross over him with his own hands. Then St. Francis, granting her prayer, took the child and raised the bandage over the sore and blessed it, making the Sign of the Cross three times over the ulcer. Then he bound it up again with his own hands and gave him back to his mother. And because it was evening, she immediately put him to bed to sleep. The next morning when she went to take her little son from the bed, she found him unbandaged, and looking at him she saw he was perfectly healed, as if he had never had any illness, except that over the spot where the ulcer had been, the flesh had grown in the form of a red rose—rather as evidence of the miracle than as a token of the ulcer, because that rose remained there throughout his whole life and often inspired him with devotion to St. Francis, who had healed him.[7]

St. Francis then remained in that town for a month, at the eager prayers of the inhabitants. During that time he performed many other miracles. And then he left there to go to St. Mary of the Angels with Brother Leo and with a good man who loaned him his donkey, which St. Francis rode.

It also happened that, because of the great cold of the winter season and the roughness of the roads, after riding all day, they were not able to reach any place where they could stay overnight. So being forced by the snow and the darkness that was overtaking them, they took shelter under the brow of an overhanging rock to spend the night.

The good man to whom the donkey belonged, being uncomfortable and poorly protected and unable to sleep on account of the cold—for there was no way of making any fire—began quietly to complain to himself and to cry. And he blamed St. Francis for having brought him to such a place. Then St. Francis, hearing this, had compassion on him, and in fervor of spirit he stretched his hand out over him and touched him. It was a marvelous thing that as soon as that hand, which had been pierced and enkindled by the Seraph, touched the man, all sense of cold left him, and so much heat came over him, interiorly and exteriorly, that he felt as if he were near the mouth of a blazing furnace. Consequently, he was immediately comforted in mind and body, and he fell asleep. And as he himself later used to declare, he slept that night until morning among the rocks and the snow more sweetly than he had ever rested in his own bed.[8]

The next day they traveled on and reached St. Mary of the Angels. And when they were near it, Brother Leo looked up and gazed toward the Place of St. Mary. And as he looked, he saw a very beautiful cross, on which there was hanging the figure of Christ Crucified, going before the face of St. Francis, who was riding ahead of him. And he clearly saw that that wonderful cross went before the face of St. Francis in such a way that when he stopped, it stopped, and when he went on, it likewise went on, and wherever St. Francis went, it preceded him. And that cross was so bright that not only did it shine in St. Francis' face, but it also illuminated the air all around, and Brother Leo could see everything in a clear light. And it lasted until St. Francis entered the Place of St. Mary. This completely amazed Brother Leo and deeply touched him with compassion and inflamed him with interior devotion.[9]

When St. Francis arrived at the Place with Brother Leo, they were made welcome by the friars with the greatest joy and affection. And from that time until his death St. Francis stayed at that Place of St. Mary most of the time. And the fame of his sanctity and his miracles spread continually throughout the Order and throughout the world, although in his very deep humility he concealed, as much as he could, the gifts and graces of God and called himself a very great sinner.

At one time Brother Leo was wondering about this, and he foolishly said to himself: "Look—this man calls himself a very great sinner in public, and he came into the Order as an adult, and he is honored so much by God, and yet in secret he never confesses any carnal sin—can he be a virgin?" And he began to feel an intense desire to know the truth about this, but he did not dare ask St. Francis about it. So he turned to God and earnestly prayed that He would give him some assurance about what he wanted to know. He prayed a great deal and merited to be heard, and he received assurance through this vision that St. Francis was truly a virgin in body. For in a vision he saw St. Francis standing on a high and exalted place where no one could go or reach, and he was told in spirit that that very high and exalted place symbolized the perfection of virginal chastity in St. Francis, which was in reasonable accord with the flesh that was to be adorned by the holy Stigmata of Christ.[10]

Seeing that because of the Stigmata his physical strength was gradually diminishing and that he was no longer able to have charge of governing the Order, St. Francis set forward the date of the General Chapter. When all its members had assembled, he humbly made his excuses to the friars for the infirmity due to which he could no longer take care of the Order as far as discharging the duties of the Generalate was concerned, although he was not renouncing the position of General, since he could not do so, as he had been made General by the Pope, and so he could not give up the position or substitute a successor without the Pope's specific permission. But he appointed Brother Peter Catani as his Vicar, commending the Order to him and to the Provincial Ministers with all possible affection.

And having done this, St. Francis felt consoled in spirit, and raising his eyes and hands toward Heaven, he spoke thus: "To You, my Lord God, I commend Your family which You have committed to me until now—for now, owing to my infirmities which You know, my very dear Lord, I can no longer have charge of it. I also commend it to the Provincial Ministers—let them be held responsible to give an account to You on Judgment Day if any friar should perish through their negligence or their bad example or their overharsh correction."

And by those words, as it pleased God, all the friars at the Chapter understood that he was speaking of the Stigmata when he excused himself because of an infirmity. And as a result of their holy affection not one of them could hold back his tears.

And henceforth he left all the care and governing of the Order in the hands of his Vicar and of the Provincial Ministers. And he used to say: "From now on, since I have given up having charge of the Order because of my infirmities, I have no other duty but to pray to God for our Order and to give a good example to the friars. And I know for sure that if my infirmity should leave me, the greatest help I could give the Order would be to pray continuously to God for it, that He may govern, defend, and preserve it."[11]

Now, as was said above, St. Francis tried as much as he could to hide from everyone's eyes the very holy wounds which Christ the Son of God had miraculously imprinted on his hands and feet and side. And after he had received them he always traveled and lived with socks on his feet, and he concealed his hands with bandages so that nothing but the tips of his fingers were visible to his companions, recalling what the angel said to the holy Tobias: "It is good to hide the secret of the King." Nevertheless he could not prevent many friars from seeing and touching them in different ways, and particularly the wound in his side, which he tried to hide with special care.

Thus a friar who was serving him once persuaded him with devout cunning to take off his habit so as to shake the dust out of it. And when St. Francis removed it in his presence, that friar clearly saw the wound in the side, and by quickly placing his hand on his chest, he touched it with three fingers and measured how long and large it was. His Vicar also saw it in a similar way at that time. But Brother Rufino had an even clearer proof of it. He was a great contemplative. St. Francis sometimes used to say of him that no man in the world was holier than he, and because of his saintliness St. Francis loved him as a dear friend and used to give in to his wishes.

This Brother Rufino obtained proof about the Stigmata, and particularly the one in the side, for himself and for others, in three ways. The first was that, as he had to wash his breeches (which St. Francis wore so long that by pulling them up well he covered the wound in the right side with them), Brother Rufino carefully examined and inspected them, and each time he found that they were bloody on the right side. Consequently he realized for sure that it was blood that issued from that wound. But St. Francis scolded him when he realized that he was laying out his breeches in order to see that spot. The second way was once when Brother Rufino was scratching St. Francis' back, in order to make more certain about it, he deliberately passed his hand over it and put his large finger into the wound in the side, whereupon St. Francis shouted aloud in great pain: "God forgive you, Brother Rufino! Why did you do that?" The third way was when, wishing to see that venerable wound with his own eyes, that same friar once said to St. Francis with affectionate cunning: "Father, I beg you to grant me the very great consolation of giving me your habit and accepting mine, for the love of charity." Now Brother Rufino did this in order that, while St. Francis was taking off his habit, he might see with his own eyes the wound in the side which he had recently touched with his fingers. And so it happened. Yielding to Brother Rufino's affectionate request, although unwillingly, St. Francis took off his habit and gave it to him and accepted his. And then, because he had only that one, while he was taking it off, he was unable to cover himself in such a way as to prevent Brother Rufino from clearly seeing that wound.

Likewise Brother Leo and many other friars saw those Stigmata of St. Francis while he was living. Although because of their holiness those friars were reliable men whose mere word could be trusted, nevertheless, in order to remove any doubt from people's minds, they swore on the Holy Book that they had clearly seen them.

Several Cardinals who were intimate friends of St. Francis also saw them, and out of reverence for the Stigmata they composed and made beautiful and inspiring hymns and antiphons and texts in prose.

The Supreme Pontiff, Pope Alexander, while preaching to

the people before all the Cardinals (among whom was the saintly Brother Bonaventure, who was a Cardinal), said and confirmed that he saw with his own eyes the holy Stigmata of St. Francis when he was alive.[12]

The Lady Jacopa dei Settesoli of Rome, who was the most prominent lady in Rome in her time and was intensely devoted to St. Francis, saw and kissed them many times with the greatest reverence before St. Francis died and after he died, because she came from Rome to Assisi at the death of St. Francis as a result of a divine revelation. And it happened this way.

Some days before his death, St. Francis was lying sick in Assisi in the Bishop's Palace. And despite all the sickness, out of devotion he would often sing certain praises of Christ with some of his companions. And if he himself was unable to sing owing to his illness, he often made his companions sing. Now the men of Assisi, fearing that such a precious treasure should happen to be carried away from Assisi, had that Palace carefully guarded day and night by armed men. And while the Saint was lying there for many days, one of his companions said to him: "Father, you know that the people of this city have great faith in you and consider you a holy man, and so they may think that if you are as they believe, you should be thinking about death in this illness of yours, and that you should be weeping rather than singing, since you are so seriously ill. For you should know that your singing and ours, which you make us perform, is heard by many people in the palace and outside, because this palace is being guarded by many armed men on account of you, and they might be scandalized. So," said this friar, "I think that we would do well to leave here and all go back to St. Mary of the Angels, as this is not the right place for us among seculars."

St. Francis answered Brother Elias, who had said this: "Dearest Brother, you know that two years ago, when we were staying in Foligno, the Lord revealed to you the end of my life. Moreover, He has also revealed to me that that end will come in a few days, during this illness. And in this same revelation God has given me assurance of the remission of all my sins and of the happiness of Paradise. Until I had that revelation, I used to weep over death and over my sins. But after that revelation was given to me, I have been so filled with joy that I cannot weep any more, but I remain in bliss and joy all the time. And that is why I sing and shall sing to the Lord, who has given me the gift of His grace and an assurance of the bliss of glory in Paradise. But regarding our leaving here I willingly agree. However, you must prepare something to carry me, because owing to my sickness I am unable to walk."[13]

The friars therefore took him up in their arms and carried him on the way toward St. Mary of the Angels, accompanied by a crowd of people. When they reached a hospital that was on the way, St. Francis asked whether they had arrived that far, because as a result of his extreme penance and former weeping, his eyesight was impaired and he could not see well. So when he was told that they were at the hospital, he said to those who were carrying him: "Set me down on the ground and turn me toward Assisi."

And standing in the road, with his face turned toward the city, he blessed it with many blessings, saying: "May the Lord bless you, holy city, for through you many souls shall be saved, and in you many servants of God shall dwell, and from you many shall be chosen for the Kingdom of Eternal Life." And after he had said those words, he had himself carried farther on, to St. Mary of the Angels.[14]

And when they arrived at St. Mary, they carried him to the infirmary, and they laid him down there to rest. Then St. Francis called one of his companions and said to him: "Dearest Brother, God has revealed to me that I am going to live until a certain day and then die from this sickness, and you know that the Lady Jacopa dei Settesoli, who is very devoted to our Order, would be extremely sad if she knew about my death and was not present. So let us notify her that if she wants to see me alive, she should come here at once."

The friar answered: "You are right, Father; because of the great devotion she has for you, she would grieve intensely if she were not present at your death."

So St. Francis said: "Go and bring the inkhorn and pen and paper, and write as I tell you." And when the friar had brought them, St. Francis dictated the letter this way: "To the Lady Jacopa, servant of God, Brother Francis, the little poor man of Christ, sends his greetings in the Lord and fellowship in the

Holy Spirit of Our Lord Jesus Christ. You must know, my very dear friend, that the Blessed Christ by His grace has revealed to me that my life will come to its end soon. So if you want to find me alive after you have seen this letter, set out and hasten to St. Mary of the Angels. For if you do not come by a certain day, you will not be able to find me alive. And bring with you some haircloth in which to wrap my body and the wax needed for the funeral. I also ask you to bring me some of those things to eat which you used to give me when I was sick in Rome."

And while this letter was being written, it was revealed to St. Francis by God that the Lady Jacopa was coming to him and was near the Place and was bringing with her all those things which he was requesting in the letter. So after he had this revelation, St. Francis suddenly said to the friar who was writing the letter: "Don't write any more, because it is not necessary, but put the letter aside."

And all the friars were very much surprised that he did not allow the letter to be finished and did not want it to be sent. And then—a little while later—there was a strong knocking at the gate of the Place. And St. Francis sent the brother porter to open it. And when he opened the gate, there was the Lady Jacopa, the greatest noblewoman of Rome, with her two sons who were senators and with a throng of companions on horseback. She had come to St. Francis and had brought with her all the things which St. Francis had included in that letter.

On entering, the Lady Jacopa went right to the infirmary and came to St. Francis. Her arrival brought him great joy and consolation, and she also rejoiced on finding him alive and talking with him. And she had the cookies fetched which she had brought to St. Francis, and she gave him some to eat.

And after he had eaten some and was very comforted, the Lady Jacopa went to the feet of St. Francis and she knelt and took those very holy feet marked and adorned with the wounds of Christ, and she kissed and bathed them with her tears with such consolation and grace that she seemed to the friars who were standing around like another Mary Magdalen weeping and embracing and kissing the feet of another Christ. And the friars were unable to draw her away from the Saint's feet.

Finally, after a long time, they nevertheless raised her up and led her aside and asked her how she had come just at the right time and so well provided with everything that St. Francis needed while alive and when he would be buried. The Lady Jacopa answered that while she was praying one night in Rome, she heard a voice from Heaven saying to her: "If you want to find Brother Francis alive, go to Assisi at once, without delay. And take with you those things which you used to give him when he was sick in Rome, and take also those things which will be needed for his burial."

"And," she said, "I did so."

Moreover, she brought such a large supply of wax that it was sufficient not only for his funeral but also for all the Masses said over his body for many days.

The Lady Jacopa stayed until St. Francis died and was buried. And she with all her company gave very great honor to his remains at his funeral, and she paid for everything that was needed. Then she returned to Rome. But some time later, out of devotion to St. Francis she came again to Assisi. And there she ended her days in saintly penance and virtuous living and died a holy death. And it was her will that she be buried in the Church of St. Francis with great devotion. And so it was done.[15]

At the death of St. Francis, not only Lady Jacopa and her sons and her company saw and kissed his glorious Stigmata, but also many citizens of Assisi. Among them was a very well-known and prominent knight named Sir Jerome, who had great doubts and was skeptical about them, as St. Thomas the Apostle was about those of Christ. In order to make himself and others sure about them, he boldly moved the nails in the hands and feet and in an obvious way touched the wound in the side, in the presence of the friars and lay people. As a result, later he was a steadfast witness of that fact, swearing on the Book that it was so and that he had so seen and touched.[16]

St. Clare with her nuns also saw and kissed the glorious Stigmata of St. Francis. They were present at his funeral.

The glorious confessor of Christ St. Francis passed from this life on Saturday, the third of October, in the year of the Lord 1226, and he was buried on Sunday. That year was the twentieth of his conversion, when he began to do penance, and it

1464

was the second year after the imprinting of the Stigmata. And it was in the forty-fifth year from his birth.

Later, in the year 1228, St. Francis was canonized by Pope Gregory IX, who came in person to Assisi to canonize him.[17]

To the praise of Christ. Amen.

And this suffices for the Fourth Consideration.

The Fifth Consideration: About Certain Apparitions to Saintly Persons Concerning the Holy Stigmata

The Fifth and last Consideration deals with certain apparitions and revelations and miracles which God performed after the death of St. Francis as a confirmation of his Stigmata and as a testimony of the day and hour when Christ gave them to him.

And in this connection it should be known that in the year of the Lord 1282, on the third day of October, Brother Philip, Minister of Tuscany, by order of Brother Bonagrazia the Minister General, commanded Brother Matthew of Castiglione Aventino, a man of great devotion and saintliness, to tell him under holy obedience what he knew about the day and hour when the sacred Stigmata were imprinted by Christ on the body of St. Francis, because he had heard that Brother Matthew had had a revelation about it. This Brother Matthew, under the obligation of holy obedience, answered him as follows:

"When I was a member of the community of Alverna during the month of May last year, one night I began to pray in the cell which has been built on the spot where it is believed that that holy apparition of the Seraph took place. And in my prayer I very fervently begged God to deign to reveal to someone the day and the hour when the sacred Stigmata were imprinted on the body of St. Francis. And as I was persevering in prayer and in this petition beyond the first watch, St. Francis appeared to me in a very bright light and said: 'Son, what are you asking God to reveal to you?' And I answered: 'Father, I am asking God to deign to reveal on what day and hour the Stigmata of the Lord's Passion were imprinted on you.'

"And he said to me: 'The Lord wishes you to know it, and

1465

I will tell you. I am indeed your Father Francis—you know me well.' Then he showed me the Stigmata of his hands, feet, and side, and said: 'The time has come when God wishes to disclose for His glory what the friars have so far not sought to know. For He who appeared to me then was not an angel but was my Lord Jesus Christ in the form of a Seraph.[1] With His hands He imprinted in my body these five wounds as He had received those same holy wounds in His body on the Cross.'

"And describing the way in which the apparition occurred, St. Francis added: 'The day before the Exaltation of the Cross an angel came to me and told me on behalf of God that I should prepare myself to be patient and to receive what God might wish to do. And I answered that I was ready to suffer and to endure whatever God might deign to do. So the next morning, that is, the day of the Exaltation of the Holy Cross, which was a Friday in that year, I came out of my cell at the break of dawn in very great fervor of spirit, and I went to pray on this spot where you are now, a place where I often prayed. And while I was praying, there came down through the air from Heaven with great rapidity a crucified Young Man in the form of a Seraph, with six wings. At this marvelous sight I humbly knelt on this spot and began to contemplate devoutly the infinite love of Jesus Crucified and the infinite pain of His Passion. And the sight of Him aroused such compassion in me that I really seemed to feel that Passion in my body. And at His presence this whole mountain was shining with a golden light like a sun. And so, coming down that way, He came close to me and stood before me and said certain words to me which I have not yet revealed to anyone. But the time is drawing near when they shall be revealed, because the Order and the friars are in great need of them. Afterward Christ vanished from my sight and returned to Heaven. And I found myself marked like this with these wounds. Now go and confidently tell these things to your Minister, because this is the work of God and not of man.' And after saying those words, St. Francis blessed me, saying: 'My son, go in the name of the Lord!' And he went back to Heaven with a great throng of very radiant men."

The above-mentioned Brother Matthew declared that he had seen and heard all these things as they are truly written above, and that he had not been sleeping but was awake and conscious. And he took an oath to that effect, with his hand on the Bible, before the said Minister in his cell in Florence, when the latter questioned him about this under obedience.[2]

Another time a certain devout and holy friar, while reading the chapter on the Stigmata in the Legend of St. Francis, began to wonder with great anxiety of mind what must have been those very secret words that the Seraph said to him when he received the holy Stigmata and which St. Francis said he would not reveal to anyone while he was living in the body. And this friar said to himself: "St. Francis did not want to say those words while he was alive, but now, since he is no longer living in the body, maybe he would tell them if he was fervently prayed to do so." Believing therefore that they would do much good, the friar decided to pray that they be revealed. And henceforth he began devoutly to pray to God and to St. Francis that they might deign to disclose to him those secret words of the Seraph. And the friar persevered in that prayer every day for eight years, and in the eighth year he merited having his prayer granted in this way.

One day after eating he went with his brethren to the church to give thanks and praise to God. And after the office was over, he remained alone to pray in a certain part of the church. And while he was praying to God and St. Francis more fervently than usual, weeping many tears and burning with a more intense desire to know those words, a friar came in and called him, saying that the guardian had ordered him to accompany him to the village to get something which the Place needed. Therefore, without doubting that obedience is more meritorious than prayer, he immediately stopped praying as soon as he heard the superior's order, and humbly and obediently hastened out with that friar who had called him. And as it pleased God, in that act of prompt obedience he earned more merit than by his long praying.

Now when they went out of the gate of the Place, they met two foreign friars who seemed to have come from a distant country. One of them looked young, and the other old and thin. And because of the rainy winter weather they were muddy and wet. When that obedient friar saw them, he felt strong compassion and charity for them, and he said to his companion: "As our errand can wait a while, dear Brother, and these foreign friars are in real need of being charitably welcomed, please let me go first and wash this older one's feet, as he needs it most, and you can wash the younger one's. And then we can go on our errand."

So the other friar yielded to his companion's charity, and they went back to the Place and gave the foreign friars an affectionate welcome, taking them into the kitchen to get warm and dry. Eight other friars of the Place were also warming themselves at the fire. And after they had been near the fire for a while, they led the foreign friars aside to wash their feet, as they had agreed to do.

And while that devout and obedient friar was washing the feet of the older friar and removing the mud—because they were all covered with mud—he looked and saw that the feet were marked with the Stigmata! In amazement and joy he kissed and embraced the feet, crying aloud: "Oh, Brother, either you are Christ or you are St. Francis!"

On hearing his surprised outcry all the friars of that Place arose and gathered around to see the Stigmata. Then that elderly friar at their request allowed all of them to see and touch and kiss them with great awe and reverence. And as they were still more moved by amazement and joy, he said to them: "Do not doubt or fear, my dearest Brothers and sons. I am your Father, Brother Francis, who, by the will of God, founded three Orders. And I have been prayed to every day for eight years by this friar who is holding my feet—and today he especially prayed to me in the church after the praises which you recited there—that I should deign to reveal to him those secret words which the Seraph said to me when he gave me the Stigmata and which I never told anyone while I was alive. But today, because of his perseverance and his prompt obedience, for which he left the consolations of prayer, I have been sent to him by command of God in order to reveal to him in your presence what he wants."

Then St. Francis turned to that friar and said: "You must know, dearest Brother, that when I was on Mount Alverna, utterly absorbed in remembering the Passion of Christ, I received in my body His holy Wounds, and then Christ said to me: 'Do you know what I have done to you? I have given you the emblems of My Passion so that you may be My standard-bearer. And just as I went down into Limbo on the day of My death and, by the virtue and merits of those Wounds, drew out of there and led to Heaven all the souls that I found there, so I grant to you henceforth, in order that you be conformed to Me in death as you were in life, that every year on the day of your death you may go to Purgatory and, by the virtue and efficacy of your Stigmata, you may draw out of there all the souls of your three Orders—that is, the Minors, Sisters, and Continent—that you find there, and may lead them to the glory of Paradise.' Now I never told those words to anyone while I lived in the world, so that I should not be accused of boastful presumption and vainglory."

And after he had said these words, St. Francis and his companion suddenly disappeared. Later many friars heard this from those eight friars who were present during that vision and those words of St. Francis. (Brother Giacomo Raneto, a lector in Rome, said in a sermon that he had heard it from one of those eight friars.)[3]

St. Francis once appeared on Mount Alverna to Brother John of Alverna, a man of great holiness, while he was praying. And he stayed and spoke with him for a long time. And finally when he wanted to leave, he said to Brother John: "Ask me what you want."

Brother John said: "Father, I beg you to tell me something I have wanted to know for a long time, and that is what you were doing and where you were when the Seraph appeared to you."

St. Francis answered: "I was praying on that spot where the Chapel of Count Simon of Battifolle is now, and I was asking my Lord Jesus Christ for two graces. The first was that I should feel in my soul and in my body, as far as possible, all that pain which He had felt within Himself during His most holy Passion. The second grace I asked was that I should likewise feel in my heart that most intense love which He enkindled within Himself so as to endure such suffering for us sinners. And then God put it in my heart that He would let me feel both the one and the other, as much as possible for a mere creature. And that was fully accomplished in me during the imprinting of the Stigmata."

Then Brother John asked him whether those secret words which the Seraph had spoken to him were really as stated by the above-mentioned friar, who declared that he had heard St. Francis say them in the presence of eight friars. St. Francis replied that it was truly as that friar said.

Now Brother John also felt encouraged by the generosity of the giver to ask still more, and he said: "Oh, Father, I most earnestly beg you to let me see and kiss your glorious Stigmata, not because I have any doubts about them, but only for my consolation and devotion—for I have always longed to do so."

And St. Francis said to him: "Here, my son, are the Stigmata which you have desired to see." And he freely showed him his hands and feet and side, and offered them to him.

On seeing them, Brother John was overcome with amazement and fell down at his feet in fright. Then St. Francis raised him up, saying: "Arise and touch me." Consoled by the Lord, he gained confidence and began to touch those sacred Stigmata and kiss them and move the nails. And then, as he himself reported, he found out by experience that what Brother Bonaventure wrote in his Legend about those sacred Stigmata was true: that when they were pressed on one side, they extended still farther on the other side.

Finally he asked: "Father, what great consolation your soul must have had when you saw the Blessed Christ come to you and give you the marks of His holy Passion! If only God would let me feel a little of that sweetness now!"

Then St. Francis answered: "Do you see these nails?"

And Brother John said: "Yes."

"Touch once more this nail in my hand," said St. Francis.

Then with great reverence and fear Brother John touched that nail. And when he touched it, a scent suddenly came forth from it, spiraling up like smoke, as incense does. And entering through Brother John's nose, it filled his soul and body with such sweetness that he was immediately rapt by God in an ecstasy and became unconscious. And after the Blessed Father disappeared, he stayed in that rapture from that hour, which was tierce, until vespers. And for the next eight days he was unable to eat, and everything he saw seemed fetid to him.

Brother John never told anyone but his confessor about that

1470

vision and intimate talk with St. Francis, until he was about to die. But when he was near death, he revealed it to many friars.[4]

A very devout and saintly friar of the Roman Province saw this wonderful vision. He was united to another friar by a bond of true affection and charity, and they loved each other after death as they had while living. For when one of them died one night and was buried the next morning in the first cloister before the entrance of the chapter room, that friar who survived, at noon on the same day, while all the friars had gone to rest, went to a corner of the chapter room in order to pray devoutly to God and St. Francis for the soul of his beloved dead companion. And while he was persevering in prayer, with tears and supplications, all of a sudden he heard the sound of many persons going through the cloister. In great fear he quickly looked at his companion's grave, and he saw St. Francis and many of his friars standing around the grave at the entrance of the chapter room. Looking beyond, he saw a great purgatorial fire in the center of the cloister and the soul of his dead companion burning in the middle of the fire. He looked around the cloister, and he saw the Lord Jesus Christ walking in procession around the cloister with a great throng of angels and saints.

And watching with intense amazement, he saw that when Christ passed before the chapter room, St. Francis knelt down with all those friars and said: "I beg You, my Most Holy Father and Lord, by that highest love and charity which You showed to the human race in Your Incarnation, to have mercy on the soul of this friar of mine that is burning in that purgatorial fire there."

Christ did not answer or grant his prayer, but went on and walked around the cloister with the throng of saints that followed Him. When He came back the second time before the chapter room, St. Francis knelt down again with his friars as before and prayed to Him thus for the soul of the dead friar: "I beg You, Most Merciful Father and Lord, by the infinite love and charity which You showed to the human race when You died on the Cross for all men, to have mercy on the soul of that friar of mine."

Again Christ passed on and did not answer. After going

1471

around the cloister the third time, He came back by the dead friar's grave. Then St. Francis knelt down with the friars as before and prayed thus to Christ: "I beg You, Most Merciful Father and Lord, by that intense pain and consolation which I felt when You imprinted these Stigmata in my flesh, to have mercy on the soul of that friar of mine that is in the fire of Purgatory!" And he showed Christ the Stigmata in his hands, feet, and side.

On being prayed to by St. Francis this third time in the name of his Stigmata, Christ immediately stopped and looked at the Stigmata. And granting his prayer, He nodded and said: "I grant to you, Brother Francis, the soul of your friar."

And thereby He certainly wished both to honor and confirm the glorious Stigmata of St. Francis and openly to signify that the souls of his friars that go to Purgatory cannot be freed from suffering and led to the glory of Paradise in any way more easily than by virtue of his holy Stigmata, in accordance with the words which Christ said to St. Francis when He imprinted them on him. Now as soon as He had uttered these words, that fire in the cloister vanished and the dead friar appeared in glory with St. Francis, and ascended into Heaven with him and with Christ and all that blessed company of rejoicing angels and saints. Consequently, the friar who was his companion and who had prayed for him felt intense joy on seeing him freed from suffering and led to Paradise. And later he told the other friars all about the vision, and together with them he praised and thanked God. (I, Brother Francis Peri, heard of this miracle from Brother Luke of Pistoia when I was in Arezzo.)[5] To the glory of Christ.

A noble baron named Landulf, of Massa di Santo Piero in the mountains near Gubbio, who was very devoted to St. Francis and finally received from his hands the habit of the Third Order, was given this assurance of St. Francis' death and his glorious Stigmata.

At the time when St. Francis' death was approaching, the devil entered into a woman of that village and cruelly tormented her. Moreover, he made her speak so intelligently in Latin that she defeated all the learned and educated men who came to debate with her. Now it happened that the devil went away from her and left her free for two days. And the third day he came back and afflicted her more cruelly than before. When the Baron Landulf heard about it, he went to this woman and asked the devil who was dwelling in her why he had left her for two days and on returning was tormenting her more severely than before.

The devil answered: "When I left her, it was because I met with all my companions who are in this region and we went in great strength to the death of that beggar Francis to dispute with him and take his soul. But as it was surrounded and defended by a throng of angels in greater numbers than we were, and it was carried to Heaven by them, we left, embarrassed by our defeat. So now I am giving back to this miserable woman what I neglected in those two days."

Then the Baron Landulf commanded him in God's name to tell the truth about the sanctity of St. Francis who, he said, was dead, and of St. Clare, who was alive. The devil replied: "I will tell you the truth about it, whether I want to or not. God the Father was so angry over the sins of the world that it seemed He would soon utter the final sentence against men and women to exterminate them from the world if they did not change for the better. But Christ, His Son, prayed for sinners and promised to renew His life and His Passion in one man— the poor little beggar Francis, through whose life and teaching He would lead many throughout the world to the path of truth and penance. And now, to show the world that He had done this in St. Francis, He wished that the Stigmata of His Passion, which He had imprinted on his body during his life, should at his death be seen and touched by many persons. Similarly, the Mother of Christ promised to renew her virginal purity and humility in a woman, Sister Clare, in such a way that through her example she would snatch many thousands of women from our hands. And so as a result of these promises God the Father was appeased and postponed His final sentence."

Then the Baron Landulf, wishing to know for sure whether the devil—who is the father of lies—was telling the truth in this matter, and especially regarding the death of St. Francis, sent one of his faithful squires to St. Mary of the Angels in Assisi to find out whether St. Francis was alive or dead. That squire on arriving there found out, and on returning reported to his master, that St. Francis had passed from this life precisely at the hour and on the day which the devil said.[6]

Omitting all the miracles of the Stigmata of St. Francis which may be read in his Legend, in concluding this Fifth Consideration it should be known that to Pope Gregory IX (as he later declared), when he was having some doubts about the wound in the side, St. Francis appeared one night, and raising his right arm a little, he uncovered the wound in his side. And he asked him for a vase, and he had one brought to him. And St. Francis had him place it under the wound in the side, and it seemed to the Pope that it really became filled to the brim with blood mixed with water which flowed from that wound. From that moment all doubt left him. And later, in agreement with all the Cardinals, he expressed his formal approval of the Stigmata of St. Francis, and gave the friars a special certificate with a hanging seal. And he did this at Viterbo in the eleventh year of his pontificate. And afterward in the twelfth year he gave another more comprehensive one.

Also Pope Nicholas III and Pope Alexander gave many privileges, whereby anyone who denied the Stigmata of St. Francis could be prosecuted as a heretic.[7]

And this suffices for the Fifth and last Consideration of the glorious Stigmata of our Father St. Francis. May God give us the grace to follow his life in this world in such a way that by virtue of his glorious Stigmata we may merit to be saved with him in Paradise!

To the glory of the Blessed Christ and His little poor Francis. Amen.

Part Three

ADDITIONAL CHAPTERS

1 *How St. Francis Abhorred the Name "Master"*

Francis, the humble imitator of Christ, knowing that the name "Master" was only appropriate for Christ by whom all things were made, used to say that he would gladly wish to do all things, but he did not want to be a master or be known by the name "Master" lest by such a name he should seem to be acting against the saying of Christ in the Gospel that forbids anyone to be called "Master," because it was better for him to be humble with his poor little knowledge than—if it were possible—to perform great deeds and presume to go against the humble words of so glorious a Master. For the name "Master" is appropriate only for the Blessed Christ, all of whose acts are perfect. And so he commanded that no one on earth should presume to be called "Master," because in Heaven there is only one true Master without any defect: the Blessed Christ who is God and man, light and life, the maker of the world, who is glorious and to be praised forever. Amen.[1]

2 *Concerning the Marvelous Statue That Spoke to St. Francis*

One night when St. Francis was devoutly praying to Almighty God in the Place of St. Mary of the Angels, a very wonderful vision appeared before his bodily eyes: a great statue similar to the one which King Nabuchodonosor saw in a dream. For it had a head of gold and a very beautiful face, and its chest and arms were of silver, its abdomen and thighs of bronze, its legs of iron, and its feet partly of iron and partly of clay, and it was dressed in sackcloth, which seemed to make it blush for shame.

Now St. Francis, gazing at the statue, was greatly amazed at its indescribable beauty and its wonderful size and also at the shame that it seemed to feel about the sackcloth in which it was dressed.

And while he was gazing with wonder at its extremely beautiful head and face, the statue itself spoke to him, saying: "Why are you so amazed? God has sent you this example so that you may learn from me what is to happen to your Order in the future.

"My golden head and very beautiful face that you see is the beginning of your Order, based on the perfection of the Gospel life. And just as the substance of gold is more valuable than all other metals, and as the position of the head and face is superior to that of the other members, so the beginning of your Order will be of such great value because of the golden fraternal charity, and of such great beauty because of the angelic purity, and of such great loftiness because of its evangelical poverty that the entire world will be astounded. And Queen Saba—that is, Holy Mother Church—will marvel and rejoice in heart when it sees in the first chosen friars of your Order such Christlike beauty and splendor of spiritual wisdom shining as in angelic mirrors. And blessed will be those who conform themselves utterly to Christ and strive to imitate the virtues and customs of that first precious metal, the golden head, by adhering more to its heavenly beauty than to the deceptive flowers of the world.

"Now the chest and arms of silver will be the second state of your Order, which will be as inferior to the first as silver is to gold. And just as silver has great value and brightness and sonorousness, so in that second state there will be many friars who will be so brilliant in Holy Scripture and the light of holiness and the sublimity of the word of God that some of them will be made popes and cardinals and many will be bishops. And because a man's strength is shown in his chest and arms, so in that time the Lord will raise up in your Order men

1476

who will be outstandingly brilliant in both knowledge and virtue and who will defend this Order and also the entire Church by knowledge and virtue from the many attacks of the devils and various attacks of faithless men. But although that future generation will be admirable, nevertheless it will not attain the very perfect state of the first friars, but compared to them it will be like silver compared to gold.

"After it there will be a third state in your Order that will be like the bronze abdomen and thigh. Because as bronze is considered of less value than silver, so those of the third state will be inferior to the first and second. And although they will spread in numbers and distance over a great part of the world, like bronze, nevertheless there will be among them some 'whose God is their belly' and for whom 'the glory' of the Order 'is in their shame,' and 'who mind' only 'earthly things.' And although, because of their knowledge, they will have an amazing eloquence 'like sounding brass,' yet alas, because they will be lovers of their belly and their body, they will be in the eyes of God (as the Apostle says) like sounding brass or a tinkling cymbal, because while uttering heavenly words and begetting spiritual offspring by showing to others the fountain of life, they themselves will be fatally arid and will adhere without interior grace to the earth. May the mercy of God succor them! Amen.

"After them will come a fourth terrible and frightening state which is now shown to you in the iron legs. For just as iron overcomes and dissolves bronze, silver, and gold, so that state will be of such ironlike hardness and depravity that the coldness and horrible blight and metallic morality of that dangerous time will sweep into oblivion whatever good the golden charity of the first friars and the silver truth of the second and the bronze, though resounding, eloquence of the third have erected in the Church of Christ. However, as the legs support the body, so those friars will support the body of the Order by some hypocritical rusty strength. And therefore both the iron belly and legs will be hidden by clothing, because those friars will have the habit of the Order and piety, but 'within they will be ravenous wolves.' But those rusty and ironlike friars serving only their belly—although they may hide it from the world, yet it will be evident to the Lord, because by the hammer of their perverse life they will reduce to nothing their most precious gifts. Therefore, like the hardest iron, they will be afflicted with the fire of tribulations and the hammer of terrible trials, so that they will be melted down not only by the fires and burning coals of the devils but also of secular authorities, in order that such powerful persons may suffer torments from powerful men. And because they sinned by irreverence and hardness, they will be cruelly tortured by irreverent men. As a result of those trials they will be stirred to such impatience that, just as iron resists all metals, they will set themselves in opposition to everyone, and thus they will stubbornly oppose not only secular authorities but also their spiritual superiors, thinking that they can resist everything, like iron. And thereby they will greatly displease God.

"Now the fifth state will be partly of iron, referring to the above-mentioned hypocrites, and partly of earth, referring to those who give themselves completely to worldly business. And as you see burnt clay and iron appearing together in the feet, although they can in no way unite, so will it be in the last state of this Order: for a great abomination and division shall arise among the earthly ambitious hypocrites who are hardened by the mire of temporal things and the desires of the flesh, for like clay and iron they cannot come together because of their great discord. And they will despise not only the Gospel and the Rule, but also with their clay and iron feet—that is, with their perverse and impure cravings—they will tread upon all the discipline of this holy Order. And just as clay and iron are separate entities, so many of them will be divided among themselves both interiorly by living in a state of contentiousness and exteriorly by adhering in a partisan way to secular despots. As a result they will arouse the hostility of everyone to such a point that they will hardly be able to enter or reside in towns or openly wear the habit. And many of them will be punished and liquidated by frightful tortures at the hands of seculars, who despise such abominable feet. All this will happen to them because they have wholly turned away from the golden head. But in those perilous days those who turn back to the warnings of that precious head shall be blessed, for the Lord will try them like gold in a furnace and will crown them and welcome them into eternity like a victim of a holocaust.

"Now this habit that I seem to be ashamed of is holy poverty. Although it is the jewel and splendor of the whole Order and the unique custodian and crown and basis of all holiness, nevertheless those degenerate sons, lacking all virtuous efforts, will, as we said, be ashamed of that most holy poverty, and putting aside their coarse habits, they will select and obtain, even by simony, expensive and ostentatious robes. But blessed and happy will be those who persevere to the end in what they have promised to the Lord!"

And after saying this, that statue vanished.

St. Francis was greatly amazed at all this, and like the good shepherd, weeping tears, he commended his present and future sheep to Almighty God.

May Our Lord Jesus Christ be praised and glorified forever! Amen.[2]

3 *How Brother Rufino Liberated a Possessed Man*

Now Brother Rufino, because of his intense concentration of mind on God and his angelic peace of soul, whenever someone called him, would answer in such a serious and gentle and strange tone that he seemed to be coming back from another world. Once when his companions called to him to go for some bread, he answered like a diviner in a trance.

And while he was begging for bread in Assisi, a tightly bound, possessed man was being led by a large group of men to St. Francis in order that he might free him from the devil. When the man saw Brother Rufino from a distance, he immediately began to shout and thrash around with such fury that he broke his bonds and leaped away from the men. They were amazed at such an extraordinary seizure and urged him to tell them why he was being tormented more than usual.

He answered: "Because that poor little friar—that obedient, meek, holy Brother Rufino going about with his sack—burns me up and crucifies me by his saintly virtues and humble prayers. And so I cannot remain in this man any longer!"

And after saying that, the devil left him at once.

When Brother Rufino heard this—as those men and the cured sick man were acting very reverently toward him—he gave praise and honor to Our Lord Jesus Christ. And he urged them in all things to glorify God and the Savior, Our Lord Jesus Christ, from whom this and all good things come and who is blessed forever. Amen.[3]

4 How St. Francis Foretold a Terrible Famine

St. Francis not only gave Brother Leo marvelous consolations during his lifetime, but he also appeared to him frequently after he died.

Once while Brother Leo was praying devoutly, St. Francis appeared to him and said: "Oh, Brother Leo, do you remember when I was in the world I predicted that a great famine would come over the whole world, and I said I knew of a certain poor little man for the love of whom God would spare the world and not send the scourge of famine as long as he was alive?"

Brother Leo answered: "I remember very well, dear Father."

And St. Francis said: "I was that creature and that poor little man for love of whom God did not send the famine among men, but out of humility I did not want to reveal it. But now you should know for sure, Brother Leo, that after I have left the world a terrible and universal famine will come over the world, so that many men will die of hunger."

And so it happened that about six or nine months after he had said those words, such a great famine spread everywhere that people ate not only the roots of plants but also the bark of trees, and a great number of them died from hunger.

The innocence of Brother Leo and the divine friendship and sublime gift of prophecy of St. Francis are evident from this.[4]

To the glory of Our Lord Jesus Christ. Amen.

Little Flowers of St. Francis

5 How Blood Came Out of a Picture of the Stigmata of St. Francis

How worthy of admiration were those wonderful Stigmata of the holy Father was demonstrated in a notable miracle which occurred in a certain friary of the Friars Preachers. For there was in that community a certain Friar Preacher who had such a heartfelt hatred for St. Francis that he could not see him in a picture or hear a word about him or really believe that he had been marked with the holy Stigmata. So when this friar was a member of the community of that convent beyond the mountains, in the refectory of which was a painting of St. Francis with the holy Stigmata, he, moved by faithlessness and hatred, secretly went and cut the sacred Stigmata out of the holy Father's picture with a knife so that not a single trace of them was to be seen.

But the next day, when the friar sat down at mealtime and glanced at the picture of St. Francis, he saw the Stigmata there in the places where he had cut them out, but looking more recent than before. He angrily thought that he had not completely cut them out the first time. And watching for a moment when no one was in the room—for he who does evil hates the light—he went and cut out the Saint's Stigmata a second time, in such a way however that he did not destroy the stone on which the picture was painted.

Now on the third day when the friar sat down at the table, he looked at the picture of St. Francis—and he saw those sacred Stigmata seeming more beautiful and new than they had ever appeared before. Then the friar, being darkened by evil and aroused by wickedness, added a third sin to his second. And he said to himself: "By God, I am going to erase those Stigmata so that they will never appear again!"

And as before he waited for a time when he would not be seen by men, forgetting that all things are bare and open to the eyes of God. Then with intense fury he took a knife and dug the marks of the Stigmata out of the picture, cutting out the color and the stone.

But just as he finished digging, blood began to flow from

the openings, and it gushed out violently and stained the friar's face and hands and habit. He was terrified and fell to the ground as if he were dead. Meanwhile the blood was flowing in streams from the openings in the wall which the unhappy man had made where the Stigmata had been.

Then the friars of the house came and found him lying there like a corpse. And they were very sorry when they realized what an evil deed he had committed. Moreover, seeing that the blood continued to flow, they tried to stop up the openings with pieces of cotton, but they could not restrain the streams of blood. So fearing that lay people would perceive it and as a result they would suffer scandal and scorn, they thought of pleading devoutly to St. Francis to help them. So the prior and all the friars in the community bared their backs before the picture of St. Francis and gave themselves the discipline and prayed, weeping tears and begging St. Francis mercifully to forgive the offense of that friar and to deign to stop the flow of blood.

And because of their humility, their prayers were immediately granted. The blood ceased flowing, and the holy Stigmata remained to be venerated in their beauty by all.

From that time the friar was exceedingly devoted to St. Francis. And as the friars of the Place of Alverna have testified, that friar went up to Mount Alverna out of devotion, and he brought some of the bloodstained cotton with him and gave it to those friars.

Moreover out of devotion he came to St. Mary of the Angels, and he very devoutly visited all the Places of St. Francis with great reverence and weeping. For wherever he could find events or relics connected with St. Francis, he would burst into tears in such a devout way that he would make others weep too. He also described all the above-mentioned miracles before many Friars Minor in Alverna and Assisi (when his companions were absent so that they should not consider these matters to reflect on their Order). By the merits of St. Francis that friar became so devoted to the Franciscans that sometimes when he could not see them, he nevertheless remained united with them by the bond of brotherly charity in God.[5]

To the glory of Our Lord Jesus Christ. Amen.

6 *How the Lady Jacopa Visited Brother Giles*

When Brother Giles was staying in Perugia, the Lady Jacopa dei Settesoli, a noble Roman lady who was very devoted to the Friars Minor, came to see him. Later a Brother Gerardino of the Order of Minors, a very spiritual man, also arrived to hear his edifying conversation.

And while several other friars were standing there, Brother Giles said these words in Italian: "Because of what a man can do, he comes to what he does not want."

Now Brother Gerardino in order to provoke Brother Giles to speak, said: "I am amazed, Brother Giles, that a man, because of what he can do, comes to what he does not want, since a man can of himself do nothing. And I can prove that in a number of ways. First, to be capable of doing something presupposes being, and a thing's functioning depends on its being, as fire warms because it is hot. But of himself a man is nothing. Therefore the Apostle said: 'If any man thinks himself to be something, whereas he is nothing, he deceives himself.' So someone who is nothing can do nothing. Consequently man can do nothing. Second, I will prove that a man can do nothing in this way: because if a man can do anything, it is either by reason of the soul alone, or by reason of the body alone, or by reason of both together. If it is by reason of the soul alone, it is certain that he can do nothing, because the soul without the body cannot gain or lose merit. If it is by reason of the body alone, he can do nothing because the body without the soul is deprived of life and form, and so cannot do anything, because all action is from form. Now if it is by reason of both together, a man can do nothing because if he could do anything, it would be by reason of the soul which is its form. But, as I have already said, if the soul without the body can do nothing, it can do still less when joined to the body, for the corruptible body is a load upon the soul. And I will give you an example of this, Brother Giles: if a donkey cannot walk without a burden, it can walk far less with a burden. And so by that example it is evident that the soul can do less when burdened with the body than it can do without it.

But it can do nothing without it. Consequently it can do nothing with it."

And he made many similar arguments to Brother Giles—in fact he made a good dozen—in order to make him talk. And all who heard those arguments were filled with admiration.

But Brother Giles replied: "You spoke badly, Brother Gerardino. Say your *mea culpa* for all of it."

Brother Gerardino said a *mea culpa*, smiling. But Brother Giles, seeing that he was not saying it sincerely, said: "That is not valid, Brother Gerardino. And when a *mea culpa* is not valid, there is nothing left for a man to gain."

Then Brother Giles said to him: "Do you know how to sing, Brother Gerardino?" And when he answered, "Yes," Brother Giles said: "Now sing with me!" And Brother Giles took from his sleeve a reed pipe such as children make, and beginning with the first note of the pipe and going on, note by note, in rhythmic words he annulled and refuted all the twelve arguments.

Beginning with the first one, he said: "I was not referring to man's being before the Creation, Brother Gerardino, because it is true that he was nothing then and could do nothing then. But I mean the being of man after the Creation, when God gave him free will, by which he could gain merit by consenting to good or lose merit by dissenting. Therefore you spoke badly and offered me a fallacy, Brother Gerardino, because St. Paul the Apostle does not refer to a lack of substance or a lack of capacity but to a lack of merit, as he says: 'If I lack charity, I am nothing.' Furthermore I was not referring to a soul without a body or to a dead body, but to a living man who can do good by consenting to grace, if he wishes to, and who can do bad by resisting grace, which is nothing else than falling away from good. Now as to your asserting that 'the corruptible body is a load upon the soul,' Scripture does not say that a man is thereby deprived of free will, so that he cannot do good or evil, but it means that his understanding and feelings are impeded and also that the soul's memory is preoccupied with temporal matters. Hence the passage continues: 'And the earthly habitation presses down the mind that muses on many things,' for they do not allow the soul to reflect freely and to seek 'the things that are above, where Christ is

1484

sitting at the right hand of God.' Therefore the potentialities of the soul are impeded in many ways on account of man's many occupations and physical cares. And so you spoke badly, Brother Gerardino."

And he likewise refuted all the other arguments. So Brother Gerardino said a sincere *mea culpa* and admitted that a creature can do something. And Brother Giles said: "Now your *mea culpa* is valid."

And then he said: "Do you want me to show you still more clearly that a creature can do something?" And climbing onto a box he cried out in a frightening voice: "O damned soul lying in hell!" Then he himself answered for the damned person in a mournful voice in a way that terrified everyone present: "Ah, me! Woe! Ah, me!" And he shrieked and moaned.

Then in another voice Brother Giles said: "Tell us, you unhappy man, why you went to hell?"

And he answered: "Because I did not avoid doing the evil that I could have avoided, and I did not do the good that I could and ought to have done."

And Brother Giles asked him: "Oh, you wicked damned soul, what would you do if you were given time to do penance?"

And he replied for him: "I would throw all the earth in the world bit by bit behind me in order to avoid an eternal punishment, because that would have an end. But my damnation will last for all eternity!"

And turning to Brother Gerardino Brother Giles said: "Do you hear, Brother Gerardino, that a creature can do something?"

Then he said: "Tell me, Gerardino, whether when a drop of water falls into the ocean, it gives its name to the ocean or the ocean to the drop?"

And the other replied that both the substance and the name of the drop are absorbed and take on the name of the ocean.

And after he said that, Brother Giles fell into a rapture before all who were there. For he realized that human nature, in relation to the nature of God, was absorbed like a drop of water into the great ocean of the Divine Infinity in the Incarnation of Our Lord Jesus Christ, who is blessed forever and ever. Amen.

Now the Lady Jacopa, after hearing and seeing these things, went away filled with joy.[6]

7 How Brother Giles Removed a Doubt Concerning the Virginity of Mary from the Heart of a Friar Preacher

At the time when the holy Brother Giles was alive, there was a certain great Master of the Order of Preachers who for many years suffered from a serious doubt concerning the virginity of the Blessed Mother of Our Lord Jesus Christ. For it seemed to him impossible that she could have been both a mother and a virgin. Otherwise he had real faith, and therefore he suffered very much from that doubt of his, and he wished to be freed from it by some enlightened man.

Now when he heard that the holy Brother Giles was a very enlightened man, he went to him. But Brother Giles, knowing in advance by the Holy Spirit about his coming and intention and spiritual conflict, went out to meet him. And before reaching him, he struck the ground with a stick that he held in his hand, and he said: "Oh, Friar Preacher, Virgin before bearing!"

And at once a very beautiful lily came up on the spot which he had struck with the stick.

Then he struck a second time, saying: "Oh, Friar Preacher, Virgin in bearing!"

And another lily sprang up.

And striking a third time, he said: "Oh, Friar Preacher, Virgin after bearing!"

And a third lily appeared. And after doing that, Brother Giles ran away.

But that Friar Preacher was immediately freed from his temptation on seeing such an amazing and novel miracle. And when he learned that it had been Brother Giles, from that moment he conceived such a devotion for him that he used to praise both him and his Order in a wonderful way.[7]

To the glory of Our Lord Jesus Christ. Amen.

8 *How Brother James Asked Brother Giles How to Act in a Rapture*

The holy and very devout lay brother James of Massa, who had been with St. Clare and many of the companions of St. Francis, had the gift of rapture, and he wished to obtain Brother Giles' advice regarding how he should act when he had such a grace.

Brother Giles answered: "Don't add. Don't take away. And avoid crowds as much as you can."

"What do you mean?" said Brother James. "Explain it to me, Reverend Father."

He replied: "When the mind is ready to be introduced into that most glorious light of God's goodness, it should not add anything by presumption or take away anything by negligence, and it should love solitude as much as possible if it wishes that the grace be preserved and increase."[8]

To the glory of Our Lord Jesus Christ. Amen.

9 *How St. Lawrence Appeared to Brother John of Alverna*

Brother John of Alverna was asked by Brother James of Falerone to pray to God concerning a certain scruple of conscience which was sorely tormenting him, namely, certain matters that pertained to the office of a priest. And before the Feast of St. Lawrence he received this answer, as he himself told it. He said that the Lord said to him: "He is a priest according to the order of God."

But when Brother James' conscience still disturbed him, he asked Brother John to pray to the Lord about it again.

Therefore during the night of the Vigil of the Feast of St. Lawrence, Brother John faithfully watched and prayed to the Lord that He might give him some certitude concerning the scruple through the merits of St. Lawrence. And while he was watching and praying, St. Lawrence appeared to him, dressed like a deacon in white vestments. And he said to Brother John:

1487

"I am the Deacon Lawrence, and he for whom you are praying is unquestionably a priest by divine ordination." And then Brother James felt perfect assurance regarding the scruple which he had had, and he was greatly consoled.

Again, while the friars were singing the *Salve Regina* in the evening, St. Lawrence appeared to Brother John as a young man wearing a red dalmatic and holding an iron grill, and said to him: "This grill has brought me glory in Heaven, and the pain of the fire has given me the fullness of God's bliss." And he added: "If you wish to enjoy the glory and bliss of God, bear with patience the suffering and bitterness of the world."

St. Lawrence remained thus visibly with him as long as the friars sang the above-mentioned antiphon. And after they went to rest, Brother John stayed in the choir with St. Lawrence. And the Saint reassured and consoled him, and then disappeared. And he left him so overflowing with affection and divine charity that he did not sleep a bit all that night of the feast, but spent the entire night experiencing marvelous consolations.

Again to this Brother John, once when he was devoutly celebrating Mass, after he had consecrated the host, all the appearance of the bread vanished before his sight, and in the twinkling of an eye Christ appeared there, dressed in a red robe and having a very beautiful red beard, and gave him such sweet consolation that if he had not remained conscious, he would have been rapt in ecstasy. And during that vision he received assurance that the Lord was propitiated by that Mass for the whole world and especially for those whom he commended to Him.[9]

To the praise and glory of Our Lord Jesus Christ. Amen.

10 *How Brother John Had the Spirit of Revelation*

When certain persons had some terrible hidden sins which no one could know except by divine revelation—some of them were dead, others were living—Brother John disclosed to the living their hidden sins by divine revelation. As a result they were converted to a life of penance.

One of them said that he had committed the sin which Brother John disclosed before Brother John had been born. And the man to whom he disclosed it told me about it.

And they admitted that what Brother John said about them was true.

It was also revealed to him that some of them who died had perished a temporal and an eternal death, and some only a temporal death. And this was demonstrated to him with certainty. And I saw a trustworthy friar who knew those persons.[10]

11   *How a Great Tyrant Was Converted and Became a Friar Minor*

This was a very clear sign that the Order of St. Francis was founded by God: that as soon as it began to increase in numbers, it began to extend to the ends of the earth. So St. Francis, striving to conform himself to Christ in all things, used to send his friars, two by two, to preach in all countries. And the Lord performed such marvels through them that "their sound has gone forth into all the earth, and their words unto the ends of the world."

Once it happened that two of those new disciples of the Saint, while traveling through a foreign land, came to a castle filled with very wicked men. In it was a certain great tyrant who was very cruel and faithless and who was the head and leader of all those robbers and bad men. He was of noble birth, but evil and vile in deeds.

When those two friars came to that castle in the evening, suffering from hunger and cold and fatigue, meekly like sheep among wolves, they asked the tyrant lord of the castle through a messenger to receive them as overnight guests, for the love of Our Lord Jesus Christ.

Inspired by God, he gave them a cordial welcome and showed them great courtesy and compassion. For he had a large fire lit and a meal prepared for them as for noblemen.

While the friars and all the others were resting, one of the friars, who was a priest and had a remarkable gift for speaking of God, noticed that none of the resting men spoke about God or the salvation of the soul but only about robberies and murders and many other evil deeds which they had committed, and that they took pleasure in the wicked and godless acts they had so far done. Therefore that friar, having received food for the body, wished to give some heavenly nourishment to his host and the others, so he said to the master: "My lord, you have shown great courtesy and charity to us, and therefore we would be very ungrateful if we did not try to repay you with some good things from God. So we ask you to have your whole household assemble in order that we may repay you with spiritual presents for the physical gifts which we have received from you."

The lord of the house agreed to their request and had everyone gather before the friars. And that friar began to speak about the glory of Paradise—how there is everlasting joy there, the society of angels, the security of the blessed, infinite glory, a wealth of heavenly treasure, eternal life, an ineffable light, untroubled peace, incorruptible health, the presence of God, and all that is good and no evil. But by their sins and their wretchedness, men lose those great gifts and go to hell, where there is everlasting suffering and sorrow, the society of devils, serpents and dragons, endless unhappiness and life without life, heavy shadows, and the presence of Lucifer; where there is trouble and anger, eternal fire and ice, worms and fury, hunger and thirst; where there is death without death, groaning, weeping, the gnashing of teeth, and an eternity of pain; where there is all that is evil, and all that is good is lacking!

"And," he said, "as I have seen and heard, all of you are hastening and running toward all that evil, for no good appears in your deeds or words. So I advise and warn you, my dear friends, not to lose those highest heavenly good things that will last forever, on account of the vile things of this world and the delights of the flesh, and not to hasten and run this way to such great and bitter sufferings!"

When that friar had spoken by the power of the Holy Spirit, the lord of the castle was stirred and his heart was moved to remorse. He threw himself down at the feet of the friars, and with all the others present he began to weep bitterly, asking and begging the friar to guide him to the way of salvation.

And after he had confessed his sins to that friar with many

tears and with sincere remorse, the friar told him that he should expiate his sins by making pilgrimages to shrines, by mortifying himself with fasting, by watching and praying, and by making generous donations to charity and other good works.

But the lord of the castle answered: "Dear Father, I have never been out of this province. And I don't know how to say the Our Father or Hail Mary or other prayers. So please give me some other penance."

Then the holy friar said: "My dear man, I want to act as your bondsman and by the charity of God intercede with Our Lord Jesus Christ for your sins, so that your soul should not perish. So now I want you to perform no other penance than to bring me tonight with your own hands some straw for my companion and myself to sleep on."

He gladly brought the straw and prepared a bed in a room where a light was burning. And as the lord of the castle reflected how that friar had spoken in such a holy and virtuous way, he realized that he was a saintly man, and he decided to investigate carefully what he did during the night. He saw that the holy friar went to bed to sleep. But when he thought that everyone was sound asleep, he silently arose in the middle of the night, and stretching out his hands to the Lord, he prayed that the sins of him for whom he had become bondsman might be forgiven.

And while he was praying, he was lifted up in the air to the ceiling of the castle, and there in the air he wept and grieved over the sins of the lord of the house, asking that they be forgiven in such a fervent way that hardly anyone has ever been seen weeping for his dead relatives or friends as that friar wept over that man's sins. And during that night he was raised in the air three times, always shedding tears of devout compassion. And the lord of the castle secretly observed all this and heard his charitable grieving and compassionate sobbing and weeping.

Therefore as soon as he arose in the morning, he threw himself down at that friar's feet and begged him with tears of compunction to guide him along the path of salvation, saying that he was firmly resolved to do whatever the friar commanded. Therefore on the advice of the holy friar, he sold all that he owned, made all the restitution that he owed, and distributed all the rest to the poor in accordance with the Gospel. And offering himself to God, he joined the Order of Friars Minor and lived a holy life with praiseworthy perseverance until he died.

And his companions and associates were inspired by remorse to change their way of life for the better. Such is the fruit that was obtained by the holy simplicity of those friars who did not preach about Aristotle or philosophy, but briefly about the pains of hell and the glory of Paradise, as is written in the holy Rule.[11]

To the praise of Our Lord Jesus Christ, who is blessed forever! Amen.

12 *How St. Francis Laid a Curse upon a Minister in Bologna*

A certain Friar Minor—Brother John of Stracchia—was the Minister of the Province of Bologna in St. Francis' time, and he was a very learned man. And without St. Francis' permission and against his will, while he was away, he founded a house of studies in Bologna.

When it was reported to the Saint that such a house of studies had been founded in Bologna, he immediately hastened there and severely reproved that Minister, saying: "You want to destroy my Order! For I want my friars to pray more than to read, according to the example of my Lord Jesus Christ."

Now after St. Francis had left Bologna, that Minister did not heed him and again organized a house of studies, as he had done before. When St. Francis heard about this, he was deeply troubled, and he laid a heavy curse on him.

Soon after he had been cursed, the Minister fell seriously ill. And he sent some friars to ask St. Francis to withdraw the curse he laid upon him.

But St. Francis answered: "Our Blessed Lord Jesus Christ has confirmed in Heaven that curse which I laid on him. And he is accursed!"

The sick Minister sadly lay in bed and grieved. And all of

a sudden a flaming drop of sulphur came down onto his body and burned up both him and his bed. And that unhappy man died amid a great stench, and his soul was seized by the devil —may Our Lord Jesus Christ who was crucified for us protect us from him! Amen.[12]

13 *How St. Francis Opposed Retaining Any of the Novices' Property*

Once the Saint's vicar, Brother Peter Catani, seeing that St. Mary of the Portiuncula was crowded with friars from other Places and that there were not enough alms to provide them with what they needed, said to St. Francis: "Father, I don't know what to do with so many friars arriving from everywhere! I haven't supplies enough to provide for them. Please allow some of the property of the novices entering the Order to be set aside for our expenses when necessary."

But St. Francis answered: "Dear Brother, put away that kind of piety which impiously goes against the Rule for the sake of anyone whatsoever!"

And Peter said: "Then what shall I do?"

St. Francis replied: "Strip the altar of the Virgin and take away its various ornaments, since you cannot provide for the needy in any other way. Believe me, the Mother of God would rather have the Gospel of her Son observed and her altar stripped than have the altar adorned and her Son scorned. The Lord will send someone who will restore to His Mother what He loaned to us."[13a]

The Saint also often uttered these complaints: "The more the friars turn away from poverty, the more the world will turn away from them. And," he said, "they shall seek and shall not find. But if they had embraced my lady Poverty, the world would nourish them, because they are given to the world for its salvation."[13b]

St. Francis often used to say to the friars: "I recommend these three words to you, namely, holy *simplicity* against an inordinate appetite for knowledge, *prayer* which the devil always tries to set aside by many exterior occupations and worries, and the *love of poverty*, not just poverty itself, the spouse of the Lord Jesus Christ and my spouse, but love and zeal for it."[13c]

14 *How Christ Complained to Brother Leo about the Friars*

Once the Lord Jesus Christ said to Brother Leo, the companion of St. Francis: "I grieve over the friars."

Brother Leo answered Him: "Why, Lord?"

"For three reasons," said the Lord; "namely, because they do not recognize My gifts which I have generously given them, as you well know, and which I bestow on them abundantly every day, while they neither sow nor reap; and because they are idle and grumble all day; and because they often provoke one another to anger, and do not return to love and do not forgive the offenses which they have received."[14a]

Once at St. Mary of the Portiuncula, reflecting that the graces obtained in prayer are lost through idle words said after prayer, St. Francis decreed this remedy against the fault of uttering idle words: "Whoever says an idle or useless word must immediately accuse himself and recite one Our Father for every idle word. And I wish him to say the Our Father for his own soul if he first accuses himself of his fault, but if he was first corrected by someone else, he should recite it for the soul of the person who corrected him."[14b]

15 *How Brother Leo Saw a Terrifying Vision in a Dream*

Once Brother Leo saw in a dream a vision of the preparation of the Last Judgment. He saw the angels blowing trumpets and various instruments and calling together a vast crowd in a field. And on one side of the field was placed a red ladder that reached from the ground to Heaven, and on the other side of the field was placed another ladder, all white, that came down from Heaven to the ground.

At the top of the red ladder appeared Christ, like an offended and very angry Lord. And St. Francis was a few steps lower, near Christ, and he went down the ladder a bit and shouted loudly and fervently, saying: "Come, my friars, come with confidence. Do not be afraid. Come and approach the Lord, for He is calling you."

On hearing St. Francis' voice and call, the friars went and climbed up the red ladder with great confidence. And when they had all gone up, some fell from the third step, some from the fourth, others from the fifth and the sixth, and all fell down, one after another, so that not one remained on the ladder.

St. Francis was moved to pity by such a fall, and like a compassionate father he prayed to the Judge for his sons, that He might receive them with mercy.

And Christ showed St. Francis His Wounds, all bleeding, and said: "Your friars have done this to Me."

And after the Saint had prayed thus for a while, he went down a few steps and called his friars who had fallen from the red ladder, and said: "Come and get up, my sons and friars. Have confidence and do not despair. Run to the white ladder and climb up, because by it you will be received into the Kingdom of Heaven."

At their father's advice, the friars ran to the white ladder. And at the top of the ladder appeared the glorious Virgin Mary, Mother of Jesus Christ, very compassionately and mercifully. And she received those friars. And without any difficulty they entered the Everlasting Kingdom.[15]

To the glory of Christ. Amen.

16 Concerning a Tribulation of the Order

The holy Brother Conrad reported—as he heard from Brother Leo—that once St. Francis was praying in St. Mary of the Angels behind the pulpit of the church. And he held out his hands toward Heaven and said: "Lord, have mercy on Your people and spare them!"

Christ appeared to him and said: "You pray well, and I willingly grant your prayer, because they mean much to me and I have paid a great price for them. Nevertheless make a pact with Me, and I will have mercy on all the people, namely, that your Order remain with Me and only with Me. Yet the time will come when it will turn away from Me, but I will sustain the Order for a while for the world's sake, which has faith in it and considers the Order its guide and its beacon. But afterward I shall give power to the devils who will everywhere arouse against it so many scandals and tribulations that they will be expelled and avoided by everyone. And if a son goes to his father's house for bread, he will strike him on the head with a stick. If the friars knew the tribulations of those days, they would begin to flee, and many of them shall flee into the wilderness, that is, those who are zealous for My honor."

And St. Francis asked the Lord: "How will they live there?"

Christ answered: "I who fed the sons of Israel in the wilderness shall feed them there with herbs. And I shall give those herbs different tastes, as formerly the manna. And afterward they shall go forth and rebuild the Order in its first perfect state.

"But woe to those who congratulate themselves on having only the appearance of conversion and who grow inert from idleness and do not steadfastly resist the temptations that are permitted for the testing of the elect, since only those who have been tried shall receive the crown of eternal life, who have meanwhile suffered from the malice of the reprobate."[16]

To the praise of Our Lord Jesus Christ.

17 *Concerning the Conversion of a Soldier*

There was a certain strong soldier who had won many victories and later became a Friar Minor. And when soldiers laughed at him because he had joined such an Order rather than the Templars or a similar Order where he could do much good and still fight battles, he replied: "I tell you that when I feel thirst, hunger, cold, and such things, the impulse of pride and concupiscence and such still attacks me. How much worse would it be if I saw my feet shod in armor and I was on a handsome horse and so on!"

And he added: "So far I was strong in fighting others—from now on I want to be strong in fighting myself!"

Thanks be to God.[17]

18   *About a Noble Friar Who Was Ashamed to Beg*

At Civitanova there was a certain friar of noble parentage named Michael who simply would not go out to beg because he was ashamed.

Now it happened that St. Francis came there, and he was told about that friar. The Saint scolded him very severely, and under holy obedience he commanded him to go alone, naked with only his breeches, to beg in a certain village that was about a mile away.

He humbly obeyed, and out of obedience went naked to beg, having set aside all shame. And he received enough bread and enough grain and other things, and he returned to the house burdened. And from that day he felt such joy and grace that as long as he lived he did not want to do anything but go and beg.[18]

19   *How a Friar Saw a Vision in Which Some Friars Minor Were Damned*

This was told by a friar who visited the Province of England. He heard from the Minister of that Province, a man of great piety and holiness, that a certain friar who was often rapt in ecstasy had once remained in a rapture for a whole day, weeping many tears.

On seeing him, the Minister said: "This friar is dying!" And he said to him: "Brother, I command you under obedience to come out of your rapture."

He immediately came back to himself and asked for some food. And after he had eaten, the Minister said to him: "I order you under obedience to tell me the cause of your weeping, as we have never seen this happen to you before—indeed it seems to be contrary to the nature of a rapture."

When the friar found that he could not avoid revealing it, he said: "I saw the Lord Jesus Christ on a high and lofty throne, surrounded by the heavenly militia, and prepared to pass judgment. And I saw not only lay persons but both clerics and religious of many different Orders being damned.

"Then I saw someone led in wearing the habit of the Friars Minor, very elegantly dressed in a very expensive habit. When he was asked about his state, he declared that he was a Friar Minor.

"Then the Judge said: 'Brother Francis, do you hear what he says? What do you say?'

"He answered: 'Away with him, Lord! For my Friars wear common materials and not such expensive ones.'

"And that unhappy man was immediately cast into hell by the devils.

"And now another came in, an important personage accompanied and honored by many great lay people. And when asked, he said he was a Friar Minor. Again the Judge spoke to St. Francis as before.

"He answered: 'Lord, my Friars seek prayer and spiritual progress, and they flee from the honors and business of worldly men.'

"The same thing happened to him as to the first.

"And now came another burdened with heavy packages of costly and useless books. And the same was done with him as with the first and second.

"And here was another who was completely preoccupied and worried about planning and building large and costly buildings. Like the others, St. Francis denied that he belonged to his Order.

"Finally there came one who was very lowly in habit and appearance. And when he was asked who he was, he confessed that he was a great sinner, unworthy of anything good, and he begged for mercy.

"St. Francis embraced him and led him into the glory of Paradise with him, saying: 'Lord, he really is a Friar Minor.'

"And that was the cause of my weeping," the friar said to his Minister.[19]

Little Flowers of St. Francis

20 *The Canticle of Brother Sun*

HERE BEGIN THE PRAISES OF THE CREATURES WHICH
ST. FRANCIS MADE FOR THE PRAISE AND HONOR OF
GOD WHEN HE WAS ILL AT SAN DAMIANO

Most High Almighty Good Lord,
Yours are the praises, the glory, the honor, and all blessings!
To You alone, Most High, do they belong,
And no man is worthy to mention You.

Be praised, my Lord, with all Your creatures,
Especially Sir Brother Sun,
By whom You give us the light of day!
And he is beautiful and radiant with great splendor.
Of You, Most High, he is a symbol!

Be praised, my Lord, for Sister Moon and the Stars!
In the sky You formed them bright and lovely and fair.

Be praised, my Lord, for Brother Wind
And for the Air and cloudy and clear and all Weather,
By which You give sustenance to Your creatures!

Be praised, my Lord, for Sister Water,
Who is very useful and humble and lovely and chaste!

Be praised, my Lord, for Brother Fire,
By whom You give us light at night,
And he is beautiful and merry and mighty and strong!

Be praised, my Lord, for our Sister Mother Earth,
Who sustains and governs us,
And produces fruits with colorful flowers and leaves!

Be praised, my Lord, for those who forgive for love of You
And endure infirmities and tribulations.
Blessed are those who shall endure them in peace,
For by You, Most High, they will be crowned!

1499

Be praised, my Lord, for our Sister Bodily Death,
From whom no living man can escape!
Woe to those who shall die in mortal sin!
Blessed are those whom she will find in Your most holy will,
For the Second Death will not harm them.

Praise and bless my Lord and thank Him
And serve Him with great humility![20]

THIS IS THE END OF THE BOOK ABOUT CERTAIN
WONDERFUL DEEDS OF ST. FRANCIS AND HIS
FIRST COMPANIONS. IN THE NAME OF OUR LORD
JESUS CHRIST, FOR THE HONOR OF OUR MOST
HOLY FATHER FRANCIS. GOD BE PRAISED!

APPENDICES

1 *The Perfect Joy (Ch. 8)*

In 1927 Father Bughetti published the following significantly different version of this famous chapter from an early fourteenth-century Latin manuscript (AFH 20, 107):

One day at St. Mary, St. Francis called Brother Leo and said: "Brother Leo, write this down."

He answered: "I'm ready."

"Write what true joy is," he said. "A messenger comes and says that all the masters of theology in Paris have joined the Order—write: that is not true joy. Or all the prelates beyond the mountains—archbishops and bishops, or the King of France and the King of England—write: that is not true joy. Or that my friars have gone to the unbelievers and have converted all of them to the faith; or that I have so much grace from God that I heal the sick and I perform many miracles. I tell you that true joy is not in all those things."

"But what is true joy?"

"I am returning from Perugia and I am coming here at night, in the dark. It is winter time and wet and muddy and so cold that icicles form at the edges of my habit and keep striking my legs, and blood flows from such wounds. And I come to the gate, all covered with mud and cold and ice, and after I have knocked and called for a long time, a friar comes and asks: 'Who are you?' I answer: 'Brother Francis.' And he says: 'Go away. This is not a decent time to be going about. You can't come in.'

"And when I insist again, he replies: 'Go away. You are a simple and uneducated fellow. From now on don't stay with us any more. We are so many and so important that we don't need you.'

"But I still stand at the gate and say: 'For the love of God, let me come in tonight.' And he answers: 'I won't. Go to the Crosiers' Place and ask there.'

1501

"I tell you that if I kept patience and was not upset—that is true joy and true virtue and the salvation of the soul."

The striking minor differences between this shorter and more realistic version and the more elaborate account of Brother James of Massa which is found in the *Actus-Fioretti*, while confirming the substance of his report, point to the priority and greater historicity of the former, which is attributed to Brother Leonard of Assisi, a companion of the Poverello who testified at his Process of Canonization.

Incidentally, the same theme is also found in the Saint's own writings (Fifth Admonition).

Most significant of all are the words, "You are a simple and uneducated fellow," that directly recall another important text in which St. Francis declared that he was a true Friar Minor only if, after preaching at a coming chapter, he could rejoice when all the friars cried out, "We don't want you to rule over us, because you are very simple and uneducated, and we are very ashamed to have a simple and contemptible person like you as our superior," and they drove him away from the meeting (2C145. B6, 5. SP-L38. SP-S64. LA104[83]. Cf. SF 44, 1–17).

Thus the famous chapter on the perfect joy of St. Francis assumes a more profound significance in this older version, for it throws new light on "the dark night of the soul" which the Little Poor Man of Assisi actually experienced when he resigned his office.

2 The Wolf of Gubbio (Ch. 21)

Chi la dice lo primo? (Who said this first?) reads a challenging note by the critical eighteenth-century Conventual historian N. Papini in the margin of a medieval manuscript account of the famous wolf of Gubbio. Since the story has been questioned by some historians—even Jörgensen did not accept it—we believe the reader will appreciate a summary of all the available evidence concerning this disputed incident.

The fully developed story first appeared in the *Actus* about a hundred years after St. Francis died. A mid-thirteenth-century chronicle of the Benedictine Monastery of San Verecondo at Vellingegno between Gubbio and Perugia supplies the following undoubtedly genuine text (AFH 1, 69–70):

In recent times the poor little man St. Francis often received hospitality in the Monastery of San Verecondo. The devout abbot and the monks welcomed him with pleasure. . . .

Weakened and consumed by his extreme mortifications, watchings, prayers, and fasting, St. Francis was unable to travel on foot and was carried by a donkey when he could not walk and especially after he was marked with the wounds of the Savior.

And late one evening while he was riding on a donkey along the San Verecondo road with a companion, wearing a coarse sack over his shoulders, some farm workers called him, saying: "Brother Francis, stay here with us and don't go farther, because some fierce wolves are running around here, and they will devour your donkey and hurt you too."

Then St. Francis said: "I have not done any harm to Brother Wolf that he should dare to devour our Brother Donkey. Good-by, my sons. And fear God."

So St. Francis went on his way. And he was not hurt.

A farmer who was present told us this.

Another early text that may or may not be relevant is the testimony of Bartholomew of Pisa in his *Conformities* (1399) that on Mount Alverna St. Francis once converted a fierce bandit. The local tradition adds that he was called *Lupo* (wolf) because of his savage cruelty, but that the Saint renamed him *Agnello* (lamb). He is reported to have become a holy friar. It was due more to him perhaps than to the wild animals that Count Orlando sent fifty soldiers to protect the two friars who explored the mountain in 1213 (LV, pp. 270–74). Could this Fra Lupo have been the Fra Lupo who accompanied St. Francis on his journey to Spain in that year and who died in Burgos in 1291 (W1291, n.19)?

In any case, the first clear reference which we have to the story of the taming of the wolf of Gubbio is in the third edition of the Latin *Legenda Sancti Francisci Versificata* by the French poet Henri d'Avranches, dating from about 1290, which reads: "It is said that through his influence one wolf especially was tamed and made peace with a town."

Moreover, the Franciscan Custody of Gubbio adopted the figure of a wolf on its seal perhaps as early as the thirteenth century. A district of the town of Gubbio also took a wolf's head as its emblem in 1349.

Late in the nineteenth century the wolf's skull, with its teeth firmly set in the powerful jaws, was reported to have been found in a small shrine on the Via Globo which was said to be over the wolf's tomb. A stone on which St. Francis preached to the people after converting the wolf is shown to visitors in the Church of San Francesco della Pace.

Finally, in January 1956, press dispatches reported that packs of famished wolves were once again terrorizing villagers in central Italy.

In a letter dated February 8, 1958, the distinguished Conventual historian Giuseppe Abate writes that he is preparing a brief study of the incident based on original research in local archives, and that he considers it "probable" owing to the "great weight" of the 1290 reference, though "perhaps a little embellished" in the *Actus*.

3   *The Mystery of the Stigmata*

As a substantial portion of this book deals with the Stigmata of St. Francis, a brief summary of basic facts and principles concerning that baffling subject may be helpful. In the sense used here, stigmata are visible or invisible wounds in the human body that are found in the same (but not necessarily exactly the same) places as those of Christ in His Passion: in the hands, feet, and left or right side, and occasionally around the head or on the shoulders and back. They usually bleed at intervals or continuously. Genuine stigmata are incurable by medical treatment and may last for years or vanish at any time.

The Church is justified in taking an attitude of extreme caution toward all reported cases of stigmatization. It applies at least six technical criteria for the recognition of genuine cases: instantaneous apparition, substantial lesions, unmodified persistence despite treatment, bleeding, absence of suppuration, and complete instantaneous cicatrization.

Genuine stigmata meeting those criteria have never been produced by experiments, despite many attempts by psychiatrists and hypnotists. However, modern research has demonstrated that mental and emotional causes can have visible effects on the skin. For instance, a mother who saw a window nearly fall on her child's neck has developed a sore on her own neck, and a hypnotized person, when told that a coin being applied to his arm is red-hot, has developed a blister on the arm. Such facts may eventually help to supply a partial explanation of the role that natural processes may play in genuine stigmatization, insofar as they play any role at all.

Actually, even the Church's foremost experts on this complex subject which involves medicine, psychiatry, and mystical theology are not in agreement on the basic nature of the stigmata. A Roman physician writing in the *Enciclopedia Cattolica,* while admitting the existence of false stigmata, presents the traditional view that the stigmata of the mystics are beyond all the rules of psychopathology and must therefore be considered preternatural phenomena. But Professor Paul Siwek, S.J., insists that "there are no convincing reasons to hold that stigmatization, considered in itself, necessarily surpasses all the powers of nature or is strictly miraculous." However, he grants that as they are an effect of ecstasy, they would be supernatural in cause if the ecstasy were a supernatural one.

Moreover, the late Father Herbert Thurston, S.J., who studied innumerable case histories of "surprising mystics," claimed that "there are visionaries who have . . . genuine stigmata, but who for all that are by no means saints," and who were "suffering from pronounced and often extravagant hysterical neuroses." It is believed that some pseudo-stigmata have been caused by the devil. Probably some of the neurotic mystics whom Father Thurston mentioned also had pseudo-stigmata. The latest enigma in this still obscure subject is the puzzling case of a non-Catholic German businessman who apparently has the stigmata without being devout!

There is no accurate count of the number of stigmatics in history. Owing to inadequate evidence, estimates covering the last seven centuries range from fifty to over three hundred cases. Relatively few have been beatified or canonized, and very few have been men. St. Francis of Assisi was probably the first stigmatic. Moreover, his Stigmata also had a feature that has never been found in any other case: the protruding nails of flesh, which could only have been produced by a miracle, in the opinion of Agostino Gemelli, O.F.M.

It is clearly the teaching of the Church that the Stigmata of St. Francis were supernatural in the sense that a direct intervention of God was involved. Moreover, the Church has honored them with a special Feast Day in the liturgy. However, mystical theology also stresses that stigmatization, when genuine and supernatural, is a charism, a purely gratuitous gift like prophecies and visions (*gratiae gratis datae*), which is not intrinsically connected with sanctity.

Nevertheless, despite all the reserve and caution with which the Church rightly approaches this little-understood phenomenon, every genuine case of stigmatization in a person whose sanctity has been acknowledged by competent authorities is evidence of extraordinary grace from God. The whole purpose of the phenomenon, as seen in the life of St. Francis and other holy stigmatics, is the vicarious participation in the Passion of Christ and the expiation of the sins of men, through the merits of the Redeemer, by voluntary intercessory suffering of soul and body.

We would certainly fail to understand not only *The Little Flowers of St. Francis* but the whole attitude of the Middle Ages toward the Poverello if we did not grasp the fact that his Stigmata were generally looked upon as the ultimate certification by God of his unparalleled conformity with Christ, as far as is possible to a mere human creature. Dante, writing at the same time as the author of the *Actus*, immortalized that attitude in the famous lines: "Then on that crag between Tiber and Arno he received from Christ the final seal" (*Paradiso* XI, 106–7).

BIBLIOGRAPHY

NOTE: A comprehensive (but little-known) current bibliography of Franciscana has been published since 1930 in *Collectanea Franciscana*, Istituto Storico dei Cappucini, Via Boncompagni 71, Rome.

I. GENERAL WORKS AND PERIODICALS

A   See *Actus* entry in next section.

AF   *Analecta Franciscana.* Quaracchi, Collegio di San Bonaventura, 1885–1941. 10 v.

AF3   *Chronica XXIV Generalium Ordinis Minorum (1209–1374) cum pluribus appendicibus.* Quaracchi, 1897. 748 pp.

AF4-5   *De Conformitate Vitae Beati Francisci ad Vitam Domini Iesu,* auctore Fr. Bartholomaeo de Pisa. Quaracchi, 1906–12. 2 v.

AFH   *Archivum Franciscanum Historicum* (Quaracchi) 1, 1908+

B   *Legenda Maior S. Bonaventurae.* AF10, pp. 557–652.

BF   *Bullarium Franciscanum,* Giovanni G. Sbaraglia, ed. v. 1–4, Rome, 1759–68; Conrad Eubel, O.F.M. Conv., ed. v. 5–7, Rome, 1848–1914; *Epitome et Supplementum* (Quaracchi, 1908).
     Carte topografiche delle diocesi italiane nei secoli XIII e XIV. Vatican City, Biblioteca Apostolica Vaticana, 1932–52.

1C   Thomas de Celano, *Vita Prima S. Francisci Assisiensis.* AF10, pp. 1–117.

2C   ———, *Vita Secunda S. Francisci Assisiensis.* AF10, pp. 127–268.

CD   *Codice Diplomatico della Verna e delle SS. Stimate di S. Francesco d'Assisi,* Saturnino Mencherini, O.F.M., ed. Florence, Tipografia Gualandi, 1924. 759 pp.

CF   *Collectanea Franciscana* (Rome) 1, 1930+

CMir   Thomas de Celano, *Tractatus de Miraculis.* AF10, pp. 269–330.

EF   *Etudes Franciscaines* (Paris) 1, 1899+
      Fortini, Arnaldo, *Nova vita di San Francesco;* new
      ed. Florence, Vallechi, 1958. 3 v.

FF   *Frate Francesco* (Assisi; Rome) 1, 1924+

FS   *Franziskanische Studien* (Muenster in W.) 1, 1914+
      Huber, Raphael M., O.F.M. Conv., *A Documented
      History of the Franciscan Order (1182–1517).* Mil-
      waukee, Wis., & Washington, D.C., 1944. v. 1.
      1028 pp.

JJ   Jörgensen, Johannes, *Saint Francis of Assisi.* Garden
      City, N. Y., Image Books, 1955. 354 pp.

LA   *La "Legenda Antiqua S. Francisci," Texte du Ms.
      1046 (M.69) de Pérouse,* Ferdinand-M. Delorme,
      O.F.M., ed.; (a) AFH 15, 1922, 23–70 & 278–
      382; (b) Paris, Editions de la France Franciscaine,
      1926. 70 pp. We cite (a) first, then (b) in paren-
      theses.

LF   *La Franceschina,* Nicola Cavanna, O.F.M., ed. Flor-
      ence, Leo S. Olschki, 1931. 2 v.

Lt   See "Little" entry in next section.

LV   *La Verna, Contributi alla Storia del Santuario (Studi
      e Documenti).* Arezzo, Cooperativa Tipografica,
      1913. 397 pp.

MF   *Miscellanea Francescana* (Foligno; Rome) 1, 1886+
      Moorman, John R. H., *The Sources for the Life of S.
      Francis of Assisi.* Manchester, Manchester Univer-
      sity Press, 1940. 176 pp.
      Oliger, Livario, O.F.M., "Spirituels." In *Dictionnaire
      de Théologie Catholique* (Paris, 1941), v. 14, col.
      2522–49.

SF   *Studi Francescani* (Florence) 1, 1914+

SP-L *Speculum Perfectionis (Redactio I),* Leonardus Lem-
      mens, O.F.M., ed. Quaracchi, 1901. 106 pp.; in his
      Documenta Antiqua Franciscana, Pars II.

SP-S *Le Speculum Perfectionis,* préparé par Paul Sabatier.
      Manchester, The University Press, 1928–31. 2 v.

3S   *Legenda Trium Sociorum.* In MF 8, 1908, 81–107;
      & 39, 1939, 325–432.

VeP   *Vita e Pensiero* (Milan) 1, 1915+
      Von Auw, Lydia, *Angelo Clareno et les Spirituels
      Franciscains.* Lausanne, Université, 1952. 59 pp.

W   Wadding, Luke, *Annales Minorum.* Quaracchi,
      1931–56. 31 v.

II. *ACTUS-FIORETTI* TEXTS AND EDITIONS

1. ACTUS

Speculum Exemplorum. Deventer, 1481 (cf. AFH 20, 1927, 109–115)

El Floreto de Sant Francisco. Sevilla, 1492.

Speculum Vitae B. Francisci et Sociorum Eius, Fabian de Igal, comp. Venice, 1504. (I have used the 1752 Györ edition.)

Chronica XXIV Generalium . . . In AF3.

Actus Beati Francisci et Sociorum Ejus, Paul Sabatier, ed. Paris, Librairie Fischbacher, 1902. LXIII, 271 pp.

De Conformitate . . . In AF4–5

Kruitwagen, Bonaventura, O.G.M., "Descriptio nonnullorum codicum MSS. quibus insunt libelli 'Speculum Perfectionis' et 'Actus B. Francisci,'" AFH 1, 1908, 300–412.

"La Question Franciscaine. Vita Sancti Francisci Anonyma Bruxellensis; d'après le Manuscrit II.2326 de la Bibliothèque Royale de Belgique," A. Fierens, ed. *Revue d'Histoire Ecclésiastique* (Louvain) 9–10, 1908–9.

Little, Andrew George, *Description of a Franciscan Manuscript Formerly in the Phillipps Library.* In British Society of Franciscan Studies *Collectanea Franciscana* (Aberdeen, 1914) v. 5, pp. 9–113.

———, *Un nouveau manuscrit franciscain, ancien Phillipps 12290, aujourd'hui dans la bibliothèque A. G. Little.* Paris, Librairie Fischbacher, 1919. 110 pp. (*Opuscules de critique historique.* Fascicule 18.)

Delorme, Ferdinand M., O.F.M., "Descriptio Codicis 23.J.60 Bibliothecae Fr. Min. Conventualium Friburgi Helvetiorum," AFH 10, 1917, 47–102.

Bughetti, Benvenuto, O.F.M., "Descriptio Novi Codicis 'Actus Beati Francisci' Exhibentis (Florentiae, Bibliotheca Nationalis Centralis II, XI, 20)," AFH 32, 1939, 412–38.

2. FIORETTI

I Fioretti di S. Francesco, Arnaldo della Torre, ed. Turin, Paravia & C., 1909. lvi, 285 pp.

———, Benvenuto Bughetti, O.F.M., ed. Florence, Adriano Salani, 1925. 423 pp.

———, Fausta Casolini, ed. Milan, Casa Editrice Giacomo Agnelli, 1926. 368 pp.

——, Filippo Graziani, O.F.M., ed. Assisi, Tipografia Porziuncola, 1931. 326 pp.

——, Mario Casella, ed. Florence, G. C. Sansoni, 1946. 143 pp.

——, Agostino Gemelli, O.F.M., ed. Milan, Società Editrice "Vita e Pensiero," 1945. 218 pp.

——, G. M. Bastianini, O.F.M. Conv., ed. Rome, A. Signorelli, 1950. 267 pp.

——, Mario Ruffini, ed. Turin, G. B. Paravia & C., 1953. 188 pp.

Gli scritti di San Francesco e "I Fioretti," Augusto Vicinelli, ed. Milan, Arnoldo Mondadori Editore, 1955. 427 pp.

The Little Flowers of the Glorious Messer St. Francis and of His Friars, W. Heywood, tr. London, Methuen, 1906. 207 pp.

The Garden Enclosed, M. Mansfield, tr. Florence, n.p., 1911. 67 pp. (Eleven *Fioretti* Additional Chapters)

Les petites fleurs de saint François d'Assise (Fioretti), traduction nouvelle d'après les textes originaux par T. de Wyzewa. Paris, Perrin & Cie., 1912. 374 pp.

Les Fioretti de saint François . . . Edition complète, Omer Englebert, tr. Paris, Editions Denoel, 1945. 420 pp.

Les Fioretti . . . traduction nouvelle d'après l'Incunable de Milan par le R. P. Godefroy, O.F.M. Cap., Paris, Editions Marcel Daubin, 1947. 314 pp.

Les Fioretti de saint François . . . Edition complète, Alexandre Masseron, tr. Paris, Editions Franciscaines, 1953. 509 pp.

Franz von Assisi. Legenden und Laude, Otto Karrer, tr. Zurich, Manesse Verlag, 1945. 811 pp.

Florecitas del glorioso señor San Francisco y de sus frailes. Madrid, Apostolado de la Prensa, 1913. xlv, 403 pp.

III. *ACTUS-FIORETTI* STUDIES

Alvisi, E., "I Fioretti di San Francesco, Studi sulla loro compilazione storica," *Archivio storico italiano* (Florence) s. 4, v. 4, 1879, 488–502.

Avanzi, Gianetto, "Le Edizioni del secolo XV dei 'Fioretti di San Francesco,' Indice Bibliografico," MF 40, 1940, 29–48.

Bughetti, Benvenuto, O.F.M., "Alcune idee fondamentali sui 'Fioretti di San Francesco,'" AFH 19, 1926, 321–33.

——, "Bibliographia," AFH 20, 1927, 386–407.

——, (Mario Negretti, pseud.), "Dai Fioretti di San Francesco secondo la lezione di un nuovo codice," FF 1, 1924, 230–43 & 374–86; 2, 1925, 133–44.

——, "Intorno ai Fioretti di San Francesco," FF 4, 1927, 235–57.

——, "Una parziale nuova traduzione degli *Actus* accopiata ad alcuni capitoli dei *Fioretti*," AFH 21, 1928, 515–52; 22, 1929, 63–113.

Camerano, Anna Maria, "Su la francescanità del traduttore dei Fioretti," FF 4, 1927, 262–64.

Cellucci, Luigi, *Le Leggende francescane del Secolo XIII nel loro aspetto artistico*. Rome, Società Editrice Dante Alighieri, 1929; see pp. 162–98.

Chiminelli, Piero, "Paolo Vergerio critico dei Fioretti," *Conscientia* (Rome) June 14, 1924.

Cuthbert, O.F.M. Cap., "The Teaching of the 'Fioretti,'" *The Catholic World* (New York) 89, 1909, 189–202.

Damiani, Quinto, O.F.M., "Origine Marchigiana dei Fioretti," SF 16, 1944, 197–99.

Facchinetti, Vittorino, O.F.M., "Attorno ai Fioretti," FF 3, 1926, 165–72.

——, *Il più bel fiore della leggenda francescana*. Quaracchi, 1918. 93 pp.

Faloci-Pulignani, Michele, "I 'Fioretti' di San Francesco," *San Francesco d'Assisi* (Assisi) 7, 1927, 57–60 & 78–83; cf. FF 4, 1927, 235; MF 26, 1926, 96; 27, 1927, 174.

Ferretti, Francesco A., "Ricerche sui Beati: Giacomo da Falerone, Giovanni da Fermo o della Verna, e sui primitivi conventi di Montolmo, di Mogliano e di Massa Fermana," SF 51, 1954, 152–73.

Garavani, Giunio, "Il Floretum di Ugolino da Montegiorgio e i Fioretti di S. Francesco. Studio storico-letterario," R. Deputazione di storia patria delle Marche *Atti e Memorie* (Ancona) n.s. 1, 1904, 169–242 & 265–315; n.s. 2, 1905, 11–58.

——, "La questione storica dei Fioretti di San Francesco e il loro posto nella storia dell'Ordine," *Rivista storico-critica delle scienze teologiche* (Rome) 2, 1906, 269–90 & 578–99.

Gardner, Edmund G., "The Little Flowers of St. Francis." In *St. Francis of Assisi: 1226–1926. Essays in Commemoration* (London, University of London Press, 1926) pp. 97–126.

Innocenti, Benedetto, O.F.M., "Teologia e Bibbia nei Fioretti di San Francesco," SF 12, 1926, 331–54.

Leandro de Bilbao, O.F.M. Cap., "Nostalgía y partidismo en 'Las Florecillas,'" *Estudios Franciscanos* (Barcelona-Sarriá) 51, 1950, 305–28.

Manzoni, Luigi, "Studi sui Fioretti di San Francesco," MF 3, 1888, 116–19, 150–52, 162–68; 4, 1889, 9–15, 78–84, 132–35.

Marconi, Angelo, O.F.M., "Attorno agli autori dei 'Fioretti,'" SF 12, 1926, 355–65.

――, "Chi fu il giardiniere dei Fioretti?" FF 4, 1927, 112–20 (cf. SF 14, 1928, 364–66 & 533).

Pace, Camillo, "L'autore del 'Floretum,'" *Rivista abruzzese di scienze, lettere ed arti* (Teramo) 19, 1904, 85–89.

Pagnani, Giacinto, O.F.M., "Contributi alla questione dei 'Fioretti di San Francesco,'" AFH 49, 1956, 3–16.

――, "Ricerche intorno al B. Liberato da Loro Piceno. A proposito di un viaggio di San Francesco a Sarnano," MF 57, 1957, fasc. 3.

Pellegrini, Leo, "I Fioretti del glorioso Messere Santo Francesco e de' suoi frati," *Annali della Scuola Normale Superiore di Pisa* (Pisa) ser. II, 21, 1952, 131–57.

Petrocchi, Giorgio, "Dagli 'Actus Beati Francisci' al volgarizzamento dei Fioretti," *Convivium* (Turin) n.s., 1954, 534–55 & 666–77; and in his *Ascesi e mistica trecentesca* (Florence, Le Monnier, 1957) pp. 85–146.

――, "Inchiesta sulla tradizione manoscritta dei 'Fioretti di San Francesco,'" *Filologia romanza* (Turin) 4, 1957, 311–25.

Quaglia, Armando, O.F.M., "Il 'Floretum' e i 'Fioretti' del Wadding," SF 50, 1953, 107–12.

――, "Perchè manca un' edizione critica dei Fioretti di San Francesco," SF 52, 1955, 216–23.

Staderini, Giuseppe, "Sulle fonti dei Fioretti di S. Francesco," Società Umbra di storia patria *Bollettino* (Perugia) 2, 1896, 339–64.

Terracini, B. A., "Appunti su alcune fonti dei Fioretti," *Bollettino critico di cose francescane* (Florence) 2, 1906, 21–30.

Tosi, Gianna, "Il 'Cursus' negli Actus Beati Francisci," R. Istituto Lombardo di scienze e lettere *Rendiconti* (Milan) ser. 2, 68, 1935, 659–68.

———, "I 'Fioretti di San Francesco' e la questione degli 'Actus Beati Francisci.' Contributo alla ricerca del testo latino dei 'Fioretti,' " *Ibid.* ser. 2, 69, 1936, 869–83.

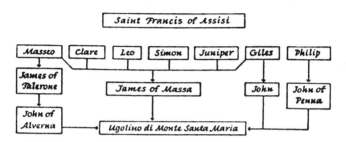

Chart Showing the Oral Tradition of the ACTUS - FIORETTI

NOTES AND REFERENCES

N.B.: Some chapter headings have been condensed. All abbreviations in the references will be found in the Bibliography.
Our subtitle combines those in the *Actus* and the *Fioretti*.

INTRODUCTION

1. It is a surprising and a regrettable fact that a complete critical biography of St. Francis has not yet been given to the world by his Order, although nearly all available early texts have been printed. Such a work is greatly needed.

2. 3S Ch. 9; cf. MF 9, 38–39; MF 39, 259–61.

3. For Ascoli: 1C62. For the friaries: AFH 1, 19–22.

4. P. Ferranti, *Memorie storiche di Amandola* (Ascoli, 1891), Pt. III, p. 165; R. Foglietti, *Le Marche dal 586–1230* (Macerata, 1907), p. 177, n.1; cf. AFH 14, 326; AFH 49, 3–7. For unpublished data re 1294 and 1342, letter from G. Pagnani, O.F.M., dated January 31, 1958.

5. Sabatier declared in a little-known lecture in London on April 4, 1908: "Those who would set him up as a kind of precursor of Protestantism would be completely wrong. . . . If I have deserved the reproach, I regret it. . . ." British Society for Franciscan Studies *Publications*, Extra Series, v. 1, p. 9.

6. AFH 11, 372.

7. See Note 4 above and AFH 49, 4–5.

8. LV, p. 121.

9. See Appendices 1 & 2; Ch. 37, Note 1; and *The Fourth Consideration on the Stigmata*, Note 15.

10. See *The Third Consideration*, Note 6.

11. First Order: 45,600. Second Order: 13,000. Third Order Regular (men and women): 70,000. Third Order Secular: 1,700,000.

12. LF 1, 5. Blessed Peter Pettinaio (d. 1289) probably knew St. Francis; cf. Dante's *Purgatory* XIII, 128.

PART ONE: THE LITTLE FLOWERS

1 *The Twelve First Companions*

1. The earliest documents mention only eleven companions when St. Francis went to Rome in 1210. Later texts evolved various lists of twelve first or chosen companions.

2 *Brother Bernard's Conversion*

1. "My God and my all!" is only in the Latin text.
2. This revelation is found only in the *Actus*.
3. In earlier versions the church is San Niccolò.
4. This chapter adds details and color to its sources: 1C24; 2C15; 2C109; B3, 3 & 5; 3S Ch. 8 (cf. MF 15, 33–43; EF 49, 476).

3 *The Humility of St. Francis and Brother Bernard*

1. The Place in the woods is the Carceri Hermitage on Mount Subasio above Assisi. The Saint's semiblindness indicates the years after his return from Egypt: 1220–24.
2. Early texts refer to this practice but not to this incident. The first friars did not wear sandals. Later they used to kiss the offended friar's feet (1C53–54. 2C155).

4 *St. Francis in Spain; The Angel and Elias*

1. St. Francis went to Spain with Bernard in 1213–14. This is the earliest mention of his visit to the famous Shrine of St. James the Apostle at Compostella (AFH 4, 796).
2. The Hermitage of Farneto, 12 miles north of Assisi.
3. The chronology is confused. A regulation restricting the eating of meat was passed in 1219 by the two Vicars appointed by the Saint when he went to Egypt, but Elias was then in Syria. The story of Elias and the angel probably evolved during the later conflicts and is considered apocryphal (AFH 2, 357).

5 *Brother Bernard in Bologna*

1. In 1211. The University of Bologna then had 10,000 students. Bernard's mission is first found in the *Actus*.
2. The earliest written Rule (now lost but embodied in the Rule of 1221) was orally approved by Pope Innocent III in 1210.
3. The judge and law professor, Niccolò di Guglielmo dei Pepoli, joined the Order in 1220 and died in 1229.

6 *The Blessing and Death of Brother Bernard*

1. Bernard's trials and death are mentioned in early texts: 2C48; LA11(108); SP-L17; SP-S107.
2. Here two distinct blessings are fused: (1) while lying sick in the Bishop's Palace in Assisi, St. Francis gave Elias a formal blessing (1C108; 2C216; cf. AFH 21, 265); (2) a few days later at the Portiuncula he gave Bernard a personal blessing (LA11[107]; SP-L17; SP-S107), which the *Actus* distorts to suggest that Bernard rather than Elias was the Saint's true heir.

7 The Forty Days' Fast

1. Probably the Lent of 1211. First recorded in the *Actus;* earlier texts mention a visit by the Saint to one of the three islands on Lake Trasimene (1C60; B8, 8). All three were inhabited by 1208. The friary existed before 1291 (BF *Epitome,* p. 194).

8 The Perfect Joy

1. Dante and Virgil "went on, the one before and the other after, as the Friars Minor walk" (*Inferno* XXIII, 2–3).

2. See Appendix 1.

9 How God Spoke Through Brother Leo

1. First found in the *Actus*. On being honored, St. Francis would have a friar "revile" him (1C53).

10 How Brother Masseo Tested St. Francis

1. First recorded in the *Actus*. Time: early years.

11 Brother Masseo Twirls Around

1. First appears in the *Actus*. A later text locates the crossroad a few miles west of Perugia, but does not mention Arezzo (LF 2, 74). The Saint visited Siena in 1211–12, 1217, and 1226.

12 How St. Francis Tested Brother Masseo

1. First found in the *Actus*. Time: early years.

13 Brother Masseo Lifted in the Air

1. The meal, Masseo's flight, and the Apostles' apparition are first recorded in the *Actus*. The chronology is confused. Francis had a special devotion to St. Peter and St. Paul (AFH 20, 22).

14 St. Francis Talking with His Companions

1. First appears in the *Actus*. Time: early years.

15 How St. Clare Ate a Meal with St. Francis

1. First found in the *Actus*. The early friars ate on the ground at the Portiuncula (LA68[33]. SP-S21). Thomas of Celano mentions Francis' reluctance to visit St. Clare (2C205), but he also states in her *Legenda* that she "imprisoned" herself in San Damiano for forty-two years. This problem has not been clarified since 1912–13 when Paschal Robinson, O.F.M., wrote that "the foundation underlying the story is likely to be the slenderest" (AFH 5, 641), while the Capuchin Father Cuthbert regarded the meal at the Portiuncula as "probable" and the fire as an "embellishment" (AFH 6, 670–80). A 14th-century text describes a meal of St. Francis with St. Clare at San Damiano (AFH 20, 106).

16   *St. Francis Should Preach*

1. The Saint may have sent another friar with Masseo (B12, 2).

2. The silencing of the swallows probably occurred at Alviano near Orvieto (1C59. B12, 4). The lay Third Order of the Penitent or Continent was founded in Florence in 1221 (AFH 14, 3–7).

3. The *Actus* adds details and symbolism to the early accounts (1C58. B12, 3). Another friar present was Gerardo da Mutina (Lt141). Franz Liszt composed a sonata on the sermon to the birds.

17   *A Young Friar Fainted*

1. Another *Actus* first. The friars slept on straw (AFH 15, 529).

18   *The Chapter at St. Mary of the Angels*

1. The *Actus* combines features of several General Chapters: Cardinal Hugolin and the Papal Court were at Perugia in 1216; St. Bonaventure (B4, 10) mentions a chapter attended by 5,000 friars (probably in 1221), whose needs were supplied by Providence. An elderly canon told Jean Pierre Olieu in 1261 that he once heard St. Dominic declare he had attended a chapter in Assisi which influenced him to stress poverty in his Order (AFH 17, 300; AFH 20, 155); the most probable year would be 1218. St. Dominic extended his previous conception of poverty about that time. For the instruments of mortification: 2C21; SP-S27.

19   *God Spoke to St. Francis; The Poor Priest's Wine*

1. In recent years scholars have written 500 pages about the events narrated in this chapter (and its parallel texts). The controversy revolves around the question: precisely where and when did St. Francis compose *The Canticle of Brother Sun?* The *Speculum Perfectionis* and the *Legenda Antiqua* of Perugia specify that he composed it during this illness at San Damiano after receiving the assurance of eternal life and before going to Rieti. The testimony of those documents has been rejected by Benedetto and Terzi in favor of the priest's house near Rieti and by Abate in favor of the Bishop's Palace in Assisi, while Fortini has defended the San Damiano tradition (MF 56, 333–415; AFH 50, 142). This student inclines to agree with Fortini.

2. The disputed question here is: exactly where was the Church of San Fabiano—at La Foresta, about 3 miles north of Rieti, or just outside that town? La Foresta had been con-

sidered the correct location since the seventeenth century until A. Sacchetti Sassetti of Rieti examined local archives and reported in 1926 that he found no reference to La Foresta before 1319, but several mentions in thirteenth-century documents of a Church and Poor Clare Convent of San Fabiano on a hillside close to Rieti. Bishop Arduino Terzi, O.F.M., recently made several important archaeological discoveries in the four Franciscan hermitages of the Valley of Rieti, which he described in his monumental work, *Memorie Francescane nella Valle Reatina* (Rome, 1955. 507 pp.). At La Foresta he claims that he found the original Chapel of San Fabiano. Since 1948 Sacchetti Sassetti has published five brochures denying the claim. While awaiting further clarification, this observer agrees with Abate and Pratesi that Sacchetti Sassetti's evidence seems more convincing (bibliography in Terzi & AFH 50, 245–50).

20 A Novice Tempted to Leave the Order
1. The time must be after St. Anthony's death in 1231.

21 The Wolf of Gubbio
1. See Appendix 2.

22 How St. Francis Freed Some Doves
1. First found in the *Actus*. The Place is the Alberino Hermitage near Siena (MF 27, 109).

23 The Devils at the Portiuncula
1. Similar incident in 2C34.

24 The Sultan and the Prostitute
1. St. Francis' interviews with the Sultan of Egypt, Malik al-Kamil (1180–1238), during a lull in the Crusaders' siege of Damietta in the Nile Delta in September 1219, are documented by contemporary writers. The Sultan was a cultured Moslem with a taste for mystical poetry, which explains his liking for Francis.

2. Another story of late origin describes a similar incident at Bari; however, such anecdotes about various Saints were current in the fourteenth century. St. Francis volunteered to enter a fire with Moslem theologians or alone (AFH 19, 572, 576).

3. The Sultan's conversion, as first described in the *Actus*, seems to be an echo of St. Bonaventure's report, based on interviews with Brother Illuminato (Francis' companion in Egypt), quoting the Moslem ruler: "'I believe that your faith is good and true.' And from that moment he always had the Christian faith imprinted in his heart" (AFH 19, 572). His Arab contemporaries criticized him for not being a fervent Moslem.

25 *St. Francis Healed a Man with Leprosy*

1. Hansen's disease (leprosy) was endemic in Europe until the Black Death of 1347, and its many victims were strictly segregated. Many Saints and religious gave them compassionate care. St. Francis wrote in his Testament that his conversion began when "the Lord led me among them," and in his First Rule he urged his friars to rejoice at associating with them. Until recently the care of victims of leprosy was almost a monopoly of Christian missionaries. Today medical science considers Hansen's disease only mildly infectious. Patients suffer more from the unjust social stigma than from the bacillus. Realizing this, St. Francis carefully avoided using the hated term "leper" when speaking to them, calling them "brother Christians." In the same spirit the 1948 and 1953 International Congresses on Leprosy strongly recommended that the objectionable words "leprosy" and especially "leper" be abandoned in popular writing.

2. The earliest texts describe several incidents involving victims of leprosy. Another version of this anecdote locates it at the Spedalaccio hospital at Collestrada between Perugia and Assisi (AFH 12, 367). Assisi had several leprosaria (AFH 43, 23).

26 *The Three Robbers*

1. Another version is known (LA111[90]. SP-L43. SP-S66. Cf. AFH 12, 343). The Hermitage of Monte Casale has been in charge of the Capuchins since 1573. The Guardian, Brother Angelo Tarlati of the Counts of Pietramàla, should not be confused with Brother Angelo Tancredi of Rieti. His vocation in 1213 is first recorded in the *Actus*. Perhaps he was the Angelo who died as chaplain of the Poor Clares in Cortona in 1237 (BF1, 38).

2. Contemporary chronicles mention a severe famine in 1227 when people ate nutshells and bark (2C53. AF 10, 164).

3. The chronology is confused: the former robber died 15 years after his conversion, i.e., about 1230, but Bernard and Giles lived until 1241–46 and 1262, respectively. This vision is first found in the *Actus*.

27 *St. Francis Converted Two Students in Bologna*

1. The Saint visited Bologna several times between 1213 and 1222; this would be an early visit. See the vivid eyewitness account of his sermon there on August 15, 1222, in JJ, p. 196.

2. Pellegrino died in 1232 at San Severino (March 27). His body was found intact in the sixteenth century.

3. Riccieri was Minister of the Marches in 1225–34. St.

Francis once patched his habit for him (SP-S16). He wrote the first Franciscan treatise on the spiritual life—a neglected jewel (MF 8, 113). For his temptation and visit to St. Francis: 1C49; SP-S2. He retired to a hermitage near Muccia and died in 1234 (March 14). The *Actus* is our main source for both friars.

28 *Brother Bernard's Gift of Contemplation*

1. Once Bernard said jokingly to Giles: "Go out for bread." Giles retorted: "Brother Bernard, it is not granted to every man to eat like the swallows, as you do" (AF 4, 182). The mountain is Mount Subasio—also the scene of the next chapter.

29 *Brother Rufino's Temptation*

1 & 2. In the *Actus* an Italian expression is used which corresponds to the English "four-letter word." Time: early years.

3. First found in the *Actus*. Another diabolic trial of Rufino, also at the Carceri, was recorded by Conrad of Offida (AF 3, 48).

30 *Brother Rufino's Sermon*

1. Appears first in the *Actus*. Time: early years.

31 *Rufino Was One of Three Chosen Souls*

1. Another *Actus* first. The friars often had evidence of the Saint's gift of reading their hearts (1C48; cf. 2C39).

32 *How Christ Appeared to Brother Masseo*

1. Another *Actus* first. The Place was probably Cibottola.

33 *How St. Clare Imprinted the Cross on Some Loaves*

1. First found in the *Actus;* not mentioned in St. Clare's earliest biography or Process of Canonization. Pope Gregory IX visited her in 1228 and 1235; Innocent IV had two interviews with her in 1253. Agnes and Ortolana were in San Damiano in 1253 (FS 35, 203 & 209). The cures are documented.

34 *How St. Louis Visited Brother Giles*

1. First appears in the *Actus*, although perhaps current in 1270–95 (MF 16, 110); not mentioned in early lives of either. There is no record of a journey to Italy by St. Louis (1215–1270), so probably another Giles was involved. Dominique Bonin, O.F.M., has suggested, with Livario Oliger concurring, that it may have been Blessed Gilles, Archbishop of Tyre (d. 1266), who was an intimate friend of the King. Another possibility is an obscure Blessed Giles who knew St. Francis, was one of the first friars in France, and was buried at Séez in Normandy (W1226, n.62); St. Louis gave that friary a thorn from the Crown of Thorns in 1252. Brother Giles' *Sayings* include the words: "If you were to go to the King of France . . ." St.

Louis was a Tertiary, and is a Patron of the Franciscan Third Order.

35 *How St. Clare Was Carried to the Church of St. Francis*
1. It was her last Christmas, 1252. Three nuns testified and her first biography states that she heard the organ and office and saw the crib in the Basilica "as if she had been present there" (AFH 13, 458, 462, 468). The *Actus* adds the reception of Communion. In direct connection with this incident, St. Clare was named the Patron Saint of television in February, 1958.

36 *Brother Leo's Vision*
1. Time: last years. There are three versions of this vision. One, rewritten by a fanatic Spiritual, has St. Francis condemn the use of the breviary by Brother Leo, a priest (AFH 20, 544).

37 *How St. Francis Was Very Kindly Received in a Home*
1. Complete Latin text found only in the Little Mss. 54 and a Barcelona codex (AFH 7, 173). The latter confirms the *Actus*. The young man may have been Blessed Guido Vagnotelli of Cortona (d. *ca.* 1245; June 16), although Wadding places the incident in the Marches (W1215, n.31).

38 *Brother Elias Was to Leave the Order*
1. Latin text in Lt55. Typical of the confused legends about Elias' death that circulated in the thirteenth century. The Latin has him die in Sicily; the Italian omits the error. The only factual elements in the chapter are his excommunication and his deathbed reconciliation with the Church; see his Biographical Sketch.

39 *St. Anthony Was Heard by Men of Different Languages*
1. In his letter authorizing Anthony to teach theology (2C164. FS 31, 135).
2. Anthony's *Legenda Prima* quotes the comment of Pope Gregory IX (probably in 1230). The pentecostal miracle appears later.

40 *How St. Anthony Preached to the Fishes*
1. Not in the earliest biographies. Another text gives the town as Padua (AFH 8, 831). The *Fioretti* condenses the *Actus*.

41 *Brother Simon of Assisi*
1. Rooks are small gregarious crows that nest in trees. Simon joined the Order in 1210, was one of the early Spirituals, and was probably exiled to the Marches. He died about 1244 at

the Brunforte friary near Sarnano. Ugolino may have known the novice (W1210, n.43).

2. Ugolino's important reference to himself is found only in Lt48 and the Barcelona codex. On its interpretation depends the dating of at least this part of the *Actus* (AFH 49, 4–5).

42 *The Wonderful Miracles of Some Holy Friars*

1. Little is known of Lucido (cf. SP-S85).

2. This Masseo of San Severino is not Masseo of Assisi.

3. Bentivoglia de Bonis had three brothers and four nephews who were Franciscans and two sisters who were Poor Clares. Trave Bonanti is now called Ponte La Trave (south of Camerino). He carried the man with leprosy to a lonely hermitage on Monte Sanvicino to the north in order to visit his spiritual father, Blessed Paul of Spoleto, whom St. Francis appointed the second Provincial of the Marches and who died in 1241 (1C77–79. W1232, n.21). Bentivoglia died in 1288 (April 6).

4. Servodeo of Urbino spent his whole life in Ancona.

5. The Crucifix is preserved in the Cathedral of Ancona.

6. See the Biographical Sketches of Peter of Montecchio and Conrad of Offida. The latter's vision occurred on the Feast of the Purification, 1289. In 1307 a commemorative picture was painted in his cell in the woods. Later a large mural of the scene placed in a new chapel became famous and was moved to the Cathedral of Treja (MF 37, 82–85).

45 *Brother John of Penna*

1. Blessed Giovanni da Penna San Giovanni was born about 1193, joined the Order about 1213, attended a Provincial Chapter at Recanati, then the General Chapter of 1217 in Assisi, where he was assigned to Languedoc in southern France with a group led by Giovanni Bonelli da Firenze. He returned to the Marches about 1242. In 1248, to settle a civil conflict in Penna San Giovanni, he wrote a recently discovered pact or *charta libertatis* of basic value in the history of Italian law. He died about 1270–75 (April 3); cult approved in 1806. Should not be confused with Giovanni da Penna (Abruzzi) who was sent to Germany in 1217 or with an architect of the Assisi Basilica of like name (MF 42, 133).

46 *Brother Pacifico and His Brother*

1. Brother Humble's full name was perhaps Umile di Monte Granaro (MF 10, 109); he died in 1234. Pacifico is not the famous "king of verses" (AFH 20, 395). Soffiano was a grotto high on the steep slopes of Monte Ragnolo, three hours'

climb from Sarnano—a striking example of early Franciscan hermitages.

2. The Place to which Humble's remains were transferred is traditionally the friary called San Liberato da Loro, but our earliest document naming it dates from 1421; see next Note.

47 *The Blessed Virgin Appeared to a Sick Friar*

1. This chapter has evolved into one of the most puzzling mysteries in all hagiography. No early Franciscan document names the holy friar of Soffiano (a marginal note on one manuscript is of very late origin). Ugolino did not recall his name, although he lived near Sarnano for three years. The first mention of the name Liberato da Loro occurs in a local civil act of 1421, when the *Clareni* friars were occupying a former hospice at the foot of Monte Ragnolo to which the name became attached; but it is not mentioned in land surveys of 1313 and 1330. One of the early leaders of the *Clareni* was Liberato da Macerata, who died in 1307. The Sarnano *Clareni* joined the Observant Franciscans in 1510. During the fifteenth and sixteenth centuries a biography of a "Beato" or "San" Liberato (Brunforte) da Loro evolved which identified him with the anonymous Soffiano friar; eventually it was included in the Franciscan breviary (October 30), but later omitted. A local cult developed around his tomb, which was said to be in the San Liberato Chapel. Persistent but unsuccessful efforts were made to have him beatified. It was falsely claimed that Pope Honorius IV had canonized him orally in 1286. The Sacred Congregation of Rites in 1697 and again in 1713 ordered pictures of the electuary cure removed and forbade any innovation in the then traditional cult. In the eighteenth century local rivalry between the citizens of Sarnano and San Ginesio produced two documents allegedly dated 1258 and 1269 which proved to be recent forgeries. This obscure conundrum has not yet received the thorough clarification which its inclusion in the *Fioretti* warrants. Until further notice it would appear that this chapter of the *Actus* is the only reliable early data available. See the articles by Giacinto Pagnani, O.F.M., in the Bibliography.

48 *The Vision of Brother James of Massa*

1. Another major *Actus* puzzle. Nearly the same text appears in Angelo of Clareno's *Chronicle of the Seven Tribulations*, written in Subiaco about 1325–28. Who then is the author, Angelo or Ugolino? Most scholars, including Sabatier (in his unpublished notes), ascribe the text to the Spiritual leader. However, this is the only reference to James of Massa in the

Chronicle, whereas Ugolino mentions him several times and knew him well. Did Ugolino perhaps visit Angelo at Subiaco on his way to Naples? Again further study is needed.

2. St. Bonaventure was not canonized until 1482 (there was no Beatification). See the Introduction for the historical background.

49 *How Christ Appeared to Brother John of Alverna*

1. The reference to his death (in 1322) was added in the *Fioretti.* See his Biographical Sketch.

2. The novicemaster was James of Falerone (see Biographical Sketches).

3. Also added in the *Fioretti.*

4. A significant early medieval instance of devotion to the Sacred Heart of Jesus (not mentioned in Margaret Williams' *The Sacred Heart in the Life of the Church*).

5. The large beech tree was blown down by the wind in 1518. A chapel was built on the spot, and the place where Christ walked is now surrounded by a low stone wall. Nearby is Brother John's cell, also transformed into a chapel.

6. The rest of the chapter appears only in the Latin text.

51 *Brother James of Falerone Appeared to Brother John*

1. The years of death of James of Falerone and James of Massa are not known with precision. Some manuscripts omit the reference to the latter in this chapter.

52 *Brother John Saw All Created Things in a Vision*

1. The entrance of Christ's Humanity into Heaven at the Ascension is meant.

53 *How While Saying Mass Brother John Fell Down*

1. An involuntary interruption of the Mass before the consecration of the wine does not involve irreverence, as the Sacrifice of the Mass requires the consecration of both species.

PART TWO: THE CONSIDERATIONS ON THE HOLY STIGMATA

The First Consideration

1. The Italian text—not the Latin—erroneously assigns this incident to 1224. Actually it took place on May 8, 1213, as Count Orlando's four sons declared in a notarized act of confirmation dated July 9, 1274 (CD p. 39). The medieval castle of the Counts of Montefeltro (often mentioned by Dante) is perched on a crag near San Marino; the village is now called San Leo.

2. The armed guard was probably sent to protect the friars from a bandit whom St. Francis later converted; see Appendix 2.

3. The *Actus* passes directly from the choice of companions to the birds' welcome (see Note 7). The Lent of St. Michael probably indicates the last stay of the Saint on Mount Alverna in 1224, but the other incidents and the itinerary belong to his first visit in 1215 (?). The first night was probably spent in the Buon Riposo Hermitage near Città di Castello.

4. The abandoned church is San Pierino, now in ruins, near Caprese (where Michelangelo was born). A similar but different attack by devils occurred near Trevi (2C122. SP-S59). The Saint's way of praying is derived from 2C95.

5. Source: 2C142, with slightly different details.

6. Source: 2C46; CMir15; B7, 12.

7. The birds' welcome is in the *Actus* (cf. LA113[93]; B8, 10). A chapel was built on the spot in 1602, after the oak tree had fallen. Mount Alverna is now a wildlife sanctuary.

The Second Consideration

1. St. Francis visited Count Orlando in his castle several times. In 1274 the latter's sons gave the friars the tablecloth and wooden dish which the Saint had used there and a leather belt he had blessed when he received the count in the Third Order (CD p. 39). A document of about 1300 states that "the Place of the holy Mount Alverna was accepted" on September 8, 1218 (*Cronica Fratris Salimbene*, Holder-Egger ed., p. 657).

2. See the text of the Saint's Rule for Hermitages in JJ, p. 184 (cf. FS 36, 213). For the poverty contract: 2C70.

3. The revelation about the rocks may belong to an early visit, and the preparation for death to that of 1224.

4. This incident occurred after the Saint received the Stigmata. See the text of his Praise and Blessing in JJ, p. 249. The precious document, with three important notes by Leo, is preserved in the Basilica of St. Francis. Sources: 2C49; 2C118; B11, 9; Lt154; cf. FS 36, 218–22.

5. Sources: A9, 32–35 & A39, 5–7; cf. B10, 4; AFH 12, 369.

6. Several versions of these and other promises regarding the future of the Order are extant (AFH 20, 556). See also *The Third Consideration*, Note 7.

7. This chasm was bridged and the Chapel of the Cross was built on the spot in 1263. Source: A9, 28–31.

8. The marks of his hands were said to be still visible in the rock in 1390 (AF 4, 164). During this fast St. Francis told Brother Leo that if the friars knew how much the devil was persecuting him, they would feel pity for him (SP-S99).

9. The friar was probably Blessed Francesco dei Malefici (d. *ca.* 1290 in Corsica). His 120-foot fall in 1273 may have been accidental, according to another version (LV, p. 82).

10. Source: 2C168; B8, 10. Falcons have nested nearby for the last seven centuries.

11. No source; a similar incident involving a zither occurred at Rieti in 1225 (LA59[24]. 2C126).

The Third Consideration

1. Source: A9, 37–67; cf. AFH 12, 392. This vision may have taken place during the Stigmatization. See *The Fifth Consideration*, Note 2.

2. Source: 1C92–93; B13, 2. The latter corrects the former.

3. The Feast of the Exaltation of the Cross falls on September 14, while the Invention (or Finding) of the Holy Cross is commemorated on May 3. The Feast of the Stigmata was assigned to September 17. For the probable source of the angel's apparition, see *The Fifth Consideration*, Note 2. The Saint's prayer may be based on the revelation to John of Alverna; see *The Fifth Consideration*, Note 4.

4. Source: 1C94–95; B13, 3. The seraphs before God's throne are similarly described in Isaias 6:2. Thomas of Celano did not specify that the seraph was Christ; later texts did (see *The Fifth Consideration*, Note 1, and *The Life of Brother Giles*, Ch. 10 & 11, with its Note 6).

5. The Latin text (A9, 69) mentions the shepherds; the Italian adds the muleteers.

6. Source: A9, 70–71. The only mention of another *Actus* writer.

7. In *The Second Consideration* (see its Note 6), an angel told the Saint that God would entrust to him the length of time which his less perfect friars would have to spend in Purgatory. Here, based on an unsubstantiated private revelation (see *The Fifth Consideration*, Note 3), this privilege is extended to all the Saint's friends—and their stay in Purgatory cannot last more than a year! As the Church has not formally approved this extraordinary claim, it would be unwise to be guided by it.

8. Source: 1C94–95; CMir4; B13, 3; cf. AFH 3, 427. The Italian text erroneously states that the heads of the nails were in the soles of the feet. See Appendix 3 on the Stigmata.

9. Source: B13, 4. Brother Illuminato Accarino of Rieti was with St. Francis in Egypt (d. 1266); should not be confused with Illuminato of Chieti, Elias' secretary and later Bishop of Assisi, who died in 1282 (LF 1, 136).

10. Source: A39, 8–10. The last paragraph is original and is the only authentic early "Farewell of St. Francis to Mount Alverna." A so-called "Farewell" found in some modern works was invented in the seventeenth century, probably by the unreliable Salvatore Vitale.

The Fourth Consideration

1. Source: B13, 5 (somewhat expanded).

2. Thomas of Celano places a similar cure in Rieti (CMir-174).

3. Source: 2C98; B10, 2.

4. Source: 1C68; B12, 11.

5. Source: 1C63; B12, 11. One of the Alverna friars was named Peter.

6. Source: 1C70; B12, 10.

7. No source.

8. Source: B13, 7. Place: near Tavernace, north of Perugia.

9. Source: A38, 5–7; cf. AF 3, 68.

10. Source: AF 3, 68 & 676; cf. MF 42, 130. Leo reported this vision in a letter (now lost) to a Minister General.

11. Source: 2C143; SP-S39. The chronology is confused: St. Francis made Peter Catani his Vicar in 1220, not 1224.

12. Source: 1C95–96; 2C135–38; B13, 8; AFH 28, 11–13.

13. Source: 1C109; LA96(64); SP-S121; A18, 1–9.

14. Source: 1C108; LA5(99); SP-S124; A18, 10–13.

15. Source: CMir37–39; AF 3, 687; LA7(101); SP-S112; A18, 14–31; with variants. The first text, written about 1250 and printed only in 1899, confirms the *Actus* account. "Brother" Jacopa dei Settesoli, b. about 1189, married Graziano Frangipani (both of prominent Roman families), had two sons, and became a widow about 1210. She met St. Francis in Rome in 1212 (?) and on several later visits. Her sons were not senators. She was present at the Saint's death and funeral. Spent her last years in Assisi, visited Brother Giles in Perugia, died probably about 1239 (the *Fioretti* errs in stating that she died in Rome and was buried at the Portiuncula); she was

buried in the Basilica of St. Francis (February 8). See references in AFH 21, 375.

16. Source: B15, 4. The prominent knight Jerome is mentioned in several Assisi documents of 1228–37 (AFH 33, 219. MF 15, 131).

17. Source: 1C116. St. Francis died on the evening of October 3, 1226. The Poor Clares were not present at his funeral in the Church of St. George, but venerated his remains at San Damiano when the funeral procession stopped there (see JJ, p. 122).

The Fifth Consideration

1. See *The Life of Brother Giles*, Ch. 11 and Note 6.

2. The text of this revelation in the Provincial's report places the three coin-offerings during the stigmatization and interprets them as symbolizing the Saint's three Orders (see *The Third Consideration*, Note 1). Conrad of Offida was in the adjoining Chapel of the Cross when Brother Matthew had this vision in May, 1281 (AF 3, 641; cf. AFH 12, 347; AFH 20, 553).

3. Other texts: AF 3, 635; AF 5, 397; SV119. See *The Third Consideration*, Note 7. Cf. LV, p. 384–89.

4. No source for the confirmation of the Purgatory revelation. John's touching the Stigmata appears in a contemporary biography.

5. Source: AFH 12, 393. The reference to the two friars in the last sentence is only in the Latin.

6. Source and texts: AFH 12, 362; AFH 20, 561; cf. AFH 17, 548.

7. Source: AF 10, 627; CD, p. 17–36 & 40–41. The Popes are Alexander IV (1254–61) and Nicholas III (1277–80).

PART THREE: ADDITIONAL CHAPTERS

N.B.: the numbers of the Notes correspond to the chapters.

1. A17; Lt74. Minister General John Parenti (1227–32) decreed that no friar should be called "master" or "lord" (*Cronica Fratris Salimbene*, Holder-Egger ed., p. 659).

2. A25; Lt15; cf. 2C82; AF 5, 163; MF 8, 97.

3. A33; Lt26; cf. AF 3, 48; AF 4, 201.

4. A38, 8–12; Lt29. See Part One, Ch. 26, n.2.

5. A40; AFH 12, 336 & 363. Another version places the incident near Avignon and has Pope Benedict XII (1334–42) go to see the mural and stop the flow of blood by vowing to institute the Feast of the Stigmata (AFH 3, 169).

6. A44. The name of the disputatious friar is corrupt. It could be Guardianus. If it is Gerardino, perhaps he was the famous Joachimist Gerardo di Borgo San Donnino, who may have visited Perugia about 1248.

7. A45.

8. A47. Note that these three chapters are not in Leo's life of Giles or in the Little Manuscript *Actus*.

9. A55; Lt43; cf. AF 3, 440.

10. A58; Lt46.

11. A60. Lt38. AF 4, 560.

12. A61; AFH 20, 102; cf. AF 3, 364. St. Francis made the friars leave the house of studies in Bologna, until Cardinal Hugolin declared it the property of the Church (2C58; SP-S6). Pietro Giovanni Stracchia, an expert in Roman law, was appointed Minister of the Province of Bologna in 1217 and suspended in 1221. Various accounts of his being cursed and his death are found in late texts.

13. A62 has 3 parts: (a) 2C67. (b) 2C70; cf. AFH 20, 103. (c) Lt146; AFH 17, 568; AFH 20, 98—these few lines are one of the brightest and fairest jewels in all Franciscan literature.

14. A63 has 2 parts: (a) SP-S52; AFH 20, 99. (b) 2C160; SP-S82.

15. A64; cf. AF 3, 71.

16. A65. AFH 17, 567. Last paragraph: 2C157.

17. A66.

18. A67. Lt94. Place: probably Civitanova north of Fermo.

19. A70. AFH 12, 350 & 400. As Chapters 61–64, 66 & 70 of Sabatier's *Actus* (our Additional Chapters 12, 13a–b, 14, 15, 17 & 19) are not in the Little Manuscript, they may not have been part of Ugolino's original *Actus*.

20. *The Canticle of Brother Sun* has in recent years been the subject of another learned controversy in addition to the one concerning the time and place of its composition (see Part One, Ch. 19, Note 1). In 1941 Luigi Foscolo Benedetto' advanced the theory that its repeated *per* meant "by" or "through," not "for," e.g., "Be praised, my Lord, by Brother Wind . . . by Sister Water." Over a dozen scholars have since debated the matter, but the majority tends to favor the traditional sense. Perhaps St. Francis, like other poets and mystics, had several senses in mind. See Giovanni Getto's *Francesco d'Assisi e il Cantico di Frate Sole* (Turin, Stab. Tip. Editoriale, 1956. 70 pp.).

The *explicit* following the poem appears in a fifteenth-century *Actus* manuscript (AFH 1, 409).

SACRUM COMMERCIUM
or
FRANCIS AND HIS
LADY POVERTY

Translated from the Latin,
with Introduction and Notes,
by Placid Hermann O.F.M.

1531

First published in *St. Francis of Assisi: His Holy Life and Love of Poverty* (Franciscan Herald Press, Chicago, 1964, pp. 125-204); Library of Congress Catalog Card Number: 64-17584; SBN: 8199-0100-8.

INTRODUCTION

For a better understanding and appreciation of the allegorical *Sacrum Commercium*, it will be helpful to present a few thoughts concerning the date of its composition and its author and concerning the background of the work and its allegorical nature.

1. *The Date of Composition and the Author*

The *Sacrum Commercium*[1] is a work of very early Franciscan origin. Six of the thirteen extant codices of the work assign the year 1227 as the year of composition in the following words added at the end of the work: "This work was completed in the month of July after the death of blessed Francis, in the year one thousand two hundred and twenty-seven after the incarnation of our Lord and Savior Jesus Christ." Some, however, do not regard this dating as absolutely conclusive in view of the fact that the other seven

---

1. The complete Latin title is *Sacrum Commercium Sancti Francisci cum Domina Paupertate*. The word *commercium* cannot be translated satisfactorily into English. Hence, the title might be given in English as *The Sacred Romance of Saint Francis with Lady Poverty*, or more briefly, as we have chosen to give it, *Francis and His Lady Poverty*.

codices do not contain this concluding sentence. Still, there is no solid evidence, either internal or external, that would persuade us to disregard this precise dating.

Some few authors have attempted to read between the lines of the work and see there a certain bitterness that would be characteristic of the later *Spirituals* and hence would like to assign a date later than 1227 for the *Sacrum Commercium*. However, the work is not at all polemical in nature and hence has no connection whatsoever with the sharp spirit of controversy that arose in the succeeding years over the matter of poverty. It is simply an allegorical presentation of Saint Francis' love for poverty and of the spirit of poverty that animated his early followers.

Various friars have been mentioned as possibly being the author of the *Sacrum Commercium*, but none can be proposed with any degree of certainty. We learn very little from the thirteen extant codices of the work; only three of them name an author. One fifteenth century codex names Brother John of Parma, minister general from 1247 to 1257, as the author. Two other codices, one of the fourteenth century, the other of the sixteenth century, name Saint Anthony of Padua as the author. The other ten codices are silent. A sixteenth-century Italian version attributes the work to Brother Crescentius of Jesi, minister general from 1244 to 1247.

Among other ancient writings that refer in one way or another to the *Sacrum Commercium*, only the *Chronica XXIV Generalium*, written about 1370 by Brother Arnald of Sarrant, attributes the work to a specific author, namely, Brother John of Parma.[2] The *Arbor vitae crucifixae Jesu* of Brother Ubertino da Casale, which quotes rather freely from the *Sacrum*

---

2. The *Chronica XXIV Generalium* text reads: Hic Generalis frater Johannes quendam libellum devotum composuit, quem intitulavit: *Commercium pauperatatis*, in quo qualiter beatus Franciscus paupertatem diligenter quaesivit et reperit et eam invitavit et desponsavit, quibusdam devotis parabolis et aenigmatibus declaravit. Apud *Analecta Franciscana*, Vol. III, p. 283, Quaracchi, 1887.

Commercium, says simply that "a certain holy doctor who professed and pursued poverty zealously" was its author. The *De conformitate vitae B. Francisci ad vitam Domini Jesu,* written by Brother Bartholomew of Pisa and containing many passages that show a thorough acquaintance with the *Sacrum Commercium,* says nothing at all about the author of the work. Some later writers, like Fr. Luke Wadding, attribute the work to Bishop John Pecham.[3] More recent writers hold for one or the other of those mentioned above, though one modern writer suggests that the name of Brother John of Parma (*Johannes Parmensis*) somehow got inserted in place of John Parenti (*Johannes Parens*), minister general from 1227 to 1232, and that the latter therefore is the author of the work.

Amid this great uncertainty concerning the author, it is a little surprising that one other friar has never been mentioned seriously as possibly being the author of the *Sacrum Commercium,* namely, Thomas of Celano.[4] Already in 1929 the Quaracchi editors of the *Sacrum Commercium*[5] offered a very tentative suggestion that a fair case might be made

---

3. John Pecham (1240-1292), an Englishman, joined the Franciscan Order and eventually became the ninth provincial of the English province. In 1279 he became bishop of Canterbury. He was an excellent poet and the author of several prose treatises, notably one on poverty. He is not usually considered seriously as the author of the *Sacrum Commercium* because the earlier date of composition is quite generally accepted.

4. Thomas of Celano entered the Franciscan Order between 1213 and 1215. He spent some time in Germany, but was back in Italy most probably for the canonization of Saint Francis in 1228 and for the translation of his remains in 1230. He died in 1260 or shortly thereafter. He wrote two lives of Saint Francis, the *Vita Prima* between 1228 and 1230 at the behest of Pope Gregory IX, the *Vita Secunda* about 1247 at the behest of the minister general Crescentius of Jesi. He also wrote a treatise on the miracles of Saint Francis *(Tractatus de Miraculis)* and a life of Saint Clare. The two sequences, the *Dies Irae* of the Requiem Mass, and the *Sanctitatis Nova Signa* of the Mass for the feast of Saint Francis, are also attributed to him.

5. The Fathers of Saint Bonaventure College, Quaracchi, Italy.

out for Thomas of Celano on the basis of the similarities between the other known works of Celano and the *Sacrum Commercium*. They did not defend their suggestion except to give some passages from Celano's works and from the *Sacrum Commercium* that exhibit a striking similarity both in idea and in wording. Their suggestion is interesting, and, because it seems to have some merit, some examples of these similarities will be given here.

Early in his *Vita Prima S. Francisci* Thomas of Celano speaks of the pre-eminence and excellence of poverty in words that recall the opening lines of the *Sacrum Commercium*:

(1) Celano's *Vita Prima*, No. 7:

Putabant homines quod uxorem ducere vellet, ipsumque interrogantes dicebant: "Uxoremne ducere vis, Francisce?" Qui respondens eis aiebat: "Nobiliorem et pulchriorem sponsam quam umquam videritis ducam, *quae caeteris forma praemineat et sapientia cunctas excellat.*"[6]

(2) The opening lines of the *Sacrum Commercium* (Prologue):

Inter ceteras praeclaras et praecipuas virtutes, quae in homine locum et mansionem praeparant Deo ac ad ipsum eundi perveniendique viam excellentiorem et expeditiorem ostendunt, sancta Paupertas quadam praerogativa *omnibus eminet et singulari gratia aliarum titulos antecellit, . . .*[7]

Many writers, in dealing with related subjects, repeat ideas they have used before, though they usually try to change

---

6. English: People thought that he wanted to take a wife, and they asked him: "Are you thinking of getting married, Francis?" Francis, answering, said: "I will take a bride more noble and more beautiful than any you have ever seen; she will excel all others in beauty and stand above all others in wisdom."

7. English: Among all the excellent and excelling virtues that prepare in man a place and a dwelling for God and show man the better and easier way of going to God and of arriving at him, holy poverty stands out above all the rest by a certain precedence and excels the glory of others by its singular grace.

the wording at least a little. The italics have been added to the sections above that seem to illustrate this point.

Again, Thomas of Celano uses the image of a *commercium* with *sancta paupertas* or *domina paupertas* several times, just as it is used in the *Sacrum Commercium*. The following passage from the *Vita Prima* (No. 35) is a good example of this. The friars have just returned from Rome in 1209 where they had received the papal approbation for their way of life and they go to a certain desolate place (*ad desertum locum*):

> Erat eis exultatio magna, cum nihil viderent vel haberent quod eos posset vane seu carnaliter delectare. Coeperunt propterea *cum sancta paupertate ibidem habere commercium.*[8]

Again, there is considerable similarity between the passage in Celano's *Vita Prima* (No. 51) that describes Francis' observance of poverty and the passage in the final paragraph (4) of the Prologue of the *Sacrum Commercium* that tells how Francis embraced poverty. These two passages read as follows:

(1) Celano:

> *Omni studio, omni sollicitudine custodiebat sanctam et dominam paupertatem,* non patiens, ne quando ad superflua perveniret, nec vasculum in domo aliquod residere, cum sine ipso utcumque posset extremae necessitatis evadere servitutem.[9]

(2) The last paragraph of the Prologue of the *Sacrum Commercium* (4):

---

8. English: There was great joy among them, because they neither saw nor had anything that could give them idle or carnal pleasure. They therefore began to dwell there familiarly with holy poverty. — The italics have been added here as in the other passages quoted.

9. English: With all care, with all solicitude he preserved holy Lady Poverty, not permitting even a vase to be kept in the house, lest he should come to have superfluous things, for without it he could still avoid the servitude of extreme necessity.

> Propterea beatus Franciscus, tamquam verus imitator et discipulus Salvatoris, in conversionis suae principio ad sanctam paupertatem quaerendam, inveniendam atque tenendam *omni studio, omni desiderio, omni deliberatione se dedit,* nil dubitans adversi, nil sinistri timens, nullum subterfugiens laborem, nullam corporis declinans angustiam, si tandem optio sibi daretur ut posset pervenire ad eam, cui Dominus tradidit claves regni caelorum.[10]

One more example should suffice. Note the similarity between the following two passages:

(1) From Celano's *Vita Secunda* (No. 55):

> Hanc [paupertatem] filiis suis dicebat perfectionis viam, *hanc aeternarum divitiarum pignus et arrham.*[11]

(2) In the *Sacrum Commercium* (65)

> De regni caelorum possessione nulla sit dubitatio, nulla sit cunctatio vobis, *quoniam arrham futurae hereditatis jam tenetis et pignus Spiritus jam suscepistis,* . . .[12]

One must not, of course, belabor similarities of this kind. Still, they do suggest the possibility that the same man wrote the several works in question when similarities like these occur so strikingly as they do in these works of Thomas of Celano and in the *Sacrum Commercium*. We do know that

---

10. English: For this reason blessed Francis, as a true imitator and disciple of the Savior, gave himself at the beginning of his conversion with all zeal, with all desire and deliberation, to seeking out, finding, and making his own this holy poverty; and in so doing he neither hesitated in adversity, nor feared any evil, nor shunned any labor, nor fled from any bodily ills, for he would be satisfied only if his desire to come to poverty, to which the Lord gave the keys of the kingdom of heaven, would be granted to him.

11. English: Poverty, he told his sons, was the way to perfection, the pledge and earnest of eternal riches.

12. English: You need have no doubt, no hesitance, about the possession of the kingdom of heaven, for you already possess an earnest of your future inheritance and you have already received the pledge of the Holy Spirit, . . .

Celano was an expert literary craftsman and an excellent poet. We can see this in his biographies and in the two sequences that are usually attributed to him, the *Dies Irae* of the Requiem Mass and the *Sanctitatis Nova Signa* of the Mass for the feast of Saint Francis. Furthermore, in view of the fact that Pope Gregory IX commissioned Thomas of Celano in 1228 to write the first biography of Saint Francis, is it not rather natural to ask if the Holy Father did not perhaps act because Celano had written, just the preceding year, the highly poetic *Sacrum Commercium?*

Yet, be that as it may, we must still content ourselves with speculation. This only can we say: so far as we can ascertain, the *Sacrum Commercium* was written in 1227 by a Franciscan whose identity is still shrouded in some mystery. Perhaps the author was John of Parma. Perhaps it was John Parenti. Or perhaps it was one of the several others tentatively proposed as its author. Or, finally, perhaps it was Thomas of Celano. But, in any case, whoever it was, the author has left us a classic in the genre of religious allegory.

2. *The Background and the Work*

Saint Francis of Assisi chose for himself and his followers a way of life that was simply a living of the holy Gospel of our Lord Jesus Christ. He did not want an elaborate rule of life; he wanted only a very brief statement of this fundamental principle that the way to God is a life in accordance with the words and deeds of our Blessed Savior as recorded in the Gospel. Accordingly, when he wrote his very first rule for his brothers, "simply and in few words,"[1] he stated very concisely that "the rule and life of the brothers

---

1. Both Thomas of Celano and Saint Bonaventure emphasize this point. Thus, Bonaventure, in his *Legenda Major* (III, 8), says: He wrote for himself and his brothers a form of life in simple words; in it, after putting down the observance of the holy Gospel as an indissoluble foundation, he added a few other things which seemed necessary for a uniform way of life. *Analecta Franciscana*, Vol. X.

is this, namely, to follow the teaching and the footsteps of our Lord Jesus Christ."[2] This, for Francis, was the will of God in his regard, as he stated in his *Testament*: "After the Lord gave me some brothers, no one showed me what I ought to do; but the Most High himself revealed to me that I was to live according to the form of the holy Gospel."[3]

The two essential points of his way of life, therefore, were these: first, to follow the teaching of our Lord Jesus Christ, that is, to live according to the words of Christ as they are revealed in the Gospel; and secondly, to follow the footsteps of our Lord Jesus Christ, that is, to imitate, in so far as is possible, the life of Christ as it is recorded in the Gospel.

Christ gave to the world a summary of Christian perfection in his *Sermon on the Mount*. Francis studied this sermon and made it, in a sense, the core of his rule of life for his brothers, as expressed in the final rule of 1223.[4] Christ praised poverty in spirit and added that to the poor in spirit belonged the kingdom of heaven. Francis made himself the poorest of the poor and commanded that his friars should appropriate nothing to themselves, neither a house, nor a place, nor any thing,[5] and that they should receive neither coins nor money, but that, on the other hand, they should go forth confidently begging alms.[6] Christ promised that the meek would possess the earth; that they who mourned would be comforted; that they who hungered and thirsted for justice would be satisfied; that the merciful would obtain mercy. Francis commanded his friars not to quarrel or contend in words or judge others, but to be meek, peaceable and modest, gentle and humble.[7]

---

2. See the reconstruction of the Primitive Rule, apud *Via Seraphica*, Placid Hermann, O.F.M., Franciscan Herald Press, p. 11.

3. The text of the *Testament* may be found in the same volume, p. 28.

4. See Saint Bonaventure's interesting study of the rule in comparison with the eight beatitudes in his *Apologia Pauperum*, Chapter 3. *Opera Omnia*, Vol. VIII.

5. Chapter VI of the Rule of 1223.

6. Chapter IV.

7. Chapter III.

He commanded them to labor earnestly to dispel idleness[8] and to bear illnesses patiently, serving one another and bearing one another's faults charitably and kindly.[9] Christ said that the clean of heart would see God. Francis commanded his friars to be chaste and pure, avoiding even the shadow of anything that could soil their purity of mind and body.[10] Christ praised peacemakers as the children of God; and he said that those who suffered persecution for justice' sake possessed the kingdom of heaven. Francis helped restore peace to his native Assisi[11] and commanded his friars to despise no one, but to love those who persecuted and calumniated them that they might be made worthy to possess the eternal kingdom.[12]

But Francis sought not only to follow the words of Christ; he wished also to imitate the life of Christ as perfectly as he could, and he willed that his friars too should "follow the footsteps of our Lord Jesus Christ."[13] Christ trod the pathways and roads of Palestine, preaching the love of his Father and the kingdom of heaven. Francis went about his native Italy, preaching to the people wherever he could find them, telling them of the love of Christ and of redemption. Christ withdrew into the mountains from time to time to pray and to meditate. Francis spent long hours and days in the wildernesses and upon the mountains in prayer and meditation. Christ suffered and died on the cross out of love for mankind, his body torn, his hands and feet pierced with nails. Francis longed to suffer with Christ out of love for Christ, and he prayed over and over that he might be per-

---

8. Chapter V.
9. Chapters VI and VII.
10. Chapter XI.
11. For example, once by singing his *Canticle of Brother the Sun* and adding a verse about peace and forgiveness he brought peace to the civil and religious authorities who were engaged in a bitter controversy.
12. Chapter X.
13. From the Primitive Rule. See footnote 2 above.

mitted to feel in his own body the intense sufferings of his Master. His prayer was answered, and one day, two years before his death, the marks of Christ's wounds appeared suddenly upon his body as he was rapt in ecstasy upon Mount La Verna. Indeed, Francis came to resemble Christ so perfectly that the people spoke of him as the *Christ of Umbria,* though of course they realized full well the essential difference between Christ and Francis.

But, with it all, there was one thing above all else in Christ that caught Francis' attention, and that was the total renunciation, the absolute poverty of Christ. *The Word was with God. The Word was God.* But when the *Word was made flesh and dwelt among us,*[14] *he emptied himself*[15] *and,* taking upon himself our own human nature, he embraced poverty and took poverty to be his spouse. When he came into the world at Bethlehem, he found his spouse, Lady Poverty, there in the cave to welcome him. Throughout his life on earth, his Lady Poverty walked at his side, loved by him above all the things of this earth. In his hour of disgrace, when he was abandoned by his chosen ones, when he was mocked, spit upon, and scourged, Lady Poverty was at his side. And when he hung upon the cross, naked, his arms outstretched, his hands and feet pierced with nails, she remained with him; she mounted the cross, as Dante says,[61] even though his mother Mary had to remain beneath the cross; and she held Christ in her arms and consoled him until he died. But, when Christ left this world to return to his Father in heaven, Lady Poverty was left an outcast in this world.

Francis was deeply impressed with what he saw of Christ's love of poverty and he was deeply grieved to see Lady Poverty no longer wanted on this earth, an outcast among men.

---

14. John 1, 1-14.
15. Philip. 2, 7.
16. The *Paradiso,* Canto XI.

He resolved, therefore, to make her his own and to take her for his bride as Christ had done. Thomas of Celano put it this way:

> Looking upon poverty as especially dear to the Son of God, though it was spurned throughout the whole world, he sought to espouse it in perpetual charity. Therefore, after he had become a lover of her beauty, he not only left his father and mother, but even put aside all things, that he might cling to her more closely as his spouse and that they might be two in one spirit.[17]

Poverty therefore became for Francis, one might almost say, the essence of his Gospel way of life, or at least the foundation upon which evangelical perfection was to be raised. It could not, of course, be the final end of his striving; the final end could only be God. But poverty was essential to his Gospel way of life and it was the rock upon which his whole spiritual life and that of his brothers was to be founded. Once, when the brothers, assembled in general chapter, asked him which virtue would render them most worthy to be called friends of Christ, "he opened to them the secret of his heart and replied: 'Know, Brothers, that poverty is the special way to salvation, for it feeds humility and is the root of perfection; its fruit is manifold, though hidden.' "[18]

Poverty meant for Francis and his first brothers much more than a mere renunciation of temporal goods. Poverty began with such a renunciation, but it went on to embrace austerity even in the simple use of things and to a deep spirit of humility. Francis gave up everything he possessed at the court of the bishop of Assisi and there became espoused to the Lady Poverty. He remained with her all his life, wanting only a tiny hermitage in which to dwell, food that was begged, clothing that was rough and poor, and the cold ground upon which to lay his head at night. He wanted

---

17. Thomas of Celano, *Vita Secunda*, No. 55.
18. Saint Bonaventure, *Legenda Major*, Chapter VII, 1.

nothing that he could call his own, only the use of the bare necessities. He remained faithful to his bride even in death, asking, when he came to die, to be laid naked upon the ground that he might die in the arms of his Lady Poverty as did his beloved Master upon the cross on Calvary. But all the while, in his austere renunciation, he considered himself, not only as nothing, but even as the greatest of sinners, for he knew that renunciation without humility is like the body without a soul. "Holy Lady Poverty," he was wont to say, "the Lord save you with your sister holy Humility."

The result of it all was that Francis became the *seraphic* saint, the seraph of love; and his early followers, walking with him in his way of austere poverty and holy humility, won for themselves the joy of possessing nothing in this life and the eternal reward for total renunciation in the kingdom of Christ. Having nothing, they possessed all things,[19] above all, Christ Crucified and his eternal love.

This is the background against which the *Sacrum Commercium* was written. There is no doubt that its author, whoever he was, understood thoroughly the Franciscan way of life and the meaning of poverty in that way of life. He was a true Franciscan. But, in addition, or perhaps because he was a true Franciscan, he was also a poet, for the *Sacrum Commercium* is poetic in quality, even though it is written in prose.

In part, at least, the *Sacrum Commercium* is an allegory; that is, it belongs to one of the several literary forms that employ concrete, picturable terms to represent what is immaterial. An allegory is an extended metaphor. It is generally narrative in form and makes use of personification and, to some extent, symbolism. In the *Sacrum Commercium* poverty becomes Lady Poverty. She dwells upon a high mountain, has had a lengthy history, is wooed by Saint Francis and his companions, and in the end joins them to be per-

---

19. II Cor. 6, 10.

petually associated with them. Persecution too is personified, as are also the vices, Avarice and Sloth. The whole works itself out in narrative form to illustrate the deep love for and devotion to poverty of Francis and his first companions, who thought of poverty as their Lady Poverty and of devotion to her as a mystical union with her.

The *Sacrum Commercium* opens with a short prologue that praises the excellence and pre-eminence of poverty, "the foundation of all other virtues and their guardian."[20] The work goes on then to show Francis seeking poverty along the highways and byways and among those who might have known her, until he is finally told to seek her upon the heights of a mountain. Francis, taking his brothers with him, ascends the mountain and at the top meets Lady Poverty. Together they salute her and then listen while she tells her own history from the garden of Paradise down to their own age. Deeply moved, Francis invites her to go with them and to dwell with them. She consents and, at the nuptial banquet that follows, they celebrate their mystical union, and Lady Poverty admonishes them to persevere to the end in their chosen way of life.

The allegorical method shows up to good effect especially in the section where Lady Poverty explains in allegorical fashion the history of poverty. First she tells how the anchorites fled to the Thebaid deserts to live there the life of poverty. She then goes on to tell how some of the early monks, though filled at first with great fervor with regard to poverty, began to relax their discipline. Her lament over the tragic growth of laxity in the matter of poverty is in accordance with historical facts, for by the time of Saint Francis, some at least of the older monastic orders had grown rich in worldly possessions and poverty was little loved among them.

The most poetic part of the book, however, is the descrip-

---

20. See the Prologue.

tion of Christ's love for poverty, brought out in the brothers' praise of Lady Poverty. Leaving behind the wealth and riches of his house in heaven, Christ came into this world seeking Lady Poverty in the dark places and in the shadow of death where she had fled, hated by all and shunned by all. He took her to himself and exalted her to the heights of the clouds. From the manger at Bethlehem to the cross on Calvary, he kept her at his side, loved her, praised and extolled her. And when he was lifted up on the cross, he drew her to himself that he might die in her arms, stripped of everything, poor and abandoned.

The whole work is highly imaginative, but it is gracefully and artistically done. It is intricately interwoven with Scriptural passages in such a way that the whole takes on the flavor and the strength of the Scriptures themselves. All in all, the *Sacrum Commercium* is one of the most literary of the writings to come out of the early days of the Franciscan Order's existence.

It should be added that the present translation was made from the Latin text of the *Sacrum Commercium* prepared by the Fathers of Saint Bonaventure's College, Quaracchi, Italy, in 1929. Furthermore, as regards the English texts of Holy Scripture, the Confraternity of Christian Doctrine version was used wherever possible. However, for many of the quotations the older Challoner-Douay translation was used because its version very often gives more precisely the meaning the author of the *Sacrum Commercium* had in mind in using the Latin Vulgate edition.

— Fr. Placid Hermann O.F.M.

CHAPTER TITLES

.

1547

THE SACRUM COMMERCIUM
or
FRANCIS AND HIS LADY POVERTY[1]

PROLOGUE

1. Among all the excellent and excelling virtues that prepare in man a place and a dwelling for God and show man the better and easier way of going to God and of arriving at him, holy poverty stands out above all the rest by a certain precedence and excels the glory of the others by its singular grace; for it is indeed the foundation of all other virtues and their guardian, and it rightly stands first both in place and in name among the other evangelical virtues.[2] The other virtues need not fear the pouring down of rain, the coming of floods, and the blowing of winds that threaten destruction, so long as they are solidly established upon this foundation of poverty.[3]

2. This is indeed as it should be, for the Son of God, *the*

---

1. The complete Latin title is *Sacrum Commercium Sancti Francisci cum Domina Paupertate*. While the English title used here is a little less poetic than the Latin title, it has the advantage of being shorter.
2. Mt. 5, 3. Poverty stands at the head of the list of the beatitudes.
3. Mt. 7, 24: Everyone therefore who hears these my words and acts upon them shall be likened to a wise man who built his house on rock. And the rain fell, and the floods came, and the winds blew and beat against that house, but it did not fall, because it was founded on rock.

Lord of hosts and *the king of glory*,[4] loved this virtue with a special predilection, sought it out, and found it, when he wrought our salvation upon this earth.[5] At the beginning of his preaching he placed this virtue as a light in the hands of those who enter the portal of faith and made it the foundation stone of his house.[6] The other virtues receive the kingdom of heaven only in promise from him; poverty, however, is already invested with it without delay. For, *blessed are the poor in spirit,* he said, *for theirs is the kingdom of heaven.*[7]

3. Very properly is the kingdom of heaven said to be the possession of those who keep nothing of the goods of this world through their own will, their inclination toward spiritual things, and their desire for eternal things. For it can only follow that a person will live on heavenly things if he cares nothing for earthly things; and he who renounces all earthly things and *counts them as dung*[8] will taste with pleasure the savory *crumbs that fall from the table* of the holy angels[9] and will deserve to taste how *sweet*[10] and how good the Lord is.[11] This is a true investing with the kingdom of heaven, a security toward the possession of that kingdom, and a kind of foretaste of future happiness.

4. Ps. 23, 10: Who is this king of glory? The Lord of hosts; he is the king of glory.
5. Ps. 73, 12: Yet, O God, my king from old, you doer of saving deeds on earth.
6. Lk. 6, 48: He is like a man building a house, who dug deep and laid a foundation upon rock.
7. Mt. 5, 3. The emphasis in this beatitude is upon the present tense ''is.''
8. Philip. 3, 8: I count them as dung that I may gain Christ.
9. Mt. 15, 27: The reference here is to the story of the Canaanite woman who asked Jesus to free her daughter beset by a devil. When he told her that he was sent only for the children of Israel and added, ''It is not fair to take the children's bread and cast it to the dogs,'' she replied: ''Yes, Lord; for even the dogs eat of the crumbs that fall from their masters' table.''
10. I Pet. 2, 3: If, indeed, you have tasted that the Lord is sweet.
11. Ps. 33, 9: Taste and see how good the Lord is.

4. For this reason Blessed Francis, as a true imitator and disciple of the Savior, gave himself at the beginning of his conversion with all zeal, with all desire and deliberation, to seeking out, finding, and making his own this holy poverty; and in so doing he neither hesitated in adversity, nor feared any evil, nor shunned any labor, nor fled from any bodily ills, for he would be satisfied only if his desire to come to poverty, to which the Lord gave *the keys of the kingdom of heaven,*[12] would be granted to him.

---

12. The words are from Mt. 16, 19: And I will give thee the keys of the kingdom of heaven. The application is to the poor of spirit of the first beatitude, *for theirs is the kingdom of heaven,* Mt. 5, 3.

CHAPTER I

Blessed Francis Seeks Out Poverty

5.   Francis began to go about *in the streets and crossings*[1] of the city, relentlessly, like a persistent hunter, diligently seeking whom his heart loved. He inquired of those standing about, he questioned those who came near to him, saying: *"Have you seen* her *whom my heart loves?"*[2] But *this saying was hidden from them,*[3] as though it were in a foreign language. Not understanding him, they said to him: "Sir, we do not know what you are saying. Speak to us in our own language and we will give you an answer."

For *there was no voice nor sense*[4] among the sons of Adam in that day that they might want to confer together or speak about poverty. They hated poverty bitterly then, as they do today, nor *could they speak peaceably*[5] about it to any one asking about it. Therefore, they answered him as they would an unknown person and they said that they knew nothing about what he was seeking.

---

1. Cant. 3, 2: I will rise then and go about the city; in the streets and crossings I will seek him whom my heart loves.
2. *Ibid.*, 3, 3.
3. Lk. 18, 34.
4. IV Kings 4, 31.
5. Gen. 37, 4.

6. *"I will go, therefore,"* said blessed Francis, *"to the great men* and the wise *and will speak to them: for they have known the way of the Lord* and *the judgment of their God;*[6] for these are perhaps *poor and foolish, that know not the way of the Lord* and *the judgment of their God."*[7]

When he had said this, they answered even more harshly: "What is this *new doctrine* that you bring *to our ears?*[8] Let this poverty that you are seeking be *with you and your posterity forever!*[9] As for us, however, let it be our good fortune to enjoy good things and to have abundant riches, for *brief and troublous is our lifetime; neither is there any remedy for man's dying.*[10] We know nothing better than how to be happy and how to eat and drink as long as we live."

7. When blessed Francis heard these things, he marvelled in his heart, and, giving thanks to God, he said: "Blessed be you, Lord God, who *didst hide these things from the wise and prudent, and didst reveal them to little ones. Yes, Father, for such was thy good pleasure.*[11] Lord, father, and sovereign ruler of my life, *leave me not to their counsels nor suffer me to fall by them,* [12] but grant me by your grace to find what I seek, *because I am your servant, the son of your handmaid."*[13]

8. Blessed Francis, therefore, leaving the city, went quickly to a certain field, where he saw from afar off two elderly men sitting there *wasted with sorrow.*[14] One of them spoke thus: *"To whom shall I have respect, but to him that is poor and of a contrite spirit and that trembleth at my words?"*[15]

6. Jer., 5, 5.
7. *Ibid.*, 5, 4.
8. Acts 17, 19.
9. Gen. 13, 15.
10. Wis. 2, 1.
11. Mt. 11, 25-26.
12. Ecclus. 23, 1.
13. Ps. 115, 16.
14. Lamen. 1, 13: He hath made me desolate, wasted with sorrow all the day long.
15. Is. 66, 2.

And the other said: *"We brought nothing into the world, and certainly we can take nothing out; but having food and sufficient clothing, with these let us be content."*[16]

9. When blessed Francis approached these men he said to them: "Tell me, I beg of you, where does Lady Poverty dwell, where does she feed, where does she lie at midday,[17] *for I am faint with love* for her?"[18]

But answering, they said: "Good Brother, we have sat here *for a time and times and a half of time,*[19] and we have often seen her pass by, for there were many who sought her. From time to time many have gone with her, but often she returned alone and naked, adorned with no jewels,[20] unescorted by any companions, clothed with no garments. She would weep bitterly and say: *'The sons of my mother have fought against me.'*[21] And we would say to her: 'Have patience, for the *righteous love thee.'*[22]

10. "And now, Brother, she has gone up into the mountain where the Lord directed her to go;[23] she dwells in the holy mountains because God loves her *more than any dwelling of Jacob.*[24] The giants cannot touch the prints of her feet[25] and the eagles cannot fly up to her neck. Poverty is the one thing that every one despises, in as much as it is not *found*

---

16. I Tim. 6, 7-8.
17. Cant. 1, 7: Tell me, you whom my heart loves, where you pasture your flock, where you give them rest at midday, lest I be found wandering after the flocks of your companions.
18. Cant. 2, 5.
19. Apoc. 12, 14.
20. Is. 61, 10: I will greatly rejoice in the Lord, and my soul shall be joyful in my God: for he hath clothed me with the garments of salvation: and with the robe of justice he hath covered me, as a bridegroom decked with a crown, and as a bride adorned with her jewels.
21. Cant. 1, 5.
22. Cant. 1, 3.
23. Mt. 28, 16: But the eleven disciples went into Galilee, to the mountain where Jesus had directed them to go.
24. Ps. 86, 2.
25. Esther 13, 13: For I would willingly and readily for the salvation of Israel have kissed even the steps of his feet.

Sacrum Commercium

in the land of them that live in delights;[26] it is therefore *hid from their eyes; the fowls of the air know it not;*[27] *God understandeth the way of it, and he knoweth the place thereof.*[28]

11. "Therefore, Brother, if you want to get to her, remove the garments of your rejoicing, and *put away every encumbrance and sin entangling you,*[29] for unless you are stripped of these things, you cannot go up to her who dwells so high above. But, because she is kind, she *is easily seen by them that love her, and is found by them that seek her.*[30] *To think therefore upon her,* Brother, *is perfect understanding: and he that watcheth for her, shall quickly be secure.*[31] Take with you some faithful companions that you may listen to their advice as you go up the mountain and be strengthened by their help, for *woe to the solitary man! For if he should fall, he has no one to lift him up.*"[32]

12. After blessed Francis had received the advice of these great men, he went and chose certain of his faithful companions and hastened with them to the mountain. And he said to his brothers: *"Come and let us go up to the mountain of the Lord, and to the house of* Lady Poverty, *that she might teach us her ways and that we might walk in her paths."*[33]

When they had considered the way up the mountain from every angle, for it was extremely steep and rough, some of them said to one another: *"Who can ascend the mountain of the Lord*[34] and who can reach its summit?"

13. Knowing this, blessed Francis said to them: *"How*

---

26. Job 28, 13.
27. Job 28, 21.
28. Job 28, 23.
29. Heb. 12, 1.
30. Wis. 6, 13.
31. Wis. 6, 16.
32. Eccles. 4, 10.
33. Is. 2, 3: Come and let us go up to the mountain of the Lord, and to the house of the God of Jacob, and he will teach us his ways, and we will walk in his paths.
34. Ps. 23, 3.

narrow the gate, Brothers, *and close the way that leads to life! And few there are who find it.*[35] *Be strengthened in the Lord and in the might of his power,*[36] for whatever is difficult will be easy for us. Put off the burdens that weigh upon your wills and cast away the freight of your sins and *gird yourselves and be valiant men.*[37] *Forgetting what is behind,* strain forward according to your abilities *to what is before.*[38] I say to you that whatever *place the sole of your foot shall tread upon* will *be yours.*[39] For *Christ the Lord is the breath of our mouth;*[40] he will draw you to the summit of the mountain *with the bands of love.*[41] Wonderful, Brothers, is the espousal with Poverty, and we may easily enjoy her embraces, for she has *become as a widow*[42] among the peoples, vile and contemptible before all, this queen of virtues. There is no one in this whole region who will dare to cry out, no one who will oppose us, no one who will be able to forbid us with any right to associate with her. *All her friends have despised her and are become her enemies.*"[43] And when he had said these things, all began to walk together after the holy Francis.

---

35. Mt. 7, 13.
36. Ephes. 6, 10.
37. I Mach. 3, 58
38. Philip. 3, 13.
39. Josue 1, 3.
40. Lamen. 4, 20.
41. Osee 11, 4.
42. Lamen. 1, 1.
43. *Ibid.,* 1, 2

CHAPTER II

The Meeting with Lady Poverty

14. While Francis and his brothers were climbing toward the summit of the mountain with very easy progress, behold, Lady Poverty, standing at the mountain's top, looked down its slopes. And seeing these men ascending with such vigor, indeed almost flying, she was greatly astonished and said: *"Who are these, that fly as clouds, and as doves to their windows?*[1] It has been a long time since I saw such men or looked upon men so unencumbered, all their burdens cast away. I will speak to them, therefore, of the things that are in my heart, lest they, like the others, repent of their strenuous climb, not seeing the abyss that lies all about them. I know that they cannot take possession of me without my consent, but I will have a reward before my Father in heaven if I give them advice concerning salvation." *And behold, a voice from the heavens*[2] came to her saying: "Fear not, daughter of Sion, for *these are the seed which the Lord has blessed*[3] and has chosen *in unaffected love.*"[4]

15. And so, Lady Poverty, reclining in her total nothing-

---

1. Is. 60, 8.
2. Mt. 3, 17,
3. Is. 60, 8.
4. II Cor. 6, 6.

ness, *welcomed* the brothers *with goodly blessings*[5] and said to them: "Tell me, Brothers, what is the reason for your coming here and why do you come with such haste from the valley of sorrows to the mountain of light? Are you perhaps seeking me who, as you see, am *a poor little one, tossed with tempest, without all comfort?*"[6]

16. But they answered and said: "We have come to you, Lady; we ask that you receive us in peace. We wish to become servants of *the Lord of hosts, for he is the king of glory.*[7] We have heard that you are the queen of virtues and, in some measure, we have learned this also by our own experience. Wherefore, kneeling at your feet, we humbly beg that you deign to dwell with us and be for us the way to come to the King of glory just as you were the way for *the Orient from on high* when he deigned to visit those who sat *in darkness and in the shadow of death.*[8] For we know that *thine* is the *power, thine is the kingdom,*[9] and that you have been placed by the King of kings over all virtues as their queen and mistress. Only grant us peace and we shall be saved, that he who redeemed us through you will also receive us through you. If you determine to save us, we will be saved indeed. [10] For he, the *King of kings and Lord of lords,*[11] the Creator of heaven and earth, desired *your splendor and your majesty.*[12] *While the king was at his repose,*[13] rich and glorious in his kingdom, he *forsook* his *house* and left his inheri-

---

5. Ps. 20, 4.
6. Is. 54, 11.
7. Ps. 23, 10.
8. Lk. 1, 78-79.
9. I Paralip. 29, 11.
10. Esther 13, 9: O Lord, Lord, almighty king, for all things are in thy power, and there is none that can resist thy will, if thou determine to save Israel.
11. Apoc. 19, 16.
12. Ps. 44, 4.
13. Cant. 1, 11.

tance;[14] for *wealth and riches* were *in his house.*[15] And coming thus *from heaven's royal throne,*[16] he very fittingly sought you out.

17.   "Your dignity therefore is great and your sublimity incomparable, since, leaving behind all the delights of the angels and the boundless excellences of which there is a great abundance in heaven, he came to seek you in the lower parts of the world, you who were lying in the *mud of the swamp,*[17] *in the dark places and in the shadow of death.*[18] You were not a little odious to all living creatures and all fled from you; and, in so far as they could, they drove you away from them. And, though some could not entirely escape you, you were not therefore less odious or less hateful to them.

18.   "But after the *Lord of hosts*[19] came and took you for his own, he exalted you among the tribes of peoples and he adorned you as a bride with a crown,[20] raising you *above the height of the clouds.*[21] But, though many surely hate you, not knowing *your power and your glory,*[22] it does you no harm, for you dwell *upon the holy mountains* by your own free will,[23] in the *firm dwelling place* of the glory of Christ.[24]

19.   "Thus the Son of the most high Father became *enamored of your beauty;*[25] while he was in the world he clung to you alone and proved that you were completely faithful in all things. For before he came upon earth from his home full of light, you prepared a place that would be satisfactory

---

14. Jerem. 12, 7.
15. Ps. 111, 3.
16. Wis. 18, 15.
17. Ps. 39, 3.
18. Ps. 87, 7.
19. Malach. 3, 1.
20. Is. 61, 10: He hath covered me, as a bridegroom decked with a crown, and a bride adorned with her jewels.
21. Is. 14, 14.
22. Ps. 62, 3.
23. Ps. 86, 1.
24. II Paral. 6, 33.
25. Wis. 8, 2.

to him, a throne upon which he would sit and a dwelling in which he would rest, namely, the most poor virgin from whom he rose to shine upon this world. Certainly, at his birth you met him in all fidelity, so that in you he might find a place that would suit him, and not in earthly delights. He was laid *in a manger*, says the evangelist, *because there was no room for* him *in the inn.*[26] And thus, always inseparable from him, you accompanied him so that throughout his life, when *he was seen upon earth and conversed with men,*[27] though the foxes had dens and the birds of the air nests, he nevertheless *had nowhere to lay his head.*[28] Then, when he opened his mouth to teach — he who of old had opened the mouths of the prophets — among the many things he said, he first of all gave praise to you and extolled you, saying: *Blessed are the poor in spirit, for theirs is the kingdom of heaven.*[29]

20. "Moreover, when he chose certain necessary witnesses of his preaching and of his glorious work for the salvation of the human race, he chose indeed not wealthy merchants but poor fishermen to show by this judgment that you were to be loved by all. In the end, that your goodness, your magnificence, your fortitude, your dignity might be made manifest to all, that all might know how you excel all other virtues, how without you there can be no virtue, how your *kingdom is not of this world*[30] but of heaven, you alone clung to the King of glory, when all his chosen and loved ones timidly abandoned him. You, however, a most faithful spouse, a most tender lover, did not for a moment leave him; what is more, you clung to him all the more faithfully the more you saw

---

26. Lk. 2, 7.
27. Baruch 3, 38.
28. Mt. 8, 20.
29. Mt. 5, 3.
30. Jn. 18, 36.

him despised by all others. Indeed, if you had not been with him, he could never have been despised thus by all.

21. "You were with him when the Jews reviled him, when the pharisees insulted him, when the chief priests cursed him; you were with him when he was buffeted, spit upon, and scourged. He who should have been respected by all was mocked by all, and you alone comforted him. You did not leave him unto death, *even to death on a cross.*[31] And on the cross itself, when he hung there naked, his arms outstretched, his hands and feet pierced, you suffered with him, so that nothing in him should appear more glorious than you. Finally, he left to you, when he went to heaven, the seal of the kingdom of heaven with which to seal the elect, that whoever would sigh for the eternal kingdom should come to you to beg it from you and to enter it through you, for no one can enter into the kingdom unless he is sealed with your seal.[32]

22. "Therefore, Lady, have compassion on us and seal us with the seal of your grace. For who is so dull, so foolish as not to love you with his whole heart, you who were thus chosen by the Most High and prepared from all eternity? Who would not revere and honor you, when he whom all the powers of heaven adore has bestowed such honor upon you? For who would not willingly adore the prints of your feet,[33] you, to whom the Lord of majesty so humbly stooped, to whom he joined himself so intimately, to whom he clung

---

31. Philip. 2, 8.

32. Apoc. 7, 2-4: And I saw another angel ascending from the rising sun, having the seal of the living God; and he cried with a loud voice to the four angels, who had it in their power to harm the earth and the sea, saying: ''Do not harm the earth or the sea or the trees, till we have sealed the servants of our God on their foreheads.'' And I heard the number of those who were sealed, a hundred and forty-four thousand sealed, ...

33. Is. 60, 14: And all that slandered thee shall worship the steps of thy feet.

with such great charity? We beg of you, therefore, Lady, that through him and because of him you despise not our petitions in our necessities but deliver us from all dangers, O glorious and eternally blessed one."[34]

---

34. Adapted from the antiphon *Sub tuum praesidium:* We fly to thy patronage, O holy Mother of God, despise not our petitions in our necessities, but deliver us from all dangers, O ever glorious and blessed Virgin.

CHAPTER III

Lady Poverty Replies to Francis and His Brothers

23. To these words of the brothers Lady Poverty replied with joyful heart, pleasant countenance, and kind words, saying: "I confess to you, my Brothers and my dearest friends, that from the time you began to speak, I have been filled with happiness; and *I overflow with joy*,[1] seeing your fervor and knowing your proposal. Your words have become for me *more precious than gold, than a heap of purest gold, sweeter also than syrup or honey from the comb*.[2] *For it is not you who are speaking, but the* Holy *Spirit who speaks through you*,[3] and his *anointing teaches you concerning all things*[4] that you speak concerning the most high King, who by his grace alone took me to be his beloved, thus taking away from the earth my reproach,[5] and made me glorious among the princes of heaven.

24. "I therefore wish to recount for you, if listening to me

---

1. II Cor. 7, 4.
2. Ps. 18, 11.
3. Mt. 10, 20.
4. I Jn. 2, 27.
5. Is. 4, 1: And in that day seven women shall take hold of one man, saying: We will eat our own bread, and wear our own apparel: only let us be called by thy name, take away our reproach.

will not bore you, the long but none the less useful history of my status, that you might learn *how you ought to walk to please God*,[6] taking care not to look back once you have willed to *put* your *hand to the plow*.[7]

"I am not inexperienced, as many think, but I am quite ancient and full of days, knowing the ordering of things, the varieties among creatures, and the fickleness of times. I know the fluctuations of the human heart, partly by the experience of years, partly by the keenness of my nature, partly by the merit of grace.

25. "I was at one time *in the paradise of my God*,[8] where man went naked; in fact I walked in man and with man in his nakedness through the whole of that most splendid paradise, fearing nothing, doubting nothing, and suspecting no evil. It was in my thoughts that I would be with him forever, for he was created just, good, and wise by the Most High and placed in that most pleasant and most beautiful place. I was rejoicing exceedingly and *playing before him all the while*,[9] for, possessing nothing, he belonged entirely to God.

26. "But alas! An unexpected evil came to pass, an evil entirely unheard of from the beginning of creation, when that unhappy one who in his glory lost his wisdom and, unable to keep his place in heaven, entered into a serpent and treacherously approached man, in `order that man might be made like unto himself, a transgressor of the divine law. That pitiable man believed the evil tempter and gave in to him; and, forgetting *the God who gave* him *birth*,[10] he imitated that first transgressor and became likewise a transgressor. He had at first been naked, Scripture says of him, but he *felt no shame*,[11] for complete innocence was in him. But once he had

---

6. I Thess. 4, 1.
7. Lk. 9, 62.
8. Apoc. 2, 7.
9. Prov. 8, 30.
10. Deut. 32, 18.
11. Gen. 2, 25.

sinned he recognized that he was naked and, being ashamed, he ran to get *fig-leaves* and made a covering for himself.[12]

27. "When therefore I saw my companion become a transgressor and covered with leaves, for he had no other covering, I went away from him, and standing afar off I began to look upon him with a tearful countenance. *I waited for him that hath saved me from pusillanimity of spirit and so* great *a storm.*[13]

"*And suddenly there came a sound from heaven*[14] that shook the whole of paradise, and a most resplendent light was sent out from heaven with it. And looking, I saw the Lord of majesty *walking in the garden in the cool of the day,*[15] alight with inexpressible and exquisite glory. Multitudes of angels accompanied him, crying out in a loud voice and saying: '*Holy, holy, holy, the Lord God of hosts, all the earth is full of* your *glory.'*[16] *Thousands of thousands ministered to him, and ten thousand times a hundred thousand stood before him.*[17]

28. "I began therefore, I confess, to grow faint with amazement and awe, quaking with fear and trembling exceedingly, and, my body chilled and my heart beating rapidly, I cried *out of the depths,*[18] saying: 'Lord, have mercy; Lord, have mercy. *Enter not into judgment with your servant, for before you no living man is just.*'[19] And he said to me: '*Go, hide yourself a little for a moment, until* my *indignation pass away.*'[20]

---

12. Gen. 3, 7. Then the eyes of both were opened, and they realized that they were naked; so they sewed fig-leaves together and made themselves coverings.
13. Ps. 54, 9.
14. Acts 2, 2.
15. Gen. 3, 8.
16. Is. 6, 3.
17. Dan. 7, 10.
18. Ps. 129, 1.
19. Ps. 142, 2.
20. Is. 26, 20.

"And immediately he called my companion, saying: 'Adam, *where are you?*'[21] And he said: '*I heard you in the garden, Lord, and I was afraid because I was naked; and I hid.*'[22] Indeed he was naked, for *going down from Jerusalem to Jericho, he fell in with robbers,*[23] and they stripped him of his goods of nature, and he lost thereby his likeness to his Creator. But the most high King, none the less most kind, gave him an opportunity to return to him and awaited his repentance.

29. "Indeed, that wretched one inclined his heart and broke forth in evil words to make excuses for his sins.[24] And thus he increased his guilt and piled up punishment, treasuring up to himself *wrath on the day of wrath* and of indignation *of the just judgment of God.*[25] He spared neither himself nor his seed after him, heaping upon all the terrible curse of death. All who stood about condemned him, and *the Lord God put him out of the Garden of Eden*[26] by a just but none the less merciful judgment. And he bade him *return to the ground* out of which he had been taken,[27] tempering much the sentence of the curse. He *made* for them *garments of skin,*[28] signifying by them man's mortality, once the garments of his innocence had been stripped from him.

30. "When I saw my companion clothed with the skins of the dead, I left him completely, because he had been cast out to multiply his labors that he might become rich. I went

---

21. Gen. 3, 9.
22. Gen. 3, 10.
23. Lk. 10, 30.
24. Ps. 140, 4: Incline not my heart to evil words; to make excuses in sins.
25. Rom. 2, 5: But according to thy hardness and unrepentant heart, thou dost treasure up to thyself wrath on the day of wrath and of revelation of the just judgment of God.
26. Gen. 3, 23.
27. Gen. 3, 19: In the sweat of your brow you shall eat bread, till you return to the ground, since out of it you were taken: for dust you are and unto dust you shall return.
28. Gen. 3, 21.

then a wanderer and a fugitive upon earth,[29] weeping and sighing greatly. From that time I did not find where to rest my foot, [30] while Abraham, Isaac, and Jacob, and the rest, received in promise riches and *a land flowing with milk and honey.*[31] *In all these I sought rest*[32] and did not find it. And all the while the Cherubim stood before the gate of Paradise with a *flaming sword, which turned every way,*[33] until the Most High came into the world from the bosom of his Father, he who sought me out most graciously.

31. "When the Most High wanted to return to his Father who had sent him, he left a testament to his faithful elect concerning me and corroborated it with an inviolable document: *Do not keep gold, or silver, or money.*[34] *Take nothing for your journey, neither a bag nor a wallet nor bread nor a staff nor shoes; neither have two tunics.*[35] *And if any one would go to law with thee and take thy tunic, let him take thy cloak as well; and whoever forces thee to go for one mile, go with him two.*[36] *Do not lay up for yourselves treasures on earth, where rust and moth consume, and where thieves break in and steal.*[37] *Do not be anxious, saying, 'What shall we eat?' or, 'What shall we drink?' or, 'What are we to put on?'*[38] *Do not be anxious about tomorrow, for tomorrow will have anxieties of its own. Sufficient for the day is its own*

---

29. Gen. 4, 12. After Cain had slain Abel, God said to Cain: When you till the soil, it shall not give its fruit to you; a fugitive and a wanderer shall you be on the earth.
30. Gen. 8, 9. An allusion to: But the dove found no place to alight, so she returned to him in the ark. The Douay version reads: But she, not finding where her foot might rest, returned to him into the ark.
31. Exod. 3, 17.
32. Ecclus. 24, 11.
33. Gen. 3, 24.
34. Mt. 10, 9.
35. This is a composite of several quotations: Mt. 10, 9; Mark. 6, 8; Lk. 9, 3.
36. Mt. 5, 40-41.
37. *Ibid.*, 6, 19.
38. *Ibid.*, 6, 31.

trouble.[39] *Everyone of you who does not renounce all that he possesses, cannot be my disciple.*[40] And many other things that are written in the same book.[41]

32. "The apostles and all the disciples observed all these things with the greatest diligence; they omitted nothing of all the things they heard from their Lord and Master, not even for an hour. They carried out the message of salvation themselves like the bravest of soldiers and like judges of the world, and they likewise preached it everywhere, the Lord cooperating and confirming their *preaching by the signs that followed.*[42] They were aflame with love; everywhere they abounded in the spirit of piety, and they devoted themselves to the needs of everyone; they took great care that it should not be said of them: they talked but did not act.[43] Wherefore one of them spoke with the greatest confidence, saying: *For I do not make bold to mention anything but what Christ has wrought through me,... being sanctified by the Holy Spirit.*[44] And another said: *Silver and gold I have none.*[45] And thus both in life and in death they all extolled me with the highest praises.

"Those who heard them strove to fulfill everything that had been told them by their teachers, and selling *their possessions and goods,* they distributed *them among all according as anyone had need.*[46] All were *together and held all things in common,*[47] *praising God and being in favor with all the*

---

39. *Ibid.,* 6, 34.
40. Lk. 14, 33.
41. That is, the book of the Gospel.
42. Mk. 16, 20.
43. An allusion to Mt. 23, 3: But do not act according to their works; for they talk but do nothing.
44. Rom. 15, 18.
45. Acts 3, 6.
46. Acts 2, 45.
47. Acts 2, 44.

people.[48] Therefore *day by day the Lord added to their company such as were to be saved.*[49]

33. "The truth of their words remained for a long time among many, at least as long as the blood of the poor Crucified One was warm in their memory and the overflowing chalice of his passion filled their hearts unto inebriation. For, if any were at any time tempted to abandon me because I was too difficult for them, remembering the wounds of the Lord by which were revealed the bowels of his mercy, they would punish themselves severely because of this temptation and cling to me all the more forcibly and embrace me with all the more fervor. I was always with them, always keeping alive in their memory the sorrows of the passion of the eternal King, so much so that, comforted not a little by my words, they willingly bore the iron that tore at their bodies and joyfully saw the sacred blood flowing from their own flesh. Enduring, this victory lasted for a long time, so that each day a thousand thousands were sealed with the seal of the most high King.[50]

34. "But alas! After not too long a time, peace was made, and that peace was more disastrous than any war. In the beginning few were sealed; toward the middle, still fewer; and at the end, very few indeed. And now certainly *in peace is my bitterness most bitter*[51] when all flee from me, all drive me away; I am needed by none, I am abandoned by all. Peace was granted me by my enemies, but not by my own; peace from strangers, but not from my own children. Indeed, *I have brought up my children, and exalted them: but they have despised me.*[52]

35. "At that time, when *the lamp* of the Lord *shined over*

---

48. Acts 2, 47.
49. *Loc. cit.*
50. An allusion to Apoc. 7, 3.
51. Is. 38, 17.
52. Is. 1, 2.

my head, and I walked by his light in the darkness,[53] the
devil raged in many who were with me, the world beckoned
to them, and the flesh was lusting in them, so much so that
many began to *love the world* and *the things that are in
the world.*[54]

36. "But the consummation of all virtues, that is, the Lady
Persecution, to whom God has given the kingdom of heaven,
just as he has given it to me, was at my side, a faithful
assistant in all things, a powerful helper, a prudent adviser;
when she saw any who grew tepid in charity, or who forgot
for a little the things of heaven and set their heart upon the
things of this earth in any way, she immediately thundered
forth, immediately moved up her army; and immediately
shame covered the faces of my sons, so much so that they
sought the name of the Lord.[55] Now, however, *my sister
has left me*[56] *and the very light of my eyes has failed me,*[57]
for, while my children have rest from persecutors, they are
torn even more cruelly by domestic and internal war, *provoking one another, envying one another*[58] in the acquisition of
riches and in an abundance of pleasures.

37. "Indeed, with the lapse of time, some began to breathe
again and to walk again by their own will along the proper
way, the way along which some had walked earlier, compelled by necessity. These all came to me begging me
earnestly with many prayers and tears to make with them
a treaty of perpetual peace and to remain with them as I
was with them of old in the days of my youth, *when the
Almighty was with me: and my servants round about me.*[59]
They were men of virtue, men of peace, *blameless in holi-*

---

53. Job 29, 3.
54. I Jn. 2, 15.
55. An allusion to Psalm 82, 17.
56. Lk. 10, 40.
57. Ps. 37, 11.
58. Gal. 5, 26.
59. Job 29, 5.

ness before God our Father,[60] persisting in *fraternal love*[61] so long as they lived in the flesh, poor in spirit, possessing nothing, rich in holiness of life, abounding in the gifts of the heavenly charismata, *fervent in spirit, rejoicing in hope, patient in tribulation,*[62] *meek and humble of heart,*[63] preserving peace of spirit, concord of life, harmony of soul, and a cheerful unity in their associations with one another. Finally, these men were devoted to God, pleasing to the angels, beloved of men, strict with themselves, gentle toward others, devout in deed, modest in walk, cheerful of countenance, earnest of heart, humble in prosperity, magnanimous in adversity, temperate at table, most simple in dress, very sparing in sleep, modest and reserved, and conspicuous by the splendor of their good deeds. My soul was joined fast with theirs, and there was one spirit and one faith in us."[64]

---

60. I Thess. 3, 13.
61. II Pet. 1, 7.
62. An adaptation of Rom. 12, 12.
63. Mt. 11, 29.
64. An adaptation of Ephes. 4, 4: One body and one Spirit, even as you were called in one hope of your calling; one Lord, one faith, one Baptism.

CHAPTER IV

Lady Poverty Continues to Speak

38. "In the end, however, there arose among us some who *were not of us,*[1] certain *children of Belial,*[2] speaking vain things, doing evil things, saying they were poor when they were not; and me, whom the noblest men loved with all their heart — about whom I have already spoken — they spurned and defiled, following *the way of Balaam, the son of Bosor, who loved the wages of wrongdoing,*[3] *men corrupt in mind and bereft of truth, supposing godliness to be gains,*[4] men who, clothing themselves with the habit of religion, did not *put on the new man,*[5] but merely covered over the old. They spoke evil of their elders and secretly sniped at the lives and morals of those who were the founders of this holy way of life, calling them indiscreet, unmerciful, cruel;[6] and me, whom these had taken to themselves, they called lazy,

---

1. I Jn. 2, 19.
2. I Kings 2, 12.
3. II Pet. 2, 15.
4. I Tim. 6, 5.
5. An adaptation of Ephes. 4, 24: Be renewed in the spirit of your mind, and put on the new man, which has been created according to God in justice and holiness of truth.
6. An allusion to Jer. 50, 42: They shall take the bow and the shield: they are cruel and unmerciful.

rough, wicked, uncultured, unfeeling, dead. It was my rival who brought all this about, my rival who, assuming the clothing of a sheep, hid with the cunning of a fox the fury of a wolf.[7]

39. "This rival is Avarice, which is said to be the immoderate desire to obtain and retain riches. Her friends are accustomed to call her by a holier name, lest they should seem to have completely abandoned me, by whose favor they have risen from the dust and have been lifted up from the dunghill.[8] They spoke civil words to me, but they thought treacherously of me.[9] And, though the desolation of *a city set on a mountain cannot be hidden*,[10] they nevertheless bestowed a name upon her, namely, Discretion or Providence, despite the fact that such discretion should rather be called confusion and such providence, the ruinous forgetfulness of all things.

"And they said to me: 'Yours is the power, yours the kingdom,[11] do not fear. It is good to continue in works of piety and to have time to bring forth good fruits, to contribute to those who are in want, to give something to the poor.'

40. "And I said to them: 'Brethren, I do not deny that what you have said is good, but *consider your own call*.[12] Do not look back. Do not descend from the *housetop to take anything from the house*. Do not go back from the field to

---

7. An allusion to Mt. 7, 15: Beware of false prophets, who come to you in sheep's clothing, but inwardly are ravenous wolves.

8. Ps. 112, 7: He raises up the lowly from the dust; from the dunghill he lifts up the poor to seat them with princes.

9. Ps. 34, 20: For civil words they speak not, but against the peaceful in the land they fashion treacherous speech.

10. Mt. 5, 14.

11. I Paral. 29, 11: Thine, O Lord, is magnificence, and power, and glory, and victory: ... thine is the kingdom, O Lord, and thou art above all princes.

12. I Cor. 1, 26.

take a cloak.[13] Do not become entangled in worldly affairs.[14] Do not become involved with the things of the world that defile and corrupt, things from which you fled through your knowledge of the Savior. For it must come about that those who become entangled in these things will be overcome and their last state will become worse than the first,[15] for, *having a semblance indeed of piety*,[16] they depart from that which was given them by a holy commandment.'

41. "When I had proposed all these things to them, *there arose a division among them.*[17] Some said, 'She is good and says what is good.' Others said, 'No, but she wishes to seduce us so that we will imitate her. She is miserable and wants us all to be miserable with her.'[18]

42. "My rival could not at that time drive me away from being near them, for there were still men among them in the great fervor and great charity of the beginning of their conversion; they were beating against heaven with their cries and piercing heaven with the persistence of their prayers,[19] going beyond their own powers in contemplation, despising all earthly things. *Then the creator of all things commanded and he that made me*, the Lord, said to me: *Let your dwelling be in Jacob, and your inheritance in Israel, and take root in my elect.*[20] I indeed did all these things most diligently.

---

13. Mt. 24, 17-18: Let him who is on the housetop not go down to take anything from his house; and let him who is in the field not turn back to take his cloak.
14. II Tim. 2, 4: No one serving as God's soldier entangles himself in worldly affairs.
15. Mt. 12, 45: Then he goes and takes with him seven other spirits more evil than himself, and they enter in and dwell there; and the last state of that man becomes worse than the first.
16. II Tim. 3, 5.
17. Jn. 10, 19.
18. An allusion to Jn. 7, 12: For some were saying, ''He is a good man.'' But others were saying, ''No, rather he seduces the crowd.''
19. An allusion to Ecclus. 35, 21: The prayer of him that humbleth himself, shall pierce the clouds.
20. Ecclus. 24, 12.

And when I was thus with them and we proceeded together along the royal road,[21] they had, because of me, *glory among the masses, and esteem from the elders;*[22] they were honored by men and called holy by them. They began to take it ill that they were called holy, and, remembering what the Son of God had said, *I do not receive glory from men,*[23] they refused utterly the glory offered them.

43. "But once they were walking in such great fervor of love for Christ, Avarice, taking the name Discretion, began to say to them: 'Do not show yourselves so unbending before men and do not despise in this way the honor they show you; but show yourselves affable to them and do not outwardly spurn the glory they offer you, but do so at most inwardly. It is good to have the friendship of kings, acquaintance with princes, and familiarity with the great, for, when they thus honor and revere you, when they rise and come to meet you, many who see this will be the more easily turned to God by their example.'

44. "They indeed, seeing the advantage of this, accepted the proffered counsel; but not guarding themselves against the snare set for them along the way, they at length embraced glory and honor with all their heart. They esteemed themselves to be also inwardly what they were proclaimed to be outwardly, placing their glory in the mouths of those who praised them, like foolish virgins giving oil to those who sold it, and like an unprofitable servant.[24]

"For others, thinking that these men were interiorly what

---

21. An allusion to Numb. 21, 22: I beseech thee that I may have leave to pass through thy land: we will not go aside into the fields or the vineyards, we will not drink waters of the wells, we will go the king's highway, till we be past thy borders.
22. Wis. 8, 10.
23. Jn. 5, 41.
24. The Latin sentence reads: *Tales se fore intus existimabant quales praedicabantur foris, ponentes gloriam suam in ore laudantium, sicut fatuae virgines in vendentibus oleum, et servus inutilis in terra.* Some manuscripts omit *virgines* and *oleum;* one omits the entire *in venden-*

they appeared to be exteriorly, freely offered their goods to them to obtain remission of their sins. These goods they at first accounted dung,[25] saying: 'We are poor and we always want to be poor; we do not want your goods, but we want you.[26] *Having food and sufficient clothing, with these let us be content,*[27] *for vanity of vanities, all things are vanity.*'[28] Wherefore men's devotion toward them increased greatly from day to day, so that many esteemed their goods less when they saw such things spurned by these holy ones.

45. "Meanwhile, when that wicked enemy of mine saw this, she began to be violently angry and to gnash her teeth; and, *grieved to the heart,*[29] she said: 'What shall I do? *Behold, the entire world has gone after her.*[30] I will take the name Providence,' she continued, '*and I will speak to their hearts,*[31] if they will but hear and forbear.'[32]

"And she did this, saying to them in humble words: '*Why do you stand here all day idle,*[33] providing nothing for yourselves for the future? What harm will it do you to have the necessaries of life, so long as you avoid having superfluous things? You would be able to work out your own salvation and the salvation of others with greater peace and quiet, if everything you really need were immediately at hand. While you have time, provide for yourselves and for those who will come after you, for men will draw back from their first generosity and from their accustomed gifts. It would be good

---

tibus oleum. But there still remains great difficulty in translating this section.

25. Philip. 3, 8.
26. An allusion to II Cor. 12, 14: And I will not be a burden to you; for I do not seek yours, but you.
27. I Tim. 6, 8.
28. Eccles. 12, 8.
29. Gen. 6, 6.
30. Jn. 12, 19.
31. Osee 2, 14.
32. An allusion to Ezech. 2, 5: If so be they at least will hear, and if so be they will forbear.
33. Mt. 20, 6.

for you to remain always as you are, but that is not possible since God daily adds to your company.[34] Would not God be pleased if you had at hand what you could give to the needy, being *mindful of the poor*,[35] since he said: *It is more blessed to give than to receive?*[36] Why do you not receive the goods that are offered to you and thereby avoid depriving the givers of their eternal reward? There is now no reason why you should be afraid of companionship with riches, since you consider them as nothing. Vice is not in the things, but in the heart, for God sees all the things he made and they are very good.[37] Good things are for the good; all things serve them, for all things were made for them.[38] O how many who have riches make but ill use of them; if you had these things, you would convert them to good use, for your purpose is holy, your desire is holy! You do not desire to make your parents wealthy, for they are rich enough; but, if you had the things that are necessary, you could live a more becoming and a more orderly life.'

"These things and others like them this fierce enemy of mine said to them. Some of them, whose conscience was already corrupt, gave their consent. Others, however, turned a deaf ear to them and refuted the arguments she proposed with penetrating answers; and, no less than the others, they rested their arguments upon the Scriptures.

46. "But when Avarice saw that she could not by herself work her desire upon these men, she changed her counsel in order to gain her end. She summoned Sloth, who is loath both to begin good works and to complete what she has be-

---

34. An allusion to Acts 2, 47: And day by day the Lord added to their company such as were to be saved.
35. Gal. 2, 10.
36. Acts 20, 35.
37. An allusion to Gen. 1, 31: And God saw all the things that he had made, and they were very good.
38. An allusion to Ecclus. 39, 30: Good things were created for the good from the beginning, so for the wicked, good and evil things.

gun; and she made an agreement with her and entered into a pact with her against them. These two were not actually too familiar with each other, nor were they even united by chance; but they willingly conspired together,[39] just as Pilate and Herod conspired of old against the Savior.

"After the pact was made, Sloth gave voice to her hatred and made an attack with her cohorts and invaded the confines of these men; and putting forth all her effort, she extinguished their charity and brought them over to lukewarmness and torpor. And thus little by little they were lead from weakness of spirit[40] to become *dead from the heart*.[41]

47. "They then began to long miserably for the *fleshpots of Egypt*,[42] which they had left behind; and what they had once despised with a generous heart, they now shamefully wanted. They were sad in walking in the way of the commandments of God,[43] and they were arid of heart in following his injunctions. They grew faint under the burden, and from lack of spirit they could hardly breathe. Rarely did they feel compunction, never true sorrow. They obeyed only with murmuring. Their thoughts were carnal, their joys dissolute. Their sorrow was feigned, their speech unguarded; their laughter came too easily. Gaiety filled their countenance; their gait was without modesty; their garments were soft and delicate, carefully cut, and even more carefully sewn. Their sleep was excessive, their food too abundant, their drink intemperate. They filled the air with trifling things, silly jokes, and idle words. They told stories, changed laws, did away with duties, and devoted themselves to administer diligently human affairs. They had no care for spiritual

---

39. Ps. 2, 2: The kings of the earth rise up, and the princes conspire together, ...
40. Ps. 54, 9: I waited for him that saved me from pusillanimity of spirit, and a storm.
41. Ps. 30, 13: I am forgotten as one dead from the heart.
42. Exod. 16, 2. Literally: for certain things of Egypt.
43. Ps. 118, 32: I will run the way of your commands when you give me a docile heart.

exercises, no interest in the salvation of souls. They spoke rarely of heavenly things, and there burned scarcely at all in them the desire for eternal things.

48. "And so, becoming obdurate, they began to envy one another, to provoke one another; and, being eager to dominate one another, one would accuse his brother of even the worst crime. They avoided things that were difficult and sought wherein they could find vain pleasure, for they were incapable of true joy. But, retaining the appearance of holiness however they could, so that they would not become entirely worthless, and speaking at least of holy things, they managed to hide their miserable life amongst the simple. But so great was their interior corruption that, not being able to contain themselves, they showed also outwardly what they really were.

49. "They began at last to fawn upon men of the world; and they began to be wedded to them, as it were, that they might empty their purses, extend their own buildings, and multiply the very things they had completely renounced. They sold their words of advice to the rich and their visits to noble ladies; and they frequented the courts of kings and princes with great eagerness, so that they might *join house to house and lay field to field*.[44] And now they are grown great and rich and strong upon the earth, because *they have proceeded from evil to evil* and *they have not known* the Lord.[45] They fell *when they were lifted up;*[46] and they sprawled upon the ground before their birth; and still they say to me, 'We are your friends.'

50. "In sorrow I grieve over certain of them who, when they were in the world were miserable and contemptible enough, but were made rich out of my wealth[47] after they came to me. When they had grown fat and wanton, they

44. Is. 5, 8.
45. Jer. 9, 3.
46. Ps. 72, 18.
47. Apoc. 18, 19.

kicked harder against me than the rest in their deriding of me.[48] They were certainly thought unworthy of life itself; they were barren with want and hunger, they ate grass and barks of trees, they were disfigured with calamity and misery.[49] Now they are not content with the common life, but they set themselves apart and without fear look after themselves;[50] living with them is quite burdensome to the rest because of their seeking after superfluous things and their striving after high places among the disciples of Christ, though in the world they had been held in contempt by persons of note. These who often lacked barley bread and water and counted it delightful to be under the briers, the children of foolish and base men, and not appearing at all upon the earth, have rolled themselves down to my miseries; they abhor me and flee far from me, and are not afraid to spit in my face.[51] I have suffered reproaches and terror from them, and they who were my familiars and continued at my side have insulted me.[52] They were ashamed of me, and the more they

---

48. An allusion to Deut. 32, 15: The beloved grew fat, and kicked.
49. An allusion to Job 30, 2-4: The strength of whose hands was to me as nothing, and they were thought unworthy of life itself. Barren with want and hunger, who gnawed in the wilderness, disfigured with calamity and misery. And they ate grass, and barks of trees, and the root of junipers was their food.
50. Several verses from Jude (verses 19 and 12) are here put together.
51. These are all verses from Job 30, 7-14 but rearranged to suit the author: They pleased themselves among these kinds of things, and counted it delightful to be under the briers. The children of foolish and base men, and not appearing at all upon the earth. Now I am turned into their song, and am become their byword. They abhor me, and flee far from me, and are not afraid to spit in my face. For he hath opened his quiver, and hath afflicted me, and hath put a bridle into my mouth. At the right hand of my rising, my calamities forthwith arose: they have overthrown my feet, and have overwhelmed me with their paths as with waves. They have destroyed my ways, they have lain in wait for me, and they have prevailed against me, and they have prevailed, and there was none to help. They have rushed in upon me, as when a wall is broken, and a gate opened, and have rolled themselves down to my miseries.
52. An adaptation of Jer. 20, 10: For I heard the reproaches of many,

knew themselves to have been enriched by my kindness to them, the more forcibly did they cast me off, and they scorned even to hear my name.

51. "Sorrowing, I was deeply grieved and I said to them: *'Return, you children* who have departed from me, *and I will heal your rebellions.*[53] Beware of all *covetousness, for that is idolatry;*[54] *a covetous man shall not be satisfied with money.*[55] *But call to mind the days gone by, in which, after you have been enlightened, you endured a great conflict of sufferings.*[56] *Be not of those who draw back unto destruction, but of those who have faith to the saving of the soul.*[57] A man making void the Law of Moses dies without mercy on the word of two or three witnesses; how much worse punishments do you think he deserves who has trodden under foot the Son of God, and has regarded as unclean the blood of the covenant through which he was sanctified, and has insulted the Spirit of grace?*[58] *Return, ye transgressors, to the heart,*[59] for a man's life does not consist in *the abundance of his possessions.'*[60]

"But they become angry and said: 'Go, wretched one, *depart from us; we desire not the knowledge of your days.'*[61]

"And I said to them: *'Have pity on me, have pity on me, at least you, my friends. Why do you persecute me without cause?*[62] Did I not tell you that my ways and your ways are not the same? See, I regret that I have seen you.'

52. *"And the word of the Lord came to me,*[63] saying: 'Re-

and terror on every side: Persecute him, and let us persecute him: from all the men that were my familiars, and continued at my side.
53. Jer. 3, 22.
54. Ephes. 5, 5.
55. Eccles. 5, 9.
56. Heb. 10, 32.
57. Heb. 10, 39.
58. Heb. 10, 28-29.
59. Is. 46, 8.
60. Lk. 12, 15.
61. Job 21, 14.
62. Job 21, 22.
63. Jer. 13, 3.

turn, O Sulamitess: return that we may behold thee.[64] These children provoke me to anger[65] and they *will not hearken to you, because they will not hearken to me.*[66] *The heart of this people is become hard of belief and provoking;*[67] *for they have not rejected you, but me.*[68] For you have taught them against your own interests and instructed them against your own good, for if they had not accepted you, they would never have become so enriched. They pretended to love you so that they might leave you, enriched with an abundance of benefits. Wherefore, *they have turned away with stubborn revolting* and *they have laid hold on lying and have refused to return.*[69] Do not believe them when they speak good things to you, for they *have despised* you and *will seek* your *life.*[70] *Do not take to you praise and supplication for them, for I will not hear you,*[71] for I have cast them out because they have rejected me.' "

---

64. Cant. 6, 12.
65. Ezech. 2, 7.
66. Ezech. 3, 7.
67. Jer. 5, 23.
68. I Kings 8, 7.
69. Jer. 8, 5.
70. Jer. 4, 30.
71. I Kings 15, 23.

CHAPTER V

Lady Poverty Admonishes Francis and His Brothers

53. "Behold, Brothers, I have disclosed to you a parable of great length. Let your *glance be directly forward*[1] so that you may see what you must do. It is extremely dangerous to look back and to deceive God. *Remember Lot's wife,*[2] and *do not believe every spirit.*[3] *But in your case, beloved, we are confident,*[4] because I see in you more than in others *better things, things that promise salvation,*[5] for you seem to have completely put off all things and to have freed yourselves entirely from every burden. The most convincing proof of this is the fact that you have come up the mountain to me, to whom few can ever attain. *But I say to you, my friends,*[6] that the malice of many has made even the virtue of the good seem suspect to me, and I have often found ravenous wolves in sheep's clothing.[7]

54. "I desire, certainly, that every one of you should be-

---

1. Prov. 4, 25.
2. Lk. 17, 32.
3. I Jn. 4, 1.
4. Heb. 6, 9.
5. *Loc. cit.*
6. Lk. 12, 4.
7. An allusion to Mt. 7, 5.

come an imitator of the holy ones who have had me for
their inheritance because of their faith and patience. But
because I fear that what happened to others might also
happen to you, I give you salutary counsel, namely, that you
do not seek to attain higher and more holy things right in
the beginning, but that you go forward gradually, under the
guidance of Christ, and thus little by little reach the highest
things. Take care lest, when the dung of worthlessness has
been placed at your roots, you be found sterile, for then there
will remain nothing but that the axe be put to you.[8] Do not
trust entirely the spirit that is now in you, for man's senses
are more prone to evil than to good, and his will easily
returns to what it was accustomed to, even though it may
have been considerably separated from it. For I know that
in your overly great fervor all things seem to you to be very
easy; but remember that it is said that *they that serve him
are not steadfast, and in his angels he found wickedness.*[9]

55.   "At first, indeed, all things will be easy for you to bear;
but a little later, when a feeling of security has sprung up,
you will become careless about the benefits you have received.
You will think that whenever you wish you will be able to
go back and recover your first consolation; but once negligence has been allowed to come in, it is not easily driven
out again. Your heart will then turn aside to other things,
but rarely will it cry out for you to return to the first things.
Thus, when you have lapsed into torpor and laziness of spirit,
you will offer easy words of excuse, saying: 'We are not able
to be strong, as we were in the beginning; times are now
different, and we do not know what it means that *when a
man ends he is only beginning.*'[10] And there will always be
in your mind a voice saying: 'Tomorrow, tomorrow we will

---

8. Lk. 13, 8: Sir, let it alone this year too, till I dig around it and
   manure it. Perhaps it may bear fruit; but if not, then afterwards
   thou shalt cut it down.
9. Job 4, 18.
10. Ecclus. 18, 5.

return to our *first husband, because it was better with* us *then than now.'*[11]

"*Behold I have foretold*[12] many things to you, Brothers, and *many things yet I have to say to you* which *you cannot bear now.*[13] But the hour will come when I will explain openly to you the things I have said."

56. At these words blessed Francis cast himself prone upon the ground, along with his brothers; and, giving thanks to God, he said: "What you say pleases us, beloved Lady, and there is nothing in what you say that can be contradicted. *The report is true which* we *heard in* our *own country* concerning your words and concerning your wisdom; and your wisdom exceeds by far *the fame which we have heard.* Blessed are your men, and blessed are your servants, who stand before you always, and hear your wisdom. Blessed be the Lord your God forever whom you have pleased; he has loved you forever and has appointed you queen to do mercy and judgment to his servants.[14] *O how good and sweet is* your *spirit,*[15] correcting those who err and admonishing those who sin.

57. "Behold, Lady, through the love of the eternal King for you and your love for him, we beg you not to defraud us of our desire,[16] but to do with us according to your kindness and mercy.[17] *For great are your* works *and hardly to be described; therefore the unruly souls* strayed from you.[18] And because you walk alone, *terrible as an army set in array,*[19]

---

11. Osee 2, 7.
12. Mt. 28, 7.
13. Jn. 16, 12.
14. An adaptation of III Kings 10, 6-9.
15. Wis. 12, 1.
16. An allusion to Ps. 77, 30: They were not defrauded of that which they craved.
17. An allusion to Ecclus. 50, 24: And now we pray to the God of all, who ... hath done with us according to his mercy.
18. Wis. 17, 1.
19. Cant. 6, 3.

the foolish cannot remain with you. But, behold, we are your servants and *the sheep of your pasture.*[20] Unto eternity and for all ages *we resolve and swear to keep your just ordinances.*"[21]

58.   At these words Lady Poverty was deeply moved[22] and, since it is characteristic of her to have mercy always and to spare, she could not contain herself any longer, and she ran and embraced them all, giving to each the kiss of peace, saying: *"Behold, I come quickly,*[23] my Brothers and my children, knowing that through you I will gain many more."

Blessed Francis was not able to restrain himself for joy, and he began to praise with a loud voice the Almighty who does not abandon those *who hope in him,*[24] saying: *"Bless the Lord, all his elect, keep days of joy, and give glory to him,*[25] *for he is good, for his mercy endureth forever."*[26]

And going down from the mountain, they led their Lady Poverty to the place where they stayed; *it was about the sixth hour.*[27]

---

20. Ps. 78, 13.
21. Ps. 118, 106.
22. An allusion to III Kings 3, 26: But the woman whose child was alive, said to the king, (for her bowels were moved upon her child,) I beseech thee, my lord, . . .
23. Apoc. 22, 7.
24. Jud. 13, 17.
25. Tob. 13, 10.
26. Ps. 135, 1.
27. Jn. 4, 6.

CHAPTER VI

The Banquet with Lady Poverty

59. When everything was ready, the brothers constrained Lady Poverty to eat with them.

But she said: "Show me first your oratory, chapter room, and cloister; your refectory, your kitchen, your dormitory and stable; show me your fine chairs, your polished tables, your great houses. I do not see any of these things. I see only that you are cheerful and happy, overflowing with joy, replete with consolation, as though you expect everything will be given to you just at your wish."

They answered, saying: "Our Lady and our Queen, we, your servants, are tired from our long journey, and you too, coming with us, have suffered not a little. Let us therefore first eat, if it please you, and thus refreshed we will fulfill all your wishes."

60. "What you say pleases me," she replied; "but now bring water so that we may wash our hands, and towels to dry them."

They very quickly brought a broken earthenware bowl filled with water, for there was not a whole one in that place.[1]

---

1. Thomas of Celano says: the friars were so solicitous about poverty that, lest they should come to possess superfluous things, they did not

And pouring the water over her hands, they looked here and there for a towel. But when they did not find one, one of the brothers gave her the tunic with which he was clothed so that she could dry her hands with it. Taking it with thanks, she magnified God in her heart because he had placed her in the midst of such men.

61.   They then took her to the place where the table was prepared. When she had come there, she looked about, and, seeing nothing but three or four crusts of barley or bran bread placed upon the grass, she was greatly astonished and said to herself: "Who has ever seen such things in the ancient generations?[2] Blessed are you, Lord God, whose is the care of all things; *for* your *power is at hand when* you will;[3] by such works you have *taught your people* to be pleasing to you."[4] They sat down and together they gave thanks to God for all his gifts.

62.   Lady Poverty then commanded the cooked food to be brought in dishes. And behold, a single dish was brought filled with cold water, that they might all dip their bread in it; there was neither an abundance of dishes there nor a variety of cooked foods.

She asked that she be given at least some uncooked, sweet-smelling herbs. But since they had no gardener and knew nothing of a garden, they gathered some wild herbs in the woods and set these before her.

She said: "Bring me a little salt to season the herbs, for they are bitter."

And they said: "Wait, Lady, and we will go to the city

---

suffer even a small bowl to be in the house. See *Vita Prima*, No. 51, *Analecta Franciscana*, Vol. X, Quaracchi, 1941.

2. This is a combination of two parts of verses from Is. 51, 9 and 66, 8. Arise, arise, put on strength, O thou arm of the Lord, arise in the days of old, in the ancient generations. — Who hath ever heard such a thing? and who hath seen the like to this?

3. An adaptation of I Par. 29, 10: Blessed art thou, the Lord God of Israel; and Wis. 12, 18: for thy power is at hand when thou wilt.

4. Wis. 12, 19: But thou hast taught thy people by such works, ...

and get some for you, if some one will give it to us."

"Well, then," she said, "give me a knife so I may cut off what is superfluous and that I may cut the bread, which is very hard and dry."

"Lady," they said to her, "we have no blacksmith to make swords for us. For now, just use your teeth in place of a knife and later we will get one for you."

"And do you have a little wine?" she asked.

But they answerd and said: "Lady, we do not have any wine, *for the chief thing for man's life is water and bread,*[5] and it is not good for you to drink wine, for the spouse of Christ must shun wine like poison."

63. But after they had been more satisfied from the glory of such great want than they would have been from an abundance of all things, they blessed the Lord in whose eyes they had found such grace; and they led Lady Poverty to the place where she might rest since she was tired. There she lay down in her total nothingness upon the bare ground.

She also begged a cushion for her head. Immediately they brought a stone and placed it under her head.

She, indeed, slept a most peaceful and sober sleep. Then she quickly arose and asked to be shown the cloister. Taking her to a certain hill, they showed her the whole world, as far as she could see, and said: "This, Lady, is our cloister."

64. Then she commanded them all to be seated around her and she spoke to them the words of life,[6] saying: "May you be blessed by the Lord God who made heaven and earth,[7] you who have received me into your home with such fulness of charity that it seemed to me today that I was with you in the paradise of God. Therefore I was *filled with comfort,*

---

5. Ecclus. 29, 27.
6. An allusion to Jn. 6, 69, where, after Jesus had made the promise of the Eucharist and then asked the apostles if they would leave too, Peter answered: To whom shall we go? Thou hast the words of eternal life.
7. An allusion to Jud. 13, 23-24.

overflowing *with joy,*[8] and I ask pardon that I was so slow in coming to you. Truly the Lord is with you, *and I did not know it.*[9] Behold, what I wished for I now see, what I desired I now possess, for I am joined on earth with those who represent for me the image of him to whom I am espoused in heaven. May the Lord bless your strength and receive the works of your hands.[10]

65. "I pray and beg you as my most dear sons that you persevere in the things that you have begun at the instigation of the Holy Spirit, not forsaking your perfection as so often happens among certain ones; but that, avoiding all the snares of darkness, you strive always for more perfect things.[11] Your profession is very exalted, above man, above virtue; and it illumines the perfection of those of old with a greater brilliance. You need have no doubt, no hesitance, about the possession of the kingdom of heaven, for you already possess an earnest of your future inheritance and you have already received the pledge of the Holy Spirit, for you are stamped with the seal of the glory of Christ,[12] and in all things, by his glory, you are like to those of that first school which he gathered together when he came into the world. For what they did in his presence, you have begun to do entirely in his absence; and there is no reason why you should be ashamed to say: '*Behold, we have left all and followed thee.*'[13]

66. "Let not the magnitude of the struggle deter you, nor the greatness of the labor, for you will have a great reward. And *looking towards the author and finisher of faith, Jesus,*

---

8. II Cor. 7, 4.
9. Gen. 28, 16.
10. An allusion to Deut. 33, 11: Bless, O Lord, his strength, and receive the works of his hands.
11. An allusion to Heb. 6, 1: Therefore, leaving the elementary teaching concerning Christ, let us pass on to things more perfect.
12. II Cor. 1, 22: Now it is God who is warrant for us and for you in Christ, who has anointed us, who has also stamped us with his seal and given us the Spirit as a pledge in our hearts.
13. Mt. 19, 27.

who for the joy set before him, endured a cross, despising shame,[14] *hold fast the confession of* your *hope without wavering.*[15] *Run with* love *to the fight set before* you.[16] Run through patience, which is extremely necessary for you, *that, doing the will of God, you may receive the promise.*[17] *For God is able*[18] to bring a happy consummation by his grace to what you have undertaken beyond your powers, for he is faithful to his promise.

67. "Let not the *spirit which now works on the unbelievers*[19] find anything in you gratifying unto himself, nothing wavering, nothing diffident, lest he find ground in you for working his wickedness against you. For *he is exceeding proud,* and *his pride and his arrogancy is more than his strength.*[20] He is in *great wrath*[21] because of you and he will turn the armament of his cunning against you and will try to pour out the poison of his malice, like one who, in his warring has conquered and cast down the rest, is saddened to see you set above him.

68. "Over your conversion, dearest Brothers, all the citizens of heaven have rejoiced with great joy and have sung new songs before the eternal King. The angels rejoice in you and because of you, for, since through you many will preserve their virginity and will be resplendent by their chastity, the ruins of the heavenly city will be repaired, where virgins are placed in greater glory, for those who neither marry nor are given in marriage *will be as angels of God in heaven.*[22] The apostles rejoice to see their own life renewed, their teaching preached, and examples given by you of out-

14. Heb. 12, 2.
15. Heb. 10, 23.
16. Heb. 12, 1.
17. Heb. 10, 36.
18. Rom. 11, 23.
19. Ephes. 2, 2.
20. Is. 16, 6.
21. Apoc. 12, 12.
22. Mt. 22, 30.

standing holiness. The martyrs are happy in the expectation that their own constancy in pouring forth their sacred blood will be renewed. The confessors dance with joy, knowing that their frequent triumphs over the enemy will be renewed in you. The virgins rejoice, following *the Lamb wherever he goes*,[23] for they know that their number is daily increased through you. Indeed, all the heavenly court is filled with joy, for they will celebrate daily feasts over new inhabitants and will be continually refreshed by the sweet odor of holy prayers rising up from this valley.

69. "I beg of you, therefore, Brothers, *by the mercy of God*,[24] for which you have been made so poor, do that for which you have come, for which you have ascended from the rivers of Babylon. Accept humbly the grace offered you; use it worthily for ever and ever unto the praise, glory, and honor of him who died for you, Jesus Christ, our Lord, who lives and reigns, conquers and rules with the Father and the Holy Spirit, the eternally glorious God, through all ages forever and ever. Amen."

This work was completed in the month of July after the death of blessed Francis, in the year one thousand two hundred and twenty-seven from the Incarnation of our Lord and Savior Jesus Christ.

---

23. Apoc. 14, 4.
24. Rom. 12, 1.

THIRTEENTH-CENTURY TESTIMONIES

1597

Translated by Paul Oligny O.F.M. from
T. Desbonnets & D. Vorreux O.F.M.,
editors, *Saint François D'Assise: Documents, Écrits et Premières Biographies*
(Paris, 1968), pp. 1433-1451.

INTRODUCTION

The writers of the Order were not the only ones who gave us information regarding the life of St. Francis. The place he held in the history of the Church is amply attested outside the narrow circle of his close friends and of his brothers. The chroniclers and memorialists of his time were not so much concerned with the personality of St. Francis as with the "Umbrian miracle" taken as a whole; for, what was especially striking was the impetus given to a gospel renewal. The hagiographers of the time emphasized the supernatural element with which Francis' life was so rich, and the result was a Golden Legend.

There are, however, a few texts that furnish, if not essential information, at least something new and picturesque. Certain modern historians often refer to them. We believe they should be made available to the reader in a translation.

Among the many documents collected by Fathers Lemmens and Golubovich,[1] there are some testimonies which merely confirm or make use of the texts that are known. We have limited ourselves to those that contribute new data or shed new light on St. Francis and his first brothers.[2]

— Fr. Damien Vorreux O.F.M.

NOTES

1. Lemmens O.F.M., *Testimonia minora saeculi XIII de S. Francisco Assisiensi* (Quaracchi, 1926), 128 pp. — G. Golubovich O.F.M., *Biblioteca bio-bibliografica della Terra Santa,* vol. I (Quaracchi, 1906).
2. A full account of the first friars' manner of life will be found in certain chroniclers such as Jordan of Giano, Thomas of Eccleston, and Salimbene. An English version of these writers will be found in *XIIIth Century Chronicles,* translated from the Latin by Placid Hermann O.F.M., with introduction and notes by Marie-Therese Laureilhe (Chicago, 1961), xvii-302 pp.

CHAPTER TITLES

THIRTEENTH-CENTURY
TESTIMONIES

1. A Sermon by St. Francis at Bologna
Thomas, archdeacon of Spalato
Historia Salonitarum
Lemmens, *Testimonia minora,* p. 10.

In that year (1222), I was residing in the Studium of Bologna; on the feast of the Assumption, I saw St. Francis preach in the public square in front of the public palace. Almost the entire city had assembled there. The theme of his sermon was: "Angels, men, and demons." He spoke so well and with such sterling clarity on these three classes of spiritual and rational beings that the way in which this untutored man developed his subject aroused even among the scholars in the audience an admiration that knew no bounds. Yet, his discourses did not belong to the great genre of sacred eloquence: rather they were harangues.[1] In reality, throughout his discourse he spoke of the duty of putting an end to hatreds and of arranging a new treaty of peace.

He was wearing a ragged habit; his whole person seemed insignificant; he did not have an attractive face. But God conferred so much power on his words that they brought back peace in many a seignorial family torn apart until then by old, cruel, and furious hatreds even to the point of assassinations. The people showed him as much respect as they did devotion; men and women flocked to him; it was a question of who would at least touch the fringe of his clothing or who would tear off a piece of his poor habit.

2. *Miracles at the Friary of San Verecondo*
Anonymous
Passion of San Verecondo, soldier and martyr
Lemmens, *Testimonia minora*, pp. 10-11.

In the months preceding his death, the blessed little poor Francis was offered hospitality more than once in the monastery of San Verecondo; there he received a gracious welcome from the abbot and his monks who venerated him. It was here that he worked the miracle of the sow which had devoured a lamb.[3]

It was also near this monastery that blessed Francis assembled his first three hundred Friars Minor in a chapter; the abbot and his monks amiably procured food and lodging for them according to their means. Sire Andrew, now a very elderly man, who happened to be there at the time, has testified that the brothers received barley bread, fine wheaten bread, winter barley, millet; drinking water, quince wine mixed with water for the sick, and a quantity of two varieties of beans.

At that time blessed Francis travelled about on a donkey; weak and exhausted from his unbelievable penances, vigils, prayers, and fastings, he no longer was strong enough to walk; from the time he had received the stigmata of the Savior, it became impossible for him to walk. Late one night he was travelling on his donkey, accompanied by one of his brothers; he had thrown a coarse sack over his shoulders as a mantle. He was on the road leading to San Verecondo when peasants called out to him: "Brother Francis, stay here with us; don't go any further: ferocious wolves prowl about in this countryside; you are running the risk of seeing your donkey devoured and you yourself attacked and wounded!" "I have done no evil to Brother Wolf," blessed Francis replied; "he will not dare devour our brother donkey. Good night, my children, and fear God!" Brother Francis continued on his way unharmed. This fact was reported to us by a peasant who was a witness to it.[4]

3. The Canonization of St. Francis
Anonymous (John of Campania, sub-deacon and notary?)
Vitae Pontificum Romanorum
Lemmens, *Testimonia minora,* p. 12.

At that time Blessed Francis shone in the city of Assisi with all the brillance of his miracles as a new star in the firmament of the Church; the saintly Pope Gregory ordered a serious inquiry into these miracles; they were screened; the report was sent to him and, on the advice of the brothers, the pope came to Assisi where on October 4,[5] the second year of his pontificate, surrounded by cardinals and prelates, vested in precious ornaments, amidst a profusion of palms and candles, in the presence of a crowd that had come from all parts of the world, he delivered a sermon which began with these words: "Like the morning star among the clouds, like the sun shining on the Temple of the Most High, this is how this man shone in the house of the Lord."[6] This was followed by a public reading of the miracles and their explanation. Then the pontiff, his eyes bathed in tears, decreed that blessed Francis, the servant of the Crucified One whose stigmata adorned his soul and body, was to be inscribed in the catalog of the saints. Three days later, the pope returned to Perugia.

4. Brother Pacificus and St. Francis
Brother Thomas of Tuscany
Gesta Imperatorum et Pontificum
Lemmens, *Testimonia minora,* p. 15.

Brother Pacificus was a man of remarkable holiness; blessed Francis called him his "sweet mother."

He owned — I saw this with my own eyes — a small board, a piece taken from a walnut tree that had formerly grown near the altar of a church in ruins. Brother Pacificus had it sawed and immediately, on the flat side of the board, the image of the Crucified One appeared not in relief but in color and as a part of the wood; it was not the work of man; divine Wisdom alone had stamped it there. Brother Pacificus venerated this image; he always carried it about with him along with a few other relics of saints.

It was Brother Pacificus who was favored with seeing the holy stigmata, which are worthy of the admiration of the whole world, on the body of blessed Francis while he was still living. He too it was who touched the wound in the side; in order to succeed in this, he used a pious stratagem dictated by the excess of his devotion.[7] And finally, when he was still pursuing the vanities of the world, he was the one who saw two swords arranged in the form of a cross come out of the saint's mouth while he was preaching.[8] Terrified by this miracle, he was converted and became one of the most faithful imitators of St. Francis.[9]

5. *The Beginnings of the Order*
Burchard of Ursperg, Premonstratensian (✝1230)
Chronicon
Lemmens, *Testimonia minora*, p. 17.

At that time the world was growing old; two Orders rose up in the Church and renewed her youth like that of an eagle; the Apostolic See confirmed both of them: the Friars Minor and the Friars Preachers. This is how they were approved.

Two sects saw the light of day in Italy: the Humiliati and the Poor Men said to be of Lyons. Pope Lucius had recently listed them among the number of heretics, for they had been found teaching dogmas contrary to the faith and of practicing superstitious observances. During their clandestine preaching which they held most of the time in very secret haunts, they deviated from the Church of God and from her hierarchy. During these days we have seen certain adepts of the Poor Men of Lyons arrive at Rome with one of their teachers, Bernard I believe;[10] they came to ask the Apostolic See for confirmation of their sect and for privileges. They claimed to be leading the life of the Apostles: they refused all ownership, even a house to reside in, and they went about from city to town. But the Lord Pope took them to task for certain strange practices: they cut off the upper part of their shoes and walked around almost barefooted; they wore mantles like religious, but had their hair cut exactly like the laity; but the most reprehensible thing about them was that men and women travelled about together, lived together most of the time in the same house, and even sometimes, it was said, slept in the same bed. All these practices, they claimed, came from the Apostles themselves.

There were others, on the contrary, who appeared after them whom the Lord Pope wished to approve; they were called "poor minors." They renounced all eccentricities and all the excesses mentioned above, but they travelled barefoot winter and summer, did not accept money or alms except in the form of food; they also accepted a habit when they absolutely needed one and if it was offered to them spontaneously; they themselves begged for nothing. Later on they noticed that the name they went by could lead to vainglory under cover of great humility, that many proudly assumed their title as poor people, a fraudulent claim; and they preferred the name "Friars Minor" to that of "Poor Minors." They were submissive in all things to the Apostolic See.

6. *Reverence for Priests*

Stephen of Bourbon, Dominican (1261)
Edit. Lecoy de la Marche, *Anecdotes historiques*,
Paris, 1877, p. 264; Lemmens, *Testimonia
minora,* pp. 93-94.

Francis was travelling in Lombardy and entered into a church to pray. A Patarine or a Manichean, a witness of Francis' renown for sanctity among the people, resolved to take unfair advantage of this influence to attract the people to his sect, destroy their faith, and reduce the priesthood to scorn. The pastor of this parish was causing scandal by living with a woman. The man, therefore, ran and said to the saint: "Tell me: if a priest maintains a concubine and thereby stains his hands, must we believe in his teaching and respect the sacraments he administers." The saint was not taken in by the trap the heretic had set; in the presence of all the parishioners he went to the priest's house, knelt down before him and said: "I do not really know whether these hands are stained as the other man claims they are. In any case, I do know that, even if they are, this in no way lessens the power and efficacy of the sacraments of God; those hands remain the channel whereby God's graces and blessings stream down on the people. That is why I kiss them out of respect for what they administer and out of respect for Him who delegated his authority to them." Francis prostrated himself before the priest, kissed his hands to the great embarrassment of the heretics and their sympathizers who were present.[11]

7. *A Sermon in the Presence of Cardinals*
Stephen of Bourbon
Lecoy de la Marche, *Anecdotes*, p. 215: Lemmens,
Testimonia minora, pp. 94-94.

I heard the following from one of our brother priests. A certain number of high-ranking prelates had assembled. They were told about St. Francis who preached to the birds and to men. They were not unaware of the fact that the saint was a man who had received little education; they summoned him and told him that they wanted to ascertain for themselves how a man who assumed this ministry preached; they settled on a date for this demonstration.[12] Then, one of the more eminent bishops, a friend of the saint, fearing that Francis would cover himself with shame, secretly summoned him to his house and offered him a soundly composed and well-written sermon. When the day came, the saint went to the designated place . . . But when he wanted to repeat the text that had been given him and which he had spent a long time learning and assimilating, his memory failed him: he could not even remember the first word. Pausing for an instant, he asked himself what he was going to do, and then, putting his trust in God, he opened a psalter. His eyes fell on this verse: "All day long I brood on this disgrace, my face covered in shame."[14] He developed this theme — not in Latin but in the language of the common people — spoke of the pride and of the bad example of those prelates who heaped shame on the whole

Church. He pointed out to them that they were the face of the Church, a face that ought to be resplendent with beauty; for, as St. Augustine said, "to be attractive, a face must have regular proportions, receive fitting attention, and be of a clear and pleasant complexion." But this face was covered with shame because of bad example. The more eminent, dignified, visible, and beautiful a part of the body is, all the more unbecoming and shameful is a stain on it. . . . And he continued along these lines to the wholesome shame and great edification of his hearers.

8. *St. Francis and the Divine Office*
Brother Leo
Manuscript Note in the Breviary of St. Francis
Lemmens, *Testimonia minora*, p. 61.

Blessed Francis procured this breviary from Brothers Angelus and Leo, his companions, and he wanted to use it as long as he enjoyed good health in order always to say the office, as is indicated in the rule. Later on, sickness prevented him from saying the office, but he wanted at least to hear it. He was faithful to this practice all his life.[15]

He also had this gospel-book copied and when sickness or some other real impediment made it impossible for him to attend Mass, he had the gospel of the day read to him. He was faithful also to this practice to the day of his death. In fact he said: "When I cannot attend Mass, I adore the Body of Christ with the eyes of the spirit in my prayer precisely as I adore it when I look at it during Mass." After it was read or heard, Blessed Francis always kissed the gospel text out of respect for the Lord.

That is why Brother Angelus and Brother Leo pleaded as best they could with Lady Benedicta, abbess of the Poor Ladies of the monastery of St. Clare and after her with all the future abbesses of the same monastery, always to preserve in the monastery of St. Clare the book from which Francis had read so often, in memory of our holy Father and out of devotion to him.

9. *Jacques de Vitry's Letter, 1216*
Lettre I (beginning of October, 1216)
R.B.C. Huygens, *Lettres de Jacques de Vitry,* Edition
critique, Leyde, 1960, pp. 75-76.

[In the midst of this corruption] I nonetheless found consolation in seeing a great number of men and women who renounced all their possessions and left the world for the love of Christ: "Friars Minor" and "Sisters Minor," as they were called.

They are held in great esteem by the Lord Pope and the cardinals. They are totally detached from temporal things and have but one passion to which they devote all their efforts: to snatch from the vanities of the world souls that are in danger and to prevail upon them to imitate their example. Thanks to God, they have already achieved important successes and made numerous conquests. Those who have heard them, say to their friends: "Come along!" and so one group brings another. As for the brothers themselves, they live the life of the primitive Church of which it is written: "The whole group of believers was united, heart and soul."[17] During the day they go into the cities and villages, giving themselves over to the active life of the apostolate; at night, they return to their hermitage or withdraw into solitude to live the contemplative life.

The women live near the cities in various hospices and refuges; they live a community life from the work of their hands,[18] but accept no income. The veneration that the clergy and laity show toward them is a burden to them, and it chagrins and annoys them.

Once a year, in a place on which they agree, the men of this Order assemble to rejoice in the Lord and eat together; and they profit greatly from these gatherings. They seek the counsel of upright and virtuous men; they draw up and promulgate holy laws and submit them for approval to the Holy Father; then they disband again for a year and go about through Lombardy, Tuscany, Apulia, and Sicily.

Very recently, the saintly Brother Nicholas, a compatriot of the pope, left the Curia to join them; but he was recalled by the pope, for he could not do without him. I am convinced that if the Lord has decided to use these simple and poor men, he has done so to save a great number of souls before the end of the world and to put to shame our prelates who are dumb dogs who do not even have the strength to bark.[19]

10. Jacques de Vitry's Letter, 1220
Lettre VI (spring, 1220)
Huygens, *Lettres,* pp. 131-133.

Sire Rainerio, the prior of St. Michael,[20] has just entered the Order of Friars Minor. They are an Order that is making great strides through the whole world, and this is so because it expressly follows the way of life of the primitive Church and of the apostles. (But, to our way of thinking, this Order constitutes a danger because it sends out not only formed religious, two by two, throughout the world, but also imperfectly formed young men who should rather be tried and subjected to strict conventual discipline for a period of time.)[21]

The master[22] of these brothers, who is also the founder of the Order, is called Francis; he is loved by God and venerated by all men. He came into our camp and, burning with zeal for the faith, he was not afraid to go into the very camp of our enemy. For several days, he preached the word of God to the Saracens, but with little success. The sultan sent for him in particular and begged him to pray to the Lord for him, the king of Egypt, so that God might show him what religion he wished him to embrace.

Colin, the Englishman, our clerk, has also entered this Order along with two other companions of ours: Master Michael and Dom Matthew to whom I had entrusted the parish of the Holy Cross. . . . And I am having a difficult time holding on to the chanter,[23] Henry, and a few others. . . .

11. Jacques de Vitry, History of the Orient
Histoire de l'Orient, chap. 32.
Golubovich, *Biblioteca,* t. 1, pp. 8-10.

Three religious orders already exist: hermits, monks, and canons; the Lord resolved to establish these foundations on a solid basis, and so in these latter times he has added a fourth religious institution to them, the beauty of a new order, the holiness of a new rule. But if we carefully consider the way of life of the early Church, we discover that it is not a new rule that has been added but rather an old one that is revived, a sick person who is cured, a dying person who is restored to life in the evening of this world which is tending toward its decline in our times, threatened as it is by the reign of the son of perdition; in this way God has resolved to prepare for himself new athletes in the face of the dangers of Antichrist; and so he wished to make his Church more secure and better protected.

This order is the one of the true poor men of the Crucified One, and also an order of preachers; they are called Friars Minor. They are lesser and more humble than all present-day religious by way of their habit, their poverty, their contempt for the world. At their head is a general superior; the subordinate superiors and all the other brothers respectfully obey his orders and regulations when he sends them into the different provinces of the world to preach and save souls. They strive with great solicitude to reproduce in themselves the religion, poverty, and humility of the primitive Church; they draw from the pure waters of the fountains of the gospel with such thirst and spiritual ardor that they are not satisfied with carrying out its precepts but work hard at observing its counsels in every way, thereby reflecting trait for trait the life of the apostles: they give up all that they own, renounce themselves, take up their cross and, naked, follow[24] the naked Christ. Like Joseph, they leave their tunic[25] behind, like the Samaritan woman, their water jar;[26] they run unimpeded, relieved of every cumbersome weight; they walk before the face of the Lord without ever turning back;[27] they forget whatever they leave behind them, straining and always marching toward the goal before them: they fly like a cloud, like doves to their cote[28] . . .

The Lord Pope approved their rule and gave them the authority to preach in all the churches they enter; out of deference they were first to request the permission of the local prelate. They were sent two by two to preach as precursors of the Face of the Lord to prepare his second coming. These poor men of Christ travel about with neither purse, haversack, bread, nor money in their belts; they have neither gold nor silver; they wear no sandals.[29] No brother of this Order has the right to own anything. They have neither monasteries, churches, fields, vineyards, animals, houses, property, nor anywhere to rest their head.[30] They have nothing to do with furs and linen, but use only woolen tunics with a capuche; they have neither capes, mantles, cowls, nor other garments. If they are invited to dinner, they eat and drink what is offered them.[31] When they are given an alms in kind, they do not keep it for future use.

Once or twice a year, at a predetermined time and place they assemble for their general chapter,[32] except those who are too far away or who would have to travel by sea. After the chapter, the superior sends them out again in groups of two or more to various regions, provinces, and cities. By their preaching as well as by the example of their holiness and their virtues they encourage a host of men, not only among the humble but also among the nobility and the rich, to despise the world; the nobles and rich leave their cities, their chateaus, their vast real estate, their wealth and — O blessed exchange! — they exchange their temporal goods for spiritual ones, then don the habit of the Friars Minor. By way of clothing they wear a coarse tunic and a cord for a belt.

They have so multiplied in such a short time that there is no province in Christendom where a few of these brothers do not reside, true mirrors reflecting before the eyes of all scorn for the vanities of the world. They refuse no one entry into their Order, except those who are already bound by marriage or profession in another order; they must not nor do they wish to receive those who are still married without the consent of their spouses or of their superiors.[33] They accept everyone else regardless of obstacles and contradictions, and with wonderful confidence; they rely on the generosity and providence of God for their nourishment. All that they give to those who come to them is a

1611

cord and a tunic, and they abandon themselves totally for the rest to the largesse of heaven. And so God gives the hundredfold to his servants in this world; on the road they travel, the Lord looks down upon them with such favor that this saying of Sacred Scripture — we are witnesses of this — is literally fulfilled for them: The Lord "loves the strangers and gives them food and clothing."[34] The people avow, they are happy when the brothers are willing to accept their hospitality or their alms.

This is true not only of the followers of Christ: even the Saracens and men plunged into the darkness of unbelief admire their humility and virtue when the brothers come among them to preach to them without fear: they receive them very gladly and give them all they need. We have seen the founder and master of this Order, the one whom all the others obey as their superior general: he was a simple unlettered man, loved by God and men; he was called Brother Francis. Spiritual fervor and ecstasy moved him to such excesses that, having arrived at the army of the Christians before Damietta in Egypt, with no fear whatsoever, fortified solely with the "shield of faith,"[35] he set out for the camp of the sultan of Egypt. The Saracens arrested him on his way. "I am a Christian," he said; "bring me to your master!" And so they brought him to him. On seeing the man of God, the sultan, that cruel beast, became sweetness itself, kept him with him for a few days and with a great deal of attention listened to him preach the Faith of Christ to him and to his followers. But in the end he was afraid of seeing some of his soldiers whom the effective words of this man would have converted to the Lord go over to the army of the Christians. He, therefore, had Francis led back to our camp with many signs of honor and with security precautions, but not without saying to him: "Pray for me, that God may reveal to me the law and the faith that is the more pleasing to him."

The Saracens gladly listened to the Friars Minor preach as long as they explained faith in Christ and the doctrine of the gospel; but as soon as their preaching attacked Mohammed and openly condemned him as a liar and traitor, then these ungodly men heaped blows upon them and chased them from their cities; they would have killed them if God had not miraculously protected his sons.

Such is this holy Order of the Friars Minor; such is this religious life of apostolic men, an admirable life that should be imitated. These are the men whom, in our opinion, the Lord has raised up in these latter times to battle against the Antichrist, the son of perdition, and against his unbelieving henchmen. They are the true bodyguards of Solomon,[36] the valiant men of Christ; they are the ones who have been designated defenders of the ramparts of Jerusalem, for day and night without interruption they devote themselves to praising God or to preaching; they shout for all they are worth and raise their voice like a trumpet. They "proclaim their faults to my people, their sins to the House of Jacob."[37] They do not withhold their sword from blood:[38] they fight, they travel through the city in all directions, they know how to bear up under hunger, like wandering dogs.[39] They are as it were the salt of the earth,[40] which seasons food and transforms it into nourishment of sweetness and salvation, preserves meat, does away with the decay of worms and the stench of vices. They are the "light of the world,"[41] that sheds light in order to lead to the truth, that inflames and enkindles fires to propagate the fervor of charity. But this Order of perfection and this cloister whose dimensions are worldwide cannot, it seems, befit the weak and the imperfect: these, in fact, sailing the sea in ships and trading on the deep waters,[42] would be shipwrecked if they did not prepare themselves by a preliminary stage in the city in order to clothe themselves first with all the strength and virtue that God gives us.

12. *Jacques de Vitry, Sermon*
Second sermon on the Friars Minor
Felder, *Spicilegium francisc.* V, Rome, 1903.

Francis spontaneously undertook to go beyond what the simple law of God demands. And so, borne upwards by the quadriga of the four gospels and of the four cardinal virtues, he climbed from perfection to perfection, following the divine Crucified One so closely that at his death one could see in the members of his body and in his side the wounds of Christ.

13. St. Francis and the Sultan of Egypt
Anonymous
Verba fr. Illuminati (Ms Vat. Ottob. lat. 522)
Golubovich, *Biblioteca,* vol. I, pp. 36-37.

The minister general [St. Bonaventure] said to us: Here are some anecdotes that Brother Illuminato who accompanied St. Francis on his visit to the sultan of Egypt told us:

One day the sultain wanted to test the faith and fervor that Blessed Francis manifested toward our crucified Lord. He had a beautiful multicolored carpet spread out on the ground; it was almost entirely decorated with motifs in the form of crosses. He said to his spectators: "Fetch that man who seems to be a true Christian; if in coming toward me he walks on the crosses of the carpet, we will say to him that he insults his Lord. If he refuses to walk on the carpet, I shall ask him why he disdains to approach me." The man full of God was called. Now, this man received his instructions for his actions as well as for his words from the very plentitude of God: he walked across the carpet from one end to the other and came near the sultan. Then the sultan, thinking that he had found a good opportunity to charge the man of God with having insulted Christ, said to him: "You Christians adore the cross as a special sign of your God: why then did you not fear to trample underfoot those crosses woven into the rug?" Blessed Francis answered him: "Thieves were also crucified along with our Lord. We have the true Cross of our Lord and Savior Jesus Christ; we adore it and show it great devotion; if the holy Cross of the Lord has been given to us, the cross of the thieves has been left to you as your share. That is why I had no scruple in walking over the symbols of brigands. . . . "

The same sultan submitted this problem to him: "Your Lord taught in his gospels that evil ·must not be repaid with evil, that you should not refuse your cloak to anyone who wants to take your tunic, etc. (Mt. 5, 40): in that case, Christians should not invade our land?" — "It seems," Blessed Francis answered, "that you have not read the gospel of our Lord Jesus Christ completely. In another place we read: if your eye causes you to sin, tear it out and throw it away (Mt. 5, 29). Here he wanted to teach us that every man, however dear and close he is to us, and even if he is as precious to us as the apple of our eye, must be repulsed, pulled out, expelled if he seeks to turn us aside from the faith and love of our God. That is why it is just that Christians invade the land you inhabit, for you blaspheme the name of Christ and alienate everyone you can from his worship. But if you were to recognize, confess, and adore the Creator and Redeemer, Christians would love you as themselves. . . . "

"All the spectators were in admiration at his answers."

NOTES

1. The harangues of a popular orator; exhortations that scorned academic methods and rules but sprang from the heart. Cf. I C 36 for the manner of preaching; I C 23 for the charism to restoring peace.
2. San Verecondo in the diocese of Gubbio.
3. Cf. 2 C 111; LM 8, 6.
4. Cf. *Actus* 23, *Fior.* 21.
5. This text was written in 1240. Celano, closer to the event, assigns it the date July 16 (I C 126).
6. Cf. Sir 50, 6-7.
7. Cf. 2 C 137-138; LM 13, 8.
8. Cf. 2, C 106.
9. Cf. LM 4, 9.
10. The name is correct: cf. Innocent III, bull *Cum inaestimabile pretium* of June 14, 1210.
11. Cf. Test. 6-10. — Another version of the words of St. Francis in another passage by Stephen of Bourbon is perhaps even more striking: "These hands have touched the Lord. Whatever they have done, they cannot make my Lord impure nor can they lessen his power. I honor his minister out of respect for the Lord. This minister may be bad as far as this man is concerned. but for me he is good."
12. Another version says the date chosen was the next day.
13. Ps. 44, 15.
14. Cf. St. Bonaventure, LM 12, 7, and *Sermon II on St. Francis, Opera* IX, p. 582.
15. Cf. Test. 29.
16. Born at Reims (Vitry-les-Reims?) around 1180; bishop of Acre; was present at the siege of Damietta; cardinal-bishop of Tusculum; died in 1240. In addition to his precious correspondence, he left an important work as historian and preacher.
17. Acts 4, 32. This detail "made a deep impression on J. de V.: he repeats it in *Letter VI* and in his *Hist. de l'Occident,* written around 1221" (Huygens).
18. Tb 2, 19; cf. I Cor 4, 12; Eph 4, 28; I Thes 4, 10; 2 Thes 3, 7-12.
19. Is 56, 10.
20. A church located at Acre. Here we have an example of a monk and even of a dignitary who left his order to join that of the Friars Minor.
21. According to Golubovich, vol. I, p. 7, n. 1, the sentence in parenthesis is interpolated: it is missing in a MS; it would be the work of a monk copyist opposed to the brothers; it clashes with the praises which J.

de V. heaps upon the budding Order. — According to Huygens, p. 132, he is a copyist favorable to the friars who, in the Ms in question, left this sentence out of the original text: J. de V. "is too much of a realist not to picture to himself the dangers that a renewal movement can create as it goes from enthusiasm to fanaticism." Compare this with the ending of the following text.

22. Even in 1219 no name had been provided for the superiors; the title "prior," used by Jacques de Vitry probably was then being introduced, just as that of master; it was prohibited in 1221 by the first rule, chap. VI.

23. John of Cambrai, mentioned in Letter IV of the same J. de V. — Unless *Chanter* here is a proper name?

24. Cf. Mt 16, 24.

25. Gn 39, 12.

26. Jn 4, 28.

27. Ez 1, 12-17.

28. Cf. Is 60, 8.

29. Cf. Lk 10, 4.

30. Lk 9, 58.

31. Cf. 2 Kgs 3, 14.

32. Cf. 2 Kgs 8, 2-5.

33. Cf. 2 Kgs 2, 3-5.

34. Dt 10, 18.

35. Cf. Eph 6, 16.

36. Wis 3, 7.

37. Is 58, 1.

38. Cf. Jer 48, 10.

39. Ps 59, 7-15.

40. Mt 5, 13.

41. Mt 5, 14.

42. Ps 107, 23.

CONCORDANCE
of the
EARLY LIVES OF ST. FRANCIS

Translated and adapted by the editor
from the Concordance in *Saint François
d'Assise, Documents, Écrits et Premières
Biographies,* rassemblés et présentés par
les PP. Théophile Desbonnets et Damien
Vorreux O.F.M. (Paris, 1968), pp. 1560-
1593.

1619

SEVEN CONCORDANCE TABLES

I. First Life by Celano (1C)
II. Second Life by Celano (2C)
III. Major Life by St. Bonaventure (LM)
IV. Minor Life by St. Bonaventure (Lmi)
V. Legend of the Three Companions (3S)
VI. Legend of Perugia (LP)
VII. Mirror of Perfection (SP)

In these tables the first column contains the numbers, not only of chapters, but also of subdivisions of chapters (by the addition of a, b, etc.). The second column (except in no. IV) indicates, by means of short sentences or abbreviated titles, the topics treated in these chapters or parts of chapters. The several columns on the right hand show where the same topics or incidents are discussed in other early lives of St. Francis. There are four right-handed columns except for the first part of the Second Life by Celano (no. II) which has five, and no. IV which is limited to the two lives by St. Bonaventure. Of the two numbers for the parts of the two lives by St. Bonaventure, the first is that of the chapter and the second that of a numbered paragraph within a chapter. The numbers given in these tables correspond to those which will be found in the text of the early biographies presented in this volume.

The first concordance of the early lives of St. Francis was prepared by A. G. Little and published in his *A Guide for Franciscan Studies* (London, 1920). A French translation appeared in *Études franciscaines,* vols. 40 and 41 (1928 and 1929), and separately as *Guide pour les études franciscaines,* translated by A. M. Rousset (Paris, 1930), pp. 61-78. However, the concordance of Fathers Desbonnets and Vorreux, now made available in English, is an original one and much more detailed. It will enable students of the life of St. Francis easily to compare the several accounts of the same events and discussions of the same topics by the different early biographers of the saint.

— M. A. H.

	1 CELANO	2C	3S	LM	Others
18b	San Damiano, monastery of the Poor Ladies	13c			
19	Eulogy of the Poor Ladies				
21a	Francis repairs St. Peter's			2 7	
21b	Arrives at the Portiuncula			2 8	
22	Gospel of the feast of St. Mathias		25a	3 1	
23a	Francis' words, ardent like a fire		25b	12 7	
23a	First sermon, at St. George's		25d		
23b	"May the Lord give you peace!"		26a	3 2	LP 67d
24	Vocation of Bernard of Quintavalle	15	27	3 3	Fior 2
25	Vocation of Giles and three others		32b	3 4	
26	"My God, have pity on me a sinner!"			3 6	
27	"I see an immense multitude coming to join us."		36	3 6	
28	"Our Order is like a fisherman casting his net."		33b		Fior 13
29	A new recruit, and the brothers are sent out			3 7	
30	Return of the brothers			3 7	
31	Four new recruits				
32a	The First Rule		46	3 8	
32b	Journey to Rome		47	3 8	
32c	Cardinal John of St. Paul		48	3 9	
33a	The Cardinal refutes objections		49	3 9	
33b	Papal approbation		53	3 9	
33c	Vision of the bent tree		52	3 8	
34a	Visit to the tombs of the Apostles			4 1	
34a	Departure for the valley of Spoleto			4 1	
34b	Appearance of the man who gives them bread				
34c	Sojourn near the town of Orte				
35	To live among men or retire into solitude			4 2	
36a	Preaching tour of towns and villages		54a	4 5	
36b	People hasten to hear Francis		54b	12 8	

	1 CELANO	2C	3S	LM	Others
37a	The face of the region is changed			4 5	
37b	Francis gives a rule of life to all		54c	4 7	LP 67
38a	"Our fraternity is the Order of Friars Minor."			6 5	
38b	Their virtues: humility		41		
38c	Their virtues: charity				
39b	Their virtues: obedience				
39c	Their virtues: poverty		to	4 7	
39d	Their virtues: work				
40a	Their virtues: patience			4 7	
40b	Their virtues: prayer				
40c	Their virtues: mortification				
41	Their virtues: peace				
42a	Rivo Torto		45	4 3	
42b	Immersion in a ditch full of ice		55a	5 3	
43	Emperor Otto passes through the region				
44	Driven away by an ass		55b	4 3	
45	"We adore you, O Christ, in all the churches."		37b	4 3	3C / 3c
46	Respect for their Father Confessor			4 4	
47	The fiery chariot			4 4	
48a	Francis' knowledge of those absent			4 10	
48b	Presence at the chapter of Arles	44b		11 9	3C 3b / Fior 27
49	Brother Riccerio delivered from a temptation			5 1	
51	Francis' frugality at his repasts		15	5 1	
52a	His manner of sleeping			5 1	
52b	"Come and see a glutton."			6 2	LP 39 / Fior 3
53	"I order you to revile me harshly."			6 1	
54	Francis confessed his faults openly				
55	He tries to reach Syria, and multiplication of food			9 5	3C 33
56	His trip to Spain			9 6	

	1 CELANO	2C	3S	LM		Others	
57a	Return to the Portiuncula and departure for Syria			9	7	Fior	24
57b	He preaches before the Sultan			12	3	3C	20
58	Sermon to the birds at Bevagna			12	4	3C	21
59	Silences the swallows at Alviano			8	8	3C	29
60a	Frees a rabbit at Greccio					3C	30
60b	The wild rabbit at the lake of Perugia						
61a	Returns a fish to the lake of Rieti			8	8	3C	24
61b	Water changed into wine at Sant' Urbano			5	10	3C	17
62	Preaching at Ascoli						
63a	Blessed bread cures illnesses					3C	19
63b	Happy delivery of a pregnant woman near Arezzo			12	11	3C	108
64	Cures effected by his cord			12	11	3C	19
65	Cure of a crippled child at Toscanella			12	9	3C	175
66	Cure of a paralytic at Narni			12	9	3C	176
67a	Cure of a blind woman at Narni			12	10	3C	121
67b	Cure of a woman's gnarled hands at Gubbio			12	10	3C	177
68	Cure of an epileptic brother			12	11	3C	195
69	An exorcism at San Gemini			12	10	3C	155
70a	An exorcism at Citta de Castello			12	10	3C	156
70b	Miracles manifest sanctity, but do not make it		1				
71	Love of solitude			3	10		
72	Conflicts with the Devil			10	3		
73	A sermon before the pope and cardinals	25					
74a	Cardinal Ugolino, protector of the Order						
74b	Meeting at Florence						
75	The Cardinal dissuades Francis from going to France	83		8	5	LP	82
76a	Compassion toward the poor and rivalry with them	85		8	5		
76b	A brother who spoke ill of a poor man			8	6	LP	89
77	Compassion for lambs						

	1 CELANO	2C	3S	LM	Others
78	A sheep bought and given to the religious of St. Severin				
79	Another story of lambs	165			
80a	Love of all creatures and praise of the Creator			8 6	
80b	Worms . . . bees				
81	Flowers . . . all nature				
82	Respect for pieces of paper with writing on them			10 6	
83	Physical and moral portrait				
84	Directions for the crib at Greccio			10 7	
85	Christmas night at Greccio			10 7	
86	Francis sings the Gospel and preaches			10 7	
87	Cures effected by the hay of the crib			10 7	3C 17
88a	Prologue of Book Two				
88b	Date of the death of St. Francis		68a		
89	Francis' progress in perfection				
91a	Departure for La Verna			13 1	
91b	Summary of his philosophy			12 2	
92	Consulting of the book of the Gospels				
93	The answer received			13 2	
94	Apparition of the Seraph	137		13 3	3C 4
95a	Description of the stigmata				3C 4
95b	The wounds seen during his lifetime				
96	Francis hides his secrets				
97	His infirmities increase				
98a	But do not stop his apostolic work			14 1	
98b	Brother Elias orders him to consult a doctor			14 1	
99	Sojourn at Rieti, near Cardinal Ugolino		69	13 3	3C 4
100	Francis predicts the Cardinal will be pope		67		Fior 18
101	The Cardinal's affection for Francis				
102	Virtues of four companions who cared for Francis				

1627

	2 CELANO	LP	SP	LM	Others
67	Better to strip the altar of the Blessed Virgin			7 4	
68	Money transformed into a serpent			7 5	
69	Poverty in garments		15		
70	Those who depart from poverty will fall into need				
71	Praise for those who seek alms	67	26	7 8	
72a	Francis' example in begging alms	60a	22d	7 7	
72b	"I will not give up the heritage of poverty."	60d	22f	7 7	
73	A meal with the bishop of Ostia	61	23	7 7	
74	Encouragement to seek alms	3	18		
75a	Do not hesitate to go begging	62a	23g		
75b	Brother "Fly"	62b	24	5 6	
76	Francis kisses the shoulder of a brother carrying alms	63	25		
77	Some knights persuaded to seek alms	59	22	7 10	
78	A piece of capon changed into a fish				
80	Conditions for admittance to the Order			7 3	
81	Brother "Fly" gives his property to relatives	20		7 3	
82	Vision concerning poverty				
83	Compassion with the poor and rivalry with them	88	17	8 5	1C 76a
84	Meeting one who was poorer	89	37	7 6	
85	A brother who spoke ill of a poor man		29	8 5	1C 76b
86	A mantle given to an old woman at Celano		30	8 5	
87	A mantle given to a poor man at Siena		31		
88	A mantle given to a poor man at Cortona		32		
89	A mantle given to a poor man at Colle				
90	Francis gives a part of his tunic to a poor man	56	38		
91	A copy of the New Testament given away	52	33	7 6	2C 196
92	A mantle given to an old woman at Rieti				
93	Apparition of three women				

2 CELANO	LP	SP	LM	Others
94c His conduct when visited by the Lord.			10 4	
95a Speaking with his Lord.	95	94	10 4	
96 Piety at the recitation of the divine office.			10 6	
97 A little vase which distracted him.			10 6	
98 Ecstasy at Borgo San Sepolcro.			10 2	
99 Behavior after prayer.			10 4	
100 The bishop of Assisi deprived of speech.	6		10 5	
101 A priest for whom Francis prayed.	36		10 5	
102 The knowledge and memory of Francis.			11 1	
103 He expounds a saying of Ezechiel.		53	11 2	
104 He explains obscure words to a cardinal.				
105 He answers a brother who urged reading.	38			
106 Vision of swords and conversion of Brother Pacifico.			4 9	
107 Testimony of a doctor concerning Francis' preaching.				
108 The demons of Arezzo.	81		6 9	
109 Vision of golden cross and vocation of Sylvester.			3 5	
110 A brother freed from a demon.				
111 The wicked sow that ate a lamb.			8 6	
112 Avoid familiarity with women.			5 5	
113a Parable of the two messengers.		86		
113b The Devil can make a hair into a beam.	96a	95c	5 5	
114a We must fear to look upon a bride of Christ.		86e		
114b Converse with women only to give good advice.			5 5	
115 "The mountain is your temptation."	21	99		
116 Temptation to lust.			5 4	
117 Seven snowmen.			5 4	
118 The good coming from temptations.				
119 Attacks of demons in the palace of a cardinal.	92	67	6 10	
121 A brother who wanted to be court chaplain.				

2 CELANO

		LP	SP	LM	Others
148	Francis and Dominic opposed to making friars bishops		43a	6 5	
149	Apostrophe to those unfaithful to this humility		43f		
150	Friendship of Francis and Dominic				
151	Obedient to a novice of one hour made guardian	106	46	6 4	
152	Obedient like a corpse		48	6 4	
153	Rarely command in virtue of vow of obedience		49		
154	Capuche of a brother thrown into the fire			6 11	
155	How a brother retracted abusive words		51	8 3	
156	"Cursed be those who destroy. . . ."			8 3	
157	Time will come when Order will have bad reputation	86	70		
158	But the Order will never die out		81a		
159	When one is a servant of God and when not		74		
160	Penance for idle words	78	82	5 6	
161	Against idleness		75	5 6	
162	Lament over idle and gluttonous brothers				
163a	Qualities of a preacher	70c			
163b	"We must honor the theologians. . . ."	71a	72c		
164a	Souls converted by the prayers of simple brothers	71c	72h	8 2	
164b	Parable of the sterile woman			8 2	
164c	Preachers who speak with elegant words				
165	Love of creatures	51	118	9 1	1C 80
166	The fire which gave Francis no pain	48	115	5 9	
167	The friendly waterfowl			8 8	
168	The falcon at La Verna			8 10	
169	The bees which used Francis' earthen vessel				
170	The pheasant			8 10	
171	The tree cricket	84		8 9	
172	Francis' love of souls			9 4	
173	A model for the Order	76	71c	9 4	

	2 CELANO	LP	SP	LM	Others
174	Francis' solicitude for his sons.		42		
175	Compassion for the sick.	5	28		
176	A sick brother's longing for grapes.				
177	Compassion for those ill in spirit.				
178	The Spanish friars.				
179	Against those who live evilly in hermitages.				
180	All are sons of the same mother.				
181	His tunic given to two brothers from France.	53	34	8 4	
182	Punishment of detractors.				
183	They try to appear good, not become good.		80a		
184	"Who can succeed you as minister general?"		80d		
185	Portrait of a minister general.				
187	Qualities of a minister provincial.		41		
188a	"Who are the ones who took the Order out of my hands?"				
188b	Why Francis did not have them removed from office.				
189	True simplicity.	19			
190	Brother John the Simple.		57		Fior 18
191	"We have promised great things. . . ."				
193	A small tonsure.				
194	Learned clerics must renounce all possessions.				
195a	Seek learning with moderation.	70c	69b	7 2	
195b	Time will come when knowledge is an occasion of ruin.	70d	72d	11 1	
195c	A lay brother who wanted a psalter.	72	4		
195d	Francis appears to a preaching brother.		69c	9 1	
196a	"For the love of God. . . ."	54a	35a		
196b	Francis wanted to cut up his tunic to aid a poor man.	54b	35b		
197	Devotion to the angels.			9 3	
198	Devotion to our Lady.	110c	114b	9 3	

	2 CELANO	LP	SP	LM		Others	
200a	"No one should be hungry on Christmas Day."	110b	114a	7	1	3S	15
200a	The great want of the Virgin Mother of Christ.			7	1		
200b	Poverty, the special way to salvation.			9	2		
201a	Devotion to the Body of Christ.	80a	65c				
201b	Francis' love of France.	79b	65b				
201c	He wished to provide precious pyxes.	80b	65e				
201d	"Wait, St. Lawrence!"						
202	Devotion to the relics of the saints.			6	7		
203	Devotion to the Cross.						
204	Solicitude for the welfare of the Poor Ladies.	45	90				
205	Why he visited them only rarely.						
206	Reprimand of those going unnecessarily to convents.						
207	A silent sermon to the Poor Ladies.						
208a	Praise of the Rule.		77				
208b	A brother who carried the Rule on his person.						
209a	The Rule: one host made of many crumbs.			4	11		
209b	No place for laziness.			14	1		
210	The care of the body.						
212	Our Sister Suffering.						
213	The Canticle of the Creatures.	43b	100	14	3		
214	Placed naked on the naked ground.			14	4		
215	A borrowed tunic.			14	5		
216	Blessing upon the whole Order.						
217a	Recalling the Last Supper.	117a	88a				
217b	Our Sister Death.		88c				
218	Vision of Brother Augustine.			14	6		
219	Francis appears to a brother.						
220	He appears to the bishop of Assisi.			14	6		
221	Prayer of Companions to St. Francis.						

III. MAJOR LIFE BY ST. BONAVENTURE

			1C	2C	3S	Others
		Prologue	1			
1	1	Birth at Assisi, bad education	17d		3d	
—	—	A poor man sent away	17d		3e	
—	—	Never refuse an alms asked for love of God	2	5a	2b	
—	—	His charming manners, his qualities				
1	2	An Assisian spreads his mantle at Francis' feet	3			
—	—	Sickness		5b	6a	
1	3	Francis clothes a poor knight	5	6a	5	
—	—	Vision of arms		6b	6b	
1	4	"Whom can you serve better?"				
—	—	Beginning of his conversion	6	9c	11b	
1	5	Francis embraces a leper	17b	11	14	
—	—	Compassion for the Passion of Christ		8a	8d	LB 37
1	6	Service of lepers		8d	8f	
—	—	Generosity toward beggars		8b	10a	
—	—	Pilgrimage to Rome		10	13c	
2	1	The crucifix of San Damiano		8	16a	
—	—	Cloth sold at Foligno		9	16b	
2	2	Sojourn at San Damiano		10	16d	
—	—	Francis hides from his father		11	17b	
—	—	Returns to Assisi		12	17f	
—	—	His father locks him up		13	18b	
—	—	His mother frees him		14	19b	
2	4	His father cites him before the bishop's court	16a	12b	19d	
—	—	Renunciation before the bishop	16b			
2	5	"I am the herald of the Great King."				
2	6	A servant in a monastery				
—	—	Service to the lepers				
—	—	Cure of a leper of Spoleto				

		MAJOR LIFE BY ST. BONAVENTURE	1C	2C	3S	Others
2	7	Repair of San Damiano..................	18a	11c	24a	
—	—	A beggar, among his old companions...		13b		
2	8	Repair of St. Peter's......	21a			
—	—	Arrival at the Portiuncula..........	21b	18b	32a	LP
—	—	The very name of Portiuncula, a prophecy.	106		56a	8
—	—	The vision told of the place.........		20	56b	
3	1	Symbolism of the repair of three churches.......	37b			
3	2	The Gospel of the feast of St. Mathias.......	22		25b	
—	—	First sermons.........	23a		25d	
3	3	"May the Lord give you peace!".......	23b		26a	LP 67d
3	3	Vocation of Bernard of Quintavalle.....	24	15	27	Fior 2
3	4	Vocation of Giles and four others.........	25		32b	
3	5	Vision of the golden cross and vocation of Sylvester.		109	30	Fior 2
3	6	"Have pity on me a sinner!".............	26			
—	—	"I see an immense multitude coming to join us."	27		36	
3	7	A new recruit, and sending out of the brothers......	29			
—	—	Return of the brothers........	30			
—	—	Four new recruits........	31			
3	8	The First Rule.........	32a			
—	—	Vision of the bent tree.......	33c		53	
3	9	Request for approbation.......	33b			
—	—	Cardinal John of St. Paul.......	32c	16a	47b	
—	—	"Pray Christ to reveal his will to me through you."		16b	49b	
3	10	Parable of the woman in the desert......		17b	50	
—	—	Vision of the Lateran, and papal approbation.......			51b	
—	—	Tonsure............			52	
4	1	Departure for the valley of Spoleto......	34a			
—	—	Appearance of the man who gave them bread....	34b			

		MAJOR LIFE BY ST. BONAVENTURE	1C	2C	3S	Others
5	4	A temptation to lust		116		
	—	Seven snowmen		117		
5	5	Guarding the senses				
	—	Avoid familiarity with women	43a	112		
	—	No conversations with women except to give advice		114b		
5	6	Out of a hair the Devil makes a beam		113b	96a	SP 95c
	—	Against idleness		129a		
	—	Brother Ass		75b	26b	SP 24
	—	Brother Fly		161		SP 75
	—	Work to avoid idleness		160	78	SP 82
	—	Penance for idle words		22	1	SP 27a
5	7	A very young brother			46	
5	8	The cause of his eye trouble			48	
5	9	The fire which did not hurt him		166		SP 115
5	10	Water changed to wine at Sant' Urbano	61b			
5	11	The angelic lute		126	24	
5	12	Darkness dispelled in the vicinity of the Po				
6	1	Francis' humility		140a		
	—	"I order you to revile me strongly."	53			Fior 3
6	2	How he confessed his own faults	54			
	—	"Come and see a glutton."	52b	133	39	SP 61
6	3	"I can still have sons and daughters."		134	104	SP 45
6	—	Against boastfulness				
6	4	"I will obey a novice of one hour made guardian."		151	106	SP 46
	—	"Like a corpse."		152		SP 48

		MAJOR LIFE BY ST. BONAVENTURE	1C	2C	LP	Others
7	10	Francis tells the knights to go begging			59	SP 22
7	11	A miracle for a doctor at Rieti		77		
7	12	Water brought from a rock		44		
7	13	Food multiplied during a voyage		46		
—		Exhortation to confidence		55		
8	1	Praise of Francis' piety				
8	2	Souls converted by the prayers of simple brothers		164a	71a	SP 72c
—		Parable of the sterile woman		164b	71c	SP 72h
8	3	Francis' joy because of the reputation of saintly friars		155d		SP 51d
—		"Cursed be those who destroy. . . ."		156	17	
—		But the Order will never die out		158	86	SP 81a
8	4	Punishment of detractors		182		
8	5	Compassion for the afflicted	76a	83		
—		A brother who spoke ill of a poor man	76b	85	89	SP 37
—		A mantle given to a poor man at Siena		87		SP 30
8	6	Francis gives to the poor what is given to him	76a	165		
—		Love of all creatures and praise of the Creator	80	111		
—		Compassion for lambs	77			
—		The wicked sow				
8	7	The sheep given to Francis				
8	8	The rabbit freed at Greccio	60	167		
—		The water fowl				
8	9	Francis returns a fish to the lake of Rieti	61a			
—		Silence imposed on the birds near Venice				
8	10	The tree cricket		84		
—		The pheasant	171			
—		The birds at La Verna	170			
—		The falcon at La Verna		168		
—		The wolves of Greccio		35		

		MAJOR LIFE BY ST. BONAVENTURE	1C	2C	LP	Others
9	1	"For the love of God...."		196a	54a	SP 35a
—	—	From the creatures, mount to God the Creator		165a		
9	2	Devotion to Jesus Crucified		201a	80a	SP 65c
9	—	Devotion to the Body of Christ		198		
9	3	Devotion to our Lady		197		
9	—	Devotion to the angels				
9	4	Devotion to SS. Peter and Paul		172	76	SP 71a
9	—	Love of souls		173		
9	5	An example for the Order	55			
9	6	Attempt to reach Syria	56			
9	7	Attempt to reach Morocco	57a			
9	8	Departure for Syria				
9	—	Accompanied by Brother Illuminatus		57b		Fior 24
9	9	He goes among the Saracens and preaches to the Sultan				
9	—	Significance of this episode				
10	1	The fervor of Francis		94a		
10	2	His faithful response to the Lord's visits		95c		
10	—	Ecstasy at Borgo San Sepolcro		98		
10	3	Love of solitude	71	122	23a	SP 59
10	—	Diabolical persecutions	72	95a		
10	4	Speaking with his God and his All				
10	—	An ecstasy		99a		
10	—	Conduct after prayer		94c		
10	—	Conduct when the Spirit visited him		99b		
10	—	Leaving in God's hands the treasure of spiritual consolations		100	6	
10	5	The bishop of Assisi deprived of speech		101	36	
10	—	A priest for whom Francis prayed		96	95	SP 94
10	6	Piety during recitation of the divine office		97		
10	—	A vase which caused distraction at prayer				

		MAJOR LIFE BY ST. BONAVENTURE	1C	2C	LP	Others
10	7	Respect for pieces of paper containing writing	82			
	—	Plans for the crib at Greccio	84			
	—	Christmas night at Greccio	85			
	—	Francis sings the Gospel and preaches	86			
	—	Cures effected by the hay of the crib	87			
11	1	The knowledge and memory of Francis		102		
	—	The quest of knowledge must be moderate		195		
11	2	Explanation of a saying from Ezechiel		103		
	—	Francis' knowledge of the Scriptures		102		
11	3	His spirit of prophecy		27		
	—	Prediction of disaster at Damietta		30		
11	4	Prediction of the death of a knight of Celano				
11	5	Canon Gedeon		41	58	
11	6	Prediction of the conversion of a husband		38	27	
11	7	Reading the conscience of a theologian				
11	8	Grumbling Brother Leonard		31	30	
11	9	Brother Riccerio freed from a temptation	49	44b		
	—	Blessing of Brother Leo		49		
11	10	A brother who was thought to be a saint		28	91	SP 102
	—	Other predictions	48a			
11	11	A brother who refused to obey the vicar	34			Fior 23
11	12	Francis leaves his cell to bless two brothers		45	31	
11	13	A brother who scandalized a young brother	39			Fior 31
11	14	Significance of this spirit of prophecy				
12	1	To live in a retreat or to preach to the people?	91b			Fior 16
12	2	Summary of Francis' philosophy				
	—	The answers of Clare and Sylvester				Fior 16
12	3	The sermon to the birds at Bevagna	58			
12	4	Silence imposed on the swallows at Alviano	59			

MAJOR LIFE BY ST. BONAVENTURE

			1C	2C	LP	Others
13	8	Some eye-witnesses of the stigmata	138			
13	9	The brother who saw the wound in Francis' side				
13	10	The stigmata: seal of Francis' sanctity				
14	1	Seven visions of the Cross culminating on La Verna	98a			
		From this time on, crucified with Christ	103			
		"Let us begin to serve God."		209b		
		No place for laziness	97			
14	2	The flesh completely submissive to the spirit				
		Increase of Francis' sufferings				
		Prayer for the time of sickness				
14	3	Lying naked upon the naked earth		214		
14	4	The loan of a tunic		215		
				217b		
14	5	As long as it takes to walk a mile		216		
		Blessing of the whole Order		217a		
		Recalling the Last Supper				
14	6	Death of Francis	110b			
		He appears to a brother	110b			
		Vision of Brother Augustine		218		
		Francis appears to the bishop of Assisi		220		
		The flight of the larks over his death chamber			117a	SP 88a
15	1	The glory of Francis after his death			110a	3C 32
15	2	All can see his stigmata	113			
15	3	The brothers experience sorrow and joy				3S 70
15	4	Crowds come running				
		A knight named Jerome has doubts about the stigmata				
15	6	The corpse is taken to San Damiano	116			
		Burial in St. George's Church	118			
15	6	After his death Francis works miracles everywhere	120a			

		1C	2C	LP	Others
MAJOR LIFE BY ST. BONAVENTURE					
15 —	His renown reaches the ears of the pope...............	121			
15 7	Investigation of his life...............	124			
15 8	Canonization...............	126			3S 71
15 9	Universal glory of St. Francis...............				

	V. THREE COMPANIONS	1C	2C	LM	Others
1	Letter to the minister general				
2a	At first called John		3a	1 1	
2b	Opinions concerning him, and prophecy of his mother		3b	1 1	
2d	His prodigality, and his frivolity	2a			
3a	His courtesy				
3b	Courteous and liberal towards the poor				
3d	A poor man sent away	17c	5a		
3e	Never refuse an alms requested for love of God	17d	4		
4	A prisoner at Perugia				
5a	Military plans	4c			
5b	Vision of arms	5	6a	1 3	
6a	He clothes a poor knight		5b	1 2	
6b	"Who can be better for you?"		6b	1 3	
7a	King of the youth of Assisi		7		
7d	"Are you thinking of getting married?"		7b		
8a	Beginning of conversion	4a			
8b	Solitary meditation	6a			
8d	Benefactor of the poor		8a	1 6	
8f	And of needy priests		8d	1 6	
9	The table of a family laden with bread for the poor				
10a	Pilgrimage to Rome		8b	1 6	
10d	God alone guides him on his way				
11a	"What you have loved carnally. . . ."				
11b	Embrace of a leper	17b	9b	1 5	
11d	Service of the lepers	17a	9c	1 6	
12a	His confidant	6d	9d		
12c	The hunchbacked woman				
12e	Praying in a grotto	6c	9b		

	THREE COMPANIONS	1C	2C	LM	Others
13b	"Are you thinking of taking a wife?"	7b	10	2	
13c	The crucifix of San Damiano.		11c	1	
13e	Oil for the lamp before the crucifix.		11a		LP 37b
14a	Contemplating the Passion.		11b		LP 37c
14c	"I must weep over the Passion of my Lord!"				
15a	Frugality: "Our Sister Ashes is chaste."	51		5	
16a	Cloth sold at Foligno.	8		2	
16b	Sojourn at San Damiano.	9			
16d	He hides from his father.	10		2	
17b	Returns to Assisi.	11		2	
17f	His father locks him up.	12		2	
18b	His mother frees him.	13		2	
19a	His father cites him before the bishop's court.	15		3	
19d	Renunciation before the bishop.	15	12b	3	
21	"Who will give me one stone. . ."			4	
22	"You will not always find such a priest. . ."		14		
23a	"You will bless. . ."		12a		
23d	"A pennysworth of sweat. . ."		12c		
24a	Begging among his former companions.		13b		
24c	He predicts coming of Poor Ladies to San Damiano.	18	13c		
25a	He wears the garment of a hermit.	21			
25b	The Gospel of the feast of St. Mathias.	22		3 1	
25d	First sermons.	23a		3 2	
26a	"May the Lord give you peace!"	23b		3 2	LP 67d
26b	A precursor in this apostolate of peace.				
26c	First fruits of his preaching.	23b		3 3	
27	Vocation of Bernard of Quintavalle.	24	15	3 5	Fior 2
30	Vocation of Sylvester.		109a	3 5	Fior 2
31b	Vision of the golden cross.		109b		

	THREE COMPANIONS	1C	2C	LM	Others
32a	Begins to reside at the Portiuncula.				
32b	Vocation of Giles.	25		2, 8	
32c	First sending out of companions.			3, 4	
33b	"Our family is like a fisherman casting out his net."	28			
33c	Exhortation to the people.				
34	Diverse opinions of his hearers.				
35a	Three new brothers.	25		3, 4	
35b	"If we have possessions, we will need arms. . . ."				
36	"Do not be disturbed by our small number. . . ."	27		3, 6	
37b	"We adore you, O Christ, in all the churches. . . ."	45		4, 3	
37c	"We are penitents from Assisi. . . ."				
38b	Hospitality received at Florence.				
40	But often badly treated.	40a		4, 7	
41	Joy at the return to the Portiuncula.				
42	A brother protects his brother.				
43	Making reparation for offenses; true poverty.				LP 55
44	Brother Giles gives his mantle to a poor man.				
45	Poverty and joy.				
46	The walk to Rome.	32b		3, 8	
47	Cardinal John of St. Paul.	32c		3, 9	
48	Offers himself as intermediary.	33a			
49a	Papal approbation.	33b			
49b	"Pray God to reveal his will to me through you."		16a	3, 9	
50	Parable of the woman in the desert.		16b	3, 9	
51b	Vision of the Lateran.		17b	3, 10	
51e	Approbation of the Rule.		17b	3, 10	
52	Commitment to obedience; tonsure; visit of Apostles' tombs.	34a		3, 10	
53	Vision of the bent tree.	35c		3, 8	
54a	Preaching tour through towns and villages.	36a		4, 5	

1653

	LEGEND OF PERUGIA	2C	SP	LM	Others
54a	"For the love of God. . ."	196a	35a	9	
54b	A piece cut from his tunic	196b	35b	1	
55	Brother Giles gives his mantle to a poor man		36		3S 44
56	Copy of New Testament given away	91	38		
57	Cure of cattle at Sant' Elia			13 6	3C 18
58	Canon Gedeon	41	22a	11 5	
59	Francis persuades some knights to go begging	77	22c	7 10	
60	He sets an example for seeking alms	72	23a	7 7	
61	A repast with the bishop of Ostia	73	23g	7 7	
62a	Do not hesitate to go begging	75a	24		
62b	Brother Fly	75b	25		
63	Francis kisses the shoulder of a begging brother	76		5 6	
64	Brother Elias finds fault with dying Francis' joy		121		
65	"What do you think of my dropsical condition?"		122		
66	Brother Riccerio asks Francis concerning his intention		2		
67a	"They shall be called Friars Minor."		26a	6 5	1C 38
67d	"May the Lord give you peace!"		26e	3 2	3S 26a
68	Francis does not enforce strict observance of poverty		2c		
69	A minister who wanted to keep books	62b	3		
70a	A novice who wanted to have a psalter	195c	4a		
70b	Do not be avid for learning		72a		
70c	"We must honor the theologians."	163b			
70d	Do not abandon your vocation under pretext of edification	195b	72b		
71a	More is accomplished by the prayers of simple brothers	164a	72h	8 2	
71b	Parable of the sterile woman	164b			
72	Reply to a novice who wanted to have a psalter		4b		
73	"Bring me my breviary."	195c	4d		
74	A Friar Minor may have only a tunic as stated in the Rule		4g		
75	"Why do you tolerate these abuses?"		71a		

	LEGEND OF PERUGIA	2C	SP	LM	Others
76	"My office is a spiritual one only."		71c		
77	Opposition to recommendations on poverty of houses.	160	11	5 6	
78	Penance for idle words.	201b	82		
79	Francis wishes to go to France.	201	65a		
80a	Reverence for the Body of Christ.		65c		
80b	"Our cell is our Brother Body."		65f		
81	The demons of Arezzo.	108			
82	The bishop of Ostia dissuades Francis from going to France.	145b	65g	6 9	1C 75
83	"We no longer want you to rule over us."	171	64	6 5	
84	The tree cricket.			8 9	
85	"I must be a model for all."	158	16	8 3	
86	The Order will never die out.		81a		
87	"My mission is to give a good example."		81c		
88	Meeting a man who was poorer.	84	17	7 6	1C 76 Fior 26
89	A brother who reviled a poor man.	85	37	8 5	
90	Conversion of the robbers.		66		
91	A brother who was thought to be a saint.	28	102	11 10	
92	Attacks of demons in a cardinal's palace.	119	67	6 10	
93	Lent in honor of St. Michael.				
94	A feather pillow.	64	98	5 2	
95	Francis' piety at the recitation of the divine office.	96	94	10 6	
96a	"Out of a hair the Devil makes a beam."	113b	95c	5 6	
96b	"Give Brother Ass his feed."	129	97		
97a	The demons are powerless against spiritual joy.	125	95a		
97b	Reprimand given to a sad brother.	120	96a		
98	Francis predicts glory that will be his after death.	109			
99	Blessing of the city of Assisi.		124		
100	"Praise to You, for our Sister Death!"				
101	Last visit of "Brother Giacoma."		112		3C 37

	LEGEND OF PERUGIA	2C	SP	LM	Others
102	Serving the lepers		44		1C 38
103	Humble reply to the bishop of Terni	141	45a		
104	"I can still have sons and daughters."	133	45c		
105	Francis resigns from office of minister general	143	39		
106	"A novice of one hour appointed as my guardian."	151	46	6 4	
107	Blessing of Brother Bernard		107a		
108	Prediction concerning Brother Bernard	48	107d		
109	Clare sees the body of Francis after death		108		
110a	Flight of the larks over Francis' death chamber		113c	14 6	3C 32
110b	"No one should suffer hunger on Christmas Day."	200	114		
110d	Our Sister Lark		113b		
111	Do not be a thief of alms		12		
112	Possessing nothing, even in common		13		
113	Christ approves the new redaction of the second Rule		1		
114	Chapter of Mats: "Not the rules of Augustine and Benedict."		68	4 10	Fior 18
115	No privilege of preaching		50		
116	Three reproaches made by Christ		52		
117a	Blessing of all the brothers	216	88a	14 5	
117b	Recalling of the Last Supper	217	88b	14 5	

	MIRROR OF PERFECTION	2C	LP	LM	Others
22a	Francis persuades some knights to go begging	77	59	7 10	
22c	He sets an example for seeking alms	72	60	7 7	
23a	A repast with the bishop of Ostia	73	61	7 7	
23g	Do not hesitate to go begging	75a	62a	6	
24	Brother Fly	75b	62b	5	
25	Francis kisses the shoulder of a begging brother	76	63	6 5	1C 38
26a	"They shall be called Friars Minor."		67a		3S 26
26e	"May the Lord give you peace!"	22	67d	5 7	
27a	"I am dying of hunger. . . ."	21	1		
27d	Rigor of discipline among the first brothers	176	2		
28	A sick brother has a longing for grapes	86	5	8 5	
29	A mantle given to an old woman at Celano	87			
30	A mantle given to a poor man at Siena	88			
31	A mantle given to a poor man at Cortona	89			
32	A mantle given to a poor man at Colle	92	52		
33	A mantle given to an old woman at Rieti	181	53		
34	Francis gives his tunic to two brothers from France	196a	54a	9 1	3S 44
35	"For the love of God."	85	55	8 5	1C 76
36	Brother Giles gives his mantle to a poor man	143	89		
37	A brother who reviled a poor man	143	105		
38	A copy of the New Testament given away	144	105		
39	Francis resigns from the office of minister general				
40	He gives up having special companions	188a			
41	"Who are the ones who have taken the Order away from me?"	175			
42	Compassion for the sick	148		6 5	
43a	Francis and Dominic opposed to making friars bishops	150			
43f	Friendship of Francis and Dominic				
44	Serving the lepers		102		
45a	Humble reply to the bishop of Terni	141	103		1C 38

	MIRROR OF PERFECTION	2C	LP	LM	Others
45c	"I can still have sons and daughters."	133	104	6 3	
46	"A novice of one hour appointed as my guardian. . . ."	151	106	6 4	
47	How to obey.	51b		6	
48	"Like a corpse. . . ."	152		6 4	
49	Only rarely command in virtue of the vow of obedience	153			
50	No special privilege for preaching		115	8 3	
51	How two brothers became reconciled	155		8	
52	Three reproaches from Christ		116	11 2	
53	Explanation of a saying by Ezechiel	103		11	
54	Submissive to the clergy	146	15		
55a	Establishment at the Portiuncula	18	8		3S 56a
55i	How the brothers lived there	19	9		
56	Francis sweeps the churches		18		
57	Brother John the Simple	190	19		
58	Francis eats with a leper		22		
59	Temptation at San Pietro de Bovara	122	23a	10 3	1C 72
60	The throne of Lucifer	123c	23c	6 6	
61	"Come and see a glutton. . . ."		39		1C 52
62a	Food prepared with lard during Lent	131	40a		
62c	A fox-skin patch	130	40c		
63	A feeling of vainglory while giving an alms	132	41		
64	"We no longer want you to rule over us!"	145b	83	6 5	
65a	Francis wishes to go to France	201b	79		
65c	Reverence for the Body of Christ	201a	80a		
65e	Precious ciboria and host-irons sent with friars	201c	80b		
65f	"Our cell is our Brother Body. . . ."		80e		1C 74
65g	The bishop of Ostia persuades Francis not to go to France		62		Fior 26
66	Conversion of the robbers		90		
67	Attacks of demons in a cardinal's palace	119	92	6 10	

A

FRANCIS OF ASSISI
RESEARCH BIBLIOGRAPHY

Comprehensive for 1939-1969
Selective for Older Materials

compiled by

RAPHAEL BROWN

1667

EXPLANATORY NOTE

A few brief notes on the sources and *technical style* of this Bibliography may be helpful to its users.

In accordance with that law of research which states that one reference leads to another, it is based primarly, of course, on the data in its own 1575 items. Secondarily, naturally, on the excellent bibliographies listed under A1-A26, especially the invaluable wealth of materials in the *Collectanea Franciscan's Bibliographia Franciscana* (A2). Other useful sources have been the major religious encyclopedias: *Enciclopedia cattolica; Lexikon für Theologie und Kirche*, 2d ed.; *Dictionnaire d'histoire et de géographie ecclésiastiques* and *Dictionaire de spiritualité ascétique et mystique* (unfortunately neither has yet treated François d'Assise); and *Dictionnaire de théologie catholique*, especially its recent *Tables générales*. Still too new to be of much help, yet richly promising for the fuure are the *Bibliotheca Sanctorum* (E103), also to appear in English; *Dictionnaire de biographie française*; and *Neue deutsche Biographie*. No doubt the *New Catholic Encyclopedia*, with articles on Francis and Clare by Lothar Hardick, OFM, will become a standard reference work.

In addition, mention should be made of the major current national bibliographies: *Bibliografia nazionale italiana, Bibliographie de la France, Deutsche Nationalbibliographie* and *Deutsche Bibliographie, Das Schweizer Buch, Nieuwsblad voor de Boekhandel, Bibliographie de Belgique*, and *Libros del mes*; as well as the various national cumulations similar to our *Cumulative Book Index*. Not least in usefulness have been two union catalogs: the National Union Catalog in the Library of Congress, on cards and in recent years in published author and subject catalogs; and the Franciscan Union Catalog at St. Bonaventure University, St. Bonaventure, N. Y.

A careful perusal of the cumulative indexes of the following periodicals (see Abbreviations) has also been rewarding: AFH, EF, MF, & DSPU; but that of IF has not been available. Still more enriching has been a systematic coverage of their pages, as well as those of the other principal Franciscan historical journals (FF, FS, IF, & SF), especially for important reviews and abstracts, from 1969 back to beyond 1939

As to *bibliographical style*, perhaps to the annoyance of some users, the principles governing the editing of this Bibliography have been deliberately Franciscan: simplicity and economy. Hence the liberal use of *contractions*, e. g. Cap for O.F.M. Cap.; 13th for thirteenth century; & for and; and of *abbreviations*, not only for periodicals and monographic series, but also for place names in imprints and even for S(aint) F(rancis) (of) A(ssisi) — see lists below.

It is hoped that the user will be helped by the equally generous number of *cross-references*, usually indicated by cf (even after a period, to avoid any possible confusion with the frequent CF); as they will lead him to other important data on the subject. For the same reason, references to outstanding *reviews* (Rev:) and *abstracts* (Abs:) have been included, often with the name or initials of the reviewer. It must be stressed that these items will frequently include significant corrections of fact and additional references.

Lastly, a single *asterisk before* an entry number (e.g. *A266) indicates that the book or article contains a useful bibliography of older materials, while two asterisks before the entry number (e.g. **A7) are used only for major bibliographies or for works having a comprehensive bibliography. For a list of the latter, see the index under Bibliographies. (Asterisks after page numbers denote a separate pagination in certain CF volumes; see list in A2.)

In the Bibliography, Notes, Appendices, and new Introduction, the system adopted for *page references*, though somewhat unorthodox, could hardly be more simple and economical: C185:37-42, for instance, means pages 37-42 in item C185 in the Bibliography.

In the still chaotic realm of *capitalization*, the rule adopted (with almost exceptionless consistency) has been to follow the more or less standard practice of each language.

The *Bibliography Subject Index* will prove helpful in finding various subjects, but it does not cover authors. The Bibliography is not included in the Index at the end of the book.

The reader will also do well to study carefully the table of *Contents* of the Bibliography, as it is much more inclusive than the brief outline of the Bibliography in the general Table of Contents in the front of the book.

This Bibliography, comprehensive for 1939 to 1963, was originally published in O. Englebert, *Saint Francis of Assisi,* new translation by E. M. Cooper, revised and augmented by I. Brady O.F.M. and R. Brown, pp. 493-601 (Franciscan Herald Press, Chicago, 1965). It is presented here in a revised form. New entries, without code numbers, have been added to update it to the year 1969. Old entries retain their code numbers, even though some have been omitted and others have been reclassified.

BIBLIOGRAPHY

CONTENTS

A. DOCUMENTATION

1671

C. LIFE

D. SPIRITUALITY

E. ORDERS

A   DOCUMENTATION

I ABBREVIATIONS

1 NAMES & PLACES IN TITLES & IMPRINTS

A   Assisi, Assise
Ba   Barcelona
Brux   Bruxelles
Chi   Chicago
Dü   Düsseldorf
F   Francesco, Francis,
     François, Franciscus,
     Franziskus (not Franz)
FA   Francesco di Assisi,
     Francis of Assisi,
     François d'Assise
Fi   Firenze
Fr/Br   Freiburg im Breisgau
L   London
Man   Manchester, England
Mi   Milano
Milw   Milwaukee
NY   New York

P   Paris
Phil   Philadelphia
Q   Quaracchi
R   Roma
S   San, Sanctus, Saint, Sankt
SF   San Francesco, Saint Francis,
     Saint François, Sankt
     Franziskus, Sanctus
     Franciscus
SFA   SF with Assisi, Assise
SMA   Santa Maria degli Angeli
     (Assisi)
To   Torino
Tü   Tübingen
Ven   Venezia
Wa   Washington
We   Werl/Westfalen
Z   Zürich

AB   *Analecta Bollandiana*
Actus   *Actus Beati Francisci et Sociorum Ejus.* See A158
AF   *Analecta Franciscana.* Q, 1885-1941. 10v. See A133,
     A134a, A191, A193, A64.

Research Bibliography

AFH	*Archivum Franciscanum Historicum.* Q, 1908-. (OFM) With *AFH Indices tomorum 1-50 (1908-1957).* Q, 1960. 435p.
AFP	*Archivum Fratrum Praedicatorum*
Anonymus Perusinus	see A126.
AHR	*American Historical Review*
AIA	*Archivo ibero-americano.* Madrid, 1914—. (OFM)
AKG	*Archiv für Kulturgeschichte*
ALKG	*Archiv für Litteratur und Kirchengeschichte des Mittelalters.* Fr/Br, 1885-1900, 7v.
Ant	*Antonianum.* R, 1926—. (OFM)
AOFM	*Acta Ordinis Fratrum Minorum.* Q, R, 1882—. (OFM)
ASF	*Les amis de saint François.* P.
ASS	*Acta Sanctorum.* See A281.
Bartholi, *Tractatus*	see F247.
BF	*Bullarium Franciscanum.* See F109.
BISI	Instituto Storico italiano per il Medio Evo *Bollettino*
Bonaventure	*Legenda Maior.* See A74.
BSFS & BSFS-ES	British Society of Franciscan Studies Publications & Extra Series
BSS	*Bibliotheca Sanctorum.* See E103.
CC	*Civiltà cattolica*
CCM	*Cahiers de civilisation médiévale*
CED	*Collection d'études et de documents sur l'histoire religieuse et littéraire du moyen âge.* Paul Sabatier, ed. P, 1893-1909. 8v. See A151, F247, A158, A133.
I *Celano*	*Thomas of Celano, Vita Prima.* See A65
II *Celano*	*Thomas of Celano, Vita Secunda.* See A67.
III *Celano*	*Thomas of Celano, Tractatus de Miraculis.* See A68.
CF	*Collectanea Franciscana.* A, R, 1931—. (Cap) cf A2.
CHR	*Catholic Historical Review*
CISSA	Congresso internazionale di scienze storiche *Atti.* R, ·1904.
CISSR	X Congresso internazionale di scienze storiche *Relazioni.* Fi, 1955.
COCR	*Collectanea Ordinis Cisterciensium Reformatorum*
Conv	*Convivium*
CVF	*Cahiers de vie franciscaine*
DA	*Dissertation Abstracts*
DASP	Deputazione Abbruzese di storia patria *Bullettino*
DBI	*Dizionario biografico degli italiani*
DDC	*Dictionnaire de droit canonique*
DHGE	*Dictionnaire d'histoire et de géographie ecclésiastiques*
DSAM	*Dictionnaire de spiritualité ascétique et mystique*
DSPM	Deputazione di storia patria per le Marche *Atti e memorie*
DSPU	Deputazione di storia patria per l'Umbria *Bollettino;* for its 1895-1954 index, see F185.

Research Bibliography

DTC & DTC-TG	*Dictionnaire de théologie catholique*; & *DTC Tables générales*
EC	*Enciclopedia cattolica*
EF	*Etudes franciscaines.* P, 1899-1938; ns 1950—. (Cap) With *Table générale des EF 1909-1928.* P, 1932. 172p.
EHR	*English Historical Review*
EstF	*Estudios franciscanos.* Ba, 1907-1911 as *Revista de EstF*; 1923-1936 as *Estudis franciscans.* (Cap)
FEC	Franciscan Educational Conference, *Report of the Annual Meeting.* Wa, 1919—.
FF	*Frate Francesco.* A, R, 1924—; ns 1954—. (OFM)
FL	*Franciscaans Leven.*
FnSs	*Franciscan Studies.* St. Bonaventure, NY, 1924—; ns 1941—. (OFM)
FNV	Fortini, *Nova vita di SFA.* Mi, 1926. See A295.
FNV I-IV	Fortini, *Nova vita di SF.* A, 1959. See A296.
FQ	*Franziskanische Quellenschriften.* We, 1956—. 7v. (OFM) See A41, E191, E120, E140, A90, A132, A105.
FrFr	*La France franciscaine.* P, 1912-1939. 22v. (OFM)
FS	*Franziskanische Studien.* Münster, We, 1914—. (OFM)
GBB	Golubovich, *Biblioteca . . .* See C94.
Giano	*Chronica Fratris Jordani.* See A133.
Gratien, *Histoire*	see E23.
GWU	*Geschichte in Wissenschaft und Unterricht*
HJ	*Historiches Jahrbuch der Görresgesellschaft*
IF	*Italia francescana.* R, 1926—. (Cap) With *Indice generale (1926-1945).* R, 1945. 103p.
Laur	*Laurentianum.* R, 1960—. (Cap)
Legenda antiqua	Delorme's *Legenda antiqua de Pérouse.* See A148.
Lex Cap	*Lexicon Capuccinum.* See A12a.
Liber exemplorum	see A221.
Little Flowers	see Fioretti; English tr. A166.
LTK	*Lexikon für Theologie und Kirche.* 2 Aufl. Fr/Br, 1957—
LS	*Luce serafica.* Ravello (Salerno).
MA	*Moyen âge*
MAH	*Mélanges d'archeologie et d'historie de l'Ecole française de Rome*
MF	*Miscellanea Francescana.* Foligno, R, 1886—. (Conv) With *Indice dei primi XXXIII volumi (1886-1930).* R, 1935. lxxivp.
MFE	*Miscellanea Francesco Ehrle.* R, 1924. 3v.
MGH-SS	*Monumenta Germaniae Historica, Scriptores*
MS	*Medieval Studies*
NCE	*New Catholic Encyclopedia.* Articles of major importance only.
NRT	*Nouvelle revue théologique*

NYT	*New York Times*
OCH	*Opuscules de critique historique.* Paul Sabatier, ed. P, 1901-1919. 3v.
Opuscula	see A28.
OR	*Osservatore romano*
OS	*Oriente serafico.* SMA. (OFM)
QF	*Quellen und Forschungen aus Italienischen Archiven und Bibliotheken*
QSF	*Quaderni di spiritualità francescana.* SMA, 1961—. (OFM)
RB	*Revue bénédictine*
RF	*Revue franciscaine.* Montréal. (OFM)
RH	*Revue historique*
RHE	*Revue d'histoire ecclésiastique*
RHF	*Revue d'historie franciscaine.* P, 1924-1931. 8v.
RIS	*Rerum Italicarum Scriptores;* ed. Muratori.
RQ	*Römische Quartalschrift*
RSB	*Rivista storica benedettina*
RSCI	*Rivista di storia della Chiesa in Italia*
RSI	*Rivista storica italiana*
RSR	*Revue des sciences religieuses*
Sabatier, *Vie*	Englebert cites 1931 ed. See A305.
SC	*Scuola cattolica*
SF	*Studi francescani.* Fi, 1914—; 1903-1911 *La Verna.* (OFM)
SFA	*San Francesco d'Assisi.* A, 1920-1930. 10v. (Conv)
SintF	*Sint Franciscus.* Brummen, Holland, 1955—(ns.). (OFM)
SISF	Società internazionale di studi francescani in Assisi *Bollettino.* A, 1904—.
SM	*Studi medievali*
SMon	*Studia Monastica*
SP	**Studia Picena**
Spec	*Speculum*
Speculum	*Speculum Perfectionis.* See A151 & A152.
SRSP	Società romana di storia patria *Archivio*
TO	*Tertius Ordo.* R, 1939—. (Cap)
Trad	*Traditio*
Tres Socii	see A143.
Verba	see A123.
VM	*Vita Minorum.* Ven, 1929—. (OFM)
VP	*Vita e pensiero*
VS	*Vie spirituelle*
VV	*Verdad y vida.* Madrid, 1943—. (OFM)
WW	*Wissenschaft und Weisheit.* M.-Gladbach, 1934— (OFM)
ZAM	*Zeitschrift für katholische Theologie*
ZKT	*Zeitschrift für Aszese und Mystik*

II BIBLIOGRAPHIES

Bibliografia storica nazionale. R, 1939—. Indispensable. **A1
Bibliographia Franciscana, "Relationes de SF." In CF (1931)— & as supplements:

   1 (1931)   98-106, 239-240, 383-407 (for 1929-30);
   3 (1933)   436-459 (1931);
   5 (1935)   125-176 (1932-33);
   9 (1939)   120-152 (1934-35);
  10 (1940)   128-160 (1936-37);
VI 12 (1942) 9*-30* (1938-39) with separate pagination;
VII 18 (1948) 23*-50* (1940-46);
VIII 20 (1950) 48*-92* (1947-48);
  IX 22 (1952) 65*-84* (1949-50);
   X -[1955-1956] 62*-92* (1951-53) published separately;
  XI -[1963] 56-132 (1954-57)   **A2
 XII -[1968] 75-139 (1958-63)

BRLEK, Michael, OFM, "De historia fontium et institutorum OFM," Ant 31 (1956) 83-91. *A3

BROWN, Raphael, "A F of A Research Bibliography," in A 291: 493-601. "The most complete and systematic bibliography ever compiled on SF," AFH 60 (1967) 255.

DI FONZO, L. Conv, "Bibliographia Franciscana, VII," MF 50 (1950) 652-656. *A4

——, "Bibliografia," BSS V (1964) 1131-1150.

ENGLEBERT, Omer, *Vie de SFA* (P 1956) App. III, "Ouvrages français sur SF," p. 408-415. *A5

——, SFA (NY 1950) App. III, "English Works & Translations on SF & His Order before Sabatier's Life of SF (1894)," p.333-335. *A6

FACCHINETTI, V., OFM, *Guide bibliografiche. SFA.* R, 1928, xlviii, 352p. Rev. AFH 24 (1931) 274. **A7

FNV IV, 7-30. Regrettably not comprehensive. *A8

HERSCHER, Irenaeus, OFM. *Franciscan Literature, A Checklist.* St. Bonaventure, NY, 1958. viii, 148p. 9000 items in one author list. **A9

ILARINO DA MILANO, Cap, "La bibliografia francescana." In *Il libro e le biblioteche. Atti del primo Congresso bibliologico francescano internazionale* (R 1950) II, 183-220; & CF 19 (1949) 224-246. Rev: AFH 45 (1952) 193-210; FS 33 (1951) 319-322; CF IX, 35*. *A10

International Guide to Medieval Studies, A Quarterly Index to Periodical Literature. Darien, Conn., 1961—. **A11

Lexicon Capuccinum. R, 1951. xlvii, 1868 col. illus. Rev: FnSs 14 (1954) 114. *A12

LITTLE, A. G., "Guide pour les études franciscaines," EF 40 (1928) 517-533; 41 (1929) 64-78 (mis à jour par le P. Gratien). *A12a

MASSERON, Alexandre, & Marion A. Habig, OFM, *The Franciscans* (Chi 1959) App. II, "Bibliography of English Franciscana. I. SF," p.480-490. *A13

OOMS, H. J., *Bibliographia de bibliographia franciscana.* Brux, 1961. xxv, 81p. *A14

Research Bibliography

——, & Ermenegildo Frascadore, OFM, "Bibliografia delle bibliografie francescane," AFH 57 (1964) 311-366, 433-528; 58 (1965) 89-136, 417-536; 60 (1967) 116-209. And separately, Q, 1967, 423p. Crit. rev.: MF 68 (1968) 370-381. **A15

PALANDRI, E., OFM, "Rassegna bibliografica sanfrancescana dell'ultimo trentennio," SF 37 (1940) 161-231. Rev: CF 11 (1941) 493. *A16

PIANA, Celestino, OFM, "Le fonti medioevali della storia e del pensiero francescano nell'ultimo settantennio." In Istituto Storico Italiano per il Medio Evo, *La Pubblicazione delle fonti del medioevo europeo negli ultimi 70 anni (1883-1953)* (R 1954) 283-312; on SF: 286, 310. CF XI, 10. **A17

PITTOLET, C., "Bibliographie franciscaine de 1920 à 1926," RHF 3 (1926) 579-591. *A18

PIZZI, F., "Per l'unificazione della bibliografia francescana," SF 45 (1949) 163-166. A19

PREZZOLINI, G., *Repertorio bibliografico della storia e della critica della letteratura italiana dal 1932 al 1942.* NY, 1946. 2v. **A20

Progress of Medieval & Renaissance Studies in the United States & Canada. Boulder, Colo., 1-25 (1923-1960). **A21

Repertoire générale de sciences religieuses. R, P, 1950-53, 4v. **A22

Repertorium fontium historiae medii aevi, primum ab Augusto Potthast digestum, nunc cura collegii historicum e pluribus nationibus emendatum et auctum. R, 1962—. Basic. **A23

SARRI, F., OFM, "Saggio bibliografico di studi francescani," SF 12 (1926) 518-546. *A24

SMOLINSKI, Arcadius, OFM, *Franciscan Literature. A Selected, Evaluated, Annotated Bibliography.* Wa, 1957. 105p. CF XI, 9. (Cath. Univ. MA thesis) *A25

VICINELLI, A., See A43: 399-407.

VITO DA CLUSONE, Cap., *Cultura e pensiero di SFA* (Modena 1952) xv-lxiv. cf D184. *A26

III THE WRITINGS OF ST. FRANCIS

1 EDITIONS

a. LATIN

BOEHMER, H., ed., *Analekten zur Geschichte des F von A.* 3. Aufl. durchgesehen von F. Wiegand. Tü, 1961. xvi, 75p. Rev: CF 33 (1963) 327. A27

Opuscula Sancti Patris F Assisiensis. Ed. 3a. Q, 1949. xvi, 209p. A28

b. ENGLISH

Memorable Words of SF, A. Masseron, ed.; M. Sullivan, tr. Chi, 1963, viii 123p. Tr. of A40. A29

SFA, His Life & Writings as Recorded by His Contemporaries . . . Tr. by Leo Sherley-Price. L & NY, 1960. 234p. Rev: CF 31 (1961) 101. A30

The Words of SF, An Anthology. Comp. by James Meyer, OFM. Chi, 1952. viii, 345p. 1966, viii, 359p. Rev: CF X, 63; FnSs 13 (1953) 209-213.   A31
The Writings of SFA. Tr. by Paschal Robinson, OFM. Phil, 1906. xxxii, 208p.   A32
The Writings of SFA. Tr. by Benen Fahy, OFM. Intr. & notes by Placid Hermann, OFM, L & Chi, 1964. 181p. Rev: CF 35 (1965) 413-414.   A33

c. FRENCH

Ainsi parlait SF. P, 1955, 255p. Rev: CF 26 (1954) 84.   A34
Les écrits de SFA, remis en langage populaire par le P. Willibrord de Paris. P, 1959. 197p. Rev: AFH 52 (1959) 472; Ant 37 (1962) 311; CF 30 (1960) 103; FS 44 (1962) 112.   A35
Le message spirituel de SFA dans ses écrits. Willibrord de Paris, Cap, ed. Blois, 1960. xvi, 367p. Rev: Ant 38 (1963) 241; AFH 53 (1960) 472; CF 31 (1961) 101.   A36
Oeuvres latines et Cantique de frère soleil. Tr., intr. & notes de Alexandre Masseron. P, 1959. 264p. Rev: AFH 52 (1959) 472; CF 30 (1960) 102.   A37
Les opuscules de SF. Texte latin & tr. fr. de l'Abbé Paul Bayart. P, 1945. viii, 263p. Rev: MF 46 (1946) 343.   A38
Les opuscules de SFA. Texte latin de Quaracchi. Intr., tr. fr. & tables du R. P. Damien Vorreux, OFM, de l'Abbé Paul Bayart & des FF. MM. de la Clarté-Dieu. P, 1956. 353p. Rev: CF 26 (1956) 308; MF 57 (1957) 305; (1945 ed. 262p.): CF 15 (1945) 227; MF 46 (1946) 343.   *A39
Paroles mémorables de SFA. Tr. & notes de Alexandre Masseron. P, 1960. 182p. Rev: CF 31 (1961) 230.. cf A29.   A40
SF d'A. Introd. et choix de textes. Damien Vorreux, OFM, ed. P, 1965. 159p.

d. GERMAN

Die Schriften des hl. F von A. Einführung, Ubersetzung, Auswertung Kajetan Esser & Lothar Hardick, OFM. 3. verb. Aufl. We, 1963. 258p. (2. verb. Aufl. 1956. 258p.; 1st ed.: 1951. xii, 204p.) Rev: AFH 47 (1954) 171; CF 22 (1952) 387-390; CF XI, 56; FS 34 (1952) 327-329. Basic.   *A41

e. ITALIAN

Gli scritti di SFA. Intr. e note di Mons. Vittorino Facchinetti, OFM. Testo riveduto e aggiornato da Fr. Giacomo Cambell, OFM. 5a ed. Mi, 1957. 211p. Rev: CF 27 (1957) 327; CF 15 (1945) 227; MF 45 (1945) 193.   A42
Gli scritti di SF, traduzione, commento e note di Mario Niccoli. R, 1967. vi-127p. Rev: CF 38 (1968) 206-207.
VICINELLI, A., *Gli scritti di S F e i Fioretti.* See A165.   *A43

f. SPANISH

San F de Asis, Escritos genuinos. Trad. e Introd. de Fray Fidel de Jesus Chauvet OFM. Mexico, 1964. 301p. Rev: AFH 58 (1965) 184-5.

2 STUDIES

CAMBELL, Jacques, OFM. "Les écrits de SFA devant la critique," FS 36 (1954) 82-109, 205-264; & We, 1954. 91p. Rev: CF XI, 58-59. Fundamental study of textual problems. **A44

——, " SF a-t-il composé une paraphrase du Pater?" FS 45 (1963) 338-342. No. *A44a

CHINI, Mario, *SF poeta*. R, 1937. 46p. Rev: CF 12 (1942) 23*. A45

DANIELE DALLARI DA BARI, Cap, "SFA 'scrittore'," IF 33 (1958) 94-102, 163-179, 188, 233-243, 328-336; 34 (1959) 11-20, 84-95, 175-183; & R, 1959. 86p. Rev: MF 62 (1962) 500-502. A46

ESSER, K., OFM, "Die älteste Handschrift der Opuscole des hl. F (cod. 338 von A)," FS 26 (1939) 120-142. cf C183: 159-174. *A47

——, "Le langage de SF," CVF 4 (1957) 116-123. A48

FALOCI-PULIGNANI, M., "Gli autografi di SF," MF 6 (1895) 33-39. With large facsimiles. A49

LAMPEN, Willibrord, OFM, "De quibusdam sententiis et verbis in opusculis S.P.N.F." AFH 24 (1931) 552-557. A50

MORETTI, G. M, (a) *I santi dalla scrittura; [esami grafologici]*. Padova, 1952. 408p. facsims. Ch. on SF in RF nov. 1953. (b) *Saints through Their Handwriting*. NY, 1964. 269p. See p. 47-49. A51

OTTAVIO DA ANGERS, Cap., "SF e il canto," IF 3 (1928) 257-268, 417-424. A52

3 INDIVIDUAL WRITINGS

(on THE CANTICLE see C144-C159; on
THE LETTER TO ALL THE FAITHFUL, D48;
on RULES see below FIRST ORDER)

a. *THE BLESSING OF BROTHER LEO*

ATTAL, Salvatore, "La benedizione di Frate Leone," MF 32 (1932) 245-248; cf CF 30 (1960) 24 n63-64; FS 36 (1954) 218-222 (Cambell); C70: 364. A53

VAN DIJK, S.J.P., OFM, "SF's Blessing of Brother Leo," AFH 47 (1954) 199-201. Abs: CF XI, 62. A54

b. *THE LETTER TO ST. ANTHONY*

BONMAN, Ottokar, OFM, "De authenticitate epistolae SF ad S. Antonianum Patavium," AFH 45 (1952) 474-492. Abs: CF X, 64. Reply to A56.
*A55

ESSER, K., OFM, "Der Brief des hl. F. an den hl. Antonius von Padua," FS 31 (1949) 135-141. Abs: CF IX, n125; cf FS 36 (1954) 244-249 (Cambell). *A56

c. *THE OFFICE OF THE PASSION*

BRACALONI, Leone, OFM, "L'ufficio composto da SFA," SF 37 (1940) 251-265. A57

Research Bibliography

DE SCHLAMPHELEER, Jacques, OFM, *L'Office de la Pâque. Commentaire de l'Officium passionis de SFA.* P, 1953 & 1963, 156p. Rev: CF 34 (1964) 185. A58

FRANCESCHINI, Ezio, "Note sull'Ufficio della passione del Signore." In QSF (SMA 1962) IV, 42-62. A59

OKTAVIAN VON RIEDEN, Cap., "Das Leiden Christi im 'Officium passionis' des hl. F.," in his "Leiden Christi . . ." (see D139), CF 30 (1960) 129-145; cf CF 33(1963) 328; WW 25 (1962) 135-142. **A60

d. THE RULE FOR HERMITAGES

ESSER, K., OFM, "Die 'Regula pro eremitoriis data' des heiligen F. von A," FS 44 (1962) 382-417. Fundamental analysis, with critical text. *A61

e. THE TESTAMENT

——, *Das Testament des heiligen F. von A.* Münster/Westf., 1949. 212p. Abs; FnSs 10 (1950) 77-81. Rev: AFH 42 (1949) 312-315 (Oliger); FS 31 (1949) 214-217 (Hardick); MF 49 (1949) 633-635. Definitive. **A62

TITO DA OTTONE, Cap., *Il Testamento di SF.* Genova, 1957. 61p. Rev: IF 33 (1958) 231. A63

VAN CORSTANJE, Auspicius, OFM, (a) *"Het Verbond van Gods armen.* Een bijbelse confrontatie met de opvattingen van Franciscun," Sint F 6 (1964), n. 2, 7-76; (b) *Gottes Bund mit den Armen. Biblische Grundgedanken bei F.* Werl, 1964. 151p. Rev: MF 64 (1964) 504-505; (c) *Un peuple de pelerins, essai d'interpretation biblique du Testament de saint François.* P, 1964. 160 p. Rev: AFH 58 (1965) 190-1; CF 35 (1965) 201-203; (d) *The Covenant with God's Poor. An Essay on the Biblical Interpretation of the Testament of SF of A.* Initial transl. by Gabriel Ready OFM. Revised and augmented edition by Stephen Anaclete Yonick OFM. Franciscan Herald Press, Chicago, 1966. xx-172 p.

IV SOURCES
1 COLLECTIONS & ANTHOLOGIES

a. LATIN

Legendae S. F. Assisiensis saeculis XIII et XIV conscriptae. AF X, Q. 1926-1941. lxxxvii, 755p. Critical edition. Rev: AFH 30 (1937) 235; 34 (1941) 420. Contains (also pub'd separately): *A64

THOMAS DE CELANO, O. Min. *Vita Prima S. F:* 1-117. A65

——, *Legenda ad usum chori:* 118-126. A66

——, *Vita Secunda S. F:* 127-168. A67

——, *Tractatus de Miraculis S. F.:* 269-330. cf A249: 20-54, 161-205. A68

IULIANUS DE SPIRA, O. Min, *Vita S. F:* 333-371. A69

——, *Officium rhythmicum S. F:* 372-388. A70

HENRICUS ABRINCENSIS, canonicus, *Legenda Versificata S. F:* 405-521. A71

(cf BIHL, M., OFM, "De 'Legenda Versificata' S. Fauctore Henrico Abrincensi," AFH 22 (1929) 3-53; cf 193-195. A71a

Research Bibliography

HELIAS, Fr., O. Min, *Epistola encyclica de transitu S. F.*: 523-528. cf C196.   A72

ANON.,   *Legenda choralis Umbra*: 543-554. cf A202.   A73

S. BONAVENTURA, O. Min, *Vita seu Legenda Maior S. F.*: 555-652.

A74

——, *Vita seu Legenda Minor S. F.*: 653-678.   A75

IACOBUS DE VORAGINE, OP,   *Vita S. F.* in eius *Legenda Aurea*: 681-693.   A76

BERNARDUS DE BESSA, O. Min,   "Liber de laudibus b. F." In AF III (Q 1897) 666-692.   A77

(cf DELORME, F.M., OFM, "A propos de Bernard de Besse," *SF* **13**, 1927, 217-228).   A78

Florilegium Franciscanum. In usum scholarum excerpsit Sam. Cavallin. Lund, 1957. 116p. Rev: CF 28 (1958) 426. 2d ed. 1965, 119p.   A79

LEMMENS, Leonardus, OFM,   (a) "Testimonia minora saeculi XIII de S.P.F." AFH 1 (1908) 68-84, cf E16:98-106, & F108:248-266. (b) 2d ed. Q, 1926. 127p. Rev: AFH 20 (1927) 154-157 (Bihl).   **A80

Via Seraphica; Selected Readings from the Early Documents & Writings Pertaining to SF & the Franciscan Order; ed. by Placid Hermann, OFM. Chi, 1959. 221p.   A81

VORREUX, Damien, OFM, "Un manuscrit inédit de la Vie de saint François par Julien de Spire: Reims, Municipale 1393," AFH 61 (1968) 201-216.

b. ENGLISH

Early Franciscan Classics. Tr. by the Friars Minor of the Franciscan Province of Saint Barbara, Oakland, California. Paterson, N.J., 1962. vii, 257p. Contains tr. of A65, A72, A112, & A133.   A82.

The Little Flowers of SF, tr. by T. Okey. *The Mirror of Perfection* by Leo of A, tr. by Robert Steele. *The Life of SF* by St. Bonaventure, tr. by Miss E. Gurney Salter. Intr. by Hugh McKay, OFM. L & NY, 1963. xi, 397p. [4th ed.] (Everyman's Library, 485)   A83

SFA, His Holy Life & Love of Poverty. The Legend of the Three Companions, tr. by Nesta de Robeck. And *The Sacrum Commercium or F & His Lady Poverty*, tr. by Placid Hermann, OFM. Chi, 1964. ix, 204p.   A83a

A New Fioretti, A Collection of Early Stories about SFA Hitherto Untranslated. Tr. & ed. by John R. H. Moorman. L, 1946. 90p. Invaluable.   *A84

SFA, The Legends & Lauds. Ed. by Otto Karrer; tr. by N. Wydenbruck. L & NY, 1948. xiv, 302p. Lacks some of notes in A86.   *A85

c. GERMAN

Franz v A: Legenden und Laude. Otto Karrer, ed. Z, 1945. 811p. illus. Rev: AFH 41 (1948) 296 (Bihl).   *A86

RUH, Kurt, *Franziskanisches Schrifttum im deutschen Mittelalter*. 2 vols. München, 1965. Rev: CF 36 (1966) 446-449.

(1946) 349. Has useful index. 4th ed. Madrid, 1965. xxxix-758p.   *A87

Research Bibliography

d. SPANISH

San F de Asis. Sus escritos. Las Florecillas. Biografías del Santo por Celano, San Buenaventura y los Tres Compañeros. Espejo de Perfección. Ed. prep. por los P. Fray Juan R. De Legísima, OFM, y Fray Lino Gómez Cañedo, OFM. 3a ed. Madrid, 1956. xxxix, 857p. illus. Rev: CF VII, n247, & XI, n168; VV 4 (1946) 349. Has useful index.   *A87

e. FRENCH

SF d'A. Documents, écrits et premières biographies, rassemblés et présentés par les Pp. Theophile Desbonnets et Damien Vorreux OFM. P, 1968. 1600 p. Rev: CF 68 (1968) 373-379.

2 MAJOR 13TH-CENTURY SOURCES
(see also A64-A80, A82)

a. THOMAS OF CELANO
(see also A65-A68, E210, E211, F210)

(1) TRANSLATIONS

SFA: First & Second Life of SF, with Selections from Treatise on the Miracles of Blessed F. Tr. from the Latin with Intr. & notes by Placid Hermann, OFM. (a) Chi, 1963. xxx, 245p. illus., map. Richly illustrated; notes based on AF X. Excellent tr. Useful index. (b) Also paperbound ed. Chi, 1964. liv, 405p. (without illus.).   *A88

Vie de SFA, tr. intr. & notes du R. P. Damien Vorreux, OFM. P, 1952. 462p. Crit. rev: EF ns6 (1955) 102; MF 52 (1952) 635-639.   *A89

Thomas von Celano. Leben und Wunder des Heiligen F von A. Einführung, Uebersetzung, Anmerkungen von Engelbert Grau, OFM. We, 1955. 621p. (FQ, 5) Rev: FS 38 (1956) 437. Fundamental work; notes based on AF X.   *A90

Fra Tommaso da Celano. Vita di SFA (Prima e Seconda) e Trattato dei miracoli. Fausta Casolini, tr. & ed. SMA, 1952 & 1960. liv, 481p. Rev: AFH 48 (1955) 147; CF 24 (1954) 402. Important intr.   *A91

Tommaso da Celano. Le due Vite e il Trattato dei miracoli di SFA. Nuova versione integrale, intr. e note di Luigi Macali, Conv. R., 1954. xxix, 563p. Rev: AFH 48 (1955) 147; MF 56 (1956) 599-601.   *A92

(2) STUDIES

CASOLINI, Fausta, "Il primo biografo francescano a sette secoli dalla morte (1260?)," FF 26 (1959) 154-161. cf her art. in EC XII, 243.   A93

——, *Profilo di fra Tommaso da Celano.* R, 1960. 75p. illus.   *A94

CHIAPPINI, Aniceto, OFM, "La sequenza 'Dies Irae, Dies Illa' di Fra Tommaso da Celano," CF 32 (1962) 116-121. Impt. refs.   *A95

COMITATO PER LE ONORANZE AL BEATO TOMMASO DA CELANO. *Numero commemorativo per il VII centenario della morte di fra Tommaso da Celano. Celano, 1960.* R, 1960. 29p. cf FF 27 (1960) 172.   A96

Research Bibliography

DE BEER, Francis, OFM, *La conversion de SF selon Thomas de Celano*. *Etude comparative des textes relatifs à la conversion en Vita I et Vita II*. P, 1963. 367p. Abs: MF 63 (1963) 380-383. Crit. rev: CF 34 (1964) 183 (OvR). Important. Rev: AFH 58 (1965) 151-154; Ant. 41 (1966) 162-164. *A97

HOONHOUT. P., *Het Latijn van Thomas van Celano Biograaf van sint F*. Amsterdam, 1947. 262p. Rev: AFH 40 (1947) 276-279; EF nsl (1950) 105. *A98

HULL, Mona C., *The Usefulness of the Original Legend of SFA in Religious Education*. Boston, 1962. vi, 281p. (Boston Univ. diss.) Abs: DA 23 (1962) 1433. *A99

MANCINI, Norberto, OFM, "Tommaso da Celano nel VII centenario della morte," IF 35 (1960) 252-257. A100

ODOARDI, Giovanni, Conv., "La patria di Tommaso da Celano, O. Min. (+ c. 1260), e le pretese falsificazioni del P. Nicolò Colagreco (+ c. 1770)," MF 68 (1968) 344-369.

SPIRITO, Silvana, *Il francescanesimo di Fra Tommaso da Celano*. SMA, 1963. 154p. cf E166. Rev: MF 64 (1964) 240-242; AFH 58 (1965) 150-151; CF 35 (1965) 206-207. *A101

VAN DEN BORNE, Fidentius, OFM, "Thomas van Celano als eerste biograaf van F," SintF 2 (1956) 183-213. Abs: CF XI, 75-76; RHE 52 (1957) 787. *A102

WDZIECZNY, Gilbert, Conv, "The Life & Works of Thomas of Celano," FnSs 26 (1945) 55-68. *A103

b. ST. BONAVENTURE

(1) TRANSLATIONS
(see also A74, A75, E174)

La vida del glorios Sant Frances. Version provençale de la Legenda Maior de s. Bonaventure. Tr. by Ingrid Arthur. Uppsala, 1955. ix-316 p.

The Greater Life of SF, & The Shorter Life of SF. Tr. by Benen Fahy, OFM with intr. & notes by Placid Hermann, OFM. Chi, 1965. 200p. A104

Saint Bonaventure. Vie de SFA. Tr. fr., intro. & notes du R. P. Damien Vorreux, OFM. P, 1951. 254p. Rev: MF 51 (1951) 635; EF ns2 (1951) 363-365. A104a

F. Engel des Sechsten Siegels. Sein Leben nach den Schriften des Heiligen Bonaventura. Intr., tr., & notes by Sophronius Clasen, OFM. We, 1962. 631p. (FQ, 7) Rev: CF 33 (1963) 442; AFH 56 (1963) 214-217 (Esser); MF 63 (1963) 129-131. Contains impt. intr., tr. of A74 & A75 & 7 sermons. Basic. Crit. rev: *Arch. Gesch. Philos.* 46 (1964) 226-233 (Schmucki). **A105

SFA, di san Bonaventura. Agostino da Melilli, Cap, tr. Bari, 1957. 213p. A100

S. Bonaventura. Vita di SF. Tr., intr. e note del P. F. Russo, Conv. R, 1951. xii, 208p. Rev: AFH 46 (1953) 99-104; CF 23 (1953) 352; MF 51 (1951) 634. A107

BRADY, Ignatius, OFM, "The Authenticity of Two Sermons of Saint Bonaventure," FnSs 28 (1968) 4-26.

Research Bibliography

(2) STUDIES

CLASEN, S., OFM, "S. Bonaventura S. F. Legendae maioris compilator," AFH 54 (1961) 241-272; 55 (1962) 3-58, 289-319. Fundamental study.
*A108

———, "Die Sendung des hl. F. Ihre heilsgeschichtliche Deutung durch Bonaventura," WW 14 (1951) 212-225. CF X, 83. *A109

———, "Einteilung und Anliegen der Legenda maior SF Bonaventuras," FS 27 (1967) 115-162.

CRESI, Domenico, OFM, "San Bonaventura biografo perfetto di SF," SF 54 (1957) 355-364. (In A258.) A110

LAURAND, L., SJ, "Le 'Cursus' dans la Légende de SF par Saint Bonaventure," RHE 11 (1910) 257-262. *A111

c. SACRUM COMMERCIUM
(see also A82, A83a, E207)

Sacrum Commercium S.F. cum domina Paupertate. Q, 1929. 77p. Rev: EF 43 (1931) 118; CF 1 (1931) 102; cf FF ns4 (1931) 218-222. A112

The Lady Poverty, A Thirteenth Century Allegory. Tr. & ed. by Montgomery Carmichael. L, 1901. 209p. A113

SF e Madonna Povertà. Raoul Manselli, ed. Fi, 1953. 97p. Rev: IF 30 (1955) 196. A114

Le sacre nozze del Beato F con Madonna Povertà. Tr. with useful intr. & notes bv Nello Vian. Mi, 1963. xxii, 70p. *A115

Der Bund hes hl. F mit der Herrin Armut. Esser, Kajetan, OFM — Grau, Engelbert, OFM We, 1966. 178p. Rev: Ant 42 (1967) 560-562; CF 38 (1968) 208-210.

COSMO, Umberto, "Il primo libro francescano." In D157:33-58. A116

ENGELS, J., "De Convivio Paupertatis cum Fratribus." In *Mélanges offerts à Mademoiselle Christine Mohrmann* (Utrecht 1963) 141-151. A117

ESSER, Kajetan, OFM, "Untersuchungen zum 'Sacrum Commercium b. F. cum Domina Paupertati,'" *Miscell. Melchor de Pobladura,* I. R, 1964. 1-33p.

SABATIER, P., "Kurze Bemerkungen zur historischen Bedeutung des Sacrum Commercium Beati F cum Domina Paupertate," FS 13 (1926) 277-282. Also in Fr. in A30:335-362. A118

SANTONI, Enrico, OFM, "SF e Madonna Povertà," FF 16 (1939) 285-292. Abs: CF VII, 11*. A119

d. LEMMENS' DOCUMENTA ANTIQUA FRANCISCANA

Documenta Antiqua Franciscana, edidit Fr. Leonardus Lemmens, OFM. Q, 1901-1902. 3v. Contains, with important intrs. & comments: *A120

Pars I. *Scripta Fratris Leonis.* (1901. 107p.). Includes: A121

A. *Vita B. Aegidii Assisiastis:* 37-62; *Verba:* 63-65; App.: 66-72. A122

B. *S.P.F. Intentio regulae:* 83-99; *Verba S.P.F.:* 100-106. A123

Pars II, *Speculum Perfectionis, Redactio I,* (1901. 107p.) 23-84. A124

Pars III. *Extractiones de Legenda Antiqua.* (1902. 75p.) A125

Research Bibliography

e. ANONYMUS PERUSINUS

VAN ORTROY, F., SJ, "La leggenda latina di SF secondo l'Anonimo Perugino," MF 9 (1902) 33-48. Latin text & comment. A126

ABATE, Giuseppe, Conv, "L'Anonimo Perugino e le sue fonti." In A147: 230-237. *A127

Note: Ghinato is preparing a critical ed. (C112:166n 12).

f. JACQUES DE VITRY
(see also F85:545-557)

Lettres de Jacques de Vitry (1160/1170-1240, évêque de Saint-Jean-d'Acre. Ed. crit. par R.B.C. Huygens. Leiden, 1960. viii, 166p. Rev: AFH 54 (1961) 227-229; SM 3s2 (1961) 240-244; Spec 36 (1961) 658-660. Definitive ed. *A128

GEMELLI, Pia, "Giacomo da Vitry e le origini del movimento francescano," Aevum 39 (1965) 474-495. Rev: AFH 61 (1968) 268-269.

McDONNELL, Ernest W., The Beguines & Beghards in Medieval Culture, With Special Emphasis on the Belgian Scene. New Brunswick, NJ, 1954. xvii, 643p. Rev: AFH 48 (1955) 153. Important. Author working on his Sermones. **A129. See also McDonnell's "Jacques de Vitry," NCE 7, 798-799.

g. FRANCISCAN CHRONICLES
(see also A230, A236, A240, E3, E16)

LAUREILHE, Marie Thérèse, Sur les routes d'Europe au XIIIe siècle; chroniques de Jourdain de Giano, Thomas d'Eccleston, et Salimbene d'Adam, traduites et commentées. P, 1959. 229p. maps. Rev: AB 79 (1961) 205-208; CF 30 (1960) 466. *A130

———, XIIIth Century Chronicles. Tr. by Placid Hermann, OFM. Chi, 1961. xvii, 302p. maps. Rev: CHR 49 (1963) 226. *A131

HARDICK, Lothar, OFM, ed. & tr. Nach Deutschland und England. Die Chroniken der Minderbrüder Jordan von Giano und Thomas von Eccleston. We, 1957. 293p. (FQ, 6) Rev: AFH 50 (1957) 445; CF 28 (1958) 233-235. *A132

Chronica Fratris Jordani. Edidit, notis et commentario illustravit H. Boehmer, P, 1908. lxxxii, 95p. Rev: AFH 2 (1909) 647-650 (Bihl). (CED, 6) cf AF I, 1-19; C10. *A133

AUWEILER, Edwin J., OFM, The "Chronica Fratris Jordani a Giano." Wa, 1917. 63p. (Cath. Univ. diss.) *A134

Chronica Fratris Nicolai Glassberger. In AF II. *A134a

Fratris Thomae vulgo dicti de Eccleston Tractatus de Adventu Fratrum Minorum in Angliam. A. G. Little, & J. Moorman, ed. Man, 1951. 115p. *A135

Eccleston, Thomas, The Coming of the Friars. L. Sherley-Price, tr. and ed. L, 1964.

Cronica fratris Salimbene de Adam Ordinis Minorum. Edidit Oswaldus Holder-Egger. Hannover, 1905-13. xxxii, 755p. (MGH SS32) Rev: AFH 1 (1908) 443-446; 6 (1913) 759-765; cf 3 (1910) 348. *A136

Salimbene. Cronica. F. Bernini, ed. Bari, 1942. 2v. Latin. A137

Salimbene de Adam. Cronica. Nuova edizione critica a cura di Giuseppe Scalia. 2 vols. Bari, 1966. 1304p. Rev: Laur. 7 (1966) 486-495.

BIHL, Michael, OFM, "Salimbene," EF 16 (1907) 520-532. A138

CAMPAGNOLA, Stanislao da, Cap, "Orientamenti critica interpretativi intorno alla 'Cronica' di Salimbene de Adam," Laur. 6 (1965) 461-491.

CLEDAT, Léon, *De fratre Salimbene et de ejus Chronicae auctoritatae.* P, 1876. 116p. A139

LAUREILHE, M. T., "Les idées religieuses des Frères Mineurs au XIIIe siècle, d'après la chronique de Salimbene," EF nsl (1950) 5-22. A140

———, "Les Frères Mineurs et les puissances de l'Europe occidental au XIIIe siècle, d'après la chronique de Salimbene," EF nsl (1950) 313-328. A141

SCIVOLETTO, N., *Fra Salimbene da Parma e la storia politica e religiosa del secolo decimoterzo.* Bari, 1950. 182p. Rev: AFH 48 (1955) 436-440; CF X, 275*. A142

3 14TH-CENTURY *LEGENDAE* & COMPILATIONS

a. THE SO-CALLED LEGEND OF THE THREE COMPANIONS
(see also A83a, A85-A87, A219)

"Legenda S. F. Assisiensis tribus ipsius sociis hucusque adscripta. Redactio antiquior iuxta Cod. Sarnanensem," Giuseppe Abate, Conv, ed., MF 39 (1939) 375-432. Best text available, though incomplete. See A147. *A143

La légende des trois compagnons. Tr. du latin par l'Abbé Louis Pichard. P, 1926. 232p. A144

La Leggenda dei Tre Compagni. Testo senese inedito del XV secolo. Appendice e discussione critica. Zefferino Lazzeri, OFM, ed. Fi, 1923. ix, 171p.
*A145

La Leggenda dei Tre Compagni. Ezio Franceschini, tr. & ed. Mi, 1957 (3a ed.) xvii, 87p. Rev: CF XI, 72; MF 47 (1947) 615-617; Ant 32 (1957) 475 (Cambell). *A146

ABATE, Giuseppe, Conv., "Nuovi studi sulla leggenda di SF detta dei 'Tre Compagni'," MF 39 (1939) 1-55, 225-262, 359-373, 635-655 (for text see A143); also R, 1939. 186p. Rev: CF 12 (1942) 9*; cf CF 29 (1959) 515. Fundamental study. **A147

CLASEN, Sophronius, OFM, "Zur Kritik van Ortroys an der 'Legenda trium sociorum,'" *Miscell. M. de Pobladura,* I. R, 1964. 35-73.

b. THE LEGENDA ANTIQUA OF PERUGIA
(see also FNV II, 479-485; A249:461-496 & C160:348-353)

"La 'Legenda Antiqua S. F.' Texte du Ms. 1046 (M. 69) de Pérouse," Ferdinand M. Delorme, OFM, ed. (a) AFH 15 (1922) 23-70, 278-382. (b) P, 1926. 70p. Rev: AB 45 (1927) 198; AFH 20 (1927) 596-598 (Bihl); EF 38 (1926) 555; RHF 1 (1924) 236-238; Note: (a) & (b) have different numbering; Englebert follows b. See Table II in A265:23-26. *A148

SFA raconté par ses premiers compagnons. Tr. fr. de la Legenda Antiqua par l'Abbé M.-J. Fagot, P, 1927 & 1946. 205p. A148a

BURKITT, P. C., "La Légende de Pérouse et le ms. 1/73 de Saint Isidore," RHF 2 (1925) 457-466. A149

Research Bibliography

GRATIEN DE PARIS, Cap, "La 'Legenda Antiqua' de Pérouse," FF 1 (1924) 142-147. A150

I Fiori dei Tre Compagni. Testi francescani latini ordinati, con introduzione e note, da fr. Jacques Campbell OFM. Versione italiana a fronte di Nello Vian. Mi, 1967. xxxii-452p. Rev: CF 38 (1969) 210-212; MF 68 (1968) 199-204; Laur. 9 (1968) 100-102.

c. THE SPECULUM PERFECTIONIS OF SABATIER
(see also C160:344-348)

Speculum Perfectionis seu S. F. Assisiensis Legenda Antiquissima, auctore fratre Leone. Nunc primum edidit Paul Sabatier. P, 1898. ccxiv, 376p. (CED, 1). *A151

Le Speculum Perfectionis, préparé par Paul Sabatier. Man, 1928-31. 2v. (BSFS 13 & 17) Rev: AFH 26 (1933) 497-518 (Bihl); RHE 25 (1929) 309-311 (Masseron). *A152. Reprinted 1965, Farnborough (Hants).

Le Miroir de la Perfection. Traduction française du *Speculum Perfectionis.* Introd. et notes de M.-Th. Laureilhe. P, 1966. 208p. Rev: AFH 60 (1967) 254-256; CF 37 (1967) 187-188; MF 68 (1968) 205-207.

SFA, His Life & Writings as Recorded by His Contemporaries. A New Version of The Mirror of Perfection . . . (see A30 & another tr. in A83). A152a

Frate Leone. Lo Specchio di Perfezione. F. Pennacchi, tr.; E. Franceschini, ed. 3a ed. Mi, 1945. xxiii, 175p. Rev: SF 39 (1942) 189-192 (Pennacchi); MF 43 (1943) 338; 49 (1949) 196; CF VII,27*. A153

Lo Specchio di Perfezione. F. Pennacchi, tr.; F. Russo, Conv, ed. R, 1950. xxvii, 248p. Rev: AFH 46 (1953) 99-103; CF 22 (1952) 79-81; MF 51 (1951) 632. A154

BIHL, Michael, OFM, "Zur Kritik des Speculum Perfectionis gelegentlich der Neuausgabe desselben von P. Sabatier," FS 22 (1935) 113-148. Abs: CF 9 (1939) 123. *A155

d. THE A.G. LITTLE MANUSCRIPT
(see also A249:3-19 & 182-194)

LITTLE, A.G. "Description of a Franciscan Manuscript Formerly in the Phillipps Library." In BSFS (Aberdeen 1914) V, 9-113. *A156

———, *Un nouveau manuscrit franciscain, ancien Phillipps 12290, aujourd'hui dans la bibliothèque A. G. Little,* P, 1919. 110p. (OCH, 18) Rev: AFH 12 (1919) 567-569 (Oliger). *A157

e. THE ACTUS-FIORETTI
(see also bibl. in A166)

(1) EDITIONS & MANUSCRIPTS

Actus Beati F et Sociorum Ejus. Paul Sabatier, ed. P, 1902. lxiii, 271p. (CED, 4) *A158

BUGHETTI, Benvenuto, OFM, "Descriptio Novi Codicis 'Actus Beati F' Exhibentis (Florentiae, Bibliotheca Nationalis Centralis II, XI, 20)," AFH 32 (1939) 412-438. *A159

KRUITWAGEN, Bonaventura, OFM, "Descriptio nonnullorum codicum

Research Bibliography

MSS. quibus insunt libelli 'Speculum Perfectionis' et 'Actus B. F.'," AFH 1 (1908) 300-412. *A160

I Fioretti di SF. Le Considerazioni sulle Stimate. La Vita di Frate Ginepro. La Vita e i Detti del Beato Egidio. Capitoli aggiunti. Il Cantico di Frate Sole. Con note del P. Benvenuto Bughetti, OFM, nuova edizione riveduta dal P. Riccardo Pratesi, OFM. Fi, 1959. 465p. Rev: AFH 53 (1960) 460-462. Useful notes. *A161

I Fioretti di SF. Le Considerazioni sulle Stimmate. II Cantico de Frate Sole. R. Pratesi & G. Sabatelli, OFM, eds. Fi, 1961. 212p. *A161a

I Fioretti di SF, con una introduzione storico-critica (& notes & bibl.) del P. Giacinto Pagnani, OFM. R, 1960. 253p. illus., map. Rev: AFH 53 (1960) 325-327 (Pratesi). Important intr. & notes. *A162

I Fioretti di SF, a cura di Giacomo V. Sabatelli OFM. Con xilografie di G. Michelucci. La Verna, 1966. 296p. Rev: CF 37 (1967) 421.

I Fioretti di SF. G. M. Bastianini, Conv, ed. R, 1950. xxii, 267p. Rev: AFH 46 (1953) 99-101; CF 21 (1951) 431-433; MF 50 (1950) 657; SF 47 (1951) 131. A163. Ed. A, 1963. 282p. Rev: CF 34 (1964) 404.

———. Agostino Gemelli, OFM, ed. Mi, 1957. 304p. 4a ed. Rev: CF XI, 74; MF 47 (1947) 617. A164

———, a cura di Guido Davico Bonino, ed. To, 1964. xv-310p. Rev: AFH 58 (1965) 156-162; CF 34 (1964) 404-405.

———, con prefazione e note di P. Luciano Canonici OFM, ed. A, 1964. xvi-191p. Rev: AFH 58 (1965) 156-162; CF 34 (1964) 404-405.

Gli scritti di SF e "I Fioretti," a cura di Augusto Vicinelli. Mi, 1955. 427p. illus. Rev: AFH 50 (1957) 120-123. Important. *A165

The Little Flowers of SF. First Complete Ed., with 20 Additional Chapters. Also The Considerations of the Holy Stigmata, The Life & Sayings of Brother Giles, The Life of Brother Juniper. A Modern English Tr. from the Latin & the Italian with Intr., Notes, & Biographical Sketches by Raphael Brown. Garden City, NY, 1958. 359p. map. Rev: AFH 52 (1959) 352. 105-item bibl. includes 36 refs. to studies. **A166

The Little Flowers of SF. With 5 Considerations on the Sacred Stigmata. Tr. with an intro. by Leo Sherley-Price. L. & Baltimore, 1959. 202p. map. (Penguin Classics, L91) A167

The Little Flowers of SF & Other Franciscan Writings. Tr. with Intr. by Serge Hughes. NY, 1964. 222p. A167a

Les Fioretti de SF. Ed. complète. Omer Englebert, tr. & ed. P, 1945. 420p. A168

Les Fioretti. Tr. nouvelle d'après l'Incunable de Milan par le R.P. Godefroy, Cap. P, 1947. 314p. Rev: CF 20 (1950) 130. A169

Les Fioretti de SF, suivis des Considérations sur les Stigmates et autres textes traditionnels. Tr., intr. et notes de Alexandre Masseron. (a) P, 1953. xxxviii, 510p. Most useful French ed. (b) P, 1963. xii, 195p. illus.; abridged juvenile ed. *A170

(2) STUDIES
(see bibl. in A166)

BROWN, Sr. M. Anthony, "Historical Value of Certain Chapters of the Fioretti," *Cord* 8 (1958) 214-220. A171

Research Bibliography

BROWN, Raphael, "Fioretti, The." NCE 5 932-933.

CLASEN, Sophronius, OFM, "Zur Problematik der Fioretti," WW 25 (1962) 214-218. Important. *A172

CRESI, Domenico, OFM, "I Fioretti di SF," SF 55 (1958) 35-50. A173

DABOVICH, Elena, "Syntaktische Eigentümlichkeiten der Fioretti." In *Syntactica und Stilistica. Festschrift für Ernst Gamillscheg* (Tü 1957) 83-109. A174

DAMIANI, Quinto, OFM, "Raffronto tra alcuni codici a stampa dei *Fioretti* e il codice di Amaretto Manelli," CF 28 (1958) 397-400. *A175

DEFRENZA, Giuseppe, "La poesia dei Fioretti," IF 34 (1957) 1-8, 73-82, 163-168, 217-224, 289-295, 380-384. A176

MARIANO da Alatri, Cap, "Genuinità del messaggio francescano dei Fioretti comprovata da un raffronto filologico con gli scritti di SF," CF 38 (1968) 5-77.

PAGNANI, Giacinto, OFM, "Il codice di Fabriano dei Fioretti di SF," SP 25 (1957) 1-23. CF XI, 79. *A177

——, "Contributi alla questione dei 'Fioretti di SF'," AFH 49 (1956) 3-16. Rev: CF XI, 78. Fundamental study, with new data on author. *A178

——, "Fioretti," DSAM V, 382-384.

——, "Ricerche intorno al B. Liberato da Loro Piceno, O. Min.," MF 58 (1958) 76-98. Important new research; cf F132, F139, F142. *A179

PELLEGRINI, Leo, "I Fioretti del glorioso Messere Santo F e de' suoi frati," *Annali della Scuola Normale Superiore di Pisa* ser. II, 21 (1952) 131-157. CF X, 67-68. *A180

PETROCCHI, Giorgio, "Dagli 'Actus Beati F' al Volgarizzamento dei Fioretti," Conv 22 (1954) 534-555, 666-677; also in his *Ascesi e mistica trecentesca* (Fi 1957) 85-146. CF XI, 78. *A181

——, "Inchiesta sulla tradizione manoscritta dei 'Fioretti di SF," *Filologia romanza* 4 (1957) 311-325. *A182

QUAGLIA, Armando, OFM, "Il 'Floretum' e i 'Fioretti' del Wadding," SF 50 (1953) 107-112. CF X, 68. See also A228. *A183

——, "'Ultime' sui Fioretti di SF," VM 30 (1959) 364-369.

——, "Il mondo ideale dei Fioretti." SF 56 (1959) 3-9. A184

——, "Perchè manca un'edizione critica dei Fioretti di SF," SF 52 (1955) 216-223. CF XI, 77. A185

TOSI, G., "Coordinazione e subordinazione nei 'Fioretti' di SF," *Archivio glottologico italiano* 27 (1935) 40-63. *A186

ZUCCA, Nazareno, "I Fioretti e il loro traduttore," *Fiamma Nova* dic. 1967, 32-33.

f. THE AVIGNON COMPILATION

SABATIER, Paul, "Compilation franciscaine d'Avignon," RHF 1 (1924) 425-431. cf A44:88-96 (Cambell). *A187

VALENTI, Tommaso, "Gl'inventari di Fr. Federico de Pernstein, O.M., Arcivescovo di Riga (1304-1341)," MF 33 (1933) 46-66; cf MF 43 (1943) 177; AFH 42 (1949) 34; AFH 41 (1948) 12. *A188

g. *MINOCCHI'S LEGGENDA ANTICA* & *RELATED DOCUMENTS*

La Leggenda Antica. Nuova fonte biografica di SFA tratta da un codice vaticano e pubblicata da Salvatore Minocchi. Fi, 1905. xxviii, 184p. cf AFH 11 (1918) 47-65; MF 49 (1949) 359n25.　A189

"Vita di SF e dei suoi compagni. Testo inedito di volgare umbro del XIV secolo," M. Faloci-Pulignani, ed., MF 8 (1901) 81-119.　A190

(For related writings of Angelo Clareno & Ubertino da Casale, see E57-E66 & E68-E73.)

h. THE CHRONICLE OF THE 24 GENERALS

Chronica XXIV Generalium Ordinis Minorum (1209-1374) [by Arnaud de [Sarrant or Samatan]. In AF 111 (Q. 1897) 1-575. cf A213.　*A191

Cronica da Ordem dos Frades Menores (1209-1285). Jose Joaquin Nunes, ed. Coimbra, 1918. 2v. Rev: AFH 11 (1918) 543-546 (Oliger).　A192

i. THE BOOK OF THE CONFORMITIES

De conformitate vitae Beati F ad vitam Domini Iesu, auctore Fr. Bartholomaeo de Pisa. In AF IV-V (Q 1906-12). Rev: AFH 6 (1913) 170.　*A193

FALOCI PULIGNANI, M.,　"Il 'Liber Conformitatum' del P. Bartolomeo da Pisa," MF 8 (1901) 137-148.　A194

GOYAU, G.,　"Les étranges destinées du Livre des Conformités." In D178: 90-147.　A195

LINDEBOOM, J.,　"De Satyren naar aanleiding van het 'Liber Conformitatum'," Akademie van Wetenschappen (Amsterdam) *Mededelingen Afdeling Letterkunde* nrd7 (1944) n6 (14p.)　A196

4　MINOR CODICES & COMPILATIONS (13TH TO 15TH CENTURIES)
(alphabetically by editor)

ALBAN STOECKLI VON HERMETSWIL, Cap, "Die Franziskuslegende des 'Passionals'," CF 7 (1937) 529-566; 8 (1938) 5-37, 165-193. cf F107.　A197

——, "Notae die Franziskuslegende des 'Passionals' praeliminaria crisis censurae 'De Legenda quadam S. F. anonyma,'" CF 7 (1937) 209-214.　A198

BIHL, M., OFM,　"De Legenda quadam S. F. anonyma et incognita nuperrime in 'Legenda Aurea' et in 'Passionali' arbitrarie detecta," AFH 28 (1935) 305-323.　*A199

HILARIN [FELDER] VON LUZERN, Cap,　"Die Mitteldeutsche Legendendichtung Passional (um 1240) und ihr Leben von Sante F und Sante Elisabeth," CF 3 (1933) 481-517. Rev: CF 5 (1935) 127-129; cf CF 9 (1939) 121.　A200

BIHL, M., OFM,　"De Legenda S. F. Neapolitana integra et nunc 'Legenda Umbra' aptius nuncupanda," AFH 28 (1935) 3-36. Abs: CF 9 (1939) 121. cf E3:19.　*A201

Research Bibliography

——, "Legenda S. F. Neapolitana supplentur ex eadem aliqua in *Vita II* deficientia," AFH 21 (1928) 240-268. *A203

ABATE, G., Conv, "La Leggenda Napoletana di SF e l'ufficio rimato di fra Giuliano da Spira secondo un codice umbro," MF 30 (1930) 129-155; & A, 1930. 91p. Abs: CF 1 (1931) 384. *A204

BIHL, M., OFM, "Narrationes VII de S. F. (In cod. Florentino Laurent. Ashburnh. 326)," AFH 17 (1924) 560-568. *A205

——, "Novus flosculus legenda S. F.," AFH 15 (1922) 202-203. A206

BUGHETTI, B., OFM, "Analecta de S. F. Assisiensi saeculo XIV ante medium collecta (e cod. Florentiae Nation. C. 9.2878)," AFH 20 (1927) 79-108. *A207

——, "Una nuova compilazione di testi intorno all vita di SF (dal cod. Universitario di Bologna, n.2697)," AFH 20 (1927) 525-562. *A208

CAMBELL, J., OFM, "Glanes franciscaines: la compilation d'Angers (Angers, bibliothèque Municipale, ms. 821)," FS 45 (1963) 41-82. *A209

——, "Glanes franciscaines. La seconde compilation de Barcelone," AIA 25 (1965) 223-298. Rev: AFH 58 (1965) 569-570; MF 65 (1965) 435-438.

——, "Glanes franciscaines. Deux manuscrits de la compilation vénetienne," FS 49 (1967) 293-349. Rev: AFH 61 (1968) 490-491.

DELORME, F. M., OFM, "Descriptio codicis 23.J.60 bibliothecae Fr. Min. Convent. Friburgi Helvetiorum," AFH 10 (1917) 47-102. A211

——, "Les Flores S. F.," MF 43 (1943) 171-178. *A212

——, "Pages inédites sur SF écrites vers 1365 par Arnaud de Sarrant Min. Prov. d'Aquitaine," MF 42 (1942) 103-131. cf A191. *A213

ELIZONDO, Jose Maria de, Cap, "Le Leyenda de SF segun la versión catalana del 'Flos Sanctorum,'" *Revista de Estudios* Franciscanos (Barcelona) abril-mayo 1910, 43p. A214.

FIERENS, A., "La Question Franciscaine, Vita S. F. Anonyma Bruxellensis, d'après le Manuscrit II.2326 de la Bibliothèque Royale de Belgique," RHE 9-10 (1908-09); & Louvain, 1909. 123p. Rev: AFH 3 (1910) 343; cf MF 40 (1940) 490. *A215

GRATIEN DE PARIS, Cap, "Sermons franciscains du Cardinal Eudes de Châteauroux (†1273)," EF 29 (1913) 171-195, 647-655; 30 (1913) 291-317, 415-437; & P, 1915. *A215a

LAMPEN, W., OFM, "Auctoris anonymi saeculi XIII Collatio de S.P.N. F," AFH 26 (1933) 549-550. A216

LAZZERI, Z., OFM, "Una piccola vita inedita di SF," *Rivista di Livorno* 1 (1926) 404-409; English tr. in NYT Feb. 13, 1927, VIII: 7. A217

LITTLE, A. G., "Flos novus Legendae S. F.," AFH 8 (1915) 675-676. A218

MARCELLINO DA CIVEZZA & Teofilo Domenichelli, OFM, *La Leggenda di SF scritta da tre suoi compagni*. R, 1894. cxxxvi, 267p. Rev: AB 19 (1900) 457. A219

MATTHAEI AB AQUASPARTA, O. Min. (d. 1302), *Sermones de S. F., de S. Antonio et de S. Clara.* Q, 1962. 222p. *A219a

OLIGER, Livarius, OFM, "Descriptio codicus S. Antonii de Urbe unacum appendice textuum de S. F.," AFH 12 (1919) 321-401. *A220

——, "Liber exemplorum Fratrum Minorum saeculi XIII. (Excerpta e Cod. Ottob. Lat. 522)," Ant 2 (1927) 202-276; cf FNV II, 59, 61; MF 49 (1949) 131. *A221

PAGNANI, Giacinto, OFM, "Frammenti della Cronaca del B. Francesco Venimbeni da Fabriano (+1322)," AFH 52 (1959) 153-177.

PENNACCHI, F., "Actus S. F in Valle Reatina. Leggenda tratta dal Codice 679 della Biblioteca Comunale di A," MF 13 (1911) 3-21; & Foligno, 1911. 63p. A222

SALVATORELLI, L., "Dante e S Francesco," DSPU 62 (1965) 235-247. Rev: AFH 61 (1968) 502.

5 LATE COMPENDIA & CHRONICLES

a. THE SPECULUM VITAE

Speculum vitae Beati F et sociorum eius. Ven, 1504. xi, 397p. (Metz, 1509; P, 15[??]; Antwerp, 1620; Köln, 1623; Györ (Raab), 1752, vi, 589p.) *A223

BIHL, M., OFM, "L'édition du 'Speculum Vitae B. F' parue à Györ en 1752 et l'origine hongroise du 'Speculum Vitae'," AFH 20 (1927) 132-153. Basic. *A224

GOYENS, F., "Les éditions du 'Speculum Vitae B. F' parues en 1620 et 1623," AFH 20 (1927) 116-131. *A225

SABATIER, P., "Description du Speculum Vitae b. F et sociorum eius (éd. de 1504)." In OCH (P 1903) VI, 298-397. *A226

b. THE SPANISH FLORETO

El Floreto de Sant Francisco. Sevilla, 1492. (R. Brown has microfilm of rare Madrid Biblioteca Nacional copy.) A227

CLASEN, Sophronius, OFM, "'El floreto de Sant Francisco.' Collectionis hispanicae de S. Francisco eiusque sociis noticiarum analysis," CF 35 (1965) 249-286. Rev: AFH 61 (1968) 492.

QUAGLIA, A., OFM, "'El Floreto': fonte storica sconosciuta di Marco da Lisbona e del Wadding," SF 54 (1957) 40-49. CF XI, 80. cf A183. *A228

c. LA FRANCESCHINA

La Franceschina. Testo volgare Umbro del secolo XV scritto dal P. Giacomo Oddi di Perugia, edito per la prima volta nella sua integrità dal P. Nicola Cavanna, OFM. Fi., 1931. 2v. cf AFH 44 (1951) 111; 51 (1958) 120.
*A229

d. THE CHRONICLES OF FRA MARIANO DA FIRENZE
(see also A178, C209, E236, F374)

MARIANUS DE FLORENTIA, O. Min., "Compendium chronicarum Fratrum Minorum," AFH 1 (1908) 98-107; 2 (1909) 92-107, 305-318, 626-641; 3 (1910) 294-309, 700-715; 4 (1911) 122-137, 318-339, 559-587; & Q, 911. 171p. *A230

CRESI, Domenico, OFM, "La vita di SF scritta da Mariano da Firenze," SF 64 (1967) no. 1, 48-90.

ABATE, G., Conv, "Le fonti storiche della cronaca di fra Mariano da Firenze." MF 34 (1934) 46-52. *A231

CANNAROZZI, Ciro, OFM, "Una fonte primaria degli 'Annales' del Wadding (II 'Fasciculus Chronicarum' di Mariano da Firenze)," SF 27 (1930) 251-285. Rev: AFH 25 (1932) 136; cf A178. *A232

——, 'Pensiero di fra Mariano da Firenze," SF 26 (1929) 4-28, 121-179, 295-326. A233

——, "Ricerche sulla vita di fra Mariano da Firenze," SF 27 (1930) 31-71 A234

CRESI, D., OFM, "Le origini dell'Ordine Minoritico nella narrazione di Mariano da Firenze," SF 56 (1959) 139-147. *A235

e. THE CHRONICLES OF MARK OF LISBON

MARCOS DE LISBOA, OFM, *Cronicas da Ordem dos Frades Menores.* Lisboa, 1557-62. 2pts. (Span. tr. Alcala, 1568; Salamanca, 1570). A236

——, *Croniche degli Ordini instituiti dal Padre SF.* Tr. by Horatio Diola. Ven, 1585. 2v. Also other eds.; for list, see Streit's *Bibliotheca Missionum* (Münster 1916) I, index. A237

——, *The Chronicle & Institution of the Order of the Seraphical Father SF.* Wm. Cape & Christopher Davenport, tr. S. Omers, 1618. 759p. A238

——, *Chronique . . .* P, 1622. 2v. in 1. A239

f. WADDING
(see also A183, A232)

WADDINGUS, Lucas, OFM, *Annales Minorum*, vols. 1-30, Q, 1931-1951; 31 —, R, 1956 —. Index Generalis. Rev: AFH 28 (1935) 273-279. A240

——, *Annales des Frères Mineurs.* P. Silvestre Castet, tr. Toulouse, 1680. 2v. in 1 (1208-1300). Abridged. A241

ABATE, G., Conv, "Un profilo storico di Fra Luca Wadding. Gli 'Annales Minorum' e la loro recente edizione," MF 40 (1940) 269-285. *A242

CASOLINI, F., *Luca Wadding, OFM, l'Annalista dei Francescani.* Mi, 1936. 282p. Rev: CF 9 (1939) 229-233; & A242. *A243

Father Luke Wadding. Commemorative Volume, Edited by the Franciscan Fathers, Dun Mhuire, Killiney. Dublin & L, 1957. 652p. illus. Rev: AFH 51 (1958) 211-215; CF 28 (1958) 116; MF 59 (1959) 260-262. *A244

PANDZIC, Basilio, OFM, "Gli 'Annales Minorum' del P. Luca Wadding," SF 54 (1957) 275-287. Useful list of editions, vols., years, & editors: 287; cf AFH 28 (1935) 579-582. *A245

MILLETT, Benignus, OFM, "Wadding, Luke" NCE 14, 761-762 (bibliography updated).

V STUDIES OF SOURCES

See A90, C219a, D156, D157, & E27; also important studies in the biographies by Beaufreton (A280), Cuthbert (A288), Fortini (A296), Joergensen (A298), Sabatier (A 303), & Sarasola (A316); likewise the articles by Abate (A147 & C33) and Cambell (A44, A209, A210).

BIGARONI, M., OFM, "La questione delle fonti." In C164:23-68 *A246

BIHL, M., OFM, "Contra duas novas hypotheses prolatas a Ioh. R. H. Moorman," AFH 39 (1946) 3-37, 279-287. cf A268. *A247

———, "De vero sensu Definitionis Capituli generalis an. 1266 Legendas antiquiores S. F. proscribentis," AFH 30 (1937) 274-281. *A248

———, "Disquisitiones Celanenses," AFH 20 (1927) 433-496; 21 (1928) 3-54, 161-205. Indispensable; analyzes A148, A156, A68. *A249

———, "La questione francescana riveduta dal signor prof. M. Barbi alla luce dell'opera dei Tre Compagni," SF 32 (1935) 6-47, 121-141. Abs: CF 9 (1939) 120. *A250

BURKITT, F. C., "SFA & Some of His Biographers." In *Franciscan Essays* (Man 1932) II, 19-40 (BSFS-ES III). CF 4 (1934) 328. A251

———, "Scripta Leonis and Speculum Perfectionis." In MFE (R 1924) III, 1-24. Rev: RHF 2 (1925) 423. *A252

———, "The Study of the Sources of the Life of SF." In D178:13-61. A253

CAVALLIN, S., "La question franciscaine comme problème philologique," *Eranos* 52 (1954) 239-270. Rev: CF XI, 75; FS 37 (1955) 325. *A254

CHIAPPINI, Aniceto, OFM, "Fr. Ioannes de Celano, OFM, S. F. Assisiensis biographus coaevus," Ant 35 (1960) 339-342. Important *A255

———, "Fr. Joannis de Celano Sermones duo saec. XIII," CF 28 (1958) 401-403. A256

CLASEN, S., OFM, & Julius van Gurp, Cap, "Nachbonaventurianische Franziskus Quellen in niederlandischen und deutschen Handschriften des Mittelalters," AFH 49 (1956) 434-482. Rev: CF XI, 77. *A257

CLASEN, S., OFM, "Die 'Legenda antiqua' des hl. F v A," *Miscellanea Mediaevalia* 3 (Ber, 1964) 86-104.

———, "Vom F der Legende zum F der Geschichte," WW 29 (1966) 15-29.

———, *Legenda antiqua s. Francisci. Untersuchungen über die nachbonaventurianischen Franziskusquellen. Legenda trium sociorum, Speculum perfectionis, Actus b. F et sociorum eius, und verwandtes Schrifttum.* Leiden, 1967. xxxii-416-62*p. Rev: CF 38 (1968) 379-392.

CRESI, D., OFM, "Discussione e documenti di storia francescana," SF 54 (1957) 351-380. Abs: CF XI, 76. cf A110. *A258

———, *Discussioni e documenti di storia francescana.* Fi, 1959. 183p. Rev: CF 29 (1959) 537. *A259

DESBONNETS, Théophile, OFM, "Recherches sur la Généalogie des Biographes primitives de Saint François," AFH 60 (1967) 273-316.

ESSER, K., OFM, "Wege zur Lözung der 'Franziskanischen Frage,'" WW 30 (1967) 238-244.

FALOCI PULIGNANI, M., "I veri biografi di SF," MF 7 (1899) 145-174. A260

FIERENS, A., "La question franciscaine. Les écrits des zélateurs de la Règle aux premiers temps de l'histoire franciscaine d'après les récentes controverses," RHE 7 (1906) 410-433; 8 (1907) 57-80. CF X, 467. *A261

FREDEGAND [CALLAEY] D'ANVERS, Cap, "De fontibus litterariis ad vitam S. F. Assisiensis speciatim pertinentibus brevis disquisitio," CF 1 (1931) 433-456. *A262

GOETZ, W., *Die Quellen zur Geschichte des hl. F. von* A. Gotha, 1904. x, 259p. *A263

LEMMENS, L., OFM, "Die Schriften des Br. Leo von A (Gest. 1271)." In MFE (R 1924) III, 25-48. *A264

LITTLE, A. G., "Some Recently Discovered Franciscan Documents & Their Relations to the Second Life by Celano & the *Speculum Perfectionis*," British Academy (L) *Proceedings* 12 (1926) 147-178. Rev: AFH 21 (1928) 127-129. Includes indispensable Tables of Parallel Passages. *A265

MARTIN DE BARCELONA, Cap, *Estudio critico de la fuentes historicas de SF y Santa Clara.* Ba, 1921. xii, 254p. Rev: AFH 15 (1922) 173-181. *A266

MASSERON, Alexandre, "Les sources de la vie de SFA." In D179:9-67. *A267

MOORMAN, John R. H., *The Sources for the Life of SFA.* Man, 1940. 176p. Despite Bihl rev. (A247) very useful; cf A84, A300. *A268 Reprint-ed 1966, Farnborough (Hants).

OKTAVIAN VON RIEDEN, Cap, *Zum kritischen Wert der bedeutenderen Quellen für die Erforschung der Geistigkeit des hl F von A.* R, 1956. Unpub'd typescript. CF 30 (1960) 7n9. *A269

OLIGER, Livarius, OFM, *De Fontibus Vitae S. F.* R, 1949. 62p. Typescript. A270

——, *Le Leggende di SF.* R, 1950. 43p. Typescript. *A271

POU Y MARTI, Jose, OFM, "Studia recentiora circa vitam S F," Ant 2 (1927)3-20. *A272

SALTER, E. G., "Sources for the Biography of SFA," Spec 5 (1930) 388-410. CF 3(1933) 453*. A273

SALVATORELLI, Luigi, "La storiografia francescana contemporanea." In CISSR III, 403-448. Abs: RHE 50 (1955) 1103. cf E55a. *A274

VAN DEN BORNE, Fidentius, OFM, *Die Franziskusforschung in ihrer Entwicklung dargestellt.* München, 1917. x, 106p. Rev: AFH 15 (1922) 175. *A275

——, "Zur Franziskusfrage," FS 6 (1919) 185-200. *A276

——, "Het probleem van de Franciscus-biografie in het licht van de moderne historische kritiek," SintF 57 (1955) 241-320. Abs: CF XI, 89; RHE 52 (1957) 369. See also A318-A321. *A277

——, "Niew licht na 50 jaren brounenstudie," Sint F 3 (1966) 18-59.

——, "Neues Licht nach 50 Jahren Quellenforschung," WW 31 (1968) 208-223.

VI MAJOR BIOGRAPHIES

AMORIM, Guiedes de, *F de Assis, renovador da humanidade; biografia.* Petropolis, 1965. 399p.

ATTAL, Francesco Salvatore (Soter), *SFA.* 2a ed. Padova, 1947. 515p. illus. Rev: (1st ed. Livorno, 1930. 517p.) CF 1 (1931) 393-395; IF 6 (1931) 347-355; 7 (1932) 101-104. CF 20 (1950) 53*; MF 49 (1949) 176-178. *A278

BARGELLINI, Piero, SF. To, 1941. 233p. illus. Rev: CF 11 (1941) 265; SF 39 (1942) 87-89. 2a ed. Brescia, 1951. 215p. CF X, 69; MF 53 (1953) 129. *A279

BEAUFRETON, Maurice, *SFA*. P, 1925. 340p. Rev: AB 44 (1926) 202; RHF 2 (1925) 418-420 (Gilson); EF 38 (1926) 549; cf A322, C45. *A280

BOASE, T. S. R., *St. F A,* with 16 lithographs by Arthur Boyd. Bloomington, Ind., 1968. 120p.

BOLLANDISTS, *Acta Sanctorum* (P 1868) L, Oct. II, 545-1004; & Dec. *Propylaeum* (Brux, 1940) 433-434. cf MF 34 (1934) 70-93. A281

BATTISTINI, Mario, "I Padri Bollandisti Henschenio e Papebrochio nelle Marche nel 1660," DSPM s4v10 (1933) 93-105. A282

———, "I Padri Bollandisti Henschenio e Papebrochio nell'Umbria nel 1660," MF 34 (1934) 53-59. Abs: CF 9 (1939) 132. A283

FALOCI PULIGNANI, M., "SF ed i Bollandisti," MF 16 (1915) 65-69. A284

———, "Corrispondenza tra il P. Suyskens ed il P. Tebaldi," MF 16 (1915) 93-123. A285

CHALIPPE, Candide, OFM, *Vie de SFA*. P, 1727; 1874, 3v. (Torino, 1787. Madrid, 1796). Based on Wadding. A286

———, (a) *The Life of SFA*. Tr. by the Congregation of the Oratory. NY, 1899. 483p. (b) *The Life & Legends of SFA*, rev'd & re-ed. by Fr. Hilarion Duerk, OFM. NY, 1918. xxxiii, 405p. Lacks notes in (a). A287

CUTHBERT OF BRIGHTON, Cap, *Life of SFA*. L & NY, 1912; 2d ed. 1913; 3d ed. 1921. xv, 536p. illus. Rev: AFH 6 (1913) 338-343 (Oliger); 18 (1925) 593; CF 3 (1933) 436-439; EF 38 (1926) 191-194; cf A328. *A288

DAL GAL, Girolamo, Conv, *SFA*. Padova, 1947. xix, 412p. Rev: MF 48 (1948) 409-412; SF 44 (1947) 122-124 (Cresi). *A289

ENGLEBERT, Omer, *Vie de SFA* (a) P, 1947, 461p. illus. Rev: MF 48 (1948) 412-414; RF (1948) 92-95 (Bonin); CF 20 (1950) 127-129. (b) Ed. rev. & corr. P, 1957. 452p. Rev: AFH 54 (1961) 431-432 (VdBorne); cf *Praeco Regis* 4 (1952) 186-190, & *Franciscana* 5 (1950) 47-62. *A290

———, *Vita di SF d'A*. G. Pampini tr. Mi, 1958.

———, *SFA*. Speyer, 1952. Rev: FS 35 (1953) 443-444 (Hardick).

———, *SFA*, tr. & ed. by Edward Hutton. L & NY, 1950. x, 352p. illus. Rev: FnSs 13 (1953) 198-206 (Brady); CF 21 (1951) 94. *A291

———, *SFA*. A Biography. A new translation by Eve Marie Cooper. Second English edition rev. and augmented by Ignatius Brady OFM and Raphael Brown. Chicago, 1965. xii-616. Rev: CF 36 (1966) 443-445; MF 67 (1967) 436-439, AFH 61 (1968) 235-237; AB 86 (1968) 226; AFH 61 (1968) 235-237; CHR 54 (1968) 122-123; EF 17 (1967) 385-386; MF 67 (1967) 436-439; Sec 42 (1967) 730-731; WW 31 (1968) 147-148.

FACCHINETTI, Mons. Vittorino, OFM, *SFA nella storia, nella leggenda, nell'arte*. (a) Mi, 1921. xlviii, 542p. illus. Rev: CC 73/3 (1922) 244-254. (b) 2da ed. arrich. e migliorata. Mi, 1926. xlviii, 542p. Sumptuously illus. Rev: AFH 20 (1927) 416-422. Important. cf A331. *A292

———, *SFA dans l'histoire, dans la legende, dans l'art*. Tr. par la Comtesse de Loppinot & F. Feugère. Vanves, 1926. lxiv, 744p. illus. Rev: RHF 4 (1927) 378-383. (Also Span. ed. Ba, 1925). *A293

Research Bibliography

FORTINI, Arnaldo, "I documenti degli archivi assisiani e alcuni punti controversi della vita di SF," AFH 43 (1950) 3-44. Abs: MF 51 (1951) 651.
*A294

——, *Nova vita di SFA*, Mi, 1926. 483p. Rev: AFH 20 (1927) 157-161 (Bihl). A295

——, *Nova vita di SF*. A, 1959. 4v in 5. Rev: AFH 53 (1960) 324-327; MF 62 (1962) 498-500. Indispensable. *A296

GHILARDI, A. — Attanasio, S. (translator), *The Life and Times of St. Francis*. Phila., 1967. 75p.

GRATIEN DE PARIS, Cap, "SFA. Essai sur sa vie et son oeuvre d'après les derniers travaux critiques," EF 18 (1907) 359-482. cf A335, D127, E23.
*A297

HARDICK, L. "Francis of Assisi, St." NCE 6, 28-31.

JOERGENSEN, Johannes, *SFA, A Biography*. (a) L & NY, 1912. Tr. by T. O'Conor Sloane. ix, 428p. (Editions & tr. in all major languages). (b) Garden City, NY, 1955, 354p.; lacks impt. app. on sources. Rev (various eds.): EF 20 (1908) 377-387 (Felder); AFH 6 (1913) 338-343 (Oliger); CW 95 (1912) 385-391 (Robinson); cf SintF 58 (1956) 25-30; abs: RHE 521 (1957) 369. cf A337. *A298

LONGPRÉ, Ephrem, OFM, "Saint François d'A," DSAM V (1964), 1271--1303.

——, *F d'A et son experience spirituelle*. P, 1966. 212p. Rev: CF 37 (1967) 186-187.

LOPES. Fernando Felix, OFM, *O Poverello S. F. de Asis*. Braga, 1951. 458p. A299

MOORMAN, JOHN R. H., *SFA*. L, 1950. 127p.; & 1963. viii, 118p. cf. D177. A300

OSCAR DE PAMEL, Cap, "La psychologie de SFA," EF 33 (1921) 489-505; 34 (1922) 327-345, 500-519; 36 (1923) 267-274. AFH 18 (1925) 421. Well documented, almost a biography. *A301

PAPINI, Niccola, Conv, *La Storia di SFA. Opera critica*. Foligno, 1825-27. 2v. cf MF 20 (1919) 56-64. Still useful. cf A341. *A302

PIAT, Stephane-J., *Saint François d'A à la découverte du Christ pauvre et crucifié*. P, 1968. 396p.

POMPEI, Alfonso, Conv, "Francesco da Assisi," BSS V (1964), 1052-1131; followed by bibl. by Lorenzo di Fonzo, 1131-1150.

SABATIER, Paul, *Vie de SFA*. P, 1894. cxxvi, 418p. (On Index.) *A303

——, *Life of SFA*. Tr. by Louis Seymour. L, 1894 (& 1942). 448p. A304

——, *Vie de SFA*. Edition définitive. P, 1931. li, 580p. Rev: AFH 25 (1933) 525-533 (Bihl); CF 2(1932) 249. *A305

——, "L'enfance et la jeunesse de SF. Etude comparative des sources." [1900-06] SM 6 (1933) 1-28; "Première partie de la vie de SFA," 7 (1934) 24-51, 165-184; 8 (1935) 72-97; 9 (1936) 150-161. *A306

——, *Etudes inédites sur SFA*. P, 1932 (& 1953). ix, 386p. Rev: AFH 25 (1932) 525-533 (cf 533-536); CF 5 (1935) 130-132. Important. A307

COSMO, U., "L'ultimo Sabatier." In D157:114-145. A308

FALOCI PULIGNANI, M., "SFA secondo Paolo Sabatier," MF 9 (1902) 65-74. A309

GOFFIN, Arnold, "Les Etudes Inédites de Paul Sabatier sur SFA," RHF 7 (1930) 129-132 (cf 134-138). A310

JOERGENSEN, J., "Paul Sabatier storico francescano," IF 3 (1928) 344-347. A311

MAUGAIN, G,. "Paul Sabatier. Notes biographiques," RHF 5 (1928) 1-22 (bibl. of Sab.'s works, 14-22); P, 1928. 22p. 2e éd. P, 1931. 28p. Rev: AFH 25 (1932) 533 *A312

ROBINSON, Paschal, OFM, "The Saint of A and M. Sabatier," *The Dolphin* (Phil) 8 (1905) 33-43, 148-165; cf A342. A313

——, *The Real SFA*. 2nd ed. rev, L, 1904. 112p. Valuable. A314

VEUTHEY, L., Conv, "Il pensiero definitivo di Sabatier sulla vita di SF e sulle sue fonti storiche," MF 33 (1933) 3-14. Abs: CF 5 (1935) 130. cf. A343. *A315

SARASOLA, Luis de, OFM, *SF de Asis*. (a) Madrid, 1929. 603p. Rev: EF 41 (1929) 440; CF 1 (1931) 388; FF ns 3 (1930) 149. (b) 2da ed. Madrid, 1960. xv, 616p. Rev: CF 31 (1961) 658. *A316

SPARACIO, Domenico, Conv, *Storia de SFA*. A, 1928. xxiv, 508p. 271 illus. Rev: AFH 22 (1929) 226-229; EF 41 (1929) 322; SFA 8 (1928) 117-119. Important. *A317

STICCO, Maria, *SFA*. Mi, 1960. 351p. 15th ed., Mi, 1967. 370p. Rev: CF 32 (1962) 165; 39 (1969) 193.

——, *The Peace of SF*, which is *SFA*, tr. by S. Attanasio. Englewood Cliffs, N. J., 1962. 283p.

VAN DEN BORNE, Fidentius, OFM, "Het 'Drama' in de moderne Franciscus biografie," SintF 58 (1956) 248-287. Abs: RHE 51 (1956) 788; CF XI; 92. *A318

——, "De Franciscus-biografie als litterair werk. Een vraagstuk van methodiek," SintF 58 (1956) 31-80. Abs: RHE 52 (1957) 370; CF XI, 90. *A319

——, "Voornamste feiten uit het leven van F in het licht van de historische kritiek," SintF 59 (1957) 163-239, 243-316. Abs: RHE 53 (1958) 1110; CF XI, 92. *A320

——, "Franciskanse beweging (XIIIe eeuw). De Gouden Eeuw," Sint F 6 (1962) afl 4, 3-58. Rev: AFH 58 (1965) 191.

CLASEN, S., OFM, "Das Schrifttum von P. Fidentius van den Borne," FS 40 (1958) 251-255. cf A275-A277. *A321

B   BACKGROUND

I TEMPORALITIES

BREZZI, P., *Roma e l'impero medioevale* (774-1252). Bologna, 1947. 663p. (Storia di Roma, 10) *B2

HEER, Friedrich, (a) *Mittelalter*. Z, 1961. 747p. illus. (b) *The Medieval World: Europe 1100-1350*. Tr. by J. Sondheimer. Cleveland, 1962. 365p. illus. (c) NY, 1963. 432p. illus. *B3

HURTER, Friederich E. von, *Geschichte Papst Innocenz der dritten und* *seiner Zeitgenossen.* Hamburg, 1892. 4v. Still useful for documented survey of institutions in last vol. (Also P, 1855, 3v.; Mi, 1857. 4v.) *B4

MORGHEN, R., *Medioevo cristiano.* 3a ed. Bari, 1962. 364p. *B5

Regesta imperii, V. Böhmer, Ficker, Winkelmann, eds. Innsbruck, 1881-1901. 3v. *B8

RENOUARD, Y., *Les villes d'Italie de la fin du Xe siècle au début du XIVe siècle.* P, 1961—. *B9

ROTA, E., et al., *Questioni di storia medioevale.* Mi, 1957. lxviii, 837p. *B10

SALVATORELLI, Luigi, *L'Italia comunale dal secolo XI alla metà del secolo XIV.* Mi, 1940. 948p. 424 illus. Basic. *B11

VERGOTTINI, G. de, *La rinascita politica medievale.* Mi, 1961. xxv, 619p. *B12

WALEY, Daniel, *The Papal State in the Thirteenth Century.* L & NY, 1961. xv, 337p. Fundamental work. cf his "Lo stato papale nel XIII secolo," RSI 73 (1961) 429-472. *B13

II MONASTICISM
1 CENOBITICAL

COUSIN, Patrice, OSB, *Précis d'histoire monastique.* P, 1959. 594p., maps. Invaluable for bibl. **B57

DE WARREN, H. B., "Le travail manuel chez les moines à travers les âges," VS Suppl. 52 (1937) [80-123]. cf D81. *B58

GROSSI, Paolo, *Le abbazie benedittine nell'alto medioevo italiano.* Fi, 1957. xxix, 168p. B59

KAPSNER, Oliver, OSB, *A Benedictine Bibliography.* 2d ed. Collegeville, Minn., 1962. 2v. **B60

LECLERCQ, Jean, OSB. (a) *L'amour des lettres et le désir de Dieu.* P. 1957. 269p. (b) *The Love of Learning & the Desire for God.* NY, 1962. 336p.; see its bibl. of his writings. Rev: Spec 37 (1962) 138-140. *B61

——, et al., *La spiritualité au moyen âge.* P, 1961. 718p. (Histoire de la spiritualité chrétienne, 2) Rev: SMon 5 (1963) 237. To appear in English. *B62

MATT, Leonard von, *Saint Benedict.* Tr. by Ernest Graf. Chi, 1961. 226p. Useful for illus. of Central Italy. cf F43. B63

PENCO, Gregorio, OSB, *Storia del monachesimo in Italia dalle origini alla fine del Medio Evo.* R, 1961. 608p. Rev: RSCI 15 (1961) 356-360. Basic. **B64

VICAIRE, Marie-Humbert, OP, *L'Imitation des apôtres, moines, chanoines, mendiants (IV-XIIIe s.).* P, 1963. 93p. Important. *B65

2 EREMITICAL

ANSON, Peter A., *The Call of the Desert.* L, 1964. xix, 278p. (New version of his 1932 *The Quest of Solitude.*) Valuable history & bibl. of Western eremiticism. **B66

BLUM, Owen J., OFM, *St. Peter Damian. His Teaching on the Spiritual Life.* Wa, 1947. 224p. (Cath. Univ. diss.) *B67

Research Bibliography

CACCIAMANI, Giuseppe, Er. Cam., *La reclusione presso l'Ordine camaldolese.* Camaldoli, 1960. 48p. *B68

DRESSLER, F., *Petrus Damiani, Leben und Werk.* R, 1954. xviii, 247p. (Studia Anselmia, 34). Basic. *B69

L'Eremitismo in Occidente nei secoli XI e XII. Atti della Settimana internazionale di studio, sett. 1962. Mi, 1964. *B70

GIABBANI, Anselmo, Er. Cam., *L'Eremo; vita e spiritualità eremitica nel monachismo camaldolese primitivo.* Brescia, 1945. xx, 238p. Basic. *B71

LECLERCQ, Jean, OSB, *Saint Pierre Damien ermite et homme d'Eglise.* R, 1960. 284p. Rev: RSCI 15 (1961) 340-344; SM 3 ser. 1 (1960) 571-574. Basic. *B72

Lettres des premiers chartreux. S. Bruno. Guigues. S. Anthelme. P, 1962. 270p. (Sources chrétiennes, 88). B73

MANSUETO DELLA SANTA, O. Cam, *Ricerche sull'idea monastica di San Pier Damiano.* Camaldoli (Arezzo), 1961. xx, 220p. With B72, fundamental. Rev: SM 3 ser. 3 (1962) 626-632. *B74

MASON, Mary E., *Active Life & Contemplative Life, A Study of the Concepts from Plato to the Present.* Milw, Wis., 1961. 137p. *B75

PAGNANI, A., OSB, *Storia dei Benedettini Camaldolesi, cenobi, eremita, monache ed oblati.* Sassoferrato, 1949. 327p. *B76

Petri Damiani Vita Beati Romualdi, a cura di Giovanni Tabacco. R, 1957. lxiv, 125p. (Fonti per la Storia d'Italia, 94). Rev: AB 78 (1960) 486. *B77

PIERDAMIANO, S., *Scritti monastici.* A cura di B. Ignesti. Siena, 1959. 2v. (Also *Lettere e discorsi.* 1956. 350p.) B78

Saint Pierre Damien et Saint Bruno Querfurt. Textes primitifs camaldules. ("La vie du bienheureux Romuald" et "La vie des Cinq Frères") Tr. par le P. L.A. Lassus. Namur, 1962. 225p. (Les Ecrits des Saints) B79

WANG, John, *St. Peter Damian as Monk.* NY, 1958. iii, 244, 12p. (Fordham Univ. diss.) *B80

3 ST. FRANCIS & MONASTICISM

(see also D13, D99, D151, E88, E205, F50, F123-F128, F258-F261, F292)

BINDANGOLI-BINI, B., "SF, la Porziuncula e i benedettini," OS 29 (1916/17) 222-250. cf F254. B81

BULLETTI, Enrico, OFM, "SF nell'Eremo di Camaldoli," *Unità Cattolica* 26 ag, 1928. Abs: FF 6 (1929) 112. B82

HUIJBEN, J., OSB, "Sint F en Sint Benedictus," FL 10 (1927) 125-143. Abs: EF 40 (1928) 312. B83

LAMPEN, W., OFM, "Utrum S.P.N.F. cognoverit regulam S. Benedicti," AFH 17 (1924) 445-448. B84

LAURI, A., "S. Benedetto e SFA nella loro regione," IF 21 (1946) 305-311; cf 3-6. CF VII, 33*. B85

LIBERATO DA STOLFI, OFM, "SF e l'Ordine di S. Benedetto," FF 26 (1959) 19-25. B86

MATURA, M. C., OFM, "SF et l'Ordre bénédictin," *Studium* 2 (1947) 171-175. CF VIII, 62*. B87

Research Bibliography
III RELIGIOUS MOVEMENTS

CLASEN, Sophronius, OFM, "Armutsbewegungen," LTK I, 883-886. *B30

——, "Poverty Movement," NCE 11, 652-653.

DE STEFANO, Antonio, "Delle origini e della natura del primitive movimento degli Umiliati," *Archivum romanicum* (Genève) 11 (1927) 31-75; cf his *Riformatori ed eretici del medioevo* (Palermo 1938) 125-208. B46

ESSER, K., OFM, "Die religiösen Bewegungen des Hochmittelalters und F von A," In *Festgabe Joseph Lortz* (Baden-Baden 1958) II, 287-315. *D198

GRUNDMANN, Herbert, *Religiöse Bewegungen im Mittelalter*. Berlin, 1935. 520p. Rev: AFH 29 (1936) 550-559 (Bihl); CF IX, 55*. Cf. B34. Reprinted with additions from **B34: *Neue Beiträge zur Geschichte der religiösen Bewegungen im Mittelalter*. Darmstadt 1961. Basic. D199a

——, "Neue Beiträge zur Geschichte der religiösen Bewegungen im Mittelalter," AKG 37 (1955) 129-182. **B34

HARDICK, L., OFM, "F, die Wende der mittelalterlichen Frömmigkeit," WW 13 (1950) 129-141. Abs: CF IX, 69*-70*. *D200

ILARINO DA MILANO, Cap, "Umiliati." In EC XII, 754-756, with rich bibl. *B47

MEERSEMAN, G. G., OP, & E. Adda, "Pénitents ruraux communautaires en Italie au XIIe siècle," RHE 49 (1954) 343-390. B48

"Movimenti religiosi popolari ed eresie del medioevo." In CISSR III, 344-365; cf. 383-402. *B39

OPTATUS VAN VEGHEL, Cap, "F gezien tegen de achterground van zijn tijd," FL 39 (1956) 14-27, 36-52, 99-110. Abs: CF XI, 95. D201

WERNER, Ernst, *Pauperes Christi; Studien zur sozial-religiösen Bewegungen im Zeitalter des Reformpapsttums*. Leipzig, 1956. 225p. *B43

WILLIBRORD DE PARIS, Cap, "Rapports de SFA avec le mouvement spirituel du XIIe siècle," EF ns12 (1962) 129-142. Important: in several ways SF was a man of the 12th century. *D204.

IV HERESIES

BORST, A., *Die Katharer*. Stuttgart, 1953. xi, 372p. (Schriften der MGH, 12) Rev: RSI 55 (1953) 574-581. Fundamental. **B29

DONDAINE, H., OP, "La hiérarchie cathare en Italie," AFP 20 (1950) 234-324. *B31

ESSER, Kajetan, OFM, "FvA und die Katharer seiner Zeit," AFH 51 (1958) 225-264. *B32

FRUGONI, A., *Arnaldo da Brescia nelle fonti del secolo XII*. R, 1954, x, 198p. cf EC I,2001; LTK I,893. *B33

GONNET, G., ed., *Enchiridion fontium Valdensium (Recueil critique des sources concernant les Vaudois au moyen âge.) Du IIIe Concile de Latran au Synode de Chanforan (1179-1532)*. Torre Pelice, 1958—. I (1179-1218) 188p. *B44

HUGON, A. A., *Bibliografia valdese*. Torre Pelice, 1953. 275p. **B45

Research Bibliography

ILARINO DA MILANO, Cap, "Le eresie medioevali (sec. XI-XV)." In *Grande antologia filosofica* (Mi 1954) IV, 1599-1689. *B35

——, "Il dualismo cataro in Umbria al tempo di SF," Atti IV Convegno di Studi Umbria, 1966 175-216. Rev: MF 68 (1968) 435-436.

KOCH, Gottfried, *Frauenfrage und Ketzertum im Mittelalter*. Berlin, 1962. 210p. (Forsch. zur mittelalt. Ges., 9) *B36

LEFF, Gordon, *Heresy in the Later Middle Ages: the Relation of Heterodoxy to Dissent, c.1250—c.1450*. Manchester & NY, 1967. 2 vols. Rev: CF 39 (1969) 189-190.

MANSELLI, R., *Studi sulle eresie del secolo XII*. R, 1953. vii, 124p. Rev: AFH 47 (1954) 431. *B37

MARIANO D'ALATRI, Cap, "L'inquisizione francescana nell'Italia centrale nel secolo XIII," CF 22 (1952) 225-250; 23 (1953) 51-165; & R, 1954. 151p. Rev: EF ns6 (1955) 230; FS 39 (1957) 93; MF 56 (1956) 610-612; SF 55 (1955) 184. *B38

SAVINI, Savino, *Il catarismo italiano ed i suoi vescovi nei secoli XIII e XIV*. Fi, 1958. 181p. *B40

SHANNON, Albert C., *The Popes & Heresy in the Thirteenth Century*. Villanova, Pa., 1949. 148p. *B41

SOEDERBERG, Hans, *La religion des cathares. Etude sur le gnosticisme de la basse antiquité et du moyen âge*. Uppsala, 1949. 301p. *B42

V GEOGRAPHY

1 MAPS

Carte topografiche delle diocesi italiane nei secoli XIII e XIV. Città del Vaticano, 1932-52. (Made for *Rationes decimarum Italiae* series; available for Latium, Marchia, Tuscia, Umbria.) Indispensable. F1

Touring Club Italiano, Carta automobilistica, 1:200,000. Mi. Foglio 13-17. Very useful. F3

United States Army Map Service, Washington, D.C. Ser. 1302, *Plastic, The World*, 1:1,000,000. No. 321 "Vesuvio." 27x30"; covers Florence-Naples-Brindisi area in plastic relief. Excellent. F4

2 MEDIEVAL ROADS & TOPOGRAPHY
(see also F1)

LUDWIG, Friedrich, *Untersuchungen uber die Reise- und Marschgeschwindigkeit im XII. und XIII. Jahrhundert*. Berlin, 1897. 193p. Basic. *F6

MILLER, Konrad, *Itineraria Romana. Römische Reisewege an der Hand der Tabula Peutingeriana*. Stuttgart, 1916. lxxv, 992p. illus., maps. Basic. *F9

PARKS, George B., *The English Traveler to Italy*. R, 1954. I. The Middle Ages (to 1525). xx, 669p. illus. *F10

PIVEC, Karl, "Italienwege der mittelalterlichen Kaiser." In *Die Brennerstrasse* (Bozen 1961) 84-110. F11

SCHROD, Konrad, *Reichstrassen und Reichsverwaltung im Königreich Italien (754-1197)*. Stuttgart, 1931. xii, 220p. *F12

SPRINGER, Otto, "Medieval Pilgrim Routes from Scandinavia to Rome,"
MS 12 (1950) 92-122. *F13

3 TRAVEL & GUIDEBOOKS

ANSON, Peter F., *The Pilgrim's Guide to Franciscan Italy*. L, 1927.
xx, 243p. illus. with fine drawings by the artist-author; bibl. Excellent. Rev:
AFH 21 (1928) 376. *F26
BRACALONI, Leone, OFM, *Terres franciscaines*. Tr. par Barthélemy
Héroux, OFM. Montréal, 1933. 294p. Articles from FF, revised; bibl. Useful.
*F27
CANONICI, Luciano, OFM, "Itinerari francescani Umbri," VM 30
(1959)-32(1961). Reprinted, revised, in *La Porziuncula*, 1962-64. Excellent.
F29
CAVANNA, Nicola, OFM, *L'Umbria francescana illustrata*. Perugia, 1910.
xv, 415p. illus., maps. Rev: AFH 3 (1910) 755-757 (Oliger). Fundamental,
with rich bibl. notes. *F30
——, *L'Ombrie franciscaine*. Tr. de T. de Wyzewa. P, 1926. xiv, 293p.
illus., maps. *F31

C   LIFE

I CHRONOLOGY

CRESI, D., OFM, "Cronologia della vita di SF," SF 55 (1958) 50-64. Rev:
MF 56 (1956) 608. Not sufficiently critical. C1
FISCHER, HERMANN, *Der hl. F. von A. während der Jahre 1219-1221.
Chronologische-historische Untersuchungen*. Fribourg, 1907. 144p. Rev: AB 13
(1912) 451-462; AFH 1 (1908) 630-633. Still useful. *C2
FORTINI, A., *Nel 750o anniversario della fondazione dell'Ordine dei Fra-
ti Minori (1209-1959). Storia, cronaca, discussioni*. SMA, 1959. 33p. illus.
Abs: AFH 53 (1960) 342. C3
GNOCCHI, Ludovico U., OFM, "In quale anno, mese e giorno il Crocifis-
so di S Damiano parlò a SF," SF 23 (1926) 274-279. C4
HERMANN, Placid, OFM, "The Chronology of SFs' Life." In A81:1-
10. C5
MANDIC, Dominik, OFM, *De legislatione antiquia OFM*. Mostar, 1924.
xvi, 140p. Rev: AFH 18 (1925) 272-278 (Bihl). *C6
——, "Kronolski pregled zivota sv. Franje Asiskoga," *Bogoslovska Smotra*
(Zagreb) 15 (1927) 36-43, 170-176, 349-357. Summary of a ms burned in
World War II. cf EF 40 (1928) 290 & 535. *C6a
PATREM, Léon, OFM, "Appunti critici sulla cronologia della vita di SF,"
MF 9 (1902) 76-101. cf AFH 1 (1908) 30. Fundamental. *C7
ROBINSON, P., OFM, "Quo anno Ordo Fratrum Minorum inceperit,"
AFH 2 (1909) 181-196. Important. *C8
TERZI, Arduino, OFM, *Cronologia della vita di SFA*. R, 1963. xvi, ·182p.
Indispensable though not sufficiently critical. *C9 Rev: AFH 58 (1965)
148-149.

VAN DER VAT, Odulf, OFM, "Das chronologische Rätsel in der Chronik des Jordanus von Giano," AFH 24 (1931) 395-398. cf A133. *C10

II HOME

ABATE, Guiseppe, Conv, *La casa dove nacque SFA, nella sua documentazione storica.* R, 1939. 56p. C11

——, *La casa dove nacque SFA nella sua nuova documentazione.* Gubbio, 1941. xxiv, 424p. illus. Also in MF 40 (1940) 321-744. Basic. **C12

——, "Storia e leggenda intorno alla nascita di SFA," MF 48 (1948) 515-549; 49 (1949) 123-153, 350-379. Valuable discussion. cf C33. *C13

——, "La casa natale di S. Francesco e la topografia d'Assisi nella prima meta del secolo XIII," DSPU 63 (1966) 5-110. Rev: AFH 61 (1968) 486-487; CF 37 (1967) 188.

ATTAL, Francesco Salvatore, *La casa dove nacque SF. Studio critico.* R, 1942. 48p. Summarizes C12. C14

——, "La casa paterna e il parentado di Santa Chiara. Falsi e falsari dei secoli XVI e XVII," MF 46 (1946) 157-197; on the casa of SF: only 170-172, 175-177. cf E216. C15

BARRADO, Arcangel, OFM, "La casa donde nació SF de Asis, patronado del Estado Español," VV 2 (1944) 471-512. *C16

BRACALONI, Leone, OFM, "Casa, casato e stemma di SF." CF 2 (1932) 520-534; 3 (1933) 81-102. Abs: CF 5 (1935) 146*. *C17

——, *La Chiesa Nuova di SF Converso, casa paterna del Santo in A.* Todi, 1943. xix, 304p. illus. *C18

——, *La Chiesa Nuova, casa paterna di SF. Capo aggiunto.* SMA, 1955. 15p. Rev: AFH 49 (1956) 227. C19

——, *La Chiesa Nuova, casa paterna di SF. Secondo capo aggiunto.* SMA, 1960. 28p. Rev: AFH 53 (1960) 341. C20

BUGHETTI, B., OFM, "Per la casa paterna di SF in A," AFH 34 (1941) 243-260, 449-455; 35 (1942) 328-337. *C21

CANALETTI GAUDENTI, Alberto, "Un parere giuridico sugli atti del Comune di A relativi alla Casa Natale di SF," MF 42 (1942) 313-317. C22

FORTINI, A., "La casa paterna di SF." FNV II, 21-90. *C23

GOLUBOVICH, G., OFM, *La storicità e autenticità della casa paterna di SFA oggi "Chiesa Nuova" e la popolare leggenda della "Stalletta." Studio critico.* Fi, 1940. xv, 112p. illus. Rev: SF 12 (1940) 151-154; 13 (1941) 237-240. *C24

JACOVELLI, A., Conv, *La casa natale di SFA intorno al 1615.* A, 1959. 20p. C25

PERALI, Pericle, "Lettera intorno alla Casa Paterna e Natale di SF, intorno ad un documento 'perentorio' ma superfluo, e intorno ad una casa dei nipoti del Santo prospiciente sulla 'Platea Nova Communis'," MF 41 (1941) 297-325J. map, facsim. Has 1395 taxlist. *C26

——, "Ottavio Ringhiere, Vescovo di A, e la casa dove nacque SF," MF 42 (1942) 277-312. C27

TERZI, A, OFM, *'La Chiesa Nuova' in A casa natale di SF.* R, 1960. 33p. map. Rev: EF ns12 (1962) 94. Quotes principal docs. *C28

III FAMILY, BIRTH, CHILDHOOD
1 BACKGROUND

ARIES, Philippe, *Centuries of Childhood, A Social History of Family Life.* Tr. by R. Baldick, NY, 1962. 447p. illus. C29

FACE, Richard D., *The Caravan Merchants & the Fairs of Champagne; a Study in the Techniques of Medieval Commerce.* Ann Arbor, Mich., 1957. lii, 175p. Abs: DA 17 (1957) 1318. Fundamental study. *C30

RENOUARD, Yves, *Les hommes d'affaires italiens du moyen âge.* P, 1949. ix, 262p. map. Rev: MA 57 (1951) 403-415. C31

SAPORI, Armando, *Le marchand italien au moyen âge.* P, 1952. lxx, 126p. Bibl: 1-115; cf B11:691-722. **C32

2 ST. FRANCIS

ABATE, G., Conv, "Storia e leggenda intorno alla nascita di SFA," MF 48 (1948) 515-549; 49 (1949) 123-153, 350-379; & R, 1949. 102p. Abs: CF VIII, 58* & CF IX, 65*. Fundamental new research on Stalletta, Pica, family, name, & birth legends. *C33

ATTAL, S., "Pietro Bernardone." In A278: 59-96. Rehabilitation. C34

BIHL, M., OFM, "De nomine S. F.," AFH 19 (1926) 469-529. Basic. *C35

FORTINI, A., FNV I/1, 102-116; II, 93-112 (chart, 100). *C36

MARINANGELI, Bonaventura, Conv, "Sulle orme di SF. Il fonte battesimale," SFA 1 (1920-1) 159-162. C37

ORTOLANI, Ciro da Pesaro, OFM, *La madre del Santo d'A.* Tolentino, 1926. 301p. Rev: FF 4 (1927) 210-213; EF 41 (1929) 322. C38

UBALD D'ALENCON, Cap, "De l'origine française de SFA," EF 10 (1903) 449-454. C39

IV YOUTH
1 GENERAL

DUGGAN, Alfred, *Growing up in 13th Century England.* NY, 1962. 213p. C40

MANACORDA, Giuseppe, *Storia della scuola in Italia. I. Il medioevo.* Mi, 1913. C40a

MEYER, Paul, "De l'expansion de la langue française en Italie pendant le moyen âge." In CISSA IV, 61-104; on SF: 68-69. C41

OZANAM, Antoine Frédéric, *Documents inédits pour servir à l'historie littéraire de l'Italie depuis le VIIIe siècle jusqu'au XIIIe.* P 1897. 418p. cf "Des écoles et de l'instruction publique en Italie aux temps barbares," 3-79. C42

SALVIOLI, G., *L'istruzione in Italia prima del mille.* Fi, 1912. 192p. C43

THOMPSON, J. W., *The Literacy of the Laity in the Middle Ages.* NY, 1939 (& 1960). 198p. cf ch. III: "Italy." *C44

Research Bibliography

2 ST. FRANCIS
(see also A306, A307:89-114; D156)

BROCART, Yves, OFM, "Une singulière nouveauté sur SFA," FF 2 (1925) 318-326. Opposes Beaufreton (A280). C45

CLASEN, Sophronius, OFM, "F, der Gottes Absicht noch nicht erkannte," WW 27 (1964) 117-128. Important. *C45a

DOMENICHELLI, Teofilo, "Il Celanese e i primi venticinque anni di SFA," *Luce e Amore* 4 (1907) 21-30. C46

FALOCI PULIGNANI, M., "Il maestro di SF," MF 22 (1921) 57-64. C47

FORTINI, A., "La giovinezza del Santo." FNV I/1, 105-149; II, 93-129. *C48

———, "SF e i Tripudianti di S. Vittorino," FF ns3 (1956) 84-88. Abs: CF XI, 93. cf FNV I/1, 164-178. C49

FREDEGAND [CALLAEY] D'ANVERS, Cap, "Come visse SFA in veste e costume secolareschi," *Rivista Internazionale di Scienze Sociali* (Roma) 106 (1926) 181-201. Basic, with C51. *C50

———, "L'allegra giovinezza di SFA. Esame critico," IF 1 (1926) 273-292. cf EF 40 (1928) 535-537; EstF 38 (1926) 356-374. cf C50. *C51

MASSERON, A., "L'enfance et la jeunesse de SF," ASF (1946-47) n.41, 4-8; n.45, 1-5. CF 20 (1950) 59*. C52

OLIGER, O., OFM, "De ultima mutatione officii S.F.," AFH 1 (1908) 45-49. *C53

3 CHIVALRY & TROUBADOURS
(see also D69, D151, F35)

BEDIER, J., "Les chansons de geste et les routes d'Italie." In his *Les légendes épiques* 2e éd (P 1917) II, 145-293. *C54

CHAYTOR, Henry J., *The Troubadours*. NY, 1912. vii, 151p. cf ch. III. *C55

D'ANCONA, A., "Le tradizioni carolingie in Italia." In his *Saggi di letteratura popolare* (Livorno 1913) 3-44. *C56

DUPIN, Henri, *La courtoisie au moyen âge (d'après les textes du XIIe et du XIIIe siècle)*. P, 1931. 167p. C57

FELDER, Hilarin, Cap. *Der Christusritter aus A. Z*, 1941. 165p. *C58

———, *Le chevalier du Christ au pays d'A*. Genève, 1943. 146p. *C59

———, *The Knight-errant of A*. Tr. by B. Bittle, Cap. Milw, 1948. 152p. Rev: (various eds.) CF 12 (1942) 557-559; Ant 17 (1942) 313; FnSs 7 (1947) 100-102; WW 12 (1949) 59-61 (Clasen). *C60

FREDEGAND [CALLAEY] D'ANVERS, Cap, *L'animo cavalleresco del Giullare di Dio*. Reggio Emilia, 1927. C61

O'CALLAGHAN, J. F., "Chivalry" NCE 3, 618-619.

OLIGER, L., OFM, "S F cognovitne pseudo-Turpinum?" Ant 2 (1927) 277-280. *C61a

VINCENTI, E., *Bibliografia antica dei trovatori*. Mi, 1963. lxiii, 179p. **C62

V MILITARY SERVICE
1 ASSISI-PERUGIA WAR

FORTINI, A., "La guerra di Perugia," FNV I/1, 151-210; "Le fazioni e la guerra di Perugia," FNV II, 131-219. *C63

GIARDINA, Camillo, "I 'boni homines' in Italia, contributo alla storia delle persone e della procedura civile e al problema dell' origine del consolato," *Riv. di storia del diritto italiano* 5 (1932) 28-98, 313-394. *C64

2 WAR IN APULIA

CALAMITA, F. P., "Chi era il conte Gentile?" MF 27 (1927) 151-152. C65

FALOCI PULIGNANI, M., "Perche SF voleva andare nelle Puglie," MF 27 (1927) 33-36; & IF 2 (1927) 325-329. Rev: C67. C66

ORZA, Mariano, *Gualteri III conte di Brienne.* Napoli, 1940. 348p. C66a

OTTAVIO DA ALATRI, Cap, "Perche F voleva andare nelle Puglie?" IF 2 (1927) 321-334. Important. *C67

VAN CLEVE, Thomas C., *Markward of Anweiler & the Sicilian Regency.* Princeton, NJ, 1937. x, 231p. Basic. **C68

VI CONVERSION

BRACALONI, Leone, OFM, (a) "Il prodigioso Crocifisso che parlò a FS," SF 36 (1939) 185-212; (b) SMA, 1958. 18p. illus. (c) Evelyn Sandberg Vavalà's masterpiece, *La Croce dipinta italiana e l'iconografia della Passione.* Verona, 1929. xiii, 943p. 585 illus. *C69

——, "SF architetto secondo Paolo Sabatier," CF 5 (1935) 353-369. *C70

DE BEER, Francis, OFM, *La conversion de SF* . . . See A97.

EDOUARD D'ALENCON, Cap, "La fenêtre de l'argent," *Annales fran-ciscaines* 16 (1889) 370-372. cf EF 40 (1928) 580. C71

ESSER, Kajetan, OFM, "Das Gebet des hl F vor dem Kreuzbild in San Damiano," FS 34 (1952) 1-11. CF X, 77*; CF 30 (1960) 16n34. Important. *C72

FALOCI PULIGNANI, M., "Il messale consultato da SF quando si con-vertì," MF 15 (1914) 32-43. cf AFH 7 (1914) 784; CF 30 (1960) 361n102. C73

FELICIANO DE VENTOSA, Cap, "SF o el triunfo de la gracia en la historia," *Nat. Gracia* 9 (1962) 35-70.

FORTINI, A., FNV I/1, 213-317; II, 221-272. C73a

LAZARO DE ASPURZ, Cap, "La via de la conversion en SFA," Laur. 8 (1967) 452-469.

VII MISSIONS
1 THE MARCHES OF ANCONA & FERMO

FOGLIETTI, Raffaele. *Le Marche dal 586 al 1230.* Macerata, 1907. F130

Research Bibliography

HUTTON, Edward, *The Cities of Romagna & the Marches.* L, 1913 (& 1925). xix, 309p. illus. Excellent. F131

PAGNANI, Giacinto, OFM, *I viaggi di SFA nell Marche.* Mi, 1962. 114p. illus., map. Rev: AFH 56 (1963) 357-359; CF 33 (1933) 329. Fundamental. *F132

STRAPPATI, Tarcisio, Conv, "Il Piceno 'Provincia stellata'," IF 34 (1959) 121-127, 131, 203-209, 265-269, 273, 344-348; 35 (1960) 51-54, 56, 128-133, 266-272, 347-352. *F133

TALAMONTI, Antonio, OFM, *Cronistoria dei Frati Minori della Provincia Lauretana delle Marche.* Sassoferrato, 1939-62. 7v. Rev: CF 9 (1939) 569; 10 (1940) 415; 13 (1943) 324-326; 20 (1950) 148; 33 (1963) 453; MF 38 (1938) 579-587 (Abate); 63 (1963) 373-385. Histories of friaries. Important. *F134

2 DALMATIA

MANDIC, Dominik, OFM, "Boravak sv. Franje Asiskoga u hrvatskim krajevima. Sur le séjour de SF dans les contrées croates," *Nova Revija (Makarska)* 5 (1926) 223-229. With French summary. cf EF 40 (1928) 537; FF ns6 (1933) 52. *C74

3 SPAIN (& CORSICA)

CHIAPPINI, Aniceto, OFM, "La Corsica francescana," *Archivio storico di Corsica* 17 (1941) 507-515. C75

ERNEST-MARIE DE BEAULIEU, Cap, "Le voyage de SF en Espagne," EF 15 (1906) 384-399; 16 (1906) 60-75; cf CF 30 (1960) 369n129. *C76

FORTI COGUL, E., "Sant Francesc d'Assis a Santes Creus," SMon 2 (1960) 223-231. C77

LOPES, Atanasio, OFM, "El viaje de SF a Espana," AIA 1 (1914) 13-45, 257-289, 433-469. Rev: AFH 4 (1911) 769; 7 (1914) 395, 798. cf CF 30 (1960) 369. Basic. *C78

ROSSETTI, Felice M., Conv, "SF ospite dei Codina," OR 7 feb, 1952: 4. CF X, 74*. C79

4 EGYPT & THE HOLY LAND

a. GENERAL

BOEHM, Ludwig, *Johann von Brienne, König von Jerusalem, Kaiser von Konstantinopel um 1170-1237.* Heidelberg, 1938. 106p. cf C68, C 82. *C80

DONOVAN, Joseph P., *Pelagius & the Fifth Crusade.* Phil, 1950. 124p. cf C84. *C81

GEROLA, Giuseppe, "Giovanni e Gualtieri di Brienne in SF di A," AFH 24 (1931) 330-340. cf MF 56 (1956) 22. On John's tomb in the Basilica. *C82

GOTTSCHALK, Hans L., *Al-Malik al-Kamil von Egypten und seine Zeit.* Wiesbaden, 1958. x, 256p. (On his personality: 23-26; on Damietta: 58-88; on SF: nothing.) Rev: AFH 52 (1959) 331-333. *C83

Research Bibliography

MANSILLA, D., "El Cardenal hispano Pelayo Gaitan (1206-1230)," *Anthologica Annua* 1 (1953) 11-66. cf C81. *C84

MAYER, Hans E., *Bibliographie zur Geschichte der Kreuzzüge.* Hannover, 1960. xxxii, 272p. **C85

OLIVER OF PADERBORN, *The Capture of Damietta.* Tr. by John J. Gavigan, Phil, 1948. ix, 112p. Rev: CHR 34 (1949) 475. *C86

RICHARD, J., "Crusaders' States" NCE 4, 500-504.

———, "Crusades" NCE 4, 504-513.

THETMARI, Magistri, *Iter ad Terram Sanctam.* T. Tobler, ed. St. Gall, 1851. 16p. C87

———, "Voyages faits en Terre Sainte par Thetmar, en 1217 . . ." In Académie royale des sciences, des lettres et des beaux-arts de Belgique *Mémoires* 26 (1851) no. 6; 61p. C88

VAN CLEVE, Thomas C., "The Fifth Crusade." In *A History of the Crusades* (Phil 1962) II, 377-428. Basic. **C89

ZACOUR, Norman F., "The Children's Crusade." *Ibid.,* 325-342.
**C90

b. EARLY FRANCISCAN MISSIONS

ANASAGASTI, Pedro de, OFM, *Francisco de Asís busca al hombre. Vocación y metodologia misioneras franciscanas.* Bilbao, 1964. 421p. Rev: AFH 58 (1965) 154-156.

BALDWIN, M. W., "Missions, History of (Medieval)" NCE 9, 933-935.

BIHL, M., OFM, "Die Franziskaner-Missionen im Morgenlande während des 13. Jahrhunderts," *Der Katholik* 35 (1907) 365-376; cf CF 30 (1960) 373n138. *C91

DE ROECK, Hildebrand, OFM, *De normis Regulae OFM circa missiones inter infideles ex vita primaeva franciscana profluentibus.* R, 1961. 125p. Rev: AFH 55(1962) 524-526. *C92

DURIGON, Natale, OFM, *L'istituzione dei missionari nell'Ordine dei Frati Minori (studio storico-giuridico).* Cairo, 1959. 134p. *C93

GOLUBOVICH, Girolamo, OFM, *Biblioteca Bio-bibliografica della Terra Santa e dell'Oriente francescano.* Q, 1906-19. Ser I, I-III. cf C97, C113. Rev: AFH 7 (1914) 132-138. Cited GBB. cf A334. **C94

GOVERNANTI, Gaudenzio, OFM, *I Francescani in Acri.* Gerusalemme, 1958. 96p. C95

HABIG, Marion A., OFM, *In Journeying Often: Franciscan Pioneers in the Orient.* St. Bonaventure, N. Y., 1953. 337p.

KRUEGER, Hilmar C., OFM, "Reactions to the First Missionaries in Northwest Africa," CHR 32 (1946) 275-301. CF VII, 44*. *C95a

ODOARDI, Giovanni, Conv, "La Custodia francescana di Terra Santa nel VI centenario della sua costituzione (1342-1942)," MF 43 (1943) 217-256.
*C96

RONCAGLIA, Martiniano, *Storia della Provincia di Terra Santa. 1. I Francescani in Oriente durante le Crociate (sec. XIII).* Cairo, 1954. xxvi, 107p. (GBB, ser. IV, Studi 1) Rev: AFH 47 (1954) 232. Useful. *C97

———, *SFA & the Middle East.* 2d ed. Tr. by Stephen A. Janto, OFM. Cairo, 1957. v, 93p. *C98

Research Bibliography

RUSSO, Francesco, Conv, *I protomartiri francescani*. Padova, 1948. 31p.
C99

La scimitarra del Miramolino: Relazione della passione dei primi martiri francescani del Marocco (1220). Tr. e pres. del P. Alberto Ghinato, OFM. R, 1962. 64p. cf AFH 23 (1930) 390. C100

SIMONUT, Noe, *Il metodo d'evangelizzazione dei Francescani tra i Mussulmani e Mongoli nei secoli XIII-XIV*. Mi, 1947. 164p. Rev: CF 21 (1951) 393. *C101

VAN DER VAT, Odulphus, OFM, *Die Anfänge der Franziskanermissionen und ihre Weiterentwicklung im nahem Orient und in den mohammedanischen Landern während des 13. Jahrhunderts*. We, 1934. xi, 267p. Rev: AFH 31 (1938) 477-486; CF 5 (1935) 277. *C102

c. ST. FRANCIS IN EGYPT & THE HOLY LAND

ANASAGASTI, Pedro de, OFM, *El alma misionera de SF de Asis*. R, 1955. 106p. Rev: CF 27 (1957) 328; EF ns7 (1956) 224. C103

BASETTI-SANI, Giulio, *Mohammed et SF*. Ottawa, 1959. 284p. Rev: CF 30 (1960) 220. *C104

DELORME, F., OFM, "Les Espagnols à la bataille de Damiette," AFH 16 (1923) 245-246. cf C84. *C105

DIOTALLEVI, Ferdinando, OFM, "SF nei suoi viaggi e nel possesso dei Luoghi Santi." In F38: 274-293. C106

FISCHER, H., "Der Aufenthalt des hl F im Orient..." In C2:20-42.
*C107

FORTINI, A., "Damiata." FNV I/2, 43-109. *C108

——, *SF in Egitto*. SMA, 1959. 71p. C109

——, *Gli ultimi Crociati, cronaca del VI centenario della Custodia di Terra Santa, celebrato in A nell'anno giubilare 1933*. Mi, 1935. 268p. C110

GABRIELI, Gabriele, *Del viaggio di SF in Egitto e del frate reatino che ve l'accompagnò. Ricerca storica*. Rieti, 1927. 21p. C111

——, "SF e il Soldano d'Egitto," *Oriente Moderno* 6 (1926) 633-643.
*C111a

GHINATO, Alberto, OFM, "S. F in Oriente Missionarius ac Peregrinus," AOFM 83 (1964) 164-181. Basic. *C112

GOLUBOVICH, Girolamo, OFM, "SF e i Francescani in Damiata," SF 12 (1926) 307-330. cf AFH 19 (1926) 559; 25 (1932) 129. See also C105.
*C113

"L'incontro d'El-Mansurah," OR 4mag, 1947: 3. CF VIII, 61*. C114

JACOPOZZI, Nazzareno, OFM, "Dove sia avvenuta la visita di SFA al Sultano Melek-el-Kamel." In 11e Congrès international de Géographie *Comptes rendus* (Cairo 1926) V, 141-156; & FF 2 (1925) 379-393. maps. Useful.
*C115

LEMMENS, Leonard, OFM, "De SF Christum praedicante coram Sultano Aegypti," AFH 19 (1926) 559-578. C116

——, "'F vir catholicus et totus apostolicus.' De primordiis missionum Ordinis Minorum," Ant 2 (1927) 21-58. *C117

NATALI, Augusto, "Gli Arabi e SF alle Crociate," IF 33 (1958) 154-162. C118

NILO, M., "SFA e l'Oriente," IF 2 (1927) 3-8. On possible Orthodox links. cf D211. C119

OKTAVIAN VON RIEDEN, Cap, "Die Sehnsucht des hl F nach dem Martyrium." In D139:365-372. Fundamental. **C120

RONCAGLIA, Martiniano, "Fonte Arabo-musulmana su SF in Oriente?" SF 50 (1953) 258-259. CF X, 74*. *C121

——, "SFA in Oriente," SF 50 (1953) 97-106. CF X, 74. Basic. *C122

ZWEMER, S. M., "F of A & Islam," Moslem World 39 (1949) 247-251. C123

VIII THE CHRISTMAS CRIB

BERLINER, Rudolf, "The Origins of the Creche," Gazette des Beaux Arts (NY) 30 (1946) 249-278. *C124

——, Die Weihnachtskrippe. München, 1955. 244p. illus. Rev: CF 27 (1957) 445-447; CF XI, 97. Abs: C133. *C125

BERNAREGGI, A., "Le fonti del presepio francescano di Greccio," SC ser. 6 3 (1924) 7-29, 99-108. Rich bibl. *C126

CANTINI, Gustavo, OFM, "L'infanzia divina nella pietà francescana," SF ns9 (1923) 283-313; cf 437-463. On post-SF evolution. C127

DAUSEND, H., OFM, "Die Weihnachtsfeier des hl F von A in Deutschland und Greccio," FS 13 (1926) 294-304. C128

DE ROBECK, Nesta, The Christmas Crib. L, 1938. 153p. Basic. *C129

GOUGAUD, L., OSB, "La crèche de Noël avant SFA," RSR 2 (1922) 26-34. Abs: AFH 19 (1926) 135. Important. *C130

GRISAR, H., SJ, "Archeologia del presepio in Roma (V-XVI secolo)," CC 59 (1908/4) 702-719; cf s16 (1895/4) 467-475. *C131

GROUSSET, René, "Le boeuf et l'âne à la Nativité du Christ," MAH 4 (1884) 334-344. *C132

MOLS, Roger, SJ, "Historie de la crèche de Noël d'après un ouvrage récent," NRT 81 (1959) 1049-1072. Abs-rev of C125. C133

OKTAVIAN VON RIEDEN, Cap, "De Kerstviering van Greccio in het licht van haar tijd," FL 40 (1957) 163-177; 41 (1958) 21-27. Rev: CF XI, 96. *C134

——, "Die Krippenfeier von Greccio in zeitgenössischer Beleuchtung," St. Fidelis 44 (1957) 8-20. Abs: CF XI, 96. Important. *C135

ROSENTHAL, Erwin, "The Crib of Greccio & Franciscan Realism," Art Bulletin (NY) 36 (1954) 57a-60a. Abs: CF XI, 125. C136

STEFANUCCI, Angelo, Storia del presepio. R, 1944. 570p. 292 illus. Rev: CF 14 (1944) 349-351. Useful but not sufficiently critical. *C137

TERZI, A., OFM, Nella selva di Greccio nacque il presepio plastico. R, 1961. 45p. 16pl. C138

TIME, Inc., "The Rich Poverty," Time (NY) Dec. 28, 1959; 34-37. C139

VAN HULST, Cesario, OFM, "Crèche," DSAM II, 2520-2526. *C140

——, De historia Praesepii Nativitatis Domini a Bethlehem usque ad Graecium. R, 1941. 200p. (diss.) *C141

YOUNG, Karl, "Officium Pastorum. A Study of the Dramatic Developments with the Liturgy of Christmas," Wisconsin Academy of Science, Arts & Letters *Transactions* 17 (1914) 299-396. *C142

IX THE STIGMATA

MELANI, Gaudenzio, OFM, *Nel crudo Sasso. S. Francesco alla Verna.* 2nd ed. La Verna, 1965. 112p. 8 plates. Rev: AFH 60 (1967) 253.

OKTAVIAN VON RIEDEN, Cap, "De Sancti F Assisiensis Stigmatum susceptione. Disquisitio historico-critica luce testimonium saeculi XIII," CF 33 (1963) 210-266, 392-422; 34 (1964) 5-62, 241-338. Masterpiece, Fundamental study with comprehensive bibl. **C143

X THE CANTICLE OF BROTHER SUN
1 MEANING

BENEDETTO, Luigi Foscolo, "Laudato si', mi' Signore, per . . ." *Pegaso* 2 (1930) 170-185. Rev: CF 1 (1931) 397. C144

——, *Il Cantico di frate Sole.* Fi, 1941. 263p. Rev: AFH 34 (1941) 236-242 (Bihl); CF 12 (1942) 71-73; MF 43 (1943) 305-314; SF 40 (1943) 185-189 (Bughetti); SM 14 (1941) 150-163. First basic study favoring per-by & S. Fabiano. *C145

BONVIN, Paul, Cap, *Cantiques des creatures de s. F.* Texte et photos. Brux, 1965. 132p, illus.

BRANCA, Vittore, "Il Cantico di frate Sole. Studio delle fonti e testo critico," AFH 41 (1948) 3-87; & Fi, 1950. 130p. Rev: CF 20 (1950) 62*; CF IX, n127; MF 52 (1952) 640. Critical ed. *C146

CAMBELL, Jacques, OFM, see A44:225-230. Favors per-for. *C147

CASELLA, Mario, "Il Cantico delle Creature," SM 16 (1943/50) 102-134. Favors per-propter. *C148

CHIMENZ, Siro A., "La poesia religiosa umbra del duecento." In *L'Umbria nella storia* (Bologna, 1954) 167-192. Abs: CF XI, 65. Favors per-through or as in Mass-Preface. C149

FUZIO, Gerolamo, *Il Cantico di SF premessa dell' Umanesimo.* Molfetta, 1965, 95p.

GETTO, Giovanni, *FA e il Cantico di Frate Sole.* To, 1956. 70p. *C150

GUERRIERI CROCETTI, Camillo, "Ancora sul Cantico di frate Sole," *Rassegna della lett. ital.* 59 (1955) 440-445. Abs: CF XI, 66. Favors per-propter. C151

MACCIONI, Enrico, *Laudes creaturarum quas b. F ad laudem et honorem Dei fecit.* Florence, 1965. Ten plates.

MATTESINI, Francesco, OFM, "Le lodi e il cantico delle creature," SF 63 (1966), n. 3, 3-15. Rev: AFH 60 (1967) 460.

MONTANO, Rocco, "Il Cantico delle Creature," *Delta* ns7/8 (1955) 107-109. Abs: CF XI, 66. Against per-by-through-for; favors an obscure mystical sense. C152

MONTEVERDI, Angelo, "Prime testimonianze di lingua e di poesia volgare in Umbria." In *L'Umbria nella storia* (Bologna, 1954) 149-163. Abs: CF VI, 64. Agrees with Pagliaro. C153

Research Bibliography

PAGLIARO, Antonio, "Il Cantico di frate Sole," *Quaderni di Roma* 1 (1947) 218-235. Abs: CF XI, 65 (with 2 later art.) Favors Preface instrumental per. C154

PAX, Elpidius, OFM, "'Bruder Feuer.' Religionsgeschichtliche und volkskundliche Hintergründe," FS 33 (1951) 238-249. Has per-durch. C155

PLATZECK, E. W., *Das Sonnenlied des Hl F von A. Eine Untersuchung seiner Gestalt und seines inneren Gehaltes nebst neuer deutscher Übersetzung.* München, 1956. 84p. Rev: CF 29 (1959) 105; FS 40 (1958) 431. C156

SABATELLI, Giacomo, OFM, "Studi recenti sul Cantico di Frate Sole," AFH 51 (1958) 3-24. Basic survey of recent studies. *C157

SCHEFFCZYK, Leo, "Der 'Sonnengesang' des hl. F v A und die 'Hymne an die Materie' des Thomas von Celano," *Geist und Leben* 35 (1962) 219-233.

SIGNER, L., *Franz von Assisi. Der Sonnengesang.* Übersetzung und Nachwort von L. Signer. Photos von K. Jud. Zürich, 1964. 40p.

SPITZER, Leo, "Nuove considerazioni sul 'Cantico di Frate Sole'," Conv 23 (1955) 257-270; "Postilla all'articolo 'Nuove .... Sole'," 24 (1956) 234-235; "Altre considerazioni sul 'Cantico di Frate Sole'," 25 (1957) 84-87. Abs: CF XI, 66-67. *C158

THILO, E. E., *S. François d'Assise. Le cantinque du Soleil.* Adaptation français, et preface d'Eric E. Thilo. Photographies de Karl Jud. Zürich, 1964. 40p.

VICINELLI, A. See A165:219-252. Outstanding literary analysis. Favors per-for. *C159

2 WHERE COMPOSED
(arranged chronologically under authors)

ABATE, G., Conv, "La nascita del Cantico di Frate Sole nel Palazzo Vescovile di A," MF 56 (1956) 333-415. Rev: RSCI 11 (1957) 262-265. Basic. *C160

ATTAL, F. S., "San Damiano e il Cantico di Frate Sole," FF 25 (1958) 139-141. Summarizes controversy; favors San Damiano. C161

BENEDETTO, L. F., *Il Cantico* . . . See C145:128-156. C162

BIGARONI, Marino, OFM, "A proposito di una rischiosa tesi sul Cantico di Frate Sole," *Accademia Properziana del Subasio Atti* 5 (1955) 46-52. Abs: CF XI, 70; RSCI 11 (1957) 262. C163

———, *Il Cantico di Frate Sole. Genesi del Cantico.* SMA, 1956. 158p. illus. Rev: AFH 50 (1957) 248; FF 23 (1956) 142; RSCI 11 (1957) 262-265. *C164

CASOLINI, F., "San Damiano o S. Fabiano?" FF 23 (1956) 25-33. C165

CAVANNA, N., OFM, "Il Santuario della Foresta presso Rieti rivendicata alla storia," SF 37 (1940) 265-273; & Fi, 1941, 11p. *C166

FORTINI, A., "Di alcune questioni riguardanti la composizione del Cantico del Sole." In E206:275-298. [1954] Rev: CF XI, 69. *C167

———, *Infondatezza di una recente critica che vorrebbe contestare al luogo* di San Damiano la gloria del Cantico del Sole. A, 1955. 24p. *C168

——, Altra ipotesi sul luogo dove fu composto il Cantico del Sole. A, 1956. 38p. *C169

——, "Questioni sulla composizione del Cantico del Sole." [1959] FNV II, 471-543. Fundamental. *C170

L.V.R. [Benigno Luciano Miglorini], Il santuario francescano di San Fabiano Papa alla Foresta. Rieti, 1949. 11p. C171

SABATELLI, Giacomo, OFM, Fatti e ipotesi sul luogo di nascita del Cantico di Frate Sole. SMA, 1959. 16p. *C172

SACCHETTI SASSETTI, Angelo, "Franciscana Reatina," SF 38 (1941) 103-108. *C174

——, Per la storia del Convento della Foresta. Rieti, 1948. 19p. C175

——, Ancora due parole sul Convento della Foresta. Rieti, 1949. 10p. C176

——, S. Fabiano della Foresta o S. Maria della Foresta? Rieti, 1955. 15p. C177

——, Nuovi documenti sul Convento della Foresta. Rieti, 1955. 23p. C178

——, Replica a Mons. Terzi sul Convento della Foresta. Rieti, 1956, 20p. C179

——, Questioncelle francescane. Rieti, 1959. 22p. Abs: AFH 53 (1960) 342. C180

——, Novissimi documenti sul convento di S. Maria della Foresta. Rieti, 1965. 12p.

——, Un 'ospite di SF a Rieti. Tebaldo Saraceno. Rieti, 1966. 7p.

TERZI, A., OFM, Memorie. [R, 1955]. Fundamental. *C181

——, Risposta al VI opuscolo del Prof. Sacchetti contro "La Foresta." R, 1956. 16p. re C177. C182

——, S. Fabiano de "La Foresta" ascoltò per primo il Cantico di Frate Sole (Supplemento al Volume "Memorie francescana nella Valle Reatina"). R, 1957. 223p. Rev: AFH 51 (1959) 219; CF XI, 68; MF 59 (1959) 253-255. Important. *C183

——, Il Poverello . . . [R, 1959]. Summarizes his case. *C184

——, Ultime battute sul luogo di nascita del Cantico di Frate Sole. R, 1960. 53p. Also important, with app. on Companions. *C185

——, Cronologia . . . [1963] See C9:126-151 & 158-171. Latest summary. *C186

——, "La Foresta," Sacello pagano, chiesina cristiana, santuario frances-cano. R, 1966. 47p.

——, Sono interpolazioni nella storia del cantico di Frate Sole le diciture "Preno S. Damiano" — vescovo "di Assisi" — podesta di Assisi. R, 1966. 15p.

XI ILLNESSES & DOCTORS
(see also C143)

ANDRESEN, Carl, "Asketische Forderung und Krankheit bei Franz von A.," Theologische Literaturzeitung 79 (1954) 129-140. Abs: CF XI, 97; CF 30 (1960) 27-29. *C186a

——, "Franz von A. und seine Krankheiten," *Wege zum Menschen* 6 (1954) 33-43. Abs: CF XI, 97; CF 30 (1960) 27. *C187

BONADIES, Antonio, *SF medico*. R, 1960. 51p. Rev: EF ns13 (1963) 225. C188

BOURNET, Albert S., *SFA, Etude sociale et médicale*. Lyon, 1893. 198p. Rev: AB 13 (1894) 301. C189

GILBERT, Judson B., *Disease & Destiny, A Bibliography of Medical References to the Famous*. L, 1962. 535p. On SF:173-174. *C190

GUALINO, L., "La morte del Santo," *Illustrazione medica italiana* 8 (1926) 201-204. Abs: EF 40 (1929) 538. C191

HARTUNG, Edward F., "SF & Medieval Medicine," *Annals of Medical History* ns7 (1935) 85-91. Well documented study of sources. *C192

LODATO, Gaetano, *La malattia d'occhi di SFA*. Mi, 1927. 8p. Rev: MF 30 (1930) 64. C192a

PARISOTTI, Orestes, *Quo morbo oculi sensum amisit F ab Assisio*. R, 1918. 26p. C193

[SCHMUCKI] Octavian v. Rieden, Cap, "De infirmitatibus SFA inde a juventute usque ad stigmatum susceptione," *Miscell. M. de Pobladura*, I. R, 1964. 99-129.

STREBEL, J., "Kulturhistorisches aus der Geschichte der Ophthalmologie und Medizindiagnose des Augenleidens des hl. F von A," *Klinische Monatsblätter für Augenheilkunde* 99 (1937) 252-260. Abs: CF 22 (1952) 81. C193a

VIVIANI, Ugo, "Sulla identificazione dei vari medici di SFA," Accademia Petrarca (Arezzo) *Atti e Memorie* ns 28-29 (1940) 221-234. cf DSPU 55 (1958) 258; FF 6 (1929) 71. C194

XII DEATH

EDOUARD D'ALENCON, Cap, "La bénédiction de SF mourant à Frère Elie," EF 9 (1903) 204-207. cf MF 9 (1902) 107. C195

BIHL, M., OFM, "De epistola encyclica Fr. Heliae circa transitum S.F.," AFH 23 (1930) 410-418. Abs: CF 1 (1931) 398. cf A72. *C196

CARMICHAEL, Montgomery, "The Gospel Read to SF in transitu," *Dublin Review* 132 (1903) 321-335; & with P.S.: "Il Vangelo letto a SF in transitu," MF 9 (1904) 149-156. C197

CERMINARA, T., OFM, "Il B. Agostino d'A," SF 29 (1932) 208-219. C198

HABIG, Marion A., OFM, *As the Morning Star, The Passing of SF*. NY, 1947. 218p. Rev: CF 21 (1951) 280; FnSs 8 (1948) 88. *C199

RENE DE NANTES, Cap, "La mort de SF," EF 18 (1907) 483-506. C200

XIII RELICS

BRACALONI, Leone, OFM, "Le sacre reliquie della Basilica di S. Chiara in A," AFH 12 (1919) 402-417. *C201

CANNAROZZI, Ciro, OFM, "Storia dell'abito col quale SFA ricevette le Sacre Stimmate," SF ns10 (1924) 262-282. cf C209. *C202

FALOCI PULIGNANI, M., "L'ultima tonaca di SF," MF 14 (1913) 73-95; illus. Abs: AFH 6 (1913) 403. *C203

FOSCO, A., "La sindone di SF," SFA 5 (1925) 158. C204

GOFFAERTS, Camille, "L'écuelle de SFA," *Revue de l'art chrétien* 4 (1893) 48-49. cf "The Soup Bowl of SF," *Dublin Review* 23 (1890) 191-192. C205

GRATIEN DE PARIS, Cap, "SFA au Musée du Trocadero," EF 38 (1926) 493-507. C206

JEAN DE COGNIN, Cap, "Une prétieuse relique de SFA: une manche de son habit," MF 32 (1932) 138-140. Abs: CF 5 (1935) 174*. C207

LAURI, Achille, "A proposito del calice di SF," *Luce serafica* 16 (1940) 216-129, CF VII, 33*. cf FNV III, 31; CF 5 (1935) 361. cf C210. C208

LAZZERI, Zeffirino, OFM, "Fra Mariano da Firenze, La storia della translazione dell'abito di SF da Montauto a Firenze," AFH 17 (1924) 545-549. cf C202. Habit on display at Ognissanti OFM church in Florence. *C209

LY, A., "Il calice di SF," OR 5ott, 1940:3. CF VII, 44*. cf C208. C210

MARINANGELI, Bonaventura, Conv, "Le reliquie di SF nella Basilica di A," SFA 3 (1922/3) 51-52, 67-69, 111-112; 4 (1924) 228-231. Basic. cf earlier series in MF 14-18 (1912-17). *C211

PARSI, Ettore, "Storia di una insigne reliquia del sangue di SF," OR 30dic, 1943:2. Abs: CF VII, 42*. cf SFA 9 (1929) 223-226; MF 34 (1954) 357. C212

Il saio delle stimmate nel suo pellegrinaggio tra le genti di Daunia, Lucania, Molise, Lupinia e Campania nell'anno 1957. Foggia. 1959. 66p. C213

STICCO, Maria, "I vestiti di SF," VP 32 (1949) 415-420. Abs: CF IX, 67*. *C214

TAMBURINI, Elisa, "Bigello," FF 16 (1939) 361-364. Abs: CF VI, 19*. C215

VALAGRA, Giuseppe, "Il sacco di SF a Montella," IF 2 (1927) 232-239. C216

XIV CANONIZATION & CULT

1 GENERAL

BIHEL, E., OFM, "S. F. fuitne angelus sexti sigilli? (Apoc. 7,2)" Ant 2 (1927) 59-90. C217

BIHL, M., OFM, "De canonizatione S. F.," AFH 21 (1928) 480-514. Basic. *C218

DELORME, F. M., OFM, "Elevations théologiques sur SF 'l'autre ange'," SF 10 (1924) 233-253. *C218a

FORTINI, A., *Il ritorno di SF. Cronaca del settimo centenario francescano.* Mi, 1937. 467p. 78 illus. Rev: CF 8 (1938) 80-83. C219

LAZZERI, Z., OFM, "La Questione francescana e il processo di canonizzazione di SF," FF ns10 (1963) 171-175. C219a

ROSSETTI, Felice M., *Alla tomba di SFA*. To, 1957. 267p. illus. Rev: CF XI, 115. *C220

SISTO DA PISA, Cap, "La invenzione del corpo di SF ad Assisi 1818-1820," IF 13 (1938) 81-92. Rev: CF VI, 18*. Not critical. C221

2 IN LITURGY
(see also C53)

Liturgia di SFA. Testi latini liturgici. Intr. di Giacomo Cambell, OFM. Versione di Fausta Casolini, TOF. Santuario della Verna (Arezzo), 1963. xxxi, 159p. Rev: CF 34 (1964) 185 (OvR). *C222

ABATE, L. G., Conv "Da chi e quando fu composto il Prefazio della Mesa di SF," MF 36 (1936) 511-514. CF 10 (1940) 142. *C223

CORNET, Bertrand, OFM, "Le 'Proles de coelo prodiit' de Grégoire IX en l'honneur de SF," EF ns2 (1950) 427-461. C224

CRESI, D., OFM, "Il Prefazio di SF in un Messale sconosciuto," Ant 35 (1960) 95-102. *C225

DIJK, S. J. D. van, "Domum portam et tumulum, Pater Francisce visita," AFH 50 (1957) 218-220.

OLIGER, L., OFM, "De Praefatione S. F. Assisiensis," Ant 11 (1936) 351-370. *C226

PAVOLINI, Francesco M., OFM, "Il Prefazio del P. SFA," VM 11 (1939) 67-71, 93-96. Abs: CF VI, 25*. C227

XV ICONOGRAPHY

ANDRISANI, Gaetano, "L'iconographie franciscaine dans l'oeuvre du Titien," EF ns12 (1962) 84-92. C233

ANHEUSER, Clemens, & P. Plaseller, *F. und seine Gefolgschaft. Philatelistische Studie über den Fr. Orden*. Saarbrücken, 1959. 96p. illus. Rev: CF 32 (1962) 195. C234

BARGELLINI, P., "Il ritratto di SF," *Città di Vita* 5 (1950) 401-404. Abs: CF IX, 81* (Bonav. Berlinghieri's.) C235

BASCAPE, Giacomo C., "Note sui sigilli dei Francescani (secoli XIII-XVI)," CF 32 (1962) 148-164; illus. cf AFH 4 (1911) 425-435. cf C248, *C236

BOVING, Remigius, "Das aktive Verhältnis des hl. Franz zur bildenden Kunst," AFH 19 (1926) 610-635. C237

BUGHETTI, B., OFM, "Vita e miracoli di SF nelle tavole istoriate dei secoli XIII e XIV," AFH 19 (1926) 636-732; 32pl. *C238

FACCHINETTI, V., OFM. See A292. Richest coll. of illus. & refs.

GUDIOL, J., "Iconography & Chronology in El Greco's Paintings of SF," *Art Bulletin* 44 (1962) 195-203. cf Paul GUINARD, "SF dans l'oeuvre de Greco," RHF 2 (1925) 1-21. C239

JULIAN, René, "Le franciscanisme et l'art italien," *Phoebus* (Basel) 1 (1946) 105-115. Important. *C240

KAFTAL, George, *SF in Italian Painting*. L, 1950. 121p. illus. Rev: CF 22 (1952) 193. *C240a

LAMY, M., "La vie de SF racontée par les artistes de la Renaissance au XIXe siècle," ASF 3 (1937) 97-100; 4 (1938) 11-14. CF VI, 29*. C241

LAZZERI, Z., OFM, "Un ritratto di SF eseguito nel 1225?" OR 20 dic, 1959:3. por. Detail of mosaic by Iacopo da Torrita in Florence Baptistery. C242

MARINO MAZZARA, S., "Il sentimento francescano di Benozzo Gozzoli," SF 7 (1921) 236-245. cf. C247. C243

MASSERON, A., "Note d'iconographie franciscaine. A propos de la fresque du baptistère de Parme." EF ns2 (1950) 463-466. C244

MARINANGELI, B., Conv, "La serie di affreschi giotteschi nella Chiesa Superiore di A," MF 13 (1911) 97-112. cf MF 49 (1949) 151n9. C245

NERI, Damiano, "Iconografia del transito di SF," SF 12 (1926) 495-517. C246

NESSI, Silvestro, "La vita di SF dipinta da Benozzo Gozzoli a Montefalco," MF 61 (1961) 467-492. Basic. *C247

RAOUL DE SCEAUX, Cap, "SF d'après les sceaux," ASF n61 (1950) 7-13. C248

REAU, Louis, *Iconographie de l'art chrétien*. P., 1955-59. 3v. in 6. On SF:t. III, pt. 1, 516-535. Useful. *C249

REMY D'ALOST, Cap, "L'oeuvre franciscaine de Rubens," EF 50 (1938) 637-659; 51 (1939) 23-54. *C250

SCHNEIDER, Reinhold, *Franziskus*. Freiburg, 1953. 17p.; 25pl.; also in English: SF. CF X, 87*. Coll. of early portraits. C251

SCHRADE, H., *Franz von A und Giotto*. Köln, 1964, 184p. *C251a

TINTORI, Leonetto, & M. Meiss, *The Painting of The Life of SF in A, with Notes on the Arena Chapel*. NY, 1962. xv, 205p. *C252

VILLAIN, Maurice, "SF et les peintres d'A," EF 49 (1937) 509-531; 50 (1938) 35-62, 172-193, 415-441; & P, nouv. éd. 1950. 232p. illus. Rev: CF VI, 29*; CF IX, 82*. *C253

FIVE OUTSTANDING MODERN ILLUSTRATORS OF THE LIFE OF ST. FRANCIS

BENLIURRE Y GIL, Jose, *SF de Asis*, comentarios del P. Antonio Torro, OFM. Valencia, 1926. xxxvii, 265p. 66 illus. (49 of SF). Rev: AFH 25 (1932) 537; EF 41 (1929) 438. C254

BOUTET DE MONVEL, Louis Maurice (1850-1913), *SFA*. P, 1921. 126p. 21 illus. C255

BURNAND, Eugene, *The Little Flowers of SF*. NY, 1919. 178p. 30 illus. C256

SEGRELLES, Jose, (a) *Florecillas de SF de Asis*. Ba, 1926. 344p. Rev: AFH 20 (1927) 408, 422; EF 41 (1929) 438. (b) *La leggenda francescana*. Mi, 1927. 49 illus. C257

SUBERCASEAUX ERRAZURIZ, Pedro, OSB. *SF d'Assise*. Intr. by J. Joergensen. Boston, 1925. xviii, 198p. 50 col. illus. Rev: Ant 2 (1927) 280 (Oliger); EF 41 (1929) 439; cf AFH 24 (1931) 271. cf his autobiography: Pedro SUBERCASEAUX, *Memorias*. Santiago de Chile, 1962. 272p. C258

Research Bibliography

XVI THE PAPACY AND FRANCIS

(1) ROME & THE CHURCH IN THE 13TH CENTURY
(see also B1-B6, B13, B31-B48)

FLICHE, A., et al., *Histoire de l'Eglise* (P 1950) X, 11-424. *F64

HERDE, Peter, *Beiträge zum päpstlichen Kanslei-und Urkundenwesen im dreizehnten Jahrhundert.* Kallmünz, 1961. xiii, 259p. *F65

HOMO, Léon, *Rome médiévale (476-1420). Histoire, civilisation, vestiges.* P, 1934. 327p. *F66

MATT, Leonard von, *Rom im Mittelalter.* Würzburg, 1960. xvi, 48pl. *Roma medioevale.* Genova, 1961. xvi, 48pl. *Medieval Rome.* Genova, 1961. xii, 48pl. F67

POTTHAST, A., *Regesta Pontificum.* Berlin, 1874. 2v. *F68

SEPPELT, F. X., *Geschichte der Päpste,* 2 Aufl. (München 1956) III, 319-411, & 614. *F70

(2) POPE INNOCENT III

BULTOT, Robert, "Mépris du monde, misère et dignité de l'homme dans la pensée d'Innocent III," CCM 4 (1961) 441-456. Basic. cf DA 14 (1954) 2069. *F71

FLICHE, Augustin, "Innocent III et la réforme de l'Eglise," RHE 44 (1949) 87-152. Fundamental. cf F74; F64:139-213. *F72

MACCARRONE, Michele, "Innocenzo III prima del Pontificato," DRSP 65 (1942) 59-134. Important. *F73

——, "Riforma e sviluppo della vita religiosa con Innocenzo III," RSCI 16 (1962) 29-72. Basic. cf F72. *F74

POWELL, James M., ed., *Innocent III, Vicar of Christ or Lord of the World?* Boston, 1963. 74p. Anthology of excerpts from leading modern historians showing evolving interpretations of Innocent's motives. *F75

SMITH, Charles E., *Innocent III, Church Defender.* Baton Rouge, La., 1951. vi, 203p. *F76

TILLMANN, Helene, *Papst Innocenz III.* Bonn, 1954. xv, 315p. Basic. *F77

(3) POPE HONORIUS III

CLAUSEN, J., *Papst Honorius III. (1216-1227); eine Monographie.* Bonn, 1895. viii, 414p. *F78

DELORME, F.M., OFM, "La bonne date de la bulle 'cum dilecti' d'Honorius III," AFH 12 (1919) 591-593. cf AFH 19 (1926) 539. *F79

FALOCI PULIGNANI, M., "Una bolla sconosciuta di Onorio III a SF," MF 27 (1927) 177-181; cf AFH 25 (1932) 146. F80

PRESSUTI, Pietro, ed., *Regesta Honorii papae III.* R, 1888-1895. 2v. *F81

(4) CARDINAL HUGOLIN — POPE GREGORY IX
(see also E19, E24, E166, E178, F96, F120-F122)

AUVRAY, Lucien, ed., *Les registres de Grégoire IX.* P, 1896-1907. 2v. *F83

Research Bibliography

BREM, Ernst, *Papst Gregor IX. bis zum Beginn seines Pontifikats*. Heidelberg, 1911. 118p. Rev: AFH 5 (1912) 752. F84

CALLEBAUT, André, OFM, "Autour de la rencontre à Florence de SF et du Cardinal Hugolin (en été 1217)," AFH 19 (1926) 530-558. Fundamental. *F85

CRISPOLTI, Virgilio, "Il VII centenario della morte di Papa Gregorio IX, commemorato nella Basilica di A (1241-21 agosto-1941)," MF 41 (1941) 411-423. F86

FELTEN, J., *Papst Gregor IX*. Fr/Br, 1886. xii, 409p. F87

LEVI, Guido, ed., "Documenti ad illustrazione del Registro del Card. Ugolino d'Ostia, legato apostolico in Toscano e Lombardia," SRSP 12 (1889) 241-326. *F88

——, *Registri dei cardinali Ugolino d'Ostia e Ottaviano degli Ubaldini*. R, 1890. xxviii, 247p. (Fonti per la storia d'Italia, 8). *F89

LIBERATO DI STOLFI, OFM, "Gregorio IX 'Padre e signore' di SF," FF 14 (1941) 249-256. F90

SIBILIA, Salvatore, *Gregorio IX (1227-1241)*. Mi, 1961. 406p. illus. *F91

THOUZELLIER, C., "La légation en Lombardie du cardinal Hugolin (1221)," RHE 45 (1950) 508-542. Basic. *F92

ZARNCKE, Lilly, *Der Anteil des Kardinals Ugolino an der Ausbildung der drei Orden des hl. Franz*. Leipzig, 1930. 144p. Rev: AFH 25 (1932) 81-85 (Bihl). Important. *F93

ZOELLIG, Benedikt, Cap, "Die Beziehungen des Kardinals Hugolino zum hl. F und zu seinem ersten Orden," FS 20 (1933) 1-33; 21 (1934) 34-79; & Münster, 1934. 79p. Rev: CF 9 (1939) 141-143. Important. *F94

(5) THE COLLEGE OF CARDINALS

"Essai de liste générale des cardinaux." In *Annuaire pontifical catholique* (P) 1928-29. Useful biographical sketches of 13th-century cardinals. F95

BERNARDINO DA SIENA, Cap, *Il cardinale protettore negli Istituti religiosi, specialmente negli Ordini francescani*. Fi, 1940. 185p. Rev: CF 10 (1940) 588. cf E3:59-76 (Brooke). *F96

GANZER, Klaus, *Die Entwicklung des auswärtigen Kardinalats im hohen Mittelalter. Ein Beitrag zur Geschichte des Kardinalcollegiums vom 11. bis 13. Jahrhundert*. Tü, 1963. xxxiv, 217p. *F98

KARTUSCH, Elfriede, *Des Kardinalskollegium in der Zeit von 1187 bis 1227*. Wien, 1948. 454p. (Wien Univ. diss.). *F100

ZIMMERMANN, Heinrich, *Die päpstliche Legationen in der ersten Hälfte des 13. Jahrhundert...(1198-1241)*. Paderborn, 1913. xv, 348p. *F101

(6) CARDINAL JOHN OF ST. PAUL

ALTANER, B., "Zur Biographie des Kardinals Johannes von St. Paul," HJ 49 (1929) 304-306. *F102

BIHL, M., OFM, "De Iohanne de S. Paulo, cardinali episcopo Sabinensi, primo S. F in Curia Romana an. 1209 fautore," AFH 19 (1926) 282-285. Basic. *F103

PASCHINI, Pio, "Il cardinale Giovanni di San Paolo." In *Studi di storia e diritto in onore di Carlo Calisse* (Mi 1940) III, 109-118. Indispensable.
*F104

WENCK, K., "Der Designationsversuch Weihnachten 1197. Kardinal Johann von St. Paul..." In *Papstum und Kaisertum* (München 1926) 456-474. *F105

(7) CARDINAL NICHOLAS DE ROMANIS

BIHL, M., "Nicolaus de Romanis (1219) fueritne primus cardinalis O. F.M.?" AFH 19 (1926) 287-289. cf AFH 54 (1961) 229. cf F105:471.
*F106

(8) ST. FRANCIS & ROME
(see also D125, D126a, D153, D199a, E3, E16)

ALBANUS AB HERMETSCHWIL, Cap, "Visio papae Innocentii III de Basilica Lateranensi collabenti secundum Legendam S. Dominici in carmine 'Passional' contentam cum fontibus franciscanis comparata," TO 22 (1961) 29-33, 146-151. cf A197. *F107

BIHL, M., OFM, "S. F. parabola in sermonibus Odonis de Ceritonia an. 1219 conscriptis," AFH 22 (1929) 584-586. Abs: CF 1 (1931) 102. Add to A80. F108

Bullarium Franciscanum, Joannes Hyacinthus Sbaralea et al., ed. R, 1759-68. v.1-4; *Bullarii Franciscani Epitome*, Conrad Eubel, Conv, ed. Q, 1908. 349p. Rev: AFH 2 (1909) 646. *F109

BULLETTI, E., OFM, "Ospedale e chiesa di S. Antonio presso il Laterano," SF 26 (1929) 267-268. Important. *F110

CECCHELLI, Carlo, "Memorie romane del Serafico," *Capitolium* 2 (1926) 329-347. illus. Basic. *F111

CERAFOGLI, G., "Il Concilio Lateranense IV e SF," OR 22dic, 1963: 7. F112

FRANCISCUS, Fr., "F en het IVe Lateraans Concilie," FL 45 (1962) 47-59, 78-94, 132-152; 46 (1963) 6-20, 40-50, 67-81, 109-123, 131-143. *F113

LIBERATO DI STOLFI, OFM, "SF e Roma," FF 15 (1938) 24-34. F114

——, *SFA e Roma.* R, 1947. 27p. Rev: CF 20 (1950) 61*. Useful.
*F115

MATANIC, Atanasio, OFM, "Papa Innocenzo III di fronte a San Domenico e SF," Ant 35 (1960) 508-527. Abs: AFH 54 (1961) 445; RSCI 15 (1961) 366. *F116

MIGUEL DE PAMPLONA, Cap, "Viajes de SF a Roma," *Verdad y Caridad* 10 (1933) 236-239, 267-269, 305-308, 338-339. Rev: CF 5 (1935) 147. F117

OLIGER, L., OFM, "SF a Roma e nella Provincia Romana." In F38: 65-112. Important. *F118

ORTH, Clement R., Conv, *The Approbation of Religious Institutes.* Wa, 1931. 171p. (Cath. Univ. diss.) Useful. *F119

SALVADORI, Giulio, "SFA nei suoi rapporti con i pontefici dell'età sua a Roma," Univ. del Sacro Cuore (Mi), *Pubblicazioni Scienze filologiche* Ser. 4 16 (1933) 321-340. Abs: CF 5 (1935) 173. cf D181. F120

STRONG, Mrs. Arthur, "SF in Rome." In D178:267-306. F121
TERZI, Arduino, OFM, *SFA a Roma.* R, 1956. xviii, 100p. illus., plans.
Rev: AFH 51 (1958) 203; CF 27 (1957) 424; MF 58 (1958) 340-342.
Indispensable. *F122

D SPIRITUALITY

I BIBLE
(see also D77, D93)

BIHEL, E., OFM, "Deux citations bibliques de SF," FrFr 12 (1929)
529-539. Abs: CF 1 (1931) 101. D1
CHIMINELLI, PIERO, "SF e la Bibbia," FF 15 (1942) 132-136, 177-
182. D2
EUGENE D'OISY, Cap, "SFA la Bible et le Saint Evangile," EF 39
(1927) 498-529, 646-656; 40 (1928) 69-80. List of scriptural passages in
SFs' works, but not based on critical ed. D3
FRANCESCHINI, Ezio, "Il Vangelo nella vita a negli scritti di SF."
In QSP (SMA 1963) VI, 71-77. D3a
LAMPEN, W., OFM, "De textibus S. Scripturae allegatis in opusculis
S.P.N. F," AFH 17 (1924) 443-445. D4
MIKL, J. M., *Die Bedeutung des Evangeliums im Leben des hl. F von A.*
Neunkirchen, 1963. xiii, 168, 13p. (Typescript Wien Kath.-Theol. diss. *D4a
STELLINI, Angelo, OFM, *Viviamo il Vangelo con S.F. d'A.* R, 1962.
155p.
VITUS A BUSSUM, Cap, "De veneratione SFA erga Sacram Scrip-
turam," TO 2 (1941) 114-120; 3 (1942) 14-19; & *Verbum Domini* 21
(1941) 161-168, 202-208. *D5

II CONTEMPLATION, MYSTICISM, & PRAYER

BLUMA, Dacian, OFM, *De vita recessuali in historia et legislatione*
OFM. R, 1959. 145p. Rev: AFH 53 (1960) 343; CF 30 (1960) 468. Fundamental. *D6
BORGESE, Maria Pia, *L'esperienza mistica di SF.* Palermo, 1930.
395p. Rev: CF 1 (1931) 395; AFH 24 (1931) 412; EF 44 (1932) 606,
cf 733-743; EF 46 (1934) 225; SF 28 (1931) 94-96. Reviews quite criti-
cal. D7
BRACALONI, L, OFM, "SF nella sua vita mistica," SF 26 (1929)
423-476. Abs: CF 1 (1931) 98. D8
——, *La spiritualità francescana.* Venice, 1949.
——, *La spiritualità francescana nei suoi corollari.* A, 1962. 218p.
BRADY, Ignatius, OFM, "The History of Mental Prayer in the Order
of Friars Minor," FnSs ns11 (1951) 317-345. *D9
BRETON, Valentine, OFM, *Franciscan Spirituality.* Chicago, 1957. 70p.
Paper, 1960.
CLASEN, S., OFM, "Das beschäuliche Leben des Eremitentums." In
D152: 176-179. *D10

Research Bibliography

CRESI, Angelo, OFM, "Il valore ascetico-mistico della perfetta letizia francescana," SF 45 (1948) 1-17. Abs: CF VIII, 71-72*. D11

CUTHBERT OF BRIGHTON, Cap, "The Mysticism of SFA. His Sacramental View of the Visible World," *Ecclesiastical Review* 87 (1932) 225-237. Abs: EF 46 (1934) 223-225. cf his *The Romanticism of SF & Other Studies . . . L*, 1924. ix, 311p. D12

DE BOER, Bertilo, OFM, "La soi-disant opposition de SFA à Saint Benoît," EF ns8 (1957) 181-194; 9 (1958) 57-65. Abs: CF XI, 62. D13

ENGEMANN, Antonellus, OFM, *Heilige Zwiesprache. Franziskanische Betrachtungsmethode.* Werl, 1964. 104p. Rev: CF 35 (1965) 203-204.

——, *The New Song: Faith, Hope, and Charity in Franciscan Spirituality.* Chicago, 1964. ix-140p.

ESSER, K., OFM, "Die 'Regula pro eremitoriis data' . . ," see A61.
*D14

GILSON, Etienne, "La conclusion de la Divine Comédie et la mystique franciscaine," RHF 1 (1924) 55-63. D15

GOAD, Harold E., "The Dilemma of SF: A Study of the Two Traditions." In D178:129-162. Abs: EF 40 (1928) 314. D16

MANACORDA, Guido, *Poesia e contemplazione.* Fi, 1947. On SF: 59-105 & 187-191. D17

MATANIC, Atanasio, OFM, *Virtù francescane. Aspetti ascetici della spiritualità francescana.* R, 1964. 119p. Rev: AFH 58 (1965) 187-188; CF 36 (1966) 198.

MEILACH, Michael D., OFM, *The Primacy of Christ.* Chicago, 1964. xii-217p.

MELCHIOR A POBLADURA, Cap, "Déserts franciscains." In DSAM IV, 539-550. Rev: CF XI, 284. Important though mostly on post-SF evolution.
*D18

MERTON, Thomas, "Franciscan Eremitism," *The Cord* 16 (1966) 356-364.

——, "F 'Dei laudator et cultor.' De orationis vi ac frequentia in eius cum scriptis tum rebus gestis," Laur. 10 (1969) 3-36.

——, "'Secretum solitudinis.' De circumstantiis externis orandi penes Sanctum Franciscum Assisiensem," CF 39 (1969) 5-58. Basic.

MEYER, Rudolf, *F. von A, Stufen des mystischen Lebens.* Stuttgart, 1951. 147p. CF XI, 101. Anthroposophical. cf D218. D19

NICHOLSON, D.H. S., *The Mysticism of SFA.* L, 1923. 393p. D20

[SCHMUCKI] Oktavian von Rieden, Cap, "Die Stellung Christi im Beten des hl F von A," WW 25 (1962) 128-145, 188-212; cf his "Leiden . . ."
(D139) *D21

——, *Saggio sulla spiritualità di S Francesco.* R, 1967. 40p.

VEUTHEY, Leo, Conv, *Union with Christ.* Chicago, 1954. ix-96p.

——, *The Our Father.* Chicago, 1955. ix-92p.

POURRAT, P., "La mystique de SF." In D179:178-203. D22

ROHR, Eric, OFM, *Der Herr und F.* Werl, 1966. 304p. Rev: CF 38 (1968) 212.

SCHWENDINGER, Fidelis, "Franziskanische Frömmigkeit. Das Beten des hl. Franz von A," WW 8 (1941) 85-93. D23

Research Bibliography

III CREATURES
(see also Canticle C144-C159; D12, D129, D146)

AMEDEE DE RENNES, Cap, *Pour la route, le jardin, l'oratoire. Thèmes de réflexions sur SF et les animaux.* Le Mons, 1945. 248p. CF VII, 41*. D24

BERNARDY, Amy A., *SF & the Animals.* Fi, 1928. D25

BIHL, M., OFM, "De praedicatione a S. F. avibus facta," AFH 20 (1927) 53-58. D91

———, "De S. F. aliisque Sanctis lepusculos foventibus," AFH 20 (1927) 206-209. D27

BROWN, Raphael, *Fifty Animal Stories of SF, As Told by His Companions. Transcribed from the Early Franciscan Chronicles.* Chi, 1958. 96p. illus. Complete but not documented. D28

———, *SF et nos frères les animaux. Cinquante histoires tirées des anciennes chroniques franciscaines.* Tr. par Serge-M. Lefébure, OFM. Montréal, 1963. 80p. illus. D29

CELLUCCI, Luigi, "Varie redazione della predica di SF agli uccelli," *Archivum romanicum* 24 (1940) 301-308. Abs: CF VII, 42*. *D30

DETTLOFF, W., OFM, "Franciscus en de dieren," SintF 2 (1956) 243-247. D31

EMIDIO DA ASCOLI, Cap, "Il sentimento della natura" & "La fraternità con le creature." In D158:211-226 & 227-256. D32

FA, protettore degli animali. Tr. dal tedesco dalla Marchesa E. del Bufalo della Valle. R, 1901. D33

JUNGE, Liselotte, *Die Tierlegende des hl. Franz von A.* Leipzig, 1932. ix, 129p. Rev: AB 53 (1935) 429-432; AFH 26 (1932) 203-206; CF 4 (1934) 411-414. Abs: FS 13 (1926) 33-53. *D34

KLINGENDER, F. D., "SF & the Birds of the Apocalypse, "Warburg & Courtauld Institutes *Journal* (L) 16 (1953) 12-23. *D35

"Sconosciuto affresco di SF che predica agli uccelli," OR 12dic, 1959:3. cf F132:53. D35

SILVESTRI, Domenico, *SF e gli animali.* R, 1927. 194p. Rev: FF 5 (1928) 395; IF 4 (1929) 189. Also R, 1928. 133p. (EF 43, 1931, 117.) D37

VITUS A BUSSUM, Cap, "L'attegiamento spirituale di SF verso il creato," IF 21 (1946) 4-12. D38

WHITE, Lynn, Jr., "Natural Science & Naturalistic Art in the Middle Ages," AHR 52 (1947) 421-435. Important. *D39

ZIMEI, Artemisia, *La concezione della natura in SFA.* R, 1929. 257p. Rev: AFH 25 (1932) 536, CC 81/4 (1930) 246-250; CF 1 (1931) 391. *D40

IV EUCHARIST
1 GENERAL

BARBERO, Giuseppe, *La dottrina eucaristica negli scritti di papa Innocenzo III.* R, 1953. xix, 226p. *D41

Research Bibliography

BROWE, Peter, SJ, *Die Verehrung der Eucharistie im Mittelalter*. München, 1933. xi, 195p. Rev: AB 54 (1936) 217. *D42

DUMOUTET, Edouard, *Corpus Domini. Aux sources de la piété eucharistique médiévale*. P, 1942. 194p. D43

———, *Le désir de voir l'hostie et les origines de la dévotion au Saint Sacrement*. P, 1926. 112p. Rev: *Irenikon* 9 (1932) 469. D44

FREDEGAND [CALLAEY] D'ANVERS, Cap, *L'origine della Festa del "Corpus Domini."* Rovigo, 1958. 100p. *D45

———, *Origine e sviluppo della festa del 'Corpus Domini.'* In *Eucaristia* (R 1957) 907-933; & *Euntes Docete* 10 (1957) 3-33. Abs: CF XI, 106. *D46

KENNEDY, V. L., OSB, "The Date of the Parisian Decree on the Elevation of the Host," MS 8 (1946) 87-96. Basic. *D47

2 ST. FRANCIS
(see also D114-D116)

CORNET, Bertrand, OFM, "Le 'De reverentia Corporis Domini', exhortation et lettre de SF," EF 6 (1955) 65-91, 167-180; 7 (1956) 20-35, 155-171; 8 (1957) 33-58. Rev: CF XI, 61. Important. *D48

ESSER, K., OFM, "Missarum sacramenta. Die Eucharistielehre des hl. F von A," WW 23 (1962) 81-108. Basic. *D49

FRANCESCHINI, Ezio, "L'Eucarestia negli scritti di SF." In QSF (SMA 1962) III, 38-49. D50

QUIRINUS VAN ALPHEN, Cap, "Het H. Sacrament des altaars en Sint F van A.," FL 22 (1939) 364-374. Abs: CF VI, 24*. D51

V LITURGY
1 GENERAL

ABATE, G., Conv, "Il primitivo breviario francescano (1224-1227)," MF 60 (1960) 47-227. Fundamental; but see D59. *D52

HANSSENS, Ioannes M., SJ, *Aux origines de la prière liturgique. Nature et genèse de l'office de Matines*. R, 1952. 130p. *D53

KENNEDY, V. L., OSB, "The Calendar of the Early Thirteenth Century Curial Missal," MS 20 (1959) 119-126. *D54

KING, Archdale A., *The Liturgies of the Religious Orders*. L, 1955. xii, 431p. Rev: COCR 18 (1956) 170-172. *D55

NUSSBAUM, Otto, *Kloster, Priestermönch und Privatmesse; ihr Verhältnis in Westen von den Anfangen bis zum hohen Mittelalter*. Bonn, 1961. 286p. Rev: CHR 49 (1963) 224; COCR 25 (1963) 71; RHE 57 (1962) 925-929; SMon 4 (1962) 428. On SF:15. cf D65, D66. *D56

PENCO, G., OSB, "Per la storia liturgica del monachesimo italico nei secoli VII-IX. Correnti ed influssi," *Rivista liturgica* 44 (1957) 168-181. *D57

SALMON, Pierre, *L'office divin, histoire de la formation du bréviaire*. P, 1959. 252p. *D58

VAN DIJK, Stephen J. P., OFM, "An Authentic Copy of the Franciscan 'Regula Breviarii'," *Scriptorium* 16 (1962) 68-76. Critical of D52. *D59

———, & J. H. Walker, *The Origins of the Modern Roman Liturgy: The Liturgy of the Papal Court & the Franciscan Order in the Thirteenth Century.* Westminster, Md., 1960. xxxi, 586p. illus. Rev: CHR 47 (1961) 215; CF 31 (1961) 235-237; *History* 46 (1961) 126 (Brooke). Fundamental. **D60

———, "The Urban & Papal Rites in Seventh & Eighth-Century Rome," *Sacris Erudiri* 12 (1961) 411-487. Summarizes D60 on p. 416-422. D61

———, *Sources of the Modern Roman Liturgy. The Ordinals of Haymo of Faversham & Related Documents (1243-1307).* Leiden, 1963. 2v. **D62

WALKER, J. H., "Early Franciscan Influence on Thirteenth Century Roman Liturgy," *Sobornost* s3,n19 (1956) 344-361. Useful. D63

2 ST. FRANCIS
(see also A52, D12, D21, D23, D48, D152)

BERTWIN, OFM, "Die Liturgie im Frömmigskeitsleben des hl. F," *S. Fidelis* 33 (1946) 139-143, 322-324. Abs: CF VII, 41*. D64

DAUSEND, Hugo, OFM, "Die Brüder dürfen in ihren Niederlassungen täglich nur eine hl. Messe lesen," FS 12 (1925) 207-212. cf RHF 4 (1927) 437. See also D56, D66. D65

OCTAVE D'ANGERS, Cap, "La messe publique et privée dans la piété de SF," EF 49 (1937) 475-486. cf CF VII, 149; CF 5 (1935) 164. cf D56, D65. *D66

VAN DIJK, S., OFM, "The Breviary of Saint Clare," FnSs 8 (1948) 25-46, 351-387. Abs: CF 21 (1951) 486*. *D67

———, "The Breviary of Saint Francis," FnSs 9 (1949) 13-40. *D68

VI MARIOLOGY

BENOIT, Ignace-M., OFM, *Le chevalier courtois de Notre-Dame-des-Anges.* Montréal, 1952. 103p. Rev: CF X, 69*. *D69

BRLEK, M., OFM, "Legislatio OFM de Immaculata Conceptione B.V.M.," Ant 29 (1954) 3-44. *D69a

BROWN, Raphael, *Our Lady & SF; All the Earliest Texts.* Chi, 1954. x, 80p. Rev. CF XI, 106. *D70

———, *Notre Dame et SF. Compilation et trad. des plus anciens textes.* Adapté de l'anglais par Romain Légaré, OFM. Montréal, 1960. 96p. Rev: EF ns10 (1960) 96. *D71

———, "SFA & Our Lady." In *The Marian Era* (Chi 1960) I, 53-55, 109-116. D72

ESSER, K., OFM, "Die Marienfrömmigkeit des hl. F von A," WW 17 (1954) 176-190. Rev: CF XI, 107. Also in D118, D119. Fundamental, with D74, D75. *D73

FELICIANO DE VENTOSA, Cap, "La devoción a Maria en la espiritualidad de SF," EstF 62 (1961) 249-274; 63 (1962) 5-21. *D74

GHINATO, Alberto, OFM, "La Madonna nella pietà e nella vita di SF." QSF (SMA 1963) V,41-56, cf 221. *D74a

[SCHMUCKI] Oktavian von Rieden, Cap, "De Seraphici Patris F habitudine erga Beatissimam Virginem Mariam," TO 15 (1954) 132-152; & in *Regina Immaculata,* Melchior a Pobladura, Cap, ed. (R 1955) 15-47. Rev: CF XI, 107; AFH 49 (1956) 228, cf 238. Definitive study. *D75

VII POVERTY

(see also A112-A119, D114-D119)

ANASTASIO DA MONTECASTELLI, Cap, "Il diritto di questua negli Ordini Mendicanti dal suo sorgere fino al Codice di Diritto Canonico," CF 21 (1951) 241-345. On SF:255-265. Basic. *D76

"De armoede van Sint F en het heilig Evangelie," SintF 57 (1955) 65-119. Abs: RHE 52 (1957) 367; cf 53 (1958) 1112. D77

AUGUSTINUS A TILS, Cap, *Der hl. F von A und die Armut.* R, 1957. Univ. Gregoriana typescript diss. D78

BRETON, Valentine, OFM, *Lady Poverty.* Chicago, 1963. 104p.

CASUTT, L., Cap, "Bettel und Arbeit nach dem hl. F v A." CF 37 (1967) 229-249.

CLASEN, S., OFM, "F und die soziale Frage," WW 15 (1952) 109-121. Abs: CF X, 76*. *D79

———, "Die Armut als Beruf: F v A," *Miscellanea Mediaevalia* 3 (Her, 1964) 73-85.

CUTHBERT OF BRIGHTON, Cap, *SF & Poverty.* NY, 1910. vii, 84p. D80

ESSER, K., OFM, "Die Handarbeit in der Frühgeschichte der Minderbrüderordens," FS 40 (1958) 145-166. Important. See also B57. *D81

———, "Leben in höchster Armut." In his *Ordo . . . ,* E16:334-345. *D81a

———, "Mysterium paupertatis. Die Armutsauffassung des hl. F von A," WW 14 (1951) 177-189. Abs: CF X, 77*. *D82

FRIEND, Julius W., *Holiness & Poverty: A Study of the Influence of the Franciscan Poverty Movement on the Early Secularist Philosophers.* Chi, 1960. 244p. Univ. of Chi diss. *D83

GHINATO, A, OFM, *La Regola e la povertà francescana nella evoluzione dell'Ordine.* R, 1953. I, 322p. *D83a

HARDICK, L, OFM, "Pecunia et denarii. Untersuchungen zum Geldverbot in den Regeln der Minderbrüder," FS 40 (1958) 192-217, 313-328; 41 (1959) 268-290; 43 (1961) 216-243. Fundamental. *D84

HUGUET, Paul, OFM, *Dame sainte pauvreté.* P, 1963. 95p. Rev: CF 34 (1964) 188. D85

———, *Richesses de la pauvreté.* P, 1962. 123p. D86

LAMBERT, Malcolm David, *Franciscan Poverty. The Doctrine of the Absolute Poverty of Christ & the Apostles in the Franciscan Order, 1210-1323.* L, 1961. 269p. Rev: AFH 55 (1962) 383-386; FS 44 (1962) 124-128 (Hardick); *Month* ns27 (1962) 148-155 (Knowles). Fundamental. *D87

LECLERC, Eloi, OFM, "La pauvreté de SF." In *La pauvreté* (P 1952) 71-84. D88

———, "The Poverty of SF," In *Poverty* (Westminster, Md. 1954) 55-68. D89

Research Bibliography

LUCA M. DA CARRE, Cap, "SF e i poveri," IF 31 (1956) 310-326
D90

MELANI, Gaudenzio, OFM, *La povertà* (Antologia). SMA, 1967. 550p.
Rev: CF 38 (1968) 211-212; MF 68 (1968) 421-422.

MITTERRUTZNER, Aug., Cap, *Der hl. F v A und die Armut. Eine genetische Darstellung seiner religiösen Anschauung von der Armut im Lichte der Quellen des 13. Jahrhunderts.* Brixen, 1961. iv-120p. Rev: CF 32 (1962) 445-460.

MOLINA, Bruce, OFM, "SFA's Attitude toward Money," Cord 12 (1962) 53-58. D91

PAUL, Jacques, "Les Franciscains et la pauvreté aux XIIIe et XIVe siècles," *Revue d'histoire de l'Église de France,* 52 (1966) 33-37.

PIAT, Stephane, J., OFM, *Riches and the Spirit.* Chicago, 1958. 254p.

PETRY, Ray C., *F of A, Apostle of Poverty.* Durham, N.C., 1941. viii, 199p. Rev: CHR 27 (1942) 109; FnSs 23 (1942) 84. Basic. *D92

REGAMEY, P. R., OP, "Poverty, Religious," NCE 11, 648-651.

SOIRON, Thaddeus, OFM, "Die Armutsideal des hl. F und die Lehre Jesu über die Armut," FS 4 (1917) 1-17. cf RHE 52 (1957) 368 (Clasen).
*D93

VITO DA BUSSUM, Cap, "Il movimento di povertà di SF e quello di Pietro Valdo," IF ns34 (1959) 225-233, 299-307. cf B44, B45. D94

——, "SFA e i poverelli," IF 9 (1934) 561-575. Anecdotes in sources. D95

VIII PRIESTHOOD & DIACONATE
(see also E92-E99)

ALBAN VON HERMETSCHWIL, Cap, "Zur Diakonatsweihe des hl F," *S. Fidelis* 28 (1941) 7-11. D96

CALLEBAUT, André, OFM, "SF lévite," AFH 20 (1927) 193-196.
*D97

CLASEN, S., OFM, "Priesterliche Würde und Würdigkeit, Das Verhältnis des hl. F zum Priestertum der Kirche," WW 20 (1957) 43-58. Abs: CF XI, 108. Basic. *D98

FRANCESCHINI, Exio, "Il Sacerdote negli scritti di SF," QSF VIII (SMA, 1964), 34-40.

LAURI, Achille, "SFA e S. Benedetto da Norcia non furono sacerdoti," *Latina Gens* 18 (1940) 234-236. D99

LECLERCQ, Jean, OSB, "On Monastic Priesthood According to the Ancient Medieval Tradition," SMon 3 (1961) 137-155. cf *Irenikon* 1963
*D100

MARIACCI, Bonaventure, OFM, "I Sacerdoti amici di SF," QSF VIII (SMA, 1964), 89-111.

QUIRINUS VAN ALPHEN, Cap, "De Priester en Sint F," *Priesterblad* 30 (1950) 130-135, 171-173, 204-206, 231-234, 307-310. Abs: CF IX, 74*.
D101

VITA DA CLUSONE, Cap, "Quando ebbe la tonsura SFA," IF 9 (1934) 15-28. Crit. rev: CF 9 (1939) 133-134. Important, with rev. *D102

Research Bibliography

IX THEOLOGY

AUSPICIUS VAN CORSTANJE, Cap, "F de Christusspeler," SintF 58 (1956) 7-24. Abs: RHE 52 (1957) 368. F as joculator Dei. D103

BACH, Kurt, "Christus am Kreuz und der hl. F." In *Ein Gabe der Freunde für Carl Georg Heise* (Berlin 1950) 103-112. D104

BENJAMIN [VAN NEERBOSCH], Cap, "De Kristus-beschouwing van Sint F," FL 19 (1936) 205-209, 272-274, 323-326. Crit. rev: CF 10 (1940) 147. D105

BERNARDS, Mattäus. "Nudus nudum Christum sequi," WW 14 (1951) 148-151. Abs: CF 28 (1958) 336. D106

BETTONI, Efrem, OFM, *Nothing for Your Journey*. Chicago, 1959. 165p.

BERNARELLO, Franco, OFM, *La fede secondo SF*. R, 1968. 93p.

BEYSCHLAG, K., *Die Bergpredigt und F von A*. Gütersloh, 1955. 243p. Rev: CF 27 (1957) 207-209 (OvR). (Erlangen Univ. thesis) D106

BUSENBENDER, Wilfrid, OFM, "Der Heilige der Inkarnation. Zur Frömmigkeit des hl. F von A," WW 15 (1952) 1-14. Abs: CF X, 76*. D107

CHAUVET, Fedele J., OFM, "La sapienza cristiana secondo SF," VM 30 (1959) 198-224 D108

CROSBY, Jeremiah (Michael), Cap, *Bearing Witness. The Place of the Franciscan Family in the Church*. Chicago, 1965. 183p.

——, *The Call and the Answer*. Chicago, 1969. xiv-165p.

DETTLOFF, Werner, OFM, "Die Geistigkeit des hl. F in der Christologie des Johannes Duns Scotus," WW 22 (1959) 17-28. D109

——, "Die Geistigkeit des hl. F in der Theologie der Franziskaner," WW 19 (1956) 197-211. Abs: CF XI, 117. D110

DOLLMANN, Alfred, OFM, *Bruder und Diener. Das Apostolat bei F und in der Frühzeit seines Ordens*. Werl, 1968. 142p.

DUKKER, Chrysostomus, OFM, *Umkehr des Herzens. Der Bussgedanke des hl. F von A*. We, 1956. 172p. Rev: CF 27 (1957) 426; FS 40 (1958) 106. *D111

——, *The Changing Heart; The Penance-concept of SFA*. Tr. by Bruce Molina, OFM. Chi, 1959. 156p. cf D114-D119. *D112

ENGEMANN, Antonellus, OFM, *Entflammt vom Heiligen Geist. Die Sieben Gaben des Hl. Geistes im Leben des hl. F*. We, 1961. 126p. Rev: FS 45 (1963) 192. *D113

ESSER, K., OFM, & Engelbert Grau, OFM, *Antwort der Liebe. Der Weg des franziskanischen Menschen zu Gott*. We, 1958. 351p. (Also 2. Aufl, 196[?]) Rev: CF 29 (1959) 512; FS 40 (1958) 433. *D114

——, *Love's Reply*. Tr. by Ignatius Brady, OFM. Chi, 1963. 258p. Tr. of D114. *D115

——, *Pour le royaume*. P, 1960. 191p. Tr. of D114. *D116

——, *La conversion du coeur*. (Both) tr. par l'Abbé Virrion. P, 1960. 127p. Tr. of D114. *D117

—— (alone), *Repair My House*. Tr. by Michael D. Meilach, OFM. Chi, 1963. 222p. Tr. from D119. Collection of WW articles. *D118

——, *Thèmes spirituels*. Tr. par Luc Mely, OFM. P, 1958. 197p. *D119

——, *Temi spirituali*. Mi, 1967. xvi-340p. Rev: CF 37 (1967) 421-422.

——, "Bindung zur Freiheit. Die Gehorsamsauffassung des hl. F von A," WW 15 (1952) 161-173. Abs: CF X, 78*. *D120

——, "Freiheit zur Liebe. Keuschheit und Jungfräulichkeit in der Auffassung des hl. F von A," WW 19 (1956) 100-108. CF XI, 114. Also in D118-D119. *D121

——, "Gehorsam und Freiheit," WW 13 (1950) 142-150. Also in D118-D119. *D122

——, "Homo alterius saeculi. Endzeitliche Heilswirklichkeit im Leben des hl. F von A," WW 20 (1957) 180-197. Abs: CF XI, 109. Also in D118-D119. *D123

——, "Die Lehre des hl. F von der Selbstleugnung," WW 18 (1955) 161-174. Abs: CF XI, 112. Also in D114-D116. *D124

——, "Sancta Mater Ecclesia Romana. Die Kirchenfrömmigkeit des hl. F von A," WW 24 (1961) 1-26; & in *Sentire Ecclesiam: das Bewusstsein von der Kirche als gestaltende Kraft der Frömmigkeit* [K. Rahner Festschrift]. Jean Danielou & H. Vorgrimler, eds. (Freiburg 1961) 218-250. Basic. *D125

——, "Wer bist Du, Herr, und wer bin ich? Das Gottesbild des hl. F von A," *Bruder Franz* 2 (1949) 146-149, 195-197. "F's visie op God," SintF 2 (1956) 288-302. Abs: CF XI, 101. Also in D159:27-42. cf B32:241-258. D126

GHINATO, Alberto, OFM, "SF nella Chiesa e per la Chiesa." In QSF (SMA 1964) VII, 22-42 cf D125. D126a

GOOSSENS, Hilarion, "De Gods- en Christus visie van Sint F," SintF 1 (1955) 7-42. D127

GRATIEN DE PARIS, Cap, (a) *SFA, sa personnalité, sa spiritualité.* Nouv. éd. rev. et augm. P, 1928. 157p. 3e éd. P, 1943. 96p. (lacks notes). Rev: AFH 25 (1932) 289; CF 3 (1933) 439-441; CF 5 (1935) 159. Also 4e éd. Blois, 1963. 87p. (b) *I Know Christ. The Personality & Spirituality of SFA.* Tr. by Paul J. Oligny, OFM. St. Bonaventure, NY, 1957. 80p. (From 1943 ed.) Excellent. *D127a

HARDICK, L., OFM et al., *The Marrow of the Gospel, A Study of the Rule of SF of A,* ed. by I Brady OFM. Chicago, 1958. xiv-346p.

HERMANN, Placid, OFM, *The Way of St. Francis.* Chicago, 1964. 172p.

KOPER, Rigobert, OFM, "F der Gottsucher," FS 40 (1958) 115-132. *D128

——, *Das Weltverständnis des hl. F von A; eine Untersuchung über das "Exivi de saeculo."* We, 1959. 156p. Rev: CF 30 (1960) 219; FS 43 (1961) 110. Important. *D129

LAMPEN, W., "De S.P. F cultu angelorum et sanctorum," AFH 20 (1927) 3-23. *D130

——, "S. F, cultor Trinitatis," AFH 21 (1928) 449-467. Basic. *D131

LONGPRE, Ephrem, OFM, *A Poor Man's Peace, the Spirit of F of A.* Chicago, 1968. ix-158.

LORSCHEIDER, Luigi, "Gesù nella vita di SF." In QSF (SMA 1961) II, 40-50. D132

LOUIS-ANTOINE, Cap, *Lire François d'Assise. Essai sur sa spiritualité d'après ses écrits.* P, 1967. 114p.

Research Bibliography

——, *Leggere F d'A.* Mi, 1969. 182p.

MATTESINI, Francesco, "La passione di Cristo nella vita di SF da S. Damiano alla Verna." In QSF (SMA 1962) IV, 32-41. D133

MAZZOTTI, Arcangelo, "La teologia dello Stimatizzato," VP 10 (1924) 604-610. D134

McDEVITT, A., "Franciscan Spirituality," NCE 6, 36-38.

MEDERLET, Eugen, *Der Hohepriester des Alls. Ein Weltbild, gewonnen aus dem Christus-Erleben des Bruders Franz von A.* Marburg, 1961. 91p. D135

MERZAGORA, A., "L'apostolo Paolo e l'Araldo del gran Re," SF 34 (1937) 321-334. D136

MESEGUER, Juan, OFM, *San Francisco en la linea conciliar. El binomio autoridad-obediencia en su vida y enseñanzas.* Murcia, 1967. 20p.

MORANT, Peter, Cap, *Unser Weg zu Gott. Das Vollkommenheitsstreben im Geiste des hl. F.* Zürich-München-Paderborn, 1965. 341p. Rev: CF 35 (1965) 414-415.

MORREAU, Abel, *On Leave from Heaven.* Chicago, 1955. viii-191.

NEYER, Paschalis, OFM, "Der hl. F und die armen Seelen seiner drei Orden." In *Kirchengeschichtliche Studien P. Michael Bihl als Ehrengabe dargeboten* (Kolmar 1941) 29-49. *D137

PETRY, Ray C., "Medieval Eschatology & SFA," *Church History* 9 (1940) 54-69. *D140

POMPEI, Alfonso, Conv, "SF e la Passione di G. Cristo in una recente indagine critica delle fonti," MF 61 (1961) 92-108. On D139. D141

SCHLUND, Erhard, OFM, "Die religiöse Gedankenwelt des hl. F," ZAM 1 (1926) 301-311; & "Das religiöse Wollen des hl F," ZAM 2 (1927) 17-33. Abs: AFH 24 (1930) 139. D142

[SCHMUCKI] Oktavian von Rieden, Cap, preparing a study of "Franziszi Gedanken zur Nachfolge Christi." Cf CF 30 (1960) 363n110. *D138

——, "Das Leiden Christi im Leben des hl. F von A. Eine quellenvergleichende Untersuchung im Lichte der zeitgenössischen Passionsfrömmigkeit," CF 30 (1960) 5-30, 129-145, 241-263, 353-397; & R, 1960. xx, 114p. Rev: AFH 54 (1961) 233; EF ns12 (1962) 94; & D141. Masterpiece. **D139

SENFTLE, Alexander, Cap, *Menschenbildung in franziskanischer Geistigkeit; die Bedeutung der franziskanischen Poenitentialehre.* Fr/Br, 1959. 126p. D143

TERSCHLUESEN, Josef, OFM, "Die Pflicht der Liebe und das Recht der Strafe. Die Strafauffassung des hl. F von A," WW 16 (1953) 90-100. Abs: CF X, 79*. D144

VERHEY, Sigismund, "Das Leben in der Busse nach F von A," WW 22 (1959) 161-174. D145

——, *Der Mensch unter der Herrschaft Gottes; Versuch einer Theologie des Menschen nach dem hl. F von A.* Dü, 1960, 212p. Rev: CF 32 (1962) 168-170 (OvR); FS 45 (1963) 199; MF 61 (1961) 129-132. *D146

VITUS A BUSSUM, Cap, "De habitudine animae S.P. F ad tres divinas personas," TO 1 (1940) 21-25, 55-59, 90-92. *D147

——, "De Spiritus Sancti donorum efficacitate in anima B.P.N. F," TO 5 (1944) 48-56. *D148

——, "F strenuus Paternitatis divinae praeco," TO 4 (1943) 19, 49, 96. *D149

X MISCELLANEOUS STUDIES

1 GENERAL

ANSCHARI A PAMEL, Cap, "La psychologie de SF," EF 33 (1921) 489-505; 34 (1922) 327-345, 500-519; & FL 6-7 (1923-24). D150

AUSEJO, Serafín de, Cap, " . . . Con brevedad de sermón, porque palabra abreviada hizo El Señor sobre la tierra," *Miscell. M. de Pobladura,* I (R, 1964) 131-149.

BERTINATO, Pierdamiano, OFM, "Il concetto di 'Lavoro' nella Regola Francescana," *Vita Minorum,* ser. 4, 35 (1964) 9-52.

CASUTT, Laurentius, Cap, (a) *Das Erbe eines grossen Herzens; Studien zum franziskanischen Ideal.* Graz, 1949. 222p. (b) "L'héritage d'un grand coeur," EF ns 5 (1954) 11-43, 205-218; 6 (1955) 5-42, 133-165; 7 (1956) 5-19. (c) *L'eredità di SF.* R, 1952. 254p. Rev: AFH 56 (1963) 225; CF IX, n177; CF X, n283; EF ns5 (1954) 227; MF 53 (1953) 130-132; MF 56 (1956) 499; WW 16 (1953) 57-61 (Clasen). Very important, with reviews; cf D156. Has chs. on SF's knightly spirit & on Francis & Benedict & Ignatius of Loyola. *D151

CERMINARA, Teofilo, *La spiritualità di SF.* Naples, 1964. 84p.

CLASEN, S., OFM, "Apostolisches oder liturgisches Franziskanertum? Die Antwort des hl F von A und seines ersten Biographen," FS 40 (1958) 167-192. Fundamental. cf D9. *D152

——, "Franz von A im Lichte der neueren historischen Forschung," GWU 3 (1952) 137-154. Abs: CF X, 72*. On sources, times, SF & Church. *D153

——, "Franz von A und Joachim von Fiore. Zur neuen F-biographie von Dimitri Merejkowski," WW 6 (1939) 68-83. cf E48. D154

——, "F der neue Moses," WW 24 (1961) 200-208. D155

——, "Kritisches zur neueren F-literatur," WW 13 (1950) 151-166. Abs: CF IX, 54. On sources, family, gay youth, influence of times (re Helder, Casutt, Grundmann). *D156

COSMO, Umberto, *Con Madonna Povertà. Studi francescani.* Bari, 1940. 303p. Rev: CF 12 (1942) 70. Collected older essays on *Sacrum Commercium* (A116), Brother Pacifico (E131), Elias (E156), Sabatier (A308), Lo Speco (F398), & Greccio (F354); also reprints of old, well-documented studies of sources. *D157

EMIDIO D'ASCOLI, Cap, *L'anima di SF.* Ascoli Piceno, 1949. 286p. Rev: CF 21 (1951) 436-438; EF ns2 (1951) 109-111; SF 47 (1951) 130. D158

ESSER, K., OFM, *F und die Seinen. Gesammelte Aufsätze.* We, 1963. 223p. Misc. essays, incl. only D126 in this Bibl. Rev: CF 34 (1964) 405-407. D159

FALCONE, Sebastian, Cap, "The Capuchin-Franciscan Goal of Capuchin Seminary Training," *Cap. Educ. Conf. I* (Wash., D.C., 1960) 100-174. Masterpiece on the spirituality of SF.

Research Bibliography

FALOCI PULIGNANI, M., *Conferenze francescane*. Città di Castello, 1924. 203p. Collected essays; list in MF 41 (1941) 499. Important. *D160

FELDER, Hilarin, Cap, (a) *Die Ideale des hl. F von A*. Paderborn, 1923. xvi, 540p. (b) *The Ideals of SFA*. Tr. by Berchmans Bittle, Cap. NY, 1925. xvi,, 518p. Other early eds. listed CF 1 (1931) 402. Rev: AFH 17 (1924) 433-437; FS 35 (1953) 451. Very useful. *D161

FORTINI, A., *F d'A e l'Italia del suo tempo*. R, 1968. 378p + 50 plates.

GEMELLI, A., OFM, (a) *SFA e la sua "Gente Poverella."* Mi, 1945. vii, 288p. Rev: CF 15 (1945) 288; MF 45 (1945) 191; SF 40 (1943) 111. (b) *The Message of SF*. Tr. by Paul J. Oligny, OFM. Chi, 1964. ix, 197p. Excellent essays. cf E20. D162

GHINATO, Alberto, OFM, *Profilo spirituale di SF tratto dai suoi scritti e dalle primitive biografie*. R, 1961. 206p. Also excellent. D163

GILSON, Etienne, (a) *La philosophie de saint Bonaventure*. 2e éd. rev. P, 1943. 419p. On SF: 37-75. (b) *The Philosophy of St. Bonaventure*. L & NY, 1938. xiii, 551p. On SF:40-86. *D164

GOBRY, Ivan, (a) *St. F d'A et l'esprit franciscain*. P, 1957. 192p. illus. (b) *Franz von A in Selbstzeugnissen und Bilddokumenten*. O von Nostitz, tr. Reinbetz b. Hamburg, 1965. 178p.

GUALINO, Lorenzo, *L'uomo di A*. To, 1932. 112p. Rev: CF 5 (1935) 132. D165

LECLERC, Eloi, OFM, (a) *Exil et tendresse*. P, 1962. 224p. Abs: MF 63 (1963) 390. (b) *Exile and Tenderness*. Chicago, 1965. xii-174. D166

———, (a) *Sagesse d'un Pauvre*. P, 1959. 143p. (b) *Wisdom of the Poverello*. Tr. by Marie Louise Johnson. Chi, 1961. 126p. Rev: CF XI, 511; CF 29 (1959) 511. D167

LEKEUX, Martial, OFM, (a) *F, qui es-tu? L'homme, son message, sa permanence*. P, 1962. 144p. Rev: CF 34 (1964) 182. (b) *F, chi sei tu?* Mi, 1964. 172p. D168

LIVERSIDGE, Douglas, *S F of A*. N. Y., 1968. v-164p. Best recent popular biography.

LORTZ, Joseph. (a) *Der unvergleichliche Heilige. Gedanken um F von A*. Dü, 1952. 80p. (b) *F l'incomparable*. P, 1956. 96p. (c) *Un Santo unico*. Alba, 1958. 163p. (d) *El Santo incomparable*. Madrid, 1964. 91p. D169 Rev: CF X, 75*; EF ns8 (1957) 97; FS 35 (1953) 444 (Hardick: "one of the most valuable studies in modern Franciscan literature").

LORTZING, J., "Franz von A als Reformator," WW 9 (1942) 61-70, 126-139. D170

LUCA M. CARRE, Cap, "Sulle vette del Francescanesimo," IF 30 (1955) 267-272. D171

MIGUEL DE ESPLUGUES de Llobregat, Cap, (a) *La vera efigie del Poverello. Assaig psicologic*. Ba, 1927. (b) *Le véritable visage du Poverello*. Tr. par A. de Falgairolle. P, 1929. 235p. Rev: CF 1 (1931) 239; cf CF 8 (1938) 491. D172

MOTTE, Ignace & Gérald Hego, OFM, (a) *La Pâque de SF*. P, 1958. 135p. Rev: EF ns 9 (1959) 118. (b) *La Pasqua di SF*. Mi, 1963. 155p. D173

Research Bibliography

PAPINI, Giovanni, "Il segreto di SF," FF 21 (1943) 18-21. cf ARSENIO DA CASORATE, Cap, "Giovanni Papini e il suo incontro con SF," IF 22 (1948) 241-258. CF VIII, 88*; & P. BARGELLINI, "Giovanni Papini terziario francescano," IF 32 (1957) 361-370. cf D183. D174

Il Patrono d'Italia. 2a ed. R, 1956. 3v. richly illus. (v.1: *Il santo della patria;* G. FORTINI. v.2: *La patria al suo santo;* A. FORTINI. v.3: *SF oggi;* I. GIORDANI.) Rev: CF XI, 122. *D175

PEPE, Gabriele, *F d'A tra medioevo e rinascimento.* Manduria (Taranto), 1965 217p.

ROGGEN, Heribert, OFM, "Saint Bonaventure comme 'Le second Fondateur' de l'OFM, par rapport a la renovation adaptie de notre Ordre," FS 49 (1967), 259-271.

———, "Saint Bonaventure second fondateur de l'OFM? EF 17 (1967) 67-79; substantially the same as the foregoing, with stylistic corrections.

ROSSETTI, Felice M., Conv, *SF e i carcerati.* Mi, 1956. 208p. Rev: CF 27 (1957) 329. D176

———, ed., *SF vivo. Testimonianze di uomini d'oggi.* A, 1952. 285p. illus. Rev: MF 53 (1953) 276. Valuable autobiographical tributes by Harold Goad, Joergensen, Arnold Lunn, Moorman, Daniel-Rops, Clare Sheridan, Eugenio Zolli, et al. D177

SFA: 1226-1926. Essays in Commemoration. W. Seton, ed. L, 1926. 332p. Several important studies on sources (see A253), spirituality (D16), Rome (F121); see also D215. *D178

SFA; son oeuvre, son influence, 1226-1926. P, 1927. 320p. illus. Includes excellent studies on sources (see A267), Book of Conformities (A195), mysticism of SF (D22), his Basilica (F273). Rev: AFH 21 (1928) 371-375. *D179

SALVADORI, Giulio, *Il vessillo sul monte.* La Verna (Arezzo), 1963. 145p. Rev: FF ns10 (1963) 142. Collected writings on SF of the saintly Tertiary professor (1862-1928). cf LIBERATO DI STOLFI, OFM, "Il francescanesimo di Giulio Salvadori," FF ns9 (1962) 63-68; & *Lettere Italiane* 15 (1963) 253. cf F120. D180

SCARAMUZZI, Diomede, OFM, *Nella luce di Cristo e di Santo F.* R, 1953. xviii, 262p. Rev: CF 24 (1954) 428. 49 articles (some from OR). D181

SCHNEIDER, Reinhold, (a) *Die Stunde des hl. Franz von A.* Heidelberg, 1950. 100p. (b) *The Hour of SFA.* Chi, 1953. xiv, 113p. CF X, 53* & 72*. D182

Universitalità del francescanesimo. A, 1950. 247p. illus. Essays by Bargellini, Fortini, Papini, et al. D183

VITO DA CLUSONE, Cap, *Cultura e pensiero di SFA; opera critico-storica.* Modena, xcii, 534p. illus. Rev: CF X, n274; CF XI, 98; MF 55 (1953) 422-427. Uncritical erudite portrait of SF as a universal genius. cf A26. *D184

———, "SFA e il lavoro," IF 8 (1933) 225-235. Survey of sources. D185

———, "La 'Forma mentis' di SFA nel giudizio degli scrittori," IF 22 (1947) 286-298. Abs: CF 20 (1950) 58*. D186

2 PEDAGOGY

BERNARELLO, Franco, *La formazione religiosa secondo la primitiva scuola francescana.* R, 1961. 94p. Rev: CF 33 (1963) 109 (OvR). *D187

BETTONI, Efrem, OFM, *La pedagogia francescana.* R, 1967. 182p. Rev: CF 38 (1968) 437-438.

FERNANDO DE MALDONADO, Cap, "La pedagogia de SFA," Laur 3 (1962) 3-40, 289-348. Fundamental. *D188

HAMMER, Robert, OFM, "SFA as an Educator & His Pedagogical Method," FEC 11 (1929) 9-40. Abs: CF 1 (1931) 404. D189

HARDICK, L., OFM, "Geistige Menschenformung durch F von A," WW 23 (1960) 147-160. *D190

HUG, Pacific, OFM, "How SF Guided His Brethren," FEC 29 (1949) 43-81. Abs: CF IX, 75*. D191

LINDEN, Raymund [von Duisburg], Cap, *Vater und Vorbild. F: Forma Minorum.* We, 1960. 311p. Rev: CF 32 (1962) 167 (OvR). *D192

PAOLO ANTONIO DA BASSANO, Cap, "SF educatore," IF 4 (1929) 3-15, 193-206, 385-397. Abs: CF 1 (1931) 99. D193

3 PREACHING
(see also F108)

BELLUCCO, B., *De sacra praedicatione in OFM.* R, 1956. xix, 134p. Rev: AFH 50 (1957) 123. *D194

BIHL, M., OFM, "De S. F. praedicante ita ut de toto corpore faceret linguam," AFH 20 (1927) 196-199. D195

˙ HOBRECHT, Hilary P., *SFA, the Model of Franciscan Preachers.* Wa, 1951. 48p. (typewritten Cath. Univ. MA thesis) *D196

4 RELATION TO MEDIEVAL SPIRITUALITY

DELARUELLE, Etienne, "L'influence de SFA sur la piété populaire." In CISSR III, 449-466. Rev: EF ns8 (1957) 98; RHE 50 (1955) 1103; CF XI, 117. *D197

GILSON, Etienne, "SF et la pensée médiévale," *Etudes italiennes* 8 (1926) 12-27. *D199

ROGGEN, Heribert, OFM, "Die Lebensform des hl. F. von A in ihrem Verhältnis zur feudalen und bürgerlichen Gesellschaft Italiens," FS 46 (1964) 1-57, 287-321; and separately, Mechelen, 1965. Rev: CF 36 (1966) 189-191; Alfonso Pompei, Conv, "L'influenze religioso-sociale di SF e della sua primitiva fraternita a nel sec. XIII," MF 66 (1966) 193-201, reviews Roggen's study.

SCHNEIDER, E., "SF et le rétablissement de l'unité spirituelle au XIIIe siècle," *Nouvelle revue historique de droit français et étranger* 60 (1939) 515-523. D202

VAN BEERS, B., "F en de Scholastiek," FL 16 (1933) 145-156. D203

5 ST. FRANCIS & NON-CATHOLICS

BROPHY, LIAM, "Non-Catholic Tributes to SF," *Catholic Digest* Dec.

1943, p. 31-32. (Ruskin & Oscar Wilde). D205

CHIMINELLI, P., "Einstein nel 'bel San Francesco' di Fiesole," FF 22 (1955) 126-128. His friendship with a friar there. D206

CONSTANTINUS [VAN SCHIEDAM], Cap, "Chassidisme, niewchassidisme en SF van Assisie," FL 14 (1931) 274-280. Abs: CF 3 (1933) 449. D207

ELENJIMITTAM, Anthony, *St. F of A, the Bhakt Yogin.* Bandra-Bombay, 1963. 141p.

EYNARD, Max, *Pietro e F.* Torre Pellice, 1951. 219p. By a Waldensian. D208

FORTINI, A., *D'Annunzio e il francescanesimo.* A, 1963. 275p. illus. Rev: FFns10 (1963) 138-141; MF 63 (1963) 388. Includes letters & interviews. D209

HESS, J., "Franz von A i n protestantischer Darstellung," *Schweizer Rundschau* 22 (1922) 1-18. D210

HEYLIGERS, A. R., "Franz von A oder die orientalische Mystik im Westen," *Internationale Kirchliche Zeitschrift* (Bern) 39 (1949) 104-114 Old-Catholic writer compares SF with Eastern Orthodox spirituality. cf. C119, D217. D211

JUILLARD, Pierre, *Le "Poverello" d'A, chantre de l'amour divin.* Genève, 1944. 163p. illus. Protestant biography; includes Rule of Les Veilleurs (Third Order) founded by Pasteur Alfred Monod in 1923. D212

LAVALLE, Guillaume, OFM, "Les littérateurs à la trace de SF," *Nos Cahiers* (later *Culture*, Montréal) 4 (1939) 344-368. D213

LUCA DA CARRE, Cap, "Il SF mutilato di Van Loon," IF 32 (1957) 254-258. Re latter's *The Arts.* D214

SETON, Walter, "The Rediscovery of SFA." In D178:245-266. D215

STEERE, Douglas Van, *On Beginning from Within.* NY, 1943. 149p. By a Quaker admirer of SF. D216

STEJN, Sergije, "Sv. Franjo Asiski i Rusija," *Nova Revija* 15 (1936) 30-48. Abs: CF 10 (1940) 150. cf Cord 4 (1954) 310-314; CF XI, 117. D217

STEINER, Rudolf, *Anthroposophical Ethics, with an Account of FA.* L, 1955(&1928). cf D19. D218

STYRA, Ambros, OFM, *F von A in der neueren deutschen Literatur.* Breslau, 1928. 182p. D219

WHITFIELD, Derek W. J., "SF & Reunion. Reflections on the Relevance of FA's Ideals to Current Oecumenical Thought," *Unitas* 11 (1959) 252-262. D220

E   ORDERS

I FRANCISCAN HISTORY

1 GENERAL & EARLY
(see also A235)

ABATE, G., Conv, "Per la storia francescana. Osservazioni e proposte," MF 37 (1937) 575-585. E1

BLASUCCI, Antonio, "Spiritualité franciscaine," DSAM 5 (1961), 1315-1347.

BRLEK, Michael, OFM, *De evolutione iuridica studiorum in Ordine Minorum (Ab initio usque ad annum 1517)*. Dubrovnik, 1942. 111p. Rev: CF 16/17 (1946/47) 350-352. E2

BROOKE, Rosalind, *Early Franciscan Government; Elias to Bonaventure*. Cambridge, Eng., 1959. xv, 313p. illus. Rev: AB 79 (1961) 205-208; AFH 53 (1960) 210-212; CF 30 (1960) 112-114; FS 41 (1959) 439-442 (Hardick); RHE 55 (1960) 572-574; 56 (1961) 676; Spec 35 (1960) 432. Fundamental. *E3

CALLEBAUT, A., OFM, "Les Provinciaux de la Province de France au XIIIe siècle," AFH 10 (1917) 289-356. *E4

CASTRO, Manuel, OFM, "Estudio bibliografico de las Constituciones Franciscanas," AIA 24 (1964) 24-304, 25 (1965) 299-340.

CENCI, Caesar, OFM, "Constitutiones Provinciales Provinciae Umbria anni 1316," AFH 56 (1963) 12-39; with list of published early Italian provincial constitutions, p. 12. cf F198, F199. *E5

CLASEN, Sophronius, OFM, "Poverty Controversy," NCE 11, 651-652.

CRESI, Domenico, OFM, *Discussioni e documenti di storia francescana*. Fi, 1959. 183p. Rev: EF ns10 (1960) 98. *E6

——, *SF e i suoi Ordini*. Fi. 1955. 335p. Rev: AFH 49 (1956) 228; Ant 31 (1956) 435-437; CF 26 (1956) 92-95; MF 56 (1956) 606-609; SF 54 (1957) 250-259. Important, with corrections in revs. *E7

——, "Statistica dell'Ordine Minoritico all'anno 1282," AFH 56 (1963) 157-162. E8

DE BEER, Francis, OFM, "La genèse de la Fraternité franciscaine (selon quelques sources primitives)," Franz. St. 49 (1967) 350-372. Rev: AFH 62 (1969) 425-426.

DI FONZO, Lorenzo, Conv, "I Francescani." In *Ordini e congregazioni religiose*, a cura di Mario Escobar (To 1952) I, 157-344. Abs: MF 54 (1954) 323. Rev: MF 53 (1953) 135. *E9

——, " 'Lezioni storiche' sull'Ordine dei Frati Minori del P. Paolo Sevesi, OFM (1942)," MF 44 (1944) 143-166. See E46. *E10

——, *Series quaedam historicio-statistica OFM Conv. 1209-1960*. R, 1961. 88p. *E11

——, "Studi, studenti e maestri nell'Ordine dei Francescani dal 1223 al 1517," MF 44 (1944) 167-195. Abs: CF 16/17 (1946/47) 352. *E12

DOUIE, D., *The Conflict between the Seculars & the Mendicants at the University of Paris in the 13th Century*. L, 1954. 30p. *E13

DUPEYRAT, Elisabeth, *De Gengis-khan à la Chine populaire, sept cents ans d'histoire franciscaine*. P, 1962. 127p. E14

EMERY, Richard W., *The Friars in Medieval France; A Catalogue of French Mendicant Convents, 1200-1550*. NY, 1962. xix, 130p. maps. *E15

ESSER, K., OFM, "Ordo Fratrum Minorum. Ueber seine Anfange und ursprünglichen Zielsetzungen," FS 42 (1960) 97-129, 297-355; 43 (1961) 171-215, 309-347. Rev: AFH 56 (1963) 224. Masterpiece. Supersedes his previous shorter surveys in FS 31 (1949) 225-246 & 39 (1957) 1-22. Replaced by the revised version in book form: *Anfänge und ursprüngliche*

Zielsetzungen des Ordens der Minderbrüder. Leiden, 1966. xvi-296. Rev: CF 36 (1966) 458-460; Ant. 42 (1967) 332-334; AFH 60 (1967) 436-441. **E16. English translation in preparation (Chicago, 1970).

———, (a) *Der Orden des hl. F. 2.* Aufl. We, 1952. 56p. (b) *The Order of SF. Its Spirit & Its Mission in the Kingdom of God.* Tr. by I. Brady, OFM. Chi, 1959. 60p. Essay, not history. E17

ESSER, K. — GRAU, E., OFM, *Franziskanisches Leben. Gesammelte* Dokumente. We, 1968. 324p. Rev: MF 68 (1968) 418-421.

FELDER, Hilarin, Cap, (a) *Geschichte der wissenschaftlichen Studien im Franziskanerorden bis um die Mitte des 13. Jahrhunderts.* Fr/Br, 1904. xi, 557p. (b) *Histoire des études dans l'Ordre de SF ...P, 1908.* vii, 574p. Rev: AFH 2 (1909) 131-136. *E18

FIDELIS ELIZONDO, Cap, "Bullae Quo Elongati Gregorii IX et Ordinem Vestrum Innocentii IV," Laur 3 (1962) 349-394. Basic. cf E24. *E19

GEMELLI, Agostino, OFM, (a) *Il francescanesimo.* 7a ed. riv. e agg. Mi, 1956. xvi, 563p. Revs of earlier eds: AFH 28 (1935) 517-527; 31 (1938) 485-487; CF 3 (1933) 105-108; CF 11 (1941) 496-499. (b) *Le message de SFA au monde moderne.* P, 1948. xviii, 483p. (c) *The Franciscan Message to the World.* L, 1934. 244p. (condensed). A classic. cf D162. *E20

GHINATO, A., OFM, *La letteratura storica francescana del primo secolo.* R, 1952. 264p. *E21

GOAD, Harold, *Greyfriars. The Story of SF & His Followers.* L, 1947. 238p. illus. Rev: AFH 41 (1948) 297-299; CF 21 (1951) 277*. E22

GRATIEN DE PARIS, Cap, (a) *Historie de la fondation et de l'évolution de l'Ordre des Frères Mineurs au XIIIe siècle.* P, 1928, xxiv, 699p. Rev: AFH 22 (1929) 187-192 (Bihl); EF 41 (1929) 345 (Cuthbert); MF 29 (1929) 93; RHE 25 (1929) 312-314. (b) *Historia de la fundación y evolución de la Orden de Frailes Menores en el siglo XIII.* Tr. del P. Victoriano M. de Larrainzar, Cap. Buenos Aires, 1947. 624p. CF 20 (1950) 401. Masterpiece. *E23

GRUNDMANN, H., "Die Bulle 'Quo elongati' Papst Gregors IX," AFH 54 (1961) 3-25. Important: critical text. cf E 19. *E24

HANLEY, Boniface, & Salvator Fink, OFM, *The Franciscans: Love at Work.* Paterson, NJ, 1962. 247p. illus. Readable current survey, not history. E25

HILARIUS A WINGENE, Cap, "Sancti F Fundatoris 'spiritus propriaque proposita,' " Laur 7 (1966) 359-381.

———, "Opinationes diversae de primordiis OFM," Laur 8 (1967) 492-511.

HOLZAPFEL, Heribert, OFM, (a) *Handbuch der Geschichte des Franziskanerordens.* Fr./Br, 1909, xxi, 732p. (b) *Manuale historiae OFM.* Fr/Br, 1909. xxi, 662p. (c) *The History of the Franciscan Order.* Tr. by Antonine Tibesar & Gervase Brinkmann, OFM. Teutopolis, Ill, 1948, xiv, 608p. Rev: AFH 2 (1909) 485-489; *Thought* 24 (1949) 748. *E26

HUBER, Raphael M., Conv, *A Documented History of the Franciscan Order from the Birth of SF to the Division of the Order under Leo X, 1182-1517.* Milw. 1944. xxxiv, 1028p. illus. Rev: CF 18 (1948) 303-306; FnSs 26 (1945) 88; 27 (1946) 93-99; MF 47 (1947) 263-266; Spec 21 (1946) 261-263. **E27

ILARINO DA MILANO, Cap, "L'incentivo escatologico nel riformismo dell'Ordine francescano." In Accademia Tudertina, 30 Convegno Storico *Atti* (Todi 1961) 55p. Abs: MF 63 (1963) 133. E28

JORDAN, Edouard "Le premier siècle franciscain. In D179:68-89. E29

———. "Les premiers franciscains et la France," *Etudes italiennes* 8 (1926) 65-84, 129-139. E30

KNOWLES, David, *The Religious Orders in England.* Cambridge, Eng, 1948. 2v. On SF: I, 114-126. Splendid. *E31

LANDINI, Lawrence, OFM, *The Causes of the Clericalization of the OFM, 1209-1260, in the Light of Early Franciscan Sources.* Chicago, 1968. xxvi-149p.

LAZARO DE ASPURZ, Cap, *Manual de historia franciscana.* Madrid, 1954. 536p. Rev: AFH 47 (1954) 461; Ant 30 (1955) 200-202; CF 25 (1955) 192-195; MF 56 (1956) 603-609. *E32

———, "Communitatis franciscalis evolutio historica," Laur 7 (1966) 91-114, 213-262. Very informative.

LEON, Achille, OFM, *Histoire de l'Ordre des Frères Mineurs. SFA et son oeuvre.* P, 1954. xviii, 395p. Rev: (1st ed.) AFH 22 (1929) 186. *E33

LYNCH, Cyprian J., "Franciscans," NCE 6, 38-46.

MacVICAR, Thaddeus, "Franciscans, Capuchins," NCE 6, 65-67.

MASSERON, Alexandre, & Marion A. Habig, OFM, *The Franciscans: SFA & His Three Orders.* Chi, 1959, xxi, 518p. illus. Rev: CF 30 (1960) 465. Includes useful statistics, lists, tables, etc. *E34

MATANIC, Atanasio, OFM, *Compendio di storia dell'Ordine dei Frati Minori. I,1: Il medioevo francescano, 1182-1517.* R, 1956. 174p. *E35

MELCHIOR DE POBLADURA, Cap, "Fondation et réformes franciscaines," DSAM 5 (1961), 1304-1314.

MENS, Alcantara, Cap, "L'Ombrie italienne et l'Ombrie brabançonne. Deux courants religieux parallèles d'inspiration commune," EF Suppl. 17 (1967), xix-78p.

MOORMAN, J. R. H., "The Foreign Element among the English Franciscans," EHR 62 (1947) 289-303. E36

———, *A History of the Franciscan Order. From its Origins to the Year 1517.* Oxford, 1968. xiv-642p. Rev: CF 39 (1969) 195-197.

ODOARDI, Giovanni, Conv, "'Inizi e sviluppi del Primo Ordine francescano nel mondo," *Città di Vita* 14 (1959) 726-739. E37

———, "Il nuovo 'Conspectus missionum' dei Frati Minori. Presentazione e rilievi critici," MF 58 (1958) 306-315. *E38

———, *SF e i Francescani. Sintesi storica del francescanesimo nei suoi tre ordini e loro varie famiglie.* 2a ed. riv. e agg. A, 1961. 95p. Rev. of 1st ed: MF 52 (1952) 307. E39

OZANAM, Antoine Frédéric, (a) *Les poètes franciscains en Italie au XIIIe siècle.* P, 1852. 440p. (b) *The Franciscan Poets in Italy of the Thirteenth Century.* NY, 1914. xvi, 333p. Still useful. E40

ROGGEN, Heribert, OFM, (a) *Geest en Leven. Evangelisch-franciskaanse orientatie.* Roeselare, 1967. 201p. (b) *Spirit and Life. The Gospel Way of Life in the Writings of St. Francis and St. Clare.* Chicago, 1970. vii-119p.

Research Bibliography

SCHMITT, Clement, OFM, "Frères mineurs." In DTC-TG VII, 1696-1733. **E41

——, Un pape réformateur et un défendeur de l'unité de l'Eglise: Benôit XII et l'ordre des Frères Mineurs (1334-1342). Q, 1959. xxxvii, 419p. Rev: CF 30 (1960) 115; RSCI 15 (1961) 498-500. Bibl. useful also for 13th century. *E42

SCUDDER, Vida D., The Franciscan Adventure. A Study in the First Hundred Years of the Order of SFA. L & NY, 1931. 409p. Rev: CF 5 (1935) 171. *E43

SESSEVALLE, François de, Histoire générale de l'Ordre de SF. Le Puy, 1935-37. 2v Rev: AFH 28 (1935) 279, 30 (1937) 239-243; Ant II (1936) 580-582 (Oliger); CF 6 (1936) 262-268; EF 47 (1935) 736-739; 50 (1938 120. cf author's letter, "A propos de l'Histoire ...," EF 50 1938 88-91. *E45

SEVESI, Paolo M., OFM, L'Ordine dei Frati Minori. Lezioni storiche (an. 1209-1517). Parte prima. Mi, 1942. xvi, 314p. Rev: CF 14 (1944) 328-330. Parte 2da, Tomo I. Mi, 1958. xix, 352p. Rev: AFH 52 (1959) 333-335; CF (1959) 535-537. Parte 2da, Tomo II. Mi, 1960 xxiii, 322p. Rev: IF 35 (1960) 146; CF 32 (1962) 188. See also E10; cf his obit., CF 34 (1964) 230. *E46

SMITH, Jeremiah, "Franciscans, Conventual," NCE 6, 68-71.

VAN DIJK, Willibrord C., "Signification sociale du franciscanisme naissant," EF n.s. 15 (1965) 84-94.

2 THE SPIRITUALS & JOACHIMISM
a. GENERAL
(see also A166:21-26 & AFH 29 (1936) 242-254)

BARTOLOMASI, Bonaventura, Conv, "Storia genuine e sincera della fondazione de' Frati Zelanti Spirituali," MF 28 (1925) 127-141, 163-175; 29 (1926) 49-61, 75-92. Written in 1823. E47

BLOOMFIELD, Morton W., "Joachim of Flora. A Critical Survey of his Canon, Teachings, Sources, Biography & Influence," Trad 13 (1957) 249-311. Masterpiece, with comprehensive bibl. **E48

CHIAPPINI, Aniceto, OFM, "I processi di Frate Andrea da Gagliano Aterno," DASP ser6 (1953-55) 45p. cf AFH 55 (1962) 286. cf E56. *E49

DOUIE, Decima L., The Nature & Effect of the Heresy of the Fraticelli. Man, 1932. 292p. Rev: RHE 29 (1933) 722-725; AFH 26 (1933) 531-535. Fundamental. *E50 See her "Fraticelli," NCE 6, 81-82, and "Spirituals, Franciscan," NCE 13, 610-611.

FREDEGAND [CALLAEY] D'ANVERS, Cap, "L'infiltration des idées franciscaines spirituels chez les Capucins." In MFE I, 388-403. *E51

FRUGONI, A., "Dai 'Pauperes eremite domini Celestini' ai 'Fraticelli de paupere vita'." In Celestiniana (R 1954) 125-167. Rev: AFH 47 (1954) 431-434. *E52

LAUGHLIN, M. F., "Joachim of Fiore," NCE 7, 990-991.

MANSELLI, R., "Dagli spirituali all'osservanza. Momenti di storia francescana," Humanitas (Brescia) 6 (1951) 1217-1228. *E53

Research Bibliography

OLIGER, L., OFM, *De secta spiritus libertatis in Umbria saec. XIV.* R, 1943. 166p. *E54

——, "Spirituels." In DTC (P 1941) XIV, 2522-2549. Basic. *E55

PASZTOR. Edith. "Il processo di Andrea da Gagliano (1337-1338)," AFH 48 (1955) 252-297. With text. cf E50. *E55a

SALVATORELLI, L., "Movimento francescano e Gioachimismo." In CISSR III, 403-448. cf A274. *E56

THADDEUS [MacVICAR] OF NEW DURHAM, Cap, *The Doctrine of the Franciscan Spirituals.* R, 1963. 84p. Rev: MF 64 (1964) 243-244; AFH 58 (1965) 166-168; Ant. 41 (1966) 165-166.

b. ANGELO CLARENO

ANGELUS A CLARINO, *Chronicon seu Historia septem tribulationum Ordinis Minorum.* Prima ed. integrale, a cura di P. Alberto Ghinato, OFM. Vol. I, Testo. R, 1959. 231p. Corrected ed. of Tocco & Ehrle texts. Notes & commentary not yet published. E57

——, "Cronaca delle tribulazioni," L. Malagoli, ed., *Didaskaleion* (To) 10 (1931) 75-236. 14th century Italian translation. E58

BATTELLI, Guido, "Il Breviloquio di fra Angelo Clareno," IF 26 (1951) 213-235. Abs: CF X, 337*. E59

BERARDINI, Lorenzo, Cap, *Frate Angelo da Chiarino alla luce della Storia.* Osimo, 1964. 315p. Rev: CF 35 (1965) 212-213.

CAMPBELL, J., "Angelus Clarenus," NCE 1, 520.

DI FONZO, Lorenzo, Conv, "Clareniana," MF 67 (1967) 392-401; summary of recent studies.

DOUCET, Victorin, OFM, "Angelus Clarinus ad Alvarum Pelagium Apologia pro vita sua," AFH 39 (1946) 63-200. Basic. *E60

OLIGER, L, OFM, ed., *Expositio Regulae Fratrum Minorum auctore Fr. Angelo Clareno.* Q, 1912. lxxx, 251p. Rev: AFH 6 (1913) 168-170 (Bihl). Basic. *E61

——, "Fra Angelo da Chiarino nel VI centenario della sua morte," FF 14 (1937) 169-176. Important. E62

[ORTOLANI], Ciro da Pesaro, OFM, *Il Clareno (studio polemico).* Macerata, 1920. cxi, 444p. Also in part in MF 15-18 (1914-1917). *E63

VON AUW, Lydia, *Angelo Clareno et les Spirituels franciscains.* Lausanne, 1952. 59p. Rev: AFH 47 (1954) 223; FS 37 (1955) 326. Important. Author is editing his Letters. *E64

——, "Clemente V ed Angelo Clareno." *Religio* 15 (1939) 119-133. *E65

——, "Quelques notes sur Angelo Clareno," BISI 66 (1954) 115-128. *E66

c. PIERRE JEAN OLIVI (OLIEU)

STADTER, E., "Das Glaubensproblem in seiner Bedeutung für die Ethik bei Petrus Johannis Olivi, OFM," FS 42 (1960) 225-296. See its comprehensive Olivi bibl: 290-296. **E67

d. UBERTINO DA CASALE

UBERTINO DA CASALE, *Arbor vitae crucifixae Jesu*. Tr. e intr. di Fausta Casolini. Lanciano, 1937. xxiv, 205p. Rev: SF 39 (1942) 89-91. Contains only Lib. I Lib. IV, cap. 9, & Lib. V, cap. 3-9; but includes all material on SF. Important.   *E68

COLASANTI, Giovanni, Conv, "I Ss Cuori di Gesu e di Maria nell' 'Arbor Vitae' (1305) di Ubertino da Casale, O. Min.," MF 59 (1959) 30-69.   *E69

FREDEGAND [CALLAEY] D'ANVERS, Cap, *L'idéalisme franciscain Spirituel au XIVe siècle. Etude sur Ubertin de Casale*. Louvain, 1911. xxviii, 280p. Rev: AFH 4 (1911) 594-599; AB 31 (1912) 371-374. Basic.
E70

——, "L'influence et la diffusion de l'*Arbor Vitae* d'Ubertin de Casale," RHE 17 (1921) 533-546. Important.   *E71

GODEFROY, Cap, "Ubertin de Casale." In DTC (P 1950) XV/2, 2031-2034.   *E72

SARRI, Francesco, OFM, "Pier di Giovanni Olivi e Ubertino da Casale Maestri di Teologia a Firenze (sec. XIII)," SF 22 (1925) 88-125. Basic.   *E73

II THE FIRST ORDER

1 MISCELLANEOUS, (CHAPTER, ETC.)

(see also E16)

BROOKE, R. B., "The Chapter of Mats." In E3:286-291.   *E74

——, "The Constitutional Position, 1217-27." In E3:106-118. cf E75.
*E74a

ESSER, K., OFM, "Das 'Ministerium generale' des hl. F von A," FS 33 (1951) 329-348. Abs: CF X, 77*. Important. cf E74a.   *E75

——, "Die regelmässigen Kapitel." In his *Ordo . . .*, E16:316-326. Basic.
*E75a

KOLTNER, Bartholomaeus, OFM, *De iuribus Ministri Provincialis in OFM ad annum 1517*. R, 1961. 124p. Rev: AFH 58 (1965) 177-179.

MARINUS VON NEUKIRCHEN, Cap, *De capitulo generali in primo Ordine Seraphico*. R, 1952. 543p. Rev: AFH 45 (1952) 462-465; MF 53 (1953) 282-284; SF 52 (1955) 321. Fundamental.   *E76

SULLIVAN, Jordan J., Cap, *Fast and Abstinence in the First Order of SF*. Wa, 1957. xvii-142p.

VITO DA CLUSONE, Cap, "Quando ebbe nome l'Ordine dei FF. Minori?" IF 8 (1933) 561-567. Important: cf Esser, "Die Name des neuen-Ordens." In his *Ordo . . .* E16:116-118.   E77

WAGNER, Elmar, OFM, *Historia Constitutionum Generalium OFM*. R, 1954. xiii-207p.

2 RULES

(see also C6, D83a, E19)

CASUTT, Laurentius, Cap, *Die älteste franziskanische Lebensform; Untersuchungen zur Regula prima sine bulla*. Graz, 1955. 172p. Rev: AFH

49 (1956) 227; CF 26 (1956) 202; FS 38 (1956) 123-125 (Hardick). Basic. *E78

———, "Die Regeln des franziskanischen Ersten Order, übertragen und eingeleitet." In *Die grossen Ordensregeln*, 2. Aufl., Hans Urs von Balthasar, ed. (Einsiedeln 1961) 261-321. Rev: (1948 ed.) CF VIII, 64*. E79

CUTHBERT OF BRIGHTON, Cap, "La Règle primitive des Frères Mineurs de SF (1209)," EF 29 (1913) 140-153; & App. I in A288:465-476. E80

ELIZONDO, Fidelis, Cap, "Bulla 'Exiit qqui seminat' Nicolai III (14 Augusti 1279)," Laur. 4 (1963) 59-119.

———, "De evangelii et regulae franciscanae obligatione usque ad Bullam 'Exivi de Paradiso' Clementis V (6 maii 1312)," Laur. 2 (1961) 226-260.

———, "De vivae vocis oraculis circa Regulam franciscanam," Laur. 1 (1960) 435-472.

———, "Doctrinales Regulae franciscanae expositiones usque ad annum 1517," Laur. 2 (1961), 449-492.

———, "Pontificiae Interpretationes Regulae franciscanae usque ad annum 1517," Laur. 1 (1960) 324-358.

ESSER, K., OFM, "Zur Textgeschichte der Regula non bullata des hl. F.," FS 33 (1951) 219-237. Abs: CF X, 64*. Basic. *E81

FLOOD, David E., OFM, *Die Regula non bullata der Minderbrüder*. We. 1967. 168p. Rev: Ant. 42 (1967) 558-560; CF 38 (1968) 207-208.

GHINATO, A., OFM, "De ordinis agendi ratione ad regulam S. F.," Ant 35 (1964) 3-48. Important. cf D83a. *E82

HARDICK, L., OFM, "Vom F-leben zur Franziskanerregel," WW 17 (1954) 27-39. Also in E91(a):55-73. Abs: CF XI, 60. *E83

MATANIC, Atanasio, OFM, *Adempiere il Vangelo. Commento letterale e spirituale della Regola di SFA.* R, 1967. 208p. Rev: CF 37 (1967) 423-424; MF 67 (1967) 446-447.

OLIGER, L., OFM, ed., *Expositio Quatuor Magistrorum super Regulam Fratrum Minorum (1241-1242).* R, 1950. xv, 203p. Rev: AFH 43 (1950) 181; CF 21 (1951) 434; EF ns 1 (1950) 361; MF 51 (1951) 630-632. Important. *E84

———, *S. F. regula anni 1223 fontibus locisque parallelis illustrata.* R, 1950. 31p. Also a reply to E86 & E87. E85

QUAGLIA, Armando, OFM, *L'originalità della Regola francescana.* Sassoferrato, 1943. x, 172p. Rev: AFH 39 (1946) 287-293; CF 16/17 (1946/47) 343-347; MF 45 (1945) 193; Ant 21 (1946) 168; SF 43 (1947) 119-131. E86

———, *Origine e sviluppo della Regola francescana.* Napoli, 1948. viii, 155p. Rev: AFH 39 (1946) 287-305; MF 52 (1952) 308-311; SF 44 (1948) 180-182. E87

———, *Originalità della Regola francescana.* 2a ed. Sassoferrato, 1959. xix, 187p. Rev: AFH 54 (1961) 220; EF 10 (1960) 85-88 (Cambell); MF 62 (1962) 502; WW 25 (1962) 230 (Clasen). Important, with critical reviews. *E88

———, "Il prologo della 'regola non bollata,'" Laur. 9 (1968) 83-91; review of Flood, D. E., above.

Seraphicae legislationis textus originales. Q, 1897. 310p.   *E89

VAN DER LUUR, Vittoricus, OFM, *Regola e vita dei Frati Minori.* SMA, 1960. xv, 403p. Rev: CF 31 (1961) 600.   *E90

(a) *Werkbuch zur Regel des heiligen F von A.* Herausgegeben von den deutschen Franziskanern. We, 1955. xvi, 434p.   (b) *The Marrow of the Gospel; A Study of the Rule of SFA,* by the Franciscans of Germany. Tr. & ed. by Ignatius Brady, OFM. Chi, 1958. xiv, 346p. Rev: CF 29 (1959) 514 (OvR); FS 40 (1958) 94-96.   (c) *La règle des Frères Mineurs, étude historique et spirituelle.* Tr. de J.-M. Genvo. P, 1961. 239p. Fundamental.
*E91

3 CLERICUS & LAICUS
(see Appendix VII & D96-D102)

ALESSANDRO DA RIPBOTTONI, Cap, "l fratelli laici nel primo Ordine francescano," *Ius Seraphicum* 1-2 (1955-1956); & R, 1956. xx, 294p. Rev: AFH 50 (1957) 447; CF 28 (1958) 113. Basic.   *E92

BOCK, Colomban, OCR, "Tonsure monastique et cléricale," *Revue de droit canonique* (Strasbourg) 2 (1952) 375-406. Basic.   *E93

BONDUELLE, J., "Convers." In DDC IV, 562-582.   *E94

BROCKHAUS, T. A., *Religious Who Are Known as Conversi.* Wa, 1946. 127p. (Cath. Univ. diss.)   *E95

HALLINGER, K., OSB, "Sui primordi dell'istituto dei fratelli conversi," *Camaldoli* (now *Vita Monastica*) n38 (1954) 115-119.   E96

——, "Woher kommen die Laienbrüder?" *Analecta S. O. Cist.* 12 (1956) 1-104. Basic.   *E97

HARDICK, L., OFM, "Gedanken zu Sinn und Tragweite des Begriffes 'Clerici'," AFH 50 (1957) 7-26. Rev: CF XI, 60. Important for SF.   *E98

LANDGRAF, A. M., "Zum Gebrauch des Wortes "Clericus' im 12. Jahrhundert," CF 22 (1952) 74-78.   E99

LAPORTE, Maurice, "Frères," DSAM 5 (1964), 1193-1203.

WILLIBRORD DE PARIS, Cap, "Frères franciscains," DSAM 5 (1964) 1210-1218.

4 FRANCISCAN BIOGRAPHY

a. COLLECTED WORKS
(see also A229)

ARTHUR DU MOUSTIER, OFM Rec. (d. 1662), *Martyrologium franciscanum,* recognitum et auctum a PP. Ignatio Beschin et Juliano Palazzolo, OFM R, 1938. xxviii, 551p. Rev: AB 59 (1941) 355-357; CF 11 (1941) 91; MF 44 (1944) 111-142 (Di Fonzo) with many corrections.   *E100

——, *Martirologio francescano,* riv., corr, ed aum. dai PP. I. Beschin e G. Palazzolo, OFM. Prima versione italiana del P. G. Palazzolo con corr. e agg. R, 1946. xi, 459p. Rev: MF 47 (1947) 267. Indispensable.   *E101

——, *Ménologe franciscaine.* Première tr. fr. d'après la réédition latine de 1939 et la version italienne de 1946. Par le P. Jacques Cambell, OFM. Rennes, 1952. 286p. (mimeogr.)   *E102

Research Bibliography

Bibliotheca Sanctorum. R, 1961—. Standard new ref. work with rich illus. & bibls. By end of 1969, v. 1-10 pub'd. *E103

Fragmenta minora. Catalogus sanctorum fratrum minorum. L. Lemmens, OFM. ed. R, 1903, xii. 54p. cf ME 34 (1934) 50. *E102

GONZALO DE CORDOBA, Fray, *Del solar franciscano. Santoral de las tres Ordenes.* Madrid, 1958. 869p. E105

HABIG, Marion A., OFM, *The Franciscan Book of Saints.* Chi, 1959. 1006p. illus. Useful tables & bibl. (English only). *E106

JACOBILLI, Lodovico, OFM, *Vite de' Santi e Beati dell'Umbria e di quelli i corpi dei quali riposano in detta Provincia.* Foligno, 1647-1656. 3v. E107

LEON DE CLARY, OFM, *Aureola serafica. Vite dei Santi e Beati dei tre Ordini di SF.* 2a ed. corr, migl., agg. dal R.P Gian-Crisostamo Guzzo,. OFM Ven, 1951-54. 6v. Rev: CF 23 (1953) 395; MF 53 (1953) 278: MF 55 (1955) 292. Useful. E108

PIETR'ANTONIO DI VENEZIA, OFM, *Leggendario francescano.* Ven, 1721-22. 12v. Old, but longer biographies than later compendia. E109

THOMA DE PAPIA, *Dialogus de gestis sanctorum Fratrum Minorum.* Ex integro edidit P. Ferdinandus M. Delorme, OFM. Q, 1923. 312p. E110

b. COMPANIONS OF ST. FRANCIS (COLLECTED WORKS)
(see Appendix VII)

FORTINI, A., "Gli uomini di A compagni del Santo," FNV II, 273-314. cf FNV I/1, 319-378; I/2, 178-211. *E111

GRAU, Engelbert, OFM, "Die ersten Brüder des hl F," FS 40 (1958) 132-144. Basic. *E112

MacDONNELL, Anne, *Sons of F.* L & NY, 1902. viii, 436p. *E113

MECCOLI, Antonio, "I compagni di SF verso la gloria degli altari?" VP 23 (1932) 640-650. Important for tombs in Basilica. E114

TERZI, A., OFM, "I compagni del Santo: Filippo, Angelo, Illuminato sono Reatini..." App. A in his *Ultime battute*... C185:27-32. *E115

c. INDIVIDUAL FRIARS

(1) BLESSED AGNELLUS OF PISA

GILBERT OF LONDON, Cap, *B. Agnellus & the English Grey Friars.* L, 1937. xiv, 134p. por. Rev: CF 9 (1939) 210. *E116

(2) BROTHER ANGELO

PRATESI, R., OFM, "Angelo da Rieti." In DBI III, 233. cf E115. *E117

(3) BLESSED BENEDICT OF AREZZO

CRESI, D., OFM, *Il beato Benedetto Sinigardi d'Arezzo e l'origine dell' Angelus Domini.* Fi, 1958. 63p. Rev: EF ns23 (1960) 222; MF 59 (1959) 543. E118

(4) BLESSED GILES OF ASSISI
(see bibl. in E121; cf F299, F303-F306)

Dicta Beati Aegidii Assisiensis. Q, 1905. 123p. E119

Research Bibliography

BEATO EGIDIO DI A., (a) *I Detti*. Intr. versione e note di Nello Vian. Brescia, 1933. lxix, 179p. Rev: AFH 28 (1935) 530; CF 5 (1935) 492-494; Ant 9 (1934) 409; Conv 5 (1933) 947. Excellent intro. & notes. 2d ed Mi, 1964. vii, 205p. *E119a. (b) *Golden Words. The Sayings of Brother Giles of A with a Biography by Nello Vian*. Trans. from the Italian by Ivo O'Sullivan OFM. Chicago, 1966. 159p.

Leben und "Goldene Worte" des Bruders Agidius. Einführung und Erläuterungen von Lothar Hardick, OFM. Uebertragen von Paul Alfred Schlüter. We, 1953, xii, 176p (FQ, 3) Rev: AFH 47 (1954) 172; CF X, 241*; FS 37 (1955) 119-122. Useful intr., notes, index. *E120

BROWN, Raphael, *Franciscan Mystic. The Life of Blessed Brother Giles of A, Companion of SF*. Garden City, NY, 1962. 221p. Rev: AFH 56 (1963) 217-220: MF 62 (1962) 511-514. Complete but not documented, though with 52-item bibl. of sources & studies. *E121

CAMBELL, Jacques, "Gilles d'Assise," DSAM 6 (1967) 379-382.

GAMBOSO, Vergilio M., Conv, *Il Beato Egidio d'A, compagno di SF*. Padova, 1962. 144p. illus. Rev: AFH 56 (1963) 220. Excellent. E122

MARIANO DA ALATRI, Cap, "Egidio da Assisi," BSS 4 (1964) 960-961.

MATTESINI, Francesco, OFM, "Ricordano un cavaliere della Tavola rotonda," SF 59 (1962) 207-212. E123

SETON, Walter W., *Brother Giles of A*. Farnborough (Hants.), 1966. vii-94p. Reprint of 1918 ed.

(5) BLESSED GUIDO OF CORTONA

BRUNI, N., *Le reliquie del beato Guido da Cortona, compagno di SF, al lume della leggenda e della scienza*. Cortona, 1947, xii, 115p. Rev: CF 21 (1951) 282*; MF 47 (1947) 621. *E124

ODOARDI, Giovanni, Conv, "Guido da Cortona," BSS 7 (1966). 505-508.

PRATESI, R., OFM, "Guido da Cortona." In EC VI, 1291. *E125

SERNINI CUCCIATTI, Ugo, *La leggenda del Beato Guido*. Cortona, 1900. 31p. Rev: AB 23 (1904) 121. E126

(6) BROTHER JUNIPER

CASOLINI, F, "Aroma di Fra Ginepro nel settimo centenario della morte (1258-1958)," FF 25 (1958) 120-123. E127

FORTINI, A., *Nel settimo centenario della morte di Frate Ginepro da (1258-1958). Cronaca delle celebrazioni di R e di A (21-22 giugno 1958)*. Ven, 1959. 34p. illus. E128

PETROCCHI, Giorgio, ed., *La vita di frate Ginepro*. Testo latino e volgarizzamento. Fi, 1960. xxxvi, 100p. Rev: AFH 53 (1960) 329. Fails to cover all extant texts. E129

(7) BROTHER LEO

GIUSEPPE DE SIMONE ·(Pinuzzo da Bonea), "Frate Pecorella del buon Dio." IF 1 (1926) 12-15, 96-101, 230-232, 293-300; 2 (1927) 204-217; 3 (1928) 182-194; & Ven, 1934. 92p. Rev: IF 9 (1934) 665. E130

Research Bibliography

(8) BROTHER PACIFICO

COSMO, Umberto, "Il re dei versi." In D157:59-81 & 128n25. *E131

MANCINI, Norberto, "Il Piceno e la letteratura delle origini. Guglielmo di Lisciano (Fra Pacifico, rei dei versi)," IF 30 (1955) 242-246. Cf FNV 1/2, 33-38.

OCTAVE D'ANGERS, Cap, "Du frère cithariste qui, à Rieti, se récusa," EF 44 (1932) 549-556. *E131a

(9) BROTHER RIZERIO OF MUCCIA

Ristampa di notizie sulla vita del Beato Rizerio e sul culto a lui dedicato. R, 1958. 82p. Reprint of G. A. ANTONUCCI's 1711 life. E132

(10) ST. ANTHONY OF PADUA
(see also A55, A56, E167)

ABATE, Giuseppe, Conv, "Quanti anni visse S. Antonio di Padovi?" *Il Santo* 7 (1967) 3-66.

ARNALDICH, Luis, OFM, *San Antonio, doctor evangelico.* Ba, 1958. 229p. E133

BENVENUTI, D. G., "Cronologia della vita di Sant Antonio di Padova (1195-1231). Esame e discussione dei documenti dei sec. XIII e XIV," MF 30 (1930) 155-157; 31 (1931) 35-37; & A, 1931. 55p. E134

CALLEBAUT, André, OFM, "Saint Antoine de Padoue. Recherches sur ses trente premières années. Notes, discussions et documents," AFH 24 (1931) 449-494. Fundamental. *E135

CLASEN, Sophronius, OFM, (a) *Antonius, Diener des Evangeliums und der Kirche.* M.-Gladbach, 1959. 136p. Many fine illus. Rev: CF 30 (1960) 226. (b) *St. Anthony, Doctor of the Gospel.* Tr. by Ignatius Brady, OFM Chi, 1961. 136p. illus. (c) *Antonius, dienaar van Evangelie en Kerk*, M-Gladbach, 1960. 136p. (d) *Sant' Antonio Dottore Evangelico.* Padua, 1963. 136p. (e) Documentation under German title in WW 23 (1960) 53-67, 108-130. Basic. *E136

——, "Die geistige Gestalt des hl. Antonius von Padua," WW 12 (1949) 45-58. *E137

——, "Die Schriften des hl. Antonius von Padua," WW 13 (1950) 104-118. *E138

——, "Lehrer des Evangeliums; über die Predigtweise des hl. Antonius von Padua," WW 16 (1953) 101-121. *E139

——, "Anthony of Padua, St." NCE 1, 595-596.

——, *Lehrer des Evangeliums. Ausgewählte Texte aus den Predigten des hl. Antonius von Padua.* Einführung, Uebersetzung, Erläuterungen. We, 1954. xii, 390p. (FQ, 4) Rev: CF 28 (1959) 106. Important. *E140

CUADRA, Pilar de, *Un Puente sobre siete siglos: San Antonio hoy. Ambientacion biografica.* Madrid, 1967. xxx-303p. Rev: MF 68 (1968) 431-433.

DA GAMA CAEIRO, Francisco Jose, *Santo Antonio de Lisboa.* vol. I: *Introducao ao estudio da obra antoniana.* Lisboa, 1967. xxxv-503p. Rev: CF 39 (1969) 202-203.

Doctor Evangelicus. Vier studies over de H. Antonius van Padua. Hertogenbosch, 1949. 132p. See E167. *E141

FACCHINETTI, V., OFM, *Antonio di Padova. Il santo, l'apostolo, il taumaturgo.* Mi, 1925. xliv, 579p. 414 illus. Rev: AFH 22 (1929) 218-220. Still the most complete work. *E142

HABIG, Marion A., OFM, *Everyman's Saint, Life, Cult and Virtues of St. Anthony of Padua.* illus. Paterson, N. J., 1953. xii-195.

HUBER, Raphael M., Conv, *St. Anthony of Padua, Doctor of the Church Universal; A Critical Study of the Historical Sources of the Life, Sanctity, Learning & Miracles of the Saint of Padua & Lisbon.* Milw, 1948. xiv, 209p. Comprehensive bibl:164-199. **E143

MESINI, Candido, OFM, "L'eremo di S. Paolo in Ponte o Monte Paolo nel quale avrebbe, soggiornato S. Antonio di Padova," AFH 55 (1862) 417-467 & 558. Claims it was near Bologna, not Forlì; important also for early Franciscan history of Bologna. *E144

PURCELL, Mary, *Saint Anthony & His Times.* Garden City, NY, 1960. 282p. Rev: RHE 56 (1961) 333. E145

RIGAULD, Jean, O. Min., *La vie de Saint Antoine de Padoue.* Tr., intr. et notes d'Alexandre Masseron. P, 1956. 153p. Rev: CF 27 (1957) 89-91.
E146

SABATELLI, Giacomo U., OFM, "Antonio da Padova, santo." In DBI (R 1961) III, 561-566. illus. 2-col. bibl. *E147

S. Antonio di Padova secondo un contemporaneo. La "Vita Prima" o "Assidua," tr., ann. e corr. di riferimenti ad altre fonti dei secoli XIII e XIV, a cura di A. F. Pavanello. Padova, 1946. 153p. Rev: SF 44 (1948) 183. *E148

S. Antonio da Padova, Prediche scelte, a cura di P. Beniamino Rossi, OFM. To, 1961. 198p. E149

S. Antonio di Padova, Le prediche, Opera omnia, a cura del P. Carlo Varotto, Conv. 5 vols. Siena, 1963-1965. Rev: CF 34 (1964) 420-421; 36 (1966) 198-199.

S. Antonio dottore della Chiesa. Atti delle settimane antoniane tenute a Roma e a Padova nel 1946. Città del Vaticano, 1947. xix, 520p. *E150

STANO, Gaetano, OFM, "Antonio di Padova." In BSS (R 1962) II, 156-179. 7-col. bibl. Basic reference study. See E103. **E151

TOUSSAERT, Jacques, *Antonius von Padua. Versuch einer kritischen Biographie.* Köln, 1967. 570p. Rev: CF 39 (1969) 200-202: WW 31 (1968) 33-51, 81-99.

VIAN, Nello, "Frate Antonio, il mio Vescovo." R, 1956. 310p. (2d ed.)
E152

WILLIBRORD DE PARIS, Cap, *Saint Antoine de Padoue, Docteur de l'Eglise. Sa vie, son oeuvre.* P, 1947. 245p. Excellent with 3 important apps. on sources, miracles, & biogs. *E153

(11) BROTHER ELIAS
(see also A72, C195, C196, D62)

ATTAL, F. S., *Frate Elia compagno di SF.* R, 1936. 186p. Rev: EF 48 (1936) 395-397; impt. crit. rev. by Fr. Cuthbert CF 6 (1936) 600-605; author's reply MF 36 (1936) 515-524. Superseded by E155. E154

——, *Frate Elia, compagno di SF*; nuova ed. riv. e ampl. Genova, 1953. 325p. illus. Rev: CF 24 (1954) 405; MF 54 (1954) 671-673. Important.
*E155

CLASEN, S., OFM, "Antonius und Elias in ihrer Bedeutung für die innere Geschichte des Franziskusordens," FS 46 (1964) 153-162.

COSMO, U., "Il dramma di frate Elia." In D157:82-113. *E156

CRIVELLUCCI, A., "La penitenza di frate Elia," *Studi storici di Pisa* 4 (1895) 41-54. cf AB 16 (1897) 351. Includes text of 1253 doc. E157

DI FONZO, L., Conv, "Elie d'A." In DHGE (P 1961) XV/1, 167-183. Basic. *E158

FORTINI, A., "Frate Elia da A architetto della Basilica di SF," MF 37 (1937) 529-545. Eulogy. E159

——, "Frate Elia." In F233:79-155. Useful for 1226-1253. E159a

——, FNV II, 299-303; & index IV, 90. Not critical; stresses A origin.
E160

GIROLAMO DA CIVITELLA, Cap, "I meriti e demeriti di Frate Elia," IF 4 (1929) 16-20, 232-246, 398-406. Abs: CF 1 (1931) 103. Objective.
*E161

GOAD, H. E., "Brother Elias as the Leader of the Assisan Party in the Order." In *Franciscan Essays* (Man 1932) II, 67-84 (BSFS-ES III). E162

MARINANGELI, B,. Conv, "Frate Elia fondatore della Provincia di Terra Santa," MF 34 (1934) 3-14. E163

ODOARDI, Giovanni, Conv, "Un geniale figlio di SF, Frate Elia di A nel settimo centenario della sua morte," MF 54 (1954) 90-139. Fundamental. *E164

POMPEI, Alfonso, "Frate Elia d'A nel giudizio dei contemporanei e dei posteri," MF 54 (1954) 539-635. Comprehensive bibl.; fundamental.
**E165

SPIRITO, S., "Etude sur deux protagonistes du mouvement franciscain au XIIIe siècle: Grégoire IX et Frère Elie," EF ns13 (1963) 181-199. Tr. from A101. E166

VAN DEN BORNE, Fidentius, OFM, "Antonius en Elias. Hun beteknis." In E141:80-132. Abs: CF 19 (1949) 270-273; MF 54 (1954) 135 & 622n294. Reaches conclusions similar to E165. Important, esp. for post-SF period. *E167

III THE SECOND ORDER

1 ST. CLARE
(see also D67, D118, D119, & F262-F265)

BEREL, Anne-Marie, *Au creux du rocher . . . Claire d'A*. Préface de Georges Goyau. P, 1960. 128p. Rev: CF ·30 (1960) 475. E168

BLASUCCI, Antonio, Conv, "Chiara da Assisi," BSS 3 (1963), 1201-1208; with special section on iconography by Emma Zocca, 1208-1217.

BRACALONI, L., OFM, "S. Chiara nell'arte." In E206:207-212. E169

BRADY, Ignatius, & Sr. M. Frances, SMIC, *The Legend & Writings of Saint Clare of A*. Intr., Tr., Studies. St. Bonaventure, NY, 1953. xiv, 177p. Based on E191. Fundamental. *E170

——, *Conferences on Saint Clare of Assisi.* St. Bonaventure, N. Y., 1966. 74p.

BRETON, Valentin-M., OFM, (a) "La spiritualità di S. Chiara." In E206:69-78. (b) "La spiritualité de Sainte Claire," EF ns6 (1955) 43-64. *E171

CALLEBAUT, André, OFM, "SF et les privilèges, surtout celui de la pauvreté concéde à Sainte Claire par Innocent III," AFH 20 (1927) 182-193. cf E193, E198, E204. *E172

CASOLINI, Fausta, *Chiara d'A rilucente specchio.* 3a ed. riv. e aum. A, 1954. xv, 294p. illus. Rev: AFH 47 (1954) 214. Excellent. *E173

CLASEN, S., OFM, "Franziskanische Christusbrautschaft. Die Stellung des hl. Bonaventura zum Orden der hl. Klara," FS 35 (1953) 313-317. *E174

CRESI, Domenico, OFM, "Cronologia di S. Chiara," SF 50 (1953) 260-267. Rev: AFH 47 (1954) 213. Important. cf E196. *E175

DANIEL-ROPS, Henri, (a) *Claire dans la clarté.* P, 1953 & 1962. 148p. (b) *The Call of St. Clare.* Tr. by A. Attanasio. NY, 1963, 144p. illus. Excellent. cf D177. E176

De ROBECK, Nesta, *St. Clare of A.* Milw, 1951. 242p. illus. Best biog. in English. Includes Rule, Testament, Process. *E177

ESSER, K., OFM, "Die Briefe Gregors IX an die hl. Klara von A," FS 35 (1953) 274-295. Abs: AFH 47 (1954) 220. *E178

FARNUM, M.A., *Saint Clare, Patroness of Television.* Pulaski, Wis., 1961. 96p. cf E185. E179

FASSBINDER, Maria, "Untersuchungen über die Quellen zum Leben der hl. Klara von A," FS 23 (1936) 296-335. *E180

FORTINI, A., *Cronache dell'Anno di santa Chiara.* Perugia, 1953. 33p. E181

——, *Nel settimo centenario della translazione del corpo di S. Chiara (A, 3 ottobre 1260-3 ottobre 1960).* SMA, 1960. 16p. Abs: MF 63 (1963) 390. E182

——, "Santa Chiara," FNV I/1, 409-453; "La famiglia di Santa Chiara," FNV II, 315-349 (chart 349); "Luoghi e persone che si ritrovano nella vita di Santa Chiara," FNV II, 384-426. Fundamental. *E183

——, "Nuove notizie intorno a S. Chiara di A," AFH 46 (1953) 3-43. Abs: AFH 47 (1954) 211. cf E183. *E184

——, *Santa Chiara patrona della televisione.* SMA, 1960. 61p. Abs: AFH 53 (1960) 480. cf E179. E185

FRANCESCHINI, Ezio, "Biografie di S. Chiara," *Aevum* 27 (1953) 455-464; & in E206:263-274. Basic critical survey. *E186

——, "I due assalti dei saraceni a S. Damiano e ad A," *Aevum* 27 (1953) 289-306. Rev: VP 37 (1954) 116. Basic; includes impt. text of A Mss. 341. *E187

——, "La notte di Natale del 1252," *Chiara d'A* 2 (1954) 69-74. E188
——, "Storia e leggenda nella vita di S. Chiara," VP 36 (1953) 394-404. Valuable critical examination of historicity of 20 incidents. Rev, with E186 & E187: AFH 47 (1954) 211-213. *E189

GALLINO, T., "La cosi detta "S. Chiara" di Simone Martini," *Chiara*

Research Bibliography

d'A 1 (1953) 89-92. Abs: CF 27 (1957) 426. E190

GRAU, Engelbert, OFM, *Leben und Schriften der heiligen Klara von A. Einf.*, Uebersetz, Erläut. We, 1952. xii, 173p. (FQ. 2) Rev: AFH 47 (1954) 218; FS 35 (1953) 137-142. 3. verb. Aufl. We, 1960. 204p. Important. cf E170. *E191

——, "Die päpstliche Bestätigung der Regel der hl. Klara," FS 35 (1953) 317-323. *E192

——, "Das Privilegium Paupertatis Innozenz' III," FS 31 (1949) 337-349. cf E172. *E193

——, "Die Regel der hl. Klara in ihrer Abhängigkeit von der Regel der Minderbrüder," FS 35 (1953) 211-274. Basic. Abs: AFH 47 (1954) 219. *E194

HARDICK Lothar, OFM, (a) *Spiritualité de sainte Claire.* Tr. par Damien Vorreux, OFM. P, 1961. 126p. Rev: AFH 55 (1962) 410; (b) *La spiritualità di S. Chiara.* Mi, 1965. 216p. E195

——, "Zur Chronologie im Leben der hl. Klara," FS 35 (1953) 174-210. Rev: AFH 47 (1954) 219. Basic; more critical than E175. *E196

——, "Clare of Assisi, St." NCE 3, 913.

J'ai connu Madame Sainte Claire. Le procès de canonisation de Sainte Claire d'A. Toulouse & P, 1961. 176p. Rev: Ant 38 (1963) 242; CF 32 (1962) 480; EF ns12 (1962) 219. Useful notes, bibl., apps., & tables. *E197

LAZZERI, Z., OFM, "La 'Forma Vitae' di S. Chiara c la Regole sue e del suo Ordine." In E206: 79-122. Crit. rev. by Hardick: FS 37 (1955) 122-124. Basic, with rev. For impt. earlier arts. & eds. of texts by Lazzeri, see AFH *Indices*, p26. *E198

LONGPRE, Ephrem, OFM, "Sainte Claire d'A (1194-1253)," EF ns4 (1953) 5-21. Fundamental; uses all impt. sources. *E199

MARIE DE SAINT-DAMIEN, *Sainte Claire d'A, lumière dans le Christ.* P, 1962. 190p. E200

OLIGER, L., OFM, "De origine regularum ordinis sanctae Clarae," AFH 5 (1912) 181-209, 413-447. Still indispensable. *E201

Il processo di S. Chiara d'A. Con una notizia di Nello Vian. Mi, 1962. xxxiv, 110p. Excellent intr. & tr. E202

"Il ricamo di S. Chiara." In E206: 145-149, illus. Two studies of an alb she made. E203

ROGGEN, Heribert, OFM, "De H. Clara en de beweging van Franciscus. Waarom nam Sint Franciscus de h. Clara op in zijn beweging en om welke reden is zij hem gevold?" *Sint Franciscus* 6 (1962) afl. 3, 22-35.

——, *Franciscaans-evangelische levensstijl volgens de h. Clara van Assisi.* Den Haag, 1966. 80p. Rev: AFH 60 (1967) 462. English translation in preparation (Chicago, 1970).

SABATIER, Paul, "Le privilège de la très haute pauvreté accordé à Saint Claire d'A par Innocent III. Son authenticité, son histoire de 1215-1253," RHF 1 (1924) 1-54. cf E172, E193, E198. *E204

SALVI, G., "La Regola di s. Benedetto nei primordi dell'ordine di S. Chiara," *Benedictina* 8 (1954) 71-121. Important. *E205

Santa Chiara d'A. Studi e cronaca del VII centenario (1253-1953). A, 1954. 722p. illus. Rev: AFH 48 (1955) 149-152; FS 37 (1955) 122-125.

Besides C167, E169, E171(a), E186, E198, includes 1253 Rule, Letters, & surveys of Order throughout the world. Fundamental. *E206

SCHNEIDER, Edouard, *Sainte Claire d'A.* Préface du R.P. Leone Bracaloni, OFM. P, 1959. 237 p. Includes tr. of *Sacrum Commercium.* Crit. rev: CF 29 (1959) 550. E207

SETON, W., "The Letters from Saint Clare to Blessed Agnes of Bohemia," AFH 17 (1924) 509-519. cf E213 & E222a. E208

SPAETLING, Luchesius, OFM, "Die geistige Gestalt der hl. Klara von A," FS 35 (1953) 145-173; cf 36 (1954) 132. Well documented. *E209

TOMASO DA CELANO, *La leggenda di Santa Chiara*... per cura di Guido Battelli. Mi, 1952. vi, 147p. Rev: AFH 47 (1954) 209. E210

——, *La leggenda di Santa Chiara d'A.* Con intr. di Arnaldo Fortini. R, 1953. xxx, 133p. illus. Rev: AFH 47 (1954) 210; MF 56 (1956) 602. cf E210. E211

——, *La leggenda di S. Chiara Vergine.* Testo latino dal cod. 338 di A. Tr di Fausta Casolini. A, 1953. xii, 94p. Rev: AFH 47 (1954) 208. E211a

VAN DIJK, S., OFM, "Il culto di S. Chiara nel Medioevo." In E206: 155-206. *E212

VYSKOCIL, J.K. & Barabas, L., OFM, "Le lettere di S. Chiara alla Beata Agnese di Praga." In E206: 123-144. With crit. text & Ital. tr. cf E222a.
*E213

2 THE HOME OF ST. CLARE

ABATE, G., Conv, "La casa paterna di S. Chiara, e falsificazioni storiche dei secoli XVI e XVII intorno alla medesima Santa e a SFA," DSPU 41 (1944) 34-160, 8pl.; & A, 1946. 128p., 8pl. Rev: CF 16/17 (1946/47) 348-350. Condensed in E216. Fundamental. *E214

——, *Nuovi studi sull'ubicazione della casa paterna di S. Chiara d'A.* A, 1954. 37p. illus. plans. Rev: EF ns9 (1959) 229; CF X, n3939. Basic *E215

ATTAL, Francesco Salvatore, "La casa paterna e il parentado di Santa Chiara. Falsi e falsari dei secoli XVI e XVII," MF 46 (1946) 157-197. Condenses E214. Important. For data on SF, see C15. *E216

FORTINI, A., "Della casa paterna di S. Chiara," AFH 48 (1955) 160-. 194; reprinted in FNV II, 351-382: "La casa paterna di Santa Chiara." Fundamental, with E215, both for the home of St. Clare & the history of San Rufino. *E217

ZOCCO, Emma, "L'identificazione della casa paterna di S. Chiara in A," MF 54 (1954) 651-656. Agrees with Abate. E218

3 EARLY POOR CLARE HISTORY & BIOGRAPHY
(see also E174, E205)

AGATHANGE DE PARIS, Cap, "L'origine et la fondation des monastères de Clarisses en Aquitaine au XIIIe siècle," CF 25 (1955) 5-52. *E219

ASCHMANN, H. F., "Poor Clares" NCE 11, 566-568.

CASOLINI, F, *Il protomonastero di S. Chiara in A. Storia e cronaca (1253-1950).* Mi, 1950. xxiv, 390p. Rev: AFH 48 (1955) 149-152; CF 21 (1951) 237-240; IF 26 (1951) 201-210; MF 51 (1951) 648-651. Basic. cf F282, F283. *E220

FASSBINDER, Maria, (a) *Die selige Agnes von Prag*. We, 1957. 180p. (b) *Princess et moniale, Agnès de Bohéme*. Tr. par G. Daubie. P, 1962. 144p. cf E213, E222a. *E221

GRATIEN DE PARIS, Cap, "L'Ordre de sainte Claire." App. in his *Histoire*... E23: 593-617. Still indispensable. *E222

VYSKOCIL, Jan Kapistran, OFM, *The Legend of Blessed Agnes of Bohemia & The Four Letters of St. Clare*. Tr. by V. Buresh. Cleveland, 1963. ix, 287p. cf E213. *E222a

IV THE THIRD ORDER
1 THE THIRD ORDER REGULAR

ESSER, Cajetan, OFM, *Life and Rule* (of the Third Order Regular). Chicago, 1967. xix-124p.

FRONCEK, M. Z. et el., '(Franciscans — Sisters" NCE 6, 46-64.

PAZZELI, Raffaele, TOR, *Il Terz' Ordine regolare di SF attraverso i secoli*. R, 1958. 383p. illus. Crit rev: AFH 52 (1959) 127-130. *E223

SECONDO, Louis, "Franciscans, Third Order Regular" NCE 6, 71-72.

2 THE THIRD ORDER SECULAR
(see also E34)

BETTEZ, Norbert M., OFM, *L'influence sociale de SFA et du Tiers Ordre franciscain*. Montréal, 1960 383p. Not critical. E224

CAOLINI, Fausta, "The History of the Third Order." *Franciscan Herald and Forum* (Chicago) 36 (1957) 257-264, 286, 301, 304-305, 316-317, 329-332, 357-358; 37 (1958) 63-67, 132-135, 178-180, 212, 205.

FANTOZZI, A., & B. Bughetti, OFM, "Il Terz' Ordine francescano in Perugia dal secolo XIII al XIX," AFH 33 (1940) 56-113, 319-365. *E225

FORTINI, A., FNV II, 456-462. E226

FREDEGAND [CALLAEY] D'ANVERS, Cap, "La diffusione e l'influenza politica del Terz' Ordine di SF nel secolo XIII. Esame critico di una frase attribuita a Pier della Vigna," IF 1 (1926) 56-67, 161-171. From E228 (a). *E227

——, (a) "Le Tiers Ordre de SFA," EF 33 (1921) 360-382, 468-488; 34 (1922) 66-85, 195-210, 367-391, 538-560; & P, 1923. 135p. (b) English tr.: *The Third Order of SFA*. Pittsburg, 1926. 109p. Still unsurpassed. *E228

HABIG, Marion A., OFM, (a) "Catholic Leadership toward Social Progress — the Third Order," FEC 17 (1935) 103-167, and *Fran. Studies*, 15 (1935). (b) *Le Tiers-Ordre en Marche,* trans. by Guillaume Lavallée, OFM. Montreal, 1937. 186p.

——, "History of the Third Order Rule and Constitutions," *Fran. Herald and Forum* (Chicago) 40 (1961) 14-19, 31, 40-44, 49, 85-90.

——, "Popes in the Third Order," *Fran. Herald and Forum* (Chicago) 41 (1962) 21-24, 53-54, 56, 83-85, 95, 121-123, 152-154, 174-177, 191, 198-202, 223, 242-246, 266-270, 298-303, 370-379.

——, (a) *New Catechism of the Third Order*. Chicago, 1962. 94p. Rev. ed., 1967. 98p. (b) *Nuevo Catecismo de la Tercera Orden*. Utuado, Puerto Rico, 1962. 94p.

HABIG, Marion A., & Mark Hegener, OFM, A *Short History of the Third Order*. Chi, 1963. 104p. illus. cf E34:401-403. E229

HALLACK, Cecily, & Peter F. Anson, *These Made Peace. Studies in the Lives of the Beatified & Canonized Members of the Third Order of SFA.* Rev. & ed. by Marion A. Habig, OFM. L & Paterson, NJ, 1957. xix, 268p. illus. Reprinted: L, 1963. Rev: CF 28 (1958) 351. Useful bibl. Basic   *E230

HARTDEGEN, Stephen, OFM, "Third Orders" NCE 14, 93-96. ¶ *Il Terz' Ordine Francescano. Lezioni di Storia, Legislazione, Apostolato.* R, 1967. xiv-478p.

MANCARELLA, Giovan B., OFM, "Una Regola in volgare dell' Ordine di Penitenza da un codice umbro del XIVe secolo," *Annali della Facoltà di Magistero* (Bari) 5 (1966) 205-223. Rev: AFH 61 (1968) 270. The Third Order Rule of 1289.

MATTESINI, Francesco, OFM, *Le origini del Terz' Ordine francescano. Regola antiqua e vita del Beato Lucchese.* Mi, 1964. vi-84p. Rev: AFH 58 (1965) 188.

MATTONE-VEZZI, E., "SFA a Poggio Bonizzo. La fondazione del Terz' Ordine," *Miscellanea storica valdelsa* 45 (1937) 16-28. E231

MEERSSEMAN, Gillis, OP, *Le dossier de l'Ordre de la Pénitence du XIIIe siècle.* Fribourg, 1961. xvi, 346p. Rev: CHR 48 (1962) 384; FS 45 (1963) 193-196 (Hardick); SM s3/3 (1962) 638-645. *E232

MOTTE, John Francis, OFM, *Face to the World.* Chicago, 1960. x-103p.

PEANO, Pierre, OFM, *Histoire du Tiers Ordre.* P, 1943. 128p. E233

ROGGEN, Heribert, OFM, *De Franciskaanse Levenbeweging. Ein historischpastorale studie.* 2 parts. Mechelen, 1966. 208p; 118p. Rev: CF 38 (1968) 213-214.

SARASOLA, Luis de, OFM, "Fraternidad de Penitencia." In A316:425-440 (1929 ed.); 361-378 (1960 ed.). Important for early origin. *E234

VAN DEN BORNE, Fidentius, OFM, *Die Anfänge des Franziskanischen Dritten Ordens.* Münster, 1925. viii, 184p. Rev: AFH 20 (1927) 164-168 (Bihl). *E235

——, "Ursprung und erste Entwicklung des Franziskanischen Dritten Ordens," FS 16 (1929) 177-192. Still useful. *E235a

VAN DEN WYNGAERT, Anastasius, OFM, "De Tertio Ordine iuxta Marianum Florentinum," AFH 13 (1920) 3-77. *E236

3 13TH CENTURY TERTIARIES
(contemporaries of St. Francis)

a. ST. ELIZABETH OF HUNGARY

ANCELET-HUSTACHE, Jeanne, *L'or dans la fournaise; vie de Sainte Elisabeth de Hongrie.* P, 1962. 142p. illus. E237

——, (a) *Sainte Elisabeth de Hongrie.* P, 1947. 444p. illus. (b) *Gold Tried by Fire: St. Elizabeth of Hungary.* Tr. by Paul J. Oligny, OFM, & Sr. Venard O'Donnell, OSF. Chi, 1963. xxx, 313p. Thoroughly documented; basic. Rev: CF 18 (1948) 361. *E238

DE ROBECK, Nesta, *Saint Elizabeth of Hungary, A Story of Twenty-four Years.* Milw, 1954. ix, 211p. illus. Rev: CF 26 (1926) 100. Excellent. *E239

Research Bibliography

KRANZ, Gisbert, *Elizabeth von Thüringen, wie sie wirklich war, 3.* Aufl. Augsburg, 1961. 64p. illus. E240

LAVATER-SLOMAN, Mary, *Triumph der Demut. Das Leben der hl. Elisabeth.* Z, 1961. 444p. E241

MARIL, Lee, ed., *Elizabeth von Thüringen; die Zeugnisse ihrer Zeitgenossen.* Einsiedeln, 1961. 174p, *E242

b. BROTHER JACOPA
(see also E113)

EDOUARD D'ALENCON, Cap, *Frère Jacqueline,* Nouv. éd P, 1927. 65p. Rev: AFH 21 (1928) 375. Basic.. *E243

FORTINI, A., FNV 11, 453-456, & index. E243a

HUMANI, Maria Castiglione, "Frate Jacopa," FF 5 (1928) 10-24, 137-142, 205-210. & re-ed. with bibl.: R, 1933. 80p. illus. Rev: FF 7 (1934) 308; CF 5 (1935) 149. *E244

MASSERON, Alexandre, "Jacqueline de Settesoli aux funérailles de SFA d'après un tableau de Sassetta," EF nsl (1950) 329-336. *E245

c. BLESSED LUCHESIO

BERTAGNA, Martino, OFM, "Note storiche e documenti intorno a S. Lucchese da Poggibonsi," AFH 62 (1969) 3-114.

DUHAMELET, Geneviève, *Lucchese, premier tertiaire franciscain (1181-1260).* P, 1959. 134p. illus. Rev: AFH 53 (1960) 481; CF 30 (1960) 345. Useful. *E246

NATALI, Augusto, "Luchesio (La vita nello sfondo dei suoi tempi, di Poggibonsi e nell'arte," IF 35 (1960) 237-247, 297-309; 36 (1961) 125-130. Basic. *E246a

Numero dedicato al settimo centenario di S. Lucchese 1260-1960. Poggibonsi (Siena), 1960. 82p. illus. E247

V ST. FRANCIS & ST. DOMINIC
(see also A80:97-99 & F116)

ALTANER, Berthold, "Die Beziehungen des hl. Dominikus zum hl. F von A," FS 9 (1922) 1-28. Rev: AFH 17 (1924) 300-302. Basic *E248

FALOCI PULIGNANI, M., "SF e San Domenico," MF 9 (1902) 13-15. *E249

FISCHER, H., "Begegnung zwischen F und Dominikus." In C2:83-108. Basic. *E250

HINNEBUSCH, William A., OP, "Poverty in the Order of Preachers," CHR 45 (1960) 436-453. On SF: 450-452. Fundamental. *E251

LIPPINI, Pietro, OP, *S. Domenico visto suoi contemporanei.* Bologna, 1966, 358p. Rev: CF 37 (1967) 420.

MATANIC, Atanasio, OFM, "Papa Innocenzo III di fronte a S. Domenico e S.F.," Ant 35 (1960) 508-527.

MATT, Leonard von, & M. H. Vicaire, OP, *St. Dominic, A Pictorial Biography.* Chi, 1957. vii, 88p. 159 illus. Splendid illus. & excellent short life. Eds. in many languages. cf E255. E252

Research Bibliography

OLIGER, L., OFM, "Ein pseudoprophetischer Text aus Spanien über die heiligen F und Dominikus (13. Jahrhundert)." In *Kirchengeschichtliche Studien P. Michael Bihl als Ehrengaben dargeboten* (Kolmar 1941) 13-28. *E253

SARASOLA, Luis de, OFM, "San F y Santo Domingo." In A316: cv-cvii (1929 ed.); 580-582 (1960 ed.). *E254

VICAIRE, M. H., OP, (a) *Histoire de Saint Dominique.* P, 1958. 2v. Rev: Spec 34 (1959) 337-341 (Hinnebusch). (b) *Geschichte des heiligen Dominikus,* Freiburg, 1962. 2v. Rev: FS 44 (1962) 330-333 (v.1). (c) *St. Dominic & His Times.* Tr. by K. Pond. NY, 1964. XI, 548p. Fundamental. On SF, see index. cf E252. **E255 See also his "Dominic, St." NCE 4, 964-965.

RECENT BOOKS

Editor's Note: The following books on St. Francis were published after the revision of this Research Bibliography was completed:

Brooke, Rosalind B., *Scripta Leonis, Rufini et Angeli, Sociorum S. Francisci: The Writings of Leo, Rufino and Angelo, Companions of St. Francis.* Oxford: Clarendon, 1970. Reviewed in *Franciscan Herald,* August, 1971, pp. 254-256.

Hansen, Warren G., *St. Francis of Assisi: Patron of Environment.* Chicago: Franciscan Herald Press, 1971.

Roggen, Heribert, O.F.M., *Spirit and Life: The Gospel Way of Life in the Writings of St. Francis and St. Clare.* Chicago: Franciscan Herald Press, 1970. A translation by the author of the original Dutch, *Geest en Leven* (Franciskaanse Samenwerking, Roeselare, Belgium, 1967).

————, *Geschichte der franziskanischen Laienbewegung,* übersetzt von Godehard Jung O.F.M., bearbeitet von Gregor Gebken O.F.M. Werl, Westf., Germany: Dietrich-Coelde-Verlag, 1971. A translation of the original Dutch, *De Franciskaanse Lekenbeweging* (Mechlin, Belgium, 1966). Reviewed in *Franciscan Herald,* October, 1971, pp. 311-315.

Von Galli, Mario, S.J., *Living Our Future: Francis of Assisi and the Church Tomorrow,* with color photos by Dennis Stock, translated by Maureen Sullivan and John Drury. Chicago: Franciscan Herald Press, 1972. A translation of the original German, *Gelebte Zukunft: Franz von Assisi* (Luzern und Frankfurt/M: Verlag C. J. Bucher, 1970).

A life of St. Francis for young people, by Ira Peck, is scheduled for publication in December, 1972, or the spring of 1973, by Scholastic Magazines and Book Services, New York, N. Y. 10036.

SUBJECT INDEX
of the
WRITINGS OF
ST. FRANCIS

1761

Subject Index of The Writings

Index of Writings

Index of Writings

INDEX OF LIVES
BY CELANO

This Index of Celano's works, prepared by Fr. Placid Hermann, refers not to pages but to numbered paragraphs. For this reason it serves, together with the Concordance, also as Index of the other lives of St. Francis in this omnibus. For instance, "Bernard of Quintavalle" in I Celano, 24 will be found also in II Celano, 15, in Three Companions, 27, in St. Bonaventure's Major Life, 3 3, and in the Fioretti 2.

INDEX OF LIVES BY CELANO

In this Index of the *First* and *Second Life* and the selections from the *Treatise on the Miracles* the Roman I stands for the *First Life;* the Roman II for the *Second* Life; the capital M for the *Miracles*. The Arabic numerals without parentheses stand for the numbers of the various paragraphs of these works, not the pages. The Arabic numerals within parentheses stand for the numbers of the footnote related to the paragraph number that immediately precedes. The occasional small p indicates the Prologue of the *First Life*.

Index of Celano's Lives

Index of Celano's Lives

Index of Celano's Lives

Index of Celano's Lives

GENERAL INDEX

Numbers in this Index indicate pages, not paragraphs or sections. St. Francis is abbreviated SF. Consult also the Subject Index of the Writings of St. Francis, the more detailed Index of Celano's Lives of St. Francis, and the Concordances.

A

Abbot, Benedictine, of Assisi, 982, 983, 1177.

Abbot of San Clemente, 775.

Abbot of San Giustino, Perugia, 445, 1014.

Abbreviations, xv.

Abruzzi, 399.

Adriatic Sea, 275, 480.

Albertino of Narni, 346.

Alessandria, city, 427.

Alexander IV, Pope (1254-1261), 734, 759, 841.

Alife, town, 767.

Alverna (La Verna), Mount, 308, 406, 696, 717, 729, 733, 952, 1028, 1069, 1256, 1429-1464.

Alviano, city, 278, 723.

Ambrose, St., 661.

Amiterno, town, 783.

Anagni, city, 774.

Ancona, Marches of, 275, 293, 350, 351, 429, 448, 681, 701, 761, 765, 920, 997, 999, 1397-1428.

Angelo Tancredi, Bro., 317, 323, 372, 474, 776, 777, 887, 1067, 1194, 1218.

Anthony of Padua, St., 269, 493, 660, 736, 772, 1390, 1391.

Antrodoco, town, 783.

Apennines (Appennino), mountains, 480.

Apulia, 233, 235, 419, 637, 665, 666, 682, 893, 894.

Arezzo, city, 282, 348, 451, 677, 679, 727, 767, 771, 1262.

Arles, Chapter of, 269, 719.

Ascoli, city, 281, 765.

Augustine, Bro., 537, 741, 772.

Augustine, St., 761, 1088.

Assisi, 229, 232, 234, 236, 272, 303, 330, 337, 338, 341, 343, 366, 374, 396, 397, 407, 412, 444, 452, 470, 514, 539, 635, 638, 641, 654, 655, 658, 686, 744, 745, 775, 893, 896, 899, 901, 907, 954, 983, 994, 1007, 1019, 1036, 1074, 1075, 1133, 1147, 1181, 1189, 1201, 1261, 1264.

B

Bagnara, city, 1035, 1040.

Bagni, town, 1147.

Barbaro, Bro., 929.

Bari, city, 419, 682.

Barletta, town, 763.

Bartholomew of Gubbio, Bro., 776.

Begging by SF, 148, 685, 844, 911, 1035, 1147.

Benedict of Piratro (Pioraco), 993, 1221.

Benevento, city, 539, 753.

Bernard of Quintavalle, Bro., 248, 252, 374, 375, 405, 448, 548, 647, 887, 916-919, 926, 1218, 1244, 1302, 1306, 1312, 1314, 1370.

1801

Bernard Viridante (Vigilante), Bro., 253.

Bernard, St., 1088.

Bernardone, Peter, father of SF, 237, 240, 241, 372, 641, 642, 671, 890, 891, 906-909, 913.

Bethlehem, 300, 301.

Bevagna, city, 277, 457, 553, 722.

Bible, Understanding of, by SF, 446-448, 711, 1175.

Bibliographies, xv, 1507, 1667.

Biographies of SF:
Celano I, 225;
Celano II, 357;
Celano, Miracles, 545;
Bonaventure, Major, 627;
Bonaventure, Minor, 789;
Bonaventure, Excerpts, 833;
Three Companions, 853;
Legend of Perugia, 887;
Mirror of Perfection, 1125;
Little Flowers, 1301;
Sacrum Commercium, 1549;
13th-Century Testimonies, 1601.

Birds and SF, 695, 841, 1070; sermon to, by SF, 277.

Birth of SF, 229, 890.

Bologna, city, 412, 726, 1132, 1312, 1367, 1492, 1601.

Bonaventure, Bro. (not St.), 768.

Bonaventure, Lord or Master (not St.), 768.

Bonaventure, St., cure of, 633; on Mount Alverna, 845.

Bonizzo of Bologna, Bro., 1087, 1125.

Book learning and SF, 1042, 1045, 1046, 1048, 1128-1131, 1196-1198, 1202.

Borgo San Sepolcro, town, 443, 706, 707, 781, 1063, 1087, 1193.

Bovara, town, 1185.

Brescia, city, 473.

Brothers of Penance (Third Order Secular of SF, Secular Franciscans), 259, 657, 837, 943.

Burial of SF, 330.

C

Calvi dell' Umbria, 770.

Campania, 780.

Campiglia, town, 438, 683.

Canonization of SF, 333, 539, 741, 954, 1603.

Canticle of Brother Sun, 1020, 1024, 1076, 1223, 1237, 1256-1259, 1264, 1499.

Capua, city, 755.

Cardinal Protector chosen by SF, 299, 383.

Castel San Gimignano, 762, 768.

Castro dei Volsci, Campania, 773.

Celano, town, 433, 713, 759, 1156, 1158.

Ceprano, town, 762.

Chapters of Friars Minor, 940, 1088, 1132, 1146, 1189, 1190, 1196, 1339.

Chapter titles of:
Writings of SF, 23;
Celano I and II, 213;
Bonaventure, Major Life, 629;
Bonaventure, Minor Life, 791;
Three Companions, 885;
Legend of Perugia, 975;
Mirror of Perfection, 1117;
Little Flowers, 1295;
Sacrum Commercium, 1547;
13th-Century Testimonies, 1600.

Charity toward the poor, of SF, 292, 365, 368, 431-438, 500-503, 639, 890, 896, 1029, 1063, 1154-1164.

Charles the Great, Emperor, 1048.

Chronology of life of SF, xi.

Churches, restored by SF, 640, 837; swept by SF, 994, 1181.

Cicada, A, and SF, 695.

Cisterna, town, 777.

Città della Pieve, 282, 352, 728, 776.

Città di Castello, 287, 727.

Clare of Assisi, St., 294, 330, 435, 657, 722, 734, 744, 837, 1084, 1223, 1246, 1332, 1334, 1380, 1383.

Collestrada, town, 435.

M

N

Addendum

While this volume was being printed, the editor received a copy of the new German translation of the *Legend of the Three Companions* by Engelbert Grau O.F.M., with a scholarly introduction by Sophronius Clasen O.F.M. (*Die Dreigefärtenlegende des Heiligen Francziskus: Die Brüder Leo, Rufin und Angelus erzählen vom Anfang seines Ordens,* Dietrich-Coelde-Verlag, Werl/Westfalen, 1972, 292 pages).

Fr. Clasen examines in detail the various theories which have been presented concerning the authorship of this *Legend* and the attempts that have been made to reconstruct the original work. Although the earliest manuscript (Sarnano) dates only from the end of the thirteenth or the beginning of the fourteenth century, Fr. Clasen in our opinion demonstrates quite conclusively that this *Legend* is not a compilation by a writer of that time, but that existing manuscripts contain the original work, though not entirely complete and intact, of Brothers Leo, Rufino, and Angelo, also that the *Legend* must be dated for the year 1246 and served as a source for Thomas of Celano when he wrote his *Second Life of St. Francis.* — M.A.H.

A NEW FIORETTI

A COLLECTION OF EARLY STORIES ABOUT SAINT FRANCIS OF ASSISI

Translated from various sources,
with Introduction and Notes,
by John R. H. Moorman, D.D.

1809

EDITOR'S NOTE

To "round off and complete our collection of all that is known of the life of the Poverello," as Bishop Moorman writes (p. 11), we have added his *A New Fioretti* at the very end of the *Omnibus* in its Third Revised Edition (1977). The proper place for this collection of 75 stories about St. Francis, taken from various sources of the thirteenth to seventeenth centuries, is after *Thirteenth-Century Testimonies* (pp. 1597-1617); but to insert it there would have required too many alterations in the reprinting of this big volume. For this reason we place it after the General Index; and *A New Fioretti's* detailed *Contents*, which not only lists all the stories but groups them under fifteen headings, will also serve as an Index for this additional little work.

A New Fioretti, listed in the Bibliography of the *Omnibus* (p. 1685) as "invaluable," was published in London, 1946. Since it is now out-of-print, we thought it would be well to reproduce it in its entirety, even though some of the stories appear elsewhere in the *Omnibus*; e.g. among the *Excerpts from the Sermons of St. Bonaventure* (no. 45 is no. 2 on p. 838, and no. 55 is no. 7 on p. 840), and among *Thirteenth-Century Testimonies* (no. 33 is on p. 1606; no. 34, on p. 1605; no. 52, on p. 1601; no. 53, on p. 1609; no. 54, on p. 1612; no. 56, on p. 1602).

Bibliographical information concerning the sources from which Bishop Moorman gathered his collection of 75 stories (he mentions the source for each story in a very helpful introductory note) is given also in the Research Bibliography of the *Omnibus* (p.. 1684-1697 and 1745); e.g. L. Lemmens' *Testimonia minora saeculi XIII* (p. 1685); Jacques de Vitry and Thomas Eccleston (p. 1689); A. G. Little Manuscript (p. 1691); *Chronica XXIV Generalium*, *De Conformitate Vitae*, and Minor *Codices* (pp. 1694-1696); *Speculum Vitae* (p. 1696); Wadding (p. 1697); Angelo of Clareno's *Expositio Regulae* and his *Historia Septem Tribulationum* (p. 1745).

Bartholomew (Rinonico) of Pisa's *De Conformitate Vitae Beati Francisci ad Vitam Domini Jesu*, written 1385-1390 and formally approved by the Franciscan General Chapter of 1399, was first printed in Milan in 1510 and again in 1513, then in Bologna in a mutilated form 1590, and lastly in a critical edition in volumes IV (1906) and V (1912) of *Analecta Franciscana*. A good essay on the sources used is in volume V, pp. xxxi-xliv. This voluminous work, consisting of three books, "is of very uneven value. . . . Side by side with fantastic legends . . . it contains much really credible and precious historical information" (Paschal Robinson in old *Catholic Encyclopedia*, II (1907), 316).

Eight volumes of *Annales Minorum* by Fr. Luke Wadding, bringing the history of the Franciscan Order down to 1540, were published at Lyons, 1625 to 1654. He had planned two more volumes, but death intervened in 1657. Though these volumes are not free of all defects, they must be acknowledged to be a compilation of exceptional accuracy. The life of St. Francis which is in the first volume has not received the recognition it deserves; it was and still is one of the best major biographies of the Poverello. The second edition of Wadding's *Annales*, consisting of 16 volumes, was published in Rome, 1731-1736; and nine additional volumes by other authors appeared 1741-1886. The third and critical edition, begun in 1931, has added seven more volumes to the 25 volumes of the second edition, the latest being volume XXXII, for the years 1671-1680, published at the Antonianum in Rome 1964. — M.A.H.

CONTENTS

CONTENTS

V.   SAINT FRANCIS AND POVERTY

VI.   SAINT FRANCIS AND THE CHURCH

VII.   SAINT FRANCIS AND THE LAITY

VIII.   THE INDULGENCE OF THE PORTIUNCULA

IX.   SAINT FRANCIS AND THE LIFE OF DEVOTION

CONTENTS

X. SAINT FRANCIS AS A PREACHER

XI. ANIMAL STORIES

XII. MIRACLE STORIES

XIII. THE INTERPRETATION OF THE RULE

XIV. LA VERNA AND THE STIGMATA

XV. SAINT FRANCIS AND THE FUTURE OF THE ORDER

INTRODUCTION

SAINT FRANCIS of Assisi was one of the greatest actors the world has ever known. His life was full of dramatic incidents from the day when he borrowed the rags of some old pauper and sat begging, in execrable French, on the steps of S. Peter's in Rome to the moment when he insisted upon his friends laying his dying body on the ashes in the little hut close to the Portiuncula outside Assisi. As a young man he loved doing spectacular things and later, as leader of a religious Order, he was constantly planning some scene which would catch the attention of even the most indifferent passer-by. It was to this end that he threw off his clothes and handed them back to his father, and that he insisted upon Brother Rufino dragging him naked through the streets of Assisi with a rope round his neck, or that he climbed on to the roof of the new building at Bologna and started throwing the tiles to the ground.

So vivid, so dramatic, a life was bound to make a deep impression upon the world, and it was no wonder that, after Francis' death in 1226, people began to demand that the story of such a life should be written down. Yet what was probably the earliest document of all was not a biography but a little allegorical work which would certainly have appealed to Saint Francis himself. It is called *The Holy Converse of the Blessed Francis with Lady Poverty*, and is a romantic story of how Francis sought out the poor, despised and hated Lady Poverty and made her his bride. In style and in language it has much in common with what Dante says of the Saint in the eleventh canto of the *Paradiso*, while the theme was one which Giotto made the subject of one of the great frescoes which adorn the roof of the Lower Church at Assisi.

But it was in no sense a *Life* of Saint Francis. For the earliest attempt to tell this story we must turn to Thomas of Celano, a learned friar who was chosen by Gregory IX to be the official biographer of the Saint. Celano had not known Saint Francis at all intimately, for, after joining the Order in 1215, he had spent most of his time in Germany. In order, therefore, to do justice to his theme and to produce a worthy biography of the Saint, he was obliged to spend some months touring Italy and interviewing those who had known the Saint most intimately and all who had any information to impart. Having collected his notes (which must have been considerable), Celano returned to Assisi to work them up into a book which would satisfy not only the friars themselves, but also the Pope who had laid this charge upon him. And apparently he succeeded, for his book held the field for fifteen years. But to us it is rather disappointing. The style is formal and stilted. There is too much of Celano and not enough of Francis. We get tired of aphorisms and moralisings. We want to see Francis in the glory of his simplicity and to be allowed to gaze with wonder and awe, without constantly being told that it is our duty so to do.

So, to our minds, the work commonly known as the *Vita Prima* or *I Celano* is in some ways the least satisfying of the early attempts to tell the story of Saint Francis. If only Celano had been a little less of a stylist and had allowed us to read the stories in the rough, homely language in which he received them from the friars, how much better it would have been. But we can hardly hope now to discover the notes upon which his work was based. Yet, unless he destroyed them, they must have been stored away somewhere for a time, and I think there is evidence that some unknown writer did come across them and use them in compiling a *Life of Saint Francis*. This is now known as the *Legend of the Three Companions*. It is short, for it appears to be no more than a fragment, but it gives us a most vivid account of the youth and conversion of the Saint and of the early years of his ministry. Compared with the work of Celano it is fresh and simple and spontaneous. If *I Celano*, with its endless quotations from theological literature, seems to emanate from some book-lined scriptorium, the *Legend* has about it something of the fresh air of the Umbrian hills.

I Celano, then, must be regarded as the first attempt to produce an official life of the Saint. It was sponsored not only by the Pope, but by Brother Elias and all those who believed that the uncompromising idealism of Saint Francis was an impossible foundation upon which to build a great religious Order. And during these years, from the death of Saint Francis in 1226 to the appointment of John of Parma as Minister General in 1248, these were the men in power, men who were moulding the Order according to the ideals and policy which they had in view. To their way of thinking it was hopeless to imagine that the Order of Friars Minor could go on as a loosely-knit band of beggars wandering all over the face of the earth with no permanent home and prohibited, by their vow of poverty, from the possession even of such books as would make their preaching most effective. Some organisation, some mitigation of the rigours which Francis had set himself, some relaxation of the demand for absolute poverty—such changes were inevitable if the Order was to continue at all.

So Gregory and Elias argued; but their arguments sounded hollow to those who had lived and suffered with Francis, who had walked barefoot with him in cold and nakedness and hunger, who had gone with him in search of the leper and the outcast and the homeless, who had learnt from him the secret of " having nothing and yet possessing all things ". To them the policy of Elias was nothing less than a betrayal of all that Francis had stood for; and, as the high officials of the Order went their way, so the inner circle of the Saint's friends withdrew more and more to mountain caves and hermitages where they could dream dreams and see visions and continue the kind of life to which they had dedicated themselves when they knelt before Francis Bernardone and swore that they would follow him in poverty and humility.

To such men Celano's *Life of Saint Francis* must have seemed a very inadequate tribute to the memory of their hero, and no doubt they longed for an opportunity of telling the world what they alone knew. Such an opportunity came in 1244. In this year the Chapter General of the Order, meeting at Genoa, issued an invitation to all the friars who had known Saint Francis to send in their reminiscences in order that a new *Life* might be put together.

Three of Saint Francis' most intimate friends—Leo, Angelo and Rufino—met together at the mountain friary of Greccio. Here, among the great woods which cover the hillsides of the Valle Reatina, they reminded one another of various incidents in the life of their Master. Here they were visited by Brothers Masseo, Illuminato, and others who had been the Saint's companions on his journeys. Here it was that Leo took up his pen and wrote down the stories in a series of rolls which were finally sent, with a covering letter, to the Minister General.

As a result of their labours and those of many other friars, a fairly large collection of material was assembled at Assisi, and once again Thomas of Celano was invited to work it up into a *Life* of Francis. The result was what is generally known as the *Vita Secunda* or *II Celano*, which now took its place along with the *Vita Prima* as the official biography of the Saint. And once again the original sources upon which Celano worked—the rolls and notes sent in by Leo and others—were left stored away in the friars' library at the Sacro Convento and at S. Damiano. Here they were found, about fifty years later, by an unknown scribe who copied them into a collection of Franciscan material which he was compiling. From this manuscript, known as the *Legenda Antiqua* of Perugia, was composed the famous *Mirror of Perfection*, that fine collection of Franciscan stories which Paul Sabatier discovered and mistakenly regarded as the oldest of all the legends.

By the year 1250 the fortunes of the strict party in the Order—the " Spirituals " as they came to be called—were in the ascendant. The glowing reminiscences of Leo, Angelo and Rufino had been incorporated into the new *Life* of Saint Francis, while the friars had recently elected as their Minister General a man whose sympathies were strongly opposed to any relaxation of the strictness of the early Rules. Humble enough to wash vegetables with his inferiors, yet a scholar who had taught in

the Schools of Bologna and Paris, John of Parma
was a splendid example of the best Franciscans of
the second generation. No wonder Brother Giles
exclaimed: " Well and opportunely have you come,
Brother John; but you have been a long time in
coming."

For seven years John of Parma presided over the
Order, visiting the provinces on foot and stirring
up the friars to a more loyal adherence to the vows
which they had made. When pressed, at the Chapter
General of 1249, to make certain new rules for the
Order, he replied: " We do not want any new
rules. Let us try to keep those we have got." No
wonder the Spirituals felt as if their deliverer had
come: no wonder that Brother James of Massa, in
his great vision of the Order, saw John of Parma
shining like the sun and sitting on the very topmost
branch of the tree. But, unfortunately, John
became interested in the strange ideas of the
Calabrian prophet, Joachim of Fiore, ideas which
the official Church knew that it could not tolerate.
So long as the Minister General was suspected of
Joachist views the Order lay under a cloud, and in
February 1255 the Pope asked John to resign.
John himself, in his humility, was willing enough to
be released from the cares and responsibilities of
office, but the friars implored him to stay on.
When he refused, they asked him to name his
successor. Without a moment's hesitation John
declared that the best man to succeed him was a
young man of thirty-six, Giovanni Fidanza, known
to history as Saint Bonaventura.

Bonaventura, the Seraphic Doctor, was one of
the outstanding figures in a period which produced
an abnormal number of great men. He was a
scholar of the first rank and a man of quite excep-

1820

tional charm and sanctity. Even those who disagreed most profoundly with his policy were forced to acknowledge his goodness and sincerity. He took over the government of the Order at a critical time and by his personality and his ability set it firmly upon the rock. So striking a contribution did he make to the fortunes of the Order that he has been claimed as its " Second Founder ".

But to the Spirituals his advent was a disaster. All hopes of a return to the simplicity and hardship of the early days were crushed. From now onwards the Order would take its place—and a place of honour—in the Church; but it was a very different place from anything which Francis had had in mind when he tramped with a few followers to Rome in 1209 and forced the Pope to recognise that there could really be nothing seriously wrong in wanting to live according to the teaching of Christ. Now, under the firm hand of Bonaventura, the future of the Order was fixed, and the Spirituals found themselves once more driven into the mountains, there to uphold the ideals to which their lives were dedicated.

By way of making a new start in the Order, the Chapter General of Narbonne in 1260 decided that a new official *Life* of Saint Francis should be written. Celano's two books had served their purpose, but something more concise and more authoritative was needed, something which would give the sort of picture of Saint Francis which the party now in power wished to perpetuate, something which could safely be put into the hands of a novice without causing him searchings of heart or making him want to rush off into the arms of the Spirituals. The responsibility for writing this new official *Life* was accepted by Bonaventura himself. His work was completed by 1262, and was accepted with acclamation by the Order. Four years later a decree was passed that all previous *Lives* of Saint Francis should be destroyed.

No one can deny that Bonaventura's *Life of Saint Francis* is a noble and beautiful work. It gives us a charming, and in many ways faithful, portrait of the Saint as the humble imitator of Christ, the example of Gospel perfection, the founder of a great Order of men (and women) dedicated to the service of God and man. It is only when we compare it with what we know of Saint Francis from other sources—all of them well known to Bonaventura himself—that we see how inadequate it is. As one critic has said : the aim of Bonaventura's *Life* was " to make the Saint ever more saintly ". So, in pursuit of this aim, homely little incidents were suppressed; Francis becomes less unconventional; strange, inexplicable traits in his character are passed over, and incidents which might appear undignified are omitted. The dirty, patched tunic of Saint Francis is washed and ironed, and a Saint is turned out worthy to take his place in even the most fastidious company. It is a very nice Saint indeed, but it is not the man whom Leo and his friends had known and loved.

With the destruction of Celano's work (and of no one knows what other precious documents) in 1266, the work of Leo, Angelo and Rufino and their companions seemed to have been in vain. Angelo, Giles and Masseo were now dead, Leo and Rufino were spending their old age at the Portiuncula, living on memories of the past, keeping alive the ideals of poverty and simplicity which they had received from Saint Francis himself. And while the new Sacro Convento up in Assisi was stirring with new life and becoming a shrine which the greatest in the world were proud to visit, down in the plain a few furtive souls found their way to the hut in which Brother Leo lived, in order to hear him tell stories of Saint Francis and describe those early days of spiritual adventure. Old men often find that the days of their youth become more and more clear to them as the years go by. Such seems to have been the experience of Brother Leo, who poured story after story into the attentive ears of the younger men who had never known the Saint and who perhaps found the official *Life* heavy and conventional.

So, gradually, a new stock of stories was being formed, and one which was greatly treasured by the Spirituals, upon whom the scourge of persecution was being laid with more and more rigour. The centre of this new tradition seems to have settled in the Marches of Ancona, where men like Conrad of Offida, James of Massa and James of Fallerone were living. Here the stories which Leo and others had told were preserved, and from this general store of material various collections were made, among them the *Actus Beati Francisci*, from which comes that most exquisite of all Franciscan documents, the *Little Flowers of Saint Francis*.

But this storehouse of the Spirituals produced other things besides this, stories which have found their way into various collections, some of which have remained hidden in unknown manuscripts until quite recent years. The translations in this book include a number of these stories, taken from various sources.[1] They, and the chapters in the first part of the *Little Flowers of Saint Francis*, have certain marked characteristics. Great emphasis is

[1] Nos. 6, 16, 18, 20, 22–26, 29, 31, 46, 47, 50, 62–64, 68–75.

laid on the ideal of absolute poverty and simplicity, the Saint's mistrust of books and scholarship is often mentioned, Brother Elias constantly appears as the " villain of the piece " and Francis frequently expresses his concern for the future of the Order. In many of them Leo is expressly mentioned as the author or source of the narrative.

The other chapters here translated are taken from various sources. There are seven from contemporary writers outside the Order—Jacques de Vitry, Thomas of Spalato, Etienne de Bourbon, O.P., and the Chronicler of St. Albans, Matthew Paris; and five from Franciscan writers of the thirteenth century—Bonaventura and the historian of the English friars, Thomas of Eccleston. Some are legal documents, and some stories from various medieval collections of Franciscan material. Another source has been the great mass of material collected by the Franciscan, Bartholomew of Pisa, during the fourteenth century, and presented to the Chapter General in 1399 as the *Book Concerning the Parallels between the Life of Saint Francis and the Life of Christ*. Bartholomew drew on many souces for his great work, including some manuscripts which are now unknown. Finally, eight chapters are from Wadding's monumental *Annales Minorum*. Luke Wadding was an Irish friar who settled in Rome early in the seventeenth century and there devoted himself to writing the history of the Order. After twenty-nine years of work he published eight volumes containing the story of the Friars Minor down to the year 1541.

The seventy-five chapters which form this collection are, therefore, taken from various sources. To describe them all as " hitherto untranslated " is not strictly accurate, for one or two have appeared in English historical works. But except for these, the stories here printed are all " new " in the sense of being unfamiliar to English readers. A few, such as the story of the birth of Saint Francis, have no great claim to historical accuracy; but by far the majority have not only a good pedigree, but fit so closely with what we know of Saint Francis from other sources as to command our respect.

Saint Francis has made so deep an impression upon our generation, and won so much love and admiration, that no apology is needed in offering this small collection of new tales. Celano's two *Lives*, the *Legend of the Three Companions, the Mirror of Perfection*, the *Life* by Bonaventura and, of course, the *Little Flowers* are all well known to English readers. The stories in this book will round off and complete our collection of all that is known of the life of the Poverello.

1825

I. STORIES OF THE EARLY YEARS

I. THE BIRTH OF SAINT FRANCIS

Those who have visited Assisi may remember being shown a small chapel which is described as the Stable where Saint Francis was born. The tradition that Francis, like Christ, was born in a stable finds no support whatever in the early legends, and cannot be traced farther back than the middle of the fifteenth century. Bartholomew of Pisa, who, in the latter years of the fourteenth century, collected every shred of evidence to give support to his comparison of the life of Francis with the life of Christ, knew nothing of it. The earliest sign of such a tradition is in a fresco by Benozzo Gozzoli painted at Montefalco in 1452. Two hundred years later the Irish Franciscan, Luke Wadding, told the story in his massive *Annales Minorum* (edition of 1731, vol. i, pp. 19–20). The story is as follows.

THERE is a curious fact about the birth of this holy man. When his mother had been in travail for several days, suffering great pain and unable to bring the child to birth, a man came to the door of the house, dressed as a pilgrim, but believed to be a divine messenger, who said that the child should be born not in a costly bed, but in a stable, and that he should lie not on silk, but on straw. He then advised them to move without delay into a stable which stood nearby. Although this seemed a mad thing to do, yet, as the pains increased, the good mother was carried to the place which had been indicated. And there, without any further help or trouble, she gave birth to her glorious son, lying in the hay. O blessed child, who, from the very first moment of your life, followed the example of Christ!

The stable has ever since been held in great esteem, and a chapel has been built there in honour of Saint Francis, called " San Francesco il Piccolo " or " Little Saint Francis ".

2. SAINT FRANCIS AND THE SIMPLETON

The *Legenda Major* of Saint Bonaventura (i, 1) tells us of a certain simpleton in Assisi who used to spread his cloak on the ground before Saint Francis when he was still quite a boy. In the *Speculum Vitae Beati Francisci* we meet this person again. See Sabatier, *Description du Speculum Vitae*, in *Opuscules de Critique Historique*, fasc. vi, p. 324, n. 4.

When Saint Francis was returning from Rome (having done great wonders on the way) and had reached Assisi, many of the townsfolk wondered whether this could possibly be the young man whom they had called " the flower of youth ", now that they saw him look so wretched, so wasted away, and so much changed. But that simpleton who had spread his cloak before him said : " I told you a little while ago that before long he would be doing great things. Now he has begun; and you will yet see greater things than these that the Lord Jesus Christ will do through him. What you see now are only human things; but wait till you see the spiritual ones. Then you will see wonders you've never heard of, flashes of lightning coming out of him so that we shall all fall down dead with fright."

3. THE EARLY FRANCISCANS

This fine description of the early friars comes from Angelo Clareno's *Expositio Regulae* (ed. L. Oliger), pp. 25–6. Clareno was one of the Spirituals, and much of his writing was concerned with the relaxations in the Order and with what he regarded as the betrayal of the Franciscan ideal. His *Expositio Regulae* was probably written about 1322.

Those who are Friars Minor know what it means to be humble with Christ and to feel that that which is highly exalted among men is an abomination with God. They have learned also to hate this fleshly life and desire to depart and to be with Christ. Crucified unto the world, they bear in their bodies and in their souls the marks of the Lord Jesus. Living with Christ in understanding and memory, in heart and mind, they seek only those things which are above, not the things of earth. Naked they bear the naked cross, following Christ and forgetting the cares of this world. As strangers and pilgrims they serve God in poverty, giving no thought for the morrow. With neither home nor shelter, cut off from the enjoyment of all earthly pleasures, they keep no store of food or of any of the necessities of life. Silver and gold they hate like poison.

Every kind of dispute they avoid like death, for peace reigns among them, and peace they proclaim —the peace of God which passeth all understanding. Living in hovels far from the haunts of men, they give themselves to prayer and lamentation for the sins of the world, pouring out their supplications to God that He may have mercy upon the transgressors. Clad in the poorest of clothes, limited to one tunic only, with bare feet or open sandals, they will accept with humility only what they need for one day, and this they either earn by the labours of their hands or else beg. They receive neither gifts nor legacies, they neither buy nor sell nor lay up treasure, they have nothing laid by, and from every kind of business, commerce, trade, industry, gain, profit or advantage, either as individuals or as a community, they are completely cut off.

As dead to the world and living only for Christ and His kingdom, they work with their hands in order that they may live as the apostles lived, honestly and without indolence. And when, as a reward for their labours, they receive less than the bare necessities of life, since they are forbidden to accept any form of money, then they must have recourse to " the table of the Lord " and must beg for alms from door to door, to the Glory of God and to the profit of those who give to them. The pains of poverty are to them the true riches, and the shame of begging becomes the greatest honour when it is done in Christ's name.

4. A DESCRIPTION OF THE FRIARS IN 1216

In a letter written at Genoa in November, 1216, Jacques de Vitry writes as follows of the Franciscans. See Golubovich, *Biblioteca Bio-bibliografica della Terra Santa*, vol. i, p. 5.

I found but one consolation in those parts, and that was that many people of both sexes, both rich and poor, leaving all for Christ, have fled from the world and are now called Friars Minor. These people are held in great esteem by the Pope and Cardinals. They occupy themselves in no worldly pursuits, but work day by day with the utmost zeal and care to draw souls away from the vanities of this wicked world. And already, by the grace of God, they have had great success and have saved many, so that one may say : " Let one loving heart set another on fire ". They live after the manner of the primitive Church, of whom it is written : " The multitude of them that believed were of one heart and soul ". By day they go into the towns and villages in order to win others by setting them an example. At night they retire to some hermitage or lonely place and give themselves up to meditation. The women are housed in certain buildings near the towns. They will accept nothing, and live entirely by manual labour. They are all greatly distressed and perturbed because, by both clergy and laity, they are esteemed more than they would wish to be.

The men of this community meet together once a year, with great profit, at some agreed place in order that they may feast together and praise God. With the advice of good men they make and publish their holy regulations, which they get confirmed by the Pope. After this, for a whole year, they are scattered abroad through Lombardy, Tuscany, Apulia and Sicily. Brother Nicholas, provincial of the lord Pope, a holy and devout man, left the papal court recently and fled to the friars; but because he was of great service to the Pope he was recalled. I personally believe that, to the disgrace of the bishops, who are like dumb dogs that won't bark, the Lord intends, before the end of the world, to save many souls by means of these poor and humble men.

5. SAINT FRANCIS CLOTHES A SICK MONK

The information given in the first part of this passage is most interesting. If it is true, it tells us something which we should never have learnt from the other sources : namely, that Saint Francis used sometimes to put his followers into existing religious houses for a time. The story comes from a manuscript at S. Antonio in Rome and is printed in *Archivum Franciscanum Histori-cum*, vol. xii, pp. 382–3.

Brother Thomas of Pavia, Provincial Minister in Tuscany, said that he had had the following narrative from a certain Brother Stephen, a good and simple man who would be incapable of saying what was not true.

He said that in the early days of the Order the Blessed Francis, when he accepted men for the Brotherhood, used to give them a habit and cord and then place them in some monastery or church, since he had no place of his own in which to put them. In so doing he used to order them to serve God faithfully and also the church where they were living, and to be loyal to it, lest they should eat the bread of idleness. And so it came about that one day he received into the Order this Brother Stephen and placed him in a certain abbey with one companion. Two years later the Blessed Francis came back to the abbey and made careful inquiry of the monks as to how Brother Stephen had behaved himself. On hearing from them all a very good account of his behaviour, he took him with him and for several years made him his special companion.

Once when they had arrived together at the house of a certain noble lady she devoutly offered the Blessed Francis a piece of coloured cloth suitable for making a priest's chasuble. The holy man accepted it, and shortly afterwards went to stay at a certain monastery. While the Blessed Francis was having an intimate talk with the Abbot, a certain lay-brother, who had been in pain for many years, lay in bed uttering the most terrible shrieks and yells and cursing everyone in the monastery for not coming to look after him. Hearing this, the Blessed Francis, with his companion, hastened to the sick man's bedside and implored him to be patient, praising the divine providence which can bring good out of evil, soothing the sick man with his words, bidding him see his faults, and showing him the most loving sympathy. And seeing him lying there, naked and wretched, he said to Brother Stephen: "Bring me that cloth which the lady gave us. We shall find plenty of chasubles if need be; but this naked creature must be clothed, or how can we fulfil the law of Christ?" The good brother brought the cloth; and Francis, with his own hands, cut out a garment and sewed it together, and, before he left the place, visited the sick man again and clothed him.

6. SAINT FRANCIS TREADS CLAY IN ORDER TO ABASE HIMSELF

There is a well-known story in the *Little Flowers of Saint Francis* of how Brother Juniper, suddenly realising that the people of Rome were coming out to meet him and to honour him, started to play see-saw with the children in order to avoid being publicly welcomed. The following story of Saint Francis and Brother Masseo is similar to that. It comes from a manuscript at Florence and is printed by Bughetti in *Archivum Franciscanum Historicum*, vol. xx, p. 108.

Once when Saint Francis was at Santa Maria degli Angeli he called Brother Masseo of Marignano and said to him: " Come, brother, let us go and preach the word of God ". And Masseo said: " Yes, let us go ". So they set out together towards Rome.

And when they were drawing near to a certain city the Bishop of the place, having heard of the sanctity of Saint Francis and getting news of his approach, arrayed himself in his episcopal robes and set out in procession from the city, accompanied by his clergy. When Francis saw what was happening he said to his companion: " O, Brother Masseo, now we are undone! " " Why is that? " asked Masseo. " O, but we are undone! " cried the Saint; " do you not realise that all these people are coming out in our honour? Whatever shall we do? Pray God, Brother Masseo, that He will deliver us from such a shameful thing." To which Masseo said: " What can we do? To run away would be a disgrace. We must do whatever is best!'' Then, as the Bishop and his clergy drew near, Francis caught sight of a heap of potter's clay just off the road, and, lifting up his tunic, he stepped into the mud and began to tread the clay with his feet. When the Bishop saw Francis thus employed he despised him as a fool and went home. But thinking it over afterwards, he began to be edified. So, after Francis had entered the city, he was received with love and reverence by the Bishop, who willingly gave him permission to preach to the people.

7. SAINT FRANCIS COMPLAINS OF ILL-TREATMENT

This very human story of Saint Francis was discovered a few years ago in a manuscript at Darmstadt and was published by Fr. Bihl in *Archivum Franciscanum Historicum*, vol. xv, pp. 202–3.

Once when Saint Francis was going on a preaching tour with Brother Leo it happened that Brother Leo began to lose heart through utter exhaustion. So, as they were passing a certain vineyard, Saint Francis went in and seized a bunch of grapes which he gave to Brother Leo to eat. But while he was so doing an angry countryman appeared on the scene and most violently beat Saint Francis with many blows.

As they were going on their way afterwards Saint Francis complained bitterly of the hard knocks which he had received on Brother Leo's account, finding it quite impossible to give thanks to God for his sufferings. When he spoke he said to Brother Leo: " Brother Leo has well eaten, but Brother Francis has been well beaten. Brother Leo has had a good meal, but Brother Francis has, with his body, well paid for it." This story comes from Brother Henry Herp.

8. SAINT FRANCIS PRAISES BROTHER BERNARD AS A TRUE DISCIPLE

The following story, which has every mark of being genuine, was printed in the English Historical Review by Dr. A. G. Little in 1915 (pp. 675–6) from a manuscript in the Royal Library at Munich. Like the previous story it shows the hardships which the friars suffered in the early days.

Once in the early days of the Order the Blessed Francis with the holy Brother Bernard, his first disciple, came to a certain town where they hoped to beg alms, and both sat down, tired, by a stone. As it was dinner-time and the pains of hunger were torturing these " poor men of Christ ", the holy father said to his companion : " By this stone, my dearest brother, let us meet again when we have both collected something to eat for the love of God ".

So they parted, and each went his way in the city, knocking on the doors of the houses, standing on the doorsteps, boldly asking for alms and reverently taking what was given to them. But that holy man Brother Bernard became so hungry with walking about that he collected together nothing at all, for, as soon as he was given any crumbs or crusts or scraps he immediately ate them, so that when he returned to the stone where they had agreed to meet he brought nothing whatever with him in the way of alms.

When Father Francis came, carrying with him the food which he had collected, he showed it to his companion and said : " See, brother, what alms God in His goodness has given me. Now set down what you have got so that we may eat together in the name of God." Then Brother Bernard was greatly perturbed and, flinging himself at the feet of the holy father, exclaimed : " O my father, let me confess my sin. Alas, I have brought nothing here, for all that I was given I ate, for I was very hungry."

When Saint Francis heard this he wept for joy, and, embracing Brother Bernard, cried out with a loud voice : "Indeed, my sweetest son, you are a much holier man than I am. You are a perfect follower of the holy Gospel, for you have laid up no store, neither have you taken any thought for the morrow, but you have cast all your care upon God."

II. SAINT FRANCIS AND THE FRIARS

9. THE VIRTUE OF FEAR

This most interesting story is to be found in a manuscript in the library of S. Antonio in Rome and has been printed by Father Oliger in *Archivum Franciscanum Historicum*, vol. xii, p. 380. It shows Saint Francis wrestling with a problem and trying to put himself in the position of the man who had so greatly disappointed him. Like so many stories, it claims to have come from Brother Leo.

BROTHER LEO, the companion of the Blessed Francis, said that there was once a friar of such holiness that he seemed to be on an equality with the Apostles themselves. Yet in the end he yielded to temptation and left the Order. But, living in the world afterwards, he still gave the appearance of being of such virtue that he seemed almost to attain to apostolic perfection.

One day when Brother Leo and some other friars were walking along a road with the Blessed Francis, the question was raised by some of the brethren as to why that brother had left the Order. But the Saint replied : " I want to read something and to ask myself some questions which I shall myself answer. Let no one speak to me until I have done." And then he said the word " Humility ", which he repeated three or four times. Then " Chastity ", "Abstinence ", " Poverty ". And in this way he ran through a number of virtues, mentioning each one several times. And with each one he asked himself : " Do you know that ? " and answered : " Yes, I know that ". Finally he said, several times over, the word " Fear ". And when he asked himself : " Do you know that ? " he answered : " No ". Then again he cried out : " Fear ", repeating the word over and over again. But when he asked himself : " Do you know that ? " again he answered : " No ". So yet again he cried : " Fear ", and at last whispered to himself : " Yes, I know Fear ". Then he added these words : " It is useless for a man to seek all virtues and leave out Fear; yet few have it, and therefore it is hard to teach them ". And finally : " It was because he had no Fear that that good brother fell and left the Order ".

10. AN EXAMPLE OF THE WISDOM OF SAINT FRANCIS

Here is a story from Wadding (*Annales Minorum*, vol. iv, p. 92). The story was told by a certain Brother Stephen to Thomas of Pavia, Provincial Minister of Tuscany, who died in 1258. The following translation is by G. G. Coulton in *From S. Francis to Dante*, pp. 72–3.

ι I, Brother Stephen, dwelt for a few months in a certain hermitage with Saint Francis and other brethren, to care for their beds and their kitchen; and this was our manner of life by command of the Founder. We spent the forenoon hours in prayer and silence, until the sound of a board struck with a mallet, like a gong, called us to dinner. Now the Holy Master was wont to leave his cell about the third hour; and if he saw no fire in the kitchen he would go down into the garden and pluck a handful of herbs, which he brought home, saying, " Cook these, and it will be well with the brethren ". And whereas at times I was wont to set before him eggs and milk-food which the faithful had sent us, with some sort of gravy stew, then he would eat cheerfully with the rest and say, " Thou hast done too much, Brother; I will that thou prepare naught for the morrow, nor do aught in my kitchen ". So I, following his precepts absolutely, in all points, cared for nothing so much as to obey that holy man; when therefore he came, and saw the table laid with divers crusts of bread, he would begin to eat gaily thereof, but presently he would chide me that I brought no more, asking me why I had cooked naught. Whereto I answered, "For that thou, Father, badest me cook none". But he would say, " Dear son, discretion is a noble virtue, nor shouldst thou always fulfil all that thy Superior biddeth thee, especially when he is troubled by any passion ".

11. ANOTHER EXAMPLE OF SAINT FRANCIS' DISCRETION

From Thomas of Eccleston, *de Adventu Fratrum Minorum in Angliam* (ed. A. G. Little), p. 106.

Brother Albert of Pisa compelled Brother Eustace de Merc to eat fish contrary to his custom, for he said that the Order lost many good men through their lack of discretion. He added also that when he was staying with Saint Francis in a certain hospice the Saint insisted upon his eating twice as much as he generally did.

12. A DISOBEDIENT FRIAR IS PUNISHED

In spite of the advice which Saint Francis gave to Brother Stephen (see above, pp. 23–24) he certainly expected to be obeyed. In § 152 of Celano's *Vita Secunda* the Saint discourses on the virtue of Obedience, comparing the truly obedient friar to a dead body. The following story from Wadding (*Annales Minorum*, vol. i, p. 280), if true, shows to what extent Francis was prepared to go in order to teach a man the duty of Obedience.

There was once a certain Friar who would not submit to the discipline of Obedience. So Francis called him one day and spoke very severely to him. Then he ordered the friars to strip him and to take him outside, where there was a big pit. In this the Saint made the man stand while the friars cast in earth as if to bury him alive. When the man was buried up to the chin, Francis said to him: " Are you dead yet, brother ? " To which the other humbly replied : " Yes, father, or at least I deserve to die for my sins ". Then the Blessed Francis ordered the friars to dig him out again, and said to him : " Get up now, brother, and if you are really dead as a good religious ought to be dead to the world and the flesh, then you will obey your superiors in everything and will never be reluctant to do what you are told, just as a corpse can't refuse to do anything ".

13. A DOMINICAN GIVES ADVICE TO SAINT FRANCIS

In later years there was much rivalry between the Franciscans and the Dominicans. Francis and Dominic, however, were friends; and in the early legends the relations between the two Orders are described as amicable. The following most interesting story is told by the Spiritual, Angelo Clareno, in his *Historia Septem Tribulationum*. It will be found in F. Tocco, *Le Due Prime Tribolazioni dell' Ordine Francescano*, pp. 42–3.

I myself met a friar who heard the Blessed Francis preach at Bologna, and others who saw him have related this fact. When the Saint was entering the city and was intending to make his way to the house in which his brethren lived, he heard that they were living delicately, far beyond the standards of the Rule. So instead of going to them he went to the house of the Dominicans, where he was well received. Now, there was there a Dominican friar of great holiness and intelligence who, when he had heard the reason why Saint Francis would not go to stay with his own brothers, was sorry for them and sought how he might persuade him to go there and pardon them if they had done wrong. But Saint Francis said to him : " It would not be at all a kindness on my part if, by accepting the hospitality of men living in iniquity, I were to condone their offence in committing this sin against the holy poverty which they have sworn to observe ". When the Dominican heard this and saw that he was not succeeding in his purpose, he said to the Blessed Francis : " For the sake of the other friars, and lest they should be brought into dishonour through your refusal, let us go to them, and then you can gently reprimand them and exert your authority. If, after that, you still feel that you can't lodge with them we will return, and in this way the good name of the brethren will be preserved and they will correct their misdemeanour." Then Saint Francis agreed to do as the Dominican suggested; and, finding the friars willing to accept the punishment which he imposed upon them, he forgave them.

14. SAINT FRANCIS AND THE TRUE MASTER

Saint Francis was always rather suspicious of scholars, and was afraid that some of the friars would try to alter the whole purpose of the community by giving up absolute poverty and settling down as a learned Order. See, for example, *Intentio Regulae*, §§ 5, 7, 10, 11; 2 *Celano*, §§ 185, 194, 195. The following incident from Clareno's *Historia Septem Tribulationum* is typical of Francis' attitude. See Tocco, *op. cit.*, p. 46.

Some French friars once came to Saint Francis and told him that at Paris the brethren had appointed as their Master a learned professor of theology who had greatly edified both clergy and laity. But when Saint Francis heard this he sighed and said : " I am afraid, brothers, that such men will end by killing my little plant. The true masters are those who set a good example to their neighbours in good works and kindness; for a man is learned just inasmuch as he works for others, he is wise just inasmuch as he loves God and his neighbour, and he is a good preacher just inasmuch as he knows how to do good works, faithfully and humbly."

15. SAINT FRANCIS CHOOSES HIS COMPANIONS FOR THE EAST

Most of the early *Lives* of Saint Francis tell of his journey to the East in 1219–20. Nothing, however, is said there about his choice of companions on this adventure. The following story from Bartholomew of Pisa (see *Analecta Franciscana*, vol. iv, p. 481) is typical of the Saint's methods in making decisions.

In the thirteenth year after his conversion the Blessed Francis proposed to go to Syria to preach to the Soldan, and many of the friars accompanied him as far as Ancona, being anxious to go with him. But Francis thought it over and realised how difficult it would be to take so many brethren overseas, though at the same time he hated to disappoint any of them. So, when they reached the harbour at Ancona, he addressed them thus : " My dearest brothers, I wish that I could satisfy you all and take you all with me, but the sailors will not hear of it. And since to start choosing one and rejecting another would only cause trouble and division, let us try to find out the will of God." Then he beckoned to a little boy, who knew none of them, and said to the brethren : " If you are agreeable, we will ask this little boy ". And when the brethren showed their consent, Francis said to the child : " Is it God's will, my son, that all these brothers should go abroad with me ? " To which the boy said : " No ". " Which, then," said the

Saint, " does God wish to go with me ? " Then the little boy touched one or two of the brethren saying : " This, and this, and that one ". In this way he touched altogether eleven brothers and said to the Blessed Francis : " These are the ones to go with you. That's God's will." Then all the brethren who had not been touched were perfectly satisfied, recognising that such was the will of God.

16. SAINT FRANCIS REBUKES BROTHER ELIAS

The literature of the Spirituals is full of stories about Brother Elias, who was regarded as a traitor. Much of the abuse poured upon him is undoubtedly undeserved, for Francis certainly loved him and admired him, even though Elias sometimes worked against him. The following story is typical of the legends about Elias which were handed round among the Spirituals. It comes from Bartholomew of Pisa, *Liber de Conformitate*, in *Analecta Franciscana*, vol. v, pp. 174–5.

The Blessed Francis once took hold of some very simple brothers and led them to the table to sit next to him. As he did so he told Brother Elias to place the other brothers as he chose. Brother Elias, who was swollen with pride, said to Francis in his reckless way : " I doubt not but that. you will destroy the whole Order with your ridiculous notions ". But Francis, glowing with spiritual fervour, said to him : " Elias, Elias, know for a certainty that you will die outside the Order ". And so it came to pass ; for, having left the Order, Elias died out of the Church altogether.

17. BROTHER ANGELO PUTS THE DEVILS TO ROUT

From Bartholomew of Pisa, *Liber de Conformitate*, in *Analecta Franciscana*, vol. iv, p. 161.

Brother Angelo, the companion of Saint Francis, was once deeply disturbed by a devil who frightened him so much that he dare not be alone. So he confided in the Blessed Francis, who told him to go to the top of a high mountain and there summon all the devils, crying : " O proud devils, come to me, all of you, and do whatever you like with me ! " This he did; but when no devil came to him he was no longer afraid.

18. A STORY OF BROTHER GILES

This, strictly speaking, has nothing to do with Saint Francis, but it is such a delightful story that it deserves to be better known. Immediately after the death of the Saint, Brother Elias devoted himself to the task of building a suitable shrine, and raised a vast sum of money in order to build, at Assisi, the great basilica of San Francesco with its two churches, magnificent frescoes, and extensive range of conventual buildings. Considering Francis' intense dislike of large buildings, it seems a strange way of honouring his memory. To the Spirituals the whole thing was regarded as a great disaster, a symbol of the vast, organised betrayal of the high ideals of Francis himself.

This story will be found in Bartholomew of Pisa in *Analecta Franciscana*, vol. iv. p. 209, and was quoted by Wadding in *Annales Minorum*, vol. ii, p. 241.

When Brother Giles once came to Assisi, the friars took him round their new home, showing him the splendid buildings which they had put up, and apparently taking great pride in them. But when Brother Giles had carefully looked at them all, he said to the brethren : " You know, brethren, there's only one thing you're short of now, and that's *wives* ! " The brothers were deeply shocked at this; so Brother Giles said to them : " My brothers, you know well enough that it is just as illegal for you to give up Poverty as to give up Chastity. After throwing Poverty overboard it is easy enough to throw Chastity as well."

III. SAINT FRANCIS AND THE RECEPTION OF NOVICES

19. SAINT FRANCIS DISCOURSES ON THE RECEPTION OF NOVICES

The following story, which will be found in Angelo Clareno's *Expositio Regulae* (ed. L. Oliger), pp. 50–1, shows Saint Francis' anxiety about the future of the Order.

SAINT FRANCIS was once asked by the friars if he would try to persuade a certain man of good life to join the Order. But he said : " It is not my business, brothers, nor yours to try to induce anyone to join our community. Our business is to preach penitence, both by the example which we give and by the words which we speak, and to draw all men to love and serve Christ and to hate and despise the world. It is for God, unto whom all hearts be open, to choose and to call those who are suitable for our way of life and to give them grace to be loyal to it. In fact, He who planted this Order in the world desires that its direction and its size and its future should be wholly left to Him. For one of the ways in which the devil will try to destroy the Order will be through bad and thoughtless admissions. Evil spirits will make all kinds of unsuitable men want to join the Order, and will stir up the minds of the Ministers so that they take in large numbers without testing either the firmness of purpose or the kind of motive or the strength of will of those whom they accept. Rather they will be swayed by such things as rank and wealth and learning and ability and reputation. And when such men have been admitted they will try to alter the whole intention of the Rule, and will consider themselves too good to keep the purity of it which is so dear to Christ. So you see that, in order to foil the cunning of the devil and to ensure the right progress of the Order, God wills that the Ministers shall accept only such men as have Christ and His Spirit in their hearts and who seek to know the things of God, for by such only will the Order continue in purity and holiness of life, and in all righteousness and perfection."

20. SAINT FRANCIS TEACHES A NOVICE HUMILITY

In the sixth fascicule of his *Opuscules de Critique Historique* Sabatier printed the *Verba Conradi* from MS. 1/25 at S. Isidoro at Rome. Conrad of Offida, the author or inspirer of this tract, died at Bastia on December 12th, 1306. Although belonging to the second generation of the friars, he had been an intimate friend of Brother Leo († 1271), whom he generally quotes as his authority. The following story will be found in *Opuscules de Critique Historique*, fasc. vi, pp. 381-3.

Brother Conrad records that in the friary at Milan was a brother who had been received into the Order by Saint Francis in this way. Two brothers were living with a learned man who, seeing them, began to ask them about their way of living. So they showed him the Rule, since it was the custom of the older friars to carry the Rule about with them wherever they went. When the learned man saw that the Rule bore the very essence of the Gospels, he, as a man taught and inspired by God and learned in all knowledge, realised that it was the work of the Holy Spirit, ordained and composed by Saint Francis at the dictation of Christ. So he said : " Brothers, I wish to join your Order ". And they answered : " My lord, we have a father, Brother Francis, who receives all who wish to follow our way of life. You must go to him at Assisi to the place called S. Mary of the Angels, and we will ask him to receive you."

So he did all that the brothers told him, and in due course came to Assisi, where he found Saint Francis and the brother who had promised to help him. Now, he came with much luggage and well dressed and mounted. When the brothers recognised him they told the Blessed Francis that a very learned man was coming to join the brotherhood. So Francis told them to bring him in to the place where he was with the brothers, and in his presence he said : " Brothers, this man wishes to become one of us. What do you think about it ? " And he began with the friar who had advised the man to come and who had spoken to Saint Francis about him. And the Blessed Francis said : " Brother, what do you think about it ? Shall I receive him ? " And he answered : " No, father, I should say not ". And Francis asked all the other brethren the same question, and they all made the same reply.

Then Francis said to the brothers : " Brethren, you have well said, for neither does it seem to me that he ought to become one of us. But if you had all told me to receive him I would have had him." Then the friar who had been the first to answer said to the blessed Francis : " Father, do you know what I think ? I think that if this man is prepared to be cook to the friars we should have him, otherwise not." Then the Blessed Francis asked all the brothers what they thought of this suggestion. And they all agreed with it. Then Francis turned to the learned clerk and said : " Well, brother, you've heard what they say. What will you do ? " But the man was speechless and astonished at what the brethren had said. First he said that he did not know what to say. But finally he said : " Yes, I am willing to be your cook and anything else that you tell me ".

Then the Blessed Francis took him into the Order and sent him to Rome to serve in the friars' kitchen, and there he stayed for a month. After that, the Blessed Francis ordered him on obedience to exercise the office of Guardian and to preach.

Thus the Blessed Francis wished the brethren to pass through the gate of humility, and thus, both wise and foolish, to go from strength to strength in pursuit of humility until the Lord should inspire those who held office in the Order to exalt them. Thus, by the grace of God and the virtue of humility (even as previously they had known something of the grace and power of God), they might lead others as much by the quality of their lives as by the force of their teaching and the power of the Spirit, and so gather a harvest of souls.

21. PLANTING CABBAGES

This charming story is told by Bartholomew of Pisa; see *Analecta Franciscana*, vol. v, p. 141.

Two young men once came to the Blessed Francis desiring to be received into the Order. But the Saint, anxious to test their obedience and to find out whether they were really willing to surrender their own wills, took them into the garden and said to them : " Come, and let us plant some cabbages; and as you see me doing, so you must do also ". So the Blessed Francis began to plant, putting the cabbages with the roots up in the air and the leaves down under the ground. Then one of the two men did as Francis was doing, but the other said : " That isn't the way to plant cabbages, father; you're putting them in upside down ! " But

Francis turned and said to him : " My son, I want you to do as I do ". And when the other still refused, thinking it all wrong, the Blessed Francis said to him : " Brother, I see that you are a very learned man; but go your way; you won't do for my Order ". So he accepted the one and refused the other.

IV. SAINT FRANCIS AND THE POOR CLARES

22. "LADIES" NOT "SISTERS"

Some very strange statements have been made from time to time upon the subject of Saint Francis and women. What is quite certain is that Francis was always highly suspicious of women and avoided their company as much as possible. He once admitted that he knew only two women by sight—presumably Saint Clare and the Roman lady, Giacomina dei Settesoli (see *II Celano*, § 112). The following story, which was printed by Father Oliger in *Archivum Franciscanum Historicum*, vol. xii, pp. 383–4, is typical of the attitude of the Saint. Most of the passage has also been translated by G. G. Coulton in *Five Centuries of Religion*, vol. ii, p. 162.

BROTHER STEPHEN used to say that the Blessed Francis would never be intimate with any woman nor would he accept familiarity from any of them. Saint Clare was the only one for whom he showed any affection. But when he spoke to her or about her he would never use her name, but called her simply "Christiana". He had always charge of her and of her convent. Nor would he ever allow any other convent to be made, although during his lifetime other houses were in fact founded by the influence of others. And when Saint Francis heard that the women who lived in these convents were called "sisters" he was greatly disturbed and is believed to have exclaimed: "God has taken away our wives, and now the devil gives us sisters".

Now the Lord Ugolino, Bishop of Ostia, who was Protector of the Order, loved these sisters very dearly. One day he said to Saint Francis as he was leaving his presence: "My brother, let me commend these ladies to you". Then Saint Francis, with a merry look, replied: "That's right, father, in future they shall not be called 'lesser sisters', but 'ladies', as you now term them in commending them to me". And from that day they were known as "ladies", not "sisters".

23. SAINT FRANCIS KEEPS THE BRETHREN IN ORDER

A continuation of the previous passage.

Soon after this there died Brother Ambrose, penitentiary of the Cistercians, to whom the Lord Ugolino had committed the care of the houses of Minoresses with the exception of the convent of Saint Clare herself. Then Brother Philip the Long got himself appointed to this office with papal authority to choose Friars Minor to look after the affairs of the convents. When the Blessed Francis heard of this he was much upset and cursed Brother Philip as a destroyer of the Order. Brother Stephen used to say that he had actually heard Saint Francis exclaim : " Hitherto the ulcer has been only in the flesh and there was hope of a cure; but now it has eaten into the very bones and has become incurable".

This Brother Stephen, at the order of Brother Philip, once visited a certain convent of Poor Clares. When, a little time afterwards, he was walking with Saint Francis from Bevagna to some other place, he asked his forgiveness for having done such a thing. Then the Saint severely reprimanded him and, for a penance, ordered him to plunge himself fully clothed into the river by the side of which they were walking. Now this was in the month of December. Thus, soaking wet and terrified of catching cold, he accompanied the Blessed Francis for two good miles until they reached the house of the brethren.

V. SAINT FRANCIS AND POVERTY

24. A FRIAR LEARNS THE JOY OF BEGGING

The older legends are, of course, full of examples of Francis' love of Poverty which also became the theme of certain allegorical works such as the *Sacrum Commercium B. Francisci*, one of the four great frescoes by Giotto over the high altar in the Lower Church of S. Francis at Assisi, and in certain stanzas of the *Paradiso*.

Francis was always particularly severe on any friars who refused to go begging. The following incident is taken from chapter 67 of the *Actus Beati Francisci*, a collection of documents from which the well-known *Fioretti* or *Little Flowers of Saint Francis* was made.

At Borgo Nuovo there was a certain brother called Michael who came of a noble family and who disliked going begging because it made him ashamed. It happened that the Blessed Francis came there one day; and, hearing about this friar, he reprimanded him very sternly and ordered him, on holy obedience, to set out alone and with nothing on except his breeches, and to go to a certain castle about a mile away and there beg for alms. And the friar obediently went in this condition and without feeling any shame. And having obtained much bread and flour and other things he returned, laden, to the house. And so overjoyed was he that he declared that he never wanted to do anything for the rest of his life except to go begging.

25. SAINT FRANCIS CURSES THE MINISTER AT BOLOGNA

Here is another story to show Saint Francis' suspicion of learning. It comes from chapter 61 of the *Actus B. Francisci* (ed. Sabatier, pp. 183–4).

A certain Friar Minor, Brother John of Sciaca, was minister of Bologna in the time of Saint

Francis, and a very learned man who, without leave
from the Saint, founded a place of study at Bologna.
When Francis heard of this he went at once to
Bologna and sharply reproved the minister, saying :
" You are trying to destroy my order ! After the
manner of Christ Jesus I have always wanted my
friars to pray rather than to read." And when he
was going away from Bologna, Francis cursed the
minister with a mighty curse. Then the minister
began to be ill, and, as his sickness increased, he
sent by the brothers for Saint Francis to ask him to
revoke his malediction. But the Saint replied :
" That curse which I put upon him has been ratified
in heaven by the Lord Jesus ". So the poor
minister lay in misery on his bed, with little consolation. And suddenly one day there came from heaven
a ball of fire and sulphur which smote right through
his body and the bed on which he was lying; and,
with a foul stench, the wretched man expired and
the devil received his soul.

26. BROTHER LEO'S DREAM

This story also concerns the fear of books and learning which
was shared by all those friars who were anxious to maintain the
literal observance of the Rule: It comes from the *Verba Conradi*
and will be found in Sabatier, *Opuscules de Critique Historique*, fasc.
vi, pp. 377–8. For other accounts of the same dream see *Actus B.
Francisci*, cap. 59, the *Chronica XXIV Generalium* in *Analecta Franciscana*, vol. iii, p. 69, and two passages in Bartholomew of Pisa's
Liber de Conformitate in *Analecta Franciscana*, vol. iv, p. 12, and vol.
v, p. 110.

The holy Brother Conrad once heard from
Brother Leo, the companion of Saint Francis, that
he (Brother Leo) woke one night in a great fright
and went to say Mattins with the Blessed Francis.
And he told the Saint that he had had a most alarming
dream. And Saint Francis said to him : " What

did you dream ? " And he said : " I seemed to be standing close to a stream, white and foaming, and many friars came to cross over, and since they were carrying books in their hands, they perished in the flood. And I also, when I wanted to cross, was holding a Breviary, and I should have been drowned in the water. So I threw the book away because otherwise I could not have crossed. Then I got over. . . ." Then the Blessed Francis answered with pain and grief : " O Brother Leo, these books are bad and will ruin the Order. I would not allow anyone to become a Friar Minor unless he is content with being able to say the ' Our Father '."

27. SAINT FRANCIS ACCUSES HIMSELF OF OVER-EATING

Another story from Wadding, *Annales Minorum*, vol. i, p. 288.

After a long struggle with the powers of darkness, Francis was once so wearied that he could go no farther. So his companions went to a certain town and asked someone, for the love of God, to lend them an ass. On hearing their request, one of the townsmen, in his rough speech, said : "Are you one of the followers of Brother Francis of Assisi, the man we hear so much good of ? " When they said that they were, and that it was for him that they wanted the ass, the man saddled his beast and brought the Saint from the church into the town in order that he might rest in his house. In the short space of time while they were between the church and the house the man was seized with a desire to make the Saint stop for a little while and to revive him with some chicken and other good things which were to be had in the town. When they finally reached the house, Francis saw on the dunghill a dead and rotten fowl, which he picked up and, pressing it to his mouth and his nose, said : " Ha ! glutton, here's some fine chicken for you ! Now eat as much as you like." Then he threw it away, and for breakfast ate nothing but some toast and water. Finally he thanked the people for all their help and blessed the house, prophesying that the family would remain there for many generations neither in great wealth nor in great poverty, but always with enough.

28. ON THE CLOTHES OF THE BRETHREN

From Angelo Clareno, *Expositio Regulae* (ed. L. Oliger) p. 72.

Although he was always ill, Francis would never, until the day of his death, go about in anything but a dirty old habit, patched with bits of sack-cloth, and barefooted, in order that he might show others that he practised what he preached. And he wanted all the friars to wear clothes of that kind, similar in material, cost and colour, and of the sort that would be considered highly undesirable by the people among whom they lived and from whom they begged their bread. Nor should the brethren be ashamed to patch their clothes with sack-cloth and other bits; for the Fathers, filled with the Holy Spirit, used regularly to clothe themselves with old and ragged garments in order that they might be one with the poverty and humility of Christ and with His fore-runner, and with all the great and holy men " who wandered about in sheepskins and goatskins, being destitute, afflicted, tormented, of whom the world was not worthy ".

29. THE FRIARS AND THE POSSESSION OF BOOKS

According to Brother Leo (see, e.g., *Intentio Regulae*, §§ 5, 7, 10, 11), Francis strictly forbade the friars to possess books, as this was contrary to their vow of absolute poverty, and would tend to convert the fraternity from a community of mendicant evangelists into a learned Order finding its spiritual home not in the slums or in the caves of the mountains, but in the universities. The struggle over this vital question exercised the friars for many years after the death of Saint Francis. The following story is typical of the kind of literature put out by the Spirituals. It will be found in an article entitled : " Una Nuova Compilazione di Testi intorno alla Vita di San Francesco dal Codice Universitario di Bologna, n. 2697 ", in *Archivum Franciscanum Historicum*, vol. xx, p. 540.

A certain very devout friar has recorded that once when he was on a journey from one place to another, or from one convent to another, he forgot to carry with him a copy of the Rule. Now, the Rule was the only thing that he ever wished to possess, being a very great lover of Holy Poverty. So when he looked and found that he had left the Rule behind, he was greatly distressed. But while he was asleep, the Blessed Francis appeared to him and rebuked him for being so upset and miserable over the loss of any material thing. To which the friar replied that what distressed him was that he would miss the spiritual consolation which he often received in reading the Rule, adding, nevertheless, that the friars ought to be careful to keep a few books, since the Rule laid upon them the duty of preaching, and also ordered them to say the Divine Office. He was therefore surprised that the Blessed Francis had rebuked him so sharply. Then the man of God spoke to him again, and when they had had some talk on these matters, he said, " Know for certain, little brother, that there is not one brother in the Order possessing books who will not be sorry, at the hour of death, that he ever had them ".

30. SAINT FRANCIS' COURAGE

Saint Francis tells us in his *Testamentum* that he had never allowed himself more than one tunic. As a result he must often have suffered a great deal from the cold during the winter months. The following story from Eccleston, *de Adventu Fratrum Minorum in Angliam* (ed. A. G. Little), p. 91, gives us an idea both of Saint Francis' love of Poverty and also of his courage.

Brother Ralph of Rheims, an Englishman, came to England after many years of hard work, and, after living for some time at Salisbury as a contemplative, he died in great content. He related how Saint Francis, when walking along a road in a biting wind, felt himself becoming faint-hearted. So he summoned up courage and, climbing a hill, took off his clothes and turned to face the wind. Then he told himself that it would be well for him if he had even one tunic.

31. THE THREE ESSENTIALS

Among the early Franciscan literature we often come upon some " saying " of Saint Francis, introduced with some such words as " Now the Blessed Francis used often to say. . . ." The aphorism which follows will be found in chapter 62, § 7, of the *Actus Beati Francisci* (ed. Sabatier), p. 186.

The Blessed Francis used often to say to the brothers : " I recommend to you these three things : first Simplicity, to counteract the excessive thirst for knowledge ; secondly Prayer, which the devil is always trying to hinder by various means ; and thirdly Love of Poverty and Holy Poverty herself ".

VI. SAINT FRANCIS AND THE CHURCH

32. SAINT FRANCIS AND INNOCENT III

Saint Francis had a number of audiences with the Pope from 1209 onwards. The story of his visit to Innocent III in this year, has been told by Celano (*I Celano*, 32–33; *II Celano*, 16–17), by the "Three Companions" (*Legenda Trium Sociorum*, cap. xii), by Saint Bonaventura (*Legenda Major*, cap. iii) and others. The following story comes from Matthew Paris (*Chronica Majora*, ed. Luard, vol. iii, p. 132). It is conceivable that Innocent III might, in jest, have told a man to go and roll in the dirt; but, if he had done so, Francis would quite certainly have taken the command literally.

WHEN the Pope had heard this petition [1] and found that it was asking for something so hard and so impossible to carry out, he looked at Brother Francis and, observing his ugly face, mean appearance, long beard, unkempt hair and black, shaggy eyebrows, he was filled with contempt and said: " Go, brother, look for some pigs, for you will find yourself more at home with them than with human beings; and go and roll yourself in the muck with them. You had better show them your Rule and occupy yourself in preaching to them." When Francis heard this he bowed his head and went straight out, and, having found some pigs, he rolled himself in the mire with them until, like them, he was totally covered with dirt from head to foot. In this condition he went back to the consistory and appeared before the Pope, saying: " My lord, I have done what you told me to do. Now perhaps you will listen to my petition." When the Pope saw what had happened he was greatly distressed and told Francis to go and get himself washed and

---

[1] That is, to be allowed to live according to the Rule which Francis had drawn up.

then return. This Francis soon did; and the Pope, moved by the petition, gave him permission to preach, and confirmed all that he had aşked for. Then he sent him away with his blessing.

33. SAINT FRANCIS PREACHES BEFORE THE CARDINALS

Saint Francis' sermon before the Pope and Cardinals is mentioned by Celano (*I Celano*, § 73). Bonaventura also refers to this event, informing us that Ugolino wrote out a sermon for Saint Francis, who, when the time came, entirely forgot what he had been told to say (*Legenda Major*, cap. xii, § 7). Two accounts of the same incident are given to us by the Dominican, Etienne de Bourbon. The longer one, which will be found in Lecoy de la Marche, *Anecdotes Historiques*, p. 215, appears to have been somewhat embellished by the writer. I here give the shorter version (*ibid.*, p. 407).

I have heard that when Saint Francis was preaching at Rome some of the prelates said to him : " We would like you to come and preach to us to-morrow ". Then one of the Cardinals, being sorry for Saint Francis and afraid that it would be too much for him, because he was a man of very little education, called him and gave him a sermon which he himself had written, sitting up all night. But when Francis was about to begin he forgot entirely what he had been told to say and, being at a loss what to do, he opened a psalter and encountered the following verse : " My confusion is daily before me, and the shame of my face hath covered me ". Then he showed them most skilfully how they, in whom the glory of the Church should shine forth as in the face of a woman, defile the Church by their evil deeds and make it an abomination to all men.

34. SAINT FRANCIS' REVERENCE FOR THE PRIESTHOOD

Saint Francis' reverence for priests is well known and finds expression in the Testament, Admonitions, etc. The following incident, which should be read in conjunction with *I Celano*, § 62, comes from the Dominican, Etienne de Bourbon. It will be found in Lecoy de la Marche, *Anecdotes Historiques*, p. 264.

I once heard the following story of the Blessed Francis when he was travelling in Lombardy. One day when he had gone into a church to pray, a certain heretic or manichee, seeing the reputation for holiness which Francis had with the people, ran to him, wishing through him to draw the allegiance of the people to himself, to upset their faith and to make the office of a priest appear contemptible. Now, the parish priest of that place happened to be a man of ill repute who kept a concubine, so the heretic said to Saint Francis : " Look here ! are we to believe what this man says and to show respect for him while he keeps a concubine and soils his hands with touching a harlot ? " The Saint, perceiving the malice of the heretic, went, before all the people, to the priest, and kneeling before him, said : " Whether or not this man's hands are as we have heard, I know not; but even if they are, I know that they cannot defile the wonder and efficacy of the Holy Sacraments. And so, because by these very hands great gifts and benefits of God are poured out upon His people, I kiss them in reverence of those things which they administer and of Him by whose authority they are given." So saying, and kneeling before the priest, he kissed his hands and put to confusion the heretics and those who supported them.

35. SAINT FRANCIS AND CARDINAL UGOLINO

Cardinal Ugolino is one of the principal characters in the story of the foundation of the Franciscan Order. He was devoted to Saint Francis, and would undoubtedly have been glad to join the Order of Francis had he encouraged him to do so. Although unpopular with the Spirituals for having co-operated with Elias in the building of the basilica and for having explained away much of the Rule and Testament in the fatal bull, *Quo elongati* (September 28, 1230), Ugolino undoubtedly did much to safeguard the future of the Order and to save it from falling into the hands of extremists. He was a large-hearted and humble-minded man, and the latter part of the following story from Bartholomew of Pisa (*Analecta Franciscana*, vol. iv, p. 454), if not historically true, is at least typical of the man.

When the Blessed Francis was once staying in the place known as " Saint Francis' Cell " [1] he was visited by the lord Cardinal Ugolino, who was afterwards Bishop of Ostia, and finally Pope Gregory IX. When the Blessed Francis saw him coming he took to his heels and fled into the very heart of the mountains. The Cardinal followed him alone and eventually managed to catch up with him. When they were together, Ugolino asked the Blessed Francis why he had run away from him, seeing that he loved him and the Order so dearly. To which Francis replied : " My lord and father, the reason why I fled was that I am but a poor man, wretched and worthless, and am put to great confusion when so noble a lord as you are condescends to speak to so poor a creature as I ". Then, after much talk together about holy things, the Cardinal said : " Tell me now, Brother Francis, for the love of God, what I ought to do ; for I cannot decide whether to remain as a Cardinal or whether to join your Order and throw over all worldly ambition. As the Lord liveth, I will do whatever you tell me."

[1] " Carcer beati Francisci." Possibly the place now known as the *Carceri*, close to Assisi on the slopes of Subasio.

Then Saint Francis said to him : " O my lord, you are a man of great wisdom and can do much good to the world by remaining as a Cardinal. Yet, at the same time, were you to join the Order it would act as a great example to the world, inspiring the hearts of many to serve Christ; for you are also a great preacher and by your eloquence many would be turned to Christ. So, as God at present gives me no guidance in this matter, I fear I am unable to tell you which of the two things you ought to do." And so Saint Francis had to leave him still undecided as to whether he should join the Order or not. But Francis prophesied that, in the fulness of time, Ugolino would become Pope; as indeed happened.

Moreover, when he had become Pope, he once put on the habit, cord and sandals and went with the friars to visit the holy places in the city of Rome. One Maundy Thursday, thus attired, he went to carry out our Lord's commandment that we should wash the feet of the poor. And while he was so doing, some of the poor men, not recognising who he was, drove him away, saying : " *You* don't know how to wash feet ! Go away, and send some of the other brothers who can make a better job of it ! " And the Holy Father got up and meekly obeyed.

36. SAINT FRANCIS SAYS GRACE

For this story see *Archivum Franciscanum Historicum*, vol. xx, p. 548.

Some Church dignitaries of Tuscany once invited the Blessed Francis to dine with them. And when the food was ready they earnestly besought the Saint to give it his blessing. But this he declined

to do until he was at last persuaded by their entreaties. And as soon as he had given his blessing
the food was immediately removed and a fresh lot
put upon the table. Afterwards many miracles
were wrought by the food which the holy father
had blessed.

VII. SAINT FRANCIS AND THE LAITY

37. SAINT FRANCIS PASSES ON PRAISE TO GOD

From Bartholomew of Pisa, *Liber de Conformitate*, in *Analecta Franciscana*, vol. iv, p. 145.

THE Blessed Francis was so much honoured for his holiness by the people that they used not only to kiss his hands, but even his feet. He, however, seemed in no way put out by such reverence; but his companions were horrified. "Brother," said one of them to him, "are you aware of what is happening? Do you not see what you are doing? The people are worshipping you, and yet you don't attempt to stop them, but seem rather to rejoice in it!" But the Blessed Francis replied: "These people never do anything out of respect for Him whom they ought to worship." Which answer only distressed the brother still further. Then Francis said to him: "Look, brother; all this reverence which is paid to me I never take to myself, but I simply pass it all on to God. And as for me, I keep myself in the dust of humility and all honour I give to God. Thus the people benefit, for it is God whom they are worshipping, though they see Him only in His creatures." And when he heard this the friar was much edified.

38. THE STORY OF MATTEO DE' ROSSI

The following delightful story will be found in Wadding's *Annales Minorum*, vol. ii, p. 35. Matteo's son, Giovanni Gaetano Orsini, became Protector of the Order, and eventually, in 1277, Pope Nicholas III (cf. *Analecta Franciscana*, vol. iii, p. 329).

When he got to Rome, the Blessed Francis made great friends with a certain nobleman called Matteo

1863

de' Rossi, a member of the ancient and puissant family of the Orsini. One day he was asked to dine with this nobleman; but, while they were waiting for him to arrive, the servants began to distribute the daily dole to the paupers who used to gather each day at noon at the palace gate. Francis, becoming aware of what was happening, secretly joined himself to the crowd and took his share. At that moment the lord Matteo came home and immediately asked what had happened to the Saint. When he could not be found, Matteo declared that he would not sit down except with the holy man. While the servants were rushing about searching for him, Matteo stood looking out of the window, when he suddenly saw him sitting among the poor in the yard. So he washed his hands, went downstairs, and, seating himself on the ground next to the man of God, he said : " Since you won't eat with me, Brother Francis, I must needs eat with you ". And so he did, rejoicing to be numbered with Christ's poor.

Hearing afterwards about the foundation of the Third Order for married men and others, he asked if he might join it and be taught how to keep its Rule. The high position of such a man did great things for the new Order, many taking heart from his example and coming to be enrolled.

39. SAINT FRANCIS AND THE THREE LITTLE BOYS

This story also comes from Wadding, *Annales Minorum*, vol. i, p. 115.

When Saint Francis was living for a time in a little house in Florence, there came one day to the door three little Florentine boys with their father and mother to see the holy man. Having rung the bell and made known the purpose of their visit, they were taken by the Blessed Francis into the garden. Here he picked five figs, which he carried to the innocent children who were watching him. Then, while with his eyes he saw their outward appearance, in the spirit he foresaw what would become of them. So to the first he gave one fig, and to the second also one fig; but to the third he gave three figs, saying : " You will one day be one of my dearest children ". Which, indeed, came about; for when the boy grew up he became a friar under the name of Angelo and proved by angelic deeds that the name was well chosen.

40. AN ENEMY IS CONVERTED

From *Archivum Franciscanum Historicum*, vol. xii, p. 382.

Brother Tebaldo said that he once witnessed and was present at the following incident. There was a certain very wicked man of Spoleto who not only refused to give any alms to the friars when they begged from him, but used to go about cursing them and heaping all manner of shame and abuse upon them. When the Blessed Francis, who was spending some time at Spoleto, heard of this, he told Brother Andrew of Siena, who was almoner there, to go to this man and try, by every possible means, to get something out of him, however small.

So Brother Andrew went and made such a nuisance of himself to the man, imploring him for the love of God to give them something, that at length the man threw him some small gift, mainly in order to be rid of the importunate friar. Brother Andrew carried this with great joy to the Blessed Francis, who rejoiced and divided it among the brethren, giving to each a tiny morsel and saying : " Let each brother say three *Paternosters* and pray for this sinner, that God may lead him into the way of goodness ". And then what happened ? Why, before the friars had risen from supper the man himself came to their house with such remorse that he threw himself at Saint Francis' feet; and, confessing that he had been blind in not appreciating the brothers, he asked their forgiveness, with tears in his eyes. And from that moment he was a changed man and became a friend of the brethren and one of their most generous supporters.

41. SAINT FRANCIS AND THE SERVANT OF THE COUNTESS

In the *Second Life of Saint Francis* by Thomas of Celano (§ 45) is a story of two friars who came to Greccio with the express purpose of seeing Saint Francis. The story which follows here is similar to that, but far more vivid. It will be found in an Italian version in a manuscript at Bologna; see *Archivum Franciscanum Historicum*, vol. xx, pp. 547-8.

A certain noble countess once sent some fishes to the Blessed Francis by the hand of two of her servants. While these men were on their way, one of them was thinking in his heart : " If I manage to see the Blessed Francis and to speak to him, then I shall know that I am saved. If I fail, then I shall know that I am lost." Having arrived at the place where the friars were living, they were most graciously received by Brother Angelo, who was then in charge of that friary. After having something to eat, the young man who had entertained this strange thought in his heart asked whether he might speak to Brother Francis. " My dearest brother," replied Brother Angelo, " we have strict commands from Brother Francis not to allow anyone who is not one of the brethren to go near him, except in great necessity. Otherwise his prayers will be interrupted. So you see it is impossible for you to see him now." When the poor boy heard this he was terribly upset and, throwing himself on the ground, burst into tears. At this Brother Angelo did his best to comfort him, asking him why he was so miserable and what was in his heart. After a long time the young man opened his heart to Brother Angelo and told him all that had happened.

Then Brother Angelo took him by the hand and led him to the place where the Blessed Francis was. When Francis saw them he cried out in great excitement to Brother Angelo: "What's all this, Brother Angelo? What's all this?" To which Brother Angelo replied: "Dear father, be patient, for it is really essential that this young man should speak to you". And Francis said: "All right; but only if it is really necessary". Then Brother Angelo explained to the Blessed Francis all that this young man had been thinking.

Then the Saint rose up and went out of the place where he had been sitting, and, running to the boy, embraced him, and, taking off his own girdle, he bound it about him from head to foot. Then, having comforted him, he said: "My dear little son, take care that you never allow such a thought to enter again into your heart, for be assured that such a temptation is both serious and dangerous". And having received Saint Francis' blessing, the young man went home so overjoyed that he could never express what he felt.

VIII. THE INDULGENCE OF THE PORTIUNCULA

The story of the granting of a plenary Indulgence for those who visit the Portiuncula Chapel outside Assisi on the second of August each year has been closely studied by Sabatier and others (see, for example, Sabatier's Introduction to his edition of Bartoli's *Tractatus de Indulgentia*). Hitherto the only plenary Indulgence had been one granted to crusaders. It is therefore no wonder that the Cardinals were horrified to discover that the Pope had granted a similar privilege to so small and insignificant a place as the little woodland chapel of the Portiuncula. Opposition to this departure from ecclesiastical custom may have encouraged the upholders of it to get whatever evidence they could before it was too late. The three following legal testimonies, all of which are printed in the *Tractatus de Indulgentia* (ed. Sabatier), pp. xliv–liv, give us a glimpse of Saint Francis pleading for his beloved Portiuncula.

42. THE TESTIMONY OF JAMES COPPOLI

THE witness of a noble knight as he heard from the mouth of the confessor of Saint Francis. Which testimony Brother Angelo, the minister, wrote down with his own hand for future reference.

The Lord James Coppoli of Perugia told me, Brother Angelo, in the presence of Brother Deodatus, custos of Perugia, and Brother Angelo, my companion, that once in the hearing of his wife and little James and another woman he asked Brother Leo, the companion of Saint Francis, whether the Indulgence of the Portiuncula was true or not. And Brother Leo said " Yes "; and then related what the Blessed Francis had himself told him, namely that he had petitioned the Pope to grant an Indulgence for this place on the anniversary of its consecration. And the Pope asked for how long he wanted it, for one year ? for three years ? At length they got as far as seven years; but still

Francis was not satisfied. Then the Pope said to him : " Well, for how long, then ? " And Francis replied : " Holy father, if it please your Holiness, my wish is that, because of the great things which God has done in this place, all those who shall come here with lowly and contrite hearts shall have remission of all their sins, and that there shall be no dispute about this ". And the Pope said : " I grant you that it shall be so ".

And when the Cardinals knew what had happened they implored the Pope to cancel it, because it would be to the prejudice of the Holy Land. But the Pope answered : " I shall certainly not cancel it now that I have granted it ". And they said : " Limit it, my lord, as much as you can ". Then the Pope decreed that the Indulgence should be available for one day in each year.

And when the Blessed Francis was going out from the presence of the Pope he heard a voice saying to him : " Francis, know that as this Indulgence has been granted on earth, so it is also ratified in heaven ". Then Francis said to Brother Leo : " Keep this a secret, and say nothing about it until the end of your life is near, for the place has not got it yet. But though this Indulgence shall be kept secret for a time, God will bring it to light and reveal it."

After a time the Lord James asked Brother Leo about it again, being anxious for fuller proof. And Brother Leo replied that it was as he had told him. And the Lady Maytana confirmed the word of the Lord James before certain witnesses. And the Lord James, priest of Santa Lucia di Colle, who is mentioned above as " little James ", ratified the same.

All this was done on the 14th of August (1277),

1869

within the octave of the Assumption, in the place where Brother Giles used to live.

43. THE TESTIMONY OF BENEDICT OF AREZZO

In the name of the Lord, Amen. I, Brother Benedict of Arezzo, was at one time with the Blessed Francis when he was still alive, and, by the mercy of God, the most holy father himself received me into the Order; and I was a friend of his companions and often, both during the lifetime of the holy father and after his death, I had conversation with his companions about the secrets of the Order. I now bear witness that I often heard from one of the companions of the Blessed Francis, Masseo of Marignano by name—an honest man and of the utmost probity—that he was with the Blessed Francis at Perugia in the presence of the lord Pope Honorius when he asked for an Indulgence for all their sins for such as came, with penitent and contrite hearts, to the church of S. Mary of the Angels, otherwise known as the Portiuncula, on the first day of August. Which Indulgence, so humbly and yet so earnestly asked for by the Blessed Francis, was at length freely granted by the lord Pope, although he made it plain that it was not the custom of the Apostolic See to grant such privileges.

In similar manner I, Brother Rayner of Mariano of Arezzo, a companion of the venerable Brother Benedict, confess that I have often heard the same thing from the said Brother Masseo, being myself one of his closest friends.

The above statements were read and published in the cell of Brother Benedict of Arezzo in the presence of Brother Compagno of Borgo, and many others. Dated: Sunday, October 31st, 1277. I,

John the Notary, was present on this occasion, and, on the orders of Brother Benedict and Brother Rayner, wrote and published the above.

44. THE TESTIMONY OF PETER ZALFANI

In the presence of Brother Angelo, minister, Brother Guido, Brother Bartolo of Perugia and of other brothers at the Portiuncula, Peter Zalfani said that he was present at the consecration of the church of S. Mary of the Portiuncula and heard the Blessed Francis preaching before the people and before seven bishops. And he had in his hand a certain parchment, and he said : " I want to send you all to Paradise. And now I make known to you an Indulgence which I have received from the mouth of the lord Pope himself. All of you, therefore, who have come here today, and all those who shall come here each year on this day with contrite hearts, shall have remission of all their sins. I tried to get this for eight days, but did not succeed."

IX. SAINT FRANCIS AND THE LIFE OF DEVOTION

45. SAINT FRANCIS IN ECSTASY

The following story was quoted by Saint Bonaventura in one of his sermons. It will be found in *Opera Omnia S. Bonaventurae* (ed. Quaracchi), vol. ix, p. 579.

ONE of the brethren was once living with the Blessed Francis outside a castle near Siena—that is to say, at Montepulciano. He said that while they were there they had nothing to eat but some dry bread. So they went and sat outside the church and ate the dry bread and drank some water. Then they went into the church, and Francis began to be filled with great exaltation. Thus he remained for a long time, until his companion began to be weary. Afterwards the brother asked him how he had felt, and the Blessed Francis replied that since his conversion he had never known such joy.

46. SAINT FRANCIS WALKS WITH CHRIST

From *Verba Conradi*, § 8, in Sabatier, *Opuscules de Critique Historique*, fasc. vi, pp. 380–1. Cf. *Analecta Franciscana*, vol. iv, p. 81.

On one occasion Brother Leo was sick of a fever one night. In the morning the Blessed Francis called him, saying : " Up, brother, and come with me ". So Brother Leo got up and went with him, but without telling him that he had suffered from a fever in the night. This he did because he did not want to miss a chance of being with the Saint. And then God showed him a vision. As he was walking along with Saint Francis he saw the Lord going before him. And the face of the Lord was turned towards the face of Saint Francis.

It is thought that whatever took place in the heart of the Blessed Francis was seen by Brother Leo.

47. SAINT FRANCIS RECEIVES ASSURANCE OF ETERNAL LIFE

Also from *Verba Conradi*, § 6 (*Opuscules de Critique Historique*, fasc. vi, pp. 378–80).

On another occasion Saint Francis said to Brother Leo : " My son, Brother Leo, there is laid up for my body in heaven a glory which no other shall have ". It is thought that the Blessed Francis said this after he had been promised Eternal Life.

The holy Conrad has told us that the Blessed Francis was always sad and lived in great grief. So one day the Lord appeared to him and said : " Why are you sad, Francis ? Have I not forgiven you all your sins ? " And Francis replied : " Yes, dear Lord, but you have not yet promised me Eternal Life ". The Lord made no reply to this ; and that is why Francis was always sad. Thus he continued for many years. And although the Lord had forgiven Francis every debt, even to the uttermost farthing, at the beginning of his conversion, the assurance of Eternal Life came to him about the time when his hands and feet and side were marked with the Stigmata. Forgiveness of all his sins was given to him at Saint Mary of the Angels. The assurance of eternal life came to him at Saint Damiano.

E

48. SAINT FRANCIS AND THE NEW TESTAMENT

In spite of his suspicion of learning, Francis does not seem to have had any objection to the friars reading the Bible. The following incident is reported by Saint Bonaventura in one of his letters. See *Opera Omnia S. Bonaventurae* (ed. Quaracchi), vol. viii, p. 334.

In order that you may know how much Saint Francis approved of Bible-reading, let me tell you what I heard from a certain friar. He told me that when a copy of the New Testament was given to the brethren, and since it was impossible for them all to read it at once, Saint Francis divided it up into single sheets and gave one page to each brother, in order that all might study it and none interfere with another.

49. SAINT FRANCIS' BREVIARY

In the convent of Santa Chiara in Assisi is preserved the Breviary of Saint Francis. In it will be found the following notes written by Brother Leo. See L. Lemmens, *Testimonia Minora Saec. XIII de S. Francisco*, p. 61. Benedicta was Abbess of Santa Chiara from 1253 to 1260 (*Acta Sanctorum*, March, vol. ii, p. 493).

The Blessed Francis acquired this Breviary from his companions, Brother Angelo and Brother Leo. When he was well he liked to say the office regularly, as is written in the Rule. And when he was ill and could not say it, he liked to hear it said. This he kept up as long as he lived. Moreover, he had the Gospels written out; and when, either through sickness or for any other obvious reason, he could not hear Mass, he had read to him the Gospel for the day as it was read in church. This he also kept up until his death. For he used to say : " When I do not hear Mass I adore the Body of Christ in mental prayer; and I worship just as much as when I see it at Mass ". And when the Blessed Francis had either read or heard the Gospel he always used to kiss the book with the utmost reverence. On this account Brother Angelo and Brother Leo implore the lady Benedicta, abbess of the Poor Clares of the church of Santa Chiara, and all future abbesses of that Convent, that, in honour and memory of the holy father, they preserve this book in their monastery, since it is one in which the Saint himself used often to read.

50. BROTHER LEO'S VISION OF THE PARCHMENT

There are two accounts of this incident, one in Bartholomew of Pisa, *Liber de Conformitate* in *Analecta Franciscana*, vol. iv, pp. 57-8, and one in *Verba Conradi* (*Opuscules de Critique Historique*, fasc. vi, p. 380). The following is taken from *Verba Conradi*. In the other version we are told that the parchment had written upon it the words : " This is the grace of God ".

Brother Leo recounts of himself, as if speaking of another, that a companion of Saint Francis once saw a great wonder. He was walking with the Saint along a road when Francis said to him : " Go back ". This he said in a moment of spiritual fervour. So the said brother turned back and left him as quickly as he could. Then he saw a parchment come down from heaven upon the head of Saint Francis and circle round his feet. As the brother was carefully watching, Francis saw the parchment and picked it up. But what became of it no one knows to this day.

51. SAINT FRANCIS MAKES A VOW

From Bartholomew of Pisa, *Liber de Conformitate*, in *Analecta Franciscana*, vol. v, p. 255.

Once Saint Francis spent a whole night in prayer saying nothing but : " O most holy Lord, I long to love Thee. O most sweet Lord, I long to love Thee." And while he was thus praying our Lord Jesus Christ appeared to him. Then Francis fell at His feet and said : " O my Lord, I have given Thee my whole heart and body, and yet I desire with all my being to do more for Thee if Thou wilt but show me how ". To which the Lord answered : " I will give thee what thou desirest. Of my own special grace I promise thee that as long as thou livest thou wilt always be either thinking or doing something good."

In the morning the Blessed Francis called Brother Angelo, who was in charge of that place, and said to him : " The Lord has appeared to me this night and has given me a great gift. And now, in order that I may the better fulfil it, I wish to entrust it to my Lord God and into your hands, making you my guardian and keeper." Brother Angelo was loth to agree to this, but finally accepted the charge. Then the Blessed Francis called six good friars together and, in their presence, vowed to God that, as long as he lived, he would think and speak and do only what was good. And Brother Angelo faithfully kept his part, but could seldom find the Saint except when he was praying. But his faith fulness was very dear to the Blessed Francis.

X. SAINT FRANCIS AS A PREACHER

52. SAINT FRANCIS PREACHES AT BOLOGNA

A great deal of Saint Francis' time was devoted to popular preaching. Yet very little is known of what he said. The following account is of peculiar interest, since it comes from an eye-witness. Thomas of Spalato (Split) has left this account of Saint Francis as a preacher in his *Historia Salonitanarum* (*Monumenta Germaniae Historica*, Scriptores, vol. xxix, p. 580).

In the same year (*i.e.*, 1222) on the Feast of the Assumption of the Mother of God, when I was a student at Bologna, I saw Saint Francis preaching in the Piazza before the Palazzo Publico, where almost the whole town was assembled. The theme of his sermon was: "Angels, men, devils". And he spoke so well and so wisely of these three rational spirits that to many learned men who were there the sermon of this ignorant man seemed worthy of no little admiration, in spite of the fact that he did not keep to the method of an expositor so much as of a revivalist. Indeed, the whole manner of his speech was calculated to stamp out enmities and to make peace. His tunic was dirty, his person unprepossessing and his face far from handsome; yet God gave such power to his words that many factions of the nobility, among whom the fierce anger of ancient feuds had been raging with much bloodshed, were brought to reconciliation. Towards him, indeed, the reverence and devotion of men were so great that men and women rushed upon him headlong, anxious to touch the hem of his garment and to carry away bits of his clothing.

53. SAINT FRANCIS IN EGYPT

In 1219 Francis went to the East in a vain attempt either to put
an end to the Crusades or to win for himself a martyr's crown.
The arrival of the Saint certainly caused something of a sensation
both among the Christians and among the infidels. The following
is an extract from a letter written by Jacques de Vitry in the spring
of 1220. It will be found in Golubovich, *Biblioteca Bio-bibliografica
della Terra Santa*, vol. i, p. 7.

Lord Rainer, prior of Saint Michael's, has gone
over to the religion of the Friars Minor. This
order has increased enormously all over the world, so
that in many ways it is following the way of the
early Church and the life of the apostles. The leader
of the order is called Brother Francis, who is so
lovable that he is held in reverence by all men.
When he came to our army he was filled with such
evangelistic zeal that he did not shrink from going
over to the camp of the enemy. There he preached
the word of God to the Saracens for many days,
and when he seemed to have made little progress,
the Soldan, King of Egypt, asked him privately to
pray to God that He would enable him to cleave to
whichever religion was most pleasing to Him.

Colin the Englishman, my clerk, has also gone
over to that order, and two other friends of his,
Master Michael and Dom Matthew, who had been
in charge of the church of Santa Croce. I am having
some difficulty in holding the precentor, and Henry
and others.

54. SAINT FRANCIS AND THE SOLDAN

The fullest account of Saint Francis' visit to the Soldan is to be
found in Saint Bonaventura's *Legenda Major*, cap. ix, and is probably based on the personal testimony of Brother Illuminato, who
was the Saint's companion on this strange journey. There is also
the account in chapter 24 of the *Fioretti* which comes from *Actus
B. Francisci*, cap. 27. The following account is interesting, as it

comes from one who had no connection with the Order. Like the previous passage, it was written by Jacques de Vitry and appears in his *Historia Orientalis*. See Golubovich, *op. cit*, vol. i, pp. 8–10.

I saw the founder and head of this Order, whom all the others obey as their Prior, a simple and ignorant man, but loved of God and of men, by name Brother Francis. To such a degree of intoxication and fervour of spirit was he seized that when he had come to the Christian army outside Damietta in Egypt he made his way to the camp of the Soldan himself, so bold was he and so strongly fortified with the shield of faith. When the Saracens captured him on the road, he said: "I am a Christian; lead me to your lord". And when they had dragged him before the Soldan, the cruel beast was turned to gentleness by the expression on the face of the man of God, so that for several days he listened most attentively to his preaching to them the faith of Christ. At length, fearing lest some of his people should be converted to the Lord by the power of his words, and so go over to the Christian army, he ordered him, with all reverence and every safeguard, to return to our camp, saying to him at the last: " Pray for me that God may reveal to me that law and that faith which is to Him most pleasing ".

XI. ANIMAL STORIES

55. SAINT FRANCIS AND THE DEER

Few things are dearer to the mind of the general reader than stories of Saint Francis' love of and influence over animals and birds. The following story was told by Saint Bonaventura in one of his sermons, and will be found in his *Opera Omnia* (ed. Quaracchi), vol. ix, p. 583.

SAINT FRANCIS had power not only over men, but also over the fishes of the sea, the birds of the air and the beasts of the field. For it is said of him that when he was once going from place to place and his path lay through a certain wood, the deer fled from him and his companion. To one of them, therefore, the Saint cried : " Why do you run away ? Stand still." And at the word of the Saint the stag stood still, and Francis went up and put his hands upon it and said : " Now go, and praise God ". The birds of the air were equally under his power. For it is recorded of him that, when he was on his travels, he found in a certain field a large number of birds singing and making a great noise. Then the Saint told them to be quiet : and immediately they were silent. Then he told them that they might sing again, and they all began to sing.

56. SAINT FRANCIS AND THE WOLVES

The account in the twenty-first chapter of the *Fioretti*, of Saint Francis taming the wolf of Gubbio, is a popular and delightful story. It received some further authenticity when, a few years ago, the skeleton of a wolf was found buried under the Franciscan Church of S. Francesco della Pace at Gubbio (Goad, *Franciscan Italy*, p. 70). The following account comes from *Legendae de Passione S. Verecundi*, edited by M. Faloci-Pulignani in *Miscellanea Francescana*, vol. x, pp. 6–7. S. Verecondo was a monastery near

Gubbio where Francis used often to stay. This mention of fierce wolves near Gubbio is most interesting taken in conjunction with the story in the *Fioretti*.

When the Blessed Francis, on account of great mortification of the flesh, and nocturnal vigils, and prayer and fasting, was wasted and weakened so that he could no longer walk—especially after he had been branded with the wounds of the Saviour—he used to ride about on a donkey. One evening when it was already getting dark he was seen, with a companion, on the road near to San Verecondo, riding upon the ass and with a rough sack thrown over his shoulders. Some farm labourers then shouted to him : " Brother Francis, stay here with us and don't go any farther, for there are fierce wolves hereabouts which will bite you and eat your donkey ". To which the Blessed Francis replied : " I have done no harm to Brother Wolf that he should want to kill and eat our donkey. Goodnight, my sons, and fear God." And so Brother Francis went safely on his way. This story was told to us by a farm-worker who was actually present.

57. SAINT FRANCIS AND THE NIGHTINGALE

From Wadding, *Annales Minorum*, vol. ii, pp. 24-5.

Once when Saint Francis was about to eat with Brother Leo he was greatly delighted to hear a nightingale singing. So he suggested to his companion that they should also sing praise to God alternately with the bird. While Leo was pleading that he was no singer, Francis lifted up his voice and, phrase by phrase, sang his duet with the nightingale. Thus they continued from Vespers to Lauds, until the Saint had to admit himself beaten by the bird.

Thereupon the nightingale flew on to his hand, where he praised it to the skies and fed it. Then he gave it his blessing and it flew away.

58. SAINT FRANCIS AND THE ASS

There are various stories of this kind, the most famous being that of Saint Francis silencing the swallows (*I Celano*, § 59). The following will be found in *Archivum Franciscanum Historicum*, vol. xii, p. 389. Another version appears in *Annales Minorum*, vol. i, p. 153; but the pious Wadding omits the delightful sentence at the end, merely telling us that the ass " listened with the utmost attention to the rest of the sermon ". Probably he did not like to leave people with a picture of Saint Francis making the crowd laugh.

Brother Tebaldo once told us something that he himself had seen. When Saint Francis was preaching one day to the people of Trevi, a noisy and ungovernable ass went careering about the square, frightening the people out of their wits. And when it became clear that no one could catch it or restrain it, Saint Francis said to it : " Brother ass, please be quiet and allow me to preach to the people ". When the donkey heard this it immediately bowed its head and, to everyone's astonishment, stood perfectly quiet. And the Blessed Francis, fearing that the people might take too much notice of this astonishing miracle, began saying funny things to make them laugh.

59. SAINT FRANCIS FRIGHTENS THE BIRDS

No story of Saint Francis is more famous than that of his preaching to the birds. The following delightful story shows that he was not always as successful in his approach to the animal world as his biographers have made out. It will be found in an Italian manuscript at Bologna and is printed in *Archivum Franciscanum Historicum*, vol. xx, pp. 546-7.

Brother Masseo has said that he was present with the Blessed Francis when he preached to the birds.

Rapt in devotion, Francis once found by the road-side a large flock of birds, to whom he turned aside to preach, as he had done before to another lot. But when the birds saw him approaching they all flew away at the very sight of him. Then he came back and began to accuse himself most bitterly, saying : " What effrontery you have, you impudent son of Peter Bernardone "—and this because he had expected irrational creatures to obey him as if he, and not God, were their Creator.

XII. MIRACLE STORIES

60. A DEAD CHILD RESTORED TO LIFE

The *Lives* of the saints generally contain a good many stories of miracles wrought by the Saint both before and after death. The Franciscan literature is no exception to this. Celano added to his *Vita Prima* a whole collection of miracle-stories, and wrote his *Tractatus de Miraculis* to supplement the *Vita Secunda*. Saint Bonaventura adds a long list of miracles to his *Legenda Major*. Naturally, therefore, we find a number of such stories scattered about among the minor Franciscan sources. Not many of them are of any great interest. The story which is here given was found in a manuscript at S. Antonio in Rome and is printed in L. Lemmens, *Testimonia Minora Saeculi XIII de S. Francisco*, pp. 51–2.

IN the name of the Lord, Amen. In the year 1278, in the time of the lord Pope Nicholas III, the following incident took place in the presence of me, a notary, and of the witnesses whose names are appended.

John, son of Peter Nicholas, having taken his Gospel oath, swore that when he was ten years old he was once given by the Blessed Francis a girdle or belt and ran with it to his father, who lived within the wall of the house of John Maximian. And while the boy was standing close to part of the wall of the house, it fell on him and killed him. In due course his body was dug out from under the stones and carried into his father's house. And when all his relations and friends had assembled together and were making great lamentation for him, news of the disaster reached the Blessed Francis. Now the boy's uncle, Nicholas, was a great friend of the Blessed Francis. So when the Saint heard the news he hastened to the house, went in secretly by the back door, and made his way to the room where

1884

the corpse was lying. Coming up to the child, he lifted him up and set him on his knee and spoke to him by name, saying : " John, did you take that girdle for me ? " Then he said to the boy : " Is anything the matter with you ? " And immediately the boy, who had been dead, said : " No ". So Saint Francis said to him : " Look how your parents are mourning for you. I don't want you to have any children to grieve for; I want you to be a child of God. So go to your parents there and say to them : ' There's nothing the matter with me. Don't be upset; God has made me well '." And the said John never had any children.

This took place in the city of Terni before the house of Antonio Raynucio in the presence of the said Antonio, John Andrew Raynaldi, John Peter Pellipari, and John Valiens, witnesses, on the 17th of April.

61. THE MIRACULOUS PLOUGHING

In the writings of Brother Leo is a famous story of how Saint Francis restored the vineyard of a priest at Rieti whose vines were trampled down by the crowd of visitors who came to see the Saint. (See *Speculum Perfectionis*, ed. Sabatier, pp. 206–7, and cf. *Fioretti*, cap. xix.) The following story comes from Wadding, *Annales Minorum*, vol. i, p. 232.

The man of God heard one day that, four miles from where he was, at the foot of the Apennines, hidden among the hills, far from the haunts of men, there was a little church dedicated to the Blessed Virgin, and beside it a ruined nunnery. This had once belonged to some Benedictine nuns, who had been driven away by war and were now at Fabriano. Hearing of this, and because of his devotion to the Virgin and of his love of solitude, the Saint was anxious to go there to see whether it would be a suitable place for a friary, so that the worship of the Blessed Virgin might be resumed and that the friars might use it as a place of meditation. So he set out with one companion; but they soon lost their way. But seeing a farmer at work, they asked him if he would show them the way. He, however, answered roughly: "What? Am I to stop ploughing and waste valuable time on you?" Then Saint Francis, in his quiet way, persuaded the man, saying that he would lose nothing by it. So he led them to the place, received their blessing and returned to the field. What was his surprise when he got back and found the whole field ploughed!

1886

XIII. THE INTERPRETATION OF THE RULE

62. THE WRITING OF THE RULE

The *Speculum Perfectionis* opens with an account of the writing of the Rule in 1223. The following, from *Verba Conradi*, § 1, gives a slightly different version of the same incidents. See *Opuscules de Critique Historique*, fasc. vi, pp. 370–4.

THE Blessed Conrad of Offida heard from the Blessed Brother Leo, the companion of Saint Francis, that during the writing of the Rule which we still observe the holy Father Francis was on a mountain-side with his two companions, Leo and Bonizo. These two were separated by about a stone's throw from the Saint, who stood below in a cave; and whatsoever the Lord revealed to Saint Francis, that he reported to the others. And Brother Bonizo dictated, while Brother Leo wrote it down. And when Saint Francis went to the lord Pope for the confirmation and sealing of the Rule, he put his hand upon the roll and swore that this was the will of God and no other. This he did two or three times.

Now, the fact is that before Francis began to write the Rule a certain cardinal who was protector of the Order said to him : " Go, brother, and ask God to show you His will, for the lord Pope and all the cardinals love you and have great faith in you, so that whatever the Lord reveals to you will be ratified and regarded as authoritative for you and the brethren ". And Saint Francis did as the cardinal had advised him.

But it happened that when the Rule was being dictated by our Lord Jesus Christ, a rumour got abroad among all the friars in Italy that Saint Francis was writing some other Rule, and the ministers were greatly alarmed. So all those that were in Italy got together and sought out Brother Elias, who was then Vicar, and said to him : " We hear that Brother Francis is making a new Rule, which we fear is going to be very severe. His standards are so high that he may well order things which we shall find intolerable. So, before it is ratified, go and tell him what we think." But Brother Elias answered : " I've already had enough rebukes from him. If you want to tell him anything, you must do it yourselves. I'm not going." But since Brother Francis had the quality of being both feared and loved by all, one of the ministers told Brother Elias that he ought to go with them.

So they went together to the place where Saint Francis was, which lay about two miles from the town of Rieti. And knowing that Francis did not wish anyone to approach him, Elias shouted out : " Praise be to God ! " When Francis heard this shout he went out and, seeing the friars, said : " What do you want ? Didn't I tell you that no one was to come here ? " To which Brother Elias replied : "All the ministers in Italy have come here because it is said that you want to make a new Rule; and they want you to make it a reasonable one, or otherwise they won't be bound by it." Then Saint Francis cried with a loud voice and said : " O Lord, answer for me ". And the Lord answered in the hearing of all the ministers and of Brother Elias, and said : " It is I who have made this Rule, Francis, not you; and I would not have you add anything to it. And my will is that all the brothers shall keep it to the letter." Then Francis said : " Do you hear that, brothers ? " So they all went back to their provinces.

And the Blessed Francis, going into the cave, held converse with God, as Moses did on Mount Sinai, face to face. And God said : ·" O Francis, make me a wall between your brethren and the world ". And so Saint Francis put into the Rule the words : " I order the brothers on obedience to have no place of their own, neither house nor any other thing; but they shall be as strangers and pilgrims and servants of God in this world ".

It is thought that the whole Rule was ordained by God. And here are the words of me, Brother Leo. That Rule, beloved, is one which we have sworn to accept, in which we must walk, and which we must keep without question; as our holy father Francis said, in his Testament : " I order all the brothers, clergy and laity, on holy obedience, not to put glosses on this Rule nor on its wording, but as the Lord gave me, etc."

The Rule was disclosed in the place called Palumma near Rieti, where the friars dwelt.

63. HONORIUS III MAKES AN ALTERATION IN THE RULE

The question of the strict observance of the Rule was one which agitated the Order during the last few years of Saint Francis' life and for many years after his death. When Saint Francis wrote the Rule in 1223, it appears that he made provision for those who wanted to keep it literally, even if their superiors tried to prevent their doing so. The following narrative from the *Legenda Vetus* is of particular interest, as it gives us some idea of the perpetual tension between the uncompromising standards of the Saint and the wise reasonableness of the ecclesiastical authorities. It will be found in *S. Francisci Legendae Veteris Fragmenta Quaedam*, edited by Sabatier in *Opuscules de Critique Historique*, fasc. iii, pp. 90–5.

When some of the friars realised from experience that they would no longer be able to live according

F

to the pure and true meaning of the Rule, because of bad customs which, in certain places, had crept in and lowered the standards which the brethren had sworn to observe; then they knew that they ought to go to the ministers about it. And Brother Leo has recorded that when Saint Francis, at Christ's command, took the second Rule to the lord Pope Honorius to be confirmed by him, the Pope, having carefully read it through, said to the Blessed Francis: "Blessed is the man who, by divine grace, can faithfully keep this Rule, for everything in it is holy and catholic and perfect. But listen to this sentence: *The brethren ought, and shall be able, to go to their ministers, and the ministers must, on obedience, willingly and freely grant them what they ask* (*i.e.*, to be allowed to observe the Rule literally). *And even if the ministers refuse, still the brethren must be allowed to keep the Rule literally, since every friar, whether a minister or not, must be subject to the Rule.* Now these words", said the Pope, "might be, for any of the brethren not well established in the love of goodness, a cause of disaster and shame and division in the Order. So I want you to alter those words so that every danger of calamity to the brethren and to the Order may be taken away."

Then the Blessed Francis replied: "It was not I who put those words into the Rule, but Christ, who knows best what is right and necessary to salvation and for the good of the Order, who also knows all that is going to happen to the Church and to the Brotherhood. So I shall not, and I cannot, alter the words of Christ. For the time is coming when the ministers and those who hold office in the Order will bring many bitter tribulations upon those who wish to keep the Rule literally. Therefore, as it is Christ's will that this Rule of His should be literally obeyed, so it ought to be your will that it should be so, and that thus it should be written in the Rule."

Then the Pope said to him : " What I shall do is this. Without in the least destroying the full sense of the words, I shall alter the wording of the Rule in this passage so that the ministers shall still feel themselves obliged to obey what Christ wills and what the Rule enjoins, while, at the same time, the brothers shall know that they have liberty to keep the Rule, fully and conscientiously; and thus no opportunity of wrong-doing shall be given to those who often seek such opportunities under pretence of keeping the Rule."

And so the Pope altered the words of that passage to the form in which they now stand in the Rule.[1]

64. SAINT FRANCIS AND THE GERMAN FRIAR

This follows the previous passage in the *Legenda Vetus* (*Opuscules*, fasc. iii, pp. 96–7).

The above is proved by a reply made by Saint Francis at Saint Mary of the Angels to a certain German friar, a Master in Theology, who had said to the Saint with great reverence : " It is my intention to keep the Gospel, and also this Rule which Christ has given to you, rigidly and faithfully for the rest of my life, God helping me. But one thing I ask of you, and it is this : that if in my time the friars desert the strict observance of the Rule as

[1] i.e., *And wherever there are brothers who know and realise that they cannot keep the Rule spiritually they ought to and they shall be able to go to their ministers. And the ministers must receive them charitably and kindly and must show them such friendliness that they can speak to them and behave before them as masters with their servants. For the ministers ought to be the servants of all the brethren.*

you, by the Holy Spirit, have warned us, then I ask that I alone, or with other friars who wish to keep it, may be allowed to separate myself from those who will not be faithful and observe it to the utmost."

When the Blessed Francis heard this he was tremendously pleased, and blessed the friar, saying : " What you ask is granted to you both by Christ and by me ". Then he put his right hand on the man's head and said : " Thou art a priest for ever after the order of Melchisedech ". Moreover the Blessed Francis added that all the promises which Christ had made to him would be fulfilled in those who tried to keep the Rule with joy, just as it stood, to the letter and without gloss.

1892

XIV. LA VERNA AND THE STIGMATA

65. LA VERNA IS GIVEN TO SAINT FRANCIS

In that part of the *Little Flowers of Saint Francis* entitled " The First Reflection on the most holy Stigmata " there is an account of how the Saint was given the mountain of La Verna, or Alvernia, by Orlando da Chiusi. This is based on chapter 9 of the *Actus Beati Francisci*, a passage which is probably to be identified with a document called *Historia Acceptionis Loci Montis Alvernae* by James of Massa, who wrote at the dictation of Brother Leo. In the fourth volume of Sbaralea's *Bullarium Franciscanum* (p. 156) is printed the following legal document connected with this event. It was formerly preserved at Borgo San Sepolcro.

In the Name of God, Amen. In the year 1274 . . . on Monday the 9th of July, in the presence of Father Giles, rector of the church of Trameggiano, and Father John, rector of the church of Campo, and of Cambio Catozzi di Chitignano, the Lord Guido, Rainerio di Gufaria and Bernardino his son and many other sworn witnesses, Orlando di Catanei, and Cungio, Bandino and Guglielmo his brothers, all sons of the Lord Orlando, formerly Count of Chiusi, gave evidence as follows . . . that the said Lord Orlando da Chiusi, a most valiant knight in the armies of the Emperor and father of the above, gave, bequeathed and conceded, freely and without any exception, to Brother Francis and his companions and brethren as well present as future, in the year 1213 on the 8th day of May, the Mount La Verna; so that the said Father Francis and his friars may live there. And by the said Mount La Verna is to be understood all the land, whether wooded, rocky or grassy, without any exception, from the brow of the mountain to its foot. . . . And because this gift was made to the

Blessed Francis and to his companions by word of mouth only and without anything in writing, therefore the said Orlando, most loving father of the young Orlando and of his brothers, when on his deathbed impressed this upon his sons and renewed the gift to the said friars, etc. Wherefore the sons of the said Orlando, wishing all to be observed and put in order according to the will of their most sweet father, have now unanimously approved, confirmed and ratified all which their father bequeathed, and they will and declare that the said friars shall always live there and that no one shall be able to turn them out or to interfere with them, and that the bequest of the said mountain shall hold good for all time.

Further, by order of the said Lord Orlando senior, they gave to the friars the following : a cloth which Father Francis used at table with the said Lord Orlando and his sons whenever he was staying with them; also a certain wooden cup in which Father Francis used to bless the bread and wine; also a leather shoe-lace belonging to the Lord Orlando which Francis blessed and tied with his own hands round the Count Orlando when he took the habit, which also worked miracles on women in childbirth, etc. . . .

Given at the Castle of Chiusi, in the palace of the said Lord Orlando and of his brothers, on the date mentioned.

66. BROTHER ELIAS' LETTER ON THE STIGMATA

At the death of Saint Francis on October 3rd, 1226, Brother Elias was Minister General of the Order, and immediately thought it his duty to publish the news that the Saint had received the Stigmata, a fact which Francis himself had taken pains to conceal during his lifetime. The following is Elias' letter written within a few hours of the death of Saint Francis. It has been printed several times—*e.g.*, by E. Lempp, *Frère Elie de Cortone*, pp. 70–1.

. . . And I now make known to you a great joy and a new thing among miracles. From the beginning of the world no such sign has been heard of, except in the Son of God, who is Christ.

Not long before his death our brother and father appeared as one crucified, bearing in his body five wounds which are the very Stigmata of Christ. For his hands and his feet had as it were the holes of nails, pierced through on both sides, remaining as wounds and having the blackness of nails. His side also seemed to be pierced, and often bled.

While the spirit still lived in him his appearance was not respected but rather despised, and there was no part of him but had undergone great suffering. From the tightening of the nerves his limbs had become rigid, as are those of a dead man; but after his death his appearance became most beautiful, shining with a wonderful light and giving joy to all who saw it. And his limbs which had been stiff became perfectly loose, so that they could be moved about according to the position in which he was lying, like those of some charming boy.

Wherefore, my brothers, let us praise the God of Heaven; and let us, in the sight of all men, confess to Him who hath showed mercy upon us. And let us keep the memory of our father and brother, Francis, to the glory and praise of God who has magnified him among men and glorified him among the angels. Pray for him, as he used to teach us, and pray to him that God may make us, with him, partakers of His grace. Amen.

67. TESTIMONY TO THE STIGMATA OF SAINT FRANCIS

Some years ago Professor Pennacchi discovered, among the municipal archives at Assisi, the following document which he published in the *Miscellanea Francescana* in 1904.

In the Name of the Lord, Amen. These are the names of those who saw the Stigmata of the Blessed Francis while he was alive and also after his death : John Simone, Bonaccurso son of Ugo di Leto, John Deoteaiute, the Lord James (Bishop's canon) saw the Stigmata only while he was living. Alberic the Notary.

These are they who saw them after death : the Lord Thomas of Raynerio, who was then Common Chamberlain, the Lord Jerome, the Lord John of Guarnerio, Hufredutius, Scalla, Alberic the Notary, the Lord Masseo Andrea di Priete, Bartolo di Donnafantina, John Guittoli, Balierus, John of Greccio.

The marks were round on the inside of the hands, on the outside elongated; and a small bit of flesh appeared like the head of a nail, bent and turned back, which lay on top of the other flesh. In the same way also in his feet were marks of nails raised up from the rest of the flesh. His right side was pierced as with a spear, the wound being closed up; and this used often to bleed so that his tunic and breeches were often stained with holy blood.

John Magnoli, Master James Pelliparii Margarite di Nocera.

XV. SAINT FRANCIS AND THE FUTURE OF THE ORDER

68. CHRIST TELLS SAINT FRANCIS OF COMING TRIBULATION

This comes from chapter 65 of the *Actus Beati Francisci*. There is a somewhat similar account in *Verba Conradi*, § 3 (*Opuscules de Critique Historique*, fasc. vi, pp. 375–6).

THE holy Brother Conrad related, as he had heard from Brother Leo, that Saint Francis was once praying at Saint Mary of the Angels behind the pulpit of the church. And he was holding out his hands towards heaven saying : " Have mercy upon thy people, O Lord; Lord, spare them ". Then Christ appeared to him saying : " You pray well; and gladly will I hear you, for I have endured much and paid a heavy price. However you must give me something and I will spare all men; your Order must continue and must be mine alone. But the time is coming when the Order will desert me, and then I will sustain it for a time because of the world, for men have put their trust in the friars, and look upon the Order as their light and their illumination. But later on I will give my authority to the devils, who will bring scandal and tribulations upon the friars so that they will be turned away and avoided by all men. And if a son shall go to the house of his father for bread he will get a box on the ears. If the brethren knew what the troubles of those days will be like they would begin to escape, and many would flee into the desert." And the Blessed Francis enquired of Christ : " Lord, how shall they live there ? " And Christ said : "As I fed the children of Israel in the desert, so will I feed them with herbs, and I will give to those herbs various flavours, as I did then to the manna; and afterwards they will return and will build again the Order as it was at the first."

69. SAINT FRANCIS FORESEES FUTURE DISTRESS

From *Verba Conradi*, § 4 (*Opuscules*, fasc vi, pp. 376–7).

On another occasion Francis was standing at prayer, and, being in great exaltation of spirit, he put his hand to his mouth to make a kind of horn and shouted as through a trumpet, "Many brothers and few brothers". And again he chanted, "The time will come when the friars shall go for bread and shall be given a box on the ears". Then the third time he sang, "The time is at hand when a friar will throw off his habit or tunic in the road and return to the world. And a worldling shall pick them up and go with them into the desert."

70. A SECOND COMING?

From *Verba Conradi*, § 2 (*Opuscules de Critique Historique*, fasc. vi, p. 374).

The Blessed Conrad heard from Brother Leo, companion of Saint Francis, that nothing that Saint Francis had done was to be compared with what he would yet do. So the Blessed Conrad asked him when this should be. But Leo replied that it would be in a time of great tribulation. What it would be he did not say, but some believe that Francis should return in the flesh because of the terrible disputes and persecutions which have arisen.

71. SAINT FRANCIS' VISION OF THE FUTURE

Also from *Verba Conradi*, § 10 (*Opuscules de Critique Historique*, fasc. vi, pp. 383-4):

Brother Leo has recorded that the holy father Francis used to say—sometimes in the presence of the Bishop of Ostia and the friars and other clergy and seculars, and sometimes when he was preaching to the people—that he knew that many of the friars, led by evil spirits, would desert the way of simplicity and poverty and accept money and legacies. They would abandon the poor little huts in the wilderness and would build large houses in the cities, where the example which they set would be one not of poverty, but of wealth and power. They would also obtain, with much cunning and worldly wisdom, all kinds of briefs and privileges from the Pope, thus not only relaxing the purity of the Rule which they had promised and which had been revealed by Christ, but destroying it altogether. Armed with these letters they would enter into litigation not only with men of the world, but with other religious, thus digging for themselves a pit into which finally they would fall, and sowing the seeds from which they would reap much trouble. And, as they deserved, Christ would send them not a shepherd, but a destroyer who would give them dire retribution of their misdeeds and of their evil thoughts and who would stir up strife and trials against them. Thus they would be entangled in their sin and would fall into the pit of their own lusts. Finally, chastised by the righteous judgment of God, they would be dragged out, and would live humbly by returning to their vows and by living according to the life-giving Rule which, before God, they promised to observe unto their life's end.

72. SAINT FRANCIS AND ANTICHRIST

Saint Francis was often thrown into great distress when he thought about the future of the Order, as many of the previous stories show. The following passage is from Bartholomew of Pisa in *Analecta Franciscana*, vol. iv, p. 437.

Brother Leo has recorded that once Saint Francis arose from prayer in great spiritual distress and said to the brothers : " Go back to the world, all of you. Take off your habits. I don't want to have an Order or to wear this habit any longer. For God has revealed to me that out of my Order shall arise Antichrist and his followers." Then Brother Masseo, who was a wise man and Francis' chief adviser, went to him and said : " Now, brother, go and ask God to show you whether there is a possibility of anything *good* coming out of the Order. Have you never seen an apple all rotten on the surface, but if you cut it open you may find, inside it, a heart that is good ? " When he had heard this the Blessed Francis said : " Yes, you are right. I will do as you suggest." And when he had prayed about this he came back full of joy and said to the brethren : " More good than bad. God has revealed to me that while the bad men in the Order are Antichrist and his followers, yet the good men in the Order will destroy them, and afterwards the whole world will be turned to Christ by their preaching."

73. THE FIENDS' COUNCIL

Many attempts were made by those who stood for a strict interpretation of the Rule to account for the relaxations which had crept in. The following story is not without interest, in that it puts the blame partly upon the practice of accepting young boys into the Order. There is nothing in the Rule about the minimum age for admission to the Order, but it is unlikely that, in the early days, anyone under the age of about eighteen would have been accepted. But in the fourteenth century the friars were sharply criticised for " stealing children ". Richard Fitzralph, Archbishop of Armagh, a violent critic of the mendicants, declared that " enticed by the wiles of the friars and by little presents, these boys (for the friars cannot circumvent men of mature age) enter the Orders, nor are they afterwards allowed, according to report, to get their liberty by leaving the Order, but they are kept with them against their will until they make profession " (see A. G. Little, *The Grey Friars in Oxford*, p. 79). As early as 1260 the Chapter General of the Franciscans, at Narbonne, had declared that, as a general rule, none were to be admitted to the Order under the age of eighteen, though boys of fifteen and upwards might, in certain circumstances, be received (see *Archiv für Literatur- und Kirchen-Geschichte*, vol. vi, p. 88). By 1316 the minimum age had been reduced to fourteen (*Archivum Franciscanum Historicum*, vol. iv, p. 277). It is interesting to see in the following passage (which comes from Bartholomew of Pisa in *Analecta Franciscana*, vol. iv, pp. 444–5) that the practice of accepting young boys was not at all approved of by some of the friars themselves.

Although observance of the Rule leads one to perfection, preserves all that is good, and makes one live an orderly life, yet by the influence and machinations of the devil it is now badly kept by many of the brothers. So the fiends, recognising the perfection and state of the Rule and the fervour of some of the early friars in keeping it, held a council in the Crucifers' Hospital on the road between Assisi and Saint Mary of the Angels. This was held at the time when the Blessed Francis was holding a General Chapter at Assisi, where there were more than five thousand of the brethren. But at the Fiends' Council there were eighteen thousand devils present, as was afterwards revealed by God to Saint Francis.

In the course of discussion on how to overthrow the friars, and when many had said their say, one devil, more cunning than all the rest, said : " These brothers who are in the Order now are still fervent in keeping the Rule, and we can do nothing against them. But the way to overthrow and destroy the Order is to find some method that seems to have nothing bad about it. And the way to do that is this : we must persuade them to accept into their Order sons of nobles and important people who will be obliged to live delicately, and so we shall lead the whole lot to the world and the flesh. And let us also induce as many others as possible—especially those who are not so keen on keeping the Rule—to live a soft life and to wear better clothes. In this way we shall win the battle against them." And all agreed to the proposals of this devil.

Now, when the Blessed Francis realised what was happening, he marvelled at the cunning of the fiends, and was so much distressed that he would scarcely speak to anyone for several days. And at last he said that God had revealed to him that He had given the Order of Friars Minor to the world to preach penitence for a hundred years. And there were three types of men who would try, to the best of their ability, to kill and destroy the Order—friars of noble birth, learned friars, and young boys. The boys would tend to destroy Discipline, the noblemen Humility, and the learned men Poverty.

And Brother Angelo once said that the Blessed Francis had told him that he thought ill of the brothers because there was so little prayer in the Order; for when the brethren met together there was no talk of God, but only of the world and of worldly things. Moreover, they build houses which are far too big (which is most displeasing to God); and charity among them is dead.

74. SAINT FRANCIS IS CHEERED BY CHRIST

A typical story from the collections made by the Spirituals. It occurs in a Florentine manuscript, and is printed in an article by Bughetti in *Archivum Franciscanum Historicum*, vol. xx, p. 97, entitled *Analecta de S. Francisco Assisiensi saeculo XIV ante medium collecta* (*e cod. Florentino C. 9. 2877*).

Once when the Blessed Francis was alone, sadly contemplating the fact that the friars were allowing their love to grow cold and were falling away from perfection, Christ Himself appeared to him and asked him why he was so sad. To whom the Blessed Francis replied : " Lord, do I not well to be sad when I think of this poor little Order which Thou hast given me, and see the brethren falling away from the path of perfection ? " But Christ said to him : " Be of good cheer, for there will always be in the Order some who will tread the way of perfection, and these I will take, at their deaths, straight to Paradise without their having to pass through Purgatory. Others there are who desire to keep the Rule, but are not allowed to do so ; and these shall go to Purgatory, but I shall commit them into thy hands to remain there as long as it shall please thee. And there are others who follow the way of the world and seek fine buildings and ease and comfort ; but do not worry about these, for I shall not worry about them either."

This was reported by a certain friar at La Verna who said that he heard it from one of the brethren who had it from the Blessed Francis himself.

75. SAINT FRANCIS TELLS BROTHER LEO TO WASH THE STONE

This incident occurs in several early Chronicles. It is here translated from the Chronica XXIV *Generalium in* Analecta Franciscana, *vol. iii, pp. 67–8.*

Once when Brother Leo and the Blessed Francis were talking to one another on the mountain of La Verna, the Saint pointed to a certain stone and said : " O Brother Leo, little sheep, wash that stone with water ". Then, when Brother Leo had done this, he said : " Wash it with wine ". When he had done that the Saint said : " Wash it with oil ". This also Brother Leo did ; and then Francis said : " Wash it with balsam ". "And how ", said Brother Leo, " am I to find any balsam here ? " Then Saint Francis said to him : " Know, O little sheep of God, that that is the stone on which the Lord once sat when He appeared before me ; and that is why I told you to wash it four times. For God then promised me four things for the Order— first, that he who loves the brethren and the Order with all his heart shall, with God's blessing, make a good end ; secondly, that everyone who unjustly persecutes the Order shall be soundly punished ; thirdly, that no brother who is evil or who continues in wickedness shall survive for long without being either dismissed or put to shame ; and fourthly, that our Order shall last to the end of the world."

1904

Francis of Assisi: Writer

Supplement to the Omnibus of Sources on St. Francis

By
Marion A. Habig O.F.M.

CONTENTS

Francis of Assisi: Writer

Manuscript collections of the writings of St. Francis began to be made soon after his death. The oldest extant manuscript containing such a collection, together with other items, is in the Municipal Library at Assisi (Codex MS 338); and it is practically certain that it dates from the middle of the thirteenth century. Another manuscript was made about 1370. The first printed collection appeared in Venice in 1504; and this was reprinted at Salamanca in 1511 and in Paris in 1512. The best known early collection was Luke Wadding's *Beati Patris Francisci Assisiatis Opuscula*, printed at Antwerp in 1623.

The first critical edition of St. Francis' writings was prepared and published by the College of St. Bonaventure at Quaracchi, near Florence, in 1904. Included were only the Latin writings—and the *Canticle of Brother Sun*, which St. Francis wrote in the vernacular, is omitted. A new English translation of the Quaracchi edition, and also of the *Canticle* by Benen Fahy, with a good Introduction and

1909

Notes by Placid Hermann, was published in 1964;[2] and this work was included in the *Omnibus of Sources* in 1973.[3]

A second critical edition of the writings of St. Francis is the masterful German work, with Latin and vernacular Italian texts, by Franciscan Kajetan Esser, *Die Opuscula des Hl. Franziskus von Assisi* (xx + 485 pp.), published in 1976 by the College of St. Bonaventure, now at Grottaferrata, near Rome. This new edition rejects as non-authentic the short prayer *Absorbeat*, mentioned by Benen Fahy (pp. 160-161) as doubtful; but two other writings, the *Paraphrase of the Our Father* and the *Letter to St. Anthony*, regarded as doubtful in Benen Fahy's English translation (pp. 159-160 and 162-164), can now be classified as authentic writings of St. Francis according to Esser.

Esser's work has also demonstrated the authenticity of five other writings of St. Francis, which were not included in the Quaracchi edition and Benen Fahy's translation. They are: (1) A *Second*

---

[2]*The Writings of St. Francis* (175 pages; same numbering of pages in the *Omnibus*), published by Burns & Oates, London, and FHP, Chicago, 1963.

[3]*St. Francis of Assisi, Writings and Early Biographies: English Omnibus of the Sources for the Life of St. Francis,* edited by Marion A. Habig (Chicago: FHP, 1973—1808 pages). The Third Revised Edition (1976) has 1904 pages and includes Bishop John R. H. Moorman's *A New Fioretti.*

Letter to Superiors (*Opuscula,* Chap. VII); (2) A *Letter to the Brothers and Sisters of Penance,* that is, the members of St. Francis' Third Order, now called "Secular Franciscans," which is a shorter and earlier form of his *Letter to All the Faithful* (Chap. VIII); (3) An *Exhortation (and Prayer) to Praise God* (Chap. XIV); (4) A *Fragment of the Rule of the Friars Minor,* antedating the one of 1221 (Chap. XVII); (5) A *Prayer before the Crucifix of San Damiano,* in the original vernacular (Chap. XX). We will have more to say about these five writings later.

The last chapter (XXVIII) of Esser's work contains the digests or precis of eight more writings dictated by St. Francis. These are found in the *Mirror of Perfection* and the *Fioretti,*[4] in the *Writings of St. Clare,*[5] and in Eccleston's Chronicle.[6]

---

[4]See *Omnibus,* pp. 1221, 1246, 1249-1250, 1318-1320.

[5]Ignatius Brady and Sr. M. Frances, *The Legend and Writings of St. Clare of Assisi,* (St. Bonaventure, N.Y. 1953); see Letter no. 3 to Agnes of Prague.

[6]Thomas of Eccleston, *De Adventu Fratrum Minorum in Anglia,* ca. 1258, translations by Fr. Cuthbert (London, 1903), E. G. Salter (London, 1926), and L. Sherley-Price (London, 1964).—Translations of the eight "dictations" and other "spoken words" reported in the early biographies can be found in *The Words of St. Francis: An Anthology,* compiled and arranged by James Meyer (FHP 1952 and 1966), and in *Memorable Words of Saint Francis,* collected and annotated by Alexandre Masseron (FHP, 1963).

Autographs of St. Francis

St. Francis dictated most of his writings in Latin to Brother Leo or one of the other friars. He learned to read and speak and write Latin when as a boy he attended the school at the church of San Giorgio in Assisi. Though his Latin was somewhat deficient, he was by no means the *idiota* or illiterate person that he called himself. He was well read in the books of the Latin Bible, both the Old and the New Testament. Some of this knowledge of the Scriptures he probably gained by daily praying the Roman Breviary, to which he bound himself when he was ordained a deacon some time between 1209 and 1216. Like many others in his day, when books had to be written by hand and were rare, Francis seems to have had a retentive memory. He was able to quote Holy Scripture, especially the Book of Psalms, without much difficulty, as is indicated in his writings. There is a certain exuberance in those writings, the frequent use of synonyms to emphasize the thought that he expressed. He never seems to have been at a loss for words.

There are extant three short writings of St. Francis which he wrote with his own hands on two small pieces of parchment. One of these, which is preserved in a reliquary at the Sacro Convento in Assisi, has on one side the *Blessing of St. Francis* or the *Blessing of Brother Leo by St. Francis*.[7] Francis

[7]Esser, *Opuscula*, pp. 134 ff; *Omnibus*, pp. 123-126.

St. Francis' Blessing of Brother Leo. (See Omnibus of Sources on St. Francis, pp. 123-126.)

quoted from memory the Old Testament blessing in Numbers 6, 24-26, leaving out the word *Dominus* (Lord) twice (verses 25 and 26), and added the name of Brother Leo (f leTo) with his signature, the Tau Cross. In a smaller hand, Brother Leo testified that Francis himself wrote the Blessing.

On the other side of this "chartula" Francis had previously written his *Praises of the Triune God* after receiving the Stigmata.[8] This song of praise and thanksgiving has been called the *Te Deum* of St. Francis. It is typical of that wholeheartedness and exuberance which characterize his writings. Francis gave the *Praises* and the *Blessing* to Brother Leo on Mount La Verna in 1224, and told him to carry them always on his person, which he did after folding the piece of parchment twice. As a result, the parchment which is 14 cm long and 10 cm wide, has suffered some damage along the folds and also on the edges. In 1974 D. Lapsanski was able to decipher the greater part of the text of the *Praises* with the help of ultraviolet rays, after the parchment had been removed temporarily from the reliquary. Esser made use of his research and reading.

Brother Leo was the recipient also of another autograph of St. Francis which is still in existence. It is an encouraging little letter that Francis wrote and

[8]Esser, *Opuscula*, pp. 142 ff; *Omnibus*, pp. 123-126; and *Saint Francis Prayer Book*, by Auspicius van Corstanje (FHP, 1978), pp. 62-64, which have a new translation of the text in Esser.

sent to him probably in 1226, the last year of Francis' life.[9]

This autograph is in good condition—after seven and a half centuries—except for brown finger marks on both sides of the parchment. It was kept in the Conventual Franciscan friary at Spoleto until the latter's secularization in 1860, when it disappeared for a time. In the 1890's it was in the possession of a priest in Spoleto, who wanted to sell it for a high price to someone in the United States. However, Pope Leo XIII acquired the relic and donated it in 1902 to the city of Spoleto, where it is preserved in a reliquary at the cathedral.

There can be no doubt about the authenticity of this autograph, says Esser. The repetition of "et" is typical of St. Francis's writing; and the use of a plural verb form *(faciatis)* instead of the singular may be an example of what Eccleston called the "bad" Latin of Francis. "The text is in an Italianized Latin," writes Esser, "or you might call it a Latinized Italian...and it is evident that the writer had no mastery of the Latin script or of the Latin language."

The original letter of Brother Francis to Brother Leo is reproduced in *The Francis Book,*[10] with "An

[9]Esser, *Opuscula,* pp. 216 ff; *Omnibus,* pp. 117-119.

[10]*The Francis Book: 800 Years with the Saint from Assisi,* compiled and edited by Roy M. Gasnick, O.F.M. (Collier Books, A Division of Macmillan Publishing Co., Inc. New York, and Collier Macmillan Publishers, London, 1980), pp. 26-27.

Analysis of St. Francis' Handwriting" by Girolamo Moretti. The handwriting proves (to Moretti) that Francis had a "quantitatively superior intelligence (that was) qualitatively capable of original concepts...(and he had) organizational abilities... firmness of character...decisiveness...knowing gentleness.

Vernacular Writings

The Latin of Francis' Letter to Brother Leo may be described as approaching the vernacular Italian which was then coming into use as the ordinary language of the people, the *volgare*. Two of St. Francis' writings at least were composed and are extant in the Italian *volgare* of his day. One, the very first of his writings, is his *Prayer before the Crucifix of San Damiano;* and the other is his *Canticle of Brother Sun.*

The San Damiano Prayer is one of those writings recognized as authentic by Esser,[11] though it was not included in the Quaracchi edition. For this reason, it is not in the *Omnibus;* but an English translation was published in the *Saint Francis Prayer Book* (p. 13). Since it is very short, we quote the entire prayer: "Most high and glorious God, lighten the darkness of my heart and give me sound faith, firm

[11]*Opuscula*, pp. 354-362. On pages 356-357 are five slightly varying Italian texts found in old manuscripts, and also some early translations into other languages.

hope, and perfect love. Let me, Lord, have the right feelings and knowledge, so that I can carry out the task that you have given me in truth."

St. Francis said this prayer not only on the occasion when the Crucified Savior spoke to him in the San Damiano chapel in 1206, but frequently thereafter—one manuscript says it was one of his daily prayers; and he taught the prayer to his first companions. The prayer shows, says Esser, that Francis had already advanced far in the science of the saints at the turning point in his life.

The Canticle of Brother Sun

The *Canticle of Brother Sun* or, more correctly, the *Canticle of the Creatures,* is Francis' literary masterpiece; and it is the first notable contribution to Italian literature. Fr. Agostino Gemelli wrote: "Thanks to St. Francis of Assisi, our (Italian) literature has a religious beginning in the hymn to life, the *Canticle of the Sun.* It is likewise a praise to God through the intermediary of creatures as well as an expression of gratitude for the beauty and usefulness of creatures themselves."[12]

In these words Father Gemelli suggested a solution to the dispute among scholars concerning the

[12]*The Message of St. Francis* (FHP, 1963), p. 72. This work is a sequel and supplement to his well known *Il Francescanesimo,* or *The Franciscan Message to the World* (Burns, Oates, and Washbourne: London, 1934, 1935).

meaning of the Italian "cun" and "per" used by Francis: "cun tucte (or cuncte) le tue creature, spetialmente messor lo frate sole...per sora luna e le stelle...per frate vento...per sor aqua...per frate focu...per sora nostra matre terra...per quelli ke perdonano...per sora nostra morte corporale." The preposition used may mean "by" or "through" or "on account of" or "for." Instead of choosing one of the meanings, there is no reason why we cannot accept all of them as having been in the mind of Francis: "Praise and thanks to the Almighty Creator, by and through and on account of and for Brother Sun, Sister Moon and the Stars, Brother Wind, Sister Water, Brother Fire, Sister Mother Earth, Those Who Forgive, Sister Death of Our Body."[13]

Francis R. and Helen E. Line have offered a similar interpretation: "It is an interesting exercise to read the *Canticle,* using first the word 'for,' then the word 'by,' and finally 'through.' All three meanings are deeply true. Each concept expands the nature of the song and the breadth of its application. God's realm widens with each such read-

[13]The original Italian text can be found in Esser, *Opuscula,* pp. 128-129; Eloi LeClerc, *The Canticle of Creatures, Symbols of Union: An Analysis of St. Francis of Assisi* (FHP, 1970), pp. 237-238; *The Francis Book: 800 Years with the Saint from Assisi,* compiled and edited by Roy M. Gasnick, O.F.M. (Collier Books, New York, and Collier Macmillan, London, 1980), p. 107.

ing. In a sense, St. Francis has given us three immortal songs in one."[14]

In the *Canticle*, therefore, Francis not only thanks God for the inanimate creatures given to man for his use, benefit, and enjoyment; but he also recognizes the fact that man, a creature endowed with intelligence and a free will, has the role of a spokesman of inanimate and irrational creatures in the praise of the Creator. However, the *Canticle* is not merely a variation of the *Canticle of the Three Youths in the Fiery Furnace* (Daniel, 3: 52-90) and Psalm 148, *A Hymn of All Creation to the Almighty Creator*; for he adds the poetical element of personifying inanimate creatures, calling them brothers and sisters. For Francis there is a fraternal communion on the part of man with all other creatures.

Eloi LeClerc finds a still deeper meaning in the *Canticle*: "The *Canticle* show Francis fraternally communing not only with the material elements of creation but also with what these elements are made to symbolize, namely with the unconscious values which are assigned to the elements and for which the latter act as a kind of language."[15] He also points out that "this fraternal communion with creatures and the enthusiastic celebration it

[14]*Man with a Song: Some Major and Minor Notes in the Life of Francis of Assisi* (FHP, 1979), p. 99. A large part of this popular book discusses or is based on the *Canticle of the Sun*. Arrangements are being made for a paper-back edition.

[15]*Op. cit.* (see note 13), p. viii.

expresses are also the language of man's opening to his whole being."[16]

According to the *Mirror of Perfection* and the *Legend of the Three Companions*, Francis did not compose the entire *Canticle* on one occasion, but added the strophe on *Those Who Forgive* to re-establish peace between the bishop and the mayor of Assisi when they were at odds with each other, and the one on Sister Death shortly before he died. Most writers on Francis have accepted this account, although Celano leaves us under the impression that all of the *Canticle* was written at the same time. Esser[17] has arrived at the conclusion that the account in the *Mirror* and the *Three Companions*, which were compiled about 150 years after the death of Francis, is a legend. He calls attention to the fact that Fortini[18] found no record of the supposed quarrel between Bishop Guido II and Mayor Oportolo Bernardi in the Archives of Assisi. It is perfectly logical and natural that Francis should add a strophe on peacemakers and on the death of the body when he composed the *Canticle*.

[16]Eloi LeClerc, *Song of Dawn* (FHP, 1977), p. ix.

[17]*Opuscula*, pp. 131-132.

[18]In his 5-volume (4 in 5) *Nova Vita di San Francesco* (1959), Arnaldo Fortini devotes an entire chapter in Volume II to the *Canticle* and tries to show that the legend in the *Mirror of Perfection* is not fiction. Cf. the one-volume English version, *Francis of Assisi* (Crossroad, New York, 1981), pp. 532-536, 577-580, 602-603.

Francis wrote the *Canticle* at San Damiano toward the end of his life, when he was a very sick man, very probably during the winter of 1224-1225. Celano says, it was after a night of physical and mental suffering when our Lord heard Francis' plea for help by assuring him of eternal life.[19] Actually Francis was putting into words what had been in his mind and heart for many years past. In the "Praises" which St. Francis composed and said daily "at every Hour (of the Divine Office) of the day and night and before the (Little) Office of the Blessed Virgin Mary," he made use of a quotation from the Apocalypse (5:13) in the following manner: "Praise him (our God) in his glory, heaven and earth, 'and every creature that is in heaven and on the earth, and such as are on the sea, and all that are in them.'"[20]

Many English translations and paraphrases of the *Canticle of Brother Sun* have been made, among them also some in verse.[21] But the latter are "free" translations, and we think a more literal versified

[19]Celano II, 213, in the *Omnibus*, p. 532.

[20]*Omnibus*, pp. 137-139. The text given by Esser, *Opuscula* (pp. 319-320) is slightly different in arrangement and wording; but he admits that the variants in the early manuscript copies of these *Praises* are such that it is quite impossible to reconstruct the exact original text.

[21]*Omnibus*, pp. 130-131; *Saint Francis Prayer Book*, pp. 94-96; *The Francis Book*, pp. 107-109. In the latter, the first (literal) translation is by Benen Fahy and is taken from the *Omnibus*; the free verse translation is found in the new English Roman Breviary, Psalter, Sunday of Week II.

translation is desirable. The *Canticle* is not only a poem—one of the world's greatest—but it is also a hymn, a song of praise. Francis and his companions often sang the *Canticle*. A version, as literal as possible, in the form of rhyming couplets would make it possible to sing all the stanzas according to one simple melody, for instance, one of the Gregorian psalm tones. We venture to offer such a versified version of the *Canticle of the Creatures*.

O Lord, most high, omnipotent and good!
We honor, praise, and bless you as we should.

For You alone can all our service claim;
And none is worthy to pronounce your Name.

To you be praise through all that you have done—
Through creatures all, and first through Brother Sun!

Of you he is a symbol, beauteous, bright;
He makes the day and gives us warmth and light.

Praise too through Sister Moon and ev'ry Star
Which you have made to shine in Heav'n afar!

Through Brothers Wind and Clouds, blue Firmament,
Through Rain and Sunshine, giving nourishment!

Through Sister Water, flowing e'er in haste,
For she is useful, humble, precious, chaste!

Be praised through Brother Fire, who lights the night,
For he is glad and strong, possesses might!

Through Sister Mother Earth and Brother Air,
Who give us life and fruits and flowers fair!

Be praised through those who love you and forgive,
In ev'ry trial and sickness patient live!

And blest are they who all in peace endure;
By you they will be crowned and made secure.

Even Sister Death to you, my Lord, gives praise,
Whose summons ev'ry living man obeys.

Who die in sin are lost; who love your Will
Shall suffer from the Second Death no ill.

Oh, praise and bless the Lord, his law observe,
And thank him, love him, always humbly serve![22]

Another poem of St. Francis (besides his *Canticle*) is his *Praises of the Virtues* or *Salute to (Salutation of) the Virtues*, in which he addresses the Virtues as though they were persons. In other words,

[22]This is the revised form of the writer's versified translation first published in *St. Anthony Messenger*, June, 1957. The *Canticle*, set to music for a soloist who sings the strophes while the people sing a refrain after each, by Franciscan Father Christopher Coelho of India, was published in *New Ritual for Public Functions, Franciscan Third Order*, compiled by Benet A. Fonck O.F.M. (FHP, 1973), pp. 102-103.

he makes use of the same poetic device of personification as in his *Canticle of Brother Sun*. These
Praises, written in Latin, certainly deserve to be
classified as poetry; but they are also a sermon,
teaching a fundamental lesson for a truly Christian
and especially a religious life. The opening lines
are:

> Hail, Queen Wisdom! The Lord save you,
> with your sister, pure, holy Simplicity!

> Lady Holy Poverty, God keep you,
> with your sister, holy Humility!

> Lady Holy Love, God keep you,
> with your sister, holy Obedience![23]

A third poem of Francis, also written in Latin, is
his *Praises of the Blessed Virgin* or *Salutation of the
Blessed Virgin*. Celano (II, 198) mentions these
Praises as one of Francis' writings: "Toward the
Mother of Jesus he was filled with an inexpressible
love, because it was she who made the Lord of
Majesty our brother. He sang special *Praises* to her,
poured out prayers to her, offered her his affections, so many and so great that the tongue of man
cannot recount them."[24] Note that Francis was wont
to *sing* these *Praises*, as he *sang* his Canticle.

[23]Esser, *Opuscula*, 413; *Omnibus*, 132; *S. F. Prayer Bk.*, 21.
[24]*Omnibus*, 521.

Some have hitherto regarded these *Praises* as a paraphrase of the Angelic Salutation (Hail Mary, which in Francis' day comprised only the first part); but Esser says this view is incorrect. This *Salutation* is Francis' own, not the Angel's and Elizabeth's. The authentic text given by Esser is slightly different from the one so regarded previously (*Omnibus,* 135). A new translation of Esser's text can be found in the *Saint Francis Prayer Book* (p. 23). There is an important addition in the first lines: "I greet you, Lady, holy Queen, holy Mary, Mother of God, Virgin *who became the Church* (*Ecclesia facta*)." Since Vatican II, theologians are emphasizing Mary's role as type and exemplar of the Church. This concept is nothing new, for we find it in the works of St. Ambrose (as Vatican II pointed out). But we are a little surprised to find it in the writings of St. Francis. In fact, he goes a step farther: Mary was *made* the Church, she *was* the Church, at the beginning, that is, at the Conception and Birth of Christ.

> I greet you, Lady, holy Queen,
> holy Mary, Mother of God,
> Virgin who became the Church,
> chosen by the most holy Father
> of heaven;
> consecrated to holiness
> through his most holy and beloved
> Son and the Holy Spirit,
> the Comforter;

in you was and is
the whole fullness of grace
and everything that is good.
I greet you, his princely dwelling.
I greet you, the tent of his covenant.
I greet you, his habitation.
I greet you, his garment.
I greet you, his handmaid.
I greet you, his mother,
    with all holy virtues, which
    through the grace and light of the
    Holy Spirit descend unto the hearts
    of believers.
    to make believers of unbelievers
    for God.

In this beautiful prayer and poem and song, addressed to the Mother of God, Francis greets her as Christ's "palatium, tabernaculum, domus, vestimentum—his princely dwelling, tent of his covenant, his habitation, his garment." There was only one ecclesiastical writer before Francis, St. Peter Damian, who used those names of the Blessed Virgin. The sermons of St. Peter Damian, the Doctor of the Church who died about a century before St. Francis was born, may have had a considerable influence on the thinking and spirituality of Francis.[25]

[25]Raphael Brown, "St. Francis of Assisi and Our Lady" in *The Marian Era,* I (FHP, 1960), 53-55, 109-116; St. Peter Damian is mentioned on p. 114. See also R. Brown's *Our Lady and St. Francis: All the Earliest Texts* (FHP, 1954).

Another Latin Prayer to the Blessed Virgin, written by Francis, is the "Antiphon" which is used repeatedly in his "Office of the Passion" (*Omnibus,* 142; *S. F. Prayer Bk.,* 34). In this prayer he is the first in the West to give to Mary the title of "Spouse of the Holy Spirit," a title which had been previously accorded to her in the East.

We have already mentioned other "Praises" of St. Francis, which are also "Prayers": The "Praises" he wrote on Mt. La Verna on one side of the "chartula" which has the *Blessing of Brother Leo* on the other side; the *Canticle of Brother Sun,* the *Praises before the Divine Office.* There is one more which has been added to Francis' authentic writings by Esser (*Opuscula,* 277). He entitles it *Exhortation to the Praise of God;* but it is also a "Prayer of Praise," consisting of a series of texts from Holy Scripture. An English translation has been published in the *Saint Francis Prayer Book* (pp. 75-76).

Worship God and honor him.

(Apoc. 14: 7)

The Lord is worthy to receive praise and glory.   (See Apoc. 4: 11)

Praise the Lord, all who worship him.

(See Ps. 22: 25)

Hail, Mary, full of grace; the Lord is with you.   (Luke 1: 28)

Praise him, heaven and earth.

(See Ps. 69: 34)

Praise the Lord, all rivers.
> (See Dan. 3: 78)

Sons of God, praise the Lord.
> (See Dan 3: 82)

This is the day that the Lord has made, let us now rejoice and sing:
> (Ps. 118: 24)

Alleluia, alleluia, alleluia, King of Israel.
> (John 12: 13)

Praise the Lord, everything that breathes.   (Ps. 150: 6)

Praise the Lord, for he is good.
> (Ps. 146: 1)

All those who read this, praise the Lord.   (Ps. 103: 21)

All creatures, praise the Lord.
> (See Ps. 103: 22)

Praise the Lord, all the birds of the air.
> (Dan. 3: 80)

All children, praise the Lord.
> (See Ps. 113: 1)

Praise the Lord, all boys and girls.
> (Ps. 148: 12)

Worthy is the Lamb that is slain to receive praise, honor and glory.
> (See Apoc. 5: 13)

Blessed is the Holy Trinity and Undivided Unity. (Mass of the Trinity)

Holy Michael the Archangel, defend us in the fight.
> (Mass of St. Michael the Archangel)

Besides the six "Prayers of Praise" which have been mentioned so far, there are other "Prayers" which St. Francis wrote in Latin. One of these is his *Paraphrase of the Our Father.* It is included as a "doubtful" writing in the Quaracchi edition (*Omnibus,* 159); but since the researches of Esser (*Opuscula,* 285), we can now say for certain that it is one of the authentic writings of St. Francis.

The *Office of the Passion,* compiled by St. Francis, is a collection of seven "psalms," one for each of the Hours, and each of them a "mosaic" of verses from various Psalms with interpolations of his own. There are some variations for Sundays, Feast Days, Advent, and the Christmas season.[26] Francis recited this *Office* daily besides the Divine Office of the Roman Breviary.

To the list of prayers written by St. Francis must be added those which form parts of other writings by him: (1) "Almighty, eternal, just, and merciful God," at the end of his *Letter to All the Friars;* (2) the long prayer, "Almighty, most high and supreme God," in Chapter 23 of his Rule of 1221; (3) "We adore you" in his Testament (cf. *Saint Francis Prayer Book*).

The so-called *Peace Prayer of St. Francis* was not written by St. Francis; but we can well name it the *Saint Francis Peace Prayer* in the same way as a certain Missal is called the "St. Joseph Missal." This very popular prayer, which is said not only by

[26]Esser, *Opuscula,* 322; *Omnibus,* 140-155; *S. F. Prayer Bk.,* 35-61.

Catholics but also other Christians and even non-Christians, admirably expresses the thought and spirit of Francis, "the Man of Peace." This is especially true if we add to the English version the missing petitions which appear in the Italian, French, and Spanish versions of the prayer; namely those for establishing *harmony* where there is *discord,* and *truth* where there is *error,* and in the second part the French addition that *we find ourselves in forgetting self.*[27]

> Lord,
> Make me an instrument of your peace:
> Where there is hatred, let me sow love;
> Where there is discord, harmony;
> Where there is injury, pardon;
> Where there is error, truth;
> Where there is doubt, faith;
> Where there is despair, hope;
> Where there is darkness, light;
> Where there is sadness, joy;
>
> O Divine Master,
> Grant that I may not so much seek:
> To be consoled, as to console;

[27]For the origin of this prayer, see the writer's article in *Franciscan Herald* (Chicago), May, 1974; and Esser, *Opuscula, 54. The complete "Peace Prayer" is in S. F. Prayer Bk.,* 105.

To be understood, as to understand;
To be loved, as to love.
For, it is in giving, that we receive;
It is in forgetting self, that we find
    ourselves;
It is in pardoning, that we are pardoned;
    and
It is in dying, that we are born to
    eternal life.

There are some who find something similar to the Peace Prayer in the second last of the *Admonitions* written by St. Francis (no. 27; *Omnibus,* 86):

Where there is Love and Wisdom,
    there is neither Fear nor Ignorance.

Where there is Patience and Humility,
    there is neither Anger nor Annoyance.

Where there is Poverty and Joy,
    there is neither Cupidity nor Avarice.

Where there is Peace and Contemplation,
    there is neither Care nor Restlessness.

Where there is the Fear of God to guard the dwelling,
    there no enemy can enter.

Where there is Mercy and Prudence,
    there is neither Excess nor Harshness.

The Admonitions

Occupying first place in both the Quaracchi and the Grottaferrata (Esser) critical editions of the writings of St. Francis are his 28 *Admonitions*.[28] They are short instructions and exhortations on such subjects as reverence for the Blessed Sacrament, the imitation of Christ, obedience, poverty of spirit, purity of heart, charity, patience, humility, true love, peacemakers. They were composed by Francis probably at different times in his life after he had founded the Order of Friars Minor, though there is a connected arrangement of the first thirteen *Admonitions* based on association of ideas. *Admonitions* numbers 14 to 28, except number 27, all begin with the words: "Blessed is (or are). . ." Some of the *Admonitions* may have been given to the Friars Minor at general chapters.

The *Admonitions,* says Esser, hold an important place in the writings of St. Francis. Esser is of the opinion that writers on the ideals and the spirit of St. Francis have not sufficiently recognized their importance. "More than other writings of St. Francis, they (the *Admonitions*) are the Saint's *Magna Charta* of a life of Christian brotherliness which is built on a radical observance of the highest poverty. In them he sketches in detail his ideal of a Christian, a servant of God, a Friar Minor."

[28]Esser, *Opuscula,* 65-121; *Omnibus,* 77-87.

The Rules of the Three Orders

St. Francis wrote three successive Rules for the Friars Minor and one for Hermitages of the Friars Minor, two paragraphs in the Rule of St. Clare, and what is now the Prologue of the new Rule of the Secular Franciscan Order (formerly called the Third Order Secular of St. Francis).

The three successive Rules for the Friars Minor were the following. The first short Rule of 1209, consisting mainly of a few passages from Holy Scripture, and approved orally by Pope Innocent III. (This Rule is no longer extant, though some attempts have been made to reconstruct it.) Then, the Rule of 1221 (23 chapters); and finally, the Rule of 1223, which was approved by a papal Bull.

In the course of time certain precepts and exhortations were added to the original Rule. For the first companions of Francis, the Gospel and the example of the founder sufficed; but as the number of Friars increased, it became necessary to add certain regulations and directives. For instance, a year of probation, the novitiate, had to be introduced before the profession of the three religious vows. At the general chapters of the Friars Minor, certain precepts were added to the Rule because they were needed in the developing organization of the growing Order.

Esser has discovered *Fragments of the Rule of the Friars Minor (Opuscula,* 300) which seem to belong to the period before 1221. It was in 1221 that Francis undertook the task of writing an orderly Rule which incorporated all the additions made since 1209 and fully expressed his concept of the kind of life that a Friar Minor should live. He gave the manuscript, which he had dictated, to Brother Caesar of Speyer, who polished the Latin and embellished it with suitable Scriptural texts. It is an excellent exposition of the ideals of Francis, but it was never submitted to the Holy See for a written approval. The reason was, no doubt, its length and the lack of the required legal terminology.

Two years later, Francis, with the help of others, rewrote the Rule to reduce it to twelve chapters and to make it acceptable for approval. The first draft was lost; and Francis had to dictate it a second time. It was no doubt discussed at the Pentecost Chapter of the Friars on June 11, 1223, and some minor changes may have been made. The Ecumenical Council of the Church held at the Lateran in 1215 had decreed that henceforth no new Rules of religious orders should receive approval and existing Rules should be used or adapted for any new Orders. Thus St. Dominic based his Rule of the Order of Preachers on the Rule of St. Augustine. However, one exception was made at the time, namely the Rule of the Friars Minor which had already received the oral approval of Pope Innocent III. A written approval was to be given later when the Rule was in its final form.

Pope Honorius III gave his approbation to the Rule of 1223 on November 29th of that year in the Bull *Solet Annuere*. The Rule with the papal Bull is preserved in the sacristy at the Sacro Convento of the Basilica of San Francesco in Assisi. The Rule of 1223 should be regarded, not as a new and different Rule, but as the final form of the Rule of 1209. That is clearly indicated in the Bull of Honorius III: "Beloved children in the Lord, moved by your pious prayers, We, in virtue of the Apostolic authority, confirm by these letters present, sanction with our protection, the Rule of your Order, approved by Pope Innocent, our Predecessor of happy memory."[29]

For the Friars Minor living in Hermitages, temporarily or permanently, Francis wrote a special little supplementary Rule (about one printed page in the *Omnibus*) between the years 1217 and 1221.[30] No more than three or four Friars were to live in a hermitage; and they were to take turns carrying out the roles of Mary and Martha.

The two paragraphs in the Rule of St. Clare which were written by St. Francis are two short messages which St. Clare received from Francis at San Damiano and which she incorporated into her

---

[29]*Omnibus*, p. 57, note 2. The texts of the Rules of 1221 and 1223, with introductions and notes, are on pp. 27-64. For the Fragmenta of the Rule antedating the one of 1221, see Esser, *Opuscula*, 300-312.

[30]Esser, *Opuscula*, 405–412; *Omnibus*, 71–73.

Rule. The first, a "Form of Life," states that the Poor Ladies or Poor Clares have embraced a manner of living that is "according to the perfection of the Gospel," and Francis promises to have the same solicitude for the Poor Ladies that he has for the Friars Minor. The second, a "Last Will," exhorts St. Clare and her Sisters to persevere in living "according to the life and poverty of our most high Lord Jesus Christ and his most holy Mother."[31]

The Prologue of the new Rule of the Third Order Secular of St. Francis or Secular Franciscan Order is one of Esser's discoveries.[32] Described by him as an earlier form of what Francis expanded into the *Letter to All the Faithful,* it is an exhortation to the Brothers and Sisters of Penance, that is, the members of his Third Order. It consists of two "chapters," one "Concerning Those Who Do Penance" and the other "Concerning Those Who Do not Do Penance."

[31] Esser, *Opuscula,* 296-299 and 448-450; *Omnibus,* 74-76.

[32] Esser, *Opuscula,* 176–192. The English version of this *Exhortation to the Brothers and Sisters of Penance* is in Esser, *Rule and Testament of St. Francis: Conferences to the Modern Followers of Francis* (FHP, 1977), pp. 217-226; and in the pamphlet *From Gospel to Life: The Rule of the Secular Franciscan Order with Commentary* (FHP, 1979). It will also be in a new manual containing a Catechism and Conferences on the new Rule, *The Rule of the Secular Franciscans* (FHP, now in press).

In the name of the Lord!

Chapter One

Concerning Those Who Do Penance

All who love the Lord with their whole heart, with their whole soul and mind, with all their strength (cf. Mk 12:30), and love their neighbors as themselves (cf. Mt 22: 39) and hate their bodies with their vices and sins, and receive the Body and Blood of our Lord Jesus Christ, and produce worthy fruits of penance:

Oh, how happy and blessed are these men and women when they do these things and persevere in doing them, because "the spirit of the Lord will rest upon them" (cf. Is 11:2) and he will make "his home and dwelling among them" (cf. Jn 14:23), and they are the sons of the heavenly Father (cf. Mt 5:45), whose works they do, and they are the spouses, brothers, and mothers of our Lord Jesus Christ (cf. Mt 12:50).

We are spouses, when by the Holy Spirit the faithful soul is united with our Lord Jesus Christ, we are brothers to him when we fulfill "the will of the Father who is in heaven" (Mt 12:50).

We are mothers, when we carry him in our heart and body (cf. 1 Cor 6:20) through divine love and a pure and sincere conscience; we give birth to him through a holy life which must give light to others by example (cf. Mt 5:16).

Oh, how glorious it is to have a great and holy Father in heaven! oh how glorious it is to have such a beautiful and admirable Spouse, the Holy Paraclete!

Oh, how glorious it is to have such a Brother and such a Son, loved, beloved, humble, peaceful, sweet, lovable, and desirable above all: Our Lord Jesus Christ, who gave up his life for his sheep (cf. Jn 10:15) and prayed to the Father saying:

"O holy Father, protect them with your name (cf. Jn 17:11) whom you gave me out of the world. I entrusted to them the message you entrusted to me and they received it. They have known that in truth I came from you, they have believed that it was you who sent me. For these I pray, not for the world (cf. Jn 17:9). Bless and consecrate them, and I consecrate myself for their sakes. I do not pray for them alone; I pray also for those who will believe in me through their word (cf. Jn 17:20) that they may be holy by being one as we are (cf. Jn 17:11). And I desire, Father, to have them in my company where I am to see this glory of mine in your kingdom" (cf. Jn 17:6-24).

Chapter Two

Concerning Those Who Do Not Do Penance

But all those men and women who are not doing penance and do not receive the Body and Blood of our Lord Jesus Christ and live in vices and sin and yield to evil concupiscence and to the wicked desires of the flesh, and do not observe what they have promised to the Lord, and are slaves to the world, in their bodies, by carnal desires and the anxieties and cares of this life (cf. Jn 8:41):

These are blind, because they do not see the true light, our Lord Jesus Christ; they do not have spiritual wisdom because they do not have the Son of God who is the true wisdom of the Father. Concerning them, it is said, "Their skill was swallowed up" (Ps 107:27) and "cursed are those who turn away from your commands" (Ps 119:21). They see and acknowledge, they know and do bad things and knowingly destroy their own souls.

See, you who are blind, deceived by your enemies, the world, the flesh and the devil, for it is pleasant to the body to commit sin and it is bitter to make it serve God because all vices and sins come out and "proceed from the heart of man" as the Lord says in the gospel (cf. Mt 7:21). And you have nothing in this world and in the next, and you thought you would possess the vanities of this world for a long time.

But you have been deceived, for the day and the hour will come to which you give no thought and which you do not know and of which you are ignorant. The body grows infirm, death approaches, and so it dies a bitter death, and no matter where or when or how man dies, in the guilt of sin, without penance or satisfaction, though he can make satisfaction but does not do it.

The devil snatches the soul from his body with such anguish and tribulation that no one can know it except he who endures it, and all the talents and power and "knowledge and wisdom" (2 Chr 1:17) which they thought they had will be taken away from them (cf. Lk 8:18; Mk 4:25), and they leave their goods to relatives and friends who take and divide them and say afterwards, "Cursed be his soul because he could have given us more, he could have acquired more than he did." The worms eat up the body and so they have lost body and soul during this short earthly life and will go into the inferno where they will suffer torture without end.

All those into whose hands this letter shall have come we ask in the charity that is God (cf. 1 Jn 4:17) to accept kindly and with divine love the fragrant words of our Lord Jesus Christ quoted above. And let those who do not know how to read have them read to them.

And may they keep them in their mind and carry them out, in a holy manner to the end, because they are "spirit and life" (Jn 6:64).

And those who will not do this will have to render "an account on the day of judgment" (cf. Mt 12:36) before the tribunal of our Lord Jesus Christ (cf. Rom 14:10).

Francis founded his Third Order in 1209, the same year in which he founded the First Order. At the time, he promised a Rule to those who became his disciples while continuing to live in the world and in their homes. This first Rule must have been very short and simple, directing the Brothers and Sisters of Penance to observe God's commandments and the Gospel counsels as literally as it was possible for persons living in the world. The *Letter to the Brothers and Sisters of Penance* may have been that first rule. A formal Rule was given to them by the Church in 1221, after fraternities of the Third Order had been established in various cities. This Rule was revised in 1289, and again in 1883. The new Rule was approved by Pope Paul VI in 1978.

St. Francis has not left any written sermons, unless the little sermon or outline for a sermon which he suggests to the Friars Minor in the Rule of 1221 (Chapter 21) can be counted as one (*Omnibus*, 46-47). Celano quotes Francis as saying: "The preacher must first draw from secret prayers what he will later pour out in holy sermons; he must first grow hot within before he speaks words that are in themselves cold" (*Omnibus*, 493). In those words of advice, Francis described his own method of preparing the sermons he preached. It is Celano again who tells us: "Francis began to preach penance to all with great fervor of spirit and joy of mind, edifying his hearers with his simple words and his greatness of heart. His words were like a burning fire, penetrating the inmost reaches of heart, and they filled the minds of all hearers with admiration" (*Omnibus*, 247).

During the last years of his life, when he could no longer travel from town to town in order to preach his Gospel message of penance (conversion) and peace and of evangelical perfection, he found a way of continuing his apostolate by writing circular letters to certain groups or classes of people.

Dr. Liam Brophy of Dublin, a Secular Franciscan journalist and poet, wrote in 1958: "If St. Francis of Assisi lived today, it is highly probable that he would be a journalist . . . We know that the Poverello realized the urgency of the problems (of his day) and that he had, besides, a reverential regard for the written word and a truly apostolic zeal for promulgating the Word of God. It seems obvious, then, that had he been born into this techical age, with its mass unrests, Communist challenges, and dire need of *pax et bonum,* he would be a top-ranking Catholic journalist.[33]

The fact is that to a certain extent—in as far as it was possible in his day—Francis was a journalist when he dictated his circular letters, and had them copied and recopied and distributed among the people for whom they were intended. This is strikingly manifest in the contents of a second *Letter to the Custodes (or Superiors) of the Friars Minor,* written by Francis and discovered by Father Esser (*Opuscula,* 172-175). It is a covering letter sent with other circular letters, and it contains instructions that the letters be multiplied by making handwritten copies and circulating them among the addressees.

Since, till now, this letter was available only in Latin, we present an English translation:

"To all the superiors of the Friars Minor who receive this letter, Brother Francis, least of the servants of God, sends greetings and holy peace in the Lord.

"Know that certain things which are very exalted and sublime in the sight of God are regarded among men as vile and mean, while other things

---

[33]*Echoes of Assisi* (FHP, 1958), p. 40.

which are esteemed and desired among men are held to be most vile and mean before God.

"Before our Lord and God, I ask you as urgently as I can to give to bishops and other clerics the letter which treats of the most holy Body and Blood of our Lord, and to keep in mind what we have recommended to you on the same subject.

"I am sending you another letter that you may give it to magistrates, consuls, and rulers. This letter contains the request that the praise of God be proclaimed publicly by the people. Make many copies of it immediately, and with great diligence present it to those for whom it is intended."[34]

This is a truly remarkable and even "modern" letter. "Make many copies immediately" of my *"Letters to the Rulers of the People"* (*Omnibus*, 115-116), Francis tells all the superiors of the Order. "Give to bishops and other clerics" copies of my letter to them, the *Letter to All Clerics* (*Omnibus*, 100-101). "Keep in mind" what I have written to you in my *Letter to All Superiors of the Friars Minor* (*Omnibus*, 112-114).

Besides these three circular letters and the covering letter, Francis wrote three others of a similar nature: the *Letter to the Brothers and Sisters of Penance*, which we have already mentioned; the *Letter to All the Friars Minor*, very probably sent

---

[34]Esser, *Opuscula*, 174.

Facsimile of the letter written by St. Francis about 1220 to Brother Leo. The original autograph is preserved since 1902 in the Cathedral of Spoleto, Italy. (See **Omnibus**, pp. 118-119.)

to the Pentecost Chapter held in 1224; and the *Letter to All the Faithful,* also very probably written during Francis' last illness. Francis writes at the beginning of the latter: "Realizing that because of my sickness and ill health I cannot personally visit each one individually, I decided to send you a letter bringing a message with the words of our Lord Jesus Christ."[35]

The first edition of the *Letter to All the Faithful* or the *Exhortation to the Brothers and Sisters in Penance* must have been written before 1221. Of two extant editions of the *Letter to All Clerics* (see Appendix II), the first was written before Pentecost, 1219, the second after March, 1220.

Besides the circular letters, Francis wrote at least four extant letters to certain individuals. We have already mentioned the one *To Brother Leo,* which Francis wrote with his own hand and is still preserved. The *Letter to St. Anthony,* which was regarded as a doubtful letter of Francis in the Quaracchi edition (*Omnibus,* 162–164) can now be included among his authentic writings (Esser, *Opuscula,* 147-154). The *Letter to a Minister* is a private letter to a certain minister provincial, written by Francis before the Pentecost Chapter of 1223 (*Omnibus,* 109-111).

[35]*Omnibus,* 93. This is a long letter, six and a half printed pages (93-99). So is the one *To All the Friars,* six printed pages (103-108). At the end of the latter is the Prayer, "Almighty, eternal, just, and merciful God."

The fourth private letter is a new discovery. It was found only after Father Esser's critical edition of the writings of Francis was published. On October 5, 1976, at Verona, Franciscan Father Giovanni Boccali found two medieval manuscripts of this letter, addressed to St. Clare and her Sisters at San Damiano, Raphael Brown, who has translated this letter,[36] thinks it is the text of the letter of which a digest is given in the *Legend of Perugia* (*Omnibus,* 1024-1025) and the *Mirror of Perfection* (*Omnibus,* 1223-1224).

> Live always in truth,
> > So that in obedience you die.
> Do not look to the life outside,
> > For that of the Spirit is better.
> I pray you with great love
> > That you have discretion as to the alms
> > Which the Lord gives you.
> Those who are weighed down by infirmities
> > And the others who labor for them,
> > All of you bear it in peace,
> > For you will see this labor as very dear,
> For you are (or will be) each a Queen
> > crowned in Heaven
> > with the Virgin Mary.

[36]R. Brown's translation was published in Esser, *The Rule and Testament of St. Francis* (FHP, 1977), p. 218. It is a short letter, only thirteen lines.

Last Will and Testament

In April or May, 1226, in Siena, St. Francis dictated to Brother Benedict of Piratro a Last Will and Testament, of which, it seems, only a digest is given in the *Mirror of Perfection*, (*Omnibus*, 1221 —only ten lines). In this Testament Francis stresses three points; he exhorts the Friars Minor to persevere especially in brotherly love, in the observance of poverty, and in obedience to ecclesiastical authority. Esser (*Opuscula*, 458) places the Siena Testament among the "dictata" of the last chapter of his critical edition of Francis' writings.

Likewise recorded in the *Mirror of Perfection* is another Testament, a "spoken" (not "dictated") discourse given by Francis at the Portiuncula "about the time of his death . . . in the presence of the Minister General and other friars." He began the discourse with these words: "I wish to entrust and bequeath the friary of St. Mary of the Portiuncula to my brethren by my Testament, in order that it may always be held in the greatest reverence and devotion by the Friars." This is the burden of the entire discourse, which seems to be chronicled in its entirety. Francis concluded it with the following words: "I wish this place to be blessed, and to remain for ever as a mirror and holy pattern for the whole Order, and as a lamp burning and shining before the throne of God and of the Blessed Virgin. For the sake of this place may God pardon the defects and faults of all the friars, and protect this Order, his little plant for ever."[37]

The Testament of St. Francis which is included among his authentic writings was dictated by him the day before or a few days before his death on October 3, 1226 (*Omnibus,* 65-70). It is more than a Testament. Francis himself calls it "a reminder, admonition, exhortation, and my testament"; and he asks that whenever the Friars Minor read the Rule "at the chapters they hold,...they should read these words also." This Testament contains some strongly worded commands and prohibitions; e.g., the words "strictly bound by obedience" and "I strictly forbid". But, as Pope Gregory IX decided in 1230 (in his Bull *Quo elongati*), the Testament did not impose on the Friars Minor any new obligations that were binding in conscience. Nevertheless, the Testament has been and "is held in great respect as an expression of the deep wisdom and spirituality of St. Francis and of his fatherly concern for those who would come after him" (Placid Hermann, in *Omnibus,*

[37]*Omnibus,* 1179-1181; also A. Masseron, *Memorable Words of Saint Francis* (FHP, 1963), pp. 110-111. No mention is made of this Testament in any collection of the Writings of St. Francis. It seems to the writer that another chapter could be added to Esser's *Opuscula,* one containing this Testament and other longer quotations of the *spoken* words of St. Francis which are found in the early biographies, e.g., Francis' description of an ideal minister general in the Second Life by Celano, nos. 185-186 (*Omnibus,* 509-511).

66). This is borne out by the fact that some excellent commentaries on the Testament have been
written and published in our own day.[38]

---

[38]Fr. Esser's commentary, a series of conferences given by him to
Franciscan Sisters in Rome, forms the second part of *The Rule and
Testament of St. Francis* (FHP, 1977). *The Covenant with God's Poor*, by
Auspicius van Corstanje O.F.M. (FHP, 1966) is "An Essay on the Biblical
Interpretation of the Testament of St. Francis of Assisi" (xx + 172 pages).

In Fr. Esser's new critical edition of the writings of St. Francis (*Opuscula,* pp. 163-165) there are two slightly varying Latin texts of the Saint's *Letter to Clerics.* St. Francis wrote the first before Pentecost, 1219, that is, before he set out on his journey to Damietta, Egypt, and the second, after March, 1220, that is, after he returned to Italy.

The alterations made in the second version of the letter are of a minor nature and do not add or subtract anything of importance in the first, except for one addition. The added phrase is: "secundum praecepta Domini et constitutiones sanctae matris Ecclesiae": and these words are exactly quoted from *Sane cum olim,* an official document issued by Pope Honorius III during the winter of 1219-1220. Francis, no doubt, learned of this papal pronouncement when he returned; and as a loyal son of Mother Church he makes use of the Pope's words to strengthen his own exhortation to give due reverence to the Blessed Sacrament and to the Word of God.

The English translation in the *Omnibus* (p. 101) is of the second version of the letter; and the added

1951

phrase is translated: "according to the law of God and the prescriptions of Mother Church."

Noteworthy is the fact that at the end of both editions of the letter Francis asks for a wider circulation of it by having copies made: "Anyone who has this writing copied, so that it may be obeyed more widely, can be sure that he has God's blessing."

APPENDIX II
Fragments of Another Rule of 1221

The definitive Rule that St. Francis gave to the Friars Minor, namely the Rule of twelve chapters which received written approval in 1223 by a papal bull was the final result of a gradual development beginning in 1209. The very short Rule which received the oral approval of Innocent III in 1209 consisted of little more than a few New Testament texts. During the decade that followed various exhortations and regulations were added so that by 1220 it was a long Rule. In that year and the next, with the help of Brother Caesar of Speyer, Francis revised and rearranged this Rule and gave it a permanent form. Because it was a spiritual rather than a legal document, Francis finally revised it once more and shortened it so that it could be given the written approval of the Holy See in 1223.

Among the authentic writings of St. Francis (*Opuscula,* pp. 301-312), Fr. Esser included three sets of fragments or excerpts which are practically the same as corresponding parts of the Rule of 1221. The differences in the texts consist of the addition or omission of a word or a few words or Scriptural texts. These citations are quite plainly from the Rule of 1221 in the form it had shortly before that year. What was then at or near the beginning of the Rule seems to have been put near the end and made chapter 22.

The first group of fragments is from a manuscript in the Library of the Cathedral at Worcester, England, which also has the Testament of St. Francis. The second collection of quotations is taken from Hugh of Digne's *Exposition of the Rule,* written in 1245-1255; and the third consists of a few references in Thomas of Celano's Second Life.

English translations of six selections from Hugh of Digne's *Exposition of the Rule* have been published in *Franciscan Readings: English Version of Vitam Alere* (Franciscan Herald Press, Chicago, 1979). On pages 31, 91, 126, Hugh of Digne expressly says he is quoting from an "earlier Rule" and, on page 60, from "the Rule even before papal approval (by a bull)." These examples will suffice for most readers; scholars will compare the Latin texts in any event.

APPENDIX III
Letter of Brother Elias

Our Father and Brother Francis departed from us and went to Christ. . . . He went from death to life. . . . He has not died. . . . Pray for him, as he asked of us, and pray to him. . . ." Thus Brother Elias, the general superior of the Friars Minor, wrote in a letter [1] announcing the death of the founder of the Order. It is a beautiful letter, a mosaic of texts and phrases from Sacred Scripture, and an important document containing the testimony of an eyewitness regarding the stigmata of St. Francis.

Most biographers of the Poverello hardly refer to this letter at all. Jörgensen mentions it briefly, calling it the first biographical work on St. Francis.

As far as we know, this letter has never before been translated into English; hence we offer a faithful version of the letter as given by Wadding, together with references to some of the biblical texts appearing in whole or in part in the letter:

[1] Only one manuscript copy of the letter seems to have been found. It is addressed to Brother Gregory, minister of the province in France, but the letter was no doubt sent also to the other ministers-provincial. In printed form and in Latin (probably the original was written in Latin), it was reproduced in Wadding's *Annales Minorum*, II, 149-150 (old edn.), 167-169 (new edn.), and in the Bollandists' *Acta Sanctorum*, Oct. II, 668-669.

*To Brother Gregory, beloved in Christ, minister
of the brethren in France, and to all of his and our
brethren, greetings from Brother Elias, a sinner.*

*Before I begin to write, I must give expression
to my sorrow, and indeed I have reason to do so. As
overflowing waters, so is my grief. For the fear I feared
has come upon me and upon you, and that which I was
afraid of has befallen me and you.*[2]

The comforter is far from us,[3] *and he who carried us like lambs in his arms*[4] *has departed into a strange
and distant country.*[5]

*Beloved of God and men, he has been taken up
into brightly shining mansions—he who taught Jacob
the law of life and conduct and gave to Israel the covenant of peace.*[6]

*For his sake we should rejoice exceedingly, but
for us there must needs be sorrow; without him darkness
envelops us, and the shadows of death enshroud us.*

*If it is a great loss for all, it is fraught with par-
ticular danger for me whom he left behind in the midst*

---

[2] "Before I eat I sigh: and as overflowing waters, so is my roaring: For
the fear which I feared, hath come upon me; and that which I was afraid
of, hath befallen me" (Job 3:24-25).

[3] "Therefore do I weep, and my eyes run down with water: because the
comforter, the relief of my soul, is far from me" (Lam. 1:16).

[4] "And I was like a foster father to Ephraim, I carried them in my arms"
(Osee 11:3).

[5] "There was a man, an householder, who planted a vineyard . . . and
went abroad" (Matt. 21:33).

[6] "And he gave him commandments . . . that he might teach Jacob his
covenant, and Israel his judgments" (Eccli. 45:6).

of darkness, oppressed and harried on all sides by countless anxieties.

Hence I beseech you, brethren, weep with me
who am immersed in deep sorrow.

We are orphans without a father; [7] we have lost
the light of our eyes. Verily, our Brother and Father
Francis was a true light to us, to those near us, and also
to those who were not associated with him by vocation
and manner of life.

He was a light, sent by the true Light, to shine
on those who sit in darkness and in the shadow of death,
and to guide their feet into the way of peace. [8] This he
did in as far as the true Sun, the Orient from on high [9]
(that is, Christ) illuminated his heart and inflamed his
will.

With ardent love he announced the kingdom of
God, imbued the children with the thoughts and senti-
ments of the fathers, taught the incredulous the wisdom
of the just, and prepared unto the Lord a perfect people
in the whole world. [10]

Even to the islands far off, his name went
abroad, [11] and all lands praise his wonderful deeds.

[7] "We are become orphans without a father" (Lam. 5:3).

[8] "To shine on those who sit in darkness and in the shadow of death,
to guide our feet into the way of peace" (Luke 1:79).

[9] "The Orient from on high has visited us" (Luke 1:78).

[10] "And he himself [John the Baptist] shall go before him in the spirit
and power of Elias, to turn the hearts of the fathers to their children
and the incredulous to the wisdom of the just; to prepare unto the Lord
a perfect people" (Luke 1:17).

[11] "Thy [Solomon's] name went abroad to the islands far off, and thou
wast beloved in thy peace" (Eccli. 47:17).

For this reason, sons and brothers, do not yield to excessive grief, for God the Father of orphans will console us with His holy consolation. When you weep, brethren, weep for yourselves, not over him.[12] For we, who are sojourning among the living, are in death, whereas he went from death to life.

Rejoice since he, another Jacob, blessed all his sons [13] before he was taken from us, and he forgave all of us who may have been guilty of some offence against him in thought or deed.

I take this occasion also to communicate to you very joyful news—a new miracle. Never yet has anyone heard of such wondrous signs except in the case of the Son of God, who is Christ the Lord.

For, a long time before his death, our Brother and Father Francis was visibly crucified; he bore on his body the five wounds, the genuine stigmata of Christ. His hands and feet were pierced through as by nails; they retained these wounds and showed the black color of nails. His side was opened as by a lance and bled frequently.

As long as his soul still was in the body, he was not handsome of appearance; but his countenance was unattractive, and none of the members of his body was spared acute sufferings. As a result of the contraction of

---

[12] "Daughters of Jerusalem, do not weep for me, but weep for yourselves and for your children" (Luke 23:28).

[13] "All these are the twelve tribes of Israel: these things their father [Jacob] spoke to them, and he blessed every one, with their proper blessings" (Gen. 49:28).

his muscles, his limbs were stiff like those of a dead person.

But now that he has died he is lovely to behold, he shines with a wonderful brilliance, and he causes all who look upon him to rejoice. His limbs, formerly stiff, are flexible and can be arranged in any position just as those of a delicate child.

Brethren, bless ye, therefore, 'the God of Heaven, give glory everywhere to Him who hath shown mercy to us.[14]

Remember our Brother and Father Francis unto the glory of God, who has made him great among men and has exalted him above the angels. Pray for him, as he asked of us, and pray to him that God may grant us His holy grace even as He granted it to him.

On the eve of Sunday, October the fourth, one hour after sunset, our Father and Brother Francis departed from us and went to Christ.

When you, dearest Brethren, receive this letter, imitate the people of Israel as they wept over their great leaders, Moses and Aaron. We may permit our tears to flow freely—we who have lost the consolation of such a Father!

It is a pious thing to rejoice with Francis, but it is pious also to weep over him.

Of a truth it is pious to rejoice with Francis, for, he has not died, since (in the morning) he went away to the market of heaven, carrying with him a purse full

---

[14] "Bless ye the God of heaven, give glory to him in the sight of all that live, because he hath shewn his mercy to you" (Tob. 12:6).

of money (his merits), and in the evening he will come back.

It is pious to weep over Francis, for, he who went about as did Aaron, who presented to us both new and old gifts out of his treasury, who consoled us in every trial—he has been taken from our midst, and we are orphans without a father.

But it is written: To thee is the poor man left: thou wilt be a helper to the orphan.[15]

Most beloved brethren, all of you, pray perseveringly that, after the little earthly vessel has been broken in the vale of the children of Adam, that highest Master-Potterer may provide another new, brightly shining vessel, who will preside over our numerous brotherhood and, like a true Machabean, will lead us on to battle.

Since it is not in vain to pray for the dead, pray to the Lord for his soul. Every priest shall read three Masses, every cleric shall pray the Psalter, the lay brothers the Pater Noster five times, and the clerics shall solemnly chant Matins in choir. Amen.

Brother Elias, a sinner.

---

[15] "To thee is the poor man left: thou wilt be a helper to the orphan" (Ps. 9:14).

MAP 3 ITALY

Grand St. Bernard
Mont Cenis
PIEMONTE
Novara
Milan
Bergamo
LOMBARDY
TRENTINO
Trent
VENETO
Vicenza
Verona
Padua
Venice
Islet near Burno
S. Francesco del Deserto
Pavia
Allesandria
Piacenza
Brescia
LIGURIA
Genoa
Pontremoli
Parma
Modena
Bologna
EMILIA
PO RIVER
VIA EMILIA
Imola
Faenza
Forli
Lucca
Pisa
Florence
Fucecchio
Livorno
ARNO RIVER
Cesena
Rimini
San Marino
San Leo
Fano
La Verna
San Sepolcro
Urbino
Cagli
Ancona
TUSCANY
Siena
Arezzo
Chiana Swamps
Gubbio
Chiusi
Perugia
Assisi
Nocera
Foligno
MARCHE
Fermo
Orvieto
LAKE OF BOLSENA
Todi
Orte
Narni
Rieti
UMBRIA
Duchy of Spoleto
NERA RIVER
SALERIA
Penne
Chieti
Viterbo
Rome
Bellegra
Subiaco
Tagliacozza
Celano
Sulmona
Monte Gargano
Foggia
LAZIO
Ceprano
Sora
ABRUZZI
Monte Cassino
Gaeta
CAMPANIA
CALORE RIVER
PUGLIA
Bari
Naples
Avellino
OFANO RIVER
BASILICATA
Brindisi
Lecce
CORSICA
SARDINIA
TYRRHENIAN SEA
ADRIATIC SEA
CALABRIA
SICILY

© 1965, Franciscan Herald Press